12·95

CONTEMPORARY
READINGS
IN CHILD
PSYCHOLOGY

CONTEMPORARY READINGS IN CHILD PSYCHOLOGY

THIRD EDITION

E. Mavis Hetherington

Department of Psychology
University of Virginia

Ross D. Parke

Department of Psychology
University of Illinois

McGRAW-HILL BOOK COMPANY

New York   St. Louis   San Francisco   Auckland   Bogotá   Caracas   Colorado Springs
Hamburg   Lisbon   London   Madrid   Mexico   Milan   Montreal   New Delhi
Oklahoma City   Panama   Paris   San Juan   São Paulo   Singapore   Sydney   Tokyo   Toronto

This book was set in Times Roman by the College Composition Unit
in cooperation with William Byrd Press.
The editors were James D. Anker and David Dunham
the designer was Amy Becker;
the production supervisor was Friederich W. Schulte.
Drawings were done by Accurate Art, Inc.
R. R. Donnelley & Sons Company was printer and binder.

CONTEMPORARY READINGS IN CHILD PSYCHOLOGY

1 2 3 4 5 6 7 8 9 0   DOCDOC   8 9 3 2 1 0 9 8

ISBN   0-07-028437-7

Contemporary readings in child psychology.

    Reprinted from various sources.
    Includes bibliographies.
    1. Child psychology.   2. Child development.
3. Hetherington, E. Mavis (Eileen Mavis), 1926–
II, Parke, Ross D. [DNLM: 1. Child Development—
collected works.   2. Child Psychology—collected
works.   WS 105 C761]
BF721.C62   1988   155.4   87-3082
ISBN 0-07-028437-7

ABOUT
THE AUTHORS

E. MAVIS HETHERINGTON is a professor of psychology at the University of Virginia. She was trained as a developmental psychologist and as a clinical psychologist at the University of California at Berkeley where she obtained her Ph.D. She is a past president of Division 7, the Developmental Psychology Division of the American Psychological Association, and currently is president of the Society for Research in Child Development. She has been editor of *Child Development*, associate editor of *Developmental Psychology*, and currently is associate editor of the *Journal of Abnormal Child Psychology*. She has authored and edited many books in the area of child development, the most recent being *Socialization, Personality and Social Development, volume IV, Handbook of Child Psychology*. Her research interests are in the areas of childhood psychopathology, personality and social development, and stress and coping in families. She is well known for her work on the effects of divorce, one-parent families, and remarriage on children's development.

ROSS D. PARKE is a professor in the Department of Psychology and the School of Medicine at the University of Illinois at Champaign-Urbana. He is a member of the governing council of the Society for Research in Child Development, and he has served on the executive committee of the Division of Developmental Psychology of the American Psychological Association as well as the executive board of the International Society for the Study of Behavioral Development. He has been associate editor of *Child Development* and is editor of *Developmental Psychology*. Professor Parke is author of *Fathers* and editor of *Recent Trends in Social Learning Theory* and most recently of *The Family, Review of Child Development Research*, vol. 7. His research has focused on early social relationships in infancy, aggression, and child abuse. He is well known for his early work on the effects of punishment and for his current work on the father's role in infancy and early childhood.

To John and Barbara and our children:
Grant, Eric, and Jason
Gillian, Timothy, Megan, Sarah, and Jennifer

CONTENTS

5. LANGUAGE AND COMMUNICATION   203

6. COGNITION AND LEARNING   248

PREFACE

The field of child psychology has undergone radical changes in the past decade, and change is still the clearest characteristic of this exciting area of study. The purpose of this book is to provide students a firsthand opportunity to share some of the recent research findings of child psychologists.

A number of themes run throughout the field of child psychology, and we have tried to choose articles that will illustrate these themes. One of the most important themes is our revised view of the child and the important role that the child plays in his or her own development. We recognize that infants and children are more capable, more influential, and more effective at earlier ages than ever before. The shift is best described by the view of the child as "competent." Recent research in infancy illustrates the shift very dramatically. Gone forever is our old view of infants as passive creatures of limited sensory, perceptual, and social capacities, awaiting the imprint of the adult world. Instead we now recognize that infants have much greater capacity to see, learn, and even socialize; the articles on infancy in this book have helped dispel our earlier myths by demonstrating the wide range of perceptual and social competence that infants display. Infants are more prepared to respond and to interact with their environment than we previously imagined. Part of the shift in our views of infancy can be credited to our revised recognition of the contribution of biological and genetic factors in child development. We have not shifted back to a one-sided biological view of development; rather we now appreciate the important interactions between genetics and environment in shaping the course of development. In this book, this interaction is illustrated in a host of different ways, including the IQ controversy, the role of nutrition in cognitive development, the influence of physical maturation on development, and the role of temperament in development.

Nor is it only our views of the *infant's* competence that have changed: children at *all levels of development* are increasingly recognized as competent, active, and influential. In both cognitive and social development, the child is viewed as an active participant. Children are curious, information-seeking, and information-processing organisms and no longer just passive actors in the learning process as the recent research represented in this book on both language and cognition illustrates so well. Similarly in the social sphere, our views of the child have changed. One shift is the recognition of the important relationship between cognitive and social development; the child's cognitive capacities are viewed as playing an influential role in shaping his or her social behavior and vice versa; social skills may play a role in modifying cognitive development.

A most dramatic change concerns our recognition of the child's role in his or her own socialization. Our unidirectional view of development, whereby adults influence children but children do not alter adult behavior, is inadequate. Children play an active role in modifying and altering adult behavior—even in early infancy. A bidirectional view of socialization is now widely accepted, with children playing an influential part in their own social and cognitive development.

There are other themes as well. A current concern is the study of the child from a developmental perspective so that the age-related changes and transformations in motor, social, and cognitive spheres can be described and understood. In this search, there are two aims: (1) to describe the nature of the child's development and (2) to explain the processes that account for the developmental progression.

These two aims have led to a recognition that a wide variety of methodological strategies are necessary. No single method will suffice. On the one hand child development specialists have been influenced by recent trends in other fields such as ethology, which emphasizes the study of the organism in its natural environment. Under this influence, there has been a renewed interest in describing the behavior of children at different ages in a variety of naturalistic settings, including homes, schools, and playgrounds. It is hoped that this trend will yield important data concerning how children in different cultures and subcultures develop in their own unique real-life environments.

At the same time, researchers continue the important task of understanding the processes of development. To a large extent, the preferred methodology for achieving this goal is the laboratory experiment. Using a well-controlled situation, this method allows the manipulation of relevant variables in order to establish clear cause-effect relationships. Increasingly, developmental psychologists are combining observational and experimental approaches; the observations yield hypotheses or clues concerning possible processes; in turn, these hunches can be systematically assessed in the laboratory. The importance of this trend is that the laboratory experiments are more likely to be testing hypotheses that will be of relevance to the ways in which children develop in their natural environment.

Just as there are multiple methods, there are multiple theories. Although the grand theoretical scheme of Piaget is still influential, child psychologists are increasingly becoming more modest and restricted in the scope of their theories. As the complexity and the multifaceted nature of development become apparent, minitheories that aim to explain smaller pieces of the developmental puzzle are becoming more popular. Theories of sex-typing, aggression, memory, and grammar development are more likely than elaborate theories aimed at explaining all social development or the total range of cognitive-language development.

Finally, child development is recognizing the culture-bound and even time-bound nature of its findings. As a number of articles in this book clearly show, no single picture of development is accurate for all cultures, social classes, or racial and ethnic groups. Children develop different skills and competencies in different cultural milieus; and no sweeping generalizations concerning children's development can be made without careful specification of a child's cultural background. Similarly, much of our knowledge about children is time-bound. Children and families are in a state of transition and change. It is our job not only to constantly monitor these changes, but to be aware of the very temporary nature of many of our ''facts'' about children.

Another theme of child psychology today is that it is influenced by and influences social policy concerning children. Just as government programs like Head Start and day-care programs alter the lives of children, the findings of child psychologists often give impetus and support to new types of government intervention on behalf of children. A significant shift over the past decade has been the increasing interdependence of child development as a scientific discipline and a government policy.

PLAN OF THE BOOK

It is the aim of this book to illustrate these contemporary themes in child psychology. An understanding of children must take into account both developmental changes that occur over the span of childhood as well as the processes underlying developmental changes and transitions. Therefore, we have organized this book to reflect this viewpoint. Our topic-oriented organization permits us to achieve both of our goals. Each chapter deals with both the processes of development as well as the ways in which children change over age.

In this third edition we have provided a balance between overviews of recent research and reports of individual research projects using a wide range of methodologies. To complement our text, Hetherington and Parke's *Child Psychology: A Contemporary Viewpoint,* we have organized this third edition of *Contemporary Readings in Child Psychology* to correspond closely to the topical organization of the text. To reflect changes made in the third edition of the textbook, we have added new sections on physical growth and maturation as well as on childhood psychopathology. However, we should emphasize that this book of readings can easily be used with any of the currently available child and development psychology textbooks.

It is our hope that you will not only learn from these articles some of the recent findings, methods, and theories of child psychology, but that through these articles you will share the excitement of our contemporary efforts to understand children.

STATISTICAL GUIDE

Many students who read this book will be unfamiliar with the common statistical terms used in research articles. To make the research articles more readable for students, we have edited those articles to minimize the number of statistical terms included. In some cases this type of editing has not been possible, but generally students can understand the hypotheses, methodology, and findings of the study without becoming enmeshed in specific statistical details which may be beyond their level of expertise.

In addition, to help students with some of the common statistical terms, we provide a brief discussion of these terms:

Mean and Median: The mean ($\overline{\text{X}}$) and median (M) are both measures of central tendency; the mean refers to the *arithmetic average* and so the mean height of children in a classroom would be the sum of the heights of individual children divided by the number of children in the class. The median, on the other hand, refers to the *middle number* when a group of values are arranged from smallest to largest. Therefore, the median height would be the height of the child who is in the middle of the group if all the students lined up from shortest to tallest.

Standard Deviation: (SD) is a measure of the variability or range of the values in a group of scores. For example, if the heights of the children in a class were all within 1 inch of each other, the standard deviation would be small; if the range was 8 inches, the standard deviation would be larger.

Correlation is an index of the relationship between two variables and is expressed in terms of the direction and size of the relationship. Height and weight are related in a positive direction since as height increases, so does weight typically rise. On the other hand, if one factor increases while the other factor decreases, the correlation is a negative one. Finally, if no relationship exists between two factors, such as eye color and IQ, then we speak of a zero order correlation. This means that changes in one factor are not related in any systematic way to changes in another factor.

Statistical Tests: A variety of tests will be found in the selections such as analysis of variance, t-tests, and chi-squares. Each of these represents different ways of determining whether differences among groups of subjects are due to chance factors. For the analysis of variance, a value of F will be given followed by another value that indicates the level of significance; for t-tests, a t value is provided, and for chi-square, a X^2 value is given. The important issue for your understanding the articles is the *level of significance* associated with each of these tests. Next we provide an explanation of this term.

Levels of Statistical Significance: The purpose of statistical tests is to permit the investigator to determine whether the results of his or her investigation were due to chance factors. For example, two groups of subjects may have received different treatments and the results of the statistical test yielded the following: p < .05 or p < .01. These values mean that the differences between the groups could have occurred by chance alone only 5 times out of 100 (*p*<.05) or 1 time out of 100 (*p* <.01). Most investigators in child psychology accept a finding as being reliable and trustworthy if the difference is at the .05 level of significance.

This is a limited survey of common statistical terms, but we trust that it will help in understanding the articles presented in this book.

REFERENCE WORKS

This list of common reference sources in child psychology will be helpful to students who wish to pursue a topic in greater depth.

Advances in child behavior and development, New York: Academic Press. A continuing series of reviews of recent research.
Flavell, J. (1985). *Cognitive development* (2nd ed.). Englewood Cliffs, N.J.: Prentice-Hall.
Minnesota symposia on child psychology (Vols. 1-10). Minneapolis: University of Minnesota Press. Vol. 11-present. Erlbaum Assoc.
Mussen, P. H. (Editor in chief). (1983). *Handbook of child psychology.*
    Vol. 1 *History, theory and methods*
    Vol. 2 *Infancy and development psychobiology*
    Vol. 3 *Cognitive development*
    Vol. 4 *Socialization, personality and social development*
New directions for child development. San Francisco: Jossey-Bass. A series of short paperbacks devoted to special topics in child development.
Osofsky, J. (Ed.) (1987). *Handbook of infant development* (Vol. 2). New York: Wiley.
Review of child development research. Chicago: University of Chicago Press. A continuing series of reviews on a wide range of current topics.
The young child: Reviews of research (Vols. 1-3). Washington: National Association for the Education of Young Children. Review of a less technical nature on a range of topics with an emphasis on applied issues.

Leading journals in child development:

Child Development
Child Language
Development Psychology
Developmental Review
Cognitive Development
International Journal of Behavioral Development
Journal of Applied Developmental Psychology
Merrill-Palmer Quarterly
Monographs of the Society for Research in Child Development
Journal of Experimental Child Psychology
Infant Development and Behavior

Thanks are extended to the following reviewers for their comments and recommendations for this third edition: Nancy Eisenberg, Arizona State University; Elissa Newport, University of Illinois; Carolyn J. Mebert, University of New Hampshire; Ross A. Thompson, University of Nebraska; and Colleen Surber, University of Wisconsin.

E. Mavis Hetherington
Ross D. Parke

CHAPTER 1

THE BIOLOGICAL BASIS OF BEHAVIOR

Some concepts, theories, and controversies in developmental psychology appear briefly, stimulate a flurry of research activity, and disappear, having made little lasting impact on the field. Others arise and may continue to provoke psychologists but only enough to be studied in a relatively unmodified and often unproductive form. Still other problems maintain a tenacious hold on the curiosity of developmental psychologists and stimulate further questions. However, the questions asked about the issues change, prompting new methods of studying them; the controversies remain but in a changed form. The interaction between biological[1] and environmental factors in development is a topic that clearly falls in the last category.

Although the historical antecedents of this subject might be said to go back to the interests of the ancient Chinese and Greeks in the relation between body types and temperament, a more modern and directly relevant antecedent is Galton's book *English Men of Science; Their Nature and Nurture*, published in 1874. Galton reported that there was an unusually high incidence of intellectually and professionally outstanding persons among the relatives of eminent scientists. Until the interest in learning theory started early in this century, and notably the rise of behaviorism in the 1930s and 1940s, the predominant emphasis was on the role of heredity as the important determinant of development, particularly intellectual development.

---

[1] In our discussion the term "biological factors" will subsume both genetic factors and changes in the anatomy or physiology of the child resulting from external agents or events.

In many ways this philosophy of biological determinism is incompatible with American social and political thought, which emphasizes equality, social mobility, and the value of education. In a culture imbued with the Horatio Alger story that a poor boy who is virtuous and works hard can be a success, and with the notion that any American can grow up to be President, the behaviorists' emphasis on experience and environment holds greater appeal. It is interesting to note that in societies holding to more rigid social structures, such as Great Britain and some of the European countries, the genetic position has found a more hospitable milieu and has been maintained more vigorously than in the United States. The following famous statement by John B. Watson, the leader of behaviorism, is more compatible with the American dream than are folksy maxims such as "Blood will tell" or "You can't make a silk purse out of a sow's ear."

> Give me a dozen healthy infants, well-formed, and my own specified world to bring them up in, and I'll guarantee to take any one at random and train him to become any type of specialist I might select—doctor, lawyer, artist, merchant-chief and yes, even beggar-man and thief, regardless of his talents, penchants, tendencies, abilities, vocations, race of his ancestors. (Watson, 1959, p. 104)

Such extreme genetic or environmentalist positions led to what was called "the nature-nurture controversy," where proponents on each side of the controversy championed either biological or experiential factors to the exclusion of others. In the past twenty years such irrational extremism has yielded to the view that behavior is determined by the interaction of biological and experiential factors, and the question of whether heredity or environment determines a characteristic is no longer being asked. Instead we are asking "how" and "when" development is affected by genetic and environmental factors and transactions between these factors.

These genetic and environmental transactions occur throughout the course of development. Therefore, the expression of the genotype, the biological inheritance of the individual, as a phenotype, the observable characteristics of an individual, is constantly being modified.

The first article in this volume, by Sandra Scarr and Kathleen McCartney, advances a provocative theory of development which suggests that experience is directed by genotypes. Genotypical differences affect differences in observable characteristics both directly and through modifying the experiences of the individual. This modification of environmental experiences by the genotype occurs through environments provided by biologically related parents, through responses elicited from others, through the behavior and attributes of the individual, and through the active selection or construction of environments that are compatible with the individual's genotype.

The impact of the environment in shaping the phenotypical expression of the genotype varies with the kind, the amount, and the timing of experiences. In addition some individuals may be genetically predisposed to being more vulnerable to certain environmental factors than are others. Some individuals and some fetuses may be more likely to alter in response to such things as drugs, malnutrition, anoxia, disease, stress, and sensory or social stimulation or deprivation. Some behaviors are also more difficult to modify than are others. Responses such as smiling, babbling, crawling, and walking in infants seem to be strongly genetically programmed. Blind infants smile at about the same time as seeing infants, the emergence of babbling occurs in a similar fashion in deaf and hearing infants, and children who spend much of their time restrained in swaddling clothes or on a cradle board crawl and walk at about the same time as infants reared under more mobile conditions. Such behaviors where there are fewer possible alternative paths from genotype to phenotype, or where the behavior is difficult to deflect under extreme variations in experience, are said to be highly "canalized" (Waddington, 1966).

At one time psychologists interested in genetic-environmental transactions were concerned with the child only after birth. It is now recognized that some of the most powerful of these transactions may occur prenatally while the infant is developing rapidly in utero and that some of the adverse effects of such transactions can be averted. Innovations in genetics and perinatology and new techniques in the detection and treatment of genetic disorders have led to an increased interest in prenatal development. The article by Greta Fein and her colleagues describes the multiple effects of environmental toxins on susceptible individuals and on the developing fetus. This article unfolds like a detective story as the investigators address such issues as variation among individuals and species in susceptibility to environmental toxins, the timing of effects, thresholds, subtle behavioral outcomes, and short- versus long-term effects of such toxins.

The complex relationship between biological factors or risk factors and experience is underscored by the last three papers in this section. Improved perinatal and neonatal care have increased the possibility for survival of high-risk infants who once would have been unlikely to survive birth or earliest infancy. Nowhere is this more apparent than in the survival rate of extremely low birthweight or premature babies. In her article, Susan Goldberg under-scores that it is not just the direct physical and neurological impact of factors such as prematurity that affect development, it is also the associated experi-ential and social factors that modify or sustain their effects. This premise, in conjunction with the Scarr and McCartney model of genetic factors shaping experiences, is interesting to consider when reading the last two articles in this section. Michael Rutter discusses the importance of individual differences in children's temperamental styles, differences which often are thought to be partially biologically based, on the way the individual responds to his or her environment and on the way others respond to the individual. Emmy Werner also emphasizes individual variation in response to adverse environments. She describes the role of protective factors that are associated with a child's resiliency in coping with stressful life situations both within and outside of the family.

In none of the articles in this section is the biological or environmental extremism prevalent twenty years ago apparent. All of the authors present a transactional model of development in which biological and environmental factors interact over the life span to shape development. Moreover, all of the articles reflect a prevalent view in contemporary psychology, that of the child playing an active role in eliciting, selecting, and shaping the experiences he or she encounters. This will be a perspective that emerges repeatedly in other articles throughout this volume.

REFERENCES

Galton, F. (1874). *English men of science: Their nature and nurture.* London: Macmillan.

Waddington, C.H. (1966). *Principles of development and differentiation.* New York: Macmillan.

Watson, J.B. (1959). *Behaviorism.* Chicago: University of Chicago Press.

How People Make Their Own Environments: A Theory of Genotype → Environment Effects

Sandra Scarr
Kathleen McCartney

INTRODUCTION

Theories of behavioral development have ranged from genetic determinism to naive environmentalism. Neither of these radical views nor interactionism has adequately explained the process of development or the role of experience in development. In this paper we propose a theory of environmental effects on human development that emphasizes the role of the genotype (heredity) in determining not only which environments are experienced by individuals but also which environments individuals seek for themselves. To show how this theory addresses the process of development, the theory is used to account for seemingly anomalous findings for deprivation, adoption, twin, and intervention studies.

For the species, we claim that human experience and its effects on development depend primarily on the evolved nature of the human genome. In evolutionary theory the two essential concepts are selection and variation. Through selection the human genome has evolved to program human development. Phenotypic variation (variation in observable characteristics) is the raw material on which selection works. Genetic variation must be associated with phenotypic variation, or there could be no evolution. It follows from evolutionary theory that individual differences depend in part on genotypic differences. We argue that genetic differences prompt differences in which environments are experienced and what effects they may have. In this view, the genotype, in both its species specificity and its individual variability, largely determines environmental effects on development, because the genotype determines the organism's responsiveness to environmental opportunities.

A theory of behavioral development must explain the origin of new psychological structures. Because there is no evidence that new adaptations can arise out of the environment without maturational changes in the organism, genotypes must be the source of new structures.

Maturational sequence is controlled primarily by the genetic program for development. As Gottlieb (1976) said, there is evidence for a role of environment in (1) maintaining existing structures and in (2) elaborating existing structures; however, there is no evidence that the environment has a role in (3) inducing new structures. In development, new adaptations or structures cannot arise out of experience per se.

The most widely accepted theories of development are vague about how new structures arise. We suggest that the problem of new structures in development has been extraordinarily difficult because of a false parallel between genotype and environment, which, we argue, are not constructs at the same level of analysis. The dichotomy of nature and nurture has always been a bad one, not only for the oft-cited reasons that both are required for development, but because a false parallel arises between the two. We propose that development is indeed the result of nature *and* nurture but that genes drive experience. Genes are components in a system that organizes the organism to experience its world. The organism's abilities to experience the world change with development and are individually variable. A good theory of the environment can only be one in which experience is guided by genotypes that both push and restrain experiences.

Behavioral development depends on both a genetic program and a suitable environment for the expression of the human, species-typical program for development. Differences among people can arise from both genetic and environmental differences, but the process by which differences arise is better described as genotype → environment effects. We propose that the genotype is the driving force behind development, because, we argue, it is the discriminator of what environments are actually experienced. The genotype determines the *responsiveness* of the person to those environmental opportunities. We do not think that development is precoded in the genes and merely emerges with maturation. Rather, we stress the role of the genotype in determining which environments are actually experienced and what effects they have on the developing person.

We distinguish here between environments to which a person is exposed and environments that are actively experienced or ''grasped'' by the person. As we all know, the relevance of environments changes with development. The toddler who has ''caught on'' to the idea that things have names and who demands the names for everything is experiencing a fundamentally different verbal environment from what she experienced before, even though her parents talked to her extensively in infancy. The young adolescent who played baseball with the boy next door and now finds herself hopelessly in love with him is experiencing her friend's companionship in a new way.

A Model of Genotypes and Environments

Figure 1 presents our model of behavioral development. In this model, the child's phenotype (P_c), or observable characteristics, is a function of both the child's genotype (G_c) and her rearing environment (E_c). There will be little disagreement on this. The parents' genotypes (G_p) determine the child's genotype, which in turn influences the child's phenotype. Again, there should be little controversy over this point. As in most developmental theories, transactions occur between the organism and the environment; here they are described by the correlation between phenotype and rearing environment. In most models, however, the source of this correlation is ambiguous. In this model, both the child's phenotype and rearing environment are influenced by the child's geno-

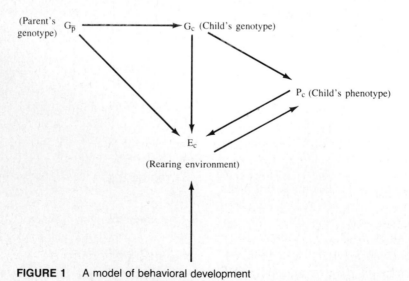

FIGURE 1   A model of behavioral development

type. Because the child's genotype influences both the phenotype and the rearing environment, their correlation is a function of the genotype. The genotype is *conceptually prior* to both the phenotype and the rearing environment.

It is an unconventional shorthand to suggest that the child's genotype can directly affect the rearing environment. What we want to represent is developmental changes in the genetic program that prompt new experiences, before the full phenotype is developed. An example could be found in the development of productive speech; the child becomes attentive to the language environment receptively months before real words are produced. Our argument is that changes in what is "turned on" in the genotype affect an emerging phenotype, both directly through maturation (G_c to P_c) and through prompting new experiences.

Also the transaction between phenotype and environment is determined by developmental changes in the genotype. We recognize that this is not a popular position, but we propose it to account for data to be discussed in the final sections of the paper.

Thus, we intend the path from G_c to E_c to represent the idea that developmental changes in phenotypes are prompted both by changes in the effective genotype and by changes in the salience of environments, which are then correlated.

The path from the child's genotype to the child's experienced environment represents maturation, which is controlled primarily by the genetic program. New structures arise out of maturation, from genotype to phenotype. Behavioral development is elaborated and maintained by the transactions of phenotype and environment, but it cannot arise de novo from this interaction. Thus, in this model, the course of development is a function of genetically controlled maturational sequences, although the rate of maturation can be affected by some environmental circumstances, such

as the effects of nutrition on physical growth (Watson & Lowrey, 1967). Behavioral examples include cultural differences in rates of development through the sequence of cognitive stages described by Piaget and other theoretical sequences (see Nerlove & Snipper, 1981).

Separation of Genetic and Environmental Effects on Development   The major problem with attempts to separate environmental from genetic effects and their combinations is that people evoke and select their own environments to a great extent. There may appear to be arbitary events of fate, such as being hit by a truck (did you look carefully in both directions?), falling ill (genetic differences in susceptibility, or a life-style that lowers resistance to disease?), but even these may not be entirely divorced from personal characteristics that have some genetic variability. Please understand that we do not mean that one's environmental fate is *entirely* determined by one's genotype—only that some genotypes are more likely to receive and select certain environments than others.

AN EVOLVING THEORY OF BEHAVIORAL DEVELOPMENT

Plomin et al. (1977) described three kinds of genotype-environment correlations that we believe form the basis for a developmental theory. The theory of genotype → environment effects we propose has three propositions:

1 The process by which children develop is best described by three kinds of genotype → environment effects: a *passive* kind, whereby the genetically related parents provide a rearing environment that is correlated with the genotype of the child (sometimes positively and sometimes negatively); an *evocative* kind, whereby the child receives responses from others that are influenced by his genotype; and an *active* kind that represents the child's selective attention to and learning from aspects of his environment that are influenced by his genotype and indirectly correlated with those of his biological relatives.

2 The relative importance of the three kinds of genotype → environment effects changes with development. The influence of the passive kind declines from infancy to adolescence, and the importance of the active kind increases over the same period.

3 The degree to which experience is influenced by individual genotypes increases with development and with the shift from passive to active genotype → environment effects, as individuals select their own experiences.

The first, *passive* genotype → environment effects arise in biologically related families and render all of the research literature on parent-child socialization uninterpretable. Because parents provide both genes and environments for their biological offspring, the child's environment is necessarily correlated with her genes, because her genes are correlated with her parents' genes, and the parents' genes are correlated with the rearing environment they provide. It is impossible to know what about the parents' rearing environment for the child determines what about the child's behavior, because of the confounding effect of genetic transmission of the same characteristics from parent to child. Not only can we not interpret the direction of effects in parent-child interaction, as Bell (1968) argued, we also cannot interpret the *cause* of those effects in biologically related families.

An example of a positive kind of passive genotype-environment correlation can be found in reading; parents who read well and enjoy reading are likely to provide their children with books; thus, the children are more likely to be skilled readers who enjoy reading, both for genetic and environmental reasons. The children's rearing environment is positively correlated with the parents' genotypes and therefore with the children's genotypes as well.

An example of a negative passive genotype-environment correlation can also be found in reading. Parents who are skilled readers, faced with a child who is not learning to read well, may provide a more enriched reading environment for that child than for another who acquires reading skills quickly. The more enriched environment for the less able child represents a negative genotype → environment effect (see also Plomin et al., 1977). There is, thus, an unreliable, but not random, connection between genotypes and environments when parents provide the opportunities for experience.

The second kind of genotype → environment effect is called evocative because it represents the different responses that different genotypes evoke from the social and physical environments. Responses to the person further shape development in ways that correlate with the genotype. Examples of such evocative effects can be found in the research of Lytton (1980), the theory of Escalona (1968), and the review of Maccoby (1980). It is quite likely that smiley, active babies receive more social stimulation than sober, passive infants. In the intellectual area, co-operative, attentive preschoolers receive more pleasant and instructional interactions from the adults around them than uncooperative, distractible children. Individual differences in responses evoked can also be found in the physical world; for example, people who are skillful at electronics receive feedback of a sort very different from those who fail consistently at such tasks.

The third kind of genotype → environment effect is the active, niche-picking or niche-building sort. People seek out environments they find compatible and stimulating. We all select from the surrounding environment some aspects to which to respond, learn about, or ignore. Our selections are correlated with motivational, personality, and intellectual aspects of our genotypes. The active genotype → environment effect, we argue, is the most powerful connection between people and their environments and the most direct expression of the genotype in experience. Examples of active genotype → environment effects can be found in the selective efforts of individuals in sports, scholarship, relationships—in life. Once experiences occur, they naturally lead to further experiences. We agree that phenotypes are elaborated and maintained by environments, but the impetus for the experience comes, we argue, from the genotype.

Developmental Changes in Genotype → Environment Effects   The second proposition is that the relative importance of the three kinds of genotype → environment effects changes over development from infancy to adolescence. In infancy much of the environment that reaches the child is provided by adults. When those adults are genetically related to the child, the environment they provide in general is positively related to their own characteristics and their own genotypes. Although infants are active in structuring their experiences by selectively attending to what is offered, they cannot do as much seeking out and niche-building as older children; thus, passive genotype → environment effects are more important for infants and young children than they are for older children, who can extend their experiences beyond the family's influences and create their own environments to a much greater extent. Thus, the effects of passive genotype → environment effects wane when the child has many extrafamilial opportunities.

In addition, parents can provide environments that are negatively related to the child's genotype, as illustrated earlier in teaching reading. Although parents' genotypes usually affect the environment they provide for their biological offspring, it is sometimes positive and sometimes negative and therefore not as direct a product of the young child's genotype as later environments will be. Thus, as stated in proposition 3, genotype → environment effects increase with development, as active replace pas-

sive forms. Genotype § environment effects of the evocative sort persist throughout life, as we elicit responses from others based on many personal, genotype-related characteristics from appearance to personality and intellect. Those responses from others reinforce and extend the directions our development has taken. High intelligence and adaptive skills in children from very disadvantaged backgrounds, for example, evoke approval and support from school personnel who might otherwise despair of the child's chances in life (Garmezy, Note 1). In adulthood, personality and intellectual differences evoke different responses in others. Similarities in personal characteristics evoke similar responses from others, as shown in the case of identical twins reared apart (Bouchard, Note 2). These findings are also consistent with the third proposition.

A Probabilistic Model   The concept of genotype → environment effects is emphasized in this emerging theory for three major reasons: the model results in a testable set of hypotheses for which disconfirmation would come from random association between genotypes and environments, it describes a developmental process, and it implies a *probabilistic* connection between a person and the environment. It is more likely that people with certain genotypes will receive certain kinds of parenting, evoke certain responses from others, and select certain aspects from the available environments; but nothing is rigidly determined. The idea of genetic differences, on the other hand, has seemed to imply to many that the person's developmental fate was preordained without regard to experience. This is absurd. By invoking the idea of genotype → environment effects, we hope to emphasize a probabilistic connection between genotypes and their environments. Although mismatches between the behaviors of parents and children certainly exist (see Nelson, 1973), we argue that on the average there are correlations of parents' characteristics and the rearing environment they provide.

There is a probable but not determinant connection between genotypes and phenotypes through the course of development in which environmental events deflect the course of the developing phenotype. A correlation remains between genotype and phenotype, even though one cannot specify in advance what environmental events will affect phenotypic development. To this conception, we add that genotypes shape many of their own experiences through evocative and active genotype → environment correlations.

THE ROLE OF THE ENVIRONMENT REVISITED

If genotypes are the driving force behind development and the determinants of what environments are experienced, does this mean that environments themselves have no effects? Clearly, environments are necessary for development and have effects on the average levels of development, but they may or may not cause variations among individuals (McCall, 1981). We argue like McCall that nature has not left essential human development at the mercy of experiences that may or may not be encountered; rather, the only necessary experiences are ones that are generally available to the species. Differences in experience per se, therefore, cannot be the major cause of variation among individuals. The major features of human development are programmed genetically and require experiences that are encountered by the vast majority of humankind in the course of living. Phenotypic variation among individuals relies on experiential differences that are determined by genetic differences rather than on differences among environmental effects that occur randomly.

Imposed Environments In developmental studies, we usually think of environments provided for a child, such as parental interaction, school curricula, and various experimental manipulations. In some cases there are passive and evocative genotype-environment correlations

that go unrecognized, as in parent-child interaction and the selection of children into school curricula. In a few cases there may be no correlation of the child's genotype with the treatment afforded an experimental group of which she is a member. On the other hand, it is impossible to ignore the attention and learning characteristics the child brings to the situation, so that the effects of environmental manipulations are never entirely free of individual differences in genotypes. Development is not necessarily constrained by genotype-environment correlations, although most often genotypes and environments are correlated in the real world, so that in fact, if not in principle, there are such constraints.

Sometimes, the influence of genotypes on environments is diminished through unusual positive or negative interventions, so that the environments experienced are less driven by genotypes and may even be negatively related to genotypes, as in the passive, familial situation. Examples of this effect can be found in studies of deprivation, adoption, and day care. Studies of children reared in isolation (Clarke & Clarke, 1976) and children reared in unstimulating institutions (Dennis & Najarian, 1951; Hunt, 1961, 1980) have demonstrated the adverse effects of deprived environments on many aspects of development. Such studies usually address average responses to these poor environments. In any case, studies of environments that are so extreme as to be outside of the normal range of rearing environments for the species have few implications for environmental variation that the vast majority of human children experience.

In contrast to the extremely poor environments in the deprivation literature, the adoption studies include only rearing environments in the range of adequate to very good. The evidence from studies of biologically related and adoptive families that vary in socioeconomic status from working to upper middle class is that most people experience what Scarr and Weinberg

(1978) have called "functionally-equivalent" environments. That is, the large array of individual differences among children and late adolescents adopted in infancy were not related to differences among their family environments—the same array of environmental differences that were and usually are associated with behavioral differences among children born to such families (Scarr, 1981; Scarr & Kidd, in press; Scarr & Weinberg, 1976, 1977, 1978). On the average, however, adopted children profit from their enriched environments, and they score above average on IQ and school achievement tests and on measures of personal adjustment.

Negative Genotype-Environment Correlations Environments provided to children that are negatively related to their genotypes can have dramatic effects on average levels of development. Extrafamilial interventions that provided unusual enrichments or deprivations can alter the developmental levels of children from those that would be predicted by their family backgrounds and estimated genotypes. Intervention theories predict these main effects (Caldwell & Richmond, 1968; Hunt, 1980).

Enriched day-care environments have been shown to enhance intellectual development of children from disadvantaged backgrounds (Ramey & Haskins, 1981; McCartney, Note 3). Similarly, less stimulating day-care environments can hamper children's intellectual and social development, even if they come from more advantaged families (McCartney, Scarr, Phillips, Grajek, & Schwarz, 1981; McCartney, Note 3).

These are, however, rather rare opportunities, or lack of same, providing negatively correlated experiences for genotypes. In the usual course of development beyond early childhood, individuals select and evoke experiences that are directly influenced by their genotypes and therefore positively correlated with their own phenotypic characteristics.

Environmental effects on averages versus individuals One must distinguish environmental events that on the average enhance or delay development for all children from those that account for *variation* among children. There can be "main effects" that account for variation among groups that are naturally or experimentally treated in different ways. Within the groups of children there still remain enormous individual differences, some of which arise in response to the treatment. It is rare that the variation *between* groups approaches the magnitude of differences *within* groups, as represented in the pervasive overlapping distributions of scores. In developmental psychology, we have usually been satisfied if the treatment observed or implemented produced a statistically reliable difference between groups, but we have rarely examined the sources of differential responsiveness within the groups.

Most often, the same treatments that alter the average performance of a group seem to have similar effects on most members of the group. Otherwise, we would find a great deal of variance in genotype-environment interactions; that is, what's sauce for the goose would be poison for the gander. For the kinds of deprivation or interventions studied most often in developmental psychology, the main effects seem not to change the rank orders of children affected. The main effects are real, but they are also small by comparison to the range of individual variation within groups so treated or not. Some children may be more responsive than others to the treatment, but we doubt that there are many situations in which disordinal interactions are the rule. Very few children lose developmental points by participating in Headstart or gain by being severely neglected in infancy. The search for aptitude-treatment interactions (Cronbach & Snow, 1977) and genotype-environment interactions (Erlenmeyer-Kimling, 1972) have not produced dramatic or reliable results.

In studies of adoptive and biologically re-lated families, the correlation of children's IQ scores with the educational level of biological parents is about .35, whether or not the parents rear their children (Scarr & Weinberg, 1977, 1978). Adopted children on the average have higher IQ scores than their biological parents as a result of the influence of their above-average adoptive parents. Taken together, these find-ings support the claim that treatments can have main effects without overcoming genetic differ-ences in children's responsiveness to those environments. Adopted children have IQ scores above those of their biological parents, yet the *correlations* of adopted children are higher with their biological than adoptive par-ents (Scarr & Weinberg, 1977, 1978). The aver-age effects of treatments, such as adoption, seem to increase the mean IQ scores, but they do not seem to affect the rank order of the children's scores with respect to their biological parents, and it is on rank orders, not means, that correlations depend. These results imply that the effect of adoptive families is to increase the scores of adopted children above those which would be predicted by their biological parents, but not to alter radically the rank order of individual differences among children they rear. And so it is, we think, with most treat-ments.

ANSWERING QUESTIONS FROM PREVIOUS RESEARCH ON TWINS AND FAMILIES

Neither extreme genetic determinism nor naive environmentalism can account for seemingly anomalous findings from research on twins and families. Three puzzling questions remain, the first of which concerns the *process* by which monozygotic (MZ) twins (twins who come from the same divided zygote or fertilized egg and who are thus genetically identical) come to be more similar than dizygotic (DZ) twins (twins who come from different zygotes and thus are no more genetically similar than other sibling pairs), and biological siblings more similar tha-nadopted siblings on all measurable character-istics, at least by the end of adolescence (Scarr & Weinberg, 1978). The second question con-cerns the declining similarities between DZ twins and adopted siblings from infancy to adolescence. The third question arises from the unexpected similarities between identical twins reared in different homes.

A theory of genotype-environment correla-tion can account for these findings by pointing to the degree of genetic resemblance and the degree of similarity in the environments that would be experienced by the co-twins and sibs.

Genetic Resemblance Determines Environmen-tal Similarity The expected degree of environ-mental similarity for a pair of relatives can be thought of as the product of a person's own genotype $\rightarrow$ environment path and the genetic correlation of the pair. On the assumption that individuals' environments are equally influ-enced by their own genotypes, the similarity in the environments of two individuals becomes a function of their genetic resemblance. These relationships can be used to answer question 1 concerning the process by which MZ twins come to be more similar than DZ twins and biological siblings more similar than adopted siblings. For identical twins, the relationship of one twin's environment with the other's geno-type is the same as the correlation of the twin's environment with her own genotype. Thus, one would certainly predict what is often observed: that the hobbies, food preferences, choices of friends, academic achievements, and so forth of the MZ twins are very similar (Scarr & Carter-Saltzman, 1980). Kamin (1974) proposed that all of this environmental similarity is imposed on MZ co-twins because they look so much alike. Theories of genetic resemblance do not speak to how close resemblances arise. We propose that the home environments provided by the parents, the responses that the co-twins evoke from others, and the active choices they make in their environments lead to striking similarities through genotypically determined correlations in their learning histories.

The same explanation applies, of course, to the greater resemblance of biological than adopted siblings. The environment of one biological sib is correlated to the genotype of the other sibling's environment because of the similarity in their genotype. The same is true for DZ twins. It should be noted however that these similarities are much less than the identical resemblances of monozygotic twins (MZ). There is a very small genetic correlation for intelligence between adopted siblings in most studies that arises from selective placement of the offspring of similar mothers in the same adoptive home. More important for this theory, however, is the selective placement of adopted children to match the intellectual characteristics of the adoptive parents. This practice allows adoptive parents to create a positive, passive genotype-environment correlation for their adopted children in early childhood, when the theory asserts that this kind of correlation is most important. In fact, the selective placement estimates from studies by Scarr and Weinberg (1977) can account for most of the resemblance between adoptive parents and their children. In addition, adoptive parents, like their biological counterparts, can provide negative genotype-environment correlations that assure that their several children will not differ too much on important skills, such as reading.

Changing Similarities Among Siblings The second question left unanswered by previous research concerned the declining similarities of dizygotic twins and adopted siblings from infancy to adolescence. It is clear from Matheny, Wilson, Dolan, and Krantz's (1981) longitudinal study of MZ and DZ twins that the DZ correlations for intelligence of .60 – .75 are higher than genetic theory would predict in infancy and early childhood. For school age and older twins, DZ correlations were the usual .55. Similarly, the intelligence correlations of a sample of late adolescent adopted siblings were zero,

compared to the .25 – .39 correlations of the samples of adopted children in early to middle childhood (Scarr & Weinberg, 1978).

Neither environmental nor genetic theories can effectively address these data. How can it be that the longer you live with someone, the less like them you become? One could evoke some ad hoc environmental theory about sibling relationships becoming more competitive, or "deidentified," but that would not account for the continued, moderate intellectual resemblance of biological siblings. Genetic theory has, of course, nothing to say about decreasing twin resemblance or any resemblance among young adoptees.

The theory put forward here predicts that the relative importance of passive versus active genotype-environment correlations changes with age. Recall that passive genotype-environment correlations are created by parents who provide children with both genes and environments, which are then correlated. Certainly in the case of DZ twins, whose prenatal environment was shared and whose earliest years are spent being treated in most of the same ways at the same time by the same parents, the passive genotype → environment effect is greater than that for ordinary sibs. Biological and adopted siblings do not, of course, share the same developmental environments at the same time because they differ in age. The passive genotype-environment correlation still operates for siblings, because they have the same parents, but to a lesser extent than for twins. (See Table 1.)

Monozygotic twin correlations for intellectual competence do not decline when active genotype-environment correlations outweigh the importance of the passive ones, because MZ co-twins typically select highly correlated environments anyway. Dizygotic pairs, on the other hand, are no more genetically related than sibs, so that as the intense similarity of their early home environments gives way to their own choices, they select environments that are

TABLE 1   THE SIMILARITY OF CO-TWIN'S AND SIBLING'S GENOTYPES AND ENVIRONMENTS DUE TO:

		Correlations in the environments of related pairs	
	Genetic Correlation	Passive genotype → environment effects in early development	Active genotype → environment effects in early development
MZ twins	1.00	High	High
DZ twins	.52	High	Moderate
Biological siblings	.52	Moderate	Moderate
Adopted siblings	.01	Moderate	Low

less similar than their previous environments and about as similar as those of ordinary sibs.

Adopted sibs, on the other hand, move from an early environment, in which mother may have produced similarity, to environments of their own choosing. Because their genotypes are hardly correlated at all, neither are their chosen environmental niches. Thus, by late adolescence, adopted siblings do not resemble each other in intelligence, personality, interests, or other phenotypic characteristics (Grotevant, Scarr, & Weinberg, 1977; Scarr, Webber, Weinberg, & Wittig, 1981; Scarr & Weinberg, 1978).

Biological siblings' early environments, like those of adopted children, lead to trait similarity as a result of passive genotype → environmental effects. As biological siblings move into the larger world and begin to make active choices, their niches remain moderately correlated because their genotypes remain moderately correlated. There is no marked shift in intellectual resemblance of biological sibs as the process of active genotype → environment influence replaces the passive one.

Identical Twins Reared Apart   The third question concerned the unexpected degree of resemblance between identical twins reared mostly apart. With the theory of genotype → environment effects, their resemblance is not surprising. Given opportunities to attend selectively to and choose from varied opportunities, identical genotypes are expected to make similar choices. They are also expected to evoke similar responses from others and from their physical environments. The fact that they were reared in different homes and different communities is not important; differences in their development could arise only if the experiential opportunities of one or both were very restricted, so that similar choices could not have been made. According to previous studies (Juel-Nielsen, 1980; Newman, Freeman, & Holzinger, 1937; Shields, 1962) and the recent research of Bouchard and colleagues at the University of Minnesota (Bouchard, Note 2), the most dissimilar pairs of MZs reared apart are those in which one was severely restricted in environmental opportunity. Extreme deprivation or unusual enrichment can diminish the influence of genotype and environment and therefore lessen the resemblance of identical twins reared apart.

SUMMARY

In summary, the theory of genotype → environment correlations proposed here describes the usual course of human development in terms of three kinds of genotype-environment correlations that posit cooperative efforts of the nature-nurture team, directed by the genetic quarterback. Both genes and environments are constituents in the developmental system, but they have different roles. Genes direct the course of human experience, but experiential opportunities are also necessary for development to occur. Individual differences can arise from restrictions in environmental opportunities to experience what the genotype would find compatible. With a rich array of opportunities, however, most differences among people arise from genetically determined differences in the experiences to which they are attracted and which they evoke from their environments.

The theory also accounts for individual differences in responsiveness to environments—differences that are not primarily interactions of genotypes and environments but roughly linear combinations that are better described as genotype-environment correlations. In addition, the theory accounts for seemingly anomalous results from previous research on twins and families.

Most important, the theory addresses the issue of process. Rather than presenting a static view of individual differences through variance allocation, this theory hypothesizes processes by which genotypes and environments combine across development to make us both human and unique.

REFERENCE NOTES

1 Garmezy, N. *The case for the single case in experimental-developmental psychology.* Paper presented at the annual meeting of the American Psychological Association, Los Angeles, August 1981.
2 Bouchard, T. *The Minnesota study of twins reared apart: Description and preliminary findings.* Paper presented at the annual meeting of the American Psychological Association, August 1981.
3 McCartney, K. *The effect of quality of day care environment upon children's language development.* Unpublished doctoral dissertation, Yale University, 1982.
4 Cole, M., & The Laboratory of Comparative Human Cognition. *Niche-picking.* Unpublished manuscript, University of California, San Diego, 1980.

REFERENCES

Bell, R. Q. A reinterpretation of the direction of effects in studies of socialization, *Psychological Review,* 1968, **75**, 81–95.

Bersheid, E., & Walster, E. Physical attractiveness. In L. Berkowitz (Ed.), *Advances in experimental social psychology.* New York: Academic Press, 1974.

Caldwell, B. M., & Richmond, I. The Children's Center in Syracuse. In L. Dittman (Ed.), *Early child: The new perspectives.* New York: Atherton, 1968.

Chomsky, N. On cognitive structures and their development: A reply to Piaget. In M. Piattelli-Palmarini (Ed.), *Language and learning: The debate between Jean Piaget and Noam Chomsky.* Cambridge, Mass.: Harvard University Press, 1980.

Chomsky, N., & Fodor, J. Statement of the paradox. In M. Piattelli-Palmarini (Ed.), *Language and learning: The debate between Jean Piaget and Noam Chomsky.* Cambridge, Mass.: Harvard University Press, 1980.

Clarke, A. M., & Clarke, A. D. B. *Early experience: Myth and evidence.* New York: Free Press, 1976.

Connolly, K. J., & Prechtl, H. F. R. (Eds.), *Maturation and development: Biological and psychological perspectives.* Philadelphia: Lippincott, 1981.

Cronbach, L. J., & Snow, R. E. *Attitudes and instructional methods.* New York: Irvington, 1977.

Dennis, W., & Najarian, P. Infant development under environmental handicap. *Psychological Monographs,* 1951, **71** (7, Whole No. 436).

Erlenmeyer-Kimling, L. Gene-environment interactions and the variability of behavior. In L. Ehrman, G. Omenn, & E. Caspair (Eds.), *Genetics, environment and behavior.* New York: Academic Press, 1972.

Escalona, S. C. *The roots of individuality.* Chicago: Aldine, 1968.

Gesell, A., & Ilg, F. L. *Infant and child in the culture of today.* New York: Harper & Bros., 1943.

Gottlieb, G. The role of experience in the development of behavior in the nervous system. In G. Gottlieb (Ed.), *Studies in the development of behavior and the nervous system.* Vol. **3** *Development and neural and behavioral specificity.* New York: Academic Press, 1976.

Grotevant, H. D., Scarr, S., & Weinberg, R. A. Patterns of interest similarity in adoptive andbiological families. *Journal of Personality and Social Psychology,* 1977, **35**, 667–678.

Hunt, J. McV. *Intelligence and experience.* New York: Ronald, 1961.

Hunt, J. McV. *Early psychological development and experience.* Worcester, Mass.: Clark University Press, 1980.

Juel-Nielsen, N. *Individual and environment: Monozygotic twins reared apart.* New York: International Universities Press, 1980.

Kamin, L.J. *The science and politics of IQ.* Potomac, Md.: Erlbaum, 1974.

Lytton, H. *Parent-child interaction: The socialization process observed in twin and single families.* New York: Plenum, 1980.

McCall, R.B. Nature-nurture and the two realms of development: A proposed integration with respect to mental development. *Child Development,* 1981, **52**, 1–12.

McCartney, K., Scarr, S., Phillips, D., Grajek, S., & Schwarz, J. C. Environmental differences among day care centers and their effects on children's development. In E. F. Zigler & E. W. Gordon (Eds.), *Day care: Scientific and social policy issues.* Boston: Auburn House, 1981.

Maccoby, E. E. *Social development.* New York: Harcourt, Brace, Jovanovich, 1980.

Matheny, A. P., Jr., Wilson, R. S., Dolan, A. B., & Krantz, J. Z. Behavioral contrasts in twinships: Stability and patterns of differences in childhood. *Child Development,* 1981, **52**, 579–598.

Murstein, B.I. Physical attractiveness and marital choice. *Journal of Personality and Social Psychology,* 1972, **22**, 8–12.

Nelson, K. Structure and strategy in learning to talk. *Monographs of the Society for Research in Child Development,* 1973, **38** (1-2, Serial No. 149).

Nerlove, S. B., & Snipper, A. S. Cognitive consequences of cultural opportunity. In R. H. Munroe, R. L. Munroe, & B. B. Whiting (Eds.), *Handbook of cross-cultural human development.* New York: Garland, 1981.

Newman, H. G., Freeman, F. N., & Holzinger, K. J. *Twins: A study of heredity and environment.* Chicago: University of Chicago Press, 1937.

Piaget, J. The psychogenesis of knowledge and its epistemological significance. In M. Piattelli-Palmarini (Ed.), *Language and learning: The debate between Jean Piaget and Noam Chomsky.*

Cambridge, Mass.: Harvard University Press, 1980.

Plomin, R., DeFries, J. C., & Loehlin, J. C. Genotype-environment interaction and correlation in the analysis of human behavior. *Psychological Bulletin,* 1977, **84**, 309–322.

Ramey, C .T., & Haskins, R. The modification of intelligence through early experience. *Intelligence,* 1981, **5**, 5–19.

Scarr, S. *IQ: Race, social class and individual differences, new studies of old problems.* Hillsdale, N.J.: Erlbaum, 1981.

Scarr, S., & Carter-Saltzman, L. Twin method: Defense of a critical assumption. *Behavior Genetics,* 1980, **9**, 527–542.

Scarr, S., & Kidd, K. K. Behavior genetics. In M. Haith & J. Campos (Eds.), *Manual of child psychology: Infancy and the biology of development.* (Vol. 2). New York: Wiley, in press.

Scarr, S., Webber, P. L., Weinberg, R. A., & Wittig, M. A. Personality resemblance among adolescents and their parents in biologically-related and adoptive families. *Journal of Personality and Social Psychology,* 1981, **40**, 885–898.

Scarr, S., & Weinberg, R. A. IQ test performance of black children adopted by white families. *American Psychologist,* 1976, **31**, 726–739.

Scarr, S., & Weinberg, R. A. Intellectual similarities within families of both adopted and biological children. *Intelligence,* 1977, **1** (2), 170–191.

Scarr, S., & Weinberg, R. A. The influence of "family background" on intellectual attainment. *American Sociological Review,* 1978, **43**, 674–692.

Scarr, S., & Weinberg, R. A. The Minnesota adoption studies: Genetic differences and malleability. *Child Development,* in this issue.

Scarr-Salapatek, S. An evolutionary perspective on infant intelligence. In M. Lewis (Ed.), *Origins of intelligence: Infancy and early childhood.* N.Y.: Plenum, 1976.

Shields, J. *Monozygotic twins brought up apart and brought up together.* London: Oxford University Press, 1962.

Waddington, C.H. *New patterns in genetics and development.* New York: Columbia University Press, 1962.

Watson, E.H., & Lowrey, G. H. *Growth and development of children.* Chicago: Year Book Medical Publishers, 1967.

Environmental Toxins and Behavioral Development

Greta G. Fein
Pamela M. Schwartz
Sandra W. Jacobson
Joseph L. Jacobson

During the 1960s, a large number of infants were born with peculiar malformations—missing ears and fingers, undeveloped limbs—that were soon discovered to have resulted from the ingestion of thalidomide by their mothers during pregnancy. Subsequent research established a surprisingly precise relationship between the time of drug consumption during pregnancy and the infant's particular malformation (Tuchmann-Duplessis, 1975). The general conclusion from this research is that developing structures are most vulnerable during the period of their most rapid development. The thalidomide incident offers a dramatic example of the effects of environmental stresses *in utero* (i.e., teratogens) on the development of the human organism.

Since the thalidomide incident, other substances have joined the list of known or suspected teratogens. Some of these are knowingly consumed (e.g., alcohol and nicotine), whereas others are unlabeled contaminants found in air or food (e.g., lead, methylmercury, and the chlorinated hydrocarbons). Although for many of these substances exposure at high levels is known to be harmful, the unsettled and more difficult question is whether chronic exposure at low and asymptomatic levels is also harmful.

In many cases of pre- or postnatal exposure to toxic substances, gross structural abnormalities and characteristic clinical signs are not present. Rather, the effects appear in less easily discernible conditions that, under low levels of exposure, may be quite subtle (Weiss & Spyker, 1974). In some instances, these conditions consist of slightly reduced birth size or an increased susceptibility to infection. In others, toxic effects appear as subtle behavioral alterations that in themselves may not be especially alarming. These alterations are of interest in teratogenic testing for several reasons. First, they may signal the early stages of an ongoing toxic process that will become more disabling with age. Second, a chemical agent that produces subtle behavioral alterations in many children may produce a major impairment in those who are especially susceptible because of genetic or other factors. Third, for the child's parents, some chemically induced behavioral effects (e.g., hyper- or hypo-irritability) may make a child difficult to care for, leading to parent-child tensions that become amplified and aggravated over time. In this context, the assessment of subtle behavioral deficits has become an important tool for determining the teratogenicity of environmentally ubiquitous chemical substances.

The need for assessing these behavioral alterations provides an unusual opportunity for psychologists to apply theoretical and methodological advances in the field to problems of considerable social consequence. In addition, as the thalidomide incident illustrates, these substances create "natural" experiments through which the mechanisms of human development can be better understood. This opportunity is accompanied by the need to establish a close working relationship with researchers in a variety of disciplines—toxicology, neuropharmacology, epidemiology, biochemistry, pediatrics, and obstetrics—each with different technical vocabularies, concepts, and research styles. Evidence of harm to human beings suggests the need for protective public policies that provoke controversies to which psychologists may not be accustomed. New evidence that a particular chemical compound is teratogenic in humans is rarely welcome. There is often a failure to distinguish the bearer of bad tidings and the tidings, and even among scientists the exchange may become vituperative (see, for example, "UK and Sweden Attack Lead Poisoning Studies," 1979).

In this article, we discuss the psychologist's emerging role in an area of study once exclusively the concern of medicine, toxicology, and related disciplines. Although psychologists are involved in the testing of a variety of pharmaceutical agents (popularly available drugs as well as prescribed medications), material for this article has been drawn largely from the literature on environmental toxins, especially those likely to endanger the born and unborn child. Because many of these toxins are widespread, tasteless, odorless, and colorless, large numbers of children and prospective parents may be exposed inadvertently and chronically. Of the many substances that have these characteristics, a few—lead, mercury, and the polychlorinated biphenyls (PCBs)—have attracted special interest because of their known toxic effects at high levels of exposure. Because these chemicals are routinely present in the environment at relatively low levels, psychologists have become increasingly involved in determining whether chronic exposure at such levels produces subtle behavioral effects.

In the following discussion, we first consider behavioral teratology in relation both to the overt disease model that once dominated the study of environmental contaminants and to the emerging multiple-effects model that better accommodates recent findings. Then we examine the notion of subtle behavioral outcomes and the importance of developmental concepts in contemporary teratogenic assessment. Finally, we discuss the essential and complementary relation between animal and human models in determining the conditions under which toxic exposure damages the immature organism.

BEHAVIORAL TERATOLOGY

In a seminal paper, Spyker (1975) defined teratology as the "study of the adverse effects of the environment...on developing systems" (p. 1836). In contrast to the traditional view that saw teratology as the study of monster-producing agents (the term itself is derived from *teratos,* monster, and *gens,* producing), Spyker's definition embodies a broader notion of the effects chemical agents might produce. These effects include morphological, maturational, reproductive, and behavioral disorders. The type of effect depends on genetic predisposition, the period in development when exposure occurs, and the period in which the assessment is made, as well as on the particular chemical, dosage, and duration of exposure. The study of teratogenic agents thus requires a concern with multiple effects and developmental processes. Within this broadened definition of teratology, behavioral teratology is that aspect of study concerned with the assessment of subtle behavioral disturbances from birth to maturity. This new domain marks a major departure from earlier conceptions of toxic effects on human beings.

Toxicity as Overt Disease

In ancient times, the poisoner and the physician, although both interested in chemical substances, pursued separate professional paths, each serving discrete and even opposing social functions. The poisoner, as state executioner and at times assassin, studied chemicals as instruments of death, carefully recording type, dose, and effect. For the assassin, it was important to discover tasteless, odorless, and colorless substances that mimicked death from natural causes. The physician, too, studied the effects of chemical compounds, more often as cures, infrequently as causes. Although the

Roman physician-philosopher Nicander (ca 200 BCE) associated "lead colic" with litharge—a lead oxide added as a sweetener and preservative to cider, wine, and fruit juices—the notion that chemical compounds might inadvertently cause human affliction was a notion whose time had not come. Almost 2,000 years later, when the industrial revolution brought large numbers of people into occupational contact with chemicals such as lead and mercury, poisoning in some industries reached epidemic proportions. Toxicology and medicine began to converge when it was discovered that mercury vapor inflicted madness on the mirror makers of Venice and the hatters of London, and that the dust of lead oxides visited cramps, paralysis, and convulsions on the painters of Paris (Bidstrup, 1964; Dana, 1848).

Physicians of the 18th and 19th centuries brought the concept of disease to the study of these chemically induced occupational disorders. If afflictions such as smallpox or typhoid fever could be cataloged as distinctive configurations of overt signs and symptoms, why not use the same procedure to catalog occupational afflictions? In the case of lead poisoning, this approach was further encouraged because lead could be readily detected in the blue-grey discoloring of teeth and gums and yellowish hue of an afflicted worker's skin. When the source of exposure could be unambiguously determined, detailed observation revealed a range of disorders associated with such exposure.

Tanquerel des Planches's classic 1838 study of Parisienne workers poisoned by the lead powder used in paint and cosmetics solidified the marriage between the study of poisons and the study of disease (Dana, 1848). Because the problem had reached epidemic proportions, Tanquerel was able to study intensively more than a thousand poisoned workers, listing symptoms and determining the working conditions responsible for them. Tanquerel claimed that there were four "diseases" of lead—colic (characterized by gastrointestinal disorders),

arthralgy (pain in the limbs, muscle contractions), paralysis (loss of voluntary motion or sensation), and encephalopathy (delirium, coma, and convulsions). In keeping with the disease model, Tanquerel argued that these diseases were distinct, independent, and specific to lead. This cataloging effort was aided by the fact that Tanquerel's hospitalized subjects were all suffering from acute poisoning. Although information about the onset of his patients' troubles was inevitably retrospective, Tanquerel conscientiously recorded the "precursors" of the poisoning—numbness in the case of lead arthralgy, sensations of lassitude, heaviness, numbness, and trembling in the case of lead paralysis. He even noted that these symptoms might provide advance warning of poisoning, although the workplace was so obviously hazardous that subtle warnings were less important than improved industrial hygiene.

Subclinical Toxicity

In the course of visits to the workplaces of his patients, Tanquerel noted that persons working side by side did not necessarily contract the overt disease and that if they did, some persons became ill sooner than others. It was puzzling to him that one attack seemed to predispose another, even though the patient appeared to have been cured. Tanquerel worried about these issues because, according to the disease model employed at the time, disease was an all-or-nothing condition; the patient either remained well or became ill, recovered or died.

The disease model of toxicity received its first major challenge over a century later, in the aftermath of the methylmercury poisoning incident in Minamata, Japan (Smith & Smith, 1975; Takeuchi, 1972b). In 1956, an unusual neurological disorder attacked persons living in this seaside village, and by 1958, when the cause was discovered, 184 persons had become overtly ill or had died. Methylmercury, discharged from a vinyl acetate plant into the water, had contaminated fish consumed by the villagers. The discharge was stopped, and the consumption of fish ceased until mercury levels in the fish returned to normal. By 1962, however, 58 new cases of Minamata poisoning were identified, and by 1974 the toll had climbed to 798 (Smith & Smith, 1975). These persons had had no clinical signs of toxicity at the time of the incident and many had not been subsequently exposed, but their disorders and autopsies revealed the pathological neural damage characteristic of methylmercury poisoning (Takeuchi, 1972a).

Influenced by the disease model, Takeuchi (1972a) described three "diseases" of methylmercury poisoning. In the *complete* type, the patient suffers ataxia, emotional instability, visual and auditory impairment, and locomotor difficulties. In the *incomplete* type, there is only one clinically evident sign. In the *latent* type, there are no clinically obvious signs at first; signs of poisoning appear later, sometimes as much as 10 years later. Thus, persons exposed to chemical agents may be initially asymptomatic—at least from the perspective of the traditional model in which toxicity is defined in terms of overt, clinically evident, well-delineated manifestations. But these persons may be only apparently asymptomatic; signs of poisoning initially detectable as subtle effects may become overt over time or at higher levels of exposure.

The Concept of Threshold

When poisons are given in incremental doses and the outcome of interest is overt disease or death, there is often a discernible dosage level below which the outcome is unlikely and above which the outcome occurs in most exposed individuals. The concept of threshold was important historically when exposure, a continuous variable, was treated as a categorical variable (e.g., the lethal dose) matched to a categorical outcome (e.g., disease or death). However, the notion of threshold becomes considerably complicated in the face of "precur-

sors" and asymptomatic toxicity. Consider precursors of lead toxicity such as Tanquerel's "lassitude" or signs of chronic, low-level methylmercury toxicity such as tremors (Hunter, Branford, & Russell, 1940). The threshold for toxicity will vary depending on the response used to assess the effect. If precursors are of interest, the threshold will be low, whereas if death is of interest, the threshold will typically be higher. Biochemical alterations often appear at relatively low levels of exposure, but these alterations may have few consequences for the functioning, longevity, or vigor of an organism (Dinman & Hecker, 1972; Needleman, 1980). At some concentration of a toxic substance, the first functional alterations appear. In low-level, chronic, methylmercury poisoning, tremors may be discernible in a person's shaky handwriting, difficulty in drinking from a glass without spilling, and in other tasks requiring fine muscle control and coordination (Bidstrup, 1964). But these signs may not be present in all exposed persons. In some, there may be general fatigue, in others an impairment of memory, and in others an inability to concentrate.

The effects of low-level, chronic, chemical exposure are of special interest in the case of 20th-century chemicals such as the PCBs. These chemicals—thermally stable, adhesive, and resistant to biodegradation—achieved widespread industrial use in products such as electrical transformers, carbonless paper, and paint. As a result of carelessness in their disposal, these chemicals are found in the soil, water, and wildlife, as well as in the bodies of humans living in industrialized nations. Since these compounds are remarkably lipophilic (i.e., fat soluble) and poorly metabolized, they become more concentrated at each level of the aquatic food chain (Swain, 1981; WHO, 1978). Relatively high levels of PCB contamination are found in fatty predatory fish (e.g., salmon) feeding in polluted waters and in the blood of persons who ingest these fish (Jacobson, Jacob son, Schwartz, & Fein, 1983; Kreiss et al., 1981; Schwartz, Jacobson, Fein, & Jacobson, 1983; Humphrey, Note 1).

PCB toxicity at high levels of exposure has been demonstrated in separate incidents in Japan and Taiwan when children and adults consumed rice oil accidentally contaminated with highly concentrated PCBs. Exposed individuals exhibited a set of clinical characteristics including chloracne, brown pigmentation of the skin, facial swelling, and sensory neuropathy known in the literature as *Yusho* disease (Higuchi, 1976; Wong & Hwang, 1981). Whether chronic low-level exposure common in industrial nations today is also harmful is as yet unknown.

For any particular chemical, what then is the lowest dose at which an adverse functional outcome occurs? The problem in establishing a minimal threshold (or "safe" level) for adverse health effects is that (a) even at the behavioral level, no single effect will appear in all persons; (b) any particular effect may be more or less pronounced, measurable in degrees as well as in its presence or absence; and (c) sensitive measures of dysfunction will yield lower thresholds than crude measures.

Multiple Effects

Tanquerel (Dana, 1848, p. 12) asked two questions, unanswered in his study and ignored until recently. First, when people are apparently exposed to the same toxin under the same conditions, "Why then is not the manifestation...in the system the same?" Second, "Why is there a greater disposition [in some people] to be attacked by one form of lead disease than by another?"

The assessment categories listed in Table 1 imply a multiple-effects model of teratogenic impact. For any given dose of a particular chemical, different individuals might exhibit different effects depending on genetic predisposition or the presence of a prior sensitizing condition. Furthermore, some individuals might exhibit multiple ailments, others only

one, and still others none. Under high levels of exposure, these multiple effects appear as a set of characteristic clinical signs (e.g., Minamata disease in the case of methylmercury poisoning, *Yusho* disease in the case of PCB poisoning).

However, under low levels of chronic exposure, the effects are unlikely to be characteristic of a particular compound. Conditions such as fatigue, apathy, emotional lability, and tremors may appear in persons exposed to a variety of toxic agents—inorganic as well as organic mercury, lead, and PCBs. Although studies of acute poisoning can indicate the domains in which effects are likely, during the preliminary stages of teratological research a variety of possible behavioral outcomes such as those indicated in Table 1 must be monitored.

Once the data are in hand, the use of univariate analyses to determine toxicity at low levels may be inappropriate, since the toxicity of a substance may only be evident when the combined impact of several small effects is evaluated. Multivariate analyses can also be used to determine the exposure levels at which these effects are likely to appear. Conceivably, scaling techniques can be used to ascertain whether, for a given chemical, these effects can be conceptualized as an ordered sequence related to degree of exposure or whether, by contrast, they reflect patterns of individual vulnerability.

In sum, even at high levels of exposure, some intoxicated persons may not display overt clinical signs of poisoning. Rather, evidence of poisoning may appear in subtle behavioral alterations and in emotional or sensorimotor difficulties discernible only when the individual is observed systematically over time in carefully designed assessment situations. At low levels of exposure, the effects may be predominantly behavioral and may differ in different individuals. For these reasons, the overt disease model of toxicity is being replaced by a multiple-effects model that includes subtle behavioral alterations and covert physical changes in addition to overt clinical signs.

TABLE 1   ASSESSMENT CATEGORIES IN THE EVALUATION OF TERATOGENIC EFFECTS

Assessment category	Illustration	Age of testing
1. Morphological characteristics	Limb or facial anomalies	Birth to maturity
2. Physical characteristics	Discoloration of the skin; facial swelling	Birth to maturity
3. Maturational landmarks	Preterm birth (neuromuscular and physical immaturity)	Birth
4. Growth	Small birth size; depressed postnatal growth	Birth to maturity
5. Reflexes	Poorly organized sucking; depressed reactions	Birth to maturity
6. Activity levels	Hypo- and hyperactivity; clinical assessment of apathy	Birth to maturity
7. Neuromuscular and sensory motor capacities	Poor hand-eye coordination (swimming in mice)	Postbirth to maturity
8. Sensory and attentional functions	Deficits in visual, auditory, or olfactory functions; numbness	Birth to maturity
9. Learning ability	Alternation and reversal learning deficits in monkeys; low IQ	Postbirth to maturity
10. Autonomic regulation	Depressed response to stress; emotional lability; tremulousness in infants	Birth to maturity
11. Sexual development	Reproductive failure; menstrual irregularities	Maturity

SUBTLE BEHAVIORAL OUTCOMES

The analogy of chemically induced illness to biological diseases suggested that when an afflicted person is removed from further exposure and the ailments subside, the person is cured. Although some biological diseases may have easily observed sequelae (e.g., the facial disfigurements of smallpox), historically these outcomes did not play a major role in the investigation of these diseases. In contrast, temporary and permanent sequelae have recently become a major issue in the study of exposure to chemical agents.

In the 1930s, informed medical opinion held that children experiencing lead encephalopathy suffered no serious consequences once the overt symptoms subsided and the children were removed from continued exposure (McKhann, 1932). This opinion was challenged by Byers and Lord (1943), the first investigators to use behavioral measures and a partial longitudinal design in the assessment of toxic outcomes. Children in the Byers and Lord study had been hospitalized for overt lead poisoning based on a combination of biological signs (e.g., lead lines on the gums, abnormal quantities in stools and urine, or lead deposits in bone revealed in roentgenograms), a known source of exposure,

and clinical symptoms. The mildest case, a 10-month-old baby who had chewed her recently painted crib, was irritable, anorexic, and anemic. The most severe cases were clearly encephalopathic. When studied two to eight years after their discharge from the hospital, all children but one were doing poorly in school, most were irritable, unpredictable, and distractible, and most did poorly on tests requiring fine sensorimotor coordination. These children were also evaluated using psychometric tests. Of the 19 children for whom IQ scores were available, 17 scored better than 80. But this rather mild retardation was typically accompanied by emotional lability, difficulty in concentrating, and variability in school performance. Of the six children whose IQ scores ranged from 95 to 106, only one did well in school. Two children were tested twice, about six years apart, and in each case, test scores dropped— 18 points for one child and 21 points for another. Although the study lacked a control group and quantitative analyses were not used, it attracted attention because it indicated that children who were not grossly abnormal might nevertheless be permanently handicapped psychologically by lead poisoning early in life. However, the children involved in this study were all to some extent symptomatic. What of exposed children who have no history of overt lead poisoning?

As recently as 1971, a whole-blood lead level of 40 ng/dl (nanograms/deciliter) or more was considered by the U.S. Surgeon General to be indicative of "undue lead absorption," and a confirmed lead level of 80 ng/dl or more was considered to represent "unequivocal lead poisoning" (Surgeon General of the United States, 1971). When it became apparent that clinically symptomatic children might have lower levels and that children who failed to display overt lead toxicity might have high body burdens (Guinee, 1972), the level indicative of undue lead absorption was lowered to 30 ng/dl (U.S. Department of Health, Education and Welfare, 1978). Using these criteria, 7% of the 2 million children screened between 1972 and 1978 were found to have undue lead absorption, with incidences above 17% in cities such as Newark, Philadelphia, Milwaukee, and St. Louis. The question still to be settled is what these biological criteria of exposure mean for an individual's functioning and development.

Numerous studies have attempted to evaluate the level of lead exposure likely to produce asymptomatic poisoning and long-term behavioral deficits (see Bornschein, Pearson, & Reiter, 1980a; Gregory & Mohan, 1977; and Ratcliffe, 1981, for different assessments of this literature). One study stands out for its well-delineated exposure groups, its consideration of confounding variables, and its use of extensive behavioral assessment (Needleman et al., 1979).

In this retrospective study, Needleman et al. used lead in the deciduous teeth of first and second graders as a cumulative measure of exposure to lead. The investigators excluded from the study children who had had overt symptoms of lead poisoning in the past. Measures used to assess subtle behavioral deficits included teachers' ratings on an 11-item scale, the Wechsler Intelligence Scale for Children-Revised (WISC-R), the Seashore rhythm test, sentence repetition, and reaction time under various delay intervals. Although high-lead children showed deficits on all these measures, the IQ difference was only a modest 4.5 points, statistically significant but perhaps of dubious biological or social significance. In response to this criticism, Needleman, Leviton, and Bellinger (1982) noted that the shift of a few points in the normal distribution had dramatic effects on the tails of the distribution. Children with elevated lead levels were substantially more likely to have IQs below 80 and less likely to have IQs above 125.

Whether these performance effects are different expressions of a common deficit or represent outcomes in different individuals cannot be determined from the analyses in this study. Moreover, a retrospective study cannot determine the age of exposure or the level at which these subtle effects occur, because the lead sequestered in bony tissue provides a cumulative measure from which information about peaks and duration cannot be obtained. Despite these problems, this study exemplifies how the measurement of subtle behavioral outcomes has come to offer a promising strategy for determining the teratogenicity of chemical agents regularly present in the environment.

DEVELOPMENTAL PROCESSES

From ancient times, lead compounds were used to terminate unwanted pregnancies; if these compounds were ingested in the proper amounts, the fetus was aborted without the woman's suffering ill effects. Thus, an 1860 study reporting 73 fetal deaths in a sample of 123 pregnant lead workers simply confirmed what was already known but not previously documented (Paul, 1860). Although 70% of the liveborn children in this study died by the age of 3, the status and development of these children was not studied. The placental passage of fetotoxic compounds and their effects on subsequent development did not become a topic of scientific inquiry until almost a century later.

Between 1950 and 1970, there occurred in different parts of the world a series of dramatic epidemics of fetal poisoning—methylmercury in Iraq, Japan, Guatemala, and Pakistan; thalidomide in northern Europe; and PCBs in Japan. Because these compounds could be convincingly identified as causal agents and because each compound produced its own set of clinical disorders, the disease model, once applied predominantly to occupationally exposed adults, was extended to unborn children. However, as these infant populations were studied, four types of evidence quickly revealed the model's limitations.

1 Doses that do not produce symptoms of poisoning in the pregnant woman may nevertheless have disastrous consequences for the unborn child. In the Minamata incident, 23 infants developed clinical signs of methylmercury poisoning shortly after birth. Autopsies performed on three who subsequently died revealed extensive neural damage and high levels of methylmercury in body tissue. Surviving infants displayed severe neurological deficits, deviant mental and motor development, retarded speech, and difficulty in chewing and swallowing. Ten years later, these children were profoundly retarded. And yet, 22 of the mothers were clinically asymptomatic during pregnancy (Harada, 1977; Takeuchi, 1972b).

2 Fetal poisoning may resemble adult poisoning in some respects but differ in other respects. In the Minamata incident, deafness, typically found in exposed adults and older children, rarely occurred in prenatally exposed newborns (Takeuchi, 1972a). But the newborns displayed more pervasive reflex anomalies than did postnatally exposed children. In the PCB incident, newborns had the facial swelling and brown discoloration but not the chloracne characteristic of poisoned adults and older children (Funatsu & Yamashita, 1972).

3 Prenatal exposure may produce long-term deficits not evident when exposure occurs postnatally. Follow-up studies of PCB-exposed infants report an average IQ of 70; sluggish, clumsy, and jerky movement; apathy and hypotonia; autonomic disturbances; and growth impairment even though clinical signs of poisoning are no longer present (Harada, 1976). These disturbances in responsiveness and neuromuscular organization are consistent with reports of slowed sensory and motor nerve conductance in exposed adults (Chia, Su, Chen, Wu, & Chu, 1981), but neither adults nor older children show long-term functional deficits (Harada, 1976).

4 The chemicals retained in adult tissue after direct exposure ceases may also be fetotoxic. Because lipid soluble compounds such as PCBs are difficult to metabolize, they are retained in body tissue for long periods of time. Although in the *Yusho* incident PCB blood levels diminished once exposure ceased, infants born several years after the exposure of their mothers showed elevated PCB blood levels, reduced birth weight, and brown pigmentation of the skin (Abe, Inoue, & Takamatsu, 1975; Harada, 1976). These findings imply what recent evidence appears to confirm. Women chronically exposed to low levels of PCBs may accumulate sufficient amounts to produce fetal poisoning (Jacobson, Jacobson, Fein, Schwartz, & Dowler, in press).

Longitudinal studies of chemicals such as PCBs and methylmercury indicate that effects may be seen at one period of development and not at another. Moreover, defects in a developmental process may not become evident until several years after exposure. In a classic study, mice exposed prenatally to low levels of methylmercury were indistinguishable from untreated animals at birth. By one month (adolescence), exposed animals showed slight growth retardation and subtle behavioral deficits in open-field and swimming tests. By 6 to 12 months of age (adulthood), overt neurological impairment measured by the appearance of coordination problems became evident. As the animals approached middle age, central nervous system involvement became obvious and behavioral tests were no longer needed to identify treated animals (Spyker, 1975).

Findings that toxic effects may first emerge several months or years after exposure underscore the importance of long-term, prospective longitudinal studies (Table 1). Some deficits associated with prenatal exposure may not be discernible until the period when language ordinarily develops, and others may first appear when a child attends school and is required to attend, persist, remember, and learn. And of course, reproductive effects cannot be assessed until adulthood. The developmental time frame in which effects appear and the particular behavioral systems affected are matters of considerable theoretical interest in developmental psychology.

For human infants, longitudinal assessment is also needed to investigate the by-products of early disturbances, especially the conditions under which a newborn disturbance creates stress in other aspects of a child's life. At issue is the problem of separating the direct effects of a toxic process from additional effects related to the parents' attempts to cope with an edgy or unresponsive infant. If there is no additional exposure after birth, if the toxic chemical is metabolized or eliminated, and if the parents respond effectively to their newborn, subsequent problems may not emerge. But if one or more of these conditions are not present, the impact of pre- or postnatal exposure may be less benign.

ANIMAL MODELS AND HUMAN STUDIES

Cats inhabiting the lead works of 19th-century Paris became ill and died. In Minamata, dogs, cats, and pigs were going mad before the first human case of poisoning was reported (Takeuchi, 1972b). For two years, experiments to induce "dancing cats disease" were performed before methylmercury was identified as the causal agent. Because the effects of toxic exposure in animals and humans are often comparable, animal models have become indispensable in teratogenic testing. Because ethical considerations do not permit the random assignment of human infants to controlled exposure conditions, only animal studies can confirm a causal relation between toxic exposure and behavioral outcome.

In human studies, doses must often be inferred from verbal reports, whereas in animal studies, the chemical can be traced from the animal's diet to its absorption in soft and hard tissue. In human studies, placental transfer must often be inferred from correlations between levels of the toxin in maternal blood and levels in the placenta and in the umbilical cord. For chemicals such as PCBs that require a large quantity of blood for laboratory analyses, the study of human populations is even more difficult.

However, the credibility of an animal model depends on the researcher's ability to produce changes in laboratory animals comparable to those occurring in acutely exposed humans (Bornschein, Pearson, & Reiter, 1980b). In the case of lead, this was not achieved until Pentschew and Garro (1966) showed that suckling rats nursing from the milk of lead-exposed dams developed disorders similar to those of children with lead encephalopathy.

The female rhesus monkey exposed to PCBs in her daily diet develops deficits similar to *Yusho* disease (Allen, Barsotti, & Carstens, 1980). Fetopathy is also more likely in the offspring of exposed than unexposed animals. At birth, the live-born progeny weighed less than controls and by two months of age developed *Yusho*-like symptomatology. Behavioral tests given between 6 and 24 months of age revealed hyperlocomotor activity and learning retardation (Bowman, Heironimus, & Allen,

1978), but when tested at 44 months of age, these animals were hypoactive relative to controls (Bowman & Heironimus, 1981). In a follow-up study in which adult female monkeys were removed from their PCB diet for a one-year period prior to conception (Allen et al., 1980), 4 of 15 infants were stillborn, even though the physical condition of the animals improved and PCB levels in maternal adipose tissue declined markedly. Also, the birth weight of the live-born infants was reduced relative to nonexposed infants, and four infants died after weaning at 4 months of age. In rhesus monkeys, as in humans (Harada, 1976), teratogenic effects appear in infants whose mothers have consumed PCB prior to, but not during, pregnancy.

Yusho-like effects are more difficult to induce in rodents, but subclinical behavioral effects appear readily. When mice consume low levels of PCB during pregnancy, some pups display neuromorphologic abnormalities at birth and subsequently develop a reflex disorder called the "spinning syndrome" (Chou, Miike, Payne, & Davis, 1979; Tilson, Davis, McLachlan, & Lucier, 1979). In addition, more subtle signs of neurobehavioral dysfunctioning can be observed in prenatally PCB-exposed mice who do not develop clinical signs of toxicity. Assessments of subtle behavioral functions indicate that exposed but asymptomatic mice show longer latencies in response to painful stimulation and difficulties in tasks requiring perceptual-motor integration, even though PCBs are no longer detectable in their body tissues (Tilson et al., 1979). A sluggish response to stress, an initially depressed response to a novel environment, and a failure to habituate have also been observed in mice exposed perinatally to doses below that associated with obvious behavioral anomalies (Storm, Hart, & Smith, 1981).

Nevertheless, extrapolation of low-level effects from animals to humans is risky on several grounds. Studies of PCBs indicate species-specific effects in addition to effects that appear to be fairly general. Species differ in their ability to eliminate PCBs, and as a result, the dose required to produce an effect will vary among species. Moreover, the sluggish response of mice and monkeys to painful stimulation may be only roughly analogous to apathy or poor autonomic control in human infants. The "spinning syndrome" in mice and patterns of hypo- or hyper-activity in monkeys may reflect adaptational disruptions that will be expressed differently in human children according to the developmental status of the child at the time of exposure and at the time of testing.

In spite of these problems, animal models are essential in teratogenic testing because (a) low-level effects can be investigated using an experimental design with random assignment, (b) significant findings indicate at least the possibility of risk to humans, and (c) the particular behavioral effects found in animals provide a basis for investigating toxic effects in humans. But the findings of this research must be corroborated in studies of humans, even though human studies are necessarily correlational and therefore unable to establish cause-effect linkages in the manner achieved by a true experiment. Attempt must be made to eliminate some plausible competing explanations of significant associations. In one of the more thorough attempts to eliminate competing explanations, Needleman et al. (1979) tested 39 nonlead variables to identify those associated with elevated lead levels in children. Lead effects persisted when these covariates were used as control variables. Although these painstaking efforts enhance the credibility of the findings, they do not eliminate all possible confounding variables.

In recognition of the correlational design required in human studies, epidemiologists use the term "risk factors" when discussing the effects of environmental toxins on humans. According to Cowan and Leviton (1980), the conclusion that a particular environmental substance is a risk factor in humans is supported by at least four considerations:

1 Subtle effects in animals exposed experimentally to low levels,

2 Evidence in chronically exposed humans of deficits comparable to those found in animals or in acutely exposed humans,

3 Consistency of findings across numerous animal and human studies performed by different investigators under different circumstances and in different population groups, and

4 The biological plausibility of a causal inference.

CONCLUDING OBSERVATIONS

In recent years, behavioral scientists have become involved in the testing of potentially harmful substances, among them those that may harm the developing embryo, fetus, infant, or child. The results of this research are of great social concern. In the case of drugs, pharmaceutical companies must affirm the safety of their products. In the case of tobacco and alcohol, farmers and manufacturers may be economically damaged by evidence of harmful effects. In the case of environmental pollutants, industries may incur extra costs if they are required to install special disposal mechanisms or clean up polluted areas.

In the case of the already outlawed PCBs, the issues are more intricate because current levels in the aquatic food chain resulted from four decades of pollution before the toxic effects of PCBs were known. Protection from the effects of environmentally ubiquitous chemicals may require studies to uncover detoxification procedures and, in the case of PCBs, temporary restrictions on fishing with consequent hardships for fishing communities. In states such as Michigan, money from the sale of fishing licenses supports state recreation areas, and in a time of budgetary crises, replacement funds are unlikely to be available. Knowledge of environmental chemical effects leads to difficult choices, judgments about different kinds of harm, and the need to evaluate the safety of chemicals never intended for human consumption (Weiss & Spyker, 1974).

PCBs have been viewed as a prototypical organic compound, similar to many other ubiquitous synthetic organic chemicals in their tendency to bioconcentrate and bioaccumulate (Swain, 1981). Some of these chemicals are still being manufactured and used in a variety of preparations such as pesticides and fire retardants. Some have never been manufactured but may serve industrial purposes in the future. Among the more than 300 chemicals found in fish from waters such as Lake Michigan, some are chemical novelties, by-products by complex interactions between chemical pollutants and natural biological processes. It is awesome to imagine a kind of ecological autonomy in which natural systems responding to xenobiotic influences of human origin produce new substances that become part of a natural laboratory of uncontrolled chemical reactions. If a long evolutionary process has provided successful species with intricate detoxification mechanisms to prevent toxic overload (e.g., in the liver), the unsettled question is whether these mechanisms will be adequate to neutralize substances that have newly entered the ecosystem. Although, when humans are involved, the research is fraught with difficulty, behavioral teratology may help to ascertain the degree to which humans will be able to adapt to this novel chemical environment.

In conclusion, the assessment of behavioral functions has become a useful tool for evaluating the teratogenicity of chemical agents. In this respect, psychologists can make a meaningful contribution to an area of social concern. Moreover, in studying teratogenic effects, general information of interest to psychology as a science may also emerge. For psychologists interested in the neurochemical and neuroanatomical basis of behavior, neurobehavioral models derived from animal experiments can be applied to the intrauterine development of humans; or studies of accidental exposure in humans might stimulate the development of new animal models. For psychologists interested in postnatal development, teratogenic studies provide an opportunity to examine behavioral development when the disruptive agent is known and effects on newborns have been identified. The boundary separating applied and basic research is largely a matter of specific versus general knowledge. For psychologists interested in behavioral teratology, the effort has already stimulated formulations likely to have important theoretical implications beyond the study of specific compounds.

REFERENCE NOTE

1 Humphrey, H. E. B. *Evaluation of changes in the level of polychlorinated biphenyls (PCB) in human tissue* (FDA Contract 223–73–2209). Lansing: Michigan Department of Public Health, 1978.

REFERENCES

Abe, S., Inoue, Y., & Takamatsu, M. Polychlorinated biphenyl residues in plasma of *Yusho* children born to mothers who had consumed oil contaminated by PCB. *Acta Medica Fukuoka*, 1975, *66*, 605–609.

Allen, J. R., Barsotti, D. A., & Carstens, L. A. Residual effects of polychlorinated biphenyls on adult nonhuman primates and their offspring. *Journal of Toxicology and Environmental Health*, 1980, *6*, 55–66.

Bidstrup, P. L. *Toxicity of mercury and its compounds*. Amsterdam. Elsevier, 1964.

Bornschein, R., Pearson, D., & Reiter, L. Behavioral effects of moderate lead exposure in children and animal models: Part 1. Clinical studies. *CRC Critical Reviews in Toxicology*, 1980, 43–100. (a)

Bornschein, R., Pearson, D., & Reiter, L. Behavioral effects of moderate lead exposure in children and animal models: Part 2. Animal studies. *CRC Critical Reviews in Toxicology*, 1980, 101–152. (b)

Bowman, R. E., & Heironimus, M. P. Hypoactivity in adolescent monkeys perinatally exposed to PCBs and hyperactive as juveniles. *Neurobehavioral Toxicology and Teratology*, 1981, *3*, 15–18.

Bowman, R. E., Heironimus, M. P., & Allen, J. R. Correlation of PCB body burden with behavioral toxicology in monkeys. *Pharmacology Biochemical Behavior*, 1978, *9*, 49–56.

Byers, R. K., & Lord, E. E. Late effects of lead poisoning on mental development. *American Journal of Diseases of Children*, 1943, *66*, 471.

Chia, L., Su, M., Chen, R., Wu, Z., & Chu, F. Neurological manifestations in polychlorinated biphenyls (PCB) poisoning. *Clinical Medicine (Taipei)*, 1981, *7*, 45–61.

Chou, S. M., Miike, T., Payne, W., & Davis, G. Neuropathology of "spinning syndrome" induced by prenatal intoxication with a PCB in mice. *Annals of the New York Academy of Sciences*, 1979, *320*, 373–395.

Cowan, L. D., & Leviton A. Epidemiologic considerations in the study of the sequelae of low level exposure. In H. L. Needleman (Ed.), *Low level lead exposure: The clinical implications of current research*. New York: Raven Press, 1980.

Dana, S. L. *Lead diseases*. Lowell, Mass.: Daniel Bixby, 1848.

Dinman, B. T., & Hecker, L. H. The dose-response relationship resulting from exposure to alkyl mercury compounds. In R. Hartung & B. D. Dinman (Eds.), *Environmental mercury contamination*. Ann Arbor, Mich.: Ann Arbor Science, 1972.

Funatsu, I., Yamashita, F., et al. Polychlorobiphenyls (PCB)-induced fetopathy. *The Kurume Medical Journal*, 1972, *19*, 43–51.

Gregory, R. J., & Mohan, P. J. Effects of asymptomatic lead exposure on childhood intelligence. *Intelligence*, 1977, *1*, 381–400.

Guinee, J. Lead poisoning. *American Journal of Medicine*, 1972, *52*, 283–288.

Harada, M. Intrauterine poisoning: Clinical and epidemiological studies and significance of the problem. *Bulletin of the Institute of Constitutional Medicine, Kumamoto University (Japan)*, 1976, *25*, 38–55.

Harada, M. Congenital alkyl mercury poisoning (congenital Minamata disease). *Paediatrician*, 1977, *6*, 58–68.

Higuchi, K. (Ed.). *PCB poisoning and pollution*. New York: Academic Press, 1976.

Hunter, D., Branford, R. R., & Russell, D. S. Poisoning by methylmercury compounds. *Quarterly Journal of Medicine*, 1940, *9*, 193.

Jacobson, J. L., Jacobson, S. W., Fein, G. G., Schwartz, P. M., & Dowler, J. K. Prenatal exposure to an environmental toxin: A test of the multiple effects model. *Developmental Psychology*, in press.

Jacobson, S. W., Jacobson, J. L., Schwartz, P. M., Fein, G. G. Intrauterine exposure of human newborns to PCBs: Measures of exposure. In F. M. D'Itri & M. Kamrin (Eds.), *PCBs: Human and environmental hazards*. Ann Arbor, Mich.: Ann Arbor Science, 1983.

Kriss, K., Zack, M. M., Kimbrough, R. D., Needham, L. L., Smrek, A. L., & Jones, B. T. Association of blood pressure and polychlorinated biphenyl levels. *Journal of the American Medical Association*, 1981, *245*, 2505–2509.

Makhanna, C. F. Lead poisoning in children: Cerebral manifestations. *Archives of Neurology and Psychiatry*, 1932, *27*, 294.

Needleman, H. L. Lead and neuropsychological functioning: Finding a threshold. In H. L. Needleman (Ed.), *Low level lead exposure: The clinical implications of current research*. New York: Raven Press, 1980.

Needleman, H., Gunnoe, C., Leviton, A., Reed, R., Peresie, H., Maher, C., & Barrett, P. Deficits in psychologic and classroom performance of children with elevated dentine lead levels. *New England Journal of Medicine*, 1979, *300*, 689–695.

Needleman, H. L., Leviton, A., & Bellinger, D. Lead-associated intellectual deficit. *New England Journal of Medicine*, 1982, *306*, 367.

Paul, C. Etude sur l'intoxication lente par les preparations de plomb; de son influence par le produit de la conception. *Archives of General Medicine*, 1860, *15*, 513–533.

Pentschew, A., & Garro, F. Lead encephalomyelopathy of the suckling rat and its implications on the porphyrenopathic nervous diseases with special reference to the permeability disorders of the nervous system's capillaries. *Acta Neuropathology*, 1966, *6*, 266.

Ratcliffe, J. M. *Lead in man and the environment*. New York: Wiley, 1981.

Schwartz, P. M., Jacobson, S. W., Fein, G. G., & Jacobson, J. L. Lake Michigan fish consumption as a source of polychlorinated biphenyls in human cord serum, maternal serum, and milk. *American Journal of Public Health*, 1983, *73*, 293–296.

Smith, W. E., & Smith, A. M. *Minamata*. New York: Holt, Rinehart & Winston, 1975.

Spyker, J. M. Assessing the impact of low level chemicals on development: Behavioral and latent effects. *Federation Proceedings*, 1975, *34*, 1835–1844.

Storm, J. E., Hart, J. L., & Smith, R. F. Behavior of mice after pre- and postnatal exposure to Arochlor 1254. *Neurobehavioral Toxicology and Teratology*, 1981, *3*, 5–9.

Surgeon General of the United States. Medical aspects of childhood lead poisoning. *Pediatrics*, 1971, *48*, 464–468.

Swain, W. R. An ecosystem approach to the toxicology of residue forming xenobiotic organic substances in the Great Lakes. In *Ecotoxicology working papers: Testing for the effects of chemicals on ecosystems*. Washington, D.C.: National Research Council, National Academy of Science, 1981.

Takeuchi, T. Approaches to the detection of subclinical mercury intoxications: Experience in Minamata, Japan. In R. Hartung & B. D. Dinman (Eds.), *Environmental mercury contamination*. Ann Arbor, Mich.: Ann Arbor Science, 1972. (a)

Takeuchi, T. Biological reactions and pathological changes in human beings and animals caused by organic mercury contamination. In R. Hartung & B. D. Dinman (Eds.), *Environmental mercury contamination*. Ann Arbor, Mich.: Ann Arbor Science, 1972. (b)

Tilson, H. A., Davis, G. J., McLachlan, J. A., & Lucier, G. W. The effects of polychlorinated biphenyls given prenatally on the neurobehavioral development of mice. *Environmental Research*, 1979, *18*, 466–474.

Tuchmann-Duplessis, H. *Drug effects on the fetus*. Littleton, Mass.: Publishing Sciences Group, 1975.

UK and Sweden attack lead poisoning studies. *Nature*, 1979, *278*, 677–678.

U.S. Department of Health, Education and Welfare. *Preventing lead poisoning in young children: A statement by the Center for Disease Control*. Atlanta, Ga.: Author, 1978.

Weiss, B., & Spyker, J. M. Behavioral implications of prenatal and early postnatal exposure to chemical pollutants. *Pediatrics*, 1974, *53*, 851–859.

Wong, K. C., & Hwang, M. Y. Children born to PCB poisoned mothers. *Clinical Medicine (Taipei)*, 1981, *7*, 83–87.

World Health Organization. Polychlorinated biphenyls and polybrominated biphenyls. *IARC monographs on the evaluation of the carcinogenic risk of chemicals to humans* (Vol. 18). Lyon, France: Author, 1978.

READING 3

Premature Birth: Consequences for the Parent-Infant Relationship

Susan Goldberg

Imagine, if you will, the sound of a young infant crying. For most adults it is a disturbing and compelling sound. If it is made by your own infant or one in your care, you are likely to feel impelled to do something about it. Most likely, when the crying has reached a particular intensity and has lasted for some (usually short) period of time, someone will pick the baby up for a bit of cuddling and walking. Usually, this terminates the crying and will bring the infant to a state of visual alertness. If the baby makes eye contact with the adult while in this alert state, the caregiver is likely to begin head-nodding and talking to the baby with the exaggerated expressions and inflections that are used only for talking to babies. Babies are usually very attentive to this kind of display and will often smile and coo. Most adults find this rapt attention and smiling exceedingly attractive in young infants and will do quite ridiculous things for these seemingly small rewards. I have used this example to illustrate that normal infant behaviors and the behaviors adults direct toward infants seem to be mutually complementary in a way that leads to repeated social interactions enjoyed by both infants and adults. Consider now the experiences of a baby whose cry is weak and fails to compel adult attention, or the baby (or adult) who is blind and cannot make the eye contacts that normally lead to social play. When the behavior of either the infant or the adult is not within the range of normal competence, the pair is likely to have difficulties establishing rewarding social interactions. Premature birth is one particular situation in which the interactive skills of both parents and infants are hampered.

Recent studies comparing interactions of preterm and full-term parent-infant pairs have found consistently different patterns of behavior in the two groups. Before we turn to these studies, it will be useful to introduce a conceptual framework for understanding parent-infant interaction and a model within which the findings can be interpreted.

A CONCEPTUAL FRAMEWORK

In most mammalian species, the care of an adult is necessary for the survival, growth, and development of the young. One would therefore expect that such species have evolved an adaptive system of parent-infant interaction which guarantees that newborns will be capable of soliciting care from adults and that adults will respond appropriately to infant signals for care. Where immaturity is prolonged and the young require the care of parents even after they are capable of moving about and feeding without assistance, one would also expect the interactive system to be organized in a way that guarantees the occurrence of social (as opposed to caregiving) interactions that can form the basis for a prolonged parent-child relationship. It is not surprising to find that when these conditions are met, the parent-infant interaction system appears to be one of finely tuned reciprocal behaviors that are mutually complementary and that appear to be preadapted to facilitate social interaction. Furthermore, as the example given earlier illustrates, both parents and infants are initiators and responders in bouts of interaction.

This view is quite different from that taken by psychologists in most studies of child development. For most of the relatively short history of developmental psychology it was commonly assumed that the infant was a passive, helpless organism who was acted upon by parents (and others) in a process that resulted in the "socialization" of the child into mature forms of behavior. In popular psychology this emphasis appeared as the belief that parents (especially mothers) were *responsible* for their child's development. They were to take the credit for successes as well as the blame for failures.

In the last fifteen years, the study of infant development has shown that the young infant is by no means passive, inert, or helpless when we consider the environment for which he or she is adapted—that is, an environment which includes a responsive caregiver. Indeed, we have discovered that infants are far more skilled and competent than we originally thought. First, the sensory systems of human infants are well developed at birth, and their initial perceptual capacities are well matched to the kind of stimulation that adults normally present to them. Infants see and discriminate visual patterns from birth, although their visual acuity is not up to adult standards. Young infants are especially attentive to visual movement, to borders of high contrast, and to relatively complex stimuli. When face to face with infants, adults will normally present their faces at the distance where newborns are best able to focus (17–22 cm) and exaggerate their facial expressions and

movements. The result is a visual display with constant movement of high contrast borders.

A similar phenomenon is observed in the auditory domain. Young infants are most sensitive to sound frequencies within the human vocal range, especially the higher pitches, and they can discriminate many initial consonants and vocal inflections. When adults talk to infants, they spontaneously raise the pitch of their voices, slow their speech, repeat frequently, and exaggerate articulation and inflection. Small wonder that young infants are fascinated by the games adults play with them!

In addition, researchers have found that when adults are engaged in this type of face-to-face play they pace their behavior according to the infant's pattern of waxing and waning attention. Thus the infant is able to "control" the display by the use of selective attention. At the same time, studies have found that babies are most likely to smile and coo first to events over which they have control. Thus, infants are highly likely to smile and gurgle during face-to-face play with adults, thus providing experiences which lead the adult to feel that he or she is "controlling" an interesting display. We will return to the notion of control and the sense of being effective as an important ingredient in parent-infant relationships.

A second respect in which infants are more skilled and competent than we might think is their ability to initiate and continue both caregiving and social interactions. Although the repertoire of the young infant is very limited, it includes behaviors such as crying, visual attention, and (after the first few weeks) smiling, which have compelling and powerful effects on adult behavior. Almost all parents will tell you that in the first weeks at home with a new baby they spent an inordinate amount of time trying to stop the baby's crying.

Crying is, at first, the most effective behavior in the infant's repertoire for getting adult attention. When social smiling and eye contact begin, they too become extremely effective in maintaining adult attention. In one study, by Moss and Robson (1968), about 80 percent of the parent-infant interactions in the early months were initiated by the infant. Thus, the normally competent infant plays a role in establishing contacts and interactions with adults that provide the conditions necessary for growth and development.

COMPETENCE MOTIVATION: A MODEL

The actual process by which this relationship develops is not clearly understood, but we can outline a plausible model that is consistent with most of the available data. A central concept in this model is that of competence motivation, as defined by White (1959). In a now-classic review of research on learning and motivation in many species, White concluded that behaviors that are selective, directed, and persistent occur with high frequency in the absence of extrinsic rewards. He therefore proposed an intrinsic motive, which he called competence motivation, arising from a need to cope effectively with the environment, to account for behavioral phenomena such as play, exploration, and curiosity. Behavior that enables the organism to control or influence the environment gives rise to feelings of efficacy that strengthen competence motivation. White pointed out that much of the behavior of young infants appears to be motivated in this manner. Why else, for example, would infants persist in learning to walk when they are repeatedly punished by falls and bruises?

At the other extreme, Seligman (1975) has demonstrated that animals, including humans, can quickly learn to be helpless when placed in an unpleasant situation over which they have no control. This learned helplessness prevents effective behavior in subsequent situations where control is possible. It has been suggested that an important part of typical parent-infant interaction in the early months is the prompt and appropriate responses of the parent to the infant's behavior, which enable the infant to feel effective. The retarded development often seen in institutionalized infants may arise from learned helplessness in a situation where, though apparent needs are met, this occurs on schedule rather than in response to the infant's expression of needs and signals for attention. There is a general consensus among researchers in infant development that the infant's early experiences of being effective support competence motivation, which in turn leads to the exploration, practice of skills, and "discovery" of new behaviors important for normal development.

I have suggested elsewhere (1977) that competence motivation is important to parents as well. Parents bring to their experiences with an infant some history that determines their level of competence motivation. However, their experiences with a particular infant will enhance, maintain, or depress feelings of competence in the parental role. Unlike infants, parents have some goals by which they evaluate their effectiveness. Parents monitor infant behavior, make decisions about caregiving or social interaction, and evaluate their own effectiveness in terms of the infant's subsequent behavior.

When parents are able to make decisions quickly and easily and when subsequent infant behavior is more enjoyable or less noxious than that which prompted them to act, they will consider themselves successful in that episode. When parents cannot make decisions quickly and easily and when subsequent infant behavior is more aversive or less enjoyable than that which led them to intervene, they will evaluate that episode as a failure. Figure 1 illustrates this process, and the following discussion is intended to clarify the model depicted.

The normally competent infant helps adults to be effective parents by being readable, predictable, and responsive. Readability refers to the clarity of the infant's signaling—that is, how easily the adult can observe the infant and conclude that he or she is tired, hungry,

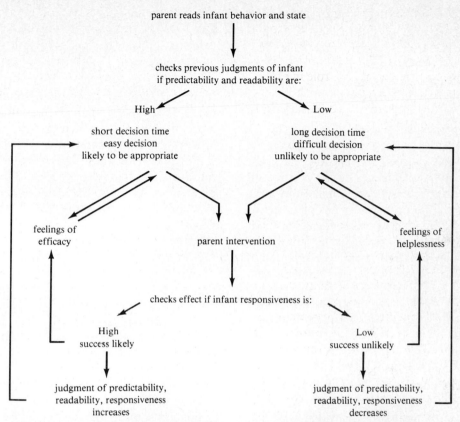

FIGURE 1   An adult who has experienced a successful interaction with an infant (left) perceives the infant as "readable" and predictable and acquires a feeling of competence in further interactions. The good and sensitive care that results causes the infant to feel more competent in turn at eliciting the appropriate responses, and thus a cycle of successful interaction is established. The reverse of this pattern is illustrated in the right side of the figure.

eager to play, etc. Although there may be some infants who are easier for everyone to read than others, readability within the parent-infant pair is a joint function of infant behavior and the adult's skill in recognizing behavior patterns.

Predictability refers to the regularity of the infant's behavior—whether sleeping, waking, feeding, and elimination follow a recognizable pattern and whether the infant repeatedly responds to similar situations in a similar fashion. Again, both infant behavior and adult behavior and sensitivity to the infant determine predict-

ability within a given pair. Responsiveness is the infant's ability to react to external stimulation, whether animate or inanimate. To the extent that an infant responds promptly and reliably to adult behavior he or she contributes directly to the adult's feelings of effectiveness as a caregiver.

The left side of Figure 1 shows that when an infant is readable and predictable the adult is able to make caregiving decisions quickly and easily and is highly likely to make decisions that lead to successful or desirable outcomes. When an adult has interacted with an infant in ways that have led to an evaluation of success, the adult is likely to perceive the infant as more readable and predictable than before. Thus, the infant who is readable, predictable, and responsive can capture an initially disinterested adult in cycles of mutually rewarding and effective interaction. Notice also that, in this part of the figure, the adult is able to respond promptly and appropriately to the infant's behavior, providing the infant with what we would describe as good or sensitive care that enhances the infant's feelings of competence. In addition, since these successes make the adult feel efficacious, he or she now has more confidence and is better able to make judgments about infant behavior and caregiving in the future. The right side of the figure illustrates the situation in which the infant is unreadable, unpredictable, and unresponsive as a joint function of poorly organized infant behavior and/or poorly developed adult skills.

PROBLEMS OF PRETERM PAIRS

Under normal conditions, the natural reciprocity of adult and infant behavior guarantees that each member of the pair is provided with frequent opportunities to feel effective. A review of what is known about preterm infants and their parents will indicate that such pairs have a greater probability of falling into the patterns on the right side of the figure than do their full-term counterparts. Most preterm pairs eventually do develop successful relationships. However, the available data also indicate that they must make compensatory adjustments to enable them to overcome initial disadvantages.

Premature infants are those who are born after fewer than 37 weeks of gestation and weigh under 2,500 g. Infants who were born small for their age or with known congenital defects are not included in the samples of the studies I am describing. The most obvious fact of premature birth is that parents are confronted with an infant who is relatively immature and may not have developed the care-

soliciting or social behaviors available to the full-term infant.

Several studies, including my own (Goldberg et al., 1978), which have systematically evaluated the behavior of preterm infants (close to term or hospital discharge), have reported that they spent less time alert, were more difficult to keep in alert states, and were less responsive to sights and sounds (a ball, a rattle, a moving face, and a voice) than the full-term comparison group. Furthermore, preterm infants who had experienced respiratory problems following birth rarely cried during the newborn examination, even though some of the procedures (e.g. undressing, testing reflexes) are mildly stressful and provoke crying from full-term infants. This suggests that these preterm infants are not likely to give adults clear distress signals.

The effectiveness of the preterm infant's cry in compelling adult attention has not been studied extensively. However, at the University of Wisconsin (Frodi et al. 1978), mothers and fathers were shown videotapes of full-term and preterm infants in crying and quiescent states. A dubbed sound track made it possible to pair the sound and the picture independently. Physiological recordings taken from the viewing parents indicated that the cry of the premature infant was physiologically more arousing than that of the full-term infant, and particularly so when paired with the picture of the preterm baby. Furthermore, ratings of the cries indicated that parents found that of the premature baby more aversive than that of the full-term infant. Thus, although the preterm infant may cry less often, this can be somewhat compensated for by the more urgent and aversive sound of these cries. If a parent is able to quiet these cries promptly, they clearly serve an adaptive function. If, however, the infant is difficult to pacify or frequently irritable, it is possible that the aversive experience will exceed the parent's level of tolerance or that he or she will experience repeated feelings of helplessness that can be damaging to the interactive relationship.

Thus far, we have assumed that the less competent behavior of the preterm infant is primarily attributable to immaturity. Often prematurity is associated with other medical problems that depress behavioral competence. In addition, the early extrauterine experiences of preterm infants in intensive-care nurseries probably do little to foster interactive competence and may, in fact, hinder its occurrence. Procedures such as tube feedings, repeated drawing of blood samples, temperature taking, and instrument monitoring often constitute a large proportion of the preterm infant's first encounters with adults. There are few data on the effects of special medical procedures, and since these procedures cannot ethically be withheld on a random schedule, this is a difficult area to study. However, numerous studies have attempted to foster early growth and development of preterm infants by adding specific kinds of experiences.

An example of a study from the first category is one in which 31 preterm infants were gently rocked for 30 minutes, three times each day, from their fifth postnatal day until they reached the age of 36 weeks postconception. They were compared to 31 unrocked preterm babies of similar gestational age, weight, and medical condition. The experimental infants were more responsive to visual and auditory stimulation and showed better motor skills as well.

Other studies have tried to treat preterm infants more like their full-term counterparts. In one study 30 preterm infants weighing 1,300–1,800 grams at birth were randomly assigned to experimental and control groups. The infants in the experimental group were given extra visual stimulation by placing mobiles over their cribs and were handled in the same manner as full-term infants for feeding, changing, and play. The control group received hospital care standard for the preterm nursery, which meant that handling was kept to a minimum.

Although initial weights and behavioral assessments had favored the control group, at 4 weeks postnatal age, the experimental group had gained more weight and showed better performance on the behavioral assessment than the controls.

Like these two examples, all of the other studies which provided extra stimulation to preterm infants showed gains in growth and/or development for the babies in the experimental group beyond those of the control group. Thus, although we do not know whether routines of intensive care interfere with early development, we do know that the behavioral competence of preterm infants can be enhanced by appropriate supplemental experiences.

On the parents' side, premature birth means that parenthood is unexpectedly thrust upon individuals who may not yet be fully prepared for it. Beyond the facts of not having finished childbirth preparation classes or having bought the baby's crib, it may be that more fundamental biological and psychological processes are disrupted. A beautiful series of studies by Rosenblatt (1969) has explored the development of maternal behavior in rats. As in humans, both male and female adult rats are capable of responding appropriately to infants. However, the hormonal state of the adult determines how readily the presence of infants elicits such behaviors. Furthermore, hormonal changes during pregnancy serve to bring female rats to a state of peak responsiveness to infants close to the time of delivery. Other animal studies indicate that experiences immediately after delivery are important for the initiation of maternal behavior. In many mammalian species removal of the young during this period may lead to subsequent rejection by the mother.

We do not have comparable hormonal studies of human mothers, but it seems likely that hormonal changes during pregnancy may serve similar functions. There is some evidence that among full-term births, immediate postpartum experiences contribute to subsequent maternal behavior. A series of studies by Klaus and Kennell (1976) and their colleagues provided some mothers with extra contact with their infants soon after birth. In comparison with control groups, these mothers were observed to stay closer to their babies, to touch and cuddle them more, and to express more reluctance to letting others care for their babies after leaving the hospital. Klaus and Kennell have summarized these studies and interpreted them as indicating that there is an optimal or "sensitive" period for initiating maternal behavior in humans. As further evidence they cite studies in which preterm infants are found to be over-represented among reported cases of child abuse, neglect, and failure to thrive. These disturbing statistics, they suggest, reflect the effects of parent-infant separation during the sensitive period.

Even if one does not accept the idea of the sensitive period as described by Klaus and Kennell (and many developmental psychologists do not), it is clear that parents whose preterm infants must undergo prolonged hospitalization have few opportunities to interact with them. Even in the many hospitals that encourage parents to visit, handle, and care for their babies in intensive care, the experiences of parents with preterm infants are in no way comparable to those of parents with full-term infants.

If you have ever visited a friend under intensive care in the hospital, you will have some idea of the circumstances under which these parents must become acquainted with their infants. Neither parents nor infants in this situation have much opportunity to practice or develop interactive skills or to experience the feelings of competence that normally accompany them. Parents also have little opportunity to learn to read, predict, or recognize salient infant behaviors. In a study conducted at Stanford University, Seashore and her colleagues (1973) asked mothers to choose themselves or one of five other caregivers (e.g. nurse, grand-

mother) as best able to meet their infants' needs in numerous caregiving and social situations. Mothers who had not been able to handle their first-born preterm infants chose themselves less often than mothers in any other group sampled.

Thus, both infants and parents in preterm pairs are likely to be less skilled social partners than their full-term counterparts, because the development of interactive capacities has been disrupted and because they have had only limited opportunities to get acquainted and to practice. In addition, during the hospital stay, parents of preterm infants already have little self-confidence and lack the feeling of competence. Ordinarily, an interactive pair in which one member has limited competence can continue to function effectively if the partner is able to compensate for the inadequate or missing skills. In the case of parent-infant pairs, because the infant's repertoire and flexibility are limited, the burden of such compensatory adjustments necessarily falls upon the parent.

OBSERVATIONS OF INTERACTIONS

Six studies to date have compared parent-infant interaction in full-term and preterm pairs. They were carried out in different parts of the country with different populations and different research methodologies. Yet there seems to be some consistency in findings that is related to the age of the infant at the time of observation (which also reflects the duration of the parent-infant relationship). Each study involved repeated observation of the same parent-infant pairs, though the number of observations and the length of the studies vary.

Those studies which observed parents and infants in the newborn period typically report that parents of preterm infants are less actively involved with their babies than parents of full-term infants, preterm infants were held farther from the parent's body, touched less, talked to less, and placed in the face-to-face position less often. Subsequent observations of the same pairs usually indicated that the differences between preterm and full-term pairs diminished with time, as parents in the preterm group became more active. Thus, it appears that the initiation of interaction patterns considered "normal" for full-term pairs is delayed in preterm pairs. In my own study (Di Vitto and Goldberg, 1979) I found that for one kind of parental behavior—cuddling the baby—the preterm infants never received as much attention as the full-term infants in spite of increases over time. Over the first four months, parents cuddled preterm infants more at later feeding observations, but they were never cuddled as much as the full-term infants at the very first (hospital) observation. Thus, the development of some kinds of interactions in the preterm group can be both delayed and depressed.

In contrast with these observations of very young infants, studies of older infants reported a very different pattern. Regardless of the observation situation (feeding, social play, or object play), preterm infants were less actively engaged in the task than were full-term infants, and their parents were more active than those of full-term infants. In one study of this type, Field (1977) placed each mother face to face with her baby, who sat in an infant seat, and asked her to "talk to your baby the way you would at home." Infant attention and parent activity were coded. Infants in the preterm group squirmed, fussed, and turned away from their mothers more than those in the full-term group, and preterm mothers were more active than full-term mothers. Instructions that decreased maternal activity ("Try to imitate everything your baby does") increased infant attention in both groups, while those that increased maternal activity ("Try to get your infant to look at you as much as possible") decreased infant attention in both groups.

Field's interpretation of these findings assumed that infants used gaze aversion to maintain their exposure to stimulation within a range that would not overtax their capacities for processing information. Thus, when mothers' activity decreased, infants were able to process the information provided without the need to reduce stimulation. Field also suggested that since the *imitation* condition provided stimulation that was matched to the infant's behavior, it might be more familiar and thus easier for the infant to process. It is possible that the greater initial fussing and gaze aversion reflected information-processing skills that were less developed than those of full-term infants.

Brown and Bakeman (1979) observed feedings in the hospital, one month after discharge, and three months after discharge. Their findings are somewhat different from the overall trend because they were similar at all observations. Behavior segments were assigned to four categories: *mother acts alone, baby acts alone, both act,* and *neither acts.* In comparing preterm and full-term pairs, they reported that preterm infants acted alone less frequently than full-term infants, while mothers of preterm infants acted alone more often than those of full-term infants. Furthermore, in preterm pairs, the *neither acts* state was most likely to be followed by *mother acts alone,* while in the full-term pairs, it was equally likely to be followed by activity by the baby or the mother.

In my own research (Di Vitto and Goldberg, 1979; Brachfeld and Goldberg, 1978) there are two sets of data consistent with these findings. First, we found that parent behavior during feedings in the hospital, and at the 4-month home and laboratory visits, was related to infant behavior in the newborn period. Regardless of their condition at birth, infants who had been difficult to rouse as newborns received a high level of functional stimulation from parents (e.g. position changes, jiggling the nipple). Infants who had been unresponsive to auditory stimulation as newborns received high levels of vocal and tactile stimulation during feedings. Thus, the parents of infants who were unresponsive as newborns appeared to work harder during feedings in the first four months than did the parents whose newborns were more responsive.

We also observed the same pairs at 8 months of age in a free-play situation. Four toys were provided and parents were asked to "do what you usually do when [name] is playing." In this situation, both at home and in the laboratory, preterm infants (particularly those who had been very young and small at birth and had respiratory problems) played with toys less and fussed more than the full-term group. Parents in the preterm group stayed closer to their babies, touched them more, demonstrated and offered toys more, and smiled less than those in the full-term group.

Another study with somewhat younger infants also fits this pattern. Beckwith and Cohen (1978) observed one wake-sleep cycle at home one month after discharge. Since babies were born and discharged at different ages, the age of the infants varied: some were relatively young, while others were closer in age to the older groups in other studies. All were born prematurely. However, Beckwith and Cohen found that mothers whose babies had experienced many early complications devoted more time to caregiving than those who had babies with fewer problems.

All these studies concur in indicating that parents with preterm infants or preterm infants with more serious early problems devote more effort to interacting with their babies than do their full-term counterparts. In most of the studies this was coupled with a less responsive or less active baby in the preterm pairs. Thus, it appears that parents adapt to the less responsive preterm baby by investing more effort in the interaction themselves. As Brown and Bakeman put it, the mother of the preterm infant "carries more of the interactive burden" than her full-term counterpart.

From our own laboratory, there is some evidence that other adults have a similar experience with preterm infants. At our regular developmental assessments at 4, 8, and 12 months, staff members rated the preterm group as being less attentive to the tasks, less persistent in solving them, and less interested in manipulating objects than the full-term group. In addition, staff members found it necessary to spend more time with the preterm group to complete the required tasks.

The consistency of these findings suggests that in pairs with a preterm infant, adults use a common strategy of investing extra time and effort to compensate for their less responsive social partner. It is important to note that while this seems to be a widely adopted strategy, it is not necessarily the most successful one. In Field's study (1977) a decrease in maternal activity evoked infant attention more effectively than an increase. In our own observations of 8-month-old infants, increased parent involvement did not reduce the unhappiness of the sick preterm group, and some play sessions had to be terminated to alleviate infant distress. Hence, while there seem to be some consistent strategies by which parents compensate for the limited skills of their preterm infants, these pairs may continue to experience interactive stress in spite of or even because of these efforts. Continuation of such unrewarding interactions, as Figure 1 indicates, is a threat to continued effective functioning of the interactive system.

The data reviewed above provide little evidence on the duration of interactive differences between full-term and preterm pairs. Among researchers in the field, there seems to be an informal consensus which holds that such differences gradually disappear, probably by the end of the first year. In my own research, a repetition of the play sessions at 12 months revealed no group differences. At 11–15 months, Leiderman and Seashore (1975) report only one difference: mothers of preterm babies smile less frequently than those of full-term babies. However, in Brown and Bakeman's study, group differences were observed as late as preschool age in rated competence in social interactions with adults (teachers) and peers. These data are too meager and scattered to support a firm conclusion on the duration of group differences. This review has focused only upon the ways in which premature birth may stress the parent-infant interaction system. Preterm infants are generally considered to be at higher risk for subsequent developmental and medical problems than their full-term counterparts. In order to understand the reasons for less than optimal developmental outcomes, it is important to bear in mind that premature births occur with high frequency among population subgroups where family stress is already high (e.g. young, single, black, lower-class mothers). Most of the research designs which would allow us to disentangle the independent contributions of each medical and social variable to long-term development are unethical, impractical, or impossible to carry out with human subjects.

The early approach to studying the consequences of prematurity was to consider each of these medical and social variables as "causes" and the physical and intellectual development of the child as the "effect." The data reviewed here indicate that we cannot think in such simple terms. Prematurity (or any other event which stresses the infant) stresses the parent-infant interaction system and indeed the entire family. The way in which the family is able to cope with these stresses then has important consequences for the child's development. A major finding of the UCLA study was that for preterm infants, as for full-term infants, a harmoniously functioning parent-infant relationship has beneficial effects on development in other areas, such as language, cognition, motor skills, and general health. Prematurity, like many other developmental phenomena, can best be understood as a complex biosocial event with multiple consequences for the child and the family.

Furthermore, in the absence of sophisticated medical technology, the vast majority of the births we have been discussing would not have produced live offspring. In evolutionary history, though it would have been adaptive for infants' initial social skills to be functional some time before birth was imminent, there was no reason for these preadapted social skills to be functioning at 6 or 7 months gestation. Premature births include only a small proportion of the population, but our ability to make such infants viable at younger and younger gestational ages by means of artificial support systems may be creating new pressures for differential selection. The fact that the majority of preterm pairs do make relatively successful adaptations indicates that the capacity to compensate for early interactive stress is one of the features of the parent-infant interaction system.

REFERENCES

Beckwith, L., and S. E. Cohen. 1978. Preterm birth: Hazardous obstetrical and postnatal events as related to caregiver-infant behavior. *Infant Behav. and Devel.* 1.

Brachfeld, S., and S. Goldberg. Parent-infant interaction: Effects of newborn medical status on free play at 8 and 12 months. Presented at Southeastern Conference on Human Development, Atlanta, GA, April 1978.

Brown, J. V., and R. Bakeman. 1979. Relationships of human mothers with their infants during the first year of life. In *Maternal Influences and Early Behavior,* ed. R. W. Bell and W. P. Smotherman. Spectrum.

Di Vitto, B., and S. Goldberg. 1979. The development of early parent-infant interaction as a function of newborn medical status. In *Infants Born at Risk,* ed. T. Field, A. Sostek, S. Goldberg, and H. H. Shuman. Spectrum.

Field, T. M. 1977. Effects of early separation, interactive deficits, and experimental manipulations on mother-infant interaction. *Child Development* 48:763–71.

Frodi, A., M. Lamb, L. Leavitt, W. L. Donovan, C. Wolff, and C. Neff. 1978. Fathers' and mothers' responses to the faces and cries of normal and premature infants. *Devel. Psych.* 14.

Goldberg, S. 1977. Social competence in infancy: A model of parent-infant interaction. *Merrill-Palmer Quarterly* 23:163–77.

Goldberg, S., S. Brachfeld, and B. Di Vitto. 1978. Feeding, fussing and play: Parent-infant interaction in the first year as a function of newborn medical status. In *Interactions of High Risk Infants and Children*, ed. T. Field, S. Goldberg, D. Stern and A. Sostek, Academic Press.

Kennell, J. H., and M. H. Klaus. 1976. Caring for parents of a premature or sick infant. In *Maternal-Infant Bonding*, ed. M. H. Klaus and J. H. Kennell. Mosby.

Klaus, M. H., and J. H. Kennell. 1976. *Maternal-Infant Bonding*. Mosby.

Leiderman, P. H., and M. J. Seashore. 1975. Mother-infant separation: Some delayed conse-quences. In *Parent-Infant Interaction*. CIBA Foundation Symp. 33. Elsevier.

Moss, H. A., and K. S. Robson. The role of protest behavior in the development of parent-infant attachment. Symposium on attachment behavior in humans and animals. Am. Psych. Assoc. Sept. 1968.

Rosenblatt, J. S. 1969. The development of maternal responsiveness in the rat. *Am. J. Orthopsychiatry* 39:36–56.

Seashore, M. J., A. D. Leifer, C. R. Barnett, and P. H. Leiderman. 1973. The effects of denial of early mother-infant interaction on maternal self-confidence. *J. Pers. and Soc. Psych.* 26:369–78.

Seligman, M. R. 1975. *Helplessness: On Development, Depression and Death*. W. H. Freeman.

White, R. 1959. Motivation reconsidered: The concept of competence. *Psych. Review* 66:297–333.

READING 4

Temperament: Concepts, Issues and Problems

Michael Rutter

The general concept of *temperament* goes back to at least mediaeval time when it was used to refer to a person's mental disposition, as determined by the combination of the four cardinal humours. Its usage today retains much of that emphasis. That is, the term usually implies reference to the basic elements of behavioural-functioning rather than to complex or idiosyncratic aspects of a person's emotional or social style; the concept applies to those elements that show substantial consistency over time and over space; and it is assumed that, to a considerable extent, the elements are constitutionally determined. Most notably, temperament refers to a preponderant style of *how* an individual does things or how he or she responds to people and to situations, rather than to *what* the individual does (i.e. the content of behaviour), or to *why* he or she does it (i.e. motivation), or to the behavioural capacities or abilities that he or she manifests (Thomas & Chess 1977).

Temperamental characteristics are abstractions, rather than directly observable discrete behaviours (Rutter et al 1964), and the questions with which we need to start therefore concern the empirical evidence that justifies the abstraction and shows its utility.

Although the concepts and terms are centuries old, the scientific study of temperamental attributes began much more recently. Gesell's (1937) analysis of film records of children—to assess characteristics such as activity level or energy output, adaptability, and liveliness of emotional expression—constituted one of the earliest studies. He concluded that...'certain fundamental traits of individuality, whatever their origin, exist early, persist late and assert themselves under varying environmental conditions'. This view contrasted starkly with the prevailing popular impression that all young babies were much alike and that individual differences in early childhood were of little importance. Over the next two decades, a steady trickle of studies indicated important individual differences in a wide range of behavioural functions in infancy and early childhood. Then, a most important stimulus to research on temperament came from the New York longitudinal study started by S. Chess, A. Thomas and H. G. Birch in the mid-1950s. One of their early papers (Chess et al 1959) included the statement...'We believe that the data indicate that the individual specific reaction pattern appears in the first few months of life, persists in a stable form thereafter, and significantly influences the nature of the child's response to all environmental events, including child care practices'. In subsequent years they somewhat modified their claims regarding temporal consistency, but the findings from their longitudinal study (see Thomas & Chess 1977) have otherwise generally supported their initial hypotheses on the importance of individual differences in temperamental characteristics. Moreover, as shown by a variety of recent reviews (Rutter 1977, Dunn 1980, Keogh & Pullis 1980, Bates 1980)—as well as by the papers in this symposium—the claims and findings from the New York study stimulated a mass of research by other investigators. We are consequently in a much stronger position now than we were 20 years ago to assess the concept of temperament. In reviewing what we know, we need to sharpen the hypotheses and clarify the issues in order to consider the utility of the current notions, and to identify the empirical questions and theoretical problems that remain to be tackled.

THE UTILITY OF THE CONCEPT OF TEMPERAMENT

The empirical evidence that points to the utility of the concept of temperament may be considered under three main headings: (a) the demonstration of behavioural individuality; (b) the findings on constitutional determinants and (c) the predictive power of temperamental measures for children's development of disorder and for children's responses to potentially stressful situations.

Behavioural Individuality

The question of behavioural individuality can be quickly dealt with in view of the entirely consistent and extensive data showing that, far from all infants being the same, babies and young children differ strikingly in their behavioural characteristics (Buss & Plomin 1975, Rutter 1977, Bates 1980, Dunn 1980, Keogh & Pullis 1980). This has been shown, for example, in features as varied as activity level, autonomic reactivity, fussiness or irritability, soothability, visual alertness, regularity of sleep-wake patterns, adaptability to change and social responsiveness. Moreover, numerous investigators have shown that these characteristics can be measured reliably by questionnaire, interview, and by observational and mechanical means.

Constitutional Basis

The question of the 'constitutional' basis of these individual differences raises more complex matters. The utility of the concept of temperament does not depend on the demonstration that it has its origins in genetically determined or any other kind of constitutional factors. If consistent individual differences in temperamental style were found, and these differences reliably predicted how children would respond to stressful situations, or how their course of later personality development would proceed, or whether they were likely to develop psychiatric problems, it would not matter if it were shown also that a child's temperament was largely shaped by early life experiences. In that case temperament would still be viewed as a relatively enduring individual characteristic that reflected the personal qualities that a child brought to a new experience he or she encountered. The behavioural features would be 'constitutional' in the sense that they reflected an intrinsic aspect of personal functioning, even though their origins were experiential rather than genetic. Nevertheless, most workers have considered it important to claim and to demonstrate that temperament has a substantial genetic component.

The evidence on this point is limited and not free from difficulties. Even so the empirical findings from twin studies (see Buss & Plomin 1975, Torgersen & Kringlen 1978, Matheny 1980, Goldsmith & Gottesman 1981) are reasonably consistent in showing that genetic factors play a significant part in individual variability for at least some temperamental features. This is most evident, perhaps, for activity level and task orientation, but it applies in varying degree to many other characteristics.

Another key aspect of the 'constitutional' notion concerns the consistency of temperamental functioning over time and space. If a feature is to be considered 'constitutional', it might be expected that the individual should exhibit the attribute in similar fashion across a range of different situations and over lengthy periods of time. In fact, this supposition is not quite so self-evident as it appears at first sight (a point to which I will return), but the evidence on consistency is still of some relevance. Several longitudinal studies have examined the question of temporal stability (Buss & Plomin 1975, Thomas & Chess 1977, Moss & Susman 1980) and found that children's temperamental style shows substantial consistency over periods of several months up to a year or so, but that correlations extending over several years between the pre-school period and middle childhood are generally quite low. The question of consistency across situations is at least as important, but there is surprisingly little evidence on the matter. There is moderate, but not high, agreement between measures based on parental reports, teacher reports and direct observations (Dunn & Kendrick 1980, Billman & McDevitt 1980, Buss et al 1980). The overall evidence therefore suggests that temperamental characteristics show some features associated with 'constitutional' variables.

Prediction to Other Aspects of Functioning

The evidence considered so far partly substantiates the notion that the abstraction of temperament has some validity, but it does not attest to its utility. That is shown by the power of temperamental measures as predictors of how children are likely to respond in various situations. It is that power that provides the main reason for regarding temperament as a crucial variable for any research in the field of developmental psychopathology.

The relevant evidence falls under three main headings. Firstly, it has been shown that children with amodal temperamental characteristics on such variables as irregularity of functioning, negative mood, non-adaptability, high emotional intensity, and low fastidiousness have a substantially increased risk of developing emotional or behavioural disorders during the next few years (see Rutter 1977, Keogh & Pullis 1980). This has been found in groups of children that might be considered both low risk (Rutter et al 1964, Thomas & Chess 1977) and high risk (Graham et al 1973) in terms of their psychosocial situation. There is also evidence linking temperamental attributes with scholastic performance (see Keogh & Pullis 1980).

Secondly, it has been found that a child's temperamental features constitute an important predictor of how that child will respond to the birth of a sibling. Dunn et al (1981) found that high emotional intensity and a tendency towards negative mood were the two temperamental features associated with adverse reactions. Little is known about the importance of temperamental variables with respect to children's responses to other potentially stressful life situations or to changes of circumstances requiring adaptation of some kind but there are various pointers to their probable relevance (see Rutter 1981a).

Thirdly, several naturalistic and experimental studies have shown that the behavioural characteristics of children have an important effect in determining how other people respond to them (see Rutter 1977, Dunn 1980). Children with different temperamental features *elicit* different behaviour from those with whom they interact. For example, in our study of families with a mentally ill parent, we found that children with adverse temperamental characteristics were twice as likely as other children to be the target of parental criticism (Rutter 1978). In contrast, easily adaptable children tended to be protected even in a stressful home environment, precisely because much of the hostility and discord was focused on other members of the family. Similarly, it has been found that weak malnourished children receive less parental attention than well-fed children and, probably because they elicit more caretaking, highly active babies are less likely to show developmental retardation in a depriving institutional environment (see Rutter 1977). Dunn found, in addition, that children's reactivity in infancy was linked with maternal responsiveness to them a year later (see Dunn 1980).

The temperamental qualities brought by a child to the interactions and situations that he or she encounters therefore play an important part in determining how that encounter proceeds and whether it is likely to result in the development of some form of maladaptive response or emotional behavioural disturbance. The empirical evidence on those points provide ample justification for regarding the concept of temperament as theoretically important and practically useful.

PROBLEMS IN MEASUREMENT

The most immediate issue that bedevils the study of temperament concerns the question of how to measure temperament—not necessarily which particular instrument or measuring device to use but, rather, how to conceptualize and operationalize the characteristics to be assessed.

Relativity

For example, some problems stem from the use of relative rather than absolute measures. Nearly all instruments (other than strictly quantitative bits of gadgetry, such as actometers or stabilimeters to assess activity level) compare children with other children on some behavioural feature. For example, the parental questionnaire developed by the New York group (Thomas & Chess 1977) includes items such as 'my child splashes hard in the bath and plays actively' or 'if my child is angry or annoyed, he gets over it quickly' or 'my child is highly sensitive to changes in the brightness or dimness of light'. Adverbs such as 'hard', 'actively', 'quickly' or 'highly' all demand a knowledge of what is the 'norm'. Almost inevitably, a person's norm consists of other children of the same age that he or she knows. The consequence is that little confidence can be placed on comparisons across ages or across sociocultural groups. A lack of difference may simply mean that the person who is rating the child has adjusted the ratings to a different set of norms.

However, for some purposes, a relative measure may be more useful, provided that there is a known and constant norm. Thus, age-standardized Intelligence Quotient scores are used to remove the massive effects of age. As Kagan (1980) points out: 'When text books say that children's intelligence is stable from 5 to 10 years of age, they do not mean that cognitive ability is stable: it is not. They mean that the differences in test scores among a cohort of children remain stable, despite dramatic changes in the abilities that accompany growth'.

Social Context

Whether or not to take social context into account constitutes a further variant of the same issue. For example, which is the higher activity level—wandering around aimlessly on the wing in a soccer match or fidgeting and squirming vigorously in a chair in front of the television set? The first may well involve greater energy output, but that is a function of the demands of the situation rather than of how the child responds to it. However, the situation may well reflect the child's *choice* of activities that suit his or her temperamental style. Precisely how to deal with social context, within a single narrow age span, is not obvious; it is even more difficult across age periods—the content of the activities of a 14-week-old baby bear little resemblance to those of a 14-year-old adolescent.

Functional Equivalence

A third question concerns the issue of functional equivalence. Crying in a six-month-old and crying in a 16-year-old, for example, are both real reflections of emotional expression. But do they have the same functional meaning, and is it sensible to regard correlations between the two as if they were reflections of continuity or discontinuity in development? Conversely, because behaviours appear different in form, does it follow that in functional (or genotypic) terms they are dissimilar? Obviously not (see Kagan 1980; Moss & Susman 1980)—developmental changes may modify or alter the particular manner in which a characteristic is manifest. But how does one determine what is functional equivalence for temperamental features?

Situations for Measurement

A further issue stems from the question of which situations or circumstance to use when attempting to assess temperament. Is it preferable to measure an individual's temperamental qualities in terms of his or her response to new situations or new demands or, rather, is it better to assess them in terms of his or her behaviour in more habitual circumstances? Of course, some characteristics (such as adaptability) can be assessed only in relation to new situations

because it is the nature of the child's response to novelty that reflects the characteristic. But that does not necessarily apply to other characteristics (such as emotional intensity). On the other hand, the routine of day-to-day activities may reduce the opportunity for individuality to be shown. But how does one decide what is novel? Is an outing to Hyde Park novel because previous outings have been to St. James' Park or do the park-like qualities of each make them comparable and hence non-novel? Is the coming of a different baby-sitter a new experience, or does it matter whether the child has previously had one or 43 baby-sitters?

Measuring Instrument

Having decided on the answers to these questions, one faces the further issue of what sort of measuring instrument to use—should it be direct observation questionnaire, interview or some form of mechanical measurement? The crucial point here concerns the need to sample behaviour over a wide range of situations and over a reasonably long span of time. Obviously, it would be pointless to attempt to assess adaptability or regularity of functioning on a single episode, because the very definition of the variable requires knowledge of a person's behaviour over time.

It was this consideration that led the New York group to choose the parent as the observer. They argued that the parent represented a potential source of extensive direct observations of the child over many situations and over a prolonged time and, hence, that if this experience could be adequately assessed it would constitute a rich and economical source of information on temperamental style. They, and those of us who have utilized interview measures (see Graham et al 1973, Thomas & Chess 1977), have relied on careful questioning about actual behaviour (rather than generalizations about supposed traits), and on detailed descriptions of specific examples in order to get an account of what the child *actually* does—an account that is as free from the biases of selective reporting or attitudinally influenced pre-judgements as skilled questioning can make it. There is no doubt that this method provides vivid and detailed accounts of temperamental style which give rise to measures that reflect individuality in the way intended.

There are, however, three main queries regarding interview assessments. The first concerns the validity of the reports. Do the differences in temperament reported by mothers simply reflect biased perceptions of their children? Dunn & Kendrick (1980) have investigated this issue, comparing mother's and observer's ratings and contrasting each with detailed observational measures. On the whole, the results are reassuring in that they indicate satisfactory validity for most variables. It seems most *un*likely that the differences are solely a function of biased perceptions, but more data are required before firm conclusions should be drawn.

The second query concerns the fact that the mother's information is necessarily limited to situations when she has been present. With older children, this is likely to mean that she has not observed behaviour in many of the situations of most interest. With pre-school children, of course, this is not as much of a problem, provided that the mother is the main caretaker (but it would be a problem with children in full-time day-care). However, to an important extent, everyone's behaviour is relatively situation-specific (see Mischel 1979, Bem & Funder 1978, Epstein 1979). The reported behaviour of the child may therefore be influenced as much by the pressure stemming from the family interaction patterns as by any qualities intrinsic to the child. The only satisfactory solution to that problem is to tap the child's behaviour by interviewing more than one informant. The third query stems from the fact that this form of detailed interviewing with cross-questioning and the eliciting of multiple examples is immensely time-consuming. Could not the whole process be streamlined by using a standard questionnaire?

Several investigators have developed questionnaires that show as much individuality as do the interview measures, with moderately satisfactory re-test reliability and with reasonable agreement between the scores on questionnaires completed by mothers and by fathers (see e.g. Persson-Blennow & McNeil 1979, Bates et al 1979). So far, so good—but there remains the major concern about whether questionnaires are more prone than interviews to the effects of perceptual or attitudinal distortions. The data on this point are sparse indeed but Bates et al (1979) found not only a low level of agreement between questionnaire measures and observational measures but also that the questionnaire measures showed associations with maternal characteristics whereas the observational measures did not. As this group points out, their finding is open to several different interpretations, depending in part on the weight attached to the observational data. The question of possible biases in questionnaire completion remains open and the matter requires further study.

Observational measures constitute a third possibility for the measurement of temperament. In some respects, they are more objective than either interview or questionnaire measures but they are the most time-consuming of all methods and are severely limited in their scope. By their nature, they can sample only one situation at a time and only certain sorts of situations at that. Because there are important situation-specificities in people's behaviour, it is only by taking *multiple* samples of behaviour that the investigator can maximize the chances of obtaining a valid appraisal of general response dispositions or temperamental attributes (Epstein 1979). For this reason, although observational data constitute valuable checks on interview and questionnaire measures, they cannot necessarily be assumed to constitute validating criteria and it is unlikely that they will prove to be the best general means of assessing temperamental features.

Categorization of Temperamental Features

Several questions need to be raised here but I shall focus on just three. The first is whether to concentrate on variations within the normal range or to focus on the few individuals showing extreme patterns. In an attempt to improve the psychometric properties of temperamental measures some investigators have rejected items applying to only small proportions of the population (Persson-Blennow & McNeil 1979) but perhaps it is precisely those extremes that predict best. The possibility requires examination.

The next two questions—how far to reduce the separate temperamental variables to a smaller number of factors or summary measures, and what criterion to use in deciding this matter—are most conveniently considered together. Different investigators have given different answers. Garside et al (1975) argued that the intercorrelations between the items (as reflected in a principal components analysis) should constitute the criterion. That is a statistically tidy solution, but is it sensible? I would suggest that it is not, for three rather different reasons: (a) especially with a questionnaire the intercorrelations are strongly influenced by the particular constructs (organization of ideas regarding behaviour) used by the rater; (b) the specific factors obtained tend to vary according to the statistical method employed and the sample studied (for example, the New York group derived factors of strikingly different composition); and (c) the fact that particular items intercorrelate with each other in a normal population may have little bearing on the grouping of items that predict best how an individual will respond to stress situations, or indeed to any other kind of outcome variable such as cognitive impairment, learning difficulties, or the development of psychiatric disorders (see

e.g. Dunn et al 1981, Rutter et al 1964, Graham et al 1973, Hertzig 1982).

An alternative approach is to consider each of the many possible temperamental variables separately. This method has been followed by most investigators, at least as the first step in statistical analysis. It has paid off in so far as individual temperamental attributes have proved useful predictors for various sorts of outcome (see the last group of references cited above). On the other hand, in several investigations particular clusters or patterns of characteristics have proved much better predictors than any single characteristic.

This repeated finding has led to a third approach—namely, the development of various composite measures such as the 'temperamental adversity' index (Rutter 1978), the 'difficult child' index (Thomas & Chess 1977, Hertzig 1982) and 'temperament risk' scores (Cameron 1978). Again, this approach has proved useful for predicting the development of emotional-behavioural problems. Nevertheless, it would be quite premature to regard any of these measures as having solved the question of how to categorize temperament. In the first place, although most of the composite measures are broadly similar, they differ in certain crucial respects and it remains uncertain which is superior. Secondly, empirical findings show that it is not always the same temperamental features that are crucial. Thus, for example, Schaffer (1966) found that high activity level was protective in a depriving institutional environment: Dunn et al (1981) found mood variables to be the best predictors of children's responses to the birth of a sibling; and Graham et al (1973) found irregularity, lack of malleability and low fastidiousness to be the attributes associated with the development of emotional-behavioural disorder in the children of mentally ill parents. It should *not* be assumed that the categorization of temperament that proves most effective for one purpose or in one situation will be equally effective in others. Nor should it be assumed that composite scores will always be more powerful than single variables (although it is likely that this will often be so). Nevertheless, the strategy of considering the categorization of temperament in terms of the groupings that best predict different sorts of outcome does seem worthwhile.

IMPLICATIONS OF TEMPERAMENTAL DIFFERENCES

Consistency

The question of consistency, of course, extends far beyond the issue of temperamental attributes in terms of the vigorous clashes over the last dozen years between trait theories and situationism theories. On the one hand, it has been argued that people's behaviour is highly inconsistent over time and place, being largely determined by situational factors (Mischel 1968). On the other, it has been asserted that genetically determined, semi-permanent personality dispositions play a major part in ensuring that people *do* behave consistently (Eysenck 1970). It is now clear that both extremes in these views must be rejected. The importance of personality traits is shown by the great individual variation in people's responses to any one situation, but the need to invoke environmental determinants is equally evident in the extent to which any person's mode of functioning alters from situation to situation (see Bem & Funder 1978, Epstein 1979). However, it is not sufficient to regard both the traits and the situations as important; a further question concerns the extent to which the two interact predictably (see Bem & Funder 1978). It would be misleadingly limiting to regard temperament as the reflection of the degree of similarity in a person's behaviour across all situations. Rather, some of the key aspects of temperament may concern the degree to which a person can adapt or modify his or her behaviour according to different environmental demands, or a person's vulnerability to certain kinds of stressors, or a tendency to respond in an unusual way to specific environments. These various kinds of ordinal and disordinal interaction effects* have been little explored up to now but the knowledge that they may be important in relation to temperamental variables has serious implications for the way in which we both assess temperament and analyse its effects.

Developmental Change

The first reports from the New York study (Chess et al 1959) claimed that temperamental patterns were established in the first few months of life and remained stable thereafter. However, these workers' own empirical findings (Thomas & Chess 1977), as well as those of others, have been consistent in showing near-zero correlations from the first year of life to age five years onwards. There are various reasons why early infancy measures are likely to show little continuity with measures in later childhood (Rutter 1970). It should be noted especially that temperamental attributes in the first few months of life tend to show less of a genetic component than do the same attributes in later infancy or early childhood (Torgersen & Kringlen 1978, Matheny 1980); and whereas temperamental variables at age three or four years have generally shown significant associations with psychiatric risk, those in the first year of life often have not (see Rutter et al 1964, Cameron 1978). Nevertheless, temperamental attributes, even at age two, three or four years have usually been found to correlate at a very modest level ($r - 0.3$) with those assessed in middle childhood. Where does that leave the notion of an enduring temperamental style? Of course, life experiences of various kinds are

*Ordinal interaction means that one variable (e.g. temperament) influences the *degree* to which a person responds to another variable (e.g. some environmental stressor) without altering the direction or type of response. In contrast, disordinal interaction means that the first variable alters the *direction* of response, so that some people react in one manner whereas others show an opposite response to the same second variable.

likely to play their part in shaping temperament and these influences will, necessarily, reduce consistency over time. But the direction and degree of developmental change themselves may be genetically conditioned—as shown by the finding from the Louisville twin study (Matheny & Dolan 1975, Wilson 1977). In addition, as noted already, phenotypic expression may alter its form over the course of development so that the simple correlation of like behaviour with like behaviour may not constitute the most appropriate test for temperamental consistency.

Genetic Influences

Up to now, the evidence regarding genetic influences on temperament has stemmed from a small number of twin studies, each based on rather different measures (not all of which have been entirely adequate for the assessment of temperament). However, there are particular problems in the use of twins for temperamental studies if interview or questionnaire measures are used. Because the measures are relative, because many parents like to emphasize the individuality of each twin, and because the other twin tends to constitute the main comparison for ratings, it is unlikely that the degree of difference within twin pairs (monozygotic or dizygotic) will be on the same scale as that between siblings or between unrelated children. There is a great need to utilize other genetic designs in addition to the twin method but, whatever the design, it will be important to examine the possibility that the genetic contribution concerns the overall *pattern* of temperamental functioning as much as the variation on each separate attribute.

Brain Damage and Mental Retardation

Although some published reports suggest that brain damage or mental retardation may be associated with a distinctive pattern of temperamental functioning, there has been little systematic study of the matter (see Thomas & Chess 1977). It is apparent already that both retarded and brain-damaged children exhibit as wide a variety of temperamental characteristics as do normal children, and that few differences are found when individual temperamental features are considered. However, Hertzig's (1982) longitudinal study of low-birthweight infants has shown a significant association between abnormalities on a neurological examination and the 'difficult child' temperamental pattern. It is well established that brain damage and mental retardation carry a markedly increased psychiatric risk, and the possibility that this increased risk is due in part to an effect on the pattern of temperamental functioning warrants further study.

Sex Differences

Numerous studies have shown that psychiatric disorder is substantially more common in boys than girls; also it has been found repeatedly that boys are more susceptible than girls to emotional-behavioural problems in association with family discord and disruption (Rutter 1981b). The reasons for this greater vulnerability of boys remain rather obscure but it would seem plausible that sex-linked temperamental differences might play a part. Accordingly, it seems surprising that most investigations have reported few, if any, signficant sex differences in temperamental variables. However, the negative findings may be a consequence of looking at each attribute separately rather than examining composite scores associated with psychiatric risk. The question of possible sex differences in overall temperamental patterns requires further study.

Modes of Operation of Temperament

Perhaps the most fundamental question concerns the manner and mechanisms by which temperamental variables exert their effect. As we have seen temperamental attributes are important predictors not only of how children respond to 'stress' situations but also of the likelihood that they will develop various types of emotional and behavioural disorder. But what do these statistical associations mean in terms of underlying mechanisms, and why are children with particular temperamental patterns more at risk than those with other temperamental features? Cameron (1978) used the geological metaphor of temperament reflecting 'fault lines' in the emerging personality so that behavioural 'earthquakes' arise in those children with 'fault lines' who experience environmental strains. However, this analogy seems both inapt and unhelpful. Why should particular temperamental patterns be regarded as 'faulty' and in what way do they put the child at risk? Dunn (1980) and Rutter (1977) suggest that children's temperamental differences may influence development through several mechanisms—including effects of these differences on how other people respond to and interact with the child; the shaping of life experiences; the determining of what is an *effective* environment for the child; the reflection of the child's social adaptive capacity i.e. malleability and adaptability in responding to altered environmental circumstances: and the rather imprecise concept of psychological vulnerability. There is a certain amount of empirical support for each of these mechanisms but the issues remain little explored up to now. We do not know, for example, how temperamental variables relate to psychophysiological measures such as autonomic reactivity or to styles of coping with stress situations.

Finally, we have only a limited understanding of the role of temperament in personality development. We use the term 'temperament' in childhood rather than 'personality' and we talk of the importance of temperamental variables in shaping the emerging personality, but just what does that mean? What is the relationship between temperamental attributes such as intensity of emotional expression and personality variables such as extraversion and neuroticism? Do the differences in terminology merely reflect differences in the concepts of the workers who introduced these various terms or are

there basic developmental processes and changes that the different terms reflect?

CONCLUSIONS

As this brief review has emphasized, the last decade has seen a burgeoning of interest in temperament. There has been an accompanying substantial growth in our knowledge and understanding of the importance of temperamental differences. Temperament constitutes a variable of considerable predictive power in developmental psychopathology, a power with both practical and theoretical implications. But many difficult issues and problems still require resolution.

REFERENCES

Bates JE 1980 The concept of difficult temperament. Merrill-Palmer Q 26:299–319

Bates JE, Freeland CAB, Lounsbury ML 1979 Measurement of infant difficultness. Child Dev 50:794–803

Bem DJ, Funder DC 1978 Predicting more of the people more of the time: assessing the personality of situations. Psychol Rev 81:485–501

Billman J, McDevitt SC 1980 Convergence of parent and observer ratings of temperament with observations of peer interaction in nursery school. Child Dev 51:395–400

Buss AH, Plomin RA 1975 A temperament theory of personality development. Wiley Interscience, New York

Buss DM, Block JH, Block J 1980 Preschool activity level: personality correlates and developmental implications. Child Dev 51:401–408

Cameron JR 1978 Parental treatment, children's temperament, and the risk of childhood behavioral problems. 2: Initial temperament, parental attitudes, and the incidence and form of behavioral problems. Am J Orthopsychiatry 48:141–147

Chess S, Thomas A, Birch HG 1959 Characteristics of the individual child's behavioral responses to the environment. Am J Orthopsychiatry 29:791–802

Dunn J 1980 Individual differences in temperament. In: Rutter M (ed) Scientific foundations of developmental psychiatry. Heinemann Medical, London. p. 101–109

Dunn J, Kendrick C 1980 Studying temperament and parent-child interaction: comparison of interview and direct observation. Dev Med Child Neurol 22:494–496

Dunn J, Kendrick C, MacNamee R 1981 The reaction of first born children to the birth of a sibling: mothers' reports. J Child Psychol Psychiatry Allied Discip 22:1–18

Epstein S 1979 The stability of behaviour. 1: On predicting most of the people much of the time. J Pers Soc Psychol 37:1097–1126

Eysenck HJ 1970 The structure of human personality. Methuen, London

Garside RF, Birch HG, Scott DM, Chambers S, Kolvin I, Tweddle EG, Barber LM 1975 Dimensions of temperament in infant school children. J Child Psychol Psychiatry Allied Discip 16:219–232

Gesell A 1937 Early evidences of individuality in the human infant. Sci Monthly 45:217–225

Goldsmith HH, Gottesman II 1981 Origins of variation in behavioral style: a longitudinal study of temperament in young twins. Child Dev 52:91–103

Graham P, Rutter M, George S 1973 Temperamental characteristics as predictors of behavior disorders in children. Am J Orthopsychiatry 43:328–339

Hertzig ME 1982 Temperament and neurologic status. In: Rutter M (ed) Behavioral syndromes of brain dysfunction in childhood. Guilford Press, New York, in press

Kagan J 1980 Perspectives on continuity. In: Brim OG, Kagan J (eds) Constancy and change in human development. Harvard University Press. Cambridge, Mass., p 26–74

Keogh BK, Pullis ME 1980 Temperament influences on the development of exceptional children. Adv Spec Educ 1:239–276

Matheny AP 1980 Bayley's infant behavior record: behavioral components and twin analyses. Child Dev 51:1157–1167

Matheny AP, Dolan AB 1975 Persons, situations and time: a genetic view of behavioral change in children. J Pers Soc Psychol 32:1106–1110

Mischel W 1969 Personality and assessment. Wiley, London

Mischel W 1979 On the interface of cognition and personality: Beyond the person-situation debate. Am Psychol 34:740–754

Moss HA, Susman EJ 1980 Longitudinal study of personality development. In: Brim OG, Kagan J (eds) Constancy and change in human development. Harvard University Press, Cambridge, Mass., p 530–598

Persson-Blennow I, McNeil TF 1979 A questionnaire for measurement of temperament in six-month old infants: development and standardization. J Child Psychol Psychiatry Allied Discip 20:1–14

Rutter M 1970 Psychological development—predictions from infancy. J Child Psychol Psychiatry Allied Discip 11:49–62

Rutter M 1977 Individual differences. In: Rutter M, Hersov L (eds) Child psychiatry: modern approaches. Blackwell Scientific Publications, Oxford, p 3–21

Rutter M 1978 Family, area and school influences in the genesis of conduct disorder. In: Hersov LA et al (eds) Aggression and anti-social behaviour in childhood and adolescence. Pergamon Press, Oxford, p 95–113

Rutter M 1981a Stress, coping and development: some issues and some questions. J Child Psychol Psychiatry Allied Discip 22:323–356

Rutter M 1981b Epidemiological-longitudinal approaches to the study of development. In: Collins WA (ed) The concept of development. (Proc 15th Minnesota Symp on Child Psychol) Erlbaum, Hillsdale, NJ, in press

Rutter M, Birch H, Thomas A, Chess S 1964 Temperamental characteristics in infancy and the later development of behavioural disorders. Br J Psychiatry 110:651–661

Schaffer HR 1966 Activity level as a constitutional determinant of infantile reaction to deprivation. Child Dev 37:595–602

Thomas A, Chess S 1977 Temperament and development. Brunner/Mazel, New York

Torgersen AM, Kringlen E 1978 Genetic aspects of temperamental differences in infants. J Am Acad Child Psychol 17:433–444

Wilson RS 1977 Mental development in twins. In: Oliverio A (ed) Genetics, environment and intelligence. North-Holland Publishing, Amsterdam, p 305–334

Resilient Children

Emmy E. Werner

Research has identified numerous risk factors that increase the probability of developmental problems in infants and young children. Among them are biological risks, such as pre- and perinatal complications, congenital defects, and low birth weight; as well as intense stress in the caregiving environment, such as chronic poverty, family discord, or parental mental illness (Honig 1984). In a 1979 review of the literature of children's responses to such stress and risks, British child psychiatrist Michael Rutter wrote:

> There is a regrettable tendency to focus gloomily on the ills of mankind and on all that can and does go wrong....The potential for prevention surely lies in increasing our knowledge and understanding of the reasons why some children are *not* damaged by deprivation....(p. 49)

For even in the most terrible homes, and beset with physical handicaps, some children appear to develop stable, healthy personalities and to display a remarkable degree of resilience, i.e., the ability to recover from or adjust easily to misfortune or sustained life stress. Such children have recently become the focus of attention of a few researchers who have asked *What is right with these children?* and, by implication, *How can we help others to become less vulnerable in the face of life's adversities?*

THE SEARCH FOR PROTECTIVE FACTORS

As in any detective story, a number of overlapping sets of observations have begun to yield clues to the roots of resiliency in children. Significant findings have come from the few longitudinal studies which have followed the same groups of children from infancy or the preschool years through adolescence (Block

and Block 1980; Block 1981; Murphy and Moriarty 1976; Werner and Smith 1982). Some researchers have studied the lives of minority children who did well in school in spite of chronic poverty and discrimination (Clark 1983; Gandara 1982; Garmezy 1981; 1983; Kellam et al. 1975; Shipman 1976). A few psychiatrists and psychologists have focused their attention on the resilient offspring of psychotic patients (Anthony 1974; Bleuler 1978; Garmezy 1974; Kauffman et al. 1979; Watt et al. 1984; Werner and Smith 1982) and on the coping patterns of children of divorce (Wallerstein and Kelly 1980). Others have uncovered hidden sources of strength and gentleness among the uprooted children of contemporary wars in El Salvador, Ireland, Israel, Lebanon, and Southeast Asia (Ayala-Canales 1984; Fraser 1974; Heskin 1980; Rosenblatt 1983). Perhaps some of the most moving testimonials to the resiliency of children are the life stories of the child survivors of the Holocaust (Moskovitz 1983).

All of these children have demonstrated unusual psychological strengths despite a history of severe and/or prolonged psychological stress. Their personal competencies and some unexpected sources of support in their caregiving environment either compensated for, challenged, or protected them against the adverse effects of stressful life events (Garmezy, Masten, and Tellegren 1984). Some researchers have called these children *invulnerable* (Anthony 1974); others consider them to be *stress resistant* (Garmezy and Tellegren 1984); still others refer to them as *superkids* (Kauffman et al. 1979). In our own longitudinal study on the Hawaiian island of Kauai, we have found them to be *vulnerable, but invincible* (Werner and Smith 1982).

These were children like Michael for whom the odds, on paper, did not seem very promising. The son of teen-age parents, Michael was born prematurely and spent his first three weeks of life in the hospital, separated from his mother. Immediately after his birth, his father was sent with the Army to Southeast Asia for almost two years. By the time Michael was eight, he had three younger siblings and his parents were divorced. His mother left the area and had no further contact with the children.

And there was Mary, born to an overweight, nervous, and erratic mother who had experienced several miscarriages, and a father who was an unskilled farm laborer with only four years of education. Between Mary's fifth and tenth birthdays, her mother had several hospitalizations for repeated bouts with mental illness, after having inflicted both physical and emotional abuse on her daughter.

Yet both Michael and Mary, by age 18, were individuals with high self-esteem and sound values, caring for others and liked by their peers, successful in school, and looking forward to their adult futures. We have learned that such resilient children have four central characteristics in common:

- an active, evocative approach toward solving life's problems, enabling them to negotiate successfully an abundance of emotionally hazardous experiences;
- a tendency to perceive their experiences constructively, even if they caused pain or suffering;
- the ability, from infancy on, to gain other people's positive attention;
- a strong ability to use faith in order to maintain a positive vision of a meaningful life (O'Connell-Higgins 1983).

PROTECTIVE FACTORS WITHIN THE CHILD

Resilient children like Mary and Michael tend to have temperamental characteristics that elicit positive responses from family members as well as strangers (Garmezy 1983; Rutter 1978). They both suffered from birth complications and grew up in homes marred by poverty, family discord, or parental mental illness, but even as babies they were described as active, affectionate, cuddly, good natured, and easy to deal with. These same children already met the world on their own terms by the time they were toddlers (Werner and Smith 1982).

Several investigators have noted *both* a pronounced autonomy and a strong social orientation in resilient preschool children (Block 1981; Murphy and Moriarty 1976). They tend to play vigorously, seek out novel experiences, lack fear, and are quite self-reliant. But they are able to ask for help from adults or peers when they need it.

Sociability coupled with a remarkable sense of independence are characteristics also found among the resilient school-age children of psychotic parents. Anthony (1974) describes his meeting with a nine-year-old girl, whose father was an alcoholic and abused her and whose mother was chronically depressed. The girl suffered from a congenital dislocation of the hip which had produced a permanent limp, yet he was struck by her friendliness and the way she approached him in a comfortable, trustful way.

The same researcher tells of another nine-year-old, the son of a schizophrenic father and an emotionally disturbed mother, who found a refuge from his parents' outbursts in a basement room he had stocked with books, records, and food. There the boy had created an oasis of normalcy in a chaotic household. Resilient children often find a refuge and a source of self-esteem in hobbies and creative interests. Kauffman et al. (1979) describes the pastimes of two children who were the offspring of a schizophrenic mother and a depressed father:

> When David (age 8) comes home from school, he and his best friend often go up to the attic to play. This area...is filled with model towns, railroads, airports and castles....He knows the detailed history of most of his models, particularly the

airplanes.... David's older sister, now 15, is extraordinarily well-read. Her other interests include swimming, her boyfriend, computers and space exploration. She is currently working on a computer program to predict planetary orbits. (pp. 138, 139)

The resilient children on the island of Kauai, whom we studied for nearly two decades, were not unusually talented, but they displayed a healthy androgyny in their interests and engaged in hobbies that were not narrowly sex-typed. Such activities, whether it was fishing, swimming, horseback riding, or hula dancing, gave them a reason to feel proud. Their hobbies, and their lively sense of humor, became a solace when things fell apart in their lives (Masten 1982; Werner and Smith 1982).

In middle childhood and adolescence, resilient children are often engaged in acts of "required helpfulness" (Garmezy, in press). On Kauai, many adolescents took care of their younger siblings. Some managed the household when a parent was ill or hospitalized; others worked part-time after school to support their family. Such acts of caring have also been noted by Anthony (1974) and Bleuler (1978) in their studies of the resilient offspring of psychotic parents, and by Ayala-Canales (1984) and Moskovitz (1983) among the resilient orphans of wars and concentration camps.

PROTECTIVE FACTORS WITHIN THE FAMILY

Despite chronic poverty, family discord, or parental mental illness, most resilient children have had the opportunity to establish a close bond with at least one caregiver from whom they received lots of attention during the first year of life. The stress-resistant children in the Kauai Longitudinal Study as well as the resilient offspring of psychotic parents studied by Anthony (1974) had enough good nuturing to establish a basic sense of trust.

Some of this nuturing came from substitute caregivers within the family, such as older

siblings, grandparents, aunts, and uncles. Such alternate caregivers play an important role as positive models of identification in the lives of resilient children, whether they are reared in poverty (Kellam et al. 1975), or in a family where a parent is mentally ill (Kauffman et al. 1979), or coping with the aftermath of divorce (Wallerstein and Kelly 1980).

Resilient children seem to be especially adept at actively recruiting surrogate parents. The latter can come from the ranks of babysitters, nannies, or student roomers (Kauffman et al. 1979); they can be parents of friends (Werner and Smith 1982), or even a housemother in an orphanage (Ayala-Canales 1984; Moskovitz 1983).

The example of a mother who is gainfully and steadily employed appears to be an especially powerful model of identification for resilient girls reared in poverty, whether they are Black (Clark 1983), Chicana (Gandara 1982), or Asian-American (Werner and Smith 1982). Maternal employment and the need for sibling caregiving seems to contribute to the pronounced autonomy and sense of responsibility noted among these girls, especially in households where the father is permanently absent.

Structure and rules in the household and assigned chores enabled many resilient children to cope well in spite of poverty and discrimination, whether they lived on the rural island of Kauai, or in the inner cities of the American Midwest, or in a London borough (Clark 1983; Garmezy 1983; Rutter 1979).

Resilient children also seem to have been imbued by their families with a sense of coherence (Antonovsky 1979). They manage to believe that life makes sense, that they have some control over their fate, and that God helps those who help themselves (Murphy and Moriarty 1976). This sense of meaning persists among resilient children, even if they are uprooted by wars or scattered as refugees to the four corners of the earth. It enables them to love despite hate, and to maintain the ability to behave compassionately toward other people (Ayala-Canales 1984; Moskovitz 1983).

PROTECTIVE FACTORS OUTSIDE THE FAMILY

Resilient children find a great deal of emotional support outside of their immediate family. They tend to be well-liked by their classmates and have at least one, and usually several, close friends and confidants (Garmezy 1983; Kauffman et al. 1979; Wallerstein and Kelly 1980; Werner and Smith 1982). In addition, they tend to rely on informal networks of neighbors, peers, and elders for counsel and advice in times of crisis and life transitions.

Resilient children are apt to like school and to do well in school, not exclusively in academics, but also in sports, drama, or music. Even if they are not unusually talented, they put whatever abilities they have to good use. Often they make school a home away from home, a refuge from a disordered household. A favorite teacher can become an important model of identification for a resilient child whose own home is beset by family conflict or dissolution (Wallerstein and Kelly 1980).

In their studies of London schools, Rutter and his colleagues (1979) found that good experiences in the classroom could mitigate the effects of considerable stress at home. Among the qualities that characterized the more successful schools were the setting of appropriately high standards, effective feedback by the teacher to the students with ample use of praise, the setting of good models of behavior by teachers, and giving students positions of trust and responsibility. Children who attended such schools developed few if any emotional or behavioral problems despite considerable deprivation and discord at home (Pines 1984).

Early childhood programs and a favorite teacher can act as an important buffer against adversity in the lives of resilient young children. Moskovitz (1983), in her follow-up study in adulthood of the childhood survivors of con-centration camps, noted the pervasive influence of such a warm, caring teacher.

Participation in extracurricular activities or clubs can be another important informal source of support for resilient children. Many youngsters on Kauai were poor by material standards, but they participated in activities that allowed them to be part of a cooperative enterprise, whether being cheerleader for the home team or raising an animal in the 4-H Club. Some resilient older youth were members of the Big Brothers and Big Sisters Associations which enabled them to help other children less fortunate than themselves. For still others emotional support came from a church group, a youth leader in the YMCA or YWCA, or from a favorite minister, priest, or rabbi.

THE SHIFTING BALANCE BETWEEN VULNERABILITY AND RESILIENCY

For some children some stress appears to have a steeling rather than a scarring effect (Anthony 1974). But we need to keep in mind that there is a shifting balance between stressful life events which heighten children's vulnerability and the protective factors in their lives which enhance their resiliency. This balance can change with each stage of the life cycle and also with the sex of the child. Most studies in the United States and in Europe, for example, have shown that boys appear to be more vulnerable than girls when exposed to chronic and intense family discord in childhood, but this trend appears to be reversed by the end of adolescence.

As long as the balance between stressful life events and protective factors is manageable for children they can cope. But when the stressful life events outweigh the protective factors, even the most resilient child can develop problems. Those who care for children, whether their own or others, can help restore this balance, either by *decreasing* the child's exposure to intense or chronic life stresses, or by *increasing* the number of protective factors, i.e., competencies and sources of support.

IMPLICATIONS

What then are some of the implications of the still tentative findings from studies of resilient children? Most of all, they provide a more hopeful perspective than can be derived from reading the extensive literature on problem children which predominates in clinical psychology, child psychiatry, special education, and social work. Research on resilient children provides us with a focus on the self-righting tendencies that appear to move some children toward normal development under all but the most persistent adverse circumstances.

Those of us who care for young children, who work with or on behalf of them, can help tilt the balance from vulnerability to resiliency if we

• accept children's temperamental idiosyncracies and allow them some experiences that challenge, but do not overwhelm, their coping abilities;
• convey to children a sense of responsibility and caring, and, in turn, reward them for helpfulness and cooperation;
• encourage a child to develop a special interest, hobby, or activity that can serve as a source of gratification and self-esteem;
• model, by example, a conviction that life makes sense despite the inevitable adversities that each of us encounters;
• encourage children to reach out beyond their nuclear family to a beloved relative or friend.

Research on resilient children has taught us a lot about the special importance of surrogate parents in the lives of children exposed to chronic or intense distress. A comprehensive assessment of the impact on siblings, grandparents, foster parents, nannies, and babysitters on the development of high risk children is elaborated upon in Werner (1984).

Outside the family circle there are other powerful role models that give emotional support to a vulnerable child. The three most frequently encountered in studies of resilient children are: a favorite teacher, a good neighbor, or a member of the clergy.

There is a special need to strengthen such informal support for those children and their families in our communities which appear most vulnerable because they lack—temporarily or permanently—some of the essential social bonds that appear to buffer stress: working mothers of young children with no provisions for stable child care; single, divorced, or teenage parents; hospitalized and handicapped children in need of special care who are separated from their families for extended periods of time; and migrant or refugee children without permanent roots in a community.

Two other findings from the studies of resilient children have implications for the well-being of all children and for those who care for them.

1 At some point in their young lives, resilient children were required to carry out a socially desirable task to prevent others in their family, neighborhood, or community from experiencing distress or discomfort. Such acts of *required helpfulness* led to enduring and positive changes in the young helpers.

2 The central component in the lives of the resilient children that contributed to their effective coping appeared to be a feeling of confidence or faith that things *will work out* as well as can be reasonably expected, and that the odds *can* be surmounted.

The stories of resilient children teach us that such a faith can develop and be sustained, even under adverse circumstances, if children encounter people who give meaning to their lives and a reason for commitment and caring. Each of us can impart this gift to a child—in the classroom, on the playground, in the neighborhood, in the family—*if* we care enough.

BIBLIOGRAPHY

Anthony, E. J. "The Syndrome of the Psychologically Invulnerable Child." In *The Child in His Family 3: Children at Psychiatric Risk*, ed. E. J. Anthony and C. Koupernik. New York: Wiley, 1974.

Antonovsky, A. *Health, Stress and Coping: New Perspectives on Mental and Physical Well-being*. San Francisco: Jossey-Bass, 1979.

Ayala-Canales, C. E. "The Impact of El Salvador's Civil War on Orphan and Refugee Children." M. S. Thesis in Child Development, University of California at Davis, 1984.

Bleuler, M. *The Schizophrenic Disorders: Long-term Patient and Family Studies*. New Haven: Yale University Press, 1978.

Block, J. H. and Block, J. "The Role of Ego-Control and Ego-Resiliency in the Organization of Behavior." In *The Minnesota Symposia on Child Psychology 13: Development of Cognition, Affect and Social Relations*, ed. W. A. Collins. Hillsdale, N.J.: Erlbaum, 1980.

Block, J. "Growing Up Vulnerable and Growing Up Resistant: Preschool Personality, Pre-Adolescent Personality and Intervening Family Stresses." In *Adolescence and Stress*, ed. C. D. Moore. Washington, D.C.: U.S. Government Printing Office, 1981.

Clark, R. M. *Family Life and School Achievement: Why Poor Black Children Succeed or Fail*. Chicago: University of Chicago Press, 1983.

Fraser, M. *Children in Conflict*. Harmondsworth, England: Penguin Books, 1974.

Gandara, P. "Passing Through the Eye of the Needle: High Achieving Chicanas." *Hispanic Journal of Behavioral Sciences* 4, no. 2 (1982): 167–180.

Garmezy, N. "The Study of Competence in Children at Risk for Severe Psychopathology." In *The Child in His Family 3: Children at Psychiatric Risk*, ed. E. J. Anthony and C. Koupernik. New York: Wiley, 1974.

Garmezy, N. "Children Under Stress: Perspectives on Antecedents and Correlates of Vulnerability and Resistance to Psychopathology." In *Further Explorations in Personality*, ed. A. I. Rabin, J, Arnoff, A. M. Barclay, and R. A. Zucker. New York: Wiley, 1981.

Garmezy, N. "Stressors of Childhood." In *Stress, Coping and Development*, ed. N. Garmezy and M. Rutter. New York: McGraw-Hill, 1983.

Garmezy, N. "Stress Resistant Children: The Search for Protective Factors." In *Aspects of Current Child Psychiatry Research*, ed. J. E. Stevenson. *Journal of Child Psychology and Psychiatry*, Book Supplement 4. Oxford, England: Pergamon, in press.

Garmezy, N.; Masten, A. S.; and Tellegren, A. "The Study of Stress and Competence in Children: Building Blocks for Developmental Psychopathology." *Child Development* 55, no. 1 (1984): 97–111.

Garmezy, N. and Tellegren, A. "Studies of Stress-Resistant Children: Methods, Variables and Preliminary Findings." In *Advances in Applied Developmental Psychology*, ed. F. Morrison, C. Lord, and D. Keating. New York: Academic Press, 1984.

Heskin, K. *Northern Ireland: A Psychological Analysis*. New York: Columbia University Press, 1980.

Honig, A. "Research in Review: Risk Factors in Infants and Young Children." *Young Children* 38, no. 4 (May 1984): 60–73.

Kauffman, C.; Grunebaum, H.; Cohler, B.; and Gamer, E. "Superkids: Competent Children of Psychotic Mothers." *American Journal of Psychiatry* 136, no. 11 (1979): 1398–1402.

Kellan, S. G.; Branch, J. D.; Agrawal; K. C.; and Ensminger, M. E. *Mental Health and Going to School*. Chicago: University of Chicago Press, 1975.

Masten, A. "Humor and Creative Thinking in Stress-Resistant Children." Unpublished Ph.D. dissertation, University of Minnesota, 1982.

Moskovitz, S. *Love Despite Hate: Child Survivors of the Holocaust and Their Adult Lives*. New York: Schocken Books, 1983.

Murphy, L. and Moriarty, A. *Vulnerability, Coping and Growth from Infancy to Adolescence*. New Haven: Yale University Press, 1976.

O'Connell-Higgins, R. "Psychological Resilience and the Capacity of Intimacy." Qualifying paper, Harvard Graduate School of Education, 1983.

Pines, M. "PT Conversation: Michael Rutter: Resilient Children." *Psychology Today* 18, no. 3 (March 1984): 60, 62, 64–65.

Rosenblatt, R. *Children of War*. Garden City, N.Y.: Anchor Press, 1983.

Rutter, M. "Early Sources of Security and Competence." In *Human Growth and Development*, ed. J. Bruner and A. Garton. New York: Oxford University, 1978.

Rutter, M. "Protective Factors in Children's Responses to Stress and Disadvantage." In *Primary Prevention of Psychopathology 3: Social Competence in Children*, ed. M. W. Kent and J. E. Rolf. Hanover, N.H.: University Press of New England, 1979.

Rutter, M.; Maughan, B.; Mortimore, P.; and Ouston, J; with Smith, A. *Fifteen Thousand Hours: Secondary Schools and Their Effects on Children*. Cambridge, Mass.: Harvard University Press, 1979.

Shipman, V. C. *Notable Early Characteristics of High and Low Achieving Low SES Children*. Princeton, N.J.: Educational Testing Service, 1976.

Wallerstein, J. S. and Kelly, J. B. *Surviving the Breakup: How Children and Parents Cope with Divorce*. New York: Basic Books, 1980.

Watt, N. S.; Anthony, E. J.; Wynne, L. C.; and Rolf, J. E., eds. *Children at Risk for Schizophrenia: A Longitudinal Perspective*. London and New York: Cambridge University Press, 1984.

Werner, E. E. *Child Care: Kith, Kin and Hired Hands*. Baltimore: University Park Press, 1984.

Werner, E. E. and Smith, R. S. *Vulnerable, but Invincible: A Longitudinal Study of Resilient Children and Youth*. New York: McGraw-Hill, 1982.

CHAPTER 2

PHYSICAL GROWTH AND MATURATION

As did those in the previous section, the three articles in this section emphasize the relation between biological, social, and psychological development.

Henry Ricciuti points out that even among the poorest families in developing countries, there are wide variations in the incidence of malnutrition occurring among families and among individuals within families living under extremely adverse circumstances. These variations are associated with the characteristics and parenting competence of the primary caregiver and the quantity and quality of social, emotional, and cognitive stimulation provided for the children. Moreover, both the behavior and appearance of the malnourished child affect the responses of others to them and alter the child's experience in developmentally salient ways.

The article by Ruth Striegel-Moore, Lisa Silberstein, and Judith Rodin addresses a different kind of malnutrition—voluntary malnutrition in the form of bulimia. Bulimics are preoccupied with weight concerns and often manifest a pattern of eating binges; induced vomiting, or purging; and periods of excessive dieting that are associated with adverse physical, social, and psychological factors. Moreover, some bulimics exhibit wide weight variations or exhibit accompanying anorexia nervosa, an eating disorder associated with severe restriction of dietary intake that may sometimes be so extreme that it may result in death. The authors focus on several questions about bulimia that are important to developmental psychologists. First, why is this disorder much more prevalent in females than in males? Second, since only a minority of females develop bulimia, what are the biological, personality, emotional, and social factors that make particular women develop this disorder? What aspects of female development at different stages of development make some women more vulnerable to developing bulimia? Third, why has there been a great increase in bulimia in recent years? This last question is of great interest to life-span developmentalists who are interested in how the development of different cohorts is shaped as subjects are exposed to different life events or experience similar events in different ways. A cohort is a group of people who go through similar experiences at the same time in their lives. Thus, we might talk of the cohort who were adolescents or young adults during the Vietnam war; or the baby boom cohorts who were born in the period of greatly increased birthrates in the late forties and fifties; or the adolescent cohort of the late seventies and eighties when teenagers were exposed to liberalized sexual mores, high rates of teenaged pregnancies, and a high incidence of drug abuse in their peer group. In this article, one of the questions being asked by the authors is, ''What is it about the female adolescent or young adult cohort of the eighties that makes them so vulnerable to developing bulimia?''

Finally, the article by David Magnusson, Hakan Stattin, and Vernon Allen examines the role of the peer group in determining whether girls who reach biological maturity early are more likely to violate social norms related to sexual behavior and alcohol and drug use. The authors find a complex interaction between biological and social factors where early maturing girls with older friends, who they believe would sanction norm violation, are most likely to indulge in antisocial behavior in adolescence. Again, we see the behavioral expression of biological factors being mediated by the social situation.

READING 6

Interaction of Adverse Environmental and Nutritional Influences on Mental Development

Henry N. Ricciuti

The major theme to be stressed in this review is that we cannot adequately evaluate the influence of nutritional factors on children's mental development without simultaneously considering the related and often major role played by the child's social environment. At the same time, if we are concerned with promoting the mental development of young children at risk of malnutrition we are most likely to be successful through programs which are concerned not only with children's nutritional and health needs, as important as these obviously are, but also with enhancing the family's capacity to provide child care and child rearing environments which are generally facilitative of psychological development.

It is well known, of course, that protein-energy malnutrition may lead to increased early childhood mortality and morbidity, and to substantial impairment of physical growth and brain development, particularly if the nutritional deficits are early, severe, and prolonged. The possibility that nutritional deprivation may also have lasting adverse effects on the development of intellectual and social competence has been a matter of heightened and continuing concern during the past ten years or so. With the increasing public concern about malnutrition as a world-wide public health problem, there was a rather widespread tendency in the late 60's and early 70's to assume, somewhat uncritically, a direct causal relationship between early protein-energy malnutrition and impaired learning and intellectual development, found to be associated in some instance with irreversible mental retardation (Ricciuti, 1970; Scrimshaw and Gordon, 1968). This assumption was based in large part on human as well as animal studies indicating impaired brain development and brain function resulting from early malnutrition (Dobbing, 1968; Winick and Rosso, 1969), and on the frequent observation that children having suffered obvious malnutrition tend to show reduced levels of intellectual functioning and school achievement. During the past few years, however, it is increasingly recognized that the relationships between nutritional deprivation and psychological development in children are quite complicated, methodologically difficult to investigate, and not yet clearly understood.

Malnutrition is most prevalent in poor populations living under adverse socioeconomic and environmental conditions, including poor housing and sanitation, exposure to disease, inadequate health care, limited food availability, restricted educational opportunities, large family size, unfavourable feeding and child care practices, etc. (Cravioto, 1970). All of these conditions are capable of playing a significant role in limiting children's growth and development, not just physically, but psychologically as well. It is extremely difficult, therefore, if not impossible, to make meaningful evaluations of the independent effect of early malnutrition *as such* on mental development apart from the influence of the various adverse social and environmental conditions just mentioned. In recent years, fortunately, increasing attention is being focussed on the manner in which the child's nutritional status and various aspects of his social environment may interact in jointly influencing the course of mental development (Ricciuti, 1977).

PRE-NATAL MALNUTRITION

It is generally recognized that malnutrition in pregnancy represents one of a number of adverse factors which may affect fetal development, and which may be manifested in varying degrees of prematurity or fetal growth retardation, and that low birth weight and/or prematurity may be indicative of subsequent risk of sub-optimal intellectual development, or even of severe neurological handicap or mental retardation, particularly if the degree of prematurity or birth weight deficits is marked, and if other serious complications are also present (Drillien, 1972).

The risk of low birth weight or prematurity is substantially increased in mothers who are relatively young (under 19 years) or old (above 35 years), whose nutritional and growth histories are relatively poor, who have had poor health care and nutrition during pregnancy, and who have had a large number of closely spaced pregnancies (Siegel and Morris, 1970). These conditions tend to be most prevalent in the poorest populations and their reduction or elimination should obviously be a matter of prime concern from a social policy or public health perspective.

What about the subsequent behavioral or intellectual traits associated with prematurity and low birth weight? Considerable evidence is available of an association between reduced levels of intellectual functioning and low birth weight, particularly in the case of very low birth weight infants (<1500 grams) (Drillien, 1972; Thompson and Reynolds, 1977).

However, the intellectual or neurological consequences of low birth weight or prematurity are greatly affected by the quality of the child's post-natal environment, which can either attentuate or increase the risk of adverse developmental outcomes (Drillien, 1964; Beckwith and Cohen, 1980). For instance, the risk of being classified as "educationally backward" in school at age 7 was found to be substantially greater for low birth weight (full term) babies who were also 5th or later born, and came from poor families (about 18%) than for babies with similar birth weight deficits who were first born

in middle-income families (about 2%) (Davie et al, 1972). Thus the risks of adverse neurological and intellectual consequences associated with low birth weight and prematurity appear to be substantially reduced with the provision of high quality care in the post-natal period, associated with favourable environmental conditions in the home strongly supportive of the child's development. Since prematurity and low birth weight occur more frequently in families living under conditions of marked socio-economic and environmental adversity, it would seem particularly important to provide special supports to such families with these high-risk infants, in order to help ensure adequate patterns of post-natal care and child rearing. To make such efforts more effective, the socio-economic and environmental stresses under which these families live should be sought to be reduced.

POST-NATAL MALNUTRITION

Early clinical malnutrition severe enough to require hospitalization occurs with some frequency in poor populations (from 5% to as much as 20% in some instances), but the most widespread nutritional problem in such populations is mild-to-moderate, chronic undernutrition reflected primarily in retardation of physical growth and development. What can be said about the effects of such undernutrition on mental development?

MILD-TO-MODERATE MALNUTRITION

It is extremely difficult to evaluate the effects of mild-to-moderate malnutrition *as such* on mental development in children without taking into account the concurrent influence of various adverse social and environmental conditions typically associated with endemic malnutrition, and capable in their own right of affecting children's intellectual development. These interpretive difficulties can be readily illustrated by two studies of pre-school children from poor families, one in Chile (Monckeberg *et al.*, 1972), the other in Nigeria (Ashem and James, 1978). In each case, the IQ level of a sub-group of poor children considered malnourished because of reduced height or weight was found to be somewhat lower than that of taller or heavier children in the same low income sample. It is very likely, however, that the former were living under generally more unfavourable socio-economic and environmental circumstances than the latter and this could have contributed appreciably to the observed IQ differences.

In summary then, very little evidence is available that the chronic, mild-to-moderate malnutrition, endemic in many economically disadvantaged populations, has a significant, direct impact on mental development, apart from the substantial influence of various socio-economic and environmental factors typically associated with undernutrition. At the same time, one has to consider the possibility that undernutrition may be implicated indirectly as one of the many factors involved in the generally adverse environments associated with sub-optimal intellectual development and school achievement.

Severe Malnutrition Studies have been made of the behavioral consequences of severe, clinical protein-energy malnutrition occurring in the first several years of life. When examined during and shortly after rehabilitation, such children typically show substantially retarded physical growth and motor development, and perform appreciably worse than control children or below norms on standard developmental tests, as well as on measure of specific intellectual and attentional competencies (Pollitt and Thomson, 1977). Retrospective studies of pre-school and school-aged children having suffered clinical malnutrition in the first few years of life also indicate that such children tend to perform less well than controls on a number of intelligence and perceptual/cognitive tests, and to do less well in school (Cravioto and Delicardie, 1970; Hoorweg, 1976). Here

too, one needs to be cautious in interpreting these findings as evidence of a direct causal link between early clinical malnutrition and subsequent sub-normal mental functioning. It is quite possible, for example, that the particular socio-environmental factors which led to the development of early clinical malnutrition in some children and not in others in the same family or in the same community may also have contributed directly to the reduced intellectual performance observed.

Despite the aforementioned uncertainties, it seems pretty clear that severe protein-calorie malnutrition occurring in the first few years of life may well be implicated as *one* of the various environmental factors leading to subsequent sub-optimal or impaired mental development. The effects appear to be more marked the more severe the nutritional deprivation, and the longer it continues without treatment. Recent studies suggest, however, that the potential long term effects of severe early malnutrition may be either greatly attenuated with continued nutritional and environmental adversity or virtually eliminated by developmentally supportive later environments.

INTERACTION BETWEEN MALNUTRITION AND SOCIO-ENVIRONMENTAL INFLUENCES

It is well recognized that severe and early protein-calorie malnutrition is most likely to occur among the poorest populations of developing countries, living under very adverse socio-economic and environmental circumstances. However, it's important to note that even under these generally stressful and adverse conditions, such severe malnutrition is not distributed uniformly among the poorest families, nor even among siblings within the same family. In a number of recent studies, it has been possible to identify variations in specific features of the child's home and family environment which may substantially increase *or* reduce the risk of malnutrition occurring in particular families. Based on research done in Jamaica (Richardson, 1974), Mexico (Cravioto and Delicardie, 1976), and India (Graves, 1978), these differentiating features appear to center in general on what we might call the primary caregiver's "mothering competence," or the degree to which child care practices provide adequate nurturance and support for growth and development even under the adverse conditions which these families confront.

These points are illustrated more specifically in the previously mentioned prospective longitudinal studies of several hundred infants born in a poor rural Mexican village, 22 of whom were severely malnourished in the first few years of life (Craviato and Delicardie, 1976). Although the families of these malnourished children did not differ from comparison families on such demographic factors as literacy, education or income level, family size, or parental age, the homes of the malnourished children were observed as early as the first year of life to be generally lower in the quantity and quality of social, emotional and cognitive stimulation provided. Also, mothers of the malnourished children seemed less inclined to be in contact with the outside world (less radio listening), less open to modernization, and were more passive and less sensitive to the young child's needs. Similar characteristics have been reported from observations of mothers who had malnourished children in India and Nepal (Graves, 1978) as well as in Jamaica (Kerr *et al.*, 1978). In a completely different setting an earlier nutrition survey of a large sample of low-income Baltimore children revealed that a sub-group of five year olds who were found to be undernourished (by dietary intake and biochemical measures) tended to come from homes characterized by more "inadequate mothering" than those of a carefully matched control group from the same population (Hepner and Maiden, 1971).

Several other studies suggest the possibility that early disturbances of mother-infant interaction (including feeding disturbances) may be predictive of subsequent sub-optimal weight gain (Pollitt and Wirtz, 1981 in press) or in more extreme instances, of subsequent "failure to thrive" or child neglect (Gray *et al.*, 1977). Another important example of the interrelatedness of nutritional and environmental circumstances affecting the child's development is found in the growing evidence that the infant or young child's altered nutritional status, as reflected in physical appearance, general demeanor, and behavior may affect the manner in which the mother or other primary caregivers respond to and care for the child, thus potentially altering the child's early experience in developmentally significant ways (Chavez *et al.*, 1975; Graves, 1978).

Recent evidence from both animal and human studies indicates that, as in the case of less severe malnutrition a supportive, growth promoting environment may substantially attenuate or even prevent the potentially unfavorable consequences of severe malnutrition. A recent study in Jamaica, for example (Richardson, 1976), indicated that severely malnourished children from families scoring relatively high on several social background factors showed only a minimal IQ reduction at 6 to 10 years of age, in comparison to the larger IQ deficits shown by children from more adverse socio-environmental home backgrounds. Similarly, Korean orphan girls judged to have been severely or moderately malnourished at 2 to 3 years of age and adopted by middle class American families achieved levels of intellectual and scholastic achievement compatible with the social status of their foster-parents (Winick *et al.*, 1975).

The findings just summarized clearly stress the importance of variations in particular aspects of family environments or family functioning which seem to make some families more or less vulnerable to the occurrence of severe malnutrition than others in the same "at risk" population, and also more or less capable of "buffering" or attenutating the potentially adverse behavioral effects of severe malnutrition when it does occur. Such information, which is just beginning to accumulate and greatly needs further expansion, should be helpful in planning effective preventive or remedial approaches aimed at families where the risk of severe malnutrition is particularly high. Similarly, a fuller understanding of the strength of those families who seem to be coping more successfully with the general socio-economic and environmental constraints confronting them may well provide valuable leads for helping those who are coping less well.

Generally speaking, these research results emphasize once again the importance of efforts to ameliorate the general socio-environmental circumstances under which many poor children live, from the perspective of prevention as well as remediation of the long term negative consequences of malnutrition and environmental deprivation. Such prevention and remediation calls for appropriate intervention measures.

RECENT INTERVENTION RESEARCH

First, insofar as birth weight and physical growth are concerned, the results certainly can be viewed as generally promising since they suggest that favorable effects on perinatal mortality, birth weight and physical growth and development can be achieved through improvement of health care and supplementation of the diets of pregnant women and children (Lechtig *et al.*, 1975, Klein, 1979; Herrera *et al.*, 1980).

In the case of infants and pre-school children with severe malnutrition of the marasmus or kwashiorkor type, it has been apparent for some time that the earlier the treatment and rehabilitation of these children, the less the risk of severe developmental impairment (Pollitt and Thomson, 1977). Some recent or current treatment programs have also incorporated procedures of care intended to ensure that the infant or toddler is not deprived of adequate social and physical stimulation. (McLaren *et*

al., 1973; Monckeberg and Ruimallo, 1979). In general, such procedures seem to offer some facilitation of the recovery process during treatment and rehabilitation, although their long term benefits are likely to be very much influenced by the nature of the enduring environments to which the children return after hospitalization.

Clearly then it is extremely important to ensure early detection, treatment, and rehabilitation of children with severe clinical malnutrition under conditions which also provide adequate stimulation and meet the children's social and emotional needs. It would seem equally important to reach these "high risk" families with health care and other supportive services intended to enhance the child care and child rearing environments in the home.

What can be said about the role of nutritional supplementation in fostering the mental development of children at risk of mild-to-moderate malnutrition? Here, the picture which has emerged thus far seems to be considerably less encouraging. For the most part, the effects of supplementation on measures of mental development are very small and rather inconsistent, suggesting that simply increasing dietary intake in mild-to-moderately-malnourished children has relatively little meaningful impact on intellectual functioning (Herrera *et al.*, 1980; Irwin *et al.*, 1979; Mora *et al.*, 1979). Similarly, while the inclusion of parent education for mothers of infants and toddlers in one project in Bogota yielded a few promising trends, the overall effects were again very modest (Mora *et al.*, 1979). It may well be that for families living under such adverse environmental circumstances, the home visiting was unable to bring about a sufficient alteration of the home environments to produce a significant impact on children's early mental development. On the other hand, a highly structured cognitively-oriented pre-school program like that employed in a project in Cali, Colombia (McKay *et al.*, 1978) appears capable of producing clear gains in intellectual skills while children are enrolled, but these gains tend to fade appreciably after the children have left the program, as has been found in many such intervention programs. However, a recent follow-up study in the U.S. suggests that children in some pre-school programs may show benefits later in terms of less need for special education, less retention in grade (Darlington *et al.*, 1980).

Despite the generally modest results achieved by these major intervention efforts thus far, it seems essential that we continue to direct major research and development efforts at the design of more effective strategies of intervention for optimizing the growth and development of children who live in adverse environments and are at risk of both malnutrition and sub-optimal intellectual development. The goal of fostering the mental development of children living in poverty is most likely to be met through *comprehensive* programs meeting the various basic needs of poor children and families. In short, the most effective intervention strategies are likely to be those which are concerned with children's nutritional and health needs, with supporting the families' capacity to provide developmentally facilitative child care and child rearing environments, and with the provision of increased opportunities for formal and informal educational experiences in day care centers or schools. In the final analysis, of course, changes of this sort are most likely to be brought about on an enduring basis through significant amelioration of the adverse social and economic circumstances under which many thousands of very poor families live in various regions of the world.

REFERENCES

Ashem, B. and James, M. D. (1978). J. Child Psychol. Psychiatry 19, 23.

Beckwith, L. and Cohen, S. E. (1980). In High-Risk Infants and Children: Adult and Peer Interactions. Chapter 9. (T.M. Field, editor), New York: Academic Press.

Chavez, A., Martinez, C. and Yachine, T. (1975). Fed. Proc., 34, 1574.

Cravioto, J. (1970). In: Malnutrition is a Problem of Ecology. (P. Gyorgy and Q. C. Kline, editors). New York: Karger.

Cravioto, J. and Delicardie, E. R. (1970). Am. J. Dis. Child, 120, 404.

Cravioto, J. and Delicardie, E. R. (1976). In: Nutrition and Agricultural Development. (N. S. Scrimshaw and M. Behar, editors). New York: Plenum Press.

Darlington, R. B. (1980). Science, 208, 202.

Davie, R., Butler, N. and Goldstein, H. (1972). From Birth to Seven: A Report of the National Child Development Study. London, England: Longman.

Drillien, C. M. (1964). Growth and Development of the Prematurely Born Infant. Edinburgh and London: Livingstone.

Drillien, C. M. (1972). Dev. Med. Child Neurol., 14, 563.

Dobbing, J. (1968). In Malnutrition, Learning and Behavior. (N. S. Scrimshaw and J. E. Gordon, editors). Cambridge, MA: Massachusetts Institute of Technology Press.

Graves, P. L. (1978). Am. J. Clin. Nutr., 31, 541.

Gray, J. D., Cutler, C. A., Dean, J. and Kempe, C. H. (1977). Child Abuse Neglect, 1, 45.

Hepner, R. and Maiden, N. C. (1971). Nutr. Rev., 29, 219.

Herrera, M. G., Mora, J. O., Christiansen, N., Ortiz, N., Clement, J., Vuori, L., Waber, D. De Paredes, B. and Wagner, M. (1980). In: Life Span Developmental Psychology: Intervention. (R. R. Turner and H. W. Reese, editors). New York: Academic Press.

Hoorweg, J. C. (1976). Protein-energy Malnutrition and Intellectual Abilities, The Hague Paris: Mouton.

Irwin, M., Klein, R., Townshend, J., Owen, W., Engle, P., Lechtig, A., Mortorell, R., Yarbrough, C., Lasky, R. and Delgado, H. (1979). In: Behavioral Effect of Energy and Protein Deficits. (J. Brozek, editor). NIH Pub. No. 79-1906.

Kerr, M., Bouges, J. and Kerr, D. (1978). Pediatrics, 62, 778.

Klein, R. E. (1979). In: Malnutrition, Environment, and Behavior: New Perspectives. (D. A.

Levitsky, editor) Ithaca, N.Y.: Cornell University Press.

Lechtig, A., Delgado, H., Lasky, R., Klein, R., Engle, P., Yarbrough, C. and Habicht, J.P. (1975). Am. J. Dis. Child., **129**, 434.

McKay, H., Sinisterra, L., McKay, H. G., Gomez, H. and Lloreda, P. (1978). Science, **200**, 270.

McLaren, D. S., Yaktin, U. S., Kanawat, A., Sabbagh, S. and Kadi, Z. (1973). J. Ment. Defic. Res., **17**, 273.

Monckeberg, F. and Ruimallo, J. (1979). In: Behavioral Effects of Energy and Protein Deficits. (J. Brozek, Editor). NIH Pub. No. 79-1906.

Monckeberg, F., Tisler, S., Toro, S., Gattas, V. and Vegal, L. (1972). Am. J. Clin. Nutr., **25**, 776.

Mora, J. O., Christiansen, N., Ortiz, N., Vuori, L. and Herrera, M. G. (1979). In: Behavioral Effects of Energy and Protein Deficits (J. Brozek, editor) NIH Pub. No. 79-1906.

Pollitt, E. and Thomson, C. (1977). In: Nutrition and the Brain. (R. J. Wurtman and J. J. Wurtman, editors). New York: Raven.

Ricciuti, H. N. (1970). In: Psychology and the Problems of Society. Washington, D.C.: American Psychological Association.

Ricciuti, H. N. (1977). In: Ecological factors in human development, (H. McGurk, editor). Amsterdam: North-Holland.

Richardson, S. A. (1974). In: Advancement in Pediatrics. (I. Schulman, editor). Chicago: Year Book Medical Publishers.

Richardson, S. A. (1976). Pediatr. Res., **10**, 57.

Scrimshaw, N. S. and Gordon, J. E. (1968). Malnutrition, Learning and Behavior. Cambridge, MA: Massachusetts Institute of Technology Press.

Siegel, E. and Morris, W. (1970) In: Maternal Nutrition and the Course of Pregnancy. Washington, D.C.: National Academy of Sciences.

Thompson, T. and Reynolds, J. (1977). J. Perinat. Med., **5**, 59.

Winick, M., Meyer, K. and Harris, R. C. (1975). Science, **190**, 1173.

Winick, M. and Russo, P. (1969). J. Pediatr., **74**, 774.

READING 7

Toward an Understanding of Risk Factors for Bulimia

Ruth H. Striegel-Moore
Lisa R. Silberstein
Judith Rodin

In its end-of-the-year review, *Newsweek* referred to 1981 as "the year of the binge purge syndrome" (Adler, 1982, p. 29). This designation reflected the public's growing awareness of a significant sociocultural phenomenon, namely, the seemingly sudden and dramatic rise of bulimia. One year earlier, bulimia had become recognized as a psychiatric disorder in its own right in the Diagnostic and Statistical Manual of Mental Disorders (DSM-III; American Psychiatric Association, 1980); this development has facilitated standardized assessment. In the last few years there has been a proliferation of literature on bulimia, as researchers and clinicians have attempted to describe the clinical picture of the disorder, to outline treatment approaches, and to identify factors associated with it.

Even though the investigative forays into bulimia have really just begun, it now seems both possible and useful to draw together the current and sometimes disparate existing pieces of knowledge about the disorder and to propose working hypotheses about its etiology. A few efforts have already been made in this direction (Garner, Rockert, Olmsted, Johnson, & Coscina, 1985; Hawkins & Clement, 1984; Johnson, Lewis, & Hagman, 1984; Russell, 1979; Slade, 1982). Our own conceptualization of this disorder both permits better understanding of the risk factors already proposed and implicates additional variables in the etiology of bulimia. We hope that as we delineate possible risk factors of bulimia, it will become clearer where our current knowledge is most lacking and therefore where research is needed. An understanding of etiology will, we hope, also facilitate the clinical treatment of bulimia.

As we think about bulimia and its recent rise, three questions in particular demand attention. First, bulimia is primarily a woman's problem, with research consistently indicating that approximately 90% of bulimic individuals are female[1] (Halmi, Falk, & Schwartz, 1981; Katzman, Wolchik, & Braver, 1984; Leon, Carroll, Chernyk, & Finn, 1985; Pope, Hudson, Yurgelun-Todd, & Hudson, 1984; Pyle et al., 1983; Wilson, 1984). Hence, a key factor that places someone at risk for developing bulimia is being a woman. One major question that demands an answer then is, simply, Why women?

Second, it appears that weight concerns and dieting are so pervasive among females today that they have become normative (Rodin, Silberstein, & Striegel-Moore, 1985). An overwhelming number of women currently feel too fat (regardless of their actual weight) and engage in repeated dieting efforts (Drewnowski, Riskey, & Desor, 1982; Garner, Olmsted, & Polivy, 1983; Herman & Polivy, 1975; Huon & Brown, 1984; Mann et al., 1983; Moss, Jennings, McFarland, & Carter, 1984; Nielsen, 1979; Nylander, 1971; Polivy & Herman, 1985; Pyle et al., 1983; Wooley & Wooley, 1984). Despite the prevalence of dieting and weight concerns among women in general, it is still a minority who develop the clinical syndrome of bulimia, thus prompting another essential question: Which women in particular?[2] In our discussion, we will be conceptualizing a continuum ranging from unconcern with weight and normal eating, to "normative discontent" with weight and moderately disregulated/restrained eating, to bulimia (Rodin, Silberstein, & Striegel-Moore, 1985). The question of "which women in particular" can be seen, therefore, as a question of which women will move along this continuum from normative concerns to bulimia.

Third, it is not women in all times and places but rather women of *this* era in Western society who are developing bulimia. Therefore, a third question is, Why now? This question has received very little empirical attention. However, the seemingly sudden and dramatic rise of bulimia over the past few years suggests that we need to consider the possible role of sociohistorical factors.

One critical aspect to the challenge of developing an etiological model of bulimia is the heterogeneity of the women who develop the disorder. Bulimic women differ with regard to their eating behavior and body weight, with some women exhibiting anorexia nervosa as well as bulimia either in the past or at present, others maintaining weight within the normal range, and others currently or in the past being obese (Beumont, George, & Smart, 1976; Garfinkel & Garner, 1982; Garner, Garfinkel, & O'Shaughnessy, 1985; Gormally, 1984; Loro & Orleans, 1981). Bulimic women can be divided into those who purge (by means of vomiting or abuse of cathartics) and those who do not resort to purging as a way of controlling their weight (Casper, Eckert, Halmi, Goldberg, & Davis, 1980; Garfinkel, Moldofsky, & Garner, 1980; Grace, Jacobson, & Fullager, 1985; Halmi et

---

[1]At present, there are insufficient data to discuss the etiology of the disorder in the 10% of bulimics who are men. Some of the risk factors specified for women may relate to men as well. Some speculation on what groups of men are most vulnerable will be considered briefly in the last section of the article.

[2]Many investigators suggest that eating disorders should be conceptualized as a spectrum spanning anorexia nervosa, bulimia, and compulsive overeating (Andersen, 1983; Szmukler, 1982; Yager, Landsverk, Lee-Benner, & Johnson, 1983). In this relatively early stage of conceptualization, it seems useful to limit our scope to bulimia. However, we will sometimes draw on the existing literature about other eating disorders when relevant. A task for the future is clearly to delineate more precisely the commonalities and differences among the eating disorders and to develop a conceptual framework that integrates them.

al., 1981). Furthermore, bulimic women vary greatly regarding the nature and extent of associated psychopathology. Some bulimic women do not exhibit any other psychiatric symptoms aside from those subsumed under the diagnosis of bulimia (Johnson, Stuckey, Lewis, & Schwartz, 1982), whereas others show multiple types of psychopathology (Garner & Garfinkel, 1985; Garner, Garfinkel, & O'Shaughnessy, 1985; Hudson, Laffer, & Pope, 1982; Hudson, Pope, & Jonas, 1984; Lacey, 1982; Wallach & Lowenkopf, 1984). The implications of this heterogeneity for identifying risk factors are crucial. A particular risk factor that may be central to the etiology of the disorder in some women may be minor or even irrelevant in the development of bulimia in other women. Furthermore, this heterogeneity argues against unidimensional models of bulimia. Any model of bulimia (e.g., biochemical or addiction models) still must consider the three questions that we are now posing.

The questions—Why women? Which women in particular? Why now?—compose the starting point for our discussion of factors placing individuals at risk for bulimia. These questions compel us to consider bulimia from a range of perspectives—sociocultural, developmental, psychological, and biological. Examining each of these perspectives in turn, we will consider the first two questions in tandem. From each perspective, we must try first to identify factors that might place women at greater risk than men for bulimia and second to understand which women in particular might be at greatest risk. Subsequently, we will consider our third question, Why now?

SOCIOCULTURAL VARIABLES

Central to an etiological analysis are the sociocultural factors that place women at greater risk than men for bulimia. We and others have reviewed data suggesting that risk increases because our society values attractiveness and thinness in particular, therefore making obesity a highly stigmatized condition (Boskind-White & White, 1983; Garner, Rockett, Olmsted, Johnson, & Coscina, 1985; Hawkins & Clement, 1984; Johnson et al, 1984; Rodin, Silberstein, & Striegel-Moore, 1985; Russell, 1979). Numerous studies suggest that this attitude affects people of all ages and that these social norms are applied more strongly to women than to men (see Rodin, Silberstein, & Striegel-Moore, 1985, for review). We begin the present analysis by asking which women in particular are affected by these sociocultural attitudes regarding attractiveness and weight, and then we suggest other significant social norms, not previously discussed, that may enhance the risk for bulimia in women.

Which Women in Particular?

How might the high value placed on thinness and the stigmatization of obesity in women have a greater impact on some women than on others, thus placing them at greater risk for bulimia? At a basic level, women at greatest risk for bulimia should be those who have accepted and internalized most deeply the sociocultural mores about thinness and attractiveness. In other words, the more a woman believes that "what is fat is bad, what is thin is beautiful, and what is beautiful is good," the more she will work toward thinness and be distressed about fatness. To explore this hypothesis, we developed a series of attitude statements based on these sociocultural values (e.g., "attractiveness increases the likelihood of professional success"). As predicted, bulimic women expressed substantially greater acceptance of these attitudes than non-bulimic women (Striegel-Moore, Silberstein, & Rodin, 1985a). Another study found that bulimic women aspired to a thinner ideal body size than did normal controls (Williamson, Kelley, Davis, Ruggiero, & Blouin, 1985). But how do women come to internalize these attitudes differently? One source of influence is the subculture within which they live. Although attitudes about thinness and obesity pervade our entire society, they also are intensified within certain strata. Women of higher socioeconomic status are most likely to emulate closely the trendsetters of beauty and fashion (Banner, 1983), and therefore not surprisingly, they exhibit greater weight preoccupation (Dornbusch et al., 1984). Obesity traditionally has been least punished (and of greatest prevalence) in the lower socioeconomic classes (Goldblatt, Moore, & Stunkard, 1965). Although as yet there are no epidemiological studies drawing representative samples across social classes, we would expect that a differential emphasis on weight and appearance constitutes an important mediating variable in a relationship between social class and bulimia. Certain environments also appear to increase risk. For example, boarding schools and colleges have been thought to "breed" eating disorders such as bulimia (Squire, 1983). Consistent with this hypothesis, one study found a dramatically higher weight gain in freshmen women during their first year in college than in women of similar socioeconomic background who did not go to college (Hovell, Mewborn, Randle, & Fowler-Johnson, 1985). Several factors may account for this observation. As predominantly middle- and upper-class environments, campuses represent those socioeconomic classes at greater risk, as just discussed. Furthermore, as stressful and semiclosed environments, campuses may serve to intensify the sociocultural pressures to be thin. The competitive school environment may foster not only academic competition but also competition regarding the achievement of a beautiful (i.e., thin) body. Women's appearance is of greater importance in dating than is men's (Berscheid, Dion, Walster, & Walster, 1971; Harrison & Saeed, 1977; Janda, O'Grady, & Barnhart, 1981; Krebs & Adinolfi, 1975; Stroebe, Insko, Thompson, & Layton, 1971; Walster, Aronson, Abrahams, & Rottmann, 1966), and we have preliminary evidence that

schools in which dating is heavily emphasized have higher prevalence rates of bulimia than schools in which the emphasis on dating is less prominent (Rodin, Striegel-Moore, & Silberstein, 1985). Other kinds of subcultures also appear to amplify sociocultural pressures and hence place their members at greater risk for bulimia. Prime examples are those subcultures in which optimal weight is specified, explicitly or implicitly, for the performance of one's vocation or avocation. Members of professions that dictate a certain body weight—for example, dancers, models, actresses, and athletes— evidence significantly greater incidence of anorexia and related eating pathology than individuals whose job performance is unrelated to their appearance and weight (Crago, Yates, Beutler, & Arizmendi, 1985; Druss & Silverman, 1979; Garner & Garfinkel, 1978, 1980; Joseph, Wood, & Goldberg, 1982; Yates, Leehey, & Shisslak, 1983). Although fewer data are available regarding the occurrence of bulimia in these subcultural groups, clinical evidence suggests that it has a high incidence level as well (Vincent, 1979). Eating pathology in these professions seems linked not to their stressful nature so much as to their emphasis on weight and appearance (Garner & Garfinkel, 1980), and the pathology typically begins after the person has entered the subculture (Crago et al., 1985) Comparative studies of athletes would help to shed light on the role of culturally mandated weight and appearance specifications as a risk factor. Our model predicts that a higher incidence of bulimia would be found in sports emphasizing a svelte body—such as gymnastics or figure skating—or attaining a certain weight class—such as wrestling—than in sports where thinness is less clearly mandated, such as tennis or volleyball. The sparse literature on the effects of athletic participation in general on body image is potentially contradictory. On the one hand, research examining self-esteem variables suggests that athletic involvement enhances self-image, sociability, and feelings of self-worth (e.g., Vanfraechem & Vanfraechem-Raway, 1978). On the other hand, studies examining weight and dieting behavior suggest that athletic activity is associated with dissatisfaction with body weight and body image, repeated dieting attempts, and dysphoric episodes (e.g., Smith, 1980). The ways in which a focus on physical strength and skills might affect body image and eating behaviors, as well as the ways in which weight concerns influence exercise patterns, are issues worthy of further study.

THE CENTRAL ROLE OF BEAUTY IN THE FEMALE SEX ROLE STEREOTYPE

Beauty ideals have varied considerably in Western cultures over the course of past centuries (Banner, 1983; Beller, 1977; Brownmiller, 1984; Rudofsky, 1971), and women have been willing to alter their bodies to conform to each historical era's ideal of beauty (Ehrenreich & English, 1978). It has been proposed that being concerned with one's appearance and making efforts to enhance and preserve one's beauty are central features of the female sex role stereotype (Brownmiller, 1984). Our language reflects the intimate connection between femininity and beauty. The word *beauty,* a derivative of the Latin word *bellus,* was originally used only in reference to women and children (Banner, 1983). This female connotation of the word beauty still exists today: The most recent revision of Webster's dictionary (Guralnik, 1982) lists as one of its definitions of beauty "a very good-looking woman."

Several studies have documented that physically attractive women are perceived as more feminine (Cash, Gillen, & Burns, 1977; Gillen, 1981; Gillen & Sherman, 1980; Unger, 1985) and unattractive women as more masculine (Heilman & Saruwatari, 1979). It has also been shown that the mesomorphic male silhouette is associated with perceived masculinity, whereas the ectomorphic female silhouette is associated with perceived femininity (Guy, Rankin, &

Norvell, 1980). Hence, thinness and femininity appear to be linked.

Interestingly, there also appears to be a relationship between certain types of eating behavior and femininity. In one study, women who were described as eating small meals were rated significantly more feminine, less masculine, and more attractive than women who ate large meals, whereas descriptions of meal size had no effect on ratings of male targets (Chaiken & Pliner, 1984). Another study suggested that women may actually restrict their food intake in the service of making a favorable impression on men (Chaiken & Pliner, 1984).

Do dieting behavior and the pursuit of the svelte body thus constitute a pursuit of femininity? For women who endorse the traditional female sex role stereotype, we would conjecture that being attractive and thin are important because, by definition, these attributes figure prominently in the traditional roles and values of womanhood. However, women who have achieved occupational success and have abandoned many traditional dictums for female behavior and roles also, it appears, worry about their weight and pursue thinness (Lakoff & Scherr, 1984). One possible reason is that thinness represents the antithesis of the ample female body associated with woman as wife and mother (Beck, Ward-Hull, & McLear, 1976). A second reason may be found in the women's orientation to success. These women set high standards for themselves, and thinness represents a personal accomplishment. At the same time, thinness may serve an instrumental and somewhat paradoxical end of furthering a woman's success in a man's world, because femininity gives a woman a "competitive edge" (Brownmiller, 1984). It also may be difficult for women to abandon femininity wholesale—and *looking* feminine, even while displaying "unfeminine" ambition and power, may serve an important function in a woman's sense of self as well as in how she appears, literally, to others.

Which Women in Particular?

Given the central role of beauty in the female sex role stereotype and the association of thinness with femininity and beauty, for which women might these dimensions increase the risk of bulimia? It might be expected that those women endorsing the female sex role most strongly would most value and pursue thinness. Clinical impressions of bulimic clients do suggest that these women show stereotypically "feminine" behavior characteristics (e.g., being dependent, unassertive, eager to please, and concerned with social approval); this suggestion leads to the hypothesis that bulimia is the result of a struggle to live up to an ideal of femininity (Boskind-Lodahl, 1976; Boskind-Lodahl & Sirlin, 1977; Boskind-White & White, 1983; Hawkins & Clement, 1984; Johnson et al., 1984). However, studies considering the relationship between bulimia and femininity, at least as measured by current masculinity-femininity scales (Bem, 1974; Spence & Helmreich, 1978), have yielded inconsistent results (Dunn & Ondercin, 1981; Hatsukami, Mitchell, & Eckert, 1981; Katzman & Wolchik, 1984; Norman & Herzog, 1983; Rost, Neuhaus, & Florin, 1982; Williamson, Kelly, Davis, Ruggiero, & Blouin, 1985). Some of these studies show a relationship, and some show no relationship between bulimia and feminine values and behaviors.

Our data suggest one way to understand the conflicting findings on the association between femininity and bulimia. We found that whereas femininity scores on the Personal Attributes Questionnaire (PAQ; Spence & Helmreich, 1978) did not relate to measures of body image and eating pathology, masculinity scores were inversely related to measures of body dissatisfaction and eating pathology (Striegel-Moore, Silberstein, & Rodin, 1985b). Masculinity as measured on the PAQ reflects such traits as being decisive, self-confident, active, and independent; in short, this construct represents a sense of competence and self-confidence. As we will explore later, self-confidence does seem to be inversely related to bulimia, although the causal direction is unclear. Femininity on the PAQ is represented by such traits as being gentle, emotional, and aware of others' feelings; it is interesting but not surprising that the presence of such traits is not consistently predictive of eating pathology.

In a recent article, Spence (1985) argued that the constructs of masculinity and femininity guiding research during the past decade have been inadequately defined. She pointed out that the terms *masculinity* and *femininity* appear to have two distinct and different meanings. First, they have an empirical meaning and are used as labels for specific qualities or events that are perceived as being more closely associated with males or females. Second, they represent theoretical constructs that refer to a person's phenomenological sense of maleness or femaleness. To date, Spence (1983) argued, no valid measure has been developed that captures these constructs. One suggestion for future measures of femininity/masculinity is to include items relevant to physical appearance.

DEVELOPMENTAL PROCESSES

A developmental perspective clarifies many issues relevant to our inquiry about the factors placing women at risk for bulimia. In this section we ask what aspects of female development might make women more vulnerable than men, and some women more vulnerable than others, to developing bulimia.

Childhood

Following from our discussion of sociocultural attitudes, it is not surprising that from early childhood girls learn from diverse agents of socialization that appearance is especially important to them as girls and that they should be concerned with it. From their families, little girls learn that one of their functions is to "pretty up" the environment, to serve as aesthetic adornment (Barnett & Baruch, 1980). Young girls learn that being attractive is intricately interwoven with pleasing and serving others and, in turn, will secure their love. Beyond the family environment, schools also teach the societal message. Significantly more of the positive feedback that boys receive from their teachers is addressed specifically to the intellectual aspects of their performance than is true for girls, whereas girls are more often praised for activities related to intellectually irrelevant aspects, such as neatness (i.e., taking care of appearances; Dweck, Davidson, Nelson, & Enna, 1978).

The mass media and children's books also teach girls about the importance of appearance. From their survey of children's readers, Women on Words and Images (1972) revealed that girls in these primers were constantly concerned about how they look, whereas boys never were. Indeed, attending to one's appearance was a major activity for the girl characters, whereas the boys were more likely to solve problems and play hard. Television teaches girls a singular feminine ideal of thinness, beauty, and youth, set against a world in which men are more competent and also more diverse in appearance (Federal Trade Commission, 1978; Lewis & Lewis, 1974; Schwartz & Markham, 1985).

Girls appear to internalize readily these societal messages on the importance of pursuing attractiveness. Developmental studies have documented that girls are more concerned than boys about looking attractive (Coleman, 1961; Douvan & Adelson, 1966). Parents, teachers, and peers all describe girls as more focused than boys on their looks, and children's fantasies and choice of toys also reflect this interest (Ambert, 1976; Nelsen & Rosenbaum, 1972; Oakley, 1972; Wagman, 1967). Whereas boys tend to choose toys involving physical and mechanical activity, girls select toys related to aesthetic adornment and nurturance (Ambert, 1976; Oakley, 1972).

In the mid-1980s bulimia does not appear to be emerging during childhood. However, it is striking how much of the groundwork seems to be laid during these early years. Two kinds of sex differences in self-concept, which will be especially pertinent to our discussion of adolescence, are already evident in grade-school children. First, when asked to describe themselves, girls as young as seven refer more to the views of other people in their self-depictions than do boys (McGuire & McGuire, 1982). For girls more than for boys it seems that self-concept is an interpersonal construct. The implications of this will be considered soon.

Second, although the role of body image in children's self-concepts has not been studied extensively, body build and self-esteem measures have been found to be correlated for girls but not boys in the fourth, fifth, and sixth grades (Guyot, Fairchild, & Hill, 1981). Furthermore, even among these grade-school children, weight was found to be critical in the relationship between body image and self-concept: The thinner the girl, the more likely she was to report feeling attractive, popular, and successful academically. In addition, studies have found that even as children, females are more dissatisfied with their bodies than are males. Although nonobese girls have a more positive attitude toward their bodies, they still express more concerns about their appearance than both nonobese and obese boys (Hammar, Campbell, Moores, Sareen, Gareis, & Lucas, 1972; Tobin-Richards, Boxer, & Petersen, 1983). Indeed Tobin-Richards, Boxer, and Petersen (1983) found that perceived weight and body satisfaction were negatively correlated with weight for girls, whereas boys valued being of normal weight and expressed equal dissatisfaction with being underweight or overweight.

Adolescence

Although girls learn from early childhood to be attentive to their appearance and even to worry about their weight, the major developmental challenge that amplifies a variety of risk factors for bulimia is adolescence. We will consider first the physical changes ushered in at puberty, because the extensive biological changes associated with this period render perceptions of the body highly salient in the adolescent's overall self-perceptions. Coming to terms with the vital adolescent question "Who am I?" involves forming a new body image and integrating the new physical self into one's self-concept.

In the context of the current sociocultural norms already described, pubertal development may create a particular problem for girls. Before puberty, girls have 10% to 15% more fat than boys, but after puberty girls have almost twice as much fat as boys (Marino & King, 1980). The reason is that girls gain their weight at puberty primarily in the form of fat tissue. In contrast, boys' weight spurt is predominantly due to an increase in muscle and lean tissue (Beller, 1977; Tanner, 1978). Given our cultural beauty ideal of the "thin, prepubertal look" for women (Faust, 1983), and the tall, muscular look for men, it is not surprising that adolescent girls express lower body esteem than adolescent boys (Simmons & Rosenberg, 1975) and greater dissatisfaction with their weight (Dornbusch et al., 1984). Whereas physical maturation brings boys closer to the masculine ideal, for most girls it means a development away from what is currently considered beautiful. Consistent with this tenet is the finding that when boys report dissatisfaction with their weight, their discontent is due to a desire to be heavier, whereas girls want to be thinner (George & Krondl, 1983; Simmons & Rosenberg, 1975; Tobin-Richards, Boxer, & Petersen, 1983).

Crisp and Kalucy (1974) and Rosenbaum (1979) found that adolescent girls were highly concerned about their looks and expressed awareness of the great value society places on physical attractiveness in women. These adolescents had a very differentiated view of their own bodies and appraised critically its various components. Interestingly, girls in the Rosenbaum (1979) study judged themselves more harshly than they thought their peers would. And consistent with our review thus far, these girls listed weight as their leading concern about their appearance. In a survey of 195 female high school juniors and seniors, 125 girls reported that they made conscious efforts to restrict their food intake in order to maintain or lose weight (Jakobovits, Halstead, Kelley, Roe, & Young, 1977).

In addition to the concrete physical changes that adolescents undergo, adolescence is clearly an era replete with challenges of both an intrapersonal and an interpersonal nature. The literature of adolescent psychology describes three primary tasks that both male and female adolescents have to master: achieving a new sense of self (involving the integration of accelerating physical growth, impending reproductive maturity, and qualitatively advanced cognitive skills); establishing peer relationships, in particular heterosexual relationships; and developing independence (Aldous, 1978; Blyth & Traeger, 1983; Douvan & Adelson, 1966; Erikson, 1968; Havighurst, 1972; Simmons, Blyth, & McKinney, 1983; Steele, 1980; Tobin-Richards et al., 1983; Wittig, 1983). Our consideration of sex differences in the ways adolescents negotiate these tasks is informed by work on the psychology of gender. Several authors have argued that women define themselves primarily in relation and connection to others, whereas for men, individuation and a sense of agency are more central in forming a sense of self (Chodorow, 1978; Gilligan, 1982; Miller, 1976).

Turning to the first task, it is consistent with Chodorow's (1978) theory that the self-images of adolescent girls seem to be more interpersonally oriented than are those of boys (Carlson, 1965; Dusek & Flaherty, 1981; Hill, Thiel, & Blyth, 1981; McGuire & McGuire, 1982). Girls also appear to be more self-conscious and insecure than boys (Bush, Simmons, Hutchinson, & Blyth, 1978; Hill & Lynch, 1983). Compared to boys, girls seem to worry more about what other people think of them, care more about being liked, and try to avoid negative reactions from others (Simmons & Rosenberg, 1975). Hill and Lynch (1983) argued that, in response to feeling insecure and in an effort to avoid negative evaluation by others, the adolescent girl becomes increasingly sensitive to and compliant with social demands and sex-role-appropriate standards. The strong message to teenage girls regarding the importance of beauty and thinness (as evidenced, for example, in the teen fashion magazines) thus intersects with heightened sensitivity to sociocultural mandates as well as to personal opinions of others. It is not surprising, then, that the adolescent girl becomes concerned with and unhappy about her pubertal increase in fat.

Following from this, we would expect that the second task of adolescence—forming peer relationships, and heterosexual relationships in particular—would also be relatively more problematic for girls than for boys. Studies support this hypothesis (Douvan & Adelson, 1966; Rosenberg & Simmons, 1975). For example, Simmons and Rosenberg (1975) found that girls were more likely than boys to rank popularity as more important than being independent or competent, and these authors found that this emphasis on popularity is correlated with a less stable self-image and a greater susceptibility to others' evaluations. Given that attractive (i.e., thin) females are rewarded in the interpersonal and especially the heterosexual domain, the wish to be popular and the pursuit of thinness may become synonymous in the mind of the teenage girl.

The third task of adolescence, establishing independence, also seems to pose a different challenge to girls than to boys. According to Gilligan (1982), females' relational orientation becomes particularly problematic for them at adolescence, when tasks of separation and individuation emerge. Gilligan reported that adolescent girls conceptualize dependence as a positive attribute, with isolation its polar oppo-

site; however, in a world that views dependence as problematic, the girls often begin to feel confused, insecure, and inadequate.

We can speculate about ways in which the adolescent girl's increasing preoccupation with weight and dieting behavior is tied to the issue of independence. When other aspects of life seem out of control, weight may appear to be one of the few areas that, allegedly, can be self-controlled (Hood, Moore, & Garner, 1982). Because our society views weight loss efforts as a sign of maturity (Steele, 1980), dieting attempts may reflect a girl's desire to show *others,* as well as herself, that she is growing up. Hence, dieting may be a part of, a metaphor for, or a displacement of movements toward independence. Alternatively, the attempts to lose weight may be a refuge from the developmental challenges regarding independence that are posed to the adolescent. Losing weight may represent an effort to defy the bodily changes signaling maturity and adulthood. A successful diet will indeed preserve the pre-pubertal look, perhaps reflecting a desire to remain in childhood (Bruch, 1973; Crisp, 1980; Leon, Lucas, Colligan, Ferdinande, & Kamp, 1985; Selvini-Palazzoli, 1978).

Adulthood

The themes of adolescence—self-concept, interpersonal relationships, and dependence/independence—clearly continue into the adult years. We will now follow these issues as women enter late adolescence and adulthood and again delineate how these tasks continue to be different for men and women.

First, let us consider the body image of adult women and men. Given a persistent indoctrination into the sociocultural emphasis on female appearance, it is not surprising that women come to use very exact barometers for measuring their own bodies. In a sample of college students, Kurtz (1969) found that women possessed a more clearly differentiated body concept—that is, they discriminated more finely among various features of the body—than men. Similarly, females have clearly defined "templates" of the ideal, extremely thin female figure (Fallon & Rozin, 1985; Fisher, 1964; Jourard & Secord, 1955) and show much less variability than males in their view of acceptable size and weight (Harris, 1983).

With these two images in mind—their own body image and the ideal body image—women measure themselves against the ideal, and most emerge from such comparisons with discrepancies that are viewed as flaws and causes for self-criticism. Fallon and Rozin (1985) asked a sample of men and women to locate their actual figure as well as their ideal figure on a display of different-sized body shapes. For females, there was a significant discrepancy between their current and their ideal figures, with a thinner figure viewed as ideal. For males, there was no significant difference between self and ideal. These sex differences have been found repeatedly in other studies as well (Leon, Carroll, et al., 1985; Striegel-Moore, McAvay, & Rodin, in press; Rodin, Striegel-Moore, & Silberstein, 1985).

There is evidence suggesting that this self-ideal discrepancy may be exaggerated for women, not only because the beauty ideal for women has become increasingly thin, but also because women tend to overestimate their body size. Many studies document women's consistent exaggeration of body size, both of the figure as a whole and of specific body parts—typically the fat-bearing areas such as waist and hips. Importantly, these estimation differences appear specific to female subjects' own bodies, because they accurately judge the size of other people's bodies and of physical objects (Button, Fransella, & Slade, 1977; Casper, Halmi, Goldberg, Eckert, & Davis, 1979; Crisp & Kalucy, 1974; Fries, 1975; Garner, Garfinkel, Stancer, & Moldofsky, 1976; Halmi, Goldberg, & Cunningham, 1977). In a study comparing the estimation errors of men and women, men were significantly more accurate than women

in estimates of their own body size (Shontz, 1963).

An issue integrally related to self-concept that has been implicit in our discussion thus far is the association between body image and self-esteem. Many self-concept theories (for an overview, see Harter, 1985) have proposed that dissatisfaction with a particular domain of one's self will result in overall lower self-esteem. In particular, it is argued that the effect of shortcomings in one domain on an individual's general level of self-esteem is determined by the relative importance of that domain in the person's self-definition. Hence, failure to succeed in an area of relatively minor importance to an individual will prove far less damaging to self-worth than inadequacy in a domain of central importance.

Surprisingly few studies have investigated the influence of body image on self-esteem. In studies that have examined this relationship, moderate, significant correlations have been found (Franzoi & Shields, 1984; Lerner, Karabenick, & Stuart, 1973; Lerner, Orlos, & Knapp, 1976; Mahoney, 1974; Secord & Jourard, 1953). Given the greater societal emphasis on attractiveness in women than in men, we would expect physical appearance to have relatively more influence on a woman's general sense of self-esteem than on a man's. Empirical studies, however, have produced conflicting results.

Some studies have supported the tenet that women's body image satisfaction is more highly correlated with self-esteem than is men's (Lerner et al., 1973; Martin & Walter, 1982; Secord & Jourard, 1953), whereas other studies have found the reverse to be true (Mahoney, 1974; Franzoi & Shields, 1984). Perhaps these contradictory findings are due to the fact that body image satisfaction has a different meaning for men and women (Franzoi & Shields, 1984). Several studies have suggested that whereas men tend to see their bodies as primarily functional and active, women seem to view their bodies along aesthetic and evaluative dimensions (Kurtz, 1969; Lerner et al., 1976; Story, 1979).

The relationship between weight, as a particular component of body image, and self-esteem in women deserves further investigation. We conjecture that dissatisfaction with weight relates to chronic low self-esteem and that, in addition, weight plays a role in more short-term and volatile fluctuations of self-esteem. In a large-scale *Glamour* magazine survey, 63% of the respondents reported that weight *often* affected how they felt about themselves, and another 33% reported that weight *sometimes* affected how they felt about themselves (Wooley & Wooley, 1984).

Thus far, we have been considering adulthood as a single entity. As theory and research on adult development have increased, earlier views of adulthood as a sustained, stable period have been replaced by conceptualizations of the entire life span as part of an ongoing developmental process (Erikson, 1968; Levinson, Darrow, Klein, Levinson, & McKee, 1978; Neugarten, 1969, 1970). Our knowledge of weight concerns, dieting, and bulimia is limited by the relatively restricted range of samples that have been studied: The majority of research has focused on the narrow band between 10th grade in high school and senior year of college. However, some initial observations about later adulthood can be made.

First, puberty is clearly not the only period in a woman's life when her biology will potentiate fat increase. During pregnancy, a healthy woman may gain 5 to 11 pounds in fat alone (National Research Council, 1970; Hytten & Leitch, 1971; Pitkin, 1976), and it is often the case that many women have difficulty losing adipose tissue after the baby is born (Beller, 1980; Cederlof & Kay, 1970; Helliovaara & Aroman, 1981). There is some evidence from cross-sectional studies that menopause may be another event in a woman's life that promotes weight gain (e.g., McKinlay & Jeffreys, 1974),

although longitudinal studies are needed to confirm this assumption. Although the precise role of sex hormones in weight regulation is still not fully understood, levels of estrogen and progesterone have been related to hunger and food intake (Dalvit-MacPhillips, 1983; Dippel & Elias, 1980).

Women also have a lower resting metabolic rate than men and thus require fewer calories for their life-sustaining functions. This sex difference is due in part to size differences between men and women, but it is also due to the higher ratio of fat to lean tissue in women. Adipose tissue is more metabolically inert than lean tissue and thus contributes to women's lower resting metabolic rate. With aging, sex differences in metabolic rate may actually increase, along with a relatively larger decrease in lean body mass and concomitant increase in fat tissue in women compared to men (Bray, 1976; Forbes & Reina, 1970; Parizkowa, 1973; Wessel, Ufer, Van Huss, & Cederquist, 1963; Young et al., 1961; Young, Blondin, Tensuan, & Fryer, 1963).

Second, it appears that middle age does not free women from assuming that their attractiveness is a key factor in their happiness. In a large-scale study of American couples, Blumstein and Schwartz (1983) observed that looks continued to be critical well beyond the early years of relationships. In particular, wives were keenly aware of the importance of their appearance to their husbands. Although the authors did not explicitly separate weight from other aspects of appearance, their case reports suggest that weight gain is a central way in which physical appearance changes over time and is a primary cause of concern.

What happens in later life? In a current longitudinal study of people over age 62, we found that the second greatest personal concern expressed by women in the sample, following memory loss, was change in body weight. Weight concerns were rarely expressed by men in the sample (Rodin, 1985). As just described, women tend to become fatter as they age, as a result of biological changes. In addition, some evidence suggests that the process of aging diminishes a woman's perceived attractiveness more than it does a man's (Hatfield & Sprecher, in press), a phenomenon dubbed by Sontag (1972) as the double standard of aging in our society.

In sum, although the data on the topic are sparse, it seems that women's battle with weight, both psychological and physical, lasts a lifetime. Clinically, we find that bulimia can have its onset well after the adolescent and young adult years. From both a clinical and a theoretical viewpoint, the study of women's concerns with weight and eating problems should examine women across the life span.

Which Women in Particular?

Having looked at the developmental trajectory followed by women in general in our society, we now consider which women during their developmental course will be pushed beyond a normative discontent into the disordered eating range.

Timing of development One developmental factor that may affect risk for bulimia is the timing of biological development. Life-span theory suggests that being "out-of-phase" (Neugarten, 1972) with one's cohorts presents a particular stressor and increases the likelihood of a developmental crisis. Research on puberty has suggested sex differences in the impact of early versus late maturation, which may be important in identifying risk factors for bulimia. Male early developers have been found to be more relaxed, less dependent, and more self-confident. They also enjoy a more positive body image and a greater sense of attractiveness than do late-developing boys (Clausen, 1975; Jones, 1965; Tobin-Richards et al., 1983).

For girls, results on the outcomes of early maturation are less clear. Although early-maturing girls have been found to enjoy greater popularity among male peers (Simmons, Blyth, & McKinney, 1983) and greater self-confidence (Clausen, 1975) than girls who develop on time or later, early-developing girls also have been reported to be less popular among female peers, to experience greater emotional distress, to perceive themselves as less attractive, and to hold a lower self-concept than their peers (Peskin, 1973; Simmons et al., 1983). Furthermore, pubertal growth may carry more explicit sexualized meanings for girls than for boys, and parents may respond to their daughters' signs of early sexual maturation with more fear and subsequent greater protectiveness than to their sons' sexual maturation (Hamburg, 1974; Seiden, 1976).

In terms of body dissatisfaction, early-developing girls seem to be particularly unhappy with their weight (Simmons et al., 1983; Tobin-Richards et al., 1983). This finding is not surprising, given that early-developing girls tend to be fatter than their peers (and tend to remain so once they have completed their pubertal growth). In Simmons et al.'s (1983) sample, weight and body image satisfaction were inversely correlated for all girls, regardless of maturational status. In fact, when weight was corrected for, the differences in body image satisfaction of early-middle-, and late-developing girls disappeared. Bruch (1981) suggested that early development may be a risk factor in anorexia nervosa. Although there are no empirical data on this issue, we conjecture that maturing faster than her peers may place a girl at risk for bulimia as well.

Personality From our depiction of female development, it becomes clear that women have a primarily relational orientation. We conjecture that if a woman's orientation toward others' needs and opinions eclipses a sense of her own needs and opinions, she will be at risk for mental health problems in general. Whereas psychiatry has long noted women's vulnerability to hysteria, agoraphobia, or depression, in our current society, women also will be at risk for bulimia. Indeed, clinicians depict bulimic women as exhibiting a strong need for social approval and avoiding conflict, and as experiencing difficulty in identifying and asserting needs (Arenson, 1984; Boskind-Lodahl, 1976; Boskind-White & White, 1983). Initial research has found that bulimic women have higher need for approval than control women (Dunn & Ondercin, 1981; Katzman & Wolchik, 1984) and also score higher on a measure of interpersonal sensitivity (Striegel-Moore, McAvay, & Rodin, 1984).

One question that arises, then, is whether there is a personality profile that places some women at greater risk for bulimia. Although the methodology of assessing personality traits in individuals who already exhibit the clinical syndrome does not permit causal inferences, let us briefly examine the major findings of this line of research. Group profiles of the Minnesota Multiphasic Personality Inventory (MMPI) obtained for bulimic women were found to show significant elevations on the clinical scales Depression, Psychopathic Deviate, Psychasthenia, and Schizophrenia (Hatsukami, Owen, Pyle, & Mitchell, 1982; Leon, Lucas et al., 1985; Orleans & Barnett, 1984; Wallach & Lowenkopf, 1984). Presenting MMPI data in the form of group profiles ignores the heterogeneity of profiles within a sample. Hatsukami et al. (1982) reported that the two most common codetypes (which together accounted for only 25% of their sample) may represent two subgroups of bulimics, one with more obsessive-compulsive problems and the other with addictive behaviors. Importantly, for 20% of the bulimic subjects, none of the clinical scales were significantly elevated; it is possible that this represents another subgroup of bulimics who do not show psychopathology in areas other than their eating disorder.

Many researchers have identified one substantial subgroup of bulimic women to be those who also report problems with alcohol or drug abuse (Leon, Carroll, et al., 1985; Mitchell, Hatsukami, Eckert, & Pyle, 1985; Pyle et al., 1983; Walsh, Roose, Glassman, Gladis, & Sadik, 1985). These observations have led some experts to conclude that bulimia is basically a substance-abuse disorder (Brisman & Siegel, 1984; Wooley & Wooley, 1981), with food either one of many substances or the only substance that is abused. A view of bulimia as a substance-abuse disorder is supported by the high incidence of substance abuse found among the members of bulimic women's immediate families (Leon, Carroll, et al., 1985; Strober, Salkin, Burroughs, & Morrell, 1982). We conjecture that the constellation of personality factors that predispose a woman to substance abuse would place her at risk also for bulimia, including an inability to regulate negative feelings, a need for immediate need gratification, poor impulse control, and a fragile sense of self (Brisman & Siegel, 1984; Goodsitt, 1983).

Another characteristic of bulimic women that has attracted considerable attention has been the high prevalence of depressive symptoms (Fairburn & Cooper, 1982; Hatsukami, Eckert, Mitchell, & Pyle, 1984; Johnson & Larson, 1982; Johnson et al. 1982; Katzman & Wolchik, 1984; Mitchell et al. 1985; Norman & Herzog, 1983; Pyle, Mitchell & Eckert, 1981; Russell, 1979; Wallach & Lowenkopf, 1984; Walsh et al., 1985; Williamson et al., 1985; Wolf & Crowther, 1983). Between 35% and 78% of bulimic patients have been reported to satisfy the DSM-III criteria for a diagnosis of affective disorder during the acute stage of illness (Gwirtsman, Roy-Byrne, Yager, & Gerner, 1983; Hatsukami et al., 1984; Herzog, 1982; Hudson et al., 1982; Hudson et al., 1984; Pope, Hudson & Jonas, 1983). This high incidence of depressive symptoms in bulimia has led to the hypothesis that bulimia is a variant of an affective disorder. However, these studies were conducted with patients, and such individuals generally report a high incidence of depressive symptoms regardless of the presenting problem (e.g., Kashani & Priesmeyer, 1983; Rabkin, Charles, & Kass, 1983). Furthermore, the symptoms of a major depressive episode or dysthymic disorder and bulimia overlap considerably, a point that has been made with respect to anorexia (Altschuler & Weiner, 1985).

Whether or not bulimia is a type of affective disorder, several possible links between bulimic and depressive symptoms may obtain. There is some evidence that depressive symptoms increase during or after binge eating and purging episodes (Johnson et al., 1982; Johnson & Larson, 1982; Russell, 1979). For some bulimic women, the binge/purge cycle serves a self-punishing purpose (Johnson et al., 1984), which is consonant with the depressive constellation. Alternatively, eating may be an antidote to depression, used as self-medication and self-nurturance. There also may be an association between depression and the onset of the binge/purge cycle. Perhaps when weight-conscious women become depressed, their customary restraint of eating weakens, thus increasing the likelihood of binging. We have described earlier the apparent association between body dissatisfaction and low self-esteem, which is a common marker of depression. At present, the question remains unanswered whether depression is a symptom secondary to bulimia, or whether a depressive syndrome places a woman at greater risk for bulimia.

Behaviorally oriented researchers have begun to examine the possibility that inadequate coping skills constitute a risk factor for bulimia (Hawkins & Clement, 1984). Several clinicians and researchers have argued that a deficit of coping skills renders a bulimic woman less able to deal effectively with stress, and binging is an expression of her inability to cope (Boskind-White & White, 1983; Hawkins & Clement, 1984; Katzman & Wolchik, 1984; Loro, 1984; Loro & Orleans, 1981).

In addition, researchers have found that women who experience more stress are at greater risk for binge eating (Abraham & Beu-mont, 1982; Fremouw & Heyneman, 1984; Pyle et al., 1981; Strober, 1984; Wolf & Crowther, 1983). We postulate that stress is not a specific risk factor but rather, in concert with the other risk factors we have discussed, may play a role in a woman's likelihood of developing bulimia. Research is needed to determine whether bulimic women compared with other women encounter a higher level of life stress, subjectively experience stressors as more stressful, or are less skilled in coping with stress.

BIOLOGICAL FACTORS

Genetic Determinants of Weight

In attempts to understand bulimia, it is crucial to examine biological and genetic factors. As discussed in the section on development, women are genetically programmed to have a proportionately higher body fat composition than men—a sex difference that appears to hold across all races and cultures (Bennett, 1984; Tanner, 1978), and the differences between the sexes in fatness increases dramatically, on the average, across the life span.

Substantial individual differences in body build and weight are genetically determined. Identical twins, even when reared apart, are significantly more similar in weight than are fraternal twins or siblings (Borjeson, 1976; Bray, 1981; Brook, Huntley, & Slack, 1975; Fabsitz, Feinleib, & Hrubec, 1978; Feinleib et al., 1977; Medlund, Cederlof, Floderus-Myrhed, Friberg, & Sorensen, 1976; Stunkard, Foch, & Hrubec, 1985). Adopted children resemble their biological parents in weight far more than they resemble their adoptive parents (Stunkard, Sorensen, et al., 1985).

One path by which heredity may influence weight is by determining the ways in which food is metabolized. Individual differences in metabolic rate seem to be of great significance in determining the efficiency of caloric expenditure (Rimm & White, 1979). Indeed, even individuals matched for age, sex, weight, and activity level can differ dramatically from each other in the amount of calories they eat while maintaining identical levels of body weight (Rose & Williams, 1961).

Which Women in Particular?

We conjecture that those women who are genetically programmed to be heavier than the svelte ideal will be at higher risk for bulimia than those women who are naturally thin. Clinical and empirical evidence suggests that a woman who is heavier than her peers may be more likely to develop bulimia (Boskind-White & White, 1983; Fairburn & Cooper, 1983; Johnson et al., 1982; Yager, Landsverk, Lee-Benner, & Johnson, 1985).

It has been suggested that in addition to the genetic predisposition to a specific body weight, a predisposition to an eating disorder may be genetically transmitted. Research on this issue is in an early stage, but initial findings suggest familial clustering of eating disorders. Studies have documented a significantly higher incidence of both anorexia nervosa and bulimia among the first-degree female relatives of anorexic patients than in the immediate families of control subjects (Gershon et al., 1983; Strober, Morrell, Burroughs, Salkin, & Jacobs, 1985). Monozygotic twins have a considerably higher concordance rate than dizygotic twins for anorexia (Crisp, Hall, & Holland, 1985; Garfinkel & Garner, 1982; Holland, Hall, Murray, Russell, & Crisp, 1984; Nowlin, 1983; Vandereyken & Pierloot, 1981). Following from this line of research with anorexic women, the question of the inheritability of bulimia now needs to be examined with bulimic patients.

The Disregulation of Body Weight and Eating Through Dieting

A significant number of women, then, face a frustrating paradox: Although society prescribes a thin beauty ideal, their own genes predispose them to have a considerably heavier body weight. Current society promotes dieting as the pathway to thinness, and as we would

expect, significantly more women than men report dieting at any time (e.g., Nielsen, 1979, Nylander, 1971). Before age 13, 80% of girls report that they have already been on a weight-loss diet, as compared to 10% of boys (Hawkins, Turell, & Jackson, 1983).

On the basis of studies investigating the physiological changes that occur as a result of dieting, many researchers now believe that dieting is not only an ineffective way to attain long-term weight loss but that it may in fact contribute to subsequent weight gain and binge eating (Polivy & Herman, 1985; Rodin, 1981; Rodin, Silberstein, & Steigel-Moore, 1985; Wardle, 1980; Wooley & Wooley, 1981). A substantial decrease in daily caloric intake will result in a reduced metabolic rate, which thus impedes weight loss (Apfelbaum, 1975; Boyle, Storlien, Harper, & Keesey, 1981; Garrow, 1978; Westerterp, 1977). The suppression of metabolic rate caused by dieting is most pronounced when basal metabolic rate is low from the outset (Wooley, Wooley, & Dyrenforth, 1979). Because women have lower metabolic rates than men, women are particularly likely to find that, despite their efforts, they cannot lose as much weight as they would like. Upon resuming normal caloric intake, a person's metabolic rate does not immediately rebound to its original pace, and in fact, a longer period of dieting will prolong the time it takes for the metabolic rate to regain its original level (Even, Nicolaidis, & Meile, 1981). Thus, even normal eating after dieting may promote weight gain.

Numerous other physiological changes due to food restriction have been reported (Bjorntorp & Yang, 1982; Faust, Johnson, Stern, & Hirsch, 1978; Fried, Hill, Nickel, & DiGirolamo, 1983; Gruen & Greenwood, 1981; Miller, Faust, Goldberger, & Hirsch, 1983; Walks, Lavan, Presta, Yang, & Bjorntorp, 1983). All of these alterations contribute to increased efficiency in food utilization and an increased proportion of fat in body composition. Hence, dieting ultimately produces effects opposite to those intended. In addition to these biological ramifications, dieting also produces psychological results that are self-defeating. Typically, a dieter feels deprived of favorite foods, and when "off" the diet, she is likely to overeat (Herman & Mack, 1975; Polivy & Herman, 1985).

Which Women in Particular?

We propose that a prolonged history of repeated dieting attempts constitutes yet another risk factor for bulimia. Animal research suggests that regaining weight occurs significantly more rapidly after a second dieting cycle than after a first (Brownell, Stellar, Stunkard, Rodin, &Wilson, 1984). We conjecture that those women who have engaged in repeated dieting attempts will be the least successful at achieving their target weights by dieting. These women may be most vulnerable, then, to attempting other weight loss strategies, including purging.

The literature on the physiological and psychological effects of dieting suggests a seemingly paradoxical picture. The more restrictively a person diets, the more likely she or he will be to crave foods (particularly foods not allowed as part of the diet) and to give in to these cravings eventually. Indeed, several studies have found a high correlation between restraint and binge eating (Hawkins & Clement, 1980, 1984; Leon, Carroll, et al., 1985; Striegel-Moore et al., 1985b). From their review of this research, Polivy and Herman (1985) concluded that food restriction may be an important causal antecedent to binging. In support of this view, the clinical literature suggests that in many cases bulimia was preceded by a period of restrictive dieting (Boskind-Lodahl & Sirlin, 1977; Dally & Gomez, 1979; Johnson et al., 1982; Mitchell et al., 1985; Russell, 1979; Wooley & Wooley, 1985).

Affective Instability

Affective instability has been proposed as another biogenetic risk factor of bulimia (Hawkins

& Clement, 1984; Johnson, Lewis, & Hagman, 1984; Strober, 1981). It is widely recognized that women have a higher incidence of affective disorders than men. If a predisposition to affective instability increases an individual's risk of bulimia, then it would represent another answer to the questions of both why women rather than men become bulimic and which women in particular.

Several family studies have revealed a high incidence rate of affective disorders among first-degree relatives of bulimic patients (Gwirtsman et al., 1983; Herzog, 1982; Hudson et al., 1982; Hudson et al., 1983; Pyle et al., 1983; Slater & Cowie, 1971; Strober et al., 1982; Yager & Strober, 1985), with one exception (Stern et al., 1984). Studies considering the incidence of bulimia in first-degree relatives of patients with an affective disorder would constitute another test of the hypothesized familial association between affective disorders and bulimia (Altschuler & Weiner, 1985). Two studies addressing this question, however, did not find increased incidence of eating disorders among the first-degree relatives of patients with an affective disorder, a result that argues against a *simple* hypothesis that affective disorders and eating disorders are merely alternate expressions of the same disposition (Gershon et al., 1983; Hatsukami et al., 1984; Strober, 1983; Yager & Strober, 1985). In the absence of twin studies, adoption studies, and sophisticated family aggregation studies, at present no conclusions regarding genetic transmission of bulimia via an affective disorder link can be made.

FAMILY VARIABLES

With a few exceptions (e.g., Boskind-White & White, 1983; Schwartz, 1982; Schwartz, Barrett, & Saba, 1985; Yager, 1982), the bulimia literature has largely ignored the potential role of family characteristics that might predispose some women to bulimia. Prospective stud ies are completely missing, and there is no comprehensive theoretical framework that would allow delineation of the relevant variables to be included in a prospective investigation of families.

In light of our review, we conjecture that certain family characteristics may amplify the sociocultural imperatives described earlier. For example, we hypothesize that a daughter's risk for bulimia is relatively increased if the family places heavy emphasis on appearance and thinness; if the family believes and promotes the myth that weight is under volitional control and thus holds the daughter responsible for regulating it; if family members, particularly females (mother, sisters, aunts), model weight preoccupation and dieting; if the daughter is evaluated critically by members of the family with regard to her weight; if the daughter is reinforced for her efforts to lose weight; and if family members compete regarding the achievement of the ideal of thinness.

Furthermore, a risk to develop bulimia may derive from how the family system operates. Clinicians have described families with a bulimic member as sharing similarities with "psychosomatic families" (Minuchin, Rosman, & Baker, 1978), including enmeshment, overprotectiveness, rigidity, and lack of conflict resolution. In addition, bulimic patients' families are reported to exhibit isolation and heightened consciousness of appearance, and they attach special meaning to food and eating (Schwartz et al., 1985). Research evaluating these assumptions is still in its infancy (Johnson & Flach, 1985; Kagan & Squires, 1985; Kog, Vandereycken, & Vertommen, in press; Kog, Vertommen, & DeGroote, in press; Sights & Richards, 1984; Strober, 1981).

WHY NOW?

In the final section, we attempt to speculate on what makes bulimia so likely at this particular time. We recognize that ease of diagnosis per se, after inclusion of the disorder in the DSM-III (American Psychiatric Association, 1980), may have contributed to the apparent increase, but we wish to focus on other sociocultural and psychological mediators that contribute to the increased risk of bulimia in this era.

Shift Toward Increasingly Thin Standard

In recent years, the beauty ideal for women has moved toward an increasingly thin standard, which has become more uniform and has been more widely distributed due to the advent of mass media. Changes in measurements over time toward increasing thinness have been documented in Miss America contestants, Playboy centerfolds, and female models in magazine advertisements (Garner, Garfinkel, Schwartz, & Thompson, 1980; Snow & Harris, 1985). During the same time period, however, the average body weight of women under 30 years of age has actually increased (Metropolitan Life Foundation, 1983; Society of Actuaries, 1959, 1979).

Lakoff and Scherr (1984) suggested that models on television and in magazines are seen as realistic representations of what people look like, as compared with painted figures who are more readily acknowledged to be artistic creations. Even though the magazine model or television actress has undergone hours of makeup preparation as well as time-consuming and rigorous workout regimens to achieve the "look," her audience thinks that the model's public persona is what she really looks like. Her "look" is then rapidly and widely disseminated, so that the public receives a uniform picture of beauty.

Effects of Media Attention on Dieting and Bulimia

We hypothesize that current sociocultural influences teach women not only what the ideal body looks like but also how to try to attain it, including how to diet, purge, and engage in other disregulating behaviors. The mass-market weight control industry almost prescribes these rituals. For example, the bestseller *Beverly Hills Diet Book* (Mazel, 1981) advocated a form of bulimia in which binges are "compensated" by eating massive quantities of raw fruit to induce diarrhea (Wooley & Wooley, 1982). In addition to the mass media making available what one might call manuals for "how to develop an eating disorder," females more directly teach each other how to diet and how to binge, purge, and starve. Schwartz, Thompson, and Johnson (1981) found that a college woman who purges almost always knows another female student who purges, whereas a woman who does not purge rarely knows someone who does.

A positive feedback loop is thus established: The more women there are with disordered eating, the more likely there are to be even more women who develop disordered eating. We certainly do not mean to imply that psychopathology is merely learned behavior—but we suggest that the public's heightened awareness of eating disorders and a young woman's likelihood of personal exposure to the behaviors may be a significant factor in the increased emergence of eating disorders in the last several years.

We have already noted how family members may model for other members both attitudes and behaviors concerning weight and eating. Interestingly, as Boskind-White and White (1983) described, the women now presenting with bulimia are the daughters of the first Weight Watchers' generation. A question for future study is, What will the daughters of the generation of bulimic women be like?

Fitness

In the past decade, along with the fitness movement, there has been a redefinition of the ideal female body, which is characterized now not merely by thinness but by firm, shapely muscles (while avoiding too much muscularity) as well. Although the possible health benefits from increased exercise are very real, the current emphasis on fitness may itself be contributing to the increased incidence of bulimia. The strong implication is that anyone who "works out" can achieve the lean, healthy-looking ideal and that such attainment is a direct consequence of personal effort and therefore worthy of pride and admiration. Conversely, the inability to achieve the "aerobics instructor look" may leave women feeling defeated, ashamed, and desperate. The pursuit of fitness becomes another preoccupation, compulsion, even obsession for many. Again, we note that women's bodies are predisposed to have a fairly high proportion of fat; indeed, female hormones are disregulated when the percentage of body fat drops below a certain level. The no-fat ideal reflects an "unnatural" standard for many women.

If the pursuit of fitness represents a step even beyond pursuit of thinness, so too does the upsurge of cosmetic surgery. From suction removal of fat to face-lifts, women in increasing numbers are seeking to match the template of beauty with ever more complicated (and expensive) procedures. The message, again, seems to be that beauty is a matter of effort and that failure to attain the beauty ideal makes one personally culpable.

Shifting Sex Roles

Perhaps, ironically, in this era when women feel capable and empowered to pursue success in professional arenas, they have a heightened sense that their efforts should attain success in the domain of beauty as well. It seems that being occupationally successful does not relieve a woman of the need to be beautiful. Indeed, the pursuit of beauty and thinness may sometimes compromise women's success in other domains, for it takes time, attention, and money and is a drain on self-esteem.

In this transitional time of rapidly shifting sex roles, it seems likely that girls more than boys are experiencing the stresses of changing roles, perhaps placing girls at greater risk for psychological distress in general. These changing roles may intersect with all of the risk factors for bulimia we have been discussing and therefore may be an important part of the answer to Why now? The messages communicated to girls are complex and quite often confusing: Work hard at school, but be sure to be popular and pretty; be a lawyer, but be feminine. Little research has been done that can illuminate these kinds of issues. Clinically, we find that bulimic women often express confusion about their roles; an interesting question for research is whether this distinguishes them from other women in general and from other women psychotherapy clients.

Steiner-Adair (1986) studied adolescent girls' images of the ideal woman and their personal goals for themselves and looked at the relationship of these views with performance on the Eating Attitudes Test (EAT), a measure of disordered eating (Garner & Garfinkel, 1979). Interestingly, all girls had a similar picture of the ideal "superwoman" (career, family, beauty), but those girls who saw the "superwoman" as consonant with their own goals had elevated eating pathology scores, whereas the non-eating-disordered girls had more modest goals for themselves. Hence, a girl's ability to put distance between the societal ideal and her own expectations for herself was associated with decreased evidence of eating disturbance. This seems analogous to our findings of a significant correlation between agreement with statements reflecting sociocultural messages regarding attractiveness, and a measure of disordered eating (Striegel-Moore, Silberstein, & Rodin, 1985a). Gilligan (1982) has argued that the process of female development in our androcentric society makes it difficult for girls and women to find and use their own "voice." We would contend that when women instead adopt the socioculturally defined voice and strive to match the unrealistically successful as well as the unrealistically thin public model, the consequences may be unhealthy.

CONCLUSIONS

We have tried to understand bulimia and point to important gaps in our knowledge by examining three questions: Why women? Which women in particular? Why now? We addressed these questions by drawing on a diverse literature in social and developmental psychology, psychology of gender, clinical psychiatry and psychology, and biological psychiatry and medicine. As we conclude our analysis of risk factors in women, it is instructive to ask how men may fit into this picture.

Though significantly fewer men than women currently show evidence of bulimia (a ratio of 1:10), bulimic men do exist and, we hypothesize, will increase in number in the near future. Indeed, bulimic men are an important group to study in the context of our risk factor model, because although men and women may share certain sociocultural, psychological, and biological risk factors, there clearly are gender differences in the variables placing an individual at risk.

Surely our society's fitness consciousness applies to men as much as, and perhaps even more than, to women. It is possible that the sexes pursue fitness for different reasons, with women focusing more on the effects exercise has on physical appearance, whereas men pursue strength and muscularity (Garner, Rockert, Olmsted, Johnson, & Coscina, 1985). However, the workout body type for men has become, it seems, a more widely aspired-to ideal, and similarly to women, more and more men today are fighting to ward off the effects of aging on their appearance. As men become more fashion conscious and more weight conscious, we would expect them to diet more. Already, diet soft drinks, light beers, and other diet products are being marketed for a male as well as a female audience. Because men rarely have the long history of dieting efforts that women do, men typically are more successful in their weight-loss efforts. However, if they succumb to repeated cycles of gaining and losing, we hypothesize that these patterns will lead to the same effects in men as they have in women and could therefore potentiate bulimia.

Beyond the general pressure on men to be conscious of physical fitness and appearance that may result in an increased risk for men to develop bulimia, certain male subcultures (similar to female subcultures) emphasize weight standards and thus place certain men at greater risk for bulimia. If our hypothesis is correct that environments that emphasize weight standards foster the development of bulimia, then we would expect to find a higher incidence of bulimia in men who participate in such environments than in men who do not. In fact, initial research does show that athletes such as wrestlers and jockeys evidence higher incidence of bulimia (Rodin, Striegel-Moore, & Silberstein, 1985) than athletes in sports that do not prescribe a certain body weight. Clinical evidence suggests that homosexual men, whose subculture promotes a thin body ideal and a heightened attentiveness to appearance and fashion (Kleinberg, 1980; Lakoff & Scherr, 1984; Mishkind, Rodin, Silberstein, & Striegel-Moore, in press), may also be at increased risk for bulimia (Herzog, Norman, Gordon, & Pepose, 1984).

The present analysis has underscored questions that remain to be investigated. As we conclude, let us briefly outline some of these agendas for future study. Initial research suggests that a description of bulimia as a single entity does not reflect adequately the heterogeneity of the population. In particular, we need diagnostic categories that allow differentiation among subgroups, which would then permit an investigation of the differential relationships among those subgroups and the various risk factors. An additional step involves clarifying the relationships among bulimia, anorexia, and obesity, and the risk factors involved in each of those syndromes. Another question deserving further attention is the place of bulimia in the spectrum of psychiatric disorders in general and in the affective disorders in particular. In addi-tion, we need to understand the risk factors that bulimia may share with other psychiatric syndromes that have been disproportionally represented by women, such as depression and agoraphobia.

Having emphasized the importance of female socialization as a major contributing factor in bulimia, we also need to examine how changes in the female sex role stereotype may affect the incidence of bulimia. Furthermore, reaching an understanding of the risk factors for bulimia in men could help expand and refine our understanding of risk factors in women as well as in men. Finally, although we have focused our attention on identifying factors that place women at risk for bulimia, it will be equally important to delineate variables that serve a protective function.

Another important task is to develop strategies for the prevention of bulimia. Numerous risk factors have been described that do not lend themselves easily to modification. Many have to do with social values and mores. Unfortunately, large-scale social changes are slow and difficult to effect. Other risk factors involve genetic determinants. Even if some factors that lead to bulimia are genetically determined or transmitted, however, the fact that they are expressed as an eating disorder rather than in some other clinical manifestation can be understood only by referring to the present sociocultural milieu and to female sex role socialization practices. As strategies for change in these areas are developed, shifts in the incidence and prevalence of bulimia may be expected to follow.

REFERENCES

Abraham, S., & Beumont, P. J. V. (1982). How patients describe bulimia or binge eating. *Psychological Medicine, 12* 625–635.

Adler, J. (1982, January). Looking back at '81. *Newsweek*, pp. 26–52.

Aldous, J. (1978). *Family careers: Developmental change in families*. New York: Wiley.

Altschuler, K. Z., & Weiner, M. F. (1985). Anorexia nervosa and depression: A dissenting view. *American Journal of Psychiatry, 142,* 328–332.

Ambert, A. M. (1976). *Sex structure.* Don Mills, Canada: Langman.

American Psychiatric Association (1980). *Diagnostic and statistical manual of mental disorders* (3rd ed.). Washington, DC: Author.

Andersen, A. E. (1983). Anorexia nervosa and bulimia: A spectrum of eating disorders. *Journal of Adolescent Health Care, 4,* 15–21.

Apfelbaum, M. (1975). Influence of level of energy intake on energy expenditure in man. Effects of spontaneous intake, experimental starvation and experimental overeating. In G. A. Bray (Ed.), *Obesity in perspective* (OBHEW Publication No. NIH 75-708, Vol. 2, pp. 145–155). Washington, DC: U.S. Government Printing Office.

Arenson, G. (1984). *Binge eating. How to stop it forever.* New York: Rawson.

Banner, L. W. (1983). *American beauty.* New York: Knopf.

Barnett, R. C., & Baruch, G. K. (1980). *The competent woman: Perspectives on development.* New York: Irvington.

Beck, J. B., Ward-Hull, C. J., & McLear, P. M. (1976). Variables related to women's somatic preferences of the male and female body. *Journal of Personality and Social Psychology, 34,* 1200–1210.

Beller, A. S. (1977). *Fat and thin: A natural history of obesity. New York: Farrar, Straus & Giroux.*

Beller, A. S. (1980). Pregnancy: Is motherhood fattening? In J. R. Kaplan (Ed.), *A woman's conflict* (pp. 139–158). Englewood Cliffs, NJ: Prentice-Hall.

Bem, S. L. (1974). The measurement of psychological androgyny. *Journal of Consulting and Clinical Psychology, 42,* 155–162.

Bennett, W. I. (1984). Dieting: Ideology versus physiology. *Psychiatric Clinics of North America, 7,* 321–334.

Berscheid, E., Dion, K. K., Walster, E., & Walster, G. (1971). Physical attractiveness and dating choice. A test of the matching hypothesis. *Journal of Experimental Social Psychology, 7,* 173–189.

Beumont, P. J., George, G. C., & Smart, D. E. (1976). "Dieters" and "vomiters and purgers" in anorexia nervosa. *Psychological Medicine, 6,* 617–622.

Bjorntorp, P., & Yang, M. U. (1982). Refeeding after tasting in the rat: Effects on body composition and food efficiency. *American Journal of Clinical Nutrition, 36,* 444–449.

Blumenstein, P. W., & Schwartz, P. (1983). *American couples.* New York: Morrow.

Blyth, D. A., & Traeger, C. M. (1983). The self-concept and self-esteem of early adolescents. *Theory Into Practice, 22,* 91–97.

Borjeson, M. (1976). The aetiology of obesity in children. *Acta Paediatrica Scandinavica, 65,* 279–287.

Boskind-Lodahl, M. (1976). Cinderella's stepsisters. *Signs: Journal of Women, Culture and Society, 2,* 342–358.

Boskind-Lodahl, M., & Sirlin, J. (1977). The gorging-purging syndrome. *Psychology Today, 10,* 50–52, 82–85.

Boskind-White, M., & White, W. C. (1983). *Bulimarexia: The binge/purge cycle.* New York: Norton.

Boyle, P. C., Storlien, L. H., Harper, A. E., & Keesey, R. E. (1981). Oxygen consumption and locomotor activity during restricted feeding and realimentation. *American Journal of Physiology, 241,* R392–397.

Bray, G. A. (1976). *The obese patient.* Philadelphia: Saunders.

Bray, G. A. (1981). The inheritance of corpulence. In L. A. Cioffi, W. P. T. James, & T. B. Van Itallie (Eds.), *Weight regulatory system: Normal and disturbed mechanisms* (pp. 185–195). New York: Raven Press.

Brisman, J., & Siegel, M. (1984). Bulimia and alcoholism: Two sides of the same coin? *Journal of Substance Abuse Treatment, 1,* 113–118.

Brook, C. G. D., Huntley, R. M. C., & Slack, J. (1975). Influence of heredity and environment in determination of skinfold thickness in children. *British Medical Journal, 2,* 719–721.

Brownell, K. D., Stellar, E., Stunkard, A. J., Rodin, J., & Wilson, G. T. (1984). *Behavioral and metabolic effects of weight loss and regain in animals and humans.* Unpublished manuscript, University of Pennsylvania, Philadelphia.

Brownmiller, S. (1984). *Femininity.* New York: Linden Press/Simon & Schuster.

Bruch, H. (1973). *Eating disorders: Obesity, anorexia nervosa and the person within.* New York: Basic Books.

Bruch, H. (1981). Developmental considerations of anorexia nervosa and obesity. *Canadian Journal of Psychiatry, 26,* 212–217.

Bush, D. E., Simmons, R., Hutchinson, B., & Blyth, D. (1978). Adolescent perceptions of sex roles in 1968 and 1975. *Public Opinion Quarterly, 41,* 459–474.

Button, E. J., Fransella, F., & Slade, P. D. (1977). A reappraisal of body perception disturbance in anorexia nervosa. *Psychological Medicine, 7,* 235–243.

Carlson, R. (1965). Stability and change in the adolescent's self-image. *Child Development, 36,* 659–666.

Cash, T. F., Gillen, B., & Burns, D. S. (1977). Sexism and "beautyism" in personnel consultant decision making. *Journal of Applied Psychology, 62,* 301–310.

Casper, R. C., Eckert, E. D., Halmi, K. A., Goldberg, S. C., & Davis, J. M. (1980). Bulimia: Its incidence and clinical importance in patients with anorexia nervosa. *Archives of General Psychiatry, 37,* 1030–1035.

Casper, R. C., Halmi, K. A., Goldberg, S. C., Eckert, E. D., & Davis, J. M. (1979). Disturbances in body image estimation as related to other characteristics and outcome of anorexia nervosa. *British Journal of Psychiatry, 134,* 60–66.

Cederlof, R., & Kay, L. (1970). The effect of childbearing on body weight. A twin control study. *Acta Psychiatrica Scandinavica,* (Suppl.) *219,* 47–49.

Chaiken, S., & Pliner, P. (1984). *Women, but not men, are what they eat: The effect of meal size and gender on perceived femininity and masculinity.* Unpublished manuscript, Vanderbilt University, Nashville, TN.

Chodorow, N. (1978). *The reproduction of mothering: Psychoanalysis and the sociology of gender.* Berkeley: University of California Press.

Clausen, J. A. (1975). The social meaning of differential physical and sexual maturation. In S. E. Dragastin & G. H. Elder, Jr. (Eds.), *Adolescence in the life cycle: Psychological change and social context* (pp. 24–48). Washington, DC: Hemisphere.

Coleman, J. S. (1961). *The adolescent society.* New York: Free Press.

Crago, M., Yates, A., Beutler, L. E., & Arizmendi, T. G. (1985). Height-weight ratios among female athletes: Are collegiate athletics the precursors to an anorexic syndrome? *International Journal of Eating Disorders, 4,* 79–87.

Crisp, A. H. (1980). *Anorexia nervosa: Let me be.* London: Academic Press.

Crisp, A. H., Hall, A., & Holland, A. J. (1985). Nature and nurture in anorexia nervosa: A study of 34 pairs of twins, one pair of triplets and an adoptive family. *International Journal of Eating Disorders, 4,* 5–27.

Crisp, A. H., & Kalucy, R. S. (1974). Aspects of the perceptual disorder in anorexia nervosa. *British Journal of Medical Psychology, 47,* 349–361.

Dally, P. J., & Gomez, J. (1979). *Anorexia nervosa.* London: William Heinemann Medical Books.

Dalvit-MacPhillips, S. P. (1983). The effect of the human menstrual cycle on nutrient intake. *Physiology and Behavior, 31,* 209–212.

Dippel, R. L., & Elias, J. W. (1980). Preferences for sweets in relationship to use of oral contraceptives in pregnancy. *Hormones and Behavior, 14,* 1–6.

Dornbusch, S. M., Carlsmith, J. M., Duncan, P. D., Gross, R. T., Martin, J. A., Ritter, P. L., & Siegel-Gorelick, B. (1984). Sexual maturation, social class, and the desire to be thin among adolescent females. *Developmental and Behavioral Pediatrics, 5,* 308–314.

Douvan, E., & Adelson, J. (1966). *The adolescent experience.* New York: Wiley.

Drewnowski, A., Riskey, D., & Desor, J. A. (1982). Feeling fat yet unconcerned: Self-reported overweight and the restraint scale. *Appetite: Journal for Intake Research, 3,* 273–279.

Druss, R. G., & Silverman, J. A. (1979). Body image and perfectionism of ballerinas. Comparison and contrast with anorexia nervosa. *General Hospital Psychiatry, 1,* 115–121.

Dunn, P., & Ondercin, P. (1981). Personality variables related to compulsive eating in college women. *Journal of Clinical Psychology, 37,* 43–49.

Dusek, J. B., & Flaherty, J. F. (1981). The development of the self-concept during the adolescent years. *Monographs of the Society for Research in Child Development, 46,* 1–67.

Dweck, C. S., Davidson, W., Nelson, S., & Enna, B. (1978). Sex differences in learned helplessness: II. The contingencies of evaluative feedback in the classroom, and III. An experimental analysis. *Developmental Psychology, 14,* 268–276.

Ehrenreich, B., & English, D. (1978). *For her own good: 150 years of the experts' advice to women.* New York: Anchor Press/Doubleday.

Erikson, E. H. (1968). *Identity: Youth and crisis.* New York: Norton.

Even, P., Nicolaidis, S., & Meile, M. (1981). Changes in efficiency of ingestants are a major factor of regulation of energy balance. In L. A. Cioffi, W. P. T. James, & T. B. Van Itallie (Eds.), *The body weight regulatory system: Normal and disturbed mechanisms* (pp. 115–123). New York: Raven Press.

Fabsitz, R., Feinleib, M., & Hrubec, Z. (1978). Weight changes in adult twins. *Acta Geneticae Medicae et Gemellologiae, 17,* 315–332.

Fairburn, C. G., & Cooper, P. J. (1982). Self-induced vomiting and bulimia nervosa. An undetected problem. *British Medical Journal, 284,* 1153–1155.

Fairburn, C. G., & Cooper, P. J. (1983). The epidemiology of bulimia nervosa. *International Journal of Eating Disorders, 2,* 61–67.

Fallon, A. E., & Rozin, P. (1985). Sex differences in perceptions of body shape. *Journal of Abnormal Psychology, 94,* 102–105.

Faust, M. S. (1983). Alternative constructions of adolescent growth. In J. Brooks-Gunn & A. C. Petersen (Eds.), *Girls at puberty* (pp. 105–125). New York: Plenum Press.

Faust, J. M., Johnson, P. R., Stern, J. S., & Hirsch, J. (1978). Diet-induced adipocyte number increase in adult rats: A new model of obesity. *American Journal of Physiology, 235,* E279–286.

Federal Trade Commission. (1978). FTC staff report on television advertising to children. Washington, DC: Author.

Feinleib, M., Garrison, R. J., Fabsitz, R., Christian, J. C., Hrubec, Z., Borhani, N. O., Kannel, W. B., Rosenman, R., Schwartz, J. T., & Wagner, J. O. (1977). The NHLBI twin study of cardiovascular disease risk factors: Methodology and summary of results. *American Journal of Epidemiology, 106,* 284–295.

Fisher, S. (1964). Sex differences in body perception. *Psychological Monographs, 78,* 1–22.

Forbes, G., & Reina, J. C. (1970). Adult lean body mass declines with age: Some longitudinal observations. *Metabolism, 19,* 653–663.

Franzoi, S. L., & Shields, S. A. (1984). The body esteem scale: Multidimensional structure and sex differences in a college population. *Journal of Personality Assessment, 48,* 173–178.

Fremouw, W. J., & Heyneman, E. (1984). A functional analysis of binge episodes. In R. C. Hawkins II, W. J. Fremouw, & P. F. Clement (Eds.), *The binge-purge syndrome* (pp. 254–263). New York: Springer.

Fried, S. K., Hill, J. O., Nickel, M., & DiGirolamo, M. (1983). Prolonged effects of fasting-refeeding on rat adipose tissue lipoprotein lipase activity. Influence of caloric restriction during refeeding. *Journal of Nutrition, 113,* 1861–1869.

Fries, H. (1975). Anorectic behavior: Nosological aspects and introduction of a behavior scale. *Scandinavian Journal of Behavior Therapy, 4,* 137–148.

Garfinkel, P. E., & Garner, D. M. (1982). *Anorexia nervosa. A multidimensional perspective.* New York: Brunner/Mazel.

Garfinkel, P. E., Moldofsky, H., & Garner, D. M. (1980). The heterogeneity of anorexia nervosa. *Archives of General Psychiatry, 37,* 1036–1040.

Garner, D. M., & Garfinkel, P. E. (1978). Sociocultural factors in anorexia-nervosa. *Lancet, 2,* 674.

Garner, D. M., & Garfinkel, P. E. (1979). The Eating Attitudes Test: An index of the symptoms of anorexia nervosa. *Psychological Medicine, 9,* 273–279.

Garner, D. M., & Garfinkel, P. E. (1980). Sociocultural factors in the development of anorexia nervosa. *Psychological Medicine, 10,* 647–656.

Garner, D. M., & Garfinkel, P. E. (Eds.). (1985). *Handbook of psychotherapy for anorexia nervosa and bulimia.* New York: Guilford.

Garner, D. M., Garfinkel, P. E., & O'Shaughnessy, M. (1985). The validity of the distinction between bulimia with and without anorexia nervosa. *American Journal of Psychiatry, 142,* 581–587.

Garner, D. M., Garfinkel, P. E., Schwartz, D., & Thompson, M. (1980). Cultural expectations of thinness in women. *Psychological Reports, 47,* 483–491.

Garner, D. M., Garfinkel, P. E., Stancer, H. C., & Moldofsky, H. (1976). Body image disturbances in anorexia nervosa and obesity. *Psychosomatic Medicine, 38,* 327–336.

Garner, D. M., Olmsted, M. P., & Polivy, J. (1983). Development and validation of a multidimensional eating disorder inventory for anorexia nervosa and bulimia. *International Journal of Eating Disorders, 2,* 15–34.

Garner, D. M., Rockert, W., Olmsted, M. P., Johnson, C., & Coscina, D. V. (1985). Psychoeducational principles in the treatment of bulimia and anorexia nervosa. In D. M. Garner & P. E. Garfinkel (Eds.), *Handbook of psychotherapy for anorexia nervosa and bulimia* (pp. 513–572). New York: Guilford.

Garrow, J. (1978). The regulation of energy expenditure. In G. A. Bray (Ed.), *Recent advances in obesity research* (Vol. 2, pp. 200–210). London: Newman.

George, R. S., & Krondl, M. (1983). Perceptions and food use of adolescent boys and girls. *Nutrition and Behavior, 1,* 115–125.

Gershon, E. S., Hamovit, J. R., Schreiber, J. L., Dibble, E. D., Kaye, W., Nurnberger, J. I., Andersen, A., & Ebert, M. (1983). Anorexia nervosa and major affective disorders associated in families: A preliminary report. In S. B. Guze, F. J. Earls, & J. E. Barrett (Eds.), *Childhood psychopathology and development* (pp. 279–284). New York: Raven Press.

Gillen, B. (1981). Physical attractiveness: A determinant of two types of goodness. *Personality and Social Psychology Bulletin, 7,* 277–281.

Gillen, B., & Sherman, R. C. (1980). Physical attractiveness and sex as determinants of trait attributions. *Multivariate Behavioral Research, 15,* 423–437.

Gilligan, C. (1982). *In a different voice: Psychological theory and women's development.* Cambridge, MA: Harvard University Press.

Goldblatt, P.B., Moore, M. E., & Stunkard, A. J. (1965). Social factors in obesity. *Journal of the American Medical Association, 192,* 1039–1044.

Goodsitt, A. (1983). Self-regulatory disorders in eating disorders. *International Journal of Eating Disorders, 2,* 51–61.

Gormally, J. (1984). The obese binge eater: Diagnosis, etiology, and clinical issues. In R. C. Hawkins II, W. J. Fremouw, & P. F. Clement (Eds.), *The binge-purge syndrome* (pp. 47–73). New York: Springer.

Grace, P. S., Jacobson, R. S., & Fullager, C. J. (1985). A pilot comparison of purging and nonpurging bulimics. *Journal of Clinical Psychology, 41,* 173–180.

Gruen, R. K., & Greenwood, M. R. C. (1981). Adipose tissue lipoprotein lipase and glycerol release in fasted Zucker (fa/fa) rats. *American Journal of Physiology, 241,* E76–E83.

Guralnik, D. B. (Ed.). (1982). *Webster's new world dictionary* (2nd ed.). New York: Simon & Schuster.

Guy, R. F., Rankin, B. A., & Norvell, M. J. (1980). The relation of sex-role stereotyping to body image. *Journal of Psychology, 105,* 167–173.

Guyot, G. W., Fairchild, L., & Hill, M. (1981). Physical fitness, sport participation, body build and self-concept of elementary school children. *International Journal of Sport Psychology, 12,* 105–116.

Gwirtsman, H. E., Roy-Byrne, P., Yager, J., & Gerner, R. H. (1983). Neuroendocrine abnormalities in bulimia, *American Journal of Psychiatry, 140,* 559–563.

Halmi, K. A., Falk, J. R., & Schwartz, E. (1981). Binge-eating and vomiting: A survey of a college population. *Psychological Medicine, 11,* 697–706.

Halmi, K. A., Goldberg, S., & Cunningham, S. (1977). Perceptual distribution of body image in adolescent girls: Distortion of body image in adolescence. *Psychological Medicine, 7,* 253–257.

Hamburg, B. (1974). Early adolescence: A specific and stressful stage of the life cycle. In G. Coelho, D. A. Hamburg, & J. E. Adams (Eds.), *Coping and adaptation* (pp. 101–126). New York: Basic Books.

Hammar, R. D., Campbell, V. A., Moores, N. L., Sareen, C., Gareis, F. J., & Lucas, B. (1972). An interdisciplinary study of adolescent obesity. *Journal of Pediatrics, 80,* 373–383.

Harris, M. B. (1983). Eating habits, restraint, knowledge and attitudes toward obesity. *International Journal of Obesity, 7,* 271–288.

Harrison, A. A., & Saeed, L. (1977). Let's make a deal: Analysis of revelations and stipulations in lonely hearts advertisements. *Journal of Personality and Social Psychology, 35,* 257–264.

Harter, S. (1985). Processes underlying the construction, maintenance and enhancement of the self-concept in children. In J. Suls & A. Greenwald (Eds.), *Psychological perspectives on the self* (Vol. 3, pp. 137–181). Hillsdale, NJ: Erlbaum.

Hatfield, E., & Sprecher, S. (in press). *Mirror, mirror: The importance of looks in everyday life.* New York: SUNY Press.

Hatsukami, D., Eckert, E., Mitchell, J. E., & Pyle, R. (1984). Affective disorder and substance abuse in women with bulimia. *Psychological Medicine, 14,* 701–704.

Hatsukami, D. K., Mitchell, J. E., & Eckert, E. (1981). Eating disorders: A variant of mood disorders? *Psychiatric Clinics of North America, 7,* 349–365.

Hatsukami, D., Owen, P., Pyle, R., & Mitchell, J. (1982). Similarities and differences on the MMPI between women with bulimia and women with alcohol or drug abuse problems. *Addictive Behaviors, 7,* 435–439.

Havighurst, R. J. (1972). *Developmental tasks and education.* New York: McKay.

Hawkins, R. C. II, & Clement, P. F. (1980). Development and construct validations of a self-report measure of binge eating tendencies. *Addictive Behaviors, 5,* 219–226.

Hawkins, R. C. II, & Clement, P. F. (1984). Binge eating: Measurement problems and a conceptual model. In R. C. Hawkins II, W. J. Fremouw, & P. F. Clement (Eds.). *The binge-purge syndrome* (pp. 229–253). New York: Springer.

Hawkins, R. C., Jr., Turell, S., & Jackson, L. J. (1983). Desirable and undesirable masculine and feminine traits in relation to students' dietary tendencies and body image dissatisfaction. *Sex Roles, 9,* 705–724.

Heilman, M. E., & Saruwatari, L. R. (1979). When beauty is beastly: The effects of appearance and sex on evaluations of job applicants for managerial and non-managerial jobs. *Organizational Behavior and Human Performance, 23,* 360–372.

Helliovaara, M., & Aromaa, A. (1981). Parity and obesity. *Journal of Epidemiology and Community Health, 35,* 197–199.

Herman, C. P., & Mack, D. (1975). Restrained and unrestrained eating. *Journal of Personality, 43,* 647–660.

Herman, C. P., & Polivy, J. (1975). Anxiety, restraint, and eating behavior. *Journal of Abnormal Psychology, 84,* 666–672.

Herzog, D. (1982). Bulimia in the adolescent. *American Journal of Diseases of Children, 136,* 985–989.

Herzog, D. B., Norman, D. K., Gordon, C., & Pepose, M. (1984). Sexual conflict and eating disorders in 27 males. *American Journal of Psychiatry, 141,* 989–990.

Hill, J. P., & Lynch, M. E. (1983). The intensification of gender-related role expectations during early adolescence. In J. Brooks-Gunn & A. C. Petersen (Eds.), *Girls at puberty* (pp. 201–228). New York: Plenum Press.

Hill, J. P., Thiel, K. S., & Blyth, D. A. (1981). *Grade and gender differences in perceived intimacy with peers among seventh- to tenth-grade boys and girls.* Unpublished manuscript, Boys Town Center for the Study of Youth Development, Richmond, VA.

Holland, A. J., Hall, A., Murray, R., Russell, G. F. M., & Crisp, A. H. (1984). Anorexia nervosa: A study of 34 twin pairs and one set of triplets. *British Journal of Psychiatry, 145,* 414–419.

Hood, J., Moore, T. E., & Garner, D. M. (1982). Locus of control as a measure of ineffectiveness in anorexia nervosa. *Journal of Consulting and Clinical Psychology, 50,* 3–13.

Hovell, M. F., Mewborn, C. R., Randle, Y., & Fowler-Johnson, S. (1985). Risk of excess weight gain in university women: A three-year community controlled analysis. *Addictive Behaviors, 10,* 15–28.

Hudson, J. I., Laffer, P. S., & Pope, H. G., Jr. (1982). Bulimia related to affective disorder by family history and response to the dexamethasone suppression test. *American Journal of Psychiatry, 137,* 605–607.

Hudson, J. I., Pope, H. G., Jr., & Jonas, J. M. (1984). Treatment of bulimia with antidepressants: Theoretical considerations and clinical findings. In A. J. Stunkard & E. Stellar (Eds.),

Eating and its disorders (pp. 259–273). New York: Raven Press.

Hudson, J. I., Pope, H. G., Jr., Jonas, J. M., Laffer, P. S., Hudson, M. S., & Melby, J. C. (1983). Hypothalamic-pituitary-adrenal axis hyperactivity in bulimia. *Psychiatry Research, 8,* 111–117.

Huon, G., & Brown, L. B. (1984). Psychological correlates of weight control among anorexia nervosa patients and normal girls. *British Journal of Medical Psychology, 57,* 61–66.

Hytten, F. E., & Leitch, I. (1971). *The physiology of human pregnancy.* Oxford: Blackwell Scientific Publications.

Jakobovits, C., Halstead, P., Kelley, L., Roe, D. A., & Young, C. M. (1977). Eating habits and nutrient intakes of college women over a thirty-year period. *Journal of the American Dietetic Association, 71,* 405–411.

Janda, L. H., O'Grady, K. E., & Barnhart, S. A. (1981). Effects of sexual attitudes and physical attractiveness on person perception of men and women. *Sex Roles, 7,* 189–199.

Johnson, C., & Flach, A. (1985). Family characteristics of 105 patients with bulimia. *American Journal of Psychiatry, 142,* 142, 1321–1324.

Johnson, C. L., & Larson, R. (1982). Bulimia: An analysis of moods and behavior. *Psychosomatic Medicine, 44,* 341–353.

Johnson, C., Lewis, C., & Hagman, J. (1984). The syndrome of bulimia. *Psychiatric Clinics of North America, 7,* 247–274.

Johnson, C. L., Stuckey, M. R., Lewis, L. D., & Schwartz, D. M. (1982). Bulimia: A descriptive survey of 316 cases. *International Journal of Eating Disorders, 2,* 3–16.

Jones, M. C. (1965). Psychological correlates of somatic development. *Child Development, 36,* 899–911.

Joseph, A., Wood, J. K., & Goldberg, S. C. (1982). Determining populations at risk for developing anorexia nervosa based on selection of college major. *Psychiatry Research, 7,* 53–58.

Jourard, S. M., & Secord, P. F. (1955). Body-cathexis and the ideal female figure. *Journal of Abnormal and Social Psychology, 50,* 243–246.

Kagan, D. M., & Squires, R. L. (1985). Family cohesion, family adaptability, and eating behaviors among college students. *International Journal of Eating Disorders, 4,* 267–280.

Kashani, J. H., & Priesmeyer, M. (1983). Differences in depressive symptoms and depression among college students. *American Journal of Psychiatry, 140,* 1081–1082.

Katzman, M. A., & Wolchik, S. A. (1984). Bulimia and binge eating in college women: A comparison of personality and behavioral characteristics. *Journal of Consulting and Clinical Psychology, 52,* 423–428.

Katzman, M. A., Wolchik, S. A., & Braver, S. L. (1984). The prevalence of frequent binge eating and bulimia in a nonclinical sample. *International Journal of Eating Disorders, 3,* 53–62.

Kleinberg, S. (1980). *Alienated affections: Being gay in America.* New York: St. Martin's Press.

Kog, E., Vandereycken, W., & Vertommen, H. (in press). Towards verification of the psychosomatic family model. A pilot study of 10 families with an anorexia/bulimia patient. *International Journal of Eating Disorders.*

Kog, E., Vertommen, H., & DeGroote, T. (in press). Family interaction research in anorexia nervosa: The use and misuse of a self-report questionnaire. *International Journal of Family Psychiatry.*

Krebs, D., & Adinolfi, A. A. (1975). Physical attractiveness, social relations, and personality style. *Journal of Personality and Social Psychology, 31,* 245–253.

Kurtz, R. M. (1969). Sex differences and variations in body attitudes. *Journal of Consulting and Clinical Psychology, 33,* 625–629.

Lacey, J. H. (1982). The bulimic syndrome at normal body weight: Reflections on pathogenesis and clinical features. *International Journal of Eating Disorders, 2,* 59–66.

Lakoff, R. T., & Scherr, R. L. (1984). *Face value: The politics of beauty.* Boston: Routledge & Kegan Paul.

Leon, G. R., Carroll, K., Chernyk, B., & Finn, S. (1985). Binge eating and associated habit patterns within college student and identified bulimic populations. *International Journal of Eating Disorders, 4,* 43–57.

Leon, G. R., Lucas, A. R., Colligan, R. C., Ferdinande, R. J., & Kamp, J. (1985). Sexual, body-image, and personality attitudes in anorexia nervosa. *Journal of Abnormal Child Psychology, 13,* 245–258.

Lerner, R. M., Karabenick, S. A., & Stuart, J. L. (1973). Relations among physical attractiveness, body attitudes, and self-concept in male and female college students. *Journal of Psychology, 85*, 119–129.

Lerner, R. M., Orlos, J. B., & Knapp, J. R. (1976). Physical attractiveness, physical effectiveness and self-concept in late adolescents. *Adolescence, 11*, 313–326.

Levinson, D. J., Darrow, C. N., Klein, E. B., Levinson, M. H., & McKee, B. (1978). *The seasons of a man's life*. New York: Knopf.

Lewis, C. E., & Lewis, N. A. (1974). The impact of television commercials on health-related beliefs and behavior in children. *Pediatrics, 53*, 431–435.

Loro, A. D. (1984). Binge eating: A cognitive-behavioral treatment approach. In R. C. Hawkins II, W. J. Fremouw, & P. F. Clements (Eds.), *The binge-purge syndrome* (pp. 183–210). New York: Springer.

Loro, A. D., & Orleans, C. S. (1981). Binge eating in obesity: Preliminary findings and guidelines for behavioral analysis and treatment. *Addictive Behaviors, 6*, 155–166.

Mahoney, E. R. (1974). Body-cathexis and self-esteem: Importance of subjective importance. *Journal of Psychology, 88*, 27–30.

Mann, A. H., Wakeling, A., Wood, K., Monck, E., Dobbs, R., & Szmukler, G. (1983). Screening for abnormal eating attitudes and psychiatric morbidity in an unselected population of 15-year old schoolgirls. *Psychological Medicine, 13*, 573–580.

Marino, D. D., & King, J. C. (1980). Nutritional concerns during adolescence. *Pediatric Clinics of North America, 27*, 125–139.

Martin, M., & Walter, R. (1982). Korperselbstbild und neurotizismus bei kindern und jugendlichen [Body image and neuroticism in children and adolescents]. *Praxis der Kinderpsychologie und Kinderpsychiatrie, 31*, 213–218.

Mazel, J. (1981). *The Beverly Hills diet*. New York: Macmillan.

McGuire, W. J., & McGuire, C. V. (1982). Significant others in self-space: Sex differences and developmental trends in the social self. In J. Suls (Ed.), *Social psychological perspectives on the self* (pp. 71–96). Hillsdale, NJ: Erlbaum.

McKinlay, S., & Jeffreys, M. (1974). The menopausal syndrome. *British Journal of Preventive and Social Medicine, 28*, 108–115.

Medlund, P., Cederlof, R., Floderus-Myrhed, B., Friberg, L., & Sorensen, S. (1976). A new Swedish Twin Registry. *Acta Medica Scandinavica* (Suppl. 600).

Metropolitan Life Foundation. (1983). *Statistical Bulletin, 64*, 2–9.

Miller, J. B. (1976). *Toward a new psychology of women*. Boston, MA: Beacon Press.

Miller, W. H., Faust, I. M., Goldberger, A. C., & Hirsch, J. (1983). Effects of severe long-term food deprivation and refeeding on adipose tissue cells in the rat. *American Journal of Physiology, 245*, E74–E80.

Minuchin, S., Rosman, B. L., & Baker, L. (1978). *Psychosomatic families: Anorexia nervosa in context*. Cambridge, MA: Harvard University Press.

Mishkind, M. E., Rodin, J., Silberstein, L. R., & Striegel-Moore, R. H. (in press). The embodiment of masculinity: Cultural, psychological, and behavioral dimensions [Special issue on men's studies]. *American Behavioral Scientist*.

Mitchell, J. E., Hatsukami, D., Eckert, E. D., & Pyle, R. L. (1985). Characteristics of 275 patients with bulimia. *American Journal of Psychiatry, 142*, 482–485.

Moss, R. A., Jennings, G., McFarland, J. H., & Carter, P. (1984). The prevalence of binge eating, vomiting, and weight fear in a female high school population. *Journal of Family Practice, 18*, 313–320.

National Research Council, Food and Nutrition Board, Committee on Maternal Nutrition. National Research Council. (1970). *Maternal nutrition and the course of pregnancy*. Washington, DC: National Academy of Sciences.

Nelsen, E. A., & Rosenbaum, E. (1972). Language patterns within the youth subculture: Development of slang vocabularies. *Merrill-Palmer Quarterly, 18*, 273–285.

Neugarten, B. L. (1969). Continuities and discontinuities of psychological issues into adult life. *Human Development, 12*, 121–130.

Neugarten, B. L. (1970). Dynamics of transition of middle age to old age: Adaptation and the life cycle. *Journal of Geriatric Psychiatry, 41*, 71–87.

Neugarten, B. I. (1972). Personality and aging process. *Gerontologist, 12,* 9.

Nielsen, A. C. (1979). Who is dieting and why? Chicago, IL: Nielsen Company, Research Department.

Norman, D. K., & Herzog, D. B. (1983). Bulimia, anorexia nervosa, and anorexia nervosa with bulimia. *International Journal of Eating Disorders, 2,* 43–52.

Nowlin, N. (1983). Anorexia nervosa in twins: Case report and review. *Journal of Clinical Psychiatry, 44,* 101–105.

Nylander, J. (1971). The feeling of being fat and dieting in a school population: Epidemiologic interview investigation. *Acta Sociomedica Scandinavica, 3,* 17–26.

Oakley, A. (1972). *Sex, gender and society.* New York: Harper & Row.

Orleans, C. T., & Barnett, L. R. (1984). Bulimarexia: Guidelines for behavioral assessment and treatment. In R. C. Hawkins II, W. J. Fremouw, & P. F. Clement (Eds.). *The binge-purge syndrome* (pp. 144–182). New York: Springer.

Parizkowa, J. (1973). Body composition and exercise during growth and development. In G. L. Rarick (Ed.), *Physical activity: Human growth and development* (pp. 98–124). New York: Academic Press.

Peskin, H. (1973). Influence of the developmental schedule of puberty on learning and ego functioning. *Journal of Youth and Adolescence, 2,* 273–290.

Pitkin, R. M. (1976). Nutritional support in obstetrics and gynecology. *Clinical Obstetrics and Gynecology, 19,* 489–513.

Polivy, J., & Herman, C. P. (1985). Dieting and binging: A causal analysis. *American Psychologist, 40,* 193–201.

Pope, H. G., Jr., Hudson, J. I., & Jonas, J. M. (1983). Antidepressant treatment of bulimia: Preliminary experience and practical recommendations. *Journal of Clinical Psychopharmacology, 3,* 274–281.

Pope, H. G., Jr., Hudson, J. I., Yurgelun-Todd, D., & Hudson, M. S. (1984). Prevalence of anorexia nervosa and bulimia in three student populations. *International Journal of Eating Disorders, 3,* 45–51.

Pyle, R. L., Mitchell, J. E., & Eckert, E. D. (1981). Bulimia: A report of 34 cases. *Journal of Clinical Psychiatry, 42.* 60–64.

Pyle, R. L., Mitchell, J. E., Eckert, E. D., Halvorson, P. A., Neuman, P. A., & Goff, G. M. (1983). The incidence of bulimia in freshman college students. *International Journal of Eating Disorders, 2,* 75–85.

Rabkin, J. G., Charles, E., & Kass, F. C. (1983). Hypertension and DSM-III depression in psychiatric outpatients. *American Journal of Psychiatry, 140,* 1072–1074.

Rimm, A. A., & White, P. L. (1979). Obesity: Its risks and hazards. In G. A. Bray (Ed.), *Obesity in America* (pp. 103–124). Washington, DC: Department of Health, Education, and Welfare.

Rodin, J. (1981). The current status of the internal-external obesity hypothesis: What went wrong. *American Psychologist, 1,* 343–348.

Rodin, J. (1985, June 30). *Yale health and patterns of living study: A longitudinal study on health, stress, and coping in the elderly.* Unpublished progress report. Yale University, New Haven, CT.

Rodin, J., Silberstein, L. R., & Striegel-Moore, R. H. (1985). Women and weight: A normative discontent. In T. B. Sonderegger (Ed.), *Nebraska symposium on motivation: Vol. 32. Psychology and gender* (pp. 267–307). Lincoln: University of Nebraska Press.

Rodin, J., Striegel-Moore, R. H., & Silberstein, L. R. (1985, July). *A prospective study of bulimia among college students on three U.S. campuses.* First unpublished progress report. Yale University, New Haven, CT.

Rose, G. A., & Williams, R. T. (1961). Metabolic studies on large and small eaters. *British Journal of Nutrition, 15,* 1–9.

Rosenbaum, M. (1979). The changing body image of the adolescent girl. In M. Sugar (Ed.), *Female adolescent development* (pp. 234–252). New York: Brunner/Mazel.

Rosenberg, F. R., & Simmons, R. G. (1975). Sex differences in the self-concept during adolescence. *Sex Roles, 1,* 147–160.

Rost, W., Neuhaus, M., & Florin, I. (1982). Bulimia nervosa: Sex role attitude, sex role behavior, and sex role-related locus of control in bulimiarexic women. *Journal of Psychosomatic Research, 26,* 403–408.

Rudofsky, B. (1971). *The unfashionable human body.* New York: Doubleday.

Russell, G. (1979). Bulimia nervosa: An ominous variant of anorexia nervosa. *Psychological Medicine, 9,* 429–448.

Schwartz, D. M., Thompson, M. G., & Johnson, C. L. (1981). Anorexia nervosa and bulimia: The socio-cultural context. *International Journal of Eating Disorders, 1,* 20–36.

Schwartz, L. A., & Markham, W. T. (1985). Sex stereotyping in children's toy advertisements. *Sex Roles, 12,* 157–170.

Schwartz, R. C. (1982). Bulimia and family therapy: A case study. *International Journal of Eating Disorders, 2,* 75–82.

Schwartz, R. C., Barrett, M. J., & Saba, G. (1985). Family therapy for bulimia. In D. M. Garner & P. E. Garfinkel (Eds.). *Handbook of psychotherapy for anorexia nervosa and bulimia* (pp. 280–307). New York: Guilford.

Secord, P. F., & Jourard, S. M. (1953). The appraisal of body-cathexis: Body-cathexis and the self. *Journal of Consulting Psychology, 17,* 343–347.

Seiden, A. M. (1976). Sex roles, sexuality and the adolescent peer group. *Adolescent Psychiatry, 4,* 211–225.

Selvini-Palazzoli, M. (1978). *Self-starvation. From individuation to family therapy in the treatment of anorexia nervosa.* New York: Aronson.

Shontz, F. C. (1963). Some characteristics of body size estimation. *Perceptual and Motor Skills, 16,* 665–671.

Sights, J. R., & Richards, H. C. (1984). Parents of bulimic women. *International Journal of Eating Disorders, 3,* 3–13.

Simmons, R. G., Blyth, D. A., & McKinney, K. L. (1983). The social and psychological effects of puberty on white females. In J. Brooks-Gunn & A. C. Petersen (Eds.), *Girls at puberty* (pp. 229–278). New York: Plenum Press.

Simmons, R. G., & Rosenberg, F. (1975). Sex, sex roles, and self-image. *Journal of Youth and Adolescence, 4,* 229–258.

Slade, P. (1982). Towards a functional analysis of anorexia nervosa and bulimia nervosa. *British Journal of Clinical Psychology, 21,* 167–179.

Slater, E., & Cowie, V. (1971). *The genesis of mental illness.* London: Oxford University Press.

Smith, N. J. (1980). Excessive weight loss and food aversion in athletes simulating anorexia nervosa. *Pediatrics, 66,* 139–142.

Snow, J. T., & Harris, M. B. (1985). *An analysis of weight and diet content in five women's interest magazines.* Unpublished manuscript, University of New Mexico, Albuquerque.

Society of Actuaries. (1959). *Build and blood pressure study.* Washington, DC: Author.

Society of Actuaries and Association of Life Insurance Medical Directors of America. (1979). *Build and blood pressure study.* Chicago, IL: Author.

Sontag, S. (1972). The double standard of aging. *Saturday Review, 54,* 29–38.

Spence, J. T. (1985). Gender identity and its implications for the concept of masculinity and femininity. In T. B. Sonderegger (Ed.), *Nebraska Symposium on Motivation: Vol. 32. Psychology and gender* (pp. 59–95). Lincoln: University of Nebraska Press.

Spence, J. T., & Helmreich, R. L. (1978). Gender, sex roles, and the psychological dimensions of masculinity and femininity. In J. T. Spence & R. L. Helmreich, *Masculinity and femininity* (pp. 3–18). Austin: University of Texas Press.

Squire, S. (1983). *The slender balance: Causes and cures for bulimia, anorexia, and the weight-loss weight-gain seesaw.* New York: Putnam.

Steele, C. I. (1980). Weight loss among teenage girls: An adolescent crisis. *Adolescence, 15,* 823–829.

Steiner-Adair, K. (1986). The body politic: Normal female adolescent development and the development of eating disorders. *Journal of the American Academy of Psychoanalysis, 14,* 95–114.

Stern, S. L., Dixon, K. N., Nemzer, E., Lake, M. D., Sansone, R. A., Smeltzer, D. J., Lantz, S., & Schrier, S. S. (1984). Affective disorder in the families of women with normal weight bulimia. *American Journal of Psychiatry, 141,* 1224–1227.

Story, I. (1979). Factors associated with more positive body self-concepts in preschool-children. *Journal of Social Psychology, 108,* 49–56.

Striegel-Moore, R. H., McAvay, G., & Rodin, J. (1984, September). *Predictors of attitudes toward body weight and eating in women.* Paper presented at the meeting of the European Association for Behavior Therapy, Brussels, Belgium.

Striegel-Moore, R. H., McAvay, G., & Rodin, J. (in press). Psychological and behavioral correlates of feeling fat in women. *International Journal of Eating Disorders*.

Striegel-Moore, R. H., Silberstein, I. R., & Rodin, J. (1985a, March). *Psychological and behavioral correlates of binge eating: A comparison of bulimic clients and normal control subjects*. Unpublished manuscript, Yale University, New Haven, CT.

Striegel-Moore, R. H., Silberstein, L. R., & Rodin, J. (1985b, August). *The relationship between femininity/masculinity, body dissatisfaction, and bulimia*. Paper presented at the meeting of the American Psychological Association, Los Angeles, CA.

Strober, M. (1981). The significance of bulimia in juvenile anorexia nervosa: An exploration of possible etiological factors. *International Journal of Eating Disorders, 1*, 28–43.

Strober, M. (1983, May). *Familial depression in anorexia nervosa*. Paper presented at the meeting of the American Psychiatric Association. New York, NY.

Strober, M. (1984). Stressful life events associated with bulimia in anorexia nervosa. *International Journal of Eating Disorders, 3*, 2–16.

Strober, M., Morrell, W., Burroughs, J., Salkin, B., & Jacobs, C. (1985). A controlled family study of anorexia nervosa. *Journal of Psychiatric Research, 19*, 239–246.

Strober, M., Salkin, B., Burroughs, J., & Morrell, W. (1982). Validity of the bulimia-restrictor distinction in anorexia nervosa. *Journal of Nervous and Mental Disease, 170*, 345–351.

Stroebe, W., Insko, C. A., Thompson, V. D., & Layton, B. D. (1971). Effects of physical attractiveness, attitude similarity, and sex on various aspects of interpersonal attraction. *Journal of Personality and Social Psychology, 18*, 79–91.

Stunkard, A. J., Foch, T. T., & Hrubec, Z. (1985). *A twin study of human obesity*. Unpublished manuscript, University of Pennsylvania, Philadelphia.

Stunkard, A. J., Sorensen, T. I. A., Hanis, C., Teasdale, T. W., Chakraborty, R., Schull, W. J., & Schulsinger, F. (1985). *An adoption study of human obesity*. Unpublished manuscript, University of Pennsylvania, Philadelphia.

Szmukler, G. L., (1982). Anorexia-nervosa: Its entity as an illness and its treatment. *Pharmacology and Therapeutics 16*, 431–446.

Tanner, J. M. (1978). *Foetus into man: Physical growth from conception to maturity*. Cambridge, MA: Harvard University Press.

Tobin-Richards, M. H., Boxer, A. M., & Petersen, A. C. (1983). The psychological significance of pubertal change. Sex differences in perceptions of self during early adolescence. In J. Brooks-Gunn & A. C. Petersen (Eds.), *Girls at puberty* (pp. 127–154). New York: Plenum Press.

Unger, R. K. (1985). Personal appearance and social control. In M. Safir, M. Mednick, I. Dafna, & J. Bernard (Eds.), *Woman's worlds: From the new scholarship* (pp. 142–151). New York: Praeger.

Vandereyken, W., & Pierloot, R. (1981). Anorexia nervosa in twins. *Psychotherapy and Psychosomatics, 35*, 55–63.

Vanfraechem, J. H. P., & Vanfraechem-Raway, R. (1978). The influence of training upon physiological and psychological parameters in young athletes. *Journal of Sports Medicine, 18*, 175–182.

Vincent, L. M. (1979). *Competing with the Sylph: Dancers and the pursuit of the ideal body form*. New York: Andrews & McMeel.

Wagman, M. (1967). Sex differences in types of daydreams. *Journal of Personality and Social Psychology, 3*, 329–332.

Walks, D., Lavan, M., Presta, E., Yang, M. U., & Bjorntorp, P. (1983). Refeeding after fasting in the rat: Effects of dietary-induced obesity on energy balance regulation. *American Journal of Clinical Nutrition, 37*, 387–395.

Wallach, J. D., & Lowenkopf, E. L. (1984). Five bulimic women. MMPI, Rorschach, and TAT characteristics. *International Journal of Eating Disorders, 3*, 53–66.

Walsh, B. T., Roose, S. P., Glassman, A. H., Gladis, M., & Sadik, C. (1985). Bulimia and depression. *Psychosomatic Medicine, 47*, 123–131.

Walster, E., Aronson, V., Abrahams, D., & Rottmann, L. (1966). Importance of physical attractiveness in dating behavior. *Journal of Personality and Social Psychology, 4*, 508–516.

Wardle, J. (1980). Dietary restraint and binge eating. *Behavioral Analysis and Modification, 4*, 201–209.

Wessel, J. A., Ufer, A., Van Huss, W. D., & Cederquist, D. (1963). Age trends of various components of body composition and functional characteristics in women aged 20–69 years. *Annals of the New York Academy of Sciences, 110,* 608–622.

Westerterp, K. (1977). How rats economize—energy loss in starvation. *Physiological Zoology, 80,* 331–362.

Williamson, D. A., Kelley, M. L., Davis, C. J., Ruggiero, L., & Blouin, D. C. (1985). Psychopathology of eating disorders: A controlled comparison of bulimic, obese, and normal subjects. *Journal of Consulting and Clinical Psychology, 53,* 161–166.

Wilson, G. T. (1984). Toward the understanding and treatment of binge eating. In R. C. Hawkins II, W. J. Fremouw, & P. F. Clement (Eds.), *The binge-purge syndrome* (pp. 264–289). New York: Springer.

Wittig, M. A. (1983). Sex role development in early adolescence. *Theory Into Practice, 22,* 105–111.

Wolf, E., & Crowther, J. H. (1983). Personality and eating habit variables as predictors of severity of binge eating and weight. *Addictive Behaviors, 8,* 335–344.

Women on Words and Images. (1972). *Dick and Jane as victims: Sex stereotyping in children's readers.* (Available from Women on Words and Images, Box 2163, Princeton, NJ 08540).

Wooley, O. W., Wooley, S. C., & Dyrenforth, S. R. (1979). Obesity and women-II. A neglected feminist topic. *Women Studies International Quarterly, 2,* 81–89.

Wooley, S. C., & Wooley, O. W. (1981). Overeating as substance abuse. *Advances in Substance Abuse, 2,* 41–67.

Wooley, S., & Wooley, O. W. (1982). The Beverly Hills eating disorder: The mass marketing of anorexia nervosa. *International Journal of Eating Disorders, 1,* 57–69.

Wooley, S. C., & Wooley, O. W. (1984, February). Feeling fat in a thin society. *Glamour,* 198–252.

Wooley, S. C., & Wooley, O. W. (1985). Intensive outpatient and residential treatment for bulimia. In D. M. Garner & P. E. Garfinkel (Eds.), *Handbook of psychotherapy for anorexia nervosa and bulimia* (pp. 391–430). New York: Guilford.

Yager, J. (1982). Family issues in the pathogenesis of anorexia nervosa. *Psychosomatic Medicine, 44,* 43–60.

Yager, J., Landsverk, J., Lee-Benner, K., & Johnson, C. (1985). *The continuum of eating disorders: An examination of diagnostic concerns based on a national survey.* Unpublished manuscript, Neuropsychiatric Institute, University of California, Los Angeles.

Yager, J., & Strober, M. (1985). Family aspects of eating disorders. In A. Francis & R. Hales (Eds.), *Annual review of psychiatry,* (Vol. 4, pp. 481–502). Washington, DC: American Psychiatric Press.

Yates, A., Leehey, K., & Shisslak, C. M. (1983). Running—An analogue of anorexia? *New England Journal of Medicine, 308,* 251–255.

Young, C. M., Blondin, J., Tensuan, R., & Fryer, J. H. (1963). Body composition studies of "older" women, thirty-seventy years of age. *Annals of the New York Academy of Science, 110,* 589–607.

Young, C. M., Martin, M. E. K., Chihan, M., McCarthy, M., Mannielo, M. J., Harmuth, E. H., & Fryer, J. H. (1961). Body composition of young women: Some preliminary findings. *Journal of the American Dietetic Association, 38,* 332–340.

Differential Maturation among Girls and its Relations to Social Adjustment: A Longitudinal Perspective

David Magnusson
Hakan Stattin
Vernon L. Allen

I. INTRODUCTION

A person's adult life situation is the result of a long developmental process involving the interaction of biological, psychological, and social factors. One serious limitation in developmental research is the underestimation of the biological role in human functioning. In this chapter we direct attention to an often ignored developmental factor—biological maturity—in the study of social adjustment over time. The chapter opens by reporting some data on the relation between biological maturity and social maladaptation in middle to late adolescence. Particular consideration is given to the role of social factors in mediating the influence of biological maturity on social behaviors. An attempt is made to determine the conditions under which we can expect the relation to occur.

A. Background of the Project

Under the title "Individual Development and Environment," a longitudinal research program was initiated by the first author in the 1960s at the Department of Psychology at the University of Stockholm (Magnusson, Duner, & Zetterblom, 1975). The first data collection took place in 1965, when subjects in the main group of the study were 10 years of age, and the project is still in progress. The subject population was all school children (1,025 boys and girls) in a mid-Sweden town of about 100,000 inhabitants who were receiving normal schooling in grade 3 of the compulsory school in 1965. Frequent data collections have been performed on this group of subjects from age 10 to adulthood.

The basic aim of the project is to investigate how person and situation factors—independently and in interplay with each other—influence the course of extrinsic and intrinsic adjustment from childhood to adulthood for a normal population.

An interactional perspective to development has explicitly guided the planning and execution of the project (Magnusson, 1985; Magnusson & Allen, 1983). Viewing the person as embedded within a complex interacting system of influences requires that we cover the broad spectrum of person and environmental factors that may be important for development. Data collection has included psychological and biological factors on the person side, and physical and social factors on the environmental side. Thus, measures of mediating psychological variables, intelligence, creativity, norms, values, social relations, manifest behaviors, and so forth, have been supplemented by measures of various biological functions of interest, with an emphasis on hormonal functioning. At the present stage of the research program, data are available for various biological, social, and psychological variables for a fairly representative sample of males and females from the age of 10 to 28.

B. Social Adaptation over Time

Having collected data repeatedly for the same individuals, it is possible to investigate trends in social adaptation over time. Results obtained in the project (Henricson, 1973; Olofsson, 1971) support other literature in the field (cf. Jessor & Jessor, 1977) that show a marked increase in breaches of norms during the teenage years.

In the early teenage years a majority of teenagers conform to their parents' standards. Over time, a greater range of contact with other persons occurs, and an increasing proportion of teenagers adhere to their peers' rather than to their parents' opinions on situations leading to breaches of norms. In one study in the project, Henricson (1973) showed that about half the subjects in the research group who were at middle adolescence had opinions on norms that were fairly consistent with those of adults. The study showed that these teenagers compromised between their parents' and their peers' standards. When peers were the dominant reference group, norm breaking was more tolerated and norm violations more frequent (Magnusson et al., 1975).

The growing number of norm violations with increase in age has been interpreted in the literature as a natural process in which the individual establishes an independent norm system. The developmental forces that operate toward conformity and conventional rules gradually lose their influence from the early years of youth.

The social processes just described mark the line of development in broad outline, but do not say anything about factors that determine variations in norm-breaking among individuals. In dealing with this issue in empirical research, the conventional procedure has been to view norm-breaking at a particular age point as an individual difference variable and to relate it to other information about the individuals under study (Brooks-Gunn & Petersen, 1983). Thus, the reason that some, rather than other, individuals break rules has been given in terms of *ecological factors* (such as housing, urban vs. rural environment, etc.), *upbringing conditions* (such as educational and economic level of the family, maladaptive parental behaviors, etc.), the *social network* (such as association with deviant peers, membership in gangs, leisure time activities, etc.), *school adjustment* (such as school motivation, achievement, etc.), and *person-bound factors* (such as cognitive capacity, emotional problems, activity level, presence of aggressive acting-out behaviors, etc.).

C. The Influence of Biological Age

The use of norm-breaking at a particular occasion as an individual difference variable contains some inherent assumptions that may not always hold true. When comparing subjects of the same chronological age with each other at one occasion and relating these individual variations to concurrent and later data, it is not certain that at the particular occasion in question we measure the same psychological processes across individuals. Research on physical growth has made it clear that the assumption of homogeneous development does not always hold true; hence, chronological age cannot be used as the only meaningful reference scale for development (Goldstein, 1979; Magnusson, 1983; Peskin, 1967).

A glance at an age-class of teenage girls shows great variations in physical maturity, with a typical range of 5 to 6 years between the earliest and the latest maturing girl. Such wide variations have psychological and social consequences for the girls, both contemporaneously and in a future perspective (Garwood & Allen, 1979; Greif & Ulman, 1982; Peskin, 1973; Stone & Barker, 1937). For boys, early maturation seems to be associated with a favorable social adjustment (Jones, 1957; Mussen & Jones, 1957). But for girls, the picture is more complex. Some findings suggest that early maturation is associated with high social status and prestige in the peer group. Other results indicate greater vulnerability to social pressures that leads to problems in social adjustment during the transition period (Andersson, Duner, & Magnusson, 1980; Davies, 1977; Frisk, Tenhunen, Widholm, & Hortling, 1966; Simmons, Blyth, Van Cleave, & Bush, 1979). One interpretation that has been offered is that very early maturation for a girl might involve difficulties in her new role as a potential adult. In this early adolescent period she has not reached the degree of emotional maturity commensurate with her physical maturity; entering into puberty later gives her time to adjust psychologically to the new situation. Thus, the transition period in the latter case would be less stressful (Peskin, 1967). Faust (1960) has drawn attention to the fact that early versus late maturation may mean different things at different periods of time in the teenage period. In her study of the relation between physical growth and social status, early-maturing girls in early adolescence were a minority of the total population and were non-normative for their age group; at this time they were the least popular girls. At late adolescence, on the other hand, they were more "in phase" with their peers, and at this age, they were ascribed the most prestigious qualities by their peers.

D. Two Models for Longitudinal Consequences of Early Biological Maturity

Though empirical data attest to the effects on behavior of differential growth rates, it is not clear how to conceptualize this impact (cf., Eichorn, 1975; Livson & Peskin, 1980). At least two models can be formulated (Magnusson & Stattin, 1982). The first model suggests persistent consequences for adjustment in future life of very early biological maturation. The model assumes that girls with different rates of maturity will perceive different reactions from their environment, so that distinctly different forms of personality and psychosocial functioning will emanate both in the short and in the long run.

According to the second model, some behaviors manifest a typical or predictable developmental pattern across time. For these behaviors, maturation may have a general impact when the girls actually enter puberty, but differences in biological growth rate will only determine the point in time at which the behavior sequence is activated. The second model predicts that individual differences among girls

is mainly due to the *timing* of the onset of the behavior in question. Hence, we would not expect differences in growth rates to have *persistent* or long-term consequences. Individual differences in behavior existing in adulthood would be determined either by person-bound factors other than age at menarche or by environmental factors unrelated to physical maturity during puberty.

Answers to the question of the source of the effects of early versus late maturation will depend on the particular kinds of consequences being investigated, the measures of physical growth that are used, the time the behavior observations are made, the cohort under investigation, and so on. For example, it is probably the case that maturity measured by ossification (a covert physiological process) will yield different results from using the age at menarche—a manifest life event that has definite psychological impact on the growing girl. Most important, however, is the recognition that the psychological and social consequences of differential biological maturation is not a simple cause-effect relation, but aspects of a complex interactive system. Effective research requires models and strategies that simultaneously incorporate social, psychological, and biological influences within the same behavioral equation.

Before describing some empirical data dealing with the connection between physical growth and social adjustment, some comments are made on the issue of differential biological maturation as it relates to the conceptualization of puberty. It is often taken for granted that the menarche marks the entrance into adulthood. In accordance with this assumption, the probable psychosocial consequences should be sought in areas that point toward future life: motherhood, work career, heterosexual relations, and so forth, or to factors characterizing the adult personality. It seems plausible, however, that much of the consequences of individual variations in biological maturity should be seen in the light of the prevailing conditions during the teenage period; how parents and the peer group respond to the girl's new situation and the meaning the girl herself gives to her own maturity relative to the variation in maturity in her reference group of peers (Scarr, 1981).

The focus of interest in the present study is on the concurrent influences that confront girls during adolescence, which means emphasizing behaviors and environmental conditions characteristic of the interval in question. In the following sections we concentrate on behaviors that characteristically take their starting point in adolescence, that are performed by a majority of teenagers, or that appear more frequently during adolescence than in any other period in the life of the individual.

As emphasized in the introduction, researchers have become increasingly aware of the complex interplay of biological, psychological, and social factors in development (Magnusson & Allen, 1983; Petersen & Taylor, 1980). In their review of the psychological impact of menarche, Greif and Ulman (1982) concluded with a plea for network analyses: "We are now ready to move beyond a simplistic dichotomy, which views menarche as a positive or negative experience, to a model which acknowledges the complexity of reactions to menarche. The use of an interactionistic perspective, with a focus on both the menarcheal girl and the environment around her, will help to elucidate the role of specific factors related to menarche" (p. 1428). The present study represents such an interactionistic approach.

E. Purpose of the Present Investigation

The data presented in the following extend over a period of 16 years (from age 10 to age 26) and cover diverse aspects of individual functioning, such as biological maturation, norm behaviors, criminal offenses, social networks, and higher education. The study illustrates how forces in one sector of the total organization of the individual have repercussions on other sectors.

The empirical portion of this chapter has three purposes.

1 The first purpose is to present data concerning the influence of biological maturity on some teenage behaviors that indicate a risk for further negative social adjustment. Norm violations in mid-adolescence are investigated for girls at varying levels of biological maturity;

2 Second, in order to elucidate the factors that mediate the influence of biological maturation on social behaviors, peer relations are introduced as a moderator factor. In the light of the role of the circle of peers as norm transmitters, expected sanctions from peers and their perceived evaluations of norm-breaking are related to behavioral differences among girls at various levels of biological maturation; and

3 To provide illustrations of the short-term changes that occur during adolescence, data on drug and alcohol use are analyzed for two occasions during the adolescent period.

II. BIOLOGICAL MATURATION AND NORMBREAKING

In the research dealing with biological factors and their role in individual development, one subproject within the longitudinal program is concerned with the synchronization of physical growth and social adjustment among adolescent girls (Magnusson & Stattin, 1982; Stattin & Magnusson, 1983). The general hypothesis is that early physical growth is paralleled by accompanying changes in social life, such that early biological maturation corresponds to an earlier display of social behaviors typical of the teenage period.

At a given point, then, individual variations in social adaptation can be understood partly from the point of view of differential maturation. Interindividual differences in social adjustment among girls at a particular age indicate that they enter the normal process of transition into new social patterns at different times. For example, girls pass through a time of liberation from parents and a time of change in norms, roles, and reference groups; but early-maturing girls pass through this phase at an earlier time than do their late-maturing peers. To the extent that social behaviors are connected with the rate of physical growth, obtained differences in adjustment among girls at a given period will represent time-lag effects.

A. Subjects and Data

The longitudinal project; "Individual Development and Environment," has been conducted as a total group investigation. A pilot and a main group of subjects have been followed by repeated data collection from their early school years into adulthood.

The subjects in the present study refer to the main group of subjects. They consist of a complete school-grade cohort—all those pupils who in 1965 (at the age of 10) attended grade 3 in a mid-Sweden town of about 100,000 inhabitants. All types of schooling within the ordinary school system that year are represented. Less than 1% of the children in the town did not attend the ordinary school system due to severe problems (e.g., severely retarded children or psychotic children). These latter children are not included in the present research. Thus, a very wide range of social and psychological upbringing conditions are included. Studies within the project have shown the group of children to be representative of pupils in the compulsory school system in Sweden (see Bergman, 1973; Magnusson et al., 1975). Data collections have been performed successively through the time in the school system. At each age level, all pupils present in the school system were included in the data collections.

The present research group consists of the girls for whom complete menarcheal data were obtained when they were about 15 years old (in grade 8) in 1970. A total of 588 were registered in the school, and data on menarche was obtained for those 509 girls who were present at school on the days the data were collected.

Most of the 509 girls in grade 8 were born in 1955; however, 1.9% were early school starters (born in 1954), and 8.4% were late school starters or pupils who had not moved in the ordinary manner up to the next class. It should be observed that the present investigation is based on those girls in grade 8 who were born in 1955 only (466 girls) in order to control for chronological age.

Age of Menarche Age at menarche was measured by an item in a questionnaire administered in April 1970, when the average age of girls was 14.10 years. The median age for the self-reported menarche was 12.86 years, which corresponds closely to national figures for the age cohort in question. For Swedish girls born in 1954–1955, Lindgren (1976) reported a median age of 12.98 years for the first menstruation using a similar data collection method. The girls were grouped into four menarcheal groups: (a) menarche before the age of 11; (b) menarche between the ages of 11 and 12; (c) menarche between the ages of 12 and 13; and (d) menarche after the age of 13.

Norm Violations Data on norm violations were collected at the average age of 14.5 years. At that time the girls answered a norm instrument asking about different situations (see Magnusson, 1981). A number of concrete norm-breaking situations were listed. For each of them the subjects were asked a number of questions concerning their own, their parents', and their peers' evaluations of breaking the norms in the situation, the expected sanctions from parents and peers if they would violate the norms in the situations, their own behavioral intentions, as well as their actual breaches of norms of this type to that point in time. An example of a situation description is the following:

They are going to have an exam, and Gunilla has not had time to prepare herself. It is important for

Gunilla to succeed. She has brought a scrap of paper with notes. She hesitates over whether to take up the note and cheat.

Subjects' answers were analyzed for the question about how many times they had actually violated rules of the type that the situations describe. Answers were given on 5-point Likert scales with the alternatives: (1) Never; (2) Once; (3) 2–3 times; (4) 4–10 times; and (5) More than 10 times (see Magnusson et al., 1975, pp. 100–103).

B. Results

Data for violations of norms *at home:* (1) Ignore parents' prohibitions, (2) stay out late without permission; *at school:* (3) cheat on an exam, (4) play truant; and *during leisure time:* (5) smoke hashish, (6) get drunk, (7) loiter in town every evening, and (8) pilfer from a shop, for girls in four menarcheal groups are summarized in Tables I and II.

Table I presents means on norm-breaking for girls in the four menarcheal groups, together with statistical tests of differences among the four groups of girls. Table II shows the percentage of girls in each of the four groups who reported *frequent* norm-breaking (four times or more) for each situation.

The results in Table I show a clear-cut association between age of biological maturation and frequency of norm-breaking, and clearly indicate that variations in norm violations at the time of the testing is highly related to the girls' physical maturation. The tests of differences in norm-breaking frequency were in most cases significant at a high level, except for one item (cheat on an exam). As can be seen in Table II, there was a considerably higher percentage of early- rather than of late-maturing girls who reported frequent violations of norms at home, at school, and during leisure time.

As can be seen from the two tables, there is a direct relation between norm-breaking and age at menarche. But it is also obvious that the relation is not linear: The earliest-developing group of girls differs markedly in mean and frequency of norm breaches from the groups of later-developing girls.

III. OLDER FRIENDS AS SOCIAL MEDIATORS

An empirically documented relation between individual variations in age at sexual maturation and frequency of norm violations in adolescence raises the question of the nature of the factors that contribute to the connection between biological maturity and social adjustment. We do not think it likely that a direct causal link exists between bodily or hormonal changes and social behavior. Rather, the effect is most likely to be mediated by an environment that changes as a consequence of changes in the individual. This proposition requires some form of social mediation of the effects of physical maturity.

An early-maturing girl will probably be considered by those in her environment as older than she actually is. The expectations and demands placed on her will be different from those placed on her late-maturing peers. One can expect the early-maturing girl to associate more with chronologically older persons, signifying new and more advanced habits and leisure-time activities. In her association with older peers the girl may encounter the more tolerant attitudes toward norm-breaking that characterize older groups of teenagers. Through association with them she will more often confront situations that may lead to rule-breaking, and also confront more positive attitudes towards norm violations.

A. Hypotheses and Method

Although a number of reasons can be given for the early-maturing girls' similarity in behavior to chronologically older peers, the most obvious one is association and identification: the early-maturing girl will seek out and be sought by others who are congruent with her own biological stage of maturity. This hypothesis

TABLE I MEANS ON NORM-BREAKING FOR FOUR MENARCHEAL GROUPS OF GIRLS

	Age at menarche					
Norm-breakup	11 years (n = 48)	11-12 years (n = 98)	12-13 years (n = 178)	13 years (n = 112)	F	P
Home						
Ignore parents' prohibitions	2.40	1.93	1.89	1.89	4.84	<.01
Staying out late without permission	2.67	2.08	1.96	1.74	9.96	<.001
School						
Cheat on an exam	2.19	2.05	2.09	2.00	0.48	ns
Play truant	2.77	2.08	1.74	1.74	12.40	<.001
Leisure time						
Smoke hashish	1.13	1.04	1.01	1.01	6.65	<.001
Get drunk	2.65	2.14	1.75	1.54	11.43	<.001
Loiter in town every evening	2.23	2.05	2.01	1.75	2.69	<.05
Pilfer from a shop	2.02	1.64	1.59	1.50	3.64	<.05
Total	2.23	1.88	1.76	1.63	10.57	<.001

Note to students: F is a statistic used to measure the difference between groups; P indicates the probability of an F that large occurring by chance; thus a P < .01 means there is less than one chance in a hundred that the differences among means on that variable occurred by chance.

suggests that for the early-maturing girl: (a) she will seek, in general, friends who are chronologically older than herself; (b) among her own age-class of girls she will seek as friends those who match her own stage of development; and (c) she will have more established relationships and more advanced heterosexual experiences with older boys than will her late-maturing peers.

Our expectations thus far suggest that friendship formation with older peers should be particularly characteristic of early-maturing girls. To the extent that tolerance of norm-breaking is evoked and maintained by association and identification with the social patterns of older teenagers, we would expect a relation between biological maturity and norm violations to occur for those girls who have close

TABLE II PERCENTAGE OF GIRLS IN DIFFERENT MENARCHE GROUPS REPORTING FREQUENT NORM-BREAKING AT AGE 14.5

	Age at menarche			
	11 years (n = 48)	11-12 years (n = 98)	12-13 years (n = 178)	13 years (n = 112)
Home				
Ignore parents' prohibitions	16.7	7.1	2.8	3.6
Staying out late without permission	27.1	12.2	5.6	4.5
School				
Cheat on an exam	17.0	5.1	5.1	7.3
Play truant	39.6	14.3	5.6	7.1
Leisure time				
Smoke hashish	12.0	4.1	1.1	.09
Get drunk	35.4	20.0	7.9	6.3
Loiter in town every evening	20.8	9.1	8.5	3.6
Pilfer from a shop	14.6	5.2	4.5	1.8

contact with older peers but not for those girls who lack this contact. This hypothesis is tested here.

Data Data on friendship formation were obtained from a questionnaire administered at the age of 14.10 years and from a sociometric instrument administered at the age of 14.5 years. Items from the questionnaire (Magnusson et al., 1975) covering dating and heterosexual experiences were used. The girls were asked whether they currently had or in the past had had stable relations with a boy, and whether they had had sexual intercourse with a boy.

The sociometric instrument measured the rated preference for a girl among her female classmates (Magnusson et al., 1975). The girls were asked to imagine that they were to be transferred to another class, and to rank all their female classmates in the order they would like them to move along. Additionally, the girls were asked whether they had chronologically older friends and how many such friends they had.

B. Older Friends as Moderators of Biological Maturation

It is evident from Table III that early-maturing girls associate with older acquaintances to a greater extent than do their late-maturing peers. There are large differences among the menarcheal groups of girls with respect to having older companions. Of the earliest maturing girls, 74% had such contacts, whereas only

39% of the latest maturing girls reported having older friends.

Does an early-maturing girl prefer her early-maturing classmates of the same chronological age? Does the late-maturing girl prefer her late-maturing schoolmates? These questions were investigated using the sociometric data. All girls assigned a rank-order value of preference for all of her same-sex classmates at age 14.5.

Data in Table IV show that the earliest and the latest developing girls tended to prefer others in terms of how they matched their own level of biological development. The earliest developed girls assigned a lower rank (i.e., the most preferred) to classmates who also were early-developing girls (5.3) than did the latest-maturing girls (8.5). There was a significant positive correlation between the preference of the earliest-maturing girls and the menarcheal age of the rating girls. Conversely, there was a significant negative correlation between the preference of the latest-maturing girls and the menarcheal age of the rating girls. The ranks assigned to these late-developing girls were lower among girls who themselves were late-maturing (6.6) than among the most early-developed girls (7.4).

Tables V and VI show that early-maturing girls are more advanced in their contacts with the opposite sex than are late-maturing girls. As can be seen in Table V, 83% of the early-maturing girls up to age 14.5 years have been or are now going steady with a boy. The same figure was lower (52.1%) for the latest-matu-

TABLE III PERCENTAGE OF GIRLS IN FOUR MENARCHEAL GROUPS WITH OLDER FRIENDS, AND THEIR MEAN MUMBER OF FRIENDS

Age at menarche	N	Girls with older friends	%	Mean number of older friends
<11	43	74.4	10	3.0
11-12	96	57.3	22.2	1.6
12-13	177	51.4	41.0	1.5
>13	116	38.8	26.9	1.0

TABLE IV MEAN RANK-ORDER PREFERENCE ASSIGNED TO CLASSMATES VARYING IN BIOLOGICAL MATURATION BY GIRLS WHO DIFFER IN BIOLOGICAL MATURATION

Girls who are "raters"	Girls who are "rated"			
	<11 yrs.	11-12yrs.	12-13 yrs.	13 yrs.
<11 yrs	5.3	7.4	6.8	7.4
11-12 yrs.	7.9	7.1	7.0	7.7
12-13 yrs.	7.4	7.6	7.0	7.2
>13 yrs.	8.5	7.3	6.7	6.6
	$r = .18^{**}$	$r = .00$	$r = .04$	$r = .12^{*}$

Note: The correlations at the bottom of the table are between menarcheal age of the rating girls and the rank-order values assigned to their rated peers. The correlations are calculated separately for each of the four menarcheal groups of rated classmates.
$^{*}p < .01.$
$^{**}p < .001.$

ring group of girls. The relation between biological maturity and dating a "steady" was highly significant (p < .001). As can be seen in Table VI, more than four times as many girls among the early-maturing have had sexual intercourse with boys as among the late-maturing girls. The relation between biological maturity and sexual experience yielded a high level of significance (*p* < .001).

All three of the factors investigated (association with older peers, association with same-age peers, and relationships with the opposite sex) showed that the early-maturing girls are more oriented toward older age groups of peers and towards same age girls who were more congruent with their early maturity. These results lead to the hypothesis that the relation between early maturation and high norm-breaking, which was demonstrated in an earlier section, is mediated by the association with more mature, older peers. If this is the case, the impact of such an association should be stronger for very early-maturing girls than for later-maturing girls.

Figure 1 shows the relation between norm-breaking and menarcheal age for girls with and for girls without older friends. The statistical analysis revealed a significant mean difference between the two groups (*p* < .01). For those girls who reported having no older friends, there was no significant difference in norm-breaking among the menarcheal groups of girls. However, a clear and significant difference in norm violations among the menarcheal groups was found for girls who reported having older friends. In accordance with the hypothesis, the difference in means between girls with and girls without older friends is mainly explained by the

TABLE V PERCENTAGE OF GIRLS IN FOUR MENARCHEAL GROUPS WHO HAVE BEEN GOING STEADY AT THE AGE OF 14.5

Age at menarche	Going steady			N	%
	No	Have been	Are now		
< 11 yrs.	17.0	44.7	38.3	47	10.4
11-12 yrs.	28.6	39.0	32.4	105	23.1
12-13 yrs.	37.6	41.1	21.0	181	39.9
> 13 yrs.	47.9	40.5	11.6	121	26.7
N	164	186	104	454	
%	36.1	41.0	22.9		

TABLE VI   PERCENTAGE OF GIRLS IN FOUR MENARCHEAL GROUPS WHO HAVE HAD
SEXUAL INTERCOURSE AT THE AGE OF 14.5

Age	Sexual intercourse			
menarche	No	Yes	N	%
< 11 yrs.	55.1	44.9	49	10.7
11-12 yrs.	64.5	35.5	107	23.2
12-13 yrs.	84.7	15.3	183	39.9
> 13 yrs.	89.2	10.8	120	26.1
N	358	101		
%	78.0	22.0		

difference between very early maturing girls *with* and very early maturing girls *without* older friends. For the other menarcheal groups, the difference was in the expected direction—hav-ing older friends was associated with more norm-breaking—but the differences were small and insignificant. For the latest maturing group of girls the means for norm-breaking were ac

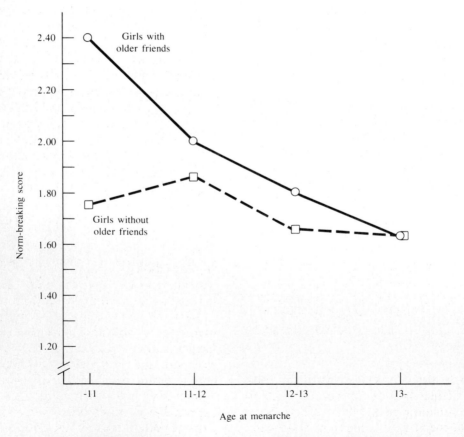

FIGURE 1   Relation between norm-breaking and menarcheal age for girls with and without older friends.

tually the same for girls with and girls without older friends.

Comments   Results up to this point may be summarized as follows. For girls at 14.5 years of age there are marked differences in norm violations that are related to the girls' physical maturation. These differences seem to be dependent on the girls' social network. The crucial characteristic of the social network is association with more mature, older friends. The main effect of having older friends was concentrated on the group of very early-maturing girls. This explains the results reported in Tables I and II, which showed that the group of very early-maturing girls differed from the other groups in both frequency and intensity of norm-breaking. In terms of vulnerability, it is particularly the very early-maturing girls who are susceptible to influences of older friends.

IV. FRIENDS AS NORM TRANSMITTERS

The role that friends play as norm transmitters—how the girls perceive their friends' opinions about norm-breaking and the sanctions they expect from friends after their own norm violations—comes into focus against the background of friends' role as social mediators for maturational influences on behavior. To throw some light on how girls interpret the norm climate among their peers and whether differences in perception in that respect can be found among girls at different levels of maturity, a further analysis was conducted to investigate: (a) girls' judgments of their peers' *evaluations* of norm-breaking; and (b) girls' *expectations of sanctions* from peers following their own norm violations.

Data   Data from the norm instrument administered at age 14.5 years were used. For each of the situations listed, data on peer evaluations and expected sanctions from peers were obtained. It was stated in the questionnaire that

"By 'peers' we mean those whose opinion you care most about, whether they are in your class, in a gang, or your best friend." After the description of a situation, the specific instruction was: "Here you should say what you think your peers think about cheating (etc.). My peers think it is..." The answers were given on 7-point scales with the alternatives: (1) "very silly," (2) "silly," (3) "rather silly," (4) "not really OK," (5) "rather OK," (6) "OK," and (7) "quite OK." For expected sanctions the following question was asked: "How do you think your peers would react, if they found out that you had cheated (etc.)?" Answers were given on 5-point scales with the alternatives: (1) "They would certainly disapprove," (2) "They would probably disapprove," (3) "I am not sure they would react," (4) "They would probably not care," and (5) "They would certainly not care."

Do girls who have different maturity levels perceive that their peers have different norm evaluations? Differences among the four menarcheal groups of girls with respect to their conceptions of peers' norms yielded nonsignificant results. A further separation of the girls into those with and those without older friends gave no support to the assumption of different levels of acceptance of norm violations among peers (girls without older friends, girls with older friends.) With respect to the expected sanctions following own norm violations, there were clear differences among the menarcheal groups: Biologically early-maturing girls expected weaker sanctions after breaches of norms than did late-maturing girls.

Because the influence of biological maturity seems to be mediated through older friends, further analyses were conducted separately for girls with and girls without older friends. For girls reporting older friends there were marked differences among the menarcheal groups in expected peer sanctions. The early-maturing girls expected weaker sanctions from their peers than did late-maturing girls. For girls

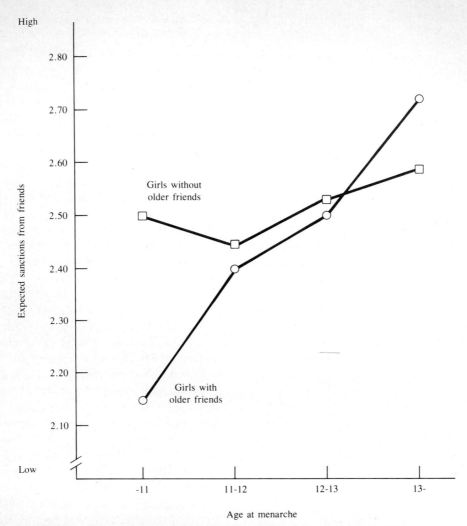

FIGURE 2   Relation between expected peer sanctions for norm-breaking and menarcheal age for girls with and without older friends.

reporting no older friends, no differences among the menarcheal groups was found. The results are graphically depicted in Fig. 2. A summary of the results in terms of correlations, including results on norm-breaking, is given in Table VII.

Notice that the relation between biological maturity and expected peer sanctions follows the same pattern as is found for the relation between biological maturity and frequency of norm violations. Early-developing girls commit norm violations to a greater extent than do late-maturing girls. They also expect weaker sanctions from peers after breaches of norms. These interconnections are, however, dependent on the presence of social mediators. Differences were found among girls with various levels of biological maturity for those girls who have older friends, but were negligible for girls without older friends.

TABLE VII   CORRELATION BETWEEN BIOLOGICAL MATURATION AND OWN NORM-BREAKING, JUDGMENT OF PEERS' NORM CLIMATE, AND EXPECTED PEER SANCTIONS FOR GIRLS WITH AND WITHOUT CHRONOLOGICALLY OLDER FRIENDS

Intercorrelations	Girls without older peers	Girls with older peers	Total group of girls
Own norm-breaking × menarcheal age	−.133	−.311***	−.252***
Peer evelutions × menarcheal age	−.087	−.097	−.111**
Peer sanctions × menarcheal age	−.065	−.248	−.195***

*p < .05.
**p < .01.
***p < .001.

V. SHORT-TERM STABILITY

The issue to be addressed in this section concerns the short-term stability of the difference in norm violations obtained for girls with different rates of maturity at the age of 14.5 years.

As they stand, the results covering mid-adolescence indicate that early-maturing girls form a group that runs a higher risk for later social maladaptation. On the other hand, we might argue that differences among the menarcheal groups at age 14.5 years are of a temporary nature, merely indicating that some girls enter the normal process of transition in norms earlier than others. In the latter case we would expect the late-maturing girls to catch up with the early-developing girls at a later point in time.

To elucidate this problem, data have been analyzed from two age points, separated by 17 months, covering use of alcohol and use of hashish, respectively. Table VIII presents data on alcohol use at the age of 14.5 years; the same type of data collected at 15.10 years are shown in Table IX. Data on hashish use at the ages 14.5 and 15.10 years are shown in Tables X and XI.

Viewed as a time sequence, these tables contain interesting information regarding trends over time for the total group of girls, and also regarding intergroup comparisons. As expected, there were more girls who had been drunk or who had smoked hashish at the latter test occasion. At age 14.5 years about 40% of the girls reported having been drunk. At age 15.10 years the same figure was 70%. At the earlier age only 3% of the girls had ever tried hashish; at the latter test occasion about 12% reported having smoked hashish.

It is particularly interesting to inspect the increase over time for the different maturational categories of girls. For the earliest maturing group, the percentage who had been drunk

TABLE VIII   PERCENTAGE OF GIRLS IN FOUR MENARCHEAL GROUPS WITH VARYING FREQUENCY OF DRUNKENNESS UP TO AGE 14.5

Age at menarche	Frequency of drunkenness					N	%
	Never	Once	2–3 times	4–10 times	> 10 times		
< 11 yrs.	37.5	12.5	14.6	18.8	16.7	48	11.0
11-12 yrs.	51.0	13.3	15.3	11.2	9.2	98	22.5
12-13 yrs.	62.1	13.0	16.9	3.4	4.5	177	40.7
> 13 yrs.	71.4	10.7	11.6	4.5	1.8	122	25.7
N	238	54	65	31	27	435	
%	59.3	12.4	14.9	7.1	6.2		

TABLE IX PERCENTAGE OF GIRLS IN FOUR MENARCHEAL GROUPS WITH VARYING FREQUENCY OF DRUNKENNESS UP TO AGE 15.10

Age at menarche	Frequency of drunkenness					N	%
	Never	Once	2–3 times	4–10 times	> 10 times		
< 11 yrs.	25.0	7.5	5.0	22.5	40.0	40	9.3
11-12 yrs.	25.7	5.9	18.8	20.8	28.7	101	23.5
12-13 yrs.	29.4	10.0	19.4	18.8	22.4	170	39.5
> 13 yrs.	35.3	9.2	20.2	11.8	23.5	119	27.7
N	128	37	78	76	111	430	
%	29.8	8.6	18.1	17.7	25.8		

more than 10 times increased from 16.7% to 40% over the 17-month period. For the latest-maturing group of girls, the percentage increased from 1.8% to 23%. For the early-maturing girls, those who had been drunk 4 to 10 times increased from 18.8% to 22.5%; and for the late-maturing girls the increase was 4.5% to 11.8%. Thus, the net increase for the categories of rather excessive drinking was about the same for early- and late-maturing girls from the age of 14.5 years to 15.10 years.

Although this net increase of excessive drinking is about the same for the menarcheal groups, a tendency can be discerned for the late-maturing girls to catch up with the earlier ones with respect to drinking. The proportion of girls moving from never having been drunk to having been drunk at least once is considerably higher for the late-maturing girls (from 28.6% to 64.7%) than for early-maturing girls (from 62.5% to 75%). Thus, in terms of moderate drinking, the "spurt" for the late-maturing girls comes during this 17-month pe-

riod. At the age of 14.5 years the relation between age at menarche and alcohol abuse was highly significant ($p < .001$); the relation was considerably weaker at 15.10 years. There was a catch-up in drunkenness over time by the late-maturing girls.

The influence of biological maturation on alcohol habits seems to be temporary and restricted to a short period in adolescence. This supports a phase displacement interpretation of the influence of biological maturity on the use of alcohol. Difference among girls can be attributed to the timing of the menarche, with late-developing girls catching up with the early developers after a short period.

By contrast, data on the use of hashish in Tables X and XI show that the influence of biological maturity persists at least during the period of time covered in this study. The equalization between the menarcheal groups found for alcohol use did not appear for smoking hashish. In fact, the opposite was true: Early-

TABLE X PERCENTAGE OF GIRLS IN FOUR MENARCHEAL GROUPS WHO HAVE SMOKED HASHISH AT 14.5 YEARS

Age at menarche	Smoke hashish		N	%
	No	Yes		
< 11 yrs.	87.5	12.5	48	11.0
11-12 yrs.	95.9	4.1	98	22.5
12-13 yrs.	98.9	1.1	178	40.8
> 13 yrs.	99.1	0.9	112	25.7
N	423	13	436	
%	97.0	3.0		

TABLE XI PERCENTAGE OF GIRLS IN FOUR MENARCHEAL GROUPS WHO HAVE SMOKED HASHISH AT 15.10 YEARS

Age at menarche	Smoke hashish		N	%
	No	Yes		
< 11 yrs.	70.5	30.0	40	9.2
11-12 yrs.	82.4	17.6	102	23.6
12-13 yrs.	89.5	10.5	171	39.5
> 13 yrs.	95.8	4.2	120	27.7
N	380	53	433	
%	87.8	12.2		

maturing girls displayed a higher net increase over the period. At the first test occasion 12.5% of the girls among the early-developing group reported having smoked hashish. At the later occasion 30% of them had tried. Among the late-maturing girls 0.9% had smoked hashish at age 14.5 years, and the corresponding figure was 4.2% at age 14.10 years. The relation between biological maturity and use of hashish was highly significant at both test occasions. Moreover, there was a higher net increase over time by the early-maturing as compared to the late-maturing girls.

VI. SUMMARY

Three issues have been empirically studied and discussed: (a) the role of biological maturation in norm-breaking behavior among girls during puberty, (b) peer relations as social mediators and modifiers in the socialization process, and finally, (c) the short-term stability of consequences for behavior of early biological maturation. These issues have been investigated by using data from a longitudinal project. The data included a broad range of psychological, biological, and social factors for a representative group of 466 girls, most of whom have been followed from age 10 to age 26.

First, it was hypothesized that early-developing girls would adopt typical teenage behaviors earlier than their late-maturing peers; thus, those interindividual differences that occur at a particular age during adolescence would be partially a function of differences in physical maturity among girls. In the present study data on norm-breaking were investigated. It was shown that variations in norm violations that occur for a group of girls at 14 years of age were related to their biological maturity. At the time of the test occasion in mid-adolescence, early-maturing girls had violated norms at home, at school, and in their leisure time considerably more frequently than their late-maturing peers.

The second issue, the impact of biological maturity on social adjustment, must be seen in the light of the role of social factors mediating this influence. A hypothesis was advanced suggesting that biological maturity is related to social adjustment processes via the characteristics of one's circle of peers. In accordance with the hypothesis, it was found that differences in norm violations among girls with different levels of maturity occurred for those girls who had formed close contacts with older and more mature peers. However, the impact of having older friends was concentrated at the group of very early maturing girls. No systematic difference among menarcheal groups in norm-breaking was found for girls without older friends. To illuminate the role of friends as norm transmitters, the girls' conceptions of their friends' norm standards and their expected sanctions from peers were investigated. With regard to norm transmission, no significant difference between early- and late-maturing girls was obtained, suggesting that girls generally are confronted by similar evaluative systems among their peers. On the other hand, the results on expected peer sanctions showed the same pattern as was found for the relation between biological maturity and norm violation frequency. That is, early-maturing girls expected weaker sanctions from their peers after norm-breaking than did late-maturing girls. When having chronologically older friends was introduced as a moderator variable, the relation between biological maturity and expected peer sanctions existed only for girls with older peers. Data on peer influences suggest, then, that how peers evaluate norms is less important than their reactions to norm violations: The latter seems to be the essential factor determining (self-reported) reactions to societal norms during puberty.

The third problem discussed in this chapter was the important question of whether individual differences in biological maturation lead to lasting individual differences in behavior. In the short-term perspective, results showed that the strong relation found at an early stage between age of the menarche and use of alcohol could be explained in terms of a socialization process that girls in general pass through at a rate that is governed by biological maturity. By the age of 15.10, the early significant relation between alcohol drinking and age at menarche had almost disappeared. For drug abuse, the results indicated, however, a lasting relation to age of menarche (over the period that was studied). This result should be extended for a longer period of time to permit a more decisive conclusion.

The results of the present study stimulate a number of points that should be discussed. Often both laymen and researchers in the field make the implicit assumption that antisocial behavior in the teenage years is the gateway to a more advanced antisocial life in adulthood. Indeed, reviews by Loeber (1982) and Loeber and Dishion (1983) found that there are often associations between early socially maladaptive behavior and later antisocial behavior. The earlier the age of onset of antisocial activities, the higher their rate, and the more contexts in which these are expressed, the higher the likelihood that antisocial behavior will become chronic.

That this continuity over time does not necessarily hold true is evident from results of the present study. The difference in frequency of norm-breaking in mid-adolescence between the early-developing girls and the late-maturing girls suggests that the early-maturing girls would remain at higher risk and maintain their higher violations of norms. However, there was only a weak tendency for these girls to have more registered criminal offenses up to age 26. Furthermore, the difference in frequency of drunkenness at mid-adolescence between the menarcheal groups of girls leveled out in later adolescence, and no difference in alcohol consumption was found at adulthood.

The lack of systematic long-term consequences suggests a somewhat different interpretation of the findings of this study. This interpretation involves taking into account simultaneously one's adaptation to adult roles and responsibilities and accommodation to the prevailing norm climate among preferred peers. Rather than viewing the higher frequency of norm-breaking among early-developing girls as a risk factor for later social maladaptation, behaviors such as ignoring of parents' prohibitions, staying out late without permission, alcohol drinking, and loitering in town in the evenings, might be interpreted as movement away from dependence on the close home environment—as the establishment of an identity as an independent and adult person. The exposure to older teenagers' more tolerant reactions to norm-breaking (especially older boys and boyfriends) constitutes an additional factor that further contributes to the early-maturing girls' greater likelihood of breaking conventional rules at this time period. Therefore, what is interpreted negatively and with a deviant connotation by the adult world may be, from the perspective of the growing girl, a logical step in her development toward an adult status. With a consolidated identity of self as adult, these behaviors are likely to diminish.

An interpretation of the higher norm-breaking frequency among early-maturing girls in mid-adolescence in terms of an acquisition of an adult social role rather than as "deviance" leads to a number of testable hypotheses. It suggests, on the one hand, that the early-maturing girl would view herself as more psychologically mature than her late-maturing peers, consider herself as adult at an earlier age, and intend to establish her own family life earlier. It also would suggest that the early-maturing girl should express greater responsibility and caring earlier—being a babysitter earlier, taking more responsibility for household activities, and so forth.

Preliminary findings point in the direction of the acquisition-of-adult-social-role hypothesis, at least with regard to the grown-up status. A question at age 14.5 asked whether the girls considered themselves as more or less mature than their classmates. For the very early-developed girls, 42% thought of themselves as more mature and only 2% said that they were less mature. The situation was quite different among the late-developing girls: only 16% considered themselves as more mature than their classmates, and nearly 20% thought of them-

selves as less mature. This relation between age at menarche and experienced maturity was significant at a high level. Table XII presents the obtained results.

On a question at the same age concerning whether they felt themselves to be different from their peers, more than half of the early-developed girls said that they felt that way, whereas a minority (17%) among the latest developed girls answered in the affirmative. On a complementary question, nearly half of the early-developed girls who considered themselves as different stated that this was so because they felt themselves more romantic than the others. On another question of whether the girls looked forward to giving birth to and bringing up their own children, two out of three girls among the earliest developed wished this very much or rather much in comparison with 42% of the latest-developed girl. Obviously, no firm conclusions can be drawn from these preliminary results. Other evidence in the literature, however, tends to support the hypothesis that difference in norm-breaking in the teenage years between the menarcheal groups of girls is not due to a deviant attitude of the early-maturing girls, but rather mirror the approximation of an adult status of these girls earlier than the late-maturing girls. For example, Simmons et al. (1983) showed that early developers were allowed greater independence from their parents than were the late developers, and that the early-maturing girls took greater responsibility for household activities by babysitting more

TABLE XII EXPERIENCED MATURITY AMONG EARLY- AND LATE- MATURING GIRLS AT AGE 14.5

Age at menarche	Do you feel yourself more or less mature than your classmates?			
	More mature	About as mature	Less mature	N
< 11 yrs.	41.7	53.6	2.1	48
11-12 yrs.	37.1	60.8	2.1	97
12-13 yrs.	20.9	75.7	3.4	177
> 13 yrs.	16.1	64.3	19.6	112

than their late-developing counterparts. Further research will clarify which of the two hypotheses, the deviant model or the acquisition-of-adult-social-role model, best represents the girls' social development from adolescence to adult life.

REFERENCES

Andersson, O., Duner, A., & Magnusson, D. (1980). *Social anpassning hos tidigt utvecklade flickor* [Social adjustment among early-maturing girls]. (Report No. 35). Stockholm: University of Stockholm, Department of Psychology. (Not available in English).

Andersson, T., Magnusson, D., & Duner, A. (1983). *Basdata—81: Livssituation i tidig vuxenalder* [Base data—81: The life situation at early adulthood]. (Report No. 49). Stockholm: University of Stockholm, Department of Psychology. (Not available in English).

Baltes, P. B. (1968). Longitudinal and cross-sectional sequences in the study of age and generation effects. *Human Development, 11,* 145–171.

Bergman, L. R. (1973). Parents' education and mean change in intelligence. *Scandinavian Journal of Psychology, 14,* 273–281.

Bergman, L. R., & Magnusson, D. (1983). *The development of patterns of maladjustment.* (Report No. 50). Stockholm: University of Stockholm, Department of Psychology.

Bergman, L. R., & Magnusson, D. (1984). *Patterns of adjustment problems at age 10.* (Report No. 615). Stockholm: University of Stockholm, Department of Psychology.

Brooks-Gunn, J., & Petersen, A. C. (Eds.). (1983). *Girls at puberty.* New York: Plenum.

Coleman, J. S. (1961). *The adolescent society.* New York: Free Press.

Davies, B. L. (1977). Attitudes towards school among early and late-maturing adolescent girls. *Journal of Genetic Psychology, 131,* 261–266.

Eichorn, D. H. (1975). Asynchronizations in adolescent development. In S. E. Dragastin & G. H. Elder (Eds.), *Adolescence in the life cycle: Psychological change and social context.* (pp. 81–96). New York: Wiley.

Faust, M. S. (1960). Developmental maturity as a determinant in prestige of adolescent girls. *Child Development, 31,* 173–184.

Frisk, M., Tenhunen, T., Widholm, O., & Hortling, H. (1966). Physical problems in adolescents showing advanced or delayed physical maturation. *Adolescence, 1,* 126–140.

Garwood, S. G., & Allen, V. L. (1979). Self-concept and identified problem differences between pre- and post-menarcheal adolescents. *Journal of Clinical Psychology, 35,* 528–537.

Gold, M., & Petronio, R. J. (1980). Delinquent behavior in adolescence. In J. Adelson (Ed.), *Handbook of adolescent psychology* (pp. 495–535). New York: Wiley.

Goldstein, H. (1979). *The design and analysis of longitudinal studies.* New York: Academic Press.

Greif, E. B., & Ulman, K. J. (1982). The psychological impact of menarche on early adolescent females: A review. *Child Development, 53,* 1413–1430.

Harnquist, K. (1961). *Manual till DBA-differentiell begavningsanalys* [Manual to DIA-differential intelligence analysis]. Stockholm: Skandinaviska Testforlaget.

Harper, J. F., & Collins, J. K. (1972). The effects of early or late maturation on the prestige of the adolescent girl. *Australian and New Zealand Journal of Sociology, 8,* 83–88.

Henricson, M. (1973). *Tonaringar och normer* [Teenagers and norms]. Stockholm: Skoloverstyrelsen. (Not available in English).

Jenicek, M., & Demirjian, A. (1974). Age at menarche in French Canadian urban girls. *Annals of Human Biology, 1,* 339–346.

Jessor, R., & Jessor, S. L. (1977). *Problem behavior and psychosocial development: A longitudinal study of youth.* New York: Academic Press.

Jones, M. C. (1957). The later careers of boys who were early- or late-maturing. *Child Development, 28,* 113–128.

Jones, M. C., & Mussen, P. H. (1958). Self-conceptions, motivations, and interpersonal attitudes of early- and late-maturing girls. *Child Development, 29,* 491–501.

Lindgren, G. (1976). Height, weight, and menarche in Swedish urban school children in relation to socio-economic and regional factors. *Annals of Human Biology, 3,* 501–528.

Livson, N., & Peskin, H. (1980). Perspectives on adolescence from longitudinal research. In J. Adelson (Ed.), *Handbook of adolescent psychology* (pp. 47–98). New York: Wiley.

Loeber, R. (1982). The stability of antisocial and delinquent child behavior: A review. *Child Development, 53,* 1431–1446.

Loeber, R., & Dishion, T. (1983). Early predictors of male delinquency: A review. *Psychological Bulletin, 94,* 68–99.

Loevinger, J. (1965). Measurement in clinical research. In B. B. Wolman (Ed.), *Handbook of clinical psychology* (pp. 78–94). New York: McGraw-Hill.

Magnusson, D. (1981). Some methodology and strategy problems in longitudinal research. In F. Schulzinger, S. A. Mednick, & J. Knop (Eds.), *Longitudinal research: Methods and uses in behavioral sciences* (pp. 192–215). Boston: Nijholt.

Magnusson, D. (in press). Implications of an interactional paradigm of research on human development. *International Journal of Behavioral Development.*

Magnusson, D., & Allen, V. L. (1983). *Human development: An interactional perspective.* New York: Academic Press.

Magnusson, D., Anderson, T., & Duner, A. (1982). Alkohol och anpassning—data fran ett longitudinellt forskningsprogram [Alcohol and adjustment—data from a longitudinal research program]. In O. Arvidsson (Ed.), *Risken att bli alkoholist* [The risk of becoming an alcoholic](pp. 140–155). Stockholm: Liber. (Not available in English).

Magnusson, D., & Duner, A. (1981). Individual development and environment. A longitudinal study in Sweden. In S. A. Mednick & A. E. Baert (Eds.). *Prospective longitudinal research: An empirical basis for the primary prevention of psychosocial disorders* (pp. 111–122). Oxford: University Press.

Magnusson, D., Duner, A., & Zetterblom, G. (1975). *Adjustment: A longitudinal study.* Stockholm: Almqvist & Wiksell.

Magnusson D., & Stattin, H. (1982). *Biological age, environment, and behavior in interaction: A methodological problem.* (Report No. 587). Stockholm: University of Stockholm, Department of Psychology.

McCall, R. B. (1977). Challenges to a science of developmental psychology. *Child Development, 48,* 333–344.

McCall, R. B., Appelbaum, M. I., & Hagerty, P. S. (1973). Developmental changes in mental performance. *Monographs of the Society for Research in Child Development, 38.*

Mussen, P. H., & Jones, M. C. (1957). Self-conceptions, motivations, and interpersonal attitudes of late- and early-maturing boys. *Child Development, 28,* 243–256.

Olofsson, B. (1971). *Vad var det vi sa? Om kriminellt och konformt beteende bland skolpojkar* [On criminal and conformity behavior among adolescent boys]. Stockholm: Utbildningsforlaget. (English summary).

Peskin, H. (1967). Pubertal onset and ego functioning. *Journal of Abnormal Psychology, 72,* 1–15.

Peskin, H. (1973). Influence of the developmental schedule of puberty on learning and ego functioning. *Journal of Youth and Adolescence, 36,* 273–290.

Petersen, A. C., & Taylor, B. (1980). The biological approach to adolescence: Biological change and psychological adaptation. *In J. Adelson (Ed.), Handbook of adolescent psychology* (pp. 117–155). New York: Wiley.

Rona, R., & Pereira, G. (1974). Factors that influence age at menarche in girls in Santiago, Chile. *Human Biology, 46,* 33–42.

Scarr, S. (1981). *Maturation and development: Biological and psychological perspectives.* London: Heinemann.

Schaie, K. W. (1965). A general model for the study of developmental problems. *Psychological Bulletin, 64,* 92–107.

Sewell, W. H., & Hauser, R. M. (1975). *Education, occupation, and earnings.* New York: Academic Press.

Shipman, W. G. (1964). Age of menarche and adult personality. *Archives of General Psychology, 10,* 155–159.

Simmons, R. G., Blyth, D. A., & McKinney, K. L. (1983). The social and psychological effects of puberty on white females. In J. Brooks-Gunn & A. C. Petersen (Eds.), *Girls at puberty* (pp. 229–272). New York: Plenum.

Simmons, R. G., Blyth, D. A., Van Cleave, E. F., & Bush, D. M. (1979). Entry into early adolescence: The impact of school structure, puberty, and early dating on self-esteem. *American Sociological Review, 44,* 948–967.

Stattin, H., & Magnusson, D. (1983). *Tonarsflickor och normbrott: Ett biologiskt utvecklings perspektiv* [Normviolations among adolescent girls: A biological perspective]. (Report No. 5). The National Council for Crime Prevention. (Not available in English).

Stone, C. P., & Barker, R. G. (1937). Aspects of personality and intelligence in post-menarcheal and pre-menarcheal girls of the same chronological age. *Journal of Comparative Psychology, 23,* 439–455.

Tanner, J. M. (1962). *Growth of Adolescence* (2nd ed.). Oxford: Blackwell Scientific Publications.

Wohlwill, J. F. (1970). The age variable in psychological research. *Psychological Review, 77,* 49–64.

CHAPTER 3

INFANCY AND EARLY DEVELOPMENT

Few areas of research have undergone so radical a change as infancy in recent times. Gone is "the booming, buzzing confusion" that William James described as the world of the infant; nor is the infant viewed any longer as passive, helpless, and at the mercy of his environment. Rather, a new and more positive view of infancy has emerged with infants, characterized as active, competent, and very early ready to make their mark on both their social and physical environment. Owing to rapid and important advances in our methodology for investigating infants, many of the capacities of the infant are just being discovered. Many perceptual and cognitive capacities are available at an earlier age than had previously been assumed. Very young infants are ready to interact with their environment in a meaningful way and through a wide range of senses—vision, hearing, smell, and taste. Nor is infant precocity limited to perceptual capacities; much evidence is accumulating to suggest that infants are prepared for their social roles as well. Infants' early preference for faces and voices over inanimate objects, as well as their predisposition to react to human speech sounds are all indicators of the infant's readiness for social interaction.

In the first article in this section, Meltzoff and Moore demonstrate the remarkable capacity of newborn infants to imitate adult facial movements. This evidence is especially interesting in light of Piaget's earlier assumptions that imitation was not possible until 8 to 12 months of age. In a similar vein, Baillargeon, Spelke, and Wasserman present new evidence which suggests that infants can achieve the important developmental landmark of object permanence by 5 months of age. This is earlier than Piaget and other theorists have suggested that this achievement is possible in infants and is further demonstration of the fact that infants seem to be much more cognitively and perceptually advanced that we have previously thought.

In the next article, Starkey and his colleagues present further indications of the cognitive and perceptual capabilities of infants. They show that 7-month-olds can match the number of objects in a visual display to the number of sounds presented in a sequence. They suggest that mathematical knowledge may be based on innate or at least very early appearing abilities of infants.

The emergence of fear of heights is a perceptual as well as an emotional puzzle that has fascinated researchers for many years. Bertenthal and Campos show that one important contributor to the emergence of fear of heights may be the onset of self-produced locomotion. The experiments suggest that the onset of locomotion such as crawling in the 7- to 9-month age period is of great significance for early perceptual and affective development.

Finally, Kagan and Klein remind us that the effects of early infant experiences are not irreversible. The human organism is adaptive and flexible and able to profit from experiences at a variety of age points. For example, early birth traumas and complications can be overcome by a stimulating and responsive child-rearing environment. Similarly, the timing of development in different cultures indicates that slowness in early development does not preclude catch-up advances at later ages. Different cultures, in short, have different timetables for development and demand certain skills at later times than in our American culture. The impressive aspect of the Kagan-Klein report is the reminder that early "deficits" can be overcome; early experience is important, but the early effects are neither inevitable nor irreversible.

Newborn Infants Imitate Adult Facial Gestures

Andrew N. Meltzoff
M. Keith Moore

Imitation has been demonstrated across a wide range of behaviors and ages in both Western and non-Western cultures (Aronfreed, 1969; Bandura, 1969; Flanders, 1968). A variety of theoretical perspectives have offered accounts of the origins of this capacity (Aronfreed, 1969; Parton, 1976; Piaget, 1945/1962).

Some theorists have asserted that imitation is based on early learning; they claim that the stimulus-response linkages manifest in imitative acts are built up through conditioning and learned associations. In this view, infants are taught to imitate simple acts in everyday interactions with their caretakers.

Although such training might explain the imitation of certain behaviors, it cannot provide a complete account of infant imitation, because young infants also copy behaviors that have not been part of any previous adult-infant interactions. Among such untrained imitative reactions, Piaget (1945/1962) singled out facial imitation as a landmark achievement. Facial imitation was regarded as a particularly important developmental milestone because, unlike manual and vocal imitation, the infant's response cannot be perceived within the same sensory modality as the model's. The stimulus and response cannot be "directly compared." In facial imitation, infants must match a gesture they see with a gesture of their own that they cannot see, a seemingly sophisticated skill that Piaget claimed was beyond the perceptual-cognitive competence of infants younger than 8–12 months of age.

There are disagreements between the learning and Piagetian accounts of imitation. However, they both maintain that young infants, without any special training in the task, should not be able to imitate facial gestures. Both assume that the capacity for facial imitation is forged through considerable postnatal experience—experience that leads infants to "link up" the model's behavior and their own unseen movements (the views differ on the kind of experience that is critical). Most modern theorists adopt some version of these views (Abravanel, Levan-Goldschmidt, & Stevenson, 1976; Gerwitz & Stingle, 1968; Kaye & Marcus, 1978; McCall, Parke, & Kavanaugh, 1977; Paraskevopoulos & Hunt, 1971; Parton, 1976; Uzgiris, 1972; Uzgiris & Hunt, 1975). Thus, whether or not writers agree with Piaget's theoretical explanation for the late development of facial imitation, there is a general acceptance of his observations that such activity is not manifest in the first few postnatal months. (See Meltzoff & Moore [1983] for a review.)

In contrast, we found that infants under 1 month of age can successfully imitate facial gestures (Meltzoff & Moore, 1977). More specifically, we showed that 12–21-day-old infants could imitate lip protrusion, mouth opening, tongue protrusion, and sequential finger movements. Three independent studies have now supported our findings of early facial imitation. Dunkeld (1978) demonstrated imitation of mouth opening, tongue protrusion, and other facial movements in infants under 4 months old. Jacobson (1979) reported that 6-week-old infants match adult tongue protrusions with tongue protrusions of their own. Burd and Milewski (Note 1) found that 2–10-week-old infants imitated not only oral gestures but also brow movements.[1]

---

[1] After this paper was accepted for publication, Field, Woodson, Greenberg, & Cohen (1982) also reported that neonates imitate "happy," "sad," and "surprised" expressions.

On the other hand, others have been unable to document early imitation (Hayes & Watson, 1981; Hamm, Russel, & Koepke, Note 2; McKenzie, Note 3). These divergent results suggest that there may be important differences in the experimental procedures utilized by the different research teams. Elsewhere we reviewed this work and specified some of the methodological shortcomings of the latter group of studies (Meltzoff & Moore, 1983). The chief problems concerned the use of experimental procedures that served to dampen the imitative effect in young infants.

We believe that the elicitation, measurement, and interpretation of neonatal imitation is facilitated by a set of procedures that we have described (Meltzoff & Moore, 1983). This experimental paradigm provides solutions to four of the major methodological issues in the study of early imitation. It describes techniques for (*a*) distinguishing imitation from a general arousal response; (*b*) guarding against shaping of the imitative response; (*c*) obtaining high resolution records of neonatal lip and tongue movements and developing valid scoring procedures for documenting these fine motor actions; and (*d*) constructing test procedures that are effective in directing the neonate's visual attention to the experimenter's facial movements.

The purpose of the present experiment was to apply this experimental paradigm to the study of newborn infants. Our 1977 results did not conclusively support the hypothesis that the ability to imitate is present at birth. The subjects were 12–21 days old. One could still argue either (*a*) that this precocious imitation is itself learned through the intricate mother-infant interaction that occurs in the first postnatal weeks, or (*b*) that it depends upon postnatal maturation of the visual system, the motor system, or the ability to coordinate these two systems. In order to assess whether either interactive experience or postnatal maturation is a necessary condition for infant imitation, we

tested whether newborn infants (0–72 hours old) could imitate two facial gestures presented by an adult model.

METHOD

Subjects The following predetermined factors were adopted as admission criteria in this study: (*a*) less than 72 hours old; (*b*) full-term (over 36 weeks' gestation); (*c*) normal birthweight (5.5–10 pounds); (*d*) fed within the last 3 hours, no rooting or other signs of hunger for 5 min immediately prior to testing; (*e*) wide-eyed, alert, and behaviorally calm for 5 min immediately prior to testing.

The subjects were 40 healthy newborns with no known visual or motor abnormalities. They ranged from 42 min to 71 hours old at the time of test, X = 32.1 hours, SD = 16.1. Other birth characteristics were: birthweight, X = 7.7 pounds, SD = 1.0, range 6.1–9.8; gestational age according to the obstetrician's EDC, X = 40.5 weeks, SD = 1.6, range 36.6–43.9; 1-min Apgar, X = 7.9, SD = 1.0, range 6–9; 5-min Apgar, X = 9.0, SD = 0.5, range 8–10. There were 18 male subjects and 22 female subjects. The maternity ward served primarily middle- and upper-middle-class whites: of the 40 subjects, 37 were white, one was black, and two were Hispanic. Over 90% of the subjects' mothers were 20 years old or older, X = 26.3 years, SD = 4.9.

Testing began on 67 additional infants who did not complete the study for the following reasons: falling asleep (30%), crying (27%), spitting or choking uncontrollably (24%), hiccuping (15%), and having a bowel movement during the test session (4%). This loss rate is typical of studies done with newborns (e.g., Kessen, Salapatek, & Haith, 1972; Mendelson & Haith, 1976; Salapatek & Kessen, 1966). The specification that an infant was sleeping, crying, etc. was not made by the experimenter during the test, but by an independent judge who evaluated the infant's state from the videotape and was kept uninformed about the infant's test condition.

Test Environment The laboratory was an isolated experimental room, out of earshot of other crying newborns, in Swedish Hospital, Seattle. The infants were examined within a large black-lined test chamber (2.0 m x 1.5 m). The room lights were extinguished during the test. A spotlight, situated above (25 cm) and behind (15 cm) the infant, was oriented toward the experimenter's face. The experimenter wore a gown made from the same black material as the background, thus reducing reflectance from his body. The luminance was approximately 0.6 log cd/m at the experimenter's face, and −1.3 log cd/m on the black background 30 cm to the right of the experimenter's face. The cameras were located outside the black test chamber with only their lenses poking through small holes. The camera operator silently focused the camera at the beginning of each test. The infants showed no tendency to fixate the camera location during the experiment. The videotape recorders were housed within a sound-dampening chamber.

Apparatus We used an infrared-sensitive video camera to photograph the infant's oral movements (Telemation TMC-1100SD with a 4352H silicon diode pickup tube and Pichel IR-75 infrared illuminator). This camera and its tape deck (Sony 3650) were devoted solely to recording a close-up picture of the infant's face. The camera was focused on the infant's lips, and the full extent of the picture was from the top of the infant's head to 2.5 cm below his or her chin. A mirror (30 cm x 30 cm) was situated behind (25 cm) and to the left (18 cm) of the infant's head. A second camera and tape deck were used to record the mirror reflection of the experimenter's face (camera: Sony 3260; tape deck: Sony 3650).

The experiment was electronically timed. The timer consisted of a digital display that was located directly above (5 cm) the infant's head, and a companion character generator that electronically mixed the elapsed time (in 0.10-sec increments) onto both videotapes.

Procedure The infants were carefully handled so that they did not see the experimenter's face until the modeling began. All the infants were tested while supported in a semiupright position by a well-padded infant seat. Once the infant was seated, the experimenter slowly moved a white cloth (46 cm x 15 cm) in the spotlight before the infant's eyes for at least 20 sec. If the infant fixated the cloth while maintaining a quiet alert state, the experimenter: (*a*) removed the cloth, (*b*) put his face in the spotlight 25 cm from the infant's eyes, and (*c*) simultaneously activated the experimental clock. The camera operator then signaled the infant's randomly determined test condition to the experimenter, and the modeling began. The experimenter thus remained uninformed about the infant's test condition until the moment he started to model the test displays.

Each infant was presented with both a mouth-opening and a tongue-protrusion gesture. For half the infants, the order of presentation was mouth opening then tongue protrusion; the remainder received the reverse order. Pilot work indicated that newborn attention and responsivity were fostered by alternating the adult's gesturing with periods in which the experimenter remained passive. Thus we used two 4-min periods. Each of these periods consisted of 12 20-sec intervals such that the experimenter alternately demonstrated the gestures (for 20 sec), then assumed a passive face (for 20 sec), and so on. At the end of this first period, the identical procedure was repeated using the new gesture. The displays were performed in a standardized fashion, at the rate of four times in a 20-sec interval with a 1-sec interact interval. (The placement of the experimental clock directly above the subject's head aided the experimenter in timing his gestures without needing to turn from the infant; see Apparatus.) There were no breaks or pauses anywhere in the test. The experimenter's behavior was thus fixed from the moment the experiment began until the end.

Response Measures The videotapes of the infant's face did not contain any record of the gesture shown to the infant. The 80 videotaped periods (40 subjects x 2 modeling periods each) were scored in random order by an observer who was uninformed about which gesture had been shown to the infant in any given period.

Both the frequency and the duration of infants' mouth openings and tongue protrusions were scored. The onset of a mouth opening was operationally defined as an abrupt jaw drop opening the mouth across the entire extent of the lips. The termination of mouth opening was defined as the return of the lips to their closed resting position. The definition of closed resting position was (*a*) lips closed and touching across the entire extent or (*b*) the minimum separation of the lips exhibited during the pretest exposure to the white cloth, for those infants who always maintained a small crack between their lips. For those cases in which a mouth began to close but had not yet reached the closed position when a second mouth opening was initiated, the first mouth opening was terminated with the initiation of the reopening. The onset of tongue protrusion was operationally defined as a clear forward thrust of the tongue such that the tongue tip crossed the back edge of the lower lip. The termination of tongue protrusion was defined as the retraction of the tip behind the back edge of the lower lip. For those cases in which the tongue was being retracted but was not yet behind the lip when a second tongue thrust occurred, the first tongue protrusion was terminated with the initiation of the second. The mouthing and tonguing that periodically occurred as part of yawning, sneezing, choking,

spitting, or hiccuping were not scored. The scorer reviewed the videotapes in real time, slow motion, and if necessary even frame by frame.

Assessments of both intra- and interscorer reliability were conducted using 15% of the data, including an equal number of periods from each type of modeling condition (mouth opening and tongue protrusion both as the first and as the second modeled gesture). The intrascorer assessments were conducted 1 week after the data had been scored the first time. The scorer was kept unaware of the trials to be used to assess reliability, which has the potential for fostering high scoring precision throughout all the trials (Reid, 1970). Pearson correlations were used to assess reliability on all the infant measures used in the subsequent analyses. The r's for the intraobserver assessments were as follows: mouth-opening frequency, .99; tongue-protrusion frequency, .99; mouth-opening duration, .99; and tongue-protrusion duration, .99; the r's for the interobserver assessments were, respectively, .92, .96, .96, and .99.

RESULTS

The experimental design allows a separation of random oral movements, general arousal, and true imitation. The two successive modeling periods involved the same experimenter, gesturing at the same rate, at the same distance from the infant. The two periods differed only in the facial gesture presented. Using this design, imitation is demonstrated if infants show significantly more tongue protrusions to the adult tongue-protrusion display than to the adult mouth-opening display and, conversely, more mouth openings to the adult mouth-opening display than to the adult tongue-protrusion display. Such a pattern of *differential* responding cannot arise from random activity or a general arousal of infant oral activity by a moving human face.

Frequency measures The frequency of infant mouth openings was greater in response to the mouth-opening display, X = 7.1, than to the tongue-protrusion display, X = 5.4, $p < .05$. Similarly, infants produced significantly more tongue protrusions in response to the tongue-protrusion display, X = 9.9, than to the mouth-opening display, X = 6.5, $p < .001$.

The pattern of imitative responding at the level of individual subjects is noteworthy. Twenty-six infants produced more mouth openings to the mouth-opening display than to the tongue display; 12 produced more mouth openings to the tongue display; and two produced an equal number of mouth openings to both displays. For the tongue-protrusion measure, 26 infants produced more tongue protrusions to the tongue-protrusion display; seven produced more tongue protrusions to the mouth display; and seven produced an equal number to both displays.

The outcome at the level of individual subjects can be analyzed in detail by taking into account the infants' mouth-opening and tongue-protrusion behaviors simultaneously. For example, each individual infant can produce a greater frequency of mouth openings to the adult mouth-opening display (+), to the adult tongue-protrusion display (−), or have an equal frequency of mouth openings to both displays (0). Similarly, each can produce a greater frequency of tongue protrusion to the tongue display (+), the mouth display (−), or have an equal frequency to both (0). Table 1 categorizes all 40 subjects in terms of their response on both behaviors considered simultaneously. The top portion of the table displays the results using the frequency measure. The results are significant, $X^2 = 38.70$, $df = 7$, $p < .001$.

The hypothesis of infant imitation can be directly examined by comparing the number of infants falling into the two most extreme cells (++ vs. −−). The infants in the ++ cell consistently matched both gestures. The infants in the −− cell consistently mismatched both gestures. Under the null hypothesis, there is an equal probability of infants falling into one or the other of these two response types. The results identify 16 infants with the ++ pattern and only one with the −− pattern.

Duration measures The same analyses were performed using the duration measure. The duration of mouth opening was longer in response to the mouth-opening display, X = 41.0, than to the tongue-protrusion display, X = 24.1, N = 40, $p < .001$, Wilcoxon test. Similarly, the duration of infant tongue protrusion was longer to the adult tongue-protrusion display, X = 10.7, than to the mouth-opening display, X = 6.5, N = 37, $p < .005$.

Again, the pattern of responding at the subject level is noteworthy. Thirty of the 40 infants had a longer duration of mouth opening to the mouth-opening display than to the tongue display; 10 had a longer duration of mouth opening to the tongue display; and none had an equal duration. For the tongue measure, 25 infants had a longer duration of tongue protrusion to the tongue-protrusion display; 12 had a longer duration of tongue protrusion to the mouth display; and three had an equal duration of tongue protrusion to both displays.

The bottom portion of Table 1 categorizes all 40 subjects using the duration measure. The one-sample X^2 test is significant, $X^2 = 62$, $df = 7$, $p < .001$. Again the equiprobable extreme cells are of particular interest; there are 20 infants who show the ++ pattern and only four who show the −− pattern.

DISCUSSION

The results demonstrate that newborns can imitate adult facial displays under certain laboratory conditions. How can we account for the fact that this phenomenon has not been commonly observed and reported by researchers in the past? Both our data and observations provide helpful clues. The first and most obvious

TABLE 1   NUMBER OF INFANTS DISPLAYING EACH OF EIGHT RESPONSE PATTERNS FOR THE FREQUENCY MEASURE AND THE DURATION MEASURE

	Response pattern								
Measure	+ +	+ 0	0 +	+ −	− +	0 −	− 0	− −	Total *N*
Frequency measure	16	5	1	5	9	1	2	1	40
Duration measure	20	2	0	8	5	0	1	4	40

Note The response patterns are shown as ordered pairs depicting the two infant behaviors in the order: mouth openings, tongue protrusions; + indicates a greater frequency (duration) of an infant behavior to the matching adult display than to the mismatching display; - indicates a greater frequency (duration) of an infant behavior to the mismatching display than to the matching display; 0 indicates an equal frequency (duration) of an infant behavior to both displays.

answer is that we tested only normal alert newborns with a procedure designed to keep them focused on the task. Newborns may not perform as systematically under less controlled circumstances.

There are also other reasons why newborn imitation might not have been commonly observed in the past, and these are of some theoretical importance. They concern the nature of the stimulus that is effective in eliciting the behavior, and the structure and organization of the infant's response.

We found in preliminary work that a constant demonstration of the target gesture was not maximally effective in eliciting imitation. Therefore, in our design the experimenter alternated between the presentation of the gesture and a passive face. We are not certain why our burst-pause procedure is the more powerful, but we can suggest three possibilities.

First, this alternation may allow the experimenter to demonstrate the gesture over a more extended period of time without the infant visually habituating to the adult display. By retaining the infants' active interest, this procedure might simply give infants more time to organize their motor response. Second, this alternation may be especially effective in isolating the modeled action. That is, the change from a burst of tongue protrusion to a passive face and back to a burst of tongue protrusion may focus the infant on what differentiates the two states. If the adult constantly and repetitively demonstrates tongue protrusion, the infant may not register the display in the same

way (Moore & Meltzoff, 1978). Third, it is possible that the alternating aspects of the demonstration have some social significance. When an infant perceives a human adult acting, then stopping acting, then stopping, this may motivate the infant to action rather than mere visual fixation. The special social significance of "turn taking" has been pointed out by several investigators (e.g., Bruner, 1975; Stern, Jaffe, Beebe, & Bennet, 1975) and may be important in eliciting imitation.

There are also aspects of the organization of the response that may have obscured newborn imitation in the past. One interesting aspects is its variability both within and between infants. All infants do not produce a given number of tongue protrusions, each individual tongue protrusion is not a fixed duration, the same form, and so on. Moreover, the imitative response does not burst forth fully formed the moment the infant fixates on the adult's gesture. Indeed, we observed that infants corrected their responses over successive efforts, often beginning by producing small approximations of the model—small tongue movements inside the oral cavity (not scored as imitation according to the operational definitions used here)—and then converging toward more accurate matches of the adult's display over successive efforts.

We next address the primary theoretical issue raised by this research: What mechanism underlies this early imitation? We previously described three possible accounts of early facial imitation: instrumental or associative learning, innate releasing mechanisms, and active inter-modal matching to target (Meltzoff & Moore, 1977).

The present data indicate that postnatal learning is not a necessary condition for facial imitation. This does not mean that infants *cannot* be conditioned to imitate, nor that the range of gestures or the meaning imputed to them might not be expanded in important ways through the experience gained in adult-infant interactions. We do not claim that a newborn is as "good" an imitator as a 1-year-old. We merely suggest that the strong view that infants have *no* capacity to imitate at birth is contradicted by the data. Evidently the capacity to imitate is available at birth and does not require extensive interactive experience, mirror experience, or "reinforcement history."

If early learning cannot account for these effects, one must consider the second possibility we proposed, namely, innate releasing mechanisms (Jacobson, 1979). There are two lines of reasoning that lead us to suggest that the concept of an innate releasing mechanism, at least as classically described (Lorenz & Tinbergen, 1938/1970; Tinbergen, 1951), is not a useful heuristic for understanding early imitation. First, young infants imitate not just one, but a range of motor acts. Here we reported imitation of two facial acts. We have previously reported that 2–3-week-old infants can imitate three oral gestures and one manual gesture (Meltzoff & Moore, 1977). Burd and Milewski (Note 1) not only confirmed our findings of early oral imitation but also extended the list of behaviors that can be successfully imitated to include brow movements. Clearly, one cannot postulate a releasing mechanism for imitation in general, and it would seem unparsimonious to conclude that every new behavior that is shown to be imitated by neonates represents another released response.

Second, the morphology and temporal organization of the imitative reaction is different from what one would expect if they were re-leased in the classical sense. A traditional hallmark of released reactions, "fixed-action patterns," is that they are stereotypic, rigidly organized reactions that "run off" independent of feedback mechanisms (Lorenz & Tinbergen, 1938/1970). Studies show that human neonates are capable of performing fairly rigid and stereotypic motor routines (Brazelton, 1973; Prechtl & Beintema, 1964). However, we do not see this kind of stereotype in these imitative reactions. Infants do not immediately produce a perfect matching response; they seem to correct their response over successive efforts. There is little in the nature and organization of the response that tempts us to describe it as a classic fixed-action pattern that is released by the adult's display.

We believe there is a need for a third alternative that does not reduce to innate releasing mechanisms or learned stimulus-response linkages. The hypothesis we favor is that this early imitation is accomplished through a more active matching process than admitted by the two other accounts. The crux of our view is that neonates can, at some level of processing, apprehend the equivalence between body transformations they see and body transformation of their own whether they see them or not. It is precisely this point that is denied by the other accounts. Both explain early imitation without postulating that the utilization of intermodal equivalences has anything to do with the infant's ability to imitate. After all, neither a "discriminative cue" nor a "sign stimulus" needs to match the response it elicits. Any two gestures could presumably be paired through reinforcement, and released behaviors need not be morphologically similar to the sign stimuli that trigger them (e.g., the chick's food-begging response is released by the adult's mandible patch, not by adult food begging).

In contrast, we postulate that infants use the equivalence between the act seen and the act done as the fundamental basis for generating the behavioral match. By our account even this early imitation involves active matching to an environmentally provided target or "model." Our corollary hypothesis is that this imitation is mediated by a representational system that allows infants to unite within one common framework their own body transformations and those of others. According to this view, both visual and motor transformations of the body can be represented in a common form and thus directly compared (Bower, 1979; Meltzoff, 1981; Meltzoff & Borton, 1979; Meltzoff & Moore, 1977, 1983). Infants could thereby relate proprioceptive/motor information about their own unseen body movements to their representation of the visually perceived model and create the match required.

The critical theoretical point is that we do not support the view that young infants have perceptual-cognitive constraints that restrict them to utilizing intramodal comparisons. Instead, we postulate that infants can recognize and use intermodal equivalences from birth onward. In our view, the proclivity to represent actions intermodally is the starting point of infant psychological development, not an end point reached after many months of postnatal development.

REFERENCE NOTES

1 Burd, A. P., & Milewski, A. E. *Matching of facial gestures by young infants: Imitation or releasers?* Paper presented at the meeting of the Society for Research in Child Development, Boston, April 1981.

2 Hamm, M., Russell, M., & Koepke, J. *Neonatal imitation?* Paper presented at the meeting of the Society for Research in Child Development, San Francisco, March 1979.

3 McKenzie, B. Personal communication, March 1979.

REFERENCES

Abravanel, E., Levan-Goldschmidt, E., & Stevenson, M. B. Action imitation: The early phase of infancy. *Child Development*, 1976, **47**, 1032–1044.

Aronfreed, J. The problem of imitation. In L. P. Lipsitt & H. W. Reese (Eds.), *Advances in child development and behavior* (Vol. **4**). New York: Academic Press, 1969.

Bandura, A. Social learning theory of identificatory processes. In D. A. Goslin (Ed.), *Handbook of socialization theory and research*. Chicago: Rand McNally, 1969.

Bower, T. G. R. *Human development*. San Francisco: W. H. Freeman, 1979.

Brazelton, T. B. *Neonatal behavioral assessment scale*. London: Heinemann, 1973.

Bruner, J. S. From communication to language—A psychological perspective. *Cognition*, 1975, **3**, 255–287.

Dunkeld, J. *The function of imitation in infancy*. Unpublished doctoral dissertation, University of Edinburgh, 1978.

Field, T. M., Woodson, R., Greenberg, R., & Cohen, D. *Science*, 1982, **218**, 179–181.

Flanders, J. P. A review of research on imitative behavior. *Psychological Bulletin*, 1968, **69**, 316–337.

Gewirtz, J. L., & Stingle, K. G. Learning of generalized imitation as the basis for identification. *Psychological Review*, 1968, **75**, 374–397.

Hayes, L. A., & Watson, J. S. Neonatal imitation: Fact or artifact? *Developmental Psychology*, 1981, **17**, 655–660.

Jacobson, S. W. Matching behavior in the young infant. *Child Development*, 1979, **50**, 425–430.

Kaye, K., & Marcus, J. Imitation over a series of trials without feedback: Age six months. *Infant Behavior and Development*, 1978, **1**, 141–155.

Kessen, W., Salapatek, P., & Haith, M. The visual response of the human newborn to linear contour. *Journal of Experimental Child Psychology*, 1972, **13**, 9–20.

Lorenz, R., & Tinbergen, N. [Taxis and instinctive behavior pattern in egg-rolling by the Graylag goose (1938).] In K. Lorenz (Ed., R. Martin, trans.), *Studies in animal and in human behavior* (Vol. I). Cambridge, Mass.: Harvard University Press, 1970. (Originally published, 1938.)

McCall, R. B., Parke, R. D., & Kavanaugh, R. D. Imitation of live and televised models by children one to three years of age. *Monographs of the Society for Research in Child Development*, 1977, **42** (5, Serial No. 173).

Meltzoff, A. N. Imitation, intermodal coordination, and representation in early infancy. In G. Butterworth (Ed.), *Infancy and epistemology*. Brighton: Harvester, 1981.

Meltzoff, A. N., & Borton, R. W. Intermodal matching by human neonates. *Nature*, 1979, **282**, 403–404.

Meltzoff, A. N., & Moore, M. K. Imitation of facial and manual gestures by human neonates. *Science*, 1977, **198**, 75–78.

Meltzoff, A. N., & Moore, M. K. The origins of imitation in infancy: Paradigm, phenomena, and theories. In L. P. Lippsitt & C. Rovee-Collier (Eds.), *Advances in infancy research* (Vol. **2**). Norwood, N.J.: Ablex, 1983.

Mendelson, M. J., & Haith, M. M. The relation between audition and vision in the human newborn. *Monographs of the Society for Research in Child Development*, 1976, **41** (4, Serial No. 167).

Moore, M. K., & Meltzoff, A. N. Object permanence, imitation, and language development: Toward a neo-Piagetian perspective on communicative and cognitive development. In F. D. Minifie & L. L. Lloyd (Eds.), *Communicative and cognitive abilities—early behavioral assessment*. Baltimore: University Park Press, 1978.

Paraskevopoulos, J., & Hunt, J. McV. Object construction and imitation under differing conditions of rearing. *Journal of Genetic Psychology*, 1971, **119**, 301–321.

Parton, D. A. Learning to imitate in infancy. *Child Development*, 1976, **47**, 14–31.

Piaget, J. *Play, dreams, and imitation in childhood* (C. Gattegno & F. M. Hodgson, trans.). New York: Norton, 1962. (Originally published 1945.)

Prechtl, R., & Beintema, D. *The neurological examination of the full-term newborn infant*. London: Heinemann, 1964.

Reid, J. B. Reliability assessment of observation data: A possible methodological problem. *Child Development*, 1970, **41**, 1143–1150.

Salapatek, P., & Kessen, W. Vision scanning of triangles by the human newborn. *Journal of Experimental Child Psychology*, 1966, **3**, 155–167.

Stern, D., Jaffe, J., Beebe, B., & Bennet, S. Vocalizing in unison and in alternation: Two modes of communication within the mother-infant dyad. *Annals of the New York Academy of Sciences*, 1975, **263**, 89–100.

Tinbergen, N. *The study of instinct*. New York: Oxford University Press, 1951.

Uzgiris, I. C. Patterns of vocal and gestural imitation in infants. In F. J. Monks, W. W. Hartup, & J. deWitt (Eds.), *Determinants of behavioral development*. New York: Academic Press, 1972.

Uzgiris, I. C., & Hunt, J. McV. *Assessment in infancy*. Urbana: University of Illinois Press, 1975.

Object Permanence in Five-Month-Old Infants

Renée Baillargeon
Elizabeth S. Spelke
Stanley Wasserman

1. BACKGROUND: PIAGET'S THEORY

For adults, an object is an entity that exists continuously in time and space: it cannot exist at two separate points in time without having existed during the interval between them, and it cannot appear at two separate points in space without having traveled from one point to the other. Do infants share this conception of objects as temporally and spatially continuous? On the basis of detailed observations of infants' reactions to object disappearances, Piaget (1954) concluded that they do not. For the young infant, Piaget maintained, each disappearance amounts to an annihilation and each reappearance to a resurrection. An object is not a permanent entity that continuous to exist while out of sight, but an ephemeral entity that is continually made and unmade: "a mere image which reenters the void as soon as it vanishes, and emerges from it for no objective reason" (p. 11).

Piaget discerned six stages in the development of the infant's object concept. He claimed that it is not until infants reach the fourth stage, at about 9 months of age, that they begin to endow objects with permanence, as evidenced by their willingness to search for hidden objects. Piaget observed that prior to stage 4, infants do not search for fully hidden objects. If an attractive toy is covered with a cloth, for example, they make no attempt to lift the cloth and grasp the toy, even though they are capable of performing each of these actions. Beginning in stage 4, however, infants do remove obstacles to retrieve hidden objects. In subsequent stages, infants come to take into account visible (stage 5) and invisible (stage 6) displacements of objects to find objects hidden in successive locations.

Why did Piaget select infants' search for hidden objects as marking the beginning of object permanence? This question is important, because Piaget observed several behaviors prior to stage 4 that are suggestive of object permanence. For example, he noted that as early as stage 1 (0–1 month), infants may look at an object, look away from it, and then return to it several seconds later, without any external cue having signaled its continued presence. In addition, Piaget observed that beginning in stage 3 (4–9 months), infants anticipate the future positions of moving objects: if they are tracking an object and temporarily lose sight of it, they look for it further along its trajectory; similarly, if they are holding an object out of sight and accidentally let go of it, they stretch their arm to recapture it.

Piaget claimed that although these and other behaviors *seem* to reveal a notion of object permanence, closer analysis indicates "how superficial this interpretation would be and how phenomenalistic the primitive universe re-

mains" (p. 11). Prior to stage 4, Piaget maintained, the infant lacks a concept of physical causality and regards all of reality as being dependent on his activity. When he acts upon an object, the infant views the object not as an independent entity but as the extension, or the product, of his action. If the object disappears from view, the infant reproduces or extends his action, because he expects that his action will again produce the object. Proof for Piaget that the infant regards the object as being "at the disposal" of his action is that if his action fails to bring back the object, he does not perform alternative actions to recover it. Beginning in stage 4, however, the infant acts very differently. For example, if a ball rolls behind a cushion and he cannot recapture it by extending his reach, he tries alternative means for recovering it: he lifts the cushion, or pulls it aside, or gropes behind it. According to Piaget, such activities indicate that the infant conceives of the ball, not as a thing at the disposal of a specific action, but as a substantial entity that is located out of sight behind the cushion and that any of several actions may serve to reveal.

2. TESTS OF PIAGET'S THEORY

In recent years, Piaget's (1954) description of the sequences of changes in infants' search behavior has been tested by numerous investigators and has been accepted with few modifications (see Gratch, 1975, 1976; Harris, 1985; Schuberth, 1983, for reviews). Nevertheless, Piaget's interpretation of this sequence has been questioned. A number of authors (e.g., Bower, 1974; Diamond and Goldman-Rakic, 1983) have suggested that young infants' failure to search for hidden objects stems not from a lack of object permanence but from an inability to perform coordinated actions. Perhaps ironically, support for this hypothesis comes from Piaget's (1952) own work on the devlopement of action. Piaget found that the capacity to act in a coordinated manner develops very slowly over the course of infancy. He noted that a major milestone is achieved at about 9 months of age, when infants begin to coordinate separate actions into means-ends sequences. In these sequences, infants perform one action in order to create the conditions under which they will be able to perform a second, independent action. Since Piaget's (1954) search task requires infants to coordinate two separate actions (one upon the occluder and one upon the object), young infants could fail this task because they are generally unable to perform such an action sequence.

A number of studies, notably by Bower (1967, 1972, 1974; Bower, Broughton and Moore, 1971; Bower and Wishart, 1972), have attempted to investigate young infants' conception of an object using methods that do not require coordinated sequences of actions. Bower's studies have yielded four findings that seem to provide evidence for object permanence in infants well below 9 months. First, 7-week-old infants were found to discriminate between disappearances that signaled the continued existence of an object (e.g., gradual occlusion), and disappearances that did not (e.g., gradual dissolution or sudden implosion) (Bower, 1967). Second, 2-month-old infants were found to anticipate the reappearance of an object that stopped behind a screen, "looking to that half of the movement path the object would have reached had it not stopped" (Bower et al., 1971, p. 183). Third, 5-month-old infants were found to show disruptions in their tracking when an object was altered while passing behind a screen: they tended to look back at the screen, as though in search of the original object (Bower, 1974; Bower et al., 1971). Finally, 5-month-old infants were found to reach for an object that had been "hidden" by darkening the room (Bower and Wishart, 1972).

Although suggestive, Bower's findings do not provide conclusive evidence for object permanence in young infants. First, methodological problems cast doubts upon the validity of the results (Gratch, 1976; Harris, 1985). Sec-

ond, the results are open to alternative interpretations that do not implicate object permanence. In particular, most of the results could be explained by Piagetian theory in terms of the extension of an ongoing action or the reproduction of a previous action. When infants reach for an object in the dark, they could simply be extending an action initiated before the lights were extinguished. Similarly, when infants anticipate the reappearance of an object, they could be extending a tracking motion begun prior to the object's disappearance. Finally, when infants look back at a screen, after a novel object has emerged from behind it, they could be repeating a prior acton of looking in that direction, with the expectation that this action will again produce the original object.

The first finding cited above cannot be explained in terms of the extension or the reproduction of an action, but it, too, is open to other interpretations. One interpretation, mentioned by Bower et al. (1971), apparently has its source in Piaget: "Piaget (personal communication) has rightly objected that the methods used were insufficient to demonstrate that the infants were responding to objects as such, rather than to perceptual configurations which contained the object as an undifferentiated element" (p. 182). Another interpretation is that infants discriminate between permanence and impermanence sequences on the basis of superficial expectations about the way objects typically disappear, rather than on the basis of a belief in object permanence. In their daily environment, infants often see objects occlude one another but they rarely, if ever, see objects implode from view or dissolve into the air. Hence, infants could respond differently to occlusions than to implosions or dissolutions because occlusions are the only type of disappearance that is familiar to them.

3. THE PRESENT EXPERIMENT

Because of the difficulties associated with Piaget's and Bower's tasks, we sought a new means of testing object permanence in young infants. Like Bower, we chose not to rely on manual search as our index of object permanence. However, we tried to find an index that could not depend on (1) the extension or reproduction of an action, or (2) knowledge about superficial properties of object disappearances.

The method we devised was rather indirect. It focused on infants' understanding of the principle that a solid object cannot move through the space occupied by another solid object ("solidity principle"). Infants' understanding of this principle was tested in a situation involving a visible object and an occluded object. If infants were surprised when the visible object appeared to move through the space occupied by the occluded object, it would suggest that they took account of the existence and the location of the occluded object. In other words, evidence that infants applied the solidity principle would also provide evidence that they possessed object permanence.

In the experiment, a box was placed on a surface behind a wooden screen. The screen initially lay flat, so that the box was clearly visible. The screen was then raised, in the manner of a drawbridge, thus hiding the box from view. Infants were shown two test events: a possible event and an impossible event. In the possible event, the screen moved until it reached the occluded box, stopped, and then returned to its initial position (see Figure 1A).In the impossible event, the screen moved until it reached the occluded box—and then kept on going as though the box were no longer there! The screen completed a full 180-degree arc before it reversed direction and returned to its initial position, revealing the box standing intact in the same location as before (see Figure 1B). To adults, the possible event is consistent with the solidity principle: the screen stops when it encounters the box. The impossible event, in contrast, violates the principle: the screen appears to move freely through the space occupied by the box. Note that adults would not perceive the event as impossible if they did not believe that the box continued to exist, in its same location, after it was occluded by the screen. To test infants' perception of these events, we used a habituation paradigm. Infants were habituated to the screen moving back and forth through a 180-degree arc, with no box present. After infants reached habituation, the box was placed behind the screen, and infants were shown the possible and impossible events. Our reasoning was as follows. If infants understood that (1) the box continued to exist, in its same location, after it was occluded by the screen, and (2) the screen could not move through the space occupied by the box,

A. Possible event

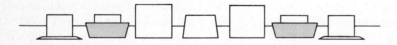

B. Impossible event

FIGURE 1   Schematic representation of the possible and impossible test events used in the principal experiments.

then they should perceive the impossible event to be novel, sur-prising, or both. On the basis of the commonly-held assumption that infants re-act to novel or surprising events with prolonged attention, we predicted that infants would look longer at the impossible than at the possible event. On the other hand, if infants did not understand that the box continued to exist after it was occluded by the screen, then they should attend to the movement of the screen without concerning themselves with the presence of the box in its path. Since the screen movement was the same in the impossible and the habituation events (in both events the screen moved through a 180-degree arc), we predicted that infants would look longer at the possible event, which depicted a novel, shorter screen movement.

There was one foreseeable difficulty with the design of our experiment. Infants might look longer at the impossible than at the possible event, not because they understood the under-lying structure of the events, but because they found the 180-degree movement intrinsically more interesting than the 120-degree move-ment. To check this possibility, we ran a control experiment that was similar to the first experiment except that the box was placed behind and to the side of the screen, out of its path of motion. Therefore, neither the 180- nor the 120-degree screen movement violated the solidity principle. We reasoned that if infants in the first experiment looked longer at the impossible event because they found the 180-degree movement intrinsically more interesting than the 120-degree movement, then infants in the control experiment should look longer at the 180-degree event. On the other hand, if infants in the first experiment looked longer at the impossible event because they viewed it as impossible, then infants in the control experi-ment should look equally at the 180- and the 120-degree events, since neither was impossi-ble, or they should look longer at the 120-degree event, since it involved a novel screen movement.

4. METHOD

4.1. Principal Experiment

4.1.1. Subjects Subjects were 21 full-term infants ranging in age from 4 months, 24 days to 5 months, 26 days (mean age: 5 months, 12 days). An additional 7 infants were eliminated from the experiment, 3 because of experimenter error and 4 because of fussiness. All infants were from the Philadelphia area. Parents were contacted by phone and were compensated for their participation.

4.1.2. Apparatus The apparatus resembled that used by Bower (1967). It involved two identical alleys containing identical screens and separated by a one-way mirror. Only one alley was visible at any one time. Shifts between the alleys were accomplished instantaneously by extinguishing the lights in one alley and illumi-nating those in the other alley. During those shifts, naive adult observers were not aware that they were shown two different alleys. It appeared merely as though one alley underwent a brief flickering of illumination.

Alleys The apparatus consisted of a large wooden box in the shape of an inverted ''L''. A one-way mirror 38 cm high and 81 cm wide divided this box to form a front and a side alley (see Figure 2). Infants faced the mirror through an opening 38 cm high and 43 cm wide at one end of the front alley. The two alleys were of the same color and dimensions: both were painted black, and both were 38 cm high, 61 cm wide, 122 cm deep on one side and 61 cm deep on the other. In addition, both alleys contained an unpainted wooden screen 28 cm high, 20 cm wide, and 1 cm thick. Each screen was attached by hinges to the floor of its respective alley and was positioned 20 cm from the side walls and 30 cm from the back wall. To one side of each screen (right in the front alley, left in the side alley) was attached a thin metal pulley, 11 cm in diameter. One half of each pulley stood above the floor of the alley, and the other half hung-beneath it. The two pulleys were operated by

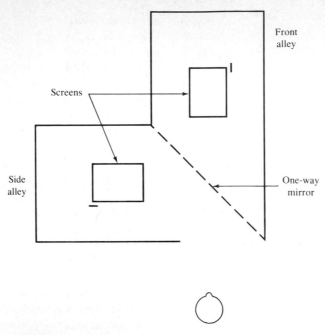

FIGURE 2   Top view of the apparatus

identical manual cranks located underneath the alleys. By means of these cranks, the two screens could be moved back and forth through a 180-degree arc.

A wooden box 15 cm high, 10 cm wide, and 10 cm thick could be introduced into the front alley through a hidden door in its back wall. This box was painted bright yellow and was decorated with small red stars. During the test, the box was centered 8 cm behind the far edge of the screen when the screen lay in its initial position on the floor of the alley, toward the infant.

Lighting Miniature bayonet light bulbs were affixed to the ceiling of each alley. Bands of black cardboard hid these light bulbs from the infant's view. More light bulbs were used in the front alley to equalize the luminance of the two alleys, because the one-way mirror considerably reduced the amount of light that reached the infant's eye from the front alley.

The lights in the two alleys were wired insuch a way that one could reverse their illumination condition by depressing a single switch. When the front alley was lit and the side alley was dark, the one-way mirror functioned as a window: infants looked through it into the front alley. When the side alley was lit and the front alley was dark, it functioned as a mirror: infants saw the side alley reflected in it. In each case, the alley that was not lit was not visible.

Experimental Chamber A wooden frame 229 cm high and 213 cm wide hung in front of the apparatus. This frame was covered with white muslin except for an opening that coincided with the opening into the front alley. Floor-length curtains hung on either side of, and perpendicular to, the muslin-covered frame. Together, the curtains and the frame formed a three-sided chamber that isolated the infant from the experimental room.

4.1.3. Events *Impossible Test Event* Two experimenters worked in concert to produce this event. The first experimenter operated thefront alley screen and controlled the illumination condition of the alleys; the second experimenter operated the side alley screen. To start, the first experimenter lit the front alley; infants could see the screen, laid flat against the floor of the alley, with the box clearly visible behind it. The first experimenter raised her screen at the approximate rate of 30 degrees per second until it had completed a 120-degree arc, at which point it made contact with the box. She then reversed the illumination condition of the alleys, so that the side alley became lit. The second experimenter, who held his screen in readiness in the 120-degree position, then lowered it to the floor of the alley, away from the infant, at the same approximate rate of 30 degrees per second. The entire process was then repeated in reverse. The second experimenter raised his screen back to the 120-degree position, at which point the primary experimenter again reversed the illumination of the alleys and then lowered her screen down to its original position against the floor of the alley.

Each full cycle of movement lasted approximately 12 seconds. The box remained occluded for about 10 of these 12 seconds: it was in view only during the first and last seconds, when the screen was raised less than 30 degrees. Cycles were repeated without stop until the recorder signaled that the trial had ended (see below). At that point, the first experimenter extinguished the lights in the alleys and brought her screen back to its starting position.

Possible Test Event This display was produced by the first experimenter alone. After lighting the front alley, she raised her screen at the same rate of 30 degrees per second until it had moved 120 degrees and contacted the occluded box; she then lowered her screen back to its initial position against the floor of the alley. Each cycle of movement—one 120-degree movement away from the infant and one 120-degree movement back toward the infant—lasted approximately 8 seconds. The box was totally occluded for about 6 of these 8 seconds. Cycles were repeated without stop until the recorder signaled that the trial had ended (see below). At that point, the first experimenter

extinguished the lights in the alley and returned her screen to its starting position.

Habituation Event. The habituation event was exactly the same as the impossible event, except that the yellow box was absent. Both alleys were used to produce this event. We sought to habituate infants to the slight changes in noise and illumination that accompanied the shifts between the alleys, to minimize the possibility that such factors would lead infants to look longer at the impossible event.

4.1.4. Procedure Each infant was seated on a parent's lap in front of the opening into the front alley. The infant's head was approximately 30 cm from the opening, 61 cm from the one-way mirror, and 152 cm from the back wall of the front alley. The parent wore occluding glasses and was instructed not to interact with the infant while the experiment was in progress.

The infant's looking behavior was monitored by two observers who viewed the infant through peepholes in the muslin frame that hung in front of the apparatus. The observers could not see the experimental events and they were not told the order in which the test events were presented. Each observer was given a button box connected to an event recorder and was instructed to depress the button when the infant looked into the opening of the display box. Inter-observer agreement for each infant was calculated on the basis of the number of seconds for which the observers agreed on the direction of the infant's gaze, out of the total number of seconds the habituation and test trials lasted. Agreement was calculated for 18 of the infants and averaged 93% per infant. The looking times of the primary observer were also registered on a clock. By monitoring this clock, another assistant, the recorder, was able to signal the ending of each trial and to determine when the habituation criterion was met (see below).

Infants were presented repeatedly with the habituation event following an infant-control procedure (after Horowitz, 1975). Each habituation trial ended when the infant looked away from the event for 2 consecutive seconds after looking at it for at least 4 consecutive seconds, or when the infant looked at the event for 120 seconds. The inter-trial interval was 3 seconds. Habituation trials continued until the infant reached a criterion of habituation: a 50% or greater decrease in looking time on 3 consecutive trials, relative to the infant's looking time on the first 3 trials. If the criterion was not met within 14 trials, the habituation phase was ended at that point. This occurred for only 1 of the 21 infants. The other infants took an average of 7.35 trials to reach criterion.

After the habituation phase, the yellow box was introduced into the front alley. Infants were given two 3-second pretest trials to call their attention to the presence of the box. During these trials, the screen lay flat against the floor of the alley, with the box standing clearly visible behind it. Following these trials, testing began. Infants were given 3 pairs of test trials, with the impossible and possible events being presented on alternate trials. Eleven infants saw the impossible event first, and 10 infants saw the possible event first. The criteria used to determine the ending of the test trials were the same as for the habituation trials.

Of the 21 infants in the experiment, 5 contributed fewer than 3 pairs of test trials to the analyses. Four infants contributed only 2 pairs, 3 because of fussiness and 1 because the primary observer could not follow the direction of his gaze. Another infant contributed a single pair: one pair was eliminated because of fussiness and one pair because of equipment failure.

4.2. Control Experiment

4.2.1. Subjects
Subjects were 22 full-term infants ranging in age from 4 months, 26 days to 5 months, 29 days (mean age: 5 months, 10 days). An additional 8 infants were eliminated from the experiment. 3 because of experimenter error, 1 because of equipment failure, and 4 because of fussiness. All infants were from the Philadelphia area. Parents were contacted by phone and were compensated for their participation.

4.2.2. Apparatus and Events
The apparatus and events were the same as in the principal experiment, except for the placement of the box during the familiarization and test trials. The yellow box in the front alley was positioned 8 cm behind and to the left of the screen so that the screen's path of movement was not obstructed. Since both the front and the side alleys were used in producing the 180-degree test event, an identical yellow box was placed 8 cm behind and to the right of the screen in the side alley.

4.2.3. Procedure
As in the principal experiment, infants were given habituation trials until they met the habituation criterion. All infants met the criterion before completing 14 habituation trials; the mean number of trials to criterion was 7.32. Following habituation, infants were given two pretest trials during which the screen lay flat against the floor of the alley, with the yellow box to one side. To minimize the possibility that infants would attend only to the box on the test trials, the pretest trials were presented using an infant-control procedure. Specifically, each pretest trial ended when theinfant looked away from the display for 2 consecutive seconds after looking at it for at least 4 cumulative seconds. Each pretest trial lasted 9.18 seconds on average. Following these trials, infants were given 3 pairs of test trials-,with the 180- and the 120-degree events being presented on alternate trials. Twelve infants saw the 180-degree event first and 10 saw the 120-degree event first. The criteria used to determine the beginning and end of the habituation and test trials were the same as in the principal experiment. Inter-observer agreement was calculated for 21 of the infants and averaged 92% per infant.

Of the 22 infants who participated in the experiment, 5 contributed fewer than 3 pairs of test trials to the analyses, due to fussiness: 4 contributed 2 pairs and 1 contributed 1 pair.

5. RESULT

5.1. Principal Experiment

The results of the principal experiment were clear-cut: infants showed a strong, consistent preference for the impossible over the possible test event. Figure 3a presents the mean looking times during the habituation and test phases of the experiment.

5.2. Control Experiment

The results of the control experiment were quite different: infants showed no overall preference between the 180- and the 120-degree test events. Figure 3b presents the mean looking times to the habituation and test events.

6. DISCUSSION

The results of the principal experiment are easily summarized: infants showed a marked preference for the impossible over the possible event. Further, infants showed this preference on all three pairs of test trials, regardless of the order in which they saw the two events. The results of the control experiment were very different: only infants who saw the 180-degre e event first showed a preference for that event,

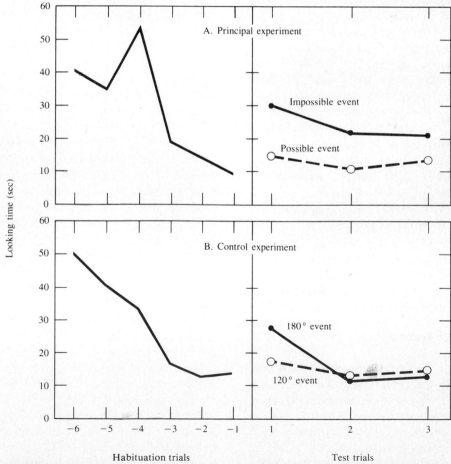

FIGURE 3   Looking times of subjects in the principal and control experiments to the habituation and test trials*

*The habituation trials are numbered backwards from the trial in which criterion was reached.

and that only on the first test pair; infants who saw the 120-degree event first looked equally at the two events on all three test pairs. These results provide evidence that infants in the principal experiment looked longer at the impossible event not because they preferred the 180-degree screen movement, but because they expected the screen to stop against the occluded box and were surprised, or puzzled, when it failed to do so.

The results of these experiments indicate that 5-month-old infants understand that an object continues to exist when occluded. These results suggest that infants who, according to Piaget's (1954) scale, have just entered stage 3 already endow objects with some permanence. Such results call into question several aspects of Piaget's description of the development of object permanence. First, they call for a reinterpretation of the behaviors—visual anticipations, interrupted prehensions, deferred actions, and so on—Piaget observed in stage 3 infants. Piaget maintained that these behaviors reflect a primitive phenomenalism, rather than a belief in object permanence: "In the present behavior patterns...the search only continues the earlier act of accommodation...the expected object is still related to the action itself" (p. 11). Since our results cannot be interpreted in terms of the extension or the reproduction of an earlier action, they provide unambiguous evidence of object permanence in stage 3 infants. As such, they suggest that Piaget was mistaken in his interpretation of stage 3 behaviors and that these behaviors are guided by a belief in object permanence, rather than by an egocentric phenomenalism.

Second, our findings call for a reinterpretation of stage 3 infants' failure to search for hidden objects. Piaget (1954) believed that these infants do not search because they do not yet view objects as permanent entities that continue to exist when concealed by other objects. Since our results indicate that infants of 5 months do confer permanence to objects, they

imply that factors other than or in addition to infants' beliefs about objects contribute to the emergence of search behavior. What might these factors be? One relevant factor might be the development of short-term memory (e.g., Bower, 1967). Young infants might fail to search for hidden objects simply because they forget their presence; as their memory improves, infants would become more likely to remember, and to search for, hidden objects. However, there are reasons to question this explanation. Piaget's observations on deferred actions suggest that stage 3 infants can remember the location of objects for several seconds at a time. In addition, the results of our first experiment suggest that infants could remember the presence of the box behind the screen for at least 3 seconds (the time it took the screen to reach the box after it was occluded) and perhaps for as long as 6 to 10 seconds (the occlusion times for the possible and the impossible events). Few search studies require retention times longer than those.

A more likely explanation for young infants' failure to search for hidden objects, one already alluded to in the introduction, is that young infants may be generally unable to coordinate separate actions into means-end sequences. This explanation appears especially plausible in light of Uzgiris's (1973) observation that infants begin to search for hidden objects at about the same age they begin to engage in reversible actions, pushing and pulling objects, crumpling and straightening them, putting them in and taking them out of containers, and so on. It is as though infants began, at 8 or 9 months, to map out their behavioral repertoire, discovering what actions produce what outcomes, and then learning to combine these actions to achieve increasingly complex goals.

We are not alone in proposing that search behavior reflects the interaction of different factors. In recent years, investigators have identified several factors that appear to play a role in the development of search behavior in stage

4, stage 5, and beyond (DeLoache, 1984; Sophian, 1984). For example, three factors that have been implicated in stage 4 infants' search errors are a deficit in memory for spatial locations (e.g., Bremner, 1978; Cornell, 1981; Cummings and Bjork, 1977; Lucas and Uzgiris, 1977), a sensitivity to proactive interference (e.g., Schacter and Moscovitch, 1983), and an inability to inhibit repetitive actions due to poor neurological control (e.g., Diamond and Goldman-Rakic, 1983).

We have questioned Piaget's claims about the time at which object permanence is attained, and the behaviors by which it is manifested. Despite these differences, however, one aspect of Piaget's (1954) theory seems exactly right to us. According to Piaget, the development of the object is intimately tied to the development of the concepts of time, space, and causality: "A world composed of permanent objects constitutes not only a spatial universe but also a world obeying the principle of causality in the form of relationships between things, and regulated in time, without continuous annihilations or resurrections" (p. 3). Like Piaget, we believe that a notion of object permanence is not an isolated conceptual attainment but an inseparable aspect of the infant's knowledge of how objects behave in time and space. Our experiments provide evidence that by 5 months of age, infants already appreciate two aspects of the behavior of objects. First, they understand that an object continues to exist when occluded, and that it exists not as a disembodied image residing somewhere behind the occluder but as a solid, three-dimensional entity occupying a specific spatial location. Second, they understand that an object can move only through space not occupied by other objects. Recently, researchers have begun to investigate infants' knowledge of other aspects of the behavior of objects. Their experiments suggest that young infants understand that objects tend to move on undeviating paths (Baillargeon, 1984), to move continuously through

space and over time (Spelke and Kestenbaum, 1984), and to begin moving only when contacted by other objects (Leslie, 1984).

From this perspective, occlusion transformations are simply a subclass of all the transformations that occur in the physical world, and the notion that objects continue to exist when occluded is only one aspect of the infant's object concept. The general problem for research is not to establish whether young infants believe objects are permanent. Rather, it is to determine what infants know about the displacements and transformations of objects, and how they attain and represent this knowledge.

REFERENCES

Baillargeon, R. (1984) Reasoning about hidden obstacles: Object permanence in 6- to 8-month-old infants. Paper presented at the Biennial Meeting of the International Conference on Infant Studies, New York, April.

Bower, T. G. R. (1967) The development of object permanence: Some studies of existence constancy. *Percep Psychophys*, 2. 411–418.

Bower, T. G. R. (1972) Object perception in infants. *Perception, I*, (1).

Bower, T. G. R. (1974) *Development in Infancy*. San Francisco: Freeman

Bower, T. G. R., Broughton, J. M., and Moore, M. K. (1971) Development of the object concept as manifested in the tracking behavior of infantsbetween 7 and 20 weeks of age. *J. exp. Child Psychol. II*, 182–193.

Bower, T. G. R., and Wishart, J. G. (1972) The effects of motor skill on object permanence. *Cog., I*, 165–172.

Bremner, J. G. (1978) Spatial errors made by infants: Inadequate spatial cues or evidence of egocentrism? *Brit. J. Psychol., 69*, 77–84.

Cornell, E. H. (1981) The effects of cue distinctiveness on infants' manual search. *J. exp. Child Psychol., 32*, 330–342.

Cummings, E. M., and Bjork, E. L. (1977) Piaget's stage IV object concept error: Evidence of perceptual confusion, state change, or failure to assimilate? Paper presented at the Meeting of the Western Psychological Association, Seattle, April.

DeLoache, J. S. (1984) Oh where, oh where: Memory-based searching by very young children. In C. Sophian (ed.). *Origins of Cognitive Skills*. Hillsdale, NJ: Lawrence Erlbaum.

Diamond, A., and Goldman-Rakic, P. (1983) Comparison of performance on a Piagetian object permanence task in human infants and rhesus monkeys: Evidence for involvement of prefrontalcortex. Paper presented at the Annual Meeting of the Society for Neuroscience, Boston, November.

Gratch, G. (1975) Recent studies based on Piaget's view of object concept development. In L. B. Cohen and P. Salapatek (eds.). *Infant Perception: From Sensation to Cognition*. Vol. II. New York: Academic Press, 51–99.

Gratch, G. (1976) A review of Piagetian infancy research: Object concept development. In W. F. Overton and J. M. Gallagher (eds.). *Knowledge and Development: Advances in Research and Theory (I)*. New York: Plenum Press.

Harris, P. L. (1985). The development of search. In P. Salapatek and L. B. Cohen (eds.). *Handbook of Infant Perception*. New York: Academic Press.

Horowitz, F. D. (ed.) (1975) Visual attention, auditory stimulation, and language discrimination in young infants. *Mono. Soc. Res. Child Dev., 39*, (5–6).

Keppel, G. (1982) *Design and Analysis: A Researcher's Handbook* (2nd edition). Englewood Cliffs, NJ: Prentice-Hall.

Leslie, A. M. (1984) Spatiotemporal continuity and the perception of causality in infants. *Perception,* in press.

Lucas, T. C., and Uzgiris, I. C. (1977) Spatial factors in the development of the object concept. *Dev. Psychol., 13*, 492–500.

Myers, J. L. (1979) *Fundamentals of Experimental Design*, 3rd edition. Boston: Allyn and Bacon.

Piaget, J. (1952) *The Origins of Intelligence in Children*. New York: International University Press.

Piaget, J. (1954) *The Construction of Reality in the Child*. New York: Basic Books.

SAS User's Guide: Statistics. 1982 Edition. Gary, NC: SAS Institute Inc., 1982.

Schacter, D. L., and Moscovitch, M. (1983) Infants, amnesics, and dissociable memory systems. In M. Moscovitch (ed.), *Infant Memory: Its Relation to Normal and Pathological Memory in Humans and Other Animals*. Volume 9 in *Advances in the Study of Communication and Affect*. New York: Plenum Press.

Schuberth, R. E. (1983) The infant's search for objects: Alternatives to Piaget's theory of concept development. In L. P. Lipsitt and C. K. Rovee-Collier (eds.), *Advances in Infancy Research*, Vol. 2. Norwood, NJ: Ablex.

Sophian, C. (1984) Developing search skills. In C. Sophian (ed.), *Origins of Cognitive Skills*. Hillsdale, NJ: Lawrence Erlbaum.

Spelke, E. S., and Kestelbaum, R. (1984) *Spatiotemporal Continuity and Object Persistence in Infancy*. Unpublished manuscript, University of Pennsylvania, Philadelphia.

Uzgiris, I. C. (1973) Patterns of cognitive development in infancy. *Merrill-Palmer Quart., 19*, 181–204.

READING 11

Detection of Intermodal Numerical Correspondences by Human Infants

Prentice Starkey
Elizabeth S. Spelke
Rachel Gelman

Before children go to school they exhibit knowledge of enumerative procedures such as counting, of numerical relationships such as equivalence, and of arithmetic operations such as addition (*1*). These observations suggest that early mathematical knowledge develops from an innate base. Here we present evidence that 7-month-old infants match the number of objects in a spatial display to the number of sounds in a temporal sequence. These findings indicate that infants can detect numerical information and that they do so by use of a mechanism that is not limited to a single modality of sensation.

Human infants discriminate among visible displays of two, three, or four dots of white light (2) and between pictures of two or three objects varying in color, shape, size, texture, and arrangement (3). Although suggestive, these experiments do not reveal whether the basis of the discrimination is numerical information as such or specific visual patterns (4). We have now addressed this issue by investigating whether infants could detect numerical correspondences between sets of visible items and sets of audible items.

The experiments used a preferential looking procedure adapted from studies of intermodal perception (5). Infants 6 to 8 months old viewed two photographic displays presented side by side. One display contained two objects, the other three. While infants watched these displays, they heard two or three drumbeats from a central location. Their time looking at the displays was subsequently recorded for 10 seconds. Infants attend preferentially to a visible object that corresponds to an accompanying sound (5). If they detect the number of items in visible and audible displays, they should look at the display of objects that matches, in number, the sequence of sounds.

Sixteen infants participated in experiment 1. They saw a variety of slide photographs of heterogeneous household items (6). Different items, in different arrangements, appeared on each slide (Fig. 1). The auditory accompaniment consisted of two or three beats (1.33 beats per second) from a drum concealed behind the projection screen. On each trial, the slides were displayed during the presentation of the sounds and for 10 seconds thereafter. Then they were removed and a new pair was displayed, thus beginning the next trial. Each infant was presented with at least 16 and no more than 32 trials (7). On each trial, the duration of looking at each of the two visible displays was recorded

during the 10-second period that followed the offset of the sound. The recordings were made by two observers who could not see the displayed slides (8).

The infants attended longer to the numerically corresponding display than to the noncorresponding display: this preference was largely limited to the second block of trials (Table 1). A majority of the infants preferred the numerically corresponding display (Table 1). In the first block of trials, infants looked longer at the three-object display regardless of the number of drumbeats sounded. These results were obtained again in experiment 2, a replication with eight additional infants (Table 1).

Experiment 3 was an investigation of whether these preferences could have been based on temporal rather than numerical information. Temporal information provided a possible basis for intermodal matching because the three-object display presumably required more scanning time than the two-object display, and the duration of the three-beat sequence was greater than that of the two-beat sequence. In this experiment, the durations of the two- and three-beat sequences were equated. The 16 infants that were observed again attended longer to the numerically corresponding display (Table 1).

When the three experiments are considered together the two-object display was attended to longer when accompanied by two drumbeats than by three and the three-object display was attended to longer when accompanied by three drumbeats than by two (9). A majority of infants preferred the numerically corresponding display. An examination of the distribution of attention of each of these infants across all trials of the experimental session revealed that several infants exhibited a pattern characterized by the presence of one or more uninterrupted runs of several trials in which the numerically corresponding display was preferred and several more infants, although they exhibited shorter runs, preferred the corresponding display on a significant number of trials (10).

Trial	Position Left	Position Right	Objects Left	Objects Right	Drumbeats (No.)
1	[1 / 2]	[1 / 2 / 3]	(1) Memo pad (2) Comb	(1) Bell pepper (2) Animal horn (3) Scissors	2
2	[1 / 2]	[1 2 3]	(1) Ribbon (2) Pipe	(1) Coin purse (2) Ring box (3) Feather	2
3	[1 / 2]	[1 / 3 2]	(1) Orange case (2) Pine burr	(1) Dark brown cloth (2) Eggbeater (3) Wooden carving A	2
4	[1 2]	[1 / 2 3]	(1) Wooden bowl (2) Lemon	(1) Glass-holder (2) Red yarn (3) Blue yoyo	2
5	[1 2]	[1 2 3]	(1) Key (2) Black disc	(1) Corkscrew (2) Jar lid (3) Glasses case	3
6	[1 2]	[1 2 3]	(1) Wig (2) Figurine	(1) Strap (2) Flute (3) Tea steeper	3
7	[1 2]	[1 / 2 3]	(1) Water glass (2) Drain plug	(1) Hair dryer cap (2) Metal cylinder (3) Wooden carving B	3
8	[2 / 1]	[3 / 1 2]	(1) Candle (2) Black case	(1) Pillow (2) Orange (3) Vase	3
9	[1 / 3 2]	[1 / 2]	(1) Memo pad (2) Comb (3) Scraper	(1) Bell pepper (2) Animal horn	2
10	[1 / 2 / 3]	[1 2]	(1) Ribbon (2) Pipe (3) Yellow rubber glove	(1) Coin purse (2) Ring box	2
11	[1 / 3 2]	[1 / 2]	(1) Orange case (2) Pine burr (3) Toy animal	(1) Dark brown cloth (2) Eggbeater	2
12	[1 / 2 3]	[1 / 2]	(1) Wooden bowl (2) Lemon (3) Blue sponge	(1) Glass-holder (2) Red yarn	2
13	[1 2 3]	[1 2]	(1) Key (2) Black disc (3) Unpainted wooden block	(1) Corkscrew (2) Jar lid	3
14	[3 / 1 2]	[1 2]	(1) Wig (2) Drain plug (3) Pink case	(1) Strap (2) Flute	3
15	[1 2 3]	[1 / 2]	(1) Water glass (2) Figurine (3) Wooden mushroom	(1) Hair dryer cap (2) Metal cylinder	3
16	[2 / 1 3]	[1 / 1 2]	(1) Candle (2) Black case (3) Pink cup	(1) Pillow (2) Orange	3

FIGURE 1 The order of displays given to one infant.

TABLE 1 ATTENTION TO AND PREFERENCES FOR NUMERICALLY CORRESPONDING DISPLAYS

Experiment	Trial block	Duration of attention (seconds)		Preference for corresponding display		
		Corresponding display	Noncorresponding display	Proportion of duration[†]	Proportion of subjects[‡]	Subjects (N)
1	1	2.11 ± 0.89	1.99 ± 0.81	0.51	0.44	7
	2	2.02 ± 0.99	1.51 ± 0.79	0.58***	0.75**	12
	1 + 2	2.06 ± 0.71	1.75 ± 0.73	0.55**	0.75**	12
2	1	2.93 ± 1.09	2.91 ± 0.84	0.50	0.50	4
	2	2.74 ± 1.38	1.92 ± 0.91	0.58***	1.00***	8
	1 + 2	2.84 ± 1.23	2.42 ± 0.57	0.54**	0.75	6
3	1	3.03 ± 0.81	2.59 ± 1.02	0.54	0.56	9
	2	2.64 ± 0.95	2.32 ± 1.06	0.54	0.56	9
	1 + 2	2.84 ± 0.77	2.46 ± 0.80	0.54***	0.75*	12
1 + 2 + 3	1	2.64 ± 0.98	2.41 ± 0.96	0.52	0.50	20
	2	2.41 ± 1.09	1.92 ± 0.98	0.57***	0.72***	29
	1 + 2	2.53 ± 0.92	2.17 ± 0.79	0.54***	0.75***	30

[†]$P_d = D_c / (D_c + D_n)$. where P_d is the mean proportion of duration averaged over trials, and D_c and D_n are the mean durations of attention averaged over the sets of corresponding displays (c) and noncorresponding displays (n). The proportion was compared with that expected by chance. 0.50: significance was assessed by one-tailed t-tests with 15 degrees of freedom (d.f.) (experiments 1 and 3). 7 d.f. (experiment 2). or 39 d.f. (overall).

[‡]$P_s = S_c / (S_c + S_n)$. where P_s is the proportion of subjects, and S_c and S_n are the numbers of subjects whose mean proportion of duration was greater on the corresponding displays (c) or the noncorresponding displays (n): significance was assessed by one-tailed sign tests.

*$P < 0.05$
**$P < 0.025$
***$P < 0.01$

The findings of these experiments shed light on the mechanisms possibly underlying the infants' ability to obtain information about number. Infants detected numerical correspondences across two very different kinds of display. In order to detect these correspondences, they must have disregarded the modality of presentation (visual or auditory) and the type of items presented (objects or events). No visual pattern matching procedure could, by itself, account for the detection of these correspondences. The infant's enumerative procedure must be more general.

It remains to be determined whether infants' numerical categories are as differentiated as those of older children and whether they are absolute (in the sense of "two" and "three") or relative (in the sense of "more numerous" and "less numerous"). It is also not known how the abilities of infants are related developmentally to those of older children. Answers to these questions may begin to elucidate the psychological foundation of number.

REFERENCES AND NOTES

1 R. Gelman and C. R. Gallistel. *The Child's Understanding of Number* (Harvard Univ. Press, Cambridge, Mass., 1978); T. P. Carpenter, J. M. Moser, T. A. Romberg, Eds. *Addition and Subtraction: A Cognitive Perspective* (Erlbaum, Hillsdale, N.J., 1982).

2 P. Starkey and R. G. Cooper, Jr., *Science* **210**, 1033 (1980); S. E. Antell and D. P. Keating. *Child Dev.* **54**, 695 (1983).

3 M. S. Strauss and L. E. Curtis. *Child Dev.* **52**, 1146 (1981); P. Starkey, E. S. Spelke, R. Gelman, in preparation. In the latter study, infants aged 6 to 9 months were presented with a subset of the visible displays described in Fig. 1 in a habituation-test procedure. Those habituated to displays containing two objects attended longer to new displays of three objects than to new displays of two objects: infants habituated to three objects did the reverse.

4 For one development of this view, see D. Klahr and J. G. Wallace [*Cognitive Development, An Information Processing View* (Erlbaum, Hillsdale, N.J., 1976)].

5 E. S. Spelke, *Cognit. Psychol.* **8**, 553 (1976).

6 Infants were seated either in an infant seat or on the lap of a parent who wore glasses that occluded his or her view of the displays. The slides were rear-projected onto a 64-cm by 89-cm screen located 60 cm from the infant. The projected displays subtended visual angles of $21.8°$ (vertical) by $25.2°$ (horizontal) and were separated by $25.2°$. The objects in each slide were presented against a white background, each spatially separated from the others. Room lighting was dim.

7 The experiment was terminated if an infant became fretful or drowsy. Eleven infants completed all 32 trials. One infant failed to complete 16 trials and was replaced. The remaining five infants completed from 17 to 29 trials. All infants were presented with 16 unique pairs of visible displays (Fig. 1). The order of presentation and the lateral position of displays within a pair were counterbalanced across infants. Each infant was presented with two drumbeats on half of the trials and with three drumbeats on the other half. For half of the infants, a particular display pair was accompanied by two drumbeats; for the rest, it was accompanied by three beats. The presentations of the materials on the first 16 trials were repeated on the second 16 trials.

8 Interobserver reliability was greater than 0.9. The observers viewed the infants through peepholes located to the left or right of the projection screen. Partitions blocked their view of the screen and hence the displays. Parents' opaque glasses did not reflect light from the displays. Moreover, two experiments revealed that the observers could neither see reflections of the displays on the infants' corneas nor analyze the infants' patterns of eye scanning to determine the number of objects on each side. Use of corneal reflections was tested in experiment 4, in which four infants were presented with the materials in Fig. 1. Eight observers (two per infant) who had also served as observers in the main experiments monitored corneal reflections from the displays and judged, as best they could, the lateral position of the two-object display. The observers' proportions of correct judgments did not differ from that expected by chance (proportion, 0.49). Use of scanning patterns was tested in experiment 3 by instructing one of the two observers present at each session to use such patterns to judge the position of the two-object display. Again, judgments were at chance level.

9 Across experiments, a preference for the two-object display when accompanied by two drumbeats was present in the first block of trials (proportion of duration, 0.54, $P < 0.05$), in the second block (proportion, 0.55, $P < 0.01$), and across both blocks (proportion, 0.55, $P < 0.01$): a preference for the three-object display when accompanied by three drumbeats was not present in the first block of trials (proportion, 0.51) but was present in the second block (proportion, 0.58, $P < 0.01$) and across both blocks (proportion, 0.54, $P < 0.01$).

10 Of the 30 infants who had an overall preference for the corresponding display, 11 exhibited one or more long uninterrupted runs as identified by a runs test [S. Siegel, *Nonparametric Statistics* (McGraw-Hill, New York, 1956)] for the presence of significantly few runs of trials in which either the corresponding display was preferred or the noncorresponding display was preferred. An additional five infants, who did not exhibit a long run, nevertheless preferred the corresponding display on a significant number of trials as indicated by a sign test.

11 Supported by NIH postdoctoral fellowship MH 07949 and by a University of Pennsylvania cognitive science fellowship to P.S., by NIH grant HD 13248 to E.S.S., and by NSF grant BNS 80-04881 to R.G. We thank R. G. Cooper, J. E. Hochberg, and the reviewers for their comments, and W. S. Born, S. Mangelsdorf, and C. Norris for assistance in conducting the research. Portions of this work were presented at the meetings of the Psychonomic Society, Philadelphia, 1981, and the International Conference on Infant Studies, Austin, Texas, 1982.

An Epigenetic Perspective on the Development of Fear

Bennett I. Bertenthal
Joseph J. Campos

INTRODUCTION

The period between 7 to 9 months of age is characterized by dramatic changes in perceptual, cognitive, social, and especially emotional development. For example, infants begin to show more effective and efficient ways of searching for hidden objects, spatial orientation undergoes a shift from the use of egocentric to objective codes, and more complex forms of imitation appear. In the affective domain, infants begin to show a sense of security through attachment, as well as a burgeoning of fear, which manifests itself in many different forms, including fear of strangers, separation from parents, fear of novel toys and animals, and fear of heights [1]. It is this last phenomenon—fear of heights—that we have studied extensively because it provides such a well-controlled opportunity for evaluating the development of fear in human infants.

There is currently much debate as to what mechanism is responsible for infants showing a developmental shift in regard to fear of heights during the second half year of life. The strong nativist position is that this event reflects the unfolding of a genetic blueprint. Alternatively, the empiricist position is that fear of heights develops as a function of specific childhood experiences, such as falls, or conceivably, as a function of more general changes in cognitive skills. No doubt, the truth lies somewhere in between these differing views. The challenge is to present a position that does more than merely suggest an interactionist perspective—it should truly specify the nature of these interactions.

In this regard, it is important to note that co-occurring with these other developmental changes between 7 and 9 months of age is the emergence of self-produced locomotion, i.e., crawling. Interestingly, a number of leading developmental theorists, such as Piaget, Mahler, and Held and Hein, have speculated on the significance of this event for early development, yet empirical research remained sparse until quite recently. As a consequence of a recent flurry of research, it is now quite clear that self-produced locomotion is functionally related to a number of developmental changes occurring during the second half year of life [2]. Our own perspective on this relation is that it reflects an epigenetic process whereby the specific experiences gained through early locomotion provide a "setting event" for the development of other skills. In the remainder of this paper we will review evidence supporting such a process in the development of fear of heights.

EMPIRICAL EVIDENCE

Our studies on fear of heights in human infants involve an apparatus known as the "visual cliff." In essence, this apparatus resembles a large glass table top supported approximately four feet off the ground. The glass surface is divided into two equal sections by a center board running across the middle of the cliff. On one side of the cliff (shallow side), a textured material is placed directly under the glass such that it appears to provide a rigid surface of support. On the other side of the cliff (deep side), the textured material is placed some distance below the glass, thus simulating an apparent drop-off. In order to adaptively respond to the apparent drop-off of the deep side of the cliff, it would seem necessary for a human infant to (1) perceive the vertical depth beyond the edge of the center-board, (2) avoid stepping off the edge, and (3) experience fear if he or she does go off the edge. Although initial studies with this apparatus suggested that avoidance of the deep side was innate and simply awaited the onset of crawling, our more recent experiments provide unequivocal evidence that this developmental shift does not emerge until sometime *after* the emergence of self-produced locomotion.

In our first experiment, we tested 92 7.3-month-old infants (48 locomotor; 48 prelocomotor) for fear of heights on the visual cliff. Fear was assessed by measuring cardiac changes of the infants while they were alternately lowered down onto the shallow and deep sides of the cliff. Converging evidence from a number of other studies in our lab as well as others provides reasonably strong support for interpreting heart rate acceleration as evidence of wariness or fear, whereas heart rate deceleration is associated with rapt attention. The results from this initial study revealed that prelocomotor infants showed no significant changes in cardiac responsiveness when lowered onto either side of the cliff. On the other hand, locomotor infants showed a significant level of cardiac acceleration when lowered onto the deep side, but no change in responsiveness when lowered onto the shallow side.

Although the preceding results suggested that locomotor experience was related to fear of heights, the evidence was by no means definitive. More recent investigations have involved experimental manipulations of locomotor experience in order to more completely establish that this experience is causally linked to the development of fear of heights and not merely confounded with more rapid maturation. One of the most important of these experiments was

designed to provide prelocomotor infants with an analogue of crawling experience. This was accomplished by recruiting prelocomotor infants who had already received a minimum of 40 hours of experience in a commercially available "walking" device. In essence, this device consists of a seat supported by a frame that is attached to wheels. Those prelocomotor infants tall enough to reach the floor with their feet are able to make themselves move while seated in this device. Since some of the infants began crawling prior to testing on the cliff, the final design of this experiment included a total of 64 infants assigned evenly to two experimental groups (artificial locomotor experience)—one prelocomotor and one locomotor (but no more than one week of crawling experience)—and to two groups of age-matched controls. As before, fear was assessed by measuring heart rate during descent onto the cliff. Without question, the most important finding to emerge from this study was that the experimental groups showed significantly greater heart rate acceleration on the deep side than did the control groups. It is also interesting to note that the group showing the greatest amount of heart rate acceleration was the group with both artificial and natural locomotor experience. On the other hand, the prelocomotor control group was the only group with absolutely no previous locomotor experience and they were also the only group to show a significant heart rate deceleration when lowered onto the deep side of the cliff. In sum, these findings provide compelling evidence for a causal, and not merely a correlative relation, between locomotor experience and fear of heights.

Further support for the existence of a functional relation between locomotion and fear of heights came in the form of a "natural deprivation" experiment. Recently, we had the opportunity to examine longitudinally an orthopedically handicapped infant who was born with two congenitally dislocated hips and at the time that testing was initiated was encased in a full body cast. Although physically handicapped, the child showed no signs of any neurological problems and was tested at 6 months of age to have a Developmental Quotient of 128 on the Bayley Scales. We began testing this infant at 6 months of age and continued until 10 months. Through the first four testings, the child's locomotion continued to be impeded by some orthopedic device, but by the last testing the infant had been crawling freely for two weeks and already seemed quite proficient. During the first four testing sessions, this infant showed no differential heart rate responsiveness upon descent onto the two sides of the cliff. At the last testing session, however, the pattern was dramatically different. Heart rate on the deep side of the cliff showed a marked acceleratory response, whereas heart rate on the shallow side showed an equally marked deceleratory shift. Although complete data has only been collected on one orthopedically handicapped infant, the findings are certainly provocative and merit additional study, especially since work on delayed locomotor experience could serve to clarify the nature of the observed functional relation. Currently, it is unclear whether locomotor experience serves as merely a facilitator of the development of fear of heights, or, alternatively, induces (and by implication is necessary for) the development of this fear. We are currently studying a larger group of orthopedically handicapped infants in collaboration with Dr. Katherine Barnard and Dr. Robert Telzrow of the University of Washington School of Medicine in order to gain additional insights into this very important issue.

CONCLUSIONS

Taken together, the results from the visual cliff studies confirm that fear of heights is function-ally linked to the acquisition of locomotor experience. Apparently, locomotor experience provides infants with an appreciation of the consequences of one's movements in the spatial layout. In contrast to passive locomotion, self-produced locomotion necessitates visual attention to where one is heading as well as the perceived transformations, or more specifically, the consequences of those movements. As a function of this increased attention, infants begin to appreciate that their own movements have consequences for the self, and thus, gradually learn to select those actions that are most adaptive, such as avoiding heights.

This perspective also allows us to understand why locomotor infants show fear when lowered onto the cliff. It is consistent with the growing evidence that fear reflects a process by which perceived events are related to the self and determined to be either consistent or inconsistent with significant goals. In the case of the cliff, avoidance of the apparent drop-off is precluded, and thus fear results. As such, these data support the point of view that goal-directed behavior and self-regulation are intimately linked to affectivity (3).

REFERENCES

1 S. Scarr and P. Salapatek, Merrill-Palmer Quarterly *16*, 53–90 (1970).
2 B. Bertenthal, J. Campos, and K. C. Barrett in: Continuities and Discontinuities in Development, R. Emde and R. Harmon, eds. (Plenum Press, New York 1984) pp. 175–210.
3 J. J. Campos and K. C. Barrett in: Cognition, Emotion and Behavior, C. Izard, J. Kagan, and R. Zajonc, eds. (Cambridge University Press, New York 1983) pp. 229–263.

READING 13

Cross-cultural Perspectives on Early Development

Jerome Kagan

Robert E. Klein

Most American psychologists believe in the hardiness of habit and the premise that experience etches an indelible mark on the mind not easily erased by time or trauma. The application of that assumption to the first era of development leads to the popular view that psychological growth during the early years is under the strong influence of the variety and patterning of external events and that the psychological structures shaped by those initial encounters have a continuity that stretches at least into early adolescence. The first part of that hypothesis, which owes much of its popularity to Freud, Harlow, and Skinner, has strong empirical support. The continuity part of the assumption, which is more equivocal, is summarized in the American adage, "Well begun is half done."

Many developmental psychologists, certain of the long-lasting effects of early experience, set out to find the form of those initial stabilities and the earliest time they might obtain a preview of the child's future. Although several decades of research have uncovered fragile lines that seem to travel both backward and forward in time, the breadth and magnitude of intraindividual continuities have not been overwhelming, and each seems to be easily lost or shattered (Kagan & Moss, 1962; Kessen, Haith, & Salapatek, 1970). A recent exhaustive review of research on human infancy led to the conclusion that "only short term stable individual variation has been demonstrated;...and demonstrations of continuity in process—genotype continuity—have been rare indeed [Kessen et al., 1970, p. 297]." Since that evaluation violates popular beliefs, the authors noted a few pages later:

In spite of slight evidence of stability, our inability to make predictions of later personality from observations in the first three years of life is so much against good sense and common observation, to say nothing of the implication of all developmental theories, that the pursuit of predictively effective categories of early behavior will surely continue unabated [p. 309].

The modest empirical support for long-term continuity is occasionally rationalized by arguing that although behaviors similar in manifest form might not be stable over long time periods, the underlying structures might be much firmer (Kagan, 1971). Hence, if the operational manifestations of these hidden forms were discerned, continuity of cognitive, motivational, and affective structures would be affirmed. However, we recently observed some children living in an isolated Indian village on Lake Atitlan in the highlands of northwest Guatemala. We saw listless, silent, apathetic infants; passive, quiet, timid 3-year-olds; but, active, gay, intellectually competent 11-year-olds. Since there is no reason to believe that living conditions in this village have changed during the last century, it is likely that the alert 11-year-olds were, a decade earlier, listless, vacant-staring infants. That observation has forced us to question the strong form of the continuity assumption in a serious way.

The data to be presented imply absence of a predictive relationship between level of cognitive development at 12–18 months of age and quality of intellectual functioning at 11 years. This conclusion is not seriously different from the repeated demonstrations of no relation between infant intelligence quotient (IQ) or developmental quotient (DQ) scores during the first year of life and Binet or Wechsler IQ scores obtained during later childhood (Kessen et al., 1970; Pease, Wolins, & Stockdale, 1973). The significance of the current data, however, derives from the fact that the infants seemed to be more seriously retarded than those observed in earlier studies, their environments markedly less varied, and the assessment of later cognitive functioning based on culture-fair tests of specific cognitive abilities rather than culturally biased IQ tests.

Moreover, these observations suggest that it is misleading to talk about continuity of any psychological characteristic—be it cognitive, motivational or behavioral—without specifying simultaneously the context of development. Consider the long-term stability of passivity as an example. The vast majority of the infants in the Indian village were homogeneously passive and retained this characteristic until they were five or six years old. A preschool child rarely forced a submissive posture on another. However, by eight years of age, some of the children became dominant over others because the structure of the peer group required that role to be filled. Factors other than early infant passivity were critical in determining that differentiation, and physical size, strength, and competence at valued skills seemed to be more important than the infant's disposition. In modern American society, where there is much greater variation among young children in degree of passivity and dominance, a passive four-year-old will always encounter a large group of dominant peers who enforce a continuing role of submissiveness on him. As a result, there should be firmer stability of behavioral passivity during the early years in an American city than in the Indian village. But the stability of that behavior seems to be more dependent on the presence of dominant members in the immediate vicinity than on some inherent force within the child.

Continuity of a psychological disposition is not solely the product of an inherited or early

acquired structure that transcends a variety of contexts. The small group of scientists who champion the view of stability—we have been among them—envision a small box of different-colored gems tucked deep in the brain, with names like intelligent, passive, irritable, or withdrawn engraved on them. These material entities guarantee that, despite behavioral disguises, an inherent set of psychological qualities, independent of the local neighborhood and knowable under the proper conditions, belongs to each individual. This belief in a distinct and unchanging mosaic of core traits—an identity—is fundamental to Western thought and is reflected in the psychological writings of Erik Erikson and the novels of popular Western writers. Only Herman Hesse, who borrowed the philosophy of the East, fails to make a brief for personal identity. *Siddhartha, Magister Ludi,* and *Narcissus and Goldmund* are not trying to discover "who they are" but are seeking serenity, and each appreciates the relevance of setting in that journey.

A secondary theme concerns the interaction of maturation and environment, an issue that has seized academic conversation because of the renewed debate surrounding the inheritance of intelligence. But there is a broader issue to probe. The majority of American psychologists remain fundamentally Lockean in attitude, believing that thought and action owe primary allegiance to experience and that reinforcements and observations of models set the major course of change. Despite Piaget's extraordinary popularity, the majority of American psychologists do not believe that maturation supplies the major impetus for psychological growth during the childhood years. We have forgotten that many years ago Myrtle McGraw (1935) allowed one twin to climb some stairs and prevented his co-twin from practicing that skill. This homely experiment occurred only a few years after Carmichael (1926) anesthetized some *Amblystoma* embryos to prevent them from swimming. The twin not allowed to climb was behind his partner in learning this skill, but he eventually mastered it. Carmichael's embryos swam perfectly when the anesthetic was pumped out of the tank. In both instances, the organisms could not be prevented from displaying species-specific properties.

Our observations in these Indian villages have led us to reorder the hierarchy of complementary influences that biology and environmental forces exert on the development of intellectual functions that are natural to man. Separate maturational factors seem to set the time of emergence of those basic abilities. Experience can slow down or speed up that emergence by several months or several years, but nature will win in the end. The capacity for perceptual analysis, imitation, language, inference, deduction, symbolism, and memory will eventually appear in sturdy form in any natural environment, for each is an inherent competence in the human program. But these competences, which we assume to be universal, are to be distinguished from culturally specific talents that will not appear unless the child is exposed to or taught them directly. Reading, arithmetic, and understanding of specific words and concepts fall into this latter category.

This distinction between universal and culturally specific competences implies a parallel distinction between absolute and relative retardation. Consider physical growth as an illustration of this idea. There is sufficient cross-cultural information on age of onset of walking to warrant the statement that most children should be walking unaided before their second birthday. A three-year-old unable to walk is physically retarded in the absolute sense, for he has failed to attain a natural competence at the normative time. However, there is neither an empirical nor a logical basis for expecting that most children, no matter where they live, will develop the ability to hunt with a spear, ride a horse, or play football. Hence, it is not reasonable to speak of absolute retardation on these skills. In those cultures where these talents are

taught, encouraged, or modeled, children will differ in the age at which they attain varied levels of mastery. But we can only classify a child as precocious or retarded relative to another in his community. The data to be reported suggest that absolute retardation in the attainment of specific cognitive competences during infancy has no predictive validity with respect to level of competence on a selected set of natural cognitive skills at age 11. *The data do not imply that a similar level of retardation among American infants has no future implication for relative retardation on culture-specific skills.*

THE GUATEMALAN SETTINGS

The infant observations to be reported here were made in two settings in Guatemala. One set of data came from four subsistence farming Ladino villages in eastern Guatemala. The villages are moderately isolated, Spanish speaking, and contain between 800 and 1,200 inhabitants. The families live in small thatched huts of cane or adobe with dirt floors and no sanitary facilities. Books, pencils, paper, and pictures are typically absent from the experience of children prior to school entrance, and, even in school, the average child has no more than a thin lined notebook and a stub of a pencil.

A second location was a more isolated Indian village of 850 people located on the shores of Lake Atitlan in the northwest mountainous region of the country. Unlike the Spanish-speaking villages, the Indians of San Marcos la Laguna have no easy access to a city and are psychologically more detached. The isolation is due not only to geographical location but also to the fact that few of the women and no more than half of the men speak reasonable Spanish. Few adults and no children can engage the culture of the larger nation, and the Indians of San Marcos regard themselves as an alien and exploited group.

The Infant in San Marcos

During the first 10–12 months, the San Marcos infant spends most of his life in the small, dark interior of his windowless hut. Since women do not work in the field, the mother usually stays close to the home and spends most of her day preparing food, typically tortillas, beans, and coffee, and perhaps doing some weaving. If she travels to a market to buy or sell, she typically leaves her infant with an older child or a relative.

The infant is usually close to the mother, either on her lap or enclosed on her back in a colored cloth, sitting on a mat, or sleeping in a hammock. The mother rarely allows the infant to crawl on the dirt floor of the hut and feels that the outside sun, air, and dust are harmful. The infant is rarely spoken to or played with, and the only available objects for play, besides his own clothing or his mother's body, are oranges, ears of corn, and pieces of wood or clay. These infants are distinguished from American infants of the same age by their extreme motoric passivity, fearfulness, minimal smiling, and above all, extraordinary quietness. A few with pale cheeks and vacant stares had the quality of tiny ghosts and resembled the description of the institutionalized infants that Spitz called marasmic. Many would not orient to a taped source of speech, not smile or babble to vocal overtures, and hesitated over a minute before reaching for an attractive toy.

An American woman who lived in the village made five separate 30-minute observations in the homes of 12 infants 8–16 months of age. If a particular behavioral variable occurred during a five-second period, it was recorded once for that interval. The infants were spoken to or played with 6% of the time, with a maximum of 12%. The comparable averages for American middle-class homes are 25%, with a maximum of 40% (Lewis & Freedle, 1972). It should be noted that the infant's vocalizations, which occurred about 6% of the time, were typically grunts lasting less than a second, rather than the prolonged babbling typical of middle-class American children. The infants cried very little because the slightest irritability led the mother to nurse her child at once. Nursing was the single, universal therapeutic treatment for all infant distress, be it caused by fear, cold, hunger, or cramps. Home observations in the eastern villages are consonant with those gathered in San Marcos and reveal infrequent infant vocalization and little verbal interaction or play with adults or older siblings. The mothers in these settings seem to regard their infants the way an American parent views an expensive cashmere sweater: Keep it nearby and protect it but do not engage it reciprocally.

One reason why these mothers might behave this way is that it is abundantly clear to every parent that all children begin to walk by 18 months, to talk by age 3, and to perform some adult chores by age 10, despite the listless, silent quality of infancy. The mother's lack of active manipulation, stimulation, or interactive play with her infant is not indicative of indifference or rejection, but is a reasonable posture, given her knowledge of child development.

COMPARATIVE STUDY OF INFANT COGNITIVE DEVELOPMENT

Although it was not possible to create a formal laboratory setting for testing infants in San Marcos, it was possible to do so in the eastern Ladino villages, and we shall summarize data derived from identical procedures administered to rural Guatemalan and American infants. Although the infants in the Ladino villages were more alert than the Indian children of San Marcos, the similarities in living conditions and rearing practices are such that we shall assume that the San Marcos infants would have behaved like the Ladino children or, what is more likely, at a less mature level. In these experiments, the Guatemalan mother and child came to a special laboratory equipped with a chair and a stage that simulated the setting in the Harvard laboratories where episodes were administered to cross-sectional groups of infants,

84 American and 80 Guatemalan, at 5½, 7½, 9½, and 11½ months of age, with 10–24 infants from each culture at each age level.

Before describing the procedures and results, it will be helpful to summarize the theoretical assumptions that govern interpretation of the infant's reactions to these episodes. There appear to be two important maturationally controlled processes which emerge between 2 and 12 months that influence the child's reactions to transformations of an habituated event (Kagan, 1971, 1972). During the first six weeks of life, the duration of the child's attention to a visual event is controlled by the amount of physical change or contrast in the event. During the third month, the infant shows prolonged attention to events that are moderate discrepancies from habituated standards. Maintenance of attention is controlled by the relation of the event to the child's schema for the class to which that event belongs. The typical reactions to discrepancy include increased fixation time, increased vocalization, and either cardiac deceleration or decreased variability of heart rate during the stimulus presentation. These conclusions are based on many independent studies and we shall not document them here (Cohen, Gelber, & Lazar, 1972; Kagan, 1971; Lewis, Goldberg, & Campbell, 1970).

However, at approximately 8–9 months, a second process emerges. The infant now begins to activate cognitive structures, called hypotheses, in the service of interpreting discrepant events. A hypothesis is viewed as a representation of a relation between two schemata. Stated in different language, the infant not only notes and processes a discrepancy, he also attempts to transform it to his prior schemata for that class of event and activates hypotheses to serve this advanced cognitive function. It is not a coincidence that postulation of this new competence coincides with the time when the infant displays object permanence and separation anxiety, phenomena that require the child to activate an idea of an absent object or person.

There are two sources of support for this notion. The first is based on age changes in attention to the same set of events. Regardless of whether the stimulus is a set of human masks, a simple black and white design, or a dynamic sequence in which a moving orange rod turns on a bank of three light bulbs upon contact, there is a U-shaped relation between age and duration of attention across the period 3–36 months, with the trough typically occurring between 7 and 12 months of age (Kagan, 1972).

The curvilinear relation between age and attention to human masks has been replicated among American, rural Guatemalan, and Kahlahari desert Bushman children (Kagan, 1971; Konner, 1973; Sellers, Klein, Kagan, & Minton, 1972). If discrepancy were the only factor controlling fixation time, a child's attention should decrease with age, for the stimulus events become less discrepant as he grows older. The increase in attention toward the end of the first years is interpreted as a sign of a new cognitive competence, which we have called the *activation of hypotheses*.

A second source of support for this idea is that the probability of a cardiac acceleration to a particular discrepancy increases toward the end of the first year, whereas cardiac deceleration is the modal reaction during the earlier months (Kagan, 1972). Because studies of adults and young children indicate that cardiac acceleration accompanies mental work, while deceleration accompanies attention to an interesting event (Lacey, 1967; Van Hover, 1971), the appearance of acceleration toward the end of the first year implies that the infants are performing active mental work, or activating hypotheses.

Since increased attention to a particular discrepancy toward the end of the first year is one diagnostic sign of the emergence of this stage of cognitive development, cultural differences in attention to fixed discrepancies during the first year might provide information on the developmental maturity of the infants in each cultural group.

METHOD

Block Episode

Each child was shown a 2-inch wooden orange block for six or eight successive trials (six for the two older ages, and eight for the two younger ages) followed by three or five transformation trials in which a 1½-inch orange block was presented. These transformations were followed by three representations of the original 2-inch block.

Light Episode

The child was shown 8 or 10 repetitions of a sequence in which a hand moved an orange rod in a semicircle until it touched a bank of three light bulbs which were lighted upon contact between the rod and the bulbs. In the five transformation trials that followed, the hand appeared but the rod did not move and the lights lit after a four-second interval. Following the transformations, the original event was presented for three additional trials.

During each of the episodes, two observers coded (a) how long the infant attended to the event, (b) whether the infant vocalized or smiled, and (c) fretting or crying. Intercoder reliability for these variables was over .90.

RESULTS

The Guatemalan infants were significantly less attentive than the Americans on both episodes, and the cultural differences were greater at the two older than at the two younger ages. Figures 1 and 2 illustrate the mean total fixation time to four successive trial blocks for the two episodes. The four trial blocks were the first three standard trials, the last three standards, the first three transformations, and the three return trials.

The American infants of all ages had longer fixation times to the block during every trial block (F ranged from 30.8 to 67.3, $df = \frac{1}{154}, p < .001$). The American infants also displayed longer fixations to the light during every trial-block (F ranged from 9.8 to 18.4, $df = \frac{1}{141}$, $p < .01$). However, it is important to note that at 11½ months, the American children maintained more sustained attention to the return of the

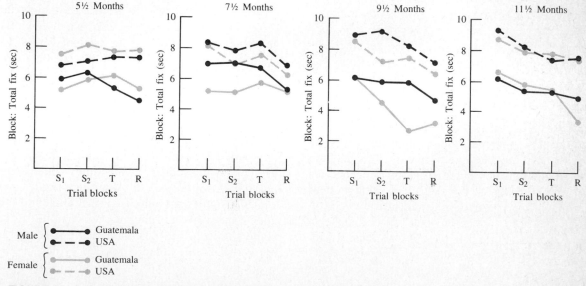

FIGURE 1 Average total fixation time to the block episode by age and culture.

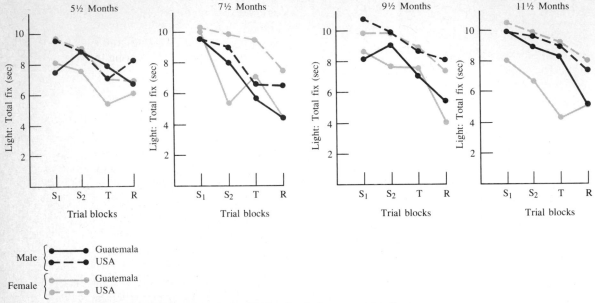

FIGURE 2   Average total fixation time to the light episode by age and culture.

standard than the Guatemalans, who showed a drop in fixation time toward the end of the episode. These data suggest that more of the American than of the Guatemalan infants had entered the stage of activation of hypotheses. Since the Ladino infants appeared more mature than the San Marcos children, it is possible that the American one-year-olds were approximately three months advanced over the San Marcos children in the cognitive function.

ADDITIONAL ASSESSMENTS OF DEVELOPMENTAL STATUS

We collected, under less formal conditions in the home, additional information on the developmental status of the San Marcos infant. Not one of the 12 infants between 8 and 16 months reached for an attractive object they watched being hidden, although many would, with considerable hesitation, reach for a visible object placed close to their hands. Furthermore, none of these 12 infants revealed facial surprise following a sequence in which they watched an object being hidden under a cloth but saw no object when that cloth was removed. These observations suggest

an absolute retardation of four months in the display of behavioral signs diagnostic of the attainment of object permanence.

A third source of data is based on observations of a stranger anxiety. Each of 16 infants between 8 and 20 months was observed following the first exposure to a strange male (the senior author). The first age at which obvious apprehension and/or crying occurred was 13 months, suggesting a five-month lag between San Marcos and American infants. Finally, the information on nonmorphemic babbling and the onset of meaningful speech supports a diagnosis of absolute retardation. There was no marked increase in frequency of babbling or vocalization between 8 and 16 months among the 12 San Marcos infants observed at home, while comparable observations in American homes revealed a significant increase in babbling and the appearance of morphemic vocalizations for some children. Furthermore, many parents remarked that meaningful speech typically appears first at 2½ years of age, about one year later than the average display of first words in American children.

These data, together with the extremely depressed, withdrawn appearance of the San Marcos infants, suggest retardations of three or more months for various psychological competences that typically emerge during the first two years of life. With the exception of one 16-month-old boy, whose alert appearance resembled that of an American infant, there was little variability among the remaining children. Since over 90% were homogeneously passive, non-alert, and quiet, it is unlikely that the recovery of intellectual functioning to be reported later was a result of the selective mortality of a small group of severely retarded infants.

RESILIENCE OF COGNITIVE DEVELOPMENT

The major theme of this article is the potential for recovery of cognitive functions despite early infant retardation. When the San Marcos child becomes mobile at around 15 months he leaves the dark hut, begins to play with other children, and provides himself with cognitive challenges that demand accommodations. Since all children experience this marked discontinuity in variety of experience and opportunity for exploration between the first and second birthday, it is instructive to compare the cognitive competence of older Guatemalan and American children to determine if differences in level of functioning are still present.

The tests administered were designed to assess cognitive processes that are believed to be part of the natural competence of growing children, rather than the culturally arbitrary segments of knowledge contained in a standard IQ test. We tried to create tests that were culturally fair, recognizing that this goal is, in the extreme, unattainable. Hence, the tests were not standardized instruments with psychometric profiles of test-retest reliabilities and criterion validity studies. This investigation should be viewed as a natural experiment in which the independent variable was degree of retardation in infancy and the dependent variables were performances on selected cognitive instruments during childhood. We assume, along with many psychologists, that perceptual analysis, recall and recognition memory, and inference are among the basic cognitive functions of children (even though they do not exhaust that set), and our tests were designed to evaluate those processes.

Tests of recall and recognition memory, perceptual analysis, and perceptual and conceptual inference were given to children in San Marcos, the Ladino villages, an Indian village close to Guatemala City and more modern than San Marcos, Cambridge, Massachusetts, and to two different groups of children living in Guatemala City. One of the Guatemala City settings, the "guarderia," was a day care center for very poor children. The second group, middle-class children attending nursery school, resembled a middle-class American sample in both family background and opportunity. Not all tests were administered to all children. The discussion is organized according to the cognitive function assessed, rather than the sample studied. The sample sizes ranged from 12 to 40 children at any one age.

Recall Memory for Familiar Objects

The ability to organize experience for commitment to long-term memory and to retrieve that information on demand is a basic cognitive skill. It is generally believed that the form of the organization contains diagnostic information regarding cognitive maturity for, among Western samples, both number of independent units of information and the conceptual clustering of that information increase with age.

A 12-object recall task was administered to two samples of Guatemalan children. One group lived in a Ladino village 17 kilometers from Guatemala City; the second group was composed of San Marcos children. The 80 subjects from the Ladino village were 5 and 7 years old, equally balanced for age and sex. The 55 subjects from San Marcos were between 5 and 12 years of age (26 boys and 29 girls).

The 12 miniature objects to be recalled were common to village life and belonged to three conceptual categories: animals (pig, dog, horse, cow), kitchen utensils (knife, spoon, fork, glass), and clothing (pants, dress, underpants, hat). Each child was first required to name the objects, and if the child was unable to he was given the name. The child was then told that after the objects had been randomly arranged on a board he would have 10 seconds to inspect them, after which they would be covered with a cloth, and he would be required to say all the objects he could remember.

Table 1 contains the average number of objects recalled and the number of pairs of conceptually similar words recalled—an index of clustering—for the first two trials. A pair was defined as the temporally contiguous recall of two or more items of the same category. A child received one point for three contiguous items, and three points for contiguous recall of four items. Hence, the maximum clustering score for a single trial was nine points. As Table 1 reveals, the children showed a level of clustering beyond chance expectation (which is between 1.5 and 2.0 pairs for recall scores of seven to eight words). Moreover, recall scores increased with age on both trials for children in both villages (F ranged from 11.2 to 27.7, $p < 0.5$), while clustering increased with age in the Ladino village ($F = 26.8$, $p < .001$ for Trial 1; $F = 3.48$, $p < .05$ for Trial 2).

TABLE 1   MEAN NUMBER OF OBJECTS AND PAIRS RECALLED

Age	Trial 1		Trial 2	
	Recall	Pairs	Recall	Pairs
Ladino village				
5	5.2	2.1	5.4	2.1
7	6.7	3.3	7.8	3.7
Indian village				
5–6	7.1	3.4	7.8	3.8
7–8	8.6	3.4	8.3	3.6
9–10	10.3	4.9	10.3	4.3
11–12	9.6	3.4	10.1	3.6

No 5- or 6-year-old in either village and only 12 of the 40 seven-year-olds in the Ladino village were attending school. School for the others consisted of little more than semiorganized games. Moreover, none of the children in San Marcos had ever left the village, and the 5- and 6-year olds typically spent most of the day within a 500-yard radius of their homes. Hence, school attendance and contact with books and a written language do not seem to be prerequisites for clustering in young children.

The recall and cluster scores obtained in Guatemala were remarkably comparable to those reported for middle-class American children. Appel, Cooper, McCarrell, Knight, Yussen, and Flavell (1971) presented 12 pictures to Minneapolis children in Grade 1 (approximately age 7) and 15 pictures to children in Grade 5 (approximately age 11) in a single-trial recall task similar to the one described here. The recall scores were 66% for the 7-year-olds and 80% for the 11-year-olds. These values are almost identical to those obtained in both Guatemalan villages. The cluster indices were also comparable. The American 7-year-olds had a cluster ratio of .25; the San Marcos 5- and 6-year-olds had a ratio of .39.[1]

Recognition Memory

The cultural similarity in recall also holds for recognition memory. In a separate study, 5-, 8-, and 11-year-old children from Ladino villages in the East and from Cambridge, Massachusetts, were shown 60 pictures of objects—all of which were familiar to the Americans but some of which were unfamiliar to the Guatemalans. After 0-, 24-, or 48-hours delay, each child was shown 60 pairs of pictures, one of which was old and the other new, and was asked to decide which one he had seen. Although the 5- and 8-year-old Americans performed significantly better than the Guatemalans, there was no statistically significant cultural difference for

[1]The cluster index is the ratio of the number of pairs recalled to the product of the number of categories in the list times one less than the number of words in each category.

TABLE 2 MEAN PERCENTAGE OF CORRECT RESPONSES

	Americans			Guatemalans		
			Age			
Delay	5	8	11	5	8	11
0 hours	92.8	96.7	98.3	58.4	74.6	85.2
24 hours	86.7	95.6	96.7	55.8	71.0	87.0
48 hours	87.5	90.3	93.9	61.4	75.8	86.2

the 11-year-olds, whose scores ranged from 85% to 98% after 0-, 24-, or 48-hour delay (Kagan et al., 1973). (See Table 2.) The remarkably high scores of the American 5-year-olds have also been reported by Scott (1973).

A similar result was found on a recognition memory task for 32 photos of faces, balanced for sex, child versus adult, and Indian versus Caucasian, administered to 35 American and 38 San Marcos children 8–11 years of age. Each child initially inspected 32 chromatic photographs of faces, one at a time, in a self-placed procedure. Each child's recognition memory was tested by showing him 32 pairs of photographs (each pair was of the same sex, age, and ethnicity), one of which was old and the other new. The child had to state which photograph he had seen during the inspection phase. Although the American 8- and 9-year-olds performed slightly better than the Guatemalans (82% versus 70%), there was no significant cultural difference among the 10- and 11-year-olds (91% versus 87%). Moreover, there was no cultural difference at any age for the highest performance attained by a single child.[2] The favored interpretation of the poorer performance of the younger children in both recognition memory studies is that some of them did not completely understand the task and others did not activate the proper problem-solving strategies during the registration and retrieval phases of the task.

It appears that recall and recognition mem-

[2]These photographs were also used in an identical procedure with 12 Kipsigis-speaking 10- and 11-year-olds from a rural village in eastern Kenya. Despite the absence of any black faces in the set, the percentage of items recognized correctly was 82 for this group of African children.

ory are basic cognitive functions that seem to mature in a regular way in a natural environment. The cognitive retardation observed during the first year does not have any serious predictive validity for these two important aspects of cognitive functioning for children 10–11 years of age.

Perceptual Analysis

The Guatemalan children were also capable of solving difficult Embedded Figures Test items. The test consisted of 12 color drawings of familiar objects in which a triangle had been embedded as part of the object. The child had to locate the hidden triangle and place a black paper triangle so that it was congruent with the design of the drawing. The test was administered to rural Indian children from San Marcos, as well as to rural Indians living close to Guatemala City (labeled Indian$_1$ in Figure 3), the Ladino villages, and two groups from Guatemala City. (See Figure 3.)

The Guatemala City middle-class children had the highest scores and, except for San Marcos, the rural children, the poorest. The surprisingly competent performance of the San Marcos children is due, we believe, to the more friendly conditions of testing. This suggestion is affirmed by an independent study in which a special attempt was made to maximize rapport and comprehension of instructions with a group of rural isolated children before administering a large battery of tests. Although all test performances were not facilitated by this rapport-raising procedure, performance on the Embedded Figures Test was improved considerably. It is important to note that no 5- or 6-year-old was completely incapable of solving some of these problems. The village differences in mean score reflect the fact that the rural children had difficulty with three or four of the harder items. This was the first time that many rural children had ever seen a two-dimensional drawing, and most of the 5-, 6-, and 7-year-olds in San Marcos had had no opportunity to play with books, paper, pictures, or cray-

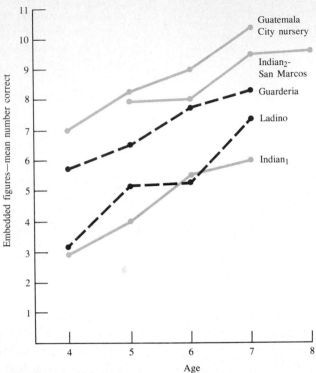

FIGURE 3   Mean number correct on the Embedded Figures Test.

ons. Nonetheless, these children solved seven or eight of the test items. Investigators who have suggested that prior experience with pictures is necessary for efficient analysis of two-dimensional information may have incorrectly misinterpreted failure to understand the requirements of the problem with a deficiency in cognitive competence. This competence seems to develop in the world of moving leaves, chickens, and water. As with recall and recognition memory, the performance of the San Marcos child was comparable to that of his age peer in a modern urban setting.

Perceptual Inference

The competence of the San Marcos children on the Embedded Figures Test is affirmed by their performance on a test administered only in San

Marcos and Cambridge and called Perceptual Inference. The children (60 American and 55 Guatemalan, 5–12 years of age) were shown a schematic drawing of an object and asked to guess what that object might be if the drawing were completed. The child was given a total of four clues for each 13 items, where each clue added more information. The child had to guess an object from an incomplete illustration, to make an inference from minimal information (see Figures 4 and 5).

There was no significant cultural difference for the children 7–12 years of age, although the American 5- and 6-year-olds did perform significantly better than the Indian children. In San Marcos, performance improved from 62% correct on one of the first two clues for the 5- and 6-year-olds to 77% correct for the 9–12-year-olds. The comparable changes for the American children were from 77% to 84% . (See Figure 6.)

---

[3]This conclusion holds for Embedded Figures Test performance, and not necessarily for the ability to detect three-dimensional perspective in two-dimensional drawings.

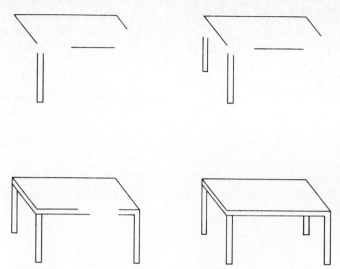

FIGURE 4   Sample item from the Perceptual Inference Test.

Familiarity with the test objects was critical for success. All of the San Marcos children had seen hats, fish, and corn, and these items were rarely missed. By contrast, many American children failed these items. No San Marcos child not attending school, and therefore unfamiliar with books, correctly guessed the book item, whereas most of those in school guessed it correctly. As with memory and perceptual analysis, the retardation seen during infancy did not predict comparable retardation in the ability of the 11-year-old to make difficult perceptual inferences.

Conceptual Inference

The San Marcos child also performed well on questions requiring conceptual inference. In this test, the child was told verbally three characteristics of an object and was required to guess the object. Some of the examples included: What has wings, eats chickens, and lives in a tree? What moves trees, cannot be seen, and makes one cold? What is made of wood, is used to carry things, and allows one to make journeys? There was improved performance with age; the 5- and 6-year-olds obtained an average

FIGURE 5   Sample item from the Perceptual Inference Test.

of 9 out of 14 correct, and the 11- and 12-year-olds obtained 12 out of 14 correct. The San Marcos child was capable of making moderately difficult inferences from both visual and verbal information.

DISCUSSION

This corpus of data implies that absolute retardation in the time of emergence of universal cognitive competences during infancy is not predictive of comparable deficits for memory, perceptual analysis, and inference during pre-adolescence. Although the rural Guatemalan infants were retarded with respect to activation of hypotheses, alertness, and onset of stranger anxiety and object permanence, the preadolescents' performance on the tests of perceptual analysis, perceptual inference, and recall and recognition memory were comparable to American middle-class norms. Infant retardation seems to be partially reversible and cognitive development during the early years and more resilient than had been supposed.

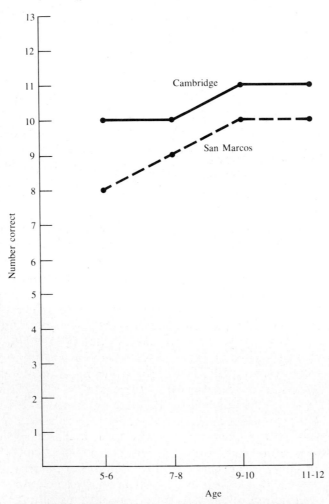

FIGURE 6   Number correct on the Perceptual Inference Test.

One potential objection to this conclusion is that the tests were too easy for the Guatemalan 11-year-olds and that is why cultural differences were absent. There are two comments that can be addressed to that issue. First, it is not intuitively reasonable to argue that the ability to remember 60 photographs of objects, classify an object from a few sketch lines, or detect the triangle hidden in a two-dimensional drawing is "easy" for children who rarely see photographs, pencils, crayons, or books. Second, we deliberately assessed cognitive functions that we believe all children should master by the time they are preadolescents. The fact that many 11-year-olds approached the ceiling on some tests is support for the basic premise of this article, namely, that infant retardation does not prevent a child from eventually developing basic cognitive competences.

This result is surprising if one believes that each child is born with a certain level of general intellectual competence that is stable from infancy through adulthood. If, on the contrary, one assumes that each stage of development is characterized by a different profile of specific competences and there is no necessary relation between early emergence of the capacities of infancy and level of attainment of the quite different abilities characteristic of childhood, then these results are more reasonable. There is no reason to assume that the caterpillar who metamorphoses a bit earlier than his kin is a better adapted or more efficient butterfly.

Consideration of why the rural Guatemalan children lagged behind the urban children on some tests during the period five through nine years of age comprises a second implication of these data. It will be recalled that on the embedded figures and recognition memory tests the performance of rural children was several years behind both the American and Guatemala City middle-class children. The differences were minimal for the object recall and perceptual inference tests. The approximately three-year lag in performance is paralleled by comparable differences between lower- and middle-class children in urban Western cities. For example, Bosco (1972) found that middle-class first and third graders were able to tolerate smaller interstimulus intervals in a backward masking procedure than lower-class children, but this difference had vanished among sixth-grade children. Similarly, Bakker (1971) compared good and poor readers from urban centers in Holland on a task that required operating simultaneously on two items of information in a temporal integration task. The poor readers performed less well than the good readers at ages six to eight, but were comparable to the good readers during the preadolescent years.

We interpret these results as indicating that the urban lower-class children, like the younger, rural Guatemalans, were not able to mobilize proper problem-solving strategies necessary for task solution, but achieved that level of competence by 11 years of age. Some of these strategies include focused attention, rehearsal of task information and instructions, awareness of and understanding the problem to be solved, maintenance of problem set, and the ability to remember critical information elements in the problem and to operate on that information. It is believed that these functions may emerge a little later in some groups of children than in others, but they are operative in all children by 11–12 years of age. In a recently completed study with Patricia Engle, we found that among rural Guatemalan children, 5 through 11 years of age, the rate of improvement in performance on three memory tasks (memory for numbers, memory for sentences, and auditory blending) was greatest between 9 and 11 years of age, whereas White (1970), using comparable data from American children, found that the greatest rate of improvement was between 5 and 7 years of age—a lag of about three years.

These data have implications for America's educational problems. There is a tendency to regard the poor test performances of economically impoverished, minority group 6-year-olds in the United States as indicative of a permanent and, perhaps, irreversible defect in intellectual ability—as a difference in quality of function rather than slower maturational rate. The Guatemalan data, together with those of Bosco and Bakker, suggest that children differ in the age at which basic cognitive competences emerge and that experiential factors influence the time of emergence. Economically disadvantaged American children and isolated rural Guatemalan children appear to be from one to three years behind middle-class children in demonstrating some of the problem-solving skills characteristic of Piaget's stage of concrete operations. But these competences eventually appear in sturdy form by age 10 or 11. The common practice of arbitrarily setting 7 years—the usual time of school entrance—as the age when children are to be classified as competent or incompetent confuses differences in maturational rate with permanent, qualitative differences in intellectual ability. This practice is as logical as classifying children as reproductively fertile or sterile depending on whether or not they have reached physiological puberty by their thirteenth birthday.

When educators note correctly that poor children tend to remain permanently behind middle-class children on intellectual and academic performance, they are referring to the relative retardation on the culturally specific skills of reading, mathematics, and language achievement described earlier. That relative retardation is the product of the rank ordering of scores on achievement and IQ tests. The fact that relative retardation on these abilities is stable from age five on does not mean that the relatively retarded children are not growing intellectually (when compared with themselves), often at the same rate as economically advantaged youngsters.

The suggestion that basic cognitive competences, in contrast to culturally specific ones, emerge at different times and that the child retains the capacity for actualization of his competence until a late age is not substantially different from the earlier conclusions of Dennis and Najarian (1957). Although the 49 infants 2–12 months of age living in poorly staffed Lebanese institutions were seriously retarded on the Cattell developmental scale (mean developmental quotient of 68 compared with a quotient of 102 for a comparison group), the 4½–6-year-olds who had resided in the same institution all their lives performed at a level comparable to American norms on a memory test (Knox Cubes) as well as on Porteus mazes and the Goodenough Draw-a-Man Test.

Of more direct relevance is Dennis's (1973) recent follow-up study of 16 children who were adopted out of the same Lebanese institution between 12 and 24 months of age—the period during which the San Marcos infant leaves the unstimulating environment of the dark hut—with an average developmental quotient of 50 on the Cattell Infant Scale. Even though the assessment of later intellectual ability was based on the culturally biased Stanford-Binet IQ test, the average IQ obtained when the children were between 4 and 12 years of age, was 101, and 13 of the 16 children had IQ scores of 90 or above.

Additional support for the inherent resiliency in human development comes from longitudinal information on two sisters who spent most of their infancy in a crib in a small bedroom with no toys.[4] The mother, who felt unable to care for her fourth child, restricted her to the room soon after birth and instructed her eight-year-old daughter to care for the child. One year later, another daughter was born, and she, too, was placed in a crib with the older sister. These two children only left the room to be fed and,

[4]The authors thank Meinhard Robinow for information on these girls.

according to the caretaker sister who is now a married woman in her twenties, the two infants spent about 23 hours of each day together in a barren crib. When the authorities were notified of this arrangement, the children were removed from the home and taken to a hospital when the younger was 2½ and the older 3½ years old. Medical records reveal that both children were malnourished, severely retarded in weight and height, and seriously retarded psychologically. After a month in the hospital, following considerable recovery, both sisters were placed in the care of a middle-class family who had several young children. The sisters have remained with that family for the last 12 years and regard the husband and wife as their parents. One of us (J. K.) tested the sisters five times when they were between 4 and 9 years of age, and recently interviewed and tested both of them over a two-day period when they were 14½ and 15½ years old.

The younger sister has performed consistently better than the older one over the last 10 years. The IQ scores of the younger girl have risen steadily from a Stanford-Binet IQ of 74 at age 4½ (after two years in the foster home) to a Wechsler Full Scale IQ of 88 at age 14. The older girl's scores have also improved, but less dramatically, from a Stanford-Binet IQ of 59 at age 5 to a Wechsler IQ of 72 at age 15. The author also administered a lengthy battery of tests, some of which were discussed earlier. On the Perceptual Inference Test, the percentage correct was 85 for the younger sister and 61 for the older sister. On the Recognition Memory for Photographs, the percentages were 94 for both. On the Embedded Figures Test, the percentages were 92 and 100, and on the recall memory for objects, the percentages were 92 and 83 for the younger and older sister, respectively. Moreover, the interpersonal behavior of both girls was in no way different from that of the average rural Ohio adolescent—a group the author came to know well after seven years of work in the area. Although there is some ambi-

guity surrounding the competence of the older girl, the younger one performs at an average level on a wide range of tests of cognitive functioning, despite 2½ years of serious isolation.

These data, together with the poor predictive relation between scores on infant developmental tests and later assessments of intellectual functioning, strengthen the conclusion that environmentally produced retardation during the first year or two of life appears to be reversible. The importance of the Guatemalan data derives from the fact that the San Marcos 11-year-olds performed so well, considering the homogeneity and isolation of their childhood environment. Additionally, there is a stronger feeling now than there was in 1957 that environmentally produced retardation during the first two years may be irreversible, even though the empirical basis for that belief is no firmer in 1972 than it was in 1957.

More dramatic support for the notion that psychological development is malleable comes from recent experimental studies with animals. Several years ago Harlow's group demonstrated that although monkeys reared in isolation for the first six months displayed abnormal and often bizarre social behaviors, they could, if the experimenter were patient, solve the complex learning problems normally administered to feralborn monkeys. The prolonged isolation did not destroy their cognitive competence (Harlow, Schiltz, & Harlow, 1969). More recently, Suomi and Harlow (1972) have shown that even the stereotyped and bizarre social behavior shown by six-month-old isolates can be altered by placing them with female monkeys three months younger than themselves over a 26-week therapeutic period. "By the end of the therapy period the behavioral levels were virtually indistinguishable from those of the socially competent therapist monkeys [Suomi & Harlow, 1972, p. 491]."

This resiliency has also been demonstrated for infant mice (Cairns & Nakelski, 1971) who experienced an initial 10 weeks of isolation from other animals. Compared with group-reared mice of the same strain, the isolated subjects were hyperreactive to other mice, displaying both extreme withdrawal and extreme aggressiveness. These investigators also attempted rehabilitation of the isolates by placing them with groups of mice for an additional 10 weeks, however, after which their behavior was indistinguishable from animals that had never been isolated.

> By the seventieth day after interchange, the effects of group therapy were complete, and animals that had been isolated for one hundred days following weaning were indistinguishable from animals that had never been isolated [Cairns & Nakelski, 1971, p. 363.].

These dramatic alterations in molar behavior are in accord with replicated reports of recovery of visual function in monkeys and cats deprived of patterned light soon after birth (Baxter, 1966; Chow & Stewart, 1972; Wilson & Riesen, 1966). Kittens deprived of light for one year recovered basic visual functions after only 10 days in the experimenter's home (Baxter, 1966); kittens who had one or both eyes sutured for close to two years were able to learn pattern discriminations with the deprived eye only after moderate training (Chow & Stewart, 1972).

If the extreme behavioral and perceptual sequelae of isolation in monkeys, cats, and mice can be altered by such brief periods of rehabilitative experience, it is not difficult to believe that the San Marcos infant is capable of as dramatic a recovery over a period of nine years. These data do not indicate the impotence of early environments, but rather the potency of the environment in which the organism is functioning. There is no question that early experience seriously affects kittens, monkeys, and children. If the first environment does not permit the full actualization of psychological competences, the child will function below his abil-ity as long as he remains in that context. But if he is transferred to an environment that presents greater variety and requires more accommodations, he seems more capable of exploiting that experience and repairing the damage wrought by the first environment than some theorists have implied.

These conclusions do not imply that intervention or rehabilitation efforts with poor American or minority group preschool children are of no value. Unlike San Marcos, where children are assigned adult responsibilities when they are strong and alert enough to assume them, rather than at a fixed age, American children live in a severely age graded system, in which children are continually rank ordered. Hence, if a poor four-year-old falls behind a middle-class four-year-old on a culturally significant skill, like knowledge of letters or numbers, he may never catch up with the child who was advanced and is likely to be placed in a special educational category. Hence, American parents must be concerned with the early psychological growth of their children. We live in a society in which the relative retardation of a four-year-old seriously influences his future opportunities because we have made relative retardation functionally synonymous with absolute retardation. This is not true in subsistence farming communities like San Marcos.

These data suggest that exploration of the new and the construction of objects or ideas from some prior schematic blueprint must be inherent properties of the mind. The idea that the child carries with him at all times the essential mental competence to understand the new in some terms and to make a personal contribution to each new encounter is only original in our time. Despite the current popularity of Kant and Piaget, the overwhelming prejudice of Western psychologists is that higher order cognitive competences and personality factors are molded completely by the environment. Locke's image of an unmarked tablet on which sensation played its patterned melody has a parallel in Darwin's failure to realize, until late in his life, that the organism made a contribution to his own evolution. Darwin was troubled by the fact that the same climate on different islands in the Galapagos produced different forms of the same species. Since he believed that climatic variation was the dynamic agent in evolution he was baffled. He did not appreciate that the gene was the organism's contributions to his own alteration. Western psychologists have been blocked by the same prejudice that prevented young Darwin from solving his riddle. From Locke to Skinner we have viewed the perfectibility of man as vulnerable to the vicissitudes of the objects and people who block, praise, or push him, and resisted giving the child any compass on his own. The mind, like the nucleus of a cell, has a plan for growth and can transduce a new flower, an odd pain, or a stranger's unexpected smile into a form that is comprehensible. This process is accomplished through wedding cognitive structures to selective attention, activation of hypotheses, assimilation, and accommodation. The purpose of these processes is to convert an alerting unfamiliar event, incompletely understood, to a recognized variation on an existing familiar structure. This is accomplished through the detection of the dimensions of the event that bear a relation to existing schemata and the subsequent incorporation of the total event into the older structure.

We need not speak in this psychological mastery, for neither walking nor breathing is performed in order to experience happiness. These properties of the motor or autonomic systems occur because each physiological system or organ naturally exercises its primary function. The child explores the unfamiliar and attempts to match his ideas and actions to some previously acquired representations because these are basic properties of the mind. The child has no choice.

The San Marcos child knows much less than the American about planes, computers, cars, and the many hundreds of other phenomena that are familiar to the Western youngster, and he is a little slower in developing some of the basic cognitive competences of our species. But neither appreciation of these events nor the earlier cognitive maturation is necessary for a successful journey to adulthood in San Marcos. The American child knows far less about how to make canoes, rope, tortillas, or how to burn an old milpa in preparation for June planting. Each knows what is necessary, each assimilates the cognitive conflicts that are presented to him, and each seems to have the potential to display more talent than his environment demands of him. There are few dumb children in the world if one classifies them from the perspective of the community of adaptation, but millions of dumb children if one classifies them from the perspective of another society.

REFERENCES

Appel, L. F., Cooper, R. G., McCarrell, N., Knight, J. S., Yussen, S. R., & Flavell, J. H. The developmental acquisition of the distinction between perceiving and memory. Unpublished manuscript, University of Minnesota at Minneapolis, 1971.

Bakker, D. J. *Temporal order in disturbed reading.* Rotterdam: Rotterdam University Press, 1972.

Baxter, B. L. Effect of visual deprivation during postnatal maturation on the electroencephalogram of the cat. *Experimental Neurology,* 1966, 14, 224–237.

Bosco, J. The visual information processing speed of lower middle class children. *Child Development,* 1972, 43, 1418–1422.

Cairns, R. B., & Nakelski, J. S. On fighting in mice: Ontogenetic and experiental determinants. *Journal of Comparative and Physiological Psychology,* 1971, 74, 354–364.

Carmichael, L. The development of behavior in vertebrates experimentally removed from the influence of external stimulation. *Psychological Review,* 1926, 33, 51–58.

Chow, K. L., & Stewart, D. L. Reversal of structural and functional effects of longterm visual deprivation in cats. *Experimental Neurology,* 1972, 34, 409–433.

Cohen, L. B., Gelber, E. R., & Lazar, M. A. Infant habituation and generalization to differing degrees of novelty. *Journal of Experimental Child Psychology,* 1971, 11, 379–389.

Cole, M., Gay, J., Glick, J. A., & Sharp, D. W. *The cultural context of learning and thinking.* New York: Basic Books, 1971.

Dennis, W. *Children of the Crèche.* New York: Appleton-Century-Crofts, 1973.

Dennis, W., & Najarian, P. Infant development under environmental handicap. *Psychological monographs,* 1957, 71(7, Whole No. 436).

Harlow, H. F., Schiltz, K. A., & Harlow, M. K. The effects of social isolation on the learning performance of rhesus monkeys. In C. R. Carpenter (Ed.), *Proceedings of the Second International Congress of Primatology.* Vol. 1. New York: Karger, 1969.

Kagan, J. *Change and continuity in infancy.* New York: Wiley, 1971.

Kagan, J. Do infants think? *Scientific American,* 1972, 226(3), 74–82.

Kagan, J., Klein, R. E., Haith, M. M., & Morrison, F. J. Memory and meaning in two cultures. *Child Development,* 1973, 44, 221–223.

Kagan, J., & Moss, H. A., *Birth to maturity.* New York: Wiley, 1962.

Kessen, W., Haith, M. M., & Salapatek, B. H. Human infancy: A bibliography and guide. In P. H. Mussen (Ed.), *Carmichael's manual of child psychology.* (3rd ed.) Vol. 1. New York: Wiley, 1970.

Konner, M. J. Development among the Bushmen of Botswana. Unpublished doctoral dissertation, Harvard University, 1973.

Lacey, J. I. Somatic response patterning in stress: Some revisions of activation theory. In M. H. Appley & R. Trumbull (Eds.), *Psychological stress: Issues in research.* New York: Appleton-Century-Crofts, 1967.

Lewis, M., & Freedle, R. *Mother-infant dyad: The cradle of meaning.* (Research bulletin RB72-22) Princeton, N.J.: Educational Testing Service, 1972.

Lewis, M., Goldberg, S., & Campbell, H. A developmental study of learning within the first three years of life: Response decrement to a redundant signal. *Monograph of the Society for Research in Child Development,* 1970, 34 (No. 133).

McGraw, M. B. *Growth: A study of Johnny and Jimmy.* New York: Appleton-Century, 1935.

Pease, D., Wolins, L., & Stockdale, D. F. Relationship and prediction of infant tests. *Journal of Genetic Psychology,* 1973, 122, 31–35.

Scott, M. S. The absence of interference effects in pre-school children's picture recognition. *Journal of Genetic Psychology,* 1973, 122, 121–126.

Sellers, M. J., Klein, R. E., Kagan, J., & Minton, C. Developmental determinants of attention: A cross-cultural replication. *Developmental Psychology,* 1972, 6, 185.

Suomi, S. J., & Harlow, H. F. Social rehabilitation of isolate reared monkeys. *Developmental Psychology,* 1972, 6, 487–496.

Van Hover, K. I. S. A developmental study of three components of attention. Unpublished doctoral dissertation, Harvard University, 1971.

White, S. H. Some general outlines of the matrix of developmental changes between 5 and 7 years. *Bulletin of the Orton Society,* 1970, 21, 41–57.

Wilson, P. D., & Riesen, A. H. Visual development in rhesus monkeys neonatally deprived of patterned light. *Journal of Comparative and Physiological Psychology,* 1966, 61, 87–95.

CHAPTER 4

EMOTIONAL DEVELOPMENT

The development of emotions in children has puzzled and fascinated investigators since Darwin published his early attempts to understand emotions in his book, *The Expression of Emotions in Man and Animals*. Over a century later, this topic is still receiving a great deal of attention. When and why do babies smile? What causes crying and laughter? Why do infants and children prefer some individuals over others or become "attached" to particular people? Why are we afraid of some things and some people? How can children be helped to overcome their fears? The articles in this section provide some tentative answers to these classic questions about children's emotional development. The development of attachment between the infant and mother is one of the most important social-emotional landmarks in infancy. As Crockenberg shows in the opening article, infant temperament as well as maternal responsiveness can affect the quality of the infant-mother emotional bond. Consistent with current views that biological differences such as infant temperament can be modified by social conditions, Crockenberg shows that the availability of social support increases the likelihood that mothers with irritable babies will develop healthy emotional relationships.

In the next article, Gunnar-VonGnechten provides impressive evidence that the ability to control a fearful event or object is an important determinant of a child's emotional reaction. If children can control the event, they respond with positive emotions; if they cannot control it, they are more likely to show a negative emotional response such as fear. The degree of control, then, is one of the important factors that determine our reactions to objects and people in our environment.

Another determinant of how children react emotionally is the nature of the information available from other people. As Sorce and his colleagues show, infants often seek information from others (e.g., their mothers) when they are uncertain about an event or a situation. Moreover the research shows that infants can use emotional expressions of others to guide their behavior in uncertain situations.

In the final article, Melamed and Siegel show how children react to medical stressors such as visits to a physician or dentist. Using these occurrences as windows for understanding the development of fear and anxiety, the authors suggest a variety of factors such as biological influences, the perceived degree of control, the nature of the mother-child relationship, and their prior experience with the stressor may predispose a child to high levels of upset during stressful experiences. Finally, Melamed and Siegel suggest ways of overcoming fears, such as exposure to fearless models. They also maintain that new and more effective ways of changing maladaptive emotional reactions can be developed by isolating how fear and anxiety develop.

READING 14

Infant Irritability, Mother Responsiveness, and Social Support Influences on the Security of Infant-Mother Attachment

Susan B. Crockenberg

INTRODUCTION

The quality of the infant-mother attachment has been defined in terms of the infant's ability to use the mother as a secure base from which to explore and as a comfort in times of distress (Ainsworth, Blehar, Waters, & Wall 1978; Sroufe & Waters 1977). Securely attached infants are confident of, insecurely attached infants anxious about their mothers' availability and responsiveness. These feelings of confidence and anxiety are reflected in their reactions to separation and in their interaction with the environment. Evidence is accumulating also that there are long-term effects of insecure attachments during the first year (Lieberman 1977; Matas, Arend, & Sroufe 1978; Waters, Wippman, & Sroufe 1979). In comparison with securely attached infants, those insecurely or anxiously attached are less competent and less sympathetic in interaction with their peers and less effective in eliciting and accepting help in problem-solving situations. In view of the far-reaching significance of the infant-mother attachment, the development of secure attachments is an issue of considerable theoretical and social import.

Conditions Affecting Attachment

Mother-Infant Interaction There is empirical as well as theoretical support for the view that the quality of infant-mother attachment is a product of the ongoing mother-infant interaction (Ainsworth et al. 1978). More specifically, infants with mothers responsive to their cues during the first few months and throughout the first year of life tend to develop secure attachments. Mothers of securely attached infants are more responsive to their infants' cries, hold their babies more tenderly and carefully, pace the interaction contingently during face-to-face interaction, and exhibit greater sensitivity in initiating and terminating feeding. Infants appear to learn what to expect from their world through their experiences with their primary caretaker. When those experiences include sensitivity and responsiveness to their cues, infants develop expectations that their caretakers will continue in the same fashion. Hence, their attachments are considered secure.

Despite a growing recognition that interaction is a reciprocal process involving both mother and infant (Sameroff 1975; Sander 1975), current research has focused almost exclusively on the mother's behavior as the precipitating event. Little attention has been given the role infant characteristics may play either in eliciting particular patterns of interaction or in determining the effect of certain mother behaviors on subsequent development.

Infant Characteristics Among others, Rutter (1979) has insisted that the infant's temperament—some organismic quality of infant functioning—affects the infant-mother attachment. If the infant is viewed as an active participant in the interaction, the infant's contribution to the evolving quality of the relationship must perforce follow. Moreover, there is evidence that infant temperamental differences are associated with the development of psychiatric disorders (Graham, Rutter, & George 1973; Thomas, Chess, & Birch 1968). Apparently the infants' characteristics either elicit maladaptive mothering (Rutter 1978) or influence the infant's response to that experience.

An issue in assessing the contribution an infant makes to the relationship arises from the rapid changes that occur during infancy due to maturation and interaction. Thus, it makes sense to examine infant characteristics neonatally and independently of the mother. The Neonatal Behavioral Assessment Scale (NBAS) (Brazelton 1973) provides such an opportunity.

One recent study (Waters, Vaughn, & Egeland 1980) administered the NBAS to 100 economically disadvantaged infants who were subsequently observed in the Ainsworth and Wittig (1969) strange-situation procedure at 1 year. Infants later classified as insecurely attached/resistant had shown signs of unresponsiveness, motor immaturity, and problems with physiological regulation. The researchers note that while these infant characteristics may not directly cause the anxious attachment, they may influence the mother and thereby the attachment relationship.

Social Context   Just as the infant's contribution to his own development must be viewed in conjunction with his mother's behavior, both occur in a broader social context (Bronfenbrenner 1979). While the context may be defined at a variety of levels, the most immediate contextual variable is the person's social support network, those people who engage in activities and exchanges of an affective and/or material nature with the individual (Cochran & Brassard 1979; Lewis & Weinraub 1976). Evidence links the adequacy of social support to amelioration of developmental crises and to the attenuation of stress effects (Gottlieb, Note 1) including the stressful life event of childbirth. Nuckolls, Cassel, and Kaplan (1972) related measures of stress to complications in pregnancy. The results revealed that for women with high levels of stress, support from kin and marital solidarity were associated with lower complication rates. Similarly, Gottlieb and Carveth (Note 2) reported that social support in the

form of frequent contacts with their spouses and physicians was the strongest predictor of low perceived stress of mothers during the first several weeks of life at home with a newborn.

It is reasonable, then, to propose that availability of social support will facilitate responsive mothering, particularly under stressful conditions, and thereby encourage secure infant-mother attachment. As Cochran and Brassard (1979) point out, however, the network may also affect the child directly, through the contact of the child with members of the network.

In summary, the quality of the infant-mother attachment appears to evolve through the transaction of mother and infant within the immediate social context. This study examines the effect of infant characteristics and mother behavior on the development of secure infant-mother attachment, and it assesses the influence of the mother's social support on her responsiveness to her baby and on the child's subsequent attachment. Assuming that an irritable infant constitutes a stress for the mother, the hypothesis is that social support will be most related to secure attachment for irritable infants.

METHOD

Forty-six Caucasian and two Asian-American mothers[1] and infants participated in the study during the first year of their child's life. All of the mothers had completed high school, 29 had 2 years of college or more. When they joined the study, all families were intact, with fathers either employed or attending college (N = 4). One-half of the families, excluding the four student families, were middle class as indicated by their placement in the first, second, and third levels of Hollingshead's (1965) occupational

---

[1]Of an original 56 infant-mother pairs, seven moved prior to 12 months and one strange-situation videotape was considered unscorable. The remaining 48 mothers agreed to participate in the collection of attachment data.

code, the remaining one-half were working class as indicated by their placement in the fourth, fifth, sixth, or seventh levels.

There were 31 firstborn and 17 second-born infants (25 males and 23 females). All were carried to term, above the tenth percentile for gestational growth, with no physical anomalies. There were 44 vaginal and four C-section deliveries. All mothers and infants were in good physical condition when they left the hospital and thus were considered low risk.

Procedures

Neonatal Behavioral Assessment Examination (NBAS) Instructions for administering and scoring the exam were followed exactly as described in Brazelton (1973), except that the pinprick aversive stimulus was eliminated, thereby reducing the maximum rating to 8 for two irritability items. The assessments were made in the infant's homes on the fifth and tenth days following birth. Scores from the peak of excitement, rapidity of buildup, and irritability items were combined in an irritability cluster identified by Kaye (1978) and averaged across the two administrations. For dichotomous analyses, infants whose irritability scores were 6.00 or greater were considered *high irritable;* those with scores below 6.00 were considered *low irritable.* An infant whose average score was 6.00 or greater was, at the minimum, consistently above the median score of 5 (4.5 on the rapidity of buildup and irritability items) for all irritability items over both administrations.

Mother-Infant Observations   Four-hour home visits, including approximately 3½ hours of observation time, were made when infants were 3 months old. A 10-sec-observe, 10-sec-record-time sampling schedule was used, with both mother and infant behavior recorded in each interval. The measure of maternal responsiveness employed in this study was the inverse of the average number of seconds before a mother responded to her infant's distress sig-

nals. For dichotomous analyses, a median split was employed. *Low-responsive* mothers were those below the median; *high-responsive* mothers were those above the median.

Social Support Interview At the 3-month observation mothers were interviewed about their sources of support and stress. They were asked who helped them when they needed it, who they talked to when they were concerned about the baby, and whether they felt they received as much (help/support) as they expected. If a mother did not volunteer the information, she was specifically asked about the help/support provided by husband, extended family, other children, friends and neighbors, and professionals. Mothers were asked also if they had experienced any stresses during those early months.

Social support was an assessment of the affective and material assistance experienced by the mother in her mother role, relative to the stresses experienced by her. This explicitly subjective approach was adopted on the assumption that the impact of an event depends on how that event is perceived and experienced by the individual (Bronfenbrenner 1979; Lewin 1951; Mead 1934). Low social support might have little impact on mothers with few additional stresses in their lives, while moderate social support might have a tremendous impact if it were coupled with many stresses. Thus, a relational measure of social support which reflected the functional adequacy of support to the needs of specific mothers was considered preferable to a simple measure of available support. Lowenthal, Thurner, and Chiriboga's (1975) finding that close interpersonal relationships differentiated individuals challenged or overwhelmed by multiple stresses lends credence to this approach.

Social support from three sources—father, older children in the family, and others (extended family, neighbors, friends, professionals)—was rated from the interview by a research assistant unfamiliar with the infant and mother data and independently by the principal investigator. Disagreements in ratings were discussed until unambiguous criteria were defined and the two raters agreed on the judgment. Support ratings for each of the three sources ranged from positive ($+1$) to negative (-1) with a neutral (0) category for instances which could not be otherwise classified. The number of stresses were also determined. An event was considered a stress if it appeared to be experienced as such by the mother. Thus, returning to work during the first 3 months would be considered a stress only if the mother indicated that this event was stressful or problematic in some way. Stresses included serious illness of the baby or other family member, loss of employment, a move to another house, other pressing responsibilities on the mother. A measure of *social support* was computed by subtracting the number of stresses from the combined support ratings; individual scores ranged from -4 to $+3$. For dichotomous analyses, scores reflecting support greater than stress ($+1$ to $+3$) were considered *high support;* scores reflecting support less than or equal to stress (-4 to and including 0 scores) were considered *low support*.

The Strange Situation Each infant and mother were seen in the Ainsworth and Wittig (1969) strange situation near the infant's first birthday.[2] The procedure lasts approximately half an hour and consists of eight episodes involving the mother, the baby, and a stranger. The stranger and the mother alternately leave and return in a standard order. Each strange situation was videotaped and all ratings were based on those records. Ratings and classifica-

tion procedures were based on Ainsworth et al. (1978) and Sroufe and Waters (1977). Proximity seeking, contact maintaining, avoidance, and resistance to the mother and crying during the reunion episodes (5 and 8) were rated. Each infant was assigned to one of three attachment categories: securely attached, anxiously attached/avoidant, anxiously attached/resistant. Reliability was established using tapes provided by Waters (Note 3). Ratings of proximity seeking, contact maintaining, resistance, and avoidance in the reunion episodes corresponded with those of Waters in 74%–94% of the ratings, mean agreement = .83. Subsequent reliability between an experienced rater and each of two independent raters was 85% and 87%, respectively, based on the scoring of the reunion episodes in five pilot tapes. Agreement was 100% for the A, B, and C classifications on those tapes. One of the two raters scored all tapes; questions were resolved by consensus between raters on 24 of the tapes.

Using this procedure, 71% (34) of the infants were classified as securely attached, 10% (5) as anxiously attached/avoidant, and 19% (9) as anxiously attached/resistant.

RESULTS

To assess the relative contribution of infant temperament, maternal responsiveness, and social support to attachment measures, hierarchical multiple-regression analyses were employed. Parity was entered first as a potential covariate, followed by neonatal irritability. Maternal responsiveness and social support were then entered in two orders: with responsiveness preceding social support and vice versa, with support preceding responsiveness.

Table 1 presents the intercorrelations of predictor variables. Neonatal irritability was associated with second born status and with responsiveness. Support and responsiveness were uncorrelated, although that relationship approached significance. Table 2 presents the

---

[2]Forty-three infants were videotaped between 12 and 13 months of age. Three infants were initially videotaped at that time but were retaped at approximately 15 months because of difficulty in scoring their strange-situation behavior. Two infants were videotaped at 10½ and 13½ months, respectively, due to moves and illness.

TABLE 1 INTERCORRELATIONS OF PREDICTOR VARIABLES

	Irritability	Responsiveness	Social support
Parity	.28*	.03	—.05
Irritability		+.29*	—.07
Responsiveness			+.25

*p < .05.

intercorrelations of outcome attachment measures. Consistent with theoretical expectations and previous research, proximity seeking and contact maintaining correlated positively with each other, negatively with avoidance and positively with resistance and crying. Resistance and avoidance were themselves uncorrelated, and correlated differently with crying. In view of the high correlations between certain variables and considering their conceptual similarity, only proximity seeking, resistance, and avoidance were subsequently analyzed.

Social support significantly predicted both avoidance and resistance after maternal responsiveness was extracted from the equations. Mothers with high social support had less resistant, less avoidant babies. In contrast, maternal responsiveness predicted proximity seeking, predicted resistance only when it was extracted prior to social support, and failed to predict avoidance. Responsive mothers had babies who showed less proximity seeking and less resistance.

Separate analyses were then calculated for those infants high and low in irritability to investigate the specific question of whether low support would have a greater impact on high irritable infants. Low social support was associated with high resistance and high avoidance only for high irritable infants.

Security of Attachment The relationships between the predictor variables and security of attachment were also investigated. Table 3 presents the frequencies of secure and insecure infants in each irritability/support subgroup. Only the relationship between social support and security of attachment was significant, $p = .003$, as 11 of the 14 anxious infants came from families with low social support. Subsequent analyses indicated that low social support was associated with anxious attachment only in the high irritable group, $p = .001$, and that high irritability was associated with anxious attachment only for the low social support group, $p = .01$. Similarly, in examining the relationship between maternal responsiveness and security of attachment, it was again found that the two were related only when social support was also low, $p = .02$. Of the 11 anxiously attached infants in the low support group, 10 had unresponsive mothers.

DISCUSSION

The adequacy of the mother's social support is clearly and consistently associated with the security of the infant-mother attachment. Low

TABLE 2 INTERCORRELATIONS OF INFANT ATTACHMENT BEHAVIORS IN THE REUNION EPISODES

	Contact maintaining	Resistance	Avoidance	Crying
Proximity seeking	.69***	.29*	—.37**	.41**
Contact maintaining		.50***	—.53***	.60***
Resistance			.02	.62***
Avoidance				—.24*

*p < .05

**p < .01

***p < .001.

TABLE 3   FREQUENCY OF SECURELY AND INSECURELY ATTACHED INFANTS IN
SOCIAL SUPPORT / IRRITABILITY SUBGROUPS

	High irritability		Low irritability	
	Low support	High support	Low support	High support
Securely attached	2	12	7	13
Anxiously attached[a]	9	1	2	2

[a]Ten of the anxiously attached infants are male, four are female.

social support was associated with high resistance, high avoidance, and with anxious attachment. Moreover, that support had its strongest effect on the irritable babies and their mothers suggests that the availability of social support is particularly critical when the family is under particular stress. This is consistent with the Nuckolls et al. (1972) and Gottlieb and Carveth (Note 2) studies cited earlier, and with Vaughn, Egeland, Sroufe and Waters's (1979) finding that shifts from secure to anxious attachment were associated with high stress in the mother's life. The apparent impact of support and stress on infants and mothers suggests again the necessity of considering the social context when attempts are made to understand development (Bronfenbrenner 1979).

It is noteworthy in contrast that less irritable infants appear somewhat impervious to the low support environments which disrupt the development of their more irritable peers. Like Rutter's (1978) temperamentally easy children who escaped the flak in discordant and quarrelsome homes, the easy babies in this study were unlikely to develop insecure attachments even when potentially unfavorable social milieus existed.

What accounts for their apparent invulnerability? Was maternal behavior toward the child unaffected by the lack of social support, or did the less irritable children simply exhibit different, more developmentally appropriate reactions to unresponsive mothering? Some of both seems to have occurred. Four low-irritable infants in the low support group had unresponsive mothers, yet they achieved secure attachments. Apparently these infants were unaffected by

their mothers' behavior by virtue of their own easy temperaments. One may speculate that when those mothers finally did respond to their infants' distress signals, the infants were able to reorganize quickly (as evidenced by the rapid calming of initially low irritable infants [Crockenberg & Smith, Note 4]) and to reenter an alert state more conducive to interaction (Dunn 1977).

The other low support mothers were moderately responsive to their less irritable infants. It is tempting to conclude, therefore, that those children simply did not bear the brunt of their mother's lack of social support. There is no doubt that these mothers felt stressed. One mother was frantic caring for an injured husband and feeding a sick cat with an eyedropper, yet she managed to respond appropriately to her baby. Possibly the mothers were "supercopers," exceptionally mature women who experienced stress but did not allow their feelings to affect their mothering. Alternately, the low irritability of the infants may have buffered them against a potentially inhospitable environment. Because they were easygoing they demanded little of their mothers. They cried infrequently and calmed quickly during the early months. It may have been easier for these stressed women to mother appropriately because appropriate mothering required relatively little.

Beyond the question of the infant's contribution to her own invulnerability, the process by which social support affects development is also at issue. As Cochran and Brassard (1979) have indicated, social networks may affect a child directly, or indirectly through the mediating influ ence of the parent. It makes intuitive sense that mothers with social support are less harried, feel less overwhelmed, have fewer competing demands on their time, and as a consequence are more available to their babies. The link between a mother's support and her responsiveness to her infant is also congruent with a general theory of altruistic behavior which posits that one is more aware of and responsive to the needs of others when one's own needs are met (Berkowitz 1972; Hoffman 1976). Findings from this study support the view that social support affects security of attachment in part through a mother's unresponsiveness: (1) The negative correlation between responsiveness and resistance is no longer significant when support is partialed prior to responsiveness; and (2) 10 of the 11 anxiously attached infants in the low support group also had unresponsive mothers. When these data are considered in conjunction with the nonsignificant correlation between support and responsiveness, it seems unlikely that a general unresponsiveness to others elicited the low support, although this possibility remains to be investigated.

Social support may have had a direct impact on the infants also. Not only did support continue to significantly predict resistance and avoidance after responsiveness was extracted from the regression, but maternal unresponsiveness was associated with anxious attachment only when support was low. Support available to the mothers in this study was frequently available to the babies as well. Grandparents provided mothers with emotional support and eager babysitters; they provided their grandchildren with doting care. In some cases grandparents were considerably more responsive than were the babies' own mothers, leading several mothers to complain that the grandparents were spoiling their children. Similarly, fathers were sometimes especially responsive to their infants. One mother described her husband as the "softie" since he couldn't bear to let the baby cry. Occasionally it was an older sibling who adopted the nurturing role

toward the baby. Like children buffered from the effects of a psychologically disturbed mother through strong, positive relationships with their father (Hetherington, Cox, & Cox 1979) or from family strife and instability through the continuity and support of grandparents (Werner & Smith, Note 5), the infants with unresponsive mothers may have been buffered by exceptionally involved grandparents, fathers, and even siblings.

The possibility that responsiveness in a person other than the mother facilitates security in the strange situation raises additional theoretical and methodological issues, however. Why should an infant feel secure with an unresponsive mother simply because another caretaker who is not present is responsive? Can we assume that an infant's security in the strange situation reflects or is generalized from that other secure attachment? An explanation of such cases may lie in the *intensity* of a child's attachment to his mother. If the attachment is low in intensity, separation in the strange situation may fail to elicit distress and that situation may therefore constitute an inappropriate context for assessing the quality of attachment. This explanation is consistent with: (1) The view that security of attachment must be inferred from behavior in a context that activates the security system (Sroufe & Waters 1977); and (2) the number of infants who show little or no distress at separation and relatively little interest in contact when their mothers are present. In the absence of experienced stress the infant may not exhibit the other behaviors (avoidance, depressed exploration) which would allow discrimination between a comfort that comes from security and a comfort born of psychological distance. One may speculate that the availability of an alternative, responsive caretaker allows the child to remain emotionally uninvolved with an unresponsive mother so that her unresponsiveness has little impact on the child's everyday functioning.

Worth noting is the absence of relationship between responsiveness and avoidance in contrast to the negative correlation between responsiveness and resistance. This juxtaposition of findings suggests that examination of other qualitative aspects of the mother-infant interaction may be necessary to explain the avoidant behavior exhibited by some infants (Tracy, Farish, & Bretherton, Note 6).

The transaction between infant and environment is well illustrated in the present study. Irritable infants growing up in contexts characterized by low support for their mothers experience less responsive mothering. Under those conditions infants developed insecure attachments. Unresponsive mothering does indeed appear to be one mechanism through which a child's trust is undermined and his attachment to his mother rendered anxious. But whether a mother behaves unresponsively appears to be influenced by the infant's irritability and her attitudes (Crockenberg & Smith, Note 4) as well as by the social support available to her as a mother. Further, the impact of her unresponsiveness seems to depend similarly on the infant's irritability and on his access to someone who is responsive to his needs (social support).

In sum, although single variables predict quality of attachment, multiple indices are necessary if we are to understand the development of secure attachments and accurately identify infants at risk for later attachment difficulties. In this study, as in others (Sigman, Cohen, & Forsythe 1980; Werner & Smith, Note 5), children who are irritable or in other ways less rewarding/more demanding of their parents are at risk for later developmental difficulty only if their environments are deficient in meeting their special needs.

REFERENCE NOTES

1 Gottlieb, B. H. The primary group as supportive milieu: applications to community psychology. In Toward an understanding of natural helping systems. Symposium presented at the meeting of the American Psychological Association, San Francisco, August 1977.

2. Gottlieb, B. H., & Carveth, W. B. The role of primary group support in mediating stress: an empirical study of new mothers. Paper presented at the meeting of the Canadian Psychological Association, Vancouver, 1977.
3. Waters, E. Personal communication, July 1978.
4. Crockenberg, S. B., & Smith, P. Antecedents of mother-infant interaction and infant temperament in the first three months of life. Paper submitted for publication, 1980.
5. Werner, E., & Smith, R. Vulnerable, but invincible: a longitudinal study of resilient children and youth. Final Report submitted to the Foundation for Child Development, 1979.
6. Tracy, R.; Farish, G.; & Bretherton, I. Exploration as related to infant-mother attachment in one-year-olds. Paper presented at the International Conference on Infant Studies, New Haven, Conn., April 1980.

REFERENCES

Ainsworth, M. D.; Blehar, M. C.; Waters, E.; & Wall, S. *Patterns of attachment*. Hillsdale, N.J.: Erlbaum, 1978.

Ainsworth, M., & Wittig, B. Attachment and exploratory behavior of one-year-olds in a strange situation. In B. Foss (Ed.), *Determinants of infant behavior*. Vol. 4, New York: Barnes & Noble, 1969.

Berkowitz, L. Social norms, feelings, and other factors affecting helping and altruism. In L. Berkowitz (Ed.), *Advances in experimental social psychology*. Vol. 6. New York: Academic Press, 1972.

Brazelton, T. *Neonatal Behavioral Assessment Scale*. Philadelphia: Lippincott, 1973.

Bronfenbrenner, U. *The ecology of human development*. Cambridge, Mass.: Harvard University Press, 1979.

Cochran, M. M., & Brassard, J. A. Child development and personal social networks. *Child Development*, 1979, **50**(3), 601–616.

Dunn, J. *Distress and comfort*. Cambridge, Mass.: Harvard University Press, 1977.

Graham, P.; Rutter, M.; & George, S. Temperamental characteristics as predictors of behavior disorders in children. *American Journal of Orthopsychiatry*, 1973, **43**, 328–339.

Hetherington, E. M.; Cox, M.; & Cox, R. Father interaction and the social, emotional and cognitive development of children following divorce. In V. C. Vaughan & T. B. Brazelton (Eds.), *The family: setting priorities.* New York: Science & Medicine Publishers, 1979.

Hoffman, M. L. Empathy, role taking, guilt, and development of altruistic motives. In T. Lickona (Ed.), *Moral development and behavior.* New York: Holt, Rinehart & Winston, 1976.

Hollingshead, A. *Two-factor index of social position.* New Haven, Conn.: Yale Station, 1965.

Kaye, K. Discriminating among normal infants by multivariate analysis of Brazelton scores: lumping and smoothing. In A. Sameroff (Ed.), Organization and stability of newborn behavior. *Monographs of the Society for Research in Child Development,* 1978, **43**(5–6, Serial No. 177), 60–80.

Lewin, K. *Field theory in social science, selected theoretical papers.* New York: Harper, 1951.

Lewis, M., & Weinraub, M. The father's role in the infant's social network. In M. E. Lamb (Ed.), *The role of the father in child development.* New York: Wiley, 1976.

Lieberman, A. F. Preschoolers' competence with a peer: relations with attachment and peer experience. *Child Development,* 1977, **48**, 1277–1287.

Lowenthal, M.; Thurner, M.; & Chiriboga, D. *Four stages of life.* San Francisco: Jossey-Bass, 1975.

Matas, L.; Arend, R. A.; & Sroufe, L. A. Continuity in adaptation: quality of attachment and later competence. *Child Development,* 1978, **49**, 547–556.

Mead, G. H. *Mind, self, and society.* Chicago: University of Chicago Press, 1934.

Nuckolls, C. B.; Cassel, J.; & Kaplan, B. H. Psychosocial assets, life crisis and the prognosis of pregnancy. *American Journal of Epidemiology,* 1972, **95**, 431–441.

Rutter, M. Family, area and school influences in the genesis of conduct disorders. In L. Hersov, M.

Berger, & D. Shaffer (Eds.), *Aggression and antisocial behavior in childhood and adolescence.* (Journal of Child Psychology and Psychiatry book series, No. 1.) Oxford: Pergamon, 1978.

Rutter, M. Maternal deprivation, 1972–1978: new findings, new concepts, new approaches. *Child Development,* 1979, **50**, 283–305.

Sameroff, A. Early influences on development: fact or fancy. *Merrill-Palmer Quarterly,* 1975, **21**, 267–294.

Sander, L. W. Infant and caretaking environment: investigation and conceptualization of adaptive behavior in a system of increasing complexity. In E. J. Anthony (Ed.), *Explorations in child psychiatry.* New York: Plenum, 1975.

Sigman, M.; Cohen, S.; & Forsythe, A. The relationship of early infant measures to later development. In S. Friedman & M. Sigman (Eds.), *Preterm birth and psychological development.* New York: Academic Press, 1980.

Sroufe, L., & Waters, E. Attachment as an organizational construct. *Child Development,* 1977, **48**, 1184–1199.

Thomas, A.; Chess, S.; & Birch, H. G. *Temperament and behavior disorders in children.* New York: New York University Press, 1968.

Vaughn, B.; Egeland, B.; Sroufe, A.; & Waters, E. Individual differences in infant-mother attachment at twelve and eighteen months: stability and change in families under stress. *Child Development,* 1979, **50**, 971–975.

Waters, E.; Vaughn, B. E.; & Egeland, B. R. Individual differences in infant-mother attachment relationships at age one: antecedents in neonatal behavior in an urban, economically disadvantaged sample. *Child Development,* 1980, **51**, 208–216.

Waters, E.; Wippmann, J.; & Sroufe, L. A. Attachment, positive affect, and competence in the peer group: two studies in construct validation. *Child Development,* 1979, **50**, 821–829.

READING 15

Changing a Frightening Toy into a Pleasant Toy by Allowing the Infant to Control Its Actions

Megan R. Gunnar-VonGnechten

Although the idea that fear in infancy may be a function of the infant's control is not new (Arsenian, 1943; Bronson, 1972; Jersild & Holmes, 1935; Rheingold & Eckerman, 1969), its validity has never been clearly demonstrated, nor has it worked its way into the mainstream of theories regarding infant fear. Several studies have indicated that fear reactions increase when limitations are placed on the infant's freedom of movement (Bronson, 1972; Morgan & Ricciuti, 1969). For example, Rheingold and Eckerman (1969) found that 10-month-old infants would explore a strange room without fear if they controlled when they entered and left the room, but would show strong fear reactions if forced to remain alone in the room. However, none of these studies demonstrated that control was the important factor because in each case the infant's freedom of movement was confounded with his/her ability to achieve proximity to his/her mother. This is a serious confound because proximity to the mother itself can reduce fear (Bowlby, 1973).

When control is discussed in regard to fear, it is typically discussed as control over avoiding or terminating the fearful event (Seligman, 1975). Numerous studies conducted with adult and animal subjects have shown that these types of control can reliably reduce fear and stress reactions (Glass & Singer, 1972; Hokanson, DeGood, Forest, & Brittain, 1971; Weiss, 1968). However, there are also some data indicating that control over initiating the occurrence of arousing and potentially frightening events may also affect fear reactions. Steiner, Beer, and Shaffer (1969), using a within-subjects design, gave rats positive brain stimulation for bar pressing. They then gave the same stimulation independent of the rat's ac-

tions and found that the rats would actively attempt to escape from the stimulation. Thus, the stimulation was perceived as pleasant when the rat controlled its initiation and aversive when the stimulation was uncontrollable. Furthermore, several studies have shown that positive responses to non-noxious events can be facilitated by allowing the infant to directly control the initiation of the event (Watson & Ramey, 1972; Yarrow, Morgan, Jennings, Gaiter, & Harmon, Note 1).

The following study was conducted to test the hypothesis that a potentially frightening event can be made into a pleasant event merely by giving 1-year-olds direct control over initiating its occurrence. In order to test this hypothesis, two groups of 12-month-old infants were shown a mechanical toy monkey that clapped cymbals together loudly when activated. One group could activate the monkey themselves by hitting a panel. Each hit to the panel caused the monkey to clap the cymbals for 3 sec. A second group served in a yoked, noncontrolling condition, in which the experimenter activated the toy. The monkey was expected to be a frightening toy for the noncontrolling infants and a pleasant toy for the infants who could control its activation.

METHOD

Subjects and Conditions

The subjects were 24 boys and 24 girls, age 12–13 months. Half of the infants of each sex were randomly assigned to a controlling condition, in which they initiated the actions of a mechanical toy monkey by hitting a panel. The other half of the infants were randomly assigned to a yoked, noncontrolling condition, in which they had no control over the toy's activation. The yoking procedure was conducted within sex such that the frequency and pattern of activations generated by a controlling infant determined the pattern of toy activations observed by a noncontrolling infant of the same sex during his/her subsequent test session. From background information obtained at the time of testing, it was determined that all the groups (2 sexes x 2 conditions) were comparable in terms of birth order, length of time walking, number who had colds, and number who were teething.

Procedure

Just prior to participating in the present study all the infants took part in a 10-minute stranger reaction test. The experimenter in the present study served as the stranger. No significant fear of strangers was observed for any of the infants, and there was no indication that group differences in reactions to the toy monkey were related to experiences during this earlier study. Following completion of the stranger episodes, the infants were taken out of the room for 5 minutes while the equipment was set up for the present study. On returning to the room, the mother placed the infant in a low infant seat equipped with a large wooden tray. The tray was bordered in front by a low table. All the infants experienced a brief (2–6 minutes) familiarization period with a pleasant musical merry-go-round toy. This toy was placed in the center of the low table and was just out of the infant's reach.

For the infants in the controlling condition, the familiarization period was used to teach them how to operate the toys by hitting a panel clamped to the upper left-hand corner of the tray. For the first minute with the merry-go-round, the experimenter and the mother demonstrated how the panel worked. Then they both moved back 3 feet from the infant and gave him/her several minutes to demonstrate competence at the task. The

criterion for competence was six consecutive directed hits to the panel. Accidental hits with the elbow or arm made while squirming were not counted and were considered to interrupt a chain of directed hits. Once the controlling infant reached criterion, the familiarization period ended. For both sexes the average time to reach criterion was approximately 3.5 minutes, including the first minute of mother and experimenter demonstrations. One infant failed to reach criterion after 6 minutes, and he was dropped from the study.

The infants in the noncontrolling condition experienced a similar sequence of events, with the exception that they did not have the panel and the experimenter turned the merry-go-round on for them approximately every 6 sec. During pretesting we attempted to equate the two groups for the time spent with the merry-go-round. However, we found that doing so often resulted in frustrating or boring the noncontrolling infants, who generally lost interest in the toy fairly quickly. (Recall that the infants could not reach the toy.) Rather than risk producing such emotions prior to showing these infants the monkey, we chose instead to terminate the familiarization period for the noncontrolling infants at the first sign that they were losing interest in looking at the merry-go-round. For both sexes this resulted in an average familiarization period of 2.5 minutes, which was about 1 minute less than that for the controlling infants. Although this minute difference may have affected the results, we are fairly confident it did not because none of the measures of reactions to the monkey was significantly correlated with the amount of time the infants spent with the merry-go-round. In fact, the correlations were all below .22.

Once the familiarization period ended, the merry-go-round was replaced by the cymbal-clapping monkey. For the first 30 sec with the monkey, all the infants remained in the infant seat. Following this they were taken out of the chair by their mothers and stood next to the tray. The mother then moved back away from the infant and the child's reactions were observed for 1 additional minute. The controlling infants were able to activate the monkey both while they were in the chair and while they were out of it. During each controlling infant's tests session, audiotapes were made of their toy activations. Each hit to the panel recorded a click on the tape. The experimenter then listened to these tapes to determine when to activate the toy monkey for the yoked, noncontrolling infants.

Two observers seated behind a one-way mirror recorded the infant's reactions to the monkey using a 6-sec, time-sampling technique. The events noted were fussing and crying, smiling and laughing, looking at the monkey, support looks to the mother (looks that did not include smiles, positive vocalizations, or other indications of pleasure), vocalizations and toy activations. These five events could occur throughout the 1.5-minute test with the monkey, thus for a total of fifteen, 6-sec coding intervals each. Four measures pertained only to the 10 coding intervals, or 1 minute, when the infant was out of the infant seat. These were touching the monkey, touching the mother, being in proximity to the monkey (within 1 foot of the monkey or the panel). The interobserver reliabilities ranged from .80 to .99 using Pearson correlations, with a mean of .94.

If any infant was clearly frightened by the monkey, as indicated by two 6-sec coding intervals of full-blown crying, the monkey was removed and the session was terminated early. To account for differences in session length, the frequency of each behavior was calculated as the percentage of coding intervals in which it occurred. The percent scores for each behavior were then analyzed using a 2 (sex) x 2 (Conditions) analysis of variance with repeated measures for the conditions factor to take into account the yoking procedure described earlier.

RESULTS

The results showed that the controlling infants did respond more positively to the monkey than did the noncontrolling infants. But, contrary to expectations, only the noncontrolling boys and not the noncontrolling girls were clearly frightened by the toy. Table 1 shows the number of sessions terminated because of strong fear reactions (full-blown crying) in each group. As can be seen, almost all of the sessions had to be terminated for noncontrolling boys, whereas few sessions had to be terminated for the infants in any of the other groups. Furthermore, it was not the case that the infants in the other groups were fussing frequently, but just not crying hard enough for the session to be terminated. This can be seen in Figure 1, which shows the percentage of intervals in which both fussing and crying occurred, with the brackets indicating the .05 confidence intervals around each mean. Negative affect was a function of both control over the toy and the infant's sex, with fussing and crying being significantly greater than zero only for the boys who could not control the toy. For boys, controlling the monkey did change it from a frightening toy to one that was not distressing. For girls the effects of control could not be determined from these data on negative affect because neither group of girls was distressed by the monkey.

For both sexes, however, smiling and laughing at the toy was a function of the infant's control over its actions (see Figure 2). Infants

TABLE 1 SESSIONS TERMINATED BECAUSE OF FULL-BLOWN CRYING

Group	n	No. terminated	% terminated
Boys			
Noncontrolling	12	9	75
Controlling	12	2	16
Girls			
Noncontrolling	12	2	16
Controlling	12	1	8

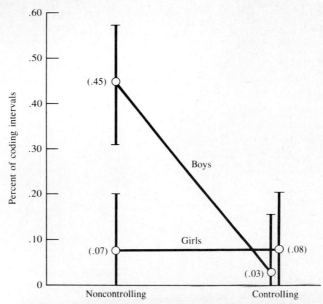

FIGURE 1   Percentage of intervals in which fussing and crying occurred. (Brackets indicate .05 confidence intervals around each mean.)

who controlled the monkey's cymbal clapping smiled and laughed more than those infants who could not control it. As indicated by the .05 confidence intervals around each mean, smiling was significantly greater than zero only for the infants who could control the toy's actions.

Combining the information on both negative and positive affect, one finds that for boys, controlling the toy changed it from a frightening toy to one that provoked positive affect. For girls, controlling the toy seemed to change it from a toy that provoked neither a significant amount of negative nor positive affect to one that clearly provoked positive emotional responses. We questioned whether the neutral affective reactions of the noncontrolling girls might actually have been an indication of some degree of wariness in the situation. Data on supportive looks toward the mother supported this possibility. For both boys and girls this measure was positively correlated with negative affect, boys $r(23) = +.52$, $p <.01$; girls $r(23) = +.49$, p

$<.01$. And there was a trend for both sexes of noncontrolling infants to look at their mothers more than controlling infants, $F(1,22) = 3.52$, $p <.10$. On the average, noncontrolling infants looked at their mothers during 25% of the coding intervals, as compared to 14% of the intervals for controlling infants.

The measures pertaining only to the time the infants were out of the infant seat presented several problems because these measures could only be obtained for those infants whose sessions were not terminated while they were still in the chair. As might be expected, the greatest loss of cases was for the group of noncontrolling boys. Only 7 of the 12 noncontrolling boys were observed for any length of time while out of the chair, as compared to 11 of the 12 controlling boys and all of the girls in both conditions. Although none of the parametric analyses on the proximity and touching measures yielded any significant differences (perhaps because of the reduced sample size and a natural selection for the bolder infants to be

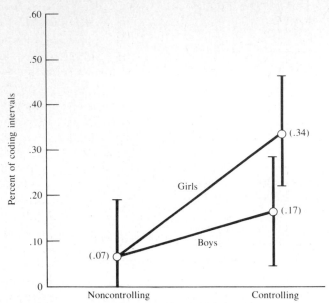

FIGURE 2   Percentage of intervals in which smiling and laughing occurred. (Brackets indicate .05 confidence intervals around each mean.)

observed while they were out of their chairs), nonparametric analyses did yield important differences.

In terms of approaching and touching the monkey, it was noted that although nearly all of the remaining controlling boys did so at least once (9 out of the 11), only 2 out of the remaining noncontrolling boys ever approached and touched the toy, $Z = 2.78$, $p < .01$. The number of girls fell somewhere in between, with half of each group touching the toy at least once. In terms of approaching and touching the mother, it was observed that only 27% of the controlling boys ever did so (3 out of 11), as compared to 57% of the noncontrolling boys (4 out of 7). Furthermore, when the reactions of the boys who did not go to their mothers was examined, it was found that two of the three noncontrolling boys had started crying immediately upon being taken out of the chair and had stood crying next to the toy until the session was terminated. This pattern of "freezing" and crying was not observed for any of the control-

ling boys. The pattern of freezing and crying was observed for one girl in the noncontrolling condition, but in general about half of the girls in each condition approached and touched their mothers during at least one of the coding intervals while they were out of the chair.

Finally, the frequency and pattern of toy activations by the controlling infants was of importance because it both reflected the controlling infants' perceptions of the monkey and, because of the yoking procedure, determined the pattern of activations observed by the noncontrolling infants. These data are shown in Table 2. If the monkey's cymbal clapping had been perceived as aversive by the controlling infants, we might expect that they would not activate the toy more than once or perhaps twice. Although 2 boys and 2 girls showed this pattern of activations, on the average both sexes activated the toy during 5 out of the 15 possible coding intervals that it was available, with the .05 t confidence interval ranging from 3 to 7 activations. The pattern of activations also

TABLE 2 FREQUENCY AND PATTERN OF TOY ACTIVATIONS BY CONTROLLING INFANTS

Sex	n	Frequency	Latency to 1st activation	Latency B/W activations[a]
Boys	12	5.25	.92	.90
Girls	12	5.33	1.75	.91

Note: Frequency determined as number of coding intervals (total possible = 15) in which the toy was activated.

[a] This measure was calculated only for the 11 boys and 10 girls who activated the toy more than once.

indicated that the cymbal clapping was not aversive to the controlling infants because the latency between activations was quite brief. Furthermore, there were no sex differences in either the frequency or pattern of toy activations generated by the controlling infants, which because of the yoking procedure, meant that there was also no sex difference in toy activations for the noncontrolling infants. Thus, the sex difference in the reactions of the noncontrolling infants cannot be accounted for by any differences in stimulation by the toy.

DISCUSSION

We can conclude that the reactions of 1-year-olds to an arousing event is a function of their control over that event. If they can control it, they respond with positive affect, whereas if they cannot control it, they are fearful, or at least neutral, and perhaps wary. Control, of course, is not the only determinant of their reactions, as indicated by the sex difference observed in the responses of the noncontrolling infants. However, these results clearly indicate that the infant's control, or lack of it, must be taken into account when attempting to predict and explain the infant's fear.

These results also raise several questions, not the least of which is the developmental issue of just when, during the first year, does control become important in regulating fear reactions? Watson and Ramey's (1972) data indicate that as early as 2 months of age, control

over initiating actions of a pleasant stimulus event facilitates more positive affective reactions to that event. And, as noted earlier, several studies have indicated that during the latter quarter of the first year, limitations on the infant's freedom of movement in strange situations can facilitate fear reactions. The answer to this developmental question will depend on the mechanisms by which control may operate to reduce fear and facilitate positive affect.

One possibility is that direct control over an event may help the infant assimilate that event and thus reduce its strangeness or discrepancy. During the sensorimotor period, the infant's schemes for events are action schemes, based on how objects or events respond to his/her motor behavior. When the occurrence of a new or strange event clearly depends on the infant's performing of his/her well-developed action schemes, it may be fairly easy for the infant to assimilate the event to that scheme and thus reduce its discrepancy. Conversely, however, the fear of strangeness may in part reflect the infant's uncertainty or inability to perceive how his/her actions will affect or control the strange object or person, as Kagan, Kearsley, and Zelazo (1975) have recently suggested.

It may also be the case that control operates to reduce fear by increasing the predictability of any given arousing event. In the present study, the infants who could initiate the actions of the monkey were also in a better position to predict when the cymbal clapping would occur than the noncontrolling infants. The possibility that this aspect of control may have played an important role is supported by work with adults and animals, indicating that prediction alone can reduce fear of noxious stimuli (Seligman, 1975).

Control may also reduce fear by allowing the infant to maintain arousal levels within manageable bounds. For example, Waters, Matas, and Sroufe (1975) found that 5–12-month-old infants who were approached by a stranger would often look away from the stranger at the point where the stranger came into close proximity. Using heart rate measures, they found that heart rate increased up to the point at which the infant looked away, at which time there was a significant decrease in arousal. Furthermore, more of the infants who used this controlling action were able to look back at the stranger and engage in positive interactions, whereas more of the infants who did not use this control or avoidance technique increased in arousal and often cried.

As these comments suggest, much more work is needed in order to understand the mechanisms by which control may act to influence the infant's affective reactions. However, the results of the present study clearly indicate that we can no longer discuss the nature of fear in infancy while ignoring the importance of the infant's control over the events he/she encounters.

REFERENCE NOTE

1 Yarrow, L. J., Morgan, G. A., Jennings, K. D., Gaiter, J. L., & Harmon, R. J. *Mastery motivation: A concept in need of measures.* Paper presented at the meeting of the Southeastern Conference on Human Development, Nashville, Tennessee, 1976.

REFERENCES

Arsenian, J. Young children in an insecure situation. *Journal of Abnormal and Social Psychology,* 1943, *38,* 235–249.

Bowlby, J. *Attachment and loss: Separation* (Vol. 2). New York: Basic Books, 1973.

Bronson, G. W. Infant's reactions to unfamiliar persons and novel objects. *Monographs of the Society for Research in Child Development,* 1972, *37*(3, Serial No. 148).

Glass, D. C., & Singer, J. W. *Urban stress: Experiments on noise and social stressors.* New York: Academic Press, 1972.

Hokanson, J. E., DeGood, D. E., Forrest, M. S., & Brittain, T. M. Availability of avoidance behaviors in modulating vascular stress responses. *Journal of Personality and Social Psychology.* 1971, *19,* 60–68.

Jersild, A. T., & Holmes, F. B. Children's fears. *Child Development Monograph,* 1935, *20.*

Kagan, J. Discrepancy, temperament, and infant distress. In M. Lewis & L. Rosenblum (Eds.), *The origins of fear,* New York: Wiley, 1974.

Kagan, J., Kearsley, R. B., & Zelazo, P. R. The emergence of initial apprehension to unfamiliar peers. In M. Lewis & L. Rosenblum (Eds.), *Peer relations and friendships.* New York: Wiley, 1975.

Morgan, G. A., & Ricciuti, H. Infants' responses to strangers during the first year. In B. M. Foss (Ed.), *Determinants of infant behavior* (Vol. 4). New York: Wiley, 1969.

Rheingold, H., & Eckerman, C. The infant's free entry into a new environment. *Journal of Experimental Child Psychology,* 1969, *8,* 271–283.

Seligman, M. *Helplessness: On depression, development and death.* San Francisco: Freeman, 1975.

Steiner, S. S., Beer, B., & Shaffer, M. M. Escape from self-produced rates of brain stimulation. *Science,* 1969, *163,* 90–91.

Waters, E., Matas, L., & Sroufe, A. Infant's reactions to an approaching stranger: Description, validation and functional significance of wariness. *Child Development,* 1975, *46,* 348–356.

Watson, J., & Ramey, C. Reactions to response-contingent stimulation in early infancy. *Merrill-Palmer Quarterly,* 1972, *18,* 219–288.

Weiss, J. M. The effects of coping response on stress. *Journal of Comparative and Physiological Psychology,* 1968, *65,* 251–260.

Maternal Emotional Signaling: Its Effect on the Visual Cliff Behavior of 1-Year-Olds

James F. Sorce
Robert N. Emde
Joseph J. Campos
Mary D. Klinnert

In human psychological research, emotional expressions are generally treated as behavioral responses or as outcomes of cognitive appraisal processes. Thus, they are viewed as external indexes of internal states. Relatively little attention has been given to the function of such displays as regulators of interpersonal behavior. This lack of attention contrasts sharply with clinical experience and everyday life, wherein the emotional reactions of another can have powerful effects on the perceiver, such as in eliciting empathy or inducing moods. It also contrasts sharply with studies in nonhuman primates where emotional signaling has been a topic of considerable interest. Facial expressions such as fear, anger, and playfulness, as well as the intensity of emotion, serve communicative functions among monkeys, as has been reviewed by Chevalier-Skolnikoff (1967) and Hinde (1974). Furthermore, the development of responsiveness to maternal facial signals among infant chimpanzees in the wild has been documented (Lawick-Goodall, 1967); in this, infants responded to postural and facial expression variations in their mothers, which indicated the moods and subsequent behavior of the latter. More recently, some theoreticians have speculated about the "catching of fears" (Bowlby, 1973) and about emotional expressions as parameters of observational learning (Bandura, 1977; Campos & Stenberg, 1981).

A major turning point for human emotions research occurred when two separate teams of investigators demonstrated the apparent universal communication value of specific emotional expressions. Cross-cultural studies of adult facial expression have shown that particular patterns are recognized reliably (such as joy, fear, anger, sadness, surprise, and disgust) and, correspondingly, there also seems to be a species-wide, intuitive capacity to express these emotions (Ekman, Sorenson, & Friesen, 1969; Izard, 1971). These findings have generated a number of lines of investigation. Among them is research leading to measurement advances in specifying the facial patterning involved in emotional signals that are recognized. In addition, it has led to research demonstrating that discrete emotional expressions occur in response to specific eliciting circumstances (Hiatt, Campos, & Emde, 1979; Stenberg, Campos, & Emde, 1983).

We believe the latter two lines of research have made possible the empirical study of the communicative and regulatory functions of emotional expressions. Our logic is as follows. If the observer can identify emotional expressions and can assume that the expressing person is reacting to relevant environmental circumstances, then it seems quite likely that the attitude and/or behavior of that observing person will be influenced by noting the other's emotional expressions (i.e., a communicative function). Beyond this, to the extent that emotional expressions influence the behavior of the observer, they can be said to be serving a *social regulatory* function.

Our human infancy research has begun to investigate the developmental roots of the social regulatory functions of facial expression. We have come to realize that a process we have called social referencing occurs when an infant is confronted with an ambiguous circumstance: the infant looks to the face of another in order to search for emotional information to help appraise or evaluate the ambiguity. The infant's subsequent behavior then reflects a revised appraisal of the environment. Accordingly, the following series of studies investigates social referencing using one ambiguous circumstance, namely a modified visual cliff. We sought to determine whether 1-year-olds confronted with this kind of ambiguous circumstance would (a) look to mother's face and (b) use the emotional information in the mother's experimentally manipulated facial pose to guide their subsequent exploratory behavior.

METHOD

Subjects were middle-class volunteers who had been recruited from birth announcements in the neighborhoods of the University and the Health Sciences Center and whose infants were normal at birth. In response to postcard inquiries, they had expressed an interest in participating in studies of normal psychological development. Subjects coming to our laboratory were included in the study if (a) they did not become distressed at any time *prior* to noticing the drop-off, (b) they spontaneously referenced mother's face after observing the drop-off (defined as an uninterrupted sequence of looking *down* at the depth and *up* to mother's face), and (c) the mother's facial signal adequately represented the pose taught during pretraining as verified by a manipulation check.

In the first three studies to be reported below, of 145 infants coming into the lab, 11% were unable to be included in the study because of distress during the warm-up, 21% because they did not engage in visual referencing of mother's face, and 8% because mother's pose was judged as inadequate when scored by an observer naive to the hypothesis of the study. Overall, therefore, 40% of the original infants were not included. Because of the question being asked, criteria for subject

inclusion from Study 4 were different; these data will be presented with the results from that study.

To create an ambiguous circumstance, we chose to manipulate depth—a physical dimension that can be varied to elicit avoidance of heights in infants, no avoidance at all, or a threshold of uncertainty. The visual cliff apparatus permits this manipulation of height quite readily (Walk, 1966). The cliff is a plexiglass-covered table divided into two halves: a shallow side under which a patterned surface is placed immediately beneath the plexiglass, and a deep side under which is placed a similar surface some varying distance beneath the plexiglass. Pilot testing revealed that setting the depth at 30 cm and placing an attractive toy (a Fisher-Price musical ferris wheel toy, model no. 969) on the deep side elicited infant pauses at the edge and frequent looks to the mother but no clear avoidance of the depth.

Before each trial, infants were placed on the shallow side of the cliff and entertained there by a previously familiarized experimenter, while mother positioned herself on the far (deep) side of the table. A second experimenter, monitoring the infant's behavior on a videotape screen from an adjacent room, was able to provide mother with instructions by means of a wireless earphone. Mother placed the attractive toy directly on the deep surface (to increase the ambiguity concerning the tactual solidity and visual transparency of the deep side) and began smiling to encourage her infant to approach the drop-off. When the infant advanced to within 38 cm of the drop-off, oriented toward the depth, and looked up to mother's face, the mother was instructed to signal her infant with one of the discrete emotions designated below.

Mothers had been trained in posing the desired facial expression in accordance with the descriptions of Izard (1980) and Ekman and Friesen (1975); they used no words, sounds, or gestures. For fear, the facial expression manipulation involved raising and drawing together of the brows, eyes open wide with sclera showing, and the mouth opened and the lips pulled back. For anger, the brows are drawn down and together, the upper eyelids are lowered, and the mouth is either open and square-shaped, or the lips are pressed together. For interest, there is a slight raising of the eyebrows, the eyes are widened slightly, and the mouth is closed and the face relaxed. For happiness, the corners of the lips are drawn back and up, the cheeks are raised, and the lower eyelids are raised but not tense. For sadness, the inner corners of the eyebrows are drawn up, the skin below the eyebrow is triangulated with the inner corner up, and the corners of the lips are drawn down.

Maternal facial expressions were scored independently by a naive rater who had achieved reliability on MAX training (Izard, 1980). All expressions during times of visual referencing were scored for the presence of components that would be expected for the given emotion according to Ekman and Friesen's *Unmasking the Face* (1975). Facial expressions met criteria of having predicted components in two or three facial zones and no components belonging to other target emotions. On those unusual occasions when only one facial zone met the predicted pattern, the posed feature had to be an indicator of the intended emotion and no other (for example, a smile or "sad brows").

A trial was terminated when the infant either crossed the deep side (touching the toy, mother, or the end wall) or when 120 s elapsed from when the infant entered the region of the dropoff. All trials employed split-screen videotape recordings, with one camera constantly focused on the infant's face and body and a second camera on the mother's face.

Tapes were scored for three infant behavioral categories: (a) *hedonic tone*—rated every 10 s on a 5-point scale ranging from a broad smile (rating of 1) through neutral interest to overt distress (rating of 5), (b) *maternal refer-*

encing—the total number of times an infant looked at mother's face after an initial instance of looking from the depth immediately to mother's face, and (c) *coping behavior*—the presence or absence of crossing the deep side, and the frequency of retreat back onto the shallow side, defined as turning his or her back to mother and moving back onto the shallow side. Reliabilities for each of these dependent variables, calculated as exact agreement between two naive judges, ranged from .80 to 1.00, with a mean of .94.

RESULTS

First Study: Happy Versus Fear Signal

The first study compared infant responses to this uncertain situation when mothers signaled either happiness or fear. Thirty-six middle-class mothers and their 12-month-old infants were randomly assigned to a smiling condition (N = 10 males, 9 females) and to a fear condition (N = 9 males, 8 females).

The mother's emotional signaling had three dramatic effects on the infants' behavior. First, it significantly influenced the infant's tendency to cross the cliff or not. When mother posed a fearful expression *none* of the 17 infants ventured across the deep side. In sharp contrast, 14 of the 19 infants who observed mothers' happy face crossed the deep side. Second, the fear pose created a negative motivational valence: 11 of the 17 infants in the fear condition retreated, whereas only 3 of the 19 infants in the joy condition retreated. Infants in the fear condition usually vacillated back and forth in the midzone of the cliff and then moved back to the shallow side. Third, the fear expression generated a significantly more negative hedonic tone in the infants. These findings are summarized in Table 1.

Second Study: Interest Versus Anger Signal

A second study was conducted to determine whether the regulatory effect of social referenc-

TABLE 1   EFFECT OF MOTHERS' FACIAL EXPRESSIONS ON INFANT BEHAVIOR

Variable	Study 1		Study 2		Study 3
	Joy (N = 19)	Fear (N = 17)	Interest (N = 15)	Anger (N = 18)	Sadness (N = 19)
Percentage of infants crossing deep side	74%	0	73%	11%	33%
Mean number of retreats per minute to shallow side	.420	1.08	.420	.72	.660
Mean rating of hedonic tone	1.62	2.12	2.00	1.92	1.92
Mean number of references per minute	3.60	2.46	5.70	2.94	4.59

ing could be observed with different emotions. Two different emotional signals, interest and anger, were used. These emotions were selected because they not only represented a positive and negative emotional signal but, like enjoyment and fear, they both seemed to provide situationally relevant messages concerning the appropriateness of crossing versus not crossing the cliff.

Thirty-three 1-year-old infants and their mothers comprised the sample for the second study, with 15 randomly assigned to the interest condition (8 males, 7 females) and 18 to the anger condition (11 males, 7 females). The instructions, training, and trial procedures as well as the subsequent data scoring techniques were identical to those reported for the first study.

Results again revealed a powerful effect of mothers' emotional signaling on infant crossing behavior (again, see Table 1). When mother posed an anger expression, only 2 of the 18 infants ventured across the deep side, while 11 of the 15 infants who observed mother's interest expression crossed the deep side. Infants who saw mother's angry expression while at the visual cliff edge tended to actively retreat by moving back onto the shallow side: 14 of the 18 infants in the anger condition retreated, and only 5 of the 15 infants in the interest condition did so. Unlike the results of the initial study, there were no significant differences in infant hedonic tone.

As discrete emotional expressions, fear and anger appear to be situationally relevant in the child's appraisal of the deep side of the cliff. Fear provides a warning that there is danger and the infant should avoid the drop-off to insure his or her safety. Anger serves as a restraint, prohibiting the infant from approaching further. Both fear and anger, however, also convey a negative hedonic tone, which might be the mediator of the avoidance behavior in both cases, independently of the discrete emotional information (Izard, 1977).

Third Study: Sadness Signal

A third study was conducted to look at the effects if mothers signaled sadness. Sadness is a fundamental emotion, which conveys a negative hedonic tone, but its discrete emotional information does not imply avoidance or prohibition. In a third study we, therefore, investigated the reactions of an additional eighteen 12-month-old infants (6 males and 12 females) on the visual cliff while their mothers posed sadness. Results indicated that 6 of the 18 infants successfully crossed the deep side when mother's face conveyed sadness. The mean number of references by infants from this group was higher than any other, suggesting that these infants might be puzzled or uncertain about the facial signal itself or its meaning in the present context, among other possibilities.

A comparison of the crossing behavior in the negative emotion conditions revealed a significant difference between sadness and fear; the difference between fear and anger was not significant. These findings suggest that the appropriateness of the context for an emotional signal must be taken into account; the most contextually appropriate emotion (fear) elicited the most consistent avoidance of heights.

Fourth Study: Fear Signal Without Uncertainty

The final study in the series addressed a separate issue related to the importance of context. In order to determine whether the expressions influenced the infant's evaluation of an ambiguous situation, or whether they were effective in controlling behavior merely because of their discrepancy or unexpectedness, we tested an additional 23 infants (11 males and 12 females) with the visual cliff table modified to consist of two shallow sides separated by a center strip .3m wide. The mothers were instructed exactly as they had been in the fear condition described above: They smiled broadly until the infant reached the center of the table, then shifted to a previously trained fear facial pose. The results obtained in this condition were quite different from the earlier study, revealing very little referencing and no effect of the facial expression on crossing behavior. Seventeen of the infants tested in this condition did not look to the mother at all and merely continued crossing to reach her or the toy. Among the six babies who referenced, two of the mothers gave poor signals, and the infants were eliminated from the study. Those four babies who looked to the mother and received a fear signal crossed to the toy in spite of her fear pose. This behavior was in marked contrast to that of the babies who saw the mothers' fear face after noticing the slight drop-off. The findings described earlier, therefore, seem interpretable as a social referencing process—the infant must seek out emotional information for that information to be maximally effective in regulating behavior.

DISCUSSION

The form of emotional communication we have referred to as social referencing appears to have a powerful and consistent effect on infant behavior. Social referencing, as we have defined it, is a process whereby an individual seeks out emotional information in order to make sense of an event that is otherwise ambiguous or beyond that individual's own intrinsic appraisal capabilities (Campos & Stenberg, 1981; Klinnert, Campos, Sorce, Emde, & Svejda, 1982). Under the conditions of our experiment, the tendency to visually reference mother and to respond according to an emotional message is already well established at 12 months of age, and it appears rather dramatic to mothers and researchers alike who view our videotapes. Under other conditions, such as the entry and approach of a stranger, social referencing effects have been shown at 10 months of age (Feinman & Lewis, 1983). Two sorts of experimental questions remain to be answered before any general application of findings about social referencing. These questions have to do with the role of *selection* of subjects and the role of *context* for social referencing.

First for selection factors. Our experiments looked at a relatively narrow set of infants. Volunteers were middle-class, and not all children were able to complete the testing. We did not include children who were crying during the warm-up phase or children who never looked at mother (except for the fourth experiment). Because of selection factors our results may, therefore, represent children who are functioning at a relatively high capacity. We need to understand more about individual differences among children who do and do not reference (e.g., Feinman & Lewis, 1983). Related to this, we need to know more about individual differences concerning internal "state" factors affecting children who may or may not attend or who may or may not be involved in appraisal. Furthermore, are there subtle differences in social referencing based on individual differences and the history of the relationship between mother and infant? A series of studies is planned to explore these questions, some of which use heartrate as a sensitive measure of change related to attentional processes and emotional state.

Now for the questions regarding context. We need to know more about situations generating "uncertainty." In our experiments, we did a considerable amount of pilot work to develop a definitive zone of uncertainty. If the "deep side" of the visual cliff was deeper, infants showed fear and avoidance; if it was shallower, they showed no uncertainty and crossing to the toy occurred without referencing. This precise adjustment was necessary to establish our experimental condition. But it is important to realize that the visual cliff is a situation that is highly controlled and one in which the infant has relatively few options, considering his or her complex behavioral repertoire. We need research involving more complex experimental situations—situations in which there are richer opportunities for behavioral regulation and coping. Recent work of Gunnar and Stone (1983) has underscored the importance of uncertainty in social referencing tasks involving unfamiliar toys. We are currently doing experiments in a variety of other uncertainty situations, which include a toy robot, a collapsing house, the approach of strangers, and a variety of social situations.

In addition to contextual questions about the setting, there are contextual questions about the emotional signal, including appropriateness. Again, it seems important to emphasize that, for reasons of experimental control, we limited the signal to a manipulation of the face alone. We now need to study other channels of communication besides the facial channel. Emotional signaling occurs through the vocalic channel of emotional communication, and it is likely that posture and gestures are also important. Research also needs to be done in more complex contexts—those in which emotional signaling occurs in multiple channels at the same time, as would be the usual case in the infant's world.

There are other interesting questions that arise from this line of research. What is the developmental onset of social referencing? What is the role of learning? Of maturation? Do emotional expressions regulate behavior by eliciting feelings in the perceiver, or are they merely cues that guide behavior? What is the relationship of social referencing to the past history of individual infants in relationship to attachment and to particular socialization experiences? What is the relationship of social referencing to empathy? What happens in situations of conflicting emotional signals?

We have emphasized future experimental approaches, but the latter questions indicate that we also need to explore naturalistic settings for the occurrence of social referencing and related phenomena. Social referencing is only one form of emotional signaling. Whatever else, these experimental effects that seem so impressive need to be understood in terms of their real-life significance.

REFERENCES

Bandura, A. (1977). *Social learning theory*. Englewood Cliffs, NJ: Prentice-Hall.

Bowlby, J. (1973). *Attachment and loss. Vol II: Separation*. New York: Basic Books.

Campos, J., & Stenberg, C. (1981). Perception, appraisal and emotion: The onset of social referencing. In M. E. Lamb & L. R. Sherrod (Eds.), *Infant social cognition* (pp. 273–314). Hillsdale, NJ: Erlbaum.

Chevalier-Skolnikoff, S. (1967). In D. Morris (Ed.), *Primate ethology*. London: Weidenfeld & Nicholson.

Ekman, P., & Friesen, W. (1975). *Unmasking the face*. Englewood Cliffs, NJ: Prentice-Hall.

Ekman, P., Sorensen, E., & Friesen, W. (1969). Pan-cultural elements in facial displays of emotion. *Science, 164,* 86–88.

Feinman, S., & Lewis, M. (1983). Social referencing at ten months: A second-order effect on infants' responses to strangers. *Child Development, 54,* 878–887.

Gunnar, M. R., & Stone, C. (1983, April). *The effects of maternal positive affect of one-year-olds reactions to toys: Is it social referencing?* Paper presented at meetings of the Society for Research in Child Development, Detroit.

Hiatt, S., Campos, J., & Emde, R. N. (1979). Facial patterning and infant emotional expression: Happiness, surprise and fear. *Child Development, 50,* 1020–1035.

Hinde, R. A. (1974). *Biological bases of human social behavior.* New York: McGraw Hill.

Izard, C. (1971). *The face of emotion.* New York: Meredith and Appleton-Century Crofts.

Izard, C. (1977). *Human emotions.* New York: Plenum.

Izard, C. (1980). *Maximally discriminative facial movement coding (MAX).* Newark, DE: University of Delaware Press.

Klinnert, M. D., Campos, J., Sorce, J., Emde, R. N., & Svejda, M. (1982). The development of social referencing in infancy. In R. Plutchik & H. Kellerman (Eds.), *Emotion: Theory, research and experience, Vol. 2: Emotion in early development.* New York: Academic Press.

Lawick-Goodall, J. van. (1967). Mother-offspring relationships in chimpanzees. In D. Morris (Ed.), *Primate ethology* (pp. 287–346). London: Weidenfeld and Nicholson.

Stenberg, C., Campos, J., & Emde, R. N. (1983). The facial expression of anger in seven-month-old infants. *Child Development, 54,* 178–184.

Walk, R. (1966). The development of depth perception in animals and human infants. *Monographs of the Society for Research in Child Development, 31,* (Whole No. 5).

READING 17

Children's Reactions to Medical Stressors: An Ecological Approach to the Study of Anxiety

Barbara G. Melamed
Lawrence J. Siegel

INTRODUCTION

This chapter advances the position that the study of how children cope with medical stress can be of considerable value in understanding the ontology of fear and anxiety. Almost all children are exposed to medical and dental procedures. These experiences, including hospitalization for surgery, outpatient diagnostic procedures, and restorative dental treatment, are often highly stressful. The pain and discomfort that occur when the child is exposed to noxious stimuli in an unfamiliar environment prompt avoidance, loss of control, and heightened arousal. Furthermore, these reactions are enhanced if separation or inadequate support from parents occurs. Such events may predispose an individual to the formation of maladaptive anxiety responses. In some children, these responses are of sufficient duration and intensity to interfere with their future adjustment to the medical and dental situation. In addition, these maladaptive anxiety responses may generalize to other settings and people. Some research suggests that over one third of all hospitalized children have long-term behavioral adjustment problems related to brief hospital experience (Vernon, Foley, & Schulman, 1967).

This paper argues for the importance of investigating specific anxiety responses to stressful medical and dental settings irrespective of the co-occurrence of these responses with other constellations of symptoms as specified in the *Diagnostic and Statistical Manual of Mental Disorders* (*DSM-III*) (1980). Many of these anxiety responses are sufficiently problematic to warrant intervention whether or not they are associated with multiple symptomatic behaviors. Of at least equal value is the potential relevance of this domain of study for the understanding of aversive emotions in children and the assessment of theories of affective pathology.

First, these settings permit an investigation of normal anxiety in children in response to naturally occurring stressors. The nature and mechanisms underlying the manifestation of anxiety in children have received little empirical investigation. For example, there are very few data regarding the expression of anxiety responses in children across the three primary modalities of verbal, physiological, and motor components (Johnson & Melamed, 1979). Furthermore, there are few developmental data available to establish the baseline of normative stress responses of children of different sexes and ages. Therefore, it is difficult to determine what is pathological.

Second, different theoretical perspectives regarding the development of fear in children can be examined by the reaction of children in the medical situation. Psychodynamic models view anxiety as a derivative of instinct, but their definitions of instinct are very different (Michels, Frances & Shear). The specific nature of the fear may be, in part, related to so-called unconscious factors, but symptoms often emerge in the context of real trauma. Whereas the psychodynamic model emphasizes the importance of innate constitutional tendencies, the learning model places greater emphasis on environmental events that elicit or maintain the conditional emotional response. The conditioning model would view the medical situation as an unconditioned stimulus. Noxious events occur repeatedly over a brief period of time, in the absence of an escape or avoidance response. Aversive emotional responses conditioned in this context may generalize to similar stimuli or persons. The social learning approach focuses on the interaction between parents and their children, on the potential roles of the parent as

a stress reducer, or in directly reinforcing fear responses, or in providing models of anxiety expression. The biological theories view the individual differences in temperament as they affect the vulnerability of children for maladaptive anxiety responses.

Finally, the vulnerability of children toward development of adult psychopathology is not necessarily predicted by behaviors that mimic adult disorders. In a recent review on developmental psychopathology, it was noted that "the strongest predictors of later pathology are not likely to be early replicas of the behavioral indicators of adult pathology. The strongest predictors likely will be adaptational failures, defined in age-appropriate terms" (Sroufe & Rutter, 1984, p. 24). The literature suggests that there are a number of factors that predispose a child to maladaptive anxiety responses during stressful experiences. Among these factors are biological and/or temperament factors, the extent to which the situation permits control over the stressor, the nature of mother-child attachments, and their previous experience with the stressor. These factors are each briefly addressed as they operate within the medical setting and are identified as components of specific theories of anxiety development.

An ecological framework, which views the child interacting in the naturalistic medical setting, can advance the integration of the theories of stressful experience within a developmental perspective. This position postulates the importance of considering cognitive abilities of children to deal with externally precipitated stressors at a given age and the nature of the mother-child attachment during the experience as predictive of adjustment.

RESPONSE TO MEDICAL STRESSORS: A PROTOTYPE FOR ANXIETY MANAGEMENT

Each year 5 million children undergo numerous medical and dental procedures. Over 45% of all children have had a hospital experience by age 7 (Davies, Butler, & Goldstein, 1972). An ecological approach to the study of childhood fears in medical and dental settings is possible because of the natural occurrence of aversive experiences. The child is confronted with experiences that allow for minimal control, unfamiliar adults, and often separation from parents. In the hospital, children are often restricted in movement, isolated from their peer group, and lack the information or ability to control their situation. Although the severity of the illness or physical dysfunction can enhance the stress with its concomitant pain, at least some portion of children's reactions can be attributed to the aversive properties of the setting itself (Traughber & Cataldo, 1982). These situations provide relatively controlled environments in which stressful stimuli that elicit anxiety-related behaviors are easily identified. Children typically have repeated contact with medical and dental procedures; thus the opportunity to study the effects of repeated experience and long-term adaptability are present.

Those individuals facing hospitalization or outpatient medical treatment ordinarily function adequately, but may become anxious to the point where emotional equilibrium is disrupted and normal coping behaviors are rendered ineffective. Following a hospital stay, approximately 32% of all children develop severe, long-term disturbances such as soiling, bedwetting, increased dependency, aggressiveness, excessive fear, sleeping or eating disturbances. For some children, hospitalization may have a beneficial effect, since 25% were rated as improved in behavior after a hospital stay (Vernon et al., 1967). Little information exists on factors that predict coping versus maladaptive behavior among children following hospitalization.

There are several other findings that suggest that medical settings are useful for investigating the formation of maladaptive anxiety disorders. For instance, those children with early traumatic dental or medical experiences have been found to show a greater incidence of somatic disturbances and neurotic tendencies (Cuthbert & Melamed, 1982; Sermet, 1974; Shaw, 1975). Evidence based on retrospective reports in the adult dental literature indicates that dental fears may be learned in childhood (Kleinknecht, Klepac, & Alexander, 1973).

The fear of injections, choking, and the sound of drilling are the three most common fears associated with visits to dentists reported consistently by children from 4 to 14. Several studies demonstrate that children who had early negative experience with doctors or surgery later have increased dental anxiety (Martin, Shaw, & Taylor, 1977). Children may become increasingly sensitized to repeated dental or medical visits (Katz, Kellerman, & Siegel, 1981; Venham, Bengston, & Cipes, 1977).

Finally, the nature and quality of the mother-child relationship prior to a hospital experience have been related to the child's in-hospital adjustment (Brown, 1979). Studies of emotional contagion (Escalona, 1953) consistently document that anxious mothers have children who are also anxious in the face of hospitalization or medical procedures. The literature on preparation of parents and their children for hospitalization and stressful medical and dental procedures was based on the assumption that reducing maternal anxiety would reduce their children's stress (Melamed & Bush, in press). However, the mechanism of change was never well specified. Interventions consisted of general psychological packages of coping skills such as relaxation or cognitive distractions. The data on mothers' absence or presence as it influences children's maladaptive behavior in face of invasive medical procedures have been much less consistent. Few studies actually observed what the mothers or fathers did in facilitating their children's coping, even though lip service has been given to the importance of assessing the quality of the parenting. In fact, two recent studies suggested that parent presence in the doctor's treatment room during the venipuncture procedure led to more intense and longer lasting crying in children than when the parent was not present, particularly with those children under the age of five (Gross, Stern, Levin, Dale, & Wojnilower, 1983; Shaw & Routh, 1982). Although the younger children exhibited more aggression, resistance, and crying whether the mothers were present or absent, older children with mothers present also cried immediately prior to the initiation of the blood test. This behavior has been interpreted as a form of protest, since the children believe that the parent will emit comforting responses at the signal of distress. Identifying those interactive patterns that enhance emotional distress during outpatient treatment or hospitalization may pinpoint those families with members who are at high risk for the development of emotional patterns indicative of anxiety disorders or somatoform disorders.

DEFINITION OF MALADAPTIVE ANXIETY RESPONSES

Expressions of fear are most often normal adaptive responses to distressing or threatening events. Whether the anxiety-related behaviors are considered maladaptive depends on a number of factors including the duration and severity of the problem and the degree to which it is disruptive to the child's life (Barrios, Hartmann, & Shigetomi, 1981; Morris & Kratochwill, 1983; Richards & Siegel, 1978). Incidence rates of phobias in the child population are dramatically lower than are incidence rates of normal fears. Reports consistently indicate that 0.5% to 2% of children have specific clinical fears (Agras, Sylvester, & Oliveau, 1969; Kennedy, 1965; Miller, Barrett, & Hampe, 1974; Rutter, Tizard, & Whitmore, 1970). Therefore, the evaluation of normal children's varied reactions during an intense stress, such as hospitalization, can be useful in understanding adaptive functioning and providing age-appropriate norms by which the children who fail to cope and show long-term behavioral disturbances can be identified. Prospective longitudinal re-

search may identify continuities in maladaptive functioning in face of other stressors.

Although fears are a common problem of normal childhood, they are often quite transient and tend to dissipate with age (McFarlane, Allen, & Honzik, 1954). Miller et al. (1974) provided a useful set of criteria for judging the dysfunctional nature of the anxiety response. They suggested that anxiety states warrant treatment when they (1) are out of proportion to the demands of the situation, (2) cannot be explained or reasoned away, (3) are beyond voluntary control, (4) lead to avoidance of the feared situation, (5) persist over an extended period of time, (6) are maladaptive, and (7) are not age or stage specific. Richards and Siegel (1978) have noted that the diagnosis of any Anxiety Disorder rests on points similar to the Miller et al. (1974) criteria for defining a phobia. Use of the label "behavior disorder," then, requires more than documentation of the fear-related behavior. It requires a judgment that the behavior exceeds certain limits of severity and disruptiveness characteristic of normal fears. Knowledge regarding age-appropriate reactions to specific stressful experiences would provide a normative baseline against which to judge the maladaptive behavior. Developmental theory must, therefore, guide the assessment process as specified in the seventh of Miller et al.'s (1974) criteria for a phobia: "Is not age or stage specific" (p. 90). Cognitive and emotional development are reciprocal processes and so the content and incidence of children's fears vary at differing stages of development. Fear results from understanding the significance of stimuli; consequently, the types of fear-eliciting stimuli change from infancy through adolescence.

Factor analytic studies have identified content categories of children's fears, based on parent ratings of children's fear. Miller, Barrett, Hampe, and Noble (1972) identified three factors in a factor analytic study using the Louisville Fear Survey Schedule: (1) fears of physical injury or personal loss (e.g., having an operation, being kidnapped, parental divorce); (2) fears of natural and supernatural dangers (e.g., fear of the dark, storms, monsters, and ghosts); and (3) fears reflecting "psychic stress" related most often to interpersonal relationships (e.g., school attendance, fears of making mistakes). Miller (1983) cites a more recent factor analysis of the same instrument by Staley and O'Donnell, who found five similar factors for ages 6 to 16. These were fears of (1) physical injury, (2) animals, (3) school, (4) night, and (5) public places.

The range of fear-eliciting stimuli broadens with increasing age (Morris & Kratochwill, 1983). Infants show fear reactions to excessive or unexpected sensory stimuli and strangers; separation anxiety is evident around the first year (Miller, 1983). Preschoolers' fears tend to focus on animals, the dark, and imaginary creatures (Bauer, 1976; Jersild & Homes, 1935; Miller, 1983). Coinciding with both school entrance and the development of concrete operational thought, school and social fears, and fears of injury predominate (Lapouse & Monk, 1959; Miller, 1983), whereas fears of animals, the dark, and imaginary creatures decline (Jersild & Holmes, 1935; Lapouse & Monk, 1959; Morris & Kratochwill, 1983). Social fears become more complex during adolescence, including anxieties concerning social alienation and the macabre (Miller, 1983).

In distinguishing between a normal and a clinical fear in children, the developmental appropriateness of the fear content needs to be assessed. Treatment for age-appropriate fears is most often not indicated, as developmental data suggest the fear may spontaneously decrease with age. However, a single symptomatic behavior reflecting anxiety response to a stressful experience such as a medical procedure may be an appropriate focus of treatment because it is maladaptive based on the criteria noted earlier. A symptom may be dysfunctional whether or not it appears as part of a syndrome or constellation of symptoms which might meet the crite-

ria for the diagnosis of Anxiety Disorder as specified in *DSM-III*. For example, among the *DSM-III* guidelines for the diagnosis of a Separation Anxiety Disorder are the presence of three of nine possible symptoms. One of these symptoms, "a persistent reluctance or refusal to go to sleep without being next to a major attachment figure or to go to sleep away from home" (p. 53), is a problem that may be manifested by children who are hospitalized for medical treatment. This symptom may sufficiently interfere with their adaptive functioning within this setting and warrant intervention irrespective of its association with other problems exhibited by the child.

The two critical reviews of the literature on children's fears (Harris & Ferrari, 1983; Winer, 1982) have revealed a tremendous gap in the understanding of the development of fears in children. Although there are many treatments available (Morris & Kratochwill, 1983), there is no research that evaluates the effective therapeutic ingredients or that takes the children's level of development into account. Melamed, Robbins, and Graves (1982) critically reviewed the treatment studies and pinpointed the need to take into account developmental factors including age, cognitive style, previous experience, as well as the quality of parenting, prior to selecting a therapeutic strategy for preparation.

LEARNING THEORY APPROACHES TO FEAR DEVELOPMENT

Learning theory provides a useful framework for investigating the etiology and maintenance of anxiety and fear in children. Learning approaches lend themselves to an operationalization of the constructs posited by the theories and, thereby, permit an adequate empirical test of the constructs.

A conceptualization of anxiety disorders that emphasizes learning has at least four separate sources that are of theoretical value. Therefore, there is no single theoretical statement regarding the development of anxiety disorders. The strength of the learning conceptualization lies, perhaps, in the successful intervention it offers, rather than in etiological explanations of the phenomenon. The success of these interventions derives from careful analysis of the current influences that maintain behavior.

Trauma is one obvious causal variable in the development of children's excessive fears. A respondent-conditioning paradigm explains the fear as a conditioned response elicited by a conditioned stimulus, a neutral stimulus that was present when the original trauma involving fear (an unconditioned response to an unconditioned stimulus) occurred. For example, a child undergoing treatment for cancer is typically exposed to a number of painful and frightening medical procedures. After several experiences with these procedures, the child may develop an anxiety response (i.e., vomiting) to the hospital setting and medical personnel that have become associated with stressful procedures. A precipitating traumatic event cannot, however, be identified in many clinical cases of children's fear (Solyom, Beck, Solyom, & Hugel, 1974). Seligman and Johnston (1973) have noted that avoidance behavior is not always mediated by fear. Classical conditioning alone, therefore, cannot account for children's fears.

Operant conditioning may often be a causal process in the acquisition of fearful behavior and is usually a critical component of its maintenance. Fearful behavior is developed and/or supported by reinforcing environmental consequences. The child may be rewarded for exhibiting fearful behavior, for example, by receiving solicitous attention from others. Avoidance behaviors, such as throwing a tantrum when the doctor enters the room, may be reinforced by postponing or avoiding the procedure.

Modeling may be a process involved in the acquisition of children's fears. A fear may be vicariously conditioned by observing a model undergo a fearful experience, or by observing a model reinforced for fearful behavior (Bandura & Rosenthal, 1966). Parental fearful behavior

and anxiety appear to be an especially potent factor in the acquisition and maintenance of children's fears (e.g., Bandura & Menlove, 1968; Bush, 1982; Shaw, 1975; Solyom et al., 1974). Thus, through observing a parent respond in a fearful manner to specific events or objects, a child may develop similar avoidance behaviors.

Respondent or operant conditioning, either directly or by modeling, thus represents learning conceptualizations of children's anxiety reactions. In addition, influential explanations of children's fears have been offered by Mowrer (two-factor learning theory, 1960) and Wolpe (1958) which explain the fear acquisition via classical conditioning, and the subsequent maintenance of the avoidance response by instrumental or operant conditioning. Although intuitively satisfying, empirical data have not supported this position. In addition to the criticisms of the classical conditioning explanation which were previously noted, one problem with the two-factor theory is the resistance of avoidance responses to extinction (Marks, 1969).

It is most likely that etiology differs across cases of children's fearful and anxious behavior. Classical or operant processes, modeled or direct, may be contributors to varying degrees and in varying combinations among children in the acquisition of the behavior. Certainly, learning processes help to sustain fearful behavior and are useful in its modification.

Predisposing Influences

Hereditary factors may possibly predispose some children to the development of an anxiety disorder. As noted by Johnson and Melamed (1979), individual differences in arousal and habituation to stimulation may be related to children's acquisition of fears. Individual differences in temperament have been demonstrated in infancy (e.g., Thomas, Chess, Birch, Hertzig, & Korn, 1963), and infants' ability to regulate their physiological states is considered an important index of their adaptability and developmental status. Thus, from birth, children vary in their reactivity and ability to adjust to environmental stimulation. In addition, some researchers have reported that psychiatric problems are more common in the families of patients with anxiety disorders (Solyom et al., 1974).

Certain stimuli appear more likely to elicit fear in humans than others (for example, fear of animals are more common than fear of objects), suggesting a genetic basis for increased reactivity to some stimuli. As previously discussed, the content of children's fears changes over the developmental course, suggesting that sensitivity to stimuli varies developmentally as well. Rachman and Hodgson (1974) have postulated that fears can be innate and maturational, such as fear of the dark, sudden noises, and the presence of strangers. Similarly, Seligman (1971) has proposed an evolutionary approach which focuses on human fears and phobias as a form of "prepared classical conditioning." He believes that there is a selective process in the development of fear-related behaviors that have an evolutionary basis. Fears or phobias may be conceptualized along a dimension of preparedness. On the one extreme of the preparedness dimension are fear responses that occur instinctively, followed by responses that occur after only a few pairings. Next are responses that occur after many pairings (unprepared responses). Responses on the other extreme of the continuum are what Seligman (1971) refers to as contraprepared (i.e., responses that occur only afer a large number of pairings). Although there is some support for this model of fear-related behaviors in adults (Hugdahl, Fredrikson, & Ohman, 1977; McNally & Reiss, 1983; Ohman, Eriksson, & Olofsson, 1975), there has been no research conducted on the preparedness of children's fears or phobias.

The following two sections illustrate how the medical situation is a useful environment in which to evaluate the manifestation of children's anxiety and fears and the processing by

which these responses are acquired and maintained.

THE STUDY OF MATERNAL-CHILD ATTACHMENT IN THE MEDICAL SETTING

The medical situation is an ideal environment to study maternal-child attachment. Separation from parents is frequently cited as a source of stress for hospitalized children (Nasera, 1978). The dental or medical situation often evokes anxiety because of separation from mothers during aversive procedures. Even when the parents are present, aversive procedures are often carried out by unfamiliar adults. This situation may be analogous to anxiety elicited by stranger approach. Some important implications from the maternal deprivation studies following Bowlby (1973) and Spitz (1950), and Bretherton and Ainsworth's (1974) stranger approach situations, relate to the degree of bonding of the parent and child (Michels et al., this volume).

Growing out of the psychoanalytic position, Bowlby (1973) recognizes the existence of constitutional factors in susceptibility to fear and includes both cognitive considerations and evolutionary notions in his theories. However, the most distinctive feature of his views resides in his arguments that a person's tendency to respond with fear is determined in large part by the perceived availability of attachment figures. In this way, most fears are considered as derivatives of separation anxiety, with the persistence of fear mainly due to the individual having developed anxious insecure attachments in early childhood as a result of disturbed family interaction.

The work of Ainsworth (1982) and Sroufe (1979) has done much to emphasize the importance of variations in the quality of attachments—with particular emphasis on the differences between secure and insecure attachments, as judged by responses during the strange situation procedures. Securely attached infants explore their environment freely when with their mothers, but following a brief separation they tend to seek closeness and comfort. Anxiously attached infants appear less secure in their mothers' presence and are acutely distressed during brief separations, but they are angry, as well as seeking closeness, on reunion. Avoidant infants, in contrast, appear undisturbed during separations, but avoid their mothers on reunion. The insecurity of their attachment is inferred from the infant's aggressive behavior toward the mother in other situations. The secure attachments constitute an adaptive norm, with insecure attachments likely to lead to maladaptive outcomes. The quality of the dyadic relationship has been shown to be an important predictor of the infant's later social development (Lewis, Feiring, McGuffey, & Jaskir, 1984; Sroufe, Fox, & Pancake, 1983); it is not regarded as something within the child or part of the child's makeup. The nature of the parenting in strange situations, such as medical visits where noxious events co-occur, may provide a prototype for the development of fear.

Few investigators have applied this notion to children above 3 years of age (Rutter, 1981). In dealing with medical emergencies, where the threat of illness exists, many mothers respond by overprotecting their children. This is seen in their encouraging dependent behavior by consistently assisting the child or displaying excessive concern when the child becomes upset or stressed. Longitudinal studies suggest that maternal overprotectiveness may be related to excessive dependency in older children (Kagan & Moss, 1962; Levy, 1943). Martin (1975) has explained the mechanism by which overly protective mothers foster the development of dependent behaviors in their children as follows:

> Separate tendencies on the part of the child may be experienced as aversive by the mother, and her attempts to restore the closeness may be reinforced by the reduction of (her) distress. The child, at the same time, may also experience forced separation as aversive, and returning to the mother may be reinforced by the reduction of his

distress...When (this) system becomes especially strong and the negative affect associated with separation behavior becomes intense,...phenomena such as school phobia may appear. (p. 487)

Lewis and Michalson (1981) studied very young children from 3 months to 3 years who were rated on five affective states: fear, anger, happiness, competence, and attachment/dependency. The children were observed across a wide range of situations including competence in meeting the task demands of a day-care program. Fearful behavior was found to be positively related to attachment/dependence and negatively to competence.

Kagan and Moss (1962) investigated the long-term effects of maternal overprotectiveness in 54 adults who had been observed in the home, school, and summer camp between the ages of 3 and 10 years. As children, the subjects were observed in terms of behavioral dimensions such as passivity, seeking nurturance, and seeking reassurance. In addition, the mothers were observed interacting with their children and were interviewed regarding their attitudes toward their children and child rearing. As adults, the subjects were interviewed regarding their dependent behaviors such as seeking support and nurturance from significant others. Kagan and Moss (1962) found that girls who had been highly protective as children tended to withdraw from stressful or challenging situations as adults. For boys, maternal protectiveness was positively related with the boys' passivity and dependence throughout childhood. Maccoby and Masters (1970) have written about the means by which parental restrictiveness is associated with a child's emotional dependency: "restrictiveness will prevent the child from acquiring autonomous skills for coping with his needs, and will therefore be associated with continued high dependency on parents and other adults" (p. 143).

Research has been undertaken in our laboratory to identify dysfunctional patterns of interaction between mothers and their children during medical stressors by developing a Dyadic Prestressor Interaction Scale (DPIS), guided by theoretical positions involving emotional contagion (Escalona, 1953; Vanderveer, 1949), crisis parenting (Kaplan, Smith, Grobstein, & Fischman, 1973; Melamed & Bush, in press), and work on attachment behavior and stranger approach (Bretherton & Ainsworth, 1974).

The emotional contagion hypothesis states that parental anxiety is communicated to the child by nonverbal as well as verbal means and that this, in turn, increases the child's anxiety level. The hypothesis is nonspecific as to exactly how or why the parental anxiety elicits child anxiety. It does have empirical support in studies correlating parental and child state anxiety in medical situations (Bailey, Talbot, & Taylor, 1973; Sides, 1977).

The crisis parenting model is more specific and emphasizes the increased importance of parenting when children face stressors. Vernon et al. (1967) found that maternal presence had a calming effect on children's (2 to 6 years old) distress during anesthesia induction but made little difference during a non-stressful procedure such as admission to the hospital. High parental anxiety at such times is thought to lead to impaired parental functioning (Duffy, 1972; Skipper, Leonard, & Rhymes, 1968) and consequently to less adequate support for the child's coping efforts. Supportive of this hypothesis, Robinson (1968) found that more fearful mothers of hospitalized children were likely to spend less time visiting, less frequently entered into conversations with the child's surgeon, and were less likely to complain or criticize aspects of their children's hospitalizations.

There are many correlational studies demonstrating that parental anxiety has a negative effect on children's adjustment to medical/dental procedures (Becker, 1972). However, this relationship is stronger in preschoolers than in older children. Many of these correlations were found for a first dental visit, but not during repeated visits (Koenigsberg & Johnson, 1972).

The relationship between Children's Manifest Anxiety Scale scores correlated positively with mothers' Taylor Manifest Anxiety Scale scores for 9- to 10-year-olds, but not for 11- to 12-year-olds (Bailey et al., 1973).

The mother-child relationship prior to hospitalization was also important to consider. Brown (1979) found that children 3 to 6 years of age, who had closer relationships with their mothers, were likely to show more distress and withdrawal during a short hospital stay than were those with poorer quality relationships. Mothers who were themselves anxious and highly accepting of the hospital authorities tended to have children who were distressed and withdrawn.

The crisis parenting hypothesis takes a closer look at the specific parenting strategies in effect during the crisis. Parental anxiety at such times may have a disorganizing influence on effective parenting behaviors. In our research program, we have undertaken an ecological approach to defining dyadic interactions.

The DPIS presented as Table 1 was devised out of the theoretical work on children in a stranger approach situation in order to operationalize the interactions (Melamed & Bush, in press). Categories of children's behavior in this situation were elaborated from the four categories used: Distress, Attachment, Exploration, and Social-Affiliative behaviors. Functional definitions were derived that would be suitable across a wide range of ages—4 to 12 years. Another six categories of parenting behaviors were derived from the parenting literature with a specific focus on the surgery preparation literature: Agitation, Ignoring, Reassurance, Information Provision, Distraction, and Restraint. All the categories except Restraint met acceptable reliability. In order to investigate combinations of parenting behavior and their relationship to the children's distress and attachment, canonical correlations were undertaken. It was found that observations about the mother's behavior accounted for 49% of the

TABLE 1 DYADIC PRESTRESSOR INTERACTION SCALE: FUNCTIONAL DEFINITIONS

Child behavior categories

Attachment
  Look at Parent: Child looking at parent
  Approach Parent: Child motorically approaching parent
  Touch Parent: Child physically touching parent
  Verbal Concern: Child verbalizing concern with the parent's continuing presence throughout the procedures

Distress
  Crying: Child's eyes watering and/or (s)he is making crying sounds
  Diffuse Motor: Child running around, pacing, flailing arms, kicking, arching, engaging in repetitive fine motor activity, etc.
  Verbal Unease: Child verbalizing fear, distress, anger, anxiety, etc.
  Withdrawal: Child silent and immobile, no eye contact with parent, in curled-up position

Exploration
  Motoric Exploration: Child locomoting around room, visually examining
  Physical Manipulation: Child handling objects in room
  Questions Parent: Child asking parent a question related to doctors, hospitals, etc.
  Interaction with Observer: Child attempting to engage in verbal or other interaction with observer

Social-Affiliative
  Looking at Book: Child is quietly reading a book or magazine unrelated to medicine or looking at its pictures
  Other Verbal Interaction: Child is verbally interacting with parent on topic unrelated to medicine
  Other Play: Child playing with parent, not involving medical objects or topics
  Solitary Play: Child playing alone with object brought into room, unrelated to medicine

Parent behavior categories

Ignoring
  Eyes Shut: Parent sleeping or has eyes shut
  Reads to Self: Parent reading quietly
  Sitting Quietly: Parent sitting quietly, not making eye contact with child
  Other Noninteractive: Parent engaging in other medically-unrelated solitary activity

Reassurance
  Verbal Reassurance: Parent telling child not to worry, that (s)he can tolerate the procedures, that it will not be so bad, etc.
  Verbal Empathy: Parent telling child (s)he understands his/her feelings, thoughts, situation; questions child for feelings
  Verbal Praise: Parent telling child (s)he is mature, strong, brave, capable, doing fine, etc.
  Physical Stroking: Parent petting, stroking, rubbing, hugging, kissing child

Distraction
  Nonrelated Conversation: Parent engaging in conversation with child on unrelated topic
  Nonrelated Play: Parent engaging in play interaction with child unrelated to medicine
  Visual Redirection: Parent attempting to attract child's attention away from medically related object(s) in the room
  Verbal Exhortation: Parent telling child not to think about or pay attention to medically related

Restraint
  Physical Pulling: Parent physically pulling child away from an object in the room
  Verbal Order: Parent verbally ordering child to change his/her current activity
  Reprimand, Glare, Swat: Parent verbally chastising, glaring at, and/or physically striking child
  Physically Holds: Parent physically holding child in place, despite resistance

Agitation
  Gross Motor: Parent pacing, flailing arms, pounding fists, stomping feet, etc.
  Fine Motor: Parent drumming fingers, tapping foot, chewing fingers, etc.
  Verbal Anger: Parent verbally expressing anger, dismay, fear, unease, etc.
  Crying: Parent's eyes watering, verbal whimpering, sobbing, wailing

TABLE 1   DYADIC PRESTRESSOR INTERACTION SCALE: FUNCTIONAL DEFINITIONS (***Continued***)

Informing
  Answers Questions: Parent attempting to answer child's medically relevant/situationally relevant questions
  Joint Exploration: Parent joining with child in exploring the room
  Gives Information: Parent attempting to impart information, unsolicited by child, relevant to medicine/the current situation, to
    the child
  Prescribes Behavior: Parent attempting to describe to the child appropriate behaviors for the examination session

observed child categories. Knowledge about the children's behaviors accounted for 36% of the variance of the parenting behaviors. All four canonicals were significant beyond the .05 level. Age, sex, type, and severity of the diagnosis did not correlate with the categories on this Dyadic Prestressor Interaction Scale.

The investigation of the mother-child interaction patterns revealed that the same strategies of information provision or distraction used by the mothers could lead to different patterns of children's behaviors depending upon other indices of maternal affect, i.e., agitation, reassurance, and ignoring. Mothers who were calm and interactive with their children, providing them with information about what to expect, were more likely to have less distressed children than mothers employing the same strategies, who were seen to be agitated or to ignore their children. Mothers who had reported higher state anxiety on the Spielberger State Trait Anxiety Inventory Test were more likely to ignore their children ($r = .35$, $p < .01$). Ignoring the child had a more detrimental effect on 4- to 6-year-old children than on 7- to 10-year-olds.

The effects of maternal reassurance also depend upon whether or not the mother is using any other parenting strategies to help her child cope with the medical visit. When reassurance is used in the absence of other strategies, children exhibit a high degree of all behaviors, including distress, attachment, exploring, and social-affiliative behaviors. Again, younger children were more likely to exhibit attachment behavior in this condition. If, on the other hand, mothers of these young children provided them

with information and were not overly reassuring, their youngsters showed more interest in exploring the examination room.

Thus, in terms of the emotional contagion theory (Escalona, 1953), it was found that agitated mothers were likely to have distressed children who were showing inhibition of attachment behaviors. These findings are similar to those reported by Bretherton and Ainsworth (1974) with younger children in the stranger approach situation. The results, furthermore, are consistent with crisis parenting, in that the behaviors of mothers who are agitated tended to be dysfunctional in the time of stress. Agitated mothers provided their children with less information relevant to the medical situation and tended to ignore them more. Mothers who used informing without agitation had children who explored the medical environment.

It is interesting that the ratings of mothers' anxiety by physicians also tended to influence how much information mothers received. Anxious mothers were given more information and were rated as less helpful in achieving their children's cooperation with medical procedures. Based on the preliminary findings from this study, a sequential analysis of the patterns of mother-child interactions will be used to help pinpoint the direction of influence in addressing the children's ability to cope with medical examinations.

INTERACTION BETWEEN TEMPERAMENT, COPING STYLES, AND ENVIRONMENTAL DEMANDS

Another factor that may mediate the child's response to the hospitalization is individual temperamental traits or behavioral styles. Temperament is defined as the child's behavioral style or emotional reactivity as he or she interacts with the environment (Willis, Swanson, & Walker, 1983). There is some evidence that these temperamental characteristics are innate and identifiable at the time of birth (Thomas & Chess, 1977).

The longitudinal research by Thomas, Chess, and Birch (1968) has demonstrated that a child's temperament is an important variable that relates to later adjustment. They identified nine dimensions of temperament including (1) level and extent of motor activity; (2) rhythmicity or degree of regularity of functions (i.e., sleep-wake cycle, hunger); (3) approach or withdrawal in response to new stimuli; (4) adaptability to new or altered situations; (5) threshold or responsiveness to stimulation; (6) intensity of reactions; (7) quality of mood; (8) distractibility; and (9) length of attention span and persistence. Five of these dimensions were found to cluster together to determine three general classes of temperament. "Difficult" children are described as displaying irregularity in biological functions, negative withdrawal responses to new stimuli, slow adaptability to change, and intense mood expressions that are generally negative. "Easy" children, on the other hand, are characterized by regularity in biological functions, positive approach responses to new stimuli, high adaptability to change, and mild or moderately intense moods that are usually positive in nature. The "slow-to-warm-up" child displays a combination of negative responses of mild intensity to new stimuli with slow adaptability after repeated contact. Furthermore, this child shows a mild intensity of reactions, whether positive or negative, and less tendency to exhibit irregularity of biological functions. Thomas et al. (1968) found that 70% of the children classified as "difficult" developed a variety of behavior problems at some later point, whereas only 18% of those children identified as "easy" developed such problems. The individual differences in children's adjustment to a hospital experience as prompted by temperament factors has yet to be investigated.

The hospital environment presents the child with many experiences over which the child has little or no control. The relationship between control over an aversive event and the amount of anxiety that it produces is a complex but critical question (Thompson, 1981). The research generated has not been tied to a single theoretical framework, although each perspective has some notion that a lack of control is basic to enhancing the anxiety state. The difficulties of finding convergence in the research literature are further increased by a confounding between the operational definitions of controllability and predictability. Although animal research (see Mineka) allows for the most careful separation of these factors, such key cognitive variables as perceived controllability, self-efficacy, desirability of outcomes, and availability of coping resources clearly demand research on humans. Unfortunately, the ethics of presenting aversive stimulation has limited research designs to brief presentation of controlled noxious stimuli such as loud tones, ischemic pressure, cold pressor task, and electric shock. Self-administration rather than experimenter administration of the noxious event has been evaluated by Staub, Tursky, & Schwartz (1971). These laboratory studies often do not take into account the process of receiving an aversive event from the anticipatory period. The legitimacy of generalizing data from laboratory studies to real-life situations has not been demonstrated, thus limiting their theoretical relevance. In fact, the diversity of presenting the aversive event and the variety of ways of measuring the anxiety reaction impede cross-study comparison. There are fewer controlled studies in which naturally occurring aversive events such as surgery and dental work have been employed. Using children who are experiencing these situations over repeated examinations places the investigator in an excellent position to study the developmental changes that occur with repeated experience at different ages.

The degree to which a medical experience is perceived as controllable by the child may be a function of the child's coping or behavioral style. Research evidence suggests that individual differences exist in information-seeking preferences. Although there has been considerable research on coping styles utilized by adults in stressful situations (e.g., Auerbach, 1977; Miller, 1983; Shipley, Butt, & Horwitz, 1978), there has been limited research in this area with children.

In one of the few studies with children, Burstein and Meichenbaum (1979) found that children who tended to avoid playing with hospital-related toys one week before surgery were more anxious about hospitalization than those who chose to play with such toys. Unger (1982) found that children who tended to deny worry actually obtained less information from videotaped models prior to impending dental procedures, and they showed more behavioral disruption than those who were low on denial. This indicates that anxiety in the face of stressors may affect information processing. Knight et al. (1979) found lower cortisol production in children who wanted to know about the upcoming hospital experience and used flexible defenses of intellectualization and isolation. The children who used denial, denial with isolation, displacement, or projection regarding the upcoming hospital experience showed maladaptive stress physiology reflected in increased cortisol production rates on the day after hospital admission.

Finally, a child's previous experience can provide information about the controllability or lack of controllability in a stressful situation and may affect the child's expectations regarding his or her ability to cope with the experience. There is, in fact, some evidence that exposure to information about medical or dental treatment in children with previous experience in these settings can reinvoke anxiety responses that had previously been conditioned to situations similar to those about which the child receives preparatory information (Faust & Melamed, 1984; Melamed, Dearborn, & Hermecz, 1983; Siegel & Harkavy, in review). These conditioned emotional responses can later interfere with the child's adaptive functioning in the medical or dental setting.

FUTURE DIRECTIONS FOR RESEARCH ON CHILDHOOD FEARS

The medical/dental prototype offers a naturalistic setting in which the principles underlying the different theoretical positions can be addressed. The data reported in this chapter suggest that one must consider transactions between the individual, with his or her biological, temperamental, and behavioral coping styles, and the particular set of stressors. The relevance of attachment figures may be important only during certain developmental phases as they may reduce or enhance the child's emotional responding.

A number of issues remain to be explored within child developmental theory that are prerequisite to the study of children's fear. What is the relationship between cognition and emotion? This review has pinpointed some research which suggests that a child's understanding and interpretation of the stressors can influence whether an emotional response, including physiological arousal and avoidance behaviors, will necessarily be prompted by a medical experience. There is little in the developmental literature regarding the preschool and older child that relates cognitive ability and emotional development, especially as fear is expressed. Lang's bioinformational theory provides a conceptual framework for understanding the cognitive events in emotion. Viewing the problem from this perspective, Hermecz and Melamed (1984) found that reinforcement of verbal reports of physiological change and descriptions of overt behavior in dental phobic children allowed for the accessing of the fear memory. This greater emotional processing was evidenced in measured physiological change. Furthermore, this procedure enhanced the congruence between semantic and physiological components of the imagery experience with therapeutic implications as an anxiety reduction procedure with children.

How does arousal level affect children's capacity to learn to cope with stress? Level of arousal has been demonstrated to influence the amount of information a child acquires from a psychological preparation procedure in the face of an impending stressor such as medical and dental treatment. Yet few studies have consistently measured the retention of information under varying levels of arousal; an understanding of the relationship would have implications for the manner in which one would teach a child to cope with a stressful event. For example, if a child is excessively aroused while being taught to cope, the child may fail to acquire the information required to effect change in his or her fear responses. Attentional factors need to be examined within this paradigm.

What are reliable indices of children's anxiety-related responses? Although the adult literature on phobias and fear has adopted a three-systems approach, the use of multidimensional assessment is still a rarity with children. In addition, the process of adaptation across the different time phases (i.e., anticipation of a medical stressor, actual procedural impact, post-medical stressor) needs to be looked at in terms of desynchronies across response systems. Differences in patterns of these responses may help operationalize such concepts as maladaptive versus adaptive anxiety. For instance, if in the face of an impending invasive procedure the child is concordant in physiological arousal and self-reported anticipatory concerns but is low on avoidance behavior and also shows adaptation across events, these conditions might predict effective coping. On the

other hand, a child showing an invariant pattern across these phases may be more vulnerable to the development of maladaptive anxiety-related behaviors.

Several research strategies that have not thus far been applied could be most useful in answering these questions. By undertaking prospective longitudinal approaches to studying children's behavior in the face of medical stress, we can evaluate predisposition for vulnerability to dysfunctional anxiety responses. The strategy taken by developmental psychopathologists as described by Sroufe & Rutter (1984) could profitably be adapted to some of these problems. For example, if normative data were collected across individuals coping with invasive medical procedures that are repeated during different phases of development, then the interaction between biological predisposition, parenting behaviors, and responses to other nonmedical stress situations can be evaluated. In addition, the subsample of children who do not develop maladaptive behaviors can also be studied to identify those factors that make them less vulnerable to stress.

REFERENCES

Agras, W.S., Sylvester, D., & Oliveau, D. The epidemiology of common fears and phobias. *Comprehensive Psychiatry, 1969.*

Ainsworth, M.D.S. Attachment: Retrospect and prospect. In C.M. Parks & J. Stevenson-Hinde (Eds.), *The place of attachment in human behavior.* London: Tavistock Press, 1982.

Auerbach, S.M. Surgery-induced stress. In R.H. Woody (Ed.), *Encyclopedia of clinical assessment (Vol. II).* San Francisco: Josey-Bass, 1977.

Bailey, P.M., Talbot, A., & Taylor, P.P. A comparison of maternal anxiety levels with anxiety levels manifested in the child dental patient. *Journal of Dentistry for Children, 1973.*

Bandura, A., & Menlove, F.L. Factors determining vicarious extinction of avoidance behavior through symbolic modeling. *Journal of Personality and Social Psychology,* 1968.

Bandura, A., and Rosenthal, T. Vicarious classical conditioning as a function of arousal level. *Journal of Personality and Social Psychology*, 1966.

Barrios, B.A., Hartmann, D.P., & Shigetomi, C. Fears and anxiety in children. In E.J. Mash & L.G. Terdal (Eds.), *Behavioral assessment of childhood disorders*. New York: Guildford Press, 1981.

Bauer, D. An exploratory study of developmental changes in children's fears. *Journal of Child Psychology and Psychiatry*, 1976.

Becker, R.D. Therapeutic approaches to psychopathological reactions to hospitalization. *International Journal of Child Psychotherapy*, 1972.

Bowlby, J. *Attachment and loss, Vol. 2: Separation: Anxiety and anger*. New York: Basic Books, 1973.

Bretherton, I., & Ainsworth, M. Responses of 1-year-olds to a stranger in a strange situation. In M. Lewis & L.A. Rosenblum (Eds.). *The origins of fear*. New York: Wiley, 1974.

Brown, B. Beyond separation. In D. Hall & M. Stacey (Eds.), *Beyond separation*. London: Routledge and Kegan Paul, 1979.

Burstein, S., & Meichenbaum, D. The work of worrying in children undergoing surgery. *Journal of Abnormal Child Psychology*, 1979.

Bush, J.P. *An observation measure of parent-child interactions in the pediatric medical clinic: Relationship with anxiety and coping style*. Unpublished doctoral dissertation proposal. University of Virginia, Charlottesville, 1982.

Cutbert, M., & Melamed, B.G. A screening device: Children at risk for dental fears and management problems, *Journal of Dentistry for Children*, 1982.

Duffy, E. Activation. In N. S. Greenfield & R.A. Sternbach (Eds.), *Handbook of psychophysiology*. New York: Holt, Rinehart, & Winston, 1972.

Escalona, S. Emotional development in the first year of life. In M.J. Senn (Ed.), *Problems of infancy and childhood*. New Jersey: Foundation Press, 1953.

Gross, A.M., Stern, R.M., Levin, R.B., Dale, J., & Wojnilower, D.A. The effect of mother-child separation on the behavior of children experiencing a diagnostic medical procedure. *Journal of Consulting and Clinical Psychology*, 1983.

Harris, S.L., & Ferrari, M. Development factors in child behavior therapy. *Behavior Therapy*, 1983.

Hermecz, D.A., & Melamed, B.B. The assessment of emotional imagery training in fearful children. *Behavior Therapy*, 1984.

Hugdahl, K., Fredrikson, M., & Ohman, A. "Preparedness" and "arousability" as determinants of electrodermal conditioning. *Behavior Research and Therapy*, 1977.

Jersild, A.T., & Holmes, F.B. Children's fears. *Child Development Monograph*, 1935.

Johnson, S.B., & Melamed, B.G. The assessment and treatment of children's fears. In B.B. Lahey & A.E. Kazdin (Eds.), *Advances in clinical child psychology* (Vol. 2). New York: Plenum, 1979.

Kagan, J., & Moss, H.A. *Birth to maturity*. New York: Wiley, 1962.

Kaplan, P.M., Smith, A., Grobstein, R., & Fischman, S.E. Family mediation of stress. *Social Work*, 1973.

Katz, E.R., Kellerman, J., & Segal, S.E. Anxiety as an affective focus in the clinical study of acute behavioral distress: A reply to Shacham and Daut. *Journal of Consulting and Clinical Psychology*, 1981.

Kennedy, W.A. School phobia: Rapid treatment of fifty cases. *Journal of Abnormal Psychology*, 1965.

Kleinknecht, R., Klepac, R., & Alexander, L. Origins and characteristics of fear of dentistry. *Journal of the American Dental Association*, 1973.

Knight, R., Atkins, A., Eagle, C., Evans, N., Finklestein, J.W., Fukushima, D., Katz, J., & Weiner, H. Psychological stress, ego defenses, and cortisol production in children hospitalized for elective surgery. *Psychosomatic Medicine*, 1979.

Koenigsberg, S., & Johnson, R. Child behavior during sequential dental visits. *Journal of the American Dental Association*, 1972.

Lang, P.J. The cognitive psychophysiology of emotion: Fear and anxiety. In A.H. Tuma & J. Maser (Eds.), *Anxiety and the Anxiety Disorders*. Hillsdale, NJ: Laurence Erlbaum Associates.

Lapouse, R., & Monk, M.A. Fears and worries in a representative sample of children. *American Journal of Orthopsychiatry*, 1959.

Levy, D.M. *Maternal overprotection*. New York: Columbia University Press, 1943.

Lewis, M., Feiring, C., McGuffey, C., & Jaskir, J. Predicting psychopathology in six-year-olds from early social relations. *Child Development*, 1984.

Lewis, M., & Michalson, L. The measurement of emotional state. In C. Izard (Ed.), *Measurement of emotion in infants and children.* New York: Cambridge University Press, 1981.

Maccoby, E. & Master, J.C. Attachment and dependency. In P.H. Mussen (Ed.), *Charmichael's manual of child psychology* (Vol. 2). New York: Wiley, 1970.

MacFarlane, J.W., Allen, L., & Honzik, M.P. *A developmental study of the behavior problems of normal children between 21 months and 14 years.* Berkeley: University of California Press, 1954.

McNally, R.J., & Reiss, S. The preparedness theory of phobias and human safety-signal conditioning. *Behavior Research and Therapy,* 1983.

Marks, I.M. *Fears and phobias.* New York: Academic Press, 1969.

Martin, B. Parent-child relations. In F.D. Horwitz (Ed.), *Review of child development research* (Vol. 4). Chicago: University of Chicago Press, 1975.

Martin, R.B., Shaw, M.A., & Taylor, P.P. The influence of prior surgical experience on the child's behavior at the initial dental visit. *Journal of Dentistry for Children,* 1977.

Melamed, B.G., & Bush, J.P. Family factors in children with acute illness. In S. Auerbach & A. Stoberg (Eds.), *Crises in families.* New York: Hemisphere Publishing Co., in press.

Melamed, B.G., Dearborn, M., & Hermecz, D.A. Necessary considerations for surgery preparation: Age and previous experience. *Psychosomatic Medicine,* 1983.

Melamed, B.G., Robbins, S., & Graves, S. Preparation for surgery and medical procedures. In C. Russo & J. Varni (Eds.), *Behavioral pediatrics.* New York: Plenum, 1982.

Michaels, R., Frances, A., & Shear, M.K. Psychodynamic models of anxiety. In A.H. Tuma & J. Maser (Eds.), *Anxiety and the anxiety disorders.* Hillsdale NJ: Laurence Earlbaum Associates.

Miller, L.C. Fears and anxiety in children. In C.E. Walder & M.S. Roberts (Eds.), *Handbook of clinical child psychology.* New York: Wiley, 1983.

Miller, L.C., Barrett, C.L., & Hampe, E. Phobias of childhood in a prescientific era. In A. Davids (Ed.), *Child personality and psychopathology: Current topics* (Vol. 1). New York: Wiley, 1974.

Miller, L.C., Barrett, C.L., Hampe, E., & Noble, H. Factor structure of childhood fears. *Journal of Consulting and Clinical Psychology,* 1972.

Morris, R.J., & Kratochwill, T.R. *Treating children's fears and phobias: A behavioral approach.* New York: Pergamon Press, 1983.

Mowrer, O.H., & Viek, P. An experimental analogue of fear from a sense of helplessness. *Journal of Abnormal Social Psychology,* 1948.

Nasera, H. Children's reactions to hospitalization and illness. *Child Psychiatry and Human Development,* 1978.

Ohman, A., Ericksson, A., & Olofsson, C. One-trial learning and superior resistance to extinction of autonomic responses conditioned to potentially phobic stimuli. *Journal of Comparative and Physiological Psychology,* 1975.

Rachman, S., & Hodgson, R.J. Synchrony and desynchrony in fear and avoidance. *Behavior Research and Therapy,* 1974.

Richards, C.S., & Siegel, L.F. Behavioral treatment of anxiety states and avoidance behaviors in children. In D. Margolin II (Ed.), *Child behavior therapy.* New York: Gardner Press, Inc., 1978.

Rutter, M. *Maternal deprivation reassessed* (2nd ed.). New York: Penguin Books, 1981.

Rutter, M., Tizard, J., & Whitmore, K. *Education, health, and behavior.* New York: Wiley, 1970.

Seligman, M.E.P. Phobias and preparedness. *Behavior Therapy,* 1971.

Seligman, M.E.P., & Johnston, J. A cognitive theory of avoidance learning. In F.J. McGuigan & D.B. Lumsden (Eds.), *Contemporary approaches to conditioning and learning.* New York: Wiley, 1973.

Sermit, O. Emotional and medical factors in child dental anxiety. *Journal of Child Psychology and Psychiatry,* 1974.

Shaw, E.G., & Rought, D.K. Effects of mothers' presence on children's reactions to aversive procedures. *Journal of Pediatric Psychology,* 1982.

Shaw, O. Dental anxiety in children. *British Dental Journal,* 1975.

Shipley, R.H., Butt, J.H., & Horwitz, B.A. Preparation to re-experience a stressful medical examination: Effect of repetitious videotape exposure and coping style. *Journal of Consulting and Clinical Psychology,* 1978.

Siegel, L.J., & Harkavy, J. The effects of filmed modeling as a prehospital preparatory on children with previous hospital experience. *Journal of Consulting and Clinical Psychology,* submitted for publication.

Skipper, J.K., Jr., Leonard, R.G., & Rhymes, J. Child hospitalization and social interaction: An experimental study of mothers' feelings of stress, adaptation, and satisfaction. *Medical Care,* 1968.

Solyom, L., Beck, P., Solyom, C., & Hugel, R. Some etiological factors in phobic neurosis. *Canadian Psychiatric Association Journal,* 1974.

Spitz, R.A. Anxiety in infancy: A study of its manifestations in the first year of life. *International Journal of Psychoanalysis,* 1950.

Sroufe, L.A. The coherence of individual development. *American Psychologist,* 1979.

Sroufe, L.A., Fox, N., & Pancake, V.R. Attachment and dependency in developmental perspective. *Child Development,* 1983.

Sroufe, L.A., & Rutter, M. The domain of developmental psychopathology. *Child Development,* 1984.

Staub, E., Tursky, B., & Schwartz, G.E. Self-control and predictability: Their effects on reactions to aversive stimulation. *Journal of Personality and Social Psychology,* 1971.

Thomas, A., & Chess, S. *Temperament and development.* New York: Brunner/Mazal, 1977.

Thomas, A., Chess, S., & Birch, H.G. *Temperament and behavior disorders in children.* New York: New York University Press, 1968.

Thomas, A., Chess, S., Birch, H.G., Hertzig, M., & Korn, S. *Behavioral individuality in early child-hood.* New York: New York University Press, 1963.

Thompson, S.C. Will it hurt less if I can control it? A complex answer to a simple question. *Psychological Bulletin,* 1981.

Traughber, B., & Cataldo, M. Biobehavioral effects of pediatric hospitalization. In J. Tuma (Ed.), *Handbook for the practice of pediatric psychology.* New York: Wiley, 1982.

Unger, M. *Defensiveness in children as it influences acquisition of fear-relevant information.* Unpublished masters thesis, University of Florida, 1982.

Vanderveer, A. The psychopathology of physical illness and hospital residence. *Quarterly Journal of Child Behavior,* 1949.

Venham, L., Bengston, D., & Cipes, M. Children's responses to sequential dental visits. *Journal of Dental Research,* 1977.

Vernon, D.T.A., Foley, J., & Schulman, J. Effect of mother-child separation and birth order on young children's responses to two potentially stressful experiences. *Journal of Personality and Social Psychology,* 1967.

Willis, D.J., Swanson, B.M., & Walker, C.E. Etiological factors. In T.H. Ollendick & M. Hersen (Eds.), *Handbook of child psychopathology.* New York: Plenum Press, 1983.

Winer, G.A. A review and analysis of children's fearful behavior in dental settings. *Child Development,* 1982.

Wolpe, J. *Psychotherapy by reciprocal inhibition.* Stanford University Press, 1958.

CHAPTER 5

LANGUAGE AND COMMUNICATION

Few achievements have captured the imagination of psychologists as much as the child's acquisition of language. A vast effort has been devoted to describing the nature of language development; in other words, how the nature of children's grammatical constructions shifts as they develop. What are the rule systems that account for the use of sentences, and how does the child's ability to use a system of rules change with development? In his article in this section, Slobin shows the remarkable similarity of children's grammar across a wide variety of different cultures. This is only one of the areas that has concerned students of language, since an analysis of the child's language that was limited to a description of the formal grammatical features of children's sentences was not enough. A second important direction of language research concerns the study of the nonlinguistic context of language. Semantics, or the study of meaning, has emerged as an important and active area of research. Children's language, in short, may be richer, more complex, and more fully understood by a consideration of the context in which the language occurs.

Closely related to this issue is the very difficult task of explaining the language achievements that previous investigators have described. How do children acquire language? This question has concerned researchers for decades. Many theories, such as biological and learning theories, have been offered. While parents probably facilitate this language learning process, it is clear that infants are ''biologically predisposed'' to respond to certain aspects of speech. In her article, Fernald shows that babies prefer to listen to ''motherese''—a pattern of speech that is characterized by high pitch and exaggerated intonation. She suggests that this pattern of speech may be more easily recognized and remembered by infants due to their sensitivity to sounds of this pitch. The study illustrates the interplay between maternal behavior—in this case the modification of mother's speech when addressing her infant—and the infant's capacity to respond to this kind of stimulation. Further evidence of the child's active role in the acquisition of language comes from the Goldin-Meadow and Mylander report. These investigators show that deaf children may acquire communication gestures that have language-like properties, even in the absence of parental models. This remarkable feat suggests that parents and adults are probably helpful, but direct parental modeling may not be critical in children's acquisition of early sign language and possibly spoken language as well.

In the next article, Grosjean explores the ways in which children develop more than one language. There are many reasons for the development of bilingualism in childhood, including the proximity of other linguistic groups, the use of a different language at school and home, or an explicit national policy to promote bilingualism. Proficiency in more than one language can be acquired by learning the languages either simultaneously or successively, and both approaches are successful routes to bilingualism. The article shows the importance of psychosocial factors, such as the use of the language in the family or in the school in determining when, to what extent, and for how long a child will be bilingual.

In the final article, Garvey illustrates the importance of a new aspect of language—pragmatics, or the study of how children learn the rules governing the use of language in communication contexts. She shows that we should not forget the obvious differences in the ways in which language varies in different settings, for different speakers, and for different audiences. Children learn to adjust their language to best suit the situational demands. In fact, a system of language that could not be easily modified to satisfy the needs of a new situation would be of very limited value in communication.

These articles survey some of the current issues and controversies in the study of language. It is very clear that our search is still not over for answers to the "when, why, and how" of language and communication development in children.

Children and Language: They Learn the Same Way All around the World

Dan I. Slobin

According to the account of linguistic history set forth in the book of Genesis, all men spoke the same language until they dared to unite to build the Tower of Babel. So that men could not cooperate to build a tower that would reach into heaven, God acted to "confound the language of all the earth" to insure that groups of men "may not understand one another's speech."

What was the original universal language of mankind? This is the question that Psammetichus, ruler of Egypt in the seventh century B.C., asked in the first controlled psychological experiment in recorded history—an experiment in developmental psycholinguistics reported by Herodotus:

"Psammetichus...took at random, from an ordinary family, two newly born infants and gave them to a shepherd to be brought up amongst his flocks, under strict orders that no one should utter a word in their presence. They were to be kept by themselves in a lonely cottage..."

Psammetichus wanted to know whether isolated children would speak Egyptian words spontaneously—thus proving, on the premise that ontogeny recapitulates phylogeny, that Egyptians were the original race of mankind. In two years, the children spoke their first word: *becos,* which turned out to be the Phrygian word for bread. The Egyptians withdrew their claim that they were the world's most ancient people and admitted the greater antiquity of the Phrygians.

Same We no longer believe, of course, that Phrygian was the original language of all the earth (nor that it was Hebrew, as King James VII of Scotland thought). No one knows which of the thousands of languages is the oldest— perhaps we will never know. But recent work in developmental psycholinguistics indicates that the languages of the earth are not as confounded as we once believed. Children in all nations seem to learn their native languages in much the same way. Despite the diversity of tongues, there are linguistic universals that seem to rest upon the developmental universals of the human mind. Every language is learnable by children of preschool-age, and it is becoming apparent that little children have some definite ideas about how a language is structured and what it can be used for:

> *Mmm, I want to eat maize.*
> What?
> *Where is the maize?*
> There is no more maize.
> *Mmm.*
> [Child seizes an ear of corn]:
> *What's this?*
> It's not our maize.
> *Whose is it?*
> It belongs to grandmother.
> *Who harvested it?*
> They harvested it.
> *Where did they harvest it?*
> They harvested it down over there.
> *Way down over there?*
> Mmm. [yes]
> *Let's look for some too.*
> You look for some.
> *Fine.*
> Mmm.
> [Child begins to hum]

The dialogue is between a mother and a two-and-a-half-year-old girl. Anthropologist Brian Stross of the University of Texas recorded it in a thatched hut in an isolated Mayan village in

Chiapas, Mexico. Except for the fact that the topic was maize and the language was Tzeltal, the conversation could have taken place anywhere, as any parent will recognize. The child uses short, simple sentences, and her mother answers in kind. The girl expresses her needs and seeks information about such things as location, possession, past action, and so on. She does not ask about time, remote possibilities, contingencies, and the like—such things don't really occur to the two-year-old in any culture, or in any language.

Our research team at the University of California at Berkeley has been studying the way children learn languages in several countries and cultures. We have been aided by similar research at Harvard and at several other American universities, and by the work of foreign colleagues. We have gathered reasonably firm data on the acquisition of 18 languages, and have suggestive findings on 12 others. Although the data are still scanty for many of these languages, a common picture of human-language development is beginning to emerge.

In all cultures the child's first word generally is a noun or proper name, identifying some object, animal, or person he sees every day. At about two years—give or take a few months—a child begins to put two words together to form rudimentary sentences. The two-word stage seems to be universal.

To get his meaning across, a child at the two-word stage relies heavily on gesture, tone and context. Lois Bloom, professor of speech, Teachers College, Columbia University, reported a little American girl who said *Mommy sock* on two distinct occasions: on finding her mother's sock and on being dressed by her mother. Thus the same phrase expressed possession in one context (*Mommy's sock*) and an agent-object relationship in another (*Mommy is putting on the sock*).

But even with a two-word horizon, children can get a wealth of meanings across:

IDENTIFICATION: See doggie.
LOCATION: Book there.
REPETITION: More milk.
NONEXISTENCE: Allgone thing.
NEGATION: Not wolf.
POSSESSION: My candy.
ATTRIBUTION: Big car.
AGENT-ACTION: Mama walk.
AGENT-OBJECT: Mama book (meaning, "Mama read book").
ACTION-LOCATION: Sit chair.
ACTION-DIRECT OBJECT: Hit you.
ACTION-INDIRECT OBJECT: Give papa.
ACTION-INSTRUMENT: Cut knife.
QUESTION: Where ball?

The striking thing about this list is its universality. The examples are drawn from child talk in English, German, Russian, Finnish, Turkish, Samoan and Luo, but the entire list could probably be made up of examples from two-year old speech in any language.

Word   A child easily figures out that the speech he hears around him contains discrete, meaningful elements, and that these elements can be combined. And children make the combinations themselves—many of their meaningful phrases would never be heard in adult speech. For example, Martin Braine studied a child who said things like *allgone outside* when he returned home and shut the door, *more page* when he didn't want a story to end, *other fix* when he wanted something repaired, and so on. These clearly are expressions created by the child, not mimicry of his parents. The matter is especially clear in the Russian language, in which noun endings vary with the role the noun plays in a sentence. As a rule, Russian children first use only the nominative ending in all combinations, even when it is grammatically incorrect. What is important to children is the *word*, not the ending; the *meaning*, not the grammar.

At first, the two-word limit is quite severe. A child may be able to say *daddy throw, throw ball,* and *daddy ball*—indicating that he understands the full proposition, *daddy throw ball*—yet be unable to produce all three words in one stretch. Again, though the data are limited, this seems to be a universal fact about children's speech.

Tools   Later a child develops a rudimentary grammar within the two-word format. These first grammatical devices are the most basic formal tools of human language: intonation, word order, and inflection.

A child uses intonation to distinguish meanings even at the one-word stage, as when he indicates a request by a rising tone, or a demand with a loud, insistent tone. But at the two-word stage another device, a contrastive stress, becomes available. An English-speaking child might say BABY chair to indicate possession, and baby CHAIR to indicate location or destination.

English sentences typically follow a subject-verb-object sequence, and children learn the rules early. In the example presented earlier, *daddy throw ball,* children use some two-word combinations (*daddy throw, throw ball, daddy ball*) but not others (*ball daddy, ball throw, throw daddy*). Samoan children follow the standard order of possessed-possessor. A child may be sensitive to word order even if his native language does not stress it. Russian children will sometimes adhere strictly to one word order, even when other orders would be equally acceptable.

Some languages provide different word-endings (inflections) to express various meanings, and children who learn these languages are quick to acquire the word-endings that express direct objects, indirect objects and locations. The direct-object inflection is one of the first endings that children pick up in such languages as Russian, Serbo-Croatian, Latvian, Hungarian, Finnish and Turkish. Children learning English, an Indo-European language,

usually take a long time to learn locative prepositions such as *on, in, under,* etc. But in Hungary, Finland, or Turkey, where the languages express location with case-endings on the nouns, children learn how to express locative distinctions quite early.

Place   Children seem to be attuned to the ends of words. German children learn the inflection system relatively late, probably because it is attached to articles (*der, die, das,* etc.) that appear before the nouns. The Slavic, Hungarian, Finnish and Turkish inflectional systems, based on noun suffixes, seem relatively easy to learn. And it is not just a matter of articles being difficult to learn, because Bulgarian articles which are noun suffixes are learned very early. The relevant factor seems to be the position of the grammatical marker relative to a main content word.

By the time he reaches the end of the two-word stage, the child has much of the basic grammatical machinery he needs to acquire any particular native language: words that can be combined in order and modified by intonation and inflection. These rules occur, in varying degrees, in all languages, so that all languages are about equally easy for children to learn.

Gap   When a child first uses three words in one phrase, the third word usually fills in the part that was implicit in his two-word statements. Again, this seems to be a universal pattern of development. It is dramatically explicit when the child expands his own communication as he repeats it: *Want that...Andrew want that.*

Just as the two-word structure resulted in idiosyncratic pairings, the three-word stage imposes its own limits. When an English-speaking child wishes to add an adjective to the subject-verb-object form, something must go. He can say *Mama drink coffee* or *Drink hot coffee,* but not *Mama drink hot coffee.* This developmental limitation on sentence span seems to be universal: the child's mental ability to express ideas grows faster than his ability to formulate the ideas in complete sentences. As the child learns to construct longer sentences, he uses more complex grammatical operations. He attaches new elements to old sentences (*Where I can sleep?*) before he learns how to order the elements correctly (*Where can I sleep?*). When the child learns to combine two sentences he first compresses them end-to-end (*the boy fell down that was running*) then finally he embeds one within the other (*the boy that was running fell down*).

Across   These are the basic operations of grammar, and to the extent of our present knowledge, they all are acquired by about age four, regardless of native language or social setting. The underlying principles emerge so regularly and so uniformly across diverse languages that they seem to make up an essential part of the child's basic means of information processing. They seem to be comparable to the principles of object constancy and depth perception. Once the child develops these guidelines he spends most of his years of language acquisition learning the specific details and applications of these principles to his particular native language.

Lapse   Inflection systems are splendid examples of the sort of linguistic detail that children must master. English-speaking children must learn the great irregularities of some of our most frequently used words. Many common verbs have irregular past tenses: *came, fell, broke.* The young child may speak these irregular forms correctly the first time—apparently by memorizing a separate past tense form for each verb—only to lapse into immature talk (*comed, falled, breaked*) once he begins to recognize regularities in the way most verbs are conjugated. These over-regularized forms persist for years, often well into elementary school. Apparently regularity heavily outranks

previous practice, reinforcement, and imitation of adult forms in influence on children. The child seeks regularity and is deaf to exceptions. [See "Learning the Language," by Ursula Bellugi, PT, December 1970.]

The power of apparent regularities has been noted repeatedly in the children's speech of every language we have studied. When a Russian noun appears as the object of a sentence (*he liked the story*), the speaker must add an accusative suffix to the noun—one of several possible accusative suffixes, and the decision depends on the gender and the phonological form of the particular noun (and if the noun is masculine, he must make a further distinction on whether it refers to a human being). When the same noun appears in the possessive form (*the story's ending surprised him*) he must pick from a whole set of possessive suffixes, and so on, through six grammatical cases, for every Russian noun and adjective.

Grasp   The Russian child, of course, does not learn all of this at once, and his gradual, unfolding grasp of the language is instructive. He first learns at the two-word stage that different cases are expressed with different noun-endings. His strategy is to choose one of the accusative inflections and use it in all sentences with direct objects regardless of the peculiarities of individual nouns. He does the same for each of the six grammatical cases. His choice of inflection is always correct within the broad category—that is, the prepositional is always expressed by *some* prepositional inflection, and dative by *some* dative inflection, and so on, just as an English-speaking child always expresses the past tense by a past-tense inflection, and not by some other sort of inflection.

The Russian child does not go from a single suffix for each case to full mastery of the system. Rather, he continues to reorganize his system in successive sweeps of over-regularizations. He may at first use the feminine ending with all accusative nouns, then use the masculine form exclusively for a time, and only much later sort out the appropriate inflections for all genders. These details, after all, have nothing to do with meaning, and it is meaning that children pay most attention to.

Bit Once a child can distinguish the various semantic notions, he begins to unravel the arbitrary details, bit by bit. The process apparently goes on below the level of consciousness. A Soviet psychologist, D. N. Bogoyavlenskiy, showed five-and six-year-old Russian children a series of nonsense words equipped with Russian suffixes, each word attached to a picture of an object or animal that the words supposedly represented. The children had no difficulty realizing that words ending in augmentative suffixes were related to large objects, and that those ending in diminutives went with small objects. But they could not explain the formal differences aloud. Bogoyavlenskiy would say, "Yes, you were right about the difference between the animals—one is little and the other is big; now pay attention to the words themselves as I say them: *lar-laryonok*. What's the difference between them?" None of the children could give any sort of answer. Yet they easily understood the semantic implications of the suffixes.

Talk When we began our cross-cultural studies at Berkeley, we wrote a manual for our field researchers so that they could record samples of mother-child interaction in other cultures with the same systematic measures we had used to study language development in middle-class American children. But most of our field workers returned to tell us that, by and large, mothers in other cultures do not speak to children very much—children hear speech mainly from other children. The isolated American middle-class home, in which a mother spends long periods alone with her children, may be a relatively rare social situation in the world. The only similar patterns we observed were in some European countries and in a Mayan village.

This raised an important question: Does it matter—for purposes of grammatical development—whether the main interlocutor for a small child is his mother?

The evidence suggests that it does not. First of all, the rate and course of grammatical development seem to be strikingly similar in all of the cultures we have studied. Further, nowhere does a mother devote great effort to correcting a child's grammar. Most of her corrections are directed at speech etiquette and communication, and, as Roger Brown has noted, reinforcement tends to focus on the truth of a child's utterance rather than on the correctness of his grammar.

Ghetto In this country, Harvard anthropologist Claudia Mitchell-Kernan has studied language development in black children in an urban ghetto. There, as in foreign countries, children got most of their speech input from older children rather than from their mothers. These children learned English rules as quickly as did the middle-class white children that Roger Brown studied, and in the same order. Further, mother-to-child English is simple—very much like child-to-child English. I expect that our cross-cultural studies will find a similar picture in other countries.

How A child is set to learn a language—any language—as long as it occurs in a direct and active context. In these conditions, every normal child masters his particular native tongue, and learns basic principles in a universal order common to all children, resulting in our adult Babel of linguistic diversity. And he does all this without being able to say how. The Soviet scholar Kornei Ivanovich Chukovsky emphasized this unconscious aspect of linguistic discovery in his famous book on child language, *From Two to Five:*

"It is frightening to think what an enormous number of grammatical forms are poured over the poor head of the young child. And he, as if it were nothing at all, adjusts to all this chaos, constantly sorting out into rubrics the disorderly elements of the words he hears, without noticing as he does this, his gigantic effort. If an adult had to master so many grammatical rules within so short a time, his head would surely burst....In truth, the young child is the hardest mental toiler on our planet. Fortunately, he does not even suspect this."

READING 19

Four-Month-Old Infants Prefer to Listen to Motherese

Anne Fernald

The intonation, or prosody, of adult speech to infants and young children is characterized by a higher pitch and wider pitch range than in normal adult conversation (Fernald & Simon, 1984; Garnica, 1977; Menn & Boyce, 1982; Stern, Spieker, Barnett, & MacKain, 1983). Such exaggerated intonation in parental speech is thought to serve several functions related to language development, including marking turn-taking episodes in mother-infant dialogue (Snow, 1977), helping the infant track and parse the speech stream (Fernald & Simon, 1984), and acoustically highlighting new linguistic information (Fernald, 1984b; Fernald & Mazzie, 1983; Gleitman & Wanner, in press). However, for the prelinguistic infant, primary functions of the exaggerated prosody of motherese may be the elicitation and maintenance of the infant's attention and the communication of affect (Fernald, 1984a; Papousek & Papousek, 1981; Sachs, 1977). In fact, mothers' specific use of rising pitch contours to engage an alert infant in social interaction (Stern, Spieker, & MacKain, 1982) and falling pitch contours to soothe a distressed infant (Fernald, Kermanschachi, & Lees, 1984; Papousek & Papousek, 1984) suggests that maternal prosody may indeed be finely tuned to infant attention and arousal level. The present study was designed to investigate experimentally infant selective listening to the exaggerated intonation of motherese.

Research on infant auditory preferences has been relatively limited in comparison with the extensive literature on selective visual attention in infancy (see Banks & Salapatek, 1983). Methodological constraints associated with basic differences between looking behavior and listening behavior may partially account for this imbalance. Visual fixation, a necessary component of visual attention, is a convenient and widely used dependent variable in infant visual-preference research, although its sufficiency as a criterion has been questioned (Haith, 1981; Posner & Rothbart, 1980). For auditory perception, however, receptor orientation to the stimulus source is not essential. Since no easily observable behavior necessarily accompanies listening, studies of infant auditory preference must rely either on indirect behavioral measures or on operant procedures. Behavioral measures used to assess infant responsiveness to auditory stimuli include smiling (Wolff, 1963), vocalization (Bankiotes, Montgomery, & Bankiotes, 1972; Brown, 1979), and motor quieting (Turnure, 1971). Operant paradigms have more commonly been used, beginning with Friedlander's (1968) Playtest procedure in which infants operate an automated device enabling them to listen to either one of a pair of auditory signals, a technique used successfully with infants from the age of 9 months (Glenn & Cunningham, 1982, 1983; Glenn, Cunningham, & Joyce, 1981). With younger infants, operant response measures used to study selective listening include sucking (DeCasper & Fifer, 1980; Mehler, Bertoncini, & Barrière, 1978; Mills & Melhuish, 1974), head turn (Jones-Molfese, 1977), and visual fixation (Colombo & Bundy, 1981; Sullivan & Horowitz, 1983).

Selective listening studies attempt to demonstrate not only that infants can discriminate between two auditory stimuli, but also that infants are more responsive to one signal than to the other. While research in infant speech perception has focused primarily on the discrimination and categorization of isolated phonetic and prosodic contrasts (see Aslin, Pisoni, & Jusczyk, 1983, for a comprehensive review), selective listening studies have tended to use longer, continuous speech samples to investigate the relative salience to the infant of other dimensions of speech such as voice quality (Bankiotes et al., 1972), normal versus distorted speech (Glenn & Cunningham, 1982; Jones-Molfese, 1977; Turnure, 1971), and repetition rate (Friedlander, 1968). Young infants choose to listen more to a female voice than to silence or white noise (Colombo & Bundy, 1981), and they are more responsive to the mother's voice than to the voice of a stranger (Brown, 1979; DeCasper & Fifer, 1981; Mehler et al., 1978; Mills & Melhuish, 1974). The salience of maternal prosody to the infant has received increasing attention (Fernald, 1984a, 1984b; Glenn et al., 1981; Sullivan & Horowitz, 1983). Mehler et al. (1978) found that 6-week-old infants recognized the mother's voice when she spoke with high inflection but not when she spoke in a monotone. Glenn and Cunningham (1983) found that infants from 9–18 months listened more to their mother's voice when she ad-dressed the infant than when she spoke to an adult.

In previous preference studies using continuous motherese speech as an auditory stimulus (Friedlander, 1968; Glenn & Cunningham, 1983), the voice presented was that of the infant's own mother. These studies did not address the question of whether the infant was responding to the familiar caretaking speech of the individual mother or rather to more general acoustic characteristics of the motherese speech register. As auditory stimuli, the exaggerated pitch contours typical of motherese may be highly salient to the young infant. The infant's perceptual, attentional, and affective responsiveness to certain acoustic dimensions of motherese speech may predispose the infant toward motherese vocalizations, relative to other forms of auditory stimulation (see Fernald, 1984a).

In the present study, a new auditory preference procedure was designed using operantly conditioned head-turns as the dependent measure. The hypothesis tested was that 4-month-old infants would demonstrate a preference for motherese speech when given the choice between listening to a variety of infant-directed and adult-directed speech samples spoken by four women unfamiliar to the subjects. That is, with the production of two alternative sets of natural speech samples under infant control, it was predicted that infants would make significantly more head-turns in the direction required to produce infant-directed speech, or motherese than in the direction required to produce normal adult speech.

METHOD

Subjects

Forty-eight 4-month-old infants (M age: 122.5 days ±5), 21 females and 27 males, participated as subjects. An additional 27 infants (M age: 121.3 days ±5), 12 females and 15 males, were tested but were excluded because of fussiness (21), experimenter error (3), or equipment failure (3). All subjects were full-term infants with no history of hearing disorders or ear infections.

Four-month-old infants were selected as subjects in this experiment because pilot-testing showed that younger infants were less able to sustain attention for the duration of the testing session, resulting in higher subject attrition.

Stimuli

Tape-recordings were made of 10 adult women as they talked to: (a) their 4-month-old infants, and (b) the adult interviewer. None of these women was the mother of an infant who participated as a subject in this study. Recordings were made in a sound-attenuated room on a full-track Nagra tape-recorder with a Sennheiser cartoid microphone. For mother–infant recordings, the infant was placed in an infant seat on a low table, while the mother sat comfortably facing the infant. The microphone was placed slightly above and behind the infant seat at a distance of about 62 cm from the mother's mouth. The mother's voice was recorded for 5 min while she played with the infant. For mother-adult recordings, the mother sat upright in her chair and spoke with the interviewer for a few minutes about a variety of topics. Again, the microphone was placed at a distance of about 62 cm from the mother's face. During the mother–adult recording, the infant was seated to the side of the mother out of her direct line of view.

The recordings of four of these women were selected for further editing. Criteria for selection were: (a) overall recording quality, (b) the absence of crying, vocalization, and audible breathing from the infant, and (c) the presence of intonationally complete phrase groups of both infant-directed and adult-directed speech, each approximately 8 s long, from the same speaker. Care was also taken to select infant-directed and adult-directed samples from a particular talker that differed from each other by no more than 400 ms. When such comparable

phrase groups from the infant-directed and adult-directed speech of four different women had been identified, they were dubbed onto a two-track tape loop. The infant-directed speech samples were recorded on one track, and the adult-directed speech samples were recorded on the other, with the onsets of the two speech samples from a particular talker precisely aligned on the two tracks of the tape. A 2-s silent interval separated each pair of speech samples from the next pair. The resulting stimulus tape consisted of four different samples of natural infant-directed speech, each approximately 8 s long, separated from one another by 2-s silent intervals, recorded on track one. Each infant-directed speech sample was aligned with a sample of natural adult-directed speech of comparable duration (400 ms) from the same talker, on track two.

Appropriate loudness levels for the two sets of stimuli were determined by asking six adult subjects, all graduate students in speech science, to make loudness-matching judgments using a modified version of the psychophysical method of adjustment (Watson, 1973). Peak signal intensities varied from 66 to 70 dB. (SPL, A-Scale), measured at the position of the infant's head with a Bruhl and Kjaer sound-level meter. Signal level was calibrated daily for the two channels on each of the two loudspeakers.

The intonation contours of the four pairs of speech samples used as auditory reinforcers are shown in Fig. 1. It should be remembered, however, that these signals contained frequencies across the full spectral range of natural speech and not just the fundamental frequency as illustrated.

Design

This experiment employed a 2 x 2 factorial design, with side of presentation of motherese (left vs. right) and training order (motherese first vs. motherese last) as between-subject variables. The dependent measure was the number of trials, out of 15, in which the infant's head-turn

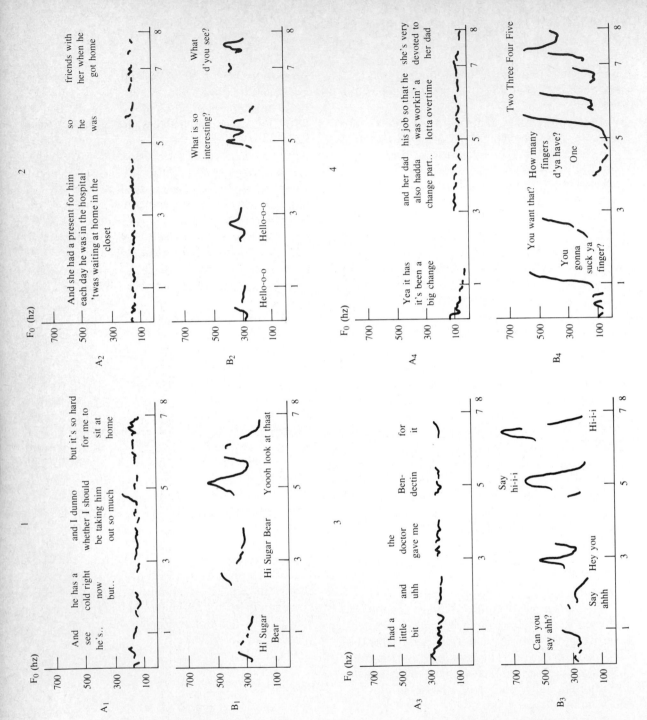

FIGURE 1　Intonation contours from the speech of four women (1–4): (A) adult-directed speech; (B) infant-directed speech, or motherese. Fundamental frequency (F₀), measured in hertz (hz), is the acoustic correlate of pitch.

was in the direction required to produce motherese. Twelve subjects were assigned randomly to each of the four groups, with the constraint that the distribution of male and female subjects was balanced throughout the groups.

Apparatus

All testing was conducted in a sound-attenuated room, approximately 3.6 x 3.6 m, separated from an adjacent control room by a one-way mirror. A testing booth was constructed of white masonite panels, 90 x 180 cm on three sides and open on the fourth side, as shown in Fig. 2. The mother, with the infant facing forward on her lap, was seated on a swivel chair in the center of the test booth. To the left and right, slightly behind the infant's head, were mounted two loud-speakers, for which 20 cm circular openings were cut in the side panels and covered with white cloth. Two small, red blinker lights were mounted on the side panels at the level of the infant's eyes but out of the field of the infant's peripheral vision when facing forward. A small green blinker light was mounted at midline on the center panel, also at eye level. Directly below the green light was a 5 cm circular opening for the lens of a video camera, connected to a video monitor in the

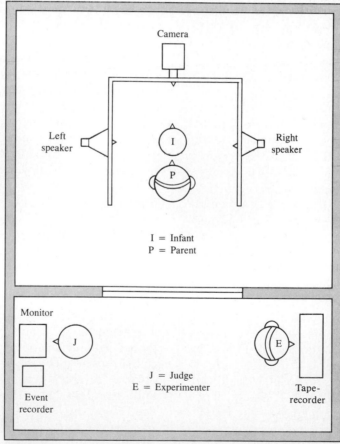

FIGURE 2   Auditory preference technique: Infant testing booth and control-room configuration.

adjacent control room. Three vertical lines were marked on the screen of the monitor, a center line indicating the position of the infant's nose when facing directly forward, and two lines to the left and right corresponding to the position of the infant's nose when the infant had made a criterion head turn ($>30°$) to one side or the other. The recorded stimuli were played on a Teac tape-recorder, with a Mackintosh amplifier for each channel located in the control room. The output of each of the two tape-recorder channels could be presented through either the left or right loudspeaker in the test booth, depending on the predetermined experimental condition. The blinker lights, which flashed at a rate of 2/s were switched on and off manually from the control room. An Esterline-Angus event recorder in the control room was used for data collection.

Procedure

The mother and infant were seated in the center of the test booth. Throughout the experiment, the mother listened over headphones to recorded music to mask the sound of the speech signals presented to the infant. The infant's head position was observed on the video monitor by a judge, who was unaware of which set of speech stimuli was being presented on which side. The responsibilities of the judge were: (a) to judge when the infant's eyes were at midline, thus enabling the infant to start a new trial; (b) to judge when the first criterion head-turn to the left or right had occurred, after the infant's eyes had returned to midline; (c) to record these judgments on three channels of the event recorder, operated by foot pedals; (d) to instruct the experimenter when, and on what side, to present a speech sample to the infant; and (e) to decide, in the case of infant fussiness, if the experiment should be terminated. The responsibilities of the experimenter were: (a) to assign each infant randomly to an experimental condition, and (b) to run the tape-recorder, switching

to the appropriate channel on the command "left" or "right" from the judge, and stopping the tape-recorder at the end of each 8-s speech sample. The experimenter monitored the sound production on headphones in order to start and stop the tape-recorder at the correct moment.

Two individuals served as judge throughout this experiment. Both observers were trained extensively in judging criterion head-turns during pilot testing. A reliability check was conducted by having the two observers judge head-turns independently during the same five testing sessions. Two judgments were considered to be in agreement if they were both in the same direction and occurred within a 2.5-s time window. The two observers showed 93.6% agreement on their head-turn judgments.

Training Trials   The experiment began with a training period in which the infant was familiarized with four of the different speech samples available on the two sides of the booth. The green center light was turned on to draw the infant's attention to midline. When the judge decided that the infant's eyes were at midline, the green center light was turned off. The judge then signaled "left" or "right" to the experimenter, depending on the predetermined training order for each subject. The experimenter then switched the tape-recorder to the appropriate channel, presenting one 8-s speech sample to the infant in the test booth, along with the red light on the corresponding side. The training period consisted of four familiarization trials; sound was presented twice to each side, in alternating order, accompanied each time by the red light on the appropriate side. After each sound presentation, the red light was switched off and the green center light was turned on, until the infant's gaze was once again at midline. When the judge decided that the infant's eyes had returned to midline, the green light was turned off, and a new training trial began. During the training period, the mother was instructed to rotate her chair to the appropriate side, if the infant did not spontaneously orient to the sound and light within a few seconds of presentation. Although the mother was unable to hear the stimuli, she was told to use the red light accompanying sound presentation as her cue to turn to the side, and the green center light as her cue to return to center. After the four training trials, the mother was instructed to keep her chair exactly centered in the test booth, making sure that the infant's legs were not shifted to one side or the other.

Test Trials Following the four training trials, sound presentation was made contingent upon a 30°-head-turn by the infant. The green center light was turned on to attract the infant's attention and turned off when the infant's eyes were judged to be at midline. The first criterion head-turn to the left or right was then rewarded with presentation of one speech sample, accompanied by the red light, on the side to which the infant had turned. The 8-s auditory reinforcer

was played to completion, regardless of whether or not the infant turned away. After each sound presentation, the infant had to return to midline in order to initiate the next trial. Completion of 15 test trials was required from each infant for inclusion in the study.

RESULTS

The score for each subject was based on the total number of trials, out of 15, in which the infant turned in the direction required to produce motherese. These data were analyzed in several ways, all showing a significantly greater number of infant head-turns toward motherese than toward adult-directed speech. These results support the major hypothesis of this study, that infants would demonstrate a preference for motherese by making significantly more head-turns in the direction required to produce infant-directed speech than in the direction required to produce adult-directed speech.

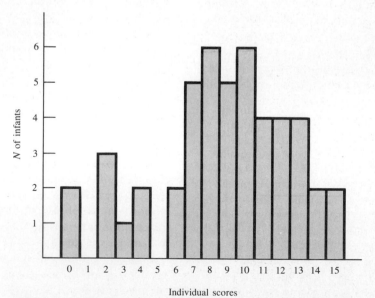

FIGURE 3 Distribution of individual scores; each score represents the number of trials out of 15 on which the infant's head-turn was in the direction of motherese.

DISCUSSION

Given the choice between listening to a variety of samples of either typical motherese speech or typical adult conversational speech, 4-month-old infants chose more often to listen to motherese. These results extend previous findings that infants are more responsive to their mother's own voice when she is addressing the infant (Glenn & Cunningham, 1983; Mehler et al., 1978). Since the speech samples used here as auditory reinforcers were produced by four different female speakers, all unfamiliar to the subjects, the results of this study demonstrate an infant preference for motherese speech rather than for the mother's voice per se.

Why should the motherese speech register be differentially attractive to infants? Infant-directed speech differs from adult-directed speech along several dimensions that might account for this infant preference. It may be the lexical usage of motherese that the infant finds familiar and appealing. In addressing infants, adults typically use a simplified lexicon, consisting primarily of monosyllabic and disyllabic words, often with special terms of affection (Ferguson, 1964). Or perhaps the intonation of speech to infants, with its exaggerated pitch level and range, slower rhythm and tempo, and relatively smooth and simple pitch contours (Fernald & Simon, 1984; Stern et al., 1983), accounts for this infant preference for motherese. In fact, Fernald and Kuhl (1981) have found fundamental frequency, or pitch, to be a primary acoustic determinant of this infant listening preference.

Fernald (1984a) has argued that the characteristic pitch contours of mothers' speech are prepotent auditory stimuli for the infant. The infant's early selective responsiveness to motherese may have its origins in innate perceptual, attentional, and affective predispositions to process sound in certain ways, as well as in the infant's experience with the speech patterns used by adults in caretaking and social interaction. For example, the fact that infant auditory sensitivity (e.g., Sinnott, Pisoni, & Aslin, 1983) and frequency discrimination abilities (Olsho, 1984) are better in the region of 500 Hz than in the region of 100 Hz suggests that speech at a higher pitch may have some perceptual advantage for the infant. Other psychoacoustic studies of auditory pattern perception in adults (e.g., Bregman, 1978; Divenyi & Hirsh, 1978) suggest that the pitch contours of motherese, simple in form and highly continuous in pitch excursion, may constitute auditory patterns that are more easily processed and remembered by the infant, when compared with the more complex and variable prosodic patterns of normal adult speech.

The salience of motherese for the infant may result not only from perceptual predispositions to process certain sounds more readily and effectively than others, but also from the infant's selective affective responsiveness to certain attributes of auditory signals. Several investigators have reported that infants show greater behavioral and cardiac responsiveness to relatively more complex auditory stimuli, such as speech, than to simpler sounds, such as continuous pure tones (e.g., Clarkson & Berg, 1983; Eisenberg, 1976). However, speech sounds are not all alike in their power to engage infant attention. Fernald, Haith, and Campos (1984) presented 4-month-old infants with rising and falling intonation contours, with either a wide pitch range as in motherese or a narrow pitch range as in normal adult speech. Infants showed consistently greater heart rate deceleration in response to the motherese pitch contours. These various findings suggest a possible psychophysiological basis for the infant's preference for human speech over other simpler auditory stimuli (Colombo & Bundy, 1981; Glenn et al., 1981) as well as for the infant's preference for the exaggerated intonation of motherese.

Such psychobiological arguments for an adaptive fit between the acoustic characteristics of adult speech to infants and the perceptual and affective processing capabilities of the infant lead to the prediction that motherese is a universal human care-taking behavior, both within and across cultures. Studies of the speech addressed to infants by fathers (e.g., Menn & Boyce, 1982; Rondal, 1980) and young children (e.g., Sachs & Devin, 1976; Shatz & Gelman, 1973) show that they also use a special register. Future research on motherese should investigate fathers' and siblings' speech to infants and infant responsiveness to prosodic modifications in male as well as female voices.

Cross-culturally, motherese speech has been widely reported, although its universality is disputed. The use of a prosodically distinctive speech register in adult speech to infants is documented in a number of European, American, African, and Asian languages (e.g., Blount & Padgug, 1976; Ferguson, 1964; Kelkar, 1964). Schieffelin (1979), however, claims that the Kaluli of Papua, New Guinea, do not use motherese and rarely address their infants directly. Yet Schieffelin also reports that Kaluli mothers commonly hold the infant up to face themselves or other people while speaking "for" the infant in a special high-pitched voice register. Perhaps this Kaluli practice is functionally equivalent to speaking motherese, providing a form of rich and varied auditory stimulation particularly appropriate for the infant. In addition to experimental research, more extensive cross-cultural observations are needed, substantiated by careful acoustic analyses, to increase our understanding of the functions and generality of motherese.

REFERENCES

Aslin, R. N., Pisoni, D. B., & Jusczyk, P. W. (1983). Auditory development and speech perception in infancy. In M. M. Haith & J. J. Campos (Eds.), *Infancy and the biology of development: Vol. 2. Carmichael's manual of child psychology* (4th ed.). New York: Wiley.

Bankiotes, F. G., Montgomery, A. A., & Bankiotes, P. G. (1972). Male and female auditory reinforcement of infant vocalizations. *Developmental Psychology, 6,* 476–481.

Banks, M. S., & Salapatek, P. (1983). Infant visual perception. In M. M. Haith & J. J. Campos (Eds.), *Infancy and the biology of development: Vol. 2. Carmichael's manual of child psychology* (4th ed.). New York: Wiley.

Blount, B. G., & Padgug, E. J. (1976). Prosodic, paralinguistic, and interactional features in parent-child speech: English and Spanish. *Journal of Child Language, 4,* 67–86.

Bregman, A. S. (1978). The formation of auditory streams. In J. Requin (Ed.), *Attention and performance VII.* Hillsdale, NJ: Erlbaum.

Brown, C. J. (1979). Reactions of infants to their parents' voices. *Infant Behavior and Development, 2,* 295–300.

Clarkson, M. G., & Berg, W. K. (1983). Cardiac orienting and vowel discrimination in newborns: Crucial stimulus parameters. *Child Development, 54,* 162–171.

Cohen, L. B. (1972). Attention-getting and attention-holding processes in infant visual preferences. *Child Development, 43,* 869–879.

Colombo, J., & Bundy, R. S. (1981). A method for the measurement of infant auditory selectivity. *Infant Behavior and Development, 4,* 219–223.

DeCasper, A. J., & Fifer, W. P. (1980). Of human bonding: Newborns prefer their mothers' voices. *Science, 208,* 1174–1176.

Divenyi, P. L., & Hirsh, I. J. (1978). Some figural properties of auditory patterns. *Journal of the Acoustical Society of America, 65,* 1369–1385.

Eisenberg, R. B. (1976). *Auditory competence in early life: The roots of communicative behavior.* Baltimore: University Park Press.

Ferguson, C. A. (1964). Baby talk in six languages. *American Anthropologist, 66,* 103–114.

Fernald, A. (1984a). The perceptual and affective salience of mothers' speech to infants. In L. Feagans, C. Garvey, & R. Golinkoff (Eds.), *The origins and growth of communication.* Norwood, NJ: Ablex.

Fernald, A. (1984b, September). *Intonation and reference*. Paper presented at the meeting of the British Psychological Society, Developmental Psychology Section, Lancaster, England.

Fernald, A., Haith, M. M., & Campos, J. J. (1984, May). *Infant cardiac orienting to motherese intonation contours*. Paper presented at the Third Biennial Retreat of the Developmental Psychobiology Research Group, Estes Park, CO.

Fernald, A., Kermanschachi, N., & Lees, D. (1984, April). *The rhythms and sounds of soothing: Maternal vestibular, tactile, and auditory stimulation and infant state*. Paper presented at the International Conference on Infant Studies, New York.

Fernald, A., & Kuly, P. K. (1981, April). *Acoustic determinants of infant preference for motherese*. Paper presented at the meeting of the Society for Research in Child Development, Boston.

Fernald, A., & Mazzie, C. (1983, April). *Pitch-marking of new and old information in mothers' speech*. Paper presented at the meeting of the Society for Research in Child Development, Detroit.

Fernald, A., & Simon, T. (1984). Expanded intonation contours in mothers' speech to newborns. *Developmental Psychology, 20,* 104–113.

Friedlander, B. Z. (1968). The effect of speaker identity, voice inflection, vocabulary, and message redundancy on infants' selection of vocal reinforcement. *Journal of Experimental Child Psychology, 6,* 443–459.

Garnica, O. (1977). Some prosodic and paralinguistic features of speech to young children. In C. E. Snow & C. A. Ferguson (Eds.), *Talking to children: Language input and acquisition*. Cambridge, England: Cambridge University Press.

Gleitman, L., & Wanner, E. (in press). Richly specified input to language learning. In: M. Arbib & O. Selfridge (Eds.), *Adaptive control of ill-defined systems*. Springer-Verlag.

Glenn, S. M., & Cunningham, C. C. (1982). Recognition of the familiar words of nursery rhymes by handicapped and nonhandicapped infants. *Journal of Child Psychology and Child Psychiatry, 23,* 319–327.

Glenn, S. M., & Cunningham, C. C. (1983). What do babies listen to most? A developmental study of auditory preferences in nonhandicapped infants and infants with Down's Syndrome. *Developmental Psychology, 19,* 332–337.

Glenn, S. M., Cunningham, C. C., & Joyce, P. F. (1981). A study of auditory preferences in nonhandicapped infants and infants with Down's Syndrome. *Child Development, 52,* 1303–1307.

Haith, M. M. (1981). *Rules that babies look by*. Hillsdale, NJ: Erlbaum.

Jones-Molfese, V. (1977). Preferences of infants for regular and distorted natural speech stimuli. *Journal of Experimental Child Psychology, 23,* 172–179.

Kelkar, A. (1964). Marathi baby talk. *Word, 20,* 40–54.

Kisbourne, M. (1978). The evolution of language in relation to lateral action. In M. Kinsbourne (Ed), *The asymmetrical function of the brain,* New York: Cambridge University Press.

Mehler, J., Bertoncini, J., & Barrière, M. (1978). Infant recognition of mother's voice. *Perception, 7,* 491–497.

Menn, L., & Boyce, S. (1982). Fundamental frequency and discourse structure. *Language and Speech, 25,* 341–383.

Mills, M., & Melhuish, E. (1974). Recognition of mother's voice in early infancy. *Nature, 252,* 123–124.

Olsho, L. W. (1984). Infant frequency discrimination. *Infant Behavior and Development, 7,* 27–35.

Papousek, H., & Papousek, M. (1981). Musical elements in the infant's vocalizations: Their significance for communication, cognition, and creativity. In L. Lipsitt (Ed.), *Advances in infancy research* (Vol. 1). Norwood, NJ: Ablex.

Papousek, M., & Papousek, H. (1984, April). *Categorical vocal cues in parental communication with presyllabic infants*. Paper presented at the International Conference on Infant Studies, New York.

Posner, M. I., & Rothbart, M. K. (1980). The development of attentional mechanisms. In J. H. Flowers (Ed.), *Nebraska symposium on motivation*. Lincoln NE: University of Nebraska Press.

Rondal, J. A. (1980). Fathers' and mothers' speech in early language development. *Journal of Child Language, 7,* 353–369.

Sachs, J. (1977). The adaptive significance of linguistic input to prelinguistic infants. In C. E. Snow, & C. A. Ferguson (Eds.), *Talking to children: Language input and acquisition.* Cambridge, England: Cambridge University Press.

Sachs, J., & Devin, J. (1976). Young children's use of age-appropriate speech styles in social interaction and role-playing. *Journal of Child Language, 3,* 81–98.

Schieffelin, B. B. (1979). Getting it together: An ethnographic approach to the study of the development of communicative competence. In: E. Ochs & B. B. Schieffelin (Eds.), *Developmental Pragmatics.* New York: Academic Press.

Shatz, M., & Gelman, R. (1973). The development of communication skills: Modifications in the speech of young children as a function of listener. *Monographs of the Society for Research in Child Development, 38*(5, Serial No. 152).

Siegel, S. (1956). *Non-parametric statistics for the behavioral sciences.* London: McGraw-Hill.

Sinnott, J. M., Pisoni, D. B., & Aslin, R. M. (1983). A comparison of pure tone auditory thresholds in human infants and adults. *Infant Behavior and Development, 6,* 3–17.

Snow, C. E. (1977). The development of conversation between mothers and babies. *Journal of Child Language, 4,* 1–22.

Stern, D. N., Spieker, S., & MacKain, K. (1982). Intonation contours as signals in maternal speech to prelinguistic infants. *Developmental Psychology, 18,* 727–735.

Stern, D. M., Spieker, S., Barnett, R. K., & MacKain, K. (1983). The prosody of maternal speech: Infant age and context related changes. *Journal of Child Language, 10,* 1–15.

Sullivan, J. W., & Horowitz, F. D. (1983). The effects of intonation on infant attention: The role of rising intonation contour. *Journal of Child Language, 10,* 521–534.

Turnure, C. (1971). Response to voice of mother and stranger by babies in the first year. *Developmental Psychology, 4,* 182–190.

Watson, C. S. (1973). Psychophysics. In B. B. Wolman (Ed.), *Handbook of general psychology.* Englewood Cliffs, NJ: Prentice Hall.

Wolff, P. (1963). Observations on the early development of smiling. In B. M. Foss (Ed.), *Determinants of infant behavior.* London: Methuen.

READING 20

Gestural Communication in Deaf Children: Noneffect of Parental Input on Language Development

Susan Goldin-Meadow

Carolyn Mylander

The deaf children in our study had hearing parents who elected to educate them by the oral method (*1*). We reported earlier (*2*) that, although these children had not been exposed to conventional sign language, they were able to develop a gestural communication system with some of the observed properties of early child language: consistent ordering of elements (the placement of words, or gestures, for certain semantic elements in consistent orders within a sentence) (*3*); differential probabilities of production of elements (the explicit production of words, or gestures, for certain semantic elements in a sentence more often than for other semantic elements) (*4*); and recursion (the concatenation of more than one proposition within a sentence) (*5*). Thus it appeared that they were able to develop a structured and productive communication system without a conventional linguistic model.

It was possible, however, that the children's hearing parents influenced the structure of this gesture system. We investigated two likely parental influences on the child's system: modeling, where the child learns the structure of his or her gestures, either by imitation or induction, from the structure of the parents' gestures; and shaping, where the structure in the child's gestures is reinforced by differential parental responses.

To determine whether the deaf children in our study might merely be imitating an adult's gestures, we videotaped four of the children and their mothers during play sessions. We classified the children's gestures as (i) spontaneous, if they were not preceded by parental gesture or were different from the parent's immediately preceding gestures, or (ii) imitated, if they were exact or partial imitations of the parent's immediately preceding gestures. Imitated gestures were found to be infrequent: 2 percent (1 of 58) of Karen's gestures, 5 percent (7 of 144) of Marvin's, 7 percent (7 of 93) of Abe's, and none (0 of 27) of Mildred's.

We next considered the possibility that the children induced a structure from their parents' gestures. We noted at the outset that gesture, not speech, was the children's primary means of communicating (only 1 to 4 percent of the children's communications contained meaningful speech); the mothers communicated by both gesture and speech (83 to 96 percent of the mothers' communications contained speech). Despite the fact that for a hearing person gesture and speech might form an integrated communication system, we chose to analyze mothers' communications from what we took to be their deaf children's point of view and therefore included only the mothers' gestures in our analyses (6).

The gestures of six deaf children and their mothers were transcribed according to a system developed earlier (2,7). Reliability—agreement between two coders in independently noting and segmenting individual gestures and assigning them to semantic categories—ranged from 83 to 100 percent. Two types of denotative signs were coded: deictic signs (pointing gestures which indicated objects) and characterizing signs (gestures whose forms were transparently related to the actions they represented—for example, a closed fist bobbed near the mouth to

TABLE 1   COMPLEX SIGN SENTENCES PRODUCED BY SIX DEAF CHILDREN OF HEARING PARENTS AND THEIR MOTHERS

| Child | Age (months) | Session first observed | | Child | | Mother | |
		Child	Mother	Complex sign sentences (N)	Total sign sentences (%)	Complex sign sentences (N)	Total sign sentences (%)
David	34 to 44	1	1	88*	26	8	12
Marvin	35 to 50	1	6	38†	23	2	6
Karen	37 to 50	1	6	31‡	22	1	4
Dennis	26 to 30	1		4§	11	0	0
Abe	27 to 45	2	5	45ǀˢ	25	1	3
Mildred	16 to 44	5	4	11¶	12	2	2

* Chi-squares were performed by comparing each child's complex sign sentences to those of his mother. $X^2(1) = 5.62$, $P < 0.02$.
† $X^2(1) = 3.79$, $P < 0.10$.
‡ $X^2(1) = 2.87$, $P < 0.10$.
§ Dennis's mother produced nine sign sentences but none was complex.
ǀˢ $X^2(1) = 8.06$, $P < 0.01$.
¶ $X^2(1) = 5.12$, $P < 0.05$.

characterize the act of eating). Deictic and characterizing signs could be concatenated to form simple sign sentences that conveyed one proposition [for example, gestures for "jar twist," indicating that the jar (object acted upon, or "patient" in the linguist's terminology) had been twisted open (act)], or complex sign sentences that conveyed at least two propositions [for example, "jar twist blow," a request that the jar (patient) be twisted open (act$_1$) and bubbles be blown (act$_2$)](8). We stress that we use linguistic terms such as sentence loosely and only to suggest that the deaf child's gesture strings share certain elemental properties with early sentences in child language.

We found that for five of the six children in our experiment the probability of producing in a two-sign sentence a sign for an intransitive actor ("boy" in the proposition "boy goes to mother") was comparable to the probability of producing a sign for a patient ("boy" in the proposition "mother hits boy"), and distinct from the probability of producing a sign for a transitive actor ("boy" in the proposition "boy hits mother") (Fig. 1). This same probability pattern was found in only two mothers, one of whom was the mother of Abe, the only child who did not convincingly show the pattern. Thus, the systems of mother and child differed in the probability of certain semantic roles (intransitive actor, patient, or transitive actor) being signed explicitly in two-sign sentences.

Furthermore, each of the six children's simple two-sign sentences could be characterized by at least one reliable construction order: patient-act, such as "grape eat" [David (N = 38) and Dennis (N = 11), P <0.01; Mildred (N = 27), P <0.05; Karen (N = 25), P <0.10; X^2 tests]; patient-recipient (recipient, the end point of a change of location), such as "cup table" [Marvin (N = 15), P <0.01; David (N = 19), P <0.001; X^2 tests]; or actor-act, such as "dog jump" [Abe (N = 11), P = 0.002; X^2 test]. In contrast, three mothers used no consistent construction orders, and the other three (mothers of Mildred, Abe, and Karen) displayed only a reliable patient-recipient construction order (N = 8, P = 0.07; binomial for each), an order not used by any of their children. Moreover, five children produced sentences following their own reliable construction orders an average of three sessions before their mothers produced any sign sentences in that order. Thus, the deaf children's reliable construction orders were not modeled by their hearing mothers' simple sign sentences.

We also analyzed use of complex sign sentences and found that all six children used complex sign sentences more frequently (9) and four used complex sign sentences earlier than did their mothers (Table 1). Taken together the data suggest that the structure of the deaf child's sign sentences was not induced from the mother's gestural model ($10,11$).

We next considered the possibility that the structure of the deaf child's sign sentences was in some way shaped by differential parental responsiveness to those sentences. Following Brown and Hanlon (12), we categorized the responses of the mothers and the experimenter to the sign sentences of four deaf subjects as either sequiturs (relevant and comprehending reactions to the child's sentence) or nonsequiturs (queries, irrelevant responses, misunderstandings, no responses, or responses of doubtful classification). We considered the child's sentence order to be preferred if it conformed to that child's reliable order and nonpreferred if it did not; for example, since Marvin reliably produced sentences with patient-recipient orders, sentences with this order were considered preferred for him, and recipient-patient sentences, nonpreferred. We found that the deaf child's sentences with preferred orders were no more likely to be followed by sequitur responses than were sentences with nonpreferred orders [49 percent (24 of 49) preferred and 47 percent (8 of 17) nonpreferred; P >0.50, Fisher's exact test with children individually tested]. Thus the child's preference for partic-

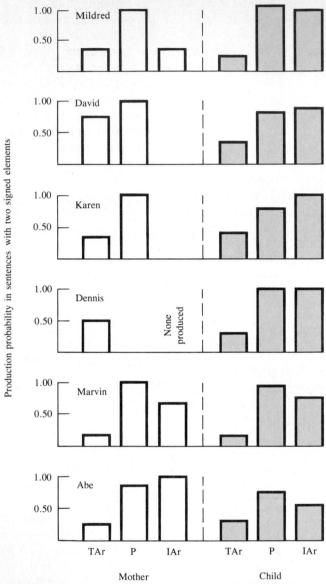

FIGURE 1   Production-probability patterns in simple sign sentences of mother and child. Probabilities were calculated only from sign sentences with two explicit semantic elements: Mildred's mother used 14 transitive sentences (the data base for the transitive actor and patient probabilities) and 4 intransitive sentences (the data base for the intransitive actor probability); her child used 22 and 2, respectively. David's mother used 10 transitive sentences and 1 intransitive sentence; her child used 54 and 16, respectively. Karen's mother used 7 transitive sentences and 1 intransitive sentence; her child used 23 and 4, respectively. Dennis's mother used 2 transitive sentences and no intransitive sentences; her child used 10 and 1, respectively. Marvin's mother used 6 transitive sentences and 8 intransitive sentences; her child used 30 and 4, respectively. Abe's mother used 8 transitive sentences and 2 intransitive sentences; her child used 29 and 19, respectively. *TAr,* transitive actor; *P,* patient; *IAr,* intransitive actor.

ular sign orders does not appear to be a function of communication pressure from the adult.

To determine whether communication pressure was shaping the deaf child's production-probability pattern we looked at sequiturs that followed sentences with preferred production-probability patterns (two-sign sentences with either an explicit patient, an explicit intransitive actor, or an implicit transitive actor) and sentences with nonpreferred patterns (two-sign sentences with either an explicit transitive actor, an implicit patient, or an implicit intransitive actor). We found that sentences with preferred production-probability patterns were no more likely to receive sequitur responses from the mother or experimenter than were sentences with nonpreferred patterns [46 percent (32 of 69) preferred and 50 percent (9 of 18) nonpreferred; $P > 0.67$, Fisher's exact test with children individually tested].

Finally, to determine whether contingent approval might have shaped the structure of the deaf children's sign sentences, we coded (12) the mother's and the experimenter's responses as approvals if they contained smiles or nods or complied with the child's request or query, and as disapprovals if they contained headshakes or frowns or did not comply with the child's request or query (sentences not responded to were not counted). We found that sentences following preferred sign orders were no more likely to be approved by mother or experimenter than were sentences following nonpreferred orders [65 percent (22 of 34) preferred and 67 percent (8 of 12) nonpreferred; $P > 0.42$, Fisher's exact test with children individually tested]. Further, approval of sentences with preferred production-probability patterns was found to be similar to that for sentences with nonpreferred patterns [73 percent (29 of 40) preferred and 83 percent (10 of 12) nonpreferred; $P > 0.25$, Fisher's exact test with children individually tested]. In sum, it appears that nei-

ther communication pressure nor contingent approval shaped the deaf children's sign orders or probabilities of sign production.

Our observations indicate that a child in a markedly atypical language learning environment can apparently develop communication with language-like properties without a tutor modeling or shaping the structural aspects of the communication. These results suggest that the child has a strong bias to communicate in language-like ways.

REFERENCES AND NOTES

1 That is, rather than learn a sign language such as American Sign Language or Signed English, the children were taught to read lips and to produce spoken English through kinesthetic cues. At the time of our study, the children (all of whom had severe to profound hearing losses) were producing only a few single words and never combined words into sentences.

2 S. Goldin-Meadow and H. Feldman, *Science* **197**, 401 (1977); H. Feldman, S. Goldin-Meadow, L. R. Gleitman, *Action, Gesture and Symbol,* A. Lock, Ed. (Academic Press, New York, 1978),pp. 349–414; S. Goldin-Meadow, *Studies in Neurolinguistics,* H. Whitaker and H. A. Whitaker, Eds. (Academic Press, New York, 1979), vol. 4, pp. 125–209.

3 D. I. Slobin, in *Studies of Child Language Development,* C. A. Ferguson and D. I. Slobin, Eds. (Holt, Rinehart &Winston, New York, 1973), pp. 175–208.

4 L. Bloom, P. Miller, L. Hood, in *The 1974 Minnesota Symposium on Child Psychology,* A. Pick, Ed. (Univ. of Minnesota Press, Minneapolis, 1975), pp. 3–55.

5 R. Brown, *A First Language* (Harvard Univ. Press, Cambridge, Mass., 1973).

6 Although the children could in principle have been getting speech input through lip reading, in fact they seemed to understand little of the English spoken to them. Indeed, the structure of the children's gesture systems did not reflect the structure of English; in particular, the children's construction orders differed from those found in canonical English sentences, and the children's

production-probability pattern was an analog of the structural case-marking pattern of ergative languages and therefore was distinct from the accusative case-marking pattern seen in English (S. Goldin-Meadow and C. Mylander, in preparation).

7 Criteria for sign sentences were the same for mother and child: if the hands did not relax between the production of two signs, these two signs were considered part of one sentence.

8 For examples of complex sentences, see S. Goldin-Meadow, in *Language Acquisition: The State of the Art,* L. R. Gleitman and E. Wanner, Eds. (Cambridge Univ. Press, New York, 1982), pp. 51–77.

9 Quantitative differences such as these are inconclusive since they suggest only that certain structures are less frequent in mother's gestures than in the child's. However, in order to argue that the child induces consistent structure from the infrequent instances of structure found in his mother's gestures, one must allow that the child is coming to the learning situation with a bias toward making those inductions.

10 Although the camera might have inhibited the mother's gesture production overall, it is unlikely that the camera affected the way in which the mother structured or failed to structure her gestures. The "camera-shy" hypothesis is further weakened by the fact that, for five mothers, the rate of single-sign production was higher for mother than for her child (although each mother's rate of production of the more complex sign sentence form was half that of her child).

11 It is possible that individuals other than parents (such as siblings or the experimenters themselves) influenced the development of the gesture system, but three of the ten deaf children had no siblings, suggesting that interaction with a sibling was not necessary to develop a structured gesture system. Experimenters made every effort not to gesture to the deaf children, and few of the children's gestures were imitations of the experimenter's gestures (2 percent, 1 of 58, overall); the experimenter produced so few gestures on videotape that analysis for structural properties was unnecessary.

12 R. Brown and C. Hanlon, *Cognition and the Development of Language,* J. R. Hayes, Ed. (Wiley, New York, 1970), pp. 11–54.

13 We thank L. Gleitman, J. Huttenlocher, M. McClintock, W. Meadow, E. Newport, M. Shatz, M. Silverstein, and T. Trabasso for comments and R. Church, E. Eichen, M. Morford, and D. Unora for videotape coding. Supported by NSF grant BNS 77-05990 and by grants from the Spencer Foundation.

READING 21

The Bilingual Child

Francois Grosjean

BECOMING BILINGUAL

Although childhood bilingualism is a worldwide phenomenon and much of adult bilingualism results from it, few studies have examined why some children become bilingual while others remain monolingual. Most children become bilingual in a "natural" way, in the sense that their parents did not actively plan their bilingualism. Such factors as movement of peoples, nationalism and political federalism, intermarriage, the plurality of linguistic groups within a region, urbanization and education inevitably lead to bilingualism in children as well as in adults. Lewis (1972) reports that in the U.S.S.R. people move from one to another republic quite extensively, and hence interethnic marriages are common. For example, in Ashkabad 29 percent of marriages between 1951 and 1965 involved men and women of different nationalities, resulting in the children acquiring two languages. This happens not only if both languages are used in the home but also if only one language—the father's, for instance—is the family language, because family members on the mother's side will communicate with the children in their native language. Another example of bilingualism in the family comes from South Africa: Malherbe (1969) reports that some 43 percent of white South African families are bilingual at home in Afrikaans and English to varying degrees.

The proximity of other linguistic groups also leads to bilingualism in the home. For example, Mkilifi (1978) reports that ten out of the fifteen Tanzanians he studied spoke the local language along with Swahili before going to school. They learned the local language first, but because both parents, especially the father, knew and used Swahili at home, they acquired that language as a second home language and as a medium of communication in the community. Mkilifi reports that this took place quite naturally, and none of the respondents realized that he or she was already speaking two distinct languages before entering primary school.

Even when the other language (the majority language or the lingua franca) is not spoken in the home by the parents themselves, it nevertheless makes its way into the house and the children are exposed to it. The language may be spoken by the parents' friends and acquaintances, older siblings and their friends, neighbors, nurses, and caretakers, not to mention television. And as the children venture outside to play or go shopping with their parents, their exposure to the other language increases. In Box 1 an Israeli Arab reports how she started to acquire Hebrew by being exposed to it inside and outside the home.

One of the main factors in childhood bilingualism is of course the school. Unless the linguistic group to which the child belongs has its own schools or has public education conducted in its own language, the children's medium of instruction in school will be some other language, such as the regional or national language. This is the case for countless minority

---

BOX 1

BILINGUALS SPEAK

Becoming bilingual

An Arabic-Hebrew-English trilingual: The very first language I spoke was Arabic, as my parents are Israeli Arabs. I first came into contact with Hebrew by watching programs on TV, and I began using it around four or five when we had to help our mother buy things from the store or when we met Jewish children at the beach or in the parks.

A Russian-English bilingual: I didn't speak a word of English when I first went to school. There was another little boy entering kindergarten with me, but our mothers separated us so that we wouldn't speak Russian between ourselves. I can't specifically remember learning English; I seem to have picked it up very quickly.

A Greek-English bilingual: I came to the United States when I was twelve years old, and I was put into an all-American class. I did not know any English then and it was a little hard in the beginning since I did not understand what the other children or the teacher were saying to me.

---

groups throughout the world: the Bretons, Basques, and Alsatians in France, most minority groups in the United States, the Greeks in Turkey, the Kurds in Iran, and so on. And if the ethnic composition of the school is quite varied, as in numerous African and Asian nations, children adopt the school language as a medium of communication among themselves. Thus, Mkilifi (1978) reports that in Tanzania, Swahili is the language of learning in the primary schools and that in most cases it alternates with the vernacular as the playground language. The position of Swahili is reinforced in the secondary schools, which are often outside the vernacular area. In these schools, meeting places of children from diverse linguistic and cultural backgrounds, Swahili becomes the primary language of communication in and out of school and is the basis of acculturation into the wider sociocultural norms and values of the country.

In the United States, an unknown number of minority Americans have become bilingual in the public school system. From the turn of the century on, children were put directly into mainstream classes and forced to sink or swim. This caused much stress and hardship and resulted in high dropout rates, but those who survived became bilingual in their home language and in English. In Box 1 two bilinguals talk about their experiences in American schools. It is important to note that such an ethnocentric approach often leads to a form of transitional bilingualism: because of the permanent pressure on the minority child to assimilate, he or she often stops using the minority language and becomes either a "covert" bilingual, concealing his or her knowledge of the minority language (Sawyer, 1978) or a monolingual in the majority language. Like many other monolingual countries, the United States is replete with members of minorities who no longer speak their minority language.

Children may also become bilingual because there is a policy in the community or in the family to make them bilingual. At the community level, different types of bilingual education programs teach the majority language but also maintain and develop the minority language. Such programs exist in the public schools of the U.S.S.R., Wales, Singapore, India, Hong Kong, Lebanon, and to some extent, Canada and the United States, and in private bilingual or international schools throughout the world. One interesting case of community-planned bilingualism, reported by Gal (1979), occurred in Oberwart, Austria, at the turn of the century. The wealthier Hungarian peasants would send their sons to live in a German-speaking village for a year and would welcome in exchange a German-speaking boy from that village for the same amount of time. This practice continued as long as the region was part of Hungary and knowledge of Hungarian was considered an asset. In fact, sending children to other regions or other countries to make them bilingual has gone on throughout history. Roman families, for example, sent their children to Greece to be educated and to learn Greek, and today, numerous exchange programs exist between schools in different countries.

At the family level, parents may decide on a particular strategy to make their child bilingual, as was the case for Ingrid in the introduction to this chapter. Their reasons range from preparing the child to go to school in the majority language (see Box 2) to enabling him or her to communicate with other family members, such as grandparents, all the way to making the child fluent in a prestigious world language, as was the case of Russian aristocrats acquiring French in Czarist Russia. The strategies used are quite diverse (Schmidt-Mackey, 1977; Arnberg, 1979). One of the earliest to be written about was the "une personne, une langue" (one person, one language) formula proposed by the French linguist Grammont to Jules Ronjat at the turn of the century. Ronjat was French and his wife German, and they decided to bring up their child as a bilingual. They agreed that Ronjat would speak only French to the boy, Louis, while his wife would speak only German to him. This strategy was highly successful, and Ronjat (1913) reports that after an initial period of mixed language, Louis quickly learned to use each language just as any native-speaking child would have done. Numerous other case studies

---

BOX 2

BILINGUALS SPEAK

Planned bilingualism in the family

A French-English bilingual: When I was a child, my parents spoke mainly French to me from birth to age four, so as not to offend my maternal grandparents who spoke only French...Later on, they gradually spoke English to me as well, while still maintaining French, so that I wouldn't have any trouble getting by in school in either language. They were successful, because I had no trouble at all in either language.

of bilingual children report the use of this learning strategy, the most famous being that of Hildegard Leopold, who learned to address her father in German and her mother in English (see the next section). Arnberg (1979) reports that a number of English-Swedish families she interviewed in Sweden had adopted this same strategy. It allowed each parent to communicate with the child in his or her native language, thereby ensuring naturalness in communication while making the child bilingual.

Another strategy adopted by parents is to use one language in the home, usually the minority language, and the other outside the home, the rule being that everyone must speak the home language at all times at home. This strategy leads to the pattern found among numerous minorities throughout the world, where the minority language is used in the home and the neighborhood, and the majority language is used at school, at work, and in the larger community. The only difference is that in this case the family has decided to enforce the home–outside the home dichotomy, whereas in general it is not enforced.

A third strategy consists of using one language with the child initially and then, at a specific age (between three and five, for instance) introducing the other language. Zierer (1977) reports on a German-Peruvian child whose parents decided that the child should become bilingual in German and Spanish before entering school. They decided that the best way to do this was to start with German, the weaker language in Peru, and to delay the learning of Spanish for at least two years. To make this approach as successful as possible, they spoke German to each other and to the child, found him some German-speaking playmates, and went so far as to ask the child's Peruvian grandmother *not* to speak to him in Spanish. At age two years and ten months, when the child's German was firmly established, they allowed him to play with Spanish-speaking children, and within four months he had learned Spanish. A

fourth strategy is to use the two languages interchangeably in and out of the family, letting such factors as topic, situation, person, and place dictate which language should be used. Finally, Schmidt-Mackey (1977) reports that some families have chosen to use a "language time" approach: one language in the morning and the other in the afternoon, or one language during the week and the other during the weekend.

How successful are these different strategies? There are no clear answers, but observers stress that the most unnatural tend to break down. For example, the "language time" approach is not very successful, because it is based on a very arbitrary factor: the time of day or the day of the week. On the other hand, the free alternation of languages is by far the most natural approach, but it suffers from the fact that the majority language may slowly become dominant as the child brings home school friends and spends more time at school and in the majority language community. As for starting with only one language and bringing in the other at the age of three or four, it can succeed only if parents take the kind of measures reported by Zierer or if the family is surrounded by a well-organized and quite large ethnic community, so that the child is exposed to the minority language in and out of the home. These same factors lead to the success of the home–outside the home language strategy; it is only when the home language is heard on radio and television, used by siblings, their friends, and the various visitors to the home that such a strategy will work.

Finally, the one person–one language approach, despite its reported success, also has potential problems. The majority language, spoken by either the father or the mother, may become dominant when the child goes to school and starts interacting with the outside community. In addition, the parent speaking the minority language may be in a difficult position when conversing with the child outside the home, especially if that language is looked down upon by the majority group. Such a situation may occur when the child is with playmates and does not wish to be singled out; in these cases, the parent often switches over to the majority language in order not to embarrass the child.

What is essential in the maintenance of the "weaker" (often the minority) language and hence in the development of bilingualism is that the child feels the *need* to use two languages in everyday life. A family relates how the home–outside the home language strategy broke down: when Cyril, a little French boy in the States, started going to an English-language day care center, he brought home English-speaking friends, he watched television, and American friends of his parents quite often came to dinner. Above all, Cyril realized that his parents spoke quite good English, and as there was no other reason for speaking French (no French-speaking grandmother or playmate, no French-speaking social activities outside the home), Cyril probably decided that the price to maintain both languages, English and French, was too high. Little by little he started speaking English to his parents and ceased to be an active bilingual, although he retained the ability to understand his first language (a very frequent phenomenon in the children of immigrants). Cyril's parents could have isolated him from the English environment, just as Zierer's family did with their child, but they either did not think it was natural or did not have the time and energy to do so. Frequent trips back to France or even the presence of a monolingual French-speaking family member probably would have been enough to maintain Cyril's bilingualism.

Arnberg (1979) concludes her study of strategies in Swedish-English families:

> The most important finding of the study was that, regardless of strategy, it is probably difficult for a child to become a true bilingual while living in a country in which one of the languages is dominant, even when the minority language is a high-status language. Most of the children who were bilingual...had either lived in an English-speaking country for several years, were attending a school in which English was the medium of instruction, or were still young enough for the English of the home to balance the dominant Swedish environment. (p. 110)

The only exception to this is if the child belongs to a cohesive linguistic minority with monolingual speakers and if the minority language is used in various social activities. If the family does not have this kind of support and cannot afford trips back to the homeland, the task of bringing up a child as a bilingual becomes quite considerable.

THE ACQUISITION OF TWO LANGUAGES

In this section we will study the processes underlying two main types of language acquisition by bilingual children: simultaneous and successive. We will use McLaughlin's (1978) age criterion to differentiate between the two types: a child who acquires two languages before the age of three is regarded as doing so simultaneously, whereas a child who acquires one language in infancy and the second after age three is considered to be doing so successively. It should be noted that the degree of bilingualism attained is not related to whether the languages are acquired simultaneously or successively. It is psychosocial factors, such as the use of the language in the family or in the school, that will condition when, to what extent, and for how long a child will be bilingual, not the age of acquisition of the two languages.

Simultaneous Acquisition

Much of the information we have about simultaneous acquisition comes from diaries kept by parents who brought up their child bilingually, most often with the one person–one language strategy. The parents have either published the diaries themselves or have given them to linguists to analyze and write up. As McLaughlin (1978) observes, such case studies are extremely informative, but they vary in quality and reliability: direct observation by parents may well lead to errors in transcription or to the misperception of ill-formed utterances. But despite these failings, they are useful documents, and much of what we know about infant bilingualism is based on them.

One of the best-known and best-documented case studies is that by Leopold (1970) concerning his daughter Hildegard. She was brought up according to the one person–one language strategy, speaking German to her father and English to her mother. Leopold (1978) reports that during her first two years, Hildegard combined her two languages into one system and was therefore not really bilingual. Her speech sounds belonged to a unified set, undifferentiated by language. She mixed English and German words and failed to separate the two languages when speaking to monolingual English or German speakers. It was only at the end of her second year that Hildegard showed the "first flicker of the later unfolding of two separate language systems," and from then on she slowly began to distinguish between them. Her knowledge of the existence of two languages was revealed in various ways: for instance, she would ask her father, "How does Mama say it?", a sly contrivance, Leopold notes, to get her dad to say an English word. When she was four, she asked: "Mother, do all fathers speak German?"—a clear indication that she was conscious of the one person–one language dichotomy. Four weeks later she asked her father: "Papa, why do you speak German?"

From the age of two to the age of five, Hildegard was dominant in English, because her exposure to that language through her mother and the surrounding English environment greatly exceeded her contacts with German. Whereas her English pronunciation was similar to that of English monolingual children, in German she had problems with rounded front vowels and with certain consonants. In addition, she gave German nouns English plural

endings, and her German grammatical constructions were very simple, often following English word order. Hildegard realized that she did not master German fully, and she refrained from saying certain things in German to avoid casting them in an English word order. By the end of her fifth year, German was by far her weaker language and was in danger of being lost. At that time, however, Hildegard spent half a year in Germany, with dramatic consequences. She became quite fluent in German, while her English receded. After four weeks in a totally German environment, she was unable to say more than a few very simple utterances in English (the parallel between Hildegard and Burling's son Stephen is striking here), and she had a pronounced German accent in English. She progressed in German very quickly and learned to invert the subject and the verb after an introductory word or clause, but certain idioms and structural aspects did remain influenced by English.

When she returned to the States, Hildegard quickly recovered her English. After two weeks she was quite fluent again, and after four weeks she was starting to have difficulties with German. The last features of German that she had acquired, such as the uvular *r* and the verb placement, were the first to be forgotten. However, after six months, Leopold noted that the reaction to English was overcome, and from then on she was really bilingual, although dominant in English. This latter language continued to influence her choice of words and idioms in German, and to a lesser degree her grammatical structures, but not her German pronunciation and morphology.

Hildegard's case is interesting because certain aspects of her development of the two languages are found repeatedly in bilingual children: the initial mixed language stage; the slow separation of the two language systems and increasing awareness of bilingualism; the influence of one language on the other when the linguistic environment favors one language; the avoidance of difficult words and constructions in the weaker language; the rapid shift from one language dominance to the other when the environment changes; the final separation of the sound and grammatical systems but the enduring influence of the dominant language on the other in the domain of vocabulary and idioms.

Before continuing, however, I should note that whether a child acquires only one language and becomes monolingual or acquires two languages and becomes bilingual, the rate and pattern of language development are the same. The first words are spoken at the same time in both monolingual and bilingual children: Doyle, Champagne, and Segalowitz (1978) report that the average age of the first word, as recalled by mothers, is 11.2 months for bilinguals and 11.6 for monolinguals. In addition, language develops similarly in both monolinguals and bilinguals: sounds easier to produce appear sooner than sounds such as fricatives (/f/, /s/, /z/, for instance) or consonant clusters (/fr/, /st/); meanings of words are overextended, so that "doggie," for example, will be used for horses and other four-legged animals as well as for dogs; utterances slowly increase in length; and simpler grammatical constructions are used before more complex ones, such as relative clauses.

Padilla and Liebman (1975) conclude their study of the language development of three English-Spanish bilingual children in the following way: "In spite of the linguistic 'load' forced on to them due to their bilingual environments, [the children] were acquiring their two languages at a rate comparable to that of monolingual-speaking children" (p. 51), and McLaughlin (1978) writes: "In short, it seems that the language acquisition process is the same in its basic features and in its developmental sequence for the bilingual child and the monolingual child. The bilingual child has the additional task of distinguishing the two language systems, but there is no evidence that this requires special language processing devices" (p. 91–92).

Successive Acquisition

Not all bilingual children acquire their two languages in a simultaneous or quasi-simultaneous manner. In fact, most are members of linguistic minorities who acquire their first language in the home and immediate community and their second language when they enter school. Some are given lessons in the second language, but most acquire it naturally by interacting with teachers, children, and other members of the majority language community. Some other children become bilingual because their parents move to another country and hence, like minority children, they find themselves speaking one language at home and the other outside it.

In this section we will briefly review how a child acquires a second language naturally, that is, by interacting with native speakers of that language. We will not consider the second-language learners who acquire their "foreign" language in the rather artificial and formal environment of the classroom. Such learning rarely results in functional and regular use of two languages.

Age of Onset of Bilingualism   Children can become bilingual at any age. In Box 1, the Russian-English bilingual spoke Russian at home in her early years and started to acquire English when she entered kindergarten. The Greek-English bilingual spoke only Greek until the age of twelve, when her family moved to the States and she became engulfed in an English-speaking environment: at school, in the community, on television, and so on. As adults, both are now active bilinguals in that they use their first and second languages in their everyday lives.

There exists a long-standing myth that the earlier a language is acquired, the more fluent a person will be in it. As both McLaughlin (1978) and Genesee (1978) report, this myth is based on a number of questionable assumptions. One of these is that young children acquire languages more quickly and with less effort than older children and adolescents. Another is linked to the notion of the critical period, as put forward by Lenneberg (1967) and others, which states that before the onset of puberty the brain is more malleable or "plastic" and hence is receptive to such tasks as language learning. In addition, they claim that the brain's hemispheric specialization for language (language lateralization) is not achieved until about the time of puberty; from then on language acquisition becomes harder and less optimal. And younger children are said to have fewer inhibitions, to be less embarrassed when they make mistakes, and hence to be better learners.

All these factors have come under considerable criticism in recent years (see Krashen, 1973; Seliger, 1978; Genesee, 1978; McLaughlin, 1978, among others). It has been shown that young children are rather unsophisticated and immature learners in that they have not yet fully acquired certain cognitive skills, such as the capacity to abstract, generalize, infer, and classify, that could help them in second-language acquisition. In addition, the notions of the critical period and of language lateralization have come under increasing attack. Krashen (1973), for example, believes that language lateralization occurs at four or five years of age and not at puberty. Seliger (1978) proposes the notion of different critical periods for different abilities, which in turn determine how completely one can acquire some aspects of language.

Finally, recent discussion has emphasized the psychosocial factors that lead to second-language acquisition. These, above all else, dictate the extent to which a second language will be acquired. Gardner and Lambert (1972) found that success in mastering a second language depends not so much on intellectual capacity or language aptitude as on the learner's attitude toward the other linguistic group and his or her willingness to identify with that group. To this should be added the motivation and, quite simply, the need, to communicate

with members of the group. For example, an eight-year-old immigrant girl who has just been put into an all-English school will probably want and, in fact, need to communicate with the other children in order to survive in that environment, and this will encourage her to acquire the language. On the other hand, if she is surrounded by other children of her minority group, she may be less motivated to communicate with the English-speaking children (especially if their attitude toward her group is negative), but she may have no choice about whether or not to acquire English if it is the medium of instruction in the school. Thus the psychosocial factors that surround language acquisition are of primary importance in determining the extent of the child's bilingualism. Other factors, such as the critical period, language lateralization, language aptitude, and intelligence, play a lesser role. This is also true of age of onset of the second language, except that by late adolescence the acquisition of a native-like pronunciation does seem to become more difficult.

Strategies in Second-Language Acquisition There has been much debate on whether similar linguistic and cognitive strategies are employed in the acquisition of a first and of a second language. It was long thought that the knowledge of a first language affected the acquisition of a second and that many of the errors made in that language were due to the direct influence or interference of the first. The French accent of French youths learning English is an example of this kind of influence. This line of thought has been called the transfer position. More recently, however, other researchers have taken the position that acquisition of a second language parallels that of the first language, and that transfer (or interference) is of minor importance. This has been termed the developmental position. McLaughlin (1978), a supporter of this position, proposes that the child learning a second language recapitulates the learning process of a native speaker of that language. He writes: "There is a unity of process that characterizes all language acquisition, whether first or second language and...this unity of process reflects the use of similar strategies of language acquisition" (p. 206).

Most proponents of this position agree that there are important differences between the first and second language learner: the latter, because he or she is older, has a better knowledge of the world, a wider range of semantic concepts, a longer memory span, and a more developed cognitive system. Nevertheless, he or she will apply very similar linguistic strategies to the second language acquisition process. For instance, the child will use simple structures (subject-verb-object, for example) before more complex ones, overextend the meanings of words, disregard irregular past tenses, overgeneralize rules, and relate word order to word meaning. Ervin-Tripp (1974) observed that English-speaking children learning French in Geneva were not using word-for-word translations from English but instead were simplifying their French constructions and using first-language-learner structures, such as simple declarative sentences or uninverted questions. Proponents of the developmental position expect to find, and often do find, more developmental errors involving simplifications and overgeneralizations than errors involving interference from the first language.

However, the picture is probably more complex than may at first appear. Mulford and Hecht (1979) report that the phonological development of English by Steinar, a six-year-old native speaker of Icelandic, could not be accounted for by either the transfer position or the developmental position alone; it was best explained by a systematic interaction between the two types. Mulford and Hecht conclude that their subject's developing English phonology is best accounted for by both transfer and developmental factors.

Hakuta and Cancino (1977) review the twists and turns that the developmental and transfer positions have gone through in the last ten years. They show how interference can be seen as the result of active hypothesis testing by the second-language learner, how both interference and developmental errors appear and disappear at varying periods during the language acquisition process, and how acquisition is in fact an interplay between the native language and the target language.

Researchers in second-language acquisition are now concentrating on isolating the social, cognitive, and linguistic strategies used. Fillmore (1976) proposes that there are three stages in the child's acquisition of a second language in a natural environment. In the first, the child establishes social relationships with the speakers of the second language; to do so, he or she engages in "interactional" rather than "informational" activities and relies heavily on fixed verbal formulas (You know what? I wanna do it, Guess what?) as well as nonverbal communication. In the second stage, the child concentrates on communicating with speakers of the language; he or she thus moves away from socially useful intact formulas to new combinations of the words in the formulas. And in the third stage, the child makes sure that the form of the language is correct.

According to Fillmore, the second-language learner will use a number of cognitive and social strategies. The five cognitive strategies she uncovered are:

Assume that what people are saying is directly relevant to the situation at hand or to what they or you are experiencing. (Metastrategy: guess.)

Get some expressions you understand and start talking.

Look for recurring parts in the formulas you know.

Make the most of what you've got.

Work on big things; save the details for later.

And the three social strategies are:

Join a group and act as if you understand what is going on, even if you don't.

Give the impression, with a few well-chosen words, that you can speak the language.

Count on your friends for help.

Fillmore points to the fact that children at first use formulaic expressions which they acquire as wholes: Look it, Wait a minute, Whose turn is it? Once they have a number of these, they start analyzing them into constituents, which they use to create new sentences. Fillmore stresses that some children who acquire a second language quite rapidly make much use of such strategies, especially those pertaining to social relationships: they seek out children who speak the language being learned, they enjoy role-playing games, and they are uninhibited when speaking their second language. Further, the important thing for them is to communicate, even if they make mistakes doing so. And often the native-speaking children will help out by including the nonnative speakers in their play and by simplifying their speech for them.

The simultaneous use of linguistic, social, and cognitive strategies allows the learner to acquire the second language. At first this may be arduous, but if the motivation to interact with speakers of the second language and the need to do so are both present—as they often are in natural second-language acquisition—then progress will be rapid and the child will soon become bilingual.

REFERENCES

Arnberg, L. 1979. Language strategies in mixed nationality families. *Scandinavian Journal of Psychology* 20:105—112.

Doyle, A., M. Champagne, and N. Segalowitz. 1978. Some issues in the assessment of linguistic consequences of early bilingualism. In *Aspects of bilingualism*, ed. M. Paradis. Columbia, S.C.: Hornbeam Press.

Ervin–Tripp, S. 1974. Is second language learning like the first? *TESOL Quarterly* 8:111-127.

Fillmore, L. 1976. The second time around: cognitive and social strategies in second-language acquisition. Ph.D. dissertation, Stanford University.

Gal, S. 1979. *Language shift: social determinants of linguistic change in bilingual Austria*. New York: Academic Press.

Gardner. R., and W. Lambert. 1972. *Attitudes and motivation in second language learning*. Rowley, Mass.: Newbury House.

Genesee, F. 1978. Is there an optimal age for starting second language instruction? *McGill Journal of Education* 13:145-154.

Hakuta, K., and H. Cancino. 1977. Trends in second language acquisition research. *Harvard Educational Review* 47:294-316.

Krashen, S. 1973. Lateralization, language learning and the critical period: some new evidence. *Language Learning* 23:63-74.

Lenneberg, E. 1967. *Biological foundations of language*. New York: Wiley.

Leopold, W. 1970. *Speech development of a bilingual child*, vols. 1–4. New York: AMS Press.

——— 1978. A child's learning of two languages. In *Second language acquisition*, ed. E. Hatch. Rowley, Mass.: Newbury House.

Lewis, E. G. 1972. *Multilingualism in the Soviet Union*. The Hague: Mouton.

Malherbe, E. 1969. Comments on "How and when do persons become bilingual?" In *Description and measurement of bilingualism*, ed. L. Kelly. Toronto: University of Toronto Press.

MacLaughlin, B. 1978. *Second-language acquisition in childhood*. Hillsdale, N.J.: Lawrence Erlbaum Associates.

Mulford, R., and B. Hecht. 1979. Learning to speak without an accent: acquisition of a second language phonology. Paper presented to the Fourth Annual Conference on Language Development, Boston University.

Mkilifi, M. 1978. Triglossia and Swahili-English bilingualism in Tanzania. In *Advances in the study of societal multilingualism*, ed. J. Fishman. The Hague: Mouton.

Padilla, A., and E. Liebman. 1975. Language acquisition in the bilingual child. *The Bilingual Review/La Revista Bilingüe* 1–2:34–55.

Ronjat, J. 1913. *Le développement du langage observé chez un enfant bilingue*. Paris: Champion.

Sawyer, J. 1978. Passive and covert bilinguals: a hidden asset for a pluralistic society. In *The bilingual in a pluralistic society*, ed. H. Key, G. McCullough, and J. Sawyer. Long Beach: California State University.

Schmidt-Mackey, I. 1977. Language stragies of the bilingual family. In *Bilingualism in early childhood*, ed. W. Mackey and T. Anderson. Rowley, Mass.: Newbury House.

Seliger, H. 1978. Implications of a multiple critical periods hypothesis for second language learning. In *Second language acquisition research*, ed. W. Ritchie. New York: Halsted Press.

Zierer, E. 1977. Experiences in the bilingual education of a child of pre-school age. *International Review of Applied Linguistics* 15:144–149.

READING 22

The Facilitation System

Catherine Garvey

Talk could not operate without a facilitation system to reduce friction and minimize the potential conflicts and embarrassments that can arise in social contact. This system reflects the speakers' ritual concerns and their pervasive awareness of interpersonal status in the transactions of daily life. The operation of this system is as ubiquitous as the societal organization it mirrors and supports. It includes the use of little markers of courtesy and concern such as *please, thank you,* and *excuse me;* displays of attentiveness and understanding during a talk engagement; selection of acceptable forms of address and phrasing of requests; and selection of topics suitable for the occasion. The speaker's manner of speaking and acting conforms not only with his achieved and ascribed status, but also with his role relationship with the others in the situation. Talk adjusts to the stable social relations between speakers and also to the more transitory ones, as when two strangers must discuss a common task or plight, or when a child adopts an authoritative tone when explaining to his mother how to play a pretend game he has devised.

Such obviously polite expressions as *please* or *excuse me* are only the tip of the ritual iceberg. Their appropriate placement in a strip of talk is a matter of considerable delicacy.

Although most parents coach young children and even prod them to produce these phrases under the conditions that call for them, the phrases are unlikely to be used reflexively in all the appropriate contexts until the child has learned their ritual functions. In the case of *excuse me* and its equivalents, *pardon me* or *sorry,* the child probably has been told that he should say "excuse me" when he has bumped into someone, when he walks in front of someone, and even when he wants to interrupt an adult's speech. Thus he could learn that *excuse me* is required for small offenses; that it should follow an accidental offense; and that if he must commit an intentional offense in order to do something necessary, *excuse me* should precede the offensive action. He will probably also sense that correctly placing *excuse me* before an offense is associated in some way with certain special ways of requesting and of asking for permission, such as saying, "May I———" or "Can I———," or "Let me———." He may even have grasped the notion that these rules are more frequently enforced if the offended person is an adult than if he is another child. But learning the proper placement of the apology requires a more generalized knowledge of what constitutes an offense in the first place and of how the relative status of the persons involved influences the gravity of an offense. This knowledge, which every normal, socialized person possesses, whether he chooses to violate the basic rules or not, the child will only slowly acquire from observation, trial and error, and from some limited rule formulation by adults that will only partially explain the principles underlying any instantiation of the tacit code of conduct.

There are at least two large areas of social convention and organization that are relevant to talk and that are often reflected in language form, that is, in the various linguistic alternatives speakers may select. One area is the differentiation and ranking of persons and the types of role relationships that are recognized. The other area is that of the commonality, the generally accepted properties and rights, of persons, or at least of all persons who are recognized as members of the group for whom the conventions are valid. The two areas are intricately interrelated, and they may be organized in different ways in different cultures and social groups. In this chapter I will discuss some of the implications for talk of person differentiation and of person "appreciation" or proper consideration. First I will describe the two areas and the points at which differentiation and appreciation operate in tandem. Next I will discuss requesting, which is a social act that sensitively reflects both fine distinctions in relationships and awareness of proper conduct with others. Finally, I will discuss how one type of request is associated with the relationships between persons and their relative status.

HOW PERSONS ARE DIFFERENT AND HOW THEY ARE THE SAME

The differentiation and relative status of persons has been described as varying on two dimensions, that of relative power and authority in which persons are superordinate, subordinate, or the same in rank, and that of relative distance, in which they are close (familiar, intimate) or more distant (unfamiliar, lacking-shared interests or attributes). Stereotypically, at least, it might be expected that parent and child would be ordered as superordinate to subordinate and would be familiar or intimate. A husband and wife might be equal in rank in one cultural group and superordinate-subordinate in another, but they would behave as intimates in both groups. A judge and a lawyer in the courtroom might exhibit behavior appropriate to a superordinate-subordinate relationship that was distant and formal, but the same two persons as friendly competitors on the tennis court would interact in a relationship of equality and familiarity. A number of languages, including German, French, and Russian, provide contrasting sets of pronouns that reflect both of these dimensions, thus incorporating the distinctions into the structure of the linguistic code.[1] Some languages, such as Javanese, provide alternative lexical forms of verbs and nouns as well as an elaborate pronoun system. Some languages, such as English, do not provide alternatives in the pronoun system but mark the distinctions by terms of address, for example, Judge Strong, Your Honor, William, Bill, and Billy. All languages provide some means by which speakers can differentiate among persons and relationships.

Languages also provide means for members of the cultural group to recognize and acknowledge the membership, or "personhood," of others and to differentiate among degrees of agency and responsibility. Fully responsible members of the culture take for granted a shared knowledge of the conventions of thought and action, and even shortcomings in someone's behavior can be excused or reinterpreted on mutually intelligible grounds.[2] Less-than-full-fledged members are dealt with, and spoken to, in a different manner. The apt phrase "speech to incompetents" was proposed by the linguist Charles Ferguson to designate the several speech styles, or registers, that exist in most cultures for talking to or with persons who are not fully accredited members.[3] "Speech to incompetents" includes the registers used to communicate with babies and young children, with the senile and the infirm, with the very ill, with pets, with prisoners, and with foreigners who have not acquired the language or cultural conventions of the members' group. Each of these registers differs from the others in a number of important ways, but they share certain characteristics that stem from members' expectations that these classes of individuals are not fully capable of engaging in "normal" communication and other common social transactions.

Members of a culture accord themselves and others, except for these less-than-full-fledged members, the full ritual consideration due to capable and responsible persons. Such persons can be trusted (except under conventionally extenuating circumstances), to observe the guidelines of the cooperative principle in action and in talk, can be expected to fulfill the given-new contract, to have a fine awareness of others' opinion of them and a desire to maintain or achieve a favorable opinion, and they will know what rightfully belongs to themselves and will accord similar rights and authority to others. They will cooperate with others in maintaining their own and others' personhood, in part by appropriately recognizing differences in relative status. Talk, along with other forms of public action, will display and confirm (or may disconfirm) this image of the self. In order to say, "Excuse me" at the right time, at the right place, and to the right person, a speaker must know what constitutes an offense against the self and thus against another person who is a comparable self. A part of this normally taken-for-granted knowledge has been explicitly stated by Erving Goffman in an essay entitled "The Territories of the Self."[4] Intrusion on or infringement of any of these territories can count as an offense and thus require an apology and/or an accounting of some sort.

THE TERRITORIES OF THE SELF

The concept of claims, of what belongs to a person, is central to social organization and to understanding social behavior. The territories of the self described by Goffman form a preserve to which a person can lay claim; that is, he is entitled to possess, control, use, or dispose of it. One's territories include not only spatial configurations, inalienable and alienable possessions, and belongings protected by institutional or legal sanctions, but also temporary, private, and psychological "possessions." The territories include one's personal space, a sort of invisible ellipse about oneself that varies with the situation and activity; the "stall," or place being used, such as a seat at table or in the theater, to which one can lay claim even if temporarily absent; use space, or "elbow room," the area needed for specific purposes such as positioning a car for parking, mopping a floor, or building a sand castle.

Less evidently physical or spatial territories include one's turn, that is, the right to be served or to talk in some order relative to others; the "sheath" of skin and clothes; possessional territory, or personal effects, which includes matters relating to one's comfort, such as sound levels, lighting, and temperature; the information preserve, which includes what one is thinking, one's private history, "good name," and correspondence. Finally, there is the conversational preserve. Part of this preserve is the right to control, to some extent, who can summon one to talk and when. To this list I will add an extremely variable, but very sensitive, preserve of the time and effort a person can expect to call his own, somewhat comparable to use space. Intruding on someone else's time requires apology or permission, such as, "Have you got a minute?" Some claims radiate out to other persons who "belong" to the self, such as wife, family, gang.

The extent of all these territories varies with the situational context, of course, and with a person's rank relative to others. Compared with adults, children enjoy less extensive rights not only in respect to space, but also in respect to information and conversation. Almost any adult can ask a child, "What's your name?" "How old are you?" or "Is Johnny Mills your brother?" An adult, however, must go to considerable trouble to assure that he does not offend an unfamiliar adult of presumably equal status if he wants to ask a similar question: "Excuse me. You look terribly familiar. Could I ask if you happen to be related to John Mills?" Showing several marks of person appreciation, the adult apologizes for intruding into the other person's conversational and informational preserves, provides an account in advance of his need to risk this offense, and then asks permission to intrude with a question that also actually conveys the request for information.

In learning about the territories of the self, an area of social knowledge that requires many years of experience to control, the child will gradually discover what constitutes an offense, what requires apology or an accounting, and when he must try to mitigate or excuse an offense before committing it. Other ritual matters are also tied to the concept of territories of the self. One function of saying "Thank you," for example, is to recognize another person's offering or giving of something that the person could rightfully claim or reserve for himself, such as giving up a seat or place in line. Person appreciation, which has been summarized in the rules "Be polite, don't impose, and give options"[5] rests, to a large extent, on knowledge of the territories of the self. But how and when does the child acquire this knowledge that every adult possesses, but which few could "explain" in so many words? Most caregivers believe that it is very important that the child learn to "ask nicely" and "be polite," but they could no more provide the child with the underlying rationale for saying "excuse me" than could the child understand such an explanation. What caregivers do is prompt the child in specific circumstances to say the proper ritual phrases, as in "Say 'Thank you.' "[6] They also make some judgments of specific offensive behavior, such as, "It's not nice to stare at people," and provide cautions about invading another's territories—"Don't bother Daddy. He's studying." And many caregivers and teachers model appropriate phrases and polite forms of requests in speaking to children, "Wouldn't you like to put the toys away now?" perhaps in hopes that children will reciprocate the courtesy. Children do learn a great deal about appropriate forms of requesting during the preschool years, as will be discussed below. There is very little direct information, however, on how children learn about the territories of the self.

It is known that children acquire the concept of possession of objects very early; *mine* and *my* are among the first linguistic formulations of the concept, and the concept can often be inferred when the child indicates an object and provides the name of the possessor, "Daddy hat." In resolving conflicts over physical possession of an object, nursery school children appear to be influenced by whether the taker has had prior possession of the object, the "prior possessor" being less vigorously resisted.[7] In respect to the concept of use space, Grace Wales Shugar and Barbara Bokus have shown that three-year-olds have a keen awareness of the boundaries of their own and their playmates' activity spaces, the areas in which they are playing and to which they have some rightful claim. A child playing with one partner was able to show an investigator by marking on the floor or placing little objects, the heretofore invisible circle of his own and his partner's play space. If the two children were playing together, the child would delineate a single, elliptical space that enclosed both, usually with most of the space between them. When the children were not engaged with one another, the child would draw a circle about himself (with a radius of about an arm's length), with himself in the center and would draw a separate, slightly smaller space for the other child. When asked where a third child could play in the room, the child would indicate another area, separated from the space assigned to self and partner together or to self and to partner independently.[8] The children also indicated the spaces differently in talk. They used deictic expressions to refer to the activity space of a separate partner or to a shared activity space, "That's her place" or "This is ours," but they favored descriptions in referring to their own separate space, "I'm working here. My store takes all this room." In another study of spontaneous play sessions, these investigators found that pairs of children used two different types of utterances in initiating interaction. If the children were farther apart, a child was likely to initiate talk by an ostensive type of utterance, "Look. See this." If the children were closer together (less than 65 centimeters), the initiation was likely to be descriptive of the speaker's activity, "Tracks and wagons for a train I'm making." These findings of both verbal differentiation and gestural indication of the relation of self and others' activity spaces and the awareness that activity was either common or independent suggest that these aspects of the territories of the self are salient for preschool-age children.

It is consonant with the general trends in development of social cognition that children begin to understand about the territories that are either perceptually given or delimited by their own actions before cognizing those territories that are less overtly marked or less related to physical action, such as the information preserve. The notion of the turn, although highly variable by situation, is one that even young children appear to recognize if the rights pertaining to the turn apply to themselves. Their concept of turn, however, is at first probably restricted to turns at acting, as in sitting on the swing or using a toy, and that is the type of situation in which caregivers urge children to take turns.

REQUESTS FOR PERMISSION

The example on page 243 illustrates how a caregiver models socially acceptable speech and attempts to guide a child's behavior. (The example also shows that the caregiver's precepts, even when followed, do not necessarily result in an experience that might reinforce the child's attempts to be polite.) Tom used a type of request that solicits permission and thereby acknowledges an addressee's authority and/or his claim to a preserve. A conflict arose between Judy (32 months) and Tom (33 months), who were alone in the playroom. Tom wanted to have a little figure of a bear that Judy was holding, which Judy refused to give him. When Tom began to cry for his mother, Judy's mother came into the room. Tom whined a couple of times and then explained his distress to Judy's mother, who directed Tom to ask nicely and reminded him of the turn-taking rule. She also used a polite version of a request to Judy in urging her to comply with Tom's request.

When Judy's mother told Tom to "ask Judy nicely" for the bear, he complied by requesting Judy's permission to have it. All requests share the essential feature that the speaker wants the addressee to do something; requests for action involve some act that the speaker desires or some behavior that will bring about a desired state of affairs. Requests for information are designed to lead the addressee to provide information in a verbal reply or a gestural equivalent. In requests for permission the addressee is asked either to allow the speaker to do or have something or to cease obstructing or preventing the speaker from doing something. Tom certainly could have complied with Judy's mother's request by issuing other polite requests, "Will you give me the bear?" or "Please give me the bear." I suspect that his choice of a request for permission in, first, a more polite-variant ("Could I have that little bear?") and, second, a somewhat less polite one ("Can I have it?") was influenced by his recognition of Judy's prior claim to the bear and/or her mother's ultimate authority in deciding who might play with what.

Mother	Tom	Judy
	(To mother) I want that little bear.	
OK, well ask Judy nicely for him. You can take turns, I know.		
	(To Judy) Could I have that little bear?	
		No, no, wait till I'm finished.
	(To Judy) But I want the little bear.	
(To Judy) Judy, if you're not playing with the little bear, why don't you give it to Tom?		
		(Judy mumbles but does not relinquish the bear.)
	(Facing mother and Judy) I want it.	
(Looks at bear and around at other toys.) Oh, there's the bear, here's something . . .		
	(Still facing both mother and Judy) Can I have it? *(Points to bear Judy has dropped.)* I wanna see the bear.	
(Mother puts another toy near Tom and leaves the room.)		
	(Temporarily distracted, he examines a toy camera.)	*(Stands, watching Tom.)*
	(As soon as the mother leaves the room, Tom turns toward Judy and the bear, and Judy moves once again to defend her claim.)	
		Tom, don't you touch my things, all right?

If young children do choose to use requests for permission for particular social reasons, then we might expect the requests to be used when the addressee was in some way obstructing the speaker from doing or having something he wanted, or when the addressee had some rightful claim to what the speaker was interested in. This proves to be the case. Among the forty-eight pairs of three- to five-year-old children we observed in the laboratory playroom, there were 121 instances of forms conventionally used for requesting permission, "Let me———," "Can I———," "May I———." Of these, 108 instances were complete, uninterrupted, and clearly addressed to the partner (rather than to a doll or an imaginary interlocutor); 87 percent of the complete instances occurred in situations in which the addressee was either physically obstructing the speaker in something he wanted to have or do, such as sitting on the car the speaker wished to drive, or appeared to have some claim to what the speaker wanted. The claim was established either by just-prior use or by the statement of a plan to use some object; for example, the addressee had just finished an imaginary phone call and turned away from the toy phone when the speaker asked, "Can I call on it now?" Some claims seemed to be related to the conventional association between the sex of the child and the particular toy; for example, a boy pointed to an ironing board that the girl had not previously touched or used and asked, "Can I have that?"

If a speaker uses a request-for-permission form, he is actually requesting the addressee's permission, but if the addressee is physically obstructing him, the speaker is also less explicitly requesting the addressee to cease the obstructive action. If the addressee must take some other action in order for the speaker to achieve his desired objective, the addressee, if cooperative, will also perform that action. Thus if the addressee was sitting on the wooden car

in the playroom and the speaker standing near it asked, "Can I ride on the car?" or "May I ride on it now?" and the addressee grants permission by saying "Yes" or "Okay," he would also either get off the car or move to the front or back, thus allowing the speaker to get on. The permission request leaves it to the addressee to determine what action is required. Almost all of the three- to five-year-olds observed in the laboratory playroom enacted this ritual interchange when one wanted to sit on the wooden car, which was the most popular toy in the room. No child simply granted permission by saying "Okay" or "Yes, you can" and then failing to move. Although the addressee complied in 70 percent of these interchanges, noncompliance often reflected the addressee's understanding that he had some prior claim to possess or dispose of the desired resource, "You can in a minute," "I'm not through yet," or, "It still my turn."

Although in the last example Tom requested Judy's permission at the initial urging of the adult, all the two-and-a-half-year-olds negotiated similar interchanges without adult prompting. In the following example, Tom (33 months) and Judy (32 months) negotiated Tom's activity in the pretend cooking that Judy had initiated. Tom approached Judy on the floor where she had set out plates and cups:

Tom	Judy
Can I play here?	
	Yeah, you can.
(Sits down by Judy and points to a plate.) Can I have some muffins?	
	Don't touch them. 'cause they're very hot.
I'm gonna put a little sugar in your muffins, all right?	
	(Judy watches as Tom pretends to sprinkle sugar on the imaginary muffins.)

Tom appears to have recognized and verbally acknowledged Judy's right to her own play space and her right to control the pretend activity in which she was engaged. Once he was allowed to join, he was still cautious, and she reminded him that she was still in charge. Not all of the two-and-a-half-year-olds' interchanges were so ritually correct, but the talk of all of these children did on occasion reveal that they could, unprompted by an adult, take into account another's claim to activity space, objects, and turns at acting. The right to ride on the wooden car, an issue in many permission requests, provided sequences of requests and rerequests that displayed the children's ability to paraphrase this well-motivated directive. Among the formulations used to gain access to the car were the following: "Can I have a turn now?" "Let me get on there?" "Hafta have a turn, please," followed by "I really should be driving this," "Can I do that, please, now?" and "When it stops I can do it?"

REQUESTS FOR ACTION

In any directive act a speaker risks infringing on another's preserve, and for adults there is potential danger of offending the other person by a presumption or of causing embarrassment to the other or to the self in the event of a refusal. Languages offer a proliferation of alternative forms for issuing directives, forms that allow the speaker to accommodate to the social situation. I will list the major options and some of the variants that are available to adult speakers of English, discuss the conventions and understandings associated with the use of directives, and then trace the development of requesting in children's talk. Although directive speech acts include requests for information, commonly formulated as questions, and requests for confirmation, agreement, sympathy, and evaluation, it is the request for action (RA), or behavioral request, that is perhaps the most ritually sensitive type. It is certainly the type that has

been the most widely studied in both children's and adults' speech, and I will restrict the following discussion to requests for action.

The basic direct linguistic form for an RA is the imperative, either positive, "Eat that," or negative, "Don't eat that." Other forms can be ranked on the dimension direct/explicit, indirect/inexplicit; in general, the greater the degree of indirectness, the more "polite" the request. The appropriateness of a particular request form depends on the relationship of the speaker and the addressee, the context of the request, and the tone of voice employed; however, it is not possible to predict that a given request form will be taken as polite or offensive without knowing the situation. The major options available to adults for requesting an action are listed below in roughly descending order of direct to indirect; possible variants that may seem more polite are listed last in each group.[9]

Imperative: Give me a glass of milk. You give me a glass of milk. Give me a glass of milk, please.

Need statement: I want a glass of milk. I need a glass of milk. I would like/I want you to give me a glass of milk.

Imbedded imperative: Will you give me a glass of milk? Can you give me a glass of milk? Would you give me a glass of milk? Could you give me a glass of milk?

Permission directive: Can I have a glass of milk? May I have/Could I have/Might I have a glass of milk?

Question directive: Is there any milk? Have you got some milk? I don't suppose you have any milk, do you?

Hint: That glass of milk sure looks good.

This listing is partial, of course; the reader can add other possibilities, such as, "You better give me a glass of milk," "Don't forget to give me a glass of milk," "Why don't you give me a glass of milk?" "Could I ask you for a glass of milk?" Also, in the home, nursery school, classroom, or wherever the standard operating procedures are familiar to all participants, reference to a rule or procedure can convey a request for action, as in, "You didn't give me a glass of milk," or "I don't see a glass of milk at my place," or simply, "Milk time," while holding out an empty glass.

Young children who have not yet mastered the more standard forms listed above have a few verbal means for conveying requests that cannot be ranked as either direct or indirect, since in the child's repertoire they do not yet contrast with other standard forms. The most common of these are: a statement with rising terminal pitch, "You read it"; the simple imperative form of the verb, "Read," or "You read"; or the name of a desired object, "Milk," perhaps with an appropriate gesture. Two other rather early forms that continue in use for several years are *you hafta* or *you gotta* plus verb, as in "You hafta read book," and an interrogative tag appended to a need statement or an imperative, "I want it, okay?" or "You sit here, all right?"

By the age of seven or eight, children are able to place the standard options and their variants in appropriate contexts and assign them to appropriate persons in different role relationships, as Claudia Mitchell-Kernan and Keith Kernan found when they asked black American children between the ages of seven and twelve to make up stories and enact them, using puppets as the characters in the role play.[10] Nurses interacted with patients; fathers with wives, sons, or daughters; and customers with salespersons; the children also interacted with each other outside the puppet play and with the investigators as well. The directive forms they used varied with the relative status of the persons, with the personal versus the transactional nature of the engagement, and with the cost in time or effort that compliance with the request demanded, for example, "Hand me that wrench" (low cost) versus "Belinda, will you go to the store for me?" (higher cost) when speaker and addressee were same-age peers. The investigators also observed that the children sometimes used inappropriate directive forms, apparently to test, negotiate, or redefine a status relationship. When a child directed an imperative RA to the investigator (normatively inappropriate recipient) and received a noncompliant response (and perhaps an objection to the rudeness), the child would rerequest in a more polite form. These observations indicate that the children understood a good deal about the social implications of directive choice. And although the relative status of the participants is an important factor in selecting the appropriate option or variant, more transitory features of the interaction, such as the cost of the requested act to the addressee and whether the act would be normally expected or counts as a favor, also influence the selection. Favors are usually requested more politely than are acts the speaker considers obligatory. Probably skill at effective use of RA options continues to be elaborated through adolescence and beyond.

What do children know or learn about the practical, everyday business of directing others and of being directed that allows them to acquire such a complex set of options and variants? No single answer is available at this time, but some features of requesting make the system a bit more learnable than it might seem to be at first glance. First, I suggested above that children are in the process of learning about the territories of the self and about what might constitute an offense or an imposition on another person. Second, many of the RA options encode some of the social understandings about the practical action of requesting and about understanding a message as a request. These understandings are: 1) that the speaker (S) wants the addressee (A) to do some desired act (DA); 2) that the

DA should be done for some purpose; 3) that *A* has the ability to do the DA; 4) that *A* is either obliged to do the DA or is willing to do it; and 5) that *S* has the right to ask or tell *A* to do the DA and that *A* is an appropriate recipient of the request. A further understanding is that if no specific time is mentioned, the DA should be done at the time of speaking. Speakers and addressees also understand that requests are only validly made for future acts and for acts that the addressee was not intending to perform anyway.[11]

These understandings are not linguistic in nature, but they are encoded in part, at least, in many of the RA options. The embedded question forms with *will you* and *can you* encode understandings 4 and 3, respectively. Need statements stress the speaker's desire but do not encode the fact that the addressee is expected to perform some act to fulfill the need. Understanding 1 is encoded in the expanded imperative, "I want you to give me a glass of milk." The children's form *you hafta* encodes the understanding of obligation, and the permission directives recognize that the addressee may have a claim that conflicts with compliance. Thus some of the social understandings that underlie requesting are encoded in talk, and they are also made more or less explicit in the talk that precedes and follows a request in the children's everyday interactions. The several meanings present to some degree in any directive act may be expressed in the RA message itself, as a preparatory message for the request, in the response to the request, or even in a reformulation of an unsuccessful directive act.

Caregivers use most of the different options in speaking with their children, although they use hints and question directives less frequently with younger children. They also encode many of the underlying understandings in replying to children's requests and in the episodes of interaction that usually accompany a request. It is not surprising that very young children most frequently use a need statement ("I want more") to make requests of caregivers, since caregivers expand a child's gestural meaning and simple demand of "Milk" by saying "Oh, you want some milk" or "Do you need more milk?" or "What do you want? Some milk?" Refusals may also encode the understandings: "I can't get it right now" or "You already have some milk, you don't need any more." Further, in preparing to make a request or in explaining the request, the caregiver often provides one of the associated meanings. Jack's mother, for example, stated the purpose, or need, for the request before using an indirect RA: "I don't have any lemonade. You wanta pour some for me?" Many similar experiences are necessary before a child begins to learn that expressing one of the associated meanings of a directive act can, under certain circumstances, count as a request. Thus the third type of help the child might receive in learning about the forms and meanings of requests derives from the negotiated nature of directive acts and the clustering of the related forms and meanings in talk exchanges with caregivers.

It is neither necessary to suppose nor probable that very young children comprehend the linguistic meanings, let alone the subtle interpersonal nuances, of the various options and variants they hear. In fact, Marilyn Shatz has shown that two-year-olds have an "action bias"; they are likely to perform a physical act if they detect an action word in an utterance and if it is possible to carry out the act the word denotes.[12] Thus, concerning comprehension of the different forms of indirect requests, probably the very young child does not understand the complete message in requests by caregivers even when his compliant behavior indicates comprehension. For example, it may matter little whether a mother says, "Can you jump?" or "Would you like to jump for me?" or "Did you see the rabbit jump?" The child is likely to respond by jumping if the situation permits. But between the ages of two and three, the child's increasing sensitivity to a speaker's intention and his growing comprehension of the linguistic meaning of phrases used in directive messages make it possible for him to learn from the often redundant linguistic and situational cues that are grouped together in negotiated directive episodes.

A complicating factor in comprehending indirect directives is that most of the more polite alternatives are indeed ambiguous. One reason they are considered more polite is that the addressee can understand and respond to them in more than one way: he is given an option, in effect. He can respond to the more literal reading and its force or to the intended directive force or to both. For example, a teacher's utterance to a nursery school child, "Would you like to play on the train?" could be understood as an offer meaning, "I'll let you play on the train," or as a polite directive meaning, "I want you to play on the train." In an experiment Kenneth Reeder asked children of two and a half and three years to decide which alternative force was intended under two different contextual conditions. In one case a puppet child and puppet teacher were facing one another, but the teacher was nearer the toy train than the child; in the other case, the child was near to and facing the train, and the teacher was farther from the train. The utterance, "Would you like to play on the train?" was interpreted as a directive in the first condition (in which the teacher would be sending the child over to the toy) and as an offer in the second condition (in which the child was already near to and looking at the train, presumably interested in it). The two-and-a-half-year-olds were reasonably consistent in this discrimination but were better at judging the offer than the directive. The three-year-olds were more consistently accurate on both judgments.[13] In everyday life children probably use not only

such spatial cues but also facial expression, tone of voice, and other information about the speaker and the situation to assess the speaker's intention and thus to clarify potentially ambiguous messages. We would expect that without such cues their performance in interpreting indirect forms would be poorer, as has been found in other experiments.

In the case of many indirect requests in everyday interchanges, older preschool children sometimes recognize both possible meanings. The embedded imperative "Can you———" can be understood as a request for information about the addressee's ability *or* as an indirect request for action. The force of the inquiry about ability may not be totally absent even if the addressee responds to the directive force. A five-year-old boy, for example, handed a girl a cloth tape measure that he had unwound and had tried unsuccessfully to roll up again. He asked her, "Can you roll this up?" Taking the tape measure, she replied, "I'll try, but if I can't, it's your problem, all right?" She recognized the directive force of his message and responded to it by acting and speaking appropriately, but she also verbally responded to the question of her ability to do the desired act. Many request options are not analyzed in this fashion, being used and understood as conventional formulas for requesting, both by children and by adults. Nonetheless, their literal meanings are potentially available to be singled out for attention, or even as the focus of a joke or flippant response, "I can, but I won't."

Children's selection of the directive options and the politeness variants also reflect their awareness of the differences among persons, and specifically, of the relative status of individuals. The differentiation of persons is marked in children's talk and in other behavior in many ways other than the choice of directive, of course, and in some instances the differentiation has little to do with the relative ranking of persons as of higher, lower, or equal status to the child. People who have different functions in the child's life may receive different types of communication. Some children, for example, reserve whining for the principal caregivers and never whine when dealing with teachers, other adult relatives, or other children. Familiarity, or lack of it, is also an important factor. A preschooler is more likely to approach and talk to a familiar adult or child than an unfamiliar one. Here I will briefly summarize how children choose the RA forms according to the rank of the addressee in relation to the speaker.

Imperative RA forms are associated with behavior control, and more indirect forms are associated with asking for favors or high benefit/high cost services. The right to control, exercise authority, or dispense favors is one defining feature of higher status, whether the right is attributable to age, size, strength, capability, or access to valued resources. Children aged three or four use the imperative primarily with younger children; they use more indirect RA forms with adults and children older than themselves. In some homes, at least, fathers receive the more polite RA options and such politeness markers as *please*, while mothers receive need statements and bare imperatives. Imperatives were the most frequent type of RA among all the peers observed in our laboratory playroom,[14] a tendency that is constant through early elementary school, where at least four-fifths of all RA directives to peers are imperative. Older peers use more of the indirect RA options, but the proportion of direct to indirect forms remains approximately the same through the third grade.[15]

Strategies for rerequesting

If a request does not at first succeed, what do children do? They can, of course, simply keep repeating the same request, perhaps more and more insistently. This tactic is certainly common enough among younger preschoolers, but its use tends to decrease with age; by third grade repetition of the same request is used less than 10 percent of the time when a first request fails. Preschoolers do, on occasion, vary their strategies, both in the case of a nonresponse and in the case of a noncompliant response, the latter being the more frequent outcome. The requester's perseverance appears to be related to the importance, or benefit to self, that he attributes to the goal of the request.

In the first example in this article Tom, prompted by an adult, used a very polite request (*could I*) to Judy. When that failed, he produced a need statement (*I want*), then another indirect request (*can I*), and finally ended with another statement of need (*I want*). Both need statements may have been meant as appeals to the adult rather than rerequests to Judy; we cannot be certain. The pattern of using a polite form, then following it when it is unsuccessful with *I want* has also been observed in the speech of Scottish children with their parents.[16] And it can be found in most transcripts of children's interactions with caregivers. Commonly, in the *I want* rerequest to parents, the substance of the initial request is reduced or diminished in some way.

Children can adapt to noncompliance in at least four ways. Which change they select depends to a large extent on their relationship with the addressee. First, they can revise the content of the request, asking for less or attempting to make the cost of the desired act appear less to the addressee. This tactic is often used to parents. Second, they can try again more politely in hopes that observance of the ritual proprieties will increase their chances of success. Even two- and three-year-olds, when prompted to do so, can increase the politeness of a request by adding *please* or softening the tone of voice, although older children command a greater variety of the conventional politeness variants and of other techniques used for persuasion. Third, they can escalate the request, making it more forceful or assertive, either selecting a more direct RA option or adding a threat or warning about what the consequences of noncompliance might be. This tactic is often used by dominant children to those less powerful. Fourth, they can accommodate to the formulation of the noncompliant response, taking into account what their partners have said. This alternative can be combined with any of the first three. Once a directive intention has been conveyed, it remains in effect throughout subsequent negotiation, and talk can be directed to the conditions relating to the request and any considerations brought up by the response. This was the tactic that Judy (31 months) finally chose when countering Tom's (32 months) failure to grant her permission directive:

Judy	Tom
(Stands beside wooden car.) Can I have a turn now?	(Driving wooden car.)
	(No response.)
I have a turn now?	
	I'm doing it right now.
When you finished?	
	I'm not finished yet.
Awright. (Continues to stand by car and look at Tom.)	
	(Drives for seconds.) Now I'm finished. (Climbs off car.)
(Gets on car.)	

Judy had at least three reasons to exert herself to the utmost to shape her rerequest-("When you finished?") to Tom's response. First, and probably foremost, he was in physical possession of the car. Second, he had not actually refused her first requests. He ignored one and gave a temporizing response to the replay; thus he did not force her by strong

opposition to escalate the strength of her request. And third, as a boy he was in some way entitled to have a say about use of the car. (Despite the number of daily trips to nursery school and on errands in cars driven by their mothers, the majority of the children we observed considered the right to drive and to tell how to drive the car as more a male than female prerogative.) Given three such coincident considerations, Judy was highly motivated to adapt her requests to her partner's response.

A final comment on the workings of talk. So much is going on at any one time in the several different systems of organization, it is surprising that it works as well as it does. In addition to the requirements of the several systems, however, there is the real motive force, that is, what the speakers are trying to do. Children are learning how to talk in the context of interpersonal exchanges motivated by objectives they may not yet understand. And yet they enter in enthusiastically and come to understand the significance of talk by virtue of talking. Not only must children be very finely attuned, or biologically adapted, to the properties of talk and to the requirements of the underlying systems, but they must also receive a good deal of help from adults, in a form they can utilize at that particular point in their development. A final example will illustrate the patience, persistence, and humor of a mother and the patience, persistence, and willingness of a child (Sarah at 26 months) as they worked through a problem of what was, essentially, a ritual observance.

Sarah, who was at the age when she might say no to her mother's suggestions, sometimes woke up feeling grumpy. She was also at the age when she was willing to say what she was told to say and to repeat under certain conditions what her mother said. On this morning her mother wanted to change her clothes and said politely, "Let's put on a shirt 'cause this one is dirty.'' Sarah replied, ''Stop it. *NO!''* The following interchange ensued:

Mother	Sarah
What did I tell you you had to practice?	
	But…yes, yes, yes.
Yes *(softly, laughing).*	
	What can I practice?
You can practice, "Yes, mommy, yes, mommy, yes, yes, yes" *(rhythmically).*	
	Yes, yes *(fades out).*
Yes, mommy, yes mommy, yes, yes, yes *(in same rhythm as before).*	
	Yes, mommy, yes, yes *(with similar rhythm).*
All right, now let's try it. Sarah, may I take off that dirty shirt, please?	
	(No response.)
What do you say?	
	Thank you.
No, you don't say "Thank you" *(Laughs.)* You say, "Yes, mommy, yes, mommy, yes, yes, yes."	
	Yes, mommy, yes mommy, yes, yes, yes *(rhythmically).*
Right now. Can you take it off or do you want me to take it off?	
	I take it. *(And she does.)*

Sarah's willingness to be led in talk helped her finally to achieve both the physical and verbal compliance her mother had intended from the outset of the episode. A previously well-learned lesson, that when an adult says, ''What do you say?'' the expected response is ''Thank you,'' temporarily interfered with the exercise. Sarah was correct, however, in realizing that her mother's general objective was to obtain compliance and that a ritually acceptable response was also required. And she was also beginning to learn, perhaps, under what condi-

tions a very polite parental request is actually an order that can't be refused.

REFERENCES

1. Roger Brown and Albert Gilman, ''The Pronouns of Power and Solidarity,'' in Thomas Sebeok, ed., *Style in Language* (Cambridge, Mass.: MIT Press, 1960).
2. John Austin, ''A Plea for Excuses,'' in *Philosophical Papers* (Oxford, Oxford University Press, 1961), chap.8.
3. Charles Ferguson, ''Baby Talk in Six Languages,'' in John Gumperz and Dell Hymes, eds., The Ethnography of Communication,'' *American Anthropologist,* 1964, 66, 11:103-114.
4. Erving Goffman, *Relations in Public* (New York: Harper and Row, 1971).
5. Robin Lakoff, ''The Logic of Politeness: or, Minding Your P's and Q's,'' *Papers from the Ninth Regional Meeting of the Chicago Linguistic Society* (1973), pp. 292-305.
6. Jean Berko Gleason and Sandra Weintraub, ''The Acquisition of Routines in Child Language,'' *Papers and Reports on Child Laguage Development,* 1975, 10, 89-96.
7. Roger Bakeman and John Brownlee, ''Social Rules Governing Object Conflicts in Toddlers and Preschoolers,'' in Kenneth Rubin and Hildy Ross, eds., *Peer Relations and Social Skills in Childhood* (New York: Springer-Verlag, 1983).
8. Grace Shugar and Barbara Bokus, ''Children's Discourse and Children's Activity in the Peer Situation,'' in Edward Mueller and Catherine Cooper, eds., *Process and Outcome in Peer Relations* (New York: Academic Press, in press).
9. Susan Ervin-Tripp, ''Is Sybil There? The Structure of Some American English Directives,'' *Language in Society,* 1976, 5, 25-66.
10. Claudia Mitchell-Kernan and Keith Kernan, ''Pragmatics of Directive Choice amoung Children,'' in Susan Ervin-Tripp and Claudia Mitchell-Kernan, eds., *Child Discourse* (New York: Academic Press, 1977), pp. 189-210.
11. William Labov and David Fanshel, *Therapeutic Discourse: Psychotherapy as Conversation* (New York: Academic Press, 1977). See especially chap. 3.

12. Marilyn Shatz, "On the Development of Communicative Understandings: An Early Strategy for Interpreting and Responding to Messages," *Cognitive Psychology*, 1978, 10, 271-301.

13. Kenneth Reeder, "The Emergence of Illocutionary Skills," *Journal of Child Language*, 1980, 7, 13-28.

14. Catherine Garvey, "Requests and Responses in Children's Speech," *Journal of Child Language*, 1975, 2, 41-63.

15. Elizabeth Levin and Kenneth Rubin, "Getting Others to Do What You Want Them to Do: The Development of Children's Requestive Strategies," in Keith Nelson, ed., *Children's Language*, vol. 4 (New York: Gardner Press, in preparation). For a detailed review of work on children's directives, see also Judith Becker, "Children's Strategic Use od Requests to Mark and Manipulate Social Status," in Stan Kuczaj, ed., *Language Development: Language, Thought, and Culture* (Hillsdale, N.J.: Lawrence Erlbaum, 1982), pp. 1-35.

16. Anthony Wooton, "Two Request Forms of Four Year Olds," *Journal of Pragmatics*, in press.

CHAPTER **6**

COGNITION AND LEARNING

The articles in this section reflect the marked and continuing increase in research on children's cognitive processes. One of the notable trends in the study of child development over the past twenty years has been the "cognizing" of psychology. This concern with the role of cognitive factors in development is found not only in traditional areas of cognitive study, such as in attention, perception, problem-solving, and learning, but also in social development. A pervasive theme of this book is how the cognitive processes or capabilities of children moderate or mediate their responses to such things as attachment, discipline, loss of a parent, behavior of teachers and peers, and a broad array of other social factors.

Although much of the original impetus to the cognitive development movement is attributable to the theory and research of Jean Piaget, most of the articles in this section reflect use of the more contemporary information-processing approach to investigating issues in cognitive development. In addition, in several of the articles, the current concern with social and ecological factors in cognitive performance is illustrated.

The first two articles in this section, by Henry Wellman and by Robert Siegler, review the evidence on how children acquire knowledge. Wellman describes how children develop concepts, a concept being defined as a cognitive category that allows people to group together perceptually distinct information, events, or items. In this section we see that children acquire a wide array of concepts that help them in understanding the physical and social worlds. Wellman discusses development of the child's concept of number as an example of a physical concept, and the child's concepts of human thinking as an example of a more social set of concepts.

Siegler addresses issues dealing with the relationship between existing knowledge and learning, the processes by which children learn that their existing knowledge is inadequate, and the process by which children construct more adequate new rules. The author uses research from a series of experiments on the development of the concept of time to support his generalizations about knowledge and learning.

The third article considers how children learn to distinguish between appearance and reality. Adults know that when a person dresses for a costume party, that person's identity does not change, or that when a performer's skin and clothing appear to change color under different-colored spotlights, in reality the person has not altered. This distinction between appearance and reality is a difficult one for young preschool children, and the developing understanding of this distinction is highly correlated with skill in solving visual perspective-taking tasks. Flavell proposes that what helps children grasp the distinction is an increased awareness that human beings are sentient subjects who have mental representations of objects and events.

In their article, Jennifer Cousins and her colleagues examine the development of children's spatial competency through children's cognitive mapping of their school campus. A hierarchical model of cognitive mapping competence is tested and validated. In the study, reversals in the developmental trends in the model are found to be related to the children's degree of familiarity with the environment. Concern with differences in children's performance in different settings leads us to the next two articles, which focus on the issue of whether the findings from a laboratory setting and those from a more naturalistic, familiar, ecologically valid setting can be generalized. The study by Sheldon Cohen and his coinvestigators is concerned with the effects of noise on attentional strategies, feelings of personal control, and physiological processes related to health. The responses of children in schools in which there were high levels of aircraft noise in contrast to those in which there were low levels of noise were congruent in some respects with children's responses to noise in the laboratory and differed in other respects. In their study of prospective memory, Ceci and Bronfenbrenner also find some marked differences related to familiarity with the setting and sex-role expectations. The results of these studies suggest that caution must be exercised in generalizing the findings from laboratory to naturalistic settings.

The final article in this section, by Scarr-Salapatek and Weinberg, has now become a classic in the study of individual differences in cognitive performance as measured by intelligence tests. Few topics have stimulated more controversy and research than that of the effects of transactions between biological and environmental factors on intellectual development. In most cases, studies in this area have involved the use of standardized tests of intelligence. Sometimes educational level, professional achievements, Piagetian tasks, and, less frequently, social problem-solving skills are also used to estimate cognitive level.

Many of the problems in interpretation of these studies rest in disparate views of what IQ scores represent; other problems are based on confusion about the concept of heritability. The layman tends to regard IQ as a measure of the innate capacity to learn, a measure that remains relatively stable throughout life. As the student will learn in reading the articles in this section, this is not true. The IQ is a measure of performance on an intelligence test, the measure being relative to the performance of a group of individuals on whom the test has been standardized. As the IQ goes above 100 it means the individual is performing better than the average person of his or her age in the standardization group; as it drops below 100 the individual is performing less well than the average person in the standardization group. The problem-solving performance measured on an intelligence test is most closely related to performance and achievement in academic settings and less closely related to competence in dealing with social situations, practical problems in everyday life, and earning power.

The student should note first that IQ is a measure of performance, not of innate capacity. This performance is a result of the interaction of many variables: innate intellectual capacity, life experiences, the environment in which the individual is raised, physical and mental condition at the time of testing, the particular items on the test, and the conditions under which the test is administered. Also the student should keep in mind that IQ is always a relative performance score. The performance of the individual should be compared to performances of those with a similar background and shared life experiences. Finally, there are considerable fluctuations in IQ scores for the same individual over the life span. This is in part attributable to the fact that very different types of items testing different cognitive competences are used with children of different ages. For the prelinguistic child under two years of age, items relying heavily on sensory or motor skills are used. With the onset of language, intelligence tests items involve more verbal skills. It has been argued that the early sensorimotor measures involve a different kind of cognitive competence than do verbal or abstract reasoning items. Some support for this position is found in the extremely low relationship between IQ scores obtained in the first two years of life and those from later ages. In addition, fluctuations in scores result because the pattern and rate of intellectual development varies for different individuals. Just as children may show plateaus and spurts in physical growth at different ages, they also show wide individual variations in patterns of cognitive development.

Scarr-Salapatek and her colleague Richard Weinberg examine the effect of cross-fostering on the IQs of black children and find that the social and cognitive environment of middle-class white adoptive homes is associated with increases in IQ in black adopted children. They propose that if high IQs are considered desirable, some restructuring of the social system within black homes is necessary to facilitate the development of intellectual skills measured by intelligence tests.

However, it should be noted that these investigators do not support the notion of interracial adoption as a preferred strategy for improving the intelligence test performance of black children. Their subsequent follow-up studies found that some of these black children placed with white parents were showing emotional problems and difficulties in adjustment that could be associated with their atypical family situation.

The articles in this section underscore the complex array of individual, biological, social, and ecological factors that must be considered in understanding cognitive development.

READING 23

The Foundations of Knowledge: Concept Development in the Young Child

Henry M. Wellman

Consider the world as described by physicists— a reality made up of atoms and molecules, of waves and frequencies, of forces and resistances. Then consider the world as it appears to us—a world of color, of number, of people and things, of plants and animals, of friends and enemies. How does the human mind transform events that have a physical reality of the first sort into the familiar world of the second sort? One crucial process in this transformation is the process of conception—the organization of information presented to the mind into an intricate array of *concepts*.

Concepts are the cognitive categories that allow people to group together perceptually distinct information, events, or items. My concept of *red* allows me to treat distinctly different colors (magenta and carmine) as similar in some ways, and also as distinct from blue or green. My concept of *chair* allows me to recognize a chair when I see one, even a new unfamiliar design. Individual concepts are further compounded and linked together. There are different colors and even different reds, all captured in a larger conceptual system of similarities and differences. These in turn are related to other concepts that carve the world into different sizes, shapes, items, and types. The term *concept* is used in several related fashions to refer to discrete, particular concepts (concepts of chair), to concepts of a more general level (the concept of furniture), and to large conceptual systems (concepts of number, of time).

The concepts possessed by the average adult are immense in scope and number. They include all the knowledge that the person uses to organize, interpret, and reason about the world. In general, concepts can be considered in two large overlapping sets. There are concepts that

aid in the understanding of the *physical world* and there are those specific to an understanding of the *social world*. Concepts of the physical world include ideas of number and amount, causes and effects, concepts of time, spatial relations, length, and weight. Also included are concepts of plants and animals, and physical systems such as weather, the seasons, gravity, and electricity. Concepts in this domain are represented in many areas of curricula—mathematics, science, music, art. Concepts of the social world, however, include the world of self, others, and social interaction. There are concepts of the variety of human behaviors (aggression, flirting, helping, competing), knowledge of a multitude of human states (fatigue, anger, dreaming, love, illness), and abilities (intelligence, creativity, retardation, memory, reasoning). In this domain would be included concepts of social roles (doctor, lawyer, boss, teacher), of the relationships between persons (friends, parents, classmate, bully), and larger social categories and institutions (races, nations, religions, and customs). Concepts of the social world also figure prominently in current curricula. All of social studies (history, civics, economics) concerns such knowledge; as does affective education (encompassing awareness and knowledge of feelings and values), moral or ethical education (utilizing concepts of good, bad, equitable, fair), and multicultural education (concerned with concepts of others, differences, tolerance).

Obviously these domains, the physical and the social, overlap, and many concepts cross-cut the two. Concepts of life and death, for example, apply to animals and plants as well as to self and others. Conceptual systems of classification apply to the physical world (e.g., biological taxa) and the social world (e.g., kinship classes). The self can be considered as a physical entity (the body) and as a social entity (the psyche).

Of course not all of these concepts and categories are possessed by the young child; much of what the adult knows must be accumulated over a long course of development. However, even the youngest children organize their world into concepts and conceptual systems. The focus of this chapter is the concepts of the young child, specifically the conceptual acquisitions of the preschooler. These early concepts are particularly important since they lay the foundation for all later knowledge and for conceptual development.

To illustrate concept development in young children, I will take as examples the development of two different conceptual systems in preschoolers. These are the child's concepts of *number* and the child's concepts of *human thinking*. Why focus on the development of these two systems? As outlined above, a list of concepts acquired by children would be immense, so any sampling of concepts must be selective. These two concepts were selected in accordance with a set of general considerations that have shaped this chapter.

The first consideration is that not all concepts are equally important or fundamental. The child's concept of *dessert* is likely to develop early, but it does not seem essential to later important developments. However, a child's conception of number is generally thought of as a crucial conceptual acquisition. Since it provides a basis for mathematics learning, it is a typical and central content in curricula for preschool children. Furthermore, number games ("One, two, buckle my shoe") are spontaneously played and invented by children themselves. A similar argument can be made for the importance of the child's conceptions of thinking. Concepts of thinking include a knowledge of human memory, dreams, reasoning, and other mental workings. Human beings are

creatures whose immediate acts and behavior are products of such internal mental processes. Thus children's knowledge of how humans reason, remember, and imagine—their knowledge of thinking broadly defined—must be an integral and major part of their larger concepts of themselves and of others.

A second consideration is that these two conceptual systems represent distinctly different types of concepts. Concepts of number are an instance of concepts of the physical world, similar to time, weight, volume, distance, and speed. In contrast, conceptions of human thinking are more related to an understanding of the social world of people, human behavior and, ultimately, society.

Finally, these two concepts are particularly rich; discussion of their development facilitates a discussion of larger issues. Perhaps the most important of these issues concerns a description of the general conceptual competence of the preschool child. All too often, preschool children have been described in negative terms. That is, studies illustrate what the child does not know or cannot do that the older elementary school child does. In Piaget's theory, for example, preschool children's conceptual systems are termed preoperational. Essentially, this stresses that they are deficient in comparison to the later, operational child. As Gelman (Gelman 1978; Gelman and Gallistel 1978) argues, such a description obscures an understanding of preschoolers in their own right. For both the concepts considered here, there is recent research that allows us to paint a more comprehensive picture of the young child's knowledge.

THE CONCEPT OF NUMBER IN THE YOUNG CHILD

Consider the standard, and now famous, number conservation task devised by Piaget (1952). A child sees two identical rows of about seven or eight marbles and correctly judges that there are the same number of marbles in each row.

Then one of the rows is spread out so that it is longer than the other. The child is now asked, does one row have more marbles than the other or are they just the same? Preschool children fail this task, typically asserting that the longer row now has more marbles. These results are very robust and can be replicated by anyone working with preschoolers; if you change the length of the row, the child believes the number of items changes. These well-known results have led to the conclusion that preschoolers have no, or at best a severely deformed, concept of number. Where older children conceive of number as a mathematical property independent of length and colors—i.e., they understand number as distinct from many number-irrelevant attributes of objects—preschoolers seem to have little idea of the true nature of number. Personal experience can also confirm this impression. Preschoolers often do not count correctly ("one, two, seven, four"), often show deficient number-based behavior (as in their use and understanding of money), and lack many number skills (even elementary ones such as addition and subtraction) that must be acquired later in school.

However, consider the following recent demonstration by Gelman (1972). A three-year-old child was shown two plates. On one plate, there was a row of three small toys (two mice and a truck) and on the other a row of two toys. The plates were covered with a can and their positions were shuffled. Over the course of a number of trials, the child had to learn to identify "the winner." The winner was always the same plate, the one with three toys. After the child could identify the winner consistently, the plates were covered for one more trial and the winner was surreptitiously changed. For some children the number of items was changed, for example one item was removed from the winner plate leaving both plates with only two items. For others the number was left unchanged but some other feature was changed, say the three items were all pushed

together or rearranged. What did young children then do when they had to pick "the winner?" A typical response to having an item removed was to judge that there was now no winner and to explain this by saying, "There was three animals. In the can (looks around). Took one. 'Cuz there's two now" (p. 84). However, a typical response to having the items pushed together was to insist that there was still a winner even while explaining, "These pushed together. When you turned 'em in the can" (p. 84). In short, in this situation young children seemed to adequately identify the number of items (3 vs. 2), spontaneously judged that number and not some other feature (such as length) defined the winner, understood that subtraction of an item changed the winner but pushing the items together did not, and explained occurrences in number-relevant manners (a toy was removed or added). The contrast between the results on Gelman's magic task and the classic Piaget number conservation task is striking and raises many questions. Most important, why do preschoolers look fairly sophisticated in Gelman's task yet deficient in many other tasks? What positive competencies with number are in fact possessed by very young children?

Table I contains a summary of information needed to answer these questions. This table lists many of the skills and components involved in an understanding of number. Some of the skills listed in the table are observable in preschoolers, others are acquired later. One important distinction indicated in Table I is that number knowledge can be divided into two distinct types (Gelman and Gallistel 1978). First, there are those skills that allow a person to tell how many items are in some given array. These are termed *number extraction* processes. Counting the items is a primary example of a number extraction skill. In addition to number extraction, there is *number reasoning*. Piaget's task, that requires the child to judge that two rows still have the same number in spite of

TABLE I   FACTORS INVOLVED IN THE ACQUISITION OF NUMBER CONCEPTS

Small sets of items (approximately 4 or fewer)	Large sets of items	Sets with no definite number
	Number extraction	
Counting:	Counting	$a, a+1, a+2 \ldots a+N$
the one-to-one principle		
the stable order principle	Generative counting	One-to-one correspondence
the cardinal principle		
the order-irrelevance principle	Estimating	
	Number reasoning	
Equality (3 = 3)	Equality	Algebraic reasoning
		$a + b = b + a$
Number-relevant transformations:	Number-relevant transformations	if $a = b$, and $b = c$
adding, subtracting		then $a = c$
Number-irrelevant transformation:	Number-irrelevant transformations	
rearrangement; substitution		
Qualitative solutions:	Qualitative solutions	
adding to increase,		
subtracting to decrease		
Quantitative solutions	Quantitative solutions	
(4−2 = 2 exactly)		

changing the lengths of the rows, involves number reasoning. Notice that it is not necessary to count the items (to extract a representation of number) to reason correctly in this task; given that one starts with identical rows, all one must know is that no items have been added or removed. Number extraction and number reasoning are distinct skills.

What number knowledge does the preschool child possess? Preschoolers possess a variety of number concepts that are found within the left-hand column of Table I. If the focus of their knowledge is very small sets of countable objects, then preschool children can be shown to know a surprising amount about numbers. Skill with large sets of items (the second column) or with uncountable sets (the third column) represent number knowledge to be acquired later.

First, following the order of Table I, begin with preschoolers' counting skills. The following is a typical demonstration of a two- or three-year-old's counting (Gelman and Gallistel 1978). The child is given small sets of items to

count. In such cases the young child may count two items as "one, two," count three items as "one, two, six," and count four items as "one, two, six, five." Though these counts are unconventional, that is the child does not use the correct sequence of standard number names, still when carefully analyzed they reveal considerable knowledge of counting. First, young children seem to know that every item to be counted should be counted just once (the one-to-one principle). In the above example two number words were used for two items, and four were used for four. Second, they know that the words used for counting should be recited in a consistent sequence (the stable order principle). The child above used "one, two, six" for three items and "one, two, six, five" for four items. The child would use "one, two, six" again if counting a different set of three. Third, children often know that the last count word that you come to in counting represents the total amount of all that you have counted (the cardinal principle). In the last example above the child would conclude there were five total items in all. Finally, they know that any set can be counted in a variety of orders—from left to right or right to left, or skipping around—and that this is irrelevant to coming up with a proper count (the order-irrelevance principle). In short, in spite of using counting systems that are not yet the same as the prescribed conventional sequence, young preschoolers' unconventional but consistent behavior indicates systematic knowledge about the goal and methods of counting.

Older children are more consistent in their counting—they make fewer errors. For example, if asked to count sets containing 4 items, approximately 60 percent of three-year-olds and 100 percent of five-year-olds consistently evidence all three of the one-to-one, stable order, and cardinal principles in their counts (Gelman and Gallistel 1978). Older children also are more conventional in their counting—they use the standard number word list to represent numbers. For example, when faced with 4 items, approximately 60 percent of three-year-olds and 90 percent of five-year-olds will say there are 4 (the conventional number) items present (Gelman and Tucker 1975). Obviously, and very importantly, older children, especially those beyond preschool, learn to make much longer counts. There would seem to be two parts to this development. First the child learns to count moderately sized arrays, arrays of from 6 to 13 or 14 items. Later yet the child learns that counting is a generative process. This occurs when children recognize and employ the rules that are used to generate larger and indefinite counts (21,22...31, 32...41,42...). The end point is the ability to extract an exact numerical representation for very large sets of items—even item sets so large that one has never had to count to such a number before.

What of number reasoning? Are young children able to reason about the numerosity of sets that they can count? Recent research suggests that the young child can reason about numbers in certain ways that represent sizable achievements in themselves, and that also set the stage for later developments. Again Gelman's work is revealing here, especially results from her magic experiments (1972), introduced earlier.

Consider the lower left-hand cell of Table I, and, first, reasoning about equality. In the magic experiments sometimes the winner was changed in number-irrelevant ways (items pushed together, a toy car substituted for a toy mouse). In these cases preschoolers typically considered the new arrangement to still be the winner. Thus they understood something of the equality of the two sets; the new set was still the winner because it had a number equal to the old winner. At other times, items were added to or subtracted from one set, sometimes resulting in equal numbered sets on the same trial. The following is a typical response to this occurrence by three-and four-year-olds: The child places the soldier on the two-mouse plate. "This is gonna be a winner plate too. Both have three things" (Gelman and Tucker 1975).

This "both have three" response indicates an understanding of equality. This "both have three" response brings up a very important point about young children's number reasoning: They seem to be able to reason only in those cases where they can compare the counted number of items directly. Thus if they can count your cookies and find three and count my cookies and find three they know that $3 = 3$ and that you and I have the same. However, if they cannot achieve a count (because there are too many items or because they are not allowed to count them), then they cannot reason about equality. For example, if each time I give Adam a cracker I also give Kathy one, an adult or older child would know that the two children must have equal amounts even if they could not count or even see the accumulated crackers. Preschoolers would not come to this conclusion. They would be able to tell this by counting both Adam's and Kathy's crackers and then comparing, but they would not know just on the basis of the obvious one-to-one correspondence of the crackers themselves.

The examples above also show the young child's understanding of number-relevant transformations—addition and subtraction of items change the winner. Similarly there is understanding of certain number-irrelevant transformation—rearrangement and item substitution (replacing a car with a mouse) does not change the winner since it does not change the number on the plate.

The reader can easily imagine how these impressive but limited abilities lead to further developments. As the child can count larger sets (column two in the table), number-reasoning can expand to more and more situations. In addition, children will eventually develop the ability to reason about numbers even when they cannot achieve a total count of the sets at all. This is what is typically referred to as *algebraic reasoning* and is represented by the last column of Table I. Algebraic reasoning is numerical reasoning independent of any specific number. For example, if I know that Adam and Kathy both have the same number of crackers and each eat half of them, then I can reason that they both have the same number of crackers left. To reason in this fashion I need never appeal to specific numbers. Similarly I could know that Joshua is twice as old as Luis who is twice as old as Dylan, and therefore know that Joshua is four times as old as Dylan, without knowing anyone's specific age. This type of number reasoning is beyond the skill—and beyond the conception—of the young child who must be able to extract some specific (small) number to apply to the sets she or he reasons about.

One other skill of the young child's number reasoning deserves mention. In the magic experiments, after the winner plate was changed the child was often given an opportunity to fix the plate so it would be a winner again. In these repair situations the children evidenced a rough idea of how to solve numerical problems. For example, suppose the winner originally had five items but now appeared with three. The typical response was to *add* items to try to fix the winner. This response shows children's understanding that subtraction can be solved (repaired) by adding. Young children in this situation could not figure out exactly how many items to add; they could only approximate it with considerable trial and error (adding some and counting, then subtracting some and counting again, etc.). This type of ability is termed *qualitative solutions* in Table I. This is to distinguish it from *quantitative solutions* that older children develop. Young children's solution attempts are qualitative because they understand the direction of change accurately; older children are quantitative however because they understand both the direction of change and the exact magnitude of change required for the solution ($4 - 2 = 2$ exactly, so precisely 2 items would need to be added to repair the winners).

While I have concentrated on Gelman's work because it provides the most detailed description of preschool children, there is other research that contributes to the above picture (see Gelman and Gallistel 1978, or Ginsburg 1977 for reviews). Also, I have dispensed with the numerous important cautions as to the limits of our knowledge. The above description is still tentative and bound to be revised as well as enriched by future work.

In summary, preschool children have an extensive conceptual system relevant to number. This includes an important number extraction skill, specifically counting, and many simple but fundamental number reasoning concepts. These skills lay the groundwork for later arithmetic and algebraic knowledge. These early skills also determine the child's ability to solve very real numerical problems. Young children's knowledge of small sets of numbers means that they often can and do notice whether they have their full share of small amounts of cookies or crackers, whether they have both mittens, and who is older than who (among their three-, four-, and five-year-old peers). Young children's need to make concrete counts in order to reason about number partly explains the prevalent use of their fingers in counting. Such aids help the child to "think about three" in order to solve number problems (Curcio, Robbins, and Ela 1971).

One other point should be made, not obvious in our discussion so far. Preschoolers seem genuinely and spontaneously interested in number or number-like properties. Counting objects, rehearsing the sequence of number names, attending to equality and inequality seem ubiquitous activities of the young child. Fortunately for the teacher, not only are young children interested in number but everyday classroom activities are rich in potential sources of number learning. Adults can use everyday tasks and events—such as dividing things up (carrot sticks, juice cups, scissors, etc.), accumulating things (both mittens, all the puzzles), making correspondences (a hat for every child, a jacket for every record), recording data (each child's height or age, days and dates, who is absent or present)—to increase the child's knowledge and curiosity about number (see Kamii 1982; Kamii and DeVries 1978).

THE CONCEPT OF THINKING IN THE YOUNG CHILD

All of us possess a reasonable idea of what basic number knowledge might be like, and this provides a needed background for understanding the number knowledge that develops in the preschool child. But, what of our second topic, conceptions of human thinking? What might a person know about human thinking broadly defined, about such mental activities as dreaming, remembering, or imagining? In answer to this question, consider for a moment the kinds of comments that adults make every day about mental processes and states. Statements like: "He's very *smart*. Are you *sure* about that? I

forgot your birthday. I just *remembered* her name. I had a strange *dream* last night. It slipped my *mind*. I didn't *understand* a word of it. I *thought* I *knew* the answer." Adults frequently refer to human thinking.

The ability to think about our own thinking is a very impressive skill. Scholars have conjectured that an ability to contemplate our own selves, to reflect on our own thoughts, hopes, and knowledge is one characteristic that distinguishes humans from lower animals. Further, the development of concepts about thinking—an ability to understand one's own thought processes and the thought processes of others—is one of the important tasks of childhood. At some point children are expected to know the difference between telling a lie and telling the truth, to know the difference between pretending to do something and actually doing it (pretending to hit a friend, in play), to judge the intentions of self and others (whether something was done on purpose or accidentally), to know the difference between dreams and reality ("Don't be afraid, it was just a dream."), and to understand that others' thoughts and beliefs are different from one's own ("He didn't *know* it was yours.").

Clearly adults and older children have acquired innumerable concepts about thinking. In order to discuss the early development of this knowledge it is useful to distinguish four broad clusters of concepts in this domain (Wellman 1982):

1 *Existence*. Adults know that thoughts and internal mental states exist, that they are not the same as external acts or events. For example, consider such concepts as those of lies, hunches, guesses, and pretending. All are based on the notion of the *difference* between a mental state and external behavior. I can know that one thing is true, but say or act as if it is not. That is, I can lie or pretend. I can be completely ignorant of the correct answer on a test, but pick the correct choice by a lucky guess. In

short, as any adult knows, mental states and external behavior are not the same.

2 *Distinct processes.* People can remember or forget, they can visualize images, they can dream, they can reason, they can concentrate or daydream, they can conjecture and guess. Clearly there are a variety of distinct mental acts; thinking takes many forms. Adults know that there are many different thought processes and understand the distinctive features of different mental acts (e.g., the differences between guessing and knowing, between dreaming and daydreaming).

3 *Integration.* While there are numerous distinctions between mental processes, the different mental processes are also similar and related. For example, adults know that all mental processes reside in the brain or mind; remove the brain and all, not some, disappear. They know that thinking, dreaming, and imagining are all internal invisible events. Yet, at the same time these are very different from other internal invisible events, such as digestion or the heart pumping blood. They know that dreaming, and fantasizing, and conjuring up mental images are all related, as are remembering, learning, knowing, and understanding; and all are different from sneezing, chewing, and wiggling your toes.

4 *Variables.* Any one mental performance is influenced by a number of other factors or variables. In remembering, for example, how much one can remember depends on how hard the task is, the nature of the items, and the memory strategies used. Adults know that long lists are harder to remember than short; that meaningful items (English words for an American) are easier to remember than meaningless ones (Russian words); and that writing yourself a note is often better than rote memory.

What does the young child know about this intriguing and varied mental world that underlies and influences all human behavior? The first and primary question is about existence.

Do young children realize that an internal mental world exists independent of overt behaviors and physical events? Some understanding of this independent existence is imperative for understanding mental concepts all of which are based on notions of the difference between mental states and external behavior and events.

Piaget (1929) investigated children's concepts of dreams and of thoughts. He concludes that young children do not discern the existence of mental processes. Instead preschoolers identify mental events with observable behaviors. They equate thinking with talking and believe that the organ of thinking is the mouth. They conceive of dreams as pictures flashed in the room while sleeping. In short, they do not view mental processes as different from related behavioral acts such as talking or watching.

More recent studies partly confirm this picture. Consider the following situations. Hakeem puts his coat in one of two closets. Later when he returns he looks in the correct closet and finds his coat. Alternately Philip's father hangs Philip's coat in one of two closets but Philip does not personally see which one. Later he returns to retrieve his coat and looks in one of the closets that turns out to be the correct one. The typical adult interpretation of these two scenarios would be to say that Hakeem, the first boy, *remembered* where his coat was, but that Philip only *guessed* where his was. However, when preschoolers are asked to interpret these two situations they judge that both boys remembered (Wellman and Johnson 1979). In other words they appear to think that remembering refers to a behavioral state of affairs—successfully finding the coat—not to the person's underlying knowledge. Other studies similarly show an interpretation of internal events in terms of external observable behaviors (Gordon and Flavell 1977; Misciones et al. 1978).

From these findings one is tempted to agree with Piaget that preschool children do not appreciate the fundamental existence of thinking as opposed to acting. But a study by

Johnson and Wellman (1980) indicates that the situation is more complex. The key problem is one of salience. Mental processes and events are unobservable—they go on inside the head. By their very nature they are less obvious than external, observable physical actions and behaviors. We cannot see people think as we can see them smile or open a door. If mental processes were made very salient would preschoolers still ignore them? Johnson and Wellman tried to make internal events maximally salient to young children. The child was shown two boxes and an object was then hidden in one of them. After viewing the hiding, the child was asked to find the object. The boxes were constructed so that the object was *not* where it ought to have been but could be secretly changed to the other box instead. In this situation, at the behavioral level the child did not succeed in finding the object. However, four-year-olds still insisted that they did *remember* where it had been and that they *knew* where it had been even though they had not found it. That is, they used appropriate mental terms to refer to their thought state (correctly knowing where it was) and not to refer to just their observable actions (incorrectly locating the object). When Johnson and Wellman (1980) tested children in the same way as reported in Wellman and Johnson (1979) and Misciones et al. (1978) they found that children again identified mental terms with behavioral acts, e.g., remembering meant simply being correct. It was only in the trick condition, where their own state of knowledge was so obvious and discrepant from the real state of things, that four-year-olds revealed an understanding of the independent existence of the mental world.

This demonstrates an impressive, if limited, conception on the part of four-and five-year-old children. They are becoming aware that there are mental processes that are sometimes independent of the external, physical world. In addition to external, physical reality there is the realm of imagination, belief, fantasies, guessing, in short the realm of thinking.

Do children of this age also know that there are a variety of distinctly different mental processes? The data here are clear. At the very least four- and five-year-olds are able to distinguish different mental events in terms of how much those events must correspond to the real world. For example, you can *remember* only things that have actually happened, but you can *guess* anything you want, whether it could or did ever really happen or not. Similarly, to say that Laura *knows* something happened usually implies that that thing really happened (Laura knows that birds fly). But you can say that Laura *thinks* something happened whether the thing happened or not (Laura thinks birds never fly). Preschool children can distinguish *know* and *remember* as mental processes that more correctly correspond to the real state of affairs from *think* and *guess* that are less dependent on the real world (Johnson and Maratsos 1977; Johnson and Wellman 1980; Wellman and Johnson 1979) and also understand that *pretend*, and *lie* refer to denials of the true states of things (McNamara, Baker, and Olson 1976; Piaget 1965). For example, if four-year-olds know that Robert always goes to school except when he is sick and are told that "Robert is pretending he is sick," then they know Robert is not really sick at all. They also know that Robert should go to school.

The above findings are with four- and five-year-olds. What about younger preschoolers? As yet there is no evidence to show that two-and-one-half- or three-year-olds also conceive of these distinctions between different mental processes. Indeed in one study three-year-olds treated *remember* and *forget* as identical (Wellman and Johnson 1979) and in another they treated *know* and *think* as identical (Johnson and Maratsos 1977). However these data could easily underestimate the conceptions of these very young children because they may not have understood what they were supposed to do in the experimental tasks.

There are some intriguing findings with two- and three-year-olds, if a slightly different question is asked: When do children understand that different people can be thinking about different things? This conception also falls under the heading of understanding distinct processes; when do children understand that my thoughts and knowledge are often distinctly different from yours? First, four- and five-year-olds do understand that different people have different thoughts. For example, four-year-olds understand that if Heather and Brian have a secret from Jill, then the three have different knowledge: Heather and Brian know the secret but Jill does not (Marvin, Greenberg, and Mossler 1976). But the most striking demonstrations with younger preschool children concentrate on the child's concepts of knowledge through vision. Specifically, with younger children the question has been, does the child know that you and I often see different things? Seeing something is one of the simplest possible forms of knowing. If I can see the ball under the table but you cannot, I know that it is there (or that it is red) whereas you do not. It is now clear that young children know that different persons have different visual knowledge. If I hold up a card between myself and a two- or three-year-old, a card that has a dog on one side and a cat on the other, the child knows that she or he sees the cat and I see the dog (Masangkay et al. 1974). The child also knows that she or he must talk about the object differently if the listener has seen it than if the listener has not (Maratsos 1973) and if it is further away and less visible to the listener as opposed to close and clear (Wellman and Lempers 1977).

In sum, young preschoolers know the basic fact that another person need not see the same object that they see. Older children of four and five further understand that even when another person sees the same object, that the other may have a different view of that object (Flavell 1978). I may see the front and you may see the side. Thus, young preschoolers know that different people see *different objects;* the older preschooler understands that different people can see *different views* of the same objects.

To this point we have considered children's concepts of the *existence* of thoughts and knowledge, and their concepts of *distinct* types of thinking and knowing. Older preschoolers also realize that different mental processes are *integrated* in certain ways. One thing they seem to know in this regard is that all mental processes similarly reside in the brain or mind. Johnson and Wellman (in press) asked children whether they needed their brains to engage in various activities: Do you need your brain to think; do you need your brain to wiggle your toes; do you need your brain to sneeze? In fact, four- and five-year-olds demonstrated a very mind-like view of the brain. They knew that thinking, remembering, dreaming, and knowing were all similar *mental* processes that required the brain whereas external behaviors, like wiggling toes, or involuntary acts, like sneezing, did not. In addition, young children clearly avoided certain misconceptions of the brain. They did not identify the brain just with the observable head, for example—they knew the brain was invisible and inside the head. They judged that you need your brain to think but not for all head acts, e.g., not to shake your head. They also believed that certain internal events were not mental events—feeling an ice cube in your closed mouth did not require the brain but dreaming did. Thus they discriminated internal mental events from other internal events.

A beginning understanding of the *variables* that influence human thinking is also apparent in preschool-age children.

Wellman (1977) tested three-, four-, and five-year-olds' understanding of the following memory-relevant variables: number of items (that more items are harder to remember than few), interference (that noisy distractions can impede memory efforts), age (that adults often remember better than young children), help (that splitting the memory task with a friend is easier than having to do it all yourself), drawing (that drawing a picture of the item to look at later, when you have to remember, will help you), time (that a short time to study the items will detract from memory performance in comparison to having ample study time), and cues (that cued recall, where someone gives you a cue for each item to remember, is easier than free recall, where you have to remember everything on your own). The vast majority of three-, four-, and five-year-olds understood the relevance of at least some of these variables. The earliest variables understood, by three-year-olds, were the influence of number of items and the effect of interference on remembering. The last variable understood, missed by some of the five-year-olds, was cues (see also Ritter 1978). Wellman (1977) also found that the same preschoolers knew that some potential variables did *not* affect memory. What the rememberer was wearing, her or his hair color, and if she or he was fat or skinny were all judged to have no influence on the person's memory performance.

Of course older children understand still more variables (Flavell and Wellman 1977). For example they know that related items (black-white) are easier to remember than unrelated ones (apple-black); they know that forming a mental image helps you remember, and that concentrating on one task can block out simultaneous attention to another. But the groundwork for this future development is clearly laid in the preschool years.

In conclusion, there is both a positive picture of what young children know about thinking broadly defined and also clear limitations to this early knowledge. On the positive side even two- and three-year-olds are beginning to form concepts of thinking. They use words such as *remember* and *think* in their everyday speech. They associate the brain with the head. And

they know that different persons have different visual knowledge. Three-year-olds know that it is harder to think about many things than one, and that distractions interfere with thinking.

Our picture of the conceptions of older preschoolers is even clearer. Four- and five-year-olds have a rudimentary but rich conception of the mental world. They understand that an internal mental world exists independent of and apart from a person's observable behaviors and acts. Relatedly they know that two peoples' thinking might be quite different, that others may not know what you are thinking or what you know. They understand fairly well the meanings of such mental terms as *remember, forget, think, know, guess, pretend,* and can distinguish among these various cognitive acts and processes. In particular, they know that some of these mental processes are more tied to the true nature of occurrences in the world (e.g., *know*) and some can be completely unrelated to reality (e.g., *guess*). They have the beginnings of an integrated knowledge of the mental world.

This picture of competence is balanced by the preschool child's limitations. Most important, the mental world has a much less central and salient place in the child's total conception of human behavior. Unless stimulated to do so, preschoolers often avoid thinking about mental occurrences. They do not ordinarily ponder the internal mediating causes of behavior, such as one's reasons or intentions. They often misunderstand mental terms as applying to less complex but observable features of persons—e.g., forgetting just means you are wrong. They also isolate the mental world. Only older children tend to see various mental processes as being integrated into all of human behavior. All in all, the elementary school child has a more consolidated, richer, and more pervasive conception of human cognition.

The preschool child is clearly more knowledgeable about the mental world than has been asserted in the past (e.g., Piaget 1929). However, these concepts are still at the cutting edge of the child's concept development. It is appropriate for teachers and parents to expect certain things of the child—for example, to remember to do or not to do certain things if told, to begin to distinguish lies from the truth, and accidents from intended misdeeds. It is useful to instruct the child in the larger implications of one's knowledge, for example, the implications of the fact that people have different minds—"He didn't know you were playing with it," "Tell him what you want." But it is inappropriate to expect the young child to have adult mastery of these concepts, to meet these expectations consistently, or to understand relevant instructions completely.

UNDERSTANDING AND FURTHERING CONCEPT DEVELOPMENT

Comparing and contrasting the concepts of number and concepts of thinking reveal some more general conclusions about concept development in the young child. The best way to organize these conclusions is by considering certain recurring themes in the investigation of concept development. The following discussion will not make clear all there is to know about concept development, but considering these themes will call attention to some larger unanswered questions (see also Flavell 1970) and to some important conclusions.

Assessment

In both areas of concept development reviewed above, the obvious major question was, what do preschool children really know? What is an accurate assessment of their conceptual accomplishments? This is an important question for both researchers and teachers. Researchers strive for an accurate understanding of the child. Teachers strive to provide information and experiences that match and build upon the child's current conceptions.

Piaget's assessment of preschoolers remains an important starting point. Both researchers

and teachers have found it extremely useful. But, Piaget's description now seems incomplete. Piaget emphasizes that preschoolers see the world primarily in terms of the external, surface features of things and events such as size, shape, and color. Preschoolers are supposed to be unable to see beyond these features to more inferred, less obvious conceptions. For example, in Piaget's number conservation task preschoolers apparently focused on how long the rows looked rather than on the numbers of items present. As this chapter has shown, despite uneven performances, preschoolers do conceive of these relatively invisible aspects of the world. They attend to and understand number and they have rudimentary but impressive conceptions of unobservable mental processes. Of course, it is important not to overstate the young child's sophistication. Piaget is certainly correct that the surface features of events have a provocative pull on the thinking of the young child. Further, the young child's knowledge is often limited to only certain helpful situations. Thus preschool concepts and knowledge include a mixture of abilities and ignorance. For investigators, as well as for parents and teachers, it is embarrassingly easy to both underestimate and at the same time overestimate the preschooler.

Current advances in our assessment of preschoolers have come from studying preschoolers in their own right, not just as negative reflections of older children. This new approach to the study of young children has meant (a) looking at preschoolers of different ages, not just a group of four-year-olds to compare to older children, (b) utilizing phenomena and events with which the child has had first-hand experience, and (c) developing procedures specifically for younger subjects—methods used with older children often require too much verbal sophistication and cooperation from the younger child. Much progress is still required. We are particularly ignorant about two- and three-year-olds, an important and formative age bridging the world of the young infant with the skills and conceptions of the relatively sophisticated older preschooler. Better understanding here will depend on future careful and creative assessment techniques.

Patterns and Sequences

One reason that accurate assessment is such a critical endeavor is that in general we do not merely want to find out if the child knows a single fact. Instead we want to appreciate the child's knowledge of many related facts and to understand how all of this knowledge fits together; what is known at the same time as what, what is known first, what only later? That is, we want to understand patterns and sequences.

In this regard the most important information in the above reviews is about patterns and sequences: arithmetic reasoning precedes algebraic reasoning; children first understand that different persons see different objects and only later understand that they also may have different views; the first knowledge of variables is that the number of things to think about influences thinking. The average ages cited above are *not* so important; individual children develop faster or slower.

Another aspect of sequences is that, once acquired, concepts can be utilized to aid in the accomplishment of other tasks and goals. Concepts of number aid the child in games or sports that require counting or keeping score, in earning and spending money, in making quantitative comparisons, and in all forms of computational behavior both in and out of school. Similarly early concepts of the thinking process are incorporated into later developments. The child must know of differences between the thoughts of different people in order to communicate accurately, to plan and evaluate her or his own acts by evaluating the consequences of what is done, and to understand and tolerate people from different backgrounds. In addition the child's developing ability to solve many problems depends on an understanding of the workings of one's own thoughts—for example that memory is limited and so must be assisted by using various strategies, that concentration affects what is learned, that a two-year-old brother is unlikely to be able to help you on some problem where an eight-year-old sister may.

Acquisition

As important as *what* concepts children possess is *how* the child acquires new knowledge. There are two related questions here. First, what accounts for the fact that five-year-olds know more about number and about thinking than three-year-olds, in the normal course of development? Second, what should adults do to aid the child's concept development?

To begin, consider two different possibilities about developing children and their experiences. In the first, adult teachers or parents are thought of as *training* the child and the child is a more or less *passive* trainee. In the second, experiences with or without adults are thought of as merely sources of *information* for the child who is an *active* seeker and interpreter of information. Following Piaget, most developmental psychologists believe that the second description more accurately characterizes the child's acquisition of major and fundamental conceptual systems such as concepts of number and of thinking.

Children do not wait for a teacher to teach them to count or that $3 = 3$, to first think about number. The child's development does not depend on certain specific training experiences such as being taught the conventional number words, or being told that more items to remember is harder than few. Instead the child is always actively striving to make sense of the world, to form miniature theories about how the world operates and to test these theories. In fact, if you think about it the world provides a rich source of information for the child where many different experiences lead to the same major conceptual conclusions. After all, almost any set of items—the child's toys or socks, etc.,—has a specific number, can be compared to other sets, can be counted, rearranged, and counted again. Similarly, there are many experiences contributing information about the mental world: dreams are *not* real, pretending to be sick is not the same as being sick, a child often has hopes or wishes for things (e.g., a birthday present) that do not come true, and even if a child starts out by assuming that the other person knows exactly what she or he knows, experience in miscommunication and missed expectations will eventually inform the child otherwise.

Does this picture of concept development mean that adults have no role to play in the child's development? No. Indeed, this picture points to the important role of providing information-rich experiences for children and in aiding them in the process of interpretation. Recall that young children at first understand the distinction between internal thought processes and external behaviors only in certain salient situations. Adults can and do increase the salience of important features of everyday events ("How many are there? Let's count them." "He doesn't know what you want. How can you tell him?"), and they can arrange special experiences to provoke the child's attention. Early childhood education programs attempt to provide such experiences, based on highlighting concepts when they are useful and meaningful to the child as part of the everyday life of the classroom. (For a good example of what this might mean in the case of teaching number concepts, see Kamii 1982; Kamii and DeVries 1978).

Through conversation and formal and informal instruction, adults also play an indispensable role in providing children with conventional knowledge. Children's concepts will develop to some extent without their knowing the conventional terms and names for them. Indeed, as we have seen, young children demonstrate considerable knowledge of counting even when still using unconventional number terms; and children reveal some understanding of thinking before correctly using *remember, think,* and *know.* However, eventual mastery of these conventions is also important, and requires feedback and instruction. Why is conventional number and language knowledge so important if concept development can proceed without it? The answer is that children's stimulation for concept development would be limited to their own personal experiences unless they can talk with others about *their* experiences. Imagine that all the knowledge you had ever acquired came directly from your own experiences. The wealth of information in books, in your past teachers' minds, in your parents' common sense, would be cut off from you. All you knew about mathematics, for example, was what was discovered on your own, unaided by what Euclid, Newton, and others discovered and passed along. In short, imagine that the entire world of social knowledge was erased from your mind. This gives a sense of the enormous importance of socially transmitted information, even if it is not the only source of information for children's theory building and interpretation.

In sum, children's active efforts benefit greatly from adult support and direction. Of course, as all teachers know, no child is constantly motivated to learn in an active way and certain children have special learning problems. External support is helpful to all and crucial to some. This can range from scheduling inviting activities when children are most rested (and more likely to attend to the conceptual features) all the way to instituting more controlled behavior modification programs. Varied educational techniques can be employed to provide individual children an environment within which ongoing active learning may most effectively operate.

Conclusions

Concept development in the young child is an extremely important topic. It is important to the child because it sets the stage for numerous later developments. Knowledge of the conceptions and misconceptions of preschoolers is important to adults—researchers, parents, educators—who seek to understand the child's potentials and limits, and to communicate with the child as friend, counselor, and teacher. Recent research, that concentrates on preschoolers in their own right, is creating an intriguing picture of the young child's impressive knowledge. The next few years should prove exciting in this regard as the broad outlines of concept development in the young child become clearer.

REFERENCES

Curcio, F.; Robbins, O.; and Ela, S. S. "The Role of Body Parts and Readiness in Acquisition of Number Conservation." *Child Development* 42 (1971): 1641–1646.

Flavell, J. H. "Concept Development." In *Carmichael's Manual of Child Psychology. Vol. 1,* ed. P. H. Mussen. New York: Wiley, 1970.

Flavell, J. H. "The Development of Knowledge about Visual Perception." In *Nebraska Symposium on Motivation. Vol. 25,* ed. C. B. Keasey. Lincoln, Neb.: University of Nebraska Press, 1978.

Flavell, J. H., and Wellman, H. M. "Metamemory." In *Perspectives on the Development of Memory and Cognition,* ed. R. Kail and J. Hagen. Hillsdale, N.J.: Lawrence Erlbaum Associates, 1977.

Gelman, R. "Logical Capacity of Very Young Children: Number Invariance Rules." *Child Development* 43 (1972): 75–90.

Gelman, R. "Cognitive Development." *Annual Review of Psychology* 29 (1978): 297–332.

Gelman, R., and Gallistel, C. R. *The Child's Understanding of Number.* Cambridge, Mass.: Harvard University Press, 1978.

Gelman, R., and Tucker, M. F. "Further Investigations of the Young Child's Conception of Number." *Child Development* 46 (1975): 167–175.

Ginsburg, H. *Children's Arithmetic.* New York: Van Nostrand, 1977.

Gordon, F. R., and Flavell, J. H. "The Development of Intuitions about Cognitive Cueing." *Child Development* 48 (1977): 1027–1033.

Johnson, C. N., and Maratsos, N. "Early Comprehension of Mental Verbs: Think and Know." *Child Development* 48 (1977): 1743–1747.

Johnson, C. N., and Wellman, H. M. "Developing Understanding of Mental States and Mental Verbs: 'Remember,' 'Know,' and 'Guess.' " *Child Development* 51 (1980): 1095–1102.

Johnson, C. N., and Wellman, H. M. "Children's Developing Conceptions of the Mind and the Brain." *Child Development,* in press.

Kamii, C. *Number in Preschool and Kindergarten: Educational Implications of Piaget's Theory.* Washington D.C.: National Association for the Education of Young Children, 1982.

Kamii, C., and DeVries, R. *Physical Knowledge in Preschool Education: Implications of Piaget's Theory.* Englewood Cliffs, N.J.: Prentice-Hall, 1978.

Maratsos, M. "Nonegocentric Communication Abilities in Preschool Children." *Child Development* 44 (1973): 697–700.

Marvin, R. S.; Greenberg, M. T.; and Mossler, D. G. "The Early Development of Conceptual Perspective Taking: Distinguishing among Multiple Perspectives." *Child Development* 47 (1976): 511–514.

Masangkay, Z. S.; McCluskey, K. A.; McIntyre, C. W.; Sims-Knight, J.; Vaughn, B. E.; and Flavell, J. H. "The Early Development of Inferences about the Visual Percepts of Others." *Child Development* 45 (1974): 357–366.

McNamara, J.; Baker, E.; and Olson, C. L. "Four-Year-Olds' Understanding of 'Pretend,' 'Forget,' and 'Know': Evidence for Proposition Operations." *Child Development* 47 (1976): 62–70.

Misciones, J. L.; Marvin, R. S.; O'Brien, R. G.; and Greenberg, M. T. "A Developmental Study of Preschool Children's Understanding of the Words 'Know' and 'Guess.' " *Child Development* 49 (1978): 1107–1113.

Piaget, J. *The Child's Conception of the World.* New York: Harcourt, Brace, 1929.

Piaget, J. *The Child's Conception of Number.* New York: Norton, 1952.

Piaget, J. *The Moral Judgement of the Child.* New York: Harcourt, Brace, 1965.

Ritter, K. "The Development of Knowledge of an External Retrieval Cue Strategy." *Child Development* 49 (1978): 1227–1230.

Wellman, H. M. "Preschoolers' Understanding of Memory-Relevant Variables." *Child Development* 48 (1977): 1720–1723.

Wellman, H. M. "A Child's Theory of Mind: The Development of Conceptions of Cognition." In *The Growth of Reflection,* ed. S. R. Yussen. New York: Academic Press, 1982.

Wellman, H. M., and Johnson, C. N. "Understanding of Mental Processes: A Developmental Study of 'Remember' and 'Forget.' *Child Development* 50 (1979): 79–88.

Wellman, H. M., and Lempers, J. D. "The Naturalistic Communicative Abilities of Two-Year-Olds." *Child Development* 48 (1977): 1052–1057.

READING 24

Five Generalizations about Cognitive Development

Robert S. Siegler

Any history of the past 20 years of research on cognitive development would document two trends. First, there was a dramatic increase in the amount of research focusing on children's understanding of natural concepts such as time, space, morality, proportionality, conservation, and classification. More than 200 articles were published on conservation alone (Siegler, 1979). Second, in this same period, research on children's learning declined precipitously. Stevenson (in press) incisively reviewed this historical trend. He noted that few studies on children's learning were published until the 1950s, when more than 200 experimental studies appeared in journals. In the 1960s, more than 1,000 studies appeared. However, in the 1970s, far fewer studies of children's learning were published, and by 1980 "it was necessary to search with diligence to uncover any articles at all" (Stevenson, in press).

Many others agree with Stevenson's assessment of the contemporary state of research on children's learning. For example, Brown (1982) commented:

> Contemporary cognitive developmentalists, myself included, appear to go to extraordinary lengths to avoid using the word 'learning.' It is not merely a problem of elaborate symbol substitutions; we no longer seem to have an area called learning at all. (p. 187)

The demise of the study of learning is not unique to developmental psychology. As Voss (1978) noted,

> Although the concept of learning may be found in cognitive psychology, it also must be conceded that the cognitive view of learning is vague, is abstract, and most important is lacking a substantive data base. (p. 13)

What caused this decline in studies of learning? Stevenson suggested two factors: the presence of charismatic figures such as Jean Piaget, who were not especially interested in learning, and experimental data that were difficult to reconcile with existing learning theories. I believe a third factor also was important: an incompatibility between the basic assumption that learning mechanisms operate in the same way regardless of context and the mounting realization that people's learning and remembering are crucially affected by what they already know. Perhaps the seminal demonstration of this interdependence was Chi's (1978) finding that 10-year-old chess experts remembered more about the placement of chess pieces on a board than adult novice players, despite the adults' having considerably longer digit spans. The finding was exceedingly difficult to explain without postulating learning and memory mechanisms whose functioning was knowledge dependent. Yet traditional learning paradigms (e.g., transposition, reversal shift, paired associate learning) explicitly attempted to preclude knowledge more complex than interitem associations acquired in the laboratory. Although there was little doubt that such classic learning mechanisms as stimulus generalization, discrimination, and extinction operated in complex knowledge domains, the ways in which they operated were far from obvious.

Fortunately, the seeds of a solution may be contained in the problem itself. In the course of studying existing knowledge of natural concepts, cognitive psychologists have developed a variety of methods for assessing conceptual understanding. These include double assessment methodologies (Wilkinson, 1982), componential approaches (Sternberg & Rifkin, 1979), information integration approaches (Wilkening, Becker, & Trabasso, 1980), and rule assessment approaches (Siegler, 1976). These methodologies for assessing knowledge increase our potential for studying learning as it interacts with knowledge. Indeed, this potential already is starting to be realized. Brown's (1982) and Voss's (1978) above-quoted laments about the decline of experiments on learning are prefaces to their new efforts to study the subject. In addition, Bowerman (1982); Brown and Van Lehn (1982); Case (in press); Chi and Koeske (in press); Collins and Stevens (1982); Fowler (1980); Inhelder, Sinclair, and Bovet (1974); Kuhn and Phelps (in press); Strauss and Stavy (1982); and numerous other investigators have begun to use assessments of existing knowledge to study children's learning.

Recent research focusing on the interaction between existing knowledge and learning suggests at least five general conclusions. The first three generalizations concern aspects of children's existing knowledge that are relevant to

the study of learning, the fourth concerns the processes by which children learn that their existing knowledge is inadequate, and the fifth concerns the processes by which they construct new rules to replace old, inadequate ones. Together, the generalizations suggest that studying existing knowledge and learning in conjunction can illuminate a number of issues of longstanding interest among developmental psychologists as well as raise new issues.

1 The rule is a useful basic unit for characterizing children's knowledge. Which rules children use can be assessed by designing problems that yield distinct patterns of performance for different rules.

2 Children adopt premastery rules in the order of their predictive accuracy, when accuracy is considered across the range of environments in which children apply the rules.

3 Children's reasoning across different concepts is more homogeneous when they have little knowledge about the concepts than when they have more.

4 When children learn is determined in large part by the interaction between their knowledge and their experience. Children learn most efficiently from experiences that indicate inadequacies in their existing rules.

5 Once children have learned that their existing knowledge is imperfect, their encoding plays a large role in constructing more advanced knowledge.

These generalizations provide a framework within which to consider how studying the relation between existing knowledge and learning can increase our understanding of development. For each generalization, one supporting example will be discussed in depth. These examples are drawn from a series of experiments that Dean Richards and I performed on the development of the concept of time. By drawing all of the detailed illustrations from a single research series, I hope to illuminate how the generalizations relate to each other. In addition, a variety of ideas and experiments relevant to each generalization will be discussed more briefly. Research on the relation between existing knowledge and learning is increasing rapidly; these brief discussions will provide an introduction to the issues that are emerging.

1. *The rule is a useful basic unit for characterizing children's knowledge. Which rules children use can be assessed by designing problems that yield distinct patterns of performance for different rules.* Sternberg (1980) noted that approaches to the study of cognition are defined in large part by their basic unit. The psychometric approach is closely associated with its basic unit, the factor; the behaviorist approach with its basic unit, the S–R bond; and the Piagetian approach with its basic unit, the scheme.

An increasingly numerous and diverse group of cognitive developmentalists have adopted rules as their basic units of analysis. Rules are if-then statements that link conditions of applicability to conclusions to be reached or actions to be taken. A wide range of knowledge and behavior can be described in terms of rules. Illustratively, Fowler (1980) wrote:

> The generic process for all cognitive change may be defined as the acquisition of rules that operationalize concepts.... Cognitive change is thus essentially a process of mental adaptation to environmental task demands that leads to learning rules about things, rules for representing concepts about things, and rules for figuring out how to manipulate and construct things. (p. 188)

Fowler's approach emphasizes the unities among problem solving, learning, and concept formation in both natural and artificial domains. It is quite different from Keil's (1981) approach, which emphasizes the role of inborn constraints in children's learning of natural concepts. Nonetheless, Keil's approach assigns a similarly basic position to rules:

> Undoubtedly there are many important differences between how a theoretical physicist ac-

quires new knowledge about quarks and how a 3-year-old learns more about a first language, but in both cases it is necessary to generate rules or hypotheses, test them, and decide whether to discard them in favor of a better alternative. (p. 217)

This use of the rule as a basic unit is far from unique to research on cognitive development. Research in linguistics (e.g., Chomsky, 1957), computer science (e.g., Lenat, 1977), instructional psychology (e.g., Collins & Stevens, 1982), and adult cognitive psychology (e.g., Levine, 1966) also has adopted the rule as a central unit of analysis.

The prevalence of theories that emphasize rule use has placed a premium on methodologies for identifying which rules people employ. Some of the most dramatic evidence for rule use has come from analyses of errors. Klima and Bellugi-Klima (1966) quoted children's speech errors in ways that compellingly illustrated the children's imperfect rules for producing negations and *wh* questions. Levine (1966) demonstrated how patterns of errors and correct answers could be used to identify people's hypotheses on artificial concept-formation problems. More recently, I have extended these error analysis approaches to a wide range of conceptual development and problem-solving tasks. The essence of the rule assessment approach that I developed for this purpose is to generate rules that people might use and then to formulate problem types that yield a distinct pattern of answers for people using each rule. To date, my colleagues and I have applied this strategy to identify children's rules on 13 tasks: balance scale, projection of shadows, probability, fullness, conservation of liquid quantity, conservation of solid quantity, conservation of number, counting of objects, Tower of Hanoi, animacy, speed, time, and distance (Klahr & Robinson, 1981; Siegler, 1976, 1981; Siegler & Klahr, 1982; Siegler & Richards, 1979; Siegler & Vago, 1978; Briars & Siegler, Note 1; Richards, Note 2).

To illustrate how the rule assessment approach works, we can examine its application to three concepts that are of interest for both theoretical and practical reasons: the concepts of time, speed, and distance. Developmental research on these concepts has a picturesque history. In 1928, Albert Einstein attended a lecture given by Jean Piaget. At the end of the lecture, Einstein posed a question: In what order do children acquire the concepts of time and speed? Almost 20 years later, Piaget published a two-volume, 500-page reply to Einstein's query (Piaget, 1946/1969, 1946/1970). In essence, Piaget claimed that children understand time and speed simultaneously, at roughly age seven, and that the two concepts develop from a common ancestor, a rudimentary spatial concept. However, a number of methodological questions have made it difficult to evaluate Piaget's claims (cf. Weinreb & Brainerd, 1975). To overcome these objections, Siegler and Richards (1979) applied the rule assessment approach to measuring children's understanding of time, speed, and also distance. The task was similar to Piaget's (1946/1969) cars task. Children were shown two parallel electric-train tracks, each with a locomotive on it. The locomotives' activities could vary along seven dimensions. The trains could start at the same or different points, stop at the same or different points, and travel the same or different distances. They could start at the same or different times, stop at the same or different times, and travel for the same or different total times. Finally, they could travel at the same or different speeds. Children were asked which train traveled for the greater time, for the longer distance, or at the faster speed.

On the basis of Piaget's (1946/1969) descriptions and our own task analyses, we expected children to use one of three rules on this task. Rule 1 children would base their judgments on the locomotives' end points; whichever train stopped farther ahead would be said to have traveled for the longer time, for the greater

distance, or at the faster speed. If the trains stopped at the same point, children would conclude that they traveled for the same time, for the same distance, or at the same speed. Rule 2 children would make the same judgments if the trains stopped at different points, but would choose the train that started farther back if the trains stopped at the same point. Rule 3 children would judge each concept in terms of the appropriate dimensions; time would be judged in terms of starting and stopping times, distance in terms of beginning and end points, and speed in terms of distance traveled per unit of time.

To test for use of these hypothesized rules, it was necessary to formulate problems that would yield distinct patterns for children using different rules. The six problem types that we devised are shown in Table 1. In the diagram at the top of the table, the lengths of the lines correspond to the relative distances traveled by the two trains. The leftmost ends of the lines correspond to the starting points and the rightmost ends to the stopping points. The numbers refer to the starting and stopping times of each train (in seconds after the onset of the trial). The letter "f" indicates which train traveled faster. Thus, in the problem-type 1 example in Table 1, the trains started at the same relative points on their tracks, and Train A finished farther up the track; Train A therefore traveled the longer distance. Train A started earlier than Train B, and they stopped at the same moment; therefore Train A traveled the longer time. Train B traveled at the faster speed. The bottom of Table 1 presents the pattern of answers that would be generated if children following various rules were asked which train traveled the longer time. For example, children who consistently followed the end point rule (Rule 1) would solve 100% of items of problem-types 1, 3, and 5 but 0% of types 2, 4, and 6.

These problem-types allowed us to assess what rule a child used. For a child to be classified as using a particular rule, at least 80% of his or her responses had to be in accord with

TABLE 1 SPECIFIC RESPONSE AND PERCENTAGE OF CORRECT ANSWERS PREDICTED BY EACH RULE FOR EACH PROBLEM TYPE ON TIME CONCEPT

		Problem type[a]					
		1	2	3	4	5	6
	Train A	0_____6	0_____9	0___9	0___6	0__f__6	0__f__5
Rule	Train B	2_f_6	0_f_5	4½_f_9	0_f_5	0___4	2__5
1		A longer (100)[b]	Equal (0)	A longer (100)	B longer (0)	A longer (100)	B longer (0)
2		A longer (100)	A longer (100)	A longer (100)	B longer (0)	A longer (100)	B longer (0)
3		A longer (100)	A longer (100)	A longer (100)	A longer (100)	A longer (100)	A longer (100)

[a]Numbers in the problems correspond to the number of seconds since the beginning of the trial. The letter F indicates which train traveled at a faster speed. Lengths and relative positions of lines correspond to distances traveled and special positions. Thus, in the example in problem-type 1, Train A starts at the beginning of the trial and travels for 6 seconds, while Train B starts 2 seconds after the trial begins and also stops at second 6. The two trains would start from parallel points, but Train A would finish farther up the track.
[b] Numbers in parentheses refer to the predicted percentage of correct answers.

the predictions of that rule. Because there were three possible responses (Train A is greater, Train B is greater, they are equal), the rules had to predict not only which items would be solved correctly but also the particular errors that children would make.

In our first experiment on children's understanding of time, speed, and distance, 5-year-olds, 8-year-olds, 11-year-olds, and adults were presented four examples of each of the six problem-types shown in Table 1. The trains' activities were identical on the items testing knowledge of each concept; the only difference was whether the experimenter's question concerned time, speed, or distance (cf. Siegler & Richards, 1979, for methodological details).

Most participants met the criterion for using a rule on each concept. On all three concepts, most 5-year-olds used the end point rule. That is, they said that the train that stopped at the more advanced point on the track was the one that had traveled faster, for the greater amount of time, and for the longer distance. At the other end of the age spectrum, almost all adults judged each concept in terms of the appropriate dimension. The 8- and 11-year-olds' performance was less homogeneous. On the distance and speed concepts, most of them used the

correct rule. On the time concept, however, many of them did not meet the criterion for using any rule, and those who did most often used a rule that had not been anticipated, the distance rule. That is, they consistently said that the train that went the farther distance was the one that had traveled for the greater time. We performed regression analyses of the distribution of errors of the "no rule" children, most of whom were 8- and 11-year-olds. These children, too, tended toward using the distance rule on the time concept; 67% of the variance in their number of errors on the 24 problems was accounted for by the prediction that children would err on those problems in which the train that traveled the larger distance did not travel for the longer time. One consequence of this rule sequence was that performance on problem-type 3 of Table 1 actually declined with age. Five-year-olds, most of whom used the end-point rule (which predicts accurately on this problem) were correct on 71% of the trials. Eleven-year-olds, who tended to use the distance rule (which predicts inaccurately on this problem) were correct on only 27%.

There are several points to note about this rule assessment method. First, the rule models predict not only whether children will answer each question correctly or incorrectly, but also the particular errors they will make. Second, the basic level of data analysis is the individual child rather than an age group. Third, the method allows detection of alternative rules that are not initially hypothesized. For example, we did not initially hypothesize that children would use the distance rule on the time concept, but we detected it because a number of children showed the same pattern of answers.

A number of other investigators have developed related assessment methodologies, in which they used patterns of errors or reaction times to infer individual childrens' rules. Consider the area of arithmetic, for example. Groen and Resnick (1977) analyzed patterns of solution times to determine preschoolers' addition rules. Riley, Greeno, and Heller (in press) analyzed patterns of errors in children's representations of addition word problems and derived three rules by which young children interpret such problems. Brown and Burton (1978) analyzed patterns of errors on multidigit subtraction problems and derived a variety of "buggy" subtraction rules, that is, subtraction algorithms that differed from the standard correct one in having one or more "bugs." Numerous other examples of approaches for determining children's rules could be drawn from Piagetian, academic, and classic problem-solving tasks (e.g., Case, 1978; Klahr & Robinson, 1981; Sternberg & Rifkin, 1979; Strauss & Stavy, 1982).

Although many researchers agree that the rule is a useful basic unit of analysis, there is less agreement on the optimal method for measuring rule use. For example, some researchers have voiced concerns about the rule assessment approach. Wilkening and Anderson (1982) wrote that "the decision tree methodology is unable to assess algebraic integration rules" (p. 215). This comment raises the issue of whether there is an inherent link between the use of decision trees and the rule assessment method-

ology, and also whether the rule assessment approach can detect the use of algebraic integration rules. The phrase "decision tree methodology" reveals one confusion. Decision trees are a language in which rules can be expressed; they are not a methodology. The rule assessment methodology has been used to examine the use of rules expressed as decision trees, flow diagrams (Siegler & Vago, 1978), and production systems (Klahr & Siegler, 1978). It has also been used with rules expressed in part as algebraic formulas (Rule 4 in Siegler, 1976). Beyond this specific confusion of languages for expressing rules and methodologies for detecting them, there is the general issue of the range of rules that the rule assessment approach can detect. Wilkening and Anderson (1982) claim that the rule assessment approach cannot detect algebraic integration rules. For example, they claim that if children are presented a balance scale with a fulcrum in the middle and weights on pegs on each side of the fulcrum, and asked to predict which side will go down, that the rule assessment approach could not detect their use of rules such as "two weights times distance equals torque," or "two weights plus distance equals torque." This claim is simply incorrect. For example, to discriminate between these two integration rules, we could present children problems such as three weights on the first peg on the left side of the fulcrum versus one weight on the fourth peg on the right. Children using the first rule would say the right side will go down; children using the second would say that the left side will. If we wanted to discriminate among additional integration rules, we could add more problem-types for which the rules would predict differently. In contrast, since the functional measurement approach assumes that rules will be an algebraic combination of the systematically manipulated dimensions, the rules it can detect are limited. If a functional measurement experiment on number conservation varied the length and density of the rows of objects, it would discover that 10-year-olds' performance fit a "length times density" equation, even if their judgments in fact were generated by reliance on the type of transformation performed (Siegler, 1981).

The range of determinate rules that can be detected by the rule assessment approach is limited only by the particular problems that are presented. These, of course, are constrained to an extent by the investigator's initial hypotheses about what rules people will use, but this is true of the information integration approach, the rule assessment approach, and any scientific methodology. It is more pertinent whether the assessment approach can distinguish among specific rules that have been hypothesized to represent people's knowledge. The rule assessment approach seems well suited to this task.

A second, related concern has been that the methodology restricts the possible behaviors that children can produce, and that these restrictions are responsible for the rules that children are classified as using. Strauss and Levin (1981) pointed to three restrictive ways in which tasks typically have been presented: The tasks are presented in a fixed fashion, there are only a few response alternatives, and children's justifications are not considered in the rule assessments. Although these descriptions accurately characterize my use of the rule assessment approach, applications by other researchers demonstrate that none of them are inherent to the methodology. Klahr and Robinson (1981) applied the rule assessment approach to a Tower of Hanoi task, using an open-ended procedure that included the active involvement of children in setting up the problems. Brown and Burton's (1978) work on subtraction strategies allowed the entire range of numbers as possible responses. Richards and Siegler (Note 3) applied the rule assessment approach to children's explanations of what attributes make an object alive. The only essential aspects of the rule assessment approach are that the rules formulated lead to unambiguous predictions on particular problems and that the problem-types

discriminate the hypothesized rules from each other.

These points of disagreement should not obscure several points of basic agreement that underlie all of the approaches. All of the investigators agree that the rule is a useful basic unit for characterizing cognitive activity. All agree that the optimal level of data analysis is the level of individual children's knowledge. They also agree that to determine what rule people are using, one should present problems on which people using different rules will respond differently. We disagree on whether continuous measurement or discrete judgment procedures are the most desirable, on the degree to which children should actively participate in setting up problems, and on the usefulness of verbal explanations as data. Determining how best to assess people's rules promises to be a lively issue in the coming years.

2. *Children adopt premastery rules in the order of their predictive accuracy, when accuracy is considered across the range of environments in which children apply the rules.* An invariant developmental sequence of knowledge states has prima facie relevance for the study of learning; it immediately raises the issue of what acquisition process produces such a regular sequence. Flavell (1972) distinguished three sources that could produce invariant sequences: the structure of the task, the structure of the environment, and the structure of the child. He suggested that investigators first try to explain invariant sequences as resulting from the structure of the task, since this explanation most often would prove applicable. If the structure of the task did not provide a satisfactory explanation, the investigator should consider the structure of the environment, the next most likely explanation. If both of these failed, the structure of the child should be considered.

Recent cognitive developmental theories can be classified in the terms of Flavell's taxonomy. Brainerd's (1978), Case's (1978), and Fischer's

(1980) theories have emphasized the structure of the task (or, more precisely, the structure of the rules used to perform the task). Chi and Rees (in press) and Carey (in press) have emphasized the order in which the environment provides opportunities to acquire knowledge. Keil (1981) and Wexler, Culicover, and Hamburger (1979) have contended that constraints inherent to human children, as well as the structure of the domain of knowledge, govern the order in which natural concepts are acquired.

In seeking to explain invariant sequences, it may be useful to distinguish between-concept sequences from within-concept sequences. Between-concept sequences involve the ordering of different concepts; for example, children always might understand speed before they understand time. Within-concept sequences involve the progression from one rule to another on a single concept; for example, children first might use the end point rule on the time concept task and later the distance rule.

Explanations that emphasize the structure of the environment and of the child may well prove to provide the most compelling explanations for between-concept sequences. Almost all explanations of within-concept sequences, however, have emphasized the structure of the rules that are used on the task. Researchers have proposed several hypotheses for how the structure of the rules might produce invariant within-concept sequences. The most frequently advanced hypothesis is that such sequences arise because earlier-developing rules are included in later-developing ones (Fischer, 1980; Flavell, 1972; Flavell & Wohlwill, 1969; Gagné, 1968). This explanation seems plausible for many within-concept sequences, but not for all of them. For example, on the time task, neither the end point rule nor the distance rule is linked by any inclusion relation to the time rule. Use of the time rule is based on information about beginning and ending times, whereas use of the end point and distance rules is based on infor-mation concerning spatial relations. Similarly, Siegler (1981) found that on tasks involving conservation of liquid and solid quantity, children first used rules based on length or height and later shifted to rules based on the type of transformation that was performed. Again, no inclusion relation between the dimensions is obvious.

An alternative explanation is that children's premastery rules are ordered by their relative predictive accuracies in the range of environments in which the children apply the rules. This view can be evaluated only if we specify both the rules that children use and the range of environments in which they apply them.

The Siegler and Richards (1979) study on the time concept provides an illustration. Given a set of randomly chosen problems involving trains moving in the same direction on parallel tracks, there almost always will be a positive relation between which train stops farther down the track and which train travels for the longer time. If the two trains travel at the same speed and begin at the same point the relation is guaranteed. However, distance traveled will more accurately predict which train travels for the longer time. Only the speeds of the two trains need to be equal to guarantee that the train that travels the longer distance also will have traveled the longer time. Only the speeds of the two trains need to be equal to guarantee that the train that travels the longer distance also will have traveled the longer time. Thus, if children use both the end point and the distance rules to judge travel time at different points in development, they should proceed from the end point to the distance rule, rather than the reverse.

What process leads children to adopt more predictively accurate rules and to reject less accurate ones? Klahr and Wallace (1976) described one inductive mechanism that could have this effect. They suggested that people maintain in memory a time line, a record of their hypotheses and the outcomes associated with each. When the predictive accuracy of a hypothesis exceeds some minimum critical consistency level, they adopt the hypothesis as their rule. They then might reset the critical consistency level to the predictive accuracy associated with the rule. If the critical consistency level of a child's current rule was below perfect predictivity, the child periodically might try other hypotheses to obtain data on how well they predicted. If a new hypothesis reliably predicted more accurately than the current rule, the child would adopt the new hypothesis as his or her rule and reset the critical consistency level to the higher point. Note that this mechanism does not imply that all children progress through the same invariant sequence, since a variety of rules may predict more accurately than the existing one. Rather, the view suggests that if a child ever uses a given pair of rules to solve a problem, he or she will do so in an invariant order (cf. Fischer, 1980, for a related view).

Within the view that premastery rules are ordered by their relative predictive accuracy in the task environments in which they are used, inclusion relations emerge simply as a special case. In an inclusion relation, the more advanced rule solves all of the problems solved by the less advanced rule and some others as well. For example, Rule 2 on the balance scale (consider weight in all cases and also consider distance when weights are equal) must follow rather than precede Rule 1 (consider weight in all cases), because Rule 2 predicts correctly on every problem that Rule 1 does and on some other problems as well. Such inclusion relations are pleasant for researchers to work with, since they obviate the messy issue of specifying the task environment to which the rules apply. However, many consistent within-concept sequences appear to exist without an inclusion relation; exploring the bases of these does require specifying the domain to which the rules are applied.

The emphasis on considering the total domain of problems to which a rule is applied suggests a simple explanation for a phenomenon of considerable recent interest among developmentalists—that of U-shaped curves. U-shaped curves are data patterns in which children first perform well on a task, then less well, and then well again. At first, such patterns appear quite mysterious. There exists a simple explanation for them, however. U-shaped curves arise when children adopt a new rule that is more predictive when the total task environment is considered but that is less predictive in a particular portion of the task environment. To illustrate, on problem-type 3 of the time concept problems described above, 5-year-olds solved 71% of items, 11-year-olds 27%, and adults 81%. Recall that the distance rule that many 11-year-olds used was in general a better predictor of travel time than the end point rule used by 5-year-olds. On problem-type 3, however, relying on end-point cues led to incorrect ones, thus accounting for the 5-year-olds' greater percentage of correct answers. Richards and Siegler (1981) demonstrated that this explanation accounted for U-shaped curves not only in rule assessment studies but also for several other well-known findings of such data patterns: Cazden's (1968) data on morphophonological rules, Weir's (1964) data on probability learning, Mehler and Bever's (1967) data on number conservation, and Gardner, Kirchner, Winner, and Perkins' (1974) data on metaphor (see Strauss and Stavy [1982] for a different view on the origins of U-shaped curves).

3. *Children's reasoning across different concepts is more homogeneous when they have little knowledge about the concepts than when they have more.* If existing knowledge and learning are related, then the broader the consistency of children's reasoning, the more encompassing the predictions that cognitive developmentalists might make about learning. It therefore seems worthwhile to search for consistent reasoning patterns that may exist in some domains of knowledge, at some points in processing, and at some levels of conceptual understanding, even if development is not in general stagelike (cf. Flavell, 1982). Fischer's (1980) theory of cognitive development is representative in two ways of many researchers' current views on the developmental synchrony issue. First, he concluded that "unevenness is the rule in development" (p. 510). Broad consistencies in reasoning, such as those envisioned by Piaget's and Kohlberg's stage theories, rarely have been found. Second, even researchers who, like Fischer, have become pessimistic about the existence of synchronies remain interested in finding them. In the same article in which he concluded that unevenness was the rule in development, Fischer proposed that limited information-processing capacity

might result in a kind of homogeneity of reasoning, as all of a child's highest accomplishments would be at a certain level of processing complexity (cf. Case, in press, and Flavell, 1982, for similar suggestions).

Another place where cognitive developmentalists might look for consistent reasoning across concepts is in children's premastery rules. The results of a number of experiments using the rule assessment approach have indicated that young children approach some quite diverse tasks in the same way. Figure 1 illustrates how great this similarity was for 5-year-olds who were presented parallel problem-types to assess understanding of three conservation and three proportionality tasks. On four of the

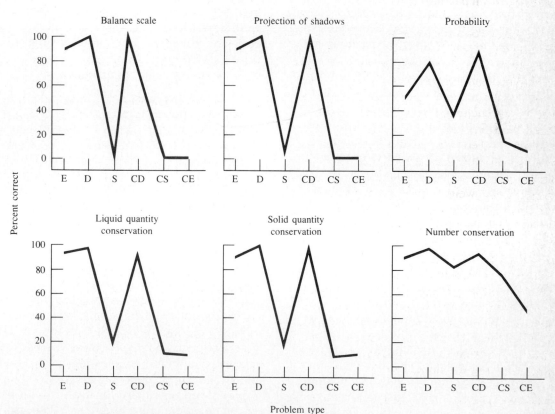

FIGURE 1   Five-year-olds' performance on six problem-solving tasks.

six tasks, almost all of the 5-year-olds based their predictions on a unidimensional rule, and on a fifth task most of them did. In predicting a balance scale's behavior, the 5-year-olds said that the side of the fulcrum with more weight would go down; in predicting the workings of a shadows projection apparatus, they said that the larger object would cast the larger shadow; on a probability task, they said that the pile of marbles with the greater number of desired-color marbles would be more likely to yield a desired-color marble (regardless of the number of undesired-color marbles in each pile); on a liquid quantity conservation task, they judged the glass with the taller liquid column to contain more water; on a solid quantity conservation task, they judged the longer piece of clay to have more clay. Siegler and Richards (1979) reported that 5-year-olds used similar rules on time, speed, and distance tasks (the train that stops farther up the track has traveled for a greater time, at a higher speed, and for more distance). Siegler and Vago (1978) obtained similar results for a fullness task (the glass with the taller liquid column is more full), as did Richards (Note 2) on an animacy task (if and only if an object is an animal, it is alive).

Why might such consistency of reasoning appear? One explanation involves fall-back rules. That is, people may have certain standard forms of reasoning on which they rely when they lack detailed procedures for solving a problem. Five-year-olds may utilize a fall-back rule of the following form: If you lack direct information about how to solve a problem on which you are to make a quantitative comparison, it is best to compare the values of the single, seemingly most important dimension and to choose the object with the greater value on that dimension as having more of whatever dimension is being asked about.

Conceptualizing young children's unidimensional approaches as reflecting fall-back rules, as opposed to capacity limitations, suggests reasons why such approaches are observed in some but not all situations. Piagetian tasks seem ideal for revealing fall-back rules. One criterion that Piaget used to select his tasks was that they not be familiar to children; he was less interested in the facts that they might know than in their reasoning in the absence of specific knowledge (Piaget, 1972). In a sense, he was interested in the children's fall-back rules. Problems selected by other criteria, such as ecological validity, would be less likely to reveal fall-back rules, since children might have developed specific procedures for dealing with them. Even task variants that place Piagetian problems in familiar contexts might obscure children's fall-back rules, if the familiar contexts suggest specific content-based approaches for children to use.

Case (Note 4) formulated descriptions of horizontal structure in children's thinking that were similar to the Siegler (1981) fall-back rules both in their general kind and in their specifics. Case's description of the underlying structure of 5- and 6-year-olds' thinking was as follows:

> Given the requirement for making a quantity judgment along DIMENSION X, set yourself the subgoal of making a judgment of relative quantity along DIMENSION Y. Then use the result obtained to make a decision about X. (p. 10)

Case cited evidence from research on young children's concepts of justice, happiness, proportionality, and success to illustrate the use of unidimensional approaches. Strauss and Stavy (1982) observed similar reasoning on the concepts of time, sweetness, and temperature. They suggested that it reflected 5- and 6-year-olds' tendency to rely on direct function logic.

Case's notion of horizontal structure rules, Strauss and Stavy's (1982) notion of direct function logic, and my notion of fall-back rules suggest a number of questions. Do children older than 5 or 6 years possess some analogous standardized procedure for dealing with newly encountered complex situations? If so, is it the same procedure as that used by 5- and 6-year-olds or a different one? Finally, do children use such approaches to reduce memory load, to check whether the simplest plausible solution works, to determine whether a frequently useful analogy can be extended to the new situation, or for some other reason? Each of these issues seems worthy of future research.

4. *When children learn is determined in large part by the interaction between their knowledge and their experience. Children learn most efficiently from experiences that indicate inadequacies in their existing rules.* Predicting the conditions under which children learn has been a longstanding goal of cognitive developmentalists. Such venerable constructs as readiness (Huey, 1908), critical periods (Riesen, 1947), the problem of the match (Hunt, 1961), behavioral prerequisites (Gagné, 1968), and aptitude-treatment interactions (Cronbach & Snow, 1977) all can be seen as efforts to predict which people will learn and when will they learn. Differential learning as a function of age, stage, and knowledge has been predicted by stage theories (Piaget, 1972), behavioral theories (Gagné, (1968), and psychometric theories (Guilford, 1967) alike.

One reason why instruction might have different effects on different children is that the instructional procedure could reveal some deficiencies in existing knowledge and not others. By assessing children's initial rules and by viewing instructional experiences in relation to those rules, we can anticipate which experiences will benefit which children. This view implies that instructional procedures are not effective or ineffective in an absolute sense. Their effectiveness depends on their relation to the learner's knowledge.

Research on the time concept illustrates this point. Siegler and Richards (Note 5; see also Richards, 1982) presented a pretest to identify 5-year-olds who used the end point rule and 11-year-olds who used the distance rule to judge time. Then they presented to each child one of the four types of feedback problems shown in Figure 2. These problems differed in whether they discriminated the distance rule, the end point rule, both, or neither from the time rule. For example, distance-discriminating problems (problem-type B in Figure 2) did not discriminate the end point rule from the time rule, since children answering on the basis of end points always would be correct. These children would have little reason to believe that their existing knowledge was imperfect. On the other hand, children using the distance rule would learn that their existing approach was inadequate, since

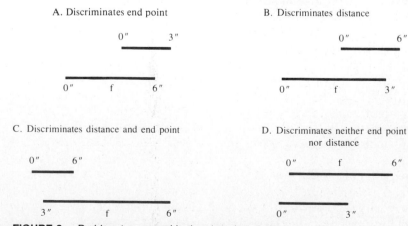

FIGURE 2 Problem types used in time-learning study.

their answers would elicit the comment ''No, the other train traveled for the longer time.'' Since 5-year-olds were selected for relying on the end point rule and 11-year-olds for relying on the distance rule, we anticipated that feedback problems that discriminated end points but not distances from time would help younger children but not older ones, whereas problems that discriminated distances but not end points from time would help older children but not younger ones.

The results supported these predictions. They also revealed how children's performance could mislead teachers into thinking that children understood concepts when in fact they did not. Consider the performance of 5-year-olds who were given the distance-discriminating problems. As shown in Figure 3, these children did very well on the feedback problems, better than the 11-year-olds on all trial blocks. However, their high percentage of correct answers masked the fact that they were not learning anything. On the posttest, 70% of them used the same end point rule with which they started. In contrast, only 15% of the 5-year-olds who received problems that discriminated end points

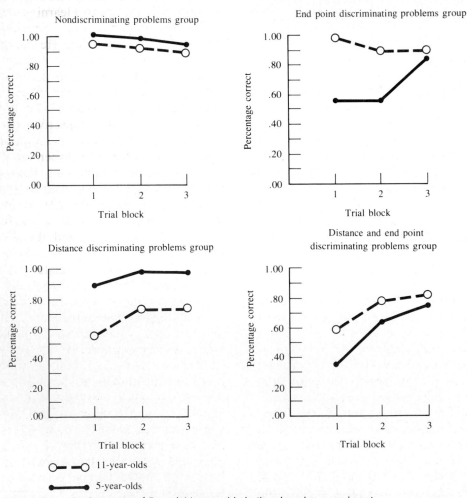

FIGURE 3   Performance of 5- and 11-year-olds in time-learning experiment.

from total times continued to use the end point rule on the posttest. A similar pattern emerged with the 11-year-olds: 55% of those who saw distance discriminated from time advanced to the time rule on the posttest, versus 20% of those whose feedback problems did not discriminate between the two dimensions. Without (a) knowledge of the children's initial rules and (b) classification of the feedback problems relative to those rules, it would have been difficult to predict which of the feedback problems would help which children to learn.

Efforts to fit instructional techniques to learners' knowledge extend far beyond simple feedback procedures and elementary physics problems. In one striking report, Collins and Stevens (1982) documented the ways in which expert teachers adjust their questions, examples, and hypothetical cases to address shortcomings of their students' existing knowledge. Many of their illustrations were drawn from efforts to teach students about the conditions under which rice can grow. Students who thought high rainfall was necessary were confronted with positive counterexamples, such as Egypt, where there is little rainfall but much water due to irrigation. Students who did not realize that warm temperature was necessary were presented with negative counterexamples, such as Oregon, which has many prerequisites for rice growing but is not warm enough. Students who knew that large quantities of water and warm temperatures were important for growing rice, but who did not realize the importance of soil quality, would be queried, "Then they grow rice in Florida?"

Collins and Stevens (1982) also observed that expert teachers have priorities that guide their decisions concerning which aspects of students' knowledge to try to improve first. They correct errors before omissions, because erroneous ideas interfere more seriously with acquisition of new information. They also correct mistaken ideas about factors that arise earlier in causal chains before mistaken ideas about factors that arise later, for much the same reason. The efficacy of such instructional priorities seems well worth testing: if learning arises from an interaction between existing knowledge and newly presented information, then it becomes important to determine which limitations of existing knowledge instructors should focus on first.

Some investigators have questioned whether existing knowledge is in fact related to learning. For example, Brainerd (1977, 1978) examined the conservation-training literature, argued that studies that claimed to have demonstrated a link between knowledge and learning confounded their measures of learning with existing knowledge, and performed a new analysis that did not reveal such a link. He concluded that "experimenters have failed to show that children learn better when they know a little bit about a certain content than when they know nothing at all" (Brainerd, 1978, p. 191).

From the present perspective, which views learning as arising from the interaction of existing knowledge and new experience, it seems more profitable to ask how the experience relates to the knowledge than to ask whether initially more knowledgeable children learn faster or slower. Depending on the fit between the existing knowledge and the instructional procedure, existing knowledge can be positively related, negatively related, or unrelated to the amount of learning. Recall the results of the time-learning experiment. Given feedback on the distance-discriminating problems, the initially more knowledgeable children (those who used the distance rule) learned more. Given feedback on the end-point discriminating problems, the initially less knowledgeable children (those who used the end point rule) learned more. Learning and knowledge were closely related, but the relation was more complex than a certain amount of existing knowledge leading to a certain amount of learning. Instead, the interaction between knowledge and learning was crucial.

5. *Once children have learned that their existing knowledge is imperfect, encoding plays a large role in their construction of more advanced knowledge.* Experiences that disconfirm children's existing rules may begin the learning process, but they do not complete it. Once existing rules are disconfirmed, children still must formulate new ones. A number of findings suggest that encoding is a critical component in the process by which new rules are formed.

Encoding is the process by which stimuli are represented in a particular situation. An encoding of a stimulus is not always identical to a person's representation of the stimulus in long-term memory. Portions of the encoding may be created at the time the stimulus is presented. For example, Pellegrino and Glaser (1982) presented college students the analogy, 15:19 :: 8:12 :: 5:?. It seems unlikely that college students' representations of the number 19 in long-term memory included the property "is 4 more than 15" prior to the presentation of this problem. In this task situation, however, 19 probably is encoded in this way. Complementarily, relevant information from long-term memory may be omitted from a particular encoding. Sternberg (1977) presented the analogy problem, Washington:1 :: Lincoln:(a) 10 or (b) 5. This problem is difficult not because the relevant information is absent from long-term memory (Whose faces are on $1 and $5 bills?), but rather because the relevant information is not included in most people's encoding of the problem.

Research from a variety of disciplines documents the role of encoding. For example, investigations of expertise in such areas as chess (Chase & Simon, 1973), go (Reitman, 1976), physics (Chi, Glaser, & Rees, 1982), and radiology (Lesgold, Feltovich, Glaser, & Wang, Note 6) indicate that the features that experts encode differ noticeably from those which less knowledgeable individuals encode. In children's cognitive development, however, encoding skills may play an especially large role. Across a wide range of situations, children are less likely to know which aspects of the stimuli should be encoded in a particular situation, and their long-term memory representations of the stimuli are likely to be less rich. That children lack knowledge about what to encode may account for the seemingly conflicting claims that young children's concepts are holistic, undifferentiated, and overly general, as well as being particularistic, exemplar based, and overly specific (Bruner, Oliver, & Greenfield, 1966; Clark, 1973; Farah & Kosslyn, 1982; Nelson, 1973; Vygotsky, 1934; Werner, 1948).

Encoding that is less than optimal may constrain ability to learn and also may influence the form that learning takes. Bransford (1979) provided the following illustration of how inadequate encoding can interfere with learning.

> Imagine that a speaker says, "Notice the sepia," while pointing to a complex painting. Unless you know that sepia refers to a color (and more specifically, to a brownish color), you will have difficulty understanding what the speaker means. Wittgenstein argues that even learning by ostensive definition (for example, hearing "This is red" while seeing someone point to a red object) presupposes that one has some knowledge of what the ostensibly defined object is supposed to be an example of (in this case color). Knowledge that a word refers to the category "color" affects one's understanding of the objects of the pointing gesture, which in turn may increase one's understanding of what counts as red. (p. 222)

Another experiment in the Siegler and Richards (Note 5) study of the time concept empirically demonstrates the role of encoding in learning. Recall that only one-half of the 11-year-olds who received feedback problems that discriminated their existing distance rule from the time rule adopted the time rule for solving temporal comparison problems. To develop hypotheses about why the other half did not do so, we performed a task analysis of the train problem.

Given that the two trains always either started or stopped at the same time, children could execute the time rule by first encoding relative starting times (which train started first or whether the trains started simultaneously), then encoding relative stopping times (which train stopped last or whether the trains stopped simultaneously), and then inserting the encoded values into one of two inference rules: If two or more events start at the same time and one stops later than the other(s), the event that stopped last took the longest time; if two or more events start at different times and they stop at the same time, the event that started first took the longest time. This analysis suggested that children's difficulty in learning might stem either from not encoding the appropriate information about starting and stopping times or from not using appropriate inference rules.

To examine these possibilities, we developed means of assessing encoding and inference processes independent of children's comparisons of time. Encoding was assessed by presenting the 11-year-old participants the usual train problems, but mixing in questions about which train started first and which train stopped last along with the usual questions about which train traveled for the greater time. Inferences were assessed by telling children the order in which the trains started and stopped, thus obviating encoding problems, and asking them to infer which train traveled the greater time. These assessments indicated that both processes were plausible sources of the children's difficulty in learning the original temporal-comparison problems. Children did not consistently encode the temporal features; they frequently erred in indicating the order in which the trains started and stopped. Even when they were told which train started first and which train stopped last, they often did not draw the correct inference about total times.

We further probed these potential sources of difficulty by training a new group of 11-year-olds in the appropriate inferences, encoding, or both. Encoding instruction involved telling the subjects to identify aloud at the beginning of each trial the train that started first (or to say that the trains started at the same time) and to identify aloud at the end of each trial the train that stopped last (or to say that they stopped at the same time). Inference training involved telling children the solutions to the problems previously used to test knowledge of inference rules and repeating the questions until they could answer them correctly.

The inference training by itself had little effect on encoding or on judgments of total time. However, the instruction in both encoding and inference led to improvements in both encoding and judgments of total time. Whereas only about one-third of children given inference instruction alone could be classified as using the time rule, more than 90% of those given instruction in both encoding and inference adopted it. Thus, changing the features that children encoded allowed them to learn from a more direct instructional procedure.

Several investigators have suggested mechanisms by which changes in encoding might influence learning. Holland and Reitman (Note 7) illustrated how a process similar to biological evolution might operate. Their model of the learner's knowledge was a set of condition-action pairings much like a production system. Each production included a string of 1's and 0's on the condition side (the system's encoding of the environment) and another string of 1's and 0's on the action side (the response the system would make, given that encoding). Each production also was associated more or less strongly with attainment of the system's goal; these associations grew in strength when the production fired as part of a sequence that led to goal attainment. Periodically, two productions with different sequences on the condition side but the same sequence on the action side were selected to be "parent productions." For example, two parent productions might be $101 \rightarrow 0\ 1\ 0$ and $0\ 0\ 0 \rightarrow 0\ 1\ 0$. The more highly associated with goal attainment a production was, the more likely that it would be chosen as a parent production. New productions were engendered by making an arbitrary cut at corresponding positions on the condition sides of the two parent productions and then combining symbols to the left of the cut in one production with symbols to the right of the cut in the other. This created productions with new encodings of the environment. In the above two productions, making a cut between the second and third position on the condition side would give birth to the productions: $0\ 0\ 1 \rightarrow 0\ 1\ 0$ and $1\ 0\ 0 \rightarrow 0\ 1\ 0$. One of these newborn productions would be chosen arbitrarily for inclusion in the production system and would replace a production that was weakly associated with goal attainment. Holland and Reitman reported that this mechanism for creating new encodings greatly increased the efficiency with which their model learned in an artifical environment. The mechanism also allowed the model to learn in a new environment in which it had no direct experience.

In Langley's (1981) BACON.3 program, new encodings contributed to learning by a process that might be labeled progressive abstraction. BACON.3 searched for consistent mathematical relations among variables that it encoded. Once it found consistent relations, it encoded them as new features and used the newly encoded features to identify yet higher-order regularities. Langley illustrated how BACON.3 induced the ideal gas law. By holding temperature and moles of gas constant and varying pressure and volume, the system initially discovered that multiplying pressure and volume yielded a constant value ($pV = K$). It then encoded pV as an entity and searched for variables that systematically related to it. By holding moles of gas constant and varying temperature, the system next discovered that pV/T also was a constant. It then encoded pV/T as a single feature. Finally, BACON.3 varied number of

moles of gas, determined the effects of the variation on the entity pV/T, noted that pV/NT was a constant, and encoded it as a single feature. In sum, both the random variation and the selection mechanism embodied in Holland and Reitman's model and the progressive abstraction mechanism embodied in Langley's model specify how improved encoding could contribute to more effective learning.

CONCLUSIONS

At the beginning of this article, I argued that advances in our methods for assessing children's existing knowledge are increasing our ability to study learning. The subsequent discussion of the five generalizations explicitly cited some potential benefits of studying existing knowledge and learning together, but left others implicit. In this concluding section, I would like to discuss these previously implicit points.

Studying learning can make us more confident of our assessments of existing knowledge. No knowledge assessment technique is infallible. If we ask children to explain their reasoning, they may not be able to tell us anything or may tell us something that does not correspond well to their nonverbal behavior. If we infer children's reasoning from their error patterns or reaction times, we run the risk of incorrect inferences, since there always are an infinite number of rules that fit any data pattern. Knowledge assessments can gain convergent validity if they predict which learning experiences will help which children, especially if the predictions would be unlikely without the knowledge assessments. This was the case in the time experiment, where we were able to predict which feedback problems would help 11-year-olds but not 5-year-olds and which would help 5- but not 11-year-olds. The experiment bolstered our confidence in the psychological reality of our claim that 5-year-olds started with an end point rule and 11-year-olds with a distance rule.

The study of learning can also increase confidence in hypothesized developmental sequences. Observing what rule children move toward when their existing rule is disconfirmed can be especially helpful. Again using the time concept to illustrate, 5-year-olds who saw the end point rule disconfirmed by feedback problems moved toward the distance rule. These children could have adopted the time rule, which was equally consistent with the feedback problems, but they did not. The fact that they adopted the distance rule rather than the time rule or some other approach strengthened our belief that children usually progress from the end point rule to the distance rule to the time rule.

Finally, the broadened assessments of existing knowledge that can result from experiments on learning can in turn broaden our perspective on how children learn. If we had not known that 11-year-olds had difficulty learning the time rule even when they were given distance-discriminating feedback problems, we would have been unlikely to assess their encoding. If we had not known that they did not encode beginning and ending times very accurately, it is unlikely that we would have attempted to influence their learning by telling them to name aloud the train that started first and the one that stopped last. Here again, the study of existing knowledge and learning proved to be mutually supportive. It seems that, in general, the broader and more precise our assessment of existing knowledge, the more we can discover about learning; the broader and more precise our understanding of learning, the more we can discover about existing knowledge.

REFERENCE NOTES

1 Briars, D., & Siegler, R. S. *A featural analysis of preschoolers' counting knowledge.* Manuscript submitted for publication, 1983.

2 Richards, D. D. *Children's concept learning: The child's concept of life.* Unpublished doctoral dissertation, Carnegie-Mellon University, 1981.

3 Richards, D. D., & Siegler, R. S. *Children's concepts of life.* Manuscript in preparation.

4 Case, R. *The search for horizontal structure in children's development.* Paper presented at the meeting of the Society for Research in Child Development, Boston, April 1981.

5 Siegler, R. A., & Richards, D. D. *Children's learning of the concept of time.* Manuscript in preparation.

6 Lesgold, A. M., Feltovich, P. J., Glaser, R., & Wang, Y. *The aquisition of perceptual diagnostic skill in radiology* (Tech. Rep.). Pittsburgh: University of Pittsburgh, Learning Research and Development Center, September 1981.

7 Holland, J. H., & Reitman, J. S. *Cognitive systems based on adaptive algorithms.* Unpublished manuscript, University of Michigan, 1981.

REFERENCES

Bowerman, M. Starting to talk worse: Clues to language acquisition from children's late speech errors. In S. Strauss (Ed.), *U-shaped behavioral growth.* New York: Academic Press, 1982.

Brainerd, C. J. Cognitive development and concept learning. An interpretive review. *Psychological Bulletin,* 1977, *81,* 919–939

Brainerd, C. J. The stage question in cognitive-developmental theory. *The Behavioral and Brain Sciences,* 1978, *1,* 173–213.

Bransford, J. D. *Human cognition: Learning, understanding, and remembering.* Belmont, Calif.: Wadsworth, 1979.

Brown, A. I. Learning and development: The problems of compatibility, access, and induction. *Human Development,* 1982, *25,* 89–115.

Brown, J. S. & Burton, R. B. Diagnostic models for procedural bugs in basic mathematical skills. *Cognitive Science,* 1978, *2,* 155–192.

Brown, J. S., & Van Lehn, K. Towards a generative theory of "bugs." In T. Romberg, T. Carpenter, & J. Moser (Eds.), *Addition and subtraction: A developmental perspective,* Hillsdale, N. J.: Erlbaum, 1982.

Bruner, J. S., Oliver, R. R., & Greenfield, P. M.

Studies in cognitive growth. New York: Wiley, 1966.

Carey, S. Are children fundamentally different kinds of thinkers and learners than adults? In S. Chipman, J. Segal, & R. Glaser (Eds.). *Thinking and learning skills.* Hillsdale, N.J.: Erlbaum, in press.

Case, R. Intellectual development from birth to adulthood: A neo-Piagetian approach. In R. S. Siegler (Ed.), *Children's thinking: What develops?* Hillsdale, N.J.: Erlbaum, 1978.

Case, R. *Intellectual development: A systematic reinterpretation.* New York: Academic Press, in press.

Cazden, C. B. The acquisition of noun and verb inflections. *Child Development,* 1968, *39,* 433–448.

Chase, W. G., & Simon, H. A. The mind's eye in chess. In W. G. Chase (Ed.), *Visual information processing.* New York: Academic Press, 1973.

Chi, M. T. Knowledge structures and memory development. In R. S. Siegler (Ed.), *Children's thinking: What develops?* Hillsdale, N.J.: Erlbaum, 1978.

Chi, M. T., Glaser, R., & Rees, E. Expertise in problem solving. In R. Sternberg (Ed.), *Advances in the psychology of human intelligence.* Hillsdale, N.J.: Erlbaum, 1982.

Chi, M. T., & Koeske, R. D. Network representation of a child's dinosaur knowledge. *Developmental Psychology,* 1983, *19,* 29–39.

Chi, M. T., & Rees, E. T. A learning framework for development. In M. T. Chi (Ed.), *Trends in memory development.* Basel: Karger, in press.

Chomsky, N. A. *Syntactic structures.* The Hague: Mouton, 1957.

Clark, E. V. What's in a word? On the child's acquisition of semantics in his first language. In T. E. Moore (Ed.), *Cognitive development and the acquisition of language.* New York: Academic Press, 1973.

Collins, A., & Stevens, A. L. Goals and strategies of inquiry teachers. In R. Glaser (Ed.), *Advances in instructional psychology.* Hillsdale, N.J.: Erlbaum, 1982.

Cronbach, L. J., & Snow, R. E. *Aptitudes and instructional methods: A handbook for research on interactions.* New York: Irvington, 1977.

Farah, M. J., & Kosslyn, S. M. Concept development. In H. W. Reese & L. P. Lipsitt (Eds.), *Advances in child development and behavior* (Vol. 16). New York: Academic Press, 1982.

Fischer, K. W. A theory of cognitive development: The control and construction of hierarchies of skills. *Psychological Review,* 1980, *87,* 477–531.

Flavell, J. H. An analysis of cognitive developmental sequences. *Genetic Psychology Monographs,* 1972, *86,* 279–350.

Flavell, J. H. On cognitive development. *Child Development,* 1982, *53,* 1–10.

Flavell, J. H., & Wohlwill, J. F. Formal and functional aspects of cognitive development. In D. Elkind & J. H. Flavell (Eds.), *Studies in cognitive development.* New York: Oxford University Press, 1969.

Fowler, W. Cognitive differentiation and developmental learning. In H. W. Resse & L. P. Lipsitt (Eds.). *Advances in child development and behavior* (Vol. 15). New York: Academic Press, 1980.

Gagné, R. M. Contributions of learning to human development. *Psychological Review:* 1968, *75,* 177–191.

Gardner, H., Kirchner, M., Winnet, E., & Perkins, D. Children's metaphoric productions and preferences. *Journal of Child Language.* 1974, *2,* 125–144.

Groen, G. J., & Resnick, L. B. Can preschool children invent addition algorithms? *Journal of Educational Psychology:* 1977, *69,* 645–652.

Guilford, J. P. *The nature of human intelligence.* New York: McGraw-Hill, 1967.

Huey, E. B. *The psychology and pedagogy of reading.* Cambridge, Mass.: MIT Press, 1908.

Hunt, J. McV. *Intelligence and experience.* New York: Ronald Press, 1961.

Inhelder, B., Sinclair, H., & Bovet, M. *Learning and the development of cognition.* Cambridge, Mass.: Harvard University Press, 1974.

Keil, F. C. Constraints on knowledge and cognitive development. *Psychological Review,* 1981, *88,* 197–227.

Klahr, D., & Robinson, M. Formal assessment of problem-solving and planning processes in preschool children. *Cognitive Psychology:* 1981, *13,* 113–148.

Klahr, D., & Siegler, R. S. The representation of children's knowledge. In H. Reese & L. P. Lipsitt

(Eds.), *Advances in child development* (Vol. 12). New York: Academic Press, 1978.

Klahr, D., & Wallace, J. G. *Cognitive development: An information processing view:* Hillsdale, N.J.: Erlbaum, 1976.

Klima, E. S., & Bellugi-Klima, U. Syntactic regularities in the speech of children. In J. Lyons & R. J. Wales (Eds.), *Psycholinguistics papers*. Edinburgh: Edinburgh University Press, 1966.

Kuhn, D., & Phelps, E. The development of problem-solving strategies. In *Advances in child development and behavior* (Vol. 17). New York: Academic Press, in press.

Langley, P. Data-driven discovery of physical laws. *Cognitive Science*. 1981, *5*, 31–54.

Lenat, D. B. The ubiquity of discovery. *Artificial Intelligence*, 1977, *9*, 257–286.

Levine, M. Hypothesis behavior by humans during discrimination learning. *Journal of Experimental Psychology*, 1966, *71*, 331–338.

Mehler, J., & Bever, T. G. Cognitive capacity of very young children. *Science*, 1967, *158*, 141–142.

Nelson, K. Structure and strategy in learning to talk. *Monographs of the Society for Research in Child Development*, 1973, *38* (Whole No. 149).

Pellegrino, J. W., & Glaser, R. Analyzing aptitudes for learning: Inductive reasoning. In R. Glaser (Ed.), *Advances in instructional psychology*. Hillsdale, N.J.: Erlbaum, 1982.

Piaget, J. [*The child's conception of time*](A. J. Pomerans, Trans.). New York: Ballantine, 1969. (Originally published, 1946.)

Piaget, J. [*The child's concept of movement and speed*](G. Holloway & M. J. Mackenzie, Trans.). New York: Ballantine, 1970. (Originally published, 1946.)

Piaget, J. *The science of education and the psychology of the child*. New York: Viking Press, 1972.

Reitman, J. S. Skilled perception in go: Deducing memory structures from inter-response times. *Cognitive Psychology*, 1976, *8*, 336–356.

Richards, D. D. Children's time concepts: Going the distance. In W. J. Friedman (Ed.), *The developmental psychology of time*. New York: Academic Press, 1982.

Richards, D. D., & Siegler, R. S. Very young children's acquisition of systematic problem-solving strategies. *Child Development*, 1981, *52*, 1318–1321.

Riesen, A. H. The development of visual perception in man and chimpanzee. *Science*, 1947, *106*, 107–108.

Riley, M. S., Greeno, J. G., & Heller, J. I. Development of children's problem-solving ability in arithmetic. In H. Ginsburg (Ed.), *The development of mathematical thinking*. New York: Academic Press, in press.

Siegler, R. S. Three aspects of cognitive development. *Cognitive Psychology*, 1976, *8*, 481–520.

Siegler, R. S. Children's thinking: The search for limits. In G. J. Whitehurst & B. J. Zimmerman (Eds.), *The functions of language and cognition*. New York: Academic Press, 1979.

Siegler, R. S. Developmental sequences within and between concepts. *Monographs of the Society for Research in Child Development*, 1981, *46*(Whole No. 189).

Siegler, R. S., & Klahr, D. When do children learn: The relationship between existing knowledge and the ability to acquire new knowledge. In R. Glaser (Ed.), *Advances in instructional psychology*. Hillsdale, N.J.: Erlbaum, 1982.

Siegler, R. S., & Richards, D. Development of time, speed, and distance concepts. *Developmental Psychology*, 1979, *15*, 288–298.

Siegler, R. S., & Vago, S. The development of a proportionality concept: Judging relative fullness, *Journal of Experimental Child Psychology*, 1978, *25*, 371–395.

Sternberg, R. J. Component processes in analogical reasoning. *Psychological Review*, 1977, *84*, 353–378.

Sternberg, R. Sketch of a componential subtheory of human intelligence. *Behavioral and Brain Sciences*, 1980, *3*, 573–614.

Sternberg, R. J., & Rifkin, B. The development of analogical reasoning processes. *Journal of Experimental Child Psychology*. 1979, *27*, 195–232.

Stevenson, H. W. Learning theories of development. In P. H. Mussen (Ed.), *Handbook of child psychology*. New York: Wiley, in press.

Strauss, S., & Levin, L. A. A commentary on R. S. Siegler, *Developmental sequences within and between concepts. Monographs of the Society for Research in Child Development*, 1981, *46*(Whole No. 189).

Strauss, S., & Stavy, R. *U-shaped behavioral growth*, New York: Academic Press, 1982.

Voss, J. F. Cognition and instruction: Toward a cognitive theory of learning. In A. M. Lesgold, J. W. Pellegrino, S. D. Fokkema & R. Glaser (Eds.), *Cognitive psychology and instruction.* New York: Plenum Press, 1978.

Vygotsky, L. S. *Thought and language.* New York: Wiley, 1934.

Weinreb, N., & Brainerd, C. J. A developmental study of Piaget's groupement model of the emergence of speed and time concepts. *Child Development,* 1975, *46,* 176–185.

Weir, M. W. Developmental changes in problem-solving strategies. *Psychological Review,* 1964, *71,* 473–490.

Werner, H. *Comparative psychology of mental development.* New York: International Universities Press, 1948.

Wexler, K., Culicover, P. W., & Hamburger, H. Learning-theoretic foundations of linguistic universals. *Theoretical Linguistics,* 1979, 2, 213–253.

Wilkening, F., & Anderson, N. H. Comparison of two rule-assessment methodologies for studying cognitive development and knowledge structure. *Psychological Bulletin,* 1982, *92,* 215–237.

Wilkening, F., Becker, J., & Trabasso, T. *Information integration by children.* Hillsdale, N.J.: Erlbaum, 1980.

Wilkinson, A. C. Partial knowledge and self-correction: Developmental studies of a quantitative concept. *Developmental Psychology,* 1982, *18,* 876–893.

READING 25

The Development of Children's Knowledge about the Appearance–Reality Distinction

John H. Flavell

Suppose someone shows a three-year-old and a six-year-old a red toy car covered by a green filter that makes the car look black, hands the car to the children to inspect, puts it behind the filter again, and asks, "What color is this car? Is it red or is it black?" (Flavell, Green, & Flavell, 1985; cf. Braine & Shanks, 1965a, 1965b). The three-year-old is likely to say "black," the six-year-old, "red." The questioner is also apt to get the same answers even if he or she first carefully explains and demonstrates the intended difference in meaning, for illusory displays, between "looks like to your eyes right now" and "really and truly is," and then asks what color it *"really* and *truly* is." At issue in such simple tasks is the distinction between how things presently appear to the senses and how or what they really and enduringly are, that is, the familiar distinction between appearance and reality. The six-year-old is clearly in possession of some knowledge about this distinction and quickly senses what

the task is about. The three-year-old, who is much less knowledgeable about the distinction, does not.

For the past half-dozen years my co-workers and I have been using these and other methods to chart the developmental course of knowledge acquisition in this area. That is, we have been trying to find out what children of different ages do and do not know about the appearance–reality distinction and related phenomena. In this article I summarize what we have done and what we think we have learned (Flavell, Flavell, & Green, 1983; Flavell et al., 1985; Flavell, Zhang, Zou, Dong, & Qi, 1983; Taylor & Flavell, 1984). The summary is organized around the main questions that have guided our thinking and research in this area.

WHY IS THIS DEVELOPMENT IMPORTANT TO STUDY?

First, the distinction between appearance and reality is ecologically significant. It assumes many forms, arises in many situations, and can have serious consequences for our lives. The relation between appearance and reality figures importantly in everyday perceptual, conceptual, emotional, and social activity—in misperceptions, misexpectations, misunderstandings, false beliefs, deception, play, fantasy, and so forth. It is also a major preoccupation of philosophers, scientists, and other scholars; of artists, politicians, and other public performers; and of the thinking public that tries to evaluate what they say and do. It is, in sum, "the distinction which probably provides the intellectual basis for the fundamental epistemological construct common to science, 'folk' philosophy, religion, and myth, of a real world 'underlying' and 'explaining' the phenomenal one" (Braine & Shanks, 1965a, pp. 241–242).

Second, the acquisition of at least some explicit knowledge about the appearance–reality distinction is probably a universal developmental outcome in our species. This knowledge seems so necessary to everyday intellectual and social life that one can hardly imagine a society in which normal people would not acquire it. To cite an example that has actually been researched, a number of investigators have been interested in the child's command of the distinction as a possible developmental prerequisite for, and perhaps even mediator of, Piagetian conservations (e.g., Braine & Shanks, 1965a, 1965b; Murray, 1968).

Third, knowledge about the distinction seems to presuppose the explicit knowledge that human beings are sentient, cognizing *subjects* (cf. Chandler & Boyce, 1982; Selman, 1980) whose mental representations of objects and events can differ, both within the same person and between persons. In the within-person case, for example, I may be aware both that something appears to be A and that it really is B. I could also be aware that it might appear to be C under special viewing conditions, or that I pretended or fantasized that it was D yesterday. I may know that these are all possible ways that I can *represent* the very same thing (i.e., perceive it, encode it, know it, interpret it, construe it, or think about it—although inadequate, the term "represent" will have to do). In the between-persons case, I may be aware that you might represent the same thing differently than I do, because our perceptual, conceptual, or affective perspectives on it might differ. If this analysis is correct, knowledge about the appearance–reality distinction is but one instance of our more general knowledge that the selfsame object or event can be represented (apprehended, experienced, etc.) in different ways by the same person and by different people. In this analysis, then, its development is worth studying because it is part of the larger development of our conscious knowledge about our own and other minds and, thus, of metacognition (e.g., Brown, Bransford, Ferara, & Campione, 1983; Flavell, 1985; Wellman, 1985) and of social cognition (e.g., Flavell, 1985; Shantz, 1983). I will return to this line of reasoning in another section of the article.

HOW CAN YOUNG CHILDREN'S KNOWLEDGE ABOUT THE APPEARANCE–REALITY DISTINCTION BE TESTED?

The development of appearance–reality knowledge in preschool children has been investigated by Braine and Shanks (1965a, 1965b), Dachler (1970), DeVries (1969), Elkind (1966), King (1971), Langer and Strauss (1972), Murray (1965, 1968), Tronick and Hershenson (1979) and, most recently and systematically, by our research group. In most of our studies we have used variations of the following procedure to assess young children's ability to think about appearance and reality (Flavell, Flavell, & Green, 1983). First, we pretrain the children briefly on the meaning of the distinction and associated terminology by showing them (for example) a Charlie Brown puppet inside a ghost costume. We explain and demonstrate that Charlie Brown "*looks like* a ghost to your eyes right now" but is "*really and truly* Charlie

Brown," and that "sometimes things look like one thing to your eyes when they are really and truly something else." We then present a variety of illusory stimuli in a nondeceptive fashion and ask about their appearance and their reality. For instance, we first show the children a very realistic looking fake rock made out of a soft sponge-like material and then let them discover its identity by manipulating it. We next ask, in random order: (a) "What is this *really* and *truly?* Is it *really* and *truly* a sponge or is it *really* and *truly* a rock?" (b) "When you look at this with your eyes right now, does it *look like* a rock or does it *look like* a sponge?" Or we show the children a white stimulus, move it behind a blue filter, and similarly ask about its real and apparent color. (Of course its "real color" is now blue, but only people who know something about color perception realize this.) Similar procedures are used to assess sensitivity to the distinction between real and apparent size, shape, events, and object presence.

HOW DO YOUNG CHILDREN PERFORM ON SIMPLE APPEARANCE–REALITY TASKS?

Our studies have consistently shown that three- to four-year-old children presented with tasks of this sort usually either answer both questions correctly, suggesting some ability to differentiate appearance and reality representations, or else give the same answer (reporting either the appearance or the reality) to both questions, suggesting some conceptual difficulty with the distinction. Incorrect answers to both questions occur only infrequently, suggesting that even the children who err are not responding randomly. There is a marked improvement with age during early childhood in the ability to solve these appearance–reality tasks: Only a few three-year-olds get them right consistently, whereas almost all six- to seven-year-olds do (Flavell et al., 1985).

Some illusory stimuli tend to elicit appearance answers to both questions (called a *phenomenism* error pattern), whereas others tend to elicit reality answers to both (*intellectual realism* pattern). The intellectual realism pattern is the more surprising one, because it contradicts the widely held view that young children respond only to what is most striking and noticeable in their immediate perceptual field (Flavell, 1977, pp. 79–80; for a review of other research on intellectual realism, see Pillow & Flavell, 1985). If the task is to distinguish between the real and apparent properties of color, size, and shape, phenomenism errors predominate. Thus, if an object that is really white or small or straight is temporarily made to look blue, big, or bent by means of filters or lenses, young children are very likely to say the object really *is* blue, big, or bent. If, instead, the task is to indicate what object(s) or event is present, really versus apparently, intellectual realism errors are likelier to predominate. For example, the fake rock is incorrectly said to look like a sponge rather than a rock; a tiny picture of a cup is incorrectly said to look like a cup rather than a spot when viewed from afar; an array consisting of a small object completely occluded by a large one is incorrectly said to look like it contains both objects rather than only the visible one; an experimenter who appears from the child's viewing position to be reading a large book, but who is known by the child really to be drawing a picture inside it, is incorrectly said to look like she is drawing rather than reading (Flavell, Flavell, & Green, 1983). Indeed, Taylor and Flavell (1984) found that significantly more phenomenism errors occurred when illusory stimuli were described to children in terms of their properties (e.g., "white" vs. "orange" liquid) than when the same stimuli were described to the same children in terms of identities ("milk" vs. "Koolaid"). We do not know yet exactly why the appearance usually seems to be more cognitively salient for young children in these property tasks and (less dependably) the reality more salient in the object/event identity tasks, although we have proposed some possible explanations (Flavell, Flavell, & Green, 1983).

HOW CAN WE FIND OUT WHETHER YOUNG CHILDREN'S DIFFICULTIES WITH THIS DISTINCTION ARE REAL OR ONLY APPARENT?

Much of our research has focused on the appearance–reality knowledge and related skills that three-year-olds possess and lack, because the early emergence of knowledge in any domain is of particular interest. (We have not yet found effective ways to test for possible cognitive precursors in children younger than three, but we hope to eventually.) As just mentioned, the evidence is now clear that many three-year-olds perform poorly even on what seem like very simple and straightforward appearance–reality tasks. Exactly how this poor performance should be interpreted is an important issue. Perhaps these tasks are valid and sensitive measures of young children's basic competence in this area, and their poor performance on them simply means that they really lack such competence. On the other hand, it is more than possible that the tasks we have been using significantly underestimate three-year-olds' capabilities. If there is one lesson to be learned from the recent history of the field of cognitive development, it is that the cognitive capabilities of young children are often seriously underestimated by the tasks developmentalists initially devise to assess those capabilities (e.g., Flavell, 1985; Flavell & Markman, 1983, pp. viii-x; Gelman, 1979). It is quite possible, therefore, that children age three or even younger really do understand the distinction. It is even imaginable that humans are in some sense born with a sensitivity to the distinction. What could one do to try to find out whether three-year-olds really lack competence in this area or only appear to?

Try Cross-Cultural Replication

We repeated as exactly as possible one of our early experiments (Flavell, Flavell, & Green, 1983, Experiment 2) in a different language and culture, namely, using Mandarin in the People's Republic of China (Flavell, Zhang, Zou, Dong, & Qi, 1983). The American children were three- to five-year-olds from Stanford University's laboratory preschool. The Chinese children were three-to five-year-olds from Beijing (Peking) Normal University's laboratory preschool. Pretraining and testing procedures, and the illusory stimuli, were the same for the two samples. We worked closely with Chinese colleagues on the translation of instructions and key terms and in the pilot testing. Error patterns, age changes, and even absolute levels of performance at each age level proved to be remarkably similar in the two subject samples. These results suggest that previously observed difficulties with our tasks cannot be due solely to some sort of simple and developmentally inconsequential misunderstanding by young American children of the English expressions "really and truly" and "looks like to your eyes right now." Rather, they suggest, as such cross-cultural replications usually do (e.g., of Piagetian phenomena), that our tasks may in fact be assessing a real and robust conceptual acquisition.

Try Making the Tasks Easier

In three recent studies (Flavell et al., 1985) we compared the difficulty for three-year-olds of "standard" and "easy" appearance–reality tasks. Standard tasks were the object-identity (fake objects) and color (objects placed behind colored filters) ones used in our previous investigations. Easy tasks were created by thinking of possible obstacles to good performance posed by the standard ones and devising tasks that eliminated or reduced these obstacles. We tried to invent tasks that still demanded some genuine if minimal knowledge of the appearance–reality distinction but that, by virtue of being stripped of certain knowledge-irrelevant processing demands, came closer than the standard ones to demanding *only* that knowledge. In short, we tried to create more sensitive assessment procedures in hopes of coaxing out nascent, hard-to-elicit appearance–reality competence.

We constructed five putatively easy color tasks using this method.

1 A small part of the target object was left uncovered when the color filter was placed over it. Consequently, visible evidence of the object's real color was still available to the children when the appearance and reality questions were asked; they did not have to remember what its real color was.

2 A liquid (milk) whose real color (white) is well known to young children was caused by use of a filter to temporarily appear to be a color (red) that they would never see in reality. We thought this might help the children both keep the real color in mind and recognize the bizarre apparent color to be a mere appearance.

3 The device that changed the object's apparent color was a familiar one known by children to have just that function (sun glasses rather than a filter). In addition, its effect on the children's momentary color experience (appearance) rather than on the object's enduring surface color (reality) was highlighted by placing it next to the children's eyes rather than next to the object.

4 The device was itself an object that possessed its own real color (a blue filter cut into the shape of a large fish) distinct from that of the object whose apparent color it changed (a small white fish that temporarily became blue-looking by chancing to "swim" behind the large one). This setup might help young children distinguish between the little fish's real color and its accidental apparent color, which really "belongs" to the big fish.

5 It is possible that the repeated juxtaposition of two different questions, one about appearance and one about reality, confuses or overtaxes three-year-olds; they might do better if simply asked what color the object behind the

filter "is." Therefore, at the very beginning of the testing session, prior to any talk about appearances and realities, we asked the single "is" question about a toy car's color described in the opening sentence of this article.

The same strategy was used to create three easier object-identity tasks.

1 After a brief conversation about dressing up for Halloween in masks and costumes, the children were questioned about the real and apparent identity of one of the experimenters after she had conspicuously put on a mask disguise. We assumed that young children would be more knowledgeable about this sort of appearance–reality discrepancy through Halloween and play experiences than with those presented by the fake objects and filters used in standard tasks.

2 The apparent identity of each object was conveyed by its sound and its real identity by its visual appearance. To illustrate, a small can (real identity) sounded like a cow (apparent identity) when turned over; the children were then asked if it sounded like a can or like a cow, and whether it really and truly was a can or a cow. We thought that appearance and reality might be easier for young children to attend to separately, and keep straight, if the two were presented via different sense modalities. In an attempt to make the task easier still, at the moment the reality question was asked the reality was perceptible (the can was still visible), but the appearance was not (the can was not still making mooing sounds)—the opposite of what happens in all standard tasks.

3 Task 3 was the same as 2, except that the nonvisual modality used was smell rather than sound. For example, one of the objects used was a cloth (real identity) that smelled like a lemon (apparent identity).

These efforts to bring to light underlying appearance–reality competence by using easier, seemingly less demanding probes for this competence were surprisingly unsuccessful. Of the five easy color tasks, only Task 1 elicited better performance than did the standard color and object-identity tasks. Children performed significantly better on the three easy object-identity tasks than on the standard object-identity tasks, but not better than on the standard color ones. Moreover, their absolute level of performance on these three tasks was not very high. Thus, the results of these studies do not support the view that the typical young preschooler can differentially represent and think about appearances and realities if only the eliciting conditions are made sufficiently facilitative and "child-friendly."

Try Teaching Appearance—Reality Knowledge

Finally we (Flavell, Green, & Flavell, 1985) have recently tried to probe for hidden competence by assessing children's response to training: in effect, to use training as a diagnostic tool (Flavell, 1985, pp. 277–278). We selected a group of 16 three-year-olds who performed very poorly on color and object-identity (fake object) pretests, trained them intensively for five to seven minutes on the meaning of real versus apparent color, and then readministered the same pretests. In this training we demonstrated, explained, defined terms, helped the child demonstrate, and gave corrective feedback on the theme that the real, true color of an object stays the same despite repeated, temporary changes in its apparent color due to the interposition of different color filters. Although we fully expected that this training would be helpful, in fact it was not. Only one of the 16 children performed well on the posttest, and he did so only on the color tasks, showing no transfer to the object-identity tasks. Braine and Shanks (1965a) had likewise been largely unsuccessful in training three-year-olds on the distinction between real and apparent size, although they used a less conceptually oriented training procedure. These results present a striking contrast to the results of the scores of studies that have tried to train conservation and other Piagetian concepts (Kuhn, 1984). Many of these studies have at least succeeded in inducing young nonconservers to behave like conservers; what remains controversial is the extent to which that trained conservation behavior reflects a real gain in genuine understanding. In contrast, the children in our study and in Braine and Shanks' (1965a) study could not be induced even to *behave* like children who understand the appearance—reality distinction. It seems reasonable to conclude, therefore, that they really did not understand it.

In summary, we have used three different research strategies to find out whether young children's difficulties with the appearance—reality distinction are real or only apparent. The results of this research strongly suggest that these difficulties are very real indeed.

WHAT RELEVANT COMPETENCIES DO YOUNG CHILDREN POSSESS AND LACK?

We can identify some relevant-seeming competencies that young children who fail simple appearance—reality tasks have already acquired. Although not sufficient in themselves to ensure understanding of the appearance—reality distinction, these competencies might be either necessary or helpful to its acquisition. By the age of three, children have become quite proficient at creating discrepancies between real and pretend identities (Bretherton, 1984; Rubin, Fein, & Vandenberg, 1983). As examples, they can pretend that a toy block is a car or make believe that they themselves are animals. Consistent with these skills in symbolic play, Estes and Wellman (H. M. Wellman, personal communication, 1984) and we (Flavell et al., 1985) have shown that most three-year-olds can consistently identify nonfake objects as being "real" and fake ones as being "not real" or "pretend," even without pretraining. We also presented three-year-olds with standard color appearance—reality task situations: that is, first show an object, then place it behind a filter that changes the object's apparent color. However, we then asked the children, not the usual appearance and reality questions, but simply whether the object will look A (its apparent color) or R (its real color) when the filter is removed. We found that many three-year-olds who performed well on this task nevertheless performed poorly on the standard color appearance–reality task. These results cannot be taken to imply that three-year-olds always maintain the object's original color in focal attention when answering reality questions, nor that they represent the object as being that color while it is behind the filter. However, these results do suggest that young children's abilities to (a) realize that the experimenter is talking about the object's color rather than the filter's color, (b) remember what color the object was before the filter was put over it, and (c) understand that it will look that same color again when the filter is removed are not sufficient to ensure good performance on color appearance–reality tasks, although they are no doubt necessary. There are undoubtedly other competencies not yet identified that also play this sort of developmental role of being necessary and facilitative but not sufficient.

What developing competencies might actually be sufficient or nearly sufficient to enable young children to grasp the appearance–reality distinction? We really do not know, but we have a hypothesis. The hypothesis is derived from the third-mentioned reason why we think this development is important to study, as described earlier in this article.

Consider the conceptual demands of appearance–reality tasks. In reality, an object cannot simultaneously be, for instance, both all blue and all white, or both a rock and a sponge. Nevertheless, to solve these tasks we have to attribute such mutually incompatible and contradictory properties and identities to the same object at the same moment in time. As adults, we easily resolve the seeming contradiction by identifying one representation of its property or identity with its present appearance and the other with its reality. We identify the one with what we see and the other with what we know. This resolution is easy for us because we are well aware that people are sentient, cognizing subjects who have internal representations of external things and can represent singular things in multiple ways. Although we are aware that external objects themselves cannot simultaneously be two different things at once, we are also aware that we can represent them as simultaneously looking like the one thing ("that's what it looks like") and really being the other ("that's what it really is").

In contrast, everything we know about meta-cognitive and social-cognitive development (e.g., Brown et al., 1983; Flavell, 1985; Shantz, 1983) suggests that young children are less cognizant of these facts about subjectivity and mental representation than older children and adults are. This is not to claim that they are wholly incognizant of these facts (see Shatz, Wellman, & Silber, 1983, and Wellman, 1985, for evidence of some early knowledge of this kind) but only to claim that they are less cognizant of them. Therefore, they might not be aware of the ongoing role of subjectivity and representational activity as they inspect the target object. Instead, they may try only to decide what single thing the object "is," as an entity out there in the world. That the object can be represented as having more than one "is," inside our heads, may be a possibility that does not, or perhaps even cannot, occur to them. (Note that identifying a fake rock as a "pretend rock," which we have just said that young children can do, does *not* require representing that object as having more than one "is"—as looking like a rock but really being a sponge.) As they become increasingly cognizant of these facts in the course of development, according to this hypothesis, the distinction between appearance and reality should become increasingly meaningful to them.

Although this hypothesis has not yet been tested directly (we are still trying to formulate it clearly), there are two pieces of evidence that are at least consistent with it. One is the fact, mentioned above, that children who err on our tasks usually do so by giving the same answer to both the appearance and the reality questions, even though the two questions sound quite different and we stress the fact during both pretraining and testing that we are asking them two different questions. It is as if, despite all efforts to help them do otherwise, they decide what the object identity or property "is" and just say it twice.

The other piece of evidence is our recent finding (Flavell et al., 1985), obtained in two separate studies using three-year-old subjects, of high positive correlations (.67 to .87) between the ability to distinguish between appearance for the self and reality (appearance–reality ability) and the ability to distinguish between appearance for the self and appearance for another person (visual perspective-taking ability). We take this finding to be supportive of our hypothesis because both tasks require the previously discussed awareness that the same object can be simultaneously represented in two different ways: appearance and reality in the appearance–reality task and two different appearances to two differently situated observers in the perspective-taking task. In the more elaborate of the two studies, 40 three-year-olds were tested in two sessions. In one session they were given five color and five shape appearance–reality tasks (standard type); in the other they saw the same 10 task displays but were asked perspective-taking questions about them. Appropriate pretraining was given at the beginning of each session. To illustrate, one of the five shape displays consisted of a bent straw that looked straight to the child who viewed it through a bottle of liquid but bent to the experimenter who, seated opposite, did not view it through the distorting bottle. As in all our studies, the child initially saw the straw without the distorting device, in its real shape. In the appearance–reality session, the three-year-olds were asked whether the straw looked bent or straight to them and whether it was really and truly bent or straight. In the perspective-taking session, they were asked whether it looked bent or straight to them and whether it looked bent or straight to the experimenter. The correlations between appearance–reality and perspective-taking scores were .67 for the color displays and .72 for the shape displays. These correlations are as high as those between color and shape appearance–reality scores (.73) and those between color and shape perspective-taking scores (.69), despite the fact that the appearance–reality and perspective-taking abilities were assessed in different experimental sessions separated by several days.

In summary, I have suggested some cognitive competencies that may variously be facilitative, necessary, or sufficient for a beginning understanding of the appearance–reality distinction. One competency hypothesized to be sufficient or nearly sufficient is an increased cognizance of subjectivity and mental representation; this competency may allow children to construe an illusory stimulus as simultaneously possessing two seemingly incompatible properties or identities—one identified with its appearance and the other with its reality. Although the hypothesis has not yet been tested directly, there exist some data that make it seem plausible.

WHAT IS THE SUBSEQUENT COURSE OF DEVELOPMENT IN THIS AREA?

According to the hypothesis proposed in the previous section, as children become increasingly cognizant of subjectivity and mental representation, both simple appearance–reality tasks and simple perspective-taking tasks should begin to make sense to them and become easily soluble. Whether this explanation of development proves to be the correct one, there is considerable evidence that tasks of both kinds do become increasingly easy to manage as youngsters approach the middle childhood years. For example, children of four and five years are much more competent at simple visual perspective-taking tasks than children of three (Flavell, Flavell, Green, & Wilcox, 1980, 1981). There is even empirical support for the more general claim that "around the ages of 4 to 6 years the ability to represent the relationship between two or more persons' epistemic states emerges and becomes firmly established" (Wimmer & Perner, 1983, p. 104). Likewise, performance on standard appearance–reality tasks improves significantly between three and five years in both American and Chinese (People's Republic of China) children (Flavell, Flavell, & Green, 1983; Flavell, Zhang et al., 1983). Finally, we have recently found that six- to seven-year-olds perform almost errorlessly on simple tasks of both types (Flavell et al., 1985). Unlike the majority of three-year-olds, six-to seven-year-olds can consistently report realities when realities are requested and appearances when appearances are requested, whether the appearances are from their own or another person's viewing position. Consistent with these results with real and apparent object identities and object properties, Harris, Donnelly, Guz, and Pitt-Watson (1985) have recently found that children of this age are also capable of understanding the distinction between real and apparent emotion.

However, our investigations (Flavell et al., 1985) also show that development is by no means complete at this age. Using groups of six- to seven-year-olds, we administered two types of more demanding tests of the ability to think and talk about appearances, realities, and appearance–reality relations: identification tasks and administration tasks. In identification tasks, they were presented with a wide variety of stimuli and were asked to identify those that exhibited discrepancies or nondiscrepancies between appearance and reality and to explain their selections. In two studies, for example, they were shown a series of 23 pairs of stimuli.

Within each pair, the stimuli differed from one another in degree of discrepancy between appearance and reality or in other ways relevant to the distinction. The subjects' job was to choose the member(s) of each pair, if any, that best exemplified an appearance–reality discrepancy and to explain their choice. In one of these studies, for instance, subjects were initially pretrained and given corrective feedback on what they were to look for. In addition, each new stimulus pair was introduced with the instruction: "Remember, we are trying to find things that don't look like what they really and truly are. Here are two things. Which one is better for the kind of things we are trying to find—this one, or this one, or are they both just about as good for the kinds of things we are trying to find?" The following items illustrate the variety of stimulus pairs used: (a) a real piece of candy and a magnet that looked like a piece of candy; (b) a bottle of cologne that looked like a tennis ball when its green base was not visible; the bottle was held so that the telltale base either was or was not visible; (c) a realistic-looking fake rock and a fake-looking fake water faucet; (d) two real flowers, one of them (an antherium) fake-looking. In the administration tasks, six- to seven-year-olds were asked to administer standard appearance–reality tasks, after having had experience taking them and following brief training on how they should be given.

The data from the identification tasks showed that the ability to identify on request stimuli exhibiting appearance–reality discrepancies and nondiscrepancies is still fragile and task-dependent at the beginning of middle childhood. On one particularly easy-looking identification task, six- to seven-year-olds did perform well but on three others, including the 23-pairs task described above, identification performance was surprisingly poor. Furthermore, they seemed to find it even more difficult to talk about appearances, realities, and appearance–reality relations. They often failed to refer to them even when asked to explain their correct stimulus choices, that is, stimuli correctly chosen as best exhibiting an appearance–reality disparity. The same difficulty was evident in the administration task data. That is, six- to seven-year-olds also tended not to mention appearances, realities, and relations between them when asked to administer the very sorts of standard appearance–reality tasks they, as subjects, found so easy to solve—even after the experimenter had explained and repeatedly demonstrated the administration procedure.

We believe that these difficulties in nonverbal identification and verbal labeling reflect genuine conceptual difficulties. Many children of this age simply seem unable to think about such notions as "looks like," "really and truly," and "looks different from the way it really and truly is" in an abstract, metaconceptual way. Although they are able to identify concrete examples of the first and second notions quite easily and of the third with considerably more difficulty, they seem to lack the knowledge and ability to reflect on and talk about, indeed, often even briefly mention, the notions themselves.

We also administered an identification task involving the 23 pairs of stimuli to 11- to 12-year-olds and college students (Flavell, Green, & Flavell, 1985). The data gave evidence of considerable knowledge development in this area subsequent to early middle childhood. They suggest that 11- to 12-year-olds, and to an even greater extent college students, have acquired a substantial body of knowledge that is both richly structured and highly accessible.

As to rich structure, older subjects seem to possess abstract and general schemas for appearances, realities, and possible relations between the two. For example, they may make abstract, general statements such as "This doesn't look like what it really is" when confronted with an appearance–reality discrepancy. These schemas permit them to identify as possible instances of the abstract category,

"appearance different from reality," many different types of appearance–reality discrepancies, including unusual and marginal ones. They can similarly identify instances of the category, "appearance same as reality," and can discriminate these from instances of the former category. They can also recognize subtle distinctions among appearance–reality task displays. In particular, they are able to identify and differentiate, with respect to these two categories, among realistic-looking nonfake objects, realistic-looking fake objects ("good fakes"), nonrealistic-looking fakes ("poor fakes"), and even fake-looking nonfakes. Consistent with our findings suggesting that appearance–reality and perspective-taking competencies are psychologically related, older subjects often draw upon their perspective-taking knowledge when thinking and talking about appearance–reality phenomena. For example, they comment spontaneously on how the appearance of a given stimulus (and therefore, perhaps, the observable appearance–reality relation) may vary with the observer's prior knowledge, previous viewing experience, or present viewing position. Finally, they can not only identify the appearances and appearance–reality discrepancies presented to them, but they can also reproduce these discrepancies, change them, or even create new ones. That is, their knowledge in this area is generative and creative as well as rich.

The appearance–reality knowledge of older subjects is also more accessible than that of younger ones, both in the sense of being (a) easily elicited by instructions and task materials and (b) readily available to conscious reflection and verbal elaboration (metaconceptual). In terms of (a), vague instructions and a few concrete examples suffice to activate their appearance–reality knowledge; they require little help from the task materials or the experimenter. In terms of (b), older subjects can describe in detail what they know and think about appearance–reality phenomena. They readily talk about their own and other people's mental events, including the expectations and inferences an object's appearance would stimulate in an observer.

In summary, the subsequent course of development in this area seems to be both lengthy and substantial. Although 6- to 7-year-olds can easily manage the simple appearance–reality tasks that 3-year-olds fail, their ability to reflect on and talk about appearances, realities, and appearance–reality relations remains very limited. In contrast, the appearance–reality and related knowledge of 11- to 12-year-olds and especially college students is both richly structured and highly accessible. In an early article on this topic, Langer and Strauss (1972) hypothesized "that the cognition of the appearance and the reality of things follows a long and varied course" (p. 106). Our evidence certainly supports their hypothesis.

WHAT NEXT?

As always, there is much more to do. One obvious task for future research in this area is to find effective ways to probe for prerequisites, protoforms, and precursors in infants and very young children. Another is to make direct tests of our current hypothesis about what mediates an elementary understanding of the appearance–reality distinction. A third is to search for other abilities that seem to require the same general type of dual representation as appearance–reality and perspective-taking ones and that may for that reason be developmentally linked to them. A possible candidate we are currently examining is the ability to represent explicitly the selfsame object as simultaneously having a real identity (e.g., that of a small piece of wood) and a temporary pretend identity (e.g., that of a car, in the child's pretend play activity).

We think linking appearance–reality and perspective-taking abilities as we have done may shed new light on both. Similarly, trying to relate pretend play to these two might further illuminate all three. Continuing in this integrative vein, there seems to be a whole family of distinctions that have a similar "feel" to them. In each, one thing is represented in two ways, and the two ways have some kind of adversative, "but" type relation between them. Familiar examples: This is x but it seems or appears (perceptually, conceptually, affectively, etc.) to be y. This seems or appears x to me but seems or appears y to you. This is x but I can imagine or pretend that it is y. Further examples: This is x but it should be y (on moral, conventional, practical, aesthetic, or other grounds). I meant x but, being an imprecise communicator, said y (Beal & Flavell, 1984; Bonitatibus & Flavell, 1985; Olson, 1981; Robinson, Goelman, & Olson, 1983). I know it is x but, deliberately lying, say it is y (Wimmer, Gruber, & Perner, 1984). I thought of doing x, but I did not actually do it (Wellman & Estes, in press). We have just begun to think about these distinctions but find them intriguing. They appear to require similar processing and therefore seem as if they might be developmentally related. But a lot more hard thinking and research will be needed to find out whether they *are—really* and *truly*.

REFERENCES

Beal, C. R., & Flavell, J. H. (1984). Development of the ability to distinguish communicative intention and literal message meaning. *Child Development, 55*, 920–928.

Bonitatibus, G. J., & Flavell, J. H. (1985). The effect of presenting a message in written form on young children's ability to evaluate its communicative adequacy. *Developmental Psychology, 21*, 455–461.

Braine, M. D. S., & Shanks, B. L. (1965a). The development of conservation of size. *Journal of Verbal Learning and Verbal Behavior, 4*, 227–242.

Braine, M. D. S., & Shanks, B. L. (1965b). The conservation of a shape property and a proposal about the origin of the conservations. *Canadian Journal of Psychology, 19*, 197–207.

Bretherton, I. (1984). *Symbolic play: The development of social understanding*. New York: Academic Press.

Brown, A. L., Bransford, J. D., Ferrara, R. A., & Campione, J. C. (1983). Learning, remembering, and understanding. In J. H. Flavell & E. M. Markman (Eds.), *Handbook of child psychology: Cognitive development* (Vol. 3, pp. 77–166). New York: Wiley.

Chandler, M., & Boyce, M. (1982). Social-cognitive development. In B. B. Wolman (Ed.), *Handbook of developmental psychology* (pp. 387–402). Englewood Cliffs, NJ: Prentice-Hall.

Daehler, M. W. (1970). Children's manipulation of illusory and ambiguous stimuli, discriminative performance, and implications for conceptual development. *Child Development, 41*, 225–241.

DeVries, R. (1969). Constancy of generic identity in the years three to six. *Society for Research in Child Development Monographs, 34*(3, Serial No. 127).

Elkind, D. (1966). Conservation across illusory transformations in young children. *Acta Psychologica, 25*, 389–400.

Flavell, J. H. (1977). *Cognitive development*. Englewood Cliffs, NJ: Prentice-Hall.

Flavell, J. H. (1985). *Cognitive development* (rev. ed.). Englewood Cliffs, NJ: Prentice-Hall.

Flavell, J. H., Flavell, E. R., & Green, F. L. (1983). Development of the appearance–reality distinction. *Cognitive Psychology, 15*, 95–120.

Flavell, J. H., Flavell, E. R., Green, F. L., & Wilcox, S. A. (1980). Young children's knowledge about visual perception: Effect of observer's distance from target on perceptual clarity of target. *Developmental Psychology, 16*, 10–12.

Flavell, J. H., Flavell, E. R., Green, F. L., & Wilcox, S. A. (1981). The development of three spatial perspective-taking rules. *Child Development, 52*, 356–358.

Flavell, J. H., Green, F. L., & Flavell, E. R. (1985). *Development of knowledge about the appearance–reality distinction*. Unpublished manuscript, Stanford University, Department of Psychology.

Flavell, J. H., & Markman, E. M. (Eds.). (1983). *Handbook of child psychology: Cognitive development* (Vol. 3), New York: Wiley.

Flavell, J. H., Zhang, X-D., Zou, H., Dong, Q., & Qi, S. (1983). A comparison between the development of the appearance–reality distinction in the People's Republic of China and the United States. *Cognitive Psychology, 15*, 459–466.

Gelman, R. (1979). Preschool thought. *American Psychologist, 34*, 900–905.

Harris, P. L., Donnelly, K., Guz, G. R., & Pitt-Watson, R. (1985). *Children's understanding of the distinction between real and apparent emotion*. Unpublished manuscript, University of Oxford, Department of Experimental Psychology, Oxford, England.

King, W. L. (1971). A nonarbitrary behavioral criterion for conservation of illusion-distorted length in five-year-olds. *Journal of Experimental Child Psychology, 11*, 171–181.

Kuhn, D. (1984). Cognitive development. In M. H. Bornstein & M. E. Lamb (Eds.), *Developmental psychology: An advanced textbook* (pp. 133–180). Hillsdale, NJ: Erlbaum.

Langer, J., & Strauss, S. (1972). Appearance, reality and identity. *Cognition, 1*, 105–128.

Murray, F. B. (1965). Conservation of illusion-distorted lengths and areas by primary school children. *Journal of Educational Psychology, 56*, 62–66.

Murray, F. B. (1968). Phenomenal-real discrimination and the conservation of illusion-distorted length. *Canadian Journal of Psychology, 22*, 114–121.

Olson, D. R. (1981, August). *A conceptual revolution in the early school years: Learning to differentiate intended meaning from the meaning in the text*. Paper presented at the meeting of the International Society for the Study of Behavioural Development.

Pillow, B. H., & Flavell, J. H. (1985). Intellectual realism: The role of children's interpretations of pictures and perceptual verbs. *Child Development, 56*, 664–670.

Robinson, E. J., Goelman, H., & Olson, D. R. (1983). Children's understanding of the relation between expressions (what was said) and intentions (what was meant). *British Journal of Developmental Psychology, 1*, 75–86.

Rubin, K. H., Fein, G. G., & Vandenberg, B. (1983). Play. In E. M. Hetherington (Ed.), *Handbook of child psychology: Vol. 4. Socialization, personality, and social development* (pp. 693–774). New York: Wiley.

Selman, R. L. (1980). *The growth of interpersonal understanding*. New York: Academic Press.

Shantz, C. U. (1983). Social cognition. In J. H. Flavell & E. M. Markman (Eds.), *Handbook of child psychology: Vol. 3. Cognitive development* (pp. 495–555). New York: Wiley.

Shatz, M., Wellman, H. M., & Silber, S. (1983). The acquisition of mental verbs: A systematic investigation of the first reference to mental states. *Cognition, 14*, 301–321.

Taylor, M., & Flavell, J. H. (1984). Seeing and believing: Children's understanding of the distinction between appearance and reality. *Child Development, 55*, 1710–1720.

Tronick, E., & Hershenson, M. (1979). Size-distance perception in preschool children. *Journal of Experimental Child Psychology, 27*, 166–184.

Wellman, H. M. (1985). The origins of metacognition. In D. L. Forrest-Pressley, G. E. MacKinnon, & T. G. Waller (Eds.), *Metacognition, cognition, and human performance*. New York: Academic Press.

Wellman, H. M., & Estes, D. (in press). Early understanding of mental entities: A reexamination of childhood realism. *Child Development*.

Wimmer, H., Gruber, S., & Perner, J. (1984). Young children's conception of lying: Lexical realism— moral subjectivism. *Journal of Experimental Child Psychology, 37*, 1–30.

Wimmer, H., & Perner, J. (1983). Beliefs about beliefs: Representation and constraining function of wrong beliefs in young children's understanding of deception. *Cognition, 13*, 103–128.

READING 26

Way Finding and Cognitive Mapping in Large-Scale Environments: A Test of a Developmental Model

Jennifer H. Cousins
Alexander W. Siegel
Scott E. Maxwell

In the last decade, the field of developmental psychology has witnessed the inception and growth of a research enterprise concerned with the development of cognitive representations of large-scale space. A considerable amount of the research conducted in the past 5 years has been focused on a model of development of cognitive mapping proposed by Siegel and White (1975). In this model, it is proposed that the development of spatial representations of large-scale space is composed of four components and is cumulative and hierarchical: landmarks are first recognized and remembered; acting in the context of these landmarks, children (or adults) construct routes along which these landmarks are first ordered and later organized according to their metric interrelationships. With additional experience and/or the development of higher-order cognitive skills (e.g., perspective taking), it is proposed that multiple routes are organized into configurations, that is, coordinated representations that can be used flexibly for environmental navigating and for other forms of spatial and nonspatial problem solving.

Using a variety of research methods, a number of researchers have found evidence of developmental differences in these component processes supportive of Siegel and White's (1975) model (Allen, Kirasic, Siegel, & Herman, 1979; Cohen & Schuepfer, 1980; Curtis, Siegel, & Furlong, 1981; Hazen, Lockman, & Pick, 1978). Allen et al. (1979) simulated a walk through an urban area with a slide presentation to children and adults to assess developmental differences in the types of landmarks subjects selected to help them remember the route. They found that adults were more likely to choose scenes that portrayed actual or potential changes in heading, defined as "critical areas of high landmark potential" (Carr & Schissler, 1969; Lynch, 1960). In the same study a separate group of adults and children from the same grade levels viewed the simulated walk and then ranked the distances among the scenes previously selected either by adults or their peers. Allen et al. (1979) found that distances among the high-landmark-potential scenes were judged more accurately than those among the low-landmark-potential scenes, suggesting that the ability to select useful landmarks may precede the development of accurate route knowledge. Cohen and Schuepfer (1980) also used slide presentations to simulate a configuration of hallways and found that landmarks were central to second graders' knowledge of the simulated environment, that sixth graders exhibited relatively well-formed route knowledge of the environment, but that only the adult subjects were able to successfully coordinate route knowledge into an accurate configuration. Hazen et al. (1978) gave children repeated walks through a playhouse and found that young children's spatial representations were routelike and poorly integrated in comparison with those of older children. Curtis et al. (1981) assessed children's configurational knowledge using a technique which combines distance and bearing estimates and found a significant increase in accuracy of configurational knowledge with age.

Although the results of these investigations support the proposed developmental differences in various components of the model, this research has not assessed each and all of the component processes in the same children. If the development of cognitive mapping follows the proposed sequence from landmark to route ordering and metric organization, to configurational representations, each child's performance on measures of these components should conform to one of a few, specifiable patterns, independent of the age of the child. This study attempted to assess the validity of

the hierarchical sequence of components of the proposed model by assessing first, fourth, and seventh graders' landmark, route (ordering and metric), and configurational knowledge of their school campus and determining the extent to which their individual performance patterns conformed to the patterns predicted by the Siegel and White (1975) model.

In most cognitive mapping research, children's cognitive mapping competence is inferred on the basis of some externalized product, which is, in effect, a second-order re-representation of spatial experience (Siegel, 1981). Much of this literature has involved the development of procedures to externalize for study and analysis the subject's internal representation. As pointed out by many researchers (Acredolo, 1977; Cohen & Schuepfer, 1980; Hardwick, McIntyre, & Pick, 1976; Herman & Siegel, 1978), both the scale of the space being investigated and the type of externalization procedures used to infer the spatial representation significantly affect the assessment of performance. Procedures which require the translation of large-scale space to small-scale space, such as sketch maps (Piaget, Inhelder, & Szeminska, 1960) or table-top models (Piaget et al., 1960); Siegel & Schadler, 1977) confound cognitive mapping abilities with the praxic or representational skills required by the procedures. Recently, Kirasic, Siegel, Allen, Curtis, & Furlong (Note 1) found evidence that even the use of multidimensional scaling procedures, which require only ordinal distance rankings on the part of the subjects, tends to underestimate adults' knowledge of landmarks and their interrelationships when compared to direct distance and bearing estimates.

Complicating the methodological issues involved with inferring and assessing internal representations is the apparent conflict of conventional wisdom and our own everyday observations regarding young children's spatial knowledge and their spatial competence. The results of age-group differences on cognitive mapping measures seem to indicate that young children are spatially incompetent, egocentric or lacking Euclidean concepts or even route-like knowledge (Cohen & Schuepfer, 1980; Piaget et al., 1960). Yet conventional wisdom suggests that young children are spatially competent in the sense that they are rather skilled way finders in their own neighborhoods by the age of four and can quite easily get to school and back home by the age of six. To date, no research has been conducted that assesses children's environmental way-finding competence in the same environment in which their cognitive mapping competence is formally inferred and assessed. A second major purpose of the present study was to assess spatial behavior within, and spatial knowledge of, the same large-scale environment.

A final issue in the literature centers on the role of environmental familiarity in the development of spatial representations. Since age of the subjects and experience within the environment are unavoidably confounded in the majority of naturalistic studies looking at cognitive mapping development, the relative effects of each have only been speculative (Anooshian & Young, 1981). The school campus selected for this study offered an unusual opportunity to assess cognitive mapping differences in three age groups with three unique levels of experience within sections of the campus. Therefore in the present study, it was of interest to compare the relative effects of age and degree of experience within the environment on each of the component measures of the proposed model (Siegel & White, 1975).

METHODS

Subjects

The subjects were 40 children attending a large private school in Houston, Texas: 16 first graders (mean chronological age (CA) 7;4, range 6;9–7;8), 12 fourth graders (mean CA 10;3, range 9;8–10;7), and 12 seventh graders (mean CA 13;5, range 12;9–13;10). At each grade level, the number of boys and girls tested was approximately equal.

Material and Apparatus

A 21.6 x 55.9-cm reduction of the architectural blueprint of the campus was used by the experimenter to mark the path traveled by the child and experimenter during the way-finding task. The blueprint was not visible to the child at any time.

Photographs (8.8 x 13.2 cm) of the buildings and scenes visible along each route were used to assess landmark and route knowledge. The photographs were taken from a height of 1.4 m and from the perspective of one facing forward while moving along each route in the direction specified and traveled. Additional photographs of environmental features which were located near but not along each route were used as decoys in the landmark task. All photographs were mounted on cardboard stands so they could be placed vertically on a table top in front of the child.

Configuration bearing estimates were obtained using a 36-cm black acrylic arrow mounted on a 35.5-cm (diameter) circular particle board compass, with 1° increments marked on the underside not visible to the child. Both pointer and compass were mounted on a tripod which allowed the pointer to be moved 360° about its axis. The child's bearing estimate was read from the underside of the compass with a hand-held mirror.

Configuration distance estimates were obtained with a 19 (wide) x 50 (long) x 9-cm (high) plywood box constructed with a metal lever and handle running along a center slot in the top of the box and extending its length. When moved along this 1 x 40-cm slot, the lever connected with an electrical current supplied by a detachable 6-volt lantern battery, and lighted one of a series of 20 lights (unnumbered) which were spaced approximately 1 cm apart alongside the slot. The child's distance estimate was taken to be the number of the light (from 1 to 20) at which the child positioned the lever.

Spatial Layout of the School

The campus was selected for its large size and number of buildings, which offered a variety of landmarks, routes, and bearing degrees and distances for the configuration tasks. A diagram of the physical layout of the school is presented in Fig. 1, which indicates the positions of landmarks, routes, sighting locations, and targets. The school was divided into two approximately equal sides by a major urban thoroughfare. School traffic flowed from one side to the other via a tunnel which ran under this street. Because of this arrangement, each task was constructed to contain elements from each side in roughly equal proportions. For example, the routes used for the way-finding, landmark, and route tasks included one route contained entirely within each side and one route which included parts of both sides and the tunnel crossing. Four sighting locations (SLs) were chosen with two in each of the north and south sides of campus. There were six targets (Ts), three on each side of the campus. Each of the targets were features along the routes in the other tasks but were not visible from any of the four SLs.

Of particular importance was the degree of experience each grade level had within the environment at the time of testing. All children had at least limited experience within both the north and south sides of the campus: Each grade attended gym and assemblies on the south side and all went to lunch and chapel on the north side of campus. However, the extent of their activities, and thus their experience, varied by grade according to which side of the campus contained their classrooms and major activities. The first graders' classrooms and all other activities except those noted above were located within the south side during the entire academic year; the seventh graders were located in the north side during the entire year; and the fourth graders were located within the north side during the fall term and within the south side in new classrooms during the spring term (at the end of which data were collected).

Procedure

Way finding. Each child was tested individually and testing began at the same point for each child (see Fig. 1). From that position, the child was told "I want you to take me to "x" the quickest or shortest way that you know how to go. I'll be walking a little behind you so that you can be the guide." This walk formed the first of three routes; from that endpoint the instructions were repeated for the next two routes. The routes were novel to the child in the sense that the children did not typically take these routes during their school day activities. The child was instructed that if s/he thought there were several ways to reach the destination, take what s/he thought was the most direct way. The mean length of the three routes was 171.5 m; (Route 1 = 131.2 m, Route 2 = 229.7 m, and Route 3 = 153.6 m). Each child received the way-finding task first. Following this, (a) the landmark and two route tasks which were administered indoors, and (b) the configuration tasks which were administered out of doors, were counterbalanced by grade.

Landmark Each child was seated at a large table in the testing room and shown eight photographs for each of the routes traveled in the way-finding task. The order of the routes presented was randomly determined. For each route there were five photographs depicting buildings and scenes visible along that route and three decoy photographs of buildings and scenes near the route but not directly visible from any point along the route. All eight photographs were presented simultaneously in a random spatial arrangement in front of the child and s/he was told "Here are some pictures of buildings and scenes on your campus. I want you to pick out the ones you would see if you

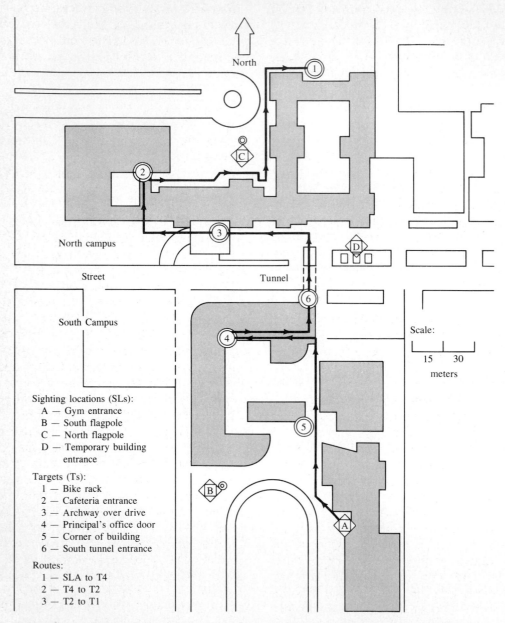

North

C

North campus

Street   Tunnel

South Campus

Scale:
15   30
meters

Sighting locations (SLs):
A — Gym entrance
B — South flagpole
C — North flagpole
D — Temporary building
        entrance

Targets (Ts):
1 — Bike rack
2 — Cafeteria entrance
3 — Archway over drive
4 — Principal's office door
5 — Corner of building
6 — South tunnel entrance

Routes:
1 — SLA to T4
2 — T4 to T2
3 — T2 to T1

FIGURE 1   Modified reduction of campus blueprint illustrating the three walks/routes used in
the way finding landmark, and route tasks, and the four sighting locations and six targets used in
the configuration tasks.

were walking from "x' to "y." If there are any pictures of things which you think you wouldn't see on this walk, put them over here" (indicating). These instructions were repeated for each of the two remaining routes.

Route Ordering The experimenter placed the five photographs of the landmarks which correctly belonged to a particular route (with the order of the route presentation again randomly determined) before the child. The child was asked to correctly order the photographs: "Here are the pictures of the buildings and things you would actually see if you were walking from "x" to "y." Now I want you to put these pictures in the order in which you would see them on this walk." The directions were repeated for the remaining two routes.

Route Scaling After the child had ordered each route to his/her satisfaction, the experimenter removed the photographs and placed them in front of the child in their correct order, one route at a time. Also placed on the table at this time was a 3.8 (wide) x 81.3-cm (long) strip of paper running the length of the table so that one end was directly in front of the child and the other end at the side opposite the child. The child was then told that the photographs were now in the correct order for that route, going from "x" to "y" and was asked to line them up along the strip of paper, one behind the other, according to their real-world distances: "I want you to put each of these pictures on this strip of paper as far apart as they would be if you were really small and were actually walking along this strip of paper. If you would walk just a little ways between the building in this picture (pointing to one of the photographs) and this building (indicating the next one), you would put this picture just behind this first one. But if you would walk a long ways between the scenes in these two pictures, you would place them further apart." The end of the strip of paper closest to the child was designated as starting

point "x" of the route. Occasionally, the instructions were repeated with modifications if the child indicated that s/he did not understand the task. This was necessary only with a few of the younger children.

Configuration *Familiarization* with the targets used in the configuration tasks occurred during the way-finding task. As the child walked the experimenter from place to place within the campus, the experimenter pointed out the targets, saying, "Later I am going to ask you where the (T) is. I will be thinking of this/these (T) right here." The experimenter touched the spot, making sure the child was paying attention, and gave a verbal label and description of the spot, for example, "this door right here to the principal's office."

Pretraining was given at the first sighting location (the order of SLs was randomly determined). For each SL, two pretraining targets had been selected, one of which was visible and one which was not. The child was instructed first to point the arrow on the tripod directly to where the visible target was and second to the occluded practice target. Additional instructions and practice were given if the child's response was grossly inaccurate on either target. This was only necessary for a few children. Next the child was given practice with the distance estimation apparatus. S/he was told that pushing the lever to the first light indicated that two objects were very close to each other, as close as s/he and the experimenter were when the experimenter was standing "here" (one yard away), and that pushing the lever all the way to the end light indicated that the two objects were as far apart as the two furthest objects (designated) on campus were apart. The experimenter then gave the child distance estimate practice using the same two practice targets, making sure that the child understood that his or her estimates were based on straight-line or crow-fly distances and not actual walking distances. Testing began when the experimenter was satisfied that the child understood both tasks, usually requiring less than 5 min.

Testing   Each child was randomly assigned to one of eight orders of the four SLs. (Due to time and distance constraints, two SLs on one side were always visited before crossing to the other side of campus and the remaining two SLs, reducing the possible order of SLs from 24 to 8.) Targets were specified randomly for each child at each SL. For each target, the child was asked to point the arrow (set at due north) to where s/he thought the target was and to move the lever to the light that indicated how far away the target was from where s/he was standing. For each child the bearing estimate was recorded in degrees (from north) and the distance estimate recorded as the number of the light adjacent to the final position of the lever. A typical experimental session took approximately 50 min.

Dependent Measures

1 *Way-finding task*. The average deviation in meters between the three routes walked and the correct routes were computed for each child. Since the instructions were to take the most direct route, negative deviations, that is, shortcuts from the sidewalk paths, were not counted as errors. Errors were computed if a wrong direction was taken (even if self-corrected) or when a less-than-direct route was taken.

2. *Landmark task*. Accuracy of landmark selection was computed for each route as the percentage of correct identifications of landmarks and decoys for that route. The average percentage of correct responses for the three routes was also computed.

3. *Route-ordering task*. The degree of agreement between the child's ordering of photographs of each route and the correct order for that route was determined by a nonparametric

correlation, Kendall's tau. A mean score was also obtained for the three routes for each child.

4. *Route-scaling task*. The accuracy of subjects' placement of photographs relative to their real-world distance was computed as the log of the ratio of estimated to actual distance and averaged across landmarks for each route. This measure has been used successfully by other researchers (Cohen, Baldwin, & Sherman, 1978) to accomplish two purposes: first, the ratio allows for the comparison of intervals of different distances, and second, the log score places over- and underestimates on the same scale. A mean score was also computed for each route.

5. *Configuration*.   (a) *Bearing   estimates*. The accuracy of bearing estimates was computed as the absolute deviation (in degrees) between the estimated and the actual bearing for each of the six targets from each of the four SLs made by each child. Mean deviations were computed for SL–target locations and a grand mean was also obtained.

(b) *Distance estimates*. Nonparametric correlations (Spearman's rho) were computed between each child's estimated distance and the actual straight-line distances.

RESULTS

Analyses of variance were performed on the dependent measures to assess the relative effects of grade and familiarity. Preliminary analyses revealed that there were no significant effects for sex, task order, or order of SLs on any measure. These were thus eliminated as variables in subsequent analyses.

The effects of grade and familiarity on performance on all dependent measures except way finding and configuration distance were assessed.

Three analyses are of interest: (1) performance on the way-finding task; (2) analyses assessing grade and familiarity differences on the landmark, route ordering and scaling, and configuration tasks; and (3) Guttman scale analysis of the individual subjects' performance patterns on each of the component measures.

Way-Finding Performance

Virtually all children at all grade levels performed without error on the way-finding task. Fourth and seventh graders performed perfectly. Only three of the 16 first graders' performance was less than perfect. Thus any differences in the cognitive mapping component measures cannot be attributed to grade related differences in way-finding skills. All children in this study were competent way finders.

Landmark Task Performance

Analysis of the mean percentage of correct identifications revealed that accuracy increased significantly with grade level. Each group performed quite accurately, with first graders on the average correctly identifying seven of eight photographs, and fourth and seventh graders responding nearly perfectly.

Visual inspection of a scatterplot of errors made on each photograph by each grade level revealed that not all photographs were equally well identified as landmarks or as decoys. In particular, one decoy photograph on Route 1 was incorrectly selected by almost half of the first graders (44%) and, in comparison, by only 8% of the older two groups. This photograph depicted the playground area in which the younger group frequently played. During the task, many of these children were overheard saying "if you stuck your neck out real far, or looked around the corner, you would see this." In actuality, the scene was about 7 m away and not visible at any point along the route. While children appeared to understand the instructions to only include those scenes *directly* visible from the route, their previous experiences within the environment may have been more powerful in some instances than the immediate task instructions, especially in the case of the younger grade level. Similar errors occurred

for photographs along other routes but to a lesser extent.

Route-Order Task Performance

While each grade performed quite accurately, accuracy significantly increased with grade level. The fourth and seventh graders again made nearly perfect responses and first graders were also quite accurate in their responses.

Route-Scaling Task Performance

Analyses of the route-scaling scores yielded a different pattern of results. There was no significant main effect for grade level on performance. However there was a significant main effect of route location as well as a significant interaction of grade and location. These results are displayed in Fig. 2. Route 1, which was located entirely within the south side of campus and was relatively unfamiliar to the oldest group, revealed a significant *negative* linear relationship between grade level and accuracy. Seventh graders made less accurate estimates (.32) than either fourth (.21) or first graders (.22). There was no significant grade effect for Route 2, which encompassed both sides of the campus. For Route 3, there was a significant positive linear trend with accuracy increasing by grade level. Seventh graders were more accurate (.24) than fourth (.29) and first graders (.32), when route metric estimates were made within the side of campus in which they had extensive experience, in which fourth graders had previous experience, and in which first graders had only limited experience.

Configuration-Bearing Task Performance

In addition to overall grade related differences, there were two questions of interest regarding performance on the configuration-bearing task: (1) whether there were differences between sightings made entirely within either side of the campus versus those made across the street "barrier" from one side of campus to the other (see Kosslyn, Pick, & Fariello, 1974); and (2) whether degree of experience within the two

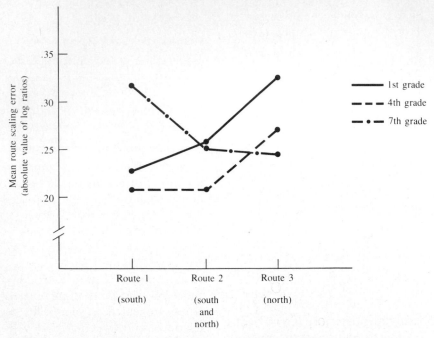

FIGURE 2   Mean route-scaling scores (log ratios) as a function of grade and route location.

sides of the campus affected performance. Deviation scores (in degrees) of estimated bearing from actual bearing from each SL to each target were thus grouped into four mean categories: south SLs to south targets (S—s), north SLs to north targets (N—n), south SLs to north targets (S—n), and north SLs to south targets (N—s). Each of the four means included was based on six bearing estimates.

Analysis of variance on these four measures revealed a significant main effect for grade, but more importantly, also a significant interaction of grade and SL-target location. There was no significant main effect of location. These results are presented in Fig. 3.

Analyses were performed on each of the four SL-target conditions to assess grade differences at each location. When bearing estimates were made entirely within the south side of campus (S—s), accuracy increased significantly with grade level. In spite of the fact that seventh

graders had only limited experience within that area, their estimates were more accurate ($\bar{X}$ = 16.6°) than either fourth ($\bar{X}$ = 19.3°) or first grade estimates ($\bar{X}$ = 29.1°). When estimates were made entirely within the north side of campus (N—n), accuracy was positively but not significantly related to grade level. Seventh ($\bar{X}$ = 15.9°) and fourth graders ($\bar{X}$ = 15.1°) performed only slightly differently and first graders made an average 28.5° bearing estimate error.

In contrast to the two within-campus SL—target location categories where positive linear relationships were found between grade and accuracy, analyses of deviation scores in the two cross-campus conditions revealed a different pattern of results. In the S—n condition, the accuracy of estimates from south SLs to north targets also were positively but not significantly related to grade level, with seventh, fourth, and first graders averaging deviations of 20, 25, and 28°, respectively. Seventh graders ($\bar{X}$ = 22°)

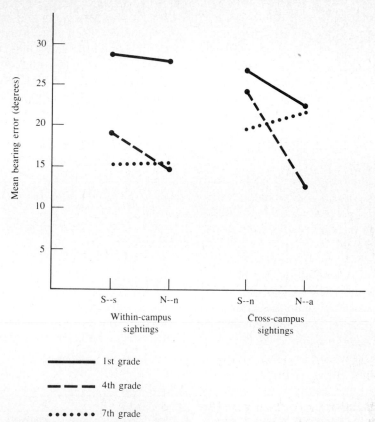

FIGURE 3 Mean deviations of bearing estimates as a function of grade and sighting location—target positions.

averaged nearly the same amount of error in their estimates as did first graders ($\bar{X}$ = 23°), when estimates were made from the more to the less familiar side of campus, while fourth graders made an average 13° error in bearing estimates in this condition.

Configuration-Distance Task Performance

The test on the configuration-distance task performance indicated a significant increase as a function of age, with seventh (.71) and fourth (.72) graders' scores again nearly equal and more accurate than first graders' scores (.59).

Guttman Scale Analysis

Guttman scale analysis was performed on the mean scores of each component measure to assess the degree to which individual performance patterns conformed to the patterns predicted by the proposed model (Siegel & White, 1975). Guttman scale analysis is a statistical procedure that seems uniquely suited for assessing the basic claim of the model: that the components in the development of cognitive mapping are attained in a cumulative unidirectional manner. Specifically, the scale analysis assesses the extent to which the components form a hierarchical set by determining how well each individual's performance on each measure of the model's components agrees with the perfect unidirectional, cumulative pattern predicted by the model. In this pattern, the measures of components proposed to develop later (e.g., configurational knowledge) should not be performed successfully (i.e., above a criterion-level of accuracy) unless measures of developmentally earlier components (e.g., landmark and route knowledge) were also above criterion levels. Each deviation from the expected pattern is counted as an error and standardized coefficients of reproducibility and scalability are statistically derived from the accumulation of errors (Goodenough, 1944).

Criterion levels for assigning subjects' performances on way finding, landmark, route order, route scaling, and configuration to either passing or failing were established on the basis of accuracy percentages.

Results of the Guttman scale analysis revealed the observed performance patterns for all subjects presented in Table 1. Each component measure is given with order of difficulty ascending from left to right. Under each component task is the number of subjects passing or failing that item. Any task which should have been passed or failed by an individual given performance on all other items is noted under the error column for that task. Each error appears twice: first under the column of the failed easier item (the developmentally earlier task), and again under the corresponding more difficult item (the developmentally later task), given in parentheses. Thirty-seven of the forty children's response patterns conformed to the pattern predicted by the model. That is, 93% of the subjects tested performed in the manner predicted. The strength of this prediction is indicated by a very high coefficient of reproducibility (.97), measuring the extent to which a subject's score is a predictor of one's response pattern. (A coefficient of reproducibility higher than .90 is generally considered to indicate a valid scale.) The coefficient of scalability (.79) assesses the extent to which the scale is truly unidirectional and cumulative, and generally should be .60 or greater (Anderson, 1966). Also given in the table is the number and percentage of subjects who passed or failed each item. No children failed or passed only the way-finding task, two children

passed only the way-finding and landmark tasks, 14 children passed only those tasks up to and including the route-order task, 16 children passed those tasks preceding and including the route-metric task, and five children passed all tasks. Three children's performance patterns did not fit the proposed sequence: two failed the landmark task yet passed the route-order task, and one failed the landmark task yet passed both route tasks. It should be noted that way-finding was not originally included as a component in the Siegel and White model (1975), but was included in this analysis as a means of testing our hypothesis regarding way finding and representational competence.

DISCUSSION

Nearly all children in this study performed perfectly on the way-finding task. That is, almost every child at each grade level exhibited rather sophisticated spatial knowledge by navigating novel and efficient routes within their environment. Yet, performance on the other cognitive mapping tasks varied significantly with grade level and, in some cases, with degree of familiarity with the environment. Few children's performances on these tasks could be characterized as perfect. This pattern of results supports the conventional wisdom regarding children's ability to navigate successfully within their environments and also confirms previous findings that older children are more skilled in cognitive mapping than younger ones. The difference in performance found between a measure of spatial knowledge in action (way finding) and the measures of spatial representational knowledge also support the notion of a competence-load tradeoff (Siegel, 1981; White & Siegel, 1976). It has become increasingly apparent in a variety of developmental studies that variations in the nature of assessment and experimental procedure result in variations in subjects' performance. In particular, variations which introduce load factors, (e.g., representa-

TABLE 1   RESULTS OF GUTTMAN SCALE ANALYSIS

Component measure	1 Way finding		2 Landmark		3 Route order		4 Route scaling		5 Configuration		Total
	Fail	Pass	Fail	Pass	Fail	Pass	Fail	Pass	Fail	Pass	
5	Error 0	5	Error 0	5	Error 0	5	Error 0	5	Error 0	Error 5	5
4	0	16	0	16	0	16	0	Error 16	16	0	16
3	0	14	0	14	0	Error 14	14	0	14	0	14
2	0	5	3	Error 2	3	(2)	4	(1)	5	0	5
1	0	0	0	0	0	0	0	0	0	0	0
Sums	0	40	3	37	3	37	18	22	35	5	40
Percent	0	100	8	93	3	93	45	55	88	13	
Errors	0	0	0	3	0	(2)	0	(1)	0	0	6

Note: Coefficient of reproducibility = .97; coefficient of scalability = .79.

tional demands), "noise," confusion regarding instructions, or the presentation of novel or unusual tasks, appear to decrease cognitive performance. These variations are particularly problematic for investigations which attempt to equate cognitive performance with some underlying cognitive competence (e.g., cognitive maps). In the present study, although most children appeared to understand task instructions after their first presentation, the number, novelty, and memory requirements of the experimental tasks suggest the presence of numerous load factors. That even the younger subjects were able to remember target locations from the way-finding task to the later configuration task reinforces the picture of competence presented by their way-finding performance. The present findings indicate the importance of increased sensitivity to load factors in future research.

The results of the Guttman scale analysis provide strong support for the developmental sequence of cognitive mapping proposed by Siegel and White (1975). Scale analysis indicated that performance patterns on the four component measures of 37 of the 40 children tested were consistent with the hierarchical pattern specified by the model. Thus, almost every child's performance, regardless of grade level, reached a criterion level of accuracy on each component measure in the manner predicted, from landmark to route order to route scaling to configuration. Further support of the developmental model was found in grade level differences on the cognitive mapping measures. These results are consistent with previous research findings which indicate that accuracy increases as a function of age. Seventh and fourth graders were consistently more accurate than first graders on measures of landmark and route-order knowledge, and in most conditions of the route scaling and configuration measures. Reversals in this developmental sequence occurred in the route-scaling and configuration-bearing

measures where performance differences appeared to be a function of degree of familiarity with the environment. An editorial reviewer has pointed out that results of the scalogram analysis may appear unlikely given the effects of familiarity upon performance and the resulting lack of consistent grade level differences on measures of route-metric and configuration-bearing knowledge. That these results indicate criterion levels of accuracy for 93% of each individual's mean performance on each task suggests that familiarity, as well as grade level, affected performance on each task in a rather consistent manner.

Familiarity and grade level interacted to predict performance on the route-scaling task. The expected relationship between grade level and accuracy was found only for the route within the side of campus experienced extensively throughout the year by seventh graders, previously by fourth graders, and limitedly by first graders. Yet, when seventh graders were asked to make metric judgments of a route within the side of campus within which they had only limited experience, their judgments were less accurate than the judgments of either the fourth or the first graders, who had more extensive experience within that area. Familiarity also influenced the accuracy of bearing estimates made from one side of campus to the other. For each group tested, accuracy appeared to be greater when estimates were made from the less familiar side of campus to targets within the more familiar side of campus.

These results are consistent with the findings of other researchers (Herman & Siegel, 1978; Allen et al., 1979) who found that a certain level of experience within the environment is necessary to construct an accurate representation of its features. The results are also consistent with the proposal that older children and adults with minimal experience within an area are able to construct configuration-like clusters of that environment before they are able to integrate all of its features into a total configuration (Hardwick et al., 1976; Siegel & White, 1975). If the development of these clusters precedes the development of configurations, it would be expected that both fourth and seventh graders, who had less than extensive (or recent) experience within one side of campus, would be able to make accurate bearing estimates within the less familiar side or from the less familiar to the more familiar side. They should not be able to make accurate estimates of the less familiar features when doing so required the integration of those features with the larger environment. Fourth graders in particular showed a large difference in accuracy between S—n and N—s estimates. It is not clear from this data, however, whether this is attributable to grade level or to their relocation from one side of the campus to the other prior to the time of testing. The apparent lack of effect of familiarity on performance of landmark and route-order tasks, and the high levels of accuracy achieved by each grade level on these tasks, suggest that even limited experience was sufficient for the acquisition of these types of representations.

This study represented an initial investigation of individual children's patterns of performance on measures of cognitive mapping components. Previous research has well documented the existence of developmental differences on cognitive mapping components between groups of children, but the present results warrant further research on within subject differences. The results of the scalogram present evidence that at one point in time nearly all children tested exhibited the predicted pattern of performance. This study did not assess the developmental sequence in each child across different time periods, that is, it was not longitudinal. The present study also attempted an exploratory analysis of the relationship between age and familiarity in a natural environment, and the results indicate the need for further investigation of this relationship. Previous research has typically confounded age and

familiarity (Curtis et al., 1981) or has tended to minimize the effect of familiarity (Annoshian & Young, 1981). The present findings indicate the type and extent of experience the individual has within the environment, for example, whether it is long term or short term, extensive or limited, previous or recent, significantly affects the accuracy of at least route and configuration knowledge and that these effects may differ developmentally. Cognitive maps exist as dynamic, functional representations of the individual's environment and, as such, reflect and differ according to the needs and agenda of the individual. Further developmental studies are needed which will address such individual differences as the extent and nature of the individual's experiences within the environment, as well as developmental differences in cognitive mapping of large-scale environments.

REFERENCES

Acredolo, L. P. Developmental changes in the ability to coordinate perspectives of a large-scale space. *Developmental Psychology,* 1977, **13**, 1–8.

Allen, G. L., Kirasic, K. C., Siegel, A. W., & Herman, J. F. Developmental issues in cognitive mapping: The selection and utilization of environmental landmarks. *Child Development,* 1979, **50**, 1062–1070.

Anderson, R. E. A computer program for Guttman scaling with the Goodenough technique. *Behavioral Science,* 1966, **11**, 235.

Anooshian, L. J., & Young, D. Developmental changes in cognitive maps of a familiar neighborhood. *Child Development,* 1981, **52**, 341–348.

Carr, S., & Schissler, D. The city as a trip: Perceptual selection and memory in the view from the road. *Environment and Behavior,* 1969, **1**, 7–36.

Cohen, R., Baldwin, L. M., & Sherman, R. C. Cognitive maps of a naturalistic setting. *Child Development,* 1978, **49**, 1216–1218.

Cohen, R., & Schuepfer, T. The representation of landmarks and routes. *Child Development,* 1980, **51**, 1065–1071.

Curtis, L. E., Siegel, A. W., & Furlong, N. E. Developmental differences in cognitive mapping: Configurational knowledge of familiar large-scale environments. *Journal of Experimental Child Psychology*, 1981, **31**, 456–469.

Goodenough, W. H. A technique for scale analysis. *Educational and Psychological Measurement*, 1944, 179–190.

Hale, G. A. On use of ANOVA in developmental research. *Child Development*, 1977, **48**, 1101–1106.

Hardwick, D. A., McIntyre, C. W., & Pick, H. L. The content and manipulation of cognitive maps in children and adults. *Monographs for the Society for Research in Child Development*, 1976, **41** (3, Serial No. 166).

Hazen, N. L., Lockman, J. J., & Pick, H. L. The development of children's representations of large-scale environments. *Child Development*, 1978, **49**, 623–636.

Herman, J. F., & Siegel, A. W. The development of cognitive mapping of the large-scale environment. *Journal of Experimental Child Psychology*, 1978, **26**, 389–401.

Kosslyn, S. M., Pick, H. L., & Fariello, G. R. Cognitive maps in children and men. *Child Development*, 1974, **45**, 707–716.

Lynch, K. *The image of the city*. Cambridge, Mass.: M.I.T. Press, 1960.

McCall, R. B., & Appelbaum, M. I. Bias in the analysis of repeated measures designs: Some alternative approaches. *Child Development*, 1973, **44**, 401–415.

Piaget, J., Inhelder, B., & Szeminska, A. *The child's conception of geometry*. New York: Basic Books, 1960.

Siegel, A. W. The externalization of cognitive maps by children and adults: In search of ways to ask better questions. In L. S. Liben, A. Patterson, & N. Newcombe (Eds.). *Spatial representation and behavior across the life span: Theory and application*. New York: Academic Press, 1981.

Siegel, A. W., & Schadler, M. Young children's cognitive maps of their classroom. *Child Development*, 1977, **48**, 388–394.

Siegel, A. W., & White, S. H. The development of spatial representations of large-scale environments. In H. W. Reese (Ed.), *Advances in child development and behavior* (Vol. 10). New York: Academic Press, 1975.

White, S. H. Cognitive competence and performance in everyday environments. *Bulletin of the Orton Society*, 1980, **30**, 29–45.

White, S. H., & Siegel, A. W. Cognitive development: The new inquiry. *Young Children*, 1976, **31**, 425–435.

REFERENCE NOTE

1 Kirasic, K. C., Siegel, A. W., Allen, G. L., Curtis, L. E., & Furlong, N. E. Externalizing maps of large-scale space. *Environment and Behavior*, in press.

READING 27

Physiological, Motivational, and Cognitive Effects of Aircraft Noise on Children

Sheldon Cohen
Gary W. Evans
David S. Krantz
Daniel Stokols

Science's contribution to social policy decisions regarding noise pollution has been primarily limited to the documentation of the impact of high-intensity sound on hearing. Acceptable noise standards used in both national and local statutes are based on research that assesses magnitude of hearing loss at varying intensities and durations of sound. Yet during the last ten years it has become clear that noise can alter nonauditory systems as well as auditory ones. Thus laboratory research has established effects of noise on cognitive, motivational, and general physiological processes. For example, noise is associated with alterations in task performance (cf. Broadbent, 1978; Loeb, 1979), decreased sensitivity to others (e.g., S. Cohen & Lezak, 1977; Mathews & Canon, 1975), and elevation of a number of nonspecific physiological responses (cf. Glass, & Singer, 1972; Kryter, 1970). Exposure to noise that is unpredictable and uncontrollable (cannot be escaped or avoided) can also reduce one's perception of control over the environment (e.g., Glass & Singer, 1972; Krantz, Glass, & Snyder, 1974). This loss of control is often accompanied by a depression of mood and a decrease in one's motivation to initiate new responses (Seligman, 1975).

One argument against serious consideration of this evidence when making policy decisions is that it is largely derived from laboratory studies. (Since laboratory subjects typically experience a single short period of exposure to high-intensity sound and are aware that their exposure is only temporary, the applicability of these findings to experiences of chronic noise exposure is questionable. Because of a lack of well-controlled studies of persons routinely living and working under noise, we are unable to say with any certainty if similar effects occur in individuals exposed to noise for prolonged periods.

Our own lack of confidence in the generality of the effects of noise that occurs in laboratory settings translates into a lack of influence in the policy-making process. Legislation restricting noise levels in industrial and community settings usually imposes a heavy economic burden on those responsible for the noise. To convince policymakers that such burdens are justified, there must be substantive evidence that community and/or industrial noise deleteriously affects health and behavior.

Naturalistic studies of the effects of noise that occurs in home, school, or office seem like the obvious alternative to investigations carried out in laboratory settings. However, such stud-ies are correlational. Subjects are not randomly assigned to noisy or quiet settings, and the settings often vary on dimensions other than noise exposure. These problems can be substantially reduced by carefully matching the noise and quiet samples on important dimensions and by statistically controlling for other possible confounds. It is always possible, however, that some unknown factor covaries with exposure to the noise setting and actually causes the effects that the investigator associates with noise. Thus, in isolation, naturalistic studies also provide insufficient evidence for a link between community noise and measures of health and behavior.

It is clear that neither laboratory nor naturalistic studies can in themselves provide what either scientists or politicians would consider convincing evidence for noise-induced effects. What is necessary is an interplay between laboratory and field methodologies. This interplay can take at least two forms. On the one hand, an effect can first be established as reliable within laboratory settings where causal links can be inferred. Then, the robustness of this relationship can be established in a number of naturalistic settings. On the other hand, by first conducting field research, it is possible to isolate important dimensions of a particular problem. At that point, laboratory studies may be useful to rule out plausible alternate explanations often inherent in naturalistic research. Laboratory and field approaches are often pursued to the exclusion of one another, but only by combining these two strategies can we begin to understand the impact of environmental variables in naturalistic settings. Moreover, only when evidence from the laboratory and field converges can a credible scientific case be presented in order to influence public policy.

This emphasis on the interplay between the laboratory and the field is consistent with Campbell and Stanley's (1966) discussion of the inevitable trade-off between well-controlled experimental settings (internal validity) and our ability to generalize across persons and settings (external validity). The laboratory provides the opportunity for an internally valid investigation, but the generality of laboratory findings is severely restricted. [Naturalistic studies provide the opportunity to generalize findings to a greater range of persons and settings but often lack the strict control of the laboratory.]

The study presented in this article examines the effects of aircraft noise on children. It is particularly concerned with exploring the generality of laboratory work on noise-induced shifts in attentional strategies, feelings of personal control, and nonauditory physiological responses related to health. Our purpose in reporting this study is twofold. First, it is presented as evidence for relationships (or lack of relationships) between aircraft noise exposure and a number of cognitive, motivational, and physiological measures. The article includes short discussions of laboratory and field research in each of the areas of concern. Second, it is presented as an example of an attempt to examine the generality of laboratory effects in a naturalistic setting. In this regard, the study employs an individual testing procedure in a field setting. It uses a matched-group design and attempts to control statistically for a number of possible alternative explanations for correlations between community noise and the various criterion variables.

OVERVIEW OF THE STUDY

The subjects were children attending the four noisiest elementary schools in the air corridor of Los Angeles International Airport. Peak sound level readings in these schools are as high as 95 dB (A), and the schools are located in an air corridor that has over 300 overflights a day—approximately one flight every 2.5 minutes during school hours (Lane & Meecham, 1974). Three control schools (quiet schools) were matched with the experimental schools for grade level, for ethnic and racial distribution of

children, for percentage of children whose families were receiving assistance under the Aid to Families with Dependent Children program, and for the occupations and education levels of parents. Thus we were able to compare samples of children attending noise schools and quiet schools who were relatively similar in terms of age, social class, and race. A statistical technique described later allowed additional control over these factors.

The study focused on effects occurring outside of noise exposure (i.e., aftereffects). Thus all tasks and questionnaires (except the achievement test records gathered from school files) were administered in a quiet setting—a noise-insulated trailer parked directly outside the school. These data were collected during two 45-minute sessions on consecutive days. Three cognitive tasks were administered during the test periods. One was designed to assess feelings of personal control and the others to determine whether the children employed some common attentional coping strategies. A questionnaire concerned with responses to noise and two blood pressure measures were also given during the testing sessions. A parent questionnaire dealing with parent response to noise, mother's and father's level of education, and the number of children in the family was sent home with each child. Scores on standardized reading and math tests and data on absenteeism were collected from school files.

The study included children from all noise-impacted third-and fourth-grade classrooms in each noise school as well as children from an equal number of classrooms in quiet schools. To ensure that performance differences between children from noise schools and those from quiet schools could not be attributed to noise-induced losses in hearing sensitivity, an audiometric pure-tone threshold screening was administered to each child. Children were screened at 25 dB for select speech frequencies (500, 1000, 2000, and 4000 Hz). Children failing to detect 25 dB tones at any one of these frequencies in either ear were not included in the study. Six percent of the noise-school children and 7 percent of the quiet-school children failed the screening. A total of 262 subjects (142 from noise schools and 120 from quiet schools) remained in the study. Individual analyses, however, sometimes contain fewer subjects because of missing data.

Data compiled from the parent questionnaire allowed us to determine the degree of similarity of the prematched noise and quiet samples. Analyses of variance indicated that there were no differences between the samples on the various social class factors. The mean number of children per family was 3.54 in the noise sample and 3.88 in the quiet sample. Levels of parent education were also equivalent, falling between some high school (scaled as 3) and high school graduate (scaled as 4). The mean level of education for fathers was 3.75 for noise-school children and 3.41 for quiet-school children, and for mothers, 3.64 and 3.35, respectively. The racial distributions, however, differed significantly with the noise group containing more blacks (32% vs 18%) and the quiet group more Chicanos (50% vs. 33%). Noise and quiet samples had nearly equal percentages of whites (32% and 29%, respectively) and of unidentifiable or mixed-race children (3% in each sample).

The two samples also differed on mobility, with children in the quiet sample having lived in their homes longer (a mean of 49.6 months vs. 41.4 months) and attended their schools for longer periods (a mean of 43.2 months vs. 36.0 months) than noise children. Length of school enrollment was not related to father's education, mother's education, or the number of children in the family. Moreover, the noise and quiet samples were relatively equal on these various social class factors across all durations of exposure. This finding suggests that the decision to continue living in the noise-impacted area was not determined by the parents' socioeconomic status. There were, how-ever, more blacks and whites in the noise group with less than 2 years' exposure than there were in the equivalent quiet group. There were no differences in racial distribution for other exposure durations.

STATISTICAL CONTROLS

A regression technique was used to compensate for differences between the noise and quiet samples on racial distribution and mobility (J. Cohen, 1968). In general, the regression analysis allows one to determine the relation between two variables while controlling (covarying or partialing out) for one or more other variables. For example, one can look at the relation between noise level and blood pressure after functionally equating the noise and quiet groups on mobility and race. All data analyses reported in this article include controls for the number of children in the child's family, the grade in school, the number of months enrolled in school (years in residence for the parent questionnaire), and race. These control factors were forced into the regression first, followed by noise and then the Noise x Months Enrolled in School interaction. The interaction indicates whether length of exposure affected the various criterion measures. Additional controls were used in the analyses of blood pressure, school achievement, and selective inattention. The use of these controls is described in appropriate sections. This conservative analysis looks at the effects of noise and the interaction between noise and length of enrollment after functionally equating the noise and quiet groups on grade, race, social class, and mobility, as well as on any additional control factors employed in a particular analysis. The various measures were analyzed in predetermined multivariate clusters created on the basis of theoretical consideration. This form of analysis helps to decrease the high probability of chance findings that occur when a large number of analyses are necessary (cf. Bock, 1975).

NOISE MEASURES

Interior sound levels (without children) were measured inside each classroom with Tracoustics (SLM S2A) sound level meters. Sound levels were monitored for a 1-hour period in the morning and a 1-hour period in the afternoon. Peak sound levels in terms of dB (A) were recorded for both morning and afternoon sessions. The overall mean peak for classrooms in noise schools was 74 dB and in quiet schools 56 dB. The highest reading in a noise-school classroom was 95 dB, while the highest reading in a quiet school was 68 dB.

The questionnaire administered to each child assessed his or her perception of classroom and home noise levels. The parent questionnaire also included questions on perception of home noise level as well as queries on how long the child had been enrolled in the present school and how long he or she had lived at their present address. Data on school enrollment were also available from school files. Noise contours (compiled by the Los Angeles International Airport) provided approximations of the sound levels outside the homes of noise-school children.

Children in noise schools reported that their classrooms were noisier and that airplanes bothered them more in the classroom than children in quiet schools did. They did not, however, report having more trouble hearing their teacher.

In regard to home noise, children from air-corridor schools were more bothered by airplane noise than their quiet-school counterparts were. However, noise-and quiet-school children did not differ in ratings of home noise.

Parents of children from the air-corridor schools indicated both that there were higher levels of noise in the home and that they were bothered more by noise than the parents of children attending quiet schools indicated. The home noise level reported by the parents of noise-school children increased with the number of years they had lived in their present residence.

EFFECTS OF NOISE

Physiological Response and Health

Aside from temporary and permanent effects on hearing, previous research provides little convincing evidence for noise-induced physical disease (cf. S. Cohen, Glass, & Phillips, 1979; Kryter, 1970). It is well established, however, that short-term exposure to relatively high sound levels in laboratory settings can alter physiological processes. Physiological changes produced by noise consist of nonspecific responses typically associated with stress reactions, including increases in electrodermal activity, catecholamine secretions, vasoconstriction of peripheral blood vessels, and diastolic and systolic blood pressure. Because such changes, if extreme, are often considered potentially hazardous to health, many feel that pathogenic effects of prolonged noise exposure are likely. Laboratory evidence that some components of the physiological response to noise do not habituate (Jansen, 1969) lends fuel to this argument, but is difficult to interpret in light of evidence from other laboratories indicating complete habituation (Glass & Singer, 1972).

A number of studies of workers in noisy industries have indicated health problems for those exposed to intense noise levels. Included are respiratory problems, such as sore throat, and allergenic, musculoskeletal, circulatory, neurological, cardiovascular, and digestive disorders (e.g., Anticaglia & Cohen, 1974; A. Cohen, 1973). However, all of the industrial noise studies are subject to serious criticism because of their failure to control for other adverse workplace or job factors, for example, task demands and risks, that often covary with the noisiness of the job (cf. S. Cohen et al., 1979; Kryter, 1970). It is also important to note that several industrial surveys have failed to find a relation between noise and ill health (e.g., Finkle & Poppen, 1948; Glorig, 1971).

There are no existing controlled studies on the impact of noise on nonauditory health in children (Mills, 1975). Recent theoretical work, however, argues that children (along with the old, individuals in institutions, and persons suffering from other sources of stress) may be particularly susceptible to noise-induced illness because they lack the ability to temporarily escape their noisy environments (S. Cohen et al., 1979). It is suggested that this inability to escape at will can cause both an increase in overall duration of noise exposure and an increase in feelings of helplessness. This effect is important, since feelings of helplessness have been implicated as possible causal factors in illness (Seligman, 1975).

Each child's resting blood pressure (systolic and diastolic) was taken on an SR-2 Physiometrics automated blood pressure recorder. To accustom the children to the blood pressure measurement technique, an initial measurement was made at the beginning of the first day of testing. A short explanation of the technique and the concept of blood pressure was given at this time, and questions were solicited and answered. This initial measurement was not recorded. Each child's blood pressure was measured again on the first day and once more on the second day. The blood pressure data are based on the mean systolic and diastolic pressures for these two measurements. The graphic output of the machine was coded after the study was completed, with coders blind to experimental condition. Each child's height and weight were also measured. Absenteeism was used as an indirect measure of health, since absence from school is often attributable to illness. These data were available from school files.

Health measures were separated into two multi-variate clusters: general health measures and blood pressure. This procedure was necessary because two of the general health measures—height and ponderosity (weight/height)—were required as controls for the blood pressure analyses (cf. Voors et al., 1976). (The ponderosity index was chosen as a measure of obesity because of its high correlation with body fat.)

The effects of noise on the general health cluster was significant. Although noise-school children were shorter and weighed less than quiet-school children, neither of these differences reached significance. Surprisingly, noise-school children attended school a higher percentage of the time (97.5% vs. 94.2%) than their quiet-school counterparts did. The effect of noise on systolic and diastolic blood pressure was significant. As is apparent from Figure 1, children from noise schools had higher blood pressure than their quiet-school counterparts did. Unadjusted means for systolic pressure were 89.68 mm for the noise group and 86.77 mm for the quiet group. Diastolic means were 47.84 mm for the noise group and 45.16 mm for the quiet group. Systolic pressure differences between noise and quiet groups are greatest during the first few years of school enrollment; differences after this point remain constant. Figure 1 reflects a similar pattern for diastolic pressure.

Helplessness

Both laboratory and community noise research suggests the possibility that high-intensity noise exposure induces feelings of helplessness. According to Seligman (1975), a psychological state of helplessness frequently results when we continually encounter events (especially aversive ones) that we can do nothing about. The state of helplessness includes a perception of lessened control over one's outcomes, a depression of mood, and a decrease in one's motivation to initiate new responses. Extreme effects of helplessness include fear, anxiety, depression, disease, and even death.

A number of researchers have induced helplessness effects in the laboratory by exposing subjects to uncontrollable bursts of noise (Hi-

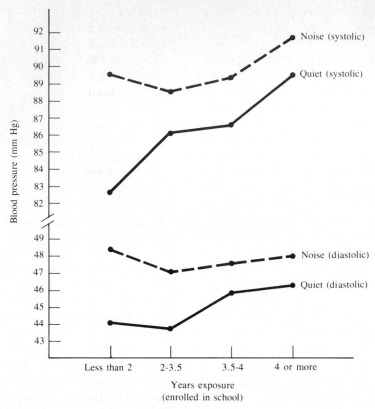

FIGURE 1 Systolic and diastolic blood pressure as a function of school noise level and duration of exposure. (Each period on the years-exposure coordinate on the figure represents approximately one quarter of the sample. For example, 25% of the sample had been enrolled in the present school less than 2 years.)

roto, 1974; Krantz et al., 1974). Moreover, survey data reporting high levels of annoyance but low levels of complaints from noise-impacted populations have similarly been interpreted as reflecting a helplessnesslike state (Herridge, 1974). This finding, however, is subject to a number of alternative explanations, and thus the helplessness interpretation is only suggestive.

Performance on a cognitive task preceded by a success or failure experience was used in the present study to examine the effect of noise on response to failure and on persistence on a difficult task. Response to failure is a standard measure of susceptibility to helplessness. Thus,

if noise-school children were more susceptible to helplessness, they would show greater effects of a failure experience than their quiet-school counterparts would. A lack of persistence (or a "giving-up" syndrome) is considered a direct manifestation of the helpless state.

Each child was given a treatment puzzle to assemble after the tester demonstrated the task with another puzzle. All puzzles were based on the same nine pieces and required the child to fill in a template of a familiar shape. One half of the children received an insoluble (failure) puzzle, and one half received a soluble (success) puzzle. The soluble puzzle was a circle, and the insoluble puzzle was a triangle. Each child was allowed to work on the treatment puzzle for 2.5 minutes. After time was up on the first puzzle, the child was given a second, moderately difficult puzzle to solve. The second (test) puzzle was the same—a square—for all (success and failure) children. The child was allowed 4 minutes to solve the second puzzle. Whether or not the puzzle was solved, time to solution and the child's persisting or giving up before the 4 minutes had elapsed were used as measures of helplessness. We expected that children from noisy schools would be more susceptible to a failure (helplessness) manipulation than children from quiet schools would be, and thus would be less likely to solve the puzzle, slower to find the solution, and more likely to give up on the second puzzle following an insoluble (failure) treatment. Moreover, children from noisy schools, irrespective of their success–failure condition, were expected to give up more often than quiet-school children.

A large proportion (34%) of the children assigned to the success condition, and thus receiving a soluble treatment puzzle, failed to solve the treatment puzzle within the 2.5 minutes allowed. Since the puzzles were considered quite simple and had been pilot tested on children of the same age group, this result was quite unexpected. Although the fact that a number of children self-selected themselves into a failure condition makes interpretation of success–failure effects impossible, comparisons between the children from noise schools and those from quiet schools, irrespective of (controlling for) their pretreatment, are still valid.

First, an examination of only those children who were assigned to the success treatment condition indicates that children from noise schools were more likely to fail to solve the treatment puzzle (41% failed) than children from quiet schools were (23% failed). Second, there were similar effects of noise on the second puzzle, which occurred irrespective of whether the child received a success (solved or not) or failure

treatment. As was the case with the first puzzle, noise-school children were more likely to fail the second puzzle (53% failed) than quiet-school children were (36% failed) and were more likely to give up than their quiet-school counterparts were. As is apparent from Figure 2, the longer a child had attended a noise school, the slower he or she was in solving the puzzle.

Although the preceding analyses indicate that children from noise schools are generally less capable of performing a cognitive task (at least puzzle solving) than children from quiet schools are, they provide only suggestive evidence that noise-school children feel or act as if they have less control over their outcomes. The strongest hint that failure on these puzzles on the part of noise-school children is related to helplessness is found in the data indicating that noise-school children were more likely to give up before their allotted time had elapsed than their quiet counterparts were. It is possible, however, that a constant proportion of children who failed on the second puzzle gave up. It would follow that the amount of giving up in the noise condition was inflated by the fact that there was a greater pool of failures. This interpretation suggests that increased giving up under the noise condition cannot necessarily be viewed as a sign of helplessness. A final analysis addresses this point. This analysis, which includes only those children who failed the second puzzle, indicates that the failures of noise-school children were associated with giving up (31% of those who failed gave up) more often than the failures of quiet-school children were (7% of those who failed gave up). Thus, even though all of these children failed to solve the puzzle, noise-school children were less likely to persist than their quiet-school counterparts were.

Attentional Processes During Noise

Human performance studies report that noise often results in a restriction (or focusing) in one's breadth of attention (Broadbent, 1971; Hockey, 1970). Cues irrelevant to task perfor-

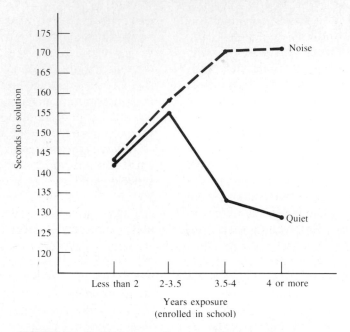

FIGURE 2   Performance on the second (test) puzzle as a function of school noise level and duration of exposure. (Each period on the years-exposure coordinate on the figure represents approximately one quarter of the sample. For example, 25% of the sample had been enrolled in the present school less than 2 years.)

mance are dropped out first, and then, if attention is further restricted, relevant task cues are eliminated. Performance improves under noise when discarded cues are those that are distracting or competing with primary task cues. Performance is adversely affected, however, when a task requires a wide breadth of attention and when focusing results in the neglect of relevant as well as irrelevant cues. Similarly, focusing can have a negative impact on interpersonal behavior when subtle social cues (e.g., another's look of distress) are dropped out, but can improve the quality of an interaction when the discarded cues are merely distracting (S. Cohen & Lezak, 1977).

There is suggestive evidence that an attentional focusing strategy will persist even after noise is terminated. A number of studies have shown post-noise effects on performance and

interpersonal behavior (e.g., Donnerstein & Wilson, 1976; Glass & Singer, 1972). These aftereffects of noise are consistent with what one would expect to occur when one uses a focusing strategy (S. Cohen, 1978). As yet, however, there is no direct evidence that attentional focusing occurs following exposure to noise in either the laboratory or the field.

Selective inattention.   A strategy that is similar (and possibly identical) to attentional focusing has been proposed by Deutsch (1964) to account for the effect of community noise on the verbal abilities of children. Deutsch suggests that children reared in noisy environments become inattentive to acoustic cues. That is, they tune out their acoustic environment. (This could be viewed as their focusing their attention on other aspects of their environment.) Children who tune out their noisy environments are not likely to distinguish between speech-relevant and speech-irrelevant sounds. Thus, they lack experience with appropriate speech cues and generally show an inability to recognize relevant sounds and their referents. The inability to discriminate sound is presumed to account, in part, for subsequent problems in learning to read. Although recent research suggests that children living and attending school in noisy neighborhoods are poorer at making auditory discriminations and in reading (Bronzaft & McCarthy, 1975; S. Cohen, Glass, & Singer, 1973), there is no direct evidence for the selective inattention mechanism. An alternative explanation is that noise masks parent and teacher speech, similarly resulting in a lack of experience with appropriate speech cues and, as a consequence, in reading deficits.

The present study attempts to assess the relation between environmental noise level and the selective inattention strategy in order (a) to determine the generality of noise-induced shifts in attention that occur in laboratory settings and (b) to test Deutsch's (1964) hypothesis. In line with the testing of the Deutsch hypothesis, the relation of the above-mentioned variables to auditory discrimination and reading achievement is also assessed.

Because children who are relatively inattentive to acoustic cues should be less affected by an auditory distractor, distractibility was used as a measure of selective inattention. Under both ambient and distracting conditions, the subjects performed a task consisting of crossing out the e's in a two-page passage from a sixth-grade reader. They were instructed to move from left to right and from top to bottom of the page, as if they were reading, and to go as fast as they could without missing any e's. Each subject worked on a short practice paragraph and then on the task for 2 minutes. Two versions (different samples of prose) were used.

In the distraction condition, the child worked on one of the versions of the task while a tape recording of a male voice read a story at a moderate volume. In the no-distraction condition, the alternative form of the task was completed under ambient sound conditions. The distraction and no-distraction tasks were administered on different testing days. Both the order of alternative versions of the task and the experimental conditions were counterbalanced. The criterion measure was performance (percentage of e's found) on the distraction task after the scores were adjusted for no-distraction performance. It was expected that the children from noise schools would be less affected by distraction than the children from quiet schools. Since selective inattention is a strategy that develops over time, it was also predicted that this tuning-out strategy would increase with increased exposure (S. Cohen et al., 1973).

Separate analyses examined the number of lines completed under distraction and the percentage of e's in the completed lines that were found under distraction. No-distraction performance (number of lines in the first analysis and percentage of e's in the second) was added as an additional control variable in order to equate the children on their ability to perform the task under quiet conditions. There were no differences between the noise group and the quiet group (nor was there an interaction) on the number of lines completed under distraction. There was, however, a significant interaction between noise–quiet and months enrolled in school, for the percentage-of-e's-found measure. As is apparent from Figure 3, the children in noise schools did better than the quiet group on the distraction task during the first 2 years of exposure and did worse after 4 years of exposure. Contrary to earlier evidence, this finding suggests that as the length of noise exposure increases, children are more, rather than less, disturbed by auditory distractors. One possible explanation for this effect is that at first, the children attempt (somewhat successfully) to

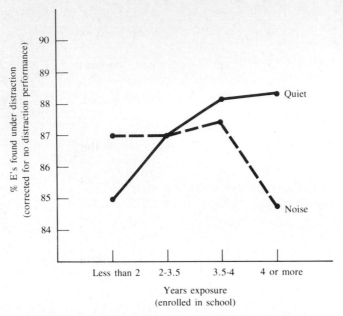

FIGURE 3 Distractibility as a function of school noise level and duration of exposure. (Each period on the years-exposure coordinate on the figure represents approximately one quarter of the sample. For example, 25% of the sample had been enrolled in the present school less than 2 years.)

cope with noise by tuning it out. Later, however, as they find that the strategy is not adequate, they give up. This interpretation is consistent with the helplessness data.

As suggested earlier, reading deficits in children from noisy neighborhoods have been attributed to noise-impacted children's selective filtering out of acoustic cues. Auditory discrimination and reading achievement were assessed in an attempt to replicate previous work and to determine whether there was an association between these measures and the children's attentional strategies. Standardized reading and math tests (administered during the second and third grades by the school system) were gathered from school files, and the Wepman Auditory Discrimination Test (Wepman, Note 1) was administered individually to children in the soundproof van. The Wepman test consists of 40 pairs of words, some of which differ from each other in either initial or final sound, for example, *sick–thick* or *map–nap*. The pairs of words are recorded on tape and presented to each child through earphones. The child is instructed to report if the two words in each pair are the same or different. Control word pairs, in which the words are the same, allow for the elimination of children who have problems with same–different judgments or who are not attending to the task.

In order to roughly equate the noise and quiet conditions on the aptitude of the children at the time they entered school, the analyses of school achievement and auditory discrimination scores included an additional control for the mean cognitive abilities of the child's class on entering the first grade. None of the multivariate or univariate analyses were significant for this cluster. Math, reading, and auditory discrimination were all unrelated to both noise and the Noise x Months Enrolled in School interaction.

Further analyses (Pearson correlations) suggest that the children who were better at auditory discriminations were also better on both the reading test, $r(231) = .19$, $p < .05$, and the math test, $r(231) = .18$, $p < .05$. There were, however, no significant relations between these variables and the selective inattention measure. The same analyses, including only noise-school children, and correlations partialing out control variables for both the entire sample and the noise sample yielded similar results. In summary, there is no evidence that aircraft noise affects reading and math skills, or that these skills are related to a selective inattention strategy.

Classroom as the Unit of Analysis Since noise would be likely to have an impact on school achievement by affecting behavior in the classroom, a second analysis of the school achievement cluster was performed with classroom, rather than individual child, as the unit of analysis. This covariance analysis treated the control factors as covariates and months enrolled in school, noise, and classrooms (nested in noise) as independent variables. This analysis is considerably more conservative than the previous analysis because the degrees of freedom in the denominator are based on the number of classrooms (37) rather than on the number of children (262). The results for the school achievement cluster were the same.

The classroom analysis was not used for the other clusters, since those measures were not achievement oriented and thus were presumed not to be classroom mediated. The subjects were also tested individually, not in the classroom. Even using this ultraconservative technique, however, a reanalysis of the other clusters indicates very similar results for the parent-questionnaire, blood pressure, and helplessness clusters. Differences between the noise group and the quiet group on the child-questionnaire and selective inattention clusters, which were significant in the previous analysis,

did not reach statistical significance with classroom used as the unit of analysis.

Quiet Homes and Noisy Schools

To determine whether or not living in a relatively quiet home (at least in terms of aircraft noise) would lessen the impact of school noise, we isolated the children living in the 20 quietest homes in the noise sample, that is, in homes with contour levels of less than 68 in terms of the Community Noise Equivalency Level (CNEL). These children were then compared (using the regression techniques described earlier) with the remainder of the noise sample and with the entire quiet sample. In no case was there a difference between these quiet-home children and the remaining children of the noise sample. In a number of cases, however, even this small group of 20 showed the effects of noise reported earlier. Thus the noise-sample children from quiet homes were less likely to solve the first helplessness task puzzles than the quiet-sample controls were. The longer a child had attended a noisy school, the less likely he or she was to solve either the first puzzle or the second puzzle. Moreover, children from quiet homes but noisy schools were more likely to fail and to give up on the second puzzle than children from quiet schools were. Further, their failures on the second puzzle were associated with giving up more often than the failures of quiet-school children were. Noise-school children from quiet homes also had both higher systolic blood pressure and higher diastolic blood pressure than children from quieter schools did. There were no effects, however, on the selective inattention task (crossing out e's under distraction condition), as reported for the entire sample.

These analyses suggest that living in a relatively quiet neighborhood did not lessen the cumulative impact of exposure to noise at school. The reason may be that the noise experienced during school attendance is sufficient to create noise effects.

AIR POLLUTION

A possible alternative explanation for differences between the noise and quiet samples is air pollution levels. Such an alternative is very unlikely. Sulfur dioxide was minimal at all the school sites, never exceeding the California standard. Ozone and nitrogen dioxide standards were exceeded, but maximum levels were slightly higher at the control schools than at the airport schools. The maximum 1-hour rates in any school area for ozone (.21 parts per million) and NO_2 (.60 ppm) were below levels that generally show any effects on human behavior or health (Morrow, 1975). Maximum carbon monoxide was slightly higher in the airport schools (30 vs. 27, 22 ppm), but average values were identical (6 ppm). The differences in maximum values of 8 ppm are negligible, and human effects from CO concentrations of less than 40 ppm are extremely rare (National Air Pollution Control Administration, 1970). Note that we have used maximum values in arguing against an air pollution alternative, thus presenting a very conservative counterargument. Average values in all cases were considerably below established standards.

CONCLUSIONS

In general, the evidence presented in this article is consistent with laboratory work on physiological response to noise and on uncontrollable noise as a factor in helplessness. Thus children from noisy schools have higher blood pressure and are more likely to give up on a task than children from quiet schools are. The development of attentional strategies predicted from laboratory work and previous field research was, on the whole, not found. Contrary to prediction, increased years of exposure led to children's being more distractible rather than less. However, a general deficit in task performance on the puzzle task and increased distractibility do seem to support the more general

hypothesis that prolonged noise exposure affects cognitive processes.

These data are most interesting, however, because of the tentative answers they provide concerning questions of adaptation to noise over time. One interpretation of the data is that they indicate some habituation of physiological stress response but show no signs of adaptation of cognitive and motivational effects. In fact, in a number of cases, increased length of exposure resulted in an increased negative impact of noise. First, the only evidence for an adaptation effect is provided by the systolic blood pressure data. On that measure, the greatest difference between the noise and quiet groups occurred during the first 2 years of exposure. As length of exposure increased, these differences leveled out but still remained substantial. Perceptions of noise and noise annoyance did not adapt. Thus children from noise schools and their parents reported more noise and being more bothered by noise. Parents, in fact, reported higher levels of noise as their length of residence in the noisy area increased. Neither the cognitive deficits on the helplessness puzzles (which actually increased over time) nor the giving-up syndrome of the children from noise schools lessened with increased length of exposure. Finally, although noise-school children were initially less affected by an auditory distractor, increased length of exposure (beyond 4 years) seemed to result in greater distractibility. Thus the preponderance of evidence suggests a lack of successful adaptation over time. The above interpretation, however, is only tentative. Although length-of-exposure differences may be due to increased exposure to noise, they may also be attributable to some unknown factors that differentiate between children who continue to live in the air corridor and those who move, or to some combination of exposure and these factors.

It should be noted that the failure of the present study to replicate the previously reported relation between community noise and reading ability (Bronzaft & McCarthy, 1975; S. Cohen et al., 1973) may be attributable to an experimental design insensitive to noise-induced differences in school achievement. In both of the earlier studies, all the students attended the same school. Moreover, in the Cohen et al. study, students from both noisy and quiet apartments were taught in the same classrooms by the same teachers. In the present study, noise-sample children and quiet-sample children attended different schools, were in different classrooms, and had different teachers. It is likely that these factors make the detection of a small effect of noise quite difficult.

Can we conclude that community noise has effects that are similar to noise-induced effects reported in the laboratory literature? The similarity of our results to those reported in laboratory settings is striking. However, we still must be cautious. Replications of these results in other settings and with other populations are required before definitive conclusions are possible. To this end, our own research program includes an ongoing replication of this study, with a population exposed to traffic noise, as well as plans to collect longitudinal data on the children attending airport schools.

What conclusions can we make in regard to public policy? From a policy point of view, these data are valuable but not sufficient. At least 8 million people in this country are exposed to aircraft noise (U.S. Environmental Protection Agency, 1974), and the vast majority of noise-impacted communities have racial and social class compositions more similar to the composition of the present sample than to that of the general population (U.S. Environmental Protection Agency, Note 5). In combination with the laboratory noise literature, these data clearly suggest lending additional weight to the possible impact of aircraft noise on psychological adjustment and on nonauditory aspects of health. Replications of these results, however,

would substantially increase their potential influence in the realms of both science and social policy.

REFERENCES

Anticaglia, J. R., & Cohen, A. Extra-auditory effects of noise as a health hazard. In P. M. Insel & R. H. Mo (Eds.), *Health and the social environment.* Toronto: Health, 1974.

Bock, R. D. *Multivariate statistical methods in behavioral research.* New York: McGraw-Hill, 1975.

Broadbent, D. E. *Decision and stress.* New York: Academic Press, 1971.

Broadbent, D. E. The current state of noise research. Reply to Poulton. *Psychological Bulletin,* 1978, **8**, 1052–1067.

Bronzaft, A. L., & McCarthy, D. P. The effects of elevated train noise on reading ability. *Environment and Behavior,* 1975, **7**, 517–527.

Campbell, D. T., & Stanley, J. C. *Experimental and quasi-experimental designs for research.* Chicago: Rand McNally, 1966.

Cohen, A. Industrial noise and medical, absence, and accident record data on exposed workers. In W. D. Ward (Ed.), *Proceedings of the International Congress on Noise as a Public Health Problem.* Washington D.C.: U.S. Government Printing Office, 1973.

Cohen, J. Multiple regression as a general data-analytic system. *Psychological Bulletin,* 1968, **70**, 426–443.

Cohen, S. Environmental load and the allocation of attention. In A. Baum, J. E. Singer, & S. Valins (Eds.) *Advances in environmental psychology.* Hillsdale, N.J., Erlbaum, 1978.

Cohen, S., Glass, D. C., & Phillips, S. Environment and health. In H. E. Freeman, S. Levine, and L. G. Reede (Eds.), *Handbook of medical sociology.* Englewood Cliffs, N.J.: Prentice-Hall, 1979.

Cohen, S., Glass, D. C., & Singer, J. E. Apartment noise auditory discrimination, and reading ability in children. *Journal of Experimental Social Psychology,* 1973, **9**, 407–422.

Cohen, S., & Lezak, A. Noise and inattentiveness to social cues. *Environment and Behavior,* 1977, **9**, 559–572.

Deutsch, C. P. Auditory discrimination and learning: Social factors. *The Merrill-Palmer Quarterly of Behavior and Development,* 1964, **10**, 277–296.

Donnerstein, E., & Wilson, D. W. Effects of noise and perceived control on ongoing and subsequent aggressive behavior. *Journal of Personality and Social Psychology,* 1976, **34**, 774–781.

Finkle, A. L., & Poppen, J. R. Clinical effects of noise and mechanical vibrations of a turbo-jet engine on man. *Journal of Applied Physiology,* 1948, **1**, 183–204.

Glass, D. C., & Singer, J. E. *Urban stress: Experiments on noise and social stressors.* New York: Academic Press, 1972.

Glorig, A. Non-auditory effects of noise exposure. *Sound and Vibration,* 1971, **5**, 28–29.

Heft, H. Background and focal environmental conditions of the home and attention in young children. *Journal of Applied Social Psychology,* 1979, **9**, 47–49.

Herridge, C. F. Aircraft noise and mental health. *Journal of Psychosomatic Reseacher,* 1974, **18**, 239–243.

Hiroto, D. S. Locus of control and learned helplessness. *Journal of Experimental Psychology,* 1974, **102**, 187–193.

Hockey, G. R. J. Effects of loud noise on attentional selectivity. *Quarterly Journal of Experimental Psychology,* 1970, **22**, 28–36.

Jansen, G. Effects of noise on physiological state. In W. D. Ward & J. E. Fricke (Eds.), *Noise as a public health problem.* Washington, D.C.: American Speech and Hearing Association, 1969.

Krantz, D. S., Glass, D. C., & Snyder, M. L. Helplessness, stress level, and the coronary prone behavior pattern. *Journal of Experimental Social Psychology,* 1974, **10**, 284–300.

Kryter, K. D. *The effects of noise on man.* New York: Academic Press, 1970.

Lane, S. R., & Meecham, W. C. Jet noise at schools near Los Angeles International Airport. *Journal of the Acoustical Society of America,* 1974, **56**, 127–131.

Loeb, M. Noise and performance: Do we know more? In J. V. Tobias (Ed.), *The proceedings of the Third International Congress on Noise as a Public Health Problem.* Washington, D.C.: American Speech and Hearing Association, 1979.

Matthews, K. E., Jr., & Canon, L. K. Environmental noise level as a determinant of helping behavior. *Journal of Personality and Social Psychology,* 1975, **32**, 571–577.

Mills, J. H. Noise and children: A review of literature. *Journal of the Acoustical Society of America,* 1975, **58**, 767–779.

Morrow, P. E. An evaluation of recent NO_x toxicity data and an attempt to derive an ambient standard for NO_x by established toxicological procedures. *Environmental Research,* 1975, **10**, 92–112.

National Air Pollution Control Administration. *Air quality criteria for carbon monoxide, AP-62.* Washington, D.C.: U.S. Government Printing Office, 1970.

Overall, J. E., & Klett, J. *Applied multivariate analysis.* New York: McGraw-Hill, 1972.

Peterson, A. P. G., & Gross, E. E., Jr. *Handbook of noise measurement.* Concord, Mass.: General Radio, 1972.

Seligman, M.P. *Helplessness: On depression, development, and death.* San Francisco: Freeman, 1975.

U.S. Environmental Protection Agency. *Levels document 550/9-74-004.* Washington, D.C.: U.S. Government Printing Office, 1974.

Voors, A. W., Foster, T. A., Frerichs, R. R., Weber, L. S., & Berenson, G. S. Studies of blood pressure in children, ages 5–14 years, in a total biracial community. *Circulation,* 1976, **54**, 319–327.

READING 28

"Don't Forget to Take the Cupcakes out of the Oven": Prospective Memory, Strategic Time-Monitoring, and Context

Stephen J. Ceci
Urie Bronfenbrenner

Until recently, researchers interested in memory have accorded attention almost exclusively to *retrospective memory,* that is, recalling information about the past. Neglected has been another function of memory important in daily life: remembering to attend to a future event, or *prospective memory* (Meacham & Leiman, 1982; Meacham & Singer, 1977).

Numerous instances of "everyday remembering" attest to the importance of prospective memory, for example, remembering to take vitamins, catch the morning bus, send a spouse an anniversary card, meet with a student, or turn off the bath water in 10 min to prevent a "flood." Yet, despite the ubiquitousness of the phenomenon in our daily lives, there have been few attempts by developmentalists to study strategies used to support prospective remembering, and their developmental and contextual determinants.

Investigations of prospective memory have, to date, focused mainly on one aspect: the use of external retrieval cues (Kreutzer, Leonard, & Flavell, 1975; Meacham & Colombo, 1980; Wellman, Ritter, & Flavell, 1975). For example, in their interview study, Kreutzer et al. (1975) asked children how they would go about remembering to bring their ice skates to school the following day. Children frequently reported that they would use an external retrieval cue to remind them, for example, placing the skates by the front door or pinning a note to their clothes.

In this study, we identify and investigate yet another strategy employed by children when called upon to perform a task at some future time. We call it *strategic time-monitoring* because its use is associated with less frequent clock-checking during a waiting period, thus releasing time for other activities. In addition to providing evidence for the use of this strategy, we examine its development as a function of the age and sex of the child, and investigate ecological factors that interact with these personal characteristics to influence efficient cognitive functioning.

Three distinct phases of strategic time-monitoring can be identified: (1) an early "calibration" phase wherein subjects engage in frequent clock-checking to "synchronize their psychological clocks" with the passage of real clock time, (2) an intermediate phase of reduced clock-checking while pursuing other activities, and (3) a "scalloping phase" wherein clock-checking sharply increases as the deadline approaches. Operationally, the use of the strategic time-monitoring strategy is manifested by a U-shaped distribution of such behavior over the course of the waiting period.

The recent work of Harris and Wilkins (1982), with adults, is consistent with the division of time-monitoring into the three phases just described. The U-shaped distribution of their subjects' clock-checks over time can be interpreted as an initial flurry of clock-checking activity in order to calibrate one's psychological clock, followed by a prolonged period of reduced clock-checking, and finally a relatively rapid burst of "last minute" clock-checks (i.e., a scalloping effect).

It remains to be demonstrated, however, that such a U-shaped distribution of clock-watching over time is indeed efficient, that it does decrease the total amount of monitoring behavior without reducing punctuality, thus releasing time for other activities. Hence,

Hypothesis 1:
In tasks requiring prospective memory, children who employ a pattern of strategic monitoring, manifested in a U-shaped distribution of clock-checking over time, will spend less total time in clock-watching but still be punctual.

As with all behavior, a child's use of strategic time-monitoring can be expected to vary as a function of the situation. In particular, we anticipated that children would be more likely to exhibit this more efficient pattern of behavior in the home than in the laboratory. This expectation was based on Bronfenbrenner's conclusion, drawn from a comparison of studies conducted in both settings (Bronfenbrenner, 1979), that the laboratory, as a typically strange and unfamiliar environment, tends to evoke higher levels of anxiety, especially in children, thereby leading to reduced efficiency in cognitive functioning. Our second hypothesis therefore reads as follows:

Hypothesis 2:
Resort to strategic time-monitoring, as manifested in a U-shaped distribution of clock-checking, will be more pronounced when tasks requiring prospective memory are presented in the familiar environment of the home as opposed to an unfamiliar laboratory setting.

Similar considerations gave rise to two corollary hypotheses. First, if children in the laboratory do not exhibit much strategic time-monitoring, what should be the pattern of their clock-checking during the waiting period? Greater anxiety tends to be accompanied by greater vigilance. Vigilance would be reflected in a constantly rising rate of clock-checking throughout the waiting period. We refer to this phenomenon as *anxious time-monitoring*. Accordingly:

Hypothesis 2a:
Anxious time-monitoring, as manifested by a constantly increasing pace of clock-checking during the waiting period, should be more pronounced in the laboratory setting than in the home.
Second, the combined effect of reduced efficiency and greater strain should result in higher overall levels of clock-checking. Hence,

Hypothesis 2b:
The total frequency of clock-checking should be greater in the laboratory than in the home. The remaining three hypotheses focus more sharply on developmental issues relating to the age and sex of the child and the manner in which these personal characteristics interact both with the nature of the task and the setting in which it is performed.

Hypothesis 3:
Since the use of more advanced cognitive strategies is expected to increase with age, resort to strategic time-monitoring will be greater among older children, with a corresponding reduction of total time spent in clock-watching. By contrast, younger children will make less use of strategic monitoring, and spend more time in clock-watching, particularly in the unfamiliar laboratory setting.
What should be the effect of age on anxious time-monitoring? On the one hand, older children, being more mature, might be expected to feel less insecure, especially in an unfamiliar situation. On the other hand, being older, they may feel a greater responsibility to accomplish the assigned task.
Because of these conflicting considerations, we could not make a specific a priori prediction on this score. Because the processes of socialization encourage different expectations for boys than girls (Maccoby & Jacklin, 1974; Shepherd-Look, 1981), we anticipated that children's time-monitoring would vary systematically as a joint function of the sex of the child and the nature of the task. Our specific hypothesis was

based on the following consideration. Tasks associated with higher expectations for a particular sex are likely to engender more anxiety than activities not regarded as sex-appropriate, with a corresponding reduction in efficiency. Our fourth hypothesis expresses this prediction in more specific form:

Hypothesis 4:

On a traditionally female sex-typed task, such as baking, girls will make less use of strategic time-monitoring. Instead, they will exhibit a more anxious pace of clock-watching than boys and spend more time in the process. Correspondingly, on a traditional male sex-typed task, such as charging a motorcycle battery, boys will exhibit the analogous pattern. Because of increasing sex-role expectations with age, these relationships should be more pronounced with older than with younger children.

Finally, on a more general plane, we assumed that the familiarity of the setting would affect not only the overall level of a particular pattern of clock-checking, but also the extent to which this pattern would be affected by other factors relating to characteristics of the child or the situation. To state our final hypothesis in more specific form:

Hypothesis 5:

The joint influence of age, sex, and nature of the task on patterns of time-monitoring will be greater in the laboratory setting than in the home.

Like Hypothesis 2, this prediction derives from Bronfenbrenner's (1979) comparative analysis of studies conducted in the laboratory versus naturalistic settings. One of the conclusions suggested in the review was that, in the less familiar setting of the laboratory, research findings were more likely to be influenced by external factors such as social class, age, and sex differences, or systematic variations in experimental procedure.

METHOD

Subjects Ninety-six children, 48 10-year-olds (mean age = 10.7 years) and 48 14-year-olds (mean age = 14.6 years) were recruited through their college-aged siblings and offered $5 either to bake cupcakes or to charge a motorcycle battery. Half of the children at each age were girls. There were no significant group differences in socioeconomic status as a function of age, sex, context, or task assignment, nor was there any among-group variation in the percentage of single-parent households or of homes where the mother was employed.

Procedure All children were tested individually. Those children asked to bake cupcakes were instructed to place them in the oven by a specified time and to remove them 30 min later (as per Jiffy Mix instructions). While waiting, the children were invited to make unlimited use of a Pac Man video machine, beginning 15 min prior to placing the cupcakes into the oven and continuing during the entire 30-min baking period. (The 15-min warm-up period was provided to familiarize children with the game.) At the start of the 30-min baking period, children's attention was directed to a wall clock, and they were instructed to remove the cupcakes 30 min from the time shown, for example, "It's now — o'clock. Be sure to let them bake exactly 30 min. So, you should remember to take them out of the oven at exactly — o'clock." (Conveniently, no children were wearing wristwatches on the day of their participation.)

The Pac Man game was always placed in an adjoining room sufficiently far from the oven to preclude the use of various external retrieval cues such as oven buzzers or the aroma of the maturing cupcakes. The game was bonded to a table top with suction cups. This was done so that the child's back would have to face the wall clock when playing Pac Man. Thus time-monitoring behaviors (turning in one's seat to check the wall clock) could easily be recorded by an unobtrusive observer who was in the room, pretending to be reading a book or magazine.

For children assigned to the motorcycle battery charging task, the same verbal instructions were employed as for the baking task, except that references to baking were replaced with references to battery charging. The children were instructed to remove the battery charger cables after the battery had been charged 30 min. They too were provided with the unlimited use of Pac Man beginning 15 min before the task began and continuing for the entire 30-min charging period.

There were two contexts for each task, with 24 children of each age and sex (six per cell) assigned at random to each setting. Half of the children did the baking or charging in their own homes, the other half in a psychophysics laboratory.

In the home, Pac Man was set up in whichever room children normally played games, provided there was a clock on the wall and a table on which the game could be affixed. All of the children in both settings in fact did play Pac Man while waiting to remove either cupcakes or the battery-charging cable.

In the home, the children's older siblings, who were undergraduates trained by the experimenters, acted as unobtrusive observers during the waiting period. While pretending to be reading in another part of the room, they recorded each instance when their younger sibling turned away from the game in order to check the time. None of the observers was informed about the purpose and design of the experiment, or the reasons for recording clock-checking, until after the study had been completed. Pilot testing of the recording procedure indicated nearly perfect reliability among a group of five of the observers who subsequently participated in the experiment. In the laboratory context, children were brought to a university psychophysics laboratory by their older

brothers or sisters. The baking or battery-charging instructions were given by an unfamiliar age-mate of their older sibling, who was also trained to record the children's clock-watching while they played Pac Man in the laboratory. The child's older sibling was not present during the experiment in the laboratory. Thus, the two contexts differed both in the physical characteristics of the setting (home furnishings vs psychophysics instrumentation) and in the familiarity of the persons present (older sibling vs. unfamiliar adult).

Debriefing Children were debriefed by their older siblings. They were informed that the primary purpose of the study had not been to bake cupcakes (or to recharge a battery) but to gain insight into how they kept track of time. It was explained that it was sometimes necessary for researchers to mislead subjects in order to gain knowledge, but that deception was never an ethically attractive way to deal with other people and was used with some reluctance by the researchers. The older siblings explained that there was no right or wrong way to monitor the passage of time. Children were encouraged to ask any questions they had concerning their participation. Finally, they were thanked for their participation and given the agreed-upon $5 stipend.

RESULTS

Pilot Studies and Preliminary Analyses As a precaution, we sought to determine whether there were any systematic age or sex differences in children's interest and/or proficiency in playing Pac Man, inasmuch as the presence of such differences could affect the capacity of the game to occupy boys' and girls' attention equally. At the outset of the study, children had been asked to indicate how frequently they played Pac Man (daily, biweekly, weekly, bimonthly, or less often) and how much they enjoyed it (*not at all* to *very much*).

In addition, gains achieved between initial and final scores, as well as the number of games they played during the waiting period, were recorded as measures of children's concentration on the game. Each of these measures was entered in a multivariate linear regression as a predictor of clock-checking for each 5-min interval. In no instance did any of these variables account for significant variation in children's clock-checking. Somewhat surprisingly, girls expressed slightly more interest in Pac Man than boys and claimed to play it equally often.

For the baking task only, all of the older siblings happened to be females. Because of the possibility of confounding by sex of older sibling, another preliminary analysis was undertaken. Since, in the battery-charging task, half of the older siblings were males, the sex of the older siblings were males, the sex of the older sibling was used as a predictor of clock-checking frequency in a discriminate function. The results indicated that, at least on this task, the sex of the older sibling was not associated with variation in the frequency of clock-checking by boys and girls.

Principal Findings With the foregoing possibilities of confounding eliminated from serious consideration, we proceed to an examination of results bearing on the main hypotheses of the study. For this purpose the effects of age, sex, context, task and time interval on children's frequencies of clock-checking were analyzed.

To turn to the findings themselves, Figures 1 and 2 depict the distribution of clock-checking during the waiting period for each of the 16 subgroups of subjects included in the experimental design. Data points along each graph show average frequencies of clock-checking for successive 5-min intervals, with the mean totals for the 30-min periods recorded at the right of each curve.

Hypothesis 1

The first hypothesis requires that strategic monitoring, as manifested by a U-shaped distribution of clock-checking, be associated with less total time looking at the clock. Evidence in support of this hypothesis is initially apparent from an inspection of Figures 1 and 2 . Perhaps the most striking feature of the two figures is the contrast in the shapes of the curves appearing in the left and right halves of each diagram. With but one exception (to be discussed below), all of the parabolas appear at the left, whereas the curves at the right are generally linear. Hence, an approximate test of the first hypothesis can be made by comparing overall time-checking scores for each successive pair of setting contrasts. As indicated by the means cited in each panel, in every paired comparison, the total amount of clock-checking was greater in the laboratory setting than in the home. In substantive terms, children observed in the home not only made greater use of strategic time monitoring, but they also spent less clock-watching time in the process.

A more precise measure and test of the first hypothesis is provided by examining this same relationship at the level of individual subjects, that is, calculating a correlation between the amount of time spent by each child in clock-checking, on the one hand, and, on the other, a measure of the extent to which the child resorted to strategic monitoring. The resulting correlation for the total sample was, as expected, rather high and negative in sign, $r = -.78$, $p < .01$.

It is instructive to calculate the analogous correlation between total time spent by each child in clock-checking and the degree of his or her anxious time-monitoring as measured by the corresponding linear regression coefficient. If our theoretical expectations are correct, the resulting correlation should again be substantial, but this time positive in sign. The obtained coefficient is in fact .67, indicating, not surpris-

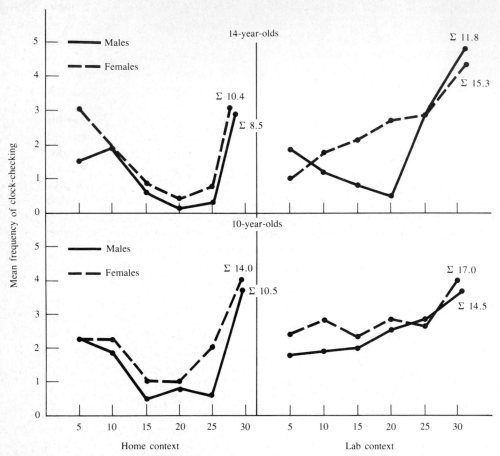

FIGURE 1 Children's clock-checking frequencies in the cupcake-baking task, late responders excluded (≥ = mean total number of clock-checks).

ingly (though not necessarily), that children who exhibited a pattern of anxious time-monitoring engaged in more clock-checking overall.

Taken together, these correlational results also constitute evidence of construct validation for our interpretation of the two principal patterns of clock-checking that have been distinguished: *strategic* and *anxious* time-monitoring.

Hypothesis 2

The consistently contrasting patterns in Figures 1 and 2 provide even stronger support for the second hypothesis and its two corollaries. Stra-

tegic monitoring was indeed more pronounced in the more familiar setting of the home, whereas anxious time-monitoring was more evident in the laboratory and resulted in more time spent in total clock-watching.

Hypothesis 3

With respect to the effects of Age, we find, as anticipated, that adolescents spent less time in clock-watching than did 10-year-olds. Their respective means for the half-hour waiting period were 11.2 and 14.1. On the average, older children also made more use of strategic time-monitoring. Further analysis, however, revealed that the age difference was significant only in the laboratory setting. The same qualification applies to the influence of Age on anxious time-monitoring, but the effect is in the opposite direction. While using a more efficient strategy of clock-checking than younger children, adolescents of both sexes nevertheless showed a stronger tendency to increase their clock-checking over time. This finding is consistent with the interpretation that older children felt a greater pressure to perform the assigned task on time. Taken together, the contrasting signs of these interaction effects also demonstrate that the two strategies of time-monitoring are not simply opposite sides

of the same coin, since they are not always correlated in the same direction.

Hypothesis 4

The effects of Age on both types of clock-watching were further qualified simultaneously by the Sex of the child and nature of the Task. Older boys, again only within the laboratory setting, tended to be most efficient and least anxious when asked to bake cupcakes. The above finding clearly speaks to the fourth hypothesis of the study: the prediction that strategic monitoring will be reduced, and the frequency and pace of clock-checking increased, on a task associated with higher sex-role expec-

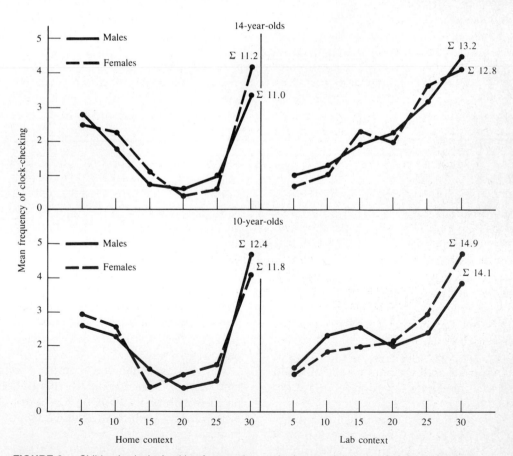

FIGURE 2 Children's clock-checking frequencies on the battery-charging task, late responders excluded ($\geq$ = mean total number of clock-checks).

tations for the group in question. There was only partial support, however, for the remainder of the hypothesis: the corresponding relationship for girls, while in the expected direction, was not statistically significant, that is, girls did not engage in reliably less clock-checking on the battery-charging task than their female peers on the baking task.

It was further anticipated that these sex-role effects would be more salient in older children than in younger children. The findings cited above are in accord with this expectation with respect to the distribution of clock-watching over time. Older boys, particularly in an unfamiliar laboratory setting, exhibited a more anxious and less efficient clock-checking strategy when requested to disconnect a battery charger (a male-typed task) than when asked to take cupcakes out of the oven (a female-typed task).

The results on the overall frequency of time-monitoring also provide corroboration for the fourth hypothesis. Boys looked at the clock more often in the battery-charging task, and girls in the baking task, particularly when the latter was conducted in the home.

Hypothesis 5

Finally, as the reader may have noted, a familiar refrain resounds throughout the last few paragraphs: the phrase "only in the laboratory." This recurrence reflects the fact that significant interaction effects were, almost without exception, limited to the laboratory setting. In accord with our final hypothesis, this finding supports the view that the laboratory, as an unfamiliar and thereby somewhat anxiety-arousing environment, is more likely to activate variation in research findings as a function of characteristics of both the person (e.g., age and sex) and the immediate situation (e.g., the nature of the task).

Taken as a whole, the results of this study indicate that, especially when observed in a familiar environment, children as young as 10 years of age can employ a fairly sophisticated

cognitive strategy for monitoring the passage of time, one that substantially reduces the overall burden of clock-checking. The question may be raised, however, whether the reduction in amount of clock-checking is achieved at some sacrifice to punctuality. Specifically, did children in fact remember to take the cupcakes out of the oven before they were burned, or to disconnect the battery cable before the battery burned out? And if some children forgot, was the failure in prospective memory related to the strategy of clock-watching that they employed?

When Prospective Memory Fails There were in fact 14 children who were more than 90 sec late in removing cupcakes from the oven or removing the battery-charger cable, and an additional seven who were between 60 and 90 sec late. Seven instances of late responding involved 10-year-olds on the baking task, six of whom were boys. All seven of these children had been assigned to the home context. Another eight instances of late responding involved 10-year-olds on the battery-charging task, five boys and three girls. All but one had been assigned to the home context. Six older children (all but one of whom were boys) responded late, three on the baking task and three on the charging task. All had been assigned to the home context. Thus, there was only a single instance of "forgetting to remember" in the laboratory context. And, overall, boys were more than three times as likely to forget as were girls (16 vs. 5).

Since nearly all of the forgetting occurred in the home and the home was also the context for most of the strategic time-monitoring, the question arises whether the latter type of behavior is indeed effective. Does it not occasionally result in failure to perform the task on time? To check on this possibility, we examined the pattern of clock-checking for the late responders as a group. As is apparent from Figure 3, these late arrivals did not engage in strategic monitor-

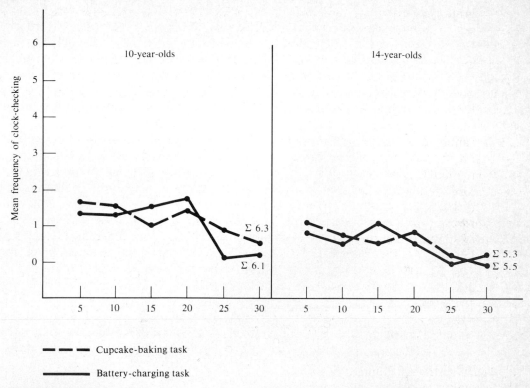

FIGURE 3   Clock-checking frequencies of "late responders" in the HOME context. No cases of late responding occurred in the LAB context ($\geq$ =mean total number of clock-checks).

ing. To a marked extent, those who responded late did not employ strategic time-monitoring.

Moreover, an inspection of Figure 3 reveals that late responders approached the task differently from their "on-time" peers. First, as previously noted, they neither engaged in strategic monitoring, nor did they increase their clock-watching over time. Instead, to the extent that they showed any variation in rate, it was to decrease the frequency of checking as they approached the deadline. Even more striking is the low overall level of clock-checking that characterized this group, a total of less than six checks for the entire 30-min waiting period compared with 10–16 checks for the sample as a whole (see Figs. 1 and 2). Given this weak and

waning pattern of response, it is not surprising that they forgot to perform the task on time.

The deviant behavior of the late responders also suggests a more general inference. A reduction in the overall level of clock-checking can apparently result from any of several processes. One of these is the use of a strategic pattern of monitoring; another may reflect a low level of effort accorded to the monitoring task. Moreover, these processes can lead to somewhat different consequences. On the one hand, the fact that none of the late responders had used a calibration strategy suggests that such a strategy insures against missing the deadline while at the same time reducing the total time expended in monitoring. On the other hand, reducing clock-watching for other reasons can result in "forgetting to remember." For example, an analysis of the relationship between late responding and the absolute frequency of clock-checking revealed that the children who checked the clock least often were the latest in removing cupcakes or battery cables. This result replicates a similar finding in an earlier study by Harris and Wilkins (1982).

The foregoing analyses of data from late responders permit an extension of our earlier generalization. Strategic monitoring not only reduces the overall burden of clock-watching, but also accomplishes this economy without risk to the effective functioning of prospective memory; one does not "forget to remember."

DISCUSSION

The principal conclusions of this experiment are most appropriately presented in the context of the specific hypotheses of the study. Thus we believe our findings clearly demonstrate that children as young as 10 years of age are able to employ fairly sophisticated cognitive strategies in support of prospective memory. Whether they in fact do so, however, depends in significant degree on the context in which prospective memory is activated. Our findings show equally clearly that children are far more likely to use a complex, time-conserving strategy in the familiar environment of the home than in the unfamiliar setting of a psychophysics laboratory. By contrast, the latter milieu evokes a pattern of response involving an escalating pace of clock-checking suggestive both of greater caution and greater anxiety. There is no evidence, however, that either of these strategies is more effective than the other in terms of achieving the ultimate goal of remembering to carry out a specified task at some future time. Those children who failed to make the deadline employed neither of the above patterns of clock-checking but rather telegraphed their failure by reducing the frequency with which they were verifying the passage of time.

There are indications, however, that the two effective strategies have rather different trade-offs. Moreover, these are trade-offs that children 10 years of age can already recognize and act upon. Thus it would appear that what we have called anxious time-monitoring insures against missing the deadline but does so at the sacrifice of intervening time that could be employed for other purposes. Strategic time-monitoring, by contrast, offers an intervening period for other activities, but possibly at some risk of failing to perform the required task on time. Our findings suggest that children perceive the request to carry out a future task as a less demanding, and perhaps less important, responsibility when the task is to be performed in the presumably more relaxed atmosphere of the home than in the less familiar and possibly more prestigious environment of the laboratory. Correspondingly, children in the latter setting, even though already capable of using a less time-consuming strategy, take precautions to insure that they will not fail to live up to expectations. It is a nice instance of Freud's principle of "anxiety in the service of the ego."

The interpretation of our results as a function of increased tension evoked by the strange and unfamiliar setting of a psychophysics laboratory requires further comment. Although not without some theoretical and empirical basis, this explanation is nevertheless an inference not grounded in any data from the experiment itself. In order to provide such direct data, we carried out an additional subexperiment making possible a further and more critical test of our a priori explanation.

A Test Case: A Halfway House between Laboratory and Home For this purpose, an additional group of 24 children were asked to perform the cupcake-baking task in a standard kitchen located in a former residential apartment of a home economics building. While waiting, children played Pac Man in an adjacent living room. In all other respects the procedure was identical with that followed in the laboratory setting. Thus we were now introducing a third context that, in terms of familiarity, was intended to be intermediate between the other two: at one extreme, one's own kitchen; then an ordinary kitchen in an unfamiliar but compatible environment (i.e., the home economics building); and, at the other extreme, the psychophysics laboratory.

The results for this intermediate context are quite straightforward, and readily summarized as follows. For the younger children, the pattern of findings in the home economics kitchen was practically indistinguishable from that for the laboratory. Thus there was little evidence of strategic monitoring, the pace of clock-checking increased with time, and the overall frequency was only slightly lower than that for the laboratory (14.5 and 15.7, respectively). It was substantially and significantly higher, however, than the corresponding figure for the home (12.3). In sharp contrast, the results for the 14-year-olds in the home economics kitchen were scarcely distinguishable from those for the home; both of these groups showed high levels of strategic monitoring, and correspondingly low frequencies of overall clock-watching (10.2 for the home economics setting and 9.5 for the home setting vs. 13.5 for the laboratory).

The foregoing findings are consistent with a hypothesis of an increase in strategic monitoring and a decrease in the frequency and pace of clock-checking as a joint function of the age of the child and the familiarity of the setting. For a 10-year-old, an unfamiliar kitchen in a home economics building at a university is no less strange than a psychophysics laboratory and has similar effects on reducing the efficiency of cognitive strategies that support remembering. But for an adolescent, an ordinary kitchen in one location is no less familiar than in another, whether the place is a home or a university

building, with the result that cognitive strategies remain efficient and unaffected.

The results of the "kitchen-on-campus" experiment also shed some light on which aspects of context evoke differences and similarities in patterns of time-monitoring. Following the usual practice in a laboratory experiment, we employed as observers in that setting research assistants who were unknown to the subjects of the study. A similar procedure was followed in the "kitchen-on-campus" experiment. Hence any differences in styles of clock-checking in these two contexts cannot be attributed to the presence of a familiar versus unfamiliar observer. Accordingly, the more anxious and less efficient pattern of time-monitoring exhibited by older children in the laboratory setting must have been induced by some features peculiar to that environment that also had special significance for youngsters of high school age. Such features might include, for example, the profusion of elaborate technical equipment or, at a more abstract level, the prestigeful and perhaps mystifying aura of science.

With respect to younger children, however, the influence of interpersonal relationships cannot be ruled out since the contrast in their pattern of monitoring in home versus out-of-home environments was confounded by the presence of an older sibling in the home setting. Hence, for this age group, the possible effect of a family member's presence on the cognitive strategies employed by the child remains an issue for future research.

The Laboratory and Ecological Validity   It is clear that, had our experiment been conducted only in the laboratory, we would have reached rather different conclusions. In particular, we would have underestimated many children's ability to employ a fairly sophisticated cognitive strategy in order to "remember not to forget." Recall that in the laboratory setting there was little evidence for strategic monitoring. Instead, children exhibited what we now recognize as comparatively high levels of clock-watching. Moreover, with the exception of older boys in the baking task, the frequency of clock-watching increased steadily during the course of the half-hour waiting period.

Over a decade ago, developmentalists voiced concern as to whether principles developed from laboratory experiments would generalize to "everyday settings" (Brown, Bransford, Ferrara, & Campione, 1983; Stevenson, 1970; White, 1970). While these arguments were not based on empirical comparisons, others have recently reported substantial differences in the effects of what is ostensibly the same behavior observed in the lab and nonlab settings (Acredolo, 1979; Bickman & Henchley, 1972; Cole, Hood, & McDermott, 1982; DeLoache, 1980; Graves & Glick, 1978; Luria, 1982; Strayer, 1980). In perhaps the seminal investigation of the lack of correspondence between laboratory and naturalistic measures of remembering, Istomina (1975) showed that children recalled approximately twice as many items from a word list when it was presented as a shopping list as opposed to a laboratory study of memory. This and other demonstrations of the noncorrespondence between naturalistic memory and laboratory remembering (e.g., Cole et al., 1982) have prompted some researchers to condemn laboratory settings, and even the analytical apparatus that experimentalists bring to the task of gathering new knowledge (e.g., Cole et al., 1982; Gergen, 1978).

In our view, the results of the present study are more properly construed not as a criticism of laboratory procedures per se, but rather as a demonstration of the limitations involved in relying exclusively on a laboratory context for clues to children's competencies on everyday tasks. Our findings point to the as yet unexploited power of the experimental laboratory as an ecological contrast that helps to highlight the distinctive features of other settings as contexts of development (Bronfenbrenner, 1977, 1979), including the development of cognitive strategies.

"Calibrating One's Psychological Clock": Fact or Fiction? It is possible to argue that the high levels of early clock-checking did not reflect children's use of the calibration strategy. After all, the deployment of the calibration strategy was only an inference. We shall contend, however, that the type of time-monitoring characteristic of high levels of early clock-checking must have been qualitatively different from the type of time-monitoring employed by children who engaged in low levels of early clock-checking. In short, more than the numbers of clock-checks were different between these groups. Otherwise, how could children with high levels of early clock-checking have been able to reduce their subsequent checking well below the levels exhibited by those with low levels of early clock-checking? It seems that the most parsimonious explanation for this turnabout in clock-checking behavior is to consider that those children who began with high levels of clock-checking were comparing the passage of real time with their subjective judgments of the length of time that had gone by; that is, they were calibrating their psychological clocks. It would appear that acquired confidence in one's estimation of time, derived through an early comparison process, was what permitted children with high levels of early clock-checking to reduce such behavior substantially during what they estimated to be the intervening period of waiting.

Caveat Lector Three shortcomings of the study need to be acknowledged. First, the present design did not permit an assessment of which aspects of the various contexts were implicated in the observed results. Further work is required to determine the importance of factors such as familiar furnishings, the presence or absence of older siblings, a "scientific" atmosphere, or some combination of these or other features in producing the observed effects. Second, one may legitimately wonder how specific the observed findings were to: (a) the use of a 30-min waiting period, (*b*) the particular tasks, (*c*) the instructions provided, and (*d*) the use of Pac Man as the intervening task. Third, some might claim that what we are calling time-monitoring is not a memory function but rather a process of attention-directing. We agree that time-monitoring is a form of attention-directing, but contend that this process is integrally involved in prospective remembering. Thus, we have referred to it as "a cognitive strategy that supports prospective memory," much like other support processes (e.g., rehearsal, metamnemonic awareness, knowledge-based strategies, etc.). That the tasks we employed entailed prospective memory can hardly be disputed; 21 out of the 96 children who participated in these tasks in fact forgot to fulfill the assigned responsibility.

CONCLUSION

The present findings would appear at first glance to run counter to the view that complex forms of memory monitoring are undeveloped in young children (see Flavell & Wellman, 1977). In this study, children as young as 10 exhibited a reasonably well-developed type of monitoring during the waiting period. Of course there is no way to be certain of our inference about what the children were doing during the waiting period, short of rerunning the experiment using clocks programmed to run faster or slower than normal—which is being done presently. Attempts through postexperimental interviews to elicit information about children's awareness of using calibration proved uninformative. To the extent that children employed a calibration strategy, they appeared to do so spontaneously, without effort or awareness, for they were unable to confirm its use during interviews. Recently, research has begun to reveal many forms of processing that are undertaken by children without awareness or effort (see Ceci, 1983, 1984, for reviews). Ceci and Howe (1982) have provided a framework and

some empirical support for the position that some forms of monitoring occur "...without intention, and neither the process of directing the attention, or the resultant product of this attention, ever became conscious....We have seen that parts of the cognitive system appear to be outside the control of the thermostat (metamemory)" (p. 162). Thus, the present findings raise the interesting specter of a fairly complex strategy being automatically deployed. If confirmed, this would help explain why young children appear to be adept at its use, as automatic processing has been shown to be age-invariant, provided that a minimal level of experience has occurred (Ceci, 1983).

In conclusion, we suggest that this series of experiments has some broader implications for research on development-in-context. First, the developmental significance of strategies employed to support retrospective memory is highlighted by the results of administering the present experiment in a nonconventional kitchen in a university building. For 10-year-olds, the kitchen may as well have been a university laboratory; for adolescents, it may as well have been their own kitchen at home. For younger children, one room at a university was as strange as another; for the adolescents, a kitchen was a kitchen regardless of where it was located, and it connoted none of the special challenge and concern experienced by young high school students exposed to the world of sophisticated science.

Even the latter, however, can lose its stirring power if the task to be performed seems unimportant. In the laboratory setting, adolescent boys steadily escalated their clock-checking lest they fail to disconnect the motorcycle battery charger on time. But when the task to be performed was remembering to remove cupcakes from the oven, there was little speedup during the waiting period; instead, the 14-year-old boys, after spending the first few minutes calibrating their psychological clocks, relaxed into a pace of less frequent monitoring until a few minutes before the expected deadline, when they again began to check the clock more often. No such temporary respite was shown by adolescent girls. For them, apparently, remembering to take cupcakes from the oven was no less challenging in a scientific setting than was disconnecting a battery charger.

None of the subtle yet psychologically significant differences in responding would have been observed, however, had the experiment been carried out solely in the home. Earlier we commented that the conclusions drawn from the study would have been different had it been conducted only in the laboratory; clearly the converse of this statement is equally true. This reciprocal relationship testifies to the scientific importance and power of the laboratory as a contrasting context for illuminating developmental processes and outcomes. Such a view of the laboratory's potential is hardly new. In a recent paper, Markova (1982) calls attention to George Herbert Mead's (1934) strong stand on this same point: "...it was Mead who vehemently defended the laboratory against those who claimed that all psychological phenomena should be explored and could be understood only in terms of individual experience. Arguing against phenomenologists and positivists at the same time, he claimed that it was wrong to overemphasize the artificiality of the experimental apparatus and technique of the psychological laboratory (Mead, 1938, p. 35). They are a necessary part of a psychological investigation because they enforce a specific and exact kind of human conduct which otherwise would not be available for investigation" (Markova, 1982, p. 197).

The repetition in the laboratory of experiments or observations conducted in a naturalistic setting like the home, or vice versa, offers rich and as yet unexploited possibilities for revealing the remarkable capabilities of children, from the earliest ages onward, to respond to their environments in ways that are cognitively complex and discriminately adaptive both to the opportunities and the risks that these environments present for the child's development.

REFERENCES

Acredolo, L. P. (1979). Laboratory versus home: The effect of environment on the 9-month-old infant's choice of spatial reference system. *Developmental Psychology, 15*, 666–667.

Bickman, L., & Henchley, T. (1972). *Beyond the laboratory: Field research in social psychology.* New York: McGraw-Hill.

Bronfenbrenner, U. (1977). Toward an experimental ecology of human development. *American Psychologist, 32*, 513–531.

Bronfenbrenner, U. (1979). *The ecology of human development: Experiments by nature and design.* Cambridge, MA: Harvard University Press.

Brown, A. L., Bransford, J. D., Ferrara, R. A., & Campione, J. C. (1983). Learning, remembering and understanding. In J. H. Flavell & E. M. Markman (Eds.), *Handbook of child psychology* (Vol. 3, pp. 77–166). New York: Wiley.

Ceci, S. J. (1983). Automatic and purposive semantic processing characteristics of normal and language/learning-disabled children. *Developmental Psychology, 19*, 427–439.

Ceci, S. J. (1984). Learning disabilities and memory development. *Journal of Experimental Child Psychology, 38*, 356–376.

Ceci, S. J., & Howe, M. J. A. (1982). Metamemory and the effects of attending, intending, and intending to attend. In G. Underwood (Ed.), *Aspects of consciousness* (Vol. 3, pp. 147–164). London: Academic Press.

Cole, M., Hood, L., & McDermott, R. (1982). Ecological niche picking: Ecological invalidity as an axiom of experimental cognitive psychology. In U. Neisser (Ed.), *Remembering in natural context* (pp. 336–341). San Francisco: W. H. Freeman.

Davis, J. A., Smith, T. W., & Stephenson, C. B. (1980). Occupational classification distributions. *General social surveys, 1972–1980: Cumulative codebook.* Chicago: National Opinion Research Center.

DeLoache, J.S. (1980). Naturalistic studies of memory for object location in very young children. In

M. Perlmutter (Ed.), *New directions for child development* (pp. 147–163). San Francisco: Jossey-Bass.

Fisher, R. (1929). *The design of experiments.* Edinburgh: Oliver & Boyd.

Flavell, J. H., & Wellman, H. M. (1977). Metamemory. In R. V. Kail & J. W. Hagen (Eds.), *Perspectives on the development of memory* (pp. 116–132). Hillsdale, NJ: Erlbaum.

Gergen, K. (1978). Experimentation in social psychology: A reappraisal. *European Journal of Social Psychology, 8,* 507–527.

Grave, Z. R., & Glick, J. (1978). The effect of context on mother-child interaction: A progress report. *Quarterly Newsletter of the Institute for Comparative Human Development, 2,* 41–46.

Harris, J., & Wilkins, A. (1982). Remembering to do things: A theoretical framework and an illustrative experiment. *Human Learning: Journal of Practical Research Applications, 1,* 1–14.

Istomina, Z. M. (1975). The development of voluntary memory in pre-school-age children. *Soviet Psychology, 13,* 5–64.

Kreutzer, M. A., Leonard, C., & Flavell, J. H. (1975). An interview study of children's knowledge about memory. *Monographs of the Society for Research in Child Development, 40,* (1, Serial No. 159).

Luria, A. R. (1982). *Language and cognition.* New York: Wiley Interscience.

Maccoby, E., & Jacklin, C. W. (1974). *The psychology of sex differences.* Stanford, CA: Stanford University Press.

Markova, I. (1982). *Paradigms, thought and language,* New York: Wiley.

Meacham, J., & Colombo, J. A. (1980). External retrieval cues facilitate prospective remembering in children. *Journal of Educational Research. 73,* 299–301.

Meacham, J., & Leiman, B. (1982). Remembering to perform future actions. In U. Neisser (Ed.), *Remembering in natural contexts* (pp. 327–335). San Francisco: W. H. Freeman.

Meacham, J. A., & Singer, J. (1977). Incentive effects in prospective remembering. *Journal of Psychology, 97,* 191–197.

Mead, G. H. (1934). *Mind, self, and society.* Chicago: University of Chicago Press.

Shepherd-Look, D. L. (1981). Sex differentiation and the development of sex roles. In B. Wolman (Ed.), *Handbook of developmental psychology.* Englewood Cliffs, NJ: Prentice-Hall.

Stevenson, H. W. (1970). Learning in children. In P. H. Mussen (Ed.), *Carmichael's manual of child psychology* (Vol. **1,** pp. 849–938). New York: Wiley.

Strayer, J. (1980). A naturalistic study of empathic behaviors and their relation to affective states and perspective-taking skills in preschool children. *Child Development, 51,* 815–822.

Wellman, H. M., Ritter, K., & Flavell, J. H. (1975). Deliberate memory behavior in the delayed reactions of very young children. *Developmental Psychology, 11,* 780–787.

White, S. H. (1970). The learning theory tradition for child psychology. In P. H. Mussen (Ed.), *Carmichael's manual of child psychology* (Vol. **1,** pp. 657–702). New York: Wiley.

Winer, B. J. (1971). *Statistical principles in experimental design* (2d ed.). New York: McGraw-Hill.

READING 29

The War over Race and IQ: When Black Children Grow Up in White Homes

Sandra Scarr-Salapatek
Richard A. Weinberg

Black children in this country, as a group, score lower on IQ tests than white children do. The difference between the two groups is about 15 points, a gap that generally corresponds to the white children's greater success in school.

The IQ difference is agreed upon by all parties in the continuing debate about race and intelligence. But there has been no resolution to the burning question of why it exists, and the efforts to explain it have generated anguish, bitterness and opprobrium among educators, makers of social policy, and laymen.

Three camps are now continuing the argument. One believes that the IQ is fixed genetically, and that efforts to change a child's score by changing his environment or giving him compensatory education must fail [see "The Differences Are Real," *pt,* December 1973]. This genetic view also maintains that IQ tests are valid because they reliably predict the academic success of all children, black and white, equally well. The second group, largely liberal and activist, retorts that black children show an IQ deficit because they live and grow in environments that are physically and intellectually impoverished. Change the environment, their argument runs, and the IQ will follow. The environmentalists consider IQ tests to be biased in favor of white middle-class children, and thus invalid measures of intelligence for minorities.

The third group, who might be called the pacifists, argues that no resolution of the debate is possible until black children are raised in exactly the same surroundings as whites. If equally rich environments close the IQ gap, then the genetic argument falls apart.

We have now completed a study on transracial adoption that provides a first look at what happens to the IQs of black children who live in white homes. Adoption changes a child's entire lifestyle around the clock, in contrast to compensatory-education programs or special classes that are wedged into the school curriculum and, at best, affect some part of the child's life between 9:00 and 3:00. If black children raised in white worlds do better on IQ tests than blacks raised in black environments, all groups in the controversy would have their answer.

WHITE PARENTS, BLACK CHILDREN

In the mid-'60s thousands of white families adopted children of other racial and nationalorigins, partly because few white infants were available for adoption, and partly because many of these families were personally committed to racial equality. We did not deal with the value judgment of whether transracial adoption is good or bad for the children and families involved; we simply seized the opportunity to see whether radical environmental change closes the IQ gap.

Over the past two years we have studied 101 white families who adopted black children. We reached them through the Minnesota Open Door Society, a group of such families, and the Adoption Unit of the Minnesota State Department of Public Welfare. In the Minneapolis area, where the black population is only 1.9 percent, black-white relationships are not as tense and troubled as they are in other states and cities. For this reason, parents can adopt children of different races easily, and the surrounding community exacts no social price, from parents or adopted children, for doing so.

A team of interviewers visited each family twice and gave every member over the age of four an IQ test: the Stanford-Binet for four-to eight-year-olds, the Wechsler Intelligence Scale for Children (WISC) for eight-to 16-year-olds, and the Wechsler Adult Intelligence Scale (WAIS) for children over 16 and their parents. The tests were all scored by an experienced psychometrician who was unaware of the children's race or adoptive status. We also interviewed the parents about the family's lifestyle, the circumstances of the adoption, and their experiences in raising children of different races.

The fathers in our transracial families tend to be professionals—ministers, engineers and lawyers. Nearly half of the mothers are employed at least part-time as secretaries, nurses, or teachers. Most of the parents are college graduates, but they are not especially wealthy. Many live in areas with a few black neighbors but most rarely see blacks in their daily lives. The households themselves often resembled miniversions of the United Nations, for a number of families adopted children of several races or nationalities in addition to having their own. The average number of children in a family was four, with a range from one to 14.

Of the 321 children in the study, 145 were natural and 176 adopted; 130 of the adoptees were black and 46 either white, Asian, or American Indian. Among the black children, 22 percent had two black parents, 52 percent had one black and one white parent, and 26 percent had one black parent and a parent of unknown or Asian ancestry.

ADOPTION AND IQ

The typical adopted child in these families—of any race—scored above the national average on standard IQ tests. But the child's age at adoption and his or her experiences before moving to the new family were strongly related to later IQ. The earlier a child was placed, the fewer disruptions in his life, and the better his care in the first few years, the higher his later IQ score was likely to be. The white adopted children, who found families earlier than any other group, scored 111 on the average; the black adopted children got IQ scores averaging 106; and the Asian and Indian children, who were adopted later than any other group, and more of whom had lived longer in impersonal institutions, scored at the national average, 100.

If the black adopted children had been reared by their natural parents, we would expect their IQ scores to average about 90. We infer these scores from the level of education and the occupations of their biological parents. The black adopted children, however, scored well above the national averages of both blacks and whites, especially if they were adopted early in life. In fact, the *lowest* score of an early-

adopted black child, 86, was close to the average for all black children in the nation.

When we compare black and white adoptees, it seems that the white children still have an IQ advantage, 111 to 106. However, the black children had lived with their adoptive families for fewer years than the white children and were younger when we tested them. Adoption at an early age increased the scores of black children to an average of 110. There was a trend for early adoption to increase the IQ scores of white children too, but we have only nine cases in that category.

True to their higher IQ scores, the black adopted children also did better at school, a real-life criterion of intellectual achievement. They scored above the average for Minnesota schoolchildren and above the national average as well on aptitude and achievement tests. In reading and math they scored in the 55th percentile; in comparison, the average ranking for all black children in the Minneapolis-St. Paul area is the 15th percentile.

The adoptive families are clearly doing something that develops intellectual skills in all of their children, adopted or not. These parents were a particularly bright group—with an average IQ of 121 for the fathers and 118 for the mothers—that is reflected in their high levels of education. Their natural children, who have lived in such enriched environments since their birth, scored above the adopted children and slightly below the parents.

	IQ scores		
	Number	Average	Range
All adopted children			
Black	130	106	68–144
White	25	111	62–143
Other	21	100	66–129
Early adopted children			
Black	99	110	86–136
White	9	117	99–138
Other	only three cases		
Natural children	144	117	81-150

THE INFLUENCES OF BIRTH VS. BREEDING

When it comes to explaining just why individual children differ in IQ, however, we still don't have a perfect way to separate genetic and environmental influences. Consider Daniel and Sara, two black children who were adopted before they were six months old. Daniel's adoptive father is a professor of biology and his mother is a high-school English teacher; both have high IQs. They had two children before adopting Daniel. The boy's black natural parents were college students. At the age of eight, Daniel tested out with an IQ of 123.

Sara's adoptive father is a minister, and her mother a housewife; their IQs are average. They have four other children, two of whom were also adopted. Sara's black mother was a nurse's aide who had a 10th-grade education, and her father a construction worker who quit high school in the 11th grade. At the age of eight, Sara's IQ was 98.

Daniel and Sara had a different biological heritage and rearing environment. Which contributed more?

Children are not dealt randomly into adoptive homes like poker hands. Adoption agencies usually try to match the backgrounds of the natural and adoptive parents. As a result, children like Daniel, whose natural parents were well-educated, tend to get placed with adoptive parents who also are bright and have professional careers. So adopted children show an intellectual ability related to that of their natural parents, even though they were not raised by them.

To answer the genetic argument that blacks have lower IQ scores than whites because of their African ancestry, we compared the IQ scores of children who had had one black parent with those who had had two. The 19 children of two black parents got an average score of 97, while the 68 with only one black parent scored 109.

One might leap to the old genetic-deficiency explanation, but the confounding problem is that the two groups had very different place-

COMPARISON OF ADOPTED CHILDREN HAVING EITHER ONE OR TWO BLACK NATURAL PARENTS

	Children with two black parents (29)	Children with one black and one white parent (68)[*]
IQ	97	109
Age at adoption (in months)	32	9
Length of time in new family (in months)	42	61
Natural mother's education (in years)	10.9	12.4
Adoptive father's IQ	119.5	121.4
Adoptive mother's IQ	116.4	119.2

[*] Note in all but two of these cases the pattern was a white woman and a black man

ment histories and their mothers differed in amount of education. The children who had two black parents were significantly older when they were adopted, had been in their new homes a shorter time when we tested them, and had had more placements before being adopted. Further, their black natural mothers had less education than the white natural mothers and probably underwent more risks during pregnancy. Prenatal problems can affect a child's intellectual ability.

Intelligence, then—at least as measured by IQ tests—is a result both of environment and genetics, but overall, our study impressed us with the strength of environmental factors. Children whose natural parents had relatively little education and presumably below-average IQs can do extremely well if they grow up in enriched surroundings. If a different environment can cause the IQ scores of black children to shift from a norm of 90 or 95 to 110, then the views advanced by the genetic determinists cannot account for the current IQ gap between blacks and whites. Our work does not rule out genetic contributions to intelligence, but it does demonstrate that a massive environmental change can increase black IQ scores to an above-average level. Social factors, such as age at placement and the adoptive family's characteristics play a strong role in accounting for this increase.

COOLING OUT THE CONTROVERSY

The touchy and troubling question is, now what? Schools, as presently run, do not have the far-reaching, intensive impact of the family in the formation and enhancement of a child's intelligence. But no one would be so arrogant or foolhardy to endorse transracial adoption as social policy, shipping black children into white homes with the same furious effort now devoted to bussing them into white schools. On the contrary, many black-action groups are now putting pressure on adoption agencies to make sure that transracial adoption does not occur.

Now we need to find out what goes on in these adoptive families that enhances IQ. From personality tests and observations of the parents we worked with, we know they are generally warm, comfortable, free of anxiety, and relaxed with children. They run democratic households in which adults and kids participate in many activities together. These factors, along with the intellectual stimulation that the children are exposed to, are doubtless involved in their children's higher IQs. We need to look for other intangibles in the things parents give their children and do with them that increase intelligence.

And after we've found all the intangibles, we may want to ask whether IQ should be an overriding middle-class value at all. Intelligence tests do measure how well a child will get on in a white middle-class schoolroom, but tell us nothing about a person's empathy, sociability and altruism, a few blessed virtues that tend to get brushed off the psychologist's test battery.

But for the moment, at least, we have evidence that the black-white IQ gap is neither inevitable nor unchangeable. Smug whites have no cause to rest on biological laurels. The question no longer is why blacks do more poorly on IQ tests than whites. The question is what we are prepared to do about it.

CHAPTER 7

SOCIAL COGNITION

Children develop an understanding not only of the physical world but also of the social world. They learn about the characteristics, behavior, and roles of themselves and others and of social groups and organizations. In some ways the development of social cognition parallels that of knowledge of the physical world, but social cognition also has its own unique developmental questions, tasks, and developmental course.

The recognition of the self is an important developmental attainment. The article by Jeanne Brooks-Gunn and Michael Lewis in this section focuses on only one aspect of the self, self recognition, though other aspects of the self, such as gender identity, self monitoring, self-control and feelings of competence, are important influences on social and emotional development. Many theorists view the interaction with the physical world as important in gaining knowledge of the self but hold that the critical factor in the development of the self is interaction in the social world. Therefore, the responses of significant people in the child's environment—parents, siblings, peers, and teachers are salient in shaping the child's self understanding.

Children must become aware not only of their own distinctive attributes of self and the way others respond to them, but they must also develop an understanding of how the traits, abilities, and behavior of others will vary in different social situations and in different roles. William Rholes and Diane Ruble present two experiments examining children's understanding of the dispositional characteristics of others. Their findings show that older children are more likely than younger children to understand that the attributes of people tend to remain the same although situations change. Surprisingly, however, it was found that even younger children (5- and 6-year-olds) understood that the characteristics of others remained stable over time. The authors offer two explanations for the finding that children younger than about age 8 tend to describe people in terms of superficial physical attributes such as appearance, clothes, hair, age, possessions, and residence rather than stable personality traits or dispositions that generalize across situations. The first is that the concept of stable personal traits is not understood by younger children; the second is that the understanding of stability in personal attributes across situations is related to the acquisition of the concept of invariance of such things as mass, volume, and number that is demonstrated in conservation studies. This is related to the appearance-reality distinction made by John Flavell in his article in the previous section. Although there may be superficial changes in appearance, activities, and situations, the individual's dispositional characteristics remain relatively stable.

Finally, Malcolm Watson examines children's developmental knowledge about social roles. Social roles are socially prescribed attributes and behaviors that are expected in a particular category of people. An understanding of social roles leads to expectations about people's behavior in those roles and behavior of the self in varying role relationships. It is important to note that people can simultaneously assume multiple roles, e.g., a woman in the role of daughter to father, wife to husband, mother to child, and employee to employer. When the demands of these roles conflict, severe stress and emotional turmoil can result. Watson proposes that there is a predictable developmental sequence involved in children's knowledge about social roles. The development of this hierarchically ordered sequence of knowledge about social roles involves the combining of social cognitive skills learned at earlier levels into a new, more advanced, complex order level that includes the previous subskills.

These three articles are representative of a burgeoning area of research merging cognitive and social development. Knowledge about the self, others, the social structure, roles, and relationships are critical mediators of social behavior.

The Development of Early Visual Self-Recognition

Jeanne Brooks-Gunn
Michael Lewis

Until quite recently, the preverbal child was believed to have little awareness of the self. The acceptance of a more active and constructionist view of the young child has led to a reconsideration of the young child's concept of the self. In the present paper, the literature on the development of visual self-recognition is reviewed with respect to five topics—(1) phylogenetic trends in the emergence of self-recognition, (2) ontogenetic changes in the first 3 years of life, (3) individual differences in the expression of self-recognition, (4) social and cognitive factors as they relate to self-recognition, (5) methodological issues associated with the measurement of self-recognition. The self-recognition findings are discussed in terms of their possible relevance for social relations, social cognition, and affective growth.

> Observation 61—Jacqueline seems not to have looked at her hands before 0; 2(30). But on this date and the following days she frequently notices her moving fingers and looks at them attentively. At 0; 3(22) her glance follows her hands which turn aside and she seems very much surprised to see them reappear.

> Observation 57—Beginning 0; 2(8) Laurent constantly pulls at his face before, during, or after sucking his fingers. This behavior slowly gains interest for its own sake and thus gives use to two distinct habits. The first consists in holding his nose. Thus at 0; 2(17) Laurent babbles and smiles without any desire to suck, while holding his nose with his right hand. (Piaget, 1963/1952/1936, pp. 93–96)

> When four and a half months old, he repeatedly smiled at my image and his own in a mirror, and no doubt mistook them for real objects; but he showed sense in being evidently surprised at my voice coming from behind him. Like all infants he much enjoyed thus looking at himself, and in less than two months perfectly understood that it was an image;

for if I made quite silently any odd grimace, he would suddenly turn around to look at me.

> When nine months old he associated his own name with his image in the looking-glass, and when called by name would turn towards the glass even when at some distance from it. (Darwin, 1877, pp. 289–290)

> Let us imagine ourselves in the position of an almost entirely helpless living organism; as yet unorientated in the world and with stimuli impinging on its nervous tissue. The organism will soon become capable of making a first discrimination and a first orientation. On the one hand, it will detect certain stimuli which can be avoided by an action of the muscles (flight)—these it ascribes to an outside world. On the other hand, it will also be aware of stimuli against which such action is of no avail...—these stimuli are the tokens of an inner world. (Freud, 1959/1915, Vol. IV, p. 62)

WHAT IS THE SELF?

Although they may seem dissimilar, the observations of Piaget, Freud, and Darwin have much in common. All were describing events in which infants were discovering their emerging sense of self, an activity that necessitates exploration of oneself, objects, and people. As our examples would suggest, the emergence of a self as separate from others appears to occur very early. Psychoanalytic theorists emphasize the tempering of instinctual desires through the gradual differentiation of self and another (Freud, 1965); sociologists stress the growing awareness of self as distinct from, but in relation to, other persons (Mead, 1934); and epistemologists discuss the changing cognitive structures which enable the child to see the social world and the self as related but distinct (Piaget, 1963).

In the present paper, we wish to explore two questions—What is the self, and how does the self emerge in the first 3 years of life? The first question has intrigued philosophers and scientists for centuries. Although we have portrayed the self as "an experimental ghost haunting social science" (Lewis & Brooks-Gunn, 1979a) and Epstein has described it as "a slippery concept whose adequate definition is irritatingly elusive" (1973, p. 404), the concept of the self has been a major theme in Western thought as evidenced by early Homeric writings (Diggory, 1966). For theorists such as Mead (1934), the self still is defined primarily by other's behavior and action toward the subject. For Epstein (1973), the self is constructed by the individuals themselves and constitutes all the attitudes and feelings that may be attributed to the subject. For genetic epistemologists, such as Merleau-Ponty (1964), Wallon (1949), and Piaget (1954), the self is derived through the knowledge both of self and other, with each developing through interaction with the social world (Lewis & Brooks-Gunn, 1981).

Even if a definition of self could be agreed upon, its developmental course in the young child might prove elusive to psychologists. Until quite recently, the preverbal child was believed to have little awareness of self, the issue being seen as phenomenological in nature or the province of ego psychology. The recent attention to the topic by developmental psychologists is based on the acceptance of the constructionist view that organisms act upon their world rather than organisms being acted upon by their world (Lewis & Brooks, 1975). Organisms, by their actions, affect their environment and actively use environmental information based upon their individual plans and cognitive organizations. Incoming stimuli are recorded and directed by deliberate action rather than being passively stored (Neisser, 1967). That children, notably young infants, make plans and test hypotheses implies an agent of these plans. Thus, the active construction of the world might be attributed to the self (Lewis & Weinraub, 1979; Lewis & Brooks-Gunn, 1979b).

The definition of the child as an active thinker, the importance of social context upon the acquisition of knowledge and development of shared symbol systems, and the differentiation of the self and others all necessitate a reconsideration of the child's concept of the self. The following review focuses on what is known about early self knowledge—procedures and criteria used to assess and infer self-knowledge as well as behavioral antecedents of, ontogenetic trends in, and cognitive and social correlates of visual self-recognition.

Most of the studies investigating the origins of self-knowledge have utilized procedures designed to study self-recognition, which is only one aspect of self-knowledge. Although other aspects of the self (self-permanence, self-control, self-regulation, and auditory or tactile self-recognition) are of equal importance, they have not received much empirical attention, in part because of the difficulty in generating nonverbal techniques for their study. The following review, then, focuses on visual self-recognition.

Visual recognition involves more than a simple discrimination of body features. To determine that a picture, mirror reflection, or movie is a representation of the self rather than another person, some rudimentary knowledge of one's own identity, identity that is continuous in time and space, is necessary (Gallup, 1977). The self may be visually experienced in different representational mediums, including mirrors, pictures, movies, and videotapes. Mirrors, the most common medium, present contingency and feature cues. By using pictures and videotape representations, contingency and feature similarity may be systematically manipulated in order to better understand what cues are necessary for self-recognition and whether developmental trends in cue salience exist.

In this review, the following topics are addressed: (1) the phylogenetic trends for visual self-recognition, (2) the ontogenetic changes and individual differences in the expression of self-recognition, (3) the relationships between self-recognition and other social and cognitive factors, and (4) the methodological issues associated with the measurement of self-recognition.

PHYLOGENETIC TRENDS IN SELF-RECOGNITION

Reactions to observing self-reflections in mirrors have been extensively studied in a variety of species. Gallup has reviewed the literature on several occasions (1968, 1977) and has distinguished between mirror-image stimulation (situations in which an organism sees its own reflection in a mirror), and self-recognition (behavior in which the self rather than the mirror is the referent). Using these definitions, reactions to a mirror may be divided into two categories—mirror-directed and self-directed behaviors.

Mirror-Directed Behavior

Mirror-image stimulation appears to have social properties. Many species act differently in the presence of a mirror than they do in isolation. For example, chickens characteristically eat more in the presence of conspecifics and in the presence of mirrors than when they are alone (Tolman, 1965). Not only do animals react as if the mirror were a social object, but they act as though it were a conspecific. The most well-known and oldest example of this involves aggressive displays toward a mirror image, reliably elicited in fish, birds, and primates (Lissman, 1932; Ritter & Benson, 1934; Schmidt, 1878). The fact that primates will search behind a mirror, presumably for the reflected image, also may be considered socially appropriate conspecific behavior. A further social discrimination is made by some species as the mirror image is usually seen as an unfamiliar rather than a familiar conspecific. When confronted

with a mirror, male macaque monkeys exhibit a facial gesture that is elicited by unfamiliar male macaques but not by familiar male conspecifics such as other colony members.

Thus, many species act as though the mirror were another organism and not the self. The reflected image is seen as another being, is treated as an unfamiliar conspecific, and does not elicit any self-directed behavior. Additionally, mirror-image stimulation elicits such high interest that it has been used as a reward in learning paradigms (Gallup, 1966; Gallup & McClure, 1971; McLean, 1964; Melvin & Anson, 1970; Thompson, 1963). These species' interest may not be related to an awareness of the contingent nature of mirror feedback, as they may be so stimulus-bound that they are unable to escape from the contingent feedback, while not being aware of or actively experimenting with the contingency itself. In brief, no phylogenetic trends have been found for mirror-directed behaviors.

Self-Directed Behavior

While mirror-directed behavior has been observed in many animals, self-directed behavior has been previously observed only in primates. Monkeys have been shown to react to their own reflections as if they were unfamiliar conspecifics and have been shown to prefer viewing conspecifics rather than mirrors (Gallup & McClure, 1971). Although the contingent action of the mirror image elicits high interest and some conspecific-appropriate behavior, it is not as interesting as the noncontingent action of another. Presumably this is due to the importance of reciprocal interaction for primates. In addition, monkeys are able to use mirrors to manipulate objects (Brown, McDowell, & Robinson, 1965) and to look at objects and persons indirectly (Tinkelpaugh, 1928). However, they do not seem to understand the nature of a reflective surface as it pertains to themselves.

The first demonstration of self-directed behavior in subhuman primates occurred in 1970, when Gallup observed four wild-born preadolescent chimpanzees' reactions to mirrors. The chimpanzees used the mirror to examine and to groom visually inaccessible parts of their bodies after only several days of experience with mirrors. As the incidence of self-directed behavior increased, other-directed behavior decreased. To investigate further the occurrence of self-directed behavior, Gallup anesthetized each animal and placed red odorless dye on the eyebrow ridge and opposite ear. Placed in front of the mirror again, all four chimpanzees directed their actions toward the marks on their faces rather than the mirror image. Not only did they touch their marked faces but they spent more time observing themselves in the marked condition than they had previously. Interestingly, two other marked chimpanzees who had no prior exposure to mirrors did not exhibit self- or mark-directed behaviors.

These findings strongly suggest that chimpanzees are able to recognize themselves in mirrors and that this recognition does not occur without some exposure to mirrors (Gallup, 1970). These findings have been replicated with other chimpanzees (Gallup, McClure, Hill, & Bundy, 1971; Hill, Bundy, Gallup, & McClure, 1970, Lethmate & Ducker, 1973) and extended to orangutans (Lethmate & Ducker, 1973). Whether or not gorillas, the other great ape species, exhibit mark recognition is open to debate (Gallup, 1979). Interestingly, no primate species other than the great apes have been found to exhibit self-recognition, even after thousands of hours of mirror experience (Gallup, 1970). Macaques, rhesus monkeys, Java monkeys, spider monkeys, capuchins, baboons, and gibbons (Gallup, 1970, 1979; Lethmate & Ducker, 1973; Benhar, Carlton, & Samuel, 1975; Pribram, as cited in Gallup, 1973) all have failed to recognize themselves in mirrors, illustrating one of the few striking discontinuities between great apes and lower primate species.[1]

In summary, phylogenetic changes occur with regard to the transition from other- to self-directed behavior. Species such as birds and fish only exhibit socially appropriate and other-directed behavior; the lower primates such as monkeys recognize the duality of mirrors for others but not for themselves and discriminate between mirror images and conspecifics; and the higher primates such as chimpanzees exhibit self-directed behavior and may be said to recognize themselves.

ONTOGENETIC TRENDS IN SELF-RECOGNITION

From the beginning of recorded history, mirrors and reflective surfaces have been used to ascertain how and what one looks like. Adults have little trouble recognizing themselves in mirrors or pictures, especially in terms of their faces. At what point in the ontogenetic sequence does recognition occur? This question will be answered by examining anecdotal accounts, infant intelligence test data, and experimental studies in three visual representations—reflective surfaces, photographic representations, and videotape/movie representations.

Self-Recognition in Mirrors

Early and Anecdotal Accounts of Self-Recognition The potency of the mirror for the young is undisputed. About 100 years ago, Preyer (1893) and Darwin (1877) both ob-

[1]Epstein, Lanza, and Skinner (1981) have demonstrated that pigeons may be trained, via a variable-ratio reinforcement schedule, to peck at a blue dot presented on a mirror. After such training, the pigeons were able to peck at a spot on themselves as seen in a mirror. The authors maintain that they have demonstrated "how at least one instance of behavior attributed to self-awareness can be accounted for in terms of environmental history (p. 696)." However, whether such training reflects self-recognition and whether such behavior would be shown to any image of a pigeon rather than the self is not explored. Since the demonstration of self–other differentiation is the issue, the results of the study, while interesting, do not speak directly to the issue of phylogenetic trends in self-recognition.

served that mirror-image stimulation elicited great interest and curiosity in their children. Darwin observed what he thought was self-recognition in his 9-month-old son. Zazzo (1948) observed his son's recognition of self in mirrors at 2½ years of age.

Infant Intelligence Tests   Almost all of the infant intelligence test developers included mirror items in their scales, although most were not interested in self-recognition per se (Bayley, 1969; Buhler, 1930; Cattell, 1940; Gesell, 1928; Gesell & Thompson, 1934; Griffiths, 1954; Stutsman, 1931). The test items may be classified into five categories—(1) regards own image, (2) social responses, (3) searching behavior, (4) other-directed behavior, and (5) verbal self-reference. Only the first two categories were represented in all of the infant tests and only Buhler, Gesell, and Stutsman included mirror-related items for infants in the second year of life. Buhler's intelligence test actively charted the development of mirror behavior with the following four skills—(1) by 8 months of age, infants regard their image with interest and smile at their reflection; (2) by 12 to 14 months, infants touch and feel the mirror image as well as grasp at the mirror reflection when an object is placed behind them; (3) by 15 to 17 months, infants respond with "astonishment" and turn around when seeing another person in the mirror (presumably, the properties of the reflective surface are being understood for the first time); (4) by 18 to 20 months, searching behind the mirror is seen. The approximate ages at which these skills appear have been verified in more recent work (Bertenthal & Fischer, 1978; Lewis & Brooks-Gunn, 1979a). Gesell (1928), Gesell and Thompson (1934), and Stutsman (1931) included self-directed behaviors as test items. For example, the Merrill–Palmer scale norms indicate that two thirds of the 2-year-olds recognized or labeled themselves when seeing themselves in mirrors (Stutsman, 1931), and the Gesell tests

indicate that the majority of 3-year-olds use their name to label themselves.

In summary, the infant intelligence tests shed little light on visual self-recognition since few items measure behaviors indicative of self-recognition, large discrepancies in the type and number of mirror items included in each scale exist, and many of the test designers did not even include items indicative of self-recognition.

Experimental Studies   The experimental literature provides a fairly precise account of how infants usually respond when seeing themselves in a mirror, how their responses change with age, and how they respond in a situation designed to elicit self-recognition. A procedure to elicit self-recognition in mirrors was developed by Amsterdam (1968) and Gallup (1970). In the Amsterdam procedure, the infant's face is marked, either with rouge or tape, and the infant's response to seeing the marked face in a mirror observed. As in Gallup's procedure, mark-directed behavior is the operational definition of self-recognition since infants must recognize that the image in the mirror is in fact the self and that the mark resides not on the image's face but on their own. At least eight groups of investigators have used variants of this procedure (Amsterdam, 1968, 1972; Ashford & Brooks, 1981; Bertenthal & Fischer, 1978; Bigelow, in press; Lewis & Brooks-Gunn, 1982; Dickie & Strader, 1974; Johnson, 1980; Lewis & Brooks-Gunn, 1979a; Mans, Cicchetti, & Sroufe, 1978). Two other methods have been used, one that contrasts infants' responses to their own mirror image to that of their twin (Dixon, 1957), and one that compares infants' responses to distorted and to flat mirrors (Modaressi & Kenny, 1977; Schulman & Kaplowitz, 1977). A variety of different behaviors have been observed, some of which are age-related and/or are indicative of self-recognition. The findings for six different behavioral categories are discussed, since different measures and behaviors seem to have different developmental courses.

Interest and Attention   In all studies, mirrors elicit a great deal of attention. Boulanger-Balleyguier (1964) observed interest in mirrors at 1 month of age. When interest in the mother, a female stranger, and one's own mirror image were compared, infants preferred to look at their own image more than the unfamiliar, but less than the familiar person. Other investigators have reported interest in mirrors occurring around 3 to 4 months of age (Amsterdam, 1972; Dixon, 1957), and the infant intelligence tests place this item at 5 to 8 months of age. Interest does not seem to be related to self-recognition.

Pleasurable Responses   The overwhelming response to a mirror is one of pleasure—smiling, vocalizing, and touching the mirror. These pleasurable behaviors have been likened to sociable responses directed to a playmate by Amsterdam (1972), Dixon (1957), and Gesell and Thompson (1938), and would be considered other-directed by Gallup (1968). The playmate analogy was originally based on Dixon's observation that his twin sons responded to their own mirror images and each other in a sociable and undistinguishable manner in the first year of life.

Pleasurable behaviors are seen in infants from 1 to 24 months of age, with Boulanger-Balleyguier (1964) reporting smiling in "advanced" 1-month olds. In terms of prevalence, Amsterdam (1972) finds the most sociable behaviors between 5 to 19 months of age, Dixon (1957) between 5 to 12 months of age, Schulman and Kaplowitz (1977) between 7 to 18 months of age, and Dickie and Strader (1974) at approximately 12 months of age. Lewis and Brooks-Gunn (1979a) report no age differences, instead finding that pleasurable responses are coupled with different behaviors at different ages—with sustained looking, kissing, and hitting at 9 months and with touching the body, touching the nose, and acting silly at 24 months. A pleasure component that is independent of

other systems may exist or affect may be in the service of different motives—pleasure or excitement in the 9-month-old, and self-recognition in the 24-month-old.

Mirror-Directed Behavior   Mirror-directed behavior has been characterized as a sociable or an other-directed response that drops out or decreases as self-recognition emerges (Amsterdam & Greenberg, 1977; Gallup, 1977). Most studies report decreases throughout the second year, at least for behavior such as kissing, hitting, and touching.

Interestingly, pointing may indicate some awareness of the mirror image as a reflection of oneself, since a point often has a "look at me" quality and may imply a distancing from the mirror, both in time and space. Pointing seems to increase in the second year of life, unlike the other mirror-directed behaviors (Lewis & Brooks-Gunn, 1979a).

Imitation   Imitative behaviors can be both other directed and self directed, since they require the infant to watch the self and act. Rhythmic movements such as bouncing, waving, and clapping are prevalent in the first year of life (Gesell & Ames, 1947; Dixon, 1957) and do not seem to be indicative of self-recognition (Amsterdam, 1972; Lewis & Brooks-Gunn, 1979a).

Self-Consciousness   Amsterdam (1972) has used the term self-conscious reaction for behaviors such as acting silly, acting coy, and appearing embarrassed when seeing the self in the mirror. Preyer (1893) found that his son acted self-consciously at approximately 17 months of age; Dixon (1957) observed similar behavior between 12 and 18 months of age; Amsterdam (1972), Schulman and Kaplowitz (1977), and Lewis and Brooks-Gunn (1979a) reported self-admiration and/or embarrassment from 15 to 24 months of age. In the last three samples, silly or coy behaviors were seen in very few infants under 15 months of age and were not the modal response until 18 months of age. Such behavior may not be seen in any situation before 1½ years of life (cf. Marvin, Marvin & Abramo-vitch, 1973).

Whether self-conscious and coy behavior is a precursor, appears concurrently, or even follows mark recognition is not known. Amsterdam's data (1972) suggest that self-consciousness is a precursor while other data suggest it may not be (Schulman & Kaplowitz, 1977). Logically, it seems that recognition of oneself might be necessary to be self-conscious of one's mirror image.

Self-Directed Behavior   Self-directed behavior may be measured by observing whether children touch any part of their bodies in response to the mark on the face or whether they touch the mark itself. Touching any part of the body may indicate self-awareness since seeing the mark in the mirror may elicit increased body focus and therefore body-directed behavior. Infants increase their body touching as a function of mark application between 9 to 24 months of age (Lewis & Brooks-Gunn, 1979a).

Mark-directed behavior appears to be a more direct measure of self-recognition since it is tied to a specific featural referent. In at least four studies, mark-directed behavior (using the mark-on-the-face technique) was never exhibited by infants younger than 15 months of age. The incidence of mark recognition in the 15- to 18-month-old group differs across studies—25% (Lewis & Brooks-Gunn, 1979a), 5% (Amsterdam, 1972), 50% (Lewis & Brooks-Gunn, 1982), and none (Schulman & Kaplowitz, 1977). Between 18 and 20 months of age a dramatic shift occurrs, with approximately three-quarters of the 18- to 24-month-olds in all studies exhibiting the phenomenon.

²The development of the mark-on-the face technique by Gallup and Amsterdam is a good example of how a similar procedure may be devised by two independent investigators at the same time.

³The relatively high incidence of mark-directed behavior in this study probably is due to the fact that all infants were 18 months of age and all testing was done in the infant's home.

Although the findings with regard to mark-directed behavior are quite consistent from study to study, they may be confounded by the particular experimental design. Several potential methodological problems should be noted. First, having the face wiped may lead to an increase in nose touching. Second, an increase in the amount of time spent in front of the mirror may be associated with an increase in the frequency of nose touching (infants may spontaneously touch their noses given a long enough observation period). Third, olfactory cues (offered by the rouge) and visual cues (parts of the nose can be seen by looking cross-eyed, down to the right or left, or alternating eyes open and closed) may elicit mark-directed behavior. To test the first two possibilities, we observed infants in front of a mirror before and after they had their faces and noses wiped (but no rouge applied). Nose-directed behavior did not occur on either the pre-or post-test condition and face-directed behavior did not increase after face wiping. To see whether the increase in behaviors from the unmarked to the marked condition was due to the use of two mirror observations, infants' responses to their marked faces without a preceding unmarked condition were observed. No differences in the incidence of mark-directed, body-directed, and imitative behavior were found between this sample and a sample that had an unmarked and marked condition (Lewis & Brooks-Gunn, 1979a). The possibility of a visual cue offered by placement of rouge on the nose is slight, as no investigators have reported cross-eyed behavior and mark placement was slightly different across studies.

Finally, the results from the two studies utilizing distorted mirror images suggest that infants do not differentiate between normal and distorted mirror images until 18 to 20 months of age, at which time infants seem to avoid their distorted image (Dickie & Strader, 1974; Modaressi & Kenny, 1977).

Self-Recognition in Moving Picture Representation

It is clear that young children are able to recognize themselves in mirrors and that ontogenetic changes occur. However, the issue of what cues are salient for self-recognition in the first 2 years of life may not be answered by the mirror paradigm. For example, infants could be responding to the social features that are common to the image and to the self (i.e., same-age, same-sex peer), to the contingent feedback offered by the mirror, to the familiarity of the perceptual features in the mirror (i.e., specific facial features common to self and image), or to some combination of these. By utilizing moving pictures, specifically a videotape feedback system, it is possible to obtain information on cue salience.

To date, only a few investigators have utilized videotape systems. Papousek and Papousek (1974) explored the saliency of eye-to-eye contact and contingency in 5-month-old infants' responses to videotapes of self and of other infants presented simultaneously. Five research groups have explored infants' responses to a simultaneous representation of the self (contingent self), a videotape of the self (noncontingent or discordant self), and a videotape of another infant in the same situation (noncontingent other). Bigelow (1975, in press) followed a small sample longitudinally from 18 to 26 months; Amsterdam and Greenberg (1977) observed 10-, 15-, and 20-month olds; Lewis and Brooks-Gunn (1979a) observed 9- to 36-month-olds; Johnson (1980) observed 12- to 26-month-olds, and Ashford and Brooks (1981) observed 4- to 25-month-olds. In another study, a person silently approached the infant from behind (with white noise covering any inadvertent noise the

---

[4]The infants were free to roam in the Amsterdam and Greenberg (1977) study so that the control was more likely to be directly in front of the TV monitor than the subject, and more direct frontal viewing was possible in the child control than the self conditions. In the other studies, subjects were placed on seats in front of a television monitor.

stranger made). The approach was live during the contingent self condition but was on the videotape during the noncontingent self and other conditions (Lewis & Brooks-Gunn, 1979a).

These studies present information relevant to three issues—(1) how infants respond to simultaneous representations of themselves in a videotape situation and whether their responses are similar to those seen in mirror studies, (2) whether or not infants respond differentially to contingent and noncontingent representations of themselves, and (3) whether or not infants respond differently to noncontingent representations of self and other.

Contingent Videotape Representations The overwhelming response to the videotape contingent representations of self is one of pleasure and interest. All infants spend a great deal of time looking at the videotapes, and the vast majority of infants smile or vocalize positively, and almost no infants cry or frown in any of the studies. Unlike the decreases in sociable behavior reported in some of the mirror studies, the videotape studies report either no change (Amsterdam & Greenberg, 1977) or an increase in smiling and vocalizing in the second year (Bigelow, 1975; Lewis & Brooks-Gunn, 1979a).

Clear developmental changes are reported for contingent play, including deliberate movements and imitation of the videotape image (Ashford and Brooks, 1981; Lewis & Brooks-Gunn, 1979a). In one study, play was exhibited by one third of the 9- to 12-month-olds, two thirds of the 15- to 18-month-olds, and almost all of the 21- to 24-month-olds (Lewis & Brooks-Gunn, 1979a).

Self-consciousness was observed by Amsterdam and Greenberg (1977), who had earlier suggested that such behavior first occurred at 15 months and became the modal response at 20 months in mirror situations (Amsterdam, 1972). Similar findings are reported for the videotape procedure, with none of the 10-month-olds, one quarter of the 15-month-olds, and all of the 20-month-olds exhibiting self-conscious behavior in the contingent self condition. Ashford and Brooks (1981) found that 22-month-olds were more likely to locate a spot on the nose when a mirror rather than a videotape situation was used (40 vs 90%); by 25 months of age the differences had disappeared.

Bertenthal and Fischer (1978) examined turning away from the mirror and toward an object suspended from the ceiling behind the infant. They found that the majority of 14-to 16-month-olds were able to perform this task. Turning toward an object and away from the videotape image occurred in one third of Johnson's (1980) 12-to 17-month-olds. Turning away from the videotape image and toward a person in the videotape contingent conditions occurred at 9 to 12 months of age in the Lewis and Brooks-Gunn study (1979a). The age differences may be due to the use of people versus objects as well as videotape versus a mirror reflection. Taken together, these findings suggest that infants are able to turn toward objects or persons at an earlier age than they are able to locate a mark on the face.

Contingent versus Noncontingent Representations The results from several studies point to the fact that infants respond differently to contingent and noncontingent representations and do so very early. Papousek and Papousek (1974) report that 5-month-olds discriminate between noncontingent eye contact and contingent–no eye contact representations of self, first preferring the latter. However, over repeated presentations, the contingent condition elicits increased attention and movement. The authors hypothesize that the infants were learning about the contingency during the testing, which might account for the increase in responding over repeated trials. Rheingold (1971) found that 5-month-old infants responded more positively to a mirror than to a moving picture of a baby (not the self). Given these findings

with young infants, it is not surprising that differentiation between contingent and noncontingent representations was found by 9 to 12 months of age in some of the videotape studies, as infants were much more likely to respond positively, to perform deliberate movements, and to turn toward the target in contingent than in noncontingent self conditions, but were more likely to watch the noncontingent than the contingent conditions (Ashford & Brooks, 1981; Bigelow, in press; Lewis & Brooks-Gunn, 1979a). Overall differentiation of contingent and noncontingent representations was not found until 20 months by Amsterdam and Greenberg (1977) using self-consciousness as the criteria, 22 months of Ashford and Brooks (1981) using deliberate movements, and 24 months by Bigelow (in press) using labeling the noncontingent self condition. Differences between studies are probably due to the different measures employed, i.e., self-conscious behavior does not seem to be part of the younger infants' repertoire, while affect, interest, and head turning are. However, that three studies pinpoint 18 to 20 months as the critical age point provides fairly consistent evidence across studies.

Self-Other Dimension Infants also responded differentially to noncontingent representations of self and other, exhibiting more positive affect and attention to another infant's videotape than their own and more imitation, deliberate movement, and turning behavior in self than in other videotape conditions (Ashford & Brooks, 1981; Bigelow, in press; Lewis & Brooks-Gunn, 1979a). Imitation of the self videotape may indicate that infants expect the videotape of themselves to respond contingently, since their usual commerce is with mirrors. The affectual and attentional preference for the other may be due to the fact that some avoidance behavior is elicited by the infant's failure to produce contingency responses in the noncontingent self condition or may be due to infants' interest in peers (McCall & Kennedy,

1980). In general, differentiation of self and other occurred between 15 to 18 and 21 to 24 months of age. Imitation and contingent play are the first behaviors to be used differentially, with turning, self-conscious behaviors, and verbal self-references emerging later (Amsterdam & Greenberg, 1977; Bigelow, in press; Johnson, 1980; Lewis & Brooks-Gunn, 1979a).

Still Pictorial Representations in Self-Recognition

Self recognition also may be assessed using still pictorial representations. Recognizing a picture of oneself as self may be a more demanding task than recognizing oneself in a videotape or a mirror, since cues, such as movement and vocalization, are not available. In addition, infants have less experience with pictures than with mirrors. In one study the majority of mothers reported that their infants saw pictures of themselves and familiar others very infrequently, and many believed that their infants could not recognize themselves in pictures but could recognize themselves in mirror images (Lewis & Brooks-Gunn, 1979a).

Preverbal children's ability to recognize themselves in pictures is best inferred from their differential responses to pictures of self and other. The "other" that is used for comparison purposes should be as similar to the self as possible, since differential responding may be elicited by person perceptions other than self-perception. For example, infants respond quite differently to adults and children in live approach sequences (Brooks & Lewis, 1976; Greenberg et al., 1973; Lewis & Brooks, 1974) so that differential responses to pictures of self and adults or even to self and older children may not be indicative of self-recognition but instead may be indicative of age differentiation. Several investigators have examined infants' responses to a picture of the self. In an early study, Zazzo (1948) reported no pictorial self-recognition in his son until the third year, and

more recently, Bigelow (1975) reported a pictorial self-recognition between 23 and 27 months of age.

Pictorial self-recognition is reported at earlier ages using 35-mm colored slides of the subject, same-sex, same-age peers, and opposite-sex, same-age peers. In our first study, the younger infants (9 to 18 months) did not respond differently to pictures of themselves and other infants although 22-month-olds smiled more at their own picture. In our second study, 9- to 12- and 12- to 24-month-olds smiled more at the self than the same-aged baby pictures, while 15- to 18-month-olds did just the opposite. That a relative decrease in smiling was exhibited to the picture of self by the 15- to 18-month-olds that was not coupled with an increase in frowning or avoidance may be related to the increased self-consciousness and/or self-knowledge of facial features seen at this time in the mirror and videotape studies. In brief, infants as young as 9- to 12-months may be capable of some differentiation between pictorial representations of self and other, although the evidence for differentiation becomes stronger in the second year (Lewis & Brooks-Gunn, 1979a).

Verbal self-referents have been used as a measure of self-recognition (Bertenthal & Fischer, 1978; Bigelow, 1975; Gesell, 1928; Johnson, 1980; Zazzo, 1948) with most placing its occurrence at approximately 24 to 30 months of age. In a study by Lewis and Brooks (1975), one quarter of the 18- and two thirds of the 22-month-olds labeled their pictures correctly.

Pictorial recognition seems to occur somewhat later than mirror or videotape recognition (Bertenthal & Fischer, 1978; Bigelow, 1975). However, these differences are confounded by the age constraints on language production. When infants are asked to point to their picture (using the subject's name) which is embedded in a set of same-age pictures, over 75% of all 18-month-olds are able to do so (Lewis & Brooks-Gunn, 1979a). As in other aspects of language development, comprehension precedes production.

Personal pronoun usage is usually placed in the third year of life (Ames, 1952; Gesell, 1928) although it has been observed at 21 to 24 months of age. Personal pronoun usage is an interesting milestone not only in the acquisition of self-knowledge but in terms of a linguistic representation of self. Although children are referred to by others as *you, he,* or *she,* and never as *I* or *me,* and hear other people refer to themselves as *I* but not *you, he,* or *she,* they do not seem to refer to themselves as *you* or to others as *I.* Autistic children and blind children have been observed using personal pronouns incorrectly, using *I* for others and *you* for self (Fraiberg & Adelson, 1976).

Charney (1978) examined when and how 18- to 30-month-olds used personal pronouns. The first personal pronoun (*I*) appeared around 22 months of age, the second and third personal pronouns (*you* and *he/she*) about 2 months later. When asked questions like "Where is my hair?" "Where is your hair?" and "Where is her hair?" toddlers responded to the second personal pronoun questions earlier than the first personal pronoun questions, even though in spontaneous conversation they used *I* correctly earlier than they used *you.* It seems that toddlers focus on the consistencies in speech, using *I* and *you* appropriately rather than just imitating others' speech. Additionally, when the self is being referred to (*I* when the child is speaking, *you* when the adult is speaking), the personal pronoun usage is more likely to be correct and to occur earlier than when another person is being referred to (*you* when the child is speaking, *I* when an adult is speaking).

AN ONTOGENETIC SEQUENCE OF VISUAL SELF-RECOGNITION

Taken together, the studies discussed suggest the following ontogenetic sequence of self-recognition in which contingency, feature recognition, and social category cues are utilized by the infant. Contingency is used quite early in the child's life, but it is the ability to recognize the self *independent* of contingency and to respond instead to feature recognition that is unique to the self. In contingent situations—mirrors and simultaneous videotapes—infants as young as 9 months of age smile, watch themselves intently, move rhythmically, and touch their bodies. These behaviors change very little over the 3- to 24-month period. Another skill of the young infant (5 to 9 months) involves adjusting their bodies to perceptual changes. Butterworth (1977) placed infants next to a tilting room so that they saw but did not experience a tilting sensation. Infants adjusted their bodies (when they were sitting or standing) to compensate for the tilt. Butterworth has suggested that this ability is indicative of the beginnings of self-controlled and self-directed behavior. Around 8 to 9 months of age, infants begin to use the mirrors to reach for objects, themselves, and other people. Around 15 months of age, infants begin to notice a mark on the face and exhibit self-conscious, coy, or silly behavior in front of the mirror. By 18 to 20 months, almost all infants respond to contingent representations appropriately and may be said to recognize themselves.

Recognition in pictures and videotapes occurs in a parallel although slower sequence. Around 9 to 12 months of age, infants may smile more at their own picture than at another infant's picture and pay more attention to another's videotape than their own. Around 15 to 18 months of age, more infants exhibit self–other differentiation in the picture and videotape studies. And, by the time verbal self-referents appear, they are used consistently for pictures and videotapes of self rather than other. By 18 to 20 months of age, self-recognition on the basis of features is clearly evident, as infants recognize their pictures and use social categories appropriately for self and other pictures. These data further suggest that self-recognition does not occur suddenly but develops gradually (Bertenthal & Fischer, 1978).

VISUAL RECOGNITION IN OLDER CHILDREN AND ADULTS

Visual self-recognition, or at least facial recognition, is almost universal in adults in societies with reflecting surfaces or pictorial representations. The only adults who have difficulty recognizing their faces are persons suffering from certain central nervous system (CNS) dysfunctions, severely mentally retarded adults, and some psychotic patients (cf. Frenkel, 1964; Harris, 1977; Shentoub, Soulaircz, & Rustin, 1954). Older children past the toddler stage are able to recognize themselves in mirrors, with the exception of the severely mentally retarded (usually those functioning under 2 years of age) and emotionally disturbed children (Hill & Tomlin, 1981; Mans et al., 1978; Shentoub et al., 1954).

Some clinicians report that psychotic patients do not recognize themselves in mirrors or pictures, presumably because of a disorganization of the self-image (Delmas, 1929), while others report recognition but difficulty in assessing self-representations (Miller, 1962). Traub and Orbach (Orbach, Traub, & Olsen, 1966; Traub & Orbach, 1964) asked normal and psychotic subjects to adjust a mirror so that no distortion was present for two different objects—themselves and a door. While normal subjects had no difficulty with either task, the psychotic subjects were able to represent the door in a distortion-free manner but were not able to do so for themselves.

Most people, both children and adults, have difficulty recognizing body parts other than the face, such as the legs or hands (Woodworth & Schlosberg, 1938, 1954). A recent study of self-recognition of photographs of hands and partial faces have been undertaken with 2½-to 5½-year-old children (Nolan & Kagan, 1980). Almost all children were able to pick out the photograph of their face with the eyes blackened out of a set. Recognition of a photograph of one's hands increased with age: 26% of the youngest versus 48% of the oldest recognized their hands with palms up. Thus, visual self-recognition is not restricted to the face.

Individual Differences in the Development of Visual Self-Recognition

How are we to explain the individual differences in self-recognition that have characterized all of the self-recognition studies? Most obvious are the striking developmental trends that have been found. However, age is not the only determinant of self-recognition, as individual differences within age groups have also been found. These differences may be related to cognitive, social, and experiential variables.

Social Experience Social experience may affect the expression of self-recognition. Mead (1934) and Merleau-Ponty (1964) have suggested that we come to know ourselves through our interactions with others and that without others, self-knowledge would not exist. Supporting evidence is found as chimpanzees reared in social isolation were unable to exhibit self-directed behavior in a mirror situation even after extensive exposure. However, two of the chimpanzees were given 3 months of group experience, after which time self-recognitory responses began to appear (Gallup et al., 1971; Hill et al., 1970). While the absence or presence of others cannot be studied in man, the number, type, and frequency of others present can. Gross measures of social experience—birth order, number of siblings, mother's education—have failed to exhibit any relationship with self-recognition (Lewis & Brooks-Gunn, 1979a).

Mirror Experience Self-recognition may be related to mirror experience. Such a relationship has been found for nontechnological peoples (Kuhler, 1927 cited in Amsterdam, 1968), and adults blind from birth (von Senden, 1960).

However, no relationship between mirror experience and self-recognition in infants has been found (Lewis & Brooks-Gunn, 1979a; Bertenthal & Fischer, 1978). This finding is limited by the fact that the data are based on mother's reports and all infants, at least in our society, have some mirror experience, usually seeing themselves at least every other day.

Cognitive Ability   The ability to infer that a mirror or videotape reflection is a representation of the self implies notions of distancing, differentiation, and schema representation. Object permanence has been thought to be important in that the notion of permanence involves the self, other persons and objects, and that sensorimotor development subsumes numerous tasks, including object permanence and self-recognition (Bertenthal & Fischer, 1978). Object permanence and self-recognition (specifically mark recognition) are highly related, but this relationship is mediated by age and disappears in covariant analyses. Thus, object permanence does not develop earlier than self-recognition, nor is the development of the latter dependent on the former (Bertenthal & Fischer, 1978; Lewis & Brooks-Gunn, 1979b). The ability to process redundant and novel stimuli also has been studied in conjunction with self-recognition, and recovery to a novel stimulus is positively related to mark recognition and imitation, even with age controlled (Lewis & Brooks-Gunn, 1979a). Thus, those infants who notice change in inanimate stimuli seem to be those who also notice change in representations of themselves (i.e., unmarked to marked mirror conditions and videotape representations of self and other). In a similar vein, 7- to 19-month-old infants who differentiated among various persons in a stranger approach situation were likely to have high recovery scores in an attention paradigm (Lewis & Brooks, 1974).

Finally, the relationship of cognition and self-recognition has been studied by examining cognitively delayed infants. Two studies have found mark-directed behavior to be quite delayed in samples of Down's syndrome, developmentally delayed, and physically impaired infants (Brooks-Gunn & Lewis, 1980; Mans et al., 1978). Handicapped infants with a developmental quotient of less than 18 months do not exhibit mark recognition.

METHODOLOGICAL CONSIDERATIONS

How do we know that children recognize themselves? With adults, one simply asks who a specific picture or reflection represents. Adults usually make the verbal distinction "That is me" or "That is not me," and by 3 years of age, most children use personal pronouns correctly (Ames, 1952; Gesell & Thompson, 1938). But what about the 2-year-old who rarely used the personal pronoun and the 9-month-old who has no verbal labels at all? Self-directed behavior, verbal labeling behavior, and differential responding to different stimulus conditions all may be indicative of self-recognition.

The occurrence of self-directed behavior implies that the child is making a distinction between the self and the representation, has some knowledge about its location in space vis-a-vis other objects or visual images, and is directing behavior toward the self in a purposeful manner. Mark recognition or touching the mark is the most compelling example of self-directed behavior.

Like self-directed behavior, verbal labeling indicates an awareness of self that is relatively clear-cut. The awareness that the picture represents the self may be mediated by a learning function; for example, parents may teach their children to label pictures. A child may know that the picture is "Susie" and that she is "Susie," but does she know that the two "Susies" represent the same person? However, the differential use of proper names, the use of the personal pronoun, and the use of an unfamiliar picture seem to make this explanation implausible.

Differential responding provides only inferential information that children are capable of the perceptual–cognitive processes necessary for differentiation of self from other. Preference procedures may allow for further inferences about self–other differentiation. That is, familiar social objects may be preferred to unfamiliar objects, the former being more likely to elicit positive affect and self-directed behaviors than the latter. Almost all of the studies support this prediction: (1) infants not only smile at the pictures of self and same-age baby different amounts of time, but smile longer at their own than at the other picture; (2) infants not only exhibit differential behavior in unmarked and marked mirror conditions, but are more likely to explore their bodies, to touch their noses, and to exhibit self-conscious and coy behavior in a marked than an unmarked condition; (3) infants not only exhibit differential behavior in contingent and noncontingent representations, but exhibit more deliberate movement, affect, self-consciousness, and turning behavior in the former than the latter; and (4) infants not only exhibit differential behavior to videotape representations of self and other, but imitate and perform deliberate movements more often in the former than the latter.

In short, what is needed is a set of convergent measures, each telling us something about the development of self-recognition. The infant who says, "That's me" or "That's Bobby" when seeing his picture and the infant who touches himself when seeing his marked face in a mirror certainly recognize themselves. But the infant who touches his body in the marked but not in the unmarked condition, the infant who looks longer at or is more positive to a picture of himself than another, and the infant who imitates a videotape of himself more than a videotape of another may also be said to have an awareness of self.

All of the studies discussed have examined self-recognition, and the inference of self-knowledge has been predicated on findings regarding recognition. Although concepts such as self-regulation, self-control, self-awareness, body images, and ego development have been discussed vis-a-vis the young child, research on these topics is sparse (cf. Escolona, 1967; Kopp, 1982; Mahler, Pine, & Bergman, 1975; Swartz, 1981; Waters & Tinsley, 1981). Another limitation of the literature is that only one modality relevant to self-recognition has been studied. Except for Butterworth's research on bodily responses to perceptual change and research on infants' reactions to their own crying behavior, modalities other than the visual one or mixed modalities have not been experimentally examined.

Another unexplored topic is the relationship between early self-recognition and later self-knowledge. Self-knowledge is complex and changes rapidly during childhood (Bannister & Agnew, 1977); such complex knowledge may not be inferred from the early self-recognition literature. Nonetheless, self-recognition, whether directly related to later measures of self-knowledge or not, still appears to be the best estimate of children's ability to differentiate themselves from their social world.

DEVELOPMENTAL IMPLICATIONS OF A THEORY OF SELF

The findings on the development of self-recognition have important implications for any theory of development since they impact on social relations and social cognition as well as on maturational and affective growth. First, by the middle of the second year of life complex social behavior becomes apparent. Not only does mark and pictorial recognition occur at this time, indicating that a fairly sophisticated sense of self exists, but emotional expressions, sex-role comprehension, empathy, and perspective taking all emerge about this time. In the second and third years of life, self-categorizations facilitate the development of complex social knowledge as well as social behavior. Three of the features that emerge early and that appear to influence subsequent social and emotional development are gender identity, knowledge of age, and feelings of efficacy or competence (Brooks-Gunn & Lewis, 1982; Lewis & Feiring, 1978). These social–cognitive abilities parallel the emergence of other cognitive abilities.

The acquisition of the self by the end of the second year not only facilitates the acquisition of social knowledge, but underlies social competence, peer relationships, gender identity, and empathy. For example, the preference for same-sex playmates is a function, at least in part, of the child's self-identity (Lewis & Weinraub, 1979). Likewise, the child's knowledge of age distinctions (derived from the perception of facial and bodily features) contributes to the development of social knowledge about social roles (Edwards & Lewis, 1979). In the emotional domain, the emerging self-concept enables children to reflect on their own emotional state, a condition we believe is necessary for the acquisition of emotional experience (Lewis & Michalson, 1983). The emergence of the self also facilitates the development of social emotions, such as empathy and deceit. For example, empathic behavior cannot emerge until the child has a concept of self and is capable of taking the role of another or being influenced by someone "like me." Thus, the self stands between the early social interactions of children and their world and later complex social behavior, social knowledge, and emotional development. It also may arise from social interaction. Few studies have explored possible connections between parent–child interactions and self-recognition. In a recent study, insecurely attached infants, as measured at 12 months using a variant of the Ainsworth Strange Situation, exhibited self-recognition earlier than securely attached infants (Lewis & Brooks-Gunn, 1982). The most parsimonious explanation may

be that children who are stressed and/or have parents who are less effective in helping them cope with stressful events need to act on their own or to monitor the environment carefully.

How the self emerges is an unresolved issue. Recently, Damon and Hart (1982) have presented a model of how self-understanding develops from infancy through adolescence. At each age level, four aspects of what we have called the categorical self and the existential self and what James (1890) deemed "me" and "I" were presented. Using their model, the research on early self-recognition addressed two conceptual features of the "me." The physical me (knowledge of physical features and name) and the active me (the awareness of self's action capabilities)—and two conceptual aspects of the "I"—continuity (based on physical features and name) and distinctiveness (contingent action, physical features, and name distinguish self from others).

Another issue involves the cognitive processes that might be involved in the emergence of the self. In general, it does not seem that self-understanding may be reduced to a set of cognitive functions (Damon & Hart, 1982). With regard to early self-recognition, a level of cognitive ability is necessary but not sufficient. We have suggested that the infant's interaction with the social world plays a role in self-recognition and more generally in self-understanding. Clearly, it is important for the emergence of the categorical self. The role of social interactions for the emergence of the existential self remain to be explored (Lewis & Brooks-Gunn, 1982). Whatever the cognitive processes, the demonstration of self-recognition allows the study of several aspects of early self-understanding.

REFERENCES

Ames, L. B. (1952). The sense of self of nursery school children as manifested by their verbal behavior. *Journal of Genetic Psychology, 81,* 193–232.

Amsterdam, B. K. (1968). *Mirror behavior in children under two years of age.* Unpublished doctoral dissertation, University of North Carolina, Chapel Hill.

Amsterdam, B. K. (1972). Mirror self-image reactions before age two. *Developmental Psychobiology,* **5**, 297–305.

Amsterdam, B., & Greenberg, L. M. (1977). Self-conscious behavior of infants: A videotape study. *Developmental Psychobiology,* **10**, 1–6.

Ashford, L. G., & Brooks, P. H. (1981, April). *Factors in the development of self-recognition.* Paper presented at the Society for Research in Child Development Meetings. Boston.

Bannister, D., & Agnew, J. (1977). The child's construing of self. In J. Cole (Ed.), *Nebraska symposium on motivation,* 1976. Lincoln: Univ. of Nebraska Press.

Bayley, N. (1969). *Bayley scales of infant development.* New York: The Psychological Corporation.

Benhar, E. E., Carlton, P. L., & Samuel, D. (1975). A search for mirror-image reinforcement and self-recognition in the baboon. In S. Kondo, M. Kawai, & A. Ehara (Eds.), *Contemporary primatology; Proceedings of the Fifth International Congress of Primatology.* Basel: Karger.

Bertenthal, B. I., & Fischer, K. W. (1978). Development of self-recognition in the infant. *Developmental Psychology,* **11**, 44–50.

Bigelow, A. (1975, June). *A longitudinal study of self-recognition in young children.* Paper presented at the Meetings of the Canadian Psychological Association, Quebec.

Bigelow, A. B. (in press). The correspondence between self and image movement as a cue to self-recognition for young children. *Journal of Genetic Psychology.*

Boulanger-Balleyguier, G. (1964, November 1). Premiers reactions devant le miroir. *Enfance,* 51–67.

Brooks, J., & Lewis, M. (1976). Infants' responses to strangers: Midget, adult and child. *Child Development,* **47**, 323–332.

Brooks-Gunn, J., & Lewis, M. (1980, March). *Self recognition in handicapped infants and toddlers.* Paper presented at the International Conference on Infant Studies, New Haven.

Brooks-Gunn, J., & Lewis, M. (1982). The development of self-knowledge. In C. B Kopp & J. B.

Krakow (Eds.), *The child: Development in a social context.* Reading, MA: Addison-Wesley.

Brown, W. L., McDowell, A. A., & Robinson, E. M. (1965). Discrimination learning of mirrored cues by rhesus monkeys. *Journal of Genetic Psychology,* **106**, 123–128.

Buhler, C. (1930). *The first year of life.* New York: John Day.

Butterworth, G. E. (1977). Object disappearance and error in Piaget's Stage IV task. *Journal of Experimental Child Psychology,* **23**, 391–401.

Cattell, P. (1940). *The Measurement of intelligence of infants and young children.* New York: The Psychological Corporation.

Charney, R. (1978). *The development of personal pronouns.* Doctoral dissertation, University of Chicago.

Damon, W., & Hart, D. (1982). The development of self-understanding from infancy through adolescence. *Child Development,* **53**, 841–864.

Darwin, C. (1877). A biographical sketch of an infant. *Mind,* **2**, 285–294.

Delmas, F. A. (1929). Le signe du miroir dans la demence precoce. *Annales Medico-Psychologiques,* **87**, 227–233.

Dickie, J. R., & Strader, W. H. (1974). Development of mirror responses in infancy. *Journal of Psychology,* **88**, 333–337.

Diggory, J. C. (1966). *Self-evaluation.* New York: Wiley.

Dixon, J. C. (1957). Development of self recognition. *Journal of Genetic Psychology,* **91**, 251–256.

Edwards, C. P., & Lewis, M. (1979). Young children's concepts of social relations: Social functions and social objects. In M. Lewis & L. Rosenblum (Eds.), *The child and its family: The genesis of behavior* (Vol. 2). New York: Plenum.

Epstein, S. (1973). The self-concept revisited, or a theory of a theory. *American Psychologist,* **28**, 404–416.

Escalona, S. (1967). *The roots of individuality.* Chicago: Aldine.

Fraiberg, S., & Adelson, E. (1976). Self representation in young blind children. In Z. Jastrzembska (Ed.), *The effects of blindness and other impairments on early development.* New York: American Foundation for the Blind.

Frenkel, R. E. (1964). Psychotherapeutic reconstruction of the traumatic amnesic period by the mirror-image projective technique. *Journal of Existentialism,* **17,** 77–96.

Freud, S. (1965). *New introductory lectures on psychoanalysis.* New York: Norton.

Freud, S. (1959). Instincts and their vicissitudes. *Collected papers.* New York: Basic Books. (Originally published 1915.)

Gallup, G. G., Jr. (1966). Mirror image reinforcement in monkeys. *Psychonomic Science,* **5,** 39–40.

Gallup, G. G., Jr. (1968). Mirror image stimulation. *Psychological Bulletin,* **70,** 782–793.

Gallup, G. G., Jr. (1970). Chimpanzees: Self-recognition. *Science,* **167,** 86–87.

Gallup, G. G., Jr. (1973). *Towards an operational definition of self-awareness.* Paper presented at the 9th International Congress of Anthropological and Ethnological Sciences, Chicago.

Gallup, G. G., Jr. (1977). Self-recognition in primates: A comparative approach to the bidirectional properties of consciousness. *American Psychologist,* **32,** 329–338.

Gallup, G. G. (1979). Self-recognition in chimpanzees and man: A developmental and comparative perspective. In M. Lewis & L. Rosenblum (Eds.), *The child and its family; The genesis of behavior* (Vol. 2). Plenum.

Gallup, G. G., Jr., & McClure, M. D. (1971). Preference for mirror-image stimulation in differentially reared rhesus monkeys. *Journal of Comparative and Physiological Psychology,* **75,** 403–407.

Gallup, G. G., McClure, M. K., Hill, S. D., & Bundy, R. A. (1971). Capacity for self-recognition in differentially reared chimpanzees. *Psychological Record,* **21,** 69–74.

Gesell, A. (1928). *Infancy and human growth.* New York: Macmillan Co.

Gesell, A., & Ames, L. (1947). The infant's reaction to his mirror image. *Journal of Genetic Psychology,* **70,** 141–154.

Gesell, A., & Thompson, H. (1938). *The psychology of early growth.* New York: Macmillan Co.

Gesell, A., & Thompson, N. (1934). *Infant behavior; Its genesis and growth.* New York: McGraw-Hill.

Greenberg, D. J., Hillman D., & Grice, D. (1973). Infant and stranger variables related to stranger anxiety in the first year of life. *Developmental Psychology,* **9,** 207–212.

Griffiths, R. (1954). *The abilities of babies.* London: University of London.

Harris, L. P. (1977). Self-recognition among institutionalized profoundly retarded males: A replication. *Bulletin of the Psychonomic Society,* **9,** 43–44.

Hill, S. D., Bundy, R. A., Gallup, G. G., Jr., & McClure, M. K. (1970). Responsiveness of young nursery-reared chimpanzees to mirrors. *Proceedings of the Louisiana Academy of Sciences* (Vol. 33, pp 77–82).

Hill, S., & Tomlin, C. (1981). Self-recognition in retarded children. *Child Development,* **52**(1), 145–150.

James, W. (1890). *The principles of psychology.* New York: Holt.

Johnson, D. B. (1980, April). *Self recognition in one- to two-year-old infants.* Paper presented at the International Conference on Infant Studies, New Haven.

Kopp, C. B. (1982). The antecedents of self recognition: A developmental perspective. *Development Psychology,* **18**(2), 199–214.

Lethmate, J., & Ducker, G. (1973). Untersuchungen zum selbsterkennen im spiegel bei orang-utans und einigen anderen offenarten. *Zeitschrift fur Tierpsychologie,* **33,** 246–269.

Lewis, M., & Brooks, J. (1974). Self, other and fear: Infants' reactions to people. In M. Lewis & L. Rosenblum (Eds.), *The origins of fear: The origins of behavior* (Vol. 2, pp. 195–227). New York: Wiley.

Lewis, M., & Brooks, J. (1975). Infants' social perception: A constructivist view. In L. Cohen & P. Solapetek (Eds.), *Infant perception: From sensation to cognition* (Vol. 2, pp. 101–143). New York: Academic Press.

Lewis, M., & Brooks-Gunn, J. (1979a). *Social cognition and the acquisition of self.* New York: Plenum.

Lewis, M., & Brooks-Gunn, J. (1979b). Toward a theory of social cognition: The development of self. In I. Uzgiris (Ed.), *New directions in child development: Social interaction and communication during infancy.* San Francisco: Jossey-Bass.

Lewis, M., & Brooks-Gunn, J. (1981). Attention and intelligence. *Intelligence,* **5**(3), 231–238.

Lewis, M., & Brooks-Gunn, J. (1982, March). *Antecedents and correlates of mark recognition in 18- to 20-month-olds.* Paper presented at the International Conference on Infant Studies, Austin.

Lewis, M., & Feiring, C. (1978). The child's social world. In R. M. Lerner & G. D. Spanier (Eds.), *Child influences on marital and family interaction: A life-span perspective*. New York: Academic Press.

Lewis, M., & Michalson, L. (1983). *Children's emotions and moods: Development, theory, and measurement*. New York: Plenum.

Lewis, M., & Weinraub, M. (1979). Origins of early sex-role development. *Sex Roles*, **5**(2), 135–153.

Lissman, H. W. (1932). Die Umwelt des Kampffisches (*Betta splendens* Regan). *Zeitschrift fur Vergleichende Physiologie*, **18**, 62–111.

Mahler, M. S., Pine, F., & Bergman, A. (1975). *The psychological birth of the human infant*. New York: Basic Books.

Mans, L., Cicchetti, D., & Sroufe, L. A. (1978). Mirror reactions of Down's syndrome infants and toddlers: Cognitive underpinnings of self-recognition. *Child Development*, **49**, 1247–1250.

McCall, R. B., & Kennedy, C. B. (1980). Attention of 4-month infants to discrepancy and babyishness. *Journal of Experimental Child Psychology*, **29**, 189–201.

McLean, P. D. (1964). Mirror display in the squirrel monkey. *Science*, **146**, 950–952.

Marvin, R. S., Marvin, C. M., & Abramovitch, L. I. (1973, March). *An ethological study of the development of coy behavior in young children*. Paper presented at the Biannual Meeting of the Society for Research in Child Development, Philadelphia, PA.

Mead, G. H. (1934). *Mind, self, and society: From the standpoint of a social behaviorist*. Chicago: Univ. of Chicago Press.

Melvin, K. B., & Anson, J. E. (1970). Image-induced aggressive display: Reinforcement in the paradise fish. *The Psychological Record*, **20**, 225–228.

Merleau-Ponty, M. (1964). *Primacy of perception*. J. Eddie (Ed.) & W. Cobb (Trans.). Evanston: Northwestern Univ. Press.

Miller, M. F. (1962). Responses of psychiatric patients to their photographed images. *Diseases of the nervous system*, **23**(6), 292–298.

Modaressi, T., & Kenny, T. (1977). Children's response to their true and distorted mirror images. *Child Psychiatry and Human Development*, **8**(2).

Neisser, U. (1967). *Cognitive psychology*. New York: Appleton.

Nolan, E., & Kagan, J. (1980). Recognition of self and self's products in preschool children. *Journal of Genetic Psychology*, **137**.

Orbach, J., Traub, A. C., & Olson, R. (1966). Psychophysical studies of body-image: II. Normative data on the adjustable body-distorting mirror. *Archives of General Psychiatry*, **14**, 41–47.

Papousek, H., & Papousek, M. (1974). Mirror image and self recognition in young human infants: I. A new method of experimental analysis. *Developmental Psychobiology*, **7**(2), 149–157.

Piaget, J. (1954). *The construction of reality in the child*. New York: Basic Books. (Original French edition, 1937.)

Piaget, J. (1963). *The origins of intelligence in children* (M. Cook, Trans.). New York: Norton. (Originally published, 1952; Original French version, 1936).

Pryer, W. (1893). *Mind of the child: Vol. 2. Development of the intellect*. New York: Appleton.

Rheingold, H. L. (1971). *Some visual determinants of smiling infants*. Unpublished manuscript.

Ritter, W. E., & Benson, S. B. (1934). "Is the poor bird demented?" Another case of "shadow boxing." *Auk*, **51**, 169–170.

Schmidt, M. (1878). Beobachtungen am Orang-Utan. *Zoologische Garten*, **19**, 230–232.

Schulman, A. H., & Kaplowitz, C. (1977). Mirror-image response during the first two years of life. *Developmental Psychobiology*, **10**, 133–142.

Shentoub, S., Soulairzc, A., & Rustin, E. (1954). Comportement de l'enfant, arriere devant le miroir. *Enfance*, **7**, 333–340.

Stutsman, R. (1931). *Mental measurement of preschool children*. Yonkers: World Book.

Swartz, J. C. (1981, April). *Measuring individual differences in self-control and self-regulation: Methods and correlates at 24 to 20 months versus 36 to 66 months of age*. Paper presented at the Society for Research in Child Development Meetings, Boston.

Tinkelpaugh, O. L. (1928). An experimental study of representational factors in monkeys. *Journal of Comparative Psychology*, **8**, 197–236.

Thompson, T. I. (1963). Visual reinforcement in Siamese fighting fish. *Science*, **141**, 55–57.

Tolman, C. W. (1965). Feeding behavior of domestic chicks in the presence of their own mirror image. *Canadian Psychologist, 6*, 227 (abstract).

Traub, A. C., & Orbach, J. (1964). Psychophysical studies of body-image: The adjustable body-distorting mirror. *Archives of General Psychiatry,* **11**, 53–66.

von Senden, M. (1960). *Space and sight: The perception of space and shape in the congenitally blind before and after operation.* Glencoe, IL: Free Press.

Wallon, H. (1949). *Les origines du caractere chez l'enfant; les precludes du sentiment de personalité* (2nd ed.). Paris: Presses Universitaires de France.

Waters, H. S., & Tinsley, V. S. (1981, April). *The development of verbal self-regulation.* Paper presented at the Society for Research in Child Development Meetings, Boston.

Woodworth, R. S., & Schlosberg, H. (1954). *Experimental psychology* (rev. ed.). New York: Holt. (Originally published, 1938.)

Zazzo, R. (1948). Images du corp et conscience du soi. *Enfance,* **1**, 29–43.

READING 31

Children's Understanding of Dispositional Characteristics of Others

William S. Rholes
Diane N. Ruble

According to attribution theory, causal attributions play an important role in organizing the social environment and directing future behavior (Heider, 1958; Kelley, 1973; Weiner, 1974). Theories of the causal attribution process typically include (*a*) the rules that attributors use to infer causality and (*b*) the nature of the causal constructs (forces) that are invoked to explain behavior. Although several developmental studies suggest that even preschool-aged children can utilize inferential rules and make attributions about behavior (for a review, see Ruble & Rholes, 1981), it is not clear that children's understanding of the nature of causal forces is the same at different ages. In fact, there is some evidence to suggest that one particularly important category, the stable personal cause, is not understood or used by younger children.

One line of evidence comes from the developmental "person perception" literature (e.g., Barenboim, 1981; Livesley & Bromley, 1973; Peevers & Secord, 1973; Scarlett, Press, & Crockett, 1971). The results of this research have been consistent in suggesting that children younger than about 8 years old rarely use stable, personal (dispositional) constructs in their descriptions of others. Instead, younger children tend to describe others in terms of "superficial" qualities, such as appearance, possessions, and place of residence. From an attributional point of view, this research implies that younger children do not conceptualize the behavior of others in terms of dispositional causal factors. There are, of course, potentially serious problems associated with the free description methodology of these studies; younger children's limited verbal abilities or differing perceptions concerning the purpose of the task, rather than their perceptions of others, may cause them to respond as they do (Feldman & Ruble, 1981). However, results of research using very different methodologies (Mohr, 1978; Rotenberg, 1982) also suggest that there may be striking developmental shifts in the tendency to perceive and understand the implications of dispositional constructs.

A second line of evidence is based on Piagetian theory. According to Inhelder and Piaget (1958), an important aspect of intellectual development is the acquisition of the concept of invariance—that is, the idea that such things as volume, mass, and number remain unchanged in spite of superficial changes in form or appearance. Some invariances are quantitative (e.g., volume), whereas others are qualitative (e.g., gender constancy). Both Flavell (1977) and Livesley and Bromley (1973) argued that the understanding of personal dispositions, such as personality traits and abilities, can be viewed as the acquisition of the concept of qualitative invariance, as it applies to persons. They speculated that, just as cognitive advances lead to the idea that gender remains constant over time and despite superficial changes in appearance, activities, and so forth, similar advances lead children to perceive constant psychological properties in the makeup of other persons.

Both the "person perception" and Piagetian perspectives suggest that, although young children may appear to make traitlike attributions in some circumstances (e.g., DiVitto & McArthur, 1978; Ruble, Feldman, Higgins, & Karlovac, 1979), they may not be referring to a characteristic that is unchanging and that has implications for future behavior. Labels such as "kind," "smart," or "mean" may instead refer more to a description of behavior than to stable causal factors.

In the present two studies, we were concerned with developmental changes in children's perceptions of stable dispositional characteristics and the implications of such dispositions for behavior in other situations (Studies 1 and 2) and over time (Study 2). In the first study, children (aged 5–6 and 9–10 years) watched a series of videotaped vignettes, which were designed to illustrate either the personality traits or abilities of an actor. The study's primary dependent measure was subjects' expectations for the actor's behavior under other, comparable circumstances. If an actor's behavior suggests *stable,* personal causes to an observer, the observer should expect the actor's behavior to remain relatively consistent with the behavior shown in the videotaped episode across a variety of situations. If, on the other hand, subjects do not perceive a behavior to represent a stable dispositional characteristic of the actor, they should have less reason to expect cross-situational consistencies in the actor's behavior. Thus, a developmental shift was expected in the tendency to form generalized expectations on the basis of the observed behavior. To address a possible alternative explanation of this outcome—that is, that younger children simply do not spontaneously label behavior with appropriate personality trait or ability terms—half of the subjects were asked questions immediately after each vignette that forced them to label the actor's behavior with such terms.

The 5–6-year-old and 9–10-year-old age groups were chosen because a previous study that concerned children's use of personality traits to describe other persons (Livesley & Bromley, 1973) suggests that important advances in children's use of traits in naturalistic situations occur at about the age of 7–8 years. Consequently, we wanted to contrast groups of children below the 7–8 age range with children above it. We chose to examine both abilities and personality traits because (*a*) we wanted to include a wider range of dispositions than either type alone would have constituted and (*b*) both are important elements in person perception. We were also interested in children's understanding of abilities because of the role played by ability attributions in theories of achievement motivation (Weiner, 1974). There was, however, no hypothesis regarding differential rates of acquisition for these two types of dispositional properties.

STUDY 1

Method

Subjects Twenty children from each of two age groups, 5–6 and 9–10 years old, who were enrolled in a parochial school in a small city in central Texas took part in the study. There were 12 females and 8 males in the younger group and 11 females and 9 males in the older group.

Procedure Subjects were tested in individual experimental sessions. In each session subjects viewed four videotaped vignettes, each of which displayed the behavior of a different child actor. Four of the vignettes illustrated abilities, and four illustrated personality traits. Half of the traits were positive (generosity and bravery), and half were negative (stinginess and fearfulness). Similarly, half of the abilities were positive (high athletic and high "intellectual-problem-solving" ability), and half were negative (low athletic and low problem-solving ability). The sex of the actor was counterbalanced with the types of behavior. Examples of the vignettes are (a) the generous vignette—a child voluntarily shares part of his lunch with another child who has nothing to eat; (b) the ungenerous vignette—a child refuses to share his lunch with another child who has nothing to eat, even though the hungry child asks him to share. Subjects viewed four vignettes in each of two experimental sessions, which were held on consecutive days. The tapes were shown in two sessions to avoid taxing the attention spans of younger children. There was only one minor difference in the two sessions; at the end of the second session, subjects were asked a set of questions (which will be described below) that were not included at the end of the first session.

The order in which the vignettes were seen was counterbalanced with all of the study's independent variables. One restriction, however, was imposed on the counterbalancing procedure. Subjects never saw both the positive and the negative instance of the same behavior in one session; for example, a subject never saw both generous and ungenerous behavior in one session.

After each tape, half of the subjects (labeling condition) were asked a set of questions that led them to characterize the actor's behavior with ability or personality trait labels. Subjects were asked first whether the actor could be characterized by the trait or ability level that the vignette had been designed to illustrate. For instance, after the generous vignette, subjects were asked whether the actor seemed to them to be "nice and kind." They responded either yes or no. Next, they were asked to rate the actor on a four-point scale that ranged from "not at all nice and kind" to "very nice and kind." This procedure served two purposes. First, it prevented subjects from ignoring the nature of the behavior they observed; they had to, at least, process the information enough to answer the labeling questions. Second, by comparing the ratings of the two age groups, one could determine whether subjects perceived the same degree of generosity, bravery, and so forth in the vignettes.

After each vignette, subjects were asked questions that measured their expectations for the actor's behavior in other, comparable circumstances. The experimenter read each subject three pairs of "stories." Subjects were told that one story in each pair described something the actor had, in fact, done, while the other described something that the actor had never done. The subjects' task was to decide which behavior had been performed by the actor that they had just seen on tape. Three different types of stories were contrasted in the pairs. "Consistent" stories depicted the same trait or ability level that had been illustrated by the actor's behavior in the vignette. For example, if a vignette showed a child sharing lunch, a "consistent" story would depict another instance of generosity. An example story is as follows: "One day Jill was playing outside when Sally asked Jill for help with the yard work she had to do. Jill went over and spent all her play time raking leaves." "Inconsistent stories" described a behavior that illustrated a trait or ability level that was opposite the one shown in the videotaped episode. If a vignette showed an actor behaving generously, an "inconsistent" story would describe an instance of ungenerous behavior, such as *not* helping with yard work. Finally, "irrelevant stories" concerned behaviors that were unrelated to the behavior that had been observed in the vignettes. Three types of story pairs were presented to subjects after each vignette: (*a*) consistent versus inconsistent stories, (*b*) consistent versus irrelevant stories, and (*c*) irrelevant versus inconsistent stories. The irrelevant stories were included to rule out the possibility that children would respond on the basis of a "halo" effect—that is, responses based on the positive or negative valence of the behavior rather than the nature of the behavior itself. Therefore, the irrelevant story in each pair was always the same valence as its consistent or inconsistent partner. A choice of a consistent story over either an inconsistent or irrelevant story or a choice of an irrelevant story over an inconsistent one was considered to indicate that a subject perceived the actor's behavior to have been caused by a stable behavioral disposition. The order of the stories in each pair was counterbalanced across subjects.

As a check on memory, subjects were asked to recall the behavior of the actors in the vignettes immediately after they had responded to the questions on the pairs of stories. To avoid making the testing session too long, subjects were asked to do this for only four randomly selected vignettes.

Finally, at the end of the second session, subjects were asked to label the behaviors depicted in the vignettes with personality trait or ability terms. This measure was designed to determine whether subjects perceived the vi-gnettes as the experimenters had intended. Subjects were first reminded of each vignette. Then, a list of three personality trait terms or three ability terms was read to them, and they were asked to select the one term that best characterized the actor. One of the three terms was the trait or ability label that the vignette had been designed to illustrate.

Results

Preliminary analyses indicated that there were no sex differences in subjects' responses to the dependent measures. Therefore, sex was not included in the analyses presented below.

Manipulation Checks   The number of stories recalled correctly was analyzed in a 2 (age groups) x 2 (types of behavior: personality or ability related) x 2 (behavior valences: positive vs. negative behavior) analysis of variance. No significant effects emerged from this analysis. More than 90% of the stories were recalled correctly by both age groups.

Ratings made by labeling-condition subjects were analyzed by separate t tests for each of the eight vignettes in order to compare the ratings of the younger and older children. These analyses revealed no significant differences between the age groups. Thus, the younger and older subjects seem to have perceived equal levels of athletic ability, generosity, stinginess, and so forth in the actors' behaviors.

Finally, the number of "correct" choices made as part of the multiple-choice procedure was computed and analyzed. This analysis also yielded no significant effects. More than 80% of the younger and older children's responses were correct. Thus, this measure, like the one above, suggests that younger and older children perceived the vignettes in similar ways.

Cross-Situational Expectations   The three types of story pairs were analyzed individually. Choices that indicated the perception of a generalized disposition (see above) were scored as

+ 1. Other choices were scored as 0. These scores were summed and analyzed by three separate 2 (age groups) x 2 (labeling vs. no-labeling conditions) x 2 (ability vs. personality related behavior) x 2 (positively vs. negatively valenced behavior) analyses of variance.

The analysis of the consistent versus inconsistent story pairs (Table 1) revealed that older children made the generalized disposition choice more often than the younger children did and that the difference between the choices of younger and older children was greater when the actor's behavior was negative. The older subjects' disposition scores were significantly higher than younger children's for all four types of behaviors (i.e., positive and negative trait and ability behaviors).

The analysis of the consistent versus irrelevant story pairs (Table 1) indicated that older children made the generalized disposition choice significantly more often than younger children when the actors' behavior involved either negative traits or low abilities. In the case of positive traits and high abilities, the age groups were not significantly different in their choices. Finally, the analysis of the irrelevant versus inconsistent story pairs (Table 1) revealed that although older children made more

generalized disposition choices than younger ones for all types of behavior, the differences between younger and older children reached statistical significance only when the actor's behavior indicated either a positive personality trait or a negative ability.

The means in Table 1 show that, on the whole, younger children made the dispositional choice about half of the time, whereas older children made this choice more than half of the time. An additional analysis was conducted to determine whether the choices of the two groups differed from the pattern of responses that one would expect if subjects' choices were made on a random basis. Subjects in each age group were first divided into two categories, those who made the dispositional choice for more than 50% of the vignettes and those who made this choice for less than 50% of the vignettes. Among the younger children, eight fell into the below-50% group, and seven fell into the above-50% group. Five subjects made the dispositional choice exactly 50% of the time. A binomial test, which included only the above-50% and below-50% groups, indicated that the younger children's responses were not significantly different from a random patterning of responses, $p > .25$. All of 20 of the older sub-

TABLE 1   STORY PAIR CHOICES FOR EACH TYPE OF PAIRING BY AGE AND TYPE AND VALENCE OF BEHAVIOR

	Personality traits		Abilities	
	Positive valence	Negative valence	Positive valence	Negative valence
Consistent versus inconsistent pair:				
5–6 years	1.15	.75	1.20	.75
9–10 years	1.85	1.90	1.95	1.90
Consistent versus irrelevant pair:				
5–6 years	1.25	1.00	1.35	.55
9–10 years	1.85	1.75	1.65	1.60
Irrelevant versus inconsistent pair:				
5–6 years	.90	1.15	1.10	.75
9–10 years	1.75	1.55	1.55	1.75

Note: These data have been collapsed across labeling conditions. Means can range between 0 and 2. Higher means indicate more frequent choice of the "generalized dispositions" alternative.

jects made the generalized dispositional choice more than 50% of the time, which was significantly different from what one would expect on the basis of chance, $p < .001$. It is still possible, however, that some of the younger children were consistently giving the "correct" answer to the prediction questions, while other younger children may have consistently given the incorrect choice. The analysis above, of course, does not indicate whether the responses of an individual subject deviate from chance. To do this, a binomial test was performed on each subject's set of 24 responses to the story pairs (three types of story pairs for each of eight behaviors). Using a $p < .05$ criterion of deviation from change, only one of the 20 younger children was found to give consistently "correct" answers, whereas 19 of the 20 older children did so. Thus, at an individual subject level of analysis, younger children's responses were again found not to deviate from what one would expect on the basis of chance, whereas older children's responses did do so.

A second individual subject analysis was conducted to determine whether any subjects gave significantly more "incorrect" answers than one would expect on the basis of chance. This analysis was conducted just like the one above. There were no younger subjects or older subjects who met a $p < .05$ criterion of deviation from chance. Thus, the subjects did not show a nonrandom pattern of incorrect answers.

Discussion

The results suggest that older children expect substantial cross-situational stability in behavior, but younger children do not. In fact, the ratings of the younger group did not differ from chance. Age differences in children's expectations were observed even when the actor's behavior was labeled and even though age differences were absent in the ratings made by subjects in the labeling condition. The differences between younger and older children's predictions, therefore, do not appear to reflect the labeling process or differential perception or memory of the stimuli. These results provide more direct support for the suggestion in previous research that younger children do not understand that behavior is caused by abiding personal factors. Though they can obviously distinguish generous from ungenerous behavior or brave from fearful behavior, younger children appear to use such labels to describe current behavior, not to characterize stable psychological factors within actors. The suggestion of a "positivity bias" provides an interesting perspective on young children's implicit theories of people's behavior and may represent a partial reason why their judgments showed a lack of generalization; that is, they do not expect negative behaviors to reoccur, especially for abilities. Such findings are consistent with previous reports that young children tend to predict future success for themselves even after a history of failure at a task (e.g., Parsons & Ruble, 1977; Rholes, Blackwell, Jordan, & Walters, 1980), but the reasons why they might ignore negative information are not clear. Perhaps an egocentric bias leads young children to impose personal, absolute standards on another's behavior; that is, they predict what they think should be done or what they think the actor would wish to do, regardless of previous information about the actor's behavior. Alternatively, they may have a more generally optimistic view of people's traits and abilities. However, if younger children's choices reflected a complete preference for positive behaviors, they should have picked the dispositional choice at least as often as older children when the actor's behavior was positive. Since they did not, assertions regarding a positivity bias must remain somewhat tentative.

One issue that is raised by the present findings concerns the appropriate characterization of the different expectations formed by younger and older children. Should the younger children's failure to form generalized expectations be characterized as "immature" or as an inaccurate perception of social behavior? On the one hand, recent studies have shown that there is a fairly substantial amount of consistency in an actor's behavior across situations (Epstein, 1979); this suggests that the older children's responses may be a more accurate reflection of social reality. However, other studies (Nisbett & Ross, 1980) have shown quite clearly that adult attributors frequently overemphasize dispositional causes of behavior and consequently expect more cross-situational stability than is warranted. Thus, it is not possible to say whose responses (those of the younger or older children) are more accurate. Clearly, it would be inappropriate to assume that the younger children are inaccurate or immature simply because they differ from the older children. But, regardless of the accuracy issue, developmental differences in the perceived stability of dispositions across situations would seem to have a marked impact on children's behavior in a wide range of areas. (See the general discussion for a further discussion of this issue.)

It might be argued that an alternative explanation of our findings is that younger children perceived the actors' traits and abilities as suffering from temporal depletion, whereas older children did not. If one runs a record-breaking mile or donates a large sum of money to charity, one is probably not likely to do so again shortly afterward. There are, however, strong reasons to reject this explanation of the present findings. First, the traits and abilities examined in our study seem unlikely to be affected by depletion; they did not involve the substantial depletion of a finite resource (such as energy or money), which would prevent future reoccurrence of similar activities. Second, the "depletion" explanation predicts that younger children's responses would be substantially biased in the direction of saying that actors would *not* engage in similar behaviors in the future (i.e., a child who shares food should be *less* likely to act altruistically in a different type of situation than a child who did not share

food). As the various binomial tests showed, however, the younger children's responses were random.

It might also be argued that, although the labeling and multiple-choice data suggested that both younger and older children were making dispositional attributions, a single instance of behavior is insufficient to induce a dispositional attribution. Even though the vignettes portrayed fairly extreme behaviors, which would seem to imply the existence of dispositions, younger children may require more "proof" that a given behavior represents a dispositional characteristic. Therefore, to address this issue a second study was conducted.

STUDY 2

Although the results of Study 1 appear quite clear, two aspects of the procedure somewhat limit the degree to which one can draw general conclusions about age differences in perception of dispositional causes. First, in spite of the positive findings regarding the manipulation checks and ability to label the behavior, it remains possible that the young children's results in Study 1 represented problems with the difficulty level of the task (e.g., utilizing the paired-story format in the response measures). Second, since the stimuli consisted of only a single instance of a given trait, it is possible that this information was an insufficient indicator of a disposition, at least for the younger children. Therefore, it seemed important to replicate the results using different stimuli and response measures.

In Study 2, subjects were again provided with information about an actor's behavior and were asked to predict how the actor might behave in other circumstances. The procedures, however, differed from those of the first study in that subjects were provided with attributional information that would allow them clearly to infer the presence of dispositional causes for the behavior of some actors and the absence of such causes for the behavior of others. Based on Kelley's (1973) theory of attribution and previous findings concerning the types of attributional information that are easiest for young children to use (DiVitto & McArthur, 1978), consistency (over time) and distinctiveness (consistency across situations) were used as attributional cues in this study. The attribution information was provided to determine whether young children would form generalized expectations about others if they were given more unambiguous disposition-related cues than were provided in Study 1. As a check on this manipulation, one group of subjects was asked standard attribution questions, rather than expectation (prediction) questions. Another major change was that a different type of perceived stability—that is, consistency of the behavior over time—was assessed as well as expectations for cross-situational stability.

In the present experiment, subjects were presented with oral descriptions of behavior followed by information that indicated that the behavior in question was either high or low in consistency or distinctiveness. The major dependent measure was subjects' expectations for the actor's behavior in other situations or in the same situation in the past. It was hypothesized that the younger subjects would not expect cross-situational consistency in an actor's behavior, even when the covariation information led them to make a dispositional attribution. (Two additional age groups, 7–8 and 18–22 year olds, were examined because we thought they would provide information about the transitional period and the "endpoint" of development, respectively.)

Method

Subjects Thirty-six subjects from each of four age groups—5–6, 7–8, 9–10, and 18–22 years—took part in the study. There were 19, 20, 19, and 21 female subjects in each of the four age groups, respectively. The younger three groups were recruited through day-care and summer day-camp programs. The oldest subjects were students in the introductory psychology course at the first author's university.

Stimulus Behaviors Behaviors were selected that could be understood by all age groups and described in a single, brief sentence. Each behavior was followed by one piece of covariation information, either high or low consistency or distinctiveness. A sample problem (of low consistency) is, "Yesterday, Sam threw the basketball through the hoop almost every time he tried. In the past, Sam has almost never thrown the ball through the hoop when he tried to." Three types of behavior were used as stimuli: (a) behaviors related to abilities, (b) behaviors describing emotional reactions (e.g., Sally liked the picture book she looked at yesterday), and (c) behaviors related to choices or preferences (e.g., Howard decided to play with the toy truck instead of the kick ball at playtime yesterday). The specific behaviors were counterbalanced with the attributional information. Thus, each behavior appeared equally often in each condition.

Procedure Subjects were tested individually at their day-care facility by a female experimenter. When children arrived for their session, they first practiced using scales like the ones that were to be used in responding to the experimental materials. Because questions about dispositional attributions might possibly contaminate responses to expectation questions (and vice versa), subjects answered only one type of question. The subjects assigned to the attribution condition (18 per age group) were told they would be asked why the central character of the story behaved as he or she did (i.e., was it because of dispositional causes). The subjects in the expectation condition (also 18 per age group) were told they would be asked (a) what they thought the actor had done in the past and (b) how they thought the actor would behave in other situations. An example of the dispositional attribution questions is, "Why do you think Sam threw the ball through the hoop so many times? Was it because Sam is just good at throwing?" Examples of the expectation questions are, "How many times do you think Sam could throw the ball through the hoop when he tried in the past?" (consistency over time), and "How many other kinds of throwing games would Sam do well at?" (consistency across situations). The attribution and expectation questions were answered on four-and five-point scales, respectively. The points on the scales were represented by squares of increasing size. The smallest square on the attribution scale was labeled "No, that's not the reason." The three successive squares were labeled "That is the reason, a little bit," "That is the reason, pretty much," and "That is the reason, very much." The squares on the expectation scale, from largest to smallest, respectively, were labeled (a) very, very much (many), (b) a lot (of times), (c) pretty much (many), (d) a few (times), and (e) not any (ever).

To avoid redundancy between the expectation questions and the information provided in the stimulus problems, children in the expectation conditions were asked about consistency over time when the stimulus problem specified the level of distinctiveness of the actor's behavior and about stability across situations when the stimulus problem specified the level of temporal consistency of the actor's behavior. This procedure was adopted because it did not seem reasonable to ask about stability over time or situations when this information was specified by the distinctiveness or consistency information contained in the stimulus problems. All of the information contained in the stories was illustrated in drawings, and both the stories and questions were read twice. Pretesting indicated that given these conditions even the youngest children could correctly recall more

than 90% of the stories, after responding to attribution or expectation questions.

Results

As in Study 1, sex of subjects was not included in the present analyses because preliminary analyses indicated there were no sex differences in the subjects' responses.

Expectations Subjects' expectations for cross-situational stability were analyzed as a function of consistency information (Table 2). It was found that high consistency led to greater expectations of cross-situational stability than did low consistency among the two oldest age groups, but not among the two youngest groups. Consistency had no significant effects on the younger subjects' expectations for stability. Thus, these results are consistent with the findings of Study 1.

Subjects' expectations for consistency over time were analyzed as a function of distinctiveness information. All age groups expected significantly greater consistency over time when distinctiveness was low than when it was high.

Attributions If the above differences in generalized expectations resulted from age differences in perceptions of the nature of the behavior, then it would be expected that the younger children would fail to utilize the consistency and distinctiveness information to make appropriate dispositional inferences. Dispositional inferences were greater given high-consistency and low-distinctiveness information, as expected. In addition, there was weaker use of the information for 7–8-year-olds than for all other age groups (see Table 2).

GENERAL DISCUSSION

The central issue addressed in these two studies concerned developmental changes in the tendency to form generalized expectations on the basis of dispositional attributions. The results

TABLE 2 DISPOSITIONAL ATTRIBUTIONS AND EXPECTATIONS FOR CONSISTENCY ACROSS SITUATIONS AND OVER TIME AS A FUNCTION OF AGE AND ATTRIBUTIONAL INFORMATION

	Age			
	5–6	7–8	9–10	18–22
Expected consistency across situations:				
High-consistency information	3.27	3.33	3.61	4.00
Low-consistency information	4.06	3.33	2.06	2.39
Expected consistency over time:				
High-distinctiveness information	3.44	2.72	2.78	3.28
Low-distinctiveness information	4.50	4.33	4.22	4.28
Dispositional attributions:				
High-consistency information	3.17	2.56	2.94	3.39
Low-consistency information	2.05	2.28	2.00	1.33
High-distinctiveness information	2.00	2.61	2.28	1.56
Low-distinctiveness information	3.11	2.94	3.72	3.33

Note: Higher numbers indicate expectations of greater consistency or stronger dispositional attributions.

overall are remarkably consistent in showing sharp developmental increases in perceptions of cross-situational stability, even though the two studies differed considerably in the stimuli and response measures employed. In Study 1, an expectation of stability was defined by a subject's choice of the behavior from a pair that was most similar to the behavior previously observed on the videotape. Only the older subjects (9–10 years) expected cross-situational stability, even though manipulation checks indicated no age differences in correctly labeling the dispositions shown. Furthermore, it is notable that the younger children failed to make stable inferences even though the information was presented on videotape; several studies have indicated that, relative to verbal stories, videotaped stimuli are powerful elicitors of often surprisingly advanced judgments about social behavior (Chandler, Greenspan, & Barenboim, 1973; Ruble et al., 1979). In Study 2, the expectations of stability were defined as a subject's prediction that the actor's behavior would be consistent across a relatively large number of new situations. Only the older subjects (9–10 and 18–22 years) expected more cross-situational stability when given information leading to a dispositional inference. These de-

velopmental effects occurred even though the youngest subjects utilized attributional information appropriately when making dispositional attributions and when making judgments of consistency over time. These results suggest younger children are able to use consistency and distinctiveness to infer causality, but the dispositional attributions that they make do not imply cross-situational consistency to them.

Interestingly, the results of Study 2 suggest, at all ages, that information implying a dispositional attribution (i.e., low distinctiveness) led to expectations of stability of the same behavior over *time*. The earlier development of stability over time is similar to that reported in other types of studies of perceived invariance, such as gender constancy (Slaby & Frey, 1975) and character constancy (Rotenberg, 1982). Thus, generalizing over situations may be more difficult than generalizing over time. It should be noted that these two kinds of generalization are quite different in some ways. One may expect consistencies over time in the same situation either because one perceives a behavior to be controlled by the constant situational stimuli or because one regards it as determined by dispositional characteristics. Expectations for cross-situational consistency, on the other hand, are difficult to form on grounds other than those of dispositional characteristics. Thus, expectations for cross-situational consistency would seem to be more directly relevant to our central question, children's understanding of the stability of dispositions. Moreover, the fact that younger children expect stability over time, but not across situations, seems to suggest that they come to understand stimulus control of behavior before they conceptualize dispositions as stable causal factors.

The present findings support and extend previous theoretical and empirical analyses of developmental changes in person perception (e.g., Barenboim, 1981; Secord & Peevers, 1974). According to Secord and Peevers (1974), there are three critical milestones in the development of children's understanding of other persons: (1) the realization that other's actions are caused by the others themselves, (2) the realization that other's actions are guided by intentions, and (3) the realization that others behave in predictable, consistent ways. This final development presupposes an understanding of stable dispositions. The results of these studies suggest that this final milestone is not usually passed until after about 7–8 years of age. Although the specific age at which the change occurs may vary considerably as a function of different stimulus factors, it is notable that this is also the age at which children show a dramatic shift in the use of personality trait terms in their descriptions of others (see Barenboim, 1981; Livesley & Bromley, 1973).

Why did younger children in our study think of behaviors in terms of stable dispositional factors less often than older children? It might be argued that younger children do not see the same similarity across contexts (e.g., generosity with food vs. helping with yard work) that older children and adults do. This possibility seems unlikely to explain the developmental shift observed, however, because Study 2 allowed for a personal definition of the different contexts (e.g., "How many other kinds of throwing games would Sam do well at?"). A more likely explanation involves information processing differences. Younger children may rarely become aware of consistent patterns in the behavior of an actor; consequently, they may not develop the *concept* of abiding personal characteristics. Behaviors relevant to inferring dispositions are typically embedded in a stream of behavior that includes many actions that are irrelevant to a given disposition, such as generosity. Moreover, individual acts of generosity typically will be separated from one another by considerable periods of time. Attributors must remember the relevant behaviors, separate them from irrelevant behaviors, and simultaneously consider behaviors that have occurred at different times in different settings in order to perceive the common theme in the other's behavior. Thus, a number of changes in information-processing skills may underlie the developmental differences that we observed. In an attempt to explain the cognitive processes involved in the development of dispositional attributions, Flavell (1977) stated that younger children may fail to perceive invariant personal dispositions in others because they focus their thought and attention almost exclusively on an actor's immediate behavior and do not typically attempt to relate an actor's immediate behavior to his or her past behavior. He referred to this tendency as "temporal centration." As a consequence of this type of centration, younger children may rarely become fully aware of consistent patterns in the behavior (e.g., consistent fearfulness in different situations) of an actor, and consequently may not develop the notion of abiding personal dispositions. The primary implication of this view is that children begin to perceive others as having stable disposition when they begin to process information about current behavior in such a way as to set it in relation to previously observed behavior.

In spite of the strength of our findings, there are at least two reasons to interpret the results cautiously. First, the 7–8-year-olds, quite unexpectedly, failed to use consistency and distinctiveness information to make dispositional attributions. Although these results do not seem to undermine the general conclusion of this research—that stability of dispositions increases with age—they do at least suggest that the expectations of the 7–8-year-olds might have shown somewhat more stability had they used the covariation cues.

The second reason to interpret our findings cautiously stems from findings of Heller and Berndt (1981), which indicate that 5–6-year-olds expect behavior to be consistent over time and across situations. There are several methodological differences between the two studies that may account for the different findings. For example, the "prediction" situations seem to have been more similar to the "observed" behavior in Heller and Berndt's study than in this one; for example, in one of their sets of stories concerning altruism, the altruistic behavior in both the observed and prediction situations involved denying oneself dessert-type foods. Thus, the conflict between our study and Heller and Berndt's may indicate that younger children can make limited generalizations across situations, but not broader ones like those in our study. Even though these discrepant findings may ultimately be explained on methodological grounds, the differing effects may point out theoretically significant boundary conditions relevant to observing the developmental changes in perceived stability.

In conclusion, our studies seem to suggest that, while younger children can make dispositional attributions, such attributions do not lead to strong expectations for cross-situational stability. Given the role of disposition-based expectancies in attribution theories (e.g., Weiner, 1974), the developmental differences shown in our studies would seem to have important implications for a wide range of behaviors, including the stability of friendships at different ages and the implications of success/failure feedback on self-perceptions of ability, achievement behavior, and learned helplessness.

REFERENCES

Barenboim, C. The development of person perception from childhood to adolescence: From behavioral comparisons to psychological constructs to psychological comparisons. *Child Development,* 1981, **52**, 129–144.

Chandler, M. J., Greenspan, S., & Barenboim, C. Judgments of intentionality in response to videotaped and verbally presented moral dilemmas: The medium is the message. *Child Development,* 1973, **44**, 315–320.

DiVitto, B., & McArthur, L. Z. Developmental differences in the use of distinctiveness, consensus, and consistency information for making causal attributions. *Developmental Psychology,* 1978, **14**, 474–482.

Epstein, S. The stability of behavior, I: On predicting most of the people much of the time. *Journal of Personality and Social Psychology,* 1979, **37**, 1097–1126.

Feldman, N. S., & Ruble, D. N. The development of person perception: Cognitive and social factors. In S. S. Brehm, S. M. Kassin, & F. X. Gibbons (Eds.), *Developmental social psychology: Theory and research.* New York: Oxford University Press, 1981.

Flavell, J. H. *Cognitive development.* Englewood Cliffs, N.J.: Prentice-Hall, 1977.

Heider, F. *The psychology of interpersonal relations.* New York: Wiley, 1958.

Heller, K. A., & Berndt, T. J. Developmental changes in the formation and organization of personality attributions. *Child Development,* 1981, **52**, 683–691.

Inhelder, B., & Piaget, J. *The growth of logical thinking from childhood to adolescence.* New York: Basic, 1958.

Kelley, H. H. The processes of causal attribution. *American Psychologist,* 1973, **28**, 107–128.

Livesley, W. J., & Bromley, B. D. *Person perception in childhood and adolescence.* London: Wiley, 1973.

Mohr, D. M. Development of attributes of personal identity. *Developmental Psychology,* 1978, **14**, 427–428.

Nisbett, R., & Ross, L. *Human inference: Strategies and shortcomings of social judgment*. Englewood Cliffs, N.J.: Prentice-Hall, 1980.

Parsons, J. E., & Ruble, D. N. The development of achievement-related expectancies. *Child Development*, 1977, **48**, 1075–1979.

Peevers, B. H., & Secord, P. F. Developmental changes in attribution of descriptive concepts to persons. *Journal of Personality and Social Psychology*, 1973, **27**, 120–128.

Rotenberg, K. Development of character constancy of self and other. *Child Development*, 1982, **53**, 505–515.

Rholes, W. S., Blackwell, J., Jordan, C., & Walters, C. A developmental study of learned helplessness. *Developmental Psychology*, 1980, **16**, 616–624.

Ruble, D. N., Feldman, N. S., Higgins, E. T., & Karlovac, M. Locus of causality and use of infor-

mation in the development of causal attributions. *Journal of Personality*, 1979, **47**, 595–614.

Ruble, D. N., & Rholes, W. S. The development of children's perceptions and attributions about their social world. In J. Harvey, R. Kidd, & W. Ickes (Eds.), *New directions in attribution theory* (Vol. 3). Hillsdale, N.J.: Erlbaum, 1981.

Scarlett, H. H., Press, A. N., & Crockett, W. H. Children's descriptions of peers: A Wernerian developmental analysis. *Child Development*, 1971, **42**, 439–453.

Secord, P. F., & Peevers, B. H. The development and attribution of person concepts. In T. Mischel (Ed.), *Understanding other persons*. Totowa, N.J.: Rowman & Littlefield, 1974.

Slaby, R. G., & Frey, K. S. Development of gender constancy and attention to same sex models. *Child Development*, 1975, **46**, 849–856.

Weiner, B. *Achievement motivation and attribution theory*. Morristown, N.J.: General Learning Press, 1974.

READING 32

Development of Social Role Understanding

Malcolm W. Watson

To carry out a successful social interaction, a person needs information about those with whom he will interact. One way of obtaining this information is to consider the social roles that each person occupies. Understanding social roles and their complementary obligations provides a person with a basis for anticipating his or her and others' behaviors and both constrains a person's behaviors to those expected in the role relation and also frees a person from the necessity of discovering the expectations of every situation independent of his or her past experiences. In short, roles provide a context for action. When the roles occupied by a person are disregarded, people may misperceive information about that person and the reasons for his or her actions. Thus, a mature conception of roles should

increase the stability and predictability of the social environment for a person.

It was just this aspect of social interactions that led sociologists and social psychologists in the late 1950s and early 1960s to formulate role theory (see Deutsch & Kraus, 1965; Mead, 1934; Sarbin & Allen, 1968). Although role theory has been out of favor in psychology because it did not generate substantial research, it did leave us with some useful definitions to describe how people conceptualize social interactions. First a *social role* can be defined as a cluster of prescribed and expected behaviors and traits that pertains to a particular category of people. The cluster of behaviors and traits for one role is determined by the relationship of that role to complementary roles, and one role is complementary to another when the two roles are normally associated and the functions of one cannot be described without reference to the other (e.g., one cannot define a husband without reference to a wife). Second, a *role intersection* can be thought of as a case when one person occupies two or more social roles simultaneously. Thus, a person may function in multiple complementary role relations (e.g., a person may simultaneously be a husband to his wife and a father to his daughter). In fact, a primary purpose of role theory was to describe how people would react when the expectations from multiple role relations were in conflict.

One major shortcoming of role theory was that it did not address the issue of the development of role concepts. Children's abilities, as well as adults', to use roles should affect their competence in social interactions, and their competence may vary with their level of role understanding. Therefore, knowledge of children's developing role concepts should help investigators to understand children's social competence, as well as to determine the importance of role relations in the social interactions of adults.

Children often spontaneously exhibit a concern over role concepts. For example, when I was a graduate student, my 5-year-old son asked me if I would still be his father when I became a psychologist. After I explained to him how a person can be both a psychologist and a father, he then asked, "Yes, but are you a teacher or a student? You teach school, and you go to classes." He then asked how I could be a teacher, a student, and a psychologist and still live at home. My son's concerns seemed to stem from his ability to understand social role relations and, therefore, attend to role expectations, and, yet, not be able to intersect multiple roles (although some graduate students might argue that such a role intersection is indeed impossible). Perhaps the real concerns of children in such situations provide the impetus for further development and reorganization of role concepts and argue for the value of assessing this development.

Although a spurt in social–cognitive research has extended the use of cognitive–developmental principles into social realms, this trend has largely neglected the domain of children's developing role concepts. Thus, until recently we have had virtually no systematic description of children's role-concept development. The purpose of this article is to review the small body of research on children's role concepts, to summarize some systematic research that we have done to describe and explain development in this domain, and to review the developmental issues and theory underlying this line of research.

RESEARCH RELATED TO CHILDREN'S ROLE CONCEPT DEVELOPMENT

Research has come largely from two domains: children's developing understanding of kinship terms and concepts and children's developing concept conservation. In perhaps the earliest study of kinship concepts, in order to study how relational understanding developed, Piaget (1928) asked children from 4 to 12 years of age a series of questions concerning family relations. For example, he asked children to tell him what a brother was. He then questioned them further as to their understanding of the reciprocal nature of two boys being brothers to each other. Although Piaget did not actually test for a specific sequence, a sequence of development can be inferred from his study. The order of development for the definitions the children gave was as follows: First, 4-year-olds gave an absolute definition of a brother—a brother is a little boy. This definition had nothing to do with relationships. Second, 5-year-olds included a one-way relation in the definition—the firstborn boy is a brother to a second-born boy, but does not have a brother himself. Third, 9-year-olds gave a definition based on reciprocal relativity—any boy is a brother to another sibling and can both be a brother and have a brother. Piaget then asked similar questions concerning children's understanding of a family. Again, we can infer three stages of definition given by the children: First, the youngest children said that all people who lived with them were family. Older children said that blood relations who were in their immediate vicinity were family, but although they accounted for some family relations, they did not yet fully understand how several family roles were related. For example, because the grandfather occupied the grandfather role, he was precluded from being the father's father at the same time and was not thought of as a member of the family. This type of thinking demonstrates an inability to understand intersections of role relations. Third, the oldest children said that all blood relations, including extended families, were family. (Elkind, 1962, has replicated some of these earlier findings by Piaget.)

In a subsequent study, Chambers and Tavuchis (1976) tested children, 7 to 9 years of age, again on labeling family roles. In addition to using questions, they used photographs and a board game as props. For example, they asked, "Here is the husband. He would say (pointing to the picture of the wife), "She is my———." What? When all the children grow up, are they still husband and wife?'' Their results suggest a developmental order similar to that found by Piaget, but, presumably because they provided the children with props and concrete examples, understanding was evidenced at younger ages.

Other studies have elaborated on Piaget's original findings. Haviland and Clark (1974) assessed children's acquisition (i.e., definitions) of kinship terms and found that semantic complexity played an important part in the order of acquisition. Nevertheless, they found development from simpler relations to more reciprocal relations. Greenfield and Childs (1977) studied the comprehension of kinship terms in a Mayan group in Mexico and also found a developmental order to the understanding of reciprocal relations. Also, children showed an early understanding of reciprocal relations in kinship roles before they could express reciprocity concepts in other tasks.

In order to determine children's speech competence, Anderson (1977, 1978) shifted from studying children's definitions as elicited by an adult to their use of language in playing various family roles. She found that by age 4, most children distinguished role and status differences as reflected in the directives and statements made in role playing for different roles.

In studies of children's sex-role and parent–child role perceptions, Emmerich (1959, 1961) and Bigner (1974) found that younger children did not take account of several dimensions in role relations simultaneously and did not define one role in terms of a complementary role, as did older children. For example, a young child may define a child role in terms of not being big, rather than in terms of its relation to an adult role. Matthews (1977) also found that 4-year-olds showed little awareness of role intersections when describing parent–child role relations or sex roles. Again, dealing with kinship roles, Moore, Cooper, and Bickhard (1977) asked 4- to 13-year-olds questions concerning their definitions of families. These questions related to the child's ability to take into account the relational nature (and intersections) of roles. They found that preschool children understood family roles based rigidly on their personal observations of behaviors. Not until children were of school age did they emphasize normative functions of family roles based on their relationships to other family roles (social roles), e.g., "A mother's still a mother no matter what she does or doesn't do, because she had a kid."

Other researchers have been interested in concept conservation rather than kinship terms per se. Sigel, Saltz, and Roskind (1967) studied children's developing conservation of roles by showing 5- to 8-year-olds pictures of people in various roles and asking them questions such as; "This father studies and becomes a doctor; is he still a father?" As age increased, the children's conservation of a father concept increased. In other words, the older children were able to hold a role concept invariant in the face of transformations. Sigel et al. defined conservation as the developing ability to identify crucial characteristics of a given role and understand how those characteristics apply even when characteristics of a different role are also present and thus change a person. Young children often overdiscriminated between roles. In other words, they could not understand how one role remained invariant when another role was added, e.g., when a father became a doctor. (What they termed conservation would be called an intersection of roles in the previous definition.)

In a recent experiment, Jordan (1980) systematically assessed the effects of various types of transformations of kinship roles on children's abilities to conserve these roles. Each type of transformation (i.e., across time, relationships, and sex roles) affected the difficulty of conservation, but children, nevertheless, showed a systematic, age-related development of conservation (or intersections) from 5 to 7 years of age.

To summarize the findings of all these studies, children developed an understanding of roles that progressed from nonrelational concepts based on salient behaviors to concepts based on role relations to concepts that included role intersections. These studies also suggest that the rate of development varies, depending on the roles and tasks studied. These ideas are not new in developmental psychology, but they provide the basis for a more systematic and complete assessment of children's role understanding, which is necessary to determine the actual developmental sequence and the underlying process that controls how transitions are made in the sequence. A valid developmental sequence is essential as a standard scale about which good questions concerning development and adjustment can be asked. In addi-

tion, any sequence should account for the findings of the studies reviewed above.

ASSESSMENT OF DEVELOPMENTAL SEQUENCES

In order to understand the method used in testing our predicted sequence, certain assumptions and developmental issues need to be clarified. First, there is a value in describing specific patterns and orders of development even though such research is mainly descriptive. Knowing systematic sequences is necessary to determine the degree of synchrony in development across domains and thus the underlying pervasiveness of cognitive structures and the possible constraints on development that determine what behaviors are most likely to occur. Most importantly and related to the above purpose, systematic observations can indeed go beyond mere description because, by predicting a specific order of steps and determining its pervasiveness compared to alternative orders, alternative explanations for the sequence are logically eliminated. Knowing a specific developmental sequence channels the explanation of underlying processes of change since any explanation must account for the specificity of the steps. Thus, the more consistent a predicted sequence is with one type of developmental process and, the more specific and concrete the steps in a sequence are, the more constrained will be any viable explanation of its development.

Using the findings regarding developing role understanding reported above, we tried to postulate a sequence that would lead to an explanation based on one type of developmental process—that of construction–inclusion. However, there were several alternatives to choose from. Flavell (1972) discussed five types of developmental sequences that were based on the functional relations between the steps in each sequence. Nevertheless, these various types seem to fall into one of two categories—either an acquisition (or construction) sequence or a deletion sequence. (Coombs & Smith, 1973, described a method of assessing both types, which they thought were likely to occur together in some domains of development.) An acquisition sequence includes cases in which one skill or behavior is simply added to already existing skills or behaviors and is cumulative (i.e., an addition sequence). Also, an acquisition sequence includes cases in which skills at one level are coordinated together and included in a higher order skill at the next level (i.e., an inclusion sequence). On the other hand, a deletion sequence includes cases in which a skill or behavior at one level is simply dropped when a new, supposedly better, skill is acquired (i.e., a substitution sequence). It remains a theoretical and empirical question whether various forms of sequences exist in different domains of development or whether one process cuts across domains. On a superficial level, it is easy to find all types of sequences (e.g., hierarchical inclusions in Piagetian class-inclusion tasks and substitutions in moral-judgment sequences), but careful analyses of specific sequences may show whether the underlying processes are truly based on acquisition, deletion, or both.

Another major issue in any assessment, is whether a sequence does reflect important developmental processes at all or is simply a measurement sequence—an artifact of the tasks used. Brainerd (1978, 1981) has argued that since so many behaviors undergo age change it is in fact trivial to find a fixed order to many tasks because no other order is conceivable. This seems to be true of many construction–inclusion sequences in which a lower level skill must be included in the higher level skill since the higher level skill is dependent on the first skill as a prerequisite for its development. This also seems to be true of many addition sequences in which one skill is simply added to already existing skills but does not require any underlying shifts in cognitive structure to explain it (e.g., a child may first seriate only 2 sticks, then 3, then 4).

Although this criticism against some sequences is valid, it tends to ignore some aspects of real-life sequences. Fischer and Bullock (1981) have argued that since in actual experimentation it is surprisingly difficult to find clear-cut hierarchical sequences, especially over a large age range, establishing developmental sequences is no trivial task (see also Bertenthal, 1981). They note, in addition, that there is usually a lack of agreement over what is added or included in an acquisition sequence. Measurement sequences may not be as easily differentiated from true developmental sequences as Brainerd has supposed. Therefore, it is an important discovery simply to find that tasks are sequential and that addition or inclusion is the underlying process rather than substitution. There are many possible hierarchical sequences of development that do not occur. For example, of the hierarchies in language production, only a small subset occurs. So, an observed developmental sequence, even though intuitive and less than profound, provides evidence for which processes and components of development are actualized and which do not occur because of constraints in maturational scheduling, differential learning, and so forth. In addition, a measurement sequence provides no information about spurts and plateaus in development as a developmental sequence can. In summary, there is no such thing as a sequence that cannot possibly result in any other way than the pattern predicted. This is always an empirical question.

Another limit on past research is that most sequences that have been reported do not test for a specific order over a relatively continuous age range but instead use age as an independent variable and simply test whether age differences in skill levels exist. However, there are more precise techniques for assessing developmental sequences that do not rely solely on the obvious fact that with age most skills are developing in young children.

One major technique is to use scalogram analysis to determine if steps in a sequence form a Guttman scale, in which any given step or skill will not occur until all previous, lower-level steps or skills have occurred (see Achenbach, 1978; Fischer & Bullock, 1981; Jackowitz & Watson, 1980; Watson & Jackowitz, in press). Such a Guttman scale demonstrates that a sequence is based on an acquisition process and focuses on the order of steps relatively independent of age. Cross-sectional samples can be used by assessing children's skills (on a pass–fail basis) for each step in a predicted sequence through the use of an independent task and assessment for each step (see Table 1). Thus, each child provides a profile of passes and failures across all the steps, and statistical analyses can assess how reproducible and scalable the sequence is across the entire sample and how consistent the sequence is when chance levels of scalability are taken into account (Green, 1956). If the developmental process is essentially one of deletion rather than acquisition (Coombs & Smith, 1973) or if the sequence is not indeed sequential and developmental, then the data will not provide the investigator with a reproducible and consistent Guttman scale.

Besides determining the ordinality of the steps, this technique allows the investigator to observe approximate intervals between the steps by comparing the differences between the mean ages of attainment of each step and by observing gaps and clustering of children at various steps. After sequentiality has been established, age is used as if it were a dependent variable to provide information about the rate in spurts and plateaus of development.

THE UNDERLYING THEORY OF THE PREDICTED SEQUENCE

In our research, we predicted a sequence of steps in children's role concept development that was based on a hierarchical, coordination model of social–cognitive skills (Watson, 1981; Watson & Fischer, 1980). This model reflects a construction–inclusion process in the acquisition of role concepts. The general model of development follows Fischer's (1980) skill theory: Children's skills in a given cognitive domain develop through a set of hierarchically organized levels that are each defined by the structural organization of the component skills. That is, skills at one level are combined with each other to form a new higher order unit that forms a new level of understanding but also includes the previous subskills. Several transformation rules describe how skills at a given level can be combined and related to form the more complex skill. Through the transformation of *compounding,* an additional component is added to a skill at the same general level (e.g., two actions of an agent or actor are expanded to include three actions). Through the transformation of *intercoordination,* two skills are combined to form a whole new unit at a higher structural level (e.g., two roles are reciprocally intercoordinated to form a unit of two comple-

TABLE 1   GENERAL MODEL FOR A GUTTMAN SCALE

Developmantal order of profiles	Task (step)				
	1	2	3	4	5
0	−	−	−	−	−
1	+	−	−	−	−
2	+	+	−	−	−
3	+	+	+	−	−
4	+	+	+	+	−
5	+	+	+	+	+

Note: A − indicates a failure and a + indicates a pass for any given step.

mentary roles). In Fischer's theory, the major intercoordinations occur in four successive levels at a given tier of understanding. Then, these four levels are repeated at a higher tier, and so on. Fischer has postulated that the tiers of understanding are a sensory–motor tier, a representational tier, and an abstract tier. Our predicted steps proceeded from Fischer's Level 3 in the Sensory–Motor tier to Fischer's Level 8 in the Abstract tier.

This general model led to a prediction that role concept development was relatively continuous, despite the separate steps we predicted, and that its origins could be observed in late infancy with the beginning developments of symbolic representation.

Although this model predicts development only in specific domains that depend on the content, props, and tasks involved for their definitions, the general inclusion process of the sequence is thought to be pervasive across areas. Thus, tasks of class inclusion, classification, and other previously researched domains should be similar in pattern, if not in rate of development, to role-concept development. However, skills such as class inclusion provide less ease in predicting the specific intercoordinations of skill units that would form the sequence than does skill theory. Not all steps would be predicted from class inclusion, for example. Another value of skill theory was that it led to a prediction of initial intercoordination at a given level and then expansion of understanding at that level. Thus, each level was represented by two or more substeps that seemed to capture the most important constructions in the sequence.

THE PREDICTED SEQUENCE

The general sequence progresses as shown in Table 2. All steps are concerned with the way basic building blocks or units are combined to form increasingly complex and abstract role concepts. The basic unit is the agent of action, and this unit can be traced through all the steps.

First, as a precursor to role understanding, the child's combination of several actions forms a conception of an agent of action independent of the child's actions, developing from Fischer's Level 3 (Sensory–Motor systems) to Level 4 (Single representations); second, a combination of agents forms the first conception of a role, based on behaviors and salient perceptual features of the agents involved, developing within Level 4; third, a combination of roles forms a conception of a complementary role relation or social role, developing from Level 4 to Level 5 (Representational mappings); fourth, a combination of role relations forms a conception of a role intersection, developing from Level 5 to Level 6 (Representational systems); fifth, a combination of role intersections forms a conception of a role network, developing from Level 6 to Level 7 (Single abstractions); sixth, a combination of role networks forms a conception of a network relation, developing from Level 7 to Level 8

TABLE 2   OVERVIEW OF THE SEQUENCE OF ROLE CONCEPT DEVELOPMENT

Order	Structure[a]
0	Action
1	Action 1 ‡ Action 2 = Independent agent
2	Agent 1 ‡ Agent 2 = Behavioral role
3	Role 1 ‡ Role 2 = Social role relation
4	Role relation 1 ‡ Role relation 2 = Role intersection
5	Intersection 1 ‡ Intersection 2 = Role network
6	Network 1 ‡ Network 2 = Network relation

(Abstract mappings). Yet at this most abstract level of understanding, children still can use the earlier conceptual skills of agents of action, social roles, and so forth. This general sequence corresponds with the findings of previous studies that show development progressing from nonrelational role concepts to role relations to role intersections but also goes beyond to role networks.

Table 3 shows the entire sequence, with the initiation and expansion steps at each level, and gives some examples of tasks used to measure each step. The first steps were expected to emerge in late infancy, and the last steps were expected to emerge in early adolescence.

The sequence begins with the onset of symbolic play in young children, in which the child combines several actions to perform some out-of-context, pretend behavior using the self only as the agent or cause of action. In Step 1, the child cannot yet represent another agent as independent of the child's own actions. Steps 2 and 3 show the child's transitions in developing a conception of independent agents as used in symbolic activities from making an agent a part of the child's actions (compounding) to Step 4, in which the child differentiates an agent from self by intercoordinating the self's actions with another agent's actions to represent and compare how other people (i.e., as independent agents), as well as the self, can perform some behavior. This defines one component of representation (see Jackowitz & Watson, 1980; Wolf, 1982). Understanding independent agency is absolutely essential for children to be able to consider that other roles even exist. Yet, at this step children still do not categorize people by roles. One child said that she knew a person was a grandmother because she herself had flown to Michigan to see her grandmother, but she did not comprehend a category of people who were all grandmothers.

In Step 5, the child combines similar categories of action for similar agents. Some agents seem to be related in the things they do, the way they dress, and what they are called (e.g., fathers). A behavioral role involves a set of behaviors related to a specific category of people. For example, one young preschooler claimed that his father was only a father when he was at home engaged in a limited set of behaviors. This is an example of an expansion of the independent agents first conceptualized at Level 4.

In Steps 6 through 8, the child begins to understand roles not only in terms of sets of behaviors but in terms of social relationships and expectations with complementary roles (e.g., fathers not only do similar things, they must have children and are expected to take care of their children). In other words, the role categories are intercoordinated to form a higher level unit—a social role relation, and then the role relations are expanded to include sequentially, and eventually simultaneously, two other complementary roles.

The following example illustrates the difference between a behavioral and a social role concept. Two brothers, one 3 and one 4½ years of age, engaged in a recurring play scenario of store keeper. The younger boy played the game by having a doll storekeeper stock the shelves and work in the store (i.e., a behavioral role). The older boy added to this game a constant interaction of the storekeeper with doll customers and his parents as customers, asking them what items they wanted, making change, and pretending to order and stock what the customers needed. This boy added the complementary interactions typical of more advanced social role relations.

In Steps 9 and 10, the child intercoordinates one social role relation with another social role relation for the same agents to form a reciprocal system—a role intersection—and then expands this intersection to include three role relations. Yet the expansion in Step 10 has the same basic structure as the role intersection of Step 9. Thus, one agent can occupy and function in two or more roles and can relate to each comple-

TABLE 3 PREDICTED SEQUENCE OF ROLE CONCEPT DEVELOPMENT

Fischer's skill level and step	Description	Assessment tasks	
		Doctor role	Family role
Level 3: Sensory–Motor systems			
1	Self as agent: A child pretends to carry out one or more behaviors, not necessarily fitting a social role	Child pretends to drink from a cup or wash himself or herself	
2	Passive other agent: A child includes another agent in one or more behaviors, not necessarily fitting a social role	Child gives a doll a drink from a cup or washes the doll, without the doll acting	
3	Passive substitute agent: A child has a substitute object act as a passive agent, as in Step 2	Child gives a block a drink from a cup or washes the block, without the block acting	
Level 4: Single representations			
4	Independent agent: A child acts as if an agent can perform one or more behaviors, not necessarily fitting a social role	Child has a doll drink from a cup or wash itself, as if it were carrying out the action itself	Child labels and describes a doll's activities
5	Behavioral role: An agent performs several behaviors fitting a role category	Child has a doll, as a doctor, use a thermometer and an otolaryngoscope	Child describes a father in terms of his typical behaviors
Level 5: Representational mappings			
6	Social role relation: One agent behaving according to one role relates to a second agent behaving according to a complementary role, i.e., one role is mapping onto another role	Child has a doctor doll examine a patient doll and respond appropriately to the patient's complaints	Child describes a father in terms of the father having children and taking care of his children
7	Shifting social roles with one common agent: Two agents perform in complementary social roles, as in Step 6, and then one of them performs a different social role with a third agent	Child has a doctor doll examine a patient doll and respond appropriately to the patient's complaints, and then child has the patient doll interact appropriately with a nurse doll	Child describes how a father has children and then how he can change to become a grandfather when he has grandchildren

#	Step / Level	Doll task example	Family role description
8	Social role with three agents: One agent in one role relates simultaneously to two other agents in complementary roles	Child has a doctor doll relate to a patient doll and be aided by a nurse doll. All dolls respond appropriately to each other	
	Level 6: Representational systems		
9	Role intersection: Two agent–complement role relations are intercoordinated so that one agent can be in two roles simultaneously and relate to both complementary roles	Child has a doctor doll examine a patient doll and also act simultaneously as father to the patient, who responds as both his patient and his daughter	Child describes how a father can be both a father to his children and a grandfather to his grandchildren simultaneously
10	Role intersection with three agents: Three agent–complement role relations are compounded so that one agent can be in three roles simultaneously and relate to the complementary roles	Child has one doll respond as a doctor and father to a second doll and as a doctor and husband to a third doll, who responds as the patient's mother and the doctor's wife	Child describes how a father can be a son, father and grandfather simultaneously in terms of the complementary roles
	Level 7: Single abstractions		
11	Role network: At least two role intersections are intercoordinated and compared to form a definition of a complex role system or network		Child compares family role relations across two generations and recognizes a family in terms of intersecting spousal and parental roles, thus forming a concept of a traditional family
12	Role network with three role intersections: At least three role intersections as in Step 11 are compounded and compared to form a more complex network		Child compares family role relations across three generations, including a future generation
	Level 8: Abstract mappings		
13	Network relation: At least two role networks are intercoordinated so that the similarities and differences between them can be recognized and a more abstract network definition is formed		Child recognizes that a spousal role (in the case of childless couples) or a parental role (in the case of single parent families) can define a family, as well as cases of traditional families
14	General network relation: Both the similarities and differences of at least three role networks are simultaneously considered, and one general network relation is abstracted		Child recognizes the essential components of both traditional and nontraditional families in terms of role relations and functions and can define families by necessary and sufficient roles and functions

Note: Portions of this table are adapted, with permission, from Watson (1981).

mentary role simultaneously (e.g., a man can be a son, a father, and a grandfather as determined by the respective complementary roles of father, son, and grandson).

In Steps 11 and 12 the child first intercoordinates one role intersection (e.g., one generation of family role relations) with another role intersection (e.g., another generation of family role relations) to define a role network or system of role intersections (e.g., spousal and parental role relations intersect across generations and make up a family network). In Step 12, the child expands the role networks to include three generations of families. It should be clear that the role intersections of the previous level are still present at this level but themselves form an intersection across sets of intersections. For example, a husband–wife role relation and a father–son role relation are intersected; then, this unit is intersected across the grandparents' and parents' families and eventually across the child's future family.

In Step 13, the child intercoordinates one role network (e.g., a traditional family with parents, children, and spouses) with another role network (e.g., a nontraditional family with only spouses or only parents and children) to recognize the similarities and differences between them, i.e., to map one onto the other so that both form a total role concept. In Step 14, the child compares the similarities and differences between more than two role networks and abstracts from all combinations to form a more general definition for all related role networks (e.g., a definition in terms of roles that will account for all types of families). This last step is simply an expansion of the network relations initiated in Step 13 and includes at least childless couples, single-parent families, and traditional families all under one concept.

ASSESSMENT OF THE PREDICTED DEVELOPMENTAL SEQUENCE

Of course, the validity of this predicted sequence, especially the specific steps at each level, remained an empirical question. As alluded to previously, the certainty of any sequence and the underlying combinations of skills cannot be accepted on logical assumptions alone. Therefore, we assessed children's levels of understanding as reflected, first, in their imitative pretending and role playing and, second, in their answers to questions concerning role relationships. In the first set of studies, we tried to elicit their highest level of competence by having an adult model demonstrate role play using realistic cardboard dolls at each step in the sequence to be tested and then encouraging each child to individually imitate the same role-playing behaviors. (In tasks involving merely an assessment of spontaneous free play, an investigator cannot be confident that the child is demonstrating his or her highest competence level since free play reflects children's preferences only.) The theme for the modeled tasks concerned the social role of medical doctor and its complements (i.e., nurse and patient). Thus, for each step, the model acted out a short story using the doctor, patient, nurse, and parent dolls (see examples for doctor roles in Table 3). Each child was expected to perform some elicited role playing on the several tasks, each of which corresponded to a separate step. With this procedure, we were able to eliminate a good deal of the extraneous verbal requirements needed to demonstrate children's understanding.

Children's role playing was scored as a pass or a fail for each step according to established criteria (summarized in Table 3). At least two observers, who were blind as to the hypotheses, always independently scored the videotapes of children's performances for the steps that they passed and failed. High interobserver reliability was consistently achieved (81 to 100% agreement of steps passed). Thus, each child produced a profile of steps passed and steps failed. By assessing all children's profiles, we could analyze the scalability of the sequence. Using Green's (1956) technique, we found an Index of Reproducibility (*Rep*) of the scale ordering, which could range from 0 to 1 (we considered .8 reproducibility or better as being indicative of high reproducibility). If *Rep* was high, we then found an Index of Consistency (*I*), which accounts for the chance level of reproducibility and can range from 0 to 1. Any *I* above .5 is evidence for a strong unidimensional scale. If the sequence formed a Guttman scale, in which any given step was not passed until all previous steps had been passed, then we would have strong evidence for the hierarchical and sequential nature of the sequence.

In the first experiment (Watson & Fischer, 1977), we tested Steps 1 through 4 of the sequence (see Table 3) in 36 children who ranged in age from 14 to 24 months. These steps were found to be scalable (Green's Index of Consistency = .58) and significantly age related. If an acquisition-deletion sequence was considered (see Coombs & Smith, 1973), the results were even stronger. Children not only acquired the steps of agent use in the predicted order, but they also stopped using them in the same order (i.e., first in–first out sequence). All but two children fit this pattern. At 14 months of age, no child demonstrated Step 4 (independent agent use), but by 24 months of age, 75% of the children demonstrated it.

In a second experiment (Watson & Fischer, 1980), we tested Steps 1, 4, 5, and 6 in the general sequence in 40 children who ranged in age from 1½ to 4 years. Again, these steps were found to be highly scalable (Green's Index of Consistency = .87) and significantly age related. At 1½ years of age, most children showed only Step 1, while, between 3 and 4 years of age, most children showed Step 5 (a behavioral role), and 70% of the 4-year-olds were able to show Step 6 (a social role relation involving the complementary roles of doctor and patient). In a third experiment (Watson & Fischer, 1980), we tested Steps 4, 5, 6, 8, 9, and 10 in the general sequence in 68 children ranging in age from 1½ to 7½ years. Again, these steps were

highly scalable (Green's Index of Consistency = .89) and age related. At age 4 or 5 years, most children showed an understanding of social roles, and, at age 6, many children were able to show Step 9 (a role intersection for doctor and father related to patient and daughter).

In another set of studies, we again tested the sequence but changed both the roles used in testing and the task requirements. If the sequence is indeed valid, it should be generalizable across many different role domains and to different tasks that may reflect role understanding. In these studies, we used family role relations for the general theme, rather than doctor–patient role relations (see Table 3 for the examples of parental and family role tasks used). Both domains of doctor–patient roles and family roles were chosen because they seemed to be of concern to preschool children. We asked the children questions concerning parental and family roles, rather than modeling role playing for the children. However, again we used the dolls as aids to help the children keep the roles and questions clear. Of course, role and task differences should likely change the rate of development (e.g., the verbal requirements of this task should have been more difficult than the previous role-playing task); however, we predicted that the same sequence would obtain.

We used the same procedure of eliciting responses for each step to be tested and scoring each task as a pass or a fail to obtain a step profile for each child. Again, high interobserver reliability was found (86–100% agreement).

We completed two experiments (Watson & Amgott-Kwan, 1983), testing 48 and 16 children, respectively, who ranged in age from 3 to 7½ years. We tested Steps 4, 5, 6, 7, 9, and 10 of the general sequence for parental role understanding (see Table 3). In both studies, the sequence was scalable (Index of Consistency = .78 and 1.) and age related. Again, between 3 and 4 years of age, children showed Step 5 (a behavioral role of father or mother); by 6 years of age, most children showed Step 6 (a social role); and, by 7½ years of age, children showed Steps 9 and 10 (role intersections). In addition, tests comparing mean ages of children who showed each step as the highest step in the previous doctor-role sequence and in the parent-role sequence indicated no significant differences between the sequences. Thus, in spite of role and task differences, both sequences of role understanding developed in close synchrony.

In a subsequent study (Watson & Amgott-Kwan, in press), we completed an additional experiment to assess an extension of the sequence through the last steps of family role understanding, as shown in Table 3. We tested 50 children, who ranged in age from 6 to 13 years. Steps 9 through 14 of the general sequence were tested. With this older age group, the sequence was also found to be scalable (Green's Index of Consistency = .87) and age related. At 6 years of age, most children showed Step 9 (role intersections for spouses and parents); by 9 years, most children showed Step 11 (a role network); and by 12 years, most children showed Step 13 (a network relation). Only a few of the oldest children showed Step 14 (a network relation for a general definition of families). Differences in the amount of experience children had with alternate family patterns influenced rate of development through the sequence but showed that the sequence was robust, nevertheless. For example, children who had had a course in their school concerning families were more likely to reach the last step (33%) than those of the same age who had not had the extra training (8%). Children from single-parent homes showed no significant differences in developmental level from children from two-parent homes.

Of the total of 258 children from all studies, 234 children (91%) scaled perfectly. In all studies, age was significantly correlated with highest step of role-concept development. These studies together suggest that the sequence is valid and generalizable across different roles and tasks and with varying samples of children. The results also imply that the underlying structural model of the developmental sequence is valid. The order of steps seemed to be based on the combinations of agents and roles, not on other factors that also varied. For example, the sequence was not based on the number of dolls used, the number of roles used, or the number of sentences uttered since these factors did not predict the sequence that was found.

In assessing spurts and plateaus in development, we found that generally children clustered at the last steps of a given level. They seemed to develop smoothly through the steps until another major reorganization was required.

THE SIGNIFICANCE OF ROLE-CONCEPT DEVELOPMENT

The findings presented above regarding children's role concept development can provide investigators not only with a clearer picture of social–cognitive development but also with a better understanding of children's developing social competence. Three areas of social competence—friendship relations, identity development, and adjustment to divorce—and their probable relation to role concept development are discussed below.

Selman (1980) has postulated and tested a sequence of stages in children's conceptions of friendship in which children seem to progress from understanding friends as (1) momentary playmates in the early preschool years to (2) viewing friendship as a one-way assistance, in which a friend gives the child what she wants, to (3) a two-way cooperation to (4) an intimate relationship of sharing common interests to eventually (5) an autonomous, interdependent relationship, which allows for other independent relations. This last level of development was not found until adolescence. Although the rates of development of role concepts and friendship concepts seem to differ, the sequences show a parallel progression. Step 1 of friendship may be related to a prerole understanding. The idea of one-way assistance in friends (Step 2) can be associated with an understanding of behavioral roles, in which the reciprocal perspective of a person in a complementary role is not taken into account. The idea of a two-way cooperation in friends (Step 3) suggests a complementary, social role relation, in which another person's expectations are intercoordinated with one's own. Step 4 of friendship may be a transition step similar to the transitions from social roles to role intersections. Autonomous, interdependent concepts of friends (Step 5) can be associated with an understanding of simultaneous role intersections, in which multiple roles are considered. The developments of friendship and role concepts probably follow the same sequence of structural development, though one may not necessarily be a prerequisite for the other and they may not develop at the same rate. However, the specific parallels suggested above may be found to exist if the tasks for assessing friendship concepts were modified to be more similar to the role concept tasks. For example, friendship concepts could be assessed through modeling and imitation of role-playing stories, which would reduce the verbal demands on the child. Then, these results could be compared with role-concept results also assessed through role playing. In this case, the sequences would be predicted to develop with a high degree of synchrony.

Another area of social competence that seems to be related to role concepts is the area of identity development. Gergen (1972) has argued that healthy adults have multiple identities and many facets to their self-concepts, but that this diversity does not seem to be a source of great conflict for them. His argument coincides with ideas found in role theory (Sarbin & Allen, 1968) that stress the multiple roles people take and the need to change behavior according to the various reciprocal role interac-

tions encountered. When people have a concept of role intersections (Step 9), they can handle the apparent conflicts.

Young children, however, may be equipped to identify with another person only to the extent that they are able to understand various possible role interactions with the other person and thus predict how another person would act in various circumstances. If a child does not know a person's full range of behaviors in social relations because the person can only be perceived in a single role (i.e., social role relations, Step 6), his or her identification with that person would be limited (e.g., a child may only identify with the mother as comforter, not with the mother as spouse, teacher, neighbor, and so forth). When the child is able to intersect role relations (Step 9), she should be able to comprehend why a person's behavior may change in different situations and how her own behavior must be adjusted (e.g., she will identify with her mother in terms of many behaviors and traits not related exclusively to the mother role). When she understands role networks (Step 11), she should be able to understand how her own identity must accommodate to the network she is in at the moment. Thus, by assessing a child's major level of role concept development and then observing her preferences and imitations of significant others, I would predict major qualitative changes and expansions in her imitations and person preferences with each new level of role concept development.

As a final area of social competence that will be discussed, changes in family structure, such as the parents' divorce, have been shown to have profound effects on children's developing social and cognitive skills (e.g., Blanchard & Biller, 1971; Hetherington, 1979; Hetherington, Cox, & Cox, 1978). Particularly relevant to the present discussion is the finding of age differences in the effects of divorce and single parents on children's coping behavior. For example, children whose fathers leave the home before the child is 5 or 6 years old tend to have more academic and sex-typing problems and problems adjusting to the divorce than children who are older when their fathers leave. These age shifts correspond to most children's shifts from social role concepts to role intersections.

Little work has been done, however, relating children's role-concept development to their reactions to their parent's divorce, and, yet, such a relation may indeed be strong. A child's understanding of role intersections (Step 9), family role networks (Step 11), and network relations (Step 13), in which spousal and parental roles are compared, might determine, in large part, how the child would interpret the divorce, where she would place the blame, and how easily she could maintain or reestablish a relationship with the parents when the family roles had been so transformed. For example, children who cannot intersect spousal and parent–child role relations may feel guilty for causing the divorce, whereas children with an understanding of role intersections could understand that the success of spousal relations is not necessarily dependent on parent–child relations. This prediction could be assessed in children experiencing divorce in their families.

In another example, one 8-year-old child in our studies, whose parents had recently divorced, was explaining what the divorce meant. He said that even though his father no longer lived with them, he was still the boy's father. He also said that his parents were no longer married, but when asked if they were all still a family, he became confused. He said, "Really, my mother and father are married because we are still a family." In this case, the child seemed to have no problems with role intersections (Step 9) (e.g., a person being both a father and a husband); however, his rationale reflected some confusion concerning the relations of spouses and parents, in which either relation alone can define a family (Step 13). I would predict that further testing involving cases like these would demonstrate that only when a child differentiated families in terms of spousal and parental role relations (Step 13) would she understand how a family could continue without the spousal relations.

CONCLUSION

In conclusion, the relationships between children's role concepts and their friendship concepts, identity development, and reactions to family changes may best be described as a set of intersecting skills in which each one may influence the others but in which all form subsets of a greater superset, which is the development of social competence. In all these cases, the child's social–cognitive skills are inextricably connected to his or her behavior. The sequence and process of social role concept development is both a prototype of these connections and seems to be one of the crucial components. The sequence of development also provides a validated example of a construction–inclusion process that may be found to cut across all social–cognitive domains.

REFERENCES

Achenbach, T. M. (1978). *Research in developmental psychology: Concepts, strategies, methods.* New York: Free Press.

Anderson, E. S. (1977). Young children's knowledge of role-related speech differences: A mommy is not a daddy is not a baby. *Papers and Reports in Child Language Development,* **13**, 83–90.

Anderson, E. S. (1978). Will you don't snore please?: Directives in young children's roleplay speech. *Papers and Reports in Child Language Development,* **15**, 140–150.

Bertenthal, B. I. (1981). The significance of developmental sequences for investigating the what and how of development. *New Directions for Child Development: Cognitive Development,* **12**, 43–54.

Bigner, J. J. (1974). Second borns' discrimination of sibling role concepts. *Developmental Psychology,* **10**, 564–673.

Blanchard, R. W., & Biller, H. B. (1971). Father availability and academic performance among 3rd grade boys. *Developmental Psychology, 4,* 301–305.

Brainerd, C. J. (1978). The stage question in cognitive–developmental theory. *The Behavioral and Brain Sciences, 1,* 173–182.

Brainerd, C. J. (1981). Stages II: A review of *Beyond universals in cognitive development. Developmental Review, 1,* 63–81.

Chambers, J. C., & Tavuchis, N. (1976). Kids and kin: Children's understanding of American kin terms. *Journal of Child Language, 3,* 63–80.

Coombs, C. H., & Smith, J. E. K. (1973). On the detection of structure in attitudes and developmental processes. *Psychological Review, 80,* 337–351.

Deutsch, M., & Kraus, R. M. (1965). *Theories in social psychology.* New York: Basic Books.

Elkind, D. (1962). Children's conceptions of brother and sister: Piaget replication study V. *Journal of Genetic Psychology, 100,* 129–136.

Emmerich, W. (1959). Young children's discrimination of parent and child roles. *Child Development, 30,* 403–419.

Emmerich, W. (1961). Family role concepts of children ages six to ten. *Child Development, 32,* 609–624.

Fischer, K. W. (1980). A theory of cognitive development: The control and construction of hierarchies of skills. *Psychological Review, 87,* 477–531.

Fischer, K. W., & Bullock, D. (1981). Patterns of data: Sequence, synchrony, and constraint in cognitive development. *New Directions for Child Development: Cognitive Development, 12,* 1–20.

Flavell, J. H. (1972). An analysis of cognitive–developmental sequences. *Genetic Psychology Monographs, 86,* 279–350.

Gergen, K. J. (1972). Multiple identity: The healthy, happy human being wears many masks. *Psychology Today, 5,* 31–35.

Green, B. F. (1956). A method of scalogram analysis using summary statistics. *Psychometrika, 1,* 79–88.

Greenfield, P. M., & Childs, C. P. (1977). Understanding sibling concepts: A developmental study of kin terms of Zinacantan. In P. Dasen (Ed.), *Cross-cultural Piagetian psychology.* New York: Gardner Press.

Haviland, S. E., & Clark, E. V. (1974). 'This man's father is my father's son': A study of the acquisition of English kin terms. *Journal of Child Language, 1,* 23–47.

Hetherington, E. M. (1979). Divorce: A child's perspective. *American Psychologist, 34,* 851–858.

Hetherington, E. M., Cox, M., & Cox, R. (1978). The development of children in mother headed families. In H. Hoffman & D. Reiss (Eds.), *The American family: Dying or developing?* New York: Plenum.

Jackowitz, E. R., & Watson, M. W. (1980). Development of object transformations in early pretend play. *Developmental Psychology, 16,* 543–549.

Jordan, V. B. (1980). Conserving kinship concepts: A developmental study in social cognition. *Child Development, 51,* 146–155.

Matthews, W. S. (1977). *Sex role perception, portrayal, and preference in the fantasy play of young children.* Paper presented at the meetings of the Society for Research in Child Development, New Orleans.

Mead, G. H. (1934). *Mind, self, and society.* Chicago: Univ. of Chicago Press.

Moore, N. V., Cooper, R. G., & Bickhard, M. H. (1977). *The child's development of the concept of family.* Paper presented at the meetings of the Society for Research in Child Development, New Orleans.

Piaget, J. (1928). Judgment and reasoning in the child (M. Warden, Trans.). London: Routledge & Kegan Paul.

Sarbin, T. R., & Allen, V. L. (1968). Role theory. In G. Lindzey & E. Aronson (Eds.), *Handbook of social psychology,* vol. 1. Reading, MA: Addison–Wesley.

Selman, R. L. (1980). *The growth of interpersonal understanding: Developmental and clinical analysis.* New York: Academic Press.

Sigel, I. E., Saltz, E., & Roskind, W. (1967). Variables determining concept conservation in children. *Journal of Experimental Psychology, 74,* 471–475.

Watson, M. W. (1981). The development of social roles: A sequence of social–cognitive development. *New Directions for Child Development: Cognitive Development, 12,* 33–42.

Watson, M. W., & Amgott-Kwan, T. (1983). Transitions in children's understanding of parental roles. *Developmental psychology,* **19,** 659–666.

Watson, M. W., & Amgott-Kwan, T. (in press). Development of family role concepts in school-age children. *Developmental Psychology.*

Watson, M. W., & Fischer, K. W. (1977). A developmental sequence of agent use in late infancy. *Child Development,* **48,** 828–836.

Watson, M. W., & Fischer, K. W. (1980). Development of social roles in elicited and spontaneous behavior during the preschool years. *Developmental Psychology,* **16,** 483–494.

Watson, M. W., & Jackowitz, E. R. (in press). Agents and recipient objects in the development of early symbolic play. *Child Development.*

Wolf, D. (1982). Understanding others: A longitudinal case study of the concept of independent agency. In G. Forman (Ed.), *Action and thought: From sensorimotor schemes to symbolic operations.* New York: Academic Press.

CHAPTER 8

THE FAMILY

The articles in this section reflect four main trends in contemporary theory and research on families:

1 An increased use of a family systems framework in studying families.
2 A concern with understanding the functioning of nontraditional families.
3 An awareness that families do not function in isolation and that to understand the family requires exploring its relationship with the larger social ecology.
4 A growing recognition that families are not static and that they must adapt to normative and nonnormative life events and to historical change.

The family has traditionally been viewed as the primary and most powerful agent of socialization of children. Interactions with parents are usually the initial and most enduring social contacts that children encounter. These early contacts with parents are likely to be critical in shaping children's self-concepts, expectations in interpersonal relations, and competence in social situations. The parents' actions, attitudes, and values which are communicated to their children also serve as a cognitive framework around which the children will organize their subsequent perceptions of social standards and appropriate social behavior.

Recent changes in theory about family processes and their role in socialization are some of the most dramatic to occur in the history of child psychology. Formerly the child was regarded as a passive object of socialization. The use of terms such as "child rearing" and "child training" reflects the dominant American behavioristic orientation in which it is believed that parents shape the

development of children in a unilateral fashion. Most contemporary psychologists now take a systems approach to studying the family. They view the
family as a multidirectional interactive system, with the behavior of each family
member modifying that of other members in the system. Children are shaping
and socializing their parents and siblings just as the parents are shaping their
children. For example, high rates of sibling conflict may lead to stress and
depression in a mother, which may impact both on her marital relationship and
her child-rearing practices. Moreover, members' experiences outside the
family—in the school, the peer group, or the workplace—may modify family
functioning and relationships.

The mutual shaping of behavior and the interaction in family relationships is
presented in the article by Mavis Hetherington on family interaction following
divorce and in the article by Glenn Elder and his colleagues showing how
family members' personal and social attributes related to the adjustment of
children to changes experienced in the Great Depression. In addition, as the
article by Robert Stewart and Robert Marvin makes clear, this interactive
interdependent pattern of family relationships exists not only between parents
and children and husband and wife but also between siblings. The caregiving
behavior of a child toward a younger sibling is related to mother-child
attachment and to conceptual skills.

In the United States the nuclear family, consisting of a working father and
nonworking mother plus one or more children, has been regarded as the most
desirable child-rearing unit. Although shifts in family roles and structure are
occurring, the majority of American children and many adults still cling to this
traditional ideal. Still, the family system is changing and alternate family forms
once viewed as deviant are becoming more frequent. Half of all American
mothers work; an increasing number of children experience their parents'
divorce, live in a one-parent household, and eventually enter into a step-family;
teenage pregnancies have become commonplace. Members of these new family
forms confront different problems and have different needs; they have different
strengths and weaknesses from those of nuclear families. Therefore, successful
family functioning, that is, those roles and relationships that lead to positive
outcomes for family members, may vary for different types of families. This is
evident in the article on teenage sexuality and childbearing by Frank Furstenberg, Richard Lincoln, and Jane Menken and in the Hetherington article on
family relationships in divorced and remarried families.

Families are dynamic; they undergo continuous change. This is to some
extent attributable to changes in family members who grow older and must
adapt to new developmental challenges in themselves and in others. This
adaptation requires an alteration in roles and relationships. In the article by
Laurence Steinberg we see the emotional, behavioral, and cognitive transformations that occur in families coping with a child's transition to adolescence.
In order to successfully negotiate this transition, family members must realign
relationships to nurture the adolescent's growing autonomy.

Some of the factors that necessitate changes in family functioning are not predictable, normative life changes such as entry into first grade, puberty, or retirement. In contrast, they are nonnormative life events such as teenage pregnancy, divorce, or remarriage that are unexpectedly encountered by individuals, or they are historical events such as war or a depression that may affect an entire cohort. Such events or life experiences may set in motion a series of related life changes with powerful long-term implications for development. Such effects are discussed in the articles by Furstenberg et al. on teenage pregnancy, by Hetherington on divorce, and by Elder on the effects of the Great Depression on families.

The contemporary developmental, ecological systems perspective on the family necessitates that the investigator ask new questions and use new research designs and methods in studying the relations between the family and development.

READING 33

The ABCs of Transformations in the Family at Adolescence: Changes in Affect, Behavior, and Cognition

Laurence Steinberg

This is an exciting time for those of us who study the family at adolescence, for several reasons. After what seems like an eternity of struggle to overthrow the "'storm and stress" model of adolescent family relationships that had dominated this area of inquiry for so many years, researchers are now beginning to examine the family at adolescence from vantage points that emphasize aspects of family relationships other than conflict, rebellion, and disagreement. In the last ten years, we have seen more and more studies examining changes in decision-making practices, in patterns of family activity, and even—God forbid—the growth of intimacy between teenagers and their parents.

Second, the focus in research on the family at adolescence has shifted away from simple correlational studies linking parent behaviors and adolescent outcomes. These correlational studies, of course, provided an important foundation upon which our current models are built. But they left open many, many important questions about *process*. Current research indicates that the study of process, as well as outcome, is a crucial part of our common research agenda. Family processes—not simply the parental behaviors—are related to psychosocial growth at adolescence. There are changes in family processes that characterize transformations in the family system as it, and its members, adapt to adolescence.

Third, the shift toward understanding family processes at adolescence has been accompanied by a movement toward a more bidirectional view of family interaction and socialization. This view, it should be said, had gained respect among scholars of childhood and infancy some years ago. It may be finally mak-

ing its way into studies of adolescence as well. Increasingly, researchers are recognizing that adolescence is not only a time of change for the young person but is likely to be a time of change for his or her parents too, who themselves may be confronting particular sets of psychosocial concerns characteristic of middle adulthood. How the changes of midlife are interconnected with transformations in the family—either as provokers or consequences of intrafamilial transformation—is a topic that warrants a great deal more investigation. Indeed, as the demographics of the population shift over the next decade, with more and more baby boomers outgrowing the game of "Trivial Pursuit" and confronting instead the not-so-trivial demands of midlife, funding agencies are likely to look more kindly upon proposals aimed at understanding not only how parents affect children, but at how adolescent children affect their middle-aged parents.

I want to explore each of these three shifts in emphasis in greater detail because they are very much related to the sorts of questions my research group has been struggling with. I will have the most to say about the first of these shifts—that is, the shift away from conflict as the dominant focus in family research. What I'd like to do today is present an alternative framework to the conflict perspective.

REALIGNMENT IN THE FAMILY: AN ALPHABETIC APPROACH

I have tentatively called the framework the ABC framework, because the pieces are alphabetical. If we step back and ask, "What is it that takes place in the family system over the course of adolescence as families adapt to the developmental changes of this era?" it seems to me that the changes one thinks of fall neatly into three interrelated, but distinct, categories. First, there are changes in how people feel about each other—what we might call transformations in the *A*ffective dimension of the adolescent-parent relationship. In this category I would place changes in the domain of conflict, intimacy, and so forth. Second, there are changes in the ways in which people behave toward each other—transformations in the *Be*havioral dimension. Here I would place changes in such phenomena as decision-making, autonomy, and privacy. And, finally, there are changes in how people conceive of each other and their relationships in the family—transformations in the *C*ognitive dimension. In this category are transformations in person perception, in social understanding and role-taking, and in conceptions of social conventions and rules in the family.

Central to the model I am proposing is the concept of *normative realignment*. By realignment I mean a set of transformations in the family that, over a period of time, produce new forms of affective, behavioral, and cognitive states. I use the term "realignment," rather than change or transformation, to suggest a process characterized by temporary periods of oscillation, perturbation, and disequilibrium. During the course of realignment, the family system moves from a stage of equilibrium established during childhood into a temporary state of disequilibrium (usually during early adolescence) and, once successfully realigned, into a new equilibrium. I use the term "normative" because there is a growing body of literature indicating that this process is fairly common at adolescence. By normative I also mean to imply that the period of disequilibrium—which many families experience as frustrating and trying—is not at all pathological. Indeed, I believe that this realignment is a necessary antecedent to healthy psychosocial growth during middle adolescence and during middle adulthood.

Affective Realignment

We know a great deal more about affective realignment in the family than about behavioral realignment, and more about realignment in the behavioral domain than in the cognitive domain. Over the past ten years, for example, we have learned several important things about the nature of affective changes in the family at adolescence. First, various investigators have demonstrated that overt conflict and rebellion are not omnipresent in the family at adolescence—at least in most families (Offer, 1969; Offer, Ostrov & Howard, 1981; Douvan & Adelson, 1966; Kandel & Lesser, 1972). Second, emotional tension in the family, when it does surface, most often takes the form of bickering about relatively minor differences of opinion, typically between adolescent and mother, presumably because mothers are more likely to be present and involved when such situations arise (Hill, 1980; Montemayor, 1983). Third, adolescents and their parents remain intimate throughout the adolescent period, although there appears to be a temporary decline in intimacy between preadolescence and early adolescence, with some recovery of adolescent-parent intimacy between middle and late adolescence (Hunter & Youniss, 1982). Fourth, early adolescence, especially around the time of puberty, may be a time of temporary disequilibrium and strain in family relationships, again, especially between adolescents and their mother (Steinberg & Hill, 1979; Steinberg, 1981; Hill, Holmbeck, Marlow, Green & Lynch, 1985a; Hill, Holmbeck, Marlow, Green & Lynch, 1985b).

Taken together, these findings suggest that, although relationships are far more pacific in the adolescent's family than orthodox theories have suggested, early adolescence may indeed be a time of important—albeit temporary—affective realignment. Moreover, it would seem that this realignment places adaptational demands on the family system. Most families cope relatively well with these demands, but some do not, and at this point in time, we need more research on why some families are better than others at negotiating this transition. One hypothesis is that authoritative families, who have all along employed more flexible and responsive child-rearing techniques, are more able to handle these adaptational demands and shift from the affective mode of childhood into the affective mode of adolescence. Actually, there is some evidence that youngsters whose families resist this realignment process evidence higher rates of problematic behavior during the adolescent years (Alexander, 1973).

Behavioral Realignment

In the behavioral domain, we know that there are important shifts in decision-making processes during early adolescence, typically, with adolescents gaining influence in family decision-making, chiefly at the expense of their mother (Steinberg, 1981). (This may be more true for middle-class families than for working-class families; at this point, all the evidence is not in [cf. Jacob, 1974].) One also suspects, although we do not have a great deal of evidence along these lines, that over time adolescents are increasingly expected to monitor and regulate their own behavior; to make certain personal decisions on their own that had previously been made by (or in consultation with) parents; and to seek (and be granted) greater autonomy and privacy over their activities, possessions, finances, rooms, leisure time, and bodies (Steinberg, 1985).

As is the case in the affective domain, early adolescence also may be a time of temporary perturbation in the behavioral domain. Families must change from a situation in which the child's life is structured and monitored by his or her parents to one in which the young person has the autonomy to come and go, to manage his or her own money, to drive the family car, or to stay out until all hours. Perturbations in the process of behavioral realignment may take the form of excessive parental authoritarianism

or permissiveness, or excessive adolescent oppositionalism or dependency. In most families, however, this state of affairs passes by the end of early adolescence.

Again, however, common sense and casual observation tell us that some families are better at negotiating this behavioral realignment than are others. Difficulties that are more than temporary can emerge when the adolescent's capacity for, or interest in, autonomous behavior is out of synchrony with the parents' willingness to grant such behavior. (Although the most commonly observed or reported pattern is one in which the adolescent desires more autonomy than the parents are willing to grant, one also hears, from time to time, of parents who wish their adolescent would be more independent than he or she is.) One hypothesis that my research group is investigating is that problems in the family are more likely to arise when a family's pattern of behavioral realignment at adolescence is markedly different from norms prevailing in the community. Demanding that a 14-year-old be home at night by 9:00 may work well in a community in which most other 14-year-olds have the same curfew, but may be problematic in a community in which the prevailing norm is 11:00, or in one in which it is 7:00.

Cognitive Realignment

The domain of cognitive realignment has, to my knowledge, not yet been studied. Yet, it seems reasonable to propose that during the transition into adolescence, family members alter their views of each other and their relationships. Although no data exist to support this proposition directly, we have sufficient evidence concerning changes in social cognition during early adolescence to hypothesize that adolescents, at the very least, most likely readjust their views of their parents and their relations with them (e.g., Hill & Palmquist, 1978; Barenboim, 1981; Schantz, 1983; Selman, 1980; Turiel, 1978). As well, it is likely that parents themselves occasionally readjust their views of, and expectations for, their children (Maccoby & Martin, 1983)—although we do not know whether or in what form these readjustments occur at adolescence. Despite the fact that the study of cognitive realignment in the adolescent's family is uncharted territory, three new series of investigations, currently underway, suggest that it may be a worthwhile avenue of inquiry. One series of studies, by Andrew Collins and his colleagues, examines parents' and adolescents' expectations for one another's behavior (Collins, 1985). A second program of research, directed by Judith Smetana, examines changes in adolescents' understanding of the social conventions that structure rules and patterns of authority in the family (Smetana, 1985). Finally, in our own program of research at Wisconsin we are examining cognitive realignment in two ways: as it is reflected in adolescents' beliefs about parental omnipotence and omniscience, and as it manifests itself in parents' conceptions of the parenting role during the adolescent years.

In all four cases, one might reasonably propose that perturbations are likely to occur during the transitional, early adolescent phase. Collins, for example, suggests that parents form expectations for their adolescents' behavior based on both generalized expectations for adolescents as a group (expectations which we know are often stereotypic and inaccurate) and on specific expectations held for their child (based on past behavior, physical cues, and so forth). He goes on to suggest that family conflict may result in part from violations of these expectations. It seems likely that such violations would more often occur during early adolescence than before or after, for it is during this period that parents and adolescents are still "feeling each other out." The cognitive realignment, thus, involves a process through which family members compare their expectations with what they actually observe and revise their expectations toward greater accuracy, either by discarding stereotypic expectations or by deriving expectations that are specific to, and more appropriate for, their particular child.

Smetana's framework also suggests that early adolescence may be an important time of cognitive realignment and, consequently, perturbation in the family system. She argues that periods of conflict are more likely to occur when adolescents are in the process of redefining and reconsidering the bases for existing patterns of regulation in the family. We know from Turiel's work on the development of social conventional understanding (Turiel, 1978), that early adolescence is often a time of transition in social conventional understanding, and thus a likely period of cognitive realignment.

My interest in adolescents' changing (or waning) beliefs in parental omniscience and omnipotence derives partly from Blos' work on individuation (1967) and partly from a conversation I had not long ago with John Hill, who suggested that an important feature of emotional autonomy during adolescence certainly must involve the child's replacing childish images of his or her parents with more mature ones. In a questionnaire we are in the process of administering to about 1,000 5th- through 9th-graders, we included items such as "My parents are almost always right;" "Even when my parents are not around, I feel like they know when I'm doing something I shouldn't do;" and "My parents know everything there is to know about me." We have not yet analyzed these data, but our hypothesis is that early adolescence is a critical time of realignment in these beliefs.

Finally, one of my associates, Susan Silverberg, is investigating changes in parental attitudes about the functions and nature of parenting during this same age period. Because of the changing competencies of the child, parents must be able to adjust their own behavior and beliefs about their role as parents. For parents, too, then, the transition requires a certain degree of cognitive realignment. We suspect that early adolescence may be an especially difficult time for parents who have invested a great deal in the parental role and who continue to define their role vis-a-vis their children primarily in terms of nurturance and protection, rather than support or guidance.

Other Features of the Model

Interrelations among Domains of Realignment Although the three domains of realignment can be distinguished from one another conceptually, in all likelihood the realignments occur at or around the same time. Assigning precedence or prominence to one over the others is, I would imagine, more an issue of theoretical faith than anything else. Those with more analytic inclinations will favor the affective domain as the driving force; those more behaviorally inclined, the behavioral domain; those with allegiances to the cognitive–developmental school, the cognitive domain. At this point I can offer no hypotheses concerning their causal interrelations; I can simply suggest that realignment in one domain is likely to provoke realignment in another, without giving prominence or temporal precedence to any one set of transformations. Thus, it seems reasonable to propose that once adolescents conceive of their parents differently, they will begin to act differently toward them and will begin to feel differently as well. By the same token, once parents conceive of their children differently, they will begin to act and feel differently toward them, too. Similarly, realignments in the affective domain likely prompt realignments in the behavioral and cognitive domains (for both adolescents and parents) and realignments in the behavioral domain likely prompt affective and cognitive realignments. In any case, how and whether these realignments are interrelated are questions that our research program is designed to examine.

Driving Forces outside the Family The model also assumes that realignment in the family at adolescence is set in motion by the biological, cognitive, and social changes of adolescence. Together and independently, Hill and I have both demonstrated that changes in both the affective and behavioral domains are linked to physical maturation around the time of puberty (Steinberg & Hill, 1979; Steinberg, 1981; Hill, Holmbeck, Marlow, Green & Lynch, 1985a; Hill, Holmbeck, Marlow, Green & Lynch, 1985b). It also seems likely that both the cognitive changes of adolescence, and the transition of youngsters into new social roles, provokes changes in the family as well. In our current research program, Silverberg and I are assessing physical maturation, reasoning abilities, and social role transitions (e.g., moving into middle school from elementary school, or into high school from middle school; the onset of heterosocial activities; taking on a job) as possible influences on the process of intrafamilial realignment. One hypothesis we will examine is that affective realignment is provoked primarily by puberty; cognitive realignment, by the development of more sophisticated reasoning abilities; and behavioral realignment, by the adolescent's movement into more adult-like social roles.

Bidirectional Realignment Unlike many conventional psychoanalytic perspectives on the family at adolescence, this framework presents transformations in the family as a series of bidirectional realignments, with all parties being forced to change affective, behavioral, and cognitive postures over the course of the transition. Thus, not only do adolescents change the way they feel about, behave toward, and think about their parents, parents also change the way they feel about, behave toward, and think about their adolescent. One important implication is that the realignment of the family at adolescence represents a developmental challenge to parents that may have consequences for their own psychosocial development. As I suggested earlier, the study of the relation between midlife development and family change at adolescence is relatively new. We know, for example, that marital satisfaction appears to be at its nadir during the children's adolescent years (e.g., Rollins & Feldman, 1970), but we have no idea why, or whether this phenomenon is related in any way to adolescence as a developmental period. (Interestingly, however, in several studies of midlife adults, mention is often made of the role adolescent children played—for better or for worse—in provoking self-examination and psychological change [Baruch, Barnett, & Rivers, 1983; Farrell & Rosenberg, 1981; Vaillant, 1977]). As a part of the investigation of parental role perceptions I mentioned earlier, Silverberg is studying the transition into adolescence from the midlife parent's perspective, including, among other questions, the relation between the physical, psychological, and social changes of adolescence; affective, behavioral, and cognitive realignment in the family; and the psychological and social changes of middle adulthood.

Perturbation versus Conflict The framework does not have as its central concern conflict. Conflict may be a characteristic feature of family life during the early adolescent years—although I know of no systematic empirical evidence demonstrating that levels of family conflict are for a fact higher in families with adolescents than in comparable families with older or younger children. But within the proposed framework, conflict is viewed as just one of many dimensions along which transformations take place; it is not the only dimension of interest, nor is it the dimension of chief importance. Moreover, the perspective provides for differentiating between temporary, normative perturbations in the family system and enduring—and atypical—conflict. In our research program we are examining parent-adolescent conflict, using a measure adapted from one of Art Robin's scales (Robin & Weiss, 1980), and its relation to the biological, cogni-

tive, and social changes of adolescence and in relation to affective, behavioral, and cognitive realignment in the family. Here we hypothesize that family conflict is not an inherent part of relationships during early adolescence, but will be most likely to be present in families who, although faced with an adolescent who has matured physically, cognitively, or socially, have nevertheless failed to realign their relationships accordingly.

CONCLUDING COMMENTS: ADOLESCENT AUTONOMY AND FAMILY REALIGNMENT

A substantial source of confusion in the literature on family relations during adolescence derives from the imprecise use—or, more accurately, the multiple uses—of the term "autonomy" (Hill & Steinberg, 1976). Many writers use autonomy to refer to an aspect of adolescent psychosocial development, while others use the term to refer to an aspect of adolescent-parent relationships. Thus, autonomy refers both to an *intrapsychic accomplishment* as well as to an *intrafamilial transformation*. Among the intrapsychic accomplishments often grouped under the general heading of autonomy are successful individuation (often referred to as *emotional autonomy*) (cf. Blos, 1967; Josselson, 1980), the development of self-reliance, independent decision-making abilities, and the capacity to resist peer pressure (often referred to as *behavioral autonomy*) (cf. Berndt, 1979; Devereux, 1970; Greenberger, 1984) and the evolution of an independent, or principled, set of moral, political, or religious beliefs (often referred to as *value autonomy*) (cf. Gallitan, 1980; Kohlberg & Gilligan, 1972; Rest, Davison, & Robbins, 1978). The intrafamilial transformations typically considered as falling into the autonomy category are the development of more egalitarian, more mutual parent-child relations (cf. White, Speisman & Costos, 1983; Youniss, 1980), the development of new patterns of decision-making (cf. Steinberg, 1981), and the development of new, more accurate levels of interpersonal perception (cf. White et al., 1983). In essence, the three domains of family realignment I have outlined today correspond to three aspects of intrafamilial autonomy referenced in the literature. (I prefer the term intrafamilial realignment, however, because it minimizes confusion between autonomy as an intrapsychic construct and autonomy as an intrafamilial one.)

In my view, there exist crucial relations between the three aspects of intrapsychic autonomy—emotional, behavioral, and value (or cognitive)—described in the literature on adolescent psychosocial development and the three domains of family realignment I have outlined today. As I think is implicit in the work of Grotevant and Cooper (e.g., Cooper, Grotevant & Condon, 1983), Speisman (White et al., 1983), and Hauser (Hauser, Powers, Noam, Jacobson, Weiss & Follansbee, 1984), the adolescent's growing sense of emotional autonomy, or individuation, is closely tied to his or her family's capacity for emotional realignment. As we have learned from the work of Bandura and Walters (1959), Baumrind (1978), and Kandel and Lesser (1972), the young person's developing capacity for behavioral autonomy is tied to the family's capacity for behavioral realignment. And, it seems reasonable to hypothesize that the growth of value autonomy during adolescence may well be tied to the family's capacity for cognitive realignment. In sum, the adolescent's psychosocial development and his or her family's capacity for adaptation, or realignment, are profoundly and inextricably linked.

REFERENCES

Alexander, J. (1973). Defensive and supportive communications in normal and deviant families. *Journal of Consulting and Clinical Psychology, 40:* 223–231.

Bandura, A. and Walters, R. (1959). *Adolescent aggression.* New York: Ronald Press.

Barenboim, C. (1981). The development of person perception in childhood and adolescence: From behavioral comparisons to psychological constructs to psychological comparisons. *Child Development, 52:* 129–144.

Baruch, G., Barnett, R., & Rivers, C. (1983). *Lifeprints.* New York: McGraw-Hill.

Baumrind, D. (1978). Parental disciplinary patterns and social competence in children. *Youth and Society, 9:* 239–276.

Berndt, T. (1979). Developmental changes in conformity to peers and parents. *Developmental Psychology, 15,* 608–616.

Blos, P. The second individuation process of adolescence. (1967). In R. S. Eissler et al. (Eds.), *Psychoanalytic study of the child* (Volume 15). New York: International Universities Press.

Collins, W. A. (1985). Cognition, affect, and development in parent-child relationships. Paper presented at the biennial meetings of the Society for Research in Child Development, Toronto, April.

Cooper, C., Grotevant, H. & Condon, S. (1983). Individuality and connectedness in the family as a context for adolescent identity formation and role-taking skill. In H. Grotevant and C. Cooper (Eds.), *Adolescent development in the family.* San Francisco: Jossey-Bass.

Devereux, E. (1970). The role of peer group experience in moral development. In J. Hill (Ed.), *Minnesota Symposium on Child Psychology* (Volume 4). Minneapolis: University of Minnesota Press.

Douvan, E. & Adelson, J. (1966). *The adolescent experience.* New York: Wiley.

Farrell, J. & Rosenberg, D. (1981). *Men at midlife.* Boston: Auburn House.

Gallitan, J. (1980). Political thinking in adolescence. In J. Adelson (Ed.), *Handbook of adolescent psychology.* New York: Wiley.

Greenberger, E. (1984). Defining psychosocial maturity in adolescence. In P. Karoly and J. Steffen (Eds.), *Adolescent behavior disorders: Foundations and contemporary concerns.* Lexington, MA: D.C. Heath.

Hauser, S., Powers, S., Noam, G., Jacobson, A., Weiss, B., and Follansbee, D. (1984). Familial contexts of adolescent ego development. *Child Development, 55:* 195–213.

Hill, J. (1980). The family. In M. Johnson (Ed.), *Toward adolescence: The middle school years.* (Seventy-ninth yearbook of the National Society for the Study of Education). Chicago: University of Chicago Press.

Hill, J., Holmbeck, G., Marlow, L., Green, T., & Lynch, M. (1985a). Menarcheal status and parent-child relations in families of seventh-grade girls. *Journal of Youth and Adolescence,* in press.

Hill, J., Holmbeck, G., Marlow, L., Green, T., & Lynch, M. (1985b). Pubertal status and parent-child relations in families of seventh-grade boys. *Journal of Early Adolescence,* in press.

Hill, J., & Palmquist, W. (1978). Social cognition and social relations in early adolescence. *International Journal of Behavioural Development, 1:* 1–36.

Hill, J., & Steinberg, L. (1976). The development of autonomy during adolescence. Paper presented at the Symposium on Research on Youth Problems Today, Fundacion Faustino Orbegoza Eizaguirre, Madrid.

Hunter, F. & Youniss, J. (1982). Changes in functions of three relations during adolescence. *Developmental Psychology, 18:* 806–811.

Jacob, T. (1974). Patterns of family conflict and dominance as a function of child age and social class. *Developmental Psychology, 10:* 1–12.

Josselson, R. (1980). Ego development in adolescence. In J. Adelson (Ed.), *Handbook of adolescent psychology.* New York: Wiley.

Kandel, D., & Lesser, G. (1972). *Youth in two worlds.* San Francisco: Jossey-Bass.

Kohlberg, L., & Gilligan, C. (1972). The adolescent as philosopher: The discovery of the self in a postconventional world. In J. Kagan & R. Coles (Eds.), *Twelve to sixteen: Early adolescence.* New York: Norton.

Maccoby, E., & Martin, J. (1983). Socialization in the context of the family: Parent-child interaction. In E. M. Hetherington (Ed.), *Handbook of child psychology* (Volume 4). New York: Wiley.

Montemayor, R. (1983). Parents and adolescents in conflict: All families some of the time and some families most of the time. *Journal of Early Adolescence, 3:* 83–103.

Offer, D. (1969). *The psychological world of the teenager.* New York: Basic Books.

Offer, D., Ostrov, E., & Howard, K. (1981). *The adolescent: A psychological self-portrait.* New York: Basic Books.

Rest, J., Davison, M., & Robbins, S. (1978). Age trends in judging moral issues: A review of cross-sectional, longitudinal, and sequential studies using the Defining Issues Test. *Child Development, 49:* 263–279.

Robin, A. & Weiss, J. (1980). Criterion-related validity of behavioral and self-report measures of problem-solving communication skills in distressed and non-distressed parent-adolescent dyads. *Behavioral Assessment, 2:* 339–352.

Rollins, B., & Feldman, H. (1970). Marital interaction over the family life-cycle. *Journal of Marriage and the Family, 32:* 20–28.

Schantz, C. (1983). Social cognition. In J. Flavell and E. Markman (Eds.), *Handbook of child psychology* (Volume 3). New York: Wiley.

Selman, R. (1980). *The growth of interpersonal understanding: Developmental and clinical analyses.* New York: Academic Press.

Smetana, J. (1985). Family rules, conventions, and adolescent-parent conflict. Paper presented at the biennial meetings of the Society for Research in Child Development, Toronto, April.

Steinberg, L. (1981). Transformations in family relations at puberty. *Developmental Psychology, 17:* 833–840.

Steinberg, L. (1985). The development of emotional autonomy in adolescence. Paper presented at the biennial meetings of the Society for Research in Child Development, Toronto, April.

Steinberg, L., & Hill, J. (1979). Patterns of family interaction as a function of age, the onset of puberty, and formal thinking. *Developmental Psychology, 14:* 683–684.

Turiel, E. (1978). The development of concepts of social structure: Social convention. In J. Glick and K. A. Clarke-Stewart (Eds.), *The development of social understanding.* New York: Gardner.

Vaillant, G. (1977). *Adaptation to life.* Boston: Little, Brown.

White, K., Speisman, J., & Costos, D. (1983). Young adults and their parents: Individuation to mutuality. In H. Grotevant and C. Cooper (Eds.), *Adolescent development in the family.* San Francisco: Jossey-Bass.

Youniss, J. (1980). *Parents and peers in social development.* Chicago: University of Chicago Press.

READING 34

Sibling Relations: The Role of Conceptual Perspective-Taking in the Ontogeny of Sibling Caregiving

Robert B. Stewart
Robert S. Marvin

In recent years child development researchers have rediscovered the sibling. Expanding the focus beyond the negative issue of sibling rivalry, much of this new research addresses the role of the older sibling as a socialization agent (e.g., Abramovitch, Corter, & Lando, 1979; Dunn & Kendrick, 1979; Lamb, 1978; Samuels, 1980; Vandell, Note 1). Although different conclusions have been drawn concerning the effect of dyad sex composition on sibling relations, a similarity found throughout these studies is that siblings engage in prosocial interaction with high frequency. This "prosocial behavior" has been measured in terms of cooperation; giving help, praise, comfort, and reassurance; sharing toys; and so on.

Stewart (1983) extended the study of sibling relations to consider the potential of the older sibling to act as a subsidiary attachment figure for an infant. He reported that 52% of his sample of 54 3- and 4-year-old children had acted to provide reassurance, comfort, and care to their younger siblings when their mothers left them alone together in a waiting-room setting. The fundamental question that emerged from the study was why only half of the sample acted as temporary caregivers.

Even though reports of shared caregiving for infants exist in the literature (e.g., Ainsworth, 1967; Schaffer & Emerson, 1964; Weisner & Gallimore, 1977), the suggestion that the older sibling might act as a subsidiary attachment figure for the infant represents a clear departure from the usual focus on mother-infant bonds in studies of Western cultures. Yet we know from the anthropological (e.g., Konner, 1976) and clinical (e.g., Minuchin, 1974) literature, as well as from

common experience, that older siblings are significant attachment figures and caregivers for a very large proportion of children. Among the most common probable settings for this relationship are: (1) the recognition by the older sibling of some danger to the younger brother or sister, and (2) a cooperative family system in which the older sibling is asked to assist or relieve the parent in caregiving while the latter is engaged in some other activity.

In this study, attachment and caregiving are viewed as distinct subsets of the more generic concept "affectional bond." Attachment and caregiving are concepts usually but not exclusively referring to complementary aspects of the relationship between a child and parent. Consistent with this distinction, Bowlby (1977) and Hinde (1979, 1982) view attachment behavior as "...behavior that results in a person attaining or retaining proximity to some other differentiated and preferred individual, who is usually conceived as stronger and/or wiser" (Bowlby, 1977, p. 207). Caregiving behavior, in complementary fashion, results in proximity with and/or security and support for a differentiated individual conceived as weaker and more vulnerable.

The present study was designed to provide further information concerning the attachment/caregiving relationship between preschool children and their infant siblings by exploring the possibility that social-cognitive developmental changes in the older child might play an important role in enabling that child to function as a caregiver and/or attachment figure for his or her infant sibling. It is interesting that children as young as 3 and 4 years are able to fill a familial role that requires so much sensitivity to the infant's feelings, the ability to interpret correctly the reasons for those feelings, and the knowledge of how to respond. It is particularly impressive since separations from mother in strange settings are still an issue of very personal concern for 3- and 4-year-old children. Perhaps the half of Stewart's sample that functioned as caregivers had a different understanding of the separation, and of their infant siblings' feelings, than did the other half.

The conceptual framework for the present study is taken from a theoretical model originally proposed by Bowlby (1969) and expanded upon by Marvin (1977) for the attenuation of mother-child attachment behavior. To summarize briefly, the model proposes that the amount of attachment behavior, and conditions under which it is displayed, will gradually change as the very young child gains more experience and becomes increasingly interested in people and activities outside the family. However, a major factor in the attenuation of this behavior is the child's developing ability to make nonegocentric inferences about his or her mother's point of view (Bowlby, 1969). This "perspective-taking" ability allows for two related and significant changes. First, the ability to make accurate inferences about another's thoughts, plans, and so on should increase the child's security in mother's absence through more accurate and detailed predictions concerning her behavior (and her return). Second, as Piaget, G. H. Mead, and others have described, these perspective-taking skills enable the child to negotiate and carry out joint, or shared, behavioral plans. Thus a child is much less likely to become upset by a separation if he and mother have negotiated and agreed upon a plan concerning what each will do during the separation, and what will happen upon reunion.

In a series of studies, Marvin and his associates (e.g., Marvin, 1977; Marvin & Greenberg, 1982; Marvin, Greenberg, & Mossler, 1976) developed a number of game-like tasks through

which they were able to demonstrate that children as young as 4 years are able to make accurate inferences about others' goals, plans, and thoughts and are able consistently to distinguish between their own point of view and that of another person. Furthermore, these same children, when about to undergo a brief separation in a novel setting, negotiated a shared plan with their mothers concerning the separation and reunion. They then tended to display no attachment behavior during either the separation or reunion. Those 3- and 4-year-old children who were unable to make nonegocentric inferences did not negotiate shared plans regarding the separation, and tended to display attachment behavior during both the separation and the reunion.

Bowlby (1969) and Marvin (1977) suggest that with the development of these perspective-taking and negotiating skills, the relationship between mother and child changes. Rather than being organized so exclusively in terms of physical contact and proximity, this relationship becomes progressively more organized in terms of a "partnership," within which mother and child cooperate across an increasingly wide range of types of interactions. In many families, caring for a younger child is one context for this partnership.

It is likely that the development of the older preschooler's caregiving skills is related to this partnership in at least two ways. First, a child who is unable to make accurate inferences about another's point of view cannot be expected to understand fully, or respond effectively to, a younger sibling's distress over separation (especially if the older sibling is also distressed). The child who has developed this skill, on the other hand, should be able to infer the reason for the infant's distress and to develop a plan to deal with it. Second, mothers should show a tendency to make use of the "partnership" when it has developed, by differentially asking this older child to assist her in caring for the infant sibling. Our question there fore becomes one of a search for an association between the child's ability to infer another's perspective, mother's tendency to request care-giving assistance, and the giving of care to a younger sibling.

METHOD

Subjects

Fifty-seven mother–older sibling–infant nuclear family subsystems were observed in this study. The infants ranged in age from 10 to 24 months ($X = 17.1$ months; mode $= 15$ months), and the older siblings from 36 to 60 months ($X = 50.6$ months; mode $= 48$ months). The difference in ages between siblings ranged from 20 to 44 months ($X = 33.5$ months; mode $= 30$ months). Fifteen dyads consisted of male infants with older brothers and 14 of male infants with older sisters; 13 consisted of female infants with older brothers and 15 of female infants with older sisters. Most (83%) of the families had only these two children; another 12% had a third older child, and 5% had another child between those observed. The sample reflected the over-representation of highly educated upper- and upper-middle-class families that has been characteristic of research conducted in university towns. Seventy-nine percent of the older children were enrolled in part-time preschool or daycare programs, and 7% of the younger children had attended part-time daycare. In all families, the mother was described as the primary caregiver for both children.

Procedures

The families were observed in a 3.0 x 3.75-m playroom/waiting room containing two chairs, a couch, a magazine stand, and numerous toys. Each family was observed in a seven-episode, 54-min attachment situation that was derived from Ainsworth's "Strange Situation" (Ainsworth & Wittig, 1969). A second playroom, also 3.0 x 3.75 m, was used in assessing the children's conceptual perspective-taking abili-

ties. This assessment was made simultaneously with Episode 2 of the attachment situation. A video camera and microphone were placed in a corner partially hidden by a screen to permit observation of this assessment procedure via closed-circuit television.

Attachment Situation   The attachment situation involves a series of seven episodes in which different combinations of people (i.e. mother, child, infant, and stranger) are present or absent. Upon arrival at the university, the families were greeted by a female research assistant whose primary responsibility was to establish rapport with all family members. While the mother completed questionnaires concerning demographic information, the assistant played with the two children in an attempt to reduce their wariness of both her and the observation room, so that she could move the older child from the observation room at the beginning of Episode 2. The schedule for the attachment situation was explained to the mothers (see Table 1), and they were instructed to act as if they were sitting in a waiting room. They were given no instructions as to what they could or could not say prior to separating from their children.

From behind a one-way window, two observers recorded the behavior of each of the families, one using a Datamyte recorder and the other paper and pencil. Behaviors in the attachment situation that were used in the statistical analyses were recorded using a "behavioral systems" framework (e.g., Bischof, 1975; Bretherton & Ainsworth, 1974; Greenberg & Marvin, 1982; Sroufe & Waters, 1977). Rather than recording discrete behaviors according to their morphology, the observer made a trained decision regarding the predictable, functional outcome of a behavior or sequence of behaviors. On the basis of this decision, each observed behavioral unit was then sequentially recorded in terms of the behavior system to which it belonged. Among the advantages of this tech-

TABLE 1   OBSERVATION SCHEDULE

Episode	Time (Min)	Objectives	Persons present		
1	3	Base rate(1)	Mother	Child	Infant
2	30	Mother-infant dyad	Mother		Infant
3	3	Base rate(2)	Mother	Child	Infant
4	7	Child as teacher	Mother	Child	Infant
5	4	Child-infant dyad		Child	Infant
6	4	Dyad with stranger		Child	Infant Stranger
7	3	Base rate(3)	Mother	Child	Infant
Total	54				

nique are that morphologically distinct but functionally equivalent behaviors can be coded identically, behavior sequences of some length can be coded as a single unit, and the organization of an *interaction* can more easily be recorded. The specific behavioral systems coded in this study included the four used in other attachment studies (e.g., Bretherton & Ainsworth, 1974), with a fifth used to record caregiving behavior:

1 *The attachment* system includes behaviors that predictably function to increase and/or maintain proximity to, or contact with, a discriminated other who is stronger and/or wiser. This system is most likely to be activated under conditions of novelty, fear, and discomfort. Behaviors coded were crying, following a departing figure, calling a departed figure, greeting a returning figure, approaching, reaching, and clinging or embracing. Since these specific behaviors sometimes serve other behavioral systems as well, coders must consider the above environmental conditions in assigning a behavior to this system (see Ainsworth, Blehar, Waters, & Wall, 1978).

2 *The caregiving* system includes behaviors that predictably function to provide material or emotional nurturance, support, or reassurance for the well-being of another who is younger and/or weaker. This system is most likely to be activated either in response to a display of attachment behavior by another, or in anticipation of or in response to a distressing or poten-

tially dangerous situation, for example, the approach of a stranger or the departure of the mother. In this study behaviors assigned to the caregiving system were approaching, hugging, kissing, caressing or holding another, offering verbal reassurances, or redirecting another's attention from distressful thoughts and/or events. Again, environmental conditions were considered in coding the behaviors, and if there was uncertainty whether a specific behavior should be coded as attachment behavior or caregiving behavior, the assumption was made that younger/weaker individuals do not provide caregiving behavior to older/wiser individuals. While this assumption may not apply in all situations, it was chosen as a sensible point of departure for this study (cf. Bowlby, 1977, p. 207).

3 *The sociable* system includes behaviors that predictably function to initiate and/or maintain playful or friendly interaction with others, whether those others are attachment figures or not. Behaviors coded were discussions of objects, exchanges of information concerning one another, sharing of or joint use of toys, laughing, and smiling (cf. Abramovitch et al., 1979; Bretherton & Ainsworth, 1974).

4 *The fear/wariness* system includes behaviors that predictably function to escape or avoid alarming stimuli or situations. Behaviors coded were gaze aversion, pouting, "cry face," crying, looking with face downcast, freezing, and fleeing. Previous research has shown that this system often is compatible with the attachment system but incompatible with the sociable and exploratory systems (e.g., Bretherton & Ainsworth, 1974; Greenberg & Marvin, 1982).

5 *The exploratory* system includes behaviors that predictably function to gain information about, and playfully manipulate, objects in the environment. Playing with toys or other objects was the most common form of this system of behaviors observed in this study. For purposes of this study, the exploratory system was further divided into classes of solitary, parallel, and coordinated play using Parten's (1932) definitions.

Three observers were involved in the actual data collection, using a variation of a "focal individual sampling technique" (Altmann, 1974). Behavior of each participant was sampled on a 30-sec, rotating basis for the duration of each episode. Observation sessions were scored "live" as they occurred. Using a Datamyte recorder, the first observer recorded behaviors in a continuous, sequential manner that yielded: (1) each behavior coded in terms of its appropriate behavior system, (2) the individual displaying the behavior, and (3) the "recipient" of that behavior. Within the 30-sec focal individual samples, discrete behavioral events were recorded at their time of onset. Precise duration (i.e., state) data could not be obtained reliably given the large number of potential codes generated by our interest in dyadic interaction involving five major systems of behavior. Therefore, the event sampling procedure was modified as follows to represent the extended duration of behaviors. Discrete events that lasted for more than 5 sec were scored repeatedly so that their duration would be represented by an increased frequency for that category. For example, a 30-sec bout of solitary play would be scored at its onset and then repeatedly every 5 sec, thus producing a total frequency score of six acts of solitary play. Events involving more than one discrete behavior of a particular system were not multiply

scored; for example, talking while sharing toys would represent one act of the sociable system. Extended bouts of a particular behavioral system that were separated by an interval of at least 5 sec in which the behavior did not occur were coded as two separate bouts. For example, an infant who cried for 20 sec, then stopped for 6 sec, and then cried for another 15 sec would be scored as having displayed two bouts of attachment behavior with frequencies of four and three acts, respectively. This scoring procedure, although producing data that in a strictly formal sense are neither frequency nor state data, does provide a meaningful way of scoring a relatively large number of behaviors of variable duration. The rule of "code-recode" with respect to a 5-sec interval for behaviors of long duration produced far more reliable data than did a procedure in which coders were required to note both the onset and termination of events. The adjusted frequency data were then analyzed in terms of behavioral acts per episode, that is, as rate data.

The second observer, using paper and pencil, recorded a less formal, "running account" of interactions throughout each episode. In addition, this observer indicated whether or not the mother at the time of her departure requested the assistance of the older sibling in caring for the infant during her absence. These running accounts were anchored to the Datamyte codings by recording exact time of occurrence. The data from the second observer were then used to supplement the statistical analyses with descriptive detail.

The third observer, also using a Datamyte recorder, duplicated the efforts of the first observer with 18 (32%) of the family subsystems, evenly distributed throughout the period of data collection. These data were used to assess coder agreement.

Conceptual Perspective-Taking Tasks Two tasks developed by Marvin and his associates (Greenberg, Marvin, & Mossler, 1977; Marvin et al., 1976) were presented to each older sibling during Episode 2 in a standard order and used to assess that child's perspective-taking ability. The first task, the Syllogisms, assessed the child's ability to carry out elementary forms of logical inference-making. These inferences are assumed to be the cognitive basis of perspective-taking activities, and performance on this task has been found to be highly correlated with performance on other perspective-taking tasks (Marvin, Note 2). Full details of the procedure are available in Greenberg et al. (1977). The child's responses to the following questions were recorded: (1) —— [an imaginary child's name] doesn't like to get wet; would he/she rather play in a puddle or read a book? (2) —— likes to get real high up; would he/she rather climb a tree or paint a picture? (3) —— likes loud noises; would he/she rather bang on a drum or put together a puzzle? (4) —— doesn't like to get dirty; would he/she rather play in the mud or play house? (5) —— is real hungry; would he/she rather play with blocks or ride a bike? The child was asked to justify his or her response on at least two of the first four questions and on the fifth question. In addition, the child's response latency was recorded. Greenberg et al. (1977) demonstrated that children who made inferences based on syllogistic reasoning were surprised and puzzled by the fifth (nonsense) question, that is, they displayed a greater latency to response, whereas children who responded egocentrically showed no such increase in latency.

The second task, the Secret Task, was designed to assess the child's ability to distinguish among perspectives within a small group of people involved in a game (Marvin et al., 1976). The task was based on the notion of a secret; that is, two participants have the same perspective, which is not known by the third person. The game involved the child and two testers, with two of these participants sharing a secret from the third. The object of the task was to assess the child's ability to distinguish accu-

rately among the three perspectives. Complete details of the procedure are contained in Marvin et al. (1976).

The responses on the perspective-taking tasks were scored using procedures developed by Marvin and his associates. On the Syllogism task, classification as a perspective-taker required that the child: (1) answer three of the first four questions with the logical answer, (2) provide at least one correct justification for these answers, (3) display an increased response latency on the final question vis-a-vis the first four, and (4) indicate that neither choice on the fifth question was logically correct (Greenberg et al., 1977). In the Secret Task, the child's responses were scored as correct if he or she indicated: (1) that the participants who shared the secret both knew what the secret was, and (2) that the person who had hidden his or her eyes did not know what it was (Marvin et al., 1976). Since in this study the Secret Task was not completed an equal number of times for each of the possible dyadic combinations, scoring was conducted only for the six trials when the child covered his or her eyes and the adult assistants shared a secret. Correct responses on four of these trials were required for the classification of perspective-taker. While this scoring system does not yield information concerning the child's ability to distinguish among all of the multiple perspectives involved in the game, it still requires that the child distinguish between two perspectives that are demonstrably different. This scoring system thus conforms to the criteria for perspective-taking described in Chandler and Greenspan (1972). In addition, Marvin et al. (1976) found all three trials to be highly intercorrelated, with the trial used in this study being the best predictor for success in the other two.

Observer Agreement

Observers were trained for 120 hours over a 5-week period using videotapes of five pilot families. On a random basis throughout the course of the study, observer agreement was assessed.

RESULTS

The results will be presented in six parts. First, we present the data from Episode 5 on the behavioral classification of older siblings as caregivers versus noncaregivers. This is followed by an analysis of the classification of those same children as perspective-takers versus non-perspective-takers. Third, data are presented, exploring the relationship between the factors of sex of child, sex of infant, caregiving, and perspective-taking. This is followed by data describing the use of older siblings as a secure base for exploration. Fifth, results are presented of an analysis of maternal requests for caregiving assistance and the older siblings' compliance. Finally, the data provided by the supplementary observer are presented to further describe the children's reactions in the strange situation.

Classification of Caregivers versus Noncaregivers

Episode 5 began with mother being requested temporarily to leave the room. Every infant responded to the departure with some degree of distress, coded as attachment behavior toward mother. Within 10 sec of mother's departure, 29 of the 57 older siblings responded to the infant with some form of caregiving behavior. Common responses, concretely recorded by the second observer, included approaching and hugging the infant, offering verbal reassurance of mother's eventual return, and carrying the infant back to the center of the room and distracting him or her with toys. The remaining 28 older siblings responded to the distress of the infants in a noninteractive, noncaregiving fashion, that is, turning their backs to the infants and concentrating on their own play, singing or talking loudly as if to drown out the infant's crying, or covering their ears and moving to the

corner of the room farthest from the infants. None of these 28 older siblings displayed any caregiving behavior toward their younger siblings during this 10-sec interval, although some (43%) did display acts of caregiving behavior somewhat later in Episode 5 or subsequently in Episode 6. Presence of caregiving behavior within this 10-sec interval was adopted as the criterion for classification of caregiver because it constitutes a conservative criterion that is consistent with the finding that promptness of response is an essential component of sensitivity to an infant's signals (Ainsworth, Bell, & Stayton, 1974). Use of this single behavioral criterion resulted in 51% of the sample of 3–5-year-old older siblings being classified as caregivers, and 49% as noncaregivers. There was no association between age of child and classification as a caregiver ($r = .043$).

Classification of Perspective-Takers

The first author, working without knowledge of the results of the caregiving classifications, scored the children's responses on the perspective-taking tasks. Thirty-one children (54%) were scored as passing on both tasks. Of the remaining 26 children, 19 failed both tasks, three passed only the Secret Task, and four marginally passed only the Syllogism task and then refused to participate further. These latter 26 children (46%) were classified as non-perspective-takers. As found by Marvin and his associates, there was a significant association between age of child and classification as a perspective-taker ($r = .474$, $p < .001$).

Relation between Perspective-Taking Ability and Caregiving Behavior

The relationship between the factors sex of child, sex of infant, child's perspective-taking level, and caregiving was examined and is presented in Table 2.

Most (72%) of the children classified as caregivers were also classified as perspective-takers, while most (64%) of the noncaregivers were classified as non-perspective-takers. In

TABLE 2 COMPARISON OF CAREGIVING BY PERSPECTIVE-TAKING, SEX OF CHILD, AND SEX OF INFANT

Child sex and infant sex	Caregiving ($N=29$)	Noncaregiving ($N=28$)
Non-perspective-takers:		
Male child:		
Male infant	0	7
Female infant	4	4
Female child:		
Male infant	3	3
Female infant	1	4
Perspective-takers:		
Male child:		
Male infant	3	5
Female infant	5	0
Female child:		
Male infant	5	3
Female infant	8	2

addition, male children with younger sisters tended to be caregivers, while those with younger brothers did not. No clear pattern was found with respect to female children, except for a slight tendency for older sisters to be caregivers more often than noncaregivers. Interestingly, collapsing over the sex of the child factor revealed that female infants were the recipients of sibling caregiving responses more often than their male counterparts.

Use of Older Sibling as a Secure Base for Exploration

During Episodes 5 and 6, the second observer described sequences of behavior indicating that many of the infants used their perspective-taking older siblings as a secure base for exploration. These descriptions were anchored, with respect to time of occurrence, to the time of Datamyte entry of corresponding infant to child attachment behaviors.

Specifically, in Episode 5, 18 of the 29 (62%) infant siblings of caregiving older children approached and maintained proximity to their older siblings, and then resumed their play. None of the 28 infant siblings of noncaregiving older children did so. Seventeen of

the dyads (94%) displaying the secure-base phenomenon included perspective-taking older siblings. It is interesting that all of the secure-base dyads maintained this relationship in Episode 6, and many of them organized their proximity in a way that left the older sibling as a physical barrier between the infant and stranger. Of the 18 instances in Episode 6, in which the older sibling served as a secure base for the infant, 10 (56%) resulted in the older sibling positioned between infant and stranger. In four cases the perspective-taking older sibling placed himself or herself between the infant and stranger, and in six cases the infant actively chose the protected position. Once this arrangement was obtained, both children appeared more at ease, that is, they resumed their exploration and play, interacted with the stranger, and so on.

Relation between Maternal Requests and Caregiving Behavior

Thirty-seven mothers (65%) requested caregiving assistance from the older siblings at the time of their departures, while 20 did not. The majority of those mothers making requests did so to children classified as perspective-takers ($N = 25$). In turn, the majority of the perspective-taking children who received requests displayed caregiving responses ($N = 18$). Of the non-perspective-taking children who received requests ($N = 12$), four displayed caregiving behavior and eight did not. Ten of the mothers who made no requests for assistance (50%) had non-perspective-taking/noncaregiving children. The remaining 10 cases of no maternal request were equally distributed among the perspective-taking/caregiving ($N = 3$), perspective-taking/noncaregiving ($N = 3$), and non-perspective-taking/caregiving ($N = 4$) subgroups. The relationship between the factors maternal request, child's perspective-taking ability, and caregiving was examined using a log linear procedure.

The analysis indicated an association between perspective-taking ability and caregiving and an association between maternal requests and perspective-taking ability. The number of mothers making requests increased dramatically if the older sibling was a perspective-taker. Indeed, 65% of the mothers overall made requests, while 81% of the mothers of perspective-taking children did so. Mothers of non-perspective-taking children were evenly split between making and not making requests.

Finally, it is important to note that the older siblings' caregiving cannot be accounted for solely on the basis of mothers' requesting this assistance.

Supplementary Descriptive Results

On the basis of the formal analyses and the supplementary observations, the differences in the reactions of the sibling dyads to the separation from the mother can be summarized descriptively as follows: Most of the non-perspective-taking older children (69%) displayed heightened fear/wariness at both the departure of the mother and the entrance of the stranger, while others (31%) did not seem distressed. These older siblings failed to provide any contingent caregiving behavior to their distressed younger siblings. In turn, infants left with these non-perspective-taking older siblings were observed either to withdraw into reduced levels of solitary play, to avert their gaze from the stranger, and/or to attempt to leave the room. Non-perspective-taking older siblings thus appeared either too distressed, or too detached, to offer comfort or reassurance to a younger sibling. The infants, in turn, displayed no attachment behavior toward these older siblings. Instead, they displayed attachment behavior toward their absent mothers and/or they withdrew in a defensive manner from the stranger.

On the other hand, as found by Marvin (1977) and Marvin and Greenberg (1982), few perspective-taking children (10%) were distressed by either their mother's departure or the stranger's entrance. When the mother left the room in Episode 5, 68% of the perspective-taking older siblings approached the distressed infant and/or offered a word of reassurance, for example, "That's OK. She'll be back in a few minutes." Many of the infant siblings (86%) of these perspective-taking older preschoolers then approached their older siblings, began to play with the toys, and remained in much closer physical proximity to the sibling than prior to mother's departure. In essence, these infants used their siblings as a secure base for exploration and play, much as they use their parental attachment figures.

The reactions of the perspective-taking older siblings to the entrance of the stranger involved only a minimal degree of wariness. This wariness often was in the form of a coy response as the children displayed an interplay of sociable and wary behaviors (cf. Bretherton & Ainsworth, 1974). Such a reaction did not prohibit these children from continuing in the role of caregiver. Many of their infant siblings also continued to use these perspective-taking older children as a secure base for exploration when the stranger entered in Episode 6.

DISCUSSION

These results clearly replicate results presented by Stewart (1983). Approximately half of the 3–5-year-old children were active in providing comfort and/or reassurance to infant siblings left in their care. The more important finding, however, was the relationship between caregiving and social cognition: those older siblings capable of making "nonegocentric" inferences about another's point of view were more likely than their "egocentric" counterparts to engage in this caregiving activity. In a corresponding fashion, mothers seemed implicitly to recognize if their older children were capable of this activity, in that mothers requested caregiving on the part of the older sibling primarily in the cases of those children who demonstrated perspective-taking ability. It is also notable that caregiving was statistically associated with perspective-taking and not with age.

These formal and descriptive results strongly support the hypotheses that, at least by the end of the preschool years, children are able to serve as subsidiary attachment figures for their infant siblings. Certainly there continue to be significant limits to this relationship, but the beginnings are there. It also makes sense that in at least two ways, this developing skill is related to the older child's ability to make inferences about another's point of view. First, this perspective-taking skill would better enable the older child to understand and react sensitively to his or her younger sibling's distress signals. Second, it is probably the mother's recognition of this perspective-taking skill that leads her to solicit this child's aid in caring for the infant.

More research is necessary in order further to explore the ontogeny of child-infant caregiving and attachment interactions as a subset of sibling relationships. It is likely that behavioral "precursors" of caregiving are present in even younger children. Furthermore, the question of individual differences is particularly interesting; for example, why some of the perspective-taking older siblings failed to display caregiving behavior toward their infant siblings. We suspect that qualitative differences in the "partnership" between mother and older sibling play an important role here, much as differences in mother-infant attachment play a role in the infant's response to separation (Ainsworth et al., 1978). It would also be interesting to explore other types of interactions between older preschoolers and their infant siblings, since attachment interactions are but one facet of their overall relationship.

In the meantime, we feel that the most important contribution of this study is the finding that the ontogeny of sibling caregiving is related to the development of the same commu-nication skills in the older child that lead to a reorganization of mother-child attachment on a cooperative, "partnership" basis (Bowlby, 1969). Developmentally, this seems most sensible, because it is only after the young child has reached the point where separations from mother are no longer so distressing that he or she could be expected to assist in ameliorating the distress of a younger sibling.

From a broader perspective, it is intriguing to view attachment behavior within a family-systems model. The results of this study illustrate the manner in which various members of the family system (mother and older sibling) cooperate within a shared plan (older sibling cares for infant while mother is absent) in a way that maintains some essential function of the family system (protecting and maintaining the security of the infant). In this way a change in the behavior of one element of the system is compensated by a change in that of another element. While the role of the father within this system has received much recent attention, a full understanding of attachment behavior will require the description and analysis both of the roles played by each family member and, more important, of the complex ways in which these roles interact with one another to maintain various definable states of family equilibrium.

REFERENCE NOTES

1 Vandell, D. L. *Encounters between infants and their preschool-aged siblings during the first year.* Unpublished manuscript, University of Texas, 1982.

2 Marvin, R. S. *Intercorrelations among perspective-taking tasks.* Unpublished data, University of Virginia, 1976.

3 Stewart, R. B., & Amaranth, P. G. *Assessing interobserver reliability for sequential data: A comparison of kappa and correlation techniques.* Paper presented at the annual meeting of the Midwestern Psychological Association, Chicago, 1983.

REFERENCES

Abramovitch, R., Corter, C., & Lando, B. Sibling interaction in the home. *Child Development,* 1979, **50**, 997–1003.

Ainsworth, M. D. S. *Infancy in Uganda: Infant care and the growth of love.* Baltimore: Johns Hopkins University Press, 1967.

Ainsworth, M. D. S., Bell, S. M., & Stayton, D. J. Infant-mother attachment and social development: "Socialization" as a product of reciprocal responsiveness to signals. In M. P. M. Richards (Ed.), *The integration of a child into a social world.* London: Cambridge University Press, 1974.

Ainsworth, M. D. S., Blehar, M. C., Waters, E., & Wall, S. *Patterns of attachment: A psychological study of the strange situation.* Hillsdale, N.J.: Erlbaum, 1978.

Ainsworth, M. D. S., & Wittig, B. A. Attachment and exploratory behavior of one-year olds in a strange situation. In B. M. Foss (Ed.), *Determinants of infant behavior* (Vol. **4**). New York: Wiley, 1969.

Altmann, J. Observational study of behavior: Sampling methods. *Behavior,* 1974, **49**, 227–267.

Bischof, N. A systems approach toward the functional connections of attachment and fear. *Child Development,* 1975, **46**, 801–817.

Bowlby, J. *Attachment and loss.* (Vol. **1**): *Attachment.* New York: Basic, 1969.

Bowlby, J. The making and breaking of affectional bonds. *British Journal of Psychiatry,* 1977, **130**, 201–210.

Bretherton, I., & Ainsworth, M. D. S. Responses of one-year-olds to a stranger in a strange situation. In M. Lewis & L. A. Rosenblum (Eds.), *The origins of fear.* New York: Wiley, 1974.

Chandler, M. J., & Greenspan, S. Ersatz egocentrism: A reply to H. Borke. *Developmental Psychology,* 1972, **7**, 104–106.

Cohen, J. A coefficient of agreement for nominal scales. *Educational and Psychological Measurement,* 1960, **20**(1), 37–46.

Dixon, W. J., & Brown, M. B. *BMDP-79: Biomedical computer programs P-series.* Berkeley: University of California Press, 1979.

Dunn, J., & Kendrick, C. Interaction between young siblings in the context of family relationships. In M. Lewis & L. Rosenblum (Eds.), *The child and its family.* New York: Plenum, 1979.

Goodman, L. A., & Kruskal, W. H. Measures of association for cross-classifications. *Journal of the American Statistical Association,* 1954, **49**, 732–764.

Greenberg, M. T., & Marvin, R. S. Reactions of preschool children to an adult stranger: A behavioral systems approach. *Child Development,* 1982, **53**, 481–490.

Greenberg, M. T., Marvin, R. S., & Mossler, D. G. The development of conditional reasoning skills. *Developmental Psychology,* 1977, **13**, 527–528.

Hinde, R. A. *Towards understanding relationships.* London: Academic Press, 1979.

Hinde, R. A. Attachment: Some conceptual and biological issues. In C. M. Parks & K. Stevenson-Hinde (Eds.), *The place of attachment in human behavior.* New York: Basic, 1982.

Konner, M. J. Maternal care, infant behavior, and development among the !Kung. In R. B. Lee & I. DeVore (Eds.), *Kalahari hunter gathers: Studies of the !Kung San and their neighbors.* Cambridge, Mass.: Harvard University Press, 1976.

Lamb, M. E. Interactions between eighteen-month-olds and their preschool-aged siblings. *Child Development,* 1978, **49**, 51–59.

Marvin, R. S. An ethological-cognitive model for the attenuation of mother-child attachment behavior. In T. Alloway, P. Pliner, & L. Krames (Eds.), *Advances in the study of communication and affect* (Vol. **3**). New York: Plenum, 1977.

Marvin, R. S., & Greenberg, M. T. Preschooler's changing conceptions of their mothers: A social-cognitive study of mother-child attachment. In D. Forbes & M. T. Greenberg (Eds.), *New directions in child development.* (Vol. **14**): *Developing plans for behavior.* San Francisco: Jossey-Bass, 1982.

Marvin, R. S., Greenberg, M., & Mossler, D. The early development of conceptual perspective taking: Distinguishing among multiple perspectives. *Child Development,* 1976, **47**, 511–514.

Minuchin, S. *Families and family therapy: A structural approach.* Boston: Harvard University Press, 1974.

Parten, M. Social participation among pre-school children. *Journal of Abnormal and Social Psychology,* 1932, **27**, 243–269.

Samuels, H. R. The effect of an older sibling on infant locomotor exploration of new environment. *Child Development,* 1980, **51**, 607–609.

Schaffer, H. R., & Emerson, P. E. The development of social attachments in infancy. *Monographs of the Society for Research in Child Development,* 1964, **29**(3, Serial No. 94).

Sroufe, L. A., & Waters, E. Attachment as an organizational construct. *Child Development,* 1977, **48**, 1184–1199.

Stewart, R. B. Sibling attachment relationship: Child-infant interactions in the strange situation. *Developmental Psychology,* 1983, **19**(2), 192–199.

Weisner, T. S., & Gallimore, R. My brother's keeper: Child and sibling caretaking. *Current Anthropology,* 1977, **18**(2), 169–190.

READING 35

Family Relations Six Years after Divorce

E. Mavis Hetherington

This paper presents part of the findings of a six year follow-up of a longitudinal study of divorce. The paper focuses on family relations six years after divorce. Children from divorced families who initially resided in mother custody households and their divorced parents were studied at two months, one year, two years and six years following divorce. A summary of the results of the first two years of the project are reported in Hetherington, Cox and Cox (1982). In this paper we will examine family functioning and parent-child relations at six years following divorce in an expanded sample of 180 families including 124 of the families from the original longitudinal study.

Most studies including this study find that the first two years following divorce might be regarded as the crisis period of divorce during which most children and many parents experience emotional distress, psychological and behavior problems, disruptions in family functioning and problems in adjusting to new roles, relationships and life changes associated with the altered family situation. However by two years following divorce the majority of parents and children are adapting reasonably well and certainly are showing great improvement since the time of the divorce. In the two year assessment period in this study some continuing problems were found in the adjustment of boys and in relations between custodial mothers and their sons. These boys from divorced families in comparison to boys in nondivorced families showed more antisocial, acting out, coercive, noncompliant behaviors in the home and in the school and exhibited difficulties in peer relations and school achievement. In contrast girls from divorced families were functioning well and had positive relations with their custodial mothers.

In considering these results two things must be kept in mind; the first is that this study involves mother custody families and there is some evidence that children may adjust better in the custody of a parent of the same sex (Warshak & Santrock, 1983; Santrock & Warshak, 1986). The second is that age of the child may be an important factor in sex differences in childrens' responses to divorce. In this study children were an average age of four at the beginning of the study, six at the two year assessment, and ten at the time of the six year assessment. Reports of more severe and long lasting disruption of behavior in boys than girls following their parents' divorce have tended to come from studies of preadolescent children. However, investigations of adolescent girls from divorced families have found problems in the heterosexual adjustment of the girls and in parent-child relations (Hetherington, 1972; Wallerstein, 1982).

A difficulty in attempting to assess the long term effects of divorce on parents and children and the factors that may mediate these outcomes is that family members may encounter widely varying family reorganizations and family experiences following divorce. For most parents and children divorce is only one in a series of family transitions that follow separation. Life in a single parent household following divorce is usually a temporary condition since 80% of men and 75% of women will remarry. About 20% of children will spend some time in a stepparent family before they are young adults. Moreover since the divorce rate is higher in remarriages than in first marriages some parents and children encounter a series of divorces, periods in a one-parent household, and remarriages.

In this paper we will examine relations between parents and a ten year old child in nondivorced families, families in which there is a divorced custodial mother, and remarried families with a divorced mother and a stepfather six years after the mother's divorce.

METHOD

Subjects

The original sample was composed of 144 middle-class white children and their parents. Half of the children were from divorced, mother-custody families, and the other half were from nondivorced families. Within each group, half were boys and half were girls. In the original study, the families were studied at 2 months, 1 year, and 2 years after divorce. The follow up to be discussed in this paper occurred 6 years after the divorce when the children were an average of 10.1 years of age. As might be expected, by this time many rearrangements in marital relations had occurred.

In the six year follow-up the subjects were residential parents and children in 124 of an original 144 families who were available and willing to continue to participate in the study. Sixty of the original divorced families and 64 of the original nondivorced families agreed to participate, although there had been many shifts in marital status in the 6 years since the study began. In the 60 available original divorced families, only 18 of the custodial mothers had remained single (10 with a target daughter and 8 with a target son), and 42 had remarried (20 with a target daughter and 22 with a target son). Two of the parents had redivorced, and there had been 6 changes in custody or residence from the mother to the father (5 sons, 1 daughter). Of the 64 originally nondivorced families, 53 were still married (30 sons, 23 daughters), 11 were divorced (7 daughters, 4 sons). It should be noted that the greater willingness to divorce in families with daughters than with sons is in accord with the findings of Block (1985) Baumrind (1986), and Glick (1979). In the newly divorced families, only one of the children, a son, was in the custody of the father. This was a well educated, middle-class, white sample. All parents had at least a high school education or advanced training beyond high school. At 6 years following divorce, the household income of the non-remarried divorced mothers was significantly lower than that of the nondivorced or remarried families. The average household income of the divorced, non-remarried mothers was $16,010, of remarried mothers was $35,162, and of nondivorced families was $36,900.

A new cohort of families was added to the group of participating original families on whom there was complete data (except for noncustodial father measures) in order to expand the size of the groups to 30 sons and 30 daughters in each of three groups—a remarried mother/stepfather group, a mother-custody, nonremarried group, and a nondivorced group—for a total of 180 families. For some analyses, the remarried group was broken down into those remarried less than 2 years and those remarried longer than 2 years. The additional subjects were matched with the original subjects on family size, age, education, income, length of marriage and, when appropriate, length of time since divorce and time of remarriage.

The cross-sectional analyses of child and parent adjustment and of the relationships among family interaction, child adjustment, parent adjustment, and marital adjustment in this paper utilize the expanded sample. Inconsistencies in the six year follow-up data reported in Hetherington, Cox, and Cox (1982) and in this paper occur because the first paper used only the original sample and this paper uses the expanded sample.

Procedure

Partial data were available in the follow-up study on 124 of the original families. For the additional families in the expanded sample only families on which all measures were available were included in the study. In all cases, including the original study, interviews, tests, and home observations of the residential parents and child were available. In 18 of the original families, complete school data, which included a peer nomination measure, were not available because of lack of willingness of the schools to participate in the study, although with 10 of these families, measures were available from teachers who were contacted directly and who agreed to participate. In addition, telephone interviews and/or take home questionnaire and test material could not be obtained for six of the noncustodial fathers. As was true in the three waves of data collection in the original study, multiple measures of family relations, stresses, and support systems, and parent and child characteristics and behavior were obtained from the child and residential parent, and when possible from the nonresidential parent. These involved standardized tests, interviews, and observations. In addition, teacher and peer evaluations of behavior, observations in school, and information from school records were obtained when possible. More details on the mea-

sures used in the first 3 waves of data collection at 2 months, 1 year, and 2 years following divorce, are available in Hetherington, Cox, and Cox (1978, 1979a, 1979b, 1982). In addition more information on the child outcome measures in wave 4, 6 years following divorce are available in Hetherington, Cox, and Cox (1985). Only the measures used in the analyses presented in this chapter will be described.

Parent Interviews Parents were interviewed separately on a structured parent interview schedule designed to assess discipline practices, the parent-child relationship, expectations for the child, sibling relations, the relationship of the child with the spouse and exspouse, the marital relationship, the relationship with the exspouse, spouse characteristics, support systems outside of the household, stresses, family roles and responsibilities, family organization, areas of desired change, satisfaction and happiness, and personality. Each of the categories were rated by two judges and the parent. In some cases the category involved the rating of only a single five point scale, however most categories involved multiple ratings. The interjudge reliabilities ranged from .58 to .95 with a mean of .83. The parent-judge reliabilities range from .40 to .94 with a mean of .67.

Child Interviews Children also were interviewed on a structured interview schedule covering many of the same topics as those in the parent interview including discipline practices; parent-child relationships; relationship with the stepparents and noncustodial parents; the quality of their parents' marital relationships; family roles and responsibility; household organization; sibling, peer, and school relations; stresses and support systems; and areas of desired change. Rating procedures were the same as in the parent interviews. Interjudge reliabilities averaged .80. When parents and children were rating the same scales mother-child reliabilities were .52 and father-child reliabilities averaged .64. As will be seen later this varied with sex of child, sex of parent and family type.

Parent Personality Inventories The parent personality measures include the Personal Adjustment Scale of the Adjective Checklist (Gough & Heilbrun, 1965), the Socialization Scale of the California Personality Inventory (Gough, 1969), Rotter's I-E Scale (Rotter, 1966), the Speilberger State-Trait Anxiety Scale (Speilberger, Gorsuch, & Lushene, 1970), and the Beck Depression Inventory (Beck, 1979).

Child Adjustment Measures Measures of child adjustment were obtained from parents, teachers, peers and the children. In the six year follow-up this included parents' and teachers' rating scales of the childrens' behavior, parents' and teachers' reports on the Child Behavior Checklist (Achenbach & Edelbrock, 1983), and on modifications of scales used in the three initial waves of the study, and a peer nomination measure based on a modification and extension of the Pupil Evaluation Inventory (Pekarik et al., 1976). In addition the child made self ratings on the Pupil Evaluation Inventory and on the Harter Perceived Competence Scale (1982).

Twenty-Four-Hour-Behavior-Checklists On 10 different occasions, residential parents and children were asked to record and report in a telephone interview whether 40 child behaviors, 20 types of parent-child conflict and 10 types of husband-wife conflict, and 10 types of parent-child interaction thought to show involvement or warmth, had occurred in the past 24 hours. Using a split-half reliability of temporal stability for the first 5 days versus the second 5 days, reliabilities average .71 for fathers, .73 for mothers, and .69 for children. Average agreement between mothers and fathers across the three dimensions was .70.

Agreement between parents and children was lower: .62 for mother and child and .60 for father and child. Children filled out this checklist only at the 6-year follow-up (time 4).

Home Observations Home observations were made on six occasions for a minimum of 3 hours. On three of these occasions, recording was done with raters present, and on three occasions the family interactions were videotaped and coded later. These tapes have been coded using three different coding systems. One was a sequential interactive code. The second was a code focussing only on the child's behavior which measured internalizing, externalizing and socially competent behaviors. This coding system is described in greater detail in Hetherington et al. (1985). Finally, the tapes were coded on global rating scales described below under observer impressions. In the sequential coding a focal subject coding system was used, where each family member served as the focal subject for 10-minute periods in rotation. The behavior of the child of interest in this study was oversampled, so that he or she served as the focal subject three times more often than did the other family members. All behaviors of the focal subject and all the reactions of other family members to the focal subject were coded at 6-second intervals. In addition each content code was coded for positive, negative or neutral affect.

Reliabilities which averaged 0.79 for agreement between categories in each 6-second unit were obtained from two coders coding 20% of the tapes. Cohen's kappas were always significantly above chance levels of agreement.

Structured Family Problem Solving Interactions Husband/wife dyads, parent/child dyads, husband/wife/target child triads, biological sibling dyads, biological/step sibling dyads when available and a group of all of the residential family members were involved in ten minute structured family problem solving interactions. Each dyad, triad or family group discussed and attempted to reach solutions about issues they previously separately had reported that were continuing problems between them. The order of these structured family problem-solving interactions was randomized and the interactions were spread across two sessions spaced over about a two week period. The coding system was similar to the sequential code used in the free home observations; however additional codes focussed on problem-solving processes were included.

Observer Impressions The investigators who had interviewed the families and observed and videotaped the families in the home in free and structured family problem-solving sessions completed a set of five point rating scales describing parents' and childrens' behavior toward each family member. They viewed the tapes after the last data gathering session and then made their ratings. In addition to rating the characteristic level of interaction for each family member on each scale, observers also rated the highest and lowest extreme level to occur at any time in any of the sessions. Thus a family member's characteristic level of hostility might be 2 but if they behaved in a particularly vicious way on one occasion they would obtain a rating of 5 on the most extreme high coding. In addition each parent's overall parenting style was characterized as authoritarian, authoritative, permissive, or disengaged. Finally, the family as a whole was rated on a set of family dimensions which will not be discussed in this paper.

Dyadic Adjustment Scale Both spouses took the Dyadic Adjustment Scale (Spanier, 1976). This scale yields an overall measure of marital satisfaction and subscales assessing satisfaction, consensus, cohesiveness and expressiveness.

School Observations In the first three time periods, each child had been observed in the classroom for 18 10-minute sessions. The child's behavior and the behavior of the person with whom the child was interacting were recorded every 6 seconds. In addition, affect during play had been assessed. The same code used in the original study combined with affect codings was used in the follow-up study. See Hetherington et al. (1979b) for more details on this procedure.

Life Experiences Survey (LES) An extension of the Sarason et al. (1978) Life Experiences Survey with 10 items added to more intensively study changes in family relations was administered to parents at time 4. Parents were asked to indicate the occurrence of certain events in the past year and in the past 6 years' time since divorce, followed by separate subjective ratings of the event as positive or negative on 7-point scales. A similar, shorter survey was constructed for children and administered at time 4. This measure was read to the children.

Analysis

Composite measures involving interview, twenty-four-hour-behavior checklist, observational measures, observer impressions and test measures were used to develop subscales of parenting behavior, husband/wife relationships and the child's relationship to parents and siblings. The dimensions of parenting behavior are presented in Table 1. Analyses were performed on the composite indices of parent and child behavior, with sex of the child and family type as the independent measures. In addition, analyses were performed for factors derived separately from mothers', fathers', and children's reports. It was thought to be important to look at reports from individual family members as well as the composite measures since variations in the perceptions of different family members are often important indicators of family dynamics and discrepant perceptions have been found

TABLE 1   DIMENSIONS OF PARENTING

Warmth/responsiveness
  Expressive affection
  Social involvement
  Instrumenal involvement
Control
  Rule setting, restrictiveness
  Firmness, firm vs. lax enforcement
  Power
Monitoring
  Monitoring strategies
  Successful monitoring
Conflict/irratability
  Coercion
  Punitiveness
  Mood
  Conflict over parental authority
  Conflict over household and personal issues
  Conflict over character development and deviance
Maturity Demands
  Maturity expectations
  Maturity demands and enforcement

to be related to family conflict (Hagan, 1986) and marital distress. The expanded sample of 30 families of boys and 30 families of girls in each of the three family groups was used in this analysis. However, the remarried group was further broken down into a remarried less than 2 years group (early remarriage, ER) and remarried more than 2 years group (late remarriage, LR); thus, there were four family groups. This was based on the assumption that families who were in the first 2 years of a remarriage would be adapting to another life transition, in contrast to families who had been in their current marital situation for more than 2 years. The analyses for residential fathers involved only three family types (early remarriage, later remarriage, and nondivorced).

RESULTS

Parent Adjustment

There were few differences in the adjustment of mothers in the remarried and nondivorced fam-

ilies with the exception that mothers in the first two years of remarriage report greater life satisfaction and marital satisfaction. They appear to be in a honeymoon period of adjustment. There are no differences between those mothers remarried for longer periods of time and nondivorced mothers. In contrast, the nonremarried, divorced mothers report less general life satisfaction, less internal control over the course of their lives, more loneliness, and more depression. Loneliness is correlated with scores for depression on the Beck Depression Inventory. The pervasive loneliness of nonremarried divorced women occurs in spite of the fact that by six years after divorce they have built up new social networks and have more contact with their families of origin than do mothers in nondivorced families. Wallerstein (1986) in a ten year follow-up of her longitudinal study of divorce also comments on the overwhelming loneliness of nonremarried women. Other studies have found that loneliness is much less marked for women who have never married. For divorced women involvement in a new intimate relationship is the critical factor that alleviates loneliness. Nonworking mothers, divorced mothers of sons, and mothers in blended families in which children from two families had been merged reported less life satisfaction, more depression and less internalized control of their fate than did other mothers. Maternal depression and state anxiety was related to more irritable and inconsistent parenting behavior and less warmth and positive responsiveness especially toward sons.

There are few differences between the personalities and adjustment of fathers in nondivorced and remarried families with the exception that newly remarried fathers report more marital satisfaction than do the other groups of fathers. In addition both groups of remarried fathers report that the relationship with their stepchildren adversely affects their marital relationship. All groups of fathers report more marital satisfaction and general life satisfaction than do mothers.

Parent-Child Relations

How do nondivorced, divorced non-remarried, and remarried mothers behave with their children? The findings suggest that mother/son relations in the divorced non-remarried families and parent-child relations in the early remarried families, particularly with stepdaughters, are problematic. It is important to note that these divorced families are what we might call stabilized divorced families. The parents have been divorced for six years and the families are well beyond the two or three year crisis period following divorce. However, divorced non-remarried mothers are continuing to exhibit many of the behaviors with their sons six years after divorce that were seen two years after divorce. Although interview and observational measures suggest that there are few differences among the three groups of mothers in the physical and verbal affection they direct toward their children, divorced mothers with sons tend to spend less time with their sons and report feeling less rapport or closeness to them. In addition, mothers in all three family types showed more expressive affection toward girls than toward boys.

It is more differences in control attempts and in punitive, coercive behaviors than in warmth and affection that distinguish divorced mothers from mothers in the other family types. Divorced mothers are ineffectual in their control attempts and give many instructions with little follow through. They tend to nag, natter and complain to their sons. Although the divorced mothers are as physically and verbally affectionate with their children as are mothers in the other family groups, they more often get involved with their sons in angry, escalating coercive cycles. Spontaneous negative start-ups, that is negative behavior initiated following neutral or positive behavior by the other person, are twice as likely to occur with moth-

ers and sons in divorced families as with those in non-divorced families. Moreover, once these negative interchanges between divorced mothers and sons occur they are likely to continue significantly longer than in any other dyad in any family type. Patterson (1982) has noted that the vast majority of normal children emit a single coercive behavior then stop. This is not the case with sons and their divorced custodial mothers. As can be seen in Table 2, the probability of continuance of a negative response is higher in the divorced mother-son dyad than in any other parent-child dyad with the exception of daughters' behavior toward stepfathers in the early stage of remarriage. It should be noted that the sons of divorced women recognize their own aggressive, non-compliant behaviors and report that their mothers have little control over their behavior; however, they also report and exhibit high levels of warmth toward their mothers. It might be best to view this relation between divorced mothers and sons as intense and ambivalent rather than purely hostile and rejecting.

Both sons and daughters in divorced families are allowed more responsibility, independence and power in decision making than are children in non-divorced families. They successfully interrupt their divorced mother and their mother yields to their demands more often than in the other family types. In some cases this greater power and independence results in an egalitarian, mutually supportive relationship. In other cases, where the emotional demands or responsibilities required by the mother are inappropriate, are beyond the capabilities of the child or interfere with normal activities of the child such as in peer relations or school activities, resentment, rebellion or psychological disturbance may follow.

Finally, divorced mothers monitor their childrens' behavior less closely than do mothers in non-divorced families. They know less about where their children are, who they are with, and what they are doing than do mothers in two

TABLE 2   PROBABILITY OF NEGATIVE RESPONSE CONTINUANCE IN FAMILY DYADS

	Nondivorced		Divorced		Remarried early		Remarried late	
	Son	Daughter	Son	Daughter	Son	Daughter	Son	Daughter
Mother interacting with child	.11	09	.26	08	.20	15	.15	13
Child interacting with mother	.12	.07	.33	.09	.21	.19	.13	.19
Sibling interacting with child	.19	.15	.27	.24	.30	.28	.20	.20
Child interacting with sibling	.18	.16	.29	.23	.29	.30	.19	.24
Stepfather interacting with child	.10	.05			.07	.03	.14	.18
Child interacting with stepfather	.03	.02			.10	.31	.06	.18

parent households. Boys in divorced families on their 24 hour behavior checklists reported being involved in more antisocial behavior that the mother did not know about than did children in any other group, although this discrepancy was also high in the mother-daughter reports in the stepfamily groups. In addition, children in the one parent households were less likely than those in the two parent households to have adult supervision in their parent's absence. Both Robert Weiss (1975) and Wallerstein and Kelly (1980) report that one way that children may cope with their parents' divorce is by becoming disengaged from the family. In this study boys from divorced families were spending significantly less time in the home with their parents or other adults and more time alone or with peers than were any of the other groups of children.

In contrast to divorced mothers and sons, there are few differences in the relationship between divorced mothers and daughters and that of mothers and daughters in nondivorced families. However, girls in divorced one parent households do have more power and are assigned more responsibilities. They do in the words of Robert Weiss (1975) "grow up faster." Mothers and daughters in mother-headed families six years after divorce express con-

siderable satisfaction with their relationship. There is an exception to this happy picture. Interview measures of pubescent status had been obtained from the parents and their children and interviewers had made ratings of pubescent status. As might be expected, few children had entered puberty by this time since they were only aged 10, however, 26 of our 90 girls were early maturers. Family conflict was higher in all three family types for these early maturing girls versus late maturing girls, however it was most marked between mothers and daughters in the single parent households. Early maturity in girls was associated with a premature weakening of the mother-child bonds. These early maturing girls, especially in the mother-headed families, were alienated and disengaged from their families, talked less to their mothers but interrupted them more and became involved in activities with older peers. Past research suggests that divorced mothers and daughters may experience problems as daughters become pubescent and involved in heterosexual activities (Hetherington, 1972). The difficulties in interactions between these early maturing girls and their divorced mothers may be precursors of more intense problems yet to come.

In looking at stepfamilies it is important to distinguish between those families in the early stages of remarriage, when they are still adapting to their new situation, and those in the later stage of remarriage, when family roles and relationships should have been worked through and established. In some ways the early stage of remarriage may be a honeymoon period where the parents at least want to make the family relationship successful. In discussing stepfamilies it becomes particularly important to identify which family members' perspective is being discussed since these vary widely. Family members agree that mothers in remarried families are as warm to their children as mothers in other types of families. However, mothers see themselves as having more control over their children's behavior than she is seen as having by either her children or the stepfather. Both interview and observational data indicate that she has greater control over her son than is found in the one parent households, but less over her daughter than is found in mothers in either of the other two family types. Control over both sons and daughters is greater for mothers who have been remarried more than two years.

In the first two years following remarriage conflict between mothers and daughters is high. In addition these daughters exhibit more demandingness, hostility, coercion and less warmth toward both parents than do girls in divorced or nondivorced families. Their behavior improves over the course of remarriage, however even two years after remarriage these girls are still more antagonistic and disruptive with their parents than are girls in the other two family types. The presence of this noxious behavior is supported by the reports of both parents and children and the observational findings. In the first two years following remarriage stepfathers reported themselves to be low on felt or expressed affection for their stepchildren although they spend time with them attempting to establish a relationship. They express less strong positive affect and show fewer negative, critical responses than do the nondivorced fathers. Biological fathers are freer in expressing affection and in criticizing their children for poor personal grooming, for not doing their homework, not cleaning up their rooms or for fighting with their siblings. However, they also are more involved and interested in the activities of their children. Initially stepfathers are far less supportive to stepsons than to stepdaughters. In the interactions in the first two years of the remarriage the stepfathers' interaction is almost that of a stranger who is attempting to be ingratiating, is seeking information, and is polite but emotionally disengaged. These stepfathers are remaining relatively pleasant in spite of the aversive behavior they encounter with their stepdaughters. However, by two years after remarriage they are more impatient. Although they try to remain disengaged they occasionally get into extremely angry interchanges with their stepdaughters. These conflicts tend to focus on issues of parental authority and respect for the mother. Stepdaughters view their stepfathers as hostile, punitive and unreasonable on matters of discipline. The interchanges between stepfathers and stepdaughters and the conflicts between divorced mothers and sons are rated as the highest on hostility of any dyad. Stepfathers make significantly fewer control attempts and are less successful in gaining control with both sons and daughters than are nondivorced fathers. Their control of stepsons but not stepdaughters is better in longer remarriages.

The situation with stepsons is very different than that with stepdaughters. Although mothers and stepfathers view sons as initially being extremely difficult, their behavior improves over time. In the families who have been remarried for over two years these boys are showing no more aggressive noncompliant behavior in the home or problem behaviors, as measured on tests such as the Childrens Behavior Checklist, than are boys in nondivorced families (see Hetherington, Cox, & Cox, 1985 for more details on the adjustment of children). However mothers, sons and teachers report these boys more positively than do stepfathers. Although stepfathers continue to view stepchildren, especially stepdaughters, as having more problems than do nondivorced fathers, they report improvement in the stepsons' behavior and exhibit greater warmth and involvement with them than with the stepdaughter. The stepsons frequently report being close to the stepfather, enjoying his company and seeking his advice and support. As was found in divorced families, monitoring of children's behavior often is not effective in stepfamilies.

Parent Typologies

One of the things that was noteable in these data was the greater variability on measures of both parents' and children's behavior in the divorced and remarried families than in the nondivorced families. It may be that stressful life transitions accentuate the diverse adaptive abilities and varied coping patterns of family members. We thought we might capture the patterning in these variations by looking at family typologies. A cluster analysis was performed on mothers in the three family types and on fathers in the divorced families and in stepfamilies. Four parenting clusters emerged for mothers and fathers. The first was a permissive parenting style which was moderately high on warmth; high on involvement; and low on coercion, control, conflict, monitoring, and maturity demands. The second was a disengaged parenting style which was low on conflict and hostility, and low on involvement, warmth, monitoring, control, and maturity demands. These are adult-oriented parents who want to minimize the amount of time, effort, and interference with their own needs that child rearing entails. It should be noted that when the child becomes demanding or inconveniences disengaged parents, things often become extremely hostile. The ratings of the most extremely

hostile behavior that occurred during interactions was highest in disengaged and authoritarian parents. The third group was an authoritarian parenting style which was high on involvement, control, conflict, and monitoring attempts, high on punitiveness and coercion and low on warmth. The fourth was an authoritative parenting group involving high warmth, involvement, monitoring, and maturity demands, moderately high but responsive control and relatively low conflict. It is apparent that with the exception of the disengaged cluster these are the same parenting typologies identified by Baumrind (1971). Table 3 presents the distribution across these four parenting typologies of mothers and fathers of boys and girls in stepfamilies, divorced and nondivorced families.

The differences among parenting types are less marked for mothers than for fathers. The largest parenting style for all groups of mothers, with the exception of divorced mothers of boys, is authoritative parenting. In contrast, fathers in stepfamilies tend to be much less authoritative and much more disengaged than are fathers in nondivorced families. Moreover, although the number of authoritative stepfathers increases over time for boys, authoritative behavior by stepfathers with daughters decreases and disengagement doubles as the remarriage goes on. In addition, even for boys after two years of remarriage, disengagement remains the predominant parenting style of stepfathers.

Both disengaged parenting and permissive parenting tend to be associated with poor impulse control, noncompliance and antisocial behavior in children. However, early delinquent behavior and low social competence was more common in the sons of disengaged parents. Authoritarian parenting in nondivorced parents and in divorced mothers was associated with moody, irritable, anxious behavior and low self-esteem in girls. In boys it is related to these same attributes but also

TABLE 3 PARENTING TYPES

	Permissive		Disengaged		Authoritarian		Authoritative	
	Mother	Father	Mother	Father	Mother	Father	Mother	Father
Nondivorced								
Boys	6	3	4	3	4	8	16	16
Girls	4	1	5	7	4	2	17	20
Divorced								
Boys	8		5		10		7	
Girls	8		3		4		15	
Remarried less than 2 years								
Boys	6	5	4	14	8	7	12	4
Girls	6	7	5	10	5	4	14	9
Remarried more than 2 years								
Boys	7	3	5	15	4	4	14	8
Girls	3	1	4	20	7	5	16	4

to impulsive, aggressive behavior in the school setting.

In general, authoritative parenting is associated with high social competence and low rates of behavior problems, especially with low externalizing problems, and especially in boys. The exception to this is in stepfathers' parenting. Both authoritative and authoritarian parenting in stepfathers is related to high rates of behavior problems in both stepdaughters and in stepsons in the first two years of remarriage. After two years authoritative parenting by stepfathers is related to fewer behavior problems and greater acceptance of the stepfather by stepsons but is not at this time significantly related to stepdaughters' behavior. The best strategy of the stepfather in gaining acceptance of the stepchildren seems to be one where there is no initial active attempt to take over and try to actively shape and control the child's behavior either through authoritarian or the more desirable authoritative techniques. Instead, a period of time first working at establishing a relationship and supporting the mother in her parenting, followed by later more active authorita-

tive parenting, leads to constructive outcomes at least for boys.

The Impact of Spousal Support on Parents' and Children's Adjustment and on Parenting Behavior

It has been suggested (Belsky, 1984) that the marital relationship and support from a spouse may affect the parents' well being, their relationship with their children and consequently their children's adjustment. It might be thought that support from the spouse would be particularly important in new stepfamilies since divorced women often are reported to suffer from economic duress, social isolation, task overload and child rearing problems. The shift to a new marital relationship might offer supports and resources from the stepfather which would help in coping with these problems. In addition it has been proposed that there is considerable stress and role ambiguity in becoming a stepfather. Support by the mother may assist the stepfather in identifying, establishing, and enjoying his new role and responsibilities.

Six types of support were examined: (1) financial support, (2) emotional support, (3) support in household maintenance, (4) direct child rearing participation in shared activities, and in emotional support of child, (5) active participation in character development and discipline, (6) support and encouragement for the spouse in his or her child rearing role. The relations between these six types of spouse support and parents' adjustment, parent-child relationships and children adjustment for mothers and fathers were examined. Financial support was based on the spouses income. Emotional support was based on a composite score which included the spouse's score on the dyadic adjustment scale (Spanier, 1976), percent of positive to positive plus negative scores on the observational measures, global ratings of warmth, and interview reports of closeness and involvement. Support in household maintenance was assessed by a composite measure involving amount of participation in household tasks and satisfaction with the amount of participation in household responsibilities. It should be noted that although these measures are moderately correlated ($p < .05$), as a single predictor of our outcome variables of interest, satisfaction with participation explains twice as much of the variance as does amount of participation. Satisfaction appears to involve an interaction between expectations and performance. Direct child rearing participation (shared activities and emotional support) was comprised of amount of time spent with the child and quality of the relationship with the child based on 24 hour behavior checklists, interview measures and molecular and global observational measures of warmth/involvement. Discipline involved giving and enforcing directions as assessed by interviews and observations. Finally, support for the spouse in his or her child rearing activities was based on interview measures and molecular and global observational measures involving approval, sympathy, or disciplinary support for the spouse in dealing with the child.

The measures of personal adjustment of the parents used in this analysis were the Beck Depression Inventory, Speilberger's State/Trait Anxiety Inventory, the Helmreich Self Esteem Inventory, the personal control scale of the Rotter I–E scale, interview measures of life satisfaction and the socialization scale of the California Personality Inventory. The assessment of the parent-child relationship involved the composite measures of warmth, control and conflict obtained from interviews, 24 hour behavior checklist and global and molecular observational measures. Finally, the child outcome measures involved measures of externalizing, internalizing and socially competent behavior based on observations, interviews, 24 hour behavior checklists and standardized tests.

The relationship among the support variables and outcome variables differed in the remarried and nondivorced families although couples remarried for more than two years were becoming more similar to the nondivorced couples. There are more relationships between spousal support and adjustment and personal well being for women than for men. For both spouses in the remarried families and for women in nondivorced families the quality of the marital relationship was related positively to life satisfaction and negatively to depression scores. For women in all three family groups (early remarried, late remarried and nondivorced) it also was related to state anxiety and for mothers in the early stages of remarriage, the quality of the marital relationship was associated with greater feelings of internalized control over the things that happened to them. Only for the mothers in the first two years of remarriage was economic support a significant predictor of maternal well being. Economic support was related not only to internalized control but also to low depression, low state anxiety and high life satisfaction, but only in this group of women. For most of the remarried women household income had more than doubled following remarriage; this may have relieved many of the stresses encountered while they were in one parent households. Many remarried women spoke of the increased options in their lives offered by their newly obtained economic security. About ten percent of these women stopped working for a short time following the remarriage but most returned to work. Twenty-three of the women in the early stages of remarriage were employed at least part time, twenty-five of those remarried more than two years were employed, twenty-five nondivorced mothers were employed, and twenty-seven of our nonremarried women were employed.

For nondivorced men, the quality of the marital relationship was related only to general life satisfaction, and this was a very modest relationship. Apparently, men's views of themselves and their life situation is largely determined by factors external to the marital relationship. Men also view their marriages and life situations more positively than do women. It may take an extremely disrupted marriage to affect masculine adjustment. However, research suggests that men are as distressed as women in response to separation and divorce and that they more often report not being aware of serious marital problems leading up to the divorce. When the marital dissolution does occur they as well as their wives are likely to experience pervasive changes in self concept, emotional distress and problems in relationships outside of the family (Hetherington, Cox, & Cox, 1982).

The effects of spousal support on three aspects of the parent-child relationship—control, warmth and conflict—were examined. None of the paternal support variables were related to maternal control in the stepfamilies remarried for less than two years, however, support by the father for the mother's childrearing practices was related to more effective maternal control especially over boys in both the longer remarried and nondivorced families, and direct participation in the rearing of boys by the father also was related to maternal control in nondivorced families. In addition, active participation in childrearing by the father and support of the mother in childrearing were both related to maternal warmth in the longer remarried and nondivorced families. Again, in the couples remarried less than two years, support of the mothers' childrearing but not active intervention led to greater maternal warmth. The quality of the marital relationship was related to maternal warmth toward children only in nondivorced families.

In nondivorced families only active participation in childrearing by the father was associated with lower conflict between mothers and sons. In the stepfamilies there occurs what might appear to be an anomalous finding. A close marital relationship is associated with high levels of conflict between mothers and their children in stepfamilies, especially their daughters. For sons this relationship is significant in the early but not later stages of remarriage. How can we explain these unexpected results? It seems likely that in the early stages of remarriage the new stepfather is viewed as an intruder or a competitor for the mother's affection. Since boys in divorced families often have been involved in coercive or ambivalent relations with their mothers, in the long run they may have little to lose and something to gain from the remarriage. In contrast, daughters in one parent families have played more responsible, powerful roles than girls in nondivorced families and have had more positive relations with their divorced mothers than have sons. They may see both their independence and their relationship with the mother threatened by the introduction of the stepfather and resent the mother for remarrying. This is seen in resistant, ignoring, critical behavior by the daughter toward her remarried mother. In addition, it is reflected in the sulky, negativistic, hostile behavior observed in stepdaughters with their stepfathers and in the girls' own reports of their negative, rejecting attitudes toward the stepfathers. It is notable that the positive behavior of the stepfather toward stepdaughters does not correlate with her acceptance of the stepfather in the early stages of remarriage. No matter how hard the stepfather tries the daughter rejects him.

For nondivorced fathers a close marital relationship, support by the mother for his child rearing participation and direct participation by the mother in child rearing are related to paternal warmth and low father–child conflict. Again, the pattern differs in the remarried families, with fathers' reports of a close marital relationship being associated with higher levels of fathers' conflict with daughters in the longer remarried families. In the early stages of remarriage stepfathers are behaving in a relatively restrained fashion while they are actively attempting to make the new family situation work. Later in remarriages there is more reciprocity of negative behavior between stepfathers and stepdaughters.

Finally let us turn to the relation between the marital relationship, spousal support and childrens' adjustment. In nondivorced families marital satisfaction, active involvement of the father in child rearing and the father's support of the mother in her child rearing role were related to less externalizing behavior in boys and greater social competence in both boys and girls. In the longer remarried families, support of the mother in her child rearing role and participation by the stepfather in child rearing not mainly as a disciplinarian but in the role of a friend and confidant also led to less externalizing behavior in boys. Boys from the small group of authoritative stepfathers in the late remarriage group had fewer total behavior problems than did boys with stepfathers in the other three parenting typologies. In contrast, active participation in child rearing by the stepfather and a close marital relationship actually led to an increase both in acting out behavior and in depression in stepdaughters. Only paternal financial support was associated with fewer total behavior problems in girls in newly remarried families.

In nondivorced families, active involvement of the mother in child rearing and her support of the father in childrearing were related to lower externalizing in boys. No other relationships between maternal support of the father and child outcomes were found.

In summary, financial support appears to be more important in the adjustment of newly remarried mothers and their daughters than in other families perhaps as a contrast with the previous state of financial deprivation experienced in a single parent household. Parental participation in household tasks had no effects on our outcome measures. The main factors affecting the adjustment of parents and children and parent–child relations appeared to be those related to marital satisfaction, direct involvement in childrearing and support for the spouse as a parent. Although marital satisfaction tends to be related to the psychological adjustment of the spouses, especially the women in all three family groups, the pattern of other relations differed in stepfamilies and nondivorced families. In stepfamilies, in contrast to nondivorced families, marital satisfaction was related to an increase in problems in parent-child relations and in childrens' adjustment, particularly with daughters. In addition, in stepfamilies support by the stepfather for the mother's parenting seems to be an efficacious strategy whereas in nondivorced families active involvement of the father in childrearing also appears to have a particularly salutary effect on mothers' parenting behavior and on the adjustment of sons.

CONCLUSION AND SUMMARY

Family relations change in the six years following divorce and these changes to some extent are related to ensuing marital arrangements. Custodial mothers who do not remarry in the six years following divorce have more emotional problems and are less satisfied with their lives than are remarried or nondivorced mothers. Even six years after divorce mothers continue to be involved in intense, ambivalent relationships and in coercive cycles with their sons whereas their relationship with their daughters is a positive one. This is reflected in the adjustment of their ten year old children. Daughters in mother custody homes with the exception of early maturing girls, are reasonably well adjusted, however sons in these families show many behavior problems, especially in noncompliant, impulsive, aggressive externalizing behavior.

When divorced mothers remarry, their psychological well being and life satisfaction increases. The marital relationship and various types of support from spouses impact on the adjustment of parents and children and on their parenting behavior. The relation of these support factors varies for parents in nondivorced, divorced and remarried families. One notable finding is that whereas marital satisfaction is related to positive parenting in nondivorced families, in the remarried families it is related to increased family conflict and behavior problems, especially in stepdaughters. Whereas boys in divorced families have more problems inside and outside of the home they gradually adapt to and may benefit from contact with a supportive stepfather. Although stepdaughters also gradually adapt to the remarriage they continue to have more problems in family relations and adjustment than do girls in nondivorced families or in families with custodial mothers who have been divorced for six years and who have not remarried.

The types of parenting patterns and their impact on children vary for children in divorced, nondivorced and remarried families. Authoritative parenting in mothers is the most common parenting style, with the exception of divorced mothers of sons. Moreover authoritative parenting is related to fewer behavior problems in children in homes with divorced nonremarried custodial mothers and in nondivorced

families. In stepfamilies a different pattern of relations occurs. Attempts by the stepfather to directly exert control, even authoritative control, over the child's behavior or disengagement early in the remarriage are associated with rejection of the stepfather by the children, and with children's problem behavior. A stepfather who first establishes a warm relationship with the stepson and supports the mother's parenting and later moves into an authoritative role has the greatest probability of gaining acceptance and facilitating the adjustment of stepsons. In contrast even when the stepfather is supportive and appropriate in responding to stepdaughters, her acceptance is difficult to gain. A troubling finding in this study is that disengaged parenting is the most common parenting style of stepfathers and disengagement with stepdaughters increases over time.

Past research (Hetherington, Cox, & Cox, 1978) has reported that coping strategies that lead to positive outcomes for one family member may adversely affect the adjustment of another member of the family during divorce. This also seems to be the case in remarriage. In order to understand the complex network of factors involved in this adjustment process it is necessary to view the family not solely in terms of intrafamilial factors as has been done in this paper but also in terms of the families larger ecological framework. This will be done in future papers ensuing from this project.

REFERENCES

Baumrind, D. (1986). Personal communication.

Baumrind, D. (1971). Current patterns of parental authority. *Developmental Psychology Monographs, 4* (1, Pt. 2).

Beck, A. T. (1967). *Depression: Causes and treatment*. Philadelphia: University of Pennsylvania Press.

Belsky, J. (1984). The determinants of parenting: A process model. *Child Development, 55,* 83–96.

Block, J. (1985). Personal communication.

Glick, P. (1979). *Who are the children in one-parent households?* Paper delivered at Wayne State University, Detroit, Michigan.

Gottman, J. M. (1979). *Marital interaction: Experimental investigations.* New York: Academic Press.

Gough, H. G. (1969). *Manual for California Personality Inventory.* Palo Alto, CA: Consulting Psychologists Press.

Gough, H. G. & Heilbrun, A.B., Jr. (1965). *The Adjective Checklist.* Palo Alto, CA: Consulting Psychologists Press.

Hagan, M. S. (April 1986). *The effect of discrepant perceptions and conflict on marital satisfaction and child adjustment in remarried versus nondivorced families.* Paper presented at the Southeastern Regional Meeting of the Society for Research in Child Development, Nashville, Tennessee.

Harter, S. (1982). The Perceived Competence Scale for Children. *Child Development, 53,* 87–97.

Hetherington, E. M. (1972). Effects of father absence on personality development in adolescent daughters. *Developmental Psychology, 7,* 313–326.

Hetherington, E. M. (1981). Children and divorce. In R. Henderson (Ed.), *Parent-child interaction: Theory, research and prospects.* New York: Academic Press.

Hetherington, E. M., Cox, M., & Cox, R. (1978). The aftermath of divorce. In J. H. Stevens, Jr. & M. Matthews (Eds.), *Mother-child, father-child relations* (pp. 110–155). Washington, DC: National Association for the Education of Young Children.

Hetherington, E. M., Cox, M., & Cox, R. (1979a). Family interaction and the social, emotional and cognitive development of children following divorce. In V. Vaughn & T. Brazelton (Eds.), *The family: Setting priorities* (pp. 89–128). New York: Science and Medicine Publishing Co.

Hetherington, E. M., Cox, M., & Cox, R. (1979b). Play and social interaction in children following divorce. *Journal of Social Issues, 35,* 26–49.

Hetherington, E. M., Cox, M., & Cox, R. (1982). Effects of divorce on parents and children. In M.E. Lamb (Ed.), *Nontraditional families: Parenting and child development* (pp. 233–288). Hillsdale, NJ: Lawrence Erlbaum.

Hetherington, E. M., Cox, M., & Cox, R. (1985). Long-term effects of divorce and remarriage on the adjustment of children. *Journal of the American Academy of Psychology, 24* (5), 518–530.

Pekarik, E. G., Prinz, R. J., Liebert, D. E., Weintraub, S., & Neale, J. M. (1976). The Pupil Evaluation Inventory. *Journal of Abnormal Child Psychology, 4,* 83–97.

Rotter, J. B. (1966). Generalized expectancies for internal versus external control of reinforcement. *Psychological Monographs, 80* (1, Whole No. 609).

Speilberger, C. D., Gorsuch, R. L., & Lushene, R. (1970). *State-Trait Anxiety Inventory.* Palo Alto, CA: Consulting Psychologists Press.

Wallerstein, J. S. (1986). Women after divorce: Preliminary report from a ten-year follow-up. *American Journal of Orthopsychiatry, 56* (1), 65–77.

Wallerstein, J. S. & Kelly, J. B. (1980). *Surviving the breakup: How children and parents cope with divorce.* New York: Basic Books.

Weiss, R. (1975). *Marital separation.* New York: Basic Books.

Resourceful and Vulnerable Children: Family Influence in Hard Times

G. H. Elder, Jr.

A. Caspi

T. van Nguyen

INTRODUCTION

Periods of drastic economic decline generally represent times of jeopardy for the welfare of children. In the Great Depression, observations pointed to a lost generation of young people. How would the large number of children growing up in families on public aid be able to withstand and possibly rise above their misfortune? Homeless, abused, and hungry children brought similar questions to mind. For all of the concern it is remarkable that we have so little evidence of uniform impairment among 'children of the Great Depression' (Elder, 1979). Even in the worst of times, some children manage to come through without undue strain or damage. But how is this achieved? What factors determine why only some children are adversely influenced by hard times? These questions are the orienting theme of our examination of factors that differentiate resourceful from vulnerable children in deprived families of the 1930s. In diverse economic situations, research on coping resources (Kasl, 1979; Kobasa, 1979) has brought greater appreciation for the resilience of individuals and their families. Within the field of developmental psychology, there is growing recognition of the need to identify and examine the adaptive and resilient individual and familial attributes that may condition the relationship of stress to children's impairment (Garmezy, Masten, & Tellegen, 1984).

This chapter examines selected personal and social resources (e.g., child's age and physical attractiveness, mother's support) that had important implications for the resilient or vulnerable status of children in two Depression cohorts (Elder, 1974; 1981): an adolescent cohort based on the Growth Study of children who were born in 1920–21 and grew up in the city of Oakland, California; and a cohort of preschool children who were born shortly before the Great Depression (1928–29) in the city of Berkeley, California. They are members of the Berkeley Guidance Study (Macfarlane, 1938).

Each cohort experienced a distinctive sequence of economic conditions and stresses. The 167 members of the Oakland cohort were children during the relatively prosperous 1920s and entered the adolescent years as the economy collapsed. They left high school just prior to war mobilization and the beginning of World War II. The 214 members of the Berkeley cohort experienced the Great Depression through the family during their early years of childhood. In many cases, hard times and family insecurity did not end until their adolescence in the Second World War. Each cohort's experience across the Depression years was recorded year by year through observations and interviews. As of 1929, three-fifths of the Oakland and Berkeley families were positioned in the middle class.

The resilience or vulnerability of children during a stressful time, such as the Great Depression brings two issues to mind: 1. the process by which economic hardship entails substantial health and developmental risks for children; and 2. factors that minimize or accentuate such risks. We begin this chapter by specifying causal paths linking family hardship to children's lives. Deprivational effects are traced through family adaptations, especially changes in father's behavior, in response to a changing environment. Next, two organizing propositions structure our analysis of conditional variations. Here we refer to variations in the causal process by which Depression hardship adversely influenced the welfare and development of children.

The first proposition centers on the personal resources of children in both cohorts, Oakland and Berkeley. We review evidence from our research on the role of children in modifying their own social environment, particularly the behavior of fathers under economic stress. Specifically, we consider the implications of children's age and sex, physical attractiveness, and temperamental characteristics (ill-tempered, irritable) before the economic crisis in shaping their family experiences and treatment by fathers.

The second proposition draws upon the resources of the Berkeley archive for an empirical test of the role of mothers in protecting children from economic stress and paternal maltreatment. The expansion of analytic models from a dyadic unit (i.e., father–child) to a family system (i.e., mother–father–child) requires knowledge of how interactions between two people influence and are influenced by a third person (e.g., Clarke-Stewart, 1978). The response of each person to the other is conditioned by their joint relationship to a third person. Thus, changes within any individual or relationship may affect all other persons and relationships. Bronfenbrenner (1979) has coined the term *second order effect* as a generic concept for these influences. Similar schemes for understanding the array of psychological influences that occur in social units larger than the dyad have been proposed by Parke, Power, and Gottman (1979) and Lewis and Feiring (1982).

The presentation of our results corresponds with progressively more complex elements in a model of the process by which families and children adapt to hard times (Moen, Kain, &

Elder, 1983): 1. Social and economic macro change is linked to children's lives through alterations in family relationships; 2. family relations take place in a reciprocal social system which involves mutual accommodation and adjustment between parent and child; and 3. parent–child relations are embedded in a network of family relationships. Thus, change in any one set of relationships inevitably influences others. We view stress in families as an interacting process. This requires identifying both the objective and subjective meanings of drastic change events; the salient attributes of families as a system of interactional personalities; and, finally, the resources individuals bring to change situations.

HARSH FATHERS IN STRESSFUL TIMES

The father's behavior during the Great Depression emerges as the critical causal link between family deprivation and children's well-being. Children were most likely to suffer adverse consequences when fathers became more explosive, tense, and emotionally unstable. Four studies using the Berkeley sample have explored the key role of fathers in mediating the influence of macroeconomic change on family relations and children's lives.

The first study examined father behavior as a link between heavy income loss and marital discord. In a second study, we extended these findings to an analysis of the arbitrary and punitive behavior of fathers during the early 1930s. A third project identified circumstances under which men were most and least likely to become explosive and unstable in stressful circumstances, and a fourth analysis traced the interplay of unstable men and unstable families across four generations. Families that suffered heavy income losses become more discordant in the marital relationship, owing largely to rising financial disputes and the more irritable, tense, and volatile state of men (Liker & Elder, 1983). The latter change represented a primary determinant of the abusive parenting behavior of men (Elder, Liker, & Cross, 1984). The more irritable men became under economic pressure, the more they tended to behave punitively and arbitrarily toward their offspring. Finally, economic stress generally accentuated the explosive behavior of men, but it did so primarily when they ranked initially high on this characteristic (Elder, Liker, & Jaworski, 1984). Hard times made explosive men more explosive.

From an intergenerational perspective, irritable, explosive husbands and fathers emerged as a primary source of family instability. In turn, family turmoil and instability increased the prospects of an irritable, unstable pattern of behavior in the lives of children (Elder, Caspi, & Downey, 1985). Within a single generation of the Berkeley study, unstable family relationships made no significant difference in the unstable behavior of men. Their causal role is intergenerational, from family of origin to the behavioral style of children and then to the latter's family behavior in adulthood. The thread of continuity extends across four generations, although its strength varies greatly according to specific conditions.

In all of the Depression research to date, we find that mothers did not become more unstable under economic stress and income loss did not directly increase their punitive or arbitrary behavior. A good many women were relatively unstable before the economic crisis and, just as for fathers, these qualities increased the likelihood of child disturbance. However, only men's behavior linked economic stress to the experience of children in the Great Depression. One possible explanation for this sex difference centers on the more personal nature of income and job loss among men than among wives and mothers. Family misfortune was often regarded as a consequence of men's losses. Women were deprived of family support when their husbands lost jobs and income, but men lost a core dimension of their social significance. Indeed, the overall pattern of men's reactions to sudden economic loss conforms to a theory of force in regaining control over life circumstances (Goode, 1971). Loss of control over one's life situation prompted efforts to regain control. Force is one means to this end.

Economic hardship was often a change agent of family life, and the father's behavior emerged as a critical link between Depression hardship and the family experience of the children. But children's characteristics also played an important role in determining their experiences in hard-pressed families. Project research has identified some attributes and behavior of children that moderated the adverse influence of economic hardship and father maltreatment on their own development and well-being.

CHILDREN AS AGENTS OF THEIR FAMILY EXPERIENCE

The interplay of family stressors and parent behavior is partly a function of the attributes and behavior of children. Increasingly, studies are showing the influence of children on the behavior of parents (Lerner & Spanier, 1978). In this section we review evidence of children as potential agents of their own family experience in the Great Depression, especially as collaborators in their treatment by deprived fathers. Using the Oakland and Berkeley cohorts, our studies identify four factors that bear upon the resourceful or vulnerable status of children and on their insulation from, or increased exposure to, parental maltreatment in hardpressed families: age, sex, physical attractiveness, and temperamental characteristics.

Age and Sex Variations

Drastic change affects people of different ages in different ways. This variability is reflected, in part, by the options and coping resources people of different ages bring to the adaptation process. The Oakland adolescents in *Children of the Great Depression* (Elder, 1974) encountered hard times when they were beyond the years of family dependency and they entered adulthood after the economy had begun to revive. By contrast, children in the Berkeley cohort, seven to eight years younger than their Oakland counterparts, were less than two years old when the economy collapsed and they remained exclusively within the family through the worst years of the decade. Figure 1 presents the key contrasts in this comparison of the two cohorts.

Cohort differences between the Oakland and Berkeley samples appear in this age contrast, and in the variable sequence of hard times and prosperity from early childhood to the adult years. Comparison of the Oakland Growth and the Berkeley Guidance samples offered a rare opportunity to examine age and sex variations in vulnerability to economic hardship. Both studies were launched within the same research institute and they relied upon similar measures of social, psychological, and family behavior. The two cohorts also shared the same ecological setting within the eastern region of the San Francisco Bay area.

Children's age and sex during the Depression crisis had implications for their roles and vulnerability within the family. In the Oakland families, adolescent boys and girls in deprived circumstances were often called upon to assume major responsibilities within and outside the household. Girls took on greater household responsibilities when their mothers worked and

a good many held paid jobs, as did boys from similar circumstances. Family change of this sort enhanced the social independence of boys. But for girls greater family involvement also meant greater exposure to family discord, tension, and abuse. From theory and research, we expected the effect of Depression hardship to be even more severe in the lives of young children (Berkeley cohort), when compared to adolescents of the Oakland cohort (Elder, 1979). Moreover, this difference should be especially pronounced among young boys in view of their known vulnerability to family stress, marital tension and the abusive behavior of fathers (Rutter, 1979).

In order to assess the effect of children's age in their family experience, we used similar measurements from the Oakland and Berkeley cohorts to construct and estimate a simple causal model. The effects of family deprivation (1929–33) and social class (1929) were estimated on scales of adolescent and adult (age 40) functioning. For both cohorts, income change was measured by comparing 1929 family income and the figure for 1933 (or the worst year). Taking into account the sharp decline in cost of living within the San Francisco Bay area (about 25% in 1933) and the correlation between income and asset loss, all families that lost at least 35% of their income were classified as economically deprived. Smaller losses placed fam-

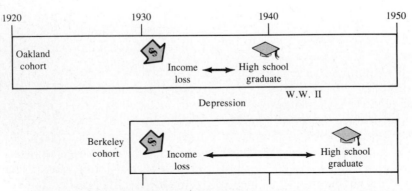

FIGURE 1 Interaction of Depression hardship and life stage. A comparison of the Berkeley and Oakland cohorts.

ilies in the nondeprived category. The two-factor Hollingshead index of family standing before the Depression (in 1929) was used in both cohorts. One factor is father's education and the other is his occupational status. California Q-sort (Block, 1971) items were available on both cohorts for the adolescent and adult years. From correlational analyses, we constructed identical sets of measures of psychosocial functioning for the two cohorts in both time periods (see Elder, 1979). The scales tapped feelings of self-inadequacy, goal orientation, passive-submissive behavior, and social competence. Some illustrative results from the analysis of self-inadequacy are summarized in Fig. 2.

In adolescence and at mid-life (age 40), the effects of family deprivation were negative primarily among the Berkeley males. The sons of deprived parents were more likely to be judged relatively low on self-adequacy, goal orientation, and social competence in adolescence, when compared with their nondeprived counterparts. By comparison, no such disadvantage was observed among the Oakland males in adolescence. Indeed, the costs of family deprivation for young boys in the Berkeley cohort were matched in some respects by the developmental gains of older boys in the Oakland cohort. In the latter group, boys from deprived homes were judged even more resilient and resourceful than the nondeprived, while in the Berkeley cohort deprived boys were consistently at a disadvantage.

Among females, the short-term effects of family deprivation were generally positive in the Berkeley (preschool) cohort and moderately negative in the Oakland (adolescent) cohort. The same pattern emerged in adulthood although it was not as pronounced. At least on psychological well-being, the Berkeley girls from deprived families had more in common with the Oakland boys than with males of similar age. In combination, these results suggest that risk factors vary in type and relative influence along the life course and between the

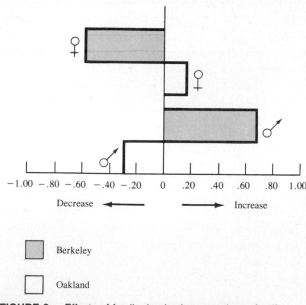

FIGURE 2 Effects of family deprivation on ratings of self-inadequacy. Metric regression coefficients (adjusted for effects of class origin, 1929).

sexes. Consistent with previous research (Rutter & Madge, 1976), family stress seems more pathogenic for boys than girls in early childhood, though not in early adolescence. During the latter period girls appear to be at greater risk than boys (cf. Werner & Smith, 1982). Acute social pressures and developmental change in early adolescence may have contributed to the psychological risk observed among adolescent girls. Other longitudinal studies (e.g., Simmons, Blyth, Van Cleave, & Bush, 1979) are beginning to identify early adolescence as a time of distinctive vulnerability for girls.

The Conditional Effects of Physical Attractiveness

Hard times caught the Oakland girls in transition to the social world of adolescence with its pressures for popularity and dating. The psychic costs of this pressure were especially acute for girls who lacked appropriate dress and material resources for social dating. Earlier analyses (Elder, 1974: Chapter 6) found that the Oakland girls, but not boys, were judged ''less well-groomed'' during early adolescence if they came from deprived families in the '30s, whether middle or working class. Some implications of this handicap appear during junior high school. On self-reports, girls from deprived families in both social classes scored higher than the nondeprived on social unhappiness and on feelings of being excluded from student activities. Mothers also perceived differences of this sort. Mothers from deprived families ranked their daughters higher on hurt feelings, worries, and self-consciousness than mothers from nondeprived families.

Some of this emotional distress may have stemmed from parental maltreatment within the family, especially from the father. Adolescent girls were less powerful from a physical standpoint than boys of similar age, and consequently they may have been more vulnerable to abusive behavior by the father. This logic ap-

plies even more readily to the least attractive girls in the Oakland cohort. In this section we review some evidence on the physical characteristics of girls that may have prompted their maltreatment by fathers in hard times.

Physical maturation often influences the way in which one is seen by others and the expectations that are held by these others (Clausen, 1975). Physically attractive children are more often the recipients of positive attributions from others. Adults also tend to assign less blame to physically attractive children, regardless of the facts (Dion, 1972). Moreover, attractive children generally think well of themselves (Sorell & Nowak, 1981). They rank high on self-confidence and assertiveness, qualities that are not characteristic of the victimized. Overall, we assumed that the least attractive members of the Oakland cohort would be at greater risk than attractive children, and that this risk was greatest among adolescent girls. Research suggests that evaluations along social dimensions are affected not only by the attractiveness level, but also by sex, with more differences appearing between attractive and unattractive females than between similarly grouped males (e.g., Bar-Tal & Saxe, 1976). Hence, we expected attractiveness to operate as a powerful conditional factor among adolescent girls in the Great Depression.

Project research (Elder, Van Nguyen, & Caspi, 1985) tends to confirm this reasoning with newly developed measures of rejecting, exploitive, and supportive behavior of fathers. All measures were constructed from parenting data in 1931–1934. The rejecting parent, indexed by four ratings, is described as ''negatively responsive to child,'' ''neglecting,'' ''rejecting,'' and ''not dependable.'' The exploitive parent, indexed by two ratings, is ''overdemanding,'' and ''exploitive.'' Parental supportiveness is indexed by a single rating. Using a general index of physical attractiveness derived from observational ratings in junior high school, we classified girls as ''unattractive'' if they had scores below the median. All other girls were placed in the "attractive" category. For each group, we estimated the effects of economic hardship on father's behavior, with adjustments for social class before the onset of Depression hardship. The results are summarized in Fig. 3.

Girls' attractiveness made a substantial difference in the parenting outcomes of economic deprivation among Oakland fathers but not among mothers. Economic hardship increased father's rejecting behavior only when daughters ranked low on physical attractiveness. In addition, if girls were unattractive, family hardship accentuated father's exploitive behavior and diminished his supportiveness. Of additional interest is the direction of observed relationships in the contrasting adolescent subgroups.

In two of the models the signs of the coefficients are reversed. Attractive girls were not simply insulated from the psychic costs of economic hardship. In some cases, hard times actually increased the supportive and benign qualities of their fathers. Comparable analyses for attractive and unattractive adolescent boys revealed no significant effects or variations of economic hardship on father's behavior toward sons. The conditional effect of physical attractiveness is restricted to adolescent girls.

The strength of this conditional outcome is especially noteworthy when we consider data limitations, in particular our reliance on reports by wives, children, and staff workers for information regarding the behavior of fathers. The Oakland fathers were never interviewed,

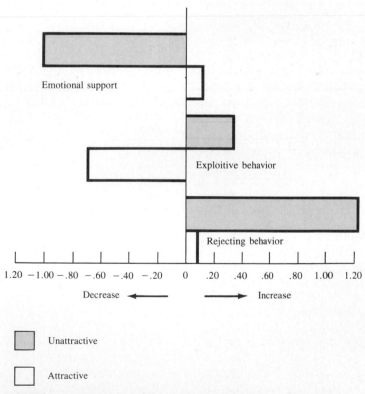

FIGURE 3 Deprivation effects on father's behavior toward daughter by her physical attractiveness. Metric regression coefficients (adjusted for effects of class origin, 1929).

whereas their wives were interviewed on three occasions, 1932, 1934, and 1936. Whatever the-full implications of this data source, they are likely to work against the attractiveness effect. According to a variety of studies of neglect and abuse in the family (Kadushin & Martin, 1981), the evidence suggests that wives and mothers are apt to underreport the paternal abuse of children. If so, the link between income loss and paternal maltreatment among relatively unattractive daughters would represent an underestimate of the actual causal relation.

Problem Child and Problem Father

Another view of the socially unattractive child is provided by behavior which has negative implications for parents. Examples include temper outbursts and quarrelsome behavior. From research completed on the Berkeley cohort (Elder et al., 1984), it is clear that young boys and girls (about 18 months old) who were observed as problematic in behavior (e.g., inclined toward tantrums, irritability, negativism) before the Depression experienced a greater risk of arbitrary and punitive treatment by father during the worst years when compared to less problematic children. The Institute staff encountered some difficulty in achieving an accurate reading on behavior at 18 months, even with the detailed reports of mother. For this reason, a problem child index was constructed as the best alternative under the circumstances. The index represents the percentage of all assessments on the child (some 35 items) that indicate some form of a behavior problem. Not surprisingly, items that had the most variance and hence dominated the index were typically overt, disruptive behaviors such as temper tantrums.

Problem boys and girls in 1930 were not distinguished by fathers with hostile feelings at that time, but three years later in the Depression they were more likely to encounter extreme and arbitrary (inconsistent) discipline by father than nonproblematic children. Extreme

behavior refers to an exaggerated disciplinary style, such as severe punishment and indifference. Arbitrary behavior refers to inconsistent disciplinary practices. Even with adjustments for the initial irritability of the fathers (1930), these correlations remain the same. In order to specify these relationships more precisely in the Depression years, we estimated the effect of a child's initial problem behavior on the father's behavior under two conditions: among fathers who were hostile toward the child before the economic crisis (in 1930) and among those who ranked below average on this scale. We expected to find the strongest effect of problem children on the arbitrary behavior of fathers in the hostile group.

Contrary to expectations, relatively hostile fathers were not locked into a cumulative exchange of problem behavior with children. This dependency was more common among initially warm or friendly fathers. The status of the problem child in 1930 was only predictive of the father's arbitrariness when the father had a positive relationship to the child in question. Upon reflection, the findings suggest that father hostility minimized a contingent relationship between father and child. That is, hostile fathers were apt to behave arbitrarily toward children *regardless* of how their children behaved. By comparison, affectionate fathers were more likely to behave arbitrarily in *response* to the problem conduct of their children. Such conduct served to elicit similar behavior from the father.

Our studies of parent–child behavior in hard times began with the premise that influence flows from parent to child and from child to parent. The results we have summarized support this premise. The effect of hard times on children in the 1930s depended on whether fathers became more arbitrary and punitive, but this process also varied according to the stimulus characteristics of the child. Factors such as the child's age, sex, physical attractiveness and temperament conditioned father–child dynamics and the effects of economic hardship. But what about mothers? They are absent from this causal sequence. The following section adds mothers to the picture of hardpressed families during the 1930s.

UNSTABLE FATHERS, PROBLEM CHILDREN, AND ECONOMIC STRESS: THE MODERATING INFLUENCE OF THE MOTHER

The Berkeley children entered the Depression crisis with different relationships to their mothers. Some were the recipients of maternal warmth and affection, while others lacked such nurturance. The implications of this pre-Depression variation are suggested by the dependency of young preschool children on their family environment and especially on the mother. Maternal responsiveness to child cues affects both immediate and long-term adaptations by children (Schaffer, 1977), and, in times of stress, the emotional support and assurance of mother can protect children from conflicts and overwhelming demands (Caplan, 1976). Using data from the Berkeley archive, we now examine the effects of family hardship and punitive fathers on the behavior of children whose mothers differ sharply on expressed affection. Following this analysis, we consider the effects of children on fathers and of fathers on children under different conditions of maternal affection.

Maternal Affection and Family Stress

Our general model defines children's temper outbursts (1933–35) as the outcome of a process whereby father instability and Depression income loss increased the likelihood of arbitrary behavior by father. The more arbitrary the discipline of father, the greater the likelihood of temper outbursts by his children. According to project research, unstable fathers and heavy income loss were especially conducive to children's temper outbursts, and this influence was largely mediated by father's arbitrary behavior (Elder et al., 1984). The important question at this point is the extent to which the affectional

support of mother moderated the influence of income loss and father instability on child behavior.

Before turning to the analysis itself, we will describe the key measures. A more detailed account can be found in Elder et al. (1984). Behavior ratings on the parents in 1930 are based on judgments by an interviewer (with the mother and father) and a home observer. An example is the index of father's instability, a measure based on the average of three behavior ratings: irritable, nervous instability, and tense-worrisome (average $r = 0.51$). The arbitrary discipline of father for 1933–35 represents an average of annual ratings on a five-point scale. Data were obtained from interviews with mothers only. Arbitrary refers at the extreme to inconsistent discipline that expresses the mood of the parent such that the "child never knows what to expect." The child temper tantrum index includes two ratings: severity and frequency of tantrums. Severe tantrums take the form of "biting, kicking, striking, throwing things and screaming." Tantrum frequency ranged from one per month to several times a day. The temper index was created by obtaining the product of severity and frequency of tantrums for 1933–35. This measure captures a key identifying characteristic of children classified as aggressive (Achenbach, 1978). Moreover, severe and frequent tantrums have been shown to be highly contingent on the disciplinary strategies of parents (Patterson, 1982).

To investigate the moderating influence of maternal sentiment, we stratified the Berkeley sample by a pre-Depression measure (1930) of mother's demonstration of affection toward the child. For purposes of analysis, we classified mothers as 'undemonstrative' if they had scores below the median and as 'affectionate' if they had scores above the median. The rating of mother's demonstrativeness is *not* significantly correlated with the antecedent variables in this model.

Mother's attitude toward the study child was found to have implications for father's behavior toward the child under conditions of severe income loss. We gain valuable information about the determinants of arbitrary parenting by treating the contrasting family subgroups separately. In particular, a family context defined by an initially undemonstrative mother is most likely to lead to the outward expression of the father's anger through physical and verbal force, especially when prompted by economic misfortune. Moreover, income loss is positively related to the temper outbursts of children only in families with an undemonstrative mother.

When measured prior to the Depression as a sentiment ranging from expressive of affection to undemonstrative, this orientation tells us a good deal about the influence of economic hardship on child disturbance and on the nature of father's action under stress. The overall pattern in homes with undemonstrative mothers suggests a lack of fatherly regulation in the household, or the absence of effective normative constraints in hard times, which are associated with child disturbance. The aversive dynamics of family stress were relatively limited when mothers were affectionate toward the study child. Family units with strong affective mother–child bonds restrained the arbitrary treatment of children by Depression fathers, and children with warm, affectionate mothers were under some protection from economic hardship. Drastic income loss increased the risk of children's problem behavior, but only in families characterized by a weak mother–child bond.

Mother's initial attitude toward the study child differentiates contrasting family trajectories under the economic pressures of the 1930s. One leads toward the maltreatment of children and their subsequent problem behavior; the other involves a more benign course in which the child is sheltered from the adverse influence of Depression hardship and the punitive hand of fathers. The contrasting dynamics of the two groups highlight the explanatory usefulness of comparing family processes under different conditions. The mother's relationship to the study child before the onset of hard times emerges as an important contextual determinant of how that child fared in Depression families. Warm affective ties to the child diminished the risk of impairment through economic pressures and the father's arbitrary behavior. Hard times were most likely to turn into bad times when children lacked the affectional and emotional support of their mothers.

Maternal Affection and Father–Child Influences

From previous results we know that children modified the nature of fathers' responses in hard times. Bearing in mind the likelihood of reciprocal influences, the analysis moves now to consider how the mother's relationship to the child modified father–child interactions. Does this process vary by the mother's initial attitude toward the child, whether negative or positive?

Different approaches are available for estimating the reciprocal influence of fathers and children in the 1930s. The 1930 father and child measures substantially affect their corresponding measures in 1933–35. Unstable fathers at Time 1 were likely to be arbitrary in the Depression and problem children were prone to temper tantrums over this time period. The evidence also supports the assumption of reciprocal influences between father and child. However the important question at this point is the extent to which the affectional support of the mother conditioned these influences. If we contrast the family subgroups (affectionate vs. undemonstrative) and examine the links between the problem behavior of the father and child in 1930 to the father's arbitrariness in 1933–35, there are no appreciable differences between the groups. For example, children classified as 'problematic' were likely to elicit the father's arbitrary behavior regardless of maternal sentiments. This significant effect, even in the face of potentially buffering or moderating influences, attests to the strength of children's capacity to influence parents.

We have noted the accentuation of father and child problem behavior when mothers were undemonstrative. We use the concept of *accentuation* to describe an increase in emphasis of an already prominent characteristic due to its reinforcement by selected contexts and settings (e.g., Feldman & Weiler, 1976). As expected, the initial problem status of father and child is magnified in the context of undemonstrative mothers. Only in families with undemonstrative mothers were problem children likely to persist in their out-of-control, aggressive behavior. The father's problem status shows a similar, though nonsignificant trend. In the 'affection' context, initial problem behaviors (both father's and child's) are less pronounced and their variation has little bearing upon the subsequent temper tantrums of children.

The findings summarized in this section underscore the critical nature of the ecological niche occupied by children and their families as well as highlighting major limitations of global descriptive research on socioeconomic factors in the lives of children and adults. All too often research proceeds no further than the demonstration of a simple association between two variables (e.g., socioeconomic stress or change with indicators of child behavior) which are assumed to be ordered in causal sequence. Project research suggests that this relationship is more accurately specified by intervening mechanisms, such as alterations in family relationships and the predictability or coherence of a home environment. Moreover, the influence of environmental stressors must be considered in terms of the family context in which they operate (e.g., Bronfenbrenner & Crouter, 1983), and personal relationships within the family should be considered in terms of a network of interactions (e.g., Hinde, 1979). These features are central to the ecological study of human development.

CONCLUSION

Drastic change and life stress do not have uniform effects on all children. Whether a given child is adversely affected by income loss depends on other variables that moderate the impact of that change. A critical question for research on stressful life events concerns the nature of those variables that determine which individuals are likely to be adversely affected by drastic change and which are likely to be spared its attendant hardships (Johnson & Sarason, 1979). What is different about the children who rise above disadvantage? What are the protective or ameliorating circumstances? Conversely, we may ask, what factors accentuate the adverse influence of stressful times on children's lives?

To understand the impact of economic hardship on the personality and behavior of children requires knowledge of adaptations chosen and played out by parents. The effects of hard times are not necessarily exercised directly. They may be produced indirectly through their disorganizing effect on family relations. Fathers represent the critical link between Depression hardship and children's experience. But the punitive and arbitrary behavior of fathers in the 1930s was expressed only when potentiating factors surpassed compensatory ones. Thus, economic loss increased the instability of fathers who were initially unstable, and thereby increased the developmental risk of young children. The risk was much less for children of initially resourceful fathers who were relatively calm under stress.

Turning to the child, project research identifies several factors that protected children from harsh parenting in Depression families. The physical attractiveness of adolescent girls proved to be a valuable asset, and this resource conditioned father's behavior toward them in hard times. Whether through impression management or implicit attribution processes, children often shaped the way they were treated, and especially their father's behavior. Moreover, under certain conditions, children's overt behavior (e.g., ill-tempered, irritable) accelerated family tensions and the risk of their maltreatment by hard-pressed fathers. Consistent with a social interactional perspective (Patterson & Reid, unpublished manuscript), our findings suggest that characteristics and reactions of victimized children often strengthened and maintained the aversive behaviors of fathers.

To explicate the nature of family dynamics in hard times requires a synthetic framework that links family members. To this end, the dyadic model orienting much of our research proved to be deficient. An exclusive focus on father–child dynamics obscures variability within particular family contexts and ignores the interplay among different family systems. In the Depression era, mothers were not as directly affected by income loss as fathers, but they played a major role in their children's development. To understand the differing, but mutually consequential, roles of father and mother in the 1930s, it is necessary to order them in relation to the sequential phases of economic crisis and family adaptation.

Fathers are prominent in our analysis of Depression families because economic misfortune was typically the first-hand experience of men. Their response to this loss intensified the social consequences of income loss. By contrast, mothers in Depression families stand out as coping and recovery figures. Following the trauma of economic crisis and the impairment of husbands and fathers, the story of family survival often centered on the role of women in the household economy and in the labor force (Elder, 1974), and, as the present findings additionally suggest, in the lives of children. Patterns of family relations (i.e., mother–child) prior to the deprivation event emerge as particularly critical determinants of subsequent family relations (i.e., father–child) and child outcomes. The influence of economic hardship, as well as father's behavior, vary by the family context in which the child resides, and stresses

in family life were often countered by the mother's nurturant relationship to the child. These findings are consistent with results from studies of families with a parent diagnosed as having a psychiatric disorder. Rutter (1979) notes that conduct disorders of children in such discordant homes were much less evident if children had a good relationship with at least one parent. Effective coping with difficult times thus represents a product of interacting persons; it is not merely individual behavior in isolation from the actions and attitudes of others.

External events, such as the Great Depression, can affect children, as well as their parents, in different ways. Drastic changes are not synonymous with stressful changes and hard times do not necessarily foreshadow bad times. The causal sequence bridging Depression hardship and children's welfare is conditioned by a host of individual and contextual factors. These factors are underscored by recognizing children as agents of their own family experience and the multiple relationships which define patterns of family adaptation in hard times.

REFERENCES

Achenbach, T. M. (1978) The child behavior profile. I: Boys aged 6 through 11. *Journal of Consulting and Clinical Psychology, 46,* 478–488

Bar-Tal, D. & Saxe, L. (1976) Perceptions of similarly attractive couples and individuals. *Journal of Personality and Social Psychology, 33,* 772–781

Block, J. (1971) *Lives through time.* Berkeley, CA: Bancroft

Bronfenbrenner, U. (1979) *The ecology of human development.* Cambridge, Mass: Harvard University Press

Bronfenbrenner, U. & Crouter, A. C. (1983) The evolution of environmental models in developmental research. In W. Kessen (Ed.), *Handbook of child psychology, Vol. I. History, theory, and methods.* New York: Wiley

Caplan, G. (1976) The family as support system. In G. Caplan & M. Killilea (Eds.), *Support systems and mutual help: Multidisciplinary explorations.* New York: Grune and Stratton

Clarke-Stewart, K. A. (1978) And daddy makes three: The father's impact on mother and young child. *Child Development, 49,* 466–478

Clausen, J. A. (1975) The social meaning of differential physical and sexual maturation. In S. E. Dragstin & G. H. Elder, Jr. (Eds.), *Adolescence in the life cycle: Psychological change and social context.* New York: Halsted

Dion, K. (1972) Physical attractiveness and evaluations of children's transgressions. *Journal of Personality and Social Psychology, 24,* 207–213

Elder, G. H., Jr. (1974) *Children of the Great Depression.* Chicago: University of Chicago Press

Elder, G. H., Jr. (1979) Historical change in life patterns and personality. In P. B. Baltes & O. G. Brim, Jr. (Eds.), *Life span development and behavior, Vol. 2.* New York: Academic

Elder, G. H., Jr. (1981) Social history in life experience. In D. H. Eichorn, J. A. Clausen, N. Haan, M. P. Honzik, & P. H. Mussen (Eds.), *Present and past in middle life.* New York: Academic

Elder, G. H., Jr., Caspi, A., & Downey, G. (1985) Problem behavior and family relationships: A multi-generational analysis. In A. Sorensen, F. Weinert, & L. Sherrod (Eds.), *Human development and the life course. Multidisciplinary perspectives.* Hillsdale, NJ: Erlbaum

Elder, G. H., Jr., Liker, J. K., & Cross, C. E. (1984) Parent–child behavior in the Great Depression: Life course and intergenerational influences. In P. B. Baltes & O. G. Brim, Jr. (Eds.), *Life span development and behavior, Vol. 6.* New York: Academic

Elder, G. H., Jr., Liker, J. K., & Jaworski, B. J. (1984) Hard times in lives: Historical influences from the 1930s to old age in postwar America. In K. McCluskey & H. W. Reese (Eds.), *Life span developmental psychology: Cohort and historical effects.* New York: Academic

Elder, G. H., Jr., Van Nguyen, T., & Caspi, A. (1985) Linking family hardship to children's lives. *Child Development, 56,* 361–375

Feldman, K. A. & Weiler, J. (1976) Changes in initial differences among major-field groups: An exploration of the "accentuation effect." In W. H. Sewell, R. M. Hauser, & D. L. Featherman

(Eds.), *Schooling and achievement in American society.* New York: Academic

Garmezy, N., Masten, A. S., & Tellegen, A. (1984) The study of stress and competence in children: A building block for developmental psychopathology. *Child Development, 55,* 97–111

Goode, W. J. (1971) Force and violence in the family. *Journal of Marriage and the Family, 33,* 624–636

Hinde, R. A. (1979) *Towards understanding relationships.* London: Academic

Johnson, J. H. & Sarason, I. G. (1979) Moderator variables in life stress research. In I. G. Sarason & C. D. Spielberg (Eds.), *Stress and anxiety, Vol. 6.* Washington: Hemisphere

Kadushin, A. & Martin, J. A. (1981) *Child abuse: An interactional event.* New York: Columbia University Press

Kasl, S. V. (1979) Changes in mental health status associated with job loss and retirement. In J. E. Barrett (Ed.), *Stress and mental disorder.* New York: Raven

Kobasa, S. C. (1979) Stressful life events, personality, and health: An inquiry into hardiness. *Journal of Personality and Social Psychology, 37,* 1–11

Lerner, R. M. & Spanier, G. B. (Eds.) (1978) *Child influences on marital and family interactions.* New York: Academic

Lewis, M. & Feiring, C. (1982) Direct and indirect interactions in social relations. In L. Lipsitt (Ed.), *Advances in infancy research, Vol, 1.* Norwood, NJ: Ablex

Liker, J. K. & Elder, G. H., Jr. (1983) Economic hardship and marital relations in the 1930s. *American Sociological Review, 48,* 343–359

Macfarlane, J. W. (1938) Studies in child guidance. I: Methodology of data collection and organization. *Monographs of the society for research in child development, 3* (serial no. 6)

Moen, P., Kain, E. L., & Elder, G. H., Jr. (1983) Economic conditions and family life: Contemporary and historical perspectives. In R. Nelson & F. Skidmore (Eds.), *American families and the economy.* Washington, DC: National Academy

Parke, R. D., Power, T. G., & Gottman, J. (1979) Conceptualizing and quantifying influence patterns in the family triad. In M. E. Lamb, S. J. Suomi & G. R. Stephenson (Eds.), *Social interaction analysis: Methodological issues.* Madison: University of Wisconsin Press

Patterson, G. R. (1982) *Coercive family process: A social learning approach.* Eugene, OR: Castalia

Patterson, G. R. & Reid, J. B. (1985) Social interactional processes within the family: The study of moment by moment family transactions in which human social development is imbedded. *Journal of Applied Developmental Psychology, 5,* 237–262

Rutter, M. (1979) Maternal deprivation, 1972–1978: New findings, new concepts, new approaches. *Child Development, 50,* 283–305

Rutter, M. (1979) Protective factors in children's responses to stress and disadvantage. In M. W. Kent & J. E. Rolf (Eds.), *Primary prevention of psychopathology, Vol. 3. Social competence in children.* Hanover, NH: University Press of New England

Rutter, M. & Madge, N. (1976) *Cycles of disadvantage: A review of research.* London: Heinemann

Schaffer, R. (1977) *Mothering.* Cambridge, MA: Harvard University Press

Simmons, R. G., Blyth, D. A., Van Cleave, E. F., & Bush, D. M. (1979) Entry into adolescence: The impact of school structure, puberty and early dating on self-esteem. *American Sociological Review, 44,* 948–967

Sorell, G. T. & Nowak, C. A. (1981) The role of physical attractiveness as a contributor to individual development. In R. M. Lerner & N. A. Busch-Rossnagel (Eds.), *Individuals as producers of their own development.* New York: Academic

Werner, E. E. & Smith, R. S. (1982) *Vulnerable but invincible: A study of resilient children.* New York: McGraw-Hill

---

READING 37

Teenage Sexuality, Pregnancy, and Childbearing

Frank F. Furstenberg, Jr.,
Richard Lincoln
Jane Menken

Contrary to popular impression, teenage childbearing in the United States has been on the decline during the past decade. Moreover, the newly discovered "epidemic" of adolescent pregnancy is not recent; elevated levels of teenage childbearing can be traced to the beginning of the baby boom after the Second World War. Nevertheless, the issue does seem to be more salient now than ever before. In this overview, we shall touch on some of the reasons. We intend to look at evidence on the social consequences of teenage childbearing for adolescent parents, their offspring, and members of their family of origin; examine briefly some of the available clues to the determinants of early parenthood; and consider some of the policy initiatives available to prevent premature childbearing or to ameliorate its deleterious effects.

TEENAGE CHILDBEARING AS A SOCIAL ISSUE

Whether we conclude that adolescent fertility is a problem of growing or diminishing significance rests largely on how we define adolescence and how we measure fertility. Table 1 presents an array of natality statistics for teenagers for the period 1950–1977. Depending on which indicator, which specific time period, and which age segment we examine, we may form quite different impressions of the current situation. The statistics can provide either some degree of reassurance or considerable cause for alarm. They demonstrate first that teenage fertility is not a rare or even an unusual event. According to 1977 rates, some 10 percent of women give birth before age 18, and more than 20 percent do so by age 20. Considered in terms of absolute numbers, adolescent (or teenage) childbearing has fallen significantly since the late 1960s and early 1970s. Even among the population younger than 18, there has been a decline recently in the number of births. One explanation for this downward trend is that the number of adolescents is not growing as rapidly as it did up to 1970. As the baby-boom children reached adolescence during the 1960s, an increase in adolescent births was inevitable unless the susceptibility of teenagers to pregnancy decreased enough to offset the numerical increase. Conversely, the teenage population has declined in size in recent years, so that even if adolescent fertility rates had remained constant, the number of births would have fallen. In fact, teenagers, especially 18- and 19-year-olds, are now less likely to have children than they used to be. Their fertility rate (the number of births per 1,000 women in the 15–19-year-old age group), has dropped off sharply since the end of the baby boom 20 years ago. Both these trends—the shrinking pool of teenagers and the decline in their birthrate—are likely to continue in the near future, suggesting that the absolute number of adolescent births may decline still further in the next few years.

If both the numbers and rates of births have fallen, then what has generated the intense concern about early childbearing in the past few years? Is adolescent parenthood a socially manufactured problem created by the mass media to generate public interest, or by government officials or private agencies in order to extend their social programs? We think not. If we look at the two lower panels of Table 1, we can see the basis for the recent focus of attention on the subject: both the absolute and the relative declines in adolescent fertility have been restricted to married teenagers. Out-of-wedlock childbearing has risen during the same period that marital childbearing among the young has fallen. While most teenagers who have babies are married when the birth occurs, if present trends continue it will not be long before most adolescent births take place outside marriage. In 1955, approximately 85 percent of the births

among the under-20 population occurred to married women; by 1977, the proportion was only 56 percent. When these figures are broken down by age, we can see that nonmarital childbearing has risen for both older and younger adolescents. Indeed, nearly 60 percent of 1977 births to females under age 18 took place out of wedlock. For the youngest teenagers, girls under 15, fertility, nearly all of it out of wedlock, increased sharply in the late 1960s and early 1970s, and only recently has declined slightly.

Fertility rates have long differed between blacks and whites in the United States. Table 2 shows that rates in the 1970s have been declining more rapidly for blacks than for whites. In fact, out-of-wedlock birthrates among white adolescents have risen sharply, suggesting that racial differences in sexual activity and pregnancy risks are diminishing. As early childbearing is seen more clearly as a problem affecting the white middle class, more vocal demands for attention and solutions are being heard.

Whether it is justified or not, out-of-wedlock births invariably generate more concern about the well-being of the mother and child than births that occur within marriage. (Later we shall show that we should be just as concerned about marital as nonmarital teenage fertility.) In fact, one might argue plausibly that the alarm surrounding early childbearing has been largely provoked by moral concern regarding the fact that an increasing number of teenagers are failing to marry when pregnancy occurs. If these teenagers did marry, or continued to drop out of school at the same very high rates that they did in the 1950s and early 1960s, the problem might well have continued to escape public notice. For many years, pregnancy was the primary reason given by young adolescent girls for leaving school. Few school systems encouraged pregnant girls to attend special classes, even when they were provided, and even fewer actively encouraged or aided young mothers to return to school. Because they were no longer visible, it was easy to ignore their

TABLE 1   SELECTED NATALITY INDICATORS FOR WOMEN UNDER 20, UNITED STATES, 1950-1977

	Year						
Age	1950	1955	1960	1965	1970	1975	1977
No. of births (in 000s)							
15–19	—	484	587	591	645	582	559
18–19	—	334	405	402	421	355	345
15–17	—	150	182	189	224	227	214
<15	—	5	7	8	12	13	11
Birthrates (per 1,000 women)							
15–19	81.6	90.3	89.1	70.4	68.3	56.3	53.7
18–19	—	—	—	—	114.4	85.7	81.9
15–17	—	—	—	—	38.8	36.6	34.5
<15	1.0	0.9	0.8	0.8	1.2	1.3	1.2
Birthrates by marital status							
Marital (per 1,000 married)							
15–19	410.4	460.2	530.6	462.3	443.7	315.8	—
Out-of-wedlock (per 1,000 unmarried)							
15–19	12.6	15.1	15.3	16.7	22.4	24.2	25.5
18–19					32.9	32.8	35.0
15–17					17.1	19.5	20.7
Ratios of out-of-wedlock births							
(per 1,000 births)							
15–19	—	142	148	208	295	382	429
18–19	—	102	107	152	224	298	344
15–17	—	232	240	327	430	514	566
<15	—	663	679	785	808	870	882

Sources: DHEW, National Center for Health Statistics, Vital Statistics, Vol. 1, 1955, 1960, 1965, 1970 and 1975;———, "Teenage Childbearing: United States, 1966-1975." Monthly Vital Statistics Report 26 (5) Supplement (September 8, 1977); ———, "Advance Report, Final Natality Statistics, 1977." Monthly Vital Statistics Report 27 (11) Supplement (February 5, 1979).

plight. However, as the policies of educational institutions were challenged in this area and more pregnant teens continued in school, the number of adolescents affected by early pregnancy became all too visible.

In addition, fewer pregnant teenagers were marrying to legitimate the birth of their child. Martin O'Connell and Maurice J. Moore report that 71 percent of unmarried white teenagers who conceived premaritally married before the birth of the child in 1963–1966. In the most recent period, 1975–1978, only 58 percent elected to marry. Among black teenagers, the percentage fell from 26 to eight.

Even though fewer premarital pregnancies are leading to marriage, more marital first births among whites (nearly half in 1975–1978) are premaritally conceived. As age at marriage has risen, relatively few nonpregnant teenagers are choosing to marry. It seems likely that a high proportion of teenage marriages are being hastened or contracted to legitimate the outcome of teenage conceptions.

Part of the concern about early childbearing probably reflects a more general apprehension about the rise in sexual activity among unmarried adolescents. Would increases in the premarital sexual activity of young people still cause public concern even if greater use of contraceptives and abortion resulted in a sharp diminution of out-of-wedlock teenage births? We believe that it would, and that the teenage parent has provided an opportunity for adults to discuss

TABLE 2 BIRTHRATES AND OUT-OF-WEDLOCK BIRTHRATES FOR WOMEN UNDER AGE 20, BY RACE, UNITED STATES, 1950-1977

Age and Race	Year						
	1950	1955	1960	1965	1970	1975	1977
A. Birthrates							
(per 1,000 women)							
15–19							
White	70.0	79.1	79.4	60.7	57.4	46.8	44.6
Black	163.5*	167.2*	156.1	140.6	147.7	113.8	107.3
18–19							
White	—	—	—	—	101.5	74.4	71.1
Black	—	—	—	—	204.9	156.0	147.6
15–17							
White	—	—	—	—	29.2	28.3	26.5
Black	—	—	—	—	101.4	86.6	81.2
10–14							
White	0.2	0.3	0.4	0.3	0.5	0.6	0.6
Black	5.1*	4.8*	4.3	4.3	5.2	5.1	4.7
Ratios of out-of-wedlock births							
(per 1,000 unmarried women)							
15–19							
White	5.1	6.0	6.6	7.9	10.9	12.1	13.6
Black	68.5*	77.6*	76.5*	75.8*	96.9	95.1	93.2

* Rates are for nonwhites.
Sources: See Table 1.

publicly the broader issue of the sexual mores and sexual instruction of the young.

Although we lack good evidence on patterns of sexual behavior among the young prior to the past decade, it is a safe assumption that youth has never even approached the ideal of premarital chastity. Historical records testify that premarital pregnancy has always been common in American society, although there were undoubtedly tremendous regional, religious and ethnic variations in adherence to sexual standards. Those variations still persist, though there is some evidence that they may break down in the future as increasing numbers of adolescents opt for a more liberal sexual code.

In part, changes in adolescent sexual behavior may be a consequence of earlier sexual maturation of both girls and boys. There is good reason to believe that age at menarche fell dramatically during this century. In the United States around 1970, the average age at menarche was just under 13; in many developing areas of the world it is still over 15, and even ranges up to 18. Most of today's young women are therefore capable of becoming pregnant at younger ages. Sexual standards may be changing partly as a response to this pattern of earlier physical maturation.

While we can only speculate about sexual behavior in the past and the future, we have learned a good deal about recent trends through the national surveys conducted by Melvin Zelnik and John F. Kantner. Their studies have shown that there has been a sharp rise in the proportion of young women who have had sexual intercourse at each age. Noteworthy is the change in sexual patterns among the white women. Although their overall level of coital experience is lower, their rate of increase is faster, suggesting that white adolescents are "catching up" to blacks. As more whites, particularly those from the middle class, are exposed to the risk of pregnancy, the problem of adolescent sexuality will attract wider interest and will command more support for intervention.

Contraception for teenagers is one form of intervention that has received considerable attention. Availability has increased and, as Zelnik and Kantner's studies have shown, contraceptive use by teenagers is indeed preventing a large number of unwanted pregnancies and births. (They estimate that 680,000 additional nonmarital pregnancies per year would occur if it were not for use of contraceptives by teenagers.) It seems likely that the increased availability of abortion has both "permitted" more sexual experimentation and, at the same time, allowed teenagers to escape the consequences of an unwanted birth. However, it is difficult to determine the changes in use of abortion among teenagers because reliable data exist only for the period since its legalization in 1973. Each year since then, nearly one-third of the women obtaining abortions have been teenagers, and the total number of abortions has increased annually. These changes in the availability of abortion and contraception may explain in part why adolescent fertility has declined in the face of increased sexual activity, as well as why proportionately fewer teenagers today marry upon becoming pregnant than did so some years ago. While abortion has served to conceal the growing sexual experience of teenagers, and to mitigate the potentially adverse effects of a rise in the adolescent birthrate, it has also drawn increased attention to teenage sexuality. In no small measure, opposition to abortion has forced attention to an issue that would previously have been swept under the rug. The controversy has pressured the public sector into action when it might have preferred to treat adolescent sexuality as a private concern, relegated to the jurisdiction of local communities, the churches, or the family. Later we will return to a more detailed discussion of the alternatives open to various parties interested in preventing premature parenthood.

THE CONSEQUENCES OF EARLY CHILDBEARING

In suggesting reasons why interest in adolescent pregnancies has mounted, we should not ignore the role of researchers in supplying information both to policy makers and to the general public through the mass media. Until 1970, only scattered studies of teenage parenthood existed. Since then, however, a consistent series of results on the consequences of teenage childbearing has emerged in this burgeoning area of research. Catherine Chilman has produced a comprehensive summary of the literature. Here we only highlight some of the relevant findings.

Much research on the consequences of adolescent childbearing has followed one of two complementary approaches. One describes the life course of women (and men) who became parents as teenagers and the ways in which their experience differs from their peers who chose to or were able to postpone the birth of their first child. Other research has attempted to separate out the experiences *caused* by early childbearing and those that followed from pre-existing circumstances that produced the pregnancy and birth in the first place. Information has come from analyses of small, often nonrepresentative samples of individuals from whom extensive data were obtained (sometimes over a period of years), and from examination of much larger groups of individuals, selected randomly from the total U.S. population, whose responses, usually to structured questions, were much less detailed. The conclusions reached by these quite different routes, where comparable, are reassuringly consistent.

TEENAGE CHILDBEARING AND HEALTH OF THE MOTHER AND CHILD

Research has regularly shown that very young mothers and their children are subject to increased health risks during pregnancy and around the time of birth. To our knowledge, however, no studies have attempted to document any longer-term effects.

Higher rates of fetal mortality are found for women under age 20. Infants of teenage mothers have higher mortality rates both in the first month of life (when mortality results primarily from problems existing at birth) and in the remainder of the first year, when environmental conditions play a greater role. The high likelihood of prematurity and low birth weight is a distinct disadvantage for infants of young mothers. Prematurity is a critical factor in infant survival and is implicated in a host of later health problems. Recent data summarized by Wendy Baldwin and Virginia Cain suggest that this disadvantage to infants can be compensated for, even in the case of very young mothers, by excellent prenatal care, but that longer-term risks to the infant's health are not so easily disposed of.

The recent increase in teenage abortions may have contributed to the reduction in the U.S. infant mortality rate by reducing the number of low-birth-weight infants. The Institute of Medicine of the National Academy of Science, in its report on legalized abortion and the public health, speculates that "it should be possible to prove an effect of increased frequency of teenage abortions on the total proportion of newborns weighing less than 2,500 grams." Data necessary for a thorough analysis are not available, but indirect observation was made by comparing the percentage decline in infant mortality rates between 1970 and 1972 in New York (9.3 percent), California (9.3 percent), and Washington (8.6 percent)—states that had liberalized their abortion laws—and the rest of the United States (6.9 percent). It is therefore possible that increased abortion has led to improved overall health of the infant population.

TEENAGE CHILDBEARING AND SCHOOLING

As one might expect from casual observation, teenage mothers, especially those under 18, are more likely to drop out of school than women who delay their first birth until they are in their 20s. Between one-half and two-thirds of all female high school dropouts cite pregnancy and/or marriage as the principal reasons that they left school. Significantly, the differences between those who drop out and those who do not are not merely a product of the young women's social background—their race, their parents' socioeconomic status, or their academic aptitude or expectations; in fact, early childbearing has a greater detrimental effect on educational attainment than any of these factors. Thus, early parenthood is a major *cause* of low educational attainment, and not just another element in a vicious cycle of poverty.

There is strong evidence that a teenage pregnancy is not merely a convenient excuse to drop out of school. Undoubtedly, an important reason why school-age mothers fail to complete their education lies in the enormous difficulties of simultaneously meeting the demands of schooling and those of child-rearing. However, in at least two studies, a majority of teenage mothers return to high school after delivery. In Frank Furstenberg's Baltimore study, the majority of the mothers also managed to graduate. As one might expect, socioeconomic and family backgrounds influence the likelihood of graduation. Additional childbearing, however, usually brings education to an abrupt halt. With each successive pregnancy, the proportion of dropouts rises. And as James Trussell and Jane Menken have shown, the likelihood of repeat pregnancies is quite high among teenage mothers.

Marriage, according to some recent evidence, may be a major complicating factor for teenagers. Women who marry as adolescents have an 80% chance of dropping out of school, whether or not they have an early birth. Among teenage mothers, those who marry are twice as likely to drop out of high school as those who remain single. These findings are quite surprising and require more of an explanation than that provided by the heavy demands of conflicting roles. Specifically, why should marriage be so much more burdensome than caring for an infant? Preexisting motivations and aspirations appear to play a part. The more educationally ambitious young mothers are more likely both to delay marriage and to postpone further childbearing. Other young mothers, including some with little interest in pursuing careers, opt for marriage and reliance on a spouse rather than preparation for employment. Unfortunately, this choice all too often works out to the women's disadvantage, since so many teenage marriages fail. Marriage may also reduce the woman's chances for additional education because of increased childbearing. Married teenagers are more likely to bear another child shortly after the first birth than those who remain single, thereby reducing even further their chances of meeting the heavy demands of schooling and motherhood.

EARLY CHILDBEARING AND MARRIAGE

A high proportion of teenagers who conceive a child out of wedlock have, at least until rather recently, married before the birth of the child. Although marriage is less likely to follow a teenage pregnancy today, many teenagers still resolve an early pregnancy by a precipitate marriage, or at least by wedding much earlier than they otherwise might have done.

Both early pregnancy and early marriage impair a couple's chance of conjugal stability. Data from census materials and surveys explicitly designed to examine the effect of nuptial and birth timing on marriage duration convincingly demonstrate that women who marry as teenagers are more likely to separate and divorce than those who marry later and conceive after wedlock. The subsequent marriages of women whose first birth was out of wedlock are more likely to be dissolved than those of women who gave birth at the same age but who married prior to delivery. Over the long term,

marriages that follow conception are more likely to be dissolved than marriages of nonpregnant brides. Some have argued that the source of marital instability lies more in early marriage than in early childbearing. There is little question that early marriages are less stable than later ones, irrespective of the woman's age at first childbirth or whether that birth occurs after marriage. It is possible, however, that an early first birth may actually promote the stability of an early marriage. The child may provide the couple with a reason to remain married in spite of the many problems associated with early marriage—psychological immaturity, lack of preparation for parental and conjugal roles, and limited socioeconomic achievement.

A significant proportion of young mothers, especially blacks, who separate do not divorce, even by five years after the couple has separated. Furstenberg has attributed this pattern in part to a feeling that there is no need for divorce unless and until another marriage is contemplated. Black women, whatever their age at marriage or childbirth, are far less likely than white women to remarry once the first union terminates. Socioeconomic status and parity may, therefore, be more important determinants of legal divorce and remarriage than the age factors considered here.

There are a number of possible reasons why a premarital pregnancy, particularly one which occurs early in life, lessens the chances of a stable marriage. First, the bonds between the young couple are often only newly formed. Additionally, a marriage in the early teens pulls the young mother away from her family of origin, often sooner than otherwise might have occurred. Many young mothers are both psychologically and economically unprepared to depart from the parental household. Indeed, a substantial minority of those who marry soon after delivery continue to live with their parents, at least for a time. Although these arrangements are partly an adaptation to economic problems, they frequently limit the young parents' commitment to the marriage, particularly when its prospects appear bleak. On the other hand, an early marriage is more likely to last when the mother marries the father of the child rather than another man, perhaps because, in this case, the bond between the parents is strengthened by their common attachment to the child.

A number of studies have demonstrated that economic resources are essential for the survival of a marriage, regardless of the partners' ages. Frequently, early parenthood forces young men and women to leave school and enter the labor market prematurely, thus eroding their prospects of long-term economic advancement. Paradoxically, couples who marry in order to provide for a child conceived out of wedlock typically are separated after a few years because the male finds himself unemployed or in a menial job with little prospect of improving his situation. Thus, it hardly matters whether marriage occurs following an early birth; most of the young women end up with the main responsibility of rearing the child.

TEENAGE CHILDBEARING AND SUBSEQUENT FERTILITY

The earlier a women's age at marriage, the greater her level and pace of subsequent childbearing. Moreover, whatever a woman's age at marriage, a premarital first birth leads to a higher level of fertility. Nevertheless, there is evidence that it is not a *premarital* birth but an *early* birth that eventuates in increased childbearing. The earlier a woman's age at first birth, the greater her fertility for up to 15 years later and the greater the proportion of out-of-wedlock and unwanted births she experiences. The consequences of early childbearing vary little by race or level of educational attainment. In fact, age at first birth accounts for about half of the racial and educational differences in completed fertility.

These results suggest a need for birth control services among all adolescents, younger and older, single and married.

It should be noted here that there is little evidence to support the argument advanced by some authors that early childbearing is the inevitable product of generous welfare payments. Several studies have found no relationship between public assistance payments and the level of teenage childbearing. The "brood-sow myth" remains popular, however, despite the fact that women on welfare have been shown to regulate their fertility as well as other women when given access to the means of birth control.

TEENAGE CHILDBEARING AND OCCUPATIONAL AND ECONOMIC ACHIEVEMENT

Adolescent childbearing seriously injures the young parents'—especially the young mother's—occupational and economic prospects. These consequences are independent of and even more severe than the disadvantages resulting from minority status or poor socioeconomic background. For women, at least, there is evidence that childbearing influences income primarily by curtailing education.

Both Furstenberg and Card and Wise found that young mothers are in a precarious economic situation—they are more likely to have relatively low incomes and less satisfactory jobs, or to require public assistance. The extremely high proportion of women living in households receiving Aid for Dependent Children who had borne a child as a teenager (61% in 1976, accounting for half of AFDC expenditures) attests to the high welfare burden associated with early childbearing.

In part, the consequences of early childbearing for economic independence may depend on the woman's marital career and on her pattern of childbearing following the first birth. For all teenage parents, irrespective of marital status, child care is essential to their efforts to find stable employment. Thus a kinship network that can provide childcare support is one of the critical conditions determining whether young mothers will work or must rely on welfare. Policy makers have been slow to recognize the important function that can be played by the family in mitigating some of the adverse effects of early childbearing on the young parent.

LONG-TERM CONSEQUENCES FOR THE CHILDREN OF EARLY CHILDBEARERS

For children of teenagers, surprisingly few consequences directly associated with parental age have been found. The children, of course, share in the social and economic disadvantages already described in detail: namely, the greater likelihood of living in a one-parent home, with a parent who is immature, badly educated, poor, or dependent on welfare. Children of teenage parents tend to become adolescent parents themselves; and they appear to be more likely to demonstrate poor cognitive development and to have more problems of social and behavioral adjustment than other children. However, family structure is apparently far more important than the age of the mother in influencing psychological and intellectual growth and maturation. The cognitive development of the child is less likely to be impaired if a teenage mother lives with other adults who share childrearing than if she lives alone. Again, whether or not a supportive network exists may be a critical determinant of the life course of teenage parents and their children.

DETERMINANTS OF TEENAGE CHILDBEARING

Once it has been ascertained that teenage childbearing has serious negative consequences, it becomes essential to pinpoint its determinants. In comparison to the relatively well-documented consequences of early parenthood, there is a paucity of information on anteced-

ents. Theories about the etiology of early childbearing have often failed to take into account the fact that parenthood is the result of social process. There has been a tendency to search for psychological or characterological factors that motivate adolescents to enter parenthood prematurely, such as the need for affection, the quest for adult status, resolution of the Oedipal conflict, the desire to escape parental control, or the inability to foresee a more gratifying future. While some of these reasons no doubt apply in some instances, the fact remains that most studies show that only a tiny minority of adolescents become parents because they want to have a child (at least at the time conception occurs). There is little evidence of self-selection for motherhood. Most become pregnant unwillingly and unwittingly, though, to be sure, once conception occurs many are reluctant to terminate the pregnancy by abortion. Adolescents typically have reasons why they want a child once they have become pregnant, but these reasons do not necessarily explain why the pregnancy initially occurred.

Too little research has been done on how and why teenagers begin to have sexual relations. The few existing studies show the powerful influence of peer groups, the difficulty that parents have in communicating and reinforcing their sexual expectations, and the competing interests of young males and females in heterosexual interaction. Clearly, many teenagers are unprepared to assume responsibility for their sexual behavior. This is partly due to the fact that the transition to nonvirginity is seldom premeditated.

It follows, then, that regular use of contraception will be relatively rare among adolescents just beginning to engage in sexual relations. Since most girls or young women do not foresee having intercourse when it first happens, most fail to take the necessary steps to prevent pregnancy. Occasionally, their male partners are equipped with a condom; typically, however, the young men do not have the same interest in contraception, since they are less affected by the consequences of an early conception. Not surprisingly, then, most studies show that only a minority of teenagers use contraception when intercourse first occurs; and, of course, as time elapses, many nonusers become pregnant. Indeed, half of teenage pregnancies occur in the first six months after intercourse is initiated.

Individuals who do receive family planning information and instruction are much less likely to experience an unplanned pregnancy. Several studies suggest, however, that many teenagers equipped with the means of contraception have difficulty using them over a sustained period. This difficulty is increased because of the intermittent nature of intercourse among teenagers—especially young teenagers—for whom intercourse is often perceived, or rationalized, as unexpected. While psychological factors undoubtedly play an important part in the rate of contraceptive compliance among teenagers, we should recognize that contraception is not easy to use, even for adults, over a lengthy period of time. Accordingly, many adults elect to become sterilized rather than encounter the risks of imperfect use or the perceived dangers associated with the pill or the IUD.

Teenagers do not have that option and are forced to make use of contraceptive methods that at best are technically effective but difficult to use. It is quite likely that if teenagers had to take a pill to become pregnant, early childbearing would quickly vanish as a major social problem. In addition, contraceptives are considerably less accessible to teenagers than to married adults. Legal restrictions against the provision of contraception to minors (at any rate, to "mature" minors) have been relaxed by action of legislatures or, more often, the courts. But many doctors and clinics still refuse to give teenagers contraceptives without their parents' consent. Embarrassment and lack of knowledge about where to go also contribute to unavailability for many teenagers. Many others have

mistaken ideas about pregnancy risks—they think they are too young, or have intercourse too seldom or at the wrong time of the month to get pregnant.

Approximately one-third of all teenage pregnancies and one-half of all pregnancies occurring to women under age 18 are terminated by abortion. If pregnancies are generally unwanted, why are abortions not more prevalent? In fact, teenagers turn to abortion much more often than older women who are more experienced contraceptors: one-third of all legal abortions are to teenagers, who represent only one-fifth of the population of reproductive-aged women. In addition, even more than is the case with contraception, abortion is not always an easily available alternative to a teenager with limited means. The Hyde amendment, which has cut off practically all federally subsidized abortions for the poor, has probably affected pregnant teenagers more than any other age group. Even before Hyde went into effect in 1977, many teenagers were denied abortions unless they had the permission of their parents. Although blanket parental consent statutes have since been declared invalid by the Supreme Court, teenagers can still be required to go through a complex and time-consuming court procedure if they wish to obtain an abortion without their parents' knowledge or consent. It is also certain that many teenagers, as do their parents, disapprove of abortion. One suspects, however, that some adolescents who decline the option of having an abortion are not fully aware of the hardships that will be imposed on them as a result of early childbearing, or feel that the price of adolescent parenthood may be offset by the advantages of motherhood.

PROSPECTS FOR THE FUTURE AND IMPLICATIONS FOR SOCIAL PROGRAMS

In this overview, we have summarized only a portion of the growing body of research on the consequences of teenage childbearing. Despite the diversity of research designs, populations studied, and measures employed, we have observed a remarkable degree of consistency in the results obtained by researchers. Early childbearing creates a distinctly higher risk of social and economic disadvantages, in great part because it complicates the transition to adulthood by disrupting schooling and creating pressures for early marriage and further fertility. We are disposed to conclude that premature parenthood is one of the social conditions that maintain the cycle of poverty.

This leads us to ask what social measures can be taken to lessen the effects of early and unplanned parenthood. As public awareness of the costs of adolescent childbearing has grown in the past decade, services have developed to equip the young parent to handle the economic and psychological demands of child care. Prenatal services providing medical care to the mother and child, special educational programs permitting the young mother to remain in school during the transition to parenthood, child care services, and contraceptive instruction are but a few measures in an arsenal of social interventions that have been devised by public and private agencies to reduce the adverse effects of early childbearing.

In 1978, the House of Representatives constituted a Select Committee on Population, which chose adolescent childbearing as one of the three main topics it considered in the area of U.S. fertility. Among its recommendations, the Committee urged the allocation of an additional $65 million in funds for family planning projects, in order to increase the number of program sites so that more adolescents at risk of unwanted pregnancy could be served. It called for "changes in service-delivery strategies" to reach more teenagers in need, the elimination of legal impediments and of factors which contribute to "lack of motivation to utilize available services." The Committee specifically recommended greater use of nontraditional approaches to birth control, such as vending machines for condoms and foam.

It asked for federal encouragement of sex education programs run by the schools as well as by private and religious groups. (A recent Gallup survey found that only 40% of 13–18-year-old boys and girls had ever had a sex education course in school, and only 30% had a course that included instruction in birth control.)

The Committee also urged the federal government to support comprehensive health and social programs for pregnant teenagers and teenage parents. It noted, however, that such comprehensive programs were far more expensive than family planning programs, and were not so clearly successful as preventive programs in dealing with undesirable social outcomes such as dropping out of school.

The Committee was not reconstituted, and there is no substitute group in Congress that considers this area its special interest. However, Congress did approve legislation in 1978 to support a network of comprehensive programs for pregnant teenage parents. The Adolescent Health Services and Pregnancy Prevention and Care Act is designed to coordinate and integrate the disparate services to teenage parents as well as to channel some additional monies to agencies for new programs. Appropriations were $1 million in its first year and $17.5 million in its second year. Assuming that the appropriations are spent, what can we expect the effect of this legislation to be on the well-being of young parents and their children?

While we believe that the bill passed by Congress represents a positive initiative on the part of the federal government, we do not hold out much hope that it will substantially alter the life chances of adolescent parents and their babies. Our research and the findings of others persuade us that the single most important obstacle facing the teenage parent is economic insecurity.

Lack of skills, minimal daycare support, and the uncertainties of the labor market conspire to create an uncertain economic future for teenage parents and their offspring. Unless jobs become more readily available, it is certain that many adolescent mothers will be compelled to turn to public assistance for support. Few are in a position to be fully supported by the child's father, who frequently cannot find work himself. Families are often willing to extend resources when they can to the young mother, but the assistance is unpredictable. Economic disadvantage erodes the possibility of a stable conjugal partnership, and marital breakup in turn jeopardizes the child's life chances.

In pointing to the need for stable and remunerative employment for teenage parents, we are well aware of the potential costs involved. Childcare services, vocational training, and public service jobs are suffering cutbacks for lack of taxpayer support. Given the political climate, it is unlikely that this trend will be reversed in the near future. Indeed, we do not look forward to much change until a labor market shortage develops in this country, an event that may not occur until the latter part of this century, when the fertility declines of recent decades begin to shrink the size of the labor force.

In the meantime, we must look to other strategies for coping with the undesirable consequences of early parenthood. We believe the most promising approach is a much more vigorous campaign to prevent most teenage childbearing, almost all of which is unwanted. There are some encouraging signs.

Schools are gradually introducing sex education courses into the curriculum, a step which is bound to provoke a host of political, ethical, and social problems in the communities involved. Thus far, most such programs are not introduced until high school, after many young people have begun sexual activity; and they do not effectively communicate to the students the risks of pregnancy or how and where they can obtain means to avoid it. (A notable exception, in two high schools in St. Paul, has been described by Laura Edwards. But even here, the effectiveness of the program in preventing pregnancy was much less when it was introduced at the high school level than when it was introduced on a pilot basis in a junior high school.) Nonetheless, as such programs increase, it appears unavoidable that parents will be encouraged, if not pushed, to share the task of providing sexual socialization to the young. Only rarely have family planners directed their attention to educating parents, who are often ill-prepared to provide guidance and instruction to their teenage offspring. It also seems clear that churches, voluntary organizations such as the Scouts, and special interest groups will need to take a more active part in equipping youth with sexual knowledge, decision-making skills and family planning services.

At present, researchers have little to say about the likely success of such public education campaigns in controlling teenage pregnancies, though only the most optimistic planners believe that family planning and sex education and contraceptive services by themselves will reduce adolescent births to an insignificant number. (We assume that the prevalence of sexual activity is not likely to decline in the immediate future, a proposition with which few experts disagree.) Given the many reservations that teenagers have about birth control, the ambivalent feelings that often accompany nonmarital sexuality, and the psychological propensity of many adolescents toward risk-taking, we may expect a substantial, though diminished, rate of premarital pregnancy in years to come.

Teenage pregnancies could probably be reduced sharply however, with the proper mixture of luck and social determination. Only good luck, coupled with an increase in research dollars, will give us a safe contraceptive method more suited to teenagers, for whom sex tends to be episodic and unexpected, than those currently available. The most likely prospect is for a postcoital contraceptive, taken either shortly after intercourse or at the time of expected menses. The Center for Population Research of the National Institute of Child Health and Human Development has announced a stepped-up program of research into such a method, but it is unlikely that a workable method will be generally available for at least 10 years.

Social determination would best be evidenced by facing the fact of increasing sexual activity by unwed teenagers at earlier and earlier ages, and not considering it a social deviation to be treated on a case-finding basis so that those who are still virgins might not be corrupted.

While we have not succeeded in preventing all teenagers from taking up smoking, we have reversed the trend of decades. This was accomplished by a massive educational program in the media and through the schools and private organizations, financed by government and private health and social service agencies. We did not limit ourselves to setting up discreet smoking clinics to which teenagers could go if they felt the urge to smoke or if they were already caught in the toils of tobacco.

Yet, this is exactly how society treats the problem of adolescent pregnancy prevention. With very few exceptions, school sex education programs do not provide young people with specific information that will help them make reasoned judgments about when to begin sexual activity, or about how and where services may be obtained that will help them prevent pregnancy. The programs do not even communicate effectively about the risk of pregnancy in relation to age and the menstrual cycle. Magazines, newspapers, television, and radio do not accompany their antismoking messages with comparable adjurements against sexual risk-taking. Church and youth groups are still more likely to provide proscriptions than prescriptions to avoid pregnancy. In order to avoid corrupting the young and sexually inexperienced, sexual information too often is not given to the teen-

ager until it is too late to prevent the first pregnancy.

That is why there has been so much emphasis on secondary pregnancy prevention—that is, prescription of birth control after the teenager is known to be sexually active because she has delivered a baby or obtained an abortion or (far less often) because she had displayed the initiative and determination to seek out professional birth control help on her own before beginning sexual activity. (Indeed, it is extraordinary that more than one million teenagers find their way each year to family planning clinics, and that a similar number obtain services from private physicians.)

If the current case-finding approach to adolescent pregnancy prevention continues, society will probably have to face the unpleasant prospect of an increasing number of abortions to teenagers each year as a necessary backup to failed contraception. Such an increase is likely to further stir controversy on the issue of legal abortion. Reasoned debate is not likely to prevail where concern over the morality of abortion is combined with concern over the sexual mores of our youth. Exhortations against sexual experimentation are not likely to reduce sexual activity among young people, and the recent federal legislation to help teenage parents and their babies is not likely to offset the severe economic and social costs of early childbearing. Our best strategy is to prevent as many unwanted pregnancies as possible in the first place. To do this, society will have to make the difficult decision to transmit the knowledge and the means of pregnancy prevention to *all* teenagers—not just those known to be sexually active. There is the chance that some, thereby, may be encouraged to experiment with sex somewhat earlier than they would have done otherwise, although there is no evidence that provision of information about sexual decision-making or contraception encourages teenagers to initiate sexual intercourse earlier than they might have done without such information.

In this brief overview of service needs, we have not given adequate space to the immense complexities of providing programs for adolescents. Generally speaking, most health and social services programs have been tailored to suit the convenience of professionals, not the clients they serve. Teenagers looking for contraceptive information and services have had to seek them out, often against considerable obstacles. At relatively low cost, family planning programs have begun to remove these barriers by making service programs more accommodating to the adolescent lifestyle. More flexible clinic hours, more attractive and congenial settings for service programs, outreach by community workers, subsidized transportation, and peer-based counseling are but a few of the innovations that have been made to reach the teenage population.

When we remember that a decade ago, few programs existed for the teenage population, and two decades ago it would have been unthinkable to equip unmarried adolescents with contraceptives, it should be clear that enormous strides have been made in the prevention of unwanted pregnancy. Though these gains have not come easily, they auger well for a more enlightened approach to teenage sexuality in the future.

REFERENCES

1 I. L. Reiss, *The Social Contract of Premarital Sexual Permissiveness,* New York, Holt, Rinehart and Winston, 1967; D. S. Smith, "The Dating of the American Sexual Revolution: Evidence and Interpretation," in Michael Gordon, ed., *The American Family in Social-Historical Perspective,* St. Martin's Press, New York, 1973.

2 J. M. Tanner, "Age at Menarche: Evidence on the Rate of Human Maturation," paper read at the second annual general meeting of the British Society for Population Studies, 1975.

3 J. Trussell and R. Steckel, "The Age of Slaves at Menarche and Their First Birth," *Journal of Interdisciplinary History,* **8**, 3 (Winter): 477, 1978.

4 DHEW, Center for Disease Control, *Abortion Surveillance 1972–1978,* published 1973–1979, Atlanta, Georgia.

5 C. S. Chilman, "Social and Psychological Aspects of Adolescent Sexuality: An Analytic Overview of Research and Theory," report prepared for National Institute of Child Health and Human Development, Contract NO1-HD-52821, by the Institute for Family Development, Center for Advanced Studies in Human Services, School of Social Welfare, University of Wisconsin, Milwaukee, 1977.

6 W. S. Baldwin and V. S. Cain, "The Children of Teenage Parents," chapter 17, below.

7 National Academy of Sciences, *Legalized Abortion and the Public Health,* Institute of Medicine Publication 75-02. The National Academy of Sciences, Washington, D.C. 1975.

8 Ibid.

9 C. S. Chilman, 1977, op. cit.; K. A. Moore, L. J. Waite, S. B. Caldwell and S. L. Hofferth, "The Consequences of Age at First Childbirth: Educational Attainment," Working Paper 1146-01, The Urban Institute, Washington, D.C., 1978; J. J. Card and L. L. Wise, "Teenage Mothers and Teenage Fathers: The Impact of Early Childbearing on the Parents' Personal and Professional Lives," chapter 13, below.

10 J. Coombs and W. W. Cooley, "Dropouts: In High School and After School," *American Educational Research Journal,* **5**: 343, 1968; K. A. Moore, L. J. Waite, S. L. Hofferth and S. B. Caldwell, "The Consequences of Age at First Childbirth: Marriage, Separation, and Divorce," Working Paper 1146-03, The Urban Institute, Washington, D.C., 1978.

11 F. F. Furstenberg, Jr., *Unplanned Parenthood: The Social Consequences of Teenage Childbearing,* The Free Press, New York, 1976; K. A. Moore, L. J. Waite, S. B. Caldwell and S. L. Hofferth, 1978, op. cit.

12 F. F. Furstenberg, Jr., 1976, op. cit.

13 K. A. Moore, L. J. Waite, S. L. Hofferth and S. B. Caldwell, 1978, op. cit.

14 F. F. Furstenberg, Jr., 1976, op. cit.

15 Ibid.; J. J. Card, "Long Term Consequences for Children Born to Adolescent Parents," Final Report, prepared for the National Institute of Child Health and Human Development, Contract

HD-72820, by the American Institutes for Research, Palo Alto, California, 1978; J. McCarthy and J. Menken, "Marriage, Remarriage, Marriage Disruption and Age at First Birth," chapter 14, below; J. J. Card and L. L. Wise, chapter 13, below; J. Menken, J. Trussell, D. Stempel and O. Babakol, unpublished manuscript, "Marriage Dissolution in the United States: Applications of Proportional Hazard Models."

16 K. A. Moore, L. S. Waite, S. L. Hofferth and S. B. Caldwell, 1978, op. cit.

17 J. McCarthy, "A Comparison of the Probability of the Dissolution of First and Second Marriages," *Demography,* **15**, 3: 345, 1978.

18 F. F. Furstenberg, Jr., 1976, op. cit.

19 M. Sauber and E. Corrigan, *The Six Year Experience of Unwed Mothers as Parents,* Community Council of Greater New York, New York, 1970.

20 Bernard, "Marital Stability and Patterns of Status Variables," *Journal of Marriage and the Family,* **28**: 421, 1966; H. Carter and P. C. Glick, *Marriage and Divorce: A Social and Economic Study,* revised edition. Harvard University Press, Cambridge, 1976; J. R. Udry, "Marital Instability by Race, Sex, Education, and Occupation Using 1960 Census Data," *American Journal of Sociology,* **72**: 203, 1966; J. R. Udry, "Marital Instability by Race and Income Based on 1960 Census Data," *American Journal of Sociology,* **72**: 673, 1967.

21 F. F. Furstenberg, Jr., 1976; op. cit.; J. J. Card and L. L. Wise, chapter 13, below.

22 C. F. Westoff and N. B. Ryder, *The Contraceptive Revolution,* Princeton University Press, Princeton, 1977.

23 L. Coombs and R. Freedman, "Premarital Pregnancy, Childspacing, and Later Economic Achievement," *Population Studies,* **24**: 389, 1970.

24 J. Trussell and J. Menken, "Early Childbearing and Subsequent Fertility," chapter 15, below.

25 P. J. Placek and G. E. Hendershot, "Public Welfare and Family Planning: An Empirical Study of the 'Brood Sow' Myth," *Social Problems,* **21**: 658, 1974.

26 F. F. Furstenberg, Jr., 1976, op. cit.

27 J. J. Card and L. L. Wise, chapter 12, below.

28 J. J. Card, 1978, op. cit.

29 J. Trussell and J. Abowd, "Teenage Mothers, Labor Force Participation and Wage Rates," in J. Menken, J. McCarthy and J. Trussell, *Sequelae to Teenage Pregnancy,* Final Report, National Institute of Child Health and Human Development, Contract NO1-HD-62858, Office of Population Research, Princeton, 1979 (mimeo).

30 F. F. Furstenberg, Jr., 1978, op. cit.

31 J. J. Card and L. L. Wise, chapter 13, below.

32 K. A. Moore and S. B. Caldwell, "The Effect of Government Policies on Out-of-Wedlock Sex and Pregnancy," chapter 7, below.

33 F. F. Furstenberg, Jr., and A. G. Crawford, "Family Support: Helping Teenage Mothers to Cope," chapter 18, below. *Teenage Pregnancy in a Family Context: Implications for Policy,* edited by Theodora Ooms. Temple University Press, Philadelphia, Pa., 1980.

34 W. Baldwin and V.S. Cain, chapter 17, below.

35 F. F. Furstenberg, Jr., 1978, op. cit.

36 G. Gallup, "Teens Claim Sex Education Classes Helpful," Gallup Youth Survey, Princeton, N.J., Oct. 4, 1978.

37 Select Committee on Population, U.S. House of Representatives, *Final Report,* Serial F., U.S. Government Printing Office, Washington, D.C. 1978.

38 L. E. Edwards, M. E. Steinman, K. A. Arnold and E. Y. Hakanson, "Adolescent Pregnancy Prevention Service in High School Clinics," chapter 25, below.

EXTRA-FAMILIAL AGENTS OF SOCIALIZATION: PEERS, DAY CARE, SCHOOLS, AND TELEVISION

Although the family is the earliest agent of socialization for children, their development is also influenced by other social agents and institutions. Schools, churches, law enforcement agencies, and many other social institutions are important influences, with the inculcation and maintenance of socially desired values and behaviors being one of their main missions. Peers, although less formally oriented toward shaping social attitudes and behavior, also remain one of the most influential forces in socialization. Finally, television, which is often viewed as merely an entertainment medium, is a powerful influence in modifying children's attitudes and behaviors. In this section we consider four of these extra-familial social agencies—peers, day care, schools, and television.

Peer interactions are encouraged early by parents, and the influence of peers increases rapidly in the preschool years. Children's views of themselves, of social standards, and of other people are modified by their experience with peers.

One of the concerns surrounding the study of peer relationships is the predictive value of these early relationships. In their article, Coie and Dodge address this important issue and find that neglected children, who are characterized as withdrawn and passive, often "recover" and become accepted by their peers. In contrast, rejected children, who are often described as aversive and aggressive in their interactions with their age-mates, tend to continue to be rejected even after five years. Peer relationships are often affected by the ways in which children are treated by their parents. In a dramatic illustration of the carry-over effects between the family and the peer systems, Main and George found marked differences in how abused and nonabused toddlers responded to distress in their age-mates. While concern, empathy, and sadness characterized the nonabused children's reaction to distress in their peers, anger, fear, or even aggression were more common in abused children.

In recent years, the number of children in day care has increased dramatically and researchers have been busy trying to assess the impact of this new form of child care on children's development. As Belsky notes in his review of the effects of day care, there have been few reports of the day-care experience having a negative impact on children. Moreover, we are moving beyond the simple "effects" question and are beginning to discover the qualities of day-care environments that are best for the development of healthy children. In his paper, Belsky highlights a number of features of the social structure of day care, such as group size and caregiver training, and how they make a positive difference on children's outcomes. As the article by Seitz, Rosenbaum, and Apfel shows, outside support such as medical and social services, including day care, can improve the functioning of impov-erished families and their children. Not only were the families who received supportive intervention more likely to become self-supporting and have higher educational attainment, their children attended school more regularly as well. The impressive results of this ten-year program underscore the importance of providing support for families, including day care for children.

Schools are rapidly changing, and one of the most exciting shifts is the introduction of the computer in the classroom. Lepper, in a thoughtful essay, explores some of the motivational issues as well as some of the social consequences of this move. While children's interest in learning and their motivation may be enhanced by the new technology, the differential effects of computers on boys and girls raises questions about the social inequities that computers may inadvertently bring about.

The rectifying of another form of inequality—the segregation of the races in the classroom—is addressed by Aronson and Bridgeman. In their article, they address the issue of desegregation and present a new approach that may produce more positive outcomes in desegregated classrooms. These investiga-tors recommend cooperation in the pursuit of common goals in contrast to classroom competitiveness as a means of improving relationships among students in desegregated classrooms. The implication of this work is that desegregation may not just be a legal reality, but it may have positive benefits for the students as well.

In the final article, Collins describes how children of different ages process or come to understand television programs. Television viewing is one of the most frequent activities of children. Because of wide variations in the use of television, statistical evidence varies about the average time children spend watching it, but it has been suggested that by the age of 18 an average child will have spent more time watching television than doing anything else except sleeping! In his article Collins shows that children's understanding of the social behaviors, roles, and relationships portrayed in typical TV programs is determined by a variety of cognitive, social, and individual factors. Clearly not all children derive the same information from the same programs, and this work underscores the close links between cognitive development and children's social understanding of televised events.

READING 38

Responses of Abused and Disadvantaged Toddlers to Distress in Agemates: A Study in the Day Care Setting

Mary Main
Carol George

This study describes reactions to the distress of agemates in 20 disadvantaged toddlers observed in a group setting. Ten had been physically abused by their parents. They were matched for age, sex, and race with 10 toddlers whose families were stressed but not physically abusive. The study is based on direct observations from the floor of day care centers attended by the children.

The first question addressed was whether disadvantaged toddlers would show concern for agemates in the group care setting. Infants and toddlers from middle-class, nonabusing homes have been observed to show concern for others in distress in both the home (Dunn & Kendrick, 1979; Zahn-Waxler, Radke-Yarrow, & King, 1979) and laboratory settings (Main, Weston, & Wakeling, 1979), but investigators have yet to focus on field observations in the group setting or to include disadvantaged toddlers in their samples.

The second question addressed by the present study was whether the abused, disadvantaged toddlers would be less likely than the nonabused, disadvantaged toddlers to show a concerned response to the distress of agemates. Recent studies of infant concern for others as related to parental attitudes and child-rearing practices would suggest this hypothesis. As opposed to the relatively nurturant and encouraging parents of toddlers who show concern for others, the parents of toddlers who fail to show concern have been described as being critical of their children and as frequently threatening them with punishment (Radke-Yarrow & Zahn-Waxler, 1982). We would expect, then, that abused toddlers would show relatively less concern for others.

This study was initiated out of our continuing concern for the apparent early development of an "abusive" behavior pattern in toddlers who have been subjected to physical abuse (Main, 1980; Main & Goldwyn, 1984). In an earlier field study involving direct coding of the social interactive behavior of abused versus nonabused toddlers in the day care setting (George & Main, 1979), we had discovered that abused toddlers resembled the available descriptions of abusing parents by being (a) avoidant of persons making friendly overtures and (b) threatening and abusive.

Shortly following the publication of our original study, we learned of a third characteristic distinguishing abusing from nonabusing parents. Frodi and Lamb (1980) reported that in contrast to nonabusing mothers, abusing mothers expressed more anger and annoyance and less sympathy in response to videotapes of crying children. In a similar laboratory study, Disbrow, Doerr, and Caulfield (1977) had also reported that child abusers reacted inappropriately and with aversion to distress in others.

The third question addressed in this study was whether abused 1- to 3-year-olds would bear further behavioral resemblance to their parents in the nature of their response to distress in others. Specifically, we expected that abused toddlers would resemble their parents in exhibiting actively angry or other aversive responses to the distress of other toddlers.

METHOD

Subjects

This study was based on reexamination of narrative reports of the social behavior of the 10 abused and 10 control children who had been observed in their day care centers in 1977. They were contacted through four metropolitan day care facilities. Two had been established for battered children. The severity of abuse in the sample ranged from severe punishment to skull fractures, broken bones, and severe burns. The two control centers specialized in serving "families under stress," but in no case was the child pervasively abused or neglected. In some cases the family was involved in intervention programs and/or therapy. The caregiver–child ratio in all four centers was 1:3 or 1:4.

The families of both the abused and control children suffered economic as well as other stresses. Fathers were present in only half the families. Fourteen of the mothers were living on welfare, and only 1 mother was educated beyond high school. (For a more complete demographic description of the participants and care centers, see George & Main, 1979.)

Procedure

Written permission to observe each toddler was obtained from parents or legal guardians. Five trained student observers made a continuous narrative account of the behavior of the children from the floor of the care centers. Each observer followed one child for 30 min. Observers were instructed to record social behavior as closely as possible. No special instructions were given regarding responses to the crying of other children. At the time of the original data collection, we had no means for the analysis of such responses. Four half-hour observations of each child were collected over a period of 3 months (for 3 of the children, only three half-hour records were available). The condition of some of the children in the abuse centers identified them as abused.

Identification of Distress Incidents A research assistant who had no knowledge of the abuse status of the children read through all the narrative records, marking all incidents in which a child other than the target child showed marked distress by crying or by indicating fright or panic. The incident and the target child's full response were extracted from the records and presented to the judges in random order. Thus, the identity of the child and his/her behavior in other contexts and incidents were made inaccessible to judges assessing the response as a particular distress incident.

Classification of Responses Two independent judges placed each incident in one of eight response categories. Four types of responses seen in this sample had been observed in previous studies of toddlers, and four other types of responses had not been reported previously. These responses were respectively labeled Group 1 and Group 2 responses. The four Group 1 categories included (a) looks (the child glances at the agemate but shows no sign of interest); (b) interest (the child merely attends closely or shows interest or curiosity); (c) mechanical physical comforting without clear concern (the child pats or otherwise acts to quiet the crying child, but the comforting is described as mechanical, or the child is not described as sad, empathic, or concerned); and (d) concerned (the child is described as responding with concern, with empathy, or with sadness; looking motherly and other expressions that could have been playful or simply imitative were excluded). The four Group 2 categories of responses were as follows: (a) fearful distress (the child shows fear, distress, or a mixture of fear and distress); (b) threatening response (the child engages in nonphysical aggressive behaviors such as making threatening faces at the crying child or verbally threatening the crying child); (c) physically attacking or malicious (the target child physically attacks the crying child by slapping, hitting, or kicking or uses physical means to worsen the state of the already distressed other child); and (d) diffuse anger. Initially the judges were told to set aside all difficult to classify, puzzling, or diffuse responses. Further examination of these responses showed that all had a quality of diffuse anger, as when an abused toddler crept toward a crying child and waved his arms in her face, his/her own face assuming a look of dissatisfaction.

Following categorization of each incident, the judges were asked to note whether they found the child's behavior disturbing or worrisome. In addition, each individual was examined for content. Group 2 responses never occurred in an incident in which a concerned response was shown. No child showed fear and aggression within the same incident. In four incidents categorized as abusive, the child alternated movements of mechanical physical comforting with attack. This combination occurred only in the case of the abused children. Finally, the diffuse anger incidents generally involved the youngest of the toddlers.

Interjudge Agreement Twenty-seven distress incidents occurred in the vicinity of the abused children (9 children), and 23 in the vicinity of the control children (9 children). Examination of incidents showed no differences in the magnitude, intensity, or nature of the distress behavior exhibited by the abused and the control toddlers. Because only 9 abused and 9 control children witnessed distress incidents, we present further results in terms of a sample of 18 children.

After the assistant had abstracted all distress incidents from the narrative records, the 50 incidents were submitted to two judges. Agreement was 94% on category placement and 88% on whether the judge found the incident disturbing. The simple distinction between physical attacks and nonphysical threatening responses was made following the final coding. The first judge was blind to the purpose of the study and was not aware that the study involved abused children. The second judge was blind to the abuse status of children involved in particular incidents but aware of the purposes of the study. For this reason, disagreements were not conferenced. Categorizations made by the first judge were taken as final.

Six reliability records had been obtained in conjunction with the initial (George & Main, 1979) study. Unfortunately for the purposes of the present study, only two distress incidents had occurred during these six half-hour periods.[1]

RESULTS

For each child, the total number of peer distress incidents observed was tallied, and the proportion of responses falling in each response category was tabulated. The mean proportion of responses falling in each category was then calculated for each group. Figure 1 compares the average abused with the average nonabused toddlers for the proportion of responses falling within each category.

No abused toddler ever exhibited a concerned response at witnessing the distress of another toddler. Five of the nine nonabused children showed concern, sadness, or empathy at least once as they observed a distressed peer in the day care setting (Fisher's exact test, $p = .015$). On the average, the 9 disadvantaged toddlers from stressed but nonabusive families responded with a concerned expression to 33.3% of the distress events that they witnessed.

Eight of the 9 abused toddlers but only 1 of the 9 controls responded with fear, physical attack, or one of the two other types of angry behavior (nonphysical aggression, diffuse anger) to the crying of other children (Fisher's exact test, $p = .002$). Three of the abused toddlers but none of the control toddlers showed fearful distress when other children cried; 1 abused toddler held out her hand with

[1]So few reliability observations were undertaken because each of the four day care centers was geared to the care of children under stress, and none of these small centers welcomed the presence of two observers focused on one infant. Training observations undertaken in normal nursery schools had, however, established high levels of interobserver reliability.

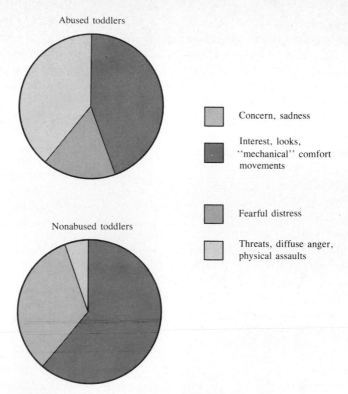

FIGURE 1   Responses to the distress of peers observed in disadvantaged, abused *versus* disadvantaged, nonabused toddlers in the day care setting. (The figures indicate the mean proportion of responses falling in each category for the 9 abused and 9 nonabused toddlers.)

fingers outspread in a typical fend-off gesture at hearing the cry of another child. Three of the abused children but none of the control children responded to the distress of peers with puzzling, diffuse anger. One abused and 1 control toddler behaved somewhat threateningly toward distressed peers. Three of the abused toddlers but none of the control toddlers responded by physically attacking the distressed child.

The percentage of responses falling in the four Group 2 categories (fearful distress, nonphysical aggression, physical attack, diffuse anger) was calculated for each child. For the control children the mean was 5.6% of incidents, as compared with a mean of 55.4% of

incidents for the abused children. The abused children did not merely fail to show concern, but as indicated, they actively responded to distress in others with patterns of behavior rarely reported in the case of normal samples. The difference between the groups was highly significant, $t(16) = 4.01$, $p = .0005$.

In several of the incidents involving aggressive or angry responses, the target child had been engaged in some form of interaction with the distressed-other toddler prior to the onset of distress. In other cases there was no immediate previous involvement. One abused toddler made a ferocious, threatening face at another toddler in distress with whom she had had no recorded previous interaction. Other abused toddlers showed diffuse anger toward children crying at a distance. Frequently the target child had deliberately or indeliberately provoked the distress of the second child, but even when the initiation was apparently accidental the responses of the abused and nonabused toddlers differed markedly.

In two comparable incidents involving pushing a swing or simply tapping a second child on the back, the second child had begun, almost incomprehensibly, to cry. The response of the nonabused toddler in this case was to frown, stare into the eyes of the other child, and say very seriously, "you shut up." However, Martin (an abused boy of 32 months) tried to take the hand of the crying other child, and when she resisted, he slapped her on the arm with his open hand. He then turned away from her to look at the ground and began vocalizing very strongly, "Cut it out! CUT IT OUT!" each time saying it a little faster and louder. He patted her, but when she became disturbed by his patting, he retreated, "hissing at her and baring his teeth." He then began patting her on the back again, his patting became beating, and he continued beating her despite her screams.

Another distress incident was deliberately initiated by an abused toddler, Kate, who struck another infant until he lay still and prone. The incident began when Kate, 28 months, deliberately swung into the infant Joey, knocking him over with her feet. When Joey lay prone on the ground in front of her, she looked "tenderly down at him" and patted him "gently on the back" a few times. Her patting, however, became very rough and she began hitting him hard. After this, she returned to her swinging while the infant lay prone and still in front of her. Kate stopped swinging to lean forward and hit him hard six or seven times further until he finally crawled away.

The judge found 9 of the 50 incidents of response to distress in other children disturbing or worrisome. No control toddler responded in a disturbing manner to the distress of another toddler. Five of the abused toddlers were involved in the 9 disturbing or worrisome incidents (Fisher's exact test, $p = .015$). Two of the worrisome incidents involved fearful distress. Thomas, an abused 1-year-old, was playing when he heard a child crying at a distance.

> Suddenly, Thomas becomes a statue. His smile fades and his face takes on a look of distress also. He sits very still, his hand frozen in the air. His back is straight, and he becomes more and more tense as the crying continues. The fingers on his hand slowly extend a bit.... The (distant) crying diminishes. Suddenly Thomas is back to normal, calm, mumbling and playing in the sand.

Four of the most disturbing incidents (3 toddlers) involved alternately comforting and attacking the abused child. In incidents observed on 2 separate days, 1 of the abused toddlers pursued and tormented a peer precisely until the peer exhibited distress, then engaged in movements of mechanical comforting, in one instance with "a square smile on her face."

DISCUSSION

Observations of toddlers studied within middle-class samples have shown an early capacity for responding to the distress of others with varying types of prosocial behaviors and with facial expressions of sadness or concern. Both the abused and the control (nonabused) toddlers in this sample came entirely from disadvantaged families. Most mothers were on welfare, and many were single. The control infants were further selected to "match" the abused infants in that their families were experiencing stress.

The first question addressed by this study was whether the early development of a concerned response to distress in others is peculiar to infants developing in relatively stress-free, economically advantaged, educated families.

The answer to this question is an unqualified negative. Despite family stress, the nonabused, disadvantaged toddlers responded with concern, empathy, or sadness to one third of the distress incidents that they witnessed in their day care settings.

The second question addressed by this study was whether abused toddlers would fail to show concern at the distress of others. Radke-Yarrow and Zahn-Waxler (1982) had shown that concern for others in toddlers is associated with relatively nurturant parenting, whereas critical and threatening parents in their white, middle-class samples had toddlers who failed to show concern. Our abused toddlers did note the distress of others, as shown in the responses of looking, showing interest, and engaging in mechanical comforting movements in response to the distress of their peers. As expected, however, no abused toddler responded to the distress of other toddlers with empathy, sadness, or concern.

The primary aim of the present report was to continue our previous search for intergenerational similarities between abuse-related behavior patterns characterizing child-abusing parents and the potential development of similar behavior patterns in their young children. This search was based on our awareness of an abused–abusing intergenerational cycle frequently cited in the child abuse literature. From the time of its first discovery, the child abuse syndrome has seemed to be associated with a history of the parent's own experience of abuse in childhood (Kempe, Silverman, Steele, Droegenmueller, & Silver, 1962; Spinetta & Rigler, 1972). Although individual reports of an abused –abusing intergenerational cycle have been based largely on clinical or retrospective accounts and/or have lacked control populations (Jayartne, 1977), recent reviews reach general agreement that abusing parents have been themselves physically or emotionally abused by parents (Parke & Collmer, 1975; Belsky, 1978, 1980).

Given the existence of an abused–abusing intergenerational cycle,[2] we need to know how early and in what ways parental abuse comes to alter the psychological state of the child so that the child also develops an abusive behavior pattern (Main & Goldwyn, 1984). Many investigators and interventionists might reasonably assume that abusive patterns of behavior appear in abuse victims only relatively late in life, for example, in adolescence or in adulthood, when parenting may provide new and excessive stresses to individuals whose own early experiences had already led to a lowered stress tolerance. In an earlier study of this same sample, however, we showed that as early as 1–3 years of age, these abused children were highly abusive toward their day care caregivers and highly avoidant of both peers and caregivers making friendly overtures. In their heightened aggressiveness and in their self-isolating tendencies, the children in this sample already seemed to bear a strong behavioral resemblance to the available descriptions of abusive parents as (a) self-isolating and (b) aggressive even beyond episodes of the abuse of a particular child (Parke & Collmer, 1975).

The impetus for the present study came from the discovery of actively aversive responses to distress in others observed in child-abusing mothers in two independent samples (Disbrow et al., 1977; Frodi & Lamb, 1980). Presented with videotapes of crying infants, abusive mothers reported relatively less sympathy and more annoyance and other aversive responses than control mothers (Frodi & Lamb, 1980). Thus, a third distinguishing characteristic of abusive parents had been discovered.

In light of the above findings, we undertook a particularly close examination of the response of young abused toddlers to the distress of peers. Previous studies of infant response to distress in others have focused on the presence

[2]It is likely that only a subset of abused children become abusive toward their own offspring. The *abused–abusing intergenerational cycle* refers only to the likelihood that an abusing parent has been similarly abused.

or absence of concern. Here, we sought rather to describe and record the full range of responses observed. We found that abused infants not only failed to respond sympathetically to the distress of peers, but they responded instead with threats, anger, and active physical attack. Indeed, fearful and angry responses to distress in others were recorded in 8 of our 9 abused toddlers over the course of no more than 2 hours of observation. Hence, in this study we have uncovered a third striking and disturbing similarity between the behavior of abusive parents and the behavior of young abused children. Not only are these infants aggressive and self-isolating, but they also respond with anger and aversion to distress in others.

Our findings regarding the response of abused toddlers to distress in others raise important questions regarding the behavior of abused individuals as parents. Are persons who were abused as infants particularly vulnerable to contexts requiring caregiving, that is, to the parenting context and other contexts in which another signals distress? Here, we have shown that a specific vulnerability to the experience of fear and anger at the distress of others can develop in abused children very early in life. Further, for 3 of these children, caregiving and aggressive behaviors seemed to stimulate one another, suggesting that these two normally highly distinct behavior patterns have the potential to become enmeshed very early in life. One of the most troubling possibilities suggested by our data is that for some parents who had been abused as children, a distressed infant could serve as a stimulus for this preexisting pattern.

REFERENCES

Belsky, J. (1978). Three theoretical models of child abuse: A critical review. *International Journal of Child Abuse and Neglect, 2,* 37–49.

Belsky, J. (1980). Child maltreatment: An ecological integration. *American Psychologist, 35,* 320–335.

Disbrow, M. A., Doerr, H., & Caulfield, C. (1977, March). *Measures to predict child abuse.* Paper presented at the biennial meeting of the Society for Research in Child Development, Detroit, Michigan.

Dunn, J., & Kendrick, C. (1979). Interaction between young siblings in the context of family relationships. In M. Lewis & L.A. Rosenblum (Eds.), *The child and its family* (pp. 143–168). New York: Plenum Press.

Frodi, A. M., & Lamb, M. E. (1980). Child abusers' responses to infant smiles and cries. *Child Development, 51,* 238–241.

George, C., & Main, M. (1979). Social interactions of young abused children: Approach, avoidance, and aggression. *Child Development, 50,* 306–318.

Jayartne, S. (1977). Child abusers as parents and children, a review. *Social Work, 22,* 5–9.

Kempe, C. H., Silverman, F. N., Steele, B. B., Droegenmueller, W., & Silver, H. K. (1962). The battered-child syndrome. *Journal of the American Medical Association, 181,* 17–24.

Main, M. (1980). Abusive and rejecting infants. In N. Frude (Ed.), *The understanding and prevention of child abuse: Psychological approaches* (pp. 19–38). London: Concord Press.

Main, M., & Goldwyn, R. (1984). Predicting rejection of her infant from mother's representation of her own experience: Implications for the abused –abusing intergenerational cycle. *Monograph of the International Journal of Child Abuse and Neglect, 8,* 203–217.

Main, M., Weston, D., & Wakeling, S. (1979, March). *Concerned attention to the crying of an adult actor in infancy.* Paper presented at the biennial meeting of the Society for Research in Child Development, San Francisco.

Parke, R., & Collmer, C. (1975). Child abuse: An interdisciplinary review. In E. M. Hetherington (Ed.), *Review of Child Development Research* (Vol. 5, pp. 509–590). Chicago: University of Chicago Press.

Spinetta, J. J., & Rigler, D. (1972). The child-abusing parent: A psychological review. *Psychological Bulletin, 77,* 296–304.

Radke-Yarrow, M., & Zahn-Waxler, C. (1982). Roots, motives and patterns in children's prosocial behavior. In J. Reykowski, J. Karylowski,

D. Bar-Tel, & E. Staub (Eds.), *The development and maintenance of prosocial behaviors: National perspectives.* New York: Plenum Press.

Zahn-Waxler, C., Radke-Yarrow, M., & King, R. A. (1979). Child rearing and children's prosocial initiations toward victims of distress. *Child Development, 50,* 319–330.

READING 39

Continuities and Changes in Children's Social Status: A Five-Year Longitudinal Study

John D. Coie
Kenneth A. Dodge

In the past few years there has been a revival of interest in sociometrics as a way of assessing peer relations. This revival has been prompted in large part by evidence that childhood social adjustment is a significant predictor of later manifestations of disorder and maladjustment (Cowen, Pederson, Babigian, Izzo, & Trost, 1973; Kohn & Clausen, 1955; Roff, 1961; Roff, Sells & Golden, 1972; Stengel, 1971; Ullman, 1957). An empirical connection between social maladjustment in childhood and maladjustment in later life carries with it the implication that childhood social maladjustment is itself a fairly stable and consistent phenomenon; those children rejected by their peers in early school years are also rejected by peers in later years. Were this to prove not to be the case, then identification of children at social risk would be a far more difficult undertaking because a determination would have to be made of the precise period in development at which social maladjustment is predictive of later adolescent or adult disorder. Of course, even with reasonably high continuity of maladjusted social status, an attempt would still be made to identify the point in development at which social maladjustment is predictive of future disorder.

Interestingly, however, there are relatively few data addressing this question of the stability of children's social adjustment with peers, particularly across the period of transition from childhood to adolescence. Witryol and Thompson (1953) reviewed the literature on the stability of social acceptance scores but this review dealt more with factors affecting the short-term stability of scores rather than the stability of individuals' social standing across longer periods of time. Thus, the time frame for most stability studies is weeks or months rather than years.

Bonney (1943) assessed the stability of social status from second to fourth grade using positive social choice nominations at monthly intervals during each of the three grade levels but only reported the correlations for single-year intervals. The correlation of social acceptance from second to third grade was .84 and from third to fourth grade there were correlations of .90, .68, and .69 for each of the three sample schools. These figures are high, relative to those for comparable periods in other studies, and may reflect the fact that each yearly score was the sum of four or more scores obtained at intervals over the year, rather than a single score.

Feinberg (1964) followed a group of 52 boys of ages 13 to 15 across a 2-year period. The boys were administered both positive and negative social choice items and Feinberg's social status score consisted of the difference between positive and negative nominations divided by the number of boys in the class. Feinberg found a stability correlation of .22 across the 2-year period, compared with a .69 correlation across a 5-month period of assessment for a sample of 246 boys.

Horrocks and Benimoff (1966) found relatively low correlations for positive nomination status across a 1-year period for a sample of 549 adolescents. Except for a .51 correlation among the 13-year-olds, the correlations were very low (.08 and −.14 for 16- and 17-year-olds, respectively, with a correlation of .25 across the entire mixed-age sample).

The most extensive longitudinal study to date was conducted by Roff et al. (1972), who followed very large samples of children from third through sixth grade in both Texas and Minnesota. The stability of sociometric scores dropped only slightly as the interval for test-retest increased and the stability of positive choice status was higher than that for negative choice status. The correlation of Liked Most scores for third to fourth grade was .52; from third to fifth grade it was .47; and from third to sixth grade it was .42. The correlations for the Liked Least scores from the same respective periods were .38, .35, and .34. The stability correlations for a combined Like Most minus Liked Least score were .53, .48, and .45 for the same time intervals (n = 1,156 children for these data).

Except for the Roff et al. (1972) study, very little is known about the longitudinal course of social status. The Roff et al. data demonstrate the relative consistency of positive and negative sociometric choice scores. As has been pointed out elsewhere (Coie, Dodge, & Coppotelli, 1982), the combination of these two dimensions into social preference (Like Most votes minus Liked Least votes) and social impact (Liked Most votes plus Liked Least votes) scores provides the basis for making more meaningful social status distinctions. One important distinction is between those who are low on both positive and negative choice dimensions, called *neglected* children, and those who are low on the positive dimension but high on the negative dimension, called *rejected* children. The former

group appear to be shy and inactive socially, whereas the latter group are quite active and have a disruptive and aggressive impact on the peer group (Coie et al., 1982; Dodge, Coie, & Brakke, 1982; Gottman, 1977; Gronlund & Anderson, 1957; Northway, 1944). A second distinction, but one involving a much smaller group of children, separates those children who receive many votes on both positive and negative dimensions, *controversial* children, from those who are only named frequently on one dimension but not the other. Although there is some disagreement about the homogeneity of the peer assessment of this controversial group (Newcomb & Bukowski, in press), Dodge (in press) has observational data on them that indicates they are a distinctive, highly visible group who have a social impact that is of strikingly mixed valence.

The present study provides an account of year-to-year continuity and change in the social status of two age-group samples of children across a 5-year period. In addition to the data on positive and negative sociometric choice, the dimensions of social preference and social impact, and the four types of social status (popular, rejected, neglected, and controversial), year-to-year data on five peer behavior description items are also described. The latter data provide some understanding of the reputation each social status group has among the peer group and may serve to clarify the basis for the relative continuity in status of some types of social adjustment.

In the methodology to be described it should be noted that nominations were made across the entire grade level rather than within classroom, or within gender and within classroom, as was the case for Roff et al. (1972). Given the extensiveness of their sample and the need to use computer punch cards in the classroom, Roff et al. were forced to restrict the potential range of sociometric choices. We adopted the present method for several reasons. The children in our study had attended the same school for a number of years but did not always continue to be grouped in the same classrooms. All the children in a grade level shared the same lunch period, recess periods, and playground times, as well as some academic activities. Thus, they knew each other reasonably well and over time maintained important friendships across classrooms. We wished to avoid having some children appear friendless when, in fact, their best friends might simply be located in a different classroom. Also, in some years a disproportionate number of troublesome, aggressive children would often be placed in one or two classrooms, while other classrooms had very few such children, if any. Forcing children to restrict their negative choices to their present classroom might thus distort the real picture of social relations in the school situation as a whole. Some children would appear more disliked than they actually were and others less so. Finally, in upper grades, children rotate among classrooms throughout the school day. Their peer group is, therefore, the entire grade.

METHOD

Subjects

All of the children in the third and fifth grades of a Durham, North Carolina, county elementary school in the academic year 1975–76 served as subjects. Data on this same sample for the Spring 1976 sociometric assessment have been reported elsewhere (Coie et al., 1982). These children were retested, when possible, in whatever school they were located each year for the next 4 years. The first group (henceforth called the *third-grade cohort*) was composed of 50 males and 46 females; 25 were black children and 71 were white (mean age of 8.9 years). The fifth-grade cohort was composed of 63 males and 59 females; 35 were black children and 77 were white (mean age of 11.0 years).

Sample Size There were 94 third graders in the first project year and data were collected on 79 of these children in Year 2 (84%), 73 in Year 3 (78%), 62 in Year 4 (66%), and 76 in Year 5 (81%). Of the 112 fifth-grade students with whom the project began in the first year, sociometric data were obtained for 106 students in the second year of the project (95%), 105 in the third year (94%), only 54 in the fourth year for reasons noted later (48%), and 89 in the fifth project year (79%).

Procedure

In the first project year, each subject was asked to complete a private sociometric interview. Before testing began, the children were assured of the strict confidentiality with which their responses would be treated. Each child was given the grade-level roster and asked to name three classmates whom he or she liked most and then the three whom he or she liked least. Following this, each child was asked to name three children who best fit each of 24 standardized behavioral descriptions. At the end of the interview, each child was reminded of the confidentiality of the responses and the importance of not discussing the interview with peers.

In the succeeding years of the project, children completed this sociometric survey in a group administration procedure in their classrooms. All children received a class-roster containing the names of all the children in their grade level. Each name was preceded by a four-digit code number for each child. The children were told that their responses were recorded in terms of these code numbers rather than by names. As in the first year, each child named three peers who were liked most and three who were liked least. All the children in the grade level were surveyed whether or not they had been surveyed in a previous year. Thus, as our original sample moved into junior high school for the seventh grade, for example, all seventh graders completed the survey. The number of children who provided the nominations on which sociometric status scores for the original sample were based expanded greatly in succeeding years of the project.

In addition to the positive and negative social choice items, the survey for Years 2 through 5 contained five of the original 24 standardized behavior descriptions. (These five were adopted on the basis of cluster analysis data indicating they best represented the original pool of 24 items. This reduction was necessary in order to fit the time consumed by the survey within the limits imposed by the school system.) These were as follows:

Cooperative. Here is someone who is really good to have as part of your group because this person is agreeable and cooperates—pitches in, shares, and gives everyone a turn.

Disruptive. This person has a way of upsetting everything when he or she gets into a group—doesn't share and tries to get everyone to do things their way.

Acts Shy. This person acts very shy with other kids, seems always to play or work by themselves. It's hard to get to know this person.

Starts Fights. This person starts fights. They say mean things to other kids, or push them, or hit them.

Leader. This person gets chosen by others as the leader. Other people like to have this person in charge.

Children were asked to name the three classmates who best fit each of these descriptions. Once again, all persons filling out the sociometric survey nominated the three grade-level peers who best fit each of these five descriptions.

In five cases, subjects from the original sample moved to a school outside the local system and it was possible to obtain sociometric data on them by conducting the survey in the classroom or homeroom within which that child was located. In those cases, nominations were made strictly within the classroom or homeroom rather than across the entire grade level and the

standard scores derived from these data served as the estimates of social status for these children.

In the fourth year of the project, the death of one of the junior high school principals and the resulting problems of administrative transition during the time sociometric testing would have taken place made it impossible to obtain social status data on a significant portion of the original fifth-grade cohort who were then in eighth grade.

Derivation of Social Status Scores The total numbers of nominations received by each child from his grade-level peers on the two sociometric items (Liked Most and Liked Least) and the five peer behavior description items were calculated and then transformed into standardized scores within each school and grade level. The standard scores for the Liked Most (LM) and Liked Least (LL) items were used to generate social preference and social impact scores. These two variables, Social Preference and Social Impact, were standardized within grade level and school for each year of the longitudinal study so that equivalent selection procedures for social status type designations were used across all years of the study.

The social preference and social impact variables defined four types of extreme social status described elsewhere (Coie et al., 1982): (a) The Popular group consisted of all of those children who received a social preference score greater than 1.0, a Liked Most standardized score of greater than 0, and a Liked Least standardized score of less than 0. (b) The Rejected group consisted of all of those children who received a social preference score of less than −1.0, and a Liked Least standardized score of less than 0. (c) The Neglected group consisted of all children who received a social impact score of less than −1.0 and Liked Most and Liked Least standardized scores of less than 0. These children differed from the rejected children in that rejected children received many nominations as being liked least, whereas the neglected children did not. (d) The Controversial group consisted of those children who received a social impact score of greater than 1.0 and who received Liked Most and Liked Least standardized scores that were each greater than 0. Thus, members of this Controversial group were all above their grade-level mean for both positive and negative sociometric nominations.

In the first year of the study, 22% of the third graders and 24% of the fifth graders were identified as popular; 22% of the third graders and 20% of the fifth graders were rejected; 20% of the third graders and 19% of the fifth graders were neglected; and 5% of the third graders and 8% of the fifth graders were controversial. The remaining children (about one-third of the population) are referred to as *average* children in this paper. Selection to a social status group was made independently of a child's gender and race.

RESULTS

Two approaches were used in conducting data analyses. In the first approach, social preference was treated as the continuous variable of primary interest. Using multiple regression, attempts were made to predict later social preference from the social preference and peer behavior description variables in preceding years. Year-to-year correlations were also computed for each of the sociometric and peer behavior description variables. In the second approach, social status categories were computed for each child in each year. Stability of social status was assessed by multidimensional contingency table analyses. Multivariate analyses of variance were then used to predict which children would maintain similar status and which children would change status groups on the basis of the peer behavior description variables.

Stability of Social Preference and Peer Behavior Description The Pearson product moment correlations of scores on the four sociometric

status variables and the five behavior description variables from the first year, with those from each of the next 4 years, are presented in Table 1. These correlations are listed separately for the two cohorts. Of the 72 correlations, 59 were significant at the .01 level. Social preference scores were significantly positively correlated across all years for each cohort, whereas social impact scores were not significantly correlated across an interval greater than 3 years. Of the five behavior description variables, the Aggression variable (starts fights) was the most stable across years. The Acts Shy variable was less stable across years among the third-grade cohort than among the fifth-grade cohort ($p <$ .05 for all but the Year 1 to Year 5 comparison for the two cohorts). Inspection of the correlations for the Shy variable, using all available scores, revealed that this variable increased in year-to-year stability as children grew older (r of Grades 3 to 4 = .35; of Grades 4 to 5 = .45; of Grades 5 to 6 = .65; of Grades 6 to 7 = .54 of Grades 7 to 8 = .89; of Grades 8 to 9 = .85). Inspection of the correlations for the other variables revealed moderately high stability for each variable across each year.

Predictions of Social Preference The pattern of correlations shown in Table 1 indicates that social preference in a given year can be predicted from social preference in previous years. We next asked the question: To what extent can this prediction be enhanced by knowledge of the peer behavior description variables? Several hierarchical multiple regression analyses were performed to answer this question. In the first step of the analyses, data from all years were used, and social preference in Year X + 1 was predicted from social preference in Year X. Subsequently, each of the five behavior descriptions in Year X were added to the regression equation in a stepwise fashion. The incremental value of the behavior descriptions in predicting social preference was assessed by comparison of the multiple R's of the regression

TABLE 1 CORRELATIONS OF SOCIAL STATUS AND PEER ASSESSMENT VARIABLE SCORES IN FIRST PROJECT YEAR WITH SCORES IN FOUR SUCCEEDING YEARS FOR COHORTS ORIGINALLY IN THIRD AND FIFTH GRADES

Variable	Cohort	Test-retest period			
		Years 1 to 2	Years 1 to 3	Years 1 to 4	Years 1 to 5
Liked Most	Third	.57*	.27	.29	.28
	Fifth	.50*	.29*	.28	.32*
Liked Least	Third	.54*	.62*	.45*	.35*
	Fifth	.71*	.27*	.51*	.32*
Social Preference	Third	.65*	.43*	.24	.36*
	Fifth	.70*	.36*	.53*	.45*
Social Impact	Third	.40*	.48*	.52*	.23
	Fifth	.44*	.16	.17	.10
Cooperative	Third	.62*	.13	.52*	.38*
	Fifth	.53*	.60*	.46*	.37*
Disruptive	Third	.63	.47*	.52*	.38*
	Fifth	.81*	.35*	.56*	.28*
Acts Shy	Third	.35*	.24	.06	.17
	Fifth	.80*	.50*	.65*	.33*
Starts Fights	Third	.83*	.58*	.65*	.44*
	Fifth	.84*	.68*	.72*	.49*
Leader	Third	.44*	.45*	.56*	.29*
	Fifth	.59*	.31*	.40*	.34*

* $p < .01$

equations. These analyses revealed that scores on the cooperative variable in Year X significantly enhanced the prediction of social preference in Year X +1 beyond the predictability obtained merely by social preference in Year X. Also, scores on the Starts Fights variable further enhanced the prediction of social preference. In all, the five peer behavior description variables enhanced the predictability of social preference in the following year by 4%, as indicated by the change in R^2 (from .22 to .26).

Similar hierarchical regression analyses were performed separately for each cohort and for each pair of years. The results consistently revealed that the behavior description variables, particularly the Cooperative and Starts Fights variables, significantly enhanced the prediction of social preference. For example, the prediction of social preference in the ninth grade from social preference in the fifth grade was enhanced by the fifth grade Starts Fights variable and was further enhanced by the Cooperates variable.

Stability of Social Status Categories In each year, children from the original sample were sorted into one of the five social status categories (Popular, Average, Rejected, Neglected, or Controversial) according to the procedure previously outlined. In order to assess the stability of social status across years, a multidimensional contingency table of frequencies was constructed in which the dimensions included status in each of Years 1 through 5, cohort, race, and sex. Information theory statistics (Attneave, 1959) were computed to assess the relationships among dimensions. The advantages of these statistics over simple bivariate chi-square statistics are that terms analogous to main effects, interactions, and residuals can be computed with these nominal data, and a measure of proportional reduction in the uncertainty of one variable that is predictable from another variable can be defined. This uncertainty reduction term is analogous to the proportion of variance accounted for by a variable in multiple regression analyses. Finally, Z scores can be calculated for individual cells to determine which cells contribute to uncertainty reduction (Sackett, 1979).

These analyses revealed that status in any given year was significantly related to status in each previous year. Status in Year 5 was significantly related to status in Year 1, and 7.8% of the uncertainty in status in Year 5 (beyond base rates) could be reduced by knowledge of status in Year 1.

Status also varied as a function of the sex and race of the subjects. Because these effects have been reported previously (Coie et al., 1982), they will be mentioned only briefly. There were tendencies for males and blacks to be overrepresented in the rejected and controversial categories and for whites to be overrepresented in the popular category. In all, 13.4% of the uncertainty in status in Year 5 could be reduced by knowledge of a child's sex, race, cohort, and status in Year 1. Tests of the interactions of these variables revealed non-significance. That is, the relation between status in Year 1 and status in Year 5 was not significantly affected by sex, race, or cohort. The meaning of these nonsignificant chi-squares is that the stability of status was not significantly different between the two cohorts, between males and females, or between whites and blacks.

The proportions of children who remained in the same status category across years are presented in Table 2. The numbers of subjects on which these proportions are calculated are also listed in this table. Finally, proportions that are larger than would be expected by chance (using a chi-square statistic) are designated by asterisks. This table reveals that status as popular is moderately stable over a 1-year period (36% of all popular children in Year X were also popular

in Year X + 1), and that stability of popularity is slightly lower over larger intervals (28% are popular after a 2-year interval, 34% after a 3-year interval, and 21% after a 4-year interval). The rejected status group is more stable than any other group. Over a 1-year interval, 45% of rejected children remained rejected. This figure is 34% after a 2-year interval, 34% after 3 years, and 30% after 4 years. Stability of rejected status is greater among the fifth-grade cohort than among the third-grade cohort. For neglected children, status is less stable than for rejected children. The percentage of children remaining neglected over a one-year interval is 25%. This figure is 27% after a 2-year interval, 22% after 3 years, and 24% after 4 years. For controversial children, status is also not as stable as for rejected children, as 31% remain controversial over a 1-year interval, 24% after 2 years, 29% after 3 years, and 14% after 4 years. Tables of the stability of status were also constructed separately for each gender and race group. It was the case that status as rejected was more stable than any other status for every one of the race and gender groups.

The high stability of rejected status suggested that it would be informative to look at the status of children who were rejected at Year 1 but who dropped out of the sample due to moving or to other reasons. Of the 12 children who were rejected in Year 1 but were no longer in the sample in Year 5, 8 had maintained rejected status each year until the point at which they left school. This was true for five of the six such children in the fifth-grade cohort. Only one of the 12 had a positive standardized social preference score (0.32) in the last year with the sample.

In order to investigate the direction of changes in social status across years, two-way tables of frequencies of each status in 1 year with each status in each subsequent year were constructed and inspected. The data in Table 3 represent the changes in status from Year 1 to Year 5. The statistical significance superscripts

TABLE 2 STABILITY OF SOCIAL STATUS TYPE AS INDEXED BY PERCENTAGE OF SUBJECTS WHO MAINTAIN STATUS ACROSS GRADE LEVELS

		Third-grade cohort							
Status type	Grade	4	(n)	5	(n)	6	(n)	7	(n)
Popular	3	44	(16)**	50	(16)**	38	(13)	16	(19)
	4			67	(12)	33	(12)	25	(12)
	5					19	(16)	29	(17)
	6							36	(14)
Rejected	3	47	(19)**	38	(16)**	23	(13)	13	(15)
	4			29	(14)	40	(10)*	33	(12)
	5					44	(9)*	17	(12)
	6							40	(10)*
Neglected	3	27	(15)	29	(14)	08	(12)	33	(15)
	4			13	(16)	08	(12)	20	(15)
	5					20	(10)	0	(10)
	6							17	(6)
Controversial	3	50	(4)**	25	(4)	50	(4)	0	(5)
	4			33	(6)	60	(5)	70	(6)
	5					25	(8)	0	(8)
	6							40	(10)**

		Fifth-grade cohort							
Status type	Grade	6	(n)	7	(n)	8	(n)	9	(n)
Popular	5	63	(27)**	30	(27)	33	(16)**	29	(21)
	6			31	(29)	20	(20)	38	(24)
	7					25	(12)	41	(17)
	8							50	(8)
Rejected	5	52	(21)**	48	(21)**	50	(6)**	42	(19)**
	6			59	(17)**	67	(3)**	46	(13)**
	7					33	(9)**	20	(20)
	8							40	(5)
Neglected	5	32	(19)	50	(20)*	25	(8)	19	(16)
	6			41	(17)	38	(8)*	31	(16)
	7					10	(10)	25	(24)
	8							29	(7)
Controversial	5	44	(9)**	0	(8)	40	(5)	22	(9)
	6			0	(7)	75	(4)**	17	(6)
	7					25	(4)	20	(5)
	8							14	(7)

Note: Scores involving Grade 7 represent the transition from elementary school to junior high school.
* $p < .05$
** $p < .01$

in Table 3 indicate the results of the two-way, single degree of freedom chi-square tests in Year 1 with status in Year 5. For example, the conclusion that children who were rejected in Year 1 had a less than chance probability of becoming popular in Year 5 was based on the two-way table defined by the dimensions of rejected versus not rejected in Year 1 and popular versus not popular in Year 5. As shown in that table, children who were rejected in Year 1 had a less than chance probability of becoming popular in Year 5. The children who were neglected in the first year spread themselves across the Neglected, Popular, and Average status categories in subsequent years. They were less likely than chance to become rejected or controversial and more likely than chance to become average. The controversial children in the first year were at increased risk of becoming rejected 4 years later, but a large proportion also became popular. They were quite unlikely to become average.

Predictions of Change in Social Status In order to determine whether the behavior description variables could enhance the prediction of which children would remain in a particular status group and which children would change status, several analyses were performed. Children who became (or remained) popular were more likely than their peers to have received high scores as cooperative and leaders, and low scores as disruptive and starting fights. Children who became (or remained) rejected had had relatively low scores as cooperative and leaders, and high scores as disrupting the group and starting fights. Children who became (or remained) neglected were those who had received high scores as shy (a marginal effect). Children who became (or remained) controversial had received relatively high ratings as cooperative, but also high ratings as disruptive and starting fights. The items Starts Fights and Leader were markedly predictive of status among boys, whereas among girls the status differences were in the same direction as among boys but were not as striking.

DISCUSSION

The year-to-year stability indices generally reflect a high degree of stability for both the sociometric indices and the peer behavior description variables. As one would expect, that stability tends to decrease with an increasing test-retest interval. However, there is a surprising degree of continuity across a 5-year period when it is considered that both cohorts shifted into junior high school during this period and that this shift resulted in a radical change in the size and composition of the peer reference group.

Unlike the Roff et al. (1972) findings, the present data suggest a greater stability to the Liked Least variable when compared to the Liked Most variable.

Except for the 1-year interval, the stability of our Liked Most variable was slightly lower than that found by Roff et al., however, the stability of our Liked Least variable was much higher than theirs. These facts may be a consequence of differences in methodology. For reasons noted previously, our use of a grade-level-wide nomination base and cross-sex nominations may result in a more accurate identification of those children who are generally troublesome for their peers. This would account for the greater stability in Liked Least scores compared to the data of Roff et al. By permitting cross-sex nominations, we may have sacrificed some stability in the Liked Most scores since older children tend to have more cross-sex friendships than do younger children (Hallinan,

TABLE 3   Proportions of Children from Year 1, by Status, Who Maintained or Changed Status by Year 5 of the Study

Status in year 1	n	Status in year 5				
		Popular	Rejected	Neglected	Controversial	Average
Popular	(38)	.21	.05**	.18	.16**	.40
Rejected	(33)	.03**	.30**	.30*	.00*	.36
Neglected	(33)	.24	.06*	.24	.00*	.45*
Controversial	(14)	.29	.36**	.07	.14	.14*
Average	(46)	.37**	.17	.13	.11	.22

Note: Scores designed with on asterisk significantly deviate from chance (using a chi-square statistic) at the .05 level. Scores with a double asterisk differ from chance at the .01 level.

1981). Except for the Year 1-to-Year 3 transition, when Year 3 was the point when the fifth-grade cohort entered junior high school, the social preference stabilities were higher for the older cohort. The only other variable for which there was a suggestion of age effects was for the Acts Shy item. This latter finding could be attributed to an increased recognition and utilization of what is essentially a low-visibility social construct as children grow older, rather than an actual increase in the stability of shyness as a behavior characteristic with increasing age; although certainly the latter is possibly the case also. With the transition into adolescence, children (Coie & Pennington, 1976) spontaneously mentioned more subtle interpersonal forms of deviance such as social withdrawal. As more and more of the peer group become aware of shyness and withdrawal, there is likely to be higher agreement about those who are shy and, as a result, the stability of this trait attribution increases.

On the other hand, the fact that scores on the Shy item at an earlier age enhanced the predictability of neglected status at a later age (although only a marginally significant finding) tends to support the validity of the earlier peer judgments of shyness. Coie and Kupersmidt (in press) also found support for the validity of these same five peer behavior descriptions in the correlations of nomination scores with behavioral observations made by unbiased, adult observers of children in group interactions. This suggests that while younger children who are viewed as shy may actually behave in ways that are commensurate with this label, many of their peers do not notice this behavior. With increasing age more children come to recognize the behavior pattern and there is increasing consensus on those who are shy.

Interestingly, the most highly stable behavior description items were the two negative behavior items, Disruptive and Starts Fights, particularly the latter. These data are consistent with those of Olweus and others (c.f. Olweus,

1979), particularly those of Olweus himself (Olweus, 1977) who found a 1-year uncorrected correlation of .81 for peer ratings of "starts fights" among a group of sixth graders and a 3-year uncorrected correlation of .65. That Olweus's ratings were made on boys within sex, whereas ours were made across sex on both boys and girls, adds to the generalizability of Olweus's conclusions.

Knowledge of the peer behavior description scores, particularly for the Cooperative and Starts Fights items, enhanced the prediction of social preference scores in 1 year from those of the previous year. Since the Cooperative and Starts Fights variables are highly correlated with social preference within year (but with opposite valence, respectively), this finding was somewhat surprising, but suggests that social behavior, or reputed behavior, is a powerful longitudinal determinant of peer status. One way in which this might happen is as a result of the combined effects of behavior and reputation in the peer group. Dodge has established (Dodge, 1980; Dodge & Frame, 1982) that while aggressive boys behave in ways likely to escalate a frustrating situation into an aggressive one, it is also true that having a reputation for being aggressive is likely to contribute to reactions among the aggressive boys' peers that in turn promote the possibility of continuing aggressive interchanges. Coie and Kupersmidt (in press) also note that boys who are established as highly popular in their peer group do not appear to be the targets of as much aversive behavior by others and are thus likely to have more benign interchanges with peers. This, in turn, should make it easier for them to continue to relate positively toward their peers and continue to enjoy both a reputation for prosocial behavior and a position of high social acceptance in the group.

When children in the two samples were assigned to social status categories for each year of the study, the degree of continuity of status was moderately high but diminished with the length of retesting interval. Only one status category was markedly higher in long-term stability than the other status categories: the Rejected category. The stability across the 3- and 4-year period into junior high school was roughly equivalent for the popular, neglected, and controversial groups, if some allowance is made for the effects of low numbers of children who fit the controversial category in any given year. The data in Table 3 indicate that across a 5-year period rejected children's status shifts in one of three directions: they become neglected, they move to more average status, or they stay rejected. The dropout data indicate that most of the rejected children who left the sample were rejected at the time they left school. Thus, the continuity of status among rejected children probably is even stronger than the data in Table 3 reflect.

It is intriguing to note that children who have neglected status in elementary school almost never become rejected or controversial in junior high school, whereas a sizeable number of children who are rejected in elementary school become neglected in junior high school. This pattern suggests that neglected status has quite a different meaning in elementary school and junior high school. In fact, as was stated in a footnote here, a less stringent criterion for neglected status was used in this paper because very few children (who do not qualify as rejected children because they do not receive high numbers of Liked Least nominations) have no one to name them as someone who is one of three liked most peers in elementary school, whereas this is an extremely common phenomenon in the junior high school years (Horrocks & Benimoff, 1966). (In fact, virtually all the neglected status children in the junior high school years of the study were those who had an absolute Liked Most score of zero.) Thus, neglected elementary school children are those who keep a very low profile and continue to be socially inoffensive on into junior high school.

The present data, coupled with evidence that rejected boys quickly reacquire rejected status when placed in groups of totally unfamiliar boys (Coie & Kupersmidt, in press), underscores the persistent nature of the rejected child's social difficulties. That there is such relatively high stability of status among rejected children, even across dramatic changes in the composition of the peer group, provides further justification for the current efforts to develop intervention programs for socially rejected children. Many social intervention programs to date have focused on isolated or withdrawn (neglected) children or low-acceptance groups composed of both neglected and rejected children (Wanlass & Prinz, 1982). Yet our stability data indicate that neglected children are quite likely to move toward more positive social status (average or popular) with the simple passage of time and without intervention. Rejected children do not appear to move toward positive social status, as a rule. Because of their tendency to be aggressive and disruptive, rejected children are likely to present more problems for clinical intervention and yet, clearly, this is the social status group most in need of help.

REFERENCES

Attneave, F. *Application of information theory to psychology: A summary of basic concepts, methods and results*. New York: Holt, Rinehart, & Winston, 1959.

Bonney, M. E. The relative stability of social, intellectual, and academic status in grades II to IV, and the interrelationships between these various forms of growth. *Journal of Educational Psychology*, 1943, *34*, 88–102.

Coie, J. D., Dodge, K. A., & Coppotelli, H. Dimensions and types of social status: A cross-age perspective. *Developmental Psychology*, 1982, *18*, 557–570.

Coie, J. D., & Kupersmidt, J. B. A behavioral analysis of emerging social status in boys' groups. *Child Development*, in press.

Coie, J. D., & Pennington, B. F. Children's perceptions of deviance and disorder. *Child Development*, 1976, *47*, 407–413.

Cowen, E. L., Pederson, A., Babigian, M., Izzo, L. D., & Trost, M. A. Long-term follow-up of early detected vulnerable children. *Journal of Consulting and Clinical Psychology*, 1973, *41*, 438–446.

Dodge, K. A. Social cognition and children's aggressive behavior. *Child Development*, 1980, *51*, 162–170.

Dodge, K. A. Behavioral antecedents of peer social status. *Child Development*, in press.

Dodge, K. A., Coie, J. D., & Brakke, N. P. Behavior patterns of socially rejected and neglected preadolescents: The roles of social approach and aggression. *Journal of Abnormal Child Psychology*, 1982, *10*, 389–409.

Dodge, K. A., & Frame, C. M. Social cognitive biases and deficits in aggressive boys. *Child Development*, 1982, *53*, 620–635.

Feinberg, M. R. Stability of sociometric status in two adolescent class groups. *Journal of Genetic Psychology*, 1964, *104*, 83–87.

Gottman, J. M. Toward a definition of social isolation in children. *Child Development*, 1977, *48*, 513–517.

Gronlund, N. E., & Anderson, L. Personality characteristics of socially accepted, socially neglected, and socially rejected junior high school pupils. *Educational Administration and Supervision*, 1957, *43*, 329–338.

Hallinan, M. T. Recent advances in sociometry. In S. R. Asher & J. M. Gottman (Eds.), *The development of children's friendships*. Cambridge: Cambridge University Press, 1981.

Horrocks, J. E., & Benimoff, M. Stability of adolescents' nominee status. *Adolescence*, 1966, *3*, 224–229.

Kohn, M., & Clausen, J. Social isolation and schizophrenia. *American Sociological Review*, 1955, *20*, 265–273.

Newcomb, A. F., & Bukowski, W. M. Social impact and social preference as determinants of children's peer group status. *Developmental Psychology*, in press.

Northway, M. L. Outsiders: A study of the personality patterns of children least acceptable to their age mates. *Sociometry*, 1944, *7*, 10–25.

Olweus, D. Aggression and peer acceptance in adolescent boys: Two short-term longitudinal studies of ratings. *Child Development*, 1977, *48*, 1301–1313.

Olweus, D. Stability of aggressive reaction patterns in males: A review. *Psychological Bulletin*, 1979, *86*, 852–875.

Roff, M. Childhood social interactions and young adult bad conduct. *Journal of Abnormal and Social Psychology*, 1961, *63*, 333–337.

Roff, M., Sells, S. B., & Golden, M. M. *Social adjustment and personality development in children*. Minneapolis: University of Minnesota Press, 1972.

Sackett, G. P. The lag sequential analysis of contingency and cyclicity in behavioral interaction research. In J. Osofsky (Ed.), *Handbook of infant development*. New York: Wiley, 1979.

Stengel, E. *Suicide and attempted suicide*. Middlesex, England: Penguin, 1971.

Ullmann, C. A. Teachers, peers, and tests as predictors of adjustment. *Journal of Educational Psychology*, 1957, *48*, 257–267.

Wanlass, R. L., & Prinz, R. J. Methodological issues in conceptualizing and treating childhood social isolation. *Psychological Bulletin*, 1982, *92*, 39–55.

Witryol, S. L., & Thompson, G. G. A critical review of the stability of social acceptability scores obtained with the partial-rank-order and the paired comparison scales. *Genetic Psychology Monographs*, 1953, *48*, 221–260.

Developmental Effects of Daycare and Conditions of Quality

Jay Belsky

The effect of daycare on children's development has been a concern of parents, scientists, and policymakers for some time. Over the past 15 years, the amount of inquiry into the effects of daycare has increased, and the focus of this research has changed.

It is possible to identify two waves of research regarding the developmental effects of childrearing outside the home.[1] In the first wave, the principal issue was whether daycare was "bad" for children, and thus the principal organizing question of daycare research was: Does rearing outside the confines of the family, in a group program, adversely affect intellectual, social, and, especially, emotional development? The results of the first wave of research revealed few, if any, necessarily deleterious consequences of daycare rearing. As a result, a second wave of research was initiated to address another issue: Under what conditions do children fare best in daycare? What types of rearing environments are most supportive of children's development?

DEVELOPMENTAL EFFECTS OF DAYCARE

Research on the effects of daycare can be organized around three topics—intellectual, emotional, and social development.[2,3]

Intellectual Development

An overwhelming majority of studies of the effects of daycare on subsequent intellectual development have indicated no differences between daycare-reared children and matched home-reared control subjects.[3] Although a number of the investigators had found initial gains in one or several test subscales, all significant differences between daycare children and matched controls disappeared during the program or soon afterward.

In contrast to this conclusion regarding children from advantaged families, it is significant that positive effects of the daycare experience on performance on standardized tests of intellectual development have been reported by a handful of investigators for those children who have been categorized as being at higher risk than the average middle-class child.[2] Although the data do not actually indicate that participation in daycare increases the intelligence of such children, they do indicate that daycare prevents the intellectual decline typically observed in children from economically disadvantaged environments over the course of early childhood.[4] To be noted, however, is the fact that most of the daycare programs in which these beneficial effects have been found were designed specifically to provide cognitive enrichment, although they varied widely in the type and degree of special enrichment provided for the children and families.[2]

Emotional Development

Historically, the mother-child bond has been of prime concern to those interested in the influence of early experience on emotional development. Psychoanalytic theory and early research on institutionalized children [5,6] suggested that any arangement that deprived the child of continuous access to the mother would impair the development of a strong maternal attachment and thereby adversely affect the child's emotional security. The typical strategy used for testing this hypothesis has involved separating the infant from his or her mother in order to create stress and then observing the child's response to the mother upon reunion. The large majority of investigations that have used such a procedure revealed few differences between daycare- and home-reared children, thereby suggesting little adverse effect of out-of-home rearing.[3]

Two recent studies[7,8] indicate, however, that daycare-reared infants are more likely to avoid, rather than to greet and approach, their mothers during a reunion following a brief but stressful separation. Whereas some investigators contend that such avoidance is characteristic of an insecure attachment relationship, others believe it simply represents an alternative style of coping with separation.[9] However, these studies may be picking up a deleterious effect of daycare, as suggested by two recent studies, one of which[10] indicates that children who begin group care in infancy are more maladjusted as preschoolers and the other of which[11] shows that, as 8- to 10-year-olds, such children display higher levels of misbehavior and greater social withdrawal.

Although still in the minority, these new findings highlighting differences between home- and daycare-reared infants lead me to modify conclusions that have been arrived at in earlier reviews.[2,3] Although most evidence indicates that extrafamilial child care exerts little influence on the child's emotional ties to his or her mother, some data are beginning to suggest that such care in the 1st year of life may have potentially adverse effects on the child's social and emotional development.

But in considering the select findings I have just summarized, it is imperative that we not lose sight of the fact that the results that distinguish daycare- from home-reared children represent more the exception than the rule. Whereas it would be totally inappropriate for my words to be taken out of context so as to suggest that we ought to be alarmed about the effects of infant daycare or fear what it is doing to our nation's children, it is important that the evidence presented be taken into careful consideration in discussions of infant daycare.

Social Development

When it comes to assessing the effects of daycare on social development, primary attention has been directed toward children's behavior toward peers and nonparental adults. With respect to peer relationships, available evidence indicates that daycare has both positive and negative effects. On the positive side, research findings indicate that daycare-reared infants and preschoolers are more sociable, that is, willing to interact with unfamiliar peers, and are more cooperative and empathic in their dealings with agemates than other children.[12-14] On the negative side, however, the data indicate that daycare-reared preschoolers are more likely to be aggressive and assertive with peers.[7,11] Considered together, the findings seem to demonstrate that children who spend a great deal of time in the presence of agemates from an early age simply become more adept at dealing with peers, relying upon both positive and negative strategies as the need arises.

When it comes to relationships with adults and the socialization of adult-like behaviors, evidence suggests that daycare-reared children are less cooperative with adults, are generally more troublesome in a classroom setting, and may be less attentive and less socially responsive.[7,15,16] However, the fact that such problematic behavior does not always, or even in the majority of studies, differentiate daycare- and home-reared children clearly indicates that such potential effects of daycare are not inevitable.

CONDITIONS OF QUALITY CARE

The preceding summary of the effects of daycare presumes, as do many comparisons of home-reared and daycare-reared children, that all daycare is alike. Any consumer knows this is not so. Thus, the basic question becomes one related to the conditions from which certain developmental consequences ensue. Is there any empiric evidence to help define the parameters of high-or low-quality rearing environments? Fortunately, there is; indeed, three approaches to specifying quality have been undertaken.

One set of studies examines the way in which regulatable dimensions of daycare, such as group size and teacher training—what I refer to as social-structure variables of daycare—relate to child development. A second set of studies attempts to link social structure with experience, since social structure is presumed to directly influence the types of day-to-day experiences children actually have in daycare. Finally, a third set of studies relates observed variation in experience, scaled on a high-to low-quality basis, to developmental outcome. Because only a single study has tried to coordinate all three pieces of this causal model (social structure →experience →development), it is most useful to discuss these investigations in blocks, weaving together results in order to generate a coherent picture.

Social Structure and Child Development

Group size, caregiver/child ratio, and caregiver training are the dimensions of daycare that have received the most systematic attention by investigators interested in learning how aspects of daycare that are subject to legislative regulation influence, or at least covary with, individual differences in the development of children reared in daycare. Findings in this area reveal that group size and caregiver training may be the most important determinants of variation in children's development, with small groups and specialized training being positively associated with child achievement.[16,17]

Social Structure and Daily Experience

If parameters of daycare structure such as group size and caregiver training are predictive of the effect that daycare will have on a child, it is probably because such aspects of daycare determine, at least in part, the nature of the child's daily experiences in care. Evidence to support this interpretation comes from studies

of the effect of group size and caregiver/child ratio on children's and caregivers' behavior. It has been observed repeatedly that in small groups, children have higher-quality experiences involving more learning and cooperation, probably because caregivers engage in more teaching and fewer controlling behaviors.[1] Most illustrative of this pattern of findings are the results of the National Day Care Study[18] which found that for children 3 to 5 years of age, group size was the single most important determinant of the quality of children's experience. In groups of fewer than 15 to 18 children, caregivers were involved in more embellished caregiving (eg, questioning, responding, praising, comforting), less straight monitoring of children, and less interaction with other adults. And in these smaller groups, children were more actively involved in classroom activities such as considering and contemplating, contributing ideas, cooperating, and persisting at tasks.

Interestingly, the National Day Care Study found that the caregiver/child ratio had little effect on the quality of *preschoolers'* experience in daycare, although it was an important determinant of *infants'* experiences. More overt distress was observed among children under 3 years of age as the number of children per caregiver increased. Additionally, in such high-ratio infant and toddler programs, staff members spent more time in management and control interactions and engaged in less informal teaching.[18,19]

Daily Experience and Child Development

Studies that speak to the way experience in daycare influences the development of children exposed to such rearing have assessed a variety of outcomes and are generally consistent in their findings. The developmental significance of the quantity and quality of caregiver involvement is best illustrated in a comprehensive investigation of 156 families with preschoolers in daycare centers on the island of Bermuda.[10]

Results revealed that variation in quality significantly predicted linguistic and social competence. In the case of language, nearly 20% of the variance was accounted for by differences in quality, whereas nearly half the variance in sociability (ie, extroversion) from a standardized measure of classroom behavior (filled out by parents and teachers) was accounted for by total quality; similarly, a measure of consideration for others also was predicted by positive aspects of the daycare milieu. In contrast, children rated as dependent tended to come from centers with low overall quality. Furthermore, poor emotional adjustment (ie, anxiety, hyperactivity, aggression), as rated by caregivers, tended to occur in centers with low levels of verbal interaction between adults and children.

CONCLUSION

The preceding analyses demonstrate that not all daycare is the same. Great variation exists in social structure, experience, and the outcomes associated with daycare exposure. Further, on the basis of the data reviewed, a case can be made for the claim that social structure influences experience, which in turn affects child development. In centers and family daycare homes in which group size is modest, caregiver-child ratios are low, and staff training is high, caregivers tend to be more stimulating, responsive, and positively affectionate, as well as less restrictive. Moreover, children who experience such care tend to be more cooperative, more intellectually capable, and more emotionally secure.

What is so intriguing about these results of investigations aimed at chronicling the conditions of quality daycare is how consistent the daycare findings are with those emanating from research on family influences on child development. Whether we look at the research on infancy or on early childhood, there is consistent evidence that certain qualities of in-home parental care promote optimal psychologic development,[20,21] and these dimensions of child-rearing are the same as those emerging from research on variation in daycare quality.

We speak of mothers being sensitive to their children in infancy: during the preschool years, Baumrind's notion of the authoritative (as opposed to permissive or authoritarian) parent[22] captures the essence of quality care. Operationally, these terms refer to parents who are involved with their children, responsive to their needs, and controlling of their behavior, but not too restrictive. Such growth-facilitating care also relies heavily on linguistic communication, which we know fosters general intellectual development, as well as the use of reasoning-based as opposed to power-assertive discipline, which we know fosters prosocial development.

This analysis suggests that it is not where the child is reared that is of principal importance, but how she or he is cared for. One's social address does not determine development, be it home or daycare center, lower-class or middle-class surroundings; rather, it is one's day-to-day experiences that shape psychologic growth. Social structure is influential because it probably determines the kinds of day-to-day experiences children will have. When group size is large and caregiver/child ratios are high, individual attention to children falls victim to the exigencies of coping with an overextended set of resources. Either restrictions and controlling behavior increase, or disregard and aimless behavior on the part of the child increase. Neither is in the child's best interest. But when the necessary human resources are available, daily experiences tend to be stimulating and rewarding, and child development is facilitated. This is as true in a daycare milieu as it is in a family environment.

REFERENCES

1 Belsky J: Two waves of day care research: Developmental effects and conditions of quality, in Ainslie R (ed): *The Child and the Day Care Setting*. New York: Praeger, 1984, pp 1–34.

2 Belsky J, Steinberg L: The effects of day care: A critical review. *Child Dev* 49:929, 1978.

3 Belsky J, Steinberg L, Walker A: The ecology of day care, in Lamb ME (ed): *Nontraditional Families: Parenting and Child Development.* Hillsdale, NJ: Erlbaum, 1982, pp 71–116.

4 Ramey C, Dorval B, Baker-Ward L: Group daycare and socially disadvantaged families: Effects on the child and the family, in Kilmer S (ed): *Advances in Early Education and Daycare.* New York: JAI Press, 1981, pp 141–173.

5 Bowlby J: *Maternal Care and Mental Health.* Geneva: World Health Organization, 1951.

6 Spitz RA: Hospitalism: An inquiry into the genesis of psychiatric conditions in early childhood. *Psychoanal Study Child* 1:53, 1945.

7 Schwarz JC, Strickland R, Krolick G: Infant day care: Behavioral effects at preschool age. *Dev Psychol* 10:502, 1974.

8 Vaughn B, Gove F, Egeland B: The relationship between out-of-home care and the quality of infant-mother attachment in an economically disadvantaged population. *Child Dev* 51:1203, 1980.

9 Clarke-Stewart KA, Fein G: Early childhood programs, in Haith M, Campos J (eds): *Handbook of Child Psychology,* ed 4, vol 2, *Infancy and Developmental Psychology.* New York: John Wiley & Sons, 1983, pp 917–1000.

10 McCartney K, Scarr S, Phillips D, et al: Environmental differences among day care centers and their effects on children's development, in Zigler EF, Gordon EW (eds): *Day Care: Scientific and Social Policy Issues.* Boston: Auburn House, 1981, pp 126–151.

11 Barton M, Schwarz JC: Day care in the middle class: Effects in elementary school. Presented at the American Psychological Association Annual Convention, Los Angeles, August 1981.

12 Clarke-Stewart KA: Assessing social development. Presented at the Biennial Meeting of the Society for Research in Child Development, San Francisco, March 1979.

13 Kagan J, Kearsley R, Zelazo P: *Infancy: Its Place in Human Development.* Cambridge, Mass: Harvard University Press, 1978.

14 Ricciuti H: Fear and development of social attachments in the first year of life, in Lewis M, Rosenblum LA (eds): *The Origins of Human Behavior: Fear.* New York: John Wiley & Sons, 1974, pp 73–106.

15 Raph J, Thomas A, Chess S, Korn S: The influence of nursery school on social interaction. *Am J Orthopsychiatry* 38:144, 1964.

16 Schwarz JC, Scarr SW, Caparulo B, et al: Center, sitter, and home day care before age two: A report on the first Bermuda infant care study. Presented at the American Psychological Association Annual Convention, Los Angeles, August 1981.

17 Ruopp R, Travers J: Janus faces day care: Perspectives on quality and cost, in Zigler EF, Gordon EW (eds): *Day Care: Scientific and Social Policy Issues.* Boston: Auburn House, 1981, pp 72–101.

18 Travers J, Ruopp R: *National Day Care Study: Preliminary Findings and Their Implications.* Cambridge, Mass: Abt Books, 1978.

19 Connell DB, Layzer JI, Goodson BD: *National Study of Day Care Centers for Infants: Findings and Implications,* unpublished, 1979.

20 Belsky J, Lerner R, Spanier G: *The Child in the Family.* Reading, Mass: Addison-Wesley, 1984.

21 Clarke-Stewart KA: *Child Care in the Family.* New York: Academic Press, 1977.

22 Baumrind D: Child care practices anteceding three patterns of preschool behavior. *Genet Psychol Monogr* 75:43, 1967.

READING 41

Effects of Family Support Intervention: A Ten-Year Follow-up

Victoria Seitz
Laurie K. Rosenbaum
Nancy H. Apfel

Much more is known about effects of programs designed to provide cognitive stimulation to children than about effects of other forms of intervention. This is particularly true with respect to long-term consequences of programs. Noteworthy examples of projects for which long-range outcome data are available are the Carolina Abecedarian Project (Ramey & Haskins, 1981), the Milwaukee Study (Garber, in press), and a group of studies whose results have been pooled and reported by the Consortium for Longitudinal Studies (Lazar & Darlington, 1982). While there are important differences among these programs, a common denominator is an emphasis on cognitive stimulation provided directly to children, usually by persons other than their parents.

Two consistent kinds of results have emerged from long-term studies of cognitive enrichment programs. First, children's performance on IQ tests has usually been increased, at least in the short term, and in some instances for several years after the program has terminated as well. Second, less relationship has been found between children's IQ test scores and their overall school or life adjustment than had been anticipated. In at least two studies, experimental children entering school with considerably higher IQs than control children have not shown commensurately better school performance (Garber & Heber, 1981; Ramey & Haskins, 1981). In other studies, experimental children have not maintained an IQ advantage over control children, but they have had significantly more successful school careers (Darlington, Royce, Snipper, Murray, & Lazar, 1980) and/or life outcomes (Schweinhart & Weikart, 1983).

Having an average or somewhat better than average IQ is thus not a sufficient cause of good later life outcomes for children from poverty-level families. Since the average level of both IQ scores and other measures in most projects falls below national norms, whether higher IQ scores are a necessary condition of good outcomes is less clear. If so, then efforts to improve children's IQs are certainly not misplaced. But it now seems safe to conclude that if children are enough at risk for educational and other adaptational failure to need intervention, they probably need more than a cognitive enrichment program.

In addition to questioning whether cognitive change is an adequate goal, it is also reasonable to ask whether children are the best targets for intervention efforts. As Bronfenbrenner (1975) and Gray and Wandersman (1980) noted in their reviews of preschool programs, the most effective were those that actively involved parents. If involving parents in programs for their children can increase effectiveness, it seems logical to explore the consequences of increasing parental involvement to the maximum possible level by having the parents, rather than their children, be the focus of the program.

We have been evaluating the effects of a program, designed and implemented by Provence and her colleagues, that exemplifies a parent-oriented approach (Provence & Naylor, 1983; Provence, Naylor, & Patterson, 1977). Probably the best label to describe it is "family support" intervention; it is similar to several more recent projects also designed to support effective family functioning in high-risk families (Field, Widmayer, Stringer, & Ignatoff, 1980;

Hardy, King, Shipp, & Welcher, 1981; Olds, 1982).

In targeting the intervention, impoverished families were chosen under the assumption that chronic stress is a significant impediment to effective family functioning, and that poverty both increases the likelihood of such stress and restricts the resources available to families to cope with it. The investigators did not view severely impoverished families as being different in some psychological way from families with more resources. In an exploratory study, however, focusing on such families increases the likelihood that the recipients of the program will actually be in need of it.

Because the program was necessarily small in size, several potential sources of interpretational difficulty were eliminated in defining the subject population. First, biological damage is a common problem in poverty-level populations, for whom almost any measure of fetal, maternal, and neonatal complications is higher than for economically advantaged populations. Attempting to remediate problems created by biological insult through a predominantly social and educational approach did not seem a wise strategy to the program designers. Therefore, the decision was made to include in the study sample only healthy infants with no known biological handicap.

A second sampling specificity was made by focusing on parents expecting a firstborn, rather than a later-born, child. A practical advantage of this decision is the elimination of many interpretational problems introduced by the presence of additional children (e.g., birth-order effects, added financial stresses). Transition to parenthood is also recognized by clinicians and researchers as being an important milestone in adult development (Dyer, 1963; Hobbs & Cole, 1976; Hobbs & Wimbish, 1977; LeMasters, 1957). Parental adjustments to the firstborn child are likely to be particularly stressful. Thus, there are also theoretical reasons for limiting a study of this kind to first-

borns in expectation of maximizing potential expected benefits to the subjects.

The data reported in the present manuscript represent findings from a 10-year follow-up of the families and children who received this family support intervention and of control children who did not. Earlier studies of this project were conducted when the children were 30 months and when they were 7 years old (Provence et al., 1977; Rescorla, Provence, & Naylor, 1982; Trickett, Apfel, Rosenbaum, & Zigler, 1982). At 30 months, experimental children showed significantly better language development relative to control children. On family measures, however, control families appeared to have an advantage: they were more likely to be self-supporting, and control children were less likely to be living without a father or surrogate father in their home. Five years later, Rescorla and her colleagues found that the experimental families had shown general upward mobility, with increases in maternal education and in the number who were self-supporting. Most had moved to better neighborhoods, and their subsequent birthrate was low (most families had only one child at the follow-up). The original control sample was not relocated at the 5-year follow-up.

In a separate study conducted at the same time, Trickett and her colleagues compared experimental families with families of randomly chosen children of the same age living in their original neighborhood. In these comparisons, experimental families had higher SES and fewer total children. Experimental mothers also were more likely to be employed. There was no differences in the presence of a father or father surrogate in the home or in maternal education. The experimental children had higher IQ scores on the Peabody Picture Vocabulary Test, better school achievement, and markedly better school attendance than did random samples of children from their original neighborhood. Testers, who were blind to the children's experimental status, also rated experimental children as being more enjoyable and easier to test.

The present study is a 10-year follow-up of the experimental families and their children. The original control families and children have also been located for this study.

DESCRIPTION OF THE INTERVENTION

As described elsewhere (Provence et al., 1977; Provence & Naylor, 1983), the Provence group's approach to family support involved social work, pediatric care, day-care, and psychological services provided in an individualized mixture tailored to what seemed to be the specific needs of each family. In receiving the four components of the program, each family interacted with a small team of persons: a home visitor (usually a social worker), pediatrician, primary day-care worker, and developmental examiner. This "family team" provided long-term continuity for each family, as at least one member could be dependably available at all times. The program began during the mother's pregnancy and continued to 30 months postpartum.

Home Visitor The role of the home visitor was to provide close personal involvement by a professionally competent person in a convenient setting for the family. Five clinical social workers, two psychologists, and one nurse served in this capacity for the project. Home visitors listened sympathetically to the parents' concerns, helped to solve immediate problems, such as reducing physical dangers or obtaining more adequate food or housing, and assisted in solving larger life problems, such as helping parents come to satisfying educational, marital, and career decisions. They also provided a liaison with other service providers in the immediate project and in the community. The families received an average of 28 such visits.

Pediatric Care Each pediatrician saw the newborn and mother at least daily during the postdelivery hospital stay and scheduled a home visit within the first week. Each made house calls if needed and responded to telephoned concerns promptly and sympathetically. The children received from 13 to 17 regular well-baby exams, which were scheduled to permit a full hour's interchange between mother and physician. Discussions of parental concerns about the infant's development could thus be held during the examinations, and parents could be assisted to learn how to be better observers of their baby's health status. Parents also were free to discuss concerns about their own lives and often did so as they became more comfortable with the pediatrician.

Day-care Day-care and/or a toddler school were provided for all but one of the children in the study for periods ranging from 2 to 28 months. On the average, the children received 13.2 months of the day-care (SD = 8.5, median = 13 months). By any conventional measure, the quality of the care was high. The staff was highly trained, and the child-caregiver ratio never exceeded three to one. Children were given ample opportunity to explore and to play, and suitable toys were carefully selected for them. Each child had a primary caregiver; thus, the principle of individualized, personalized care was extended to children in day-care as well as to their parents in the other services that were provided. The staff actively tried to achieve continuity between their child-care practices and those of the parents, discussing any problems with parents in an effort to work out mutually agreeable methods of handling them. The primary focus was on the children's emotional and social development (e.g., helping the children learn to handle aggression, dealing with problems of separation from the parents, and fostering good peer interactions).

Developmental Examinations The children received from seven to nine regularly scheduled developmental examinations, using the Yale Child Development Schedule (which is similar to the Bayley Scales of Infant Development). The parent again spent this time with the examiner and child and had an opportunity to observe the child's abilities. Without making any direct effort to teach facts about development, the examiner could nevertheless capitalize on the parent's interest and curiosity about the significance of the child's performance. Parents also had the opportunity to witness the examiner's techniques for handling difficult behavior and to discuss their concerns about it.

In short, the intervention employed a teamwork approach providing continuity of care by familiar and skilled professionals; it focused on the social and emotional adjustment of the parents and children, and its aim was to strengthen parents in their caregiving ability and their ability to solve their own life problems.

METHOD

Subjects

Recruitment The experimental sample consists of 18 children from 17 families who resided in a depressed inner-city area in a northeastern city in 1968–1970. The control sample consists of 18 children from 18 families living in the same area in 1971. The identification of families as potential subjects was made from clinic records of the population of women who were registered for obstetrical care in the women's clinic of a large city hospital located in the same inner-city area. Families were considered eligible for the project if their clinic record indicated the following: (*a*) the pregnancy would result in the mother's firstborn child, (*b*) there were no serious complications of pregnancy, (*c*) the families resided in the inner city and had incomes below the federal poverty level, and (*d*)

the mothers were not markedly retarded or acutely psychotic. Beginning in late 1968, all registrants whose records satisfied these criteria were interviewed, and, if they were not planning to leave the area in the forseeable future, they were invited to join the project. In order to recruit 20 families, it was necessary to interview 25 (for an 80% acceptance rate). Reasons for declining included plans to move away, as well as disinterest; no record was kept of the exact reasons offered. Recruitment ceased early in 1970 when the twentieth family had accepted the invitation to join.

One child was stillborn, and one was born with a biological handicap. A third family withdrew during the project. The number of families receiving the full program thus was 17. One of these families had a second child in 1971, and the child was added to the sample.

As a control group for assessing the effects of the program, the project staff recruited a sample of 18 30-month-old children after the project had ended. The clinic records beginning with April 1971 were searched in the same manner as had been used to identify the experimental subjects. From the pool of mothers who met the original criteria, and who would have been invited to participate in the project had it continued, potential control children were matched with the experimental children on sex, income level of the family, number of parents in the home, and ethnicity of the mother. All potential control children were full-term and healthy at birth. Some of the control families could not be located, having moved without leaving sufficient forwarding addresses in the 30 months since the birth of their child. Three families who were located declined to participate. All such lost controls were replaced by the next appropriate name from the records. In order to recruit 18 families, it was necessary to contact 28 (for a 64% recruitment rate). Since the two experimental families who did not deliver healthy infants would not have been considered for potential control subjects, the recruitment rate for experimental families can be considered to be 17 families out of 23 interviewed (74%) who had healthy babies and who both accepted and completed the project. The recruitment rate for the control sample is thus slightly lower than that for the experimental sample.

Description   In the experimental group, 12 of the children are black, two are Hispanic (from a single family), two are white, and two are of mixed race (white mother, black father). In the control group, 12 children are black, two are Hispanic, and four are white. Within each group, 11 of the children are boys, and seven are girls. The birthdates of the experimental children range from December 1968 through March 1970, with all but three births occurring in 1969. The birthdates of the control children range from May through December 1971. With one exception, the control children had not received any group day-care prior to 30 months (one child began attending a day-care program at age 2).

Fathers   While the project's services were available to fathers as well as to mothers, only six of the 17 fathers agreed to participate. In all these cases, the parents were either married or living in a stable common-law marriage. The project staff worked intensively with two of these fathers; they had variable contact with the other four, all of whom were working. None of the 11 nonparticipating fathers was reliably available to the mother or assumed a consistent parental role with the child. In two cases, the parents' divorce was pending during the pregnancy. Three fathers were married to other women, two had broken off with the mother when the pregnancy was discovered, two had only occasional contact with the mother, and two fathers had left town (Provence & Naylor, 1983).

Design

Because this was a quasi-experimental study, special consideration is given to examining fac-

tors affecting its internal validity (Cook & Campbell, 1979). The present design employed a simple time lag, in which the same recruitment procedures were applied to the same population with a time gap between recruitment periods. The necessary assumption for this procedure to yield a valid control group is that the nature of the population did not change over the time involved. According to city records, the ethnic and socioeconomic characteristics of the neighborhoods and the population size and density did not change markedly over the 2 years between recruitments. There also were no major shifts in number of patients served by the hospital clinic whose records were used to identify potential recruits. Thus the assumption of no significant change appears reasonable.

A small, and similar, number of potential subjects in each group declined to participate. It is thus likely that there was little differential bias due to this factor. The project staff, however, had difficulty locating some control subjects, as the location effort was not made until the children were 30 months old. Since transient persons in this area tend to be the most seriously disadvantaged residents (Seitz, Apfel, & Rosenbaum, 1983), it is likely that, by substituting easier-to-find subjects for lost ones, the project staff established a control group that was somewhat more advantaged than the intervention families. The early data on these subjects also suggest that was the case (Provence et al., 1977). This control group may thus provide a somewhat conservative test of the effects of the intervention.

While in some instances matching introduces misleading biases into samples (Campbell & Erlebacher, 1970; Yando, Seitz, & Zigler, 1979), in the present study it shoule not have done so. None of the variables used for matching required selection of subjects who were unrepresentatively rare in the population of hospital patients from which the sample was taken. Thus this was not a case where the best-functioning subjects from one population were chosen for comparison with the worst cases from the other. Rather, the matching probably increased the power of the study by focusing on a particularly well-defined group of both experimental and control mothers: impoverished women who were expecting a firstborn child, who were not adolescents, who had sought prenatal care from a public clinic, who had no serious complications of pregnancy, and who delivered healthy infants.

Measures

Data in the present report are based on the Peabody Individual Achievement Test (PIAT; Dunn & Markwardt, 1970), the Wechsler Intelligence Scale for Children (WISC-R; Wechsler, 1974), interviews with children's teachers and guidance counselors, and interviews with the parents.

Children's Performance Measures The PIAT and WISC-R were administered individually to the children by trained examiners who were unfamiliar with the purpose of the study and with the group assignment of the children. For the school interviews, neither the respondent nor the interviewer was aware of the group identity of the children. Because families are likely to identify themselves during lengthy interviews, no special effort was made to conduct home interviews by persons blind to group membership.

Teacher Ratings Teachers rated 12 attributes of the child's personality and classroom behavior, half relating to positive and half relating to negative characteristics. Negative items were selected from problems reported by Achenbach and Edelbrock (1981) to be relatively common for children in the age range of 8–12 years (e.g., "lying or cheating," "unhappy, sad, or depressed"; at least 25% of boys or girls in the normative population were reported as demonstrating each selected problem). Positive attributes were chosen from a teacher

interview employed by Yando and her colleagues (Yando et al., 1979), including such items as "is liked by other children," and "energetic, lively, and enthusiastic." The 12 items were presented in counterbalanced order beginning and ending with a positive attribute. As in the Achenbach and Edelbrock questionnaire, each item was rated as 0 ("item not true of child"), 1 ("item somewhat or sometimes true of child"), or 2 ("item very true or often true of child").

Need for Special Services A person within the school who knew the child well was interviewed. This individual was usually the child's classroom teacher. For children in junior high school, information was also obtained from a school counselor. Respondents were asked to indicate whether the child had received any special services of a remedial, enriched-program, psychological, or any other nature. If the child received services, the number of times per week, the number of total sessions, and whether the services were individual or group based was ascertained. For children receiving services, the respondent was asked to judge whether they were actually needed by the child and whether or not they appeared to be effective. For children not receiving services, the respondent was asked to judge whether the child needed any services not currently being provided.

RESULTS

Complete data were obtained for 14 of the 17 matched pairs of families and their children. Partial data were obtained for all remaining intervention and for one of the remaining control families. Two control families, both with girls as firstborns, could not be located. Analyses were performed only with data from the matched pairs. The more complete intervention sample data do not, however, yield different conclusions from those reported for the sample for whom matched control subjects were found. Because the matching variables did not introduce any significant correlation between intervention and control groups, ordinary t tests were performed.

Maternal Education

Data are available for 15 of the 17 pairs of families (five of the seven pairs of girls' families and all of the 10 firstborn boys' families). The two groups did not differ significantly in education at the birth of their first child or 30 months later (averaging approximately 11–11.5 years of education at each time). As Table 1 shows, in the present follow-up, the experimental mothers had completed significantly more years of education than had the control mothers. The number of experimental mothers who had completed some education beyond high school rose from one of the 15 mothers at the birth of the first child to 10 of the 15 at the recent follow-up. For control mothers, the comparable numbers were two of the 15 when their first child was born to six of the 15 at the recent follow-up.

Family Size

Data are available for the same 15 pairs of families just described. Because the control children are younger, the number of children per family was calculated for each pair equating for the age of the control child. As shown in Table 1, the average number of children per family when the firstborn child was approximately 10 years old was smaller for the experimental than for the control families ($p = .06$). In each group, the range of number of children was from one to three.

Information on the median years to birth of the second child was available for all of the families in the study. The intervention mothers waited a median of 9 years before having a second child, compared with a median of 5 years for the control mothers.

The effect size for number of children was large (Cohen, 1977), with the group means differing by 7/10 of their pooled standard deviation. With the present sample sizes, the probability of a beta error incurred in failing to reject the null hypothesis is greater than .40 (Cohen, 1977). It thus seems advisable to regard the reduced family size as a statistically reliable result.

Marital Status and Family Type

For the same 15 pairs of families, at the birth of their first child, five mothers in each group were married. The two groups were also comparable when their children were 30 months old (four of 15 intervention and seven of 15 control mothers were married). As Table 1 shows, in the 1982 follow-up, the two groups were still similar. Overall, in 30% of the families, the mother was married to the biological father of her firstborn child. The two groups did not differ significantly in this regard. The two groups did differ in overall family configuration. As may be seen in Table 1, all of the intervention families were nuclear families (mother and child or children, or mother, husband, and child or children). In

TABLE 1   SUMMARY OF COMPARISONS OF INTERVENTION AND CONTROL FAMILIES

Measure	Intervention group			Control group			Probability of difference
	Mean	SD	Proportion	Mean	SD	Proportion	
Maternal education (in years)	13.00	1.50	...	11.70	1.80	...	$t(28) = 2.35, p < .05$
No. of children	1.67	.62	...	2.20	.86	...	$t(28) = 1.95, p = .06$
No. of mothers married	...	...	9(15)	...	...	7(15)	N.S.
No. of nuclear families	...	...	15(15)	...	...	9(15)	$x^2(1) = 7.25^a, p < .01$
No. of self-supporting families	...	...	13(15)	...	...	8(15)	$x^2(1) = 3.84, p < .05$

Note: Numbers in parentheses refer to total sample size.
[a] Chi-square values corrected for small sample size by method of Rhoades and Overall (1982).

six of the control families, the parent(s) shared an extended household with other adult relatives.

Socioeconomic Status

An estimate of socioeconomic status was made from the interview data, which included detailed questions about the parents' employment history to the present. If at least one adult in the family was employed on a full-time basis, or if the number of jobs held by the parents equaled a full-time job, the family was regarded as being self-supporting.[1] This is a more stringent criterion than has been used in earlier studies of this project, in that it excludes part-time or temporary employment and being supported by parents from the definition of being self-supporting. Since the adults in these families are now in their 30s, we have considered that a good outcome means financial independence from their own parents as well as from welfare and other outside sources of support.

For the 15 pairs of families, eight of the intervention and 10 of the controls had been self-supporting by this definition when their firstborn child was 30 months old (i.e., at the end of the intervention period). This slight difference was not significant. At the 1982 follow-up, most of the intervention families were self-supporting, while about half of the 15 control families were.[2] The total number of persons who were not family-supported was six (two mothers and four children) in the intervention and 25 (seven mothers, two fathers, and 16 children) in the control group.

To estimate costs associated with these findings, the assumption was made that the absence

[1] This criterion also reflects the true dichotomy found for this outcome. Only one family reported having a part-time job. In all other cases, parents either reported having full-time employment or none at all.

[2] One intervention family not included in the analysis was known to be self-supporting. No current data were available for the other family, who resided out of state. This family was self-supporting when interviewed 5 years ago.

of obvious gainful employment means that a person's expenses for shelter, food, and clothing must be available from some outside source. State welfare guidelines provide a baseline estimate of such costs, although perhaps a conservative one. (They do not include costs of medical care or food stamps.) Costs of support were estimated based on 1983 welfare standards for the State of Connecticut, regardless of the family's actual place of residence. These yearly values were $4,298 for a family of two persons, $5,280 for a family of three, and $6,201 for a family of four. The average dollar costs of support, based on the above formula, were $700 per year for the intervention and $2,705 per year for the control families. The means of the two groups differed significantly, $t(28) = 2.13$, $p < .05$.

Parenting Style

Comparisons were made of responses to interview questions regarding the number of hours of television watching per day, hours of homework per day, and number and frequency of household chores the parent reported they permitted or required of their child.

The two groups were nearly identical in their self-reported parenting practices in these areas. The groups did differ, however, in the degree to which their involvement in their children's schooling was self-initiated. While almost all mothers reported that they consulted with their child's teacher at least once during the school year, control mothers were more likely than experimental mothers to have done so only in response to a teacher's specific request. The two groups of mothers also differed in their view of what was most satisfying about their child. In response to the question of what the child had done that most pleased the parent, experimental mothers usually reported an act showing the child's concern or affection for them or other family members; few control mothers did so.

Children's IQ Test Performance

Data were available for 14 of the 18 matched pairs of children. (The Hispanic children were not given the WISC-R, and data for one additional control child of each sex were missing; data were thus available for nine of the 11 pairs of boys and five of the seven pairs of girls.) Table 2 summarizes the results of comparisons of these groups. As Table 2 shows, experimental and control children did not differ significantly on the full-scale WISC-R IQ. (They also did not differ on the verbal or performance scaled scores.) Within each group, boys scored lower than did girls.

Correlations were calculated between the number of months of day-care children had received and their IQ test scores. From 30 months of age until entering school, experimental and control children had received similar amounts of day-care (averaging approximately 14 months in each group). For both experimental and control children, there was no significant correlation between amount of day-care— whether prior to 30 months, after 30 months, or total amount of day-care—and later IQ scores.

Months of day-care during the intervention phase were significantly related to the children's language DQ at 30 months ($r = +.57$ for the 15 children for whom current IQ data were obtained). The correlation between months of day-care and these children's 12-year-old WISC-R verbal IQ was significantly lower ($r = -.20$) than the earlier correlation.

Academic Achievement

Data on the PIAT were available for the same children as were WISC-R data. As shown in Table 2, within each group, girls performed better than did boys. Because of the age difference between groups, comparisons were made using percentile ranks. If children had failed a grade, their performance was compared with norms for the grade they should have been attending. The mean percentile rank for the total PIAT performance did not differ significantly across groups, and girls performed better than did boys. The correlation between children's IQ test scores and their performance on the PIAT was significant and of similar magnitude in both groups ($r = .70$ for intervention, r

TABLE 2   SUMMARY OF COMPARISONS OF INTERVENTION AND CONTROL GROUP CHILDREN

	Intervention		Control		
Measure	Mean	SD	Mean	SD	Probability of difference
Boys:					
WISC-R full-scale IQ	91.7	15.2	93.3	13.8	N.S.
Achievement (PIAT percentile rank)	41.0	28.0	32.0	28.0	N.S.
Positive teacher ratings (Sum)	8.1	2.6	5.7	2.9	N.S.
Negative teacher ratings (Sum)	1.4	1.8	6.6	3.1	$t(18) = 3.46, p < .01$
Number of negative school services	.4	.5	1.9	1.4	$t(20) = 3.36, p < .01$
Girls:					
WISC-R full-scale IQ	98.0	9.2	103.8	16.7	N.S.
Achievement (PIAT percentile rank)	51.0	23.0	56.0	28.0	N.S.
Positive teacher ratings (Sum)	8.6	2.4	10.6	1.7	N.S.
Negative teacher ratings (Sum)	3.4	2.3	1.8	3.0	N.S.
Number of negative school services	0	0	0	0	N.S.
Both sexes					
No. with serious absenteeism	0(15)[a]		4(15)		$x^2(1) = 4.46[b], p < .05$
No. with good current school adjustment	10(16)		4(16)		$x^2(1) = 4.42, p < .05$

[a] Numbers in parentheses refer to total group.
[b] Chi-square values corrected for small sample size by method of Rhoades and Overall (1982).

= .81 for control subjects, $p < .01$ in each case). The relationship between months of day-care and PIAT score was nonsignificant in each group.

Teacher Interview Data

The two scores chosen for analysis were the sum of the six ratings on positive attributes and the sum of the six ratings on negative attributes. Each score ranged from 0 to 12; the two scores were moderately negatively correlated ($r = -.39$, $p < .05$). Correlations among the six positive items and among the six negative items were too high to justify considering results for individual items separately.

Teacher interview data were available for 10 of 11 pairs of boys and five of seven pairs of girls. As Table 2 shows, for the girls there were no significant differences in teacher ratings. Control boys, however, were rated much more negatively by their teachers than were experimental boys.

School Attendance

Data on school attendance were available for the same 15 of 18 pairs of children for whom teacher interview data were available. On the average, experimental children missed 7.3 days of school during the school year, while control children missed 13.3 days of school. The variances were significantly different, and a square root transformation did not stabilize the variances. We therefore analyzed these data nonparametrically, defining serious absenteeism as missing without valid excuse 20 or more days of school (a cutoff defined as representing truancy by the school system). As Table 2 shows, the groups differed significantly on this measure.

Remedial and Supportive School Services

School service data were available for all of the 11 pairs of boys and for five of the seven pairs of girls. With one exception (a control girl receiving a gifted students' program), all services were of a remedial or supportive nature. As Table 2 shows, experimental and control

boys differed significantly on this measure. Four intervention boys received one service each; eight control boys received from one to four services each.

Costs of services were determined using the hourly compensation paid in the city school system for social workers, math and reading tutors, special education teachers, speech and language tutors, home-bound tutors, etc., and the number of hours the child received of each service during the school year. For group services, the costs were divided by the number of children in the group. Costs of school-requested psychological evaluations, court hearings, and other outside services were obtained from the institutions involved. On the average, the 11 control boys received services during the school year costing $1,570 above the normal cost per pupil in the city schools, while the additional services provided to the corresponding experimental boys averaged $450 per child. With a square root transformation, the variances of the two groups were homogeneous. The means of the two groups differed significantly, $t(20) = 2.09$, $p < .05$. The median additional costs for the 11 experimental and 11 control boys provide a similar picture ($0 and $1,030 for experimental and control boys, respectively).

Combined Index of Current School Adjustment

To describe current school adjustment, a single indicator was selected from each of the four kinds of outcomes just described. The following information was scored on a simple yes/no basis: (1) Poor Achievement: Was the child's PIAT performance a year or more below the child's actual grade in school? (2) Absenteeism: Did the child have 20 or more unexcused absences during the school year? (3) Classroom Behavioral Problems: Did the child's teacher describe the child as having serious problems of acting out (e.g., "lying or cheating" or "disobedient")? (4) School Services: Was the child receiving school services of a negative kind? As

Table 2 shows, the two groups differed significantly in the number of children who were free of problems in any of these areas. Many more intervention than control children had good current school adjustment.

Other Analyses

Effects of Father Presence or Absence The availability of a father or father figure in the home did not differ across experimental and control groups. Since this factor may affect school adjustment, especially for boys, its effects were examined by pooling across experimental and control subjects, and comparing those boys whose biological father lived in the home ($N = 5$) with those for whom this was not true ($N = 17$) on all measures of children's performance. Similar comparisons were made for boys having a father figure in the home (stepfather or grandfather, $N = 15$) versus those for whom this was not true ($N = 7$). None of the comparisons was significant, and the direction of the differences did not consistently favor any group.

Effects of Being Self-Supporting Within the control group, comparisons were made between the children from the eight families who were self-supporting (five boys, three girls) and the seven who were not (five boys, two girls). The two groups did not differ in IQ. They did differ significantly in school achievement, school attendance, and teacher's ratings of negative characteristics, with children from self-supporting families showing better school adjustment than did children whose families were not self-supporting. The two groups did not differ in the extent to which boys received special services, either in number or cost ($M = \$1,591$ vs. $M = \$1,611$ for self-supporting vs. non-self-supporting families, respectively; medians $= \$1,196$ vs. $\$1,369$).

Correlations between Project Utilization and Outcomes As noted earlier, the experimental families varied in the number of home visits they received and in the number of months their children attended the day-care program. These two measures of project utilization were negatively related to each other ($r = -.61$, $p < .01$). Correlations were calculated between each of these measures and each quantitative outcome measure. Chi-square analyses were performed to assess the relationship between a median split on each variable and qualitative outcomes. None of these relationships was statistically significant.

DISCUSSION

The results of the present study suggest that early, intensive family support intervention has significant potential for improving long-range family functioning in at least certain kinds of impoverished families. While much remains to be determined about targeting, timing, and specific procedures that are effective, the present findings suggest that the general strategy of focusing on families is a promising one.

Too few fathers participated to permit an evaluation of whether this kind of program is well designed to strengthen marriages or to meet paternal as well as maternal needs. A replication with a sample of married couples would be necessary to answer this question. In the present study, many of these first-time mothers had been essentially abandoned during their pregnancy by the father of their child. The family support for these women was, of necessity, maternal and child support. While little can be said about the effects of this program on fathers, there is a great deal of information about its effects on overall family functioning, on the children's social and emotional adjustment, and on the quality of the mother-child relationship.

Family Functioning

The 10-year follow-up data, employing the original matched control groups, support the conclusion reached by the authors of a 5-year follow-up (Trickett et al., 1982) that parents changed dramatically in response to this program. The intervention appears to have had lasting consequences for the families' socioeconomic status. Approximately 10 years after the project ended, almost all of the intervention families were self-supporting, while only about half of the control families were. Since the two groups did not differ in marital status or in the number of two-parent families (whether married or not), being self-supporting was not an artifact of the number of adults in the household.

The number of control families who are presently self-supporting is at best equal to the number who were self-supporting 10 years ago (if both missing families are self-supporting). In contrast to this static picture, the intervention families have shown a slow, steady rise in becoming financially self-sufficient. There were no immediate effects of the program on this outcome: the number of intervention families supported by welfare at the start and end of the intervention was unchanged (Rescorla et al., 1982). The long-term findings seem to be an example of a sleeper effect (Seitz, 1981).

In proposing a possible causal mechanism by which this slow, steady change occurred, we hypothesize that the intervention affected the mother's childbearing decisions very early, and that this fact was central to the other changes that have been found. As was the case for employment, the difference in education between the two groups did not occur when the children were very young. Thus, there was not an immediate cause-effect relationship of mothers obtaining more education during the 30 months of intervention. During the firstborn's later preschool years, however, the intervention mothers tended to delay subsequent childbearing (waiting a median of 9 years before having a second child). Having fewer children to care for and support and not having more than one preschooler at home almost certainly

makes it easier for a woman to further her education or to seek employment.

It may be that women with limited vision of what they could accomplish were helped to see their potential more fully as encompassing employment as well as motherhood. The present intervention was intensive, personalized, and delivered in an explicitly nurturant manner. In this regard it resembles procedures employed in many maternal and infant care centers (U.S. Department of Health, Education, and Welfare, 1975) and those employed by Hardy and her colleagues (1981) in an experimental study of intervention with teenage mothers. The results of all three projects are consistent in suggesting that comprehensive medical and social support services, delivered in a personalized, nurturant way to impoverished women, result in reduced subsequent childbearing and increased maternal return to school. This is clearly a promising lead, well worth pursuing in future intervention studies.

Child Effects

Social Development and School Adjustment
There was no evidence of lasting cognitive change produced by this program. Rather, the principal effects for children occurred among boys and were related to socialization and school adjustment. Teachers who had known the children 9 months rated intervention boys as being socially well-adjusted. In contrast, most of the control boys were described as being disobedient, usually to a serious degree, and as not getting along well with other children. Slightly over half were also described as "unhappy, sad, or depressed" and as having problems with lying or cheating. Such negative descriptions were supported by parental reports as well. Mothers reported that several of the control boys had shown such predelinquent behavior as stealing, being expelled from school for fighting, and staying out all night without reporting their whereabouts. The finding of

better social adjustment for intervention children is similar to findings reported by Trickett and her colleagues in the 5-year follow-up, when persons who tested the children rated their social characteristics highly. For reasons we discuss below, we believe these differences in socialization reflect long-standing differences in the quality of the parent-child relationship.

The average difference of over $1,000 a year per boy in need for school services does not appear to be artifactual in any way. Experimental and control children were attending comparable kinds of schools with similar educational resources. Since the experimental and control families did not differ in the availability of a father in the home, comparisons between the two groups of children are not confounded by this factor. Finally, the effects for control children of their family's being self-supporting essentially mirrored the experimental versus control group results, with the important exception of children's need for school services. Evidently, the experimental boys' ability to adjust to school without requiring costly school services is not simply the result of their families' better overall societal adaptation as reflected in their being self-supporting.

The finding of lessened need for school services among intervention children is in agreement with results reported by the Consortium for Longitudinal Studies (Lazar & Darlington, 1982), but, in the present study, this result occurred only for boys. Because of the very small sample size for girls, the possibility of inadequate statistical power exists. However, differences between experimental and control girls did not even approach statistical significance. One possible explanation is that the present intervention and control samples were initially relatively better functioning than the less selected samples studied by the Consortium (e.g., all of the children were full-term and healthy at birth). Such girls may not need intervention to function adequately in school, at least in the early grades. It is also possible that

girls may wait until their teenage years, or until they become mothers themselves, to display serious adjustment problems. Dropping out of school, or becoming a teenage mother, for example, are indices that were not yet appropriate for the 10- and 11-year-old control girls in the present study.

The intervention children (both boys and girls) had good school attendance, a finding that was true for them when they were younger as well (Trickett et al., 1982). In contrast, over a quarter of the control children (equally divided between boys and girls) were officially truant. School absence has been found in other studies to predict serious life outcomes such as delinquency for boys (Loeber & Dishion, 1983; Mitchell & Rosa, 1981; Robins & Hill, 1966) and teenage pregnancy for girls (Osofsky & Osofsky, 1978; Seitz et al., 1983). Because of the small sample, we are not prepared to interpret the school attendance findings in a predictive manner. At this point, we consider it simply as cause for concern for the control children.

Relationship between IQ and School Adjustment Our findings suggest that raising IQs perhaps should not be the first goal of efforts to improve poor children's educability. As others have noted (Cowen, Gesten, & Weissberg, 1980; Kellam, Ensminger, & Turner, 1977), children's school adjustment difficulties can be categorized into the three areas of achievement problems, shyness or withdrawal, and aggression or acting-out. What the present intervention appears to have accomplished was to eliminate the need for services other than those related to school achievement difficulties for low-IQ children. No intervention boy with an IQ score above 80 required services, and all needed services for lower-IQ boys were remedial in nature. Among control boys, even for those with IQs above their group median of 93, the majority were receiving services, directed toward both learning and behavioral problems (e.g., placement in a classroom for emotionally disturbed children, or "home-bound" tutoring following suspension from school). The lack of practical benefits associated with higher IQ scores suggests that unless the problems of the child's family are adequately addressed, it seems doubtful that a few extra IQ points can bring much lasting life advantage to a child.

It remains possible, however, that effective intervention might be able to provide both family support and cognitive enrichment, perhaps resulting in improved social-emotional development as well as higher IQs. As has been found with many other interventions, the present project's day-care produced short-term cognitive benefits. At 30 months, the intervention children showed a linguistic advantage over the control children; the correlation between months of day-care and language test performance at that time was also positive and significant (Rescorla et al., 1982). It is noteworthy that the correlation between months of early day-care and *current* IQ is negative in sign. A reasonable interpretation of this change is that the project staff most actively promoted enrollment in day-care for children whose homes were most limiting, that the day-care experience stimulated these children's language development, but that their home environments were not changed in the ability to promote subsequent cognitive growth. These IQ findings thus leave open the question of whether extending the day-care program might have resulted in longer-lasting IQ and school achievement benefits for the children.

Parent-Child Bond

We tentatively postulate that the causal link between the intervention program and the children's better social and school adjustment is to be found in the greater parental nurturance brought about by the program. We did not measure early mother-child interactions and cannot therefore determine whether intervention strengthened the parent-child bond, which

then led to the better emotional development and to the long-term behavioral differences now evident in these children. However, this was the explicit aim of the program, and this kind of causal chain appears to be a plausible one. Many studies indicate that various kinds of family support can reduce the stress of new parenthood and facilitate the development of secure mother-infant attachments (Bronfenbrenner, 1979; Cochran & Brassard, 1979; Crockenberg, 1981; Gottlieb, 1981; Mueller, 1980; Powell, 1979). There is also evidence that a strong mother-child bond has beneficial consequences for children in their preschool years, including better social development (Belsky, 1981; Lieberman, 1977; Matas, Arend, & Sroufe, 1978; Rutter, 1978; Sroufe, Fox & Pancake, 1983; Waters, Wippman, & Sroufe, 1979). The present findings suggest that a good parent-child relationship carries benefits for the child into later years as well.

There is no question that current mother-child relationships are better in intervention than in control families. The mothers' interview responses indicate that the intervention children have an investment in pleasing their mothers and that they show their affection in very satisfying ways. The parents also express interest in the child's hobbies and activities. The sense of this finding is best given in the mothers' own words. Parents had been asked, "Think about the last time———did something that pleased you. What was it?" Typical responses were: "Helping me with the house, so I could study"; "When I was sick, he took care of me"; "On mother's day, she gave me a rose and cooked breakfast"; "He made me candle holders at school"; and "His baseball—they were the champs and———pitched. We jumped and screamed and went for pizza."

Very few control mothers gave responses suggesting pleasure in their relationship with their child. Typical responses referred to some accomplishment, such as: "When he got promoted"; "She got all A's except for a C in music"; and "When she passed this year." Others reported household chores: "He cleaned house before vacation"; "Cleaning up on her own." And two mothers replied: "Can't think of anything"; and "He hasn't pleased me in a long time."

The experimental mothers' active stance in dealing with schools is also suggestive of confidence and competence in the parental role. Almost all of these mothers initiated contact with teachers and solicited information to monitor the education of their children. We hypothesize that this style arose from their earlier interactions with the day-care staff, interactions that developed an expectation that there should be information exchange between parents and the institutions caring for their children. That they have continued this practice so many years after the program ended also suggests that they feel competent to deal with whatever information such exchanges reveal. In contrast, control mothers appeared to be operating under the premise that "no news is good news" in regard to their children's academic life.

Because of the age differences between intervention and control children, we have postponed a fuller comparison of the parental interview data until the control families are reinterviewed. We will examine parental style and children's school achievement more completely when same-age data are available.

Replication

As many researchers have documented, there are many reasons why a parent's capacity to nurture may be compromised. Living in a stressful environment, having limited support available from others, lacking knowledge about what is normal in child development, having babies who are unusually difficult, and having received inadequate nurturance themselves may all cause parents to be unable to support their child's optimal development. Intervention programs that address any one of these problems are likely to result in benefits for children

and families. Programs designed to address combinations of problems are likely to be even more effective.

For this reason, we would argue that comprehensiveness, or coordination, of all services likely to be needed should be a cornerstone of family support intervention. While a laboratory research paradigm might suggest attempting to separate components in order to contrast them (e.g., day-care for children vs. home visits for parents), in our opinion, this is not a promising research strategy. Attempting to determine which component of a program is most important may be akin to testing whether surgery is more important than medication in treating illness: in some cases one treatment will be more efficacious than the other; in some cases, both should be used. In the present project, utilization of the day-care and home-visit components was negatively correlated, reflecting the fact that what one family needed was not necessarily needed or wanted by another. Also, neither component alone significantly predicted any later outcome.

Questions that could more productively be examined within an experimental paradigm include issues of timing and targeting. Beginning a parent-oriented program at 6 weeks postpartum may have quite different effects from beginning it just prior to the child's delivery (Larson, 1980). Providing family support for married couples might yield different results from those for single mothers, and the same may be true for experienced rather than first-time parents. Focusing on the parent's needs and the child's emotional development might be the first phase of an intervention that then provided either cognitive enrichment for the child or continued general family support during the child's later preschool years.

Financial Considerations

As Naylor (1982) has noted, the true financial benefits of the project are probably cumulative over many years; they would thus be considerably higher than the value we were able to calculate for a single year. It is probably against such cumulative costs that a cost-benefit analysis should be made. The cost of the program was $7,500 per family in 1970–72 dollars over the 30 months of the intervention (Naylor, 1982). In 1982 dollars, such costs translate to approximately $20,000 per family for the full period of intervention.[3] Because it is difficult to assess socioeconomic status reliably (Mueller & Parcel, 1981), before crediting a family with being self-supporting, we chose to use the relatively stringent criterion of full-time employment of a publicly verifiable nature. Our estimates of what it costs to support a family in the absence of earned income were conservative, since they did not include medical care and food stamps. Because of the larger family sizes among the control families, the actual dollar costs of needed extrafamilial support were considerably higher (approximately $30,000 more) for the control than for the intervention group this 1 year alone. For school services, the total difference of approximately $10,000, when added to the figure for extrafamilial support needs, suggests a total 1-year differential of approximately $40,000. Thus, in comparison with costs, the project currently appears to be paying itself off at the rate of at least two families per year.

The results also indicate that providing services over a long period of time need not make parents permanently dependent on them. In fact, the opposite may be the case. A central theme in all the findings of this study is the increased self-reliance of the project families. This is true in their employment, in their having become independent from their parents, in their active involvement in their children's schooling, and in their children's lessened need for special services. Just as independence in children is fostered by appropriately meeting their

[3]1970 dollars were multiplied by a factor of 2.73 to estimate 1982 dollars, based on the change in the consumer price index for all services, including educational services (*Statistical Abstracts* of the U.S., 1982–1983).

legitimate early dependency needs, it may be that addressing the problems of troubled new parents increases the likelihood that their family will later be able to function independently and well.

What the project staff in the present study provided might be described as social work, as psychotherapy, as the humanized delivery of medical care, as quality day-care, or even as substitute parenting for distressed young parents. What remains to be accomplished in future research is the clarification of many issues of program design, targeting, and timing. But what seems no longer in doubt is that interventions can be implemented that can greatly enhance parent and child development in families at risk and that the cost of failing to do so is high in both financial and human terms.

REFERENCES

Achenbach, T. M., & Edelbrock, C. S. (1981). Behavioral problems and competencies reported by parents of normal and disturbed children aged 4–16. *Monographs of the Society for Research in Child Development*, **46**(1, Serial No. 188).

Belsky, J. (1981). Early human experience: A family perspective. *Developmental Psychology*, **17**, 3–23.

Bronfenbrenner, U. (1975). Is early intervention effective? In M. Guttentag & E. L. Struening (Eds.), *Handbook of evaluation research* (Vol. **2**, pp. 519–603). Beverly Hills, CA: Sage.

Bronfenbrenner, U. (1979). *The ecology of human development*. Cambridge, MA: Harvard University Press.

Campbell, D. T., & Erlebacher, A. (1970). How regression artifacts in quasi-experimental evaluations can mistakenly make compensatory education look harmful. In J. Hellmuth (Ed.), *The disadvantaged child: Vol. 3. Compensatory education: A national debate* (pp. 185–210). New York: Brunner/Mazel.

Cochran, M. M., & Brassard, J. A. (1979). Child development and personal social networks. *Child Development*, **50**, 601–616.

Cohen, J. (1977). *Statistical power analysis for the behavioral sciences* (rev. ed.). Hillsdale, NJ: Erlbaum.

Cook, T. D., & Campbell, D. T. (1979). *Quasi-experimentation: Design and analysis issues for field settings.* Chicago: Rand McNally.

Cowen, E. L., Gesten, E. L., & Weissberg, R. P. (1980). An interrelated network of preventatively oriented schoolbased mental health approaches. In R. H. Price & P. Pulitzer (Eds.), *Evaluation and action in the community context* (pp. 173–210). New York: Academic Press.

Crockenberg, S. D. (1981). Infant irritability, mother responsiveness, and social influences on the security of the infant-mother attachment. *Child Development, 52,* 857–865.

Darlington, R. B., Royce, J. M., Snipper, A. S., Murray, H. W., & Lazar, I. (1980). Preschool programs and later school competence of children from low-income families. *Science, 208,* 202–204.

Dunn, L. M., & Markwardt, F. C. (1970). *Peabody Individual Achievement Test manual.* Circle Pines, MN: American Guidance Service.

Dyer, E. (1963). Parenthood as crisis: A restudy. *Marriage and Family Living, 25,* 488–496.

Field, T. M., Widmayer, S. M., Stringer, S., & Ignatoff, E. (1980). Teenage, lower-class, black mothers and their preterm infants: An intervention and developmental follow-up. *Child Development, 51,* 426–436.

Garber, H. L. (in press). The Milwaukee Project. *American Journal of Mental Deficiency.*

Garber, H. L., & Heber, R. (1981). The efficacy of early intervention with family rehabilitation. In M. J. Begab, H. C. Haywood, & H. L. Garber (Eds.), *Psychosocial influences in retarded performance:* Vol. 2. *Strategies for improving competence* (pp. 71–88). Baltimore, MD: University Park Press.

Gottlieb, B. H. (Ed.). (1981). *Social networks and social support.* Beverly Hills, CA: Sage.

Gray, S. W., & Wandersman, L. P. (1980). The methodology of home-based intervention studies: Problems and promising strategies. *Child Development, 51,* 993–1009.

Guilford, J. P. (1965). *Fundamental statistics in psychology and education* (4th ed.). New York: McGraw-Hill.

Hardy, J. B., King, T. M., Shipp, D. A., & Welcher, D. W. (1981). A comprehensive approach to adolescent pregnancy. In K. G. Scott, T. Field, & E. Robertson (Eds.), *Teenage parents and their offspring* (pp. 265–282). New York: Grune & Stratton.

Hobbs, D., & Cole, S. (1976). Transition to parenthood: A decade replication. *Journal of Marriage and the Family, 38,* 723–731.

Hobbs, D., & Wimbish, J. (1977). Transition to parenthood by black couples. *Journal of Marriage and the Family, 39,* 677–689.

Kellam, S. G., Ensminger, M. E., & Turner, R. J. (1977). Family structure and the mental health of children. *Archives of General Psychiatry, 34,* 1012–1022.

Larson, C. P. (1980). Efficacy of prenatal and postpartum home visits on child health and development. *Pediatrics, 66,* 191–197.

Lazar, I., & Darlington, R. (1982). Lasting effects of early education: A report from the Consortium for Longitudinal Studies. *Monographs of the Society for Research in Child Development, 47*(2, Serial No. 195).

LeMasters, E. (1957). Parenthood as crisis. *Marriage and Family Living, 19,* 352–355.

Lieberman, A. F. (1977). Preschooler's competence with a peer: Relations with attachment and peer experience. *Child Development, 48,* 1277–1287.

Loeber, R., & Dishion, T. (1983). Early predictors of male delinquency: A review. *Psychological Bulletin, 94,* 68–99.

Matas, L., Arend, R. A., & Sroufe, L. A. (1978). Continuity in adaptation: Quality of attachment and later competence. *Child Development, 49,* 547–556.

Mitchell, S., & Rosa, P. (1981). Boyhood behavior problems as precursors of criminality: A fifteen-year follow-up study. *Journal of Child Psychology and Psychiatry, 22,* 19–33.

Mueller, C. W., & Parcel, T. L. (1981). Measures of socioeconomic status: Alternatives and recommendations. *Child Development, 52,* 13–30.

Mueller, D. P. (1980). Social networks: A promising direction for research on the relationship of the social environment to psychiatric disorder. *Social Science and Medicine, 40,* 147–161.

Naylor, A. (1982). Child day care: Threat to family

life or primary prevention? *Journal of Preventive Psychiatry, 1*, 431–441.

Olds, D. L. (1982). The prenatal/early infancy project: An ecological approach to prevention of developmental disabilities. In J. Belsky (Ed.), *In the beginning: Readings on infancy* (pp. 270–285). New York: Columbia University Press.

Osofsky, J. D., & Osofsky, H. J. (1978). Teenage pregnancy: Psychosocial considerations. *Clinical Obstetrics and Gynecology, 21*, 1161–1173.

Powell, D. R. (1979). Family-environment relations and early childrearing: The role of social networks and neighborhoods. *Journal of Research and Development in Education, 13*, 1–11.

Provence, S., & Naylor, A. (1983). *Working with disadvantaged parents and children: Scientific issues and practice.* New Haven, CT: Yale University Press.

Provence, S., Naylor, A., & Patterson, J. (1977). *The challenge of daycare.* New Haven, CT: Yale University Press.

Ramey, C. T., & Haskins, R. (1981). The causes and treatment of school failure: Insights from the Carolina Abecedarian Project. In M. J. Begab, H. C. Haywood, & H. L. Garber (Eds.), *Psychosocial influences in retarded performance:* Vol. **2**. *Strategies for improving competence* (pp. 89–112). Baltimore, MD: University Park Press.

Rescorla, L. A., Provence, S., & Naylor, A. (1982). The Yale Child Welfare Research Program: Description and results. In E. F. Zigler & E. W. Gordon (Eds.), *Day care: Scientific and social policy issues* (pp. 183–199). Boston: Auburn.

Rhoades, H. M., & Overall, J. E. (1982). A sample size correction for Pearson chi-square in 2 x 2 contingency tables. *Psychological Bulletin, 91*, 418–423.

Robins, L. N., & Hill, S. Y. (1966). Assessing the contribution of family structure, class and peer group to juvenile delinquency. *Journal of Criminal Law, Criminology, and Police Science, 57*, 325–334.

Rutter, M. (1978). Family, area and school influences in the genesis of conduct disorders. In L. Hersov, M. Berger, & D. Shaffer (Eds.), *Aggression and antisocial behavior in childhood and adolescence* (pp. 49–74). (*Journal of Child Psychology and Psychiatry* Book Series, No. 1). Oxford: Pergamon.

Schweinhart, L. J., & Weikart, D. (1983). The effects of the Perry Preschool Program on youths through age 15—A summary. In Consortium for Longitudinal Studies (Ed.), *As the twig is bent...Lasting effects of preschool programs* (pp. 71–101). Hillsdale, NJ: Erlbaum.

Seitz, V. (1981). Intervention and sleeper effects: A reply to Clarke and Clarke. *Developmental Review, 1*, 361–373.

Seitz, V., Apfel, N. H., & Rosenbaum, L. K. (1983). *Schoolaged mothers: Infant development and maternal educational outcome.* Paper presented at the biennial meeting of the Society for Research in Child Development, Detroit.

Sroufe, L. A., Fox, N. E., & Pancake, V. R. (1983). Attachment and dependency in developmental perspective. *Child Development, 54*, 1615–1627.

Trickett, P. K., Apfel, N. H., Rosenbaum, L. K., & Zigler, E. F. (1982). A five-year follow-up of participants in the Yale Child Welfare Research Program. In E. F. Zigler & E. W. Gordon (Eds.), *Day care: Scientific and social policy issues* (pp. 200–222). Boston: Auburn.

U.S. Department of Health, Education, and Welfare. (1975). *The maternal and infant care projects: Reducing risks for mothers and babies.* (DHEW Publication No. [HSA]75-5012). Washington, DC: Government Printing Office.

Waters, E., Wippman, J., & Sroufe, L. A. (1979). Attachment, positive affect, and competence in the peer group: Two studies in construct validation. *Child Development, 50*, 821–829.

Wechsler, D. (1974). *Manual for the Wechsler Intelligence Scale for Children (Revised).* New York: Psychological Corp.

Winer, B. J. (1971). *Statistical principles in experimental design* (2d ed.). New York: McGraw-Hill.

Yando, R. M., Seitz, V., & Zigler, E. F. (1979). *Intellectual and personality characteristics of children: Social class and ethnic group differences.* Hillsdale, NJ: Erlbaum.

READING 42

Microcomputers in Education: Motivational and Social Issues

Mark R. Lepper

By the end of this century, it has been predicted, most of our children's education will take place via the computer (e.g., Bork, 1980; Kleiman, 1984; Papert, 1980). This article seeks to present a set of research issues raised by the imminent widespread introduction of powerful personal computers into the lives of children. In contrast to most previous discussions in this area, however, its central focus will be on motivational and social-psychological issues rather than cognitive and instructional issues.

By way of introduction, consider three relatively mundane, but still important, presuppositions. The first of these, by now a truism, is that technological changes frequently have important social and psychological consequences. Over the past 30 years, we have seen a growing awareness of the interdependence of technological advances and social change. Again and again in this century, we have seen major shifts in social patterns and cultural values that have followed from the introduction of technological innovations. The social consequences of the introduction of affordable personal automobiles, high-speed air travel, mainframe computers, and commercial television provide only the most obvious recent examples.

A second introductory point is that the social consequences of technological advances occur on many different levels. The invention of the internal combustion engine and the personal automobile did not simply lead to an increased ability for each of us to travel long distances more quickly and easily; it also contributed heavily to the development of suburbia and the corresponding decay of our inner cities. It led to the rise of the shopping center and the supermarket and precipitated the decline of many independent neighborhood businesses. It gave prominence to the oil industry in ways that

significantly shifted the balance of international relations. It contributed to the increased isolation of the nuclear family, changed the social environment in which children are raised, and so forth.

Significant technological advances, in short, have both primary, intended consequences and a variety of often more revolutionary, frequently more important, secondary or derived consequences. To paraphrase Isaac Asimov, what must be foreseen is not just the automobile, but smog and the parking problem; not just the radio, but the soap opera and the situation comedy; not just the television, but the rise of the advertising industry and the creation of the football widow and the TV dinner.

The third point of background is that we are currently on the edge of a revolution in technology that may eventually prove much more sweeping and significant than any other technological advance in the last 200 years—the revolution that is likely to occur as powerful microcomputers begin to infiltrate our lives, in business and industry, in our homes, and in our schools (Condry & Keith, 1983; Deken, 1982; Evans, 1979; Levin & Kareev, 1981; Taylor, 1980). Today, for under $1,000, one can purchase a portable personal computer with more computational power than could have been delivered 30 years ago by a $10,000,000 machine the size of an average living room. It is informative to consider what the current state of the automobile industry would be had similar progress been made over the past 30 years in that domain (Evans, 1979). Had improvements in efficiency and reductions in the cost of automobiles followed patterns similar to the computer industry, each of us would be able to buy a Rolls-Royce today for roughly $2.75; it would get nearly 3,000,000 miles to the gallon and would deliver enough power to tow an aircraft carrier. In short, recent changes in the power and cost of computer technology have been truly astonishing, and we seem to be on the edge of a period of rapidly increasing and widespread distribution of this technology.

The research challenge is obvious. What will be the social–psychological consequences of this technological revolution? How will we know them? Who is, or should be, keeping score?

OVERVIEW OF BASIC RESEARCH ISSUES

This article focuses on four classes of questions of potential theoretical significance and social interest. Of these questions, two involve basic theoretical questions for which the study of the design of educational software happens to provide a particularly appropriate laboratory. The first concerns the study of the determinants of intrinsic motivation: How might one optimize the motivational appeal of educational materials in order to sustain children's interest in instructional programs? What effects will the introduction of highly motivating computer-based materials have on children's later intrinsic interest in and reactions to more traditional forms of instruction? The second, closely related, issue concerns the relationship between the motivational appeal and the instructional value of such programs: How do different techniques for enhancing children's interest and motivation increase, or decrease, the educational value of the materials being presented?

A third general class of research questions involves many of these same issues, considered on an even broader scale. It involves the study of computer-based learning as a laboratory for examining competing, often antithetical, educational philosophies embodied in the design of different sorts of educational software for children. Finally, a fourth set of questions arise in the larger domain of social policy considerations. These issues concern the ways in which the spread of microcomputers may affect the process of social development, enhance social equality or inequality, or influence family relationships. They are explored briefly in the concluding section of this article.

The Research Window

Before turning to these substantive issues, however, one more introductory remark must be made. Much (though not all) of the research suggested here can only be done now or in the relatively near future, the next 2 or 5 or 8 years. Now, one can still find children without previous computer experience and can vary the nature of their introduction to this medium systematically and study the consequences. Soon it will be too late for this. Once the technology has become truly ubiquitous, it will no longer be possible for us to study some of the most interesting questions raised by this new technology.

The analogy to research on the social and cognitive effects of television is instructive (e.g., Hornik, 1981; Liebert, Neale, & Davidson, 1973; Murray, 1980). When commercial television was first introduced, only a few far-sighted individuals were able to foresee its potentially great impact on our society. By the time psychologists had agreed upon what the important questions were, virtually every home had one or more sets, and children were already spending substantial amounts of time in front of the tube (Schramm, Lyle, & Parker, 1961). Once this was true, it became difficult to study many of the most interesting questions concerning television's effects on children. Possible research procedures were highly constrained. The researcher had to rely largely on correlational procedures—comparing self-selected populations of high and low viewers of various sorts—knowing full well that these populations differed on a variety of other potentially important and potentially confounding variables. Alternatively, the researcher could take an experimental approach, but even in the best cases

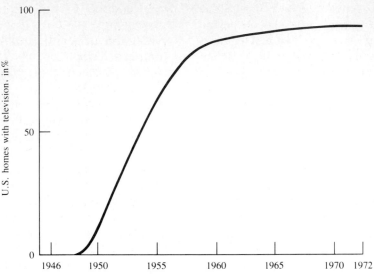

FIGURE 1   Percentage of U.S. homes with television by year.

this approach was likely to involve an intervention of perhaps 20 to 30 hours of controlled viewing set against a backdrop of several thousand hours of prior uncontrolled viewing. These constraints on research possibilities made it virtually impossible to examine several types of fundamental questions (Hornik, 1981).

The period between television's appearance as a novelty in every fifth or sixth home and its virtually universal acceptance, we should note, was little more than 5 years. Figure 1, adapted from Liebert, Neale, and Davidson (1973), displays the distribution curve for home television sets dramatically. Comparably steep distribution curves have been seen more recently for electronic calculators and other recent technological advances (e.g., Nilles et al., 1981).

The point of this analogy should be evident. If we do not act quickly, we may miss the "research window" on microcomputers, as we did with television. Although current projections concerning the spread of microcomputers suggest a somewhat slower growth curve for personal computers than for television or electronic calculators, the fact that microcomputers may become available to children not only at home but also in school, in the public library,

and at summer camp should make us concerned about the time we have left before the population of computer-naive children vanishes (cf. Levin & Kareev, 1981).[1]

DETERMINANTS OF INTRINSIC MOTIVATION

What, then, are the questions that deserve our research attention in the present interval before early exposure to computers becomes universal? One set of issues of simultaneous theoretical and practical significance concerns the determinants of intrinsic motivation: What are the factors that determine when a child will find a set of educational materials to be highly moti-

[1]The fact that this technology may become available to children in many different social settings is of considerable practical significance. It suggests, in particular, that expectations of educational impact should not be limited to the narrower questions of how or how quickly this new technology will be incorporated into our system of formal schooling—questions on which previous, overly optimistic, predictions of technological revolutions in education have typically floundered (Walker, 1983). The instructional and motivational issues raised in this article, it should also be noted, apply equally to the design of educational programs implemented on larger mini- or mainframe computers. The present focus on microcomputers is intended merely to highlight the immediacy and increasing importance of these issues as this technology becomes more widely available.

vating? Clearly, the advent of microcomputers as educational tools has made issues of motivational appeal salient. If one examines the types of programs that are being written for children these days, presumably with educational aims, it is evident that many programs try to use the computer to enhance student motivation.

Suppose that one wished to teach children about the addition and subtraction of fractions with unlike denominators and to provide children with practice at solving such problems. One possibility would be to design a simple "drill and practice" program that would present a child with a sequence of fractions problems and provide praise, or corrective feedback, after each answer the child enters. Such programs are widespread. A generic example appears in the top panel of Figure 2. An alternative approach might involve a different strategy. Suppose one were to present the same sequence of problems to the child in the form of an instructional computer "game" designed to stimulate the child's intrinsic motivation. Such programs, though less common, are not at all unusual. The middle and bottom panels of Figure 2 display two versions of such educational games, "Fractions Basketball" and "Torpedo," respectively, taken from the excellent mathematics curriculum developed by the PLATO Project at the University of Illinois (Dugdale & Kibbey, 1980). In each instance, the goal is to present children with an identical series of problems to be solved, but in these latter cases these problems are presented in a game-like context presumably designed to enhance and maintain children's motivation.

What effects might such procedures have? Does the presentation of educational activities in the form of such games significantly enhance students' intrinsic motivation? For which children does it do so? And, most important, what are the processes by which such variations in the format for presenting problems might influence children's intrinsic interest (cf. Malone, 1980, 1981)?

In addition to simply making these issues salient, there are several important respects in which the design of intrinsically motivating computer-based educational programs for children provides an ideal laboratory for studying the factors that determine intrinsic motivation. First, the design of intrinsically motivating software provides a common context in which the concepts and principles initially developed within several historically distinct research traditions can be systematically and simultaneously studied (Malone & Lepper, in press).

One large class of theorists, for example, has discussed intrinsic motivation primarily in terms of concepts such as challenge, competence, effectance, or mastery motivation (e.g., Csikszentmihalyi, 1975; Harter, 1978, 1981; Kagan, 1972; White, 1959, 1960). Here the focus is on humans as problem solvers. In this view, tasks and activities are intrinsically motivating to the extent that they engage individuals in a process of seeking to solve problems and accomplish goals that require the exercise of valued personal skills. From this point of view, the critical variables influencing intrinsic interest are things such as the goal structure of the activity (e.g., the clarity, multiplicity, and hierarchical structure of goals), the difficulty of accomplishing those goals given the initial skills and knowledge of the learner (e.g., most theories posit some optimal level of difficulty), and the relevance of these goals to valued personal abilities (e.g., a dependence on skill, rather than luck).

A second class of theorists, by contrast, has taken a slightly different approach, focusing on concepts such as curiosity, incongruity, complexity, or discrepancy (e.g., Berlyne, 1960, 1966; Hunt, 1961, 1965; Kagan, 1972). The relevant image in this instance is of humans as information processors. We derive pleasure, by this account, from activities and events that provide us with some optimal (intermediate) level of surprise, incongruity, complexity, or discrepancy as a function of our initial skills and

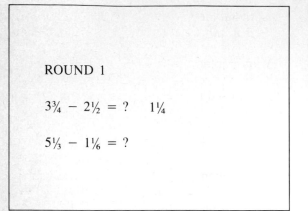

ROUND 1

$3\frac{3}{4} - 2\frac{1}{2} = ?$ $1\frac{1}{4}$

$5\frac{1}{3} - 1\frac{1}{6} = ?$

Here are your scores for today:

Number of Problems
    Attempted   40

Number of Problems
    Correct   36

Percent Correct   90%

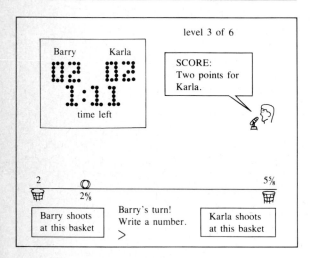

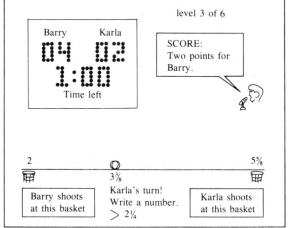

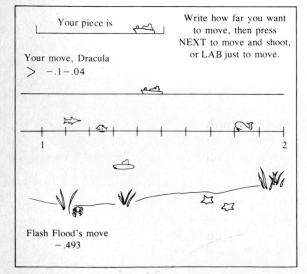

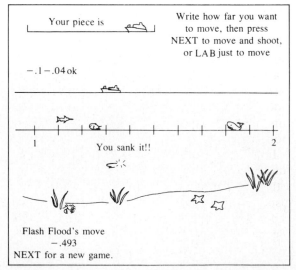

FIGURE 2 Examples of educational computer programs involving drill (top panel) versus game (lower panels) formats.

expectations. The crucial determinants of intrinsic interest, from this perspective, include factors such as novelty, complexity, variability, figurality, uncertainty, and all the rest of Berlyne's (1960) "collative variables."

Yet a third general approach to these issues has focused on concepts of perceived control and self-determination (e.g., Condry, 1977; de-Charms, 1968; Deci, 1975, 1981; Nuttin, 1973). In this view, humans are actors who seek to exercise and validate a sense of control over the external environment. Activities evoke intrinsic interest, in this model, when they provide us with the opportunity to exert control, to determine our own fate, or at least to maintain the perception that we are doing so. For these theorists, variables such as the responsiveness of the environment, contingencies between actions and outcomes, high levels of choice, and perceived personal freedom assume importance.

The important point in this brief review of past research is not that these approaches are incompatible, or even that they are necessarily distinctive. Rather, it is that historically these traditions have largely developed independently, each producing its own set of research paradigms and findings and doing so in a way that has made comparative research extraordinarily difficult. What microcomputers will add to these debates is a laboratory in which variables relevant to each of these models can be systematically studied—a laboratory in which it is possible to manipulate variables relevant to each of these traditional models and to examine their effects on a set of common measures of subsequent intrinsic motivation.

In addition to this basic laboratory function, educational software also provides a propitious setting for studying intrinsic motivation in other respects. First, this medium makes clear the importance of yet a fourth set of factors that appears to have highly significant motivational effects but fits very poorly into any of our traditional models of intrinsic motivation—factors that influence what might be called fantasy involvement. Under this heading would fall the use of graphics, characters, story plots, sound effects, and all the other technical devices that may be used to evoke a playful set, an identification with fictional characters, and an involvement in a world of fantasy (cf. Singer, 1973). The opportunities the computer provides for the creation of interactive stories, animated action sequences, and exciting audio and visual effects may help us in understanding these little-investigated determinants of intrinsic motivation (Malone, 1981; Malone & Lepper, in press).

Two other, more mundane characteristics of the computer also contribute to its utility in serving as a laboratory for studying intrinsic motivation. On the one hand, the fact that each of these factors can easily be varied systematically within a given educational program provides the opportunity for the exercise of a very high level of experimental control. On the other hand, the necessity for specifying a theoretical model that is required to translate abstract concepts into programmable terms should itself improve the level of current theoretical formulations considerably.

Consider the simple, and very prevalent, notion of maintaining an optimal level of difficulty. If children do prefer tasks of moderate difficulty, as many models suggest, then in order for a program to maintain its appeal over time, a series of activities of gradually increasing difficulty will be required. These tasks must keep pace with the child's increasing ability as he or she progresses through the program. The illusion of simplicity in such a prescription, however, becomes quickly apparent as soon as one attempts to embody such a model in a concrete computer program. To take a simple illustration, one can find current educational programs with carefully constructed problem sequences designed to present children with increasingly challenging problems as they demonstrate mastery over earlier units. So far, in theory, so good. One major difficulty with some of these programs, however, arises when children are not informed of this careful sequencing of problems. Rather than enhancing motivation, such programs may often undermine it by leading children to perceive themselves as incapable of succeeding. As one child engaged in one of these programs commented, "Every time I think I've got it, I just miss more of them." Putting abstract principles into concrete programs, then, may often teach us unexpected lessons about the variables that are truly important in motivating children (Malone & Lepper, in press).

INTRINSIC MOTIVATION AND LEARNING

If a first major research issue raised by computer-based instruction is the study of what makes educational activities intrinsically motivating, a second major issue is closely related: What are the effects of differences in motivational appeal on instructional effectiveness? Do educational activities that are "fun" produce learning that is in any sense "better," or "worse," than would be obtained if the same content were presented in some less enjoyable format?

Note that there are two relevant and interesting but quite theoretically distinct issues to be addressed here. The first concerns the effects of motivational appeal on subsequent learning, given what might be called "variable exposure." That is, if one assumes that children are free to choose when and whether to engage in a particular activity, as they might be at home or at the library computer, then motivation may have effects on learning that occur simply as a function of differences in amount of exposure or that ubiquitous educational variable "time-on-task" (cf. Rosenshine, 1976; Stallings, 1980). Such effects may be important in practical terms, but they may not always evoke theoretical interest.

Theoretically important issues do arise, however, when we consider a second case in which overt exposure is "controlled," as it might be in a more highly structured school context in which each child is allotted a given block of time for work at the computer and might be assigned to work with one type of program or another. Here the question would be whether the devices and techniques used to enhance intrinsic motivation also further, or perhaps interfere with, learning the relevant educational content contained in these programs.

Surprisingly, we know very little about this very fundamental question of how motivation affects learning. There are a number of variables that might be hypothesized to determine the character of such effects, but at present there are few data for guidance (Lepper & Malone, in press). The kinds of factors that might deserve investigation include the following: (a) how differing motivational features may influence the direction and intensity of the child's attention to the materials (cf. Kahneman, 1973; Simon, 1967); (b) whether differences in motivational appeal may prompt differences in the child's depth of involvement in the activity (cf. Corno & Mandinach, 1983; Kintsch, 1977; Salomon, 1983); (c) whether variations in motivational features produce concomitant variations in level of arousal (cf. Spence, 1956; Zajonc, 1965); and (d) whether the addition of motivational embellishments provides or prompts an effective means for representing abstract problems (cf. Kintsch, 1977).

Once again, the basic point is not that the study of educational software is the only domain in which such issues might be addressed. Nor should it be assumed that the study of such issues in this domain will yield any "simple" answers (cf. Lepper & Malone, in press). To the extent that existing translations of straightforward computer-assisted instruction (CAI) lessons into instructional games frequently involve the embedding of problems in some fantasy context, for example, additional performance goals besides the attainment of correct answers may be introduced. Such additional goals may either enhance or detract from the educational value of the materials.

To take one simple illustration from existing software, there is a large class of allegedly educational games that involve small-scale "economic simulations," in which children are given the chance to run a bicycle store, manage a lemonade stand, or rule a small kingdom. The notion behind these games is that they will provide the children with both practice in mental arithmetic and some feeling for simple economic principles such as the law of supply and demand, the value of advertising, and so on. In fact, however, most of them share one simple and frequently "fatal" flaw—they allow the children to accumulate earnings or riches over an endless series of trials. As a result, if students have only a limited amount of time to spend on these games, the most efficient way for them to accumulate wealth may be to spend as little time thinking about the choices the program provides as possible. Instead, as soon as the students discover even a single moderately successful combination, a "mindless" repetition of the same figures as fast as their fingers can fly will allow them to amass a considerable hypothetical fortune.

The point, once again, is a simple one: The study of such activities and when and why they succeed or fail provides a rich and compelling natural laboratory in which to address some theoretical issues of more general importance. Although these questions are of interest in their own right, it is possible to view them in yet a broader and potentially even more fascinating context, which brings us to the third general set of issues that the study of educational applications of microcomputers raises—the comparative study of divergent philosophies of education embodied in different approaches to the design of educational software for children.

EXAMINING DIVERGENT EDUCATIONAL PHILOSOPHIES

These divergent philosophies differ in both their goals and their methods for achieving common goals. Each can be seen in existing instructional software. Each has its own vocal adherents.

Achieving Traditional Curriculum Goals

Consider, first, the set of approaches that attempts to teach traditional curriculum content but uses the microcomputer to make the learning of that traditional content more efficient, more lasting and effective, or simply more enjoyable.

Individualized Drill and Practice A first approach, characteristic in many respects of much of the early CAI work, involves the use of the computer as a tool for providing efficient information transfer, coupled with individualized drill and practice (e.g., Atkinson, 1972; Kulik, Bangert, & Williams, 1983; Suppes, 1965, 1966, 1980; Suppes & Morningstar, 1969). Note that even in this least exotic use of the computer, there are several potentially important advantages to the use of the computer over traditional classroom methods. First, the computer provides immediate responsive feedback and sustained attention to the child. Second, the computer provides the opportunity for several sorts of feedback not typically available in the classroom, such as feedback concerning the child's speed of response or immediate evidence on the quality of performance relative to past social norms or the child's own prior performance. Third, the computer affords the opportunity for highly individualized instruction. Both the problems to be presented and the additional instruction to be provided can easily be made contingent on the child's mastery of, and patterns of errors on, previous problems. Moreover, as microcomputer equipment becomes more sophisticated, increasingly complex models of the student can be incorporated into more "intelligent" tutoring systems (Sleeman & Brown, 1982).

Motivational Enhancement via Educational Games Clearly, this first approach may be contrasted with a second that involves an attempt to stimulate children's interest through the construction of educational games and game-like activities of the type illustrated earlier in Figure 2. Rather than simply presenting relevant problems in abstract form (e.g., determining the length of the hypotenuse of a right triangle given knowledge of the lengths of sides AB and AC), a courseware designer in this second tradition might attempt to present such problems in a more intrinsically interesting fashion. The child might be asked, for example, to aid Captain Kirk in determining the distance setting needed for the tractor beam to reach the dilithium crystals, knowing the distance from Kirk to the crystals and to the Enterprise directly overhead. Although the formal mathematical problem is identical in both cases, the motivational effects of these two approaches may be quite different (Davis, Dugdale, Kibbey, & Weaver, 1977).

Within this second category, however, there are also potentially significant variations in the techniques used to enhance motivation. One dimension along which current educational programs of this sort vary dramatically is the degree of relationship between motivational and instructional features. At one extreme, game-like graphics, sound effects, and the like ("bells and whistles," in the trade) are used simply as one form of extrinsic reward for successful performance. In this model, attainment of some predetermined standard of performance produces exciting audiovisual effects. The relationship between the problems presented and the special effects is entirely arbitrary, and the fantasy elements are exogenous. As one example, in the program illustrated in the top panel of Figure 3, successful choices of

the appropriate prefix reveal successive portions of a fire-breathing dragon.

At the other extreme are programs in which special effects are used to create a fantasy context into which the solution of a series of educational activities may be integrated and in which the fantasy elements are endogenous. In this model, the presentation of problems is integrated into an imagined scenario from which the problems naturally arise. The lower half of Figure 3 provides one illustration. In this program, taken again from the Illinois PLATO curriculum (Dugdale & Kibbey, 1980), problems involving basic fraction skills are presented in the context of serving customers frequenting a pizza parlor run by the student. Again, as the technology becomes more advanced, more intellectually complex and challenging versions of instructional games will become possible (Brown, 1984).

At one end of this dimension, special effects and educational content are entirely independent. In the first case, the revelation of the dragon could have been used as a reward with any set of problems in mathematics, language arts, or social studies. At the other pole, there is some integral relationship between the problems posed and the special effects employed; slicing and serving pizza inherently involves concepts and problems involving fractions. Other cases fall at intermediate points on the continuum. In both of the educational games presented in Figure 2, for example, several different sorts of mathematical operations might be taught using the framework embodied in these programs, but the range of possibilities remains relatively limited.

Although there are few data on this score, it seems likely that these different techniques designed to enhance children's motivation may have significantly different effects (Lepper & Malone, in press; Malone & Lepper, in press). Drawing on previous literature concerning the differential effects of extrinsic versus intrinsic

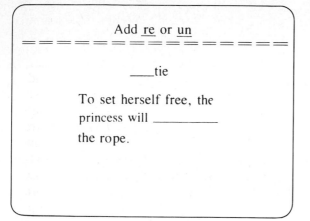

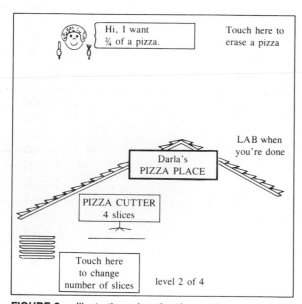

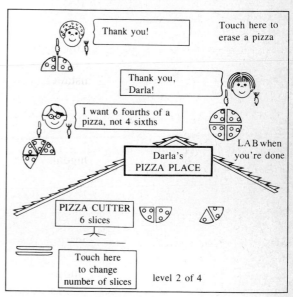

FIGURE 3 Illustrative educational computer games involving exogenous (top panel) versus endogenous (bottom panel) fantasies.

motivation (e.g., Deci, 1975; Lepper, 1983; Lepper & Greene, 1978a), for example, one might predict greater subsequent intrinsic interest in the subject matter presented when there is an integral relationship between instructional content and imaginary context. Even the immediate motivational appeal of such programs may be greater when the fantasy is ''endogenous'' (i.e., when there is a natural relationship be-

tween context and content) rather than ''exogenous'' (Malone, 1981). Similarly, one might expect the imagined context to serve as a more effective learning device when the relationship of problems to context is nonarbitrary. In each of these instances, however, there is an assumption that there are significant benefits to the strategy of employing special effects in an attempt to increase students' motivation.

Educational Simulations Both this motivational enhancement and the earlier drill and practice approaches to traditional curriculum content may be compared, however, to a third general approach—one that involves an attempt to create educational simulations or "microworlds" (cf. Lawler, 1982; Papert, 1980), designed to promote more active, inductive, or discovery-based learning.[2] In this third model, an imaginary environment is presented in which the student confronts some series of problems, frequently in the form of choices to be made by a particular character or object under the control of the student. By observing the contingencies between actions and outcomes built into such simulations, the student is led to abstract basic principles of relevance to the operation of the real-world environment or context after which the simulation is modeled.

Again, however, such programs vary along several dimensions. Perhaps the most obvious of these, for present purposes, is the "directedness" of the simulation. On the one hand, many simulations are designed to achieve highly specific and limited educational aims. The top panel of Figure 4 shows one such directed or focused simulation, drawn from the materials prepared by the Minnesota Educational Computing Corporation (MECC). In this program, the food chain in a typical North American lake is embodied in a simulation in which students, taking the role of a particular fish, are confronted with a series of choices such as whether to attack, flee, or ignore another fish of a different species. The consequences of students' choices in each situation are designed to

reflect the likely results of such actions in the real world. A child who engages in this simulation over a series of trials, then, might be expected to gain knowledge of predator–prey relationships and other aspects of the ecology of Northern American lakes.

Many other educationally oriented simulations, by contrast, have a much more exploratory and less directed character. In these cases, typically, educational aims are less directly specified, and the variety of choices and possibilities open to students is likely to be greater. The bottom panel of Figure 4 contains one example developed by the U. C. Irvine Physics Computer Development Project (Bork, 1980). In this program, students studying the mechanics of eclipses can experiment with a wide variety of relative positions of the sun, earth, and moon, receiving responsive feedback after each choice. Other such programs provide simulations of a high school electronics laboratory or plot the trajectories of missiles fired into space.

Both types of programs share a common assumption about education—that there is something significantly beneficial about active, inductive, exploratory learning that outweighs the relative "inefficiency" of such approaches for achieving highly specified goals, compared with more direct, didactic approaches. Such issues are, of course, direct descendants of those raised in earlier debates concerning the merits of discovery-based learning in other noncomputerized domains (e.g., Bruner, 1962, 1966; Shulman & Keislar, 1966). Clearly, one could teach students about food chains and ecological niches in the North American lakes in a very explicit and directive manner, probably in considerably less time than it will take the students to absorb this material from the simulation presented. On the other hand, there is a fairly widespread belief that children may learn the material "better" and in a more meaningful fashion when they have "discovered" the relevant facts and principles on their own. They

[2]It is not my intention here to argue for a sharp distinction between educational games and instructional simulations or microworlds. Indeed, it appears that the characteristics typically used to distinguish among these concepts are largely a matter of degree (e.g., the degree of structure versus freedom in the activity; the number, complexity, and diversity of response options available to the user, etc.). Despite the conceptual overlaps among these categories, however, these terms have historically developed somewhat different connotations concerning goals and underlying philosophies of instruction that are reflected in their separate treatment here.

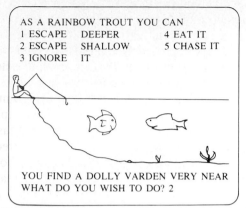

AS A RAINBOW TROUT YOU CAN
1 ESCAPE   DEEPER   4 EAT IT
2 ESCAPE   SHALLOW   5 CHASE IT
3 IGNORE   IT

YOU FIND A DOLLY VARDEN VERY NEAR
WHAT DO YOU WISH TO DO? 2

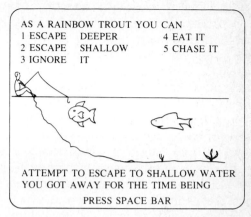

AS A RAINBOW TROUT YOU CAN
1 ESCAPE   DEEPER   4 EAT IT
2 ESCAPE   SHALLOW   5 CHASE IT
3 IGNORE   IT

ATTEMPT TO ESCAPE TO SHALLOW WATER
YOU GOT AWAY FOR THE TIME BEING
PRESS SPACE BAR

Suppose we take a position far out in space, looking down on the earth-moon-sun system from above the north pole of the earth.

The observer on earth is located at the small box.

To make the circles visible, we've made the moon and earth much larger than they would appear on a photograph.

Suppose the observer, in the location indicated, sees a full moon. Use the crosshairs to point to a possible location of the sun. Type S when you want to proceed.

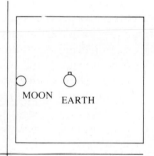

MOON   EARTH

Type S when you've selected your position.

For your choice of the sun position light would travel from the sun to the moon along these lines.

The situation you have indicated does indeed occur. But consider what the observer sees under such circumstances. The earth blocks out some of the light.

Is the face of the moon fully illuminated under these circumstances.
?NO

That is correct.
This is the relatively rare occurrence where the earth's shadow does fall on the moon, a lunar eclipse.

To continue push return■

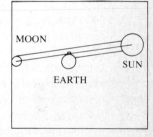

MOON
EARTH   SUN

FIGURE 4   Sample educational simulations.

may also retain this information better, understand it more completely, or be able to make use of it more effectively in situations outside of the immediate context in which the material was acquired (Lawler, 1982; Levin & Kareev, 1981; Papert, 1980).

Again, the reemergence of these classic issues in the arena of computer-based instruction provides the stimulus for a new look at these issues. The sustained attentiveness of the computer and its ability to provide immediate responsive feedback, along with its ability to track and record students' progress, may make it a particularly effective medium for encouraging and studying the process of discovery-based inductive learning.

Other Educational Tools A final opportunity that computers afford for enhancing traditional instruction lies in their use as tools to make easier (or possible) tasks that would otherwise require great time or effort. Thus, the computer can provide facilities for word processing, collection of on-line data, access to major data banks, and programs for statistical analysis or music composition that could be employed in a variety of content areas.

From a research perspective, such opportunities raise two sets of questions.

On the one hand, one may examine the consequences of introducing such facilities into "natural" classroom or home environments. If word processing programs were available in English classes, for example, would children be motivated to write more, would they revise their work more frequently, would they share their work with their friends more readily, or would they engage in more collaborative writing projects (Kane, 1983; Levin & Kareev, 1981)? On the other hand, one may also examine the consequences of more deliberate attempts to integrate and employ the computer in programs designed to achieve specified educational objectives. One could, for example, try to make deliberate use of the availability of word processing facilities to create lessons designed to teach young children higher order lessons about the process of writing and successive revision than they would otherwise encounter.

Expanding the Curriculum

Although all of the foregoing approaches share a common general goal of enhancing instruction in traditional curriculum areas, that is, to make learning of traditional content more effective, more motivating, or more efficient, a second set of approaches begins with the somewhat different goal of adding to and expanding traditional instruction to include skills and topics not now a part of our standard classroom agenda. This second category is, at the moment, largely focused on programs that attempt to teach children to program the computer themselves. Again, however, there are several specific approaches within this general category.

Programming as an end.   Many people seek to teach children programming for its own sake, because they see this skill as inherently valuable in an increasingly computerized society. From this perspective, the acquisition of programming skills is viewed as an end in itself. "Computer literacy" is the byword. The primary goal of such programs is to augment training in traditional subjects with training in this newly developed but potentially critical intellectual ability (e.g., Luehrmann, 1979, 1980).

Programming as a Means   Others make different arguments for teaching young children to program, arguments that rest on the general assumption that the computer provides a unique educational medium for teaching children a variety of skills of thinking and problem solving that are not well captured or explicitly included in our common definition of the standard curriculum. Learning to program, this latter group would argue, is indirectly valuable in several different respects.

First and foremost, proponents of this approach argue, learning to program the computer may lead to the acquisition of general and inherently valuable planning and problem-solving skills that should increase children's ability to solve problems in other settings having no direct connection with the computer at all. Thus, the process of learning to formalize a conceptual model, to decompose a complex problem into smaller and more manageable chunks, to employ a flow chart or a decision tree to anticipate and evaluate alternatives, and perhaps most important to "debug" a program (i.e., to isolate and correct conceptual errors when initial efforts go awry) will provide the child with strategies and heuristics for problem solving that will prove valuable in many domains (e.g., Lawler, 1982; Papert, 1980).

Second, the acquisition of the ability to program may allow children to harness the power of the computer to engage in active, self-directed, exploratory learning in domains of interest that lend themselves to simulation or formalization (e.g., Dwyer, 1974, 1980). For example, knowledge of programming may permit children to experiment with hypothetical and even counterfactual modes of thinking and to perform and observe the results of thought experiments that can be visually represented or computationally performed via the computer. As a concrete example, one might imagine a student writing or adapting a program that simulates the motions of the planets in our solar system according to known gravitational principles and then experimenting with that program to ask what would happen if the law of gravity followed a simple inverse-distance function or were not directly proportional to the mass of the objects involved.

Finally, a child learning to program may also acquire indirectly, and perhaps painlessly and without anxiety, a considerable amount of mathematical knowledge and intuition (Papert, 1972). The concrete and responsive environment the computer provides may prove a particularly felicitous context for children to begin to learn about concepts such as functions, variables, and conditional statements. Graphics systems designed to facilitate children's learning of basic programming skills may similarly help to provide young pupils with a deeper intuitive understanding of underlying principles and regularities in the realm of geometry. Hence, one may wish to teach programming not only because it is an inherently valuable skill, but also because it may accomplish these other goals in an active and highly motivating fashion.

The best-known example of this second general approach to the teaching of programming is embodied in the Logo programming language and the accompanying Logo philosophy, propounded by Seymour Papert, Harold Abelson, Andrea diSessa, and their colleagues at MIT (e.g., Abelson & diSessa, 1980; Papert, 1980; Papert, Watt, diSessa, & Weir, 1979). Logo is a computer language that has recently been adapted for use on several microcomputers. It is a high-level programming language that incorporates list-processing principles originally developed by researchers in the field of artificial intelligence. What makes this language of particular interest in the present context, however, is the fact that it was designed, in part, to facilitate the introduction of young children to computer programming. Thus it contains a number of features (such as a graphics microworld that requires an understanding of only a handful of primitive commands to produce interesting effects, conceptually unlimited extensibility of the primitive command system, complete modularity of procedures, and immediate execution capabilities) that are intended to make it potentially understandable for even very young children.

In its most well-known current use with children, Logo is designed to provide the novice user with access to a programmed microworld known as "turtle graphics." In this mode of operation, children are taught to write programs that control the movements of a cybernetic "turtle" (actually a triangular cursor displayed on the monitor), enabling this turtle to make drawings on the screen. Knowledge of only a half-dozen primitive commands, such as forward and back, left and right, permits the child to produce large and exciting graphic effects that provide immediate feedback concerning his or her efforts to control the turtle's actions in this programmed environment. Planning and controlling the turtle's moves, in turn, encourages the development of more sophisticated programming skills. Logo encourages active and relatively unstructured exploration in a context in which children can make use of their own personal knowledge of the physical world. By putting themselves in the turtle's place, children learn to design and debug their programs. In this fashion, an attempt is made to induce "deep" connections between the child's intuitive understanding of the physical world and fundamental concepts and principles in mathematics and physics (e.g., Abelson & diSessa, 1980; diSessa, 1977, 1982; Lawler, 1981; Papert, 1972, 1980).

In addition, Logo is designed to promote cumulative mastery by permitting the child to designate previously generated procedures or subroutines as "commands" that can later be employed, once defined, as primitives in other more complex procedures. By repeating and combining programs that produce simple figures, interesting and complex designs can be easily created, as illustrated in Figure 5, from Papert, Watt, diSessa, and Weir (1979). More significantly, complicated graphics projects can be accomplished by decomposing these problems into smaller and more easily programmed chunks, as shown in Figure 6 from the same source.

In part, the development of Logo can be viewed as an attempt to provide one instantiation of a philosophy of dynamic and exploratory education, based on a Piagetian model of learning through action (Papert, 1980). Whether exposure to programming in Logo, under present classroom conditions, will produce the generalized cognitive gains its proponents suggest is a source of considerable current research and controversy. In all probability, such effects will prove to be neither as robust or general as proponents would claim, nor as evanescent as opponents would argue (e.g., Clements & Gullo, in press; Milojkovic, 1983; Pea & Kurland, in press).

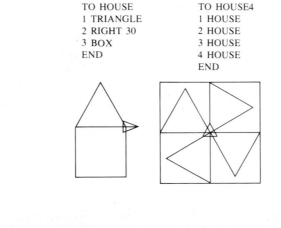

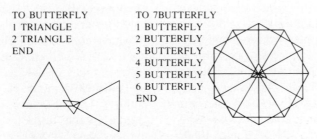

FIGURE 5 Illustrative Logo programs involving simple combinations and repetitions of component modules.

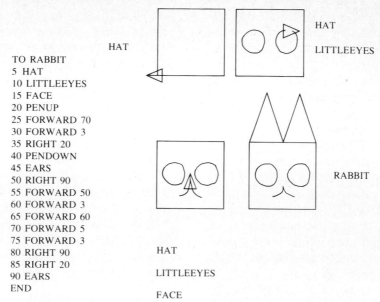

```
TO RABBIT
5  HAT
10 LITTLEEYES
15 FACE
20 PENUP
25 FORWARD 70
30 FORWARD 3
35 RIGHT 20
40 PENDOWN
45 EARS
50 RIGHT 90
55 FORWARD 50
60 FORWARD 3
65 FORWARD 60
70 FORWARD 5
75 FORWARD 3
80 RIGHT 90
85 RIGHT 20
90 EARS
END
```

FIGURE 6   Sample Logo program providing a more sophisticated example of modular problem solving.

Comparing Competing Philosophies

Given the divergent philosophies and goals represented in the preceding discussions, one obvious further set of research issues involves an attempt to evaluate and compare the contrasting claims that these different positions make. What are the central presuppositions and expectations underlying these different approaches? How can they be evaluated empirically? Let us examine two concrete examples.

Instructional Drills versus Educational Games

Consider the differences between a classical "drill and practice" model and a "motivational embellishment" approach to teaching some particular set of traditional curriculum units via the microcomputer. Suppose one were to compare, for instance, two of the programs illustrated earlier in Figures 2 and 3 for teaching children fractions—the first a relatively unadorned CAI program, the second a motivationally enriched version presenting comparable material in the form of problems arising as the student manages a pizza parlor—using an identical series of problems and rules governing feedback and progress through the problem series. Here the goals of both approaches are the same, but the methods quite different. Each approach, in addition, leads to quite different, and often explicitly conflicting, empirical predictions (Lepper & Malone, in press).

A first set of issues here concerns the effects of embedding instruction in the context of an educational game on children's initial learning of the material presented. Clearly, the two schools are not in agreement. To proponents, the addition of motivational features is expected to enhance attention and produce superior learning. To critics, the addition of these extraneous features seems more likely to prove distracting and impair initial learning. At the very least, from this second perspective, the use of such features should make learning significantly less efficient per unit of time invested.

Similar competing claims exist regarding children's later retention of, or ability to transfer to new domains, the material they have learned by using the computer. For advocates, the availability of an involving and concrete frame of reference may promote retention and transfer. For the skeptics, embedding instructional material in the context of a game may limit children's ability to apply that knowledge in the absence of supporting "props" and "crutches."

What about the effects of such a strategy on children's motivation? Certainly on this issue there is less disagreement between the two positions regarding the likelihood that one can enhance children's motivation as they work at the computer by using such computer games. Note, however, that this question remains an empirical issue, and one to which the "obvious" answer may be incorrect (Malone, 1980, 1981; Malone & Lepper, in press).

Even if one assumes that games can be created that will have enhanced motivational appeal on the computer, however, there remains an even more significant motivational question: What effects will the use of such motivational techniques have on children's later intrinsic interest in the subject taught, when they are no longer using the computer? Again, there is considerable disagreement. From one perspective, the use of artificial technical devices to "fool" the child into thinking that this work is fun may prove effective in the short term, but in the long run this strategy of sugarcoating learning will backfire. Because the teacher cannot replicate the fun and games of the computer, children will come to find routine classroom work dull and boring. They may persist less, show decreased attention spans, and learn less from traditional classroom instruction. From the other perspective, of course, such motivational enrichment strategies are expected to have quite general positive effects (cf. Lepper & Gilovich, 1982). Children should come to like the subject more and should prove more, rather than less, attentive and interested when the subject arises in other domains. Indeed, by using such techniques one may be able to build generalized positive attitudes toward learning, even among children who have not previously been successful in their regular classrooms.

Who is right? More reasonably, for which children, on which measures, or under what circumstances is one technique superior to the other? These are the sorts of empirical questions that require research attention. These questions are not only of immediate relevance to the issue of how computer-based courseware should be designed, but they are also relevant to deeper theoretical issues. Such issues are the subject of current debate not only in the context of courseware development (e.g., D'Attore, 1981; Thornburg, 1981) but also outside the domain of computer-based instruction (e.g., Baker, Herman, & Yeh, 1981).

Exploratory Learning versus Didactic Instruction   Other equally important and equally controversial issues are raised by the current debate between proponents of exploratory, discovery-based, inductive learning and proponents of more highly structured, didactic instruction. Both in the domain of educational simulations and the domain of teaching children programming, sharply contrasting educational philosophies are evident in the approaches taken by different groups (cf. Shulman & Keislar, 1966).

To the adherents of inductive, exploratory, Piagetian learning, the virtues of self-directed discovery arising from a sustained involvement in an educationally rich simulation, microworld, or programming environment are substantial. Not only will such an experience heighten students' motivation; it will also produce deeper, more lasting, more meaningful learning (e.g., Brown, 1984; Bruner, 1961, 1966; diSessa, 1982; Lawler, 1981, 1982; Papert, 1972, 1980). Equally clear, however, is the challenge posed by supporters of a more explicitly didactic approach (e.g., Becker, 1971; Engelmann, 1968; Skinner, 1968). They propose that the same knowledge, strategies, and powerful ideas children acquire inductively could be taught more efficiently and effectively with a more directive and structured approach to instruction. The tension and the interesting research issues involve the potential trade-off between "mere efficiency" of possibly superficial learning and the "depth" of learning presumed to arise when students themselves discover, induce, and interact with intellectually powerful ideas.

The discovery learning approach is, of course, intuitively appealing and has been so for many centuries. Plato, in *The Republic,* was among the first to offer the opinion that "No compulsory learning can remain in the soul" (1935, p. 232). "Anything we would have children learn," John Locke (1693/1892) suggested, "should not be presented to them as business...you must make what you would have them do a recreation to them and not a business" (pp. 110–111). This model of active, exploratory learning appeals to our sense of how great discoveries are made by experts and inventors in many fields and to our sense of wonder at the enormous intellectual achievements made by the young child who learns to speak and navigate his or her environment in the relative absence of explicit, didactic instruction (Moore & Anderson, 1969). Does everyday academic learning, by ordinary children, follow a similar course?

Clearly, one central issue here concerns the meaning of deep versus superficial learning. Traditionally, such a distinction has concerned variables such as the transfer of learning to new domains, the retention of material learned, and the later accessibility of that knowledge (though this is neither an exhaustive nor a sufficient list).

Even this limited view of the question, however, is sufficient to suggest some features of the learning process that might be expected to influence such variables. One major set of features concerns the degree of internal versus external control provided over the focus of attention at the task, the organization of information gained, the pacing of task engagement, and the selection of problems for study. Increased levels of internal control over these parameters, of the sort presumed to occur in an exploratory learning environment, for example, may have positive effects on learning and memory to the extent that they encourage heuristic and constructive information processing (Bruner, 1966; Condry & Chambers, 1978; Corno & Mandinach, 1983). Alternatively, self-direction could decrease the efficiency of learning if the student is led to nonoptimal allocations of attention and effort, compared to some more highly structured instructional system (Atkinson, 1972).

Discovery-based learning environments may also differ in the extent to which they provide clear and constructive feedback or the extent to which they present useful representations for the knowledge they contain. The value of a discovery-based learning environment should also depend, in short, on the extent to which it prompts thoughtful, elaborate processing (cf. Corno & Mandinach, 1983; Moore & Anderson, 1969; Salomon, 1983).

In addition to these information-processing concerns, consideration must be given to issues of motivation that parallel those considered earlier. Proponents of discovery learning typically argue, and adherents of more didactic approaches sometimes concede, that learning is more enjoyable and intrinsically motivating when students have personal control over the goals, pacing, and difficulty level of their activities (Condry & Chambers, 1978; Lepper & Greene, 1978b). The central instructional question that follows, once again, is whether such potential motivational differences have important consequences for learning or retention.

Such issues are not limited to the context of learning with computers, as the array of research on discovery learning during the 1960s illustrates (Shulman & Keislar, 1966). Nor, as the mixed results of prior research attest, are these issues likely to be amenable to simplistic solutions. The novel possibilities offered by computer-based learning lie in the potential of this medium for the creation of rich and responsive learning environments in which questions about the relative strengths and shortcomings of these two approaches may be more crisply defined and systematically studied (Brown, 1983; Cronbach, 1966; McLaughlin, 1982).

SOCIAL AND POLICY ISSUES

Finally, there are a number of more general social-developmental and social policy issues raised by this new technology. Let us examine, briefly, those that seem particularly salient.

Social Equity

Perhaps the most important policy issues raised by this new technology involve the effects of the spread of this technology on equality of access and equality of outcome between the privileged and the underprivileged segments of our society. Clearly, if events are left entirely to the pressures of the marketplace, one might imagine a number of powerful ways in which the introduction of this technology will be likely to increase the gap between the advantaged and the disadvantaged. Selectivity in the availability of the hardware (e.g., which families or schools will have the money to purchase even an inexpensive microcomputer), the nature of the software purchased (e.g., whether Space Invaders and Asteroids or elementary algebra and symbolic logic games are purchased for the home or school library), and the degree of parent or teacher assistance available to the child may all work to make "the rich richer and the poor poorer" (Lepper, Daley, Chen, Hess, Kuspa, & Walker, 1984; Podemski, Husk, & Jones, 1983).

Moreover, it is possible that even if access to the technology at each of these levels were entirely equivalent, the divergence between high- and low-aptitude children would still increase. In some of the early CAI programs, for example, it seemed that the more able students benefited more from any constant level of access to well-designed educational programs that permitted students to proceed at their own speed (e.g., Atkinson, 1972). Alternatively, the use of motivationally enriched instructional materials may prove a particularly effective approach for precisely those children who are not now being effectively motivated by traditional classroom instruction. If so, one might expect a reduction of variance in performance attributable to individual differences in children's motivation. Indeed, recent meta-analytic findings suggest that, in practice, gains from computer-assisted instruction at the secondary-school level may be greatest for low- and average-ability students (Kulik et al., 1983).

A second, closely-related equity issue concerns potential gender differences in children's responses to this medium, and the causes and consequences of such differences. If one were to examine, today, young children's participation in the variety of optional computer programming courses, educational games programs, and summer camps, one would often find very large sex differences in participation, with boys participating more frequently than girls. The ratio of boys to girls involved with computers appears to increase, moreover, the more advanced, effortful, or costly the level of involvement (Hess & Miura, in press; Kiesler, Sproull, & Eccles, 1983; Lepper et al., 1984). Why is this, and if we believe that computer literacy will become an increasingly important resource for children in the future, what can be done about it?

Clearly this phenomenon is complex and the result of a variety of factors, many of which may not be easy to overcome. One contributing factor, however, may be that many of the supposedly motivating educational activities that are currently on the market are simply more appealing to boys. For example, one large class of presumably educational games involves the same themes of war and violence that are so prevalent in video arcade games, and another large class of programs involves largely male sex-typed sports (e.g., baseball, basketball, and football). Both themes are much more characteristic of the activities that boys prefer, quite apart from the computer context (cf. Pulaski, 1973). In the game of "Spelling Baseball," for instance, the child's reward for superior performance is the opportunity to see his or her own baseball team outscore the computer's team. When one watches children exposed to such games, it is hard to avoid the conclusion that these choices are not optimal for interesting girls in the world of computers.

Social Development

A second general set of issues involves what might be called the social-developmental effects of this new technology. How will this new medium, for example, affect children's social interactions and social abilities? Will the influx of home computers create, as some fear, a generation of introverted social isolates, 8-year-old "hackers" and video-game addicts? Or will it, instead, promote levels of sustained, cooperative interaction among children of a sort rarely seen outside of formally organized recreational programs, as some recent observations suggest (e.g., Hawkins, 1983)? What will happen to the family? If, in the future, more work is done at home, will this strengthen parent–child bonds? Or will the computer become the ultimate babysitter, entertaining, free, and always available? How will children view computers and interactions with others via computers or other telecommunications systems? Will their perceptions of human nature be affected? Will they come to learn that computers are dependable and consistently friendly, whereas real people are moody and often unpleasant? In any case, it seems likely that there will be some important effects on the course of social development (Condry & Keith, 1983; Deken, 1982; Turkle, 1984).

Displacement

Similarly, one may ask what kinds of activities will be "displaced" by the computer (Hornik, 1981; Lin & Lepper, 1984). Will spontaneous reading levels drop further, or will the computer be more likely to displace other potentially less instructive activities, such as passive television viewing? Will children spend less time engaged in active sports or informal play activities?

Educational Goals

Finally, there are a number of ways in which the availability of inexpensive computers may influence our thinking about the goals of education and the skills that children should be taught. It seems hard to believe that this new technology will not eventually force us to reconsider the structure of our basic elementary school curriculum. To what extent will it be important in the future, to take just one example, for children to be able to do basic mental arithmetic quickly? Without prejudging the issue, because it turns out to be quite complex, the eventual universal availability of calculators and computers will undoubtedly raise the issue of how much effort should be invested in teaching children how to do things proficiently in their heads that could be done a hundred times faster at the touch of some relevant keys. Will the 3Rs, in short, ultimately be replaced by the 4Cs—comprehension, composition, calculation, and computing?

SUMMARY

In short, the technology is here, and the time for research is now. There seems to be relatively little disagreement that the influx of this new and powerful technology is likely to have more important effects on the lives and the social and psychological functioning of children than any other technological advance in the past century (cf. Deken, 1982; Evans, 1979). There is considerable and quite heated debate, however, concerning the nature of the effects that are likely to occur—the potential benefits, or possible costs, of early computer access (e.g., Bork, 1980; Dwyer, 1974; Papert, 1980; Suppes, 1980; Taylor, 1980; Turkle, 1984; Walker, 1983; Weizenbaum, 1976; Zimbardo, 1980). To advocates, this technology offers possibilities for enhancing children's intellectual abilities and their intrinsic motivation for learning; for increasing children's perceptions of personal competence and self-esteem; and for promoting an internal locus of control, increased persistence in problem solving, and heightened feelings of independence. To critics, this technology is viewed instead as likely to produce impulsive and distractible children; to stifle creativity and undermine intrinsic motivation outside of the computer context; and to promote social isolation, dehumanization, and decreased social interaction skills among frequent users.

In part, these disagreements reflect attention to different aspects of the wide variety of uses to which computers may be put in the lives of children. They also reflect, however, fundamental theoretical disagreements about basic empirical questions. At present, there is virtually no research concerning such issues. What little comparative research has been done on the effects of this technology is almost entirely focused on purely cognitive and instructional questions (Taylor, 1980). Yet it seems critical to examine the larger issues now, before this technology becomes such an integral part of our daily lives that it will be, as was the case with research on commercial television, too late to ask critical questions.

REFERENCES

Abelson, H., & diSessa, A. A. (1980). *Turtle geometry: The computer as a medium for exploring mathematics*. Cambridge, MA: MIT Press.

Atkinson, R. C. (1972). Ingredients for a theory of instruction. *American Psychologist, 27,* 921–931.

Baker, E. L., Herman, J. L., & Yeh, J. P. (1981).

Fun and games: Their contribution to basic skills instruction in elementary school. *American Educational Research Journal, 18,* 83–92.

Becker, W. C. (1971). Teaching concepts and operations, or how to make kids smart. In W. C. Becker (Ed.), *An empirical basis for change in education* (pp. 401–423). Chicago: Science Research Associates.

Berlyne, D. E. (1960). *Conflict, arousal, and curiosity*. New York: McGraw-Hill.

Berlyne, D. E. (1966). Curiosity and exploration. *Science, 153,* 25–33.

Bork, A. (1980). Preparing student-computer dialogs: Advice to teachers. In R. P. Taylor (Ed.), *The computer in the school: Tutor, tool, tutee* (pp. 15–52). New York: Teachers College Press.

Brown, J. S. (1983). Learning-by-doing revisited for electronic learning environments. In M. A. White (Ed.), *The future of electronic learning* (pp. 13–32). Hillsdale, NJ: Erlbaum.

Brown, J. S. (1984). Process versus product—a perspective on tools for communal and informal electronic learning. Unpublished manuscript, Xerox PARC.

Bruner, J. S. (1961). The act of discovery. *Harvard Educational Review, 31,* 21–32.

Bruner, J. S. (1962). *On knowing: Essays for the left hand*. Cambridge, MA: Harvard University Press.

Bruner, J. S. (1966). *Toward a theory of instruction*. Cambridge, MA: Harvard University Press.

Clements, D. H., & Gullo, D. F. (in press). Effects of computer programming on young children's cognition. *Journal of Educational Psychology*.

Condry, J. C. (1977). Enemies of exploration: Self-initiated versus other-initiated learning. *Journal of Personality and Social Psychology, 35,* 459–477.

Condry, J., & Chambers, J. (1978). Intrinsic motivation and the process of learning. In M. R. Lepper & D. Greene (Eds.), *The hidden costs of reward* (pp. 61–84). Hillsdale, NJ: Erlbaum.

Condry, J., & Keith, D. (1983). Educational and recreational uses of computer technology. *Youth and Society, 15,* 87–112.

Corno, L., & Mandinach, E. B. (1983). The role of cognitive engagement in classroom learning and motivation. *Educational Psychologist, 18,* 88–108.

Cronbach, L. J. (1966). The logic of experiments on discovery. In L. S. Shulman & E. Keislar (Eds.), *Learning by discovery: A critical appraisal* (pp. 77–91). Chicago: Rand McNally.

Csikszentmihalyi, M. (1975). *Beyond boredom and anxiety.* San Francisco: Jossey-Bass.

D'Attore, A. (1981). Computer-aided instruction, boon or bust? *Compute!, 3*(12), 18–20.

Davis, R., Dugdale, S., Kibbey, D., & Weaver, C. (1977). Representing knowledge about mathematics for computer-aided teaching: Part II—The diversity of roles that a computer can play in assisting learning. In E. W. Elcock & D. Michie (Eds.), *Machine representations of knowledge* (pp. 387–421). Dordrecht, the Netherlands: D. Reidel.

deCharms, R. (1968). *Personal causation.* New York: Academic Press.

Deci, E. L. (1975). *Intrinsic motivation.* New York: Plenum.

Deci, E. L. (1981). *The psychology of self-determination.* Lexington, MA: Heath.

Deken, J. (1982). *The electronic cottage.* New York: William Morrow.

diSessa, A. A. (1977). *On "learnable" representations of knowledge: A meaning for the computational metaphor* (Logo Memo No. 47). Cambridge, MA: MIT Press.

diSessa, A. A. (1982). Unlearning Aristotelian physics: A study of knowledge-based learning. *Cognitive Science, 6,* 37–75.

Dugdale, S., & Kibbey, D. (1980). *Fractions curriculum of the PLATO elementary school mathematical project.* Urbana-Champaign, IL: Computer-Based Education Research Laboratory.

Dwyer, T. A. (1974). Heuristic strategies for using computers to enrich education. *International Journal of Man-Machine Studies, 6,* 137–154.

Dwyer, T. (1980). The significance of solo-mode computing for curriculum design. In R. P. Taylor (Ed.), *The computer in the classroom: Tool, tutor, tutee* (pp. 104–112). New York: Teachers College Press.

Engelmann, S. (1968). The effectiveness of direct verbal instructions on I.Q. performance and achievement in reading and arithmetic. In J. Hellmuth (Ed.), *The disadvantaged child* (Vol. 3, pp. 339–361). New York: Brunner/Mazel.

Evans, D. (1979). *The micro millenium.* New York: Viking.

Harter, S. (1978). Effectance motivation reconsidered: Toward a developmental model. *Human Development, 1,* 34–64.

Harter, S. (1981). A new self-report scale of intrinsic versus extrinsic orientation in the classroom: Motivational and informational components. *Developmental Psychology, 3,* 300–312.

Hawkins, J. (1983, April). Learning Logo together: The social context. Paper presented at the annual meeting of the American Educational Research Association, Montreal, Canada.

Hess, R. D., & Miura, I. T. (in press). Gender and socioeconomic differences in enrollment in computer camps and classes. *Sex Roles.*

Hornik, R. (1981). Out-of-school television and schooling; Hypotheses and methods. *Review of Educational Research, 51,* 193–214.

Hunt, J. McV. (1961). *Intelligence and experience.* New York: Ronald Press.

Hunt, J. Mc.V. (1965). Intrinsic motivation and its role in psychological development. In D. Levine (Ed.), *Nebraska Symposium on Motivation* (Vol. 13, pp. 189–282). Lincoln, NE: University of Nebraska Press.

Kagan, J. (1972). Motives and development. *Journal of Personality and Social Psychology, 22,* 51–66.

Kahneman, D. (1973). *Attention and effort.* Englewood Cliffs, NJ: Prentice-Hall.

Kane, J. H. (1983, April). Computers for composing. Paper presented at the annual meeting of the American Educational Research Association, Montreal, Canada.

Kiesler, S., Sproull, L., & Eccles, J. S. (1983, March). Second-class citizens? *Psychology Today,* pp. 41–48.

Kintsch, W. (1977). *Memory and cognition.* New York: Wiley.

Kleiman, G. M. (1984). *Brave new schools: How computers can change education.* Reston, VA: Reston.

Kulik, J. A., Bangert, R. L., & Williams, G. W. (1983). Effects of computer-based teaching on secondary school students. *Journal of Educational Psychology, 75,* 19–26.

Lawler, R. W. (1981). The progressive construction of mind. *Cognitive Science, 5,* 1–30.

Lawler, R. W. (1982). Designing computer microworlds. *Byte, 7,* 138–160.

Lepper, M. R. (1983). Extrinsic reward and intrinsic motivation: Implications for the classroom. In J. M. Levine & M. C. Wang (Eds.), *Teacher and student perceptions: Implications for learning* (pp. 281–317). Hillsdale, NJ: Erlbaum.

Lepper, M. R., Daley, H., Chen, M., Hess, R., Kuspa, L., & Walker, D. (1984). *Computers and education: The social equity issues.* Manuscript in preparation, Stanford University.

Lepper, M. R., & Gilovich, T. (1982). Accentuating the positive: Eliciting generalized compliance from children through activity-oriented requests. *Journal of Personality and Social Psychology, 42,* 248–259.

Lepper, M. R., & Greene, D. (Eds.). (1978a). *The hidden costs of reward.* Hillsdale, NJ: Erlbaum.

Lepper, M. R., & Greene, D. (1978b). Overjustification research and beyond: Toward a means-end analysis of intrinsic motivation. In M. R. Lepper & D. Greene (Eds.), *The hidden costs of reward* (pp. 109–148). Hillsdale, NJ: Erlbaum.

Lepper, M. R., & Malone, T. W. (in press). Intrinsic motivation and instructional effectiveness in computer-based education. In R. E. Snow & M. C. Farr (Eds.), *Aptitude, learning, and instruction: III. Conative and affective process analyses.* Hillsdale, NJ: Erlbaum.

Levin, J. A., & Kareev, Y. (1981). *Personal computers and education: The challenge to the schools.* Unpublished manuscript, University of California at San Diego.

Liebert, R. M., Neale, J. M., & Davidson, E. S. (1973). *The early window: Effects of television on children and youth.* New York: Pergamon.

Lin, S., & Lepper, M. R. (1984). Correlates of children's usage of videogames and computers. Unpublished manuscript, Stanford University.

Locke, J. (1892). *Some thoughts concerning education.* Cambridge, England: Cambridge University Press. (Original work published 1693).

Luehrmann, A. (1979). Technology in science education. In D. K. Devinger & A. R. Molnar (Eds.), *Technology in science education: The next ten years* (pp. 19–27). Washington, DC: National Science Foundation.

Luehrmann, A. (1980). Pre-and post-college computer education. In R. P. Taylor (Ed.), *Computers in the schools: Tool, tutor, tutee* (pp. 141–148). New York: Teachers College Press.

Malone, T. W. (1980). *What makes things fun to learn? A study of intrinsically motivating computer games.* Unpublished doctoral dissertation, Stanford University.

Malone, T. W. (1981). Toward a theory of intrinsically motivating instruction. *Cognitive Science, 4,* 333–369.

Malone, T. W., & Lepper, M. R. (in press). Making learning fun: A taxonomy of intrinsic motivation for learning. In R. E. Snow & M. C. Farr (Eds.), *Aptitude, learning, and instruction: III. Conative and affective process analyses.* Hillsdale, NJ: Erlbaum.

McLaughlin, B. (1982). *An experimental comparison of discovery and didactic computerized instructional strategies in the learning of computer programming.* Unpublished manuscript, National Institutes of Health.

Milojkovic, J. D. (1983). *Children learning computer programming: Cognitive and motivational consequences.* Unpublished doctoral dissertation, Stanford University, Stanford, CA.

Moore, O. K., & Anderson, A. R. (1969). Some principles for the design of clarifying educational environments. In D. Goslin (Ed.), *Handbook of socialization theory and research* (pp. 571–613). Chicago: Rand McNally.

Murray, J. P. (1980). *Television and youth: 25 years of research and controversy.* Boystown, NE: The Boys Town Center for the Study of Youth Development.

Nilles, J. M., Carlson, F. R., Jr., Gray, P., Hayes, J. P., Holmen, M. G., White, M. J., Akkud, C. B., & Gordon, C. B. (1981). *A technology assessment of personal computers.* Unpublished manuscript, University of Southern California.

Nuttin, J. R. (1973). Pleasure and reward in human motivation and learning. In D. E. Berlyne & K. B. Madsen (Eds.), *Pleasure, reward, preference* (pp. 243–274). New York: Academic Press.

Papert, S. (1972). Teaching children to be mathematicians vs. teaching about mathematics. *International Journal of Mathematical Education in Science and Technology,* 249–262.

Papert, S. (1980). *Mindstorms: Children, computers, and powerful ideas*. New York: Basic Books.

Papert, S., Watt, D., diSessa, A., & Weir, S. (1979, September). *Final report of the Brookline LOGO Project, Part II: Project summary and data analysis* (LOGO Memo No. 53). Cambridge, MA: Artificial Intelligence Laboratory.

Pea, R. D., & Kurland, D. M. (in press). On the cognitive effects of learning computer programming: A critical look. *New Ideas on Psychology*.

Plato. (1935). *The republic*. London, England: J. M. Dent.

Podemski, R. S., Husk, S., & Jones, A. B. (1983). Micros and the disadvantaged. *Electronic Learning, 2*, 20–22.

Pulaski, M. A. (1973). Toys and imaginative play. In J. L. Singer (Ed.), *The child's world of make-believe* (pp. 74–103). New York: Academic Press.

Rosenshine, B. (1976). Classroom instruction. In N. L. Gage (Ed.), *The psychology of teaching methods* (pp. 335–371). Chicago, IL: University of Chicago Press.

Salomon, G. (1983). The differential investment of mental effort in learning from different sources. *Educational Psychologist, 18,* 42–50.

Schramm, W., Lyle, J., & Parker, E. B. (1961). *Television in the lives of our children*. Stanford, CA: Stanford University Press.

Shulman, L. S., & Keislar, E. R. (Eds.). (1966). *Learning by discovery: A critical appraisal*. Chicago: Rand-McNally.

Simon, H. A. (1967). Motivational and emotional controls of cognition. *Psychological Review, 74,* 29–39.

Singer, J. L. (1973). *The child's world of make-believe*. New York: Academic Press.

Skinner, B. F. (1968). *The technology of teaching*. New York: Appleton-Century-Crofts.

Sleeman, D., & Brown, J. S. (Eds.). (1982). *Intelligent tutoring systems*. New York: Academic Press.

Spence, K. W. (1956). *Behavior theory and conditioning*. New Haven: Yale University Press.

Stallings, J. (1980). Allocated academic learning time revisited, or beyond time on task. *Educational Researcher, 9,* 10–16.

Suppes, P. (1965). Computer-based mathematics instruction. *Bulletin of the Study Group for Mathematics Learning, 3,* 7–22.

Suppes, P. (1966). The uses of computers in education. *Scientific American, 215,* 206–221.

Suppes, P. (1980). The future of computers in education. In R. P. Taylor (Ed.), *The computer in the school: Tutor, tool, tutee*. (pp. 248–261). New York: Teachers College Press.

Suppes, P., & Morningstar, M. (1969). Computer-assisted instruction. *Science, 166,* 343–350.

Taylor, R. P. (Ed.). (1980). *The computer in the school: Tutor, tool, tutee*. New York: Teachers College Press.

Thornburg, D. D. (1981). Computers and society: Some speculations on the well-played game. *Compute!, 3*(14), 12–16.

Turkle, S. (1984). *The second self: Computers and the human spirit*. New York: Simon & Schuster.

Walker, D. F. (1983). Reflections on the educational potential and limitations of microcomputers. *Phi Delta Kappan, 65,* 103–107.

Weizenbaum, J. (1976). *Computer power and human reason: From judgment to calculation*. San Francisco: W. H. Freeman.

White, R. W. (1959). Motivation reconsidered: The concept of competence. *Psychological Review, 66,* 297–333.

White, R. W. (1960). Competence and the psychosexual stages of development. In M. R. Jones (Ed.), *Nebraska symposium on motivation* (Vol. 8, pp. 97–141). Lincoln, Nebraska: University of Nebraska Press.

Zajonc, R. B. (1965). Social facilitation. *Science, 149,* 269–274.

Zimbardo, P. G. (Ed.). (1980, August). The hacker papers. *Psychology Today*, pp. 62–74.

READING 43

Jigsaw Groups and the Desegregated Classroom: In Pursuit of Common Goals

Elliot Aronson
Diane Bridgeman

There were high hopes when the Supreme Court outlawed school segregation a quarter of a century ago. If black and white children could share classrooms and become friends, it was thought that perhaps they could develop relatively free of racial prejudice and some of the problems which accompany prejudice. The case that brought about the court's landmark decision was that of Oliver Brown *vs*. the Board of Education of Topeka, Kansas; the decision reversed the 1896 ruling (Plessy *vs*. Ferguson) which held that it was permissible to segregate racially, as long as equal facilities were provided for both races. In the Brown case, the court held that psychologically there could be no such thing as "separate but equal." The mere fact of separation implied to the minority group in question that its members were inferior to those of the majority.

The Brown decision was not only a humane interpretation of the Constitution, it was also the beginning of a profound and exciting social experiment. As Stephan (1978) has recently pointed out, the testimony of social psychologists in the Brown case, as well as in previous similar cases in state supreme courts, suggested strongly that desegregation would not only reduce prejudice but also increase the self-esteem of minority groups and improve their academic performance. Of course the social psychologists who testified never meant to imply that such benefits would accrue automatically. Certain preconditions must be met. These preconditions were most articulately stated by Gordon Allport in his classic, *The Nature of Prejudice*, published the same year as the Supreme Court decision:

> Prejudice...may be reduced by equal status contact between majority and minority groups in the pursuit of common goals. The effect is greatly enhanced if this contact is sanctioned by institutional supports (i.e., by law, custom or local atmosphere), and provided it is of a sort that leads to the perception of common interests and common humanity between members of the two groups. (Allport, 1954, p. 281)

THE EFFECTS OF DESEGREGATION

A quarter of a century after desegregation was begun, an assessment of its effectiveness is not encouraging. One of the most careful and thoroughgoing longitudinal studies of desegregation was the Riverside project conducted by Harold Gerard and Normam Miller (1975). They found that long after the schools were desegregated, black, white and Mexican-American children tended not to integrate but to hang together in their own ethnic clusters. Moreover, anxiety increased and remained high long after desegregation occurred. These trends are echoed in several other studies. Indeed, the most careful, scholarly reviews of the research show few, if any, benefits (see St. John, 1975; Stephan, 1978). For example, according to Stephan's review, there is no single study that shows a significant increase in the self-esteem of minority children following desegregation; in fact, in fully 25% of the studies desegregation is followed by a significant decrease in the self-esteem by young minority children. Moreover, Stephan reports that desegregation reduced the prejudice of whites toward blacks in only 13% of the school systems studied. The prejudice of blacks toward whites increased in about as many cases as it decreased. Similarly, studies of the effects of desegregation on the academic performance of minority children present a mixed and highly variable picture.

What went wrong? Let us return to Allport's prediction. Equal status contact in pursuit of common goals, sanctioned by authority will produce beneficial effects. We will look at each of these three factors separately.

1 *Sanction by authority.* In some school districts there was clear acceptance and enforcement of the ruling by responsible authority. In others the acceptance was not as clear. In still others (especially in the early years) local authorities were in open defiance of the law. Pettigrew (1961) has shown that desegregation proceeded more smoothly and with less violence in those localities where local authorities sanctioned integration. But such variables as self-esteem and the reduction of prejudice do not necessarily change for the better even where authority clearly sanctions desegregation. While sanction by authority may be necessary, it is clearly not a sufficient condition.

2 *Equal status contact.* The definition of equal status is a trifle slippery. In the case of school desegregation, we could claim that there is equal status on the grounds that all children in the fifth grade (for example) have the same "occupational" status, i.e., they are all fifth grade students. On the other hand, if the teacher is prejudiced against blacks, she/he may treat them less fairly than she/he treats whites, thus lowering their perceived status in the classroom. (See Gerard and Miller, 1975.) Moreover, if, because of an inferior education (prior to desegregation) or because of language difficulties, black or Mexican-American students perform poorly in the classroom, this could also lower their status among their peers. An interesting complication was introduced by Elizabeth Cohen (1972). While Allport (1954) predicted that positive interactions will result if cooperative equal status is achieved, expectation theory, as developed by Cohen, holds that even in such an environment biased expectations by both whites and blacks may lead to sustained white dominance. Cohen reasoned that both of these groups accept the premise that the majority group's competence results in dominance and superior achievement. She suggested that alternatives be created to reverse these often unconscious expectations. According to Cohen, at least a temporary exchange of majority and minority roles is therefore required as a prelude to equal status. In one study, for example (Cohen and Roper, 1972), black children were instructed in building radios and in how to teach this skill to others. Then a group of white children and the newly trained black children viewed a film of themselves building the radios. This was followed by some of the black children teaching the whites how to construct radios while others taught a black administrator. Then all the children came together in small groups. Equal status interactions were found in the groups where black children had taught whites how to construct the radios. The other group, however, demonstrated the usual white dominance. We will return to this point in a moment.

3 *In pursuit of common goals.* In the typical American classroom, children are almost never engaged in the pursuit of common goals. During the past several years, we and our colleagues have systematically observed scores of elementary school classrooms, and have found that, in the vast majority of these cases, the process of education is highly competitive. Children vie with one another for good grades, the respect of the teacher, etc....This occurs not only during the quizzes and exams but in the informal give and take of the classroom where, typically, children learn to raise their hands (often frantically) in response to questions from the teacher, groan when someone else is called upon, revel in the failure of their classmates, etc.

This pervasive competitive atmosphere unwittingly leads the children to view one another as foes to be heckled and vanquished. In a newly desegregated school, all other things being equal, this atmosphere could exacerbate whatever prejudice existed prior to desegregation.

A dramatic example of dysfunctional competition was demonstrated by Sherif, et al. (1961) in their classic "Robber's Cave" experiment. In this field experiment, the investigators encouraged intergroup competition between two teams of boys at a summer camp; this created fertile ground for anger and hostility even in previously benign, noncompetitive circumstances—like watching a movie. Positive relations between the groups were ultimately achieved only after both groups were required to work cooperatively to solve a common problem.

It is our contention that the competitive process interacts with "equal status contact." That is to say, whatever differences in ability existed between minority children and white children prior to desegregation are emphasized by the competitive structure of the learning environment, and since segregated school facilities are rarely equal, minority children frequently enter the newly desegregated school at a distinct disadvantage which is made more salient by the competitive atmosphere.

It was this reasoning that led Aronson and his colleagues (1975, 1978) to develop the hypothesis that interdependent learning environments would establish the conditions necessary for the increase in self-esteem and performance and the decrease in prejudice that were expected to occur as a function of desegregation. Toward this end they developed a highly structured method of interdependent learning and systematically tested its effects in a number of elementary school classrooms. The aim of this research program was not merely to compare the effects of cooperation and competition in a classroom setting. This has been ably demonstrated by other investigators dating as early as Deutsch's (1949) experiment. Rather, the intent was to devise a cooperative classroom structure which could be utilized easily by classroom teachers on a long term sustained basis and to evaluate the effects of this intervention via a well controlled series of field experiments. In short, this project is an action research program aimed at developing and evaluating a classroom atmosphere which can be sustained by the classroom teachers long after the researchers have packed up their questionnaires and returned to the more cozy environment of the social psychological laboratory.

The method is described in detail elsewhere (Aronson, et al., 1978). Briefly, students are placed in six-person learning groups. The day's lesson is divided into six paragraphs such that each student has one and only one segment of the written material. Each student has a unique and vital part of the information which, like the pieces of a jigsaw puzzle, must be put together for any of the students to learn the whole picture. The individual must learn his/her own section and teach it to the other members of the group. The reader will note that in this method each child spends part of her time in the role of expert. Thus, the method incorporates Cohen's findings (previously discussed) within the context of an equal status contact situation.

Working with this "jigsaw" technique, children gradually learn that the old competitive behaviors are no longer appropriate. Rather, in order to learn all of the material (and thus perform well on a quiz), each child must begin to listen to the others, ask appropriate questions, etc....The process opens the possibility for children to pay attention to one another and begin to appreciate one another as potentially valuable resources. It is important to emphasize that the motivation of the students is not necessarily altruistic; rather, it is primarily self-interest which, in this case, happens also to produce outcomes which are beneficial to others.

EXPERIMENTS IN THE CLASSROOM

Systematic research in the classroom has produced consistently positive results. The first experiment to investigate the effects of the jigsaw technique was conducted by Blaney, Stephan, Rosenfield, Aronson and Sikes (1977). The schools in Austin, Texas, had recently been desegregated, producing a great deal of tension and even some interracial skirmishes throughout the school system. In this tense atmosphere, the jigsaw technique was introduced in ten fifth grade classrooms in seven elementary schools. Three classes from among the same schools were also used as controls. The control classes were taught by teachers who, while using traditional techniques, were rated very highly by their peers. The experimental classes met in jigsaw groups for about 45 minutes a day, three days a week for six weeks. The curriculum was basically the same for the experimental and control classes. Students in the jigsaw groups showed significant increases in their liking for their groupmates both within and across ethnic boundaries. Moreover, children in jigsaw groups showed a significantly greater increase in self-esteem than children in the control classrooms. This was true for Anglo children well as ethnic minorities. Anglos and blacks showed greater liking for schools in the jigsaw classrooms than in traditional classrooms. (The Mexican American students showed a tendency to like school *less* in the jigsaw classes; this will be discussed in a moment.)

These results were essentially replicated in a Ph.D. dissertation by Geffner (1978) in Watsonville, California—a community consisting of approximately 50% Anglos and 50% Mexican-Americans. As a control for the possibility of a Hawthorne effect, Geffner compared the behavior of children in classrooms using the jigsaw and other cooperative learning techniques with that of children in highly innovative (but not interdependent) classroom environments as well as with traditional classrooms. Geffner found consistent and significant gains within classrooms using jigsaw and other cooperative learning techniques. Specifically, children in these classes showed increases in self-esteem as well as increases in liking for school. Negative ethnic stereotypes were also diminished, i.e., children increased their positive general attitudes toward their own ethnic group as well as toward members of other ethnic groups—to a far greater extent than children in traditional and innovative classrooms.

Changes in academic performance were assessed in an experiment by Lucker, Rosenfield, Sikes and Aronson (1977). The subjects were 303 fifth and sixth grade students from five elementary schools in Austin, Texas. Six classrooms were taught in the jigsaw manner, while five classrooms were taught traditionally by highly competent teachers. For two weeks children were taught a unit on colonial America taken from a fifth grade textbook. All children were then given the same standardized test. The results showed that Anglo students performed just as well in jigsaw classes as they did in traditional classes (means = 66.6 and 67.3 respectively) minority children performed significantly better in jigsaw classes than in traditional classes (means = 56.5 and 49.7 respectively). The difference for minority students was highly significant. Only two weeks of jigsaw activity succeeded in narrowing the performance gap between Anglos and minorities from more than 17 percentage points to about 10 percentage points. Interestingly enough, the jigsaw method apparently does *not* work a special hardship on high ability students: students in the highest quartile in reading ability benefited just as much as students in the lowest quartile.

UNDERLYING MECHANISMS

Increased Participation

We have seen that learning in a small interdependent group leads to greater interpersonal attraction, self-esteem, liking for school, more positive inter-ethnic and intra-ethnic perceptions and, for ethnic minorities, an improvement in academic performance. We think that some of our findings are due to more active involvement in the learning process under conditions of reduced anxiety. In jigsaw, children are required to participate. This increase in participation should enhance interest, which would result in an improvement in performance as well as an increased liking for school—all other things being equal. But all other things are sometimes not equal. For example, in the study by Blaney, et al. (1977) there was some indication from our observation of the groups that many of the Mexican-American children were experiencing some anxiety as a result of being required to participate more actively. This seemed to be due to the fact that these children had difficulty with the English language which produced some embarrassment in working with a group dominated by Anglos. In a traditional classroom, it is relatively easy to "become invisible" by remaining quiet, refusing to volunteer, etc....Not so in jigsaw. This observation was confirmed by the data on liking for school. Blaney, et al. found that Anglos and blacks in the jigsaw classrooms liked school better than those in the traditional classrooms, while for Mexican-Americans the reverse was true. This anxiety could be reduced if Mexican-American children were in a situation where it was not embarrassing to be more articulate in Spanish than in English. Thus, Geffner (1978), working in a situation where both the residential and school population was approximately 50% Spanish-speaking, found that Mexican-American children (like Anglos and blacks) increased their liking for school to a greater extent in the cooperative groups than in traditional classrooms.

Increases in Empathic Role-Taking

Only a small subset of our results is attributable to increases in active participation in and of itself. We believe that people working together in an interdependent fashion increase their ability to take one another's perspective. For example, suppose that Jane and Carlos are in a jigsaw group. Carlos is reporting and Jane is having difficulty following him. She doesn't quite understand because his style of presentation is different from what she is accustomed to. Not only must she pay close attention, but in addition, she must find a way to ask questions which Carlos will understand and which will elicit the additional information that she needs. In order to accomplish this, she must get to know Carlos, put herself in his shoes, empathize.

Bridgeman (1977) tested this notion. She reasoned that taking one another's perspective is required and practiced in jigsaw learning. Accordingly, the more experience students have with the jigsaw process, the greater will their role-taking abilities become. In her experiment, Bridgeman administered a revised version of Chandler's (1973) role-taking cartoon series to 120 fifth grade students. Roughly half of the students spent eight weeks in a jigsaw learning environment while the others were taught in either traditional or in innovative small group classrooms. Each of the cartoons in the Chandler test depicts a central character caught up in a chain of psychological cause and effect, such that the character's subsequent behavior was shaped by and fully comprehensible only in terms of the events preceding them. In one of the sequences, for example, a boy who had been saddened by seeing his father off at the airport began to cry when he later received a gift of a toy airplane similar to the one which had carried his father away. Midway into each sequence, a second character is introduced in the role of a late-arriving bystander who witnessed the resultant behaviors of the principal character, but was not privy to the causal events. Thus, the subject is in a privileged position relative to the story character whose role the subject is later asked to assume.

The cartoon series measures the degree to which the subject is able to set aside facts known only to him or herself and adopt a perspective measurably different from his or her own. For example, while the subject knows why the child in the above sequence cries when he receives the toy airplane, the mailman who delivered the toy is not privy to this knowledge. What happens when the subject is asked to take the mailman's perspective?

After eight weeks, students in the jigsaw classrooms were better able to put themselves in the bystander's place than students in the control classrooms. For example, when the mailman delivered the toy airplane to the little boy, students in the control classrooms tended to assume that the mailman knew the boy would cry; that is, they behaved as if they believed that the mailman knew that the boy's father had recently left town on an airplane—simply because they (the subjects) had this information. On the other hand, students who had participated in a jigsaw group were much more successful at taking the mailman's role—realizing that the mailman could not possibly understand why the boy would cry upon receiving a toy airplane.

Attributions for Success and Failure

Working together in the pursuit of common goals changes the "observer's" attributional patterns. There is some evidence to support the notion that cooperation increases the tendency for individuals to make the same kind of attributions for success and failure to their partners as they do for themselves. In an experiment by Stephan, Presser, Kennedy and Aronson (1978) it was found (as it has been in several experiments by others) that when an individual succeeds at a task he tends to attribute his success dispositionally (e.g., skill) but when he fails he tends to make a situational attribution (e.g., luck). Stephan, et al. went on to demonstrate that individuals engaged in an *interdependent* task make the same kinds of attributions to their

partner's performance as they do for their own. This was not the case in competitive interactions.

Effects of Dependent Variables on One Another

It is reasonable to assume that the various consequences of interdependent learning become antecedents for one another. Just as low self-esteem can work to inhibit a child from performing well, anything that increases self-esteem is likely to produce an increase in performance among those underachievers. Conversely, as Franks and Marolla (1976) have indicated, increases in performance should bring about increases in self-esteem. Similarly, being treated with increased attention and respect by one's peers (as almost inevitably happens in jigsaw groups) is another important antecedent of self-esteem according to Franks and Marolla. There is ample evidence for a two-way causal connection between performance and self-esteem (see Covington and Beery, 1976; Purkey, 1970).

OTHER COOPERATIVE TECHNIQUES

In recent years a few research teams utilizing rather different techniques for structuring cooperative behavior have produced an array of data consistent with those resulting from the jigsaw technique. For example, Stuart Cook and his colleagues at the University of Colorado (1978) have shown that interracial cooperative groups in the laboratory underwent a significant improvement in attitudes about people of other races. In subsequent field experiments, Cook and his colleagues found that interdependent groups produced more improved attitudes to members of previously disliked racial groups than was present in non-interdependent groups. It should be noted, however, that no evidence for generalization was found; i.e., the positive change was limited to the specific members of the interdependent group and did not extend to the racial group as a whole.

Working out of the University of Minnesota, Johnson and Johnson (1975) have developed the "Learning Together" model which is a general and varied approach to interdependent classroom learning. Basically, Johnson and Johnson have found evidence for greater cross-ethnic friendship ratings, self-esteem and higher motivation in their cooperative groups than in control conditions. They have not found an increase in academic performance, however.

In a different vein, Slavin (1978), DeVries (1978) and their colleagues at Johns Hopkins University have developed two highly structured techniques that combine within-group cooperation with across-group competition. These techniques, "Teams Games and Tournaments" (TGT) and "Student Teams Achievement Divisions" (STAD) have consistently produced beneficial results in lower class, multi-racial classrooms. Basically, in TGT and STAD, children form heterogeneous five-person teams; each member of a team is given a reasonably good opportunity to do well by dint of the fact that she competes against a member of a different team with similar skills to her own. Her individual performance contributes to her team's score. The results are in the same ball park as jigsaw: children participating in TGT and STAD groups show a greater increase in sociometric, cross-racial friendship choices and more observed cross-racial interactions than control conditions. They also show more satisfaction with school than the controls do. Similarly, TGT and STAD produces greater learning effectiveness among racial minorities than the control groups.

It is interesting to note that the basic results of TGT and STAD are similar to those of the jigsaw technique in spite of one major difference in procedure: while the jigsaw technique makes an overt attempt to minimize competition, TGT and STAD actually promote competitiveness and utilize it across teams—within the context of intrateam cooperation. We believe that this difference is more apparent than real.

In most classrooms where jigsaw has been utilized the students are in jigsaw groups for less than two hours per day. The rest of the class time is spent in a myriad of process activities, many of which are competitive in nature. Thus, what seems important in both techniques is that *some* specific time is structured around cooperativeness. Whether the beneficial results are produced *in spite* of a surrounding atmosphere of competitiveness or *because* of it—is the task of future research to determine.

CONCLUSIONS

We are not suggesting that jigsaw learning or any other cooperative method constitutes the solution to our interethnic problems. What we have shown is that beneficial effects occur as a result of structuring the social psychological aspects of classroom learning so that children spend at least a portion of their time in pursuit of common goals. These effects are in accordance with predictions made by social scientists in their testimony favoring desegregating schools some 25 years ago. It is important to emphasize the fact that the jigsaw method has proved effective even if it is employed for as little as 20% of a child's time in the classroom. Moreover, other techniques have produced beneficial results even when interdependent learning was purposely accompanied by competitive activities. Thus, the data do not indicate the placing of a serious limit on classroom competition, or interfering with individually guided education. Interdependent learning can and does coexist easily with almost any other method used by teachers in the classroom.

REFERENCES

Aronson, E., Blaney, N., Sikes, J., Stephan, C., and Snapp, M. Busing and racial tension: The jigsaw route to learning and liking, *Psychology Today,* 1975, *8,* 43–59.

Aronson, E., Stephan, C., Sikes, J., Blaney, N., and Snapp, M. *The Jigsaw Classroom,* Sage Publications, Inc., Beverly Hills, California, 1978.

Aronson, E., Bridgeman, D. L., and Geffner, R. The effects of a cooperative classroom structure on students' behavior and attitudes. In D. Bar-Tal and L. Saxe (Eds.) *Social Psychology of Education: Theory and Research,* Washington, D.C.: Hemisphere, 1978.

Blaney, N. T., Stephan, C., Rosenfield, D., Aronson, E., and Sikes, J. Interdependence in the classroom: A field study, *Journal of Educational Psychology,* 1977, *69,* 139–146.

Bridgeman, D. L. The influence of cooperative, interdependent learning on role taking and moral reasoning: A theoretical and empirical field study with fifth grade students. Unpublished Doctoral Dissertation, University of California, Santa Cruz, 1977.

Chandler, M. J. Egocentrism and antisocial behavior: The assessment and training of social perspective-taking skills, *Developmental Psychology,* 1973, *9,* 326–332.

Cohen, E. Interracial interaction disability, *Human Relations,* 1972, *25,* (1), 9–24.

Cohen, E. and Roper, S. Modification of interracial interractions disability: An application of status characteristics theory, *American Sociological Review,* 1972, *6,* 643–657.

Cook, S. W. Interpersonal and attitudinal outcomes in cooperating interracial groups, *Journal of Research and Development in Education,* 1978, *12,* 97–113.

Covington, M. V. and Beery, R. G. *Self-worth and School Learning,* New York: Holt, Rinehart and Winston, 1976.

Deutsch, M. An experimental study of the effects of cooperation and competition upon group process, *Human Relations,* 1949, *2,* 199–231.

DeVries, D. L., Edwards, K. J., and Slavin, R. E. Bi-racial learning teams and race relations in the classroom: Four field experiments on Teams-Games-Tournament, *Journal of Educational Psychology,* 1978, *70,* 356–362.

Franks, D. D. and Marolla, J. Efficacious action and social approval as interacting dimensions of self-esteem: A tentative formulation through construct validation, *Sociometry,* 1976, *39,* 324–341.

Geffner, R. A. The effects of interdependent learning on self-esteem, inter-ethnic relations, and intra-ethnic attitudes of elementary school children: A field experiment. Unpublished Doctoral Dissertation, University of California, Santa Cruz, 1978.

Gerard, H. and Miller, N. *School Desegregation,* New York: Plenum, 1975.

Johnson, D. w. and Johnson, R. T. *Learning Together and Alone.* Englewood Cliffs, New Jersey: Prentice-Hall, Inc., 1975.

Lucker, G. W., Rosenfield, D., Sikes, J., and Aronson, E. Performance in the interdependent classroom: A field study, *American Educational Research Journal,* 1977, *13,* 115–123.

Pettigrew, T. Social psychology and desegregation research, *American Psychologist,* 1961, *15,* 61–71.

Purkey, W. W. *Self-Concept and School Achievement.* Englewood Cliffs, New Jersey: Prentice-Hall, 1970.

Sherif, M., Harvey, O. J., White, J., Hood, W., and Sherif, C. *Intergroup Conflict and Cooperation: The Robber's Cave Experiment.* Norman, Oklahoma: University of Oklahoma Institute of Intergroup Relations, 1961.

Slavin, R. E. Student teams and achievement divisions, *Journal of Research and Development in Education,* 1978, *12,* 39–49.

Stephan, C., Presser, N. R., Kennedy, J. C., and Aronson, E. Attributions to success and failure in cooperative, competitive and interdependent interactions, *European Journal of Social Psychology,* 1978, *8,* 269–274.

Stephan, W. G. School desegregation: An evaluation of predictions made in Brown vs. The Board of Education, *Psychological Bulletin,* 1978, *85,* 217–238.

St. John, N. *School Desegregation: Outcomes for Children.* New York: John Wiley and Sons, 1975.

READING 44

Social Antecedents, Cognitive Processing, and Comprehension of Social Portrayals on Television

W. Andrew Collins

Television, invented and propagated to entertain, has gradually become the focus of more popular and scientific attention in the study of children than any other socialization force except family and school. As has been the case with several other topics in the study of social development (see Sears, 1975), interest in television has emerged from circumstances that are partly ecological and demographic, partly historical-political, and partly scientific. From the perspective of social effects on children, the impetus can be stated simply: Television has been thought to convey to children a unique variety and volume of social models that could socialize attitudes, behaviors, and expectations about social life. The extensive research literature on television and children (Comstock et al., 1978) largely reflects the deterministic tone of this statement; the predominant questions have been whether and in what ways children generally are affected by television viewing. Much less attention has been given to the responses of children of varying ages, abilities, and social backgrounds to social models that commonly occur on television.

In this chapter I review some recent research on developmental and individual differences in children's understanding of the social behaviors, roles, and relationships portrayed in typical programs. A major premise of these studies is that the effects of televised social models are partly determined by cognitive, social, and individual characteristics that affect children's representations of what they see. The research itself involves examining children's processing across a variety of television programs, with the goal of specifying some sources and effects of variability in comprehension. Later in the chapter I will discuss how analysis of naturally occurring social stimuli may be of value in the study of social cognition and social behavior.

VIEWS ON THE EFFECTS OF TELEVISION

Relatively few of the large number of studies on the effects of television have focused on the child as a viewer (for reviews see Comstock et al., 1978; Stein & Friedrich, 1975). Rather, the field has been influenced by its sociological forebears toward a "dominant-image" view (e.g., Gerbner, 1972; Liebert, Neale, & Davidson, 1973) concerned primarily with the incidence of certain types of content, like violence. In this view the frequency of a behavior's occurrence, not the viewer's perception of its function or significance within a narrative, is socially influential; the most frequently occurring images determine the major effects of television. Viewers, whether children, youth, or adults, are commonly pictured as passive recipients of a series of salient images, from which they make no attempt to extract unique social meanings. The most influential psychological formulation in the past decade of research on television and children, Bandura's theory of observational learning (e.g., Bandura, 1965, 1969; Goranson, 1970), has often been assimilated to a dominant-image view, despite Bandura's (e.g., Bandura, 1977) recent focus on retention processes and the relevance of the context of modeled action to performance.

A more differentiated view of effects appears in other psychological perspectives on television and children (e.g., Comstock et al., 1978; Feshbach & Singer, 1971; Leifer, Gordon, & Graves, 1974; Liebert, Neale, & Davidson, 1973; Maccoby, 1964; Siegel, 1975; Stein & Friedrich, 1975). Rather than being determined primarily by salient social models (e.g., violence, prosocial behavior), postviewing behavior is also seen partly as a function of extra-presentation age and social-group correlates of postviewing behaviors. For example, postviewing aggressive behavior may be influenced by (1) the results of antecedent social learning (e.g., internalization of social and moral values, previous direct or vicarious experience with the observed behaviors) and (2) states and circumstances subsequent to viewing (e.g., opportunities for behavior and their circumstances, including provocation, existing or expected sanctions, and emotional arousal). These correlates of outcome behaviors are assumed to heighten or reduce viewers' motivations to adopt salient social behaviors from television programs; the implicit equation is one in which the separate motivational factors are weighted and combined to determine an outcome. In short, age-related and individual differences in outcomes are largely seen as the result of variation in the nature and extent of socialization of pertinent behavioral and emotional tendencies.

THE ROLE OF COMPREHENSION

Emphases on the occurrence of certain types of models and motivational factors in the social outcomes of viewing have largely overshadowed issues of whether and how children process social models in typical programs. Yet television portrayals are considerably more complex and more subject to vagaries in comprehension than the laboratory analogs in most research on basic modeling processes. Younger, less cognitively skilled viewers may process these complex materials differently or less adequately than older viewers. Furthermore, besides predicting certain categories of social actions, antecedent social experiences may influence children's attention to, and retention of, portrayals of television characters and events, which in turn mediate the social influ-

ence of many television programs (Omanson, 1979).

An example illustrates this point. A commonly portrayed character in many typical entertainment programs is the "double-dealer," who superficially appears benevolent but is subtly and gradually revealed to be malevolent. Preschool and young grade school viewers may well fail to comprehend the duplicity in such a characterization (Collins & Zimmermanm, 1975) and in many instances may evaluate the character's behavior more positively than the plot warrants. According to prevailing theories of behavioral effects, a duplicitous character would probably thus be more readily emulated than one for whom contextual cues were more consistently negative. Young viewers in particular would be more affected by such a model than older, more experienced viewers, who would be apt to recognize the pertinent negative cues, discount the apparently positive ones, and evaluate the character negatively.

Other factors besides developmental ones may also affect children's comprehension. Children who are especially familiar with an ambiguous character's social role and the circumstances of the portrayed behavior are in a better position to weigh apparently conflicting cues. For example, in one instance of pilot research, some young children were interviewed after seeing a plot in which the focal characters in a plot were a duplicitous white plain-clothes policeman and a Hispanic community organizer, whose laudable intentions were confounded by a contentious manner. White children viewed the Hispanic character more negatively than the policeman, and justified their evaluation by citing matters of appearance and interpersonal style. Non-white children, however, seemed to recognize the underlying goals of the Hispanic character in their explanations and judge him more positively. In other views of children's responses to social models, social factors like class or ethnic background have been considered important correlates of the viewer's tendency to engage in the modeled behaviors. Imitation of the minority character by minority children might be attributable either to a strong base-line tendency for members of the same social group to engage in a behavior or a motivation to emulate the behavior of a model with whom they could readily identify. In our view, the effects of the similarity between model and viewer in the present example probably also reflect more cognitive components, such as the attention-directing function of similarity and preference (cf. Bartlett, 1932; Krebs, 1970) and the facilitative effects of prior knowledge on the processing of the particulars of the plot in which the model is portrayed. In the remainder of the chapter, I will discuss some research findings relevant both to age-related strategies for processing information from complex programs and to the ways in which a child's prior relevant social experiences affect comprehension of social information on television.

DEVELOPMENTAL ASPECTS OF COMPREHENSION

At this point, more extensive evidence is available about developmental differences in comprehension of typical television programs than about the differential effects of individual experience and predispositions. Most information about developmental aspects of processing comes from studies of children's understanding of dramatic programs produced for adults. These narrative programs—action-adventure programs, family dramas, situation comedies— are devised with sufficient complication to keep adult viewers interested; the particulars of the plots are often subtle, inexplicit, and interspersed with extraneous or tangentially relevant material. We have focused on the extent to which children of different ages retain two kinds of information from these complex television plots: (1) *explicit events* that occur in single scenes of the program, particularly those that are essential to the sense of the plot, and (2)

implicit information that is not explicitly mentioned or depicted but is implied by the relations between scenes. For example, consider the following two hypothetical explicit events: Character *A* observes Character *B* steal something; later, *B* jumps *A* from behind as *A* enters a room. The causal relation between these two events (that *B* jumped *A* because *A* witnessed the theft he committed) is only implicit in the program and must be inferred by the viewer. We have been especially interested in this process of *temporal integration,* in which viewers must infer the relations among discretely presented units of information across time (Collins, 1977).

The measures used to assess comprehension are developed in several steps. The first task is an event analysis similar to that suggested by Warren, Nicholas, and Trabasso (1979) and by Omanson (1979), in which the essential elements of the plot and the relations among them are represented. Subsequently, panels of adults are asked to rate the importance of the content items and also to retell the story, including the essential elements. These panels generally show considerable agreement (across studies, between .76 and .94) about the essential items of content in programs. Next, children are asked open-ended questions about the plot to elicit words and phrases that are likely to be understandable to children when referring to the programs. Finally, multiple-choice recognition items are written to cover the essential information in the narrative, using wordings for stems and for both correct and incorrect alternatives that come from the children's responses in the pretest interviews.

One example may clarify the nature of the recognition measure. An explicit content item might concern a violent act ("When Luke was walking in the alley he...saw a man steal some money"). Another might concern a later act of violence ("When Luke walked into the office, another man...jumped on him from behind"). A subsequent question then concerns the cause of the fight ("Someone jumped on Luke...because Luke knew he had stolen the money"). The first two questions deal with explicit content; the third, with an inference about the implicit cause–effect relation between them. The measure thus taps children's abilities to verify the occurrence of on-screen events and the implicit relations among them. In addition, choices of incorrect alternatives, which are constructed to represent specific comprehension errors, permit both an analysis of difficulties in understanding programs and an assessment of the effects of guessing and response bias. Other nonrecognition procedures, selected according to the purpose of individual studies, are used to supplement the recognition measure.

Comprehension of Explicit and Implicit Content

This approach has been used in several studies of children's comprehension. A brief review of one (Collins et al., 1978) illustrates the research strategy and exemplary findings. The stimulus program was an hour-long action-adventure show composed of two parallel subplots edited into four different versions. One version, the *simple* version, consisted of one of the plots. The second, or *complex*, version of the program contained the same plot, and in addition intermingled it with the second subplot, which was not necessary for comprehension of the basic story line. The third and fourth versions were *jumbled* renderings, in which scenes from the simple and complex versions were randomly ordered. This manipulation, which was designed to permit examination of effects of plot organization and complexity on processing by children of different ages, is described here to illustrate the stimulus variations over which the general comprehension patterns we found have been obtained.

In the experiment, one of these four versions was shown to second-, fifth-, and eighth-grade children ($N = 292$). After viewing, the children completed a recognition-items test about dis-

crete scenes in the show and about the causal relationships that existed among the scenes. Second-graders remembered a significantly smaller proportion of the explicit content than did older children, adolescents, and adults. On these items, second-graders recalled an average of only 66% of the content that adults had judged as essential to the plot; fifth-graders recalled 84% of these scenes, and eighth-graders recalled 92%. These age differences occur regardless of plot length; and they parallel age trends reported in studies of situation comedies (Collins, 1970; Newcomb & Collins, 1979) and other action-adventure programs, including a period Western (Collins, in preparation). Even when they do remember important explicit events, however, younger children often fail to grasp the interscene relations that also carry important information. Performance on the recognition measure of implicit information—the content that is not explicitly presented but is implicit in the relationships between discrete scenes—is shown in Figure 1. Second-graders had an overall mean score of fewer than half (47%) of the inference items adults had agreed upon as essential, and fifth- and eighth-graders scored 67% and 77%, respectively. However, as Figure 1 shows, children's ability to make the inferences required for understanding implicit information varied with the version of the stimulus program they watched. It is clear from both boys' and girls' data that fifth- and eighth-graders comprehended best in the two ordered conditions. This pattern is also apparent in the data for girls at the second-grade level, although their mean scores are markedly lower than those of older children. However, second-grade boys in all four conditions perform at chance level on this measure of inferences.

Second-graders' poor performance on the recognition inference items does not appear to be only an artifact of their poor knowledge of individual scenes. The conditional probabilities for correct inferences provide evidence of this,

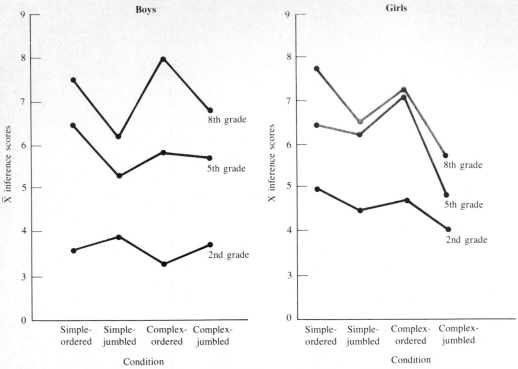

FIGURE 1   Boys' and girls' mean scores for inferences about the content of four versions of
an action-adventure drama. (Data from Collins, Wellman, Keniston, & Westby, 1978.)

given that the children knew at the time they
were tested either both of the relevant premise
scenes, only one of them, or neither one. It was
possible to determine from questionnaire measures and supplementary interview probes
whether individual children knew the two discrete scenes or the *premises* on which each of
the inference items was based. The shaded bars
in Figure 2 represent the probability that inference items were answered correctly, given that
children knew both requisite pieces of discrete
information. Clearly, the likelihood of correctly
integrating important information about the plot
across temporally separate discrete scenes is
relatively small for second-graders; the probability is less than 50%, just greater than chance.
The probabilities for fifth- and eighth-graders
are considerably higher (68 %and 75%, respectively). By contrast, the likelihood of correct
inferences when there is evidence at testing that

children know only one, or neither, of the
premise scenes (shown in Figure 2 by the
shaded bars) is just greater than chance at all
three grade levels. Thus, given knowledge of
the discrete, explicit scenes, older children are
more likely than younger children to infer the
implied relationships among them.

Developmental differences of the sort described here have been replicated in studies of a
number of different types of commercial dramatic
television programs. As do developmental differences in comprehension of other kinds of materials, these age-related patterns appear to reflect
emergence of strategies for "going beyond the
information given." We have attempted in recent
studies (Collins, in preparation; Purdie, Collins,
& Westby, 1979) to examine whether this characterization is an apt one by tracing the course of
processing during viewing. Briefly described, the
procedure involves interrupting viewing at differ-

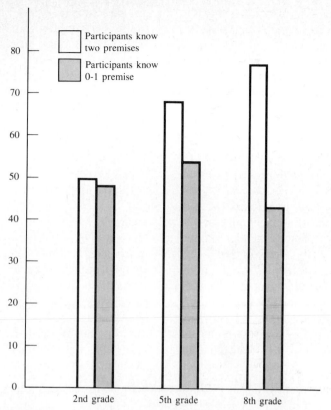

FIGURE 2   Conditional probabilities of correct inferences about relations between program events, given that both premises of the inference are known or that only one or neither of the premises is known. (Data from Collins, Wellman, Keniston, & Westby, 1978.)

ent points for different subgroups of children and then testing the children's knowledge of explicit content and inferences up to the point of interruption. Viewing is resumed after testing; and all children answer recognition items and interview questions about the remainder of the show when the program is over. One group of children sees the entire program without interruption and is then tested on the full battery of recognition items to provide a check on possible contamination of postinterruption answers in the other three conditions.

The interruption procedure revealed that children tested on content they had seen only minutes before performed no better than chil-

dren who were asked the same questions at a later time. Apparently the comprehension difficulties of young grade school viewers are not attributable simply to forgetting; nor do they result from the interferences of intervening information, when children are tested without interruption at the end of a lengthy program. Rather, throughout the program the recognition of explicit content and inferences of implicit relationships was poorer for second-graders than for fifth- and eighth-graders.

Processing Social Cues

From this vantage point, let us now turn to some research in which we examined age-related comprehension of cues relevant to the evaluation of a televised social model, namely, motives for an antisocial act and the causal relation between motives and aggression.

In this study (Purdie, Collins, & Westby, 1979) the stimulus program was an edited version of a commercial-network action-adventure drama. The plot involved a man searching for his former wife to prevent her from presenting damaging testimony against him in a kidnapping case. He finds the house where she is hiding and shoots at her. His goal is thwarted by the arrival of law officers, and he is taken away in handcuffs. In editing, the main events of the plot were retained, but some extraneous materials and all commercials were deleted. We manipulated narrative sequences by creating one version in which the temporal distance between relevant premise scenes was reduced. Thus, in the *distal-motive version,* the protagonist's motives and aggression appeared in scenes that were approximately four minutes apart. In the *proximal-motive version,* motive and aggression information were presented in immediate sequence. One or the other of the two versions was then shown to 200 randomly selected second- and fifth-grade girls and boys.

As in our other research, there were pronounced grade differences on the recognition measure of comprehension. At both grade levels, however, children who saw the motive and aggression cues next to each other understood the implicit motive-aggression relationship better than children who saw the cues separated from each other. Apparently, reducing the distance between relevant cues facilitated integration of information about the protagonist's motive and aggression, especially for the second-graders. The conditional probability for correct inference items, given that children answered both discrete premises correctly, was .52 for proximal-motive viewers in the second grade, whereas distal-motive-condition second-graders made correct inferences at chance level (.29). Fifth-graders' probabilities were higher

and essentially equal in both viewing conditions. Both age groups performed at chance level when only one, or neither, explicit premise was known.

These variations in children's recognition of explicit and implicit information about the motives and action of the character in the program influenced their impressions of the goodness or badness of the aggressor. Evaluations were assessed using a graduated-squares procedure (Costanzo et al., 1973), in which six size-graduated squares are labeled from "very bad" to "very good." Children point to the square that shows how good or how bad the character is. Children who answered all three motive-aggression inference questions correctly were significantly more negative in their evaluations of the aggressor than were children who understood two or fewer inferences. Whether motives and aggression were proximally or distally portrayed also affected evaluation. At both grades, distal-motive viewers evaluated the character less negatively then proximal-motive viewers, particularly following portrayal of the aggressive action. Thus, children's inferences about critical links were related to evaluative responses that potentially affect adoption of observed behaviors.

Children's Representations of Programs

Thus far the emphasis has been on what children fail to understand from typical portrayals. Let us now take another perspective on the problem: granted that—compared to older viewers—young grade school children comprehend less of the essential explicit and implicit content of programs, what *do* they take away from typical portrayals of characters and events? Recent analyses indicate that representations of programs are heavily affected by the knowledge about persons and sequences of events that children bring to viewing.

For example, in the study just described (Collins et al., 1978) two-thirds of the second-, fifth-, and eighth-graders were interrupted at

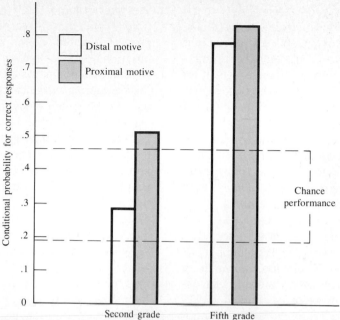

FIGURE 3   Conditional probabilities for correct responses by second- and fifth-grade children in the distal-motive and proximal-motive viewing conditions.

one or the other of two points that had previously been agreed upon by adult raters as suspense points, or scenes after which something noteworthy obviously was going to happen. During these interruptions, the children were asked what they thought was going to happen next and why, and their predictions were coded according to whether or not they mentioned events from the program in explaining their answers. (The predictions were not coded for accuracy.) The majority of the fifth- and eighth-graders (78% and 68%, respectively) predicted events that invoked, or followed from, the sequence of plot occurrences prior to interruption. For example, following a scene in which a murderer meets a panhandler who resembles the man he had killed, *relevant* predictions often involved the likelihood that the murderer would confuse the man with his earlier victim and provoke further mayhem ("He'll think he didn't kill the wino and will go after this guy"). Second-graders rarely (28% of the

cases) predicted events that followed from the earlier events of the shows. Instead, they appeared to answer on the basis of the immediately preceding scene alone.

A typical prediction made by these children was simply that the villain would give the old panhandler some money. In many instances, of course, the common action sequences that young children cite are high-probability occurrences that can aid in understanding observed behavior. They are examples of what have been called *schemata* (e.g., Bartlett, 1932; Neisser, 1976) or *scripts* (Schank & Abelson, 1977), that is, groupings of actions that are called into play when key parts of the action or characteristic settings are encountered. For example, in the instance of the killer and the panhandler, knowing that someone asks for money may initially suggest a sequence in which a handout is granted (even though it is inconsistent with the traits of the character in question here).

How do such expectations about social events enter into comprehension of social narratives? At this point only a speculative account can be offered. In constructing a representation, mature viewers may use increasingly more specialized action sequences. At one level comprehension may be based on various standard sequences that are evoked by details of the portrayal. For example, from seeing police in uniforms, even a young child could understand that the plot was a police story and could infer that police were chasing someone who was guilty of some transgressions and so forth. Thus, certain types of program-elicited *common knowledge* are likely to be represented in children's understanding. On the other hand, certain variations or embellishments on these simple sequences represent more *program-specific knowledge,* or more specialized understandings, that would probably be typical only of older children. Applying these distinctions to the stimulus program studied by Collins and his associates (1978), the show probably evoked *common knowledge* about (1) policeman, (2) a murder committed by one of the characters, (3) this same person's being shot or apprehended by the police in the end, and (4) buying groceries (which the protagonist did repeatedly in order to cash his forged checks; buying groceries is likely to be understood even by young children [Nelson, 1978]). *Program-specific knowledge* included information that (1) some nonuniformed characters were policemen, (2) the murder at the beginning occurred because the victim surprised the villain during a theft (a motive inference), and (3) the purpose behind buying groceries was cashing "fake" checks to get money.

These categories of content recently have been examined by Collins and Wellman (1980) in interview protocols from the children who participated in the study by Collins and his associates (1978). The children had been asked to retell the narrative so that "someone would be able to tell what happened in the show."

Wellman first had adults code content propositions from these interviews into either the program-elicited common knowledge or the program-specific knowledge categories (proportion of agreements was .98). He then noted the frequency with which children mentioned one or the other category of content in their narratives. As Table 1 shows, among second-graders the mean proportion of children who mentioned the content that fit scripts readily known by all age groups was 81%, but the mean proportion of these younger children who mentioned more specialized knowledge was only 16%. Fifth- and eighth-graders were just as likely as younger children to mention common knowledge, but many more older viewers mentioned program-specific knowledge. The relevant mean proportions in fifth and eighth grades were 55% and 98%, respectively, compared to 16% for second-graders. Thus, for viewers whose expectations coincide with what the actors do, think, and feel, both the explicit and implicit events in a television portrayal are probably relatively easy, because observations can be assimilated readily. For viewers who lack pertinent schemata or scripts, comprehension is probably more difficult.

In the study by Collins and his associates (1978), however, younger children mentioned some details just as frequently as older children but fewer program-specific details; and their comprehension of the program was generally poorer. Perhaps young viewers, even when they know many relevant scripts, apply them less flexibly than older children in comprehending new experiences. That is, once a script has been instantiated by a salient cue (e.g., the label "police" or seeing uniformed characters), younger children may behave as though the program simply follows a standard script; as a result, they may fail to notice or may ignore ways in which the program varies from the script. Consequently, central explicit and implicit details or particular narratives may be short-circuited by rigid expectations of actors

TABLE 1   PROPORTIONS OF CHILDREN WHO MENTIONED COMMON-KNOWLEDGE AND PROGRAM-SPECIFIC CONTENTS IN RETELLING THE TELEVISED NARRATIVE

Grade	Common-knowledge content				Program-specific content		
	Police	Murder	Bad guy caught	Buying groceries	Show premise	Villain's crime	Forgery
Second	9/17	12/17	15/15	16/17	2/17	3/17	1/17
Fifth	10/19	14/19	19/19	19/19	7/19	12/19	12/19
Eighth	3/14	12/14	12/14	14/14	13/14	14/14	14/14

and actions. More knowledgeable viewers may more readily recognize the significance of departures from scripts and process them as significant aspects of stories that override action scripts.

This view of age-related differences in comprehension difficulty is a working hypothesis for future research. The tendency to short-circuit attention to unique, essential features of dramatic plots may be consequential for social learning in cases where reliance on early instantiated, limited knowledge could result in misleading impressions of actors and their behavior. For example, in the case of the double-dealing character in the preceding sequence, behavioral and appearance cues may initially instantiate a script for benevolent behavior, although in the details of the program the character is actually revealed, subtly and by small increments, to be malevolent instead.

INDIVIDUAL DIFFERENCES IN SOCIAL KNOWLEDGE AND COMPREHENSION

Recently, evidence has emerged in our research indicating that prior social experiences may underlie individual variations, as well as developmental differences, in children's comprehension. These individual differences may be especially pronounced within younger age groups, whose comprehension of the explicit content of programs is often poor. In a recently published study (Newcomb & Collins, 1979), individual differences were found in the understanding of typical televised social portrayals. The experiment involved equal numbers of children from both lower-socioeconomic and middle-

socioeconomic samples (SES) at the second, fifth, and eighth grades. One set of children, including all these subgroups, viewed an edited version of a commercial network show featuring middle-class characters; the second set of participants saw a show with a similar plot line featuring lower-class characters. Family composition and the complexity of the programs were similar, and the two recognition measures constructed for the study were of similar degrees of difficulty.

When the children were tested for understanding of the events, the inferred causes of action, and the emotions of the characters, second-grade children performed best when the social-class milieu portrayed in the program was similar to their own. Figure 4 shows these results. Middle-SES second-graders who viewed the middle-class show inferred more about the causes of actions and the feelings and emotions of the characters than lower-SES youngsters who watched the middle-class shows; and lower-SES second-graders who watched the lower-class characters inferred more of the same kind of information from that plot than did the middle-class children who watched the lower-class program. These effects do not appear at the fifth- and eighth-grade levels. Thus, for the younger children, with more limited cognitive skills for understanding television programs, seeing the action portrayed in settings similar to their own backgrounds helped them acquire relevant information from the program; their difficulties in comprehending shows, which have been attributed to developmental factors, were most evident when the types of roles, characters, and

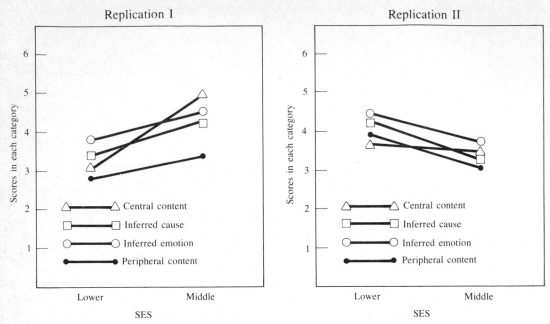

FIGURE 4   Mean correct answers on explicit- and implicit-content recognition items for middle- and lower-SES second-graders who watched middle-class characters (Replication I) or working-class characters (Replication II). (Data from Newcomb & Collis, 1979.)

settings portrayed in the program were unfamiliar. Thus, if TV characters and events do not conform to social expectations, young viewers may be even less than ordinarily likely to understand actions, motives, and feelings in television programs.

Despite the salutary effects of pertinent social experiences for second-graders, however, preadolescent and adolescent viewers in the study again appeared to use selective and inferential strategies more effectively than the younger children. Even the best-performing second-graders were still significantly less accurate than fifth- and eighth-graders. Furthermore, conditional probabilities were again computed to determine whether, if the children knew the central explicit contents of the scenes, they were also likely to know the implicit content—the causes of actions and the emotional states of actors. These probabilities were significantly higher for fifth-graders than for

second-graders, indicating that information implied by on-screen events was more likely to be grasped by older viewers than by younger ones.

Other evidence of individual differences in comprehension comes from a recently completed study (List, Collins, & Westby, 1981) of the effects of sex-role stereotypes on comprehension of conventional versus nonconventional sex-role portrayals in television dramas. In this research, third-graders' degree of sex-role stereotyping was assessed. Their comprehension of explicit content and inferences after viewing both a conventional and a nonconventional portrayal of a female character were then tested in a within-subjects design using recognition procedures. Understanding of the two programs was clearly affected by children's sex-role expectations. When high-stereotype children made errors of comprehension, the errors significantly reflected traditional sex-role expectations, whereas low-stereotype viewers more often made errors consonant with less-traditional expectations. These findings cannot be explained by differences in ability between the two groups nor by differential difficulty of the two programs or measures. Furthermore, a separate group of high- and low-stereotype third-graders who answered the recognition items without having seen the programs chose among the alternative answers at chance level. Sex-role expectations apparently were cued by the content of the programs and, in turn, influenced children's perceptions of plot events. Thus, social expectations as commonplace as sex-role stereotypes affect children's representations of content in television programs.

CONCLUSIONS

I have attempted to outline here some aspects of children's representations of television portrayals of social models. In the view I have proposed, the social stimuli purveyed by television are at the center of a causal configuration, in which what children select and remember about the portrayals they observe are shaped by prior social and cognitive growth, and the resulting representations in turn mediate the social effects of viewing. The evidence to date indicates that, after watching typical dramatic programs, grade-school and preadolescent children construct representations that vary considerably in how accurately and completely they reflect the content of portrayals. Furthermore, their evaluations of the portrayed characters and actions appear to vary concomitantly with comprehension.

Age-related differences in cognitive strategies for processing social content across the time span of typical dramatic narratives clearly contribute to variation in representation of acts and the contexts in which they occur. In addition, variability in social understanding depends heavily on viewers' prior knowledge of a variety of social experiences. Pre-viewing experiences, circumstances, and states have long

been recognized as pertinent to the prediction of behavior after viewing; but judging from our evidence, the effects of these factors may partly reflect their influence on the way in which the social portrayals themselves are understood and remembered.

At present there is little basis for saying how social knowledge is represented and how it enters into comprehension of social portrayals. The most extensive evidence comes from theory and research on prose narratives (Bower, 1978a; Bower, Black, & Turner, 1979; Mandler & Johnson, 1977; Warren, Nicholas, & Trabasso, 1979; Schank & Abelson, 1977; Stein & Glenn, 1979), but few details are known and several contending perspectives presently guide research efforts (Omanson, 1979). The most detailed account of the role of prior knowledge in understanding stories is the scripts approach (Schank & Abelson, 1977), in which prior knowledge, in the form of stereotypes of event sequences, enables inferences about gaps in the linkages between the actions or states of the story characters. These scripts, which are abstracted from previous experiences in similar situations, make possible hierarchical representations of plots. One difficulty, as Bower (1978b) notes, is that scripts may often not be clearly distinguishable from a conceptually cumbersome aggregation of similar experiences elicited in different circumstances. Schank and Abelson (1977), however, emphasize the abstract, categorical quality of scripts. Like other views of the role of schemata in processing of social information (e.g., Cantor & Mischel, 1977; Hastie, in press; Judd & Kulik, in press; Taylor & Crocker, in press), the scripts formulation implies hierarchical information structures in which the highest, most abstract levels are supported by a rich store of specific experiences or bits of information at lower levels. Such structures affect both encoding (Bower, 1977; Markus, 1977; Rogers, Kuiper, & Kirker, 1977) and retrieval (Cantor & Mischel, 1977; Hastie, in press; Zadny & Gerard, 1974) of information about newly encountered persons and events. Neisser's (1976) characterization applies generally to current views of the effects of structures in social information processing:

A schema is like a *format* in a computer programming language. Formats specify that information must be of a certain sort if it is to be interpreted coherently.... Information can be picked up only if there is a developmental format ready to accept it. Information that does not fit such a format goes unused. Perception is inherently selective. (p. 55)

Little attention has been given to the assessment of relevant schemata in studies of social cognition. In most research, manipulations have been introduced to activate certain commonly available schemata, which have then been observed to affect memory for a stimulus (e.g., Cantor & Mischel, 1977; Taylor & Crocker, in press). Recently, however, Bower, Black, and Turner (1979) and Nelson (1978), the latter working with children, have attempted to specify knowledge of scripts in memory and language tasks, and social psychologists (e.g., Markus, 1977; Rogers, Kuiper, & Kirker, 1977) have also examined the nature of certain social schemata and their role in the processing of new stimuli. Their strategies are potentially applicable to comprehension of important aspects of social portrayals in television narratives. One focus of future research should be further specification of the nature and representation of social knowledge and its role in children's processing of social stimuli like television programs.

In addition to knowledge about social interactions and events, two other kinds of general knowledge also affect comprehension of televised narratives and thus continue to be central to our analysis of children's processing. One is knowledge of the usual form and structure of stories. In recent research on prose stories (e.g., Mandler & Johnson, 1977; Poulsen et al., 1978; Stein & Glenn, 1979), preschool and young grade school children's relatively poor recall of story details has appeared to be related to a less adequate general structure according to which story details might be parsed. More recently, Sedlak (1979) has suggested that young children fail to comprehend the actions and events in a narrative because they assume different interpretations of the various actors' intentions or plans. Sedlak's approach is congruent with recent dissertation research by Wilensky (1978), in which the importance of perceived goals and intentions to narrative comprehension is further specified. Both approaches specify inferential steps that characterize the processing of narratives by older children, but are used less reliably by younger ones.

A third kind of knowledge that affects processing of audiovisually presented narratives is familiarity with certain cinematic conventions (Tada, 1969). Baggett (1979) has recently found that an audiovisually presented narrative had identifiable structure and meaningful breakpoints that corresponded semantically to the breakpoints in a prose version of the same narratives. The way in which information was conveyed in the two media differed markedly, however. Formal features of programs, such as camera angles and the use of background music, and visual techniques for compressing time and signaling breaks in action carry considerable information for viewers whose experience permits their meaning to be recognized. At present, however, little is known about the interaction of social knowledge and knowledge of the presentation conventions common to television programs.

Potential Effects of Comprehension on Behavior

Implications of variations in comprehension of television portrayals for behavioral effects on children and adolescents have been addressed in relatively few studies, and those in which direct measures of both comprehension and behavior have been taken (e.g., Leifer & Roberts, 1972) have yielded null findings. In this regard, the literature parallels discouraging empirical efforts in the areas of attitude–behavior relationships (e.g., Ajzen & Fishbein, 1977) and social-cognition–behavior correspondences (e.g., Shantz, 1975). Nevertheless, several researchers have found behavioral differences that are suggestive of links between children's representations of programs and subsequent behavior. Such links should be further examined. For example, Collins, Berndt, and Hess (1974) found that kindergarten and second-grade children who had watched an action-adventure program had difficulty remembering the relationship of the motive and consequence cues to the aggressive action. Although such cues appear to moderate the behavioral effects of observed aggression (Bandura, 1965; Berkowitz & Geen, 1967; Berkowitz & Rawlings, 1963), kindergartners and second-graders in the research remembered the aggressive scene but only infrequently knew its links with the motives and consequences. Collins (1973) further reported behavioral differences that ostensibly reflect cognitive processing differences such as those previously described. This research involved inserting commercials between scenes of negative motives and negative consequences for aggression and the violent scene itself. Under this condition, third-graders' postviewing tendencies to choose aggressive responses increased, in comparison to children of the same age who saw the three scenes in immediate sequence. Although no measure of comprehension was available, the task of inferring relations between aggressive action and the pertinent motive and consequence cues was probably more difficult for the first group than for the second, a result, most likely, of the temporal separation imposed by the commercials. There was no evidence of behavioral differences among the sixth- and tenth-graders who saw both types of programs.

It is impossible to estimate what part of the variance in the social impact of television is due to incomplete or distorted comprehension of what children see; comprehension is only one factor in a very complex equation for television effects. However, we have found marked variability of children's comprehension of socially pertinent content during the middle-childhood and adolescent years; and we can point to suggestive evidence of concomitant effects on behavior in the laboratory. These two empirical thrusts indicate that social-cognitive components of the viewing process should become a term in the effects equation that guides future research.

IMPLICATIONS FOR THE STUDY OF SOCIAL COGNITION

The formulation advanced here of the source and nature of difficulties in children's understanding of common social models emerged from studies of television portrayals. In our research, we have noted a number of instances in which predictions about the effects of social models are different from, or more differentiated than, those that would be made from extant social-modeling formulations. Perhaps social-cognitive analyses of other natural social stimuli could similarly supplement and inform research on children's social cognition. In several other instances, like Lepper's (this volume) studies of messages to children in classrooms, social-cognitive analyses have been enriched by in vivo investigations of the stimuli typically encountered by children. It may be profitable to diversify our analytic efforts to examine the range and nature of social-cognitive tasks involved in children's typical social experiences. Such analyses, in fine-tuned oscillation with laboratory work, would be useful both in constructing more accurate laboratory analogs and in testing the sufficiency of the analogs once they have been constructed. Perhaps, with appropriate adjustments for the nature of the phenomena under study, social-cognition researchers could experience some of the benefits that social-behavior scholars have enjoyed as a result of renewed involvement in studies of children in natural settings.

A corollary to the need for in vivo research on social cognition is the need to give explicit attention to the social antecedents of social-cognitive functioning, or—the other way around—the social-cognitive sequelae of social experiences. Thus far in our own research we have relied on differential studies, investigating comprehension of social portrayals as a function of group differences in social class, attitudes and expectations, and behavioral tendencies. We have little sense of the ways in which mundane social experiences are represented in memory and then enter into construing new social experiences. In other social-cognitive domains, more is known about the effects of specific experiences on social cognition: Lepper and Ruble (this volume) have examined social contingencies that appear to be correlated with certain attributional processes, for example. Despite several generations of research on parent–child and peer relations, however, we still know relatively little about the nature and functioning of the social-cognitive sequelae of primary social interactions with parents and with different configurations of peers. Nor do we know how, or to what extent, television portrayals affect expectations about more or less common social occurrences. Judging from the few studies to date, problems like these may be more central to the social-cognition–behavior relationship than had previously been recognized. Perhaps better understanding of the effects of social experience on social cognition will enable us to specify more adequately the ways in which social cognition affects social behavior.

REFERENCES

Ajzen, I., & Fishbein, M. Attitude-behavior relations: A theoretical analysis and review of empirical research. *Psychological Bulletin*, 1977, *84*, 888–918.

Austin, V., Ruble, D., & Trabasso, T. Recall and order effects as factors in children's moral judgments. *Child Development*, 1977, *48*(2), 470–474.

Baggett, P. Structurally equivalent stories in movie and text and the effect of the medium on recall. *Journal of Verbal Learning and Verbal Behavior*, 1979, *18*(3), 333–356.

Bandura, A. Influence of models' reinforcement contingencies on the acquisition of imitative responses. *Journal of Personality and Social Psychology*, 1965, *1*(6), 589–595.

Bandura, A. A social-learning theory of identificatory processes. In D. A. Goslin (Ed.), *Handbook of socialization theory and research*. Chicago: Rand McNally, 1969.

Bandura, A. *Social learning theory*. New York: Wiley, 1977.

Bartlett, F. C. *Remembering*. Cambridge: Cambridge University Press, 1932.

Berkowitz, L., & Geen, R. The stimulus qualities of the target of aggression: A further study. *Journal of Personality and Social Psychology*, 1967, *5*, 364–368.

Berkowitz, L., & Rawlings, E. Effects of film violence on inhibitions against subsequent aggression. *Journal of Abnormal and Social Psychology*, 1963, *66*(5), 405–412.

Bower, G. H. *On injecting life into deadly prose*. Paper presented to the meeting of the Western Psychological Association, Seattle, 1977.

Bower, G. Experiments on story comprehension and recall. *Discourse Processes*, 1978, *1*, 211–231. (a)

Bower, G. Representing knowledge development. In R. Siegler (Ed.), *Children's thinking: What develops?* pp. 349–362. Hillsdale, N.J.: Erlbaum, 1978. (b)

Bower, G. H., Black, J. B., & Turner, T. J. Scripts in memory for text. *Cognitive Psychology*, 1979, *11*, 177–220.

Cantor, N., & Mischel, W. Traits as prototypes: Effects on recognition memory. *Journal of Personality and Social Psychology*, 1977, *35*, 38–48.

Collins, W. A. Learning of media content: A developmental study. *Child Development*, 1970, *41*(4), 1133–1142.

Collins, W. A. The effect of temporal separation between motivation, aggression and consequences: A developmental study. *Developmental Psychology*, 1973, *8*(2), 215–221.

Collins, W. A. *Temporal integration and inferences about televised social behavior.* Paper presented as part of a symposium on Cognitive Processing of Television Content: Perspectives on the Effects of Television on Children, at the biennial meeting of the Society for Research in Child Development, New Orleans, March 1977.

Collins, W. A., & Wellman, H. M. *Social scripts and developmental changes in representations of televised narratives.* Unpublished manuscript, Institute of Child Development, University of Minnesota, 1980.

Collins, W. A. *Developmental and individual differences in children's responses to television.* Manuscript in preparation.

Collins, W. A., Berndt, R., & Hess, V. Observational learning of motives and consequences for television aggression: A developmental study. *Child Development,* 1974, *45,* 799–802.

Collins, W. A., Wellman, H., Keniston, A., & Westby, S. Age-related aspects of comprehension of televised social content. *Child Development,* 1978, *49,* 389–399.

Collins, W. A., & Zimmerman, S. A. Convergent and divergent social cues: Effects of televised aggression on children. *Communication Research,* 1975, *2,* 331–347.

Comstock, G., Chaffee, S., Katzman, N., McCombs, M., & Roberts, D. *Television and human behavior.* New York: Columbia University Press, 1978.

Costanzo, P., Coie, J., Grumet, J., & Farnill, D. A reexamination of the effects of intent and consequence on children's moral judgments. *Child Development,* 1973, *44,* 154–161.

Feldman, N. S., Klosson, E. C., Parsons, J. E., Rholes, W. S., & Ruble, D. N. Order of information presentation and children's moral judgments. *Child Development,* 1976, *47,* 556–559.

Feshbach, S., & Singer, R. *Television and aggression: An experimental field study.* San Francisco: Jossey-Bass, 1971.

Gerbner, G. Violence in television drama: A study of trends and symbolic functions. In G. Comstock & E. Rubinstein (Eds.), *Television and social behavior* (Vol. 1). Washington, D.C.: U.S. Government Printing Office, 1972.

Goranson, R. E. Media violence and aggressive behavior: A review of experimental research. In R. Berkowitz (Ed.), *Advances in experimental social psychology,* pp. 2–31. New York: Academic Press, 1970.

Hastie, R. Schematic principles in human memory. In E. T. Higgins, C. P. Herman, and M. P. Zanna (Eds.), *The Ontario Symposium on Personality and Social Psychology: Social cognition.* Hillsdale, N.J.: Erlbaum, in press.

Judd, C. M., & Kulik, J. Schematic effects of social attitudes upon information processing and recall. *Journal of Personality and Social Psychology,* in press.

Krebs, D. L. Altruism: An examination of the concept and a review of the literature. *Psychological Bulletin,* 1970, *73,* 258–302.

Leifer, A., Gordon, N., & Graves, S. Children's television: More than mere entertainment. *Harvard Educational Review,* 1974, *44,* 213–245.

Leifer, A., & Roberts, D. Children's responses to television violence. In J. Murray, C. Rubenstein, & G. Comstock (Eds.), *Television and social behavior* (Vol. 2). Washington, D.C.: U.S. Government Printing Office, 1972.

Liebert, R., Neale, J., & Davidson, E. *The early window: Effects of television on children and youth.* Elmsford: N.Y.: Pergamon Press, 1973.

List, J., Collins, W. A., & Westby, S. *Comprehension and inferences from traditional and nontraditional sex-role portrayals.* Unpublished manuscript, University of Minnesota, 1981.

Maccoby, E. Effects of the mass media. In M. Hoffman & L. W. Hoffman (Eds.), *Review of child development research* (Vol. 1), pp. 323–348. Chicago: University of Chicago Press, 1964.

Mandler, J., & Johnson, N. Remembrance of things parsed: Story structure and recall. *Cognitive Psychology,* 1977, *9,* 111–151.

Markus, H. Self-schemata and processing information about the self. *Journal of Personality and Social Psychology,* 1977, *35,* 63–78.

Neisser, U. *Cognition and reality.* San Francisco: Freeman, 1976.

Nelson, K. How children represent knowledge of their world in and out of language: A preliminary report. In R. Siegler (Ed.), *Children's thinking: What develops?* pp. 255–274. Hillsdale, N.J.: Erlbaum, 1978.

Newcomb, A. F., & Collins, W. A. Children's comprehension of family role portrayals in televised dramas: Effects of socioeconomic status, ethnicity, and age. *Developmental Psychology,* 1979, *15*(4), 417–423.

Omanson, R. *The narrative analysis.* Unpublished doctoral dissertation, University of Minnesota, 1979.

Poulsen, D., Kintsch, E., Kintsch, W., & Premack, D. *Children's comprehension and memory for stories.* Unpublished manuscript, University of Colorado, 1978.

Purdie, S., Collins, W. A., & Westby, S. *Children's processing of motive information in a televised portrayal.* Unpublished manuscript, Institute of Child Development, University of Minnesota, 1979.

Rogers, T. B., Kuiper, R. G., & Kirker, W. S. Self-reference and the encoding of personal information. *Journal of Personality and Social Psychology,* 1977, *35,* 677–688.

Schank, R., & Abelson, R. *Scripts, plans, goals, and understanding.* Hillsdale, N.J.: Erlbaum, 1977.

Sears, R. Your ancients revisited: A history of child development. In E. M. Hetherington (Ed.), *Review of child development research* (Vol. 5), pp. 1–73. Chicago: University of Chicago Press, 1975.

Sedlak, A. J. Developmental differences in understanding plans and evaluating actors. *Child Development,* 1979, *50*(2), 536–560.

Shantz, C. U. The development of social cognition. In E. M. Hetherington (Ed.), *Review of child*

development research (Vol. 5). Chicago: University of Chicago Press, 1975.

Siegel, A. Communicating with the next generation. *Journal of Communication,* 1975, *25,* 14–24.

Stein, A., & Friedrich, L. Impact of television on children and youth. In E. M. Hetherington (Ed.), *Review of child development research* (Vol. 5), pp. 183–256. Chicago: University of Chicago Press, 1975.

Stein, N., & Glenn, C. An analysis of story comprehension in elementary school children. In R. Freedle (Ed.), *Advances in discourse processes* (Vol. 2). Hillsdale, N.J.: Erlbaum, 1979.

Tada, T. Image-cognition: A developmental approach. In *Studies of Broadcasting,* pp. 105–173. Tokyo: Nippon Hoso Kyokai, 1969.

Taylor, S., & Crocker, J. Schematic bases of social information processing. In E. T. Higgins, C. P. Herman, and M. P. Zanna (Eds.), *The Ontario Symposium on Personality and Social Psychology: Social cognition.* Hillsdale, N.J.: Erlbaum, in press.

Warren, W., Nicholas, D., & Trabasso, T. Event chains and inferences in understanding narratives. In R. Freedle (Eds.), *Advances in discourse processes* (Vol. 2). Hillsdale, N.J.: Erlbaum, 1979.

Wilensky, R. *Understanding goal-based stories.* Research Report No. 140, Yale University, Department of Computer Sciences, 1978.

Zadny, J., & Gerard, H. B. Attributed intentions and informational selectivity. *Journal of Experimental Social Psychology,* 1974, *10,* 34–52.

10

TARGETS OF SOCIALIZATION: MORAL DEVELOPMENT, SEX TYPING, AGGRESSION, AND ACHIEVEMENT

The beliefs, values, and attitudes which guide socialization, and the means of inculcating standards and developing desired behavior in children vary among cultures. The social norms and skills regarded as appropriate differ for members of an isolated Eskimo village, for nomadic desert Berber families, or for the recently discovered people of the primitive Tasaday tribe living in the jungles of the Philippines. Even within a culture such as that of the United States there are wide subcultural variations in social standards and socialization practices. Behavior regarded as desirable differs in Appalachian mountain hollows, in a black rural Southern village, in a New York Puerto Rican ghetto, or in a Midwest farming community.

In spite of these disparities in social standards there are certain classes of behaviors that are targets of socialization in almost every culture. In every society children are expected to become increasingly independent and able to care for themselves. They are encouraged to set and attain some achievement goals whether they are learning to read and write, to be a skilled hunter with a bow and arrow, to be a nuclear physicist, or to brew fine fermented beer. In each society members are expected to develop some degree of self-control, to inhibit or express aggression in a socially acceptable manner, to delay gratification of needs until an appropriate situation arises, and to restrain themselves from performing grossly antisocial behaviors. In addition, not only are individuals expected to exhibit self-control but they are socialized to perform prosocial behaviors such as sharing, helping, being cooperative, and showing expressions of sympathy.

In many, but not all, cultures the norms and modes of expression of social standards vary for men and women. There may be different expectations and goals for the training of independence, achievement, self-control, and prosocial behavior in the socialization of boys and girls. Across a broad range of cultures including that of the dominant American culture these sex-role standards take the form of what Parsons has called an "expressive" role for females and an "instrumental" role for males (Parsons, 1970). Women are expected to be more sensitive and skilled in interpersonal relations, more dependent and nurturant, and freer to express tender emotions than are men. Men are expected to be more aggressive, competitive, independent, able to solve problems, and to inhibit expression of affect that might be interpreted as weakness. It can well be asked if either of these stereotypes is descriptive of a fully competent, well-adjusted individual. Aggressiveness may have had some adaptive evolutionary value for primitive man and nurturance for females but in contemporary society surely a well-functioning individual of either sex should be able to feel and express affection and care for others, be able to solve problems, and be moderately assertive and self-sufficient. This has led to the position that rather than being socialized in accord with sex-role standards, children should be socialized in an androgynous fashion which aims for the same goals of competence in men and women.

In selecting articles for this section we have attempted to include those that cover behaviors that are the main targets of socialization. Hoffman begins this section with a discussion of moral thought, feeling, and behavior. Ruble, Balaban, and Cooper present a cognitive developmental analysis of the effects of televised sex-stereotypic information on children's behavior and attitudes. Their study illustrates the role of cognitive development in the emergence of sex typing as well as the potent role that television plays in the maintenance of sex role stereotypes. In their article Ginsburg and Miller demonstrate sex differences in childrens' risk-taking behaviors and show that girls are less likely than boys are to take risks.

Aggression continues to be a topic of concern to developmental psychologists as well as to parents and teachers. Children learn aggressive behaviors from a variety of sources. As Cummings, Iannotti, and Zahn-Waxler show, exposure to conflict between adults is associated with increased aggression between peers, as well as elevated levels of distress. Even young children are responsive to the interpersonal conflicts and hostility of adults.

In his analysis, Dodge shows that understanding the role of cognitive factors is important in understanding aggression. Aggressive boys were more likely than their nonaggressive peers to assume that another child's action was intentionally hostile. Aggressive children may see the world as a more belligerent and negative place than do less aggressive children.

Children's achievement behavior is another important target of socialization. Carol Dweck and Janine Bempechat provide a framework for understanding how children's cognitions contribute to the development of achievement behavior. Stevenson, Lee, and Stigler on the other hand, illustrate the role of cultural factors in achievement in their study of Japanese, Chinese, and American children.

Again we urge the student to think of the outcomes of socialization being associated with a network of interacting factors. Moral development, sex typing, aggression, self-control, and achievement are not shaped by parents alone, or by peers alone, or by schools or mass media. They are shaped to some extent by all the factors, with some agents having more impact in certain situations and at certain times in the life span. In addition, although by now it must sound rather like an old record to the reader, children are active participants in the socialization process. They are not passive recipients of the demands and behavior of others. They shape the world and people about them, they interpret and process social information, and they respond in an individualistic fashion.

REFERENCE

Parsons, T. *Social structure and personality*. New York: Free Press, 1970.

READING 45

Development of Moral Thought, Feeling, and Behavior

Martin L. Hoffman

Research on moral development has proceeded without letup for over half a century. One reason for the sustained interest is the obvious social significance of the topic in an urban industrialized society that is characterized by increasing crime, declining religious involvement, and events like Watergate, Jonestown, and the Kitty Genovese murder, which are brought home by the mass media. More fundamentally, morality is the part of personality that pinpoints the individual's very link to society, and moral development epitomizes the existential problem of how humans come to manage the inevitable conflict between personal needs and social obligations.

The legacy of Freud and Durkheim is the agreement among social scientists that most people do not go through life viewing society's moral norms (e.g., honesty, justice, fair play) as external, coercively imposed pressures. Though initially external and often in conflict with one's desires, the norms eventually become part of one's motive system and affect behavior even in the absence of external authority. The challenge is to discover what types of experience foster this internalization. The research, which initially focused on the role of parents, has now expanded to include peers and the mass media as well as cognitive development and arousal of affects such as empathy and guilt. The aim here is to pull together relevant findings and theories, drawing heavily from previous critical reviews (Hoffman, 1977, 1978, 1980).

CHILD-REARING PRACTICES AND MORALINTERNALIZATION

Since the parent is the most significant figure in the child's life, every facet of the parent's role—disciplinarian, affection giver, model—has been studied.

Discipline and Affection

Moral internalization implies that a person is motivated to weigh his or her desires against the moral requirements of a situation. Since one's earliest experience in handling this type of conflict occurs in discipline encounters with parents, and since discipline encounters occur often in the early years—about 5–6 times per hour (see, e.g., Wright, 1967)—it seems reasonable that the types of discipline used by parents will affect the child's moral development. Affection is important because it may make the child more receptive to discipline, more likely to emulate the parent, and emotionally secure enough to be open to the needs of others.

A large body of research done mainly in the 1950s and 1960s dealt with correlations between types of discipline and moral indices such as resisting temptation and feeling guilty over violating a moral norm. The findings (reviewed by Hoffman, 1977) suggest that moral internalization is fostered by (a) the parent's frequent use of inductive discipline techniques, which point up the harmful consequences of the child's behavior for others, and (b) the parent's frequent expression of affection outside the discipline encounter. A morality based on fear of external punishment, on the other hand, is associated with excessive power-assertive discipline, for example, physical punishment, deprivation of privileges, or the threat of these. There is also evidence that under certain conditions—when the child is openly and unreasonably defiant—the occasional use of power assertion by parents who typically use induction may contribute positively to moral internalization (Hoffman, 1970a).

The mid-1960s saw a shift from correlational to experimental research. In the most frequently used paradigm the child is first trained, or "socialized," by being presented with several toys. When the child handles the most attractive one, he or she is punished (e.g., by an unpleasant noise, the intensity and timing of which varies). The child is then left alone and observed surreptitiously. Resistance-to-temptation scores are based on whether or not, how soon after the experimenter left, and for how long the child plays with the forbidden toy. Recently, a verbal component had been added—a simple prohibition or a complex, inductionlike reason. The general findings are that (a) with no verbal component, intensity and timing of punishment operate as they do in animals—the child deviates less when training consists of intense punishment applied at the onset of the act; (b) with a verbal component, these effects are reduced; and (c) the verbal component is more effective with mild than severe punishment and with older than younger children.

Both types of research are limited. Thus it may seem as plausible to infer from the correlations that the child's moral internalization contributes to the parent's use of inductions as it is to infer the reverse. I have argued, however, that although causality cannot automatically be inferred from correlations, in this case the evidence warrants doing so (Hoffman, 1975a), at least until the critical research employing appropriate (e.g., cross-lagged longitudinal) designs has been done. The experimental research, on the other hand, lacks ecological validity, since the socialization process is telescoped. In addition, the distinction between moral action and compliance with an arbitrary request is blurred, since compliance is used as the moral index. Compliance is also a questionable index in light of Milgram's finding that it may at times lead to immoral action. Despite these flaws, the experiments are useful because they may tell something about the child's im-

mediate response to discipline, and as such, the findings are compatible with the correlational research (Hoffman, 1977).

I recently proposed a theoretical explanation of the findings (Hoffman, Note 1). Briefly, it consists of the following points: (a) Most discipline techniques have power-assertive and love-withdrawing properties, which comprise the motive-arousal component needed to get the child to stop and pay attention to the inductive component that may also be present. (b) The child may be influenced cognitively and affectively, through arousal of empathy and guilt, by the information in the inductive component and may thus experience a reduced sense of opposition between desires and external demands. (c) Too little arousal and the child may ignore the parent; too much, and the resulting fear or resentment may prevent effective processing of the inductive content. Techniques having a salient inductive component ordinarily achieve the best balance. (d) The ideas in inductions (and the associated empathy and guilt) are encoded in "semantic" memory and are retained for a long time, whereas the details of the setting in which they originated are encoded in "episodic" memory and are soon forgotten. (e) Eventually, lacking a clear external referent to which to attribute the ideas, they may be experienced by the child as originating in the self.

Parent as a Model

It has been assumed since Freud that children identify and thus adopt the parents' ways of evaluating one's own behavior. The intriguing question is, Why does the child do this? Psychoanalytic writers stress anxiety over physical attack or loss of the parent's love. To reduce anxiety, the child tries to be like the parent—to adopt the parent's behavioral mannerisms, thoughts, feelings, and even the capacity to punish oneself and experience guilt over violating a moral standard. For other writers, the child identifies to acquire desirable parent characteristics (e.g., privileges, control of resources, power over the child).

The research, which is sparse, suggests that identification may contribute to aspects of morality reflected in the parent's words and deeds (e.g., type of moral reasoning, helping others). It may not contribute to feeling guilty after violating moral standards (Hoffman, 1971), however, perhaps because parents rarely communicate their own guilt feelings to the child, children lack the cognitive skills needed to infer guilt feelings from overt behavior, and children's motives to identify are not strong enough to overcome the pain of self-criticism.

In the early 1960s Bandura suggested that identification is too complex a concept; imitation is simpler, more amenable to research, yet equally powerful as an explanatory concept. Numerous experiments followed. Those studying the effects of adult models on moral judgment and resistance to temptation in children (reviewed by Hoffman, 1970b) are especially pertinent. The results are that (a) children will readily imitate an adult model who yields to temptation (e.g., leaves an assigned task to watch a movie), as though the model serves to legitimize the deviant behavior, but they are less likely to imitate a model who resists temptation. (b) When a child who makes moral judgments of others on the basis of consequences of their acts is exposed to an adult model who judges acts on the basis of intentions, the child shows an increased understanding of the principle of intentions, and the effect may last up to a year.

It thus appears that identification may contribute to the adoption of visible moral attributes requiring little self-denial, which may become internalized in the sense that the child uses them as criteria of right and wrong in judging others, but it may not contribute to the use of moral standards as an evaluative perspective for examining his or her own behavior.

PEER INFLUENCE

Despite the interest, there is little theorizing and still less research on the effects of peers. The theories boil down to three somewhat contradictory views about the effects of unsupervised peer interaction: (1) Since gross power differentials do not exist, it allows everyone the kind of experiences (role taking, rule making, rule enforcing) needed to develop a morality based on mutual consent and cooperation among equals (Piaget, 1932). (2) It may release inhibitions and undermine the effects of prior socialization—a view reflected in Golding's novel *Lord of the Flies* and Le Bon's (1895/1960) notions about collective behavior. (3) Both 1 and 2 are possible, and which one prevails depends, among other things, on the hidden role of adults (Hoffman, 1980). For example, 1 may operate when the children come from homes that are characterized by frequent affection and inductive discipline. Parents may also play a more direct, "coaching" role, as when they do not just take their child's side in an argument with a peer but sometimes provide perspective on the other child's point of view.

The research indicates that parental influence wanes and peer groups become more influential as children get older (Devereux, 1970). The direction of the influence is less clear. Some studies report broad areas of agreement between peer and adult values (e.g., Langworthy, 1959). Others show disagreement—radical disagreement, as in the finding by Sherif et al. (1961) that newly formed unsupervised groups of preadolescent boys may undermine the preexisting morality of some members, or modest differences in emphasis, as in high school subcultures stressing athletics and popularity rather than academic achievement (see, e.g., Coleman, 1961). There is no evidence that children are more apt to endorse peer-sponsored misbehavior as they get older, and that this may reflect a growing disillusionment with the good will of adults rather than an increasing loyalty to peers, whose credibility may actually decline (Bixenstine, DeCorte, & Bixenstine, 1976). Finally, the peer-model research (reviewed by Hoffman, 1970b) suggests that exposure to a peer who behaves aggressively or yields to temptation and is not punished increases the likelihood that a child will do the same; if the model is punished, the subject behaves as though there were no model. These findings suggest that if children deviate from adult moral norms without punishment, as often happens outside the home, this may stimulate a child to deviate; if they are punished, however, this may not serve as a deterrent. The immediate impact of peer behavior may thus be more likely to weaken than to strengthen one's inhibitions, at least in our society.

SEX-ROLE SOCIALIZATION AND MORAL INTERNALIZATION

Contrary to Freud and others, females appear to be more morally internalized than males, and their moral values are also more humanistic (Hoffman, 1975b). The difference may be due partly to the fact that parents of girls more often use inductive discipline and express affection (Zussman, 1978). More broadly, since females have traditionally been socialized into the "expressive" role (Johnson, 1963)—to give and receive affection and to be responsive to other people's needs—they are well equipped to acquire humanistic moral concerns. Boys are also socialized this way, but as they get older they are increasingly instructed in the "instrumental" character traits and skills needed for occupational success, which may often conflict with humanistic moral concerns (e.g., Burton, Note 2, found that under high achievement pressure, parents may communicate that it is more important to succeed than to be honest). Since females may now be receiving more instrumental socialization than formerly, the sex difference in morality may soon diminish.

TELEVISION

The burgeoning work on effects of television on aggression and helping is tangential to mainstream research on moral development, but any assessment of social influences would be incomplete without reference to it. It may also be useful to provide an alternative to the frequent assumption that important effects have been demonstrated (see, e.g., Murray, 1973; Stein & Friedrich, 1975). To begin, the correlations between watching violent television programs and behaving aggressively are inconclusive because the causality is unclear. The one study that used a cross-lagged design and found that a childhood preference for violent programs relates to aggressive behavior in adolescence (Eron, Huesmann, Lefkowitz, & Walder, 1972) may have serious flaws (see, e.g., Kaplan, 1972).

Numerous experiments done mainly in the 1960s showed that children exposed to a live or filmed model behaving aggressively—or helping or sharing—are apt to behave like the model shortly afterward. It thus appeared that the content of television programs might affect children's moral development. To demonstrate this convincingly, however, may require controlling the television viewing of children and observing their social behavior over an extended time in a natural setting. This has been done in four studies. I will summarize one (Friedrich & Stein, 1973). For four weeks, children in a summer nursery school watched three 20-minute episodes per week of an aggressive (*Batman* or *Superman*), neutral, or prosocial (*Mister Rogers' Neighborhood*) program. Measures of interpersonal aggression (physical and verbal) and prosocial behavior (cooperation and nurturance) were based on observations made during free play for two weeks before, during, and following the exposures. The only expected effect found in the postexposure period was a decline in prosocial behavior by middle-class children who saw the aggressive film. It was also found, however, contrary to expectations, that lower-class girls who saw the aggressive film showed an increase in prosocial behavior, and the total sample showed an increase in aggression when exposed to either the aggressive or prosocial film. It is difficult to make sense of these findings, as well as those obtained in the other three studies (see review by Hoffman, Note 3). Further research is needed, perhaps using more subtle measures of aggression and prosocial behavior. It is possible, however, that even the most sophisticated designs may not reveal long-term effects because the effects may be overridden by one's overall television experience (including newscast violence), not to mention one's actual socialization experiences as well as other pressures and frustrations to which one is exposed, which may be impossible to control. The measurable effects of television on behavior may thus be largely momentary.

COGNITIVE DEVELOPMENT AND MORAL THOUGHT

Piaget's view that cognitive development contributes to moral development continues to stimulate research. Children's moral judgment, for example, has been found to relate positively to their cognitive level, as shown in solving mathemathics and physics problems, and to their ability to take the role of others (Kurdek, 1978).

Piaget thought that children under 7 or 8 years of age are egocentric and thus often miss crucial aspects of moral action (e.g., intentions). Recent research that minimizes the cognitive and linguistic demands on subjects, however, shows that even 4-year-olds consider intentions when the amount of damage is controlled (Keasey, 1978). They can also allocate rewards in a way that coordinates other children's needs and contributions in simple group tasks (Anderson & Butzin, 1978). And they recognize that norms about the human consequences of action are more important than social conventions; for example, they resist attempts to convince them that it would be all right to hit someone if the rules said so, but they are more flexible about dress codes (Turiel, 1978).

Kohlberg (1969) saw morality as developing in a series of six stages, beginning with a premoral one in which the child obeys to avoid punishment and ending with a universal sense of justice or concern for reciprocity among individuals. Each stage is a homogenous, value-free, moral cognitive structure or reasoning strategy; moral reasoning within a stage is consistent across different problems, situations, and values. Each stage builds on, reorganizes, and encompasses the preceding one and provides new perspectives and criteria for making moral evaluations. People in all cultures move through the stages in the same order, varying only in how quickly and how far they progress. The impetus for movement comes from exposure to moral structures slightly more advanced than one's own. The resulting cognitive conflict is resolved by integrating one's previous structure with the new one.

Kohlberg's theory has been criticized as follows (Hoffman, 1970b, 1980; Kurtines & Greif, 1974): The stages do not appear to be homogeneous or to form an invariant sequence. There is no evidence that exposure to appropriate levels of moral reasoning inevitably leads to forward movement through the stages or that it leads to "structural" rather than value conflict. Though low positive correlations exist between moral reasoning and moral behavior, the stages are not associated with distinctive patterns of behavior. These problems may be due to the manner of scoring moral reasoning, and future research with the new scoring system (Kohlberg, Colby, Speicher-Dubin, & Lieberman, Note 4) may produce different results. The theory has also been criticized for neglecting motivation which may be needed to translate abstract moral concepts into action (Peters, 1971), and for having a western, a male, and a "romantic individualistic" bias (Hogan, 1975; Samson, 1978; Simpson, 1974).

Cognitive conflict may underlie the previously noted finding that adult models affect children's moral judgments (see "Parent as Model" section above). Since the subjects' understanding of intentions was increased and the effect lasted long, they were not mindlessly imitating the model. Rather, they probably knew the difference between accidental and intended action initially (as noted, even 4-year-olds know this) but were influenced by the more severe consequences in the accident stories. Exposure to adults who repeatedly assign more weight to intentions despite the disparity in consequences must therefore have produced cognitive conflict, which may have led the subjects to change their minds. This interpretation does not assume that cognitive conflict always leads to progressive change, since models who espouse consequences, the less mature response, might have similar effects.

Whether or not cognitive-conflict theory is confirmed, it has called attention to people's active efforts to draw meaning from experience. It has also led to a new approach to moral education (Kohlberg, 1973): Different moral stages are assumed to be represented in the classroom; in discussing moral dilemmas lower-stage children are thus exposed to higher-stage reasoning, and in the course of handling the resulting conflict their moral levels advance. This approach appeals to educators partly because they are not expected to make moral judgments or state their values. They need only present moral dilemmas, foster discussion, and occasionally clarify a child's statement. In actual practice, the children are also encouraged to participate in decisions about making rules and assigning punishments for violating them. Should the program be effective, it will therefore still remain for research to determine whether cognitive conflict is necessary.

EMPATHY AND PROSOCIAL BEHAVIOR

Empathy, the vicarious emotional response to another person, has long interested social think-ers. Philosophers like David Hume and Adam Smith and early personality theorists like Stern, Sheler, and McDougall all saw its significance for social life. Despite the interest, there has been little theory or research. The topic is discussed below in some detail, nevertheless, because it bears on the affective side of morality, which has long been neglected. The focus thus far has been on the response to someone in distress, since this seems central to morality. A brief summary of a developmental theory of empathic distress (Hoffman, 1975c, 1978) follows.

When empathically aroused, older children and adults know that they are responding to something happening to someone else, and they have a sense of what the other is feeling. At the other extreme, infants may be empathically aroused without these cognitions. Thus, the experience of empathy depends on the level at which one cognizes others. The research suggests at least four stages in the development of a cognitive sense of others: for most of the first year, a fusion of self and other; by 11–12 months, "person permanence," or awareness of others as distinct physical entities; by 2–3 years, a rudimentary awareness that others have independent inner states—the first step in role taking; by 8–12 years, awareness that others have personal identities and life experiences beyond the immediate situation.

Empathy thus has a vicarious affective component that is given increasingly complex meaning as the child progresses through these four stages. I now describe four levels of empathic distress that may result from this coalescence of empathic affect and the cognitive sense of the other: (1) The infant's empathic response lacks an awareness of who is actually in distress (e.g., an 11-month-old girl, on seeing a child fall and cry, looked like she was about to cry herself and then put her thumb in her mouth and buried her head in her mother's lap, which is what she does when she is hurt). (2) With person permanence, one is aware that another person and not the self is in distress, but the other's inner states are unknown and may be assumed to be the same as one's own (e.g., an 18-month-old boy fetched his own mother to comfort a crying friend, although the friend's mother was also present). (3) With the beginning of role taking, empathy becomes an increasingly veridical response to the other's feelings in the situation. (4) By late childhood, owing to the emerging conception of self and other as continuous persons with separate histories and identities, one becomes aware that others feel pleasure and pain not only in the situation but also in their larger life experience. Consequently, though one may still respond empathically to another's immediate distress, one's empathic response is intensified when the distress is not transitory but chronic. This stage thus combines empathically aroused affect with a mental representation of another's general level of distress or deprivation. If this representation falls short of the observer's standard of well-being, an empathic distress response may result even if contradicted by the other's apparent momentary state, that is, the representation may override contradictory situational cues.

With further cognitive development, one can comprehend the plight of an entire class of people (e.g., poor, oppressed, retarded). Though one's distress experience differs from theirs, all distress has a common affective core that allows for a generalized empathic distress capability. Empathic affect combined with the perceived plight of an unfortunate group may be the most advanced form of empathic distress.

These levels of empathic response are assumed to form the basis of a motive to help others; hence their relevance to moral development. A summary of the research follows: (a) Very young children (2–4 years) typically react empathically to a hurt child, although they sometimes do nothing or act inappropriately (Murphy, 1937; Zahn-Waxler, Radke-Yarrow, & King, 1979). (b) Older children and adults react empathically too, but this is usually fol-lowed by appropriate helping behavior (see, e.g., Leiman, Note 5; Sawin, Note 6). (c) The level of empathic arousal and the speed of a helping act increase with the number and intensity of distress cues from the victim (see, e.g., Geer & Jarmecky, 1973). (d) The level of arousal drops following a helping act but continues if there is no attempt to help (see, e.g., Darley & Latané, 1968).

These findings fit the hypothesis that empathic distress is a prosocial motive. Some may call it an egoistic motive because one feels better after helping. The evidence suggests, however, that feeling better is usually not the *aim* of helping (see, e.g., Darley & Latané, 1968). Regardless, any motive for which the arousal condition, aim of ensuing action, and basis for gratification in the actor are all contingent on someone else's welfare must be distinguished from obvious self-serving motives like approval, success, and material gain. It thus seems legitimate to call empathic distress a prosocial motive, with perhaps a quasi-egoistic dimension.

Qualifications are in order. First, though helping increases with intensity of empathic distress, beyond a certain point empathic distress may become so aversive that one's attention is directed to the self, not the victim. Second, empathic distress and helping are positively related to perceived similarity between observer and victim: Children respond more empathically to others of the same race or sex and, with cognitive development, to others perceived as similar in abstract terms (e.g., similar "personality traits"). These findings suggest that empathic morality may be particularistic, applied mainly to one's group, but they also suggest that moral education programs which point up the similarities among people, at the appropriate level of abstraction, may help foster a universalistic morality.

Despite the qualifications, a human attribute like empathy that can transform another's misfortune into distress in the self demands the attention of social scientists and educators for its relevance both to moral development and to bridging the gap between the individual and society.

GUILT

The reemergence of interest in affective and motivational aspects of morality includes a revived interest in guilt. I have suggested a relation between guilt and empathy (Hoffman, 1976), summarized as follows: The attribution research suggests a human tendency to make causal inferences about events. One can thus be expected to make inferences about the cause of a victim's distress, which serve as additional inputs in shaping one's affective empathic response. If one is the cause of the distress, one's awareness of this may combine with the empathic affect aroused to produce a feeling of guilt (not the Freudian guilt which results when repressed impulses enter consciousness).

I have been constructing a developmental theory of guilt that highlights the importance of empathic distress and causal attribution (Hoffman, in press-b). Space permits mentioning only that the guilt stages correspond roughly to the empathy stages described above and that some gaps in the theory reflect a lack of research on certain aspects of cognitive development such as the awareness that one has choice over one's actions and that one's actions have an impact on others, as well as the ability to contemplate or imagine an action and its effects (necessary for anticipatory guilt and guilt over omission).

A summary of the findings follows: (a) A full guilt response appears in children as young as 6 years (Thompson & Hoffman, in press), and a rudimentary one appears in some 2-year-olds (Zahn-Waxler et al., 1979). (b) As noted earlier, discipline that points up the effects of the child's behavior on others contributes to guilt feelings. (c) Arousal of empathic distress appears to intensify guilt feelings (Thompson &

Hoffman, in press). (d) Guilt arousal is usually followed by a reparative act toward the victim or toward others (see, e.g., Regan, 1971) or, when neither is possible, a prolongation of the guilt. (e) Guilt arousal sometimes triggers a process of self-examination and reordering of values, as well as a resolution to act less selfishly in the future (Hoffman, 1975b). It is interesting that this response, which should contribute to moral development, might be missing in children who are too "good" to transgress and thus may not have the experience of guilt. The findings suggest, somewhat paradoxically, that guilt, which results from immoral action, may operate as a moral motive.

CONCLUDING REMARKS

To pull together the findings and most promising concepts, I suggest three somewhat independent moral internalization processes, each with its own experiential base:

1 People often assume that their acts are under surveillance. This fear of ubiquitous authority may lead them to behave morally even when alone. The socialization experiences leading to this orientation may include frequent power-assertive and perhaps love-withdrawing discipline, which results in painful anxiety states becoming associated with deviant behavior. Subsequently, kinesthetic and other cues produced by the deviant act may arouse anxiety, which is avoided by inhibiting the act. When the anxiety becomes diffuse and detached from conscious fears of detection, this inhibition of deviant action may be viewed as reflecting a primitive form of internalization (perhaps analogous to the Freudian superego).

2 The human capacity for empathy may combine with the cognitive awareness of others and how others are affected by one's behavior, resulting in an internal motive to consider others. As contributing socialization experiences, the research suggests exposure to inductive

discipline by parents who also provide adequate affection and serve as models of prosocial moral action (e.g., they help and show empathic concern for others rather than blame them for their plight). Reciprocal role taking, especially with peers, may also heighten the individual's sensitivity to the inner states aroused in others by one's behavior; having been in the other's place helps one know how the other feels in response to one's behavior.

3 People may cognitively process information at variance with their preexisting moral conceptions and construct new views that resolve the contradiction. When they do this, they will very likely feel a special commitment to—and in this sense internalize—the moral concepts they have actively constructed.

These processes are not stages. The first, in one form or another (e.g., anxiety over retribution by God), may be pervasive in all ages and most cultural groups. The second may also occur in all ages, though primarily in humanistically oriented groups. The third may be true mainly among adolescents in groups for whom intellectually attained values are important.

The three processes may develop independently, since their presumed socialization antecedents differ. They may sometimes complement one another, as when the rudimentary moral sense originating in the child's early capacity for empathy and in discipline encounters contributes direction for resolving moral conflicts in adolescence. They may sometimes be noncomplementary, as when an early, anxiety-based inhibition prevents a nonmoral behavior from occurring later, when its control might be acquired through moral conflict resolution. Perhaps the processes are best viewed as three components of a moral orientation, with people varying as to which one predominates, and individual differences being due to cognitive abilities and socialization. A mature orientation in our society would then be based predominantly on empathic and cognitive pro-

cesses, and minimally on anxiety. The challenge is to find ways to foster this morality. Whether this is possible in the context of the prevailing competitive-individualistic ethic is problematic. The finding by Burton (Note 2) noted earlier highlights the dilemma confronting parents who want to socialize children for both morality and achievement.

To test hypotheses implicit in the processes suggested above and to gain new knowledge as well may require complex designs including close observations of children's behavioral, cognitive, and affective responses to a socialization agent. A longitudinal dimension will also be needed to permit cross-lagged or other analyses for assessing causality and finding out which of the agent's actions are responsible for the child's moral growth. To do all this in a single study is a tall order, but it should be feasible with the aid of new procedures such as Zahn-Waxler et al.'s (1979) method of observing children's behavior in and out of discipline encounters, over long periods of time, Cheyne and Walters' (1969) use of telemetered heart-rate data to assess children's emotional responses to simulated discipline techniques, and Leiman's (Note 5) use of videotaped facial expression to tap empathic arousal. If techniques like these were appropriately combined and modified for use in naturalistic or laboratory settings as needed, I would anticipate new levels of knowledge about how affect and cognition interact in moral development.

REFERENCE NOTES

1 Hoffman, M. L. *Parental discipline and moral internalization: A theoretical analysis* (Developmental Report 85). Ann Arbor: University of Michigan, 1976.

2 Burton, R. V. *Cheating related to maternal pressures for achievement.* Unpublished manuscript, State University of New York at Buffalo, Department of Psychology, 1972.

3 Hoffman, M. L. *Imitation and identification in children*. Unpublished manuscript, University of Michigan, Department of Psychology, 1978.

4 Kohlberg, L., Colby, A., Speicher-Dubin, B., & Lieberman, M. *Standard form scoring manual*. Unpublished manuscript, Harvard University, Moral Education Research Foundation, 1975.

5 Leiman, B. *Affective empathy and subsequent altruism in kindergartners and first graders*. Paper presented at the meeting of the American Psychological Association, Toronto, September 1978.

6 Sawin, D. B. *Assessing empathy in children: A search for an elusive construct*. Paper presented at the meeting of the Society for Research in Child Development, San Francisco, March 1979.

REFERENCES

Anderson, N. H., & Butzin, C. A. Integration theory applied to children's judgments of equity. *Developmental Psychology*, 1978, *14*, 593–606.

Bixenstine, E. V., DeCorte, M. S., & Bixenstine, B. A. Conformity to peer-sponsored misconduct at four grade levels. *Developmental Psychology*, 1976, *12*, 226–236.

Cheyne, J. A., & Walters, R. H. Intensity of punishment, timing of punishment, and cognitive structure as determinants of response inhibition. *Journal of Experimental Child Psychology*, 1969, *7*, 231–244.

Coleman, J. S. *The adolescent society*. New York: Free Press of Glencoe, 1961.

Darley, J. M., & Latané, B. Bystander intervention in emergencies: Diffusion of responsibility. *Journal of Personality and Social Psychology*, 1968, *8*, 377–383.

Devereux, E. C. The role of peer-group experience in moral development. In J. P. Hill (Ed.), *Minnesota symposia on child psychology* (Vol. 4). Minneapolis: University of Minnesota Press, 1970.

Eron, L. D., Huesmann, L. R., Lefkowitz, M. M., & Walder, L. O. Does television violence cause aggression? *American Psychologist*, 1972, *27*, 253–263.

Friedrich, L. K., & Stein, A. H. Aggressive and prosocial television programs and the natural behavior of preschool children. *Monographs of the Society for Research in Child Development*, 1973, *38*(4, Serial No. 151).

Geer, J. H., & Jarmecky, L. The effect of being responsible for reducing another's pain on subject's response and arousal. *Journal of Personality and Social Psychology*, 1973, *26*, 232–237.

Hoffman, M. L. Conscience, personality, and socialization techniques. *Human Development*, 1970, *13*, 90–126. (a)

Hoffman, M. L. Moral development. In P. H. Mussen (Ed.), *Carmichael's handbook of child psychology* (Vol. 2). New York: Wiley, 1970. (b)

Hoffman, M. L. Identificatioin and conscience development. *Child Development*, 1971, *42*, 1071–1082.

Hoffman, M. L. Developmental synthesis of affect and cognition and its implications for altruistic motivation. *Developmental Psychology*, 1975, *11*, 607–622. (a)

Hoffman, M. L. Moral internalization, parental power, and the nature of parent-child interaction. *Developmental Psychology*, 1975, *11*, 228–239. (b)

Hoffman, M. L. Sex differences in moral internalization. *Journal of Personality and Social Psychology*, 1975, *32*, 720–729. (c)

Hoffman, M. L. Empathy, role-taking, guilt, and development of altruistic motives. In T. Likona (Ed.), *Moral development: Current theory and research*. New York: Holt, Rinehart & Winston, 1976.

Hoffman, M. L. Moral internalization: Current theory and research. In L. Berkowitz (Ed.), *Advances in experimental social psychology* (Vol. 10). New York: Academic Press, 1977.

Hoffman, M. L. Empathy, its development and prosocial implications. In C. B. Keasey (Ed.), *Nebraska symposium on motivation* (Vol. 25). Lincoln: University of Nebraska Press, 1978.

Hoffman, M. L. Adolescent morality in developmental perspective. In J. Adelson (Ed.), *Handbook of adolescent psychology*. New York: Wiley-Interscience, 1980.

Hoffman, M. L. Empathy, guilt, and social cognition. In W. Overton (Ed.), *Relation between social and cognitive development*. Hillsdale, N.J.: Erlbaum, in press. (b)

Hogan, R. Theoretical egocentrism and the problem of compliance. *American Psychologist*, 1975, *30*, 533–540.

Johnson, M. J. Sex role learning in the nuclear family. *Child Development*, 1963, *34*, 319–333.

Kaplan, R. M. On television as a cause of aggression. *American Psychologist,* 1972, *27,* 968–969. (Comment)

Keasey, C. B. Children's developing awareness and usage of intentionality and motives. In C. B. Keasey (Ed.), *Nebraska symposium on motivation* (Vol. 25). Lincoln: University of Nebraska Press, 1978.

Kohlberg, L. The cognitive-developmental approach. In D. A. Goslin (Ed.), *Handbook of socialization theory and research.* Chicago: Rand McNally, 1969.

Kohlberg, L. The contribution of developmental psychology to education—Examples from moral education. *Educational Psychologist,* 1973, *10*(1), 2–14.

Kurdek, L. A. Perspective-taking as the cognitive basis of children's moral development: A review of the literature. *Merrill-Palmer Quarterly,* 1978, *24,* 3–28.

Kurtines, W., & Greif, E. B. The development of moral thought: Review and evaluation of Kohlberg's approach. *Psychological Bulletin,* 1974, *31,* 453–470.

Langworthy, R. L. Community status and influence in a high school. *American Sociological Review,* 1959, *24,* 537–539.

Le Bon, G. *The crowd: A study of the popular mind.* New York: Viking Press, 1960. (Originally published, 1895).

Murphy, L. B. *Social behavior and child personality.* New York: Columbia University Press, 1937.

Murray, J. P. Television and violence: Implications of the Surgeon General's research program. *American Psychologist,* 1973, *28,* 472–478.

Peters, R. S. Moral development: A plea for pluralism. In T. Mischel (Ed.), *Cognitive development and epistemology.* New York: Academic Press, 1971.

Piaget, J. *The moral judgment of the child.* New York: Harcourt, 1932.

Regan, J. W. Guilt, perceived injustice, and altruistic behavior. *Journal of Personality and Social Psychology,* 1971, *18,* 124–132.

Samson, E. E. Scientific paradigms and social values: Wanted—A scientific revolution. *Journal of Personality and Social Psychology,* 1978, *36,* 1332–1343.

Sherif, M., Harvey, O. J., White, B. J., Hood, W. R., & Sherif, C. *Intergroup conflict and cooperation: The Robber's Cave Experiment.* Norman, Okla.: University Book Exchange, 1961.

Simpson, E. L. Moral development research: A case study of scientific cultural bias. *Human Development,* 1974, *17,* 81–106.

Stein, A. H., & Friedrich, L. K. The impact of television on children and youth. In E. M. Hetherington, J. W. Hagen, R. Kron, & A. H. Stein (Eds.), *Review of child development research* (Vol. 5). Chicago: University of Chicago Press, 1975.

Thompson, R., & Hoffman, M. L. Empathic arousal and guilt feelings in children. *Developmental Psychology,* in press.

Turiel, E. Distinct conceptual and developmental domains: Social convention and morality. In C. B. Keasey (Ed.), *Nebraska symposium on motivation* (Vol. 25). Lincoln: University of Nebraska Press, 1978.

Wright, H. F. *Recording and analyzing child behavior.* New York: Harper & Row, 1967.

Zahn-Waxler, C., Radke-Yarrow, M., & King, R. M. Childrearing and children's prosocial initiations toward victims of distress. *Child Development,* 1979, *50,* 319–330.

Zussman, J. U. Relationship of demographic factors to parental discipline techniques. *Developmental Psychology,* 1978, *14,* 685–686.

READING 46

Gender Constancy and the Effects of Sex-typed Televised Toy Commercials

Diane N. Ruble
Terry Balaban
Joel Cooper

Numerous studies have shown that television programs and commercials are presented in a way that is overwhelmingly consistent with sex stereotypes (Stein & Friedrich 1975; Sternglanz & Serbin 1974). Since children watch 3–4 hours of television a day (Lyle & Hoffman 1972), its potential impact on the development of children's gender-related attitudes and behaviors is enormous. It is well demonstrated that, under the appropriate conditions, people will imitate the behavior of others (Bandura 1969; Mischel 1966). Thus, it seems important to ask the question: Does watching television promote sex-stereo-typed behavior and attitudes in boys and girls?

In order to address this question, a more basic theoretical problem needs to be examined. One of the most significant and controversial theoretical issues in the area of gender development concerns the role of same-sex modeling (Barkley, Ullman, Otto, & Brecht 1977; Masters, Ford, Arend, Grotevant, & Clark 1979; Perry & Bussey 1979). Both major theories of sex-role development—social learning theory (e.g., Mischel 1966, 1970) and cognitive-developmental theory (e.g., Kohlberg 1966; Kohlberg & Ullian 1974)—argue that same-sex modeling is a crucial process; however there is some debate concerning the timing of this process. According to social learning theory, information provided by readily available same-sex models in the home and in the media, together with reinforcement for sex-appropriate behavior serve as the major impetus for the acquisition of sex-typed behaviors occurring during the preschool years. In contrast, according to cognitive-developmental theory, a child's notion of gender develops in stages until, at about 5–6 years of age, he or she recognizes that gender is an invariant property of an individual—that is, that a person will always be male or female regardless of superficial transformations, such as hairstyle or clothing. This stage of gender constancy is thought to be critical; specifically it is assumed that children become interested in same-sex models and perceive sex-appropriate behaviors as reinforcing because of the newly acquired sense of the inevitability of their gender, rather than the reverse. Thus, although sex-typed behavior is clearly present prior to 5 years of age (Maccoby & Jacklin 1974; Ruble & Ruble, in press), the attainment of gender constancy may be a special point in sex-role development. That is, it may represent a shift in the role of the child from being relatively passively influenced by sex-role reinforcement and information to actively seeking it out.

Consistent with Kohlberg's (1966) formulation, stages of gender constancy have been identified, which have been shown to have characteristics of developmental stages and to be related to Piagetian measures of the constancy of physical objects occurring at approximately 5–7 years of age in middle-class children (DeVries 1969; Emmerich, Goldman, Kirsh, & Sharabany 1977; Marcus & Overton 1978; Slaby & Frey 1975). Unfortunately, however, there is only tentative and indirect support for the idea that children at the age associated with gender constancy are more attentive to same-sex models (Bryan & Luria

1978; Grusec & Brinker 1972; Slaby & Frey 1975). Furthermore, totally absent from the literature is any evidence concerning behavioral effects of such processes. Only a few of the many modeling studies show that children differentially imitate same-sex models (e.g., Barkley et al. 1977), but most of this research was with preschool children who are presumably pre-gender constant. Thus, a crucial question remains: Does the apparent heightened attention to same-sex models during later stages of gender constancy translate into heightened behavioral responsiveness at this time?

The purpose of the present study was to examine this key but, to date, missing link in the evaluation of theories of sex-role development by means of a developmental analysis of the effects of televised sex-stereotyped information on children's behavior. Because play behavior has served as a central focus in studies of early sex-role development and because television commercials are a major source of same-sex models of play, the stimulus selected for the study was a TV toy commercial.

Children saw a commercial of a toy, pretested to be "neutral" in terms of sex-role appropriateness (i.e., for boys and girls equally). Two commercials were filmed of the same neutral toy, so that one made the toy seem appropriate for girls and the other made it seem appropriate for boys. It was predicted that children who were "low" in gender constancy would not be affected by the sex-role information in the commercial: Males and females in this stage would play with the toy for similar amounts of time, when later given the chance, and would report similar perceptions of the appropriateness of the toy for girls versus boys. In contrast, it was predicted that the behavior and perceptions of children who were "high" in gender constancy would be differentially affected by the sex-role information in the different commercial conditions.

METHOD

Subjects

The children were 50 males and 50 females, ranging in age from 44 months to 77 months (X 60). The subjects were obtained from various nursery schools and kindergartens in the central New Jersey area. The parents were informed of the purpose and procedures of the study, but were asked not to divulge the purpose to their children.

Stimulus materials

Two commercials were prepared about a toy, which pretesting had shown was perceived by children as being appropriate for both boys and girls. These commercials depicted this neutral toy—the Fisher-Price Movie Viewer—as being appropriate either for males or for females, by showing either two boys or two girls playing with the toy. Identical narrations were dubbed in, with either a male or a female voice corresponding to the sex of the models. The commercial consisted of one model playing with the toy, then showing the second model how to play with the toy. The second model then played with the toy, while the first model looked on. Each commercial was 1 min long and was edited into the middle of a 5-min Bugs Bunny cartoon.

Procedures

One of two experimenters (a male and a female) escorted the subjects one at a time from their classrooms to the experimental room, located on the school premises. The room was divided by an apparatus which contained a one-way mirror. En route, the experimenter explained that the child was going to see a cartoon. Upon arrival, the child was asked to sit down and watch the cartoon while the experimenter went to make a phone call. The experimenter turned on the videotape player and left the room, entering the adjacent section. The time spent-viewing the commercial was recorded. Forty-children saw "same-sex" models, 40 saw opposite-sex models, and 20 saw no commercial (control).

When the cartoon ended, the experimenter entered the viewing room and explained that he or she had to leave again for a few minutes, but that the child was free to play with any of the toys in the room. One of the toys was the Fisher-Price Movie Viewer. Another was a stacking toy (pretested to be similar in interest value to the viewer and, like the viewer, to be appropriate for both sexes). A book and some poker chips were also provided. The experimenter then left the room and entered the adjacent observation section, where he or she scored the child's play behavior patterns for 5 min by marking which toy the child was playing with at 6-sec intervals. Interrater reliabilities were high; the average percentage of agreement for 10 observer reliability tests was .96.

Upon the experimenter's return, the children were asked to answer a few questions. First, the children were trained to use a measure of attractiveness consisting of three faces drawn with progressively broader smiles, and were asked to indicate how much they liked the viewer and the stacking toy by pointing to the appropriate face. Next, a question was posed to assess whether the children perceived the viewer as more appropriate for one sex or the other. The experimenter said, "I have a little brother and a little sister about your age, and their birthdays are coming up. Who do you think would like this toy more, my brother or my sister?" (The order of asking about the brother and sister was counterbalanced across subjects.)

To assess recall, children were then asked: (1) which toy was in the commercial, and (2) whether boys or girls or both were in the commercial. Responses were scored as correct or incorrect for both recall measures. The next set of questions assessed the extent to which the children were aware of sex-stereotypic labels applied to four toys. The children were

asked, "Who would like this toy more—boys, girls, or both boys and girls"—for a nurse kit, a dish set, an airplane, and a truck. At this time, the children were shown a brief (8 sec) clip of each of the two commercials and asked to identify which one they had seen. They were also asked to identify the models as boys, girls, or boys and girls.

Finally, the gender-constancy interview was administered, using the procedure described by Slaby and Frey (1975). Props for the interview included a set of four dolls (a man, a woman, a girl, a boy) and four black-and-white photos (two adult males and two adult females). The scale consists of a series of questions and counter-questions, grouped into three sets of gender-constancy questions: (1) nine identity questions (e.g., "Is this a woman or a man? Is this a [opposite sex of subject's first response]?)"; (2) two stability questions (e.g., "When you grow up, will you be a mommy or a daddy?"); and (3) three consistency questions (e.g., "If you played [opposite sex of subject] games, would you be a boy or a girl?"). Following the procedure of Slaby and Frey (1975), questions were scored "plus" (correct) only if the subjects answered both the question and the counter-question correctly; otherwise, it was scored "minus" (incorrect).

The children were divided into high- and low-gender-constancy groups by means of a median split across commercial conditions, based on the number of questions answered correctly. This modification of the Slaby and Frey categorization system based on sets of questions was deemed necessary because it was expected that the differential effects of same-sex models on behavior would occur within the higher stages of gender constancy. Thus, assignment to gender-stage levels was based on a more finely differentiated analysis of the children's responses to the three gender-consistency questions than was used in the original study. The basis for assignment and the percentages and ages of boys and girls at each level are presented in Table 1. The present breakdown is consistent with the Slaby and Frey study in that the four levels were sequentially ordered.

RESULTS

Behavioral measure

The major hypothesis concerned the amount of time spent playing with the viewer. Only high-gender-stage children spent less time playing with the viewer when they saw opposite-sex models in the commercial than when they saw same-sex models ($p < .025$) or no commercial ($p < .05$), as expected (see Fig. 1). In addition, high-gender-stage children spent significantly less time with the viewer than low-gender-stage ones in the opposite-sex model condition ($p < .01$). The only other significant contrast showed that low-gender-stage children spent more time with the viewer when they saw an opposite-sex model than when they saw no commercial ($p < .05$).

The only other significant result was a main effect for sex, $p < .05$. Overall, boys spent more 6-sec intervals with the viewer ($X = 20.1$) than did girls ($X = 14.5$). It is noteworthy that the sex of the subject did not interact with the other variables, since Slaby and Frey found that only high-gender-constant boys selectively attended to same-sex models. However, in the present study the pattern of differences between same-sex and opposite-sex model conditions was very similar for boys and girls.

Verbal measures

A secondary hypothesis concerned verbally reported perceptions regarding the sex appropriateness of the viewer. Children were asked whether the experimenter's brother or sister would like the viewer more. As expected, children who viewed the opposite-sex commercial were more likely than children in the other two groups to say that opposite-sex siblings would like the viewer more. However, this result must be interpreted in terms of a significant commercial-condition x gender-stage interaction, as shown in Figure 2. Consistent with predictions, post hoc comparisons revealed that the high-gender-stage/opposite-sex model condition differed from all other cells ($p < .05$). There were no other significant main effects or interactions.

Attention and recall

Several checks on the children's attention to and memory of the key manipulations were included in the study. Analyses were conducted on these data to determine if there were any differences across conditions that might have influenced the effects reported above. Almost all of the children correctly recalled the toy and most (70%) spontaneously remembered correctly the sex of the children in the commercials. In addition, 87.5% of the children correctly identified which commercial they had seen, after being shown the short clips. Finally, all except three children were able to correctly identify the sex of the children in the commercial. Thus, it appears that neither attention nor memory factors can account for the interaction effects on behavior and perceived appropriateness described earlier.

DISCUSSION

The findings of the present study provide a direct link between television viewing and sex-typed behavior; and equally important, they demonstrate an important connection between the child's cognitive-developmental level and the impact of gender-related information provided by television. A single viewing of a commercial portraying a gender-neutral toy in a context that made it seem appropriate for only one sex had a dramatic impact on children's subsequent behavior with that toy—but only for children who were aware of the constancy of their gender.

TABLE 1   BOYS AND GIRLS AND AGES OF CHILDREN ANSWERING THE GENDER CONSTANCY QUESTIONS OR QUESTION SETS "CORRECTLY" AS A FUNCTION OF GENDER LEVEL CATEGORIES (%)

| | | | Question set | | | Total Children (%) | | | Age (mo.) | |
| | | | Gender consistency | | | | | | | |
Gender level	Gender identity	Gender stability	Motivation	Games	Clothing	Boys	Girls	Combined	Range	X
Low:										
	−	−	−	−	−	4	3	7	44-64	52
1	+	−	−	−	−	…	…	…	…	…
	+	+	−	−	−	24	29	53	44-74	59
	+	+	+	−	−	…	…	…	…	…
2	+	+	−	+	−	…	…	…	…	…
High:										
	+	+	+	+	−	8	8	16	52-77	60
3	+	+	+	−	+	…	…	…	…	…
4	+	+	+	+	+	14	9	23	44-77	62

Specifically, for low-gender-stage children, viewing the commercials seemed to produce a simple modeling effect—relative to the control group they played more with the toy when they saw a commercial, even if opposite-sex children were playing with the toy. In contrast, for high-gender-stage children, viewing opposite-sex children playing with the toy led to an avoidance of that toy during the subsequent play period. The effects of the commercial conditions on children's verbal perceptions of the sex-appropriateness of the viewer paralleled the behavioral data. The one inexplicable element in the pattern of the results was the discrepancy in the play behavior of the control subjects such that low-gender-stage children tended to play less with the toy than high-gender-stage children. However, because this difference was not statistically significant and because it did not appear in the perceived appropriateness measure, it would not seem to pose a serious qualification to our major conclusions.

It is important to note that the effects in the present study are not due to simple maturational effects associated with age. Covariance analyses showed no effect of age on these variables; and there were no differences across gender stages in attention, recognition, or recall variables. Thus, the present results, together with the Slaby and Frey (1975) report of a relationship between constancy and attention to same-sex models, suggest that gender constancy may, indeed, represent a stage in development in which children actively seek information about what is appropriate for their sex and act in accordance with it.

The different results obtained for the sex-stereotyping measure provide additional insight into the underlying processes involved. Specifically, in direct constrast to the results for the behavioral and verbal measures concerning the viewer, age but not gender stage was significantly related to children's ability to correctly label sex-stereotypic toys. This pattern of results indicates the importance of recognizing that different processes are likely to be involved in different aspects of sex-role development. For example, it may be that age represents a variable primarily associated with increasing experience with sex-typed labels and reinforcement for using them correctly. On the other hand, the ability to

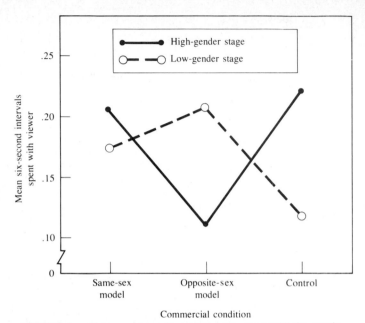

FIGURE 1   Mean number of 6-sec intervals spent with the movie viewer as a function of high/low gender-constancy stage and commercial condition. The cell N's for the same-sex, opposite-sex, and control modeling conditions are 24, 25, and 11, respectively, for the low-gender-stage group; and 16, 15, and 8, respectively, for the high-gender-stage group.

regulate one's own behavior in terms of such labels may depend on changes associated with gender stage.

An anecdote may help clarify this point. One of the older male children correctly applied a "female" label to the dish set. However, the child then asked if he could play with the toy. The fact that the female label was not interfering with the boy's desire to play with the toy seems to indicate that the label was not highly meaningful to the child, as a cue to how he himself should be behaving. Because this child was at the low gender stage, he may not have seen the need to regulate his own behavior in terms of the sex-typed label of the dish set.

This distinction between the relatively passive learning process associated with age or experience and the relatively active learning process associated with stage of gender constancy may help explain some apparent inconsistencies in previous literature. For example, in contrast to the cognitive-developmental hypothesis, Marcus and Overton (1978) failed to find a relationship between gender constancy and preferences for sex-typed activities. Although they explain their findings by reinterpreting the cognitive-developmental predictions, it may also be that their measure was not sensitive to the active information seeking associated with gender constancy. Indeed, as with the sex-stereotyping measure in the present finding, their preference measure was related to age but not gender stage.

Finally, the fact that sex-stereotyped toy commercials may have a powerful influence on children's play behavior at this stage has impli-

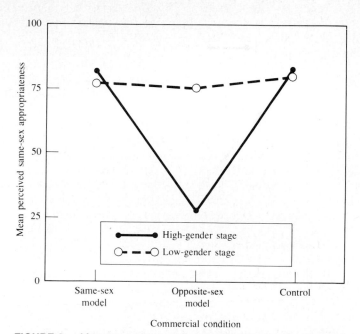

FIGURE 2   Mean perceived appropriateness of the movie viewer for a same-sex sibling as a function of high/low gender-constancy stage and commercial condition. Cell sizes are the same as for the behavioral measure.

cations beyond its influence on immediate sex-role differentiation. The kinds of toys and activities that are "appropriate" for boys versus girls differ greatly in structural properties. For example, one survey found that, in contrast to "boys' " toys, girls' toys are not made to be constructed, taken apart, or repaired (Mitchell 1973). Several recent studies have reported data suggesting that the type of toy or activity children spend time with may affect personality characteristics, such as compliance, cognitive development, and spatial and verbal skills (e.g., Serbin & Connor 1979; Carpenter, Huston-Stein, & Baer, Note 1). Thus, the sex-related behaviors learned during this period of socialization may have broad and long-lasting implications. Clearly, sex-stereotypic information directed toward children during this period of development must be carefully considered.

REFERENCE NOTE

1 Carpenter, C. J.; Huston-Stein, A.; & Baer, D. M. The relation of children's activity preference to sex-typed behavior. Paper presented at the annual meeting of the American Psychological Association, Toronto, August 1978.

REFERENCES

Bandura, A. Social learning theory of identificatory processes. In D. A. Goslin (Ed.), *Handbook of socialization theory and research*. Chicago: Rand McNally, 1969.

Barkley, R. A.; Ullman, D. G.; Otto, L.; & Brecht, J. M. The effects of sex typing and sex appropriateness of modeled behavior on children's imitation. *Child Development*, 1977, **48**, 721–725.

Bryan, J. W., & Luria, Z. Sex-role learning: a test of the selective attention hypothesis. *Child Development*, 1978, **49**, 13–23.

DeVries, R. Constancy of gender identity in the

years three to six. *Monographs of the Society for Research in Child Development*, 1969, **34** (3, Serial No. 127).

Emmerich, W.; Goldman, K. S.; Kirsh, B.; & Sharabany, R. Evidence for a transitional phase in the developmental of gender constancy. *Child Development*, 1977, **48**, 930–936.

Grusec, J. E., & Brinker, D. B. Reinforcement for imitation as a social learning determinant with implications for sex-role development. *Journal of Personality and Social Psychology*, 1972, **21**, 149–158.

Kohlberg, L. A cognitive-developmental analysis of children's sex-role concepts and attitudes. In E. E. Maccoby (Ed.), *The development of sex differences*. Stanford, Calif.: Stanford University Press, 1966.

Kohlberg, L., & Ullian, D. Z. Stages in the development of psychosexual concepts and attitudes. In R. C. Friedman, R. M. Richart, & R. L. Vande Wiele (Eds.), *Sex differences in behavior*. New York: Wiley, 1974.

Lyle, J., & Hoffman, H. R. Explorations of patterns of television viewing by preschool-age children. In F. A. Rubenstein, G. A. Cornstock, & J. P. Murray (Eds.), *Television and social behavior*. Vol. **4**. Washington, D.C.: Government Printing Office, 1972.

Maccoby, E. E., & Jacklin, C. N. *The psychology of sex differences*. Stanford, Calif.: Stanford University Press, 1974.

Marcus, D. E., & Overton, W. F. The development of cognitive gender constancy and sex role preferences. *Child Development*, 1978, **49**, 434–444.

Masters, J. C.; Ford, M. E.; Arend, R.; Grote-

vant, H. D.; & Clark, L. V. Modeling and labeling as integrated determinants of children's sex-typed imitative behavior. *Child Development*, 1979, **50**, 364–371.

Mischel, W. A social learning view of sex differences in behavior. In E. E. Maccoby (Ed.), *The development of sex differences*. Stanford, Calif.: Stanford University Press, 1966.

Mischel, W. Sex-typing and socialization. In P. H. Mussen (Ed.), *Carmichael's manual of child psychology*. New York: Wiley, 1970.

Mitchell, E. The learning of sex roles through toys and books. *Young Children*, 1973, **118**, 226–231.

Perry, D. G., & Bussey, K. The social learning theory of sex differences: imitation is alive and well. *Journal of Personality and Social Psychology*, 1979, **37**, 1699–1712.

Ruble, D. N., & Ruble, T. L. Sex stereotypes. In A. G. Miller (Ed.), *In the eye of the beholder: contemporary issues in stereotyping*. New York: Holt, Rinehart & Winston, in press.

Serbin, L. A., & Connor, J. M. Sex-typing of children's play preferences and patterns of cognitive performance. *Journal of Genetic Psychology*, 1979, **134**, 315–316.

Slaby, R. G., & Frey, K. S. Development of gender constancy and selective attention to same-sex models. *Child Development*, 1975, **46**, 849–856.

Stein, A. H., & Friedrich, C. K. The impact of television on children and youth. In E. M. Hetherington (Ed.), *Review of child development research*. Vol. **5**. Chicago: University of Chicago Press, 1975.

Sternglanz, S. H., & Serbin, L. A. Sex-role stereotyping in children's television programs. *Developmental Psychology*, 1974, **10**, 710–715.

READING 47

Sex Differences in Children's Risk-taking Behavior

Harvey J. Ginsburg
Shirley M. Miller

A widely held belief in our society is that males demonstrate a greater willingness to take risks or chances than females (Appenfels & Hays 1961). However, this belief has not been strongly documented. Some indirect support for this assumption has stemmed from three-sources: (*a*) elementary school children conceptualize the typical boy as more daring than thetypical girl (Tuddenham 1951b); (*b*) boldness has been found to be positively correlated with popularity for males and negatively correlated for girls (Tuddenham 1951a); and (*c*) a greater propensity for taking risks has been implicated as a plausible factor underlying the finding that boys have a higher frequency and greater severity of childhood accidents than girls (Douglas & Bloomfield 1956; Suchman & Schertzer 1960).

A very limited amount of direct evidence has been gathered to substantiate the belief that males engage in more risk-taking behavior than females. For example, Maccoby and Jacklin (1974) focus their entire discussion of sex differences in risk taking on a study by Slovic (1966) and a subsequent replication by Kopfstein (1973).

Slovic set up a booth at a county fair where children could pull levers to win M&M candy. One of the levers was a randomly assigned "disaster switch"; if a child continued to play the game and eventually pulled this lever, all the candy won up to that point would be lost. Slovic reported that 11- to 16-year-old males were more willing to continue the game and take the risk of losing than females. No sex difference was found among 6- to 10-year-old children who participated in this study. Similarly, Kopfstein reported no sex difference for 9-year-old children. Based on this limited evidence, Maccoby and Jacklin concluded their discussion of sex differences in risk taking by simply stating, "We do not know if there is a consistent but age specific tendency for boys to take more risks" (p. 142).

However, the summary provided by Maccoby and Jacklin failed to note an important aspect of the sample of children in the Slovic study. Although 6- to 10-year-old girls and boys did not differ in their willingness to risk losing M&Ms by continuing to play the game, nearly twice as many boys ($N = 226$) initially volunteered to play the game as girls ($N = 135$). Slovic suggested that if less daring girls were

unwilling to participate in the game to begin with, the magnitude of sex differences on the experimental task may have been significantly reduced. Therefore, his failure to find a sex difference on the experimental task may have occurred as a consequence of this sample bias. The present study was performed in an effort to determine sex-related differences in risk taking among young children.

METHOD

A total of 480 3- to 11-year-old children were unobtrusively observed for three 30-min periods in four risk-taking situations at the San Antonio Zoological Gardens. Two observers made independent frequency counts of boys and girls at each of the selected locations.

The total frequency counts were divided into two age groups, 3- to 6-year-old and 7- to 11-year-old children to ascertain any age-related sex differences in risk-taking behavior. The observers estimated the ages of the children in the study. To check the accuracy of these estimates, the observers in a separate sample of children independently estimated the ages of children using the following categories: younger than 3 years, from 3 to 6 years, from 7 to 11 years, and older than 11 years. The observers' abilities to categorize correctly the ages of the children were 90% and 95%, respectively.

Risk taking behavior was observed at the following locations.

Elephant rides.—Several children and adults climb onto a large saddle mounted on an adult elephant and ride around a circular path for approximately 2 min. Admission for the ride is 50 cents. Children who were accompanied by an adult were excluded from the frequency count.

Burro exhibit.—An adult burro is available for children to pet or feed. They must climb or lean over a fenced enclosure in order to reach the burro. A sign on the fence reads, "Careful, he bites!" and a graphic illustrates the burro biting the hand of someone who attempts to feed the animal. A frequency count was made of the girls and boys who leaned over the fence and touched the burro without adult assistance.

The children's petting zoo.—Children enter a gate in order to pet and feed a variety of domestic animals (sheep, goats, etc.). A frequency count was made of children who attempted to feed the animals without adult assistance. The animal food could be purchased for 10 cents at several dispensers outside the entry gate.

The river bank.—The San Antonio River runs through the zoo and adjoining park. At one point, the river has a steep concrete embankment. A frequency count was made of the boys and girls who attempted to climb the embankment and walk on a narrow ledge above it.

RESULTS

Baseline observations were made at the entrance to the zoo to ensure that the number of boys and girls who visited the zoo was equal. Of 300 children sampled at the entry gate, 157 girls (86 3- to 6-year-olds, 71 7- to 11-year-olds) and 143 boys (77 3- to 6-year-olds, 66 7- to 11-year-olds) entered the zoo grounds. Thus, no preexisting difference in the total numbers of boys and girls visiting the zoo could have resulted in the differences between sexes observed in the risk-taking situations. Nearly all of the girls (97%) and boys (94%) were accompanied by an adult.

The numbers of boys and girls, as well as younger and older children, taking risks are given in table 1. Chi square analyses were computed separately for each situation to examine for sex effects, age effects, and interaction effects. Significantly more boys than girls rode elephants ($X^2 = 16.47, p < .001$), touched the burro ($X^2 = 8.01, p < .01$), fed the animals ($X^2 = 6.43, p < .02$), and

TABLE 1   RISK TAKING BEHAVIOR BY AGE AND SEX OF CHILD

	Boys		Girls	
Situation	**3–6**	**7–11**	**3–6**	**7–11**
Elephant rides	58 (24)	94 (39)	37 (15)	52 (22)
Burro exhibit	24 (25)	43 (45)	10 (11)	18 (19)
Petting zoo	22 (27)	36 (43)	11(13)	14 (17)
River bank	11 (18)	34 (56)	3 (5)	13 (21)

Note: Numbers shown in parentheses are percentages.

climbed the river embankment ($X^2 = 14.77, p < .001$). Similarly, older children were more likely than younger children to ride the elephants ($X^2 = 11.22, p < .001$), pet the burro ($X^2 = 3.48, p < .05$), and climb the river embankment ($X^2 = 18.97, p < .001$). (Older children were not more likely to feed the animals.) No significant age x sex interactions were found for any of the situations.

Each measure of risk taking involved children who performed the behavior without adult assistance. Thus, the extent to which parental roles shaped these behaviors was beyond the scope of this study. Differential parental encouragement of males or females to participate in risks in these particular situations or in other related situations was not assessed. Whether or not these sex differences were due to parents rewarding boys more than girls for risk-taking behavior was not examined in this study. Therefore, though evidence for a sex difference in risk taking was found, the relative importance of familial and cultural learning in determining this sex difference was not investigated.

The purely descriptive nature of the data reported in this study apply to the kind of biosocial analysis described by Unger (1979). She noted that a major problem with many studies of sex differences is that the term "sex difference" is used as an explanation rather than as a description. It is important not to ascribe unwarranted causal inference to the descriptive differences in risk-taking behavior found in this study. Freedman (1979) has provided an appropriate context for viewing data obtained within the framework of studying sex differences. He has carefully described the application of a holistic rather than causal approach which may be used to interpret biosocial behavior patterns of the kind described in this study.

Block (1976) has suggested that Maccoby and Jacklin may have conservatively estimated the general extent of sex differences. Their failure to carefully scrutinize the subject sample in the Slovic study may be indicative of their conservative appraisal of sex differences in risk-taking behavior. The 2:1 ratio of boys and girls who were willing to play Slovic's game of chance closely parallels the male-to-female ratio found in our study of risk taking at the zoo. Thus, although the quality of the risk behavior may not differ between boys and girls among those who make the decision to take a risk, it appears that more boys than girls decide to take risks.

REFERENCES

Appenfels, E. J., & Hays, A. B. Cultural factors affecting accidents among children. *Behavioral approaches to accident research*. New York: Association for the Aid of Crippled Children, 1961.

Block, J. H. Issues, problems and pitfalls in assessing sex differences. *Merrill-Palmer Quarterly*, 1976, **22**, 283–308.

Douglas, J. W. B., & Bloomfield, J. M. *Children under five*. Fair Lawn, N.J.: Essential Books, 1956.

Freedman, D. G. *Human sociobiology: a holistic approach*. New York: Free Press, 1979.

Kopfstein, D. Risk-taking behavior and cognitive style. *Child Development*, 1973, **44**, 190–192.

Maccoby, E. E., & Jacklin, C. N. *The psychology of sex differences*. Stanford, Calif.: Stanford University Press, 1974.

Slovic, P. Risk-taking in children: age and sex differences. *Child Development*, 1966, **37**, 169–176.

Suchman, E. A., & Schertzer, A. L. *Current research in childhood accidents*. New York: Association for the Aid of Crippled Children, 1960.

Tuddenham, R. D. Studies in reputation, III: correlates of popularity among elementary school children. *Journal of Educational Psychology*, 1951, **42**, 257–276. (a)

Tuddenham, R. D. Studies in reputation, I: sex and grade differences in school children's evaluation of their peers. *Psychological Monographs*, 1951, **66** (No. 333). (b)

Unger, R. K. Toward a redefinition of sex and gender. *American Psychologist*, 1979, **34**, 1085–1094.

READING 48

Influence of Conflict between Adults on the Emotions and Aggression of Young Children

E. Mark Cummings
Ronald J. Iannotti
Carolyn Zahn-Waxler

The present research was designed to explore the following questions. Are young children affected by negative emotions that are not directed toward them but that they witness and hence may experience none the less? More specifically, is children's social and emotional functioning altered by exposure to anger and quarrels between others? Is there a cumulative effect of exposure to such environmental stressors? And finally, can stable, individual styles of reaction be identified in young children? Such questions represent the intersection of at least two areas of research. One concerns the influence on children of others' emotions, moods, and interpersonal problems. The other concerns the development of aggression, possibly problem aggression, in young children. Background anger may be conceptualized simultaneously as an indirect rearing influence, an environmental stressor, and a stimulus that might be expected to elicit aggression. In this study an experimental manipulation of background anger was introduced to explore some of these issues.

Aggressive styles may begin in early childhood (Hay & Ross, 1982; Loeber, 1982; Olweus, 1979) and, once established, may be difficult to change (Patterson, 1979). This suggests the importance of identifying conditions in the lives of young children that contribute to the early development of aggression. Biological determinants of aggression in children have been studied principally in relation to hormone variations (e.g., Olweus, Mattsson, Schalling, & Loow, 1980). Among the most commonly hypothesized environmental influences on aggression are television violence (see reviews in Pearl, Bouthilet, & Lazar, 1982), aggressive models (Bandura, 1973), and specific parent-child rearing and discipline practices (Patterson & Cobb, 1971; Sears, Maccoby, & Levin, 1957). Children's aggression might be influenced by still other characteristics of their emotional environments. For example, exposure to anger between others might result in a contagion of negative emotions (Lewin, Lippitt, & White, 1939; Sullivan, 1940) or transfer of excitation (Zillmann, 1971). This latter influence has been little studied.

The literature on marital discord is relevant both for examining how children cope with anger between others and how their own levels of aggression might be influenced. Several studies suggest connections between marital discord and a variety of conduct problems and emotional difficulties in young children (e.g., Baruch & Wilcox, 1944; Gassner & Murray, 1969; Johnson & Lobitz, 1974; Porter & O'Leary, 1980; Rutter, 1970). In some instances children of divorce are studied (Anthony, 1974; Hetherington, 1979; Wallerstein & Kelly, 1980),

and outcomes might also reasonably be attributed to effects of separation from the father or mother. However, marital discord in intact homes also may have negative developmental outcomes; and even in cases of divorce, the turmoil and conflict in the home may be a more significant influence than separation of the parents (McCord, McCord, & Thurber, 1962; Power, Ash, Schoenberg, & Sorey, 1974; Rutter, 1971; Rutter, 1979).

There are, however, few observational studies of young children's reactions to anger. Cummings, Zahn-Waxler, and Radke-Yarrow (1981) used mothers trained to be observers of 1- to 2½-year-old children's reactions to anger and to provide data on multiple, discrete events of fighting in the home setting. Anger between others, when witnessed by young children, was found to be a highly arousing stimulus. Children were stressed and distressed by others' physical and verbal quarrels as early as 1 year of age. Exposure to background anger also had apparent cumulative effects: The more fighting between parents, the more distressed were the children. Aggression in response to others' anger was infrequent. There are several possible explanations: (a) The assessments focused more on immediate than on delayed reactions to anger events; (b) the children were very young; and (c) the angry persons were commonly family members, often adults, and hence there may have been few convenient targets for aggression. An additional interpretive problem in this research derives from the problems with objectivity a family member might have in reporting intimate details of family conflicts.

Procedures of direct observation were used in the present research to further explore children's emotions and aggression upon witnessing conflict between others. Changes were introduced into the background affective environment of a play session involving 2-year-old peers. At different times, pairs of children were exposed to friendly, affiliative interactions or to a pointedly angry quarrel between two unfamiliar adults. We reasoned that exposure to unfamiliar adults trained to simulate anger would provide greater experimental control and would allow detailed examination of the effects of witnessing anger under relatively benign conditions outside the family setting. The study was designed to permit examination of (a) delayed as well as immediate effects of exposure to anger, (b) cumulative effects of such exposure, and (c) reactions to anger that reflect both internalizing (e.g., distress) versus externalizing (e.g., aggression) patterns of coping. One group of children experienced the experimental interventions on two occasions in order to assess cumulative effects of background anger. New playmates for the children experiencing a second exposure to anger constituted a replication sample for examining the effects of initial exposure to background anger. A control group of children did not experience the simulations of emotions.

Based on the marital discord literature and the work of Cummings et al. (1981), we expected to see heightened distress during exposure to others' anger. Based on the modeling and television literature, we expected also increases in aggression following exposure to anger. However, because many of the remaining questions were more exploratory and because the study was not designed to provide stringent tests of any given theory, a conservative analytic stance was adopted, and no formal directional predictions were made. That is, two-tailed tests of significance were used throughout.

METHOD

Subjects and Experimental Groups

Two-year-old toddlers (M age $= 27$ months, $SD = 3.8$) and their mothers were seen in an apartment-like setting in a research laboratory. With few exceptions, the subjects were from intact, middle-class homes. Individual peer dyads and their mothers participated in each ob-

servation session. Familiar peers were used in order to maximize representativeness of children's day-to-day social interactions.

Forty-seven children (26 boys and 21 girls) took part in two experimental sessions. In the first session, they were approximately equally divided between same-and opposite-sex pairings. In the second session, 1 month later, children were matched with new children of the opposite sex from the partner seen the first time. The 43 new children (22 boys and 21 girls) thus participated in one experimental session.[1] Twenty children (10 boys and 10 girls) equally distributed in same-sex and opposite-sex pairings constituted a control group. Thus, three groups of children were compared: (a) A group that was initially exposed to background anger (1A) and then exposed to a repetition of anger in a second session to assess cumulative influences (1B); (b) a replication sample (2) for group 1A who were the children participating in just one experimental session; and (c) a control group of children never exposed to the anger stimulation (C).

Procedure

Observation Sessions Procedures were carried out in a room furnished as a living room–kitchenette. The play setting was patterned after a typical peer play session in the home with mothers accessible but not highly involved. At the start of each session mothers were asked to sit on a sofa located at one side of the living room and were given a variety of paper-and-pencil tasks. They were asked not to

---

[1]Due to disruptions in schedules, subject mobility, and unanticipated changes in friendship patterns of both children and mothers, the familiar peer pairing was not achieved for 12 of the children. In two instances, a child was paired in the second session with a child who had been part of another pair in the first session. This contributed to the slight variation in the Ns for different analyses. The unfamiliar peers were evenly distributed across comparison groups. All analyses reported in the results section are based on the total sample. Statistical analyses were also conducted using familiar peers only. The results were virtually identical to those reported for the larger group.

initiate interactions with children or to interrupt children's interactions with each other, unless something occurred that made them uncomfortable or that they felt was dangerous. A standard set of toys (a rocking horse, a ball, a pull toy, a stacking toy, a doll, a hammer and ball toy, and a toy telephone) were placed on the living room floor before the start of each session.

Children were permitted to explore these surroundings freely throughout the session. Children were exposed to others' angry and affectionate interactions within the context of a six-period sequence, which is outlined in Table 1. The changes in the emotional environment that were introduced were as follows: (a) In Period 2 two actors interacted in a pleasant and friendly fashion; (b) in Period 4 the same two actors interacted angrily; and (c) in Period 6 the actors reconciled their earlier argument. In periods before and after the simulations (Periods 1, 3, & 5) there were no planned background emotion events. The sequence was intended to typify one set of conditions that children commonly experience, that is, routine play activity that may become interspersed with, or disrupted by, pleasant and unpleasant emotional experiences of others. The study was not de-

signed to provide definitive conclusions about variations in children's reactions in relation to different sequencing, ordering, and variations in background emotions.

Simulations of affection and anger followed a script but with an emphasis on behaving naturally and projecting the desired emotions. Simulations took place at a kitchenette located at the opposite side of the room from the usual location of children (2m to 4m away). They began when both simulators reached the kitchenette and continued until they were given a signal to leave. In Period 2 simulators greeted the mothers and children and then cooperated in a friendly fashion while getting juice for the children, coffee for the parents, and straightening up the kitchen. During this time they engaged in warm and friendly conversation. In Period 4 they had a verbal argument while washing the dishes in which each actor accused the other of not doing her share of the work around the laboratory. The background anger condition started when one person entered in an obvious huff. The other person came in several seconds later, slamming the door behind her, and began complaining loudly to the one who had entered first. The angry verbal dialogue continued throughout this period as they washed juice and coffee dishes and straightened up the room. At no point was there physical contact nor did they try to grab or take things from each other. In the Period 6 simulation, the simulators greeted each other with a show of affection, apologized, and reconciled. Simulators were never unfriendly to mothers or children; their expressions of anger were confined to their interactions with each other. The simulators were always women (six white and two black). Sessions were videotaped from behind one-way mirrors. Subsequent assessments of children's emotions and behaviors were based upon theme videotape records. The sequencing and timing of control conditions exactly matched experimental conditions except that background-neutral affect conditions were sub-

TABLE 1 EXPERIMENTAL MANIPULATIONS OF BACKGROUND EMOTIONS

Condition	Description	Length
No emotion	No background interaction	5 min
Background of positive emotion	Adults talk in a warm and friendly fashion in the background	5 min
No emotion	No background interaction	5 min
Background of anger	Adults interact angrily in the background	5 min
No emotion	No background interaction	5 min
Background of postive emotion	The background interaction is again friendly as the adults reconcile their differences	2 min

stituted where they were background-positive affect or anger conditions in experimental sessions. In background-neutral affect conditions, actors engaged in matter-of-fact communications similar in duration to those done during the simulations.

Two major sets of measurements were used to examine children's reactions to background emotions: (a) the emotions evidenced during the simulations and (b) the aggression shown throughout the periods. Independent observers/coders were used for the two different coding systems. Every decision in coding was collaborative in the sense that two observers adjudicated disagreements. Interobserver reliability was checked for each measure by having two different pairs of observers score 25% of the sessions. These calculations, based on the formula (agreements/agreements and disagreements) for discrete categories or Pearson product-moment correlation coefficients for continuous categories, are given in parentheses below.

Children's Distress in Relation to Background Emotion Conditions

To isolate distress associated with background conditions from other distress, only responses were scored in which children stopped playing and became preoccupied with the simulators. This may have missed other forms of induced distress, and it precluded statistical comparisons of distress across *all* six periods as well. But this strategy was adopted because it increased the likelihood that the distress responses recorded were, in fact, due to background emotion conditions. Categories of distress were coded as follows:

Distress evident in body posture or movement. (a) Freezing (85%). The child freezes in place without movement or with only absentminded movement of fingers or hands for an extended period. This was not merely motionlessness; there had to be a clear sense that the child was tense, anxious, fixed in place. (b)

Shutting out or denial of distress (100%). The child covers or hides his or her face, or head, or puts his or her hands over his or her ears. (c) Seeking mother (100%). The child, after looking at the simulators, or freezing in place, goes over and seeks physical contact from the mother.

Distress in the face. (a) Serious or concerned expression (85%). An expression of anxiety or concern is evident on the child's face. Subtle looks of concern could not be scored from the videotapes, and sometimes children looked the wrong way, so the total incidence of this response is undoubtedly underestimated.

Distress in the voice or cry. (a) Crying (100%). The child begins to cry, fret, or whimper. (b) Verbal concern (85%). The child expresses a desire to escape from the situation, e.g., "Go home now." (c) Scolding (100%). The child comments disapprovingly, for example, "Bad ladies." (d) Mediating (100%). The child in some way tries to interrupt or terminate the behavior of the simulators, for example, "Stop."

Aggression and Background Emotion Events

Aggression was scored throughout the observation sessions. It was coded when children attacked others (hitting, kicking, pushing, or throwing) or physically attempted to take another's possessions. Children's verbalizations were often too indefinite, for example, "ball" or poorly articulated, for example, "meeugh" to be scored with certainty as aggressive. For each incident, the initiator and recipient were distinguished (93%).

Aggression incidents began when a child first attacked another, or reached for another's possession, and ended with the last act of aggression, protest, or resistance. If children ceased conflict but had not moved on to other activities, 30 s were allowed to elapse to determine if the episode would resume; the incident was scored as continuing if they became reengaged in the same conflict during this period. The correlation between independent raters for duration of aggression was .97. Several qualitative aspects of aggression were coded. The intensity of aggression was scored on the following rating scale: (1) *minimally aggressive* (taking another's possession or physically attacking another, but the aggression leaves a subjectively weak impression), (2) *moderately aggressive* (salient physical or object-related aggression), (3) *highly aggressive* (intense, potentially dangerous aggression; eliciting an immediate desire to intervene). Each child then received a score for each aggression incident in which he or she was characterized as aggressive (a rating of 1) or intensely aggressive (a rating of 2 or 3). Intensity of aggression could be reliably discriminated (89%). Aggression of extended duration, for example, in which the child started a long fight was scored. The criterion was a fight longer than three fourths of the fights in Period 1, namely 18 s or more. Escalation of aggression (91%) was coded if the child became more hostile as the fight proceeded by hitting harder or by hitting and shoving in what was originally a manageable object conflict. Expressions of emotion during aggression, evidenced as (a) anger (angry vocalizing or facial expressions; 96%) or (b) distress (crying, facial or verbal expressions of distress; 95%) were also scored. Children were given scores for each period based on cumulative frequencies or durations of responses.

Assessments of Stability of Aggression An attempt was made to assess stability of aggression by comparing peer aggression in Session 2 with a composite measure of peer aggression in Session 1 and aggression toward an adult in Session 2. A standard conflict setting for the children who participated in two sessions was used to examine aggression toward an adult. After the observation session ended in Visit 2, a female experimenter entered with three new toys, sat down in front of the child on the floor, and requested that he or she choose a toy for play. The child was allowed to play freely with

the toy until he or she was clearly enjoying it, usually several seconds. Then the experimenter said, "It's my turn," took the toy from the child, and began to play with it with great enjoyment for a minute. The toy was moved out of reach if the child tried to take it back. At the end of 1 minute, the experimenter said, "It's your turn now," and gave the toy back to the child. Each child was rated as aggressive or nonaggressive on this task, based on an earlier described definition of aggression, (reliability = 100%). These scores were combined with ratings of the child as aggressive or nonaggressive, based on a global judgment following Session 1 (reliability = 96%), to provide a composite measure of aggression (Epstein, 1979). Based on children's reactions in these two situations, three groups of individuals were identified: (a) highly aggressive children (11 boys and 5 girls), (b) nonaggressive, passive children (4 boys and 6 girls), and (c) children who were moderate (or not extreme) either in their aggressiveness or their lack of aggressiveness (11 boys and 10 girls).

RESULTS

Children's Distress in Relation to Backgrounds of Anger and Positive Emotion

Group Comparisons of Distress Reactions to Simulations Distress responses of children to simulations of anger and positive emotion are shown in Figure 1 for each of the four comparison conditions. The dependent variable is the frequency of different distress responses in each of the conditions where background emotions were simulated.

Distress responding varied across conditions for each of the three experimental groups (1A, 1B, & 2). For each experimental group, greater distress was induced by background anger than by either of the background positive emotion conditions. Distress responding did not change across the parallel

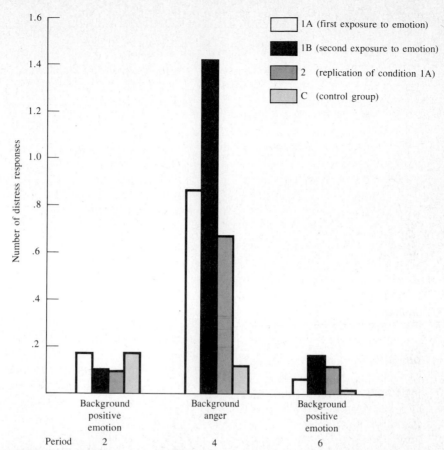

FIGURE 1   Mean frequency of children's distress responses during background conditions of anger or positive emotion between adults.

time periods for the control group. The incidence of different distress responses to background anger is shown in Table 2. Distress was most evident in children's body posture or movement but was also sometimes shown in the voice or cry or in the face. A comparison of children's distress responses to positive emotion yielded percentages of zero in virtually all categories: Eighty-five percent of the children showed no distress in response to positive emotion (comparable to 90% of children in the control condition). The few children who were reactive to the simulation of positive emotion or the control condition

showed it primarily in the form of momentary freezing.

Frequency of Distress during First versus Second Exposure to Anger   These analyses compared distress responding for children who took part in two experimental sessions. Children showed more distress when exposed to background anger a second time. There was also stability across sessions: Children who were more distressed by a first exposure to background anger also tended to be more distressed by a second exposure, r (45) = .63, $p < .001$.

TABLE 2   DISTRESS IN REACTION TO BACKGROUND ANGER

Distress response	Group			
	1A: First exposure to anger	1B: Second exposure to anger	2: Replication sample for 1A	3: Control (no exposure to anger)
Distress evident in body posture or movement	35.7	60.9	44.8	10.0
Freezing	33.6	54.6	29.4	10.0
Shutting out	2.1	10.5	13.2	0
Seeking mother	12.6	12.6	8.8	0
Distress in face	16.8	33.6	15.4	0
Distress in voice or cry	14.7	23.1	4.4	0
Crying	6.3	8.4	2.2	0
Verbal concern	2.1	8.4	0	0
Scolding	6.3	2.1	2.2	0
Mediating	4.2	6.3	0	0
No distress	57.5	36.2	53.5	90.0

Note: Scores reflect percentages of children evidencing responses during exposure to background anger and may exceed 100% due to multiple responses.

Background Anger and Aggression in Children

Children's Aggression Following Exposure to Background Anger and Positive Emotion   Aggression by period for each experimental group and the control groups is presented in Figure 2. Aggression scores were calculated separately for each child in a dyad based on the cumulative duration of aggression incidents that they initiated. Correlations between peers' aggression scores based on this method of calculation were all nonsignificant. (Aggression scores based on dyads yielded findings parallel to those to be described below, but because of our interest in individual differences analyses based only on the individuals' scores are presented.)

The major purpose of these analyses was to determine whether exposure to backgrounds of anger between others heightened children's levels of aggression during peer interaction. There was a marginally significant periods effect for children in Group 1A, a nonsignificant effect for children in Group 2 and a significant effect for children in Group 1B. When children from Groups 1A and 2 were combined for analysis (both groups represented first time exposure to

the simulations of emotion) there was a significant periods effect. Aggression did not change across periods for the control group, and none of the parallel comparisons between periods were significant. Planned comparisons of the significant effects indicated that they were primarily the result of increases in children's aggression following exposure to the anger simulation, as can be seen in Figure 2.

A subsidiary purpose of these analyses was to explore whether exposure to backgrounds of warm, friendly interaction (positive emotion condition) had the effects of altering, possibly reducing, levels of aggression among children. Planned comparisons parallel to those conducted for the anger simulation provided little evidence in support of this hypothesis. Clearly the effect of background anger as a facilitator of children's aggression was much stronger than the effect of a background of positive emotions in dampening aggression.

Hostility of Aggression in Relation to Exposure to Background Anger   Levels of intense aggression for each comparison group are illustrated in Figure 3. The significant effects were

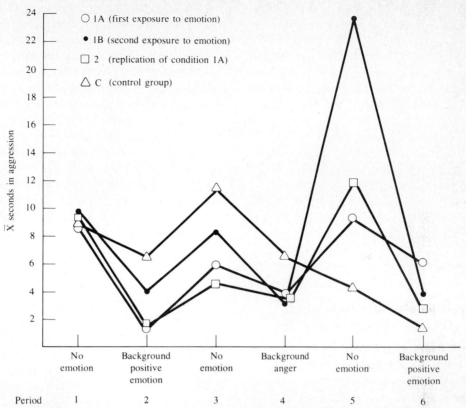

○ 1A (first exposure to emotion)
● 1B (second exposure to emotion)
□ 2 (replication of condition 1A)
△ C (control group)

FIGURE 2   Mean number of seconds in aggression in children before, during, and after background conditions of anger or positive emotion between adults.

entirely due to increases in intense aggression following exposure to the anger simulation.

Sex Differences in Responding to Background Anger   These analyses were conducted for children who participated in two sessions. The dependent variables were average aggression scores across periods and distress during the simulations, summed across sessions. Girls were more distressed by simulation of emotion conditions than boys. Comparisons by condition showed that girls were significantly more distressed by background anger than boys, but there were no significant sex differences in specific comparisons of responding to a background of positive emotion. Boys were more aggressive than girls following exposure to

background anger, but not in the periods prior to exposure to anger. Parallel sex differences in patterns of intense aggression were identified as well in the postanger period. These significant sex differences were evident only when session scores were combined.

Differences Between Children High, Moderate, and Low on Aggression in Their Responses to Background Anger   Distress and aggression scores in Session 2 for children categorized as high, moderate, and low in aggression were analyzed. Means are presented in Table 3. There were significant differences between the three subtypes of children on the amount of distress they showed during background anger. During the anger simulation, the children earlier classified as low in aggression were more likely than the children in the other two groups to show distress, respectively. There were also significant differences between the three subtypes of children on the amount of aggression they showed following anger. Children categorized as high on aggression were more predisposed toward aggression following a second exposure to background anger than children in the other two categories. These differences did not emerge in any of the periods prior to the provocation to aggression.

Finally, there were differences between the different subtypes of children in qualitative features of their aggression in the postanger

period. Children categorized as high on aggression were more often intensely aggressive than either the middle group or the low-aggression group. They also became involved in more extended conflicts after witnessing others' anger than either the middle group or the low-aggressive group and were more likely than low-aggressive children to escalate aggression and engage in emotional aggression. Thus, when a composite measure reflecting both aggression toward an adult (in Session 2) and aggression toward a peer (in Session 1) was examined in relation to peer aggression in Session 2 following the anger provocation, there was evidence of significant continuity or stabil-

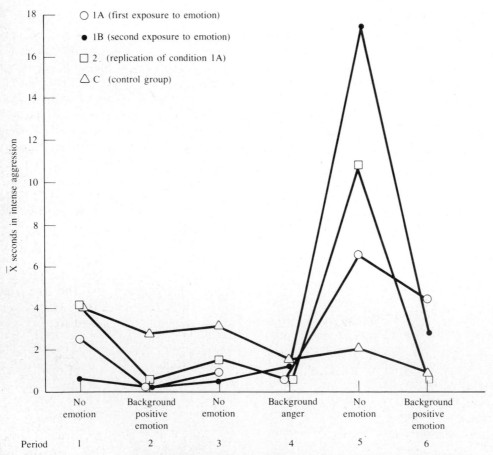

FIGURE 3   Mean number of seconds of intense aggression in children before, during, and after background conditions of anger or positive emotion between adults.

TABLE 3   COMPARISONS OF CHILDREN HIGH, MODERATE, AND LOW IN AGGRESSION IN RESPONDING TO BACKGROUND EMOTION CONDITIONS

Condition	Nonaggressive children	Moderately aggressive children	Aggressive children
	Mean frequency of distress		
Background postive emotion	0	.14	0.13
Background anger	2.30	1.33	1.13
Background positive emotion	0.20	0.19	0.13
	Mean s spent in aggression		
Entry	7.80	8.95	12.00
Background positive affect	1.30	5.29	4.88
No emotion	0.90	7.95	13.00
Background anger	0	4.62	3.19
No emotion	7.70	10.57	50.19
Background positive affect	0.20	5.76	6.56

ity in aggression. A more robust and independent test of whether there are stable styles of aggression in early childhood will require multiple assessments of aggression in contexts and settings that are still more varied and widely separated in time.

DISCUSSION

The purpose of this study was to explore how the emotions and interactions of children are influenced by the ambient affective environment. Young children exposed to a background of conflict and anger between adults were influenced markedly by this environmental stressor. The most immediate effect of anger between adults was to heighten children's distress, an influence that became even more pronounced with repeated exposure to conflict. This provides a replication and an experimental confirmation of findings from naturalistic home studies of young children (Cummings et al., 1981; Cummings, Zahn-Waxler, & Radke-Yarrow, 1984). In the latter studies, distress was a prominent reaction to anger in the home, especially in toddlers. Children's distress became exacerbated when they were exposed to high levels of parental conflict. Children whose parents fought frequently also tended to show

complex prosocial response patterns, such as attempts to mediate, reconcile, and distract the angry partners. This pattern of caregiving began to characterize the reactions of more of the children and to replace the more overt distress reactions as the children become older. In the research reported here the prosocial pattern was less evident, probably because the persons in conflict were not family members and were unknown to the child.

The present study also graphically documented the potential for conflict to produce aggression in children who witness it. This is consistent with research on the influences on children of aggressive models and of television and family violence. Furthermore, it indicates that even very young children are influenced by conflict between others. The mechanisms by which anger between others stimulates aggression cannot be determined from this research design, but processes linked with emotional reactivity are suggested. Exposure to anger could result in contagion of emotion, or there may be a transfer of excitation that results in communicated aggressive behavior. The arousal of distress may stress children and make them less tolerant of frustration or sensitize children to interpret further stressful events in a more negative light. Children's aggression also may reflect delayed anger that is part of the release of inhibition that occurs in the course of recovery from distress. Furthermore, conflict between others may provide permission for the behavioral expression of aggressive impulses. From a socio-biological perspective, anger in the external environment may signal danger to the organism and hence elicit protective and defensive maneuvers. Each of these processes could lower the threshold for long and highly aggressive displays. Our data indicate that children did not simply learn specific aggressive behaviors or imitate the specific actions they witnessed. The adults' quarrel was verbal and hence did not provide models for children's acts of physical aggression. Thus, children's aggression following exposure to anger simulations did not appear to be a function of modeling in the strict sense of the concept.

There were suggestions of stable patterns of individual differences in children's emotional reactivity and aggression. Children classified as aggressive based on other preceding and concurrent laboratory measures were particularly likely to show aggression after they had witnessed anger. This, too, is consistent with the literature on television violence. Television violence has been shown to have a greater impact on the aggression of aggressive children than on the aggression of other children (Friedrich & Stein, 1973; McIntyre & Teevan, 1972; Robinson & Backman, 1972; Steur, Applefield, & Smith, 1971). The suggestion of continuity in styles of aggression identified here is consistent with early stable patterns of conflict identified by Hay and Ross (1982). The extent to which these continuities in aggression reflect biological, constitutional, or environmental influences is an open, empirical question. If just one repetition of an aversive environmental event like anger produces such marked increases in children's reactions, it is reasonable to hypothesize a strong influence of the affective environment on children who are exposed to pervasive, chronic conditions of anger and turmoil. Meyersberg and Post (1979) have provided a useful framework for addressing some of these issues in an integration of concepts from biological psychiatry, behavioral psychology, and neopsychoanalytic tradition. They advance a complex model that details how traumatic environmental stimuli (e.g., parental conflict, depression, stress) might produce significant changes in children's social, emotional, and biochemical functioning.

Background anger will be an enduring feature of young children's lives in some families. We may speculate on what will be the more long-term outcomes of such experiences with conflict between others. Our earlier studies indicated that children were unlikely to aggress openly when exposed to anger and were likely to aid in conflict resolution as they grew older. This orientation is adaptive in many respects. However, assumption of the role of caregiver, mediator, or peacemaker may also create an unhealthy role reversal if the child regularly intervenes for a parent. A common theme in the literature on divorce and marital discord is the guilt or unrealistic sense of responsibility that children are sometimes believed to assume for their parents' problems. Moreover, though the child's aggressive impulses that are stimulated by others' anger may remain unexpressed in that setting they are, nonetheless, experienced. These aggressive impulses may then become internalized (and expressed as anger toward self) or externalized and sometimes expressed as displaced aggression in other settings (Emery, 1982).

In the literature much emphasis has been placed on relations between family discord and conduct disorders or aggression in boys. In the current study, too, boys more than girls reacted to the argument between the adults with aggression. Such findings have been interpreted sometimes to suggest that boys are less resistant and more vulnerable to the effects of family or marital discord than girls. However, an alternative explanation is that girls and boys are equally disturbed by discord, but girls show it in a way that is less noticeable and less problematical to others. Consistent with our own findings, Emery (1982) has recently argued that girls may show their disturbances in a manner more "appropriate" to their sex, namely, by becoming distressed, anxious, or withdrawn. Again, the causal mechanisms remain unidentified.

The distress or anxiety that appears so immediately and pervasively in children during conflict between others may be a mediating variable that variously functions to determine whether children will become avoidant *or* aggressive *or* prosocial depending upon many other factors. Why, for certain children, does anger (in the form of aggression) appear to be part of their process of recovery from distress? Why does this anger or aggression emerge as a delayed reaction to others' anger, whereas distress is so quickly apparent? How long is the "recovery" period? We are only beginning to understand how others' anger is experienced, processed, and channeled, both in the short term and in the long run. More information is needed on how the nature of the relationship of the child with the person(s) in conflict influences the ways in which that anger will be experienced. Among other variables that may be important are (a) the duration and chronicity of anger incidents, (b) the extent to which anger is accompanied by other emotions (e.g., distress, sadness) or physical violence, and (c) the extent to which the anger is overtly versus covertly expressed. What is the influence, for example, of the "silent" treatment, subtle sarcasm, or tension that "can be cut with a knife"? Finally, there is a need to explore whether other kinds of distress stimuli similarly provoke aggression in children. Studies of young children's reactions to distress cries and pain in others yield higher levels of prosocial behavior and lower levels of aggression than were found here (Zahn-Waxler, Radke-Yarrow, & King, 1979; Zahn-Waxler & Radke-Yarrow, 1982), but more research is needed.

This study informs us that very young children are emotionally influenced by the quarrels of others, but some vexing practical concerns remain unsettled. For example, to what extent should children be shielded from background anger? Conflict is a significant part of life, and the development of effective coping strategies requires some exposure to conflict (and hopefully to resolution of conflict as well). But how much anger can be tolerated or experienced safely is unknown and clearly, at some point, it becomes a detrimental experience. The extensiveness of the upset and aggressive behavior seen in youngsters in the present study highlights the negative outcomes of too much background anger. Thus, whereas much attention has been paid to television violence as an instigator of aggression (Pearl et al., 1982), there is another similar, perhaps more powerful influence on aggression in the home, an influence that is not so easily turned off as a television set.

REFERENCES

Anthony, E. J. (1974). Children at risk from divorce: A review. In E. J. Anthony & C. Koupernik (Eds.), *The child in his family*. (Vol. 3, pp. 461–478). New York: Wiley.

Bandura, A. (1973). *Aggression: A social learning analysis*. Englewood Cliffs, N.J.: Prentice-Hall.

Baruch, D. W., & Wilcox, J. A. (1944). A study of sex differences in pre-school children's adjustment coexistent with interparent tensions. *Journal of Genetic Psychology, 64*, 21–303.

Cummings, E. M., Zahn-Waxler, & Radke-Yarrow, M. (1981). Young children's responses to expressions of anger and affection by others in the family. *Child Development, 52*, 1274–1282.

Cummings, E. M., Zahn-Waxler, C., & Radke-Yarrow, M. (1984). Developmental changes in children's reactions to anger in the home. *Journal of Child Psychology and Psychiatry, 25*, 63–74.

Emery, R. E. (1982). Interparent conflict and the children of discord and divorce. *Psychological Bulletin, 92*, 310–330.

Epstein, S. (1979). The stability of behavior: On predicting most of the people much of the time. *Journal of Personality and Social Psychology, 37,* 1097–1126.

Friedrich, L. K., & Stein, A. H. (1973). Aggressive and prosocial television programs and the natural behavior of preschool children. *Monographs of the Society of Research in Child Development, 38,* (4, Serial No. 151).

Gassner, S., & Murray, F. J. (1969). Dominance and conflict in the interactions between parents of normal and neurotic children. *Journal of Abnormal Psychology, 74,* 33–41.

Hay, D. F., & Ross, H. S. (1982). The social nature of early conflict. *Child Development, 53,* 105–113.

Hetherington, E. M. (1979). Divorce: A child's perspective. *American Psychologist, 34,* 851–858.

Johnson, S. M., & Lobitz, C. K. (1974). The personal and marital adjustment of parents as related to observed child deviance and parenting behavior. *Journal of Abnormal Child Psychology, 2,* 193–207.

Keppel, G. (1973). *Design and analysis: A researcher's handbook.* Englewood Cliffs, NJ: Prentice-Hall.

Lewin, K., Lippitt, R., & White, R. K. (1939). Patterns of aggressive behavior in experimentally created "social climates." *Journal of Social Psychology, 10,* 271–299.

Loeber, R. (1982). The stability of antisocial and delinquent child behavior: A review. *Child Development, 53,* 1431–1446.

McCord, J., McCord, W., & Thurber, E. (1962). Some effects of paternal absence on male children. *Journal of Abnormal and Social Psychology, 64,* 361–369.

McIntyre, J. J., & Teevan, J. J. (1972). Television violence and deviant behavior. In G. A. Comstock & E. A. Rubinstein (Eds.), *Television and social behavior (Vol. 3). Television and adolescent aggressiveness* (pp. 383–435). Washington, DC: U. S. Government Printing Office.

Meyersberg, H. A., & Post, R. M. (1979). A holistic developmental view of neural and psychological processes. *British Journal of Psychiatry, 135,* 139–155.

Olweus, D. (1979). Stability of aggressive reaction patterns in males: A review. *Psychological Bulletin, 86,* 852–875.

Olweus, D., Mattsson, A., Schalling, D., & Loow, H. (1980). Testosterone, aggression, physical and personality dimensions in normal adolescent males. *Psychosomatic Medicine, 42,* 253–269.

Patterson, G. R., & Cobb, J. A. (1971). Stimulus control for classes of noxious behavior. In J. F. Knutson (Ed.), *The control of aggression: Implications from basic research* (pp. 72–129). Chicago: Aldine.

Patterson, G. (1979). Treatment for children with conduct problems: A review of outcome studies. In S. Feshbach & A. Fraczek (Eds.), *Aggression and behavior change: Biological and social processes* (pp. 83–138). New York: Praeger Publishers.

Pearl, D., Bouthilet, L., & Lazar, J. (Eds.), (1982). *Television and behavior: Ten years of scientific progress and implications for the 1980's: Technical reviews* (Vol. 2). Washington, DC: U. S. Government Printing Office.

Porter, B., & O'Leary, K. D. (1980). Marital discord and childhood behavior problems. *Journal of Abnormal Child Psychology, 8,* 287–295.

Power, M. J., Ash, P. M., Schoenberg, E., & Sorey, E. C. (1974). Delinquency and the family. *British Journal of Social Work, 4,* 17–38.

Robinson, J. P., & Backman, J. G. (1972). Television viewing habits and aggression. In G. A. Comstock & E. A. Rubinstein (Eds.), *Television and social behavior: Vol 3. Television and adolescent aggressiveness* (pp. 372–382). Washington, DC: U. S. Government Printing Office.

Rutter, M. (1970). Sex differences in children's responses to family stress. In E. J. Anthony, & C. Koupernick (Eds.), *The child in his family* (pp. 165–196). New York: Wiley.

Rutter, M. (1971). Parent-child separation: Psychological effects on the children. *Journal of Child Psychology and Psychiatry and Allied Disciplines, 12,* 233–260.

Rutter, M. (1979). Maternal deprivation. 1972–1978: New findings, new concepts, new approaches. *Child Development, 50,* 283–305.

Sears, R. R., Maccoby, E. E., & Levin, H. (1957), *Patterns of child rearing.* Evanston, IL: Row, Peterson.

Steuer, F. B., Applefield, J. M. & Smith, R. (1971). Televised aggression and the interpersonal aggression of preschool children. *Journal of Experimental Child Psychology, 11,* 442–447.

Sullivan, H. S. (1940). *Conceptions of modern psychiatry*. London: Tavistock Press.

Wallerstein, J. S., & Kelly, J. B. (1980). *Surviving the breakup*. New York: Basic Books.

Zahn-Waxler, C., Radke-Yarrow, M., & King, R. A. (1979). Child rearing and children's prosocial initiations towards victims of distress. *Child Development, 50*, 319–330.

Zahn-Waxler, C., & Radke-Yarrow, M. (1982). The development of altruism: Alternative research strategies. In N. Eisenberg-Berg (Ed.), *The development of prosocial behavior* (pp. 109–137). New York: Academic Press.

Zillmann, D. (1971). Excitation transfer in communication-mediated aggressive behavior. *Journal of Experimental Social Psychology, 7*, 419–434.

READING 49

Social Cognition and Children's Aggressive Behavior

Kenneth A. Dodge

The application of concepts from the literature on the development of social cognition to the problem of inappropriate and persistent aggression among certain children provides the basis for two connected studies constituting this investigation. These studies deal specifically with children's defensive aggression, that is, aggression which is a hostile and assertive response to perceived threat or intentional frustration. Defensive aggression is differentiated from instrumental aggression, which is injurious behavior intended to gain an independent reward and which may be altered by the appropriate manipulation of reward and punishment (Hartup 1974; Rule 1974).

The moral-judgment literature is abundant with studies demonstrating the importance of social cognitions in inhibiting defensive aggression. When a person perceives that a peer is *intentionally* causing a negative outcome, that person's modal response is aggression against the peer. When a person perceives that a peer causes a negative outcome *accidentally*, his modal response is inhibition of aggression. This finding holds for adults (Burnstein & Worchel 1962; Pastore 1952) and for children (Mallick & McCandless 1966; Rule, Nesdale, & McAra 1974; Shantz & Voydanoff 1973). Since a child's ability to differentiate the intentions of

others and his ability to integrate that intention information into his own behavior are milestones which are thought to be developmentally acquired (Flavell 1977; Heider 1958; Piaget 1965), it has been hypothesized that variations in defensive aggressive behavior in children may be related to variations in cognitive development (Feshbach 1970; Hartup 1974). That is, the 10-year-old child who persistently responds with aggression to a nonintentional negative outcome may be doing so because of a *cue-utilization deficiency* related to a lag in his ability to integrate intention information into his behavior.

An alternate explanation of persistent aggressive responding to nonintentional negative outcomes by a certain child is that this child is not deficient in *cue utilization,* but rather engages in *cue distortion*. This hypothesis is that the child makes a distortion in the perception of intention which is related to his expectation about the intentions of others. If a child strongly expects that a peer will behave with hostile intent, then he may be likely to perceive the peer's behavior as hostile, particularly when the behavior produces a negative outcome. This perception may justify the child's retaliatory aggressive behavior from his own point of view.

This process of making an inaccurate attribution in the direction of one's expectations has been identified as a "complementary apperceptive projection" by Murray (1933). He suggested that the likelihood of one making a misperception of this kind increases with the ambiguity of the stimulus. Translated to the inappropriately aggressive child, it may be hypothesized that, given a negative outcome, this child will be most likely to mistakenly attribute a hostile intention to a peer (and consequently, to retaliate aggressively) when the peer's behavior seems ambiguously intended.

As a test of these hypotheses, in the first study of the present investigation, known aggressive and nonaggressive children in three grades were presented with a negative outcome which was the consequence of the behavior of a peer who had acted with hostile intent, benign intent (accidental behavior), or ambiguous intent. The child's behavioral responses were recorded by a video camera and constituted the dependent measure.

STUDY 1

Method

Selection of Subjects Samples of 15 aggressive and 15 nonaggressive boys in each of grades 2, 4, and 6 (90 boys in all) of a semi-rural lower-middle-class school were selected on the joint bases of peer nominations and teacher assessments. Subjects selected by this method have been found to differ in their actual aggressive behavior, both in the classroom and on the playground (Dodge and Coie, Note 1). Informed consent for all phases of participation, including consent to videotape children, was obtained from parents of all participating children. Through a sociometric interview and with the aid of grade-level rosters, the 326 children in these grades were asked to nominate three peers who fit a particular behavioral description. Two of the descriptions were about con-

sistent aggressive behavior ("This child starts fights," and "This child upsets everything when he gets in a group"). Also, children were asked to nominate three peers whom they liked most and three peers whom they liked least. Scores for each nomination category were computed for each child by summing the numbers of nominations received from all peers. Teachers were asked to privately assess each of their students by rating, on a scale of 1 to 9, each child's behavior in the areas of social relations, initiation of fights, and total involvement in fights.

In order to be selected as "aggressive," a boy had to be placed above the median of his teacher's ratings on each of the aggression questions and below the median on the favorability of social relations question. From this pool, the 15 boys in each grade whose peer nomination scores for aggression were highest, *and* whose cooperation and liking scores were low, were selected as the aggressive sample. Only males were selected since the total pool of aggressive children was predominantly male. The "nonaggressive" sample of boys was matched to the aggressive sample by race. One-third of the sample was black, paralleling the overall racial composition of the school. The nonaggressive sample was similarly selected on the basis of teacher ratings and peer nominations, but for prosocial and nonaggressive behavior.

Overview of Experimental Design Subjects were exposed to a frustrating negative outcome during the course of a puzzle-assembling task in which a prize could be won. A negative outcome (destruction of the subject's puzzle) was instigated by an unseen peer who, through simulated "live" audio information, was heard to be acting with a hostile intent, with a benign intent, or ambiguously. Assignment to condition was random. The boy was then given an opportunity to retaliate by destroying the unseen peer's puzzle. His verbal and behavioral responses were recorded by a video camera and constituted the dependent measure in a 3 x 2 x 3 (grade level of subject x status of subject x experimental condition) factorial experiment.

Procedure Each boy was escorted into a research trailer which was divided into two rooms and was told by the white female experimenter that he could win a prize by performing well in a puzzle-assembling task. He was told that another boy, in the adjoining room, would also be working at this task, even though they were not competing against each other. By means of a contrived demonstration, the boy was led to believe that a microphone and speaker system had been connected between the two rooms, which allowed the two boys to communicate openly with each other. The "other boy" was actually a tape-recording of scripts read by a 9-year-old boy. The tape player was operated by a technician in the other room.

The experimenter then went on to explain the task to the child. He could win one of three prizes of differing value, or no prize, depending on how many pieces of his puzzle were assembled at the end of the task. The boy would have a limited amount of time and was to work as rapidly as possible on the 50-piece jigsaw puzzle, which was large and simple enough that all children could assemble at least some pieces. Boys unfamiliar with the task were given time to practice. The experimenter then began timing the boy's efforts. When the boy had assembled 13 puzzle pieces, she announced that they would stop for a break. She told the subject she wanted the boys to look at each other's puzzles, so she left the room with his partially completed puzzle, which was in a wooden tray. A few seconds later the tape player was turned on, and the subject was led to believe he heard the experimenter talk to the other boy. She told the other boy to look at the puzzle while she left the room. The subject then heard one of three recordings by the fictitious other boy.

In the hostile condition, the other boy made the following statement, in a hostile voice: "Gee, it looks like he's got a lot done. Well, I don't like it. I don't want him to win that dumb prize, so there, I'll mess it up. [Crashing sounds are heard.] There...that'll do it." In the benign condition, the other boy stated, in a friendly voice: "Gee it looks like he's got a lot done. I think I'll help him put some more pieces together. Hey, there's one. I'll put it here. [Crashing sounds are heard.] Oh, no, hey, I didn't mean to drop it. I didn't mean it." In the ambiguous condition, the other boy made only the following statement, in a nondescriptive voice: "Gee it looks like he's got a lot done." [After a long pause, crashing sounds are heard.]

Following this sequence, the experimenter was heard to return to the room and collect the two puzzles. Moments later, she returned to the subject's room with both puzzles. The subject's puzzle had been disassembled, and the other boy's puzzle was partially completed. She told the subject to look over the two puzzles while she was gone, and then she left the room. At all stages of the experiment, the experimenter remained blind to the status of the child and to the experimental condition.

Following the experimenter's departure, a video recorder filmed the subject's behavior through a one-way mirror and recorded his voice for the next 3 min. Subjects were not made aware of the filming. The subject's behavior during this period constituted the dependent measure. Following this period, the experimenter returned to the room and told the child that the task was over. The experimenter awarded him the best prize for his positive performance on the task, thereby reinforcing the child for his *performance* and not the *outcome*, and escorted him back to the classroom. He was asked to not tell other children about the task.

While cognizant of ethical considerations, the experimenter did not inform the child that his behavior had been videotaped, or that the task had been "rigged." This information was withheld so that children would not be tempted to "divulge the trick" to peers and because it was felt that the information would only confuse the children. Both parents and school personnel had given fully informed consent for this procedure.

As an informal check on the credibility of the manipulation, the experimenter questioned the child about the procedure as she escorted him back to the classroom. No children appeared to disbelieve the reality of the procedure. Teachers acted as a check on the experimenter's request that each child not tell other children about the procedure. By anecdotal accounts of teachers, all children appeared to honor this request.

Observer Coding and Reliability Two observers independently coded the occurrences of each child's behavior in seven categories, which were derived after observation of the range in behaviors displayed: (A) disassembled one or more pieces of the other's puzzle, (B) expressed verbal hostility, (C) showed indirect hostility (such as hitting the wall, pounding the table, or making a fist), (D) assembled one's own puzzle, (E) attempted a neutral communication with the other child, (F) made a positive verbal statement, and (G) helped assemble the other's puzzle. The percentage of times in which both coders agreed whether or not a particular category of behavior occurred was calculated as the measure of observer reliability. The median agreement for the seven categories was 97%, with a range of 94%–100%.

In addition, an a priori single measure which assessed the affective valence of the child's behavior was derived from the seven observer categories. If the observer had recorded an occurrence of any of the aggressive categories (A, B, or C), the child received a score of 3. A child received a score of 2 if no valenced behavior was recorded, and a score of 1 if he had demonstrated positive behavior (categories F or G), in absence

of aggressive behavior. Cases in which the two observers disagreed on this coding were resolved by a joint review, so that 100% agreement was reached for this measure.

Results and Discussion

These data show that all groups of children reacted to the hostile condition with aggression and to the benign condition with relative restraint from aggression. The aggressive group of boys were more likely than their nonaggressive peers to display aggression, as one might predict. Interestingly, they were also more likely to help the peer, but only when the situation called for it, as in the benign condition. The latter finding suggests that the boys in the aggressive group were not blindly aggressive, but were highly discriminating and were reacting to the interpersonal stimuli to a greater extent than were nonaggressive boys. The "increased reactivity" of aggressive boys is a finding which is distinct from a hypothesis of "increased activity" in these children and which could be explored further in other studies. (See Table 1.)

Neither a main effect of grade level nor an interaction of grade level with experimental condition was found for the aggression score, indicating that in all three grades children displayed aggression when the peer was hostile and refrained from aggression when the peer was benign. This finding differs from the data of Shantz and Voydanoff (1973) but is consistent with the findings of other researchers (Berndt 1977; Darley, Klossen, & Zanna 1978) who have studied children's verbal responses in various hypothetical situations. The present data extend those findings to boys' behavioral responses in actual interpersonal situations, and suggest that, when the intentions of another are defined clearly, young boys (7 years of age) incorporate intention cues into their ongoing behavior in the same fashion as do older boys. However, it remains plausible to speculate that age effects might have been found had even younger boys served as subjects.

TABLE 1 PERCENTAGES OF SUBJECTS IN EACH CONDITION DISPLAYING VARIOUS BEHAVIORS, STUDY 1

Subjects	Behavior category						
	A	B	C	D	E	F	G
Aggressive:							
Hostile peer	47	60	33	33	27	13	0
Ambiguous peer	20	13	33	20	20	53	7
Benign peer	0	7	13	20	27	13	53
Nonaggressive:							
Hostile peer	40	27	13	7	0	7	0
Ambiguous peer	7	7	0	27	0	47	7
Benign peer	0	0	0	20	0	7	20

Note: A = disassemble puzzle, B = verbal hostility, C = indirect hostility, D = assemble own puzzle, E = neutral communication with peer, F = positive verbal behavior, G = help assemble peer's puzzle.

The present data show that, when a peer's intention is stated clearly, aggressive boys alter their retaliatory behavior according to that intention as appropriately as do nonaggressive boys. These data do not support the cue-utilization-deficiency hypothesis. When the intention of the peer remains ambiguous, aggressive and nonaggressive boys diverge in their behavioral reactions. Aggressive boys react as if the peer had acted with hostile intent, that is, with aggression, while nonaggressive boys behave as if the peer had acted benignly, that is, by refraining from aggression. These data support the cue-distortion hypothesis that aggressive and nonaggressive boys differ in their perceptions of the intentions of peers in ambiguous circumstances. However, in this study, only behavioral reactions of the subjects were measured. The attributions made by the boys must be inferred. In order to more directly assess specifically the attributions of these children in negative outcome ambiguous circumstances, a second study was run. This study employed an interview methodology in which children were asked to respond to hypothetical events. They were asked to attribute reasons for a negative outcome which was hypothetically inflicted upon them by a peer. Also, they were asked to state their probable behavioral response. According to the cue-distortion hypothesis, aggressive boys would be more likely than nonaggressive boys to attribute a hostile intention to the peer and would therefore be more likely to state that they would respond aggressively to the peer.

It may be suggested that characteristics of the specific peer who caused the negative outcome in this second study could additionally affect the attributions of these children. A study by Zadney and Gerard (1974) has shown that predetermined attributes of a person could affect others' interpretations of his behavior. It may be hypothesized that if a peer is known to be aggressive, then children will be more likely to attribute hostile intentions to him in an ambiguous situation than if the peer is known to be nonaggressive. To test this hypothesis, the status of the actors in the second study was manipulated by using the names of actual known aggressive and nonaggressive boys as actors.

STUDY 2

Method

Subjects The same children who served in study 1 also served in study 2. The two studies were administered at separate times, in random order, by independent experimenters, so that the children did not associate the two studies.

Procedure This study was conducted as an interview in which each child was brought to a private room and assured of the confidentiality of his responses, which were tape recorded. The child was asked a series of four questions about each of four peers. In each series, the interviewer told subjects one of two hypothetical stories in which a peer was involved in a negative outcome for the child. In one story, the child was to imagine that he was sitting at a lunch table. As the peer (identified by name) approached the table, a carton of milk on the peer's tray spilled all over the child's back. In the other story, the child was to imagine that he was on the playground playing catch with a ball. When the peer got the ball, he threw it, and it hit the child in the back, hurting him. Each of the two stories was worded so that the intention of the peer was left ambiguous. The child's task was to describe how the incident might have happened. His responses were probed in a non-leading direction until the child responded about the intentionality of the peer. Subsequently, he was asked how he would respond behaviorally and two additional questions about the peer.

Selection of Peer Targets The four peers who were targets of each series of questions were selected because they had been identified by the subject as aggressive or nonaggressive during the course of the above-mentioned peer nomination interviews which were conducted 6 weeks prior to the experimental interview by independent administrators. Two aggressive peer targets were chosen from the subject's nominations for the "starts fights" and "disrupts group" categories. Two nonaggressive peer targets were chosen from the subject's nominations to the "cooperates in a group" category. When subjects had made more than two nominations for a category the nominated peers who also happened to be subjects in the study were selected as targets for the stories.

No peer name was used as a target figure in a category opposite to the category in which he was a subject. In other words, no aggressive subject served as a nonaggressive target, and vice versa.

Experimental Design and Dependent Measures The study followed a 2 x 3 x (2 x 2) factorial design in which subject status (aggressive vs. nonaggressive) and grade level (2, 4, or 6) were between-subject factors and target status (aggressive vs. nonaggressive) and story content (lunch vs. playground) were within-subject factors. Subjects were interviewed in random order. Target status and story content were factorially combined into four conditions and were presented to subjects in an order which was counterbalanced across all subjects. The first dependent measure was the subject's attribution about the intention of the peer target and was scored as 1 if intentional and 2 if accidental. The second dependent measure was the subject's stated behavioral response, which was scored as 1 if aggressive retaliation and as 2 if no aggressive retaliation. In the third question, the subject was asked what he thought the peer target would do next after the negative outcome, and his response was scored as 1 if he said the peer would continue to aggress, 2 if he said the peer would do nothing, and 3 if he said the peer would act benevolently. In the fourth question, the subject was asked if he would trust the peer by allowing himself to be placed in a position to let the act be repeated. His response was scored as 1 if he said yes he would trust the peer, and 2 if he said no he would not trust the peer. Since all interviews were tape recorded, an independent coder was able to check the reliability of the interviewer's coding of responses. This coder listened to 20 tapes and agreed with the interviewer in over 95% of the cases. Thus, the interviewer's coding was used for all subjects.

Results and Discussion

Mean scores of subjects' responses to the four questions are displayed in table 2. As the results of the first study would have one predict, aggressive subjects attributed a hostile intention to the peer 50% more often than did nonaggressive subjects. Aggressive subjects also predicted that the target would continue to behave aggressively more often than did nonaggressive subjects, and they said that they would not trust the target in the future more often than did nonaggressive subjects.

These findings support the major hypothesis. In a hypothetical, negative-outcome, ambiguous circumstance, aggressive boys are more likely than nonaggressive boys to attribute a hostile intention to the peer instigator of the behavior. They also expect continued hostility from the peer and will not trust him. It is worth noting that when subjects attributed a hostile intention to the peer, they also said they would retaliate aggressively in 60% of the cases. When they attributed a benign intention to the peer, they retaliated in only 26% of the cases. This difference is significant. Apparently, even in this ambiguous circumstance the subject's attributions about the intention of the peer is highly predictive of his stated response.

The status of the peer target who instigated the behavior had an even more sizable effect on subjects' attributions and stated behavior than did the status of the subject. As Table 2 shows, aggressive targets were attributed a hostile intention five times more often than were nonaggressive targets. This effect held true at all grade levels (all t tests were significant at the .05 level), although the disparity between attributions for aggressive and nonaggressive targets was greater among sixth graders and fourth graders than among second graders, as revealed by a significant interaction of grade with target status. In other words, being labeled as aggressive has an increasingly negative effect on children's attributions about a peer as he gets older.

The status of the peer target also had a significant effect on subjects' hypothetical reactions to the negative outcome in the story. Subjects proposed aggressive retaliation more often against aggressive targets than against nonaggressive targets. Subjects predicted that aggressive targets would be more likely to continue behaving in aggressive ways than would nonaggressive targets. Subjects also refused to trust aggressive targets more often than nonaggressive targets. These data amply demonstrate the importance of a peer's reputation in the determination of a child's attributions about the peer's behavior and in that child's behavior toward the peer. Specifically, children who are known to be aggressive are more likely than others to be attributed hostile intentions, to be the objects of aggressive retaliation, and to be expected to continue to aggress. Also, they are

TABLE 2 MEAN SCORES OF AGGRESSIVE AND NONAGGRESSIVE SUBJECTS' RESPONSES TO INTERVIEW QUESTIONS ABOUT AGGRESSIVE AND NONAGGRESSIVE PEERS, STUDY 2

Subjects	Question			
	1: Attributions of hostility	2: Aggressive retaliation	3: Prediction of aggression	4: Lack of trust in peer
Aggressive:				
Aggressive target	1.40	1.48	1.86	1.46
Nonaggressive target	1.10	1.31	1.38	1.14
Nonaggressive:				
Aggressive target	1.31	1.39	1.70	1.30
Nonaggressive target	1.03	1.20	1.17	1.06

less likely to be trusted by their peers than are their nonaggressive counterparts.

GENERAL DISCUSSION

The two studies reported provide complementary data concerning the attributions and behavior of aggressive and nonaggressive boys. In the first study, it was found that both aggressive and nonaggressive boys in each of three grades could differentiate their retaliatory behavior in a negative-outcome situation according to the clearly stated intention of the peer instigator of the outcome. This finding does not support the hypothesis that aggressive boys lack the ability to integrate intention cues into their behavior. Only when the peer's intentions were ambiguous in producing a negative outcome did aggressive and nonaggressive boys' responses differ. The aggressive boys reacted with aggression, as if the peer had acted with a hostile intent, while the nonaggressive boys reacted with restraint from aggression, as if the peer had acted benignly.

This difference in the behavior of aggressive and nonaggressive boys in the ambiguous circumstance may have broad implications about the naturally occurring interpersonal behavior of these children. First, aggression in the ambiguous circumstance may bring negative reactions from peers who believe that aggression is not warranted in that situation. Lesser (1959) reported that warranted aggression (such as that elicited by the present hostile condition) was actually positively correlated to popularity among children of this age range while unwarranted aggression was linked to social rejection. Aggressive responding in the ambiguous circumstance, if considered unwarranted by peers, may bring about social rejection. Second, it is reasonable to assume that since many naturally occurring peer interactions are filled with ambiguous, or multi-intentioned circumstances the present ambiguous experimental

condition approximates many of the actual situations in which boys find themselves. It is in these situations that aggressive boys are more likely than others to aggress against peers.

Data from the second study show that aggressive and nonaggressive boys differ in their attributions about a peer who ambiguously instigates a negative outcome. Aggressive boys are relatively more likely to attribute a hostile intention to the peer, to expect continued aggression from the peer, and to mistrust the peer. In addition, the second study demonstrates the overwhelming importance of a child's reputation in determining attributions made about his behavior and in determining how others will behave toward him. Children known to be aggressive were more often than others attributed hostile intentions in ambiguous circumstances. They were more often the objects of aggression. Peers expected continued aggression from them and refused to trust them. Unfortunately for these children, the data suggest that the negative consequences associated with this label may actually increase over time, even when differences in the attributions and behavior of aggressive and nonaggressive children have *not* changed.

Based on the present data, a cyclical relationship between attributions and aggressive behavior may be proposed. Given a negative outcome in the context of unclear intentions, an aggressive child may be likely to attribute a hostile intention to a peer who is responsible for this negative event. This attribution may confirm his general image of peers as hostile and may increase the likelihood of his interpreting future behavior by the peer as hostile. Consequently, he may retaliate against the peer with what he feels is justified aggression. Subsequently, the peer, who has become the recipient of a negative outcome, may attribute a hostile intention to the aggressive child. This attribution confirms the peer's view of the child as being inappropriately aggressive in general and increases the peer's likelihood of interpreting future behavior by the aggressive child as being hostile. Consequently, the peer may aggress against the aggressive child, which could start the cycle over again.

Given a series of negative outcomes, which is inevitable, the cycle could turn into a self-perpetuating spiral of increased hostile attributions, aggressive behavior, and social rejection. Indeed, data from the second study showed that the effects of being labeled as aggressive increased with age. Older children suffered more negative consequences of their label than did younger children. Certainly, this label becomes known to the child himself and may serve to incite and justify his continued aggressive behavior as he grows up.

Supportive evidence for the proposed cyclical process has been found in studies in related behavioral areas. Snyder, Tanke, and Berscheid (1977) showed that, in a dyadic interaction, when person A was led to expect (by the experimenter) that person B would be friendly, then A unwittingly behaved toward the naive B in such a way as to cause B to actually become friendly. An implication of this study is that B's behavior will actually confirm A's expectation and cause him to respond accordingly, thus perpetuating the cycle. The durability of the expectations that could be built by such a process was demonstrated in a longitudinal study by Campbell and Yarrow (1961) in which it was inferred that changes in a child's behavior did not always change his social label.

The present investigation has shown that attributions and behavior may interact in a way that could perpetuate their relationship. For children who are developing aggressive styles of social interaction, this relationship could make behavioral change for them very difficult. The present data do not explain how children initially become aggressive, but do suggest a way in which defensive aggressive behavior is maintained and strengthened.

REFERENCE NOTE

1 Dodge, K. A., and Cole, J. D. Behavioral patterns among socially rejected, average, and popular fifth graders. Paper presented at the Biennial Southeastern Conference on Human Development, Atlanta, April 1978.

REFERENCES

Berndt, T. J. The effect of reciprocity in norms on moral judgments and causal attribution. *Child Development,* 1977, **48**, 1322–1330.

Burnstein, E., & Worchel, P. Arbitrariness of frustration and its consequences for aggression in a social situation. *Journal of Personality,* 1962, **30**, 528–540.

Campbell, J. D., & Yarrow, M. R. Perceptual and behavioral correlates of social effectiveness. *Sociometry,* 1961, **24**, 1–20.

Darley, J. M.; Klossen, E. C.; & Zanna, M. P. Intentions and their contexts in the moral judgments of children and adults. *Child Development,* 1978, **49,** 66–74.

Feshbach, S. Aggression. In P. Mussen (Ed.), *Carmichael's manual of child psychology.* New York: Wiley, 1970.

Flavell, J. H. *Cognitive Development.* Englewood Cliffs, N.J.: Prentice-Hall, 1977.

Hartup, W. W. Aggression in childhood: developmental perspectives. *American Psychologist,* 1974, **29**, 336–341.

Heider, F. Perceiving the other person. In R. Tagiuri and L. Petrullo (Eds.), *Person perception and interpersonal behavior.* Stanford, Calif.: Stanford University Press, 1958.

Lesser, G. S. The relationship between various forms of aggression and popularity among lower class children. *Journal of Educational Psychology,* 1959, **50**, 20–25.

Lunney, G. H. Using analysis of variance with a dichotomous dependent variable: an empirical study. *Journal of Educational Measurement,* 1970, **7**, 263.

Mallick, S. K., & McCandless, B. R. A study of catharsis of aggression. *Journal of Personality and Social Psychology,* 1966, **4**, 591–596.

Murray, H. A. The effect of fear upon estimates of maliciousness of other personalities. *Journal of Social Psychology,* 1933, **4**, 310–329.

Pastore, N. The role of arbitrariness in the frustration-aggression hypothesis. *Journal of Abnormal and Social Psychology*, 1952, **47**, 728–731.

Piaget, J. *The moral judgment of the child*. New York: Free Press, 1965.

Rule, B. G. The hostile and instrumental functions of human aggression. In W. W. Hartup and J. deWit (Eds.), *Determinants and origins of aggressive behaviors*. The Hague: Mouton, 1974.

Rule, B. G.; Nesdale, A. R.; & McAra, M. J. Children's reactions to information about the in-

tentions underlying an aggressive act. *Child Development*, 1974, **45**, 794–798.

Shantz, D. W., & Voydanoff, D. A. Situational effects on retaliatory aggression at three age levels. *Child Development*, 1973, **44**, 149–153.

Snyder, M.; Tanke, E. D.; & Berscheid, E. Social perception and interpersonal behavior: on the self-fulfilling nature of social stereotypes. *Journal of Personality and Social Psychology*, 1977, **35**, 656–666.

Zadney, J., & Gerard, H. B. Attributed intentions and informational selectivity. *Journal of Experimental Social Psychology*, 1974, **10**, 34–52.

READING 50

Children's Theories of Intelligence: Consequences for Learning

Carol S. Dweck
Janine Bempechat

Motivational factors can have pronounced and far-reaching effects on children's learning and performance. They determine such critical things as whether children seek or avoid challenges and whether they persist in the face of obstacles—in short, whether children actually pursue and master the skills they value and are capable of mastering. Interestingly, facilitating and debilitating motivational tendencies are often independent of actual ability, as measured either by prior performance on a given task, school grades, or standardized intellectual assessments, such as IQ tests (Crandall, 1969; Dweck & Licht, 1980; Weiner, 1972). This implies that even among the most highly capable students are those who are apt to show impairment in the face of challenge. It also means that among children who are not particularly proficient are those who thrive on challenge. Why might this happen?

In this chapter we examine beliefs about intelligence that are unrelated to measures of intelligence but that appear to promote or interfere with learning. Specifically, we focus on children's theories of intelligence and show how the different theories may dictate children's choice of achievement goals and may determine their success in reaching those goals.

We begin by describing our past research on the patterns of cognition, affect, and behavior that appear to facilitate or impair performance in achievement situations. Following this, we show how these patterns may stem from different theories of intelligence—intelligence as an "entity" or trait that is judged vs. intelligence as a dynamic repertoire of skills that is increased through one's efforts. We suggest that the view of intelligence as a judgeable entity orients children toward competence judgments (toward looking smart, or, "performance" goals), whereas the view of intelligence as a quality that grows orients children toward competence building (toward getting smarter, or, "learning" goals). Further, we suggest it is the former view that renders children vulnerable to debilitation in the face of obstacles, and the latter view that spurs persistence even when children believe themselves to be unskilled at the task at hand. We then describe a series of recent studies that provides evidence that children's beliefs about the nature of intelligence do in fact predict the goals they choose to pursue (learning or performance) and the achievement patterns they display (facilitating or debilitating).

Finally, we explore the educational implications of these findings: What practices might foster the different theories of intelligence, and how might teachers' own theories dictate these practices? For example, what strategies (e.g., types of tasks or feedback regimes) would teachers holding different theories employ to make children feel smart? How might some of these strategies produce effects that are virtually the opposite of what was intended?

We turn now to the patterns that we have repeatedly observed in achievement situations.

PATTERNS OF PERFORMANCE IN ACHIEVEMENT SITUATIONS

In a variety of studies in classrooms and laboratory settings in which children have been asked either to master new academic materials (e.g., certain principles of psychology), learn novel skills, or perform already demonstrated skills, we have repeatedly observed coherent, organized patterns of behavior that come into play and appear to either facilitate or impair performance. These patterns become particularly pronounced in the face of obstacles. That is, under conditions in which difficulty is experienced, some children become incapable of performing effectively, even on problems they had previously solved with relative ease. In contrast, other children bring to bear on the task new levels of concentration and effort. These pronounced individual differences, although experimentally manipulable (Dweck, Davidson, Nelson, & Enna, 1978), emerge reliably in the absence of clear cues (Diener & Dweck, 1978, 1980; Dweck, 1975; Dweck & Reppucci, 1973; Licht & Dweck, 1981). Moreover, it has been a continual source of interest

to us that the tendency to display the facilitating or debilitating pattern in the face of difficulty appears to be virtually independent of the child's level of ability—either as assessed by such standardized measures as IQ or achievement tests or by measures of task performance prior to encountering obstacles.

These affect-cognition-behavior patterns were examined in detail in a series of studies conducted by Diener and Dweck (1978, 1980), and this research serves as the basis for the discussion that follows. Briefly, fifth and sixth graders were trained to perform a three-dimension, two-choice visual discrimination task. The stimuli were systematically varied so that each child's hypothesis-testing strategy could be inferred from his or her choices, classified according to level of sophistication, and tracked for changes in sophistication over all problems (cf. Gholson, Levine, & Phillips, 1972). Children were given a total of twelve problem sets. All children, with training, succeeded in solving the first eight problems (success trials), but failed to reach solution on the next four problems (failure trials). In order to tap salient moment-to-moment cognition and affect, children were instructed, following the seventh problem set, to verbalize aloud as they performed.

Table 1 presents these verbalization results. However, before continuing, two points should be addressed. First, children were divided into two groups prior to the individual sessions on the basis of their responses to an attribution questionnaire (The Intellectual Achievement Responsibility [IAR] scale of Crandall, Katkovsky & Crandall, 1965.) Although these responses are extremely reliable predictors of reactions to failure, as we will see they are likely to be reflective of even more basic, underlying beliefs. Second, we are very sensitive to the issue of confronting children with such difficult tasks, and have perfected procedures involving mastery experiences that ensure that each child leaves the situation feeling

TABLE 1 NUMBER OF HELPLESS AND MASTERY-ORIENTED CHILDREN WITH VERBALIZATIONS IN EACH CATEGORY

Category of verbalizations	Group			
	Helpless	Mastery-oriented	$x^2(df=1)$	p
Ineffectual task strategy	14	2	12.27	.001
Attributions to lack of ability	11	0	13.46	.001
Self-instructions	0	12	15.00	.001
Self-monitoring	0	25	42.86	.001
Statements of positive affect	2	10	6.00	.025
Statements of negative affect	20	1	26.46	.001
Statements of positive prognosis	0	19	27.8	.001
Solution-irrelevant statements	22	0	34.74	.001

Adapted from Diener, C.I., & Dweck, C.S., 1978. An analysis of learned helpnessness: Continuous changes in performance, strategy, and achievement cognitions following failure. *Journal of Personality and Social Psychology*, 1978, *36*, p. 459. Copyright 1978 by the American Psychological Association. Adapted by permission.

his or her performance was highly commendable. Indeed, this mastery procedure is similar to ones that have been shown to have beneficial effects on children's subsequent persistence in the face of failure (e.g., Dweck, 1975).

To return to our data, two distinct patterns emerged. As we will see, one pattern appears to be organized around evaluations of ability and the other appears to be organized around the acquisition of ability. The first, the "learned helpless" pattern (cf. Seligman, Maier & Solomon, 1971) is accompanied by marked debilitation in the face of obstacles. Despite their prior successes, children who displayed this pattern tended to react to difficulties as though they were insurmountable: They very quickly began to interpret their errors as indicative of insufficient ability and as predictive of future failure. That is, they began to make attributions for their errors to a lack of ability (e.g., "I never did have a good 'rememory' ") and for many of them, errors were readily viewed as implying some rather permanent and generalized incompetence (e.g., "I'm not smart enough") (see Weiner, 1972, 1974). This type of self-denigration occurred even though, moments before, their performance had been quite excellent, and even though they had not really attempted very much in the way of alternative strategies or increased effort.

Nevertheless, in line with their attributions to lack of ability, these children showed increased impairment of their problem-solving strategies, increased negative affect, and negative prognosis for subsequent outcomes. Whereas by the end of training, all children were using effective strategies and a sizable proportion were using the top level strategy employed by children their age, by the fourth trial 60 to 70% had lapsed into stereotypical or perseverative choice patterns, ones that could never yield solution. Furthermore, when children were asked whether they thought they could now solve one of the problems they had solved before if it were to be readministered, 100% of the "mastery-oriented" children replied in the affirmative, whereas only 65% of the helpless children did so.

It is also interesting to note the striking differences between the helpless children and their mastery-oriented counterparts in recall for success and failure. As depicted in Table 2, helpless children recalled having successfully solved significantly fewer problems and having failed to solve significantly more problems than the mastery-oriented children. In short, helpless children rapidly question their ability in the face of obstacles, perceiving past successes to be few and irrelevant, and perceive future effort to be futile.

TABLE 2 RECALL OF SUCCESSES AND FAILURES BY HELPLESS AND MASTERY-ORIENTED CHILDREN

Type of problem and actual number	Helpless	Mastery-oriented	p Value of difference
Success (=8)	5.14	7.51	p<.01
Failure (=4)	6.14	3.71	p<.01

The second pattern, called "mastery-oriented," is characterized by intensified effort in the face of difficulty. Children who displayed this pattern seemed to focus at once on how to overcome their errors. Indeed, they did not tend to leap to or even seek attributions for failure, and much of their behavior indicated that they did not really consider themselves to be failing. Specifically, their verbalizations consisted primarily of self-instructions and self-monitoring designed to aid performance (e.g., "OK, now I really need to concentrate," "I should slow down and try and figure this out"). In addition, these "mastery-oriented" children maintained positive affect and a positive prognosis about task outcomes. Some expressed what appeared to verge on delight at the chance to confront a challenge or gain new skills. Furthermore, many children not only maintained but improved their problem-solving strategies over the "failure" trials: They taught themselves new and more sophisticated strategies in their attempt to master the task. In sharp contrast to the helpless children, who were no longer using the top level strategy by the end of the failure trials, an additional 25% of the mastery-oriented children had begun to use this strategy by the end of these trials. Interestingly, some proportion of the mastery-oriented children lapsed temporarily into ineffective patterns, but then climbed out and began to strategize anew. In short, these children appeared to view the skill required by the task as one that they could acquire by applying themselves. Moreover, they appeared to give themselves the time and the leeway to do so.

Thus, although both groups of children received identical problems and feedback, the evidence suggests that they were structuring the situation quite differently—either as a *performance* situation that involved evaluations of competence, a display or demonstration of that competence, or as a *learning* situation that provided an opportunity to increase competence.

What might underlie these different ways of structuring achievement situations? These different views imply an emphasis on very different conceptions of competence: competence as a stable, general, "judgeable" entity or as a repertoire of dynamic, acquirable skills. And, indeed, our current research is suggesting that children's conceptions of intellectual competence—their personal theories of intelligence, play an important role in these achievement patterns.

CHILDREN'S THEORIES OF INTELLIGENCE

Our research has indicated that children hold two functional or operating theories of intelligence. The one they tend to emphasize is the one that appears to guide their behavior in novel achievement settings. We propose that these implicit theories are beliefs around which achievement behavior, affect, and cognitions are organized.

The first theory, which we have called an "entity" theory, involves the belief that intelligence is a rather stable, global trait. Children favoring this theory tend to subscribe to the idea that they possess a specific, fixed amount of intelligence, that this intelligence is displayed through performance, and that the outcomes or judgments indicate whether they are or are not intelligent. The second theory, which we call an "instrumental-incremental" theory, involves the belief that intelligence consists of an ever-expanding repertoire of skills and knowledge, one that is increased through one's own instrumental behavior. By middle to late grade school, children understand aspects of both theories, but tend to focus on one in thinking about intelligence. (For related observations see Harari & Covington, 1981; Marshall, Weinstein, Middlestadt, & Brattesani, 1980; Surber, 1982. For treatment of conceptions of mind and intelligence from a more "cognitive" point of view see Goodnow, 1980; Sternberg, Conway, Ketron, & Bernstein, 1981; Wellman, 1981.) That is, although instrumental theorists realize that individuals may differ in the rate at which they acquire skills, they focus on the idea that anyone can become smarter (more skillful and more knowledgeable) by investing effort. Entity theorists also realize that virtually everyone can increase their skills or knowledge, but they do not believe that people can become smarter. It is important to note that some children may act in accordance with different theories in different skill areas (e.g., physical vs. intellectual skills). In addition, situational factors may create strong tendencies to adopt one theory over the other. For example, a critical exam may make entity considerations highly salient. Yet, in the absence of strong cues, we find striking individual differences in which theory children tend to endorse and use as a guide for their behavior (M. Bandura & Dweck, 1981).

We have assessed these differences by presenting children with several pairs of contrasting notions about the meaning of smartness. Each pair of ideas pits an essential component of the entity view against an essential component of the incremental view of intelligence. The extent to which children endorse one of the two perspectives is taken to indicate their favored theory of intelligence. For example, inherent in the entity view is the belief that intelligence is essentially static, whereas the incremental theory implies that intelligence can be increased by one's own actions. Thus, one item poses the choice: "You can learn new

things, but how smart you are stays pretty much the same" vs. "Smartness is something you can increase as much as you want to."

Essentially, then, children with an entity theory are those who tend to view intelligence as an attribute they possess that is relatively global and stable, that can be judged as adequate or inadequate, and that is both limited and limiting. In contrast, children with an incremental theory tend to view intelligence as something they produce—something with great potential to be increased through their efforts.[1]

Predictions

When one considers the differences inherent in the two definitions of intelligence, one is led to predict that entity and incremental theorists would adopt different goals in achievement situations. That is, the tendency to conceive of intelligence as a judgeable entity would seem likely to incline one towards seeking positive judgments and/or avoiding negative ones, toward goals that involve "looking smart"—*performance* goals. In contrast, the tendency to conceive of intelligence as a body of skills that grows through one's efforts would seem likely to incline one toward seeking to increase one's skills, toward the goal of "becoming smarter"—*learning* goals (see Dweck & Elliott, 1983 and Nicholls, 1981 for an extensive discussion of achievement goals).

It is important to note that these various goals need not be mutually exclusive and, indeed, may often be held simultaneously. Some

---

[1]An intriguing issue, and one we are investigating, concerns the extent to which entity and incremental theories may serve as the basis for conceptualizing other major domains. That is, are these two theories alternative ways of viewing a variety of personal attributes, not simply intelligence? Indeed, most of the attributes that are generally considered to constitute basic qualities of the "self" are amenable to these alternative conceptualizations (e.g., artistic or physical competence, physical appearance, or morality). That is, they may be seen as rather fixed traits that can be judged to be adequate or inadequate or as dynamic qualities that can be cultivated by actions or increased through effort.

situations allow one both to learn and to perform well. Therefore, we are not suggesting that entity theorists do not wish to develop skills or increase their knowledge, or that incremental theorists are always unconcerned with global judgments that others might make. We are proposing, however, that the two theories of intelligence create a differential likelihood of adopting one goal over others, particularly when they come into conflict. And they do, because the same tasks that maximize learning are often poor tasks for looking smart and vice versa. Tasks most suitable for learning are often ones that are difficult, involve errors, confusion, or revelations of ignorance, and require a lengthy presolution period. In contrast, tasks that are often best-suited for performance goals are ones that appear to be difficult or are difficult for others, but are relatively easy for the individual—tasks that yield rapid solutions with little effort, or at least tasks on which one is fairly certain one can outperform others.

Thus, entity theorists should adopt goals that tend to involve positive judgments of their intelligence or avoid negative judgments of their intelligence. If they feel confident of their ability, this should lead them to aim toward the former and, under these conditions, to display mastery-oriented behavior. Low confidence should make them aim toward the latter, to attempt to conceal their perceived lack of ability from an evaluator, and to be vulnerable to the helpless pattern in the face of failure. In contrast, incremental theorists should be more likely to choose goals that involve learning. Unlike entity theorists, who focus on the documentation of competence, children with an incremental view should focus on the acquisition of competence. Because within a learning framework, encountering obstacles does not signify lack of ability, these children should display the mastery-oriented pattern in the pursuit of their goals.

Therefore, we would actually predict *two* facilitating (mastery-oriented) patterns: a performance-oriented one and a learning-oriented one. When might these two types of mastery-oriented children differ? One would predict this to occur when the different goals come into conflict, that is, when a choice must be made between learning and performing. For example, if the acquisition of some valued skill or knowledge involved a likely display of errors or confusion, mastery-oriented entity theorists might be more likely than incrementalists to sacrifice that opportunity, particularly if a less "risky" option were available. Indeed, our findings suggest that this distinction between the two types of mastery-orientation is in fact a useful one.

In the following section, we present research evidence for the hypothesis that children's theories of intelligence predict their choice of achievement goals, and that their achievement goals predict their achievement patterns.

Research Evidence

Table 3 both summarizes the foregoing discussion and provides the structure within which we will place our research findings. Let us look first at the second column, labeled "performance goal expectancy." This refers to the child's subjective probability of obtaining positive and avoiding negative competence judgments, and, in conjunction with the third column "goal choice" is intended to represent the idea that this estimate will be a determining factor in goal choice within an entity theory, but not within an incremental theory.

We assume that performance goal expectancies are the result of a series of judgments on the part of the child. For example, the child may make some assessment of his or her present skill or aptitude, may consider this in relation to such factors as the perceived task requirements, may use this information to predict some level of performance, may then ask whether the predicted performance will reach his or her standards, and so on (see Dweck & Elliott, 1983). Although we will not

TABLE 3   THEORIES OF INTELLIGENCE, CHOICE OF ACHIEVEMENT GOALS, AND TYPE OF ACHIEVEMENT PATTERN

Theory of intelligence	Performance goal expectancy	Achievement goal choice	Achievement pattern
		Performance goals:	
Entity theory	High	→ Obtaining a favorable competence judgment	→ Mastery-oriented
	Low	→ Avoiding a negative competence judgment	→ Helpless
		Learning goal:	
Incremental theory	High	→ Increasing competence	→ Mastery oriented
	Low	→	

Note: See Dweck & Elliott (1983) for a more complete discussion of the distinction between the two performance goals, and of the conditions under which the goal of avoiding a negative judgment would spur approach vs avoidance behavior.

scrutinize this process, it is important to note that actual competence, however defined, does not necessarily translate directly into performance goal expectancies. In fact, for girls, a *negative* relationship is sometimes found between measures of actual skill and measures of expectancies. In the face of unfamiliar tasks, the more able girls may be the ones who are most likely to underestimate their skills, overestimate task difficulty, and adopt excessively high performance standards (see Crandall, 1969; Dweck, Goetz & Strauss, 1980; Frieze, Fisher, Hanusa, McHugh, & Valle, 1978; Lenney, 1977; Montanelli & Hill, 1969; McMahan, 1972; Nicholls, 1975; Parsons, 1982; Small, Nakamura & Ruble, 1973; Stipek & Hoffman, 1980).

To continue, the child's perceptions of present competence and his or her performance expectancies should figure very differently in the two types of theories and goals. As noted, we propose these factors to play a critical role in determining task choice and achievement pattern within the context of an entity theory. That is, high expectancies will predict choice of tasks that will enable the child to look smart and will predict a mastery-oriented pattern in the face of obstacles. Low expectancies will predict choice of tasks that will allow the child to avoid looking incompetent (if this choice is provided), and will predict debilitation in the face of obstacles. In either case, children with entity theories will tend to avoid

difficult learning tasks that involve the risk of appearing incompetent.

However, when children have an incremental theory and are oriented toward learning goals, perceived skill and performance expectancy should play a less important role. For these children, such factors do not preclude the possibility of satisfactory gains. That is, even what might be considered poor performance by normative standards may well involve some noteworthy skill acquisition. Although we are not suggesting that these children would tend to embark on unrealistic ventures, we do predict that those who favor an incremental theory and learning goals would, regardless of perceived skill, tend to choose challenging tasks that maximize acquisition and to pursue them in a mastery-oriented manner.

In a study by Bandura and Dweck (1981), entity and incremental theorists were identified (on the basis of their responses to the contrasting notions of ability described earlier) and were presented with stimulus discrimination problems similar to those used in the Diener and Dweck research. Prior to working on the problems, however, they were asked a series of questions relating to their performance expectancies and their goals and concerns in the situation, as well as to how they would react to different outcomes. Thus, although all children were confronted with "objectively" the same situation, entity and incremental theorists were expected to structure the situation in terms of different goals.

As predicted, there were clear differences in their goal choices. Children were presented with the stem "I hope these problems are...," and were given learning versus performance goals to rank order. In line with our analysis, the learning option ("hard, new, and different so I can try to learn from them") was ranked significantly higher by the incremental theorists (regardless of performance expectancies) than by the entity theorists. In order to assess further their differing goals in the situation, six different achievement goals or concerns were described. Entity and incremental theorists again differed, as predicted, in the degree to which they endorsed four of the six goals. Specifically, entity theorists showed significantly more concern than incremental theorists with "not making mistakes," as well as with "how smart a teacher (or adult) who saw your work thinks you are." In contrast, incremental theorists were significantly more likely to focus on "how much you feel you'll learn from the problems," and to be concerned that "the problems might be too easy for me." In short, there appears to be a difference between entity and incremental theorists in the achievement goals they emphasize: Incremental theorists are more concerned than entity theorists with meeting challenges and increasing competence (becoming smarter) as opposed to obtaining positive judgments of competence and avoiding negative ones (looking smart). This relationship between children's theories of intelligence and their goals and concerns has been replicated with a large sample of Junior High School children as well.

This differential focus on learning versus evaluation is further illustrated by differences in reported affect (Bandura & Dweck, 1981). For example, children were asked:

> Now think about how you'd feel if you solved these problems right away without having to try much at all. Here are some of the ways other kids

say they'd feel if the problems were real easy for them. Some kids say they'd feel kind of proud they solved them so fast, some say they'd feel relieved that the problems weren't too hard, some say they'd feel disappointed that they weren't harder, and others say they'd probably feel bored. Think about how you'd feel if the problems were easy for you.

Incremental theorists reported significantly more often than entity theorists that they would be *disappointed* or *bored* as opposed to *relieved* or *proud* if the problems were easy and required little effort. The different emphases of the two types of theorists is perhaps most strikingly illustrated by their responses to the following question about the problems they were about to attempt:

> Kids say different things about what would make them feel smartest. Some kids say they'd feel smartest if these problems were easy for them but hard for other kids. Some kids say they'd feel smartest if they worked hard on the problems and make a lot of mistakes, but learned something. Which thing would make you feel smartest?

Some children tended to find only one of the options plausible—but they differed in which one it happened to be. Incremental theorists were more likely than the entity theorists to feel smartest when they confront a challenging task and learn something new. Children with an entity view feel smartest when the task allows them to appear more competent than others. Or, considering these free responses from another study (with E. Elliott) in which we asked children:

> *Question:* Sometimes kids feel smart in school, sometimes not. When do you feel smart?
>
> *Incremental:* When I don't know how to do it and it's pretty hard and I figure it out without anybody telling me.
>
> When I'm doing school work because I want to learn how to get smart.
>
> When I'm reading a hard book.

Entity: When I don't do mistakes.

When I turn in my papers first.

When I get easy work.

As can be seen, quite disparate, even opposite, experiences appear to make entity and incremental theorists feel smart.

The proposed conceptualization is also receiving support from our experimental work relating achievement goals to the achievement patterns children display. Using the Deiner and Dweck paradigm, Elliott and Dweck (1981) differentially oriented children toward the achievement goals of increasing competence vs obtaining positive judgments of competence or avoiding negative judgments of competence by (1) highlighting either the learning or the performance aspects of the situation (i.e., value of the skill vs. degree of external evaluation), and by (2) simultaneously manipulating children's confidence of performing well (via feedback on a pretest said to be predictive of future performance). Children's goal choices (learning vs performance) and task performance were then assessed.

For all children, the "performance" task was presented basically in this manner:

In this box we have problems of different levels. Some are hard, some are easier. If you pick this box, although you won't learn new things, it will really show me what kids can do. [Children were also given a choice of difficulty levels: moderately easy, moderate, or moderately difficult].

The "learning" task was depicted as follows:

If you pick the task in this box you'll probably learn a lot of new things. But you'll probably make a bunch of mistakes, get a little confused, maybe feel a little dumb at times—but eventually you'll learn some useful things.

Following their task choices, children were all given the same series of discrimination problems to solve. (For those who chose perfor-

mance tasks, the task actually administeredwas described as being of moderate difficulty and as being consonant with their choice. So that this could be done, children had been asked to make two selections in choosing among the three difficulty levels. Thus, moderately difficult tasks always represented either one of their actual choices or the average of their two choices.) They were requested to verbalize as they worked on the problems; strategies and verbalizations were monitored and scored as in the Diener and Dweck research.

The results showed the predicted relationships. When children were oriented toward skill acquisition, their "performance" expectancy was largely irrelevant: They adopted the learning goal and displayed a mastery-oriented pattern. That is, children in this condition were more concerned with acquiring new skills than with exhibiting or concealing their present ones. In contrast, when children were oriented toward evaluation, the goal they adopted (seeking positive judgments or avoiding negative ones) and the achievement pattern they displayed (mastery-oriented or helpless) were highly dependent on their expectation of performing well or poorly. Indeed, the great majority of children in the evaluation-oriented condition sacrificed altogether the opportunity for new learning that involved a display of errors or confusion. Instead, depending on their expectancy, they selected performance tasks that would allow them to obtain judgments of competence (by succeeding on difficult tasks) or to avoid judgments of incompetence (by succeeding on easier tasks).

What was most striking was the degree to which the manipulations created the entire constellation of performance, cognition, and affect characteristic of the naturally occurring achievement patterns. For example, children who were given an evaluation orientation and a low performance expectancy showed the same strategy deterioration, negative ability attributions, and negative affect that characterized the helpless children in our earlier studies (Diener & Dweck, 1978; 1980).

We have just completed a study (Dweck, Tenney, & Dinces, 1982) in which children's theories of intelligence were manipulated by means of a reading passage about intelligence (embedded in a series of passages), in which the accomplishments of notable individuals (Albert Einstein, Helen Keller, and the child Rubik's Cube champion) were presented in either an entity or incremental context. The structure, content, tone, and interest value of the two passages were highly similar, except that they presented and illustrated different definitions of smartness. Great care was taken to avoid attaching any goals to the theories, that is, to avoid any mention or implication of learning vs performance goals. Yet, when the children were asked, as a separate task, to select the type of problems they wished to work on when the experimenter returned, our preliminary analyses suggest that their choices reflected the theory to which they had been exposed.

In summary, our research to date has provided encouraging support for the notion that children's implicit theories of intelligence influence the goals they seek to pursue and the persistence they display in pursuit of those goals. If it is true that children's theories play a major role in achievement strivings, it becomes important to examine the conditions that foster the different conceptions of intelligence. For example, how do teachers convey what it means to be smart? How might teachers' own theories of intelligence lead to differential teaching and feedback practices?

Practices that May Foster Different Theories of Intelligence

How do children get messages about the meaning of smartness? We propose that teachers themselves have implicit theories of intelligence, and that these theories may guide their practices, such as feedback techniques or selection and assignment of tasks.

We assume that most teachers would wish their students to feel intelligent (or not feel unintelligent) and to learn effectively. In the discussion that follows, we examine how entity and incremental perspectives might dictate very different teaching regimes designed to accomplish these aims—how different teaching strategies flow "intuitively" from the two views. We also use available research evidence to judge what consequences these practices actually have for children's beliefs about their abilities, and thus whether the practices would in fact foster what teachers intend them to foster.

Teachers who define intelligence as a quality or trait that a child possesses are likely to categorize students, for example, as smart, average, or not smart. They may nonetheless wish all children to feel smart, to have confidence in their abilities. Within this "entity" orientation, what would teachers do to accomplish this end? A likely strategy would be to fill children with success and shield them from errors. For example, such teachers might give each child tasks that could be performed with a minimum of struggle and confusion resulting in a maximum of praise. The implicit belief here would be that the accumulation of successes untarnished by failures would lead children to conclude they are intelligent. This inference would then arm them against debilitation when setbacks might occur.

Yet it is precisely this regime of programmed success that has been shown to be ineffective in promoting persistence, and to foster, if anything, greater debilitation in the face of obstacles (Dweck, 1975). In such an environment, or in other environments that do not protect them, these children would be likely to interpret setbacks as failure. Some children (the "less bright" ones) may even begin to label themselves as failures simply because they are consistently assigned easy work, may be praised for work that does not seem particularly noteworthy (Meyer, Bachman, Biermann, Hempelmann, Ploger, & Spiller, 1979), or may even receive praise for intellectually-irrelevant aspects of their work when the intellectual content is questionable (cf. Dweck, Davidson, Nelson, & Enna, 1978; Eisenberger, Kaplan, & Singer, 1974; Paris & Cairns, 1972). It may also be the case that when these children do encounter obstacles or commit errors, teachers are apt to gloss over the errors or supply the answer in a well-meant attempt to prevent discomfort. However, this means that the teacher fails to convey to the children that they can overcome obstacles, and fails to model the strategies for doing so (see Bandura, 1980; Brophy & Good, 1974).

What about the "smart" children—i.e., the ones who perform the tasks quickly and easily, who finish first? These are the very conditions under which entity theorists say they feel smartest; however, as our research has suggested, to the extent that children become dependent on such conditions in order to feel smart, this regime may lead them to avoid challenges and may increase susceptibility to self-doubts and impaired performance when obstacles are encountered. Thus, quite contrary to teacher's intentions, practices designed to make children feel smart within an entity framework may render children more vulnerable to maladaptive patterns.

In contrast, teachers who view a child's intelligence as an ever-growing quality that is increased through the child's own efforts would likely provide for all children challenging, long-term tasks that require planning and persistence in search of resolution. Children may not always be sure exactly where they are, where they are going, or when they will get there, but coping with uncertainly becomes intriguing rather than threatening, a direct source of competence feelings rather than self-doubt. These, "incremental," teachers would be available as models and guides in the process of learning, rather than judges of the products of performance (see Bruner, 1961, 1965; Covington, 1980; Nicholls, 1981). In fact, it might be the

less proficient children who would receive the most instruction in how to strategize in the face of obstacles. Research evidence suggests that when errors are capitalized upon as vehicles for teaching children how to deal with failure, they tend to react to difficulty with renewed effort (Andrews & Debus, 1978; Chapin & Dyck, 1976; Dweck, 1975). Indeed, "incremental" teachers might show a reverse teacher expectancy effect, with the less proficient children receiving more attention and showing greater gains [Brophy and Good (1974) report that some teachers show a facilitating pattern of interaction (more explanations, encouragement, etc.) with "brighter" children and some with "less bright" children. It would be most interesting to determine whether these teachers differed in their theories of intelligence].[2]

In sum, teachers' beliefs about children's intelligence may lead them to adopt different teaching practices. We have suggested that for teachers with an entity perspective, the consequences of their practices may be quite discrepant with the intended consequences. For as long as we can remember it has been fashionable to criticize educators for undermining children's confidence in their abilities by exposing them to failures, criticism, negative social comparison and the like. And, it is clear that such practices often warrant criticism. However, we are led to the hypothesis that seemingly positive experiences may also have deleterious effects—that certain practices designed to make children feel smart in the short run may prevent them from becoming smarter in the long run.

Entity vs. Incremental Theory: What is Adaptive?

Although our research findings and the earlier discussion may give the impression that it is good to have an incremental orientation and

---

[2]Indeed, a series of studies has been designed to examine how teachers' theories might influence their practices, and whether these practices (when programmed in an experimental situation) do in fact foster the predicted beliefs and behavior in children.

bad to have an entity orientation, it is clear that what is good or bad (i.e., adaptive, maladaptive) depends very much on the environment in which the child is asked to perform. Indeed, many grade school classrooms may foster and favor entity theories. In such an "entity" environment, where the emphasis is on performance and judgment, the child may be provided with little other justification for engaging in school tasks. Lessons are to be learned not for their own value or interest, but as a means of gaining the teacher's approval of one's work and, ultimately, oneself. An incremental child may indeed not be as "good" a child in such an environment. Lacking a more profound justification for learning, and being less interested in attaining positive judgments than in acquiring skills, he or she may put little effort into school tasks and may come to be viewed as an "underachiever." Under such circumstances, it may be considered to be more adaptive to have an entity orientation. That is, the best way to be successful in such an environment—the best way to continually obtain a teacher's positive judgment—may be not to question the validity of assignments and to perform well when asked to do so.

If this type of environment were typical of the ones children would confront in the future, then perhaps in some ways an entity theory might represent good training for that future. However, in many cases, this orientation may be adaptive only in the short run, and may render a child less suited for later pursuits, particularly ones that call for independent choice, long-term planning, perseverance, and the maintenence of confidence in the face of unclear outcomes or actual setbacks. Children with entity views will be at a sharp disadvantage when faced with these circumstances. Indeed, as the school environment changes to include more difficult courses and to afford a greater degree of latitude in course choice, one would expect differential challenge-seeking from entity and incremental theorists. Similar-

ly, when career choices are perceived to differ in the degree of risk for failures or negative evaluation, one would predict differential choice as a function of theory. An incremental orientation, it would seem, would lead children to generate a larger set of options, to make decisions based on interests or values, not fear of failure, and to pursue the chosen goal with greater vigor.

ACKNOWLEDGMENT

The authors acknowledge the support of Grant BNS 79-14252 from the National Science Foundation, Grant MH 31667 from the National Institute of Mental Health, and a Research Scientist Development Award from the National Institute of Mental Health to the first author, as well as Doctoral Fellowships 453-81-0178 and 452-82-8178 from the Social Sciences and Humanities Research Council of Canada to the second author.

REFERENCES

Andrews, G. R., & Debus, R. L. Persistence and the causal perception of failure: Modifying cognitive attributions. *Journal of Educational Psychology,* 1978, *70,* 154–166.

Bandura, A. The self and mechanisms of agency. In J. Suls (Ed.), *Social psychological perspectives on the self.* Hillsdale, N.J.: Lawrence Eribaum Associates, 1980.

Bandura, M., & Dweck, C. S. *Children's theories of intelligence as predictors of achievement goals.* Unpublished manuscript, Harvard University, 1981.

Brophy, J. E., & Good, T. *Teacher-student relationships: Causes and consequences.* New York: Holt, Rinehart & Winston, 1974.

Bruner, J. S. The act of discovery. *Harvard Educational Review,* 1961, *31,* 21–32.

Bruner, J. S. The growth of mind. *American Psychologist,* 1965, *20,* 1007–1017.

Chapin, M., & Dyck, D. G. Persistence in children's reading behavior as a function of a length and attribution retraining. *Journal of Abnormal Psychology,* 1976, *85,* 511–515.

Covington, M. V. Strategic thinking and fear of failure. Chapter for *NIE-LRDC Proceedings,* October 1980.

Crandall, V. C. Sex differences in expectancy of intellectual and academic reinforcement. In C. P. Smith (Ed.), *Achievement-related motives in children,* New York: Russell Sage, 1969.

Crandall, V. C., Katkovsky, W., & Crandall, V. J. Children's beliefs in their own control of reinforcements in intellectual-academic situations. *Child Development,* 1965, *36,* 91–109.

Diener, C. I., & Dweck, C. S. An analysis of learned helplessness: Continuous changes in performance, strategy, and achievement cognitions following failure. *Journal of Personality and Social Psychology,* 1978, *36,* 451–462.

Diener, C. I., & Dweck, C. S. An analysis of learned helplessness: II. The processing of success. *Journal of Personality and Social Psychology,* 1980, *39,* 940–952.

Dweck, C. S. The role of expectations and attributions in the alleviation of learned helplessness. *Journal of Personality and Social Psychology,* 1975, *31,* 674–685.

Dweck, C. S., Davidson, W., Nelson, S., & Enna, B. Sex differences in learned helplessness: II. The contingencies of evaluative feedback in the classroom and III. An experimental analysis. *Developmental Psychology,* 1978, *14,* 268–276.

Dweck, C. S., & Elliott, E. S. Achievement motivation. In P. Mussen (gen. Ed.), and E. M. Hetherington (vol. Ed.), *Carmichael's manual of child psychology: Social and personality development.* New York: Wiley, 1983.

Dweck, C. S., Goetz, T. E., & Strauss, N. L. Sex differences in learned helplessness: IV. An experimental and naturalistic study of failure generalization and its mediators. *Journal of Personality and Social Psychology,* 1980, *38,* 441–452.

Dweck, C. S., & Licht, B. G. Learned helplessness and intellectual achievement. In J. Garber & M. E. P. Seligman (Eds.), *Human helplessness: Theory and applications.* New York: Academic Press, 1980.

Dweck, C. S., & Reppucci, N. D. Learned helplessness and reinforcement responsibility in children. *Journal of Personality and Social Psychology,* 1973, *25,* 109–116.

Dweck, C. S., Tenney, Y., & Dinces, N. Unpublished data, Harvard University, 1982.

Eisenberger, R., Kaplan, R. M., & Singer, R. D. Decremental and nondecremental effects of noncontingent social approval. *Journal of Personality and Social Psychology,* 1974, *30,* 716–722.

Elliott, E. S., & Dweck, C. S. *Children's achievement goals as determinants of learned helpless and mastery-oriented achievement patterns: An experimental analysis.* Unpublished manuscript, Harvard University, 1981.

Frieze, I. H., Fisher, J., Hanusa, B., McHugh, M. C., & Valle, V. A. Attributions of the causes of success and failure as internal and external barriers to achievement in women. In J. Sherman & F. Denmark (Eds.), *Psychology of women: Future directions for research.* New York: Psychological Dimensions, 1978.

Gholson, B., Levine, M., & Phillips, S. Hypotheses, strategies, and stereotypes in discrimination learning. *Journal of Experimental Child Psychology.* 1972, *13,* 423–446.

Goodnow, J. J. Concepts of intelligence and its development. In N. Warren (Ed.), *Studies in cross-cultural psychology,* Vol. 2, London: Pergamon, 1980.

Harari, O., & Covington, M. V. Reactions to achievement behavior from a teacher and student perspective: A developmental analysis. *American Educational Research Journal,* 1981, *18,* 15–28.

Lenney, E. Women's self confidence in achievement settings. *Psychological Bulletin,* 1977, *84,* 1–13.

Licht, B. G., & Dweck, C. S. *Determinants of academic achievement: The interaction of children's achievement orientations with skill area.* Manuscript submitted for publication, 1981.

Marshall, H. H., Weinstein, R. S., Middlestadt, S. & Brattesani, K. A. *"Everyone's smart in our class." Relationship between classroom characteristics and perceived differential teacher treatment.* Paper presented at the American Educational Research Association, Boston, April 1980.

McMahan, I. D. *Sex differences in expectancy of success as a function of task.* Paper presented at The Eastern Psychological Association, Boston, April 1972.

Meyer, W., Bachmann, M., Biermann, U., Hempelmann, M., Plöger, F., & Spiller, H. *The informational value of evaluative behavior: Influences of praise and blame on perceptions of ability.* Unpublished manuscript, University of Bielefeld, 1979.

Montanelli, D. S., & Hill, K. T. Children's achievement expectations as a function of two consecutive, reinforcement experiences, sex of subject, and sex of experimenter. *Journal of Personality and Social Psychology,* 1969, *13,* 115–128.

Nicholls, J. G. Causal attributions and other achievement related cognitions. Effects of task outcome, attainment value, and sex. *Journal of Personality and Social Psychology,* 1975, *31,* 379–389.

Nicholls, J. G. Quality and equality in intellectual development. *American Psychologist,* 1979, *34,* 1071–1084.

Nicholls, J. G. *Striving to demonstrate and develop ability: A theory of achievement motivation.* Unpublished manuscript, Purdue University, 1981.

Paris, S. G., & Cairns, R. B. An experimental and ethological analysis of social reinforcement with retarded children. *Child Development,* 1972, *43,* 717–729.

Parsons, J. E. Expectancies, values, and academic behaviors. In J. T. Spence (Ed.), *Assessing achievement.* San Francisco: W. H. Freeman, 1982.

Seligman, M. E. P., Maier, S. F., & Solomon, R. L. Unpredictable and uncontrollable aversive

events. In F. R. Brush (Ed.), *Aversive conditioning and learning.* New York: Academic Press, 1971.

Small, A., Nakamura, C. Y., & Ruble, D. N. *Sex differences in children's outer directedness and self-perceptions in a problem-solving situation.* Unpublished manuscript, University of California at Los Angeles, 1973.

Sternberg, R., Conway, B. E., Ketron, J. L., & Bernstein, M. People's conceptions of intelligence. *Journal of Personality and Social Psychology,* 1981, *41,* 37–55.

Stipek, D. J., & Hoffman, J. M. Children's achievement-related expectancies as a function of academic performance histories and sex. *Journal of Educational Psychology,* 1980, *72,* 861–865.

Surber, C. F. The development of achievement-related judgment processes. In J. Nicholls (Ed.), *The development of achievement motivation.* Greenwich, Conn.: JAI Press, 1982.

Weiner, B. (Ed.). *Theories of motivation: From mechanism to cognition.* Chicago: Markham, 1972.

Weiner, B. (Ed.). *Achievement motivation and attribution theory.* Morristown, N.J.: General Learning Corporation, 1974.

Wellmann, H. M. The child's theory of mind: The development of conceptions of cognition. In S. R. Yussen (Ed.), *The growth of insight in the child.* New York: Academic Press, 1981.

READING 51

Mathematics Achievement of Chinese, Japanese, and American Children

Harold W. Stevenson
Shin-Ying Lee
James W. Stigler

Poor scholastic performance by American children has focused attention on education, especially in mathematics and science. Funds for research on how to improve teaching have been allocated and commissions formed, such as a National Research Council committee exploring a research agenda for precollege education in mathematics, science, and technology. Recommendations to be made by this committee and others that have preceded it concentrate on the nation's secondary schools. The wisdom of this emphasis is questionable. Results emerging from a large cross-national study of elementary school children suggest that Americans should not focus solely on improving the performance of high school students. The problems arise earlier. American children appear to lag behind children in other countries in reading and mathematics as early as kindergarten and continue to perform less effectively during the years of elementary school. When differences in achievement arise so early in the child's formal education, more must be involved than inadequate formal educational practices. Improving secondary education is an important goal, but concentrating remedial efforts on secondary schools may come too late in the academic careers of most students to be effective.

Our research deals with the scholastic achievement of American, Chinese, and Japanese children in kindergarten and grades 1 and 5. Children were given achievement tests and a battery of cognitive tasks. The children and their mothers and teachers were interviewed, and observations were made in the children's classrooms. These procedures have yielded an enormous array of information (1–5). In this article, we focus on the discussion of achievement in mathematics and factors that may contribute to the poor performance of American children in that area.

ACHIEVEMENT TESTS

Comparative studies of children's scholastic achievement are hindered by the lack of culturally fair, interesting, and psychometrically sound tests and research materials. It was necessary to construct material in order to test children in Taiwan, Japan, and the United States for our study. A team of bilingual researchers from each culture constructed tests and other research instruments with the aim of eliminating as much as possible any cultural bias (1, 2).

Mathematics tests were based on the content of the textbooks used in the three cities in which we conducted our research. Analyses were made of each mathematical construct and

operation and of the time that it was introduced in the textbook. The test for kindergarten children contained items assessing basic concepts and operations included in the curricula from kindergarten through the third grade. The mathematics test constructed for elementary school children contained 70 items derived from concepts and skills appearing in the mathematics curricula through grade 6. Some items required only computation, and others required application of mathematical principles to story problems.

Reading tests were based on analyses of the words, grammatical structures, and story content of the readers used in the three cities. There were separate tests for kindergarten and for elementary school children. The kindergarten test tapped letter and word recognition and contained comprehension items of gradually increasing difficulty. The reading test for grades 1 through 6 consisted of three parts: sight reading of vocabulary, reading of meaningful text, and comprehension of text.

Tests were constructed for administration to one child at a time. The tests were not timed. The testing procedure required that the child continue in the test to the point where over a quarter of the items at a grade level were failed. The mathematics tests and the kindergarten reading test were given 6 months after the beginning of the school year. Reading tests were given 2 months earlier in grades 1 and 5. Carefully written instructions in all three languages and personal contact with the supervisors of the examiners helped produce testing procedures that were as comparable as possible in the three cities (7).

SELECTING THE CHILDREN

Children in only one city in each country were studied. In the United States, we selected children in the Minneapolis metropolitan area. Several factors led to this choice, the most important being that the residents of this area tend to come from native-born, English-speaking, economically sound families. Few are from a minority background. These factors, we assumed, would provide an advantageous cultural, economic, and linguistic environment for learning in school. If problems were found in Minneapolis, we assumed they would be compounded in other American cities where a greater proportion of the children speak English as a second language, come from economically disadvantaged homes, and have parents whose cultural backgrounds diverge from the typically middleclass milieu to which American elementary school curricula generally are addressed.

The Japanese city that we chose as being most comparable to Minneapolis was Sendai, which is located in the Tohoku region several hundred miles northeast of Tokyo. It, too, is a large, economically successful city, with little heavy industry and with an economic and cultural status in Japan similar to that of Minneapolis in the United States. Taipei was the Chinese city in which it was most feasible for us to conduct our research, in terms of language, size, colleagues, and other factors.

Ten schools in each city were selected to provide a representative sample of the city's elementary schools (6). Because we wanted to test children shortly after they entered elementary school and also near the end of their elementary education, we randomly chose two firstgrade and two fifth-grade classrooms in each school. The age of school entrance is the same in all three countries and elementary school attendance is mandatory. From each classroom we randomly chose six boys and six girls. This procedure resulted in a sample of 240 first-graders and 240 fifth-graders from each city.

Kindergartens in Taiwan and Japan are mainly privately owned and attendance is not compulsory. Nevertheless, more than 98 percent of the 5-year-olds in Sendai and over 80 percent of the 5-year-olds in Taipei attend kindergarten for at least a full year. All Minneapolis children attend kindergarten. Children in

the study came from 24 kindergarten classes in each city. In order to ensure that the samples of kindergarten and elementary school children in Taipei and Sendai would be comparable, the kindergartens chosen were among those attended by children from the ten elementary schools. Six boys and six girls were randomly chosen from each classroom, yielding a sample in each city of 288 children for study. A representative sample of 24 kindergarten classrooms was selected in the Minneapolis metropolitan area.

MATHEMATICS ACHIEVEMENT

The American children's scores were lower than those of the Japanese children in kindergarten and at grades 1 and 5, and lower than those of the Chinese children's at grades 1 and 5 (Table 1). Average scores for boys and girls did not show statistically significant differences from each other at any of the three grade levels.

Figure 1 shows graphically the result of transforming each child's score into a z score, which represents the departure in standard deviation units from the mean of a distribution derived from the scores of the children in all three cities at each grade level. Scores were then recombined according to country, and the mean score of children in each country was determined. Consistently superior performance of the Japanese children and

TABLE 1   MEAN SCORES (±SD) ON THE MATHEMATICS TESTS FOR KINDERGARTEN (K) AND GRADES 1 AND 5˙ SCHEFFE METHOD CONTRASTS: UNITED STATES < JAPAN AT KINDERGARTEN, GRADE 1, AND GRADE 5 ($P<0.001$); UNITED STATES < TAIWAN AT GRADE 1 AND GRADE 5 ($P<0.01$). SAMPLE SIZES FOR UNITED STATES, TAIWAN, AND JAPAN, RESPECTIVELY: KINDERGARTEN, 288, 286, AND 280; GRADE 1, 237, 241, AND 240; AND GRADE 5, 238, 241, AND 239.

Grade	United States	Taiwan	Japan
K	37.5 ± 5.6	37.8 ± 7.4	42.2 ± 5.1
1	17.1 ± 5.3	21.2 ± 5.5	20.1 ± 5.2
2	44.4 ± 6.2	50.8 ± 5.7	53.3 ± 7.5

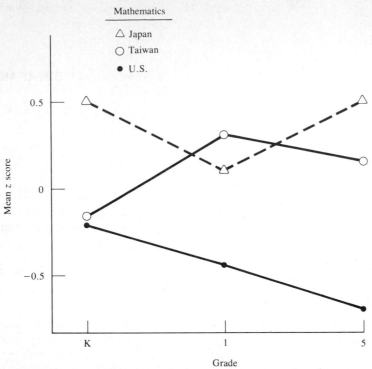

FIGURE 1   Children's performance on the mathematics test. (Standard deviations for kindergarten, grade 1, and grade 5 were as follows: Japan, 0.77, 0.93, and 1.00; Taiwan, 1.10, 0.98, and 0.76; United States, 0.83, 0.96, and 0.83).

rapid improvement in the scores of the Chinese children from kindergarten through fifth grade are evident. Scores of the American children display a consistent decline compared to those of the Chinese and Japanese children.

Another way of considering the data is in terms of the performance in each classroom. Data for the first-and fifth-grade children are presented in Fig. 2. Each line represents one classroom. The height of the line represents the average score for the 12 children tested in each of the 20 classrooms in each city, and the width of the line represents the range of scores within each classroom. The z scores were obtained in a manner similar to that just described, except that the raw scores for both first- and fifth-graders were combined into a single distribution

from which the z score for each child was computed. The z scores were then compiled for each classroom.

A high degree of overlap appears in the distributions of scores for the first-grade classrooms in the three cities. At the fifth-grade level there is a clear separation. The highest average score of an American fifth-grade classroom was below that of the Japanese fifth-grade classroom with the lowest average score. In addition, only one Chinese classroom showed an average score lower than the American classroom with the highest average score. Equally remarkable is the fact that the lowest average score for a fifth-grade American classroom was only slightly higher than the average score for the best first-grade Chinese classroom.

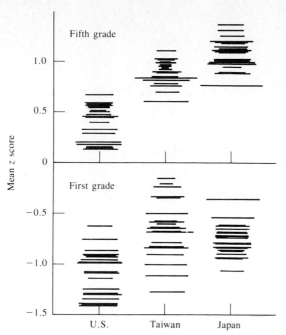

FIGURE 2   Performance in each classroom on the mathematics test.

Viewed in still another way, the data indicate that among the 100 top scorers on the mathematics test at grade 1, there were only 15 American children. At grade 5, only one American child appeared among the 100 top scorers from the total sample of approximately 720 children. On the other hand, among the children receiving the 100 lowest scores at each grade, there were 58 American children at grade 1 and 67 at grade 5.

The low level of performance of American children was not due to a few exceptionally low-scoring classrooms nor to a particular area of weakness. They were as ineffective in calculating as in solving word problems. The search for an adequate explanation of these findings will be a long one, for many factors are involved in producing such large differences in performance. Some of the most obvious alternatives are discussed below, including the children's

cognitive abilities and several factors related to school and home.

READING ACHIEVEMENT AND COGNITIVE ABILITIES

A look at results for the reading test helps clarify whether low levels of achievement generally characterized the academic performance of American children. Although reading scores show statistically significant differences among the three cities, the differences were less extreme than those in mathematics. Chinese children had the highest average scores and Japanese children the lowest. Average scores for the American children consistently were in the middle. Data presented in Fig. 3 from the vocabulary portion of the reading test illustrate these results.

Solving mathematics problems is one aspect of cognitive functioning. Perhaps differences in mathematics scores reflect differences in general intelligence among children in the three cultures. Although Lynn (8) has suggested that Japanese children display general cognitive superiority to American children, his study had numerous methodological problems, such as selective sampling of children in Japan (9). The cognitive tasks constructed especially for evaluating the intellectual functioning of Japanese, Chinese, and American children in this study offer data related to these cross-national comparisons. The tasks included performance tasks, such as perceptual speed, coding, and spatial abilities, and verbal tasks, such as vocabulary, verbal memory, and general information.

We found no evidence to support Lynn's suggestion; American children did not receive lower average scores than the Chinese and Japanese children during kindergarten or at grades 1 or 5. In fact, American children obtained the highest scores on many of the tasks during kindergarten and first grade. By the fifth

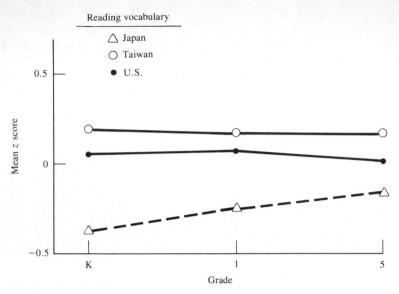

FIGURE 3   Children's performance on the vocabulary portion of the reading test. (Standard deviations for kindergarten, grade 1, and grade 5 were as follows: Taiwan, 0.99, 1.06, and 0.84; United States, 0.98, 1.12, and 1.07; Japan, 0.84, 0.72, and 1.05).

grade there was no overall difference in the total scores received by the children in the three cities (3).

LIFE IN SCHOOL

Our information about the children's experiences in school is based on extensive observations made in each elementary school classroom. Each classroom was visited according to a schedule in which the time of observation was randomized during a period of several weeks. The observer's attention was focused on the children for some of the observations and on the teacher for others. Behavior was coded according to an objective coding system (4). The number of hours of observation was 1353 in Minneapolis, 1600 in Taipei, and 1200 in Sendai.

Learning depends, in part, on the amount of time spent in practicing the material to be learned. We therefore looked at the percentage of time devoted to academic activities, and especially to mathematics. American first-graders were engaged in academic activities a smaller percentage of time than the Chinese and Japanese children: 69.8 percent for the American children, 85.1 percent for the Chinese children, and 79.2 percent for the Japanese children. By fifth grade, differences between the American and the Chinese and the Japanese children were greater than at the lower grades. American children spent 64.5 percent of their classroom time involved in academic activities. Chinese children spent 91.5 percent, and Japanese children, 87.4 percent. Assuming that our observations provide a representative picture of what went on in Minneapolis fifth-grade classrooms, we estimate that 19.6 hours per week (64.5 percent of the 30.4 hours the American children spend in school) were devoted to academic activities. This is less than half the estimate of 40.4 hours (91.5 percent of 44.1 hours that Chinese children attend school) devoted to academic activities in the fifth-grade Chinese classrooms, and not much less than half of the

32.6 hours (87.4 percent of 37.3 hours that Japanese children attend school) in the Japanese classrooms.

In both grades 1 and 5, American children spent less than 20 percent of their time on the average studying mathematics in school. This was less than the percentage for either Chinese or Japanese children. At the fifth grade, language arts (including reading) and mathematics occupied approximately equal amounts of time for the Chinese and Japanese children, but the American children spent more than twice as much time on language arts (40 percent) as on mathematics (17 percent) (Fig. 4). In some of the American classrooms, no time was devoted to work in mathematics during the approximately 40 randomly selected hours when an observer was present. The high variability

among American classrooms in the time allocated to the various academic subjects can be readily explained. There are precisely defined curricula in Taiwan and Japan, and teachers are expected to adhere closely to these curricula. American teachers are allowed to organize their classrooms much more according to their own desires; hence, there is greater variability among classrooms.

The leader of a classroom activity in which a child was engaged could be the teacher, another adult, such as a teacher's aide, or a child. Asian and American classrooms had strikingly different patterns of leadership. Children in Taipei were led by the teacher nearly 90 percent of the time; in Sendai, more than 70 percent of the time. Children in Minneapolis, in contrast, spent less than half their time in classrooms

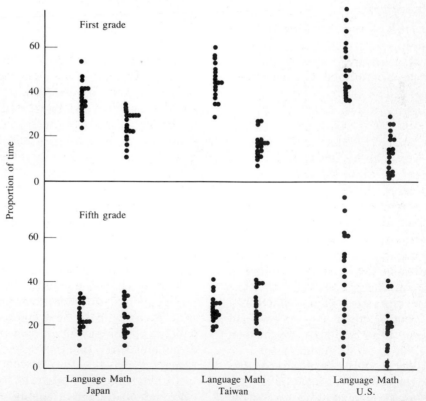

FIGURE 4 Proportion of time spent in each classroom on language arts and mathematics from classroom observations.

where they were led by the teacher. Children can learn without a teacher. Nevertheless, it seems likely that they could profit from having their teacher as a leader more than half of the time.

Moreover, American teachers spent proportionally much less time imparting information (21 percent) than did the Chinese (58 percent) or Japanese (33 percent) teachers. These are sobering results. American children were in school approximately 30 hours a week. This means that they were receiving information from the teacher for approximately 6 hours a week (0.21 times 30). Computing similar estimates for Chinese and Japanese classrooms gives values of 26 hours for Chinese children and 12 hours for Japanese children. American teachers actually spent somewhat more time giving directions than in imparting information (26 percent compared to 21 percent).

There were other interesting differences in the ways children spent their time in school. For example, we sometimes found that a child who was known to be at school was not present in the classroom. The child could be at the school office, on an errand for the teacher, in another classroom, or in the library. This occurred 18.4 percent of the time that an American fifth-grader was to be observed, but less than 0.2 percent of the time in Taipei and Sendai classrooms.

The comparatively low levels of achievement of the American children in mathematics appear to be attributable in part to the fact that they are not receiving amounts of instruction comparable to those received by children in Taiwan and Japan. These cross-national differences become even more profound when they are extended over the school year. Chinese and Japanese children spend half a day at school on Saturdays and have fewer holidays than do American children. As a result, American children attend school an average of 178 days a year; Chinese and Japanese children attend school for 240 days. In addition, Japanese fifth-graders were estimated by their mothers to spend an average of 1 hour more each day, and the Chinese children, 2 hours more each day at school than the American children. Taken together, these data point to enormous differences in the amounts of schooling young children receive in the three countries.

HOMEWORK

Learning occurs at home as well as at school. But our data indicate that neither American parents nor teachers of elementary school children tend to believe that homework is of much value. As a consequence, American children spend much less time on homework than do Japanese children, and both groups spend vastly less time on homework than do Chinese children. American mothers estimated that on weekdays their first-graders spent an average of 14 minutes a day on homework; the daily average for Chinese first-graders was 77 minutes, and for Japanese, 37 minutes. For fifth-graders, the estimate for the American children was 46 minutes a day; for the Chinese and Japanese fifth-graders the estimates were 114 and 57 minutes a day, respectively. On weekends, American children studied even less: an estimated 7 minutes on Saturday and 11 minutes on Sunday. The corresponding values for Chinese children were 83 and 73 minutes, and for the Japanese children, 37 and 29 minutes—and this was in addition to the half day in school on Saturday. American children also were given less help when they were doing their homework, according to their mothers' estimates. Someone, usually the mother, assisted the fifth-grade children with their homework an average of 14 minutes a day. The Chinese children were assisted by some family member an average of 27 minutes a day, and the Japanese children, 19 minutes a day.

Parental concern about a child's schoolwork was evident in another simple index, the possession of a desk. Only 63 percent of the

American fifth-graders, but 98 percent of the Japanese and 95 percent of the Chinese fifth-graders had desks. When the Chinese and Japanese children were not occupied with homework, they were given other opportunities to practice by solving the problems appearing in the workbooks purchased for them by their parents. Only 28 percent of the parents of American fifth-graders, but 58 percent of the Japanese and 56 percent of the Chinese parents bought their children workbooks in mathematics. The discrepancy was even more pronounced in the purchase of workbooks in science, which were purchased by only 1 percent of the American parents, but by 29 percent of the Japanese and 51 percent of the Chinese parents.

How did children in the three cities react to doing homework? Taipei children said they liked homework; children in Minneapolis said they did not like homework; and the attitudes of the Sendai children were somewhere in between. When asked to choose among an array of five frowning, neutral, or smiling faces to express their attitudes about homework, more than 60 percent of the Chinese fifth-graders chose a smiling face, more than 60 percent of the Japanese children chose a smiling or neutral face, and 60 percent of the American children chose a frowning face. Although 30 percent of the American children chose a smiling face at first grade, the percentage was half that among fifth-graders.

One indication of what teachers thought about homework appeared in their ratings of the value of homework and 15 other activities directed at helping children do well in school. Ratings given to the value of homework by American teachers placed it 15th among 16 items—lowest except for physical punishment. Chinese and Japanese teachers were much more positive; the average rating given by Chinese teachers on a 9-point scale was 7.3; by Japanese teachers, 5.8; and by American teachers, 4.4.

The small amounts of homework assigned to American children were not in conflict with the mothers' beliefs about how much schoolwork their child should be assigned. Among American mothers, 69 percent said that the amount of homework was "just right." Nor were the Chinese and Japanese mothers dissatisfied with the large amounts of homework assigned to their children; 82 percent of the Chinese mothers and 67 percent of the Japanese mothers thought the amount was "just right."

MOTHERS' EVALUATIONS

When asked to rate their child's achievement in mathematics, American mothers gave their children favorable evaluations. Ratings were made on nine-point scales, each anchored by five defining statements, ranging from "much below average" to "much above average." Although mothers were asked to compare their child with "other children of his or her age," the mean rating made by the American mothers for their child's ability in mathematics was 5.9, higher than the average rating of 5.2 of the Chinese mothers and similar to the average of 5.8 of the Japanese mothers.

Mothers were also asked to rate children on several cognitive abilities, each defined by several words or a short phrase. Great care was taken to select words and phrases that express the same nuances of meaning in the three languages. American mothers consistently gave their children the highest average ratings and Japanese mothers gave their children the lowest. For example, on ratings of a child's intellectual ability, the average rating given by American mothers was 6.3, much above the 5.0 that would indicate an average level of ability. The average rating given by the Japanese mothers was 5.5, and by the Chinese mothers, 6.1.

Despite the positive bias of the American mothers, the rank order of their ratings was in line with the children's performance. The correlation between the mothers' ratings of the children's abilities in mathematics and the fifth-graders' scores on the mathematics test was 0.50 in Minneapolis, 0.37 in Taipei, and 0.54 in Sendai. The high ratings made by American mothers must be attributed to an excessively positive attitude, rather than to a failure to perceive a child's status in relation to other children. Conversely, the low ratings of Japanese mothers appear to reflect an effort to be more realistic in their evaluations.

The optimism of the American mothers was reflected in other ways. They were pleased with the job the schools were doing in educating their children: 91 percent judged that the school was doing an "excellent" or "good" job. Only 42 percent of the Chinese mothers and 39 percent of the Japanese mothers were this positive. Instead, the majority of the Chinese and Japanese mothers considered that the schools were doing a "fair" job.

The high esteem the American mothers had for their children's cognitive abilities extended to their satisfaction with their children's current academic performance. More than 40 percent of the American mothers described themselves as

being "very satisfied" (Fig. 5). Fewer than 6 percent of the Chinese and Japanese mothers were this positive.

When asked if there were things about their children's education that could be improved, 45 percent of the American mothers of fifth-graders who suggested improvements could be made emphasized improvement in academic subjects. The subject that they thought should get more emphasis was reading (48 percent of the suggestions). Mathematics and science were seldom mentioned (<6 percent of the suggestions). The subjects mentioned most frequently by the Japanese mothers were reading and mathematics. Chinese mothers, on the other hand, believed that more emphasis should be given to music, art, and gym.

The positive attitudes of the mothers did not mean that American children liked school. In rating how well they liked school, 52 percent of the American children, compared to 86 percent of the Chinese fifth-graders, chose a smiling face. (The question was not asked in Japan.)

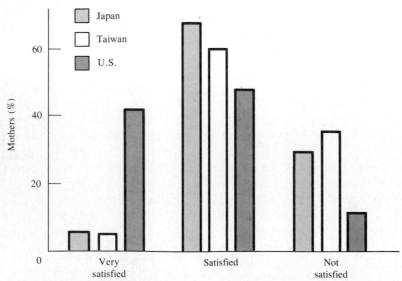

FIGURE 5 Mothers' attitudes toward children's academic performance.

Critics of Chinese and Japanese education often suggest that the high demands placed on children result in ambivalence or dislike of school. This does not seem to be the case in elementary schools. It is the American children who regard elementary school less positively. Expressing a dislike for school may be a socially acceptable reaction among American school children. Even young children in Taiwan and Japan are aware of the fact that education is highly prized in the Chinese and Japanese cultures. The emphasis on scholastic achievement may lead to the intense competition that is often said to characterize secondary schools in Taiwan and Japan, but negative consequences were not evident during the elementary school years. In fact, the children in all three cities appeared to be cheerful, enthusiastic, vigorous, and responsive. Although some of these characteristics may be more vividly expressed in classrooms in Minneapolis, they are readily apparent to the observer who follows Chinese and Japanese children through their school day.

PARENTAL BELIEFS

Experiences that parents provide their children may be strongly influenced by their general beliefs about the components of success. For example, parents who emphasize ability as the most important requisite for success may be less disposed to stress the need to work hard than would parents who believe success is largely dependent on effort.

In exploring cultural differences in beliefs about the relative importance of factors leading to success in school, we asked the mothers to rank effort, natural ability, difficulty of the schoolwork, and luck or chance by importance in determining a child's performance in school. They were then asked to assign a total of ten points to the four factors. Japanese mothers assigned the most points to effort, and American mothers gave the largest number of points to ability (Fig. 6). The willingness of Japanese and Chinese children to work so hard in school may be due, in part, to the stronger belief on the part of their mothers in the value of hard work.

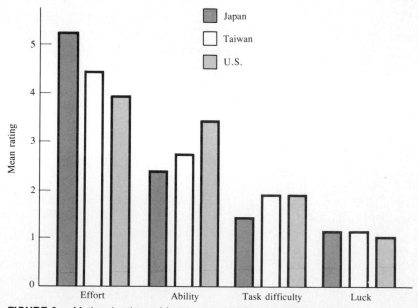

FIGURE 6   Mothers' ratings of factors contributing to academic success.

OUTSIDE ASSISTANCE

It has been suggested that the scholastic performance of young Chinese and Japanese children is due in part to outside tutoring. Articles about the *juku,* the cram schools of Japan, and the *buxiban,* the after-hours schools in Taiwan, have appeared in American newspapers. These seem to be phenomena associated with later years of schooling, for few mothers said that their elementary school children attended such classes. Children in all three of the cities that we studied were enrolled in after-school lessons or classes, but these were not necessarily ones that would help the children with their schoolwork. American children most frequently took lessons in various types of sports. Among Chinese children, the most popular lessons were in sports and calligraphy, and among Japanese children, the most popular lessons were in art and calligraphy. The percentage of children taking lessons in mathematics was higher in Sendai (7 percent) than in Taipei (2 percent), but not higher than the percentage in Minneapolis (8 percent).

THE TEACHERS

The number of hours teachers spent with the children each week did not show statistically significant differences among the three countries, despite the fact that the hours were spread out over 5.5 days a week in Taiwan and Japan, and only 5 days in the United States. American and Japanese teachers estimated that they spent 28 hours a week teaching, and the Chinese teachers, 30 hours. The amount of time spent at school did differ greatly—an average of 51 hours for the Japanese teachers, 47 hours for the Chinese teachers, and 42 hours for the American teachers. This means that American teachers have little time when they are at school for activities other than those where they are directly responsible for the children in their classroom, a factor that may help explain the complaints of American teachers that they are overworked.

American teachers frequently said that if they could shed some of their nonacademic functions, they could spend more of their time actually teaching. A large amount of classroom time is spent in unproductive activities that can be attributed, in part, to the American teachers being asked to take on too many functions other than teaching, including the roles of counselor, family therapist, and surrogate parent. This diversion of energy is perhaps the most common problem of American elementary school teachers, and is one that was seldom mentioned by the teachers in Taipei and Sendai. Such problems are not due to there being a greater number of children in the American classrooms, for the average number of children in the Minneapolis elementary school classrooms was 21, whereas it was 47 in Taipei and 39 in Sendai.

Whether increased time for teaching would result in improved instruction in mathematics and science is questionable. When asked whether there were ways in which they would change the curriculum if they were free to do so, nearly a quarter of the American teachers had no suggestions. The two most frequent suggestions related to academic subjects involved placing more emphasis on "basics" (13 percent) and increasing the time available for reading, spelling, and language instruction (18 percent). Only one American teacher expressed a desire to spend more time on mathematics.

CURRENT DATA

The data for the elementary school children were collected in 1980, and for the kindergarten children in 1984. A follow-up study also was undertaken in 1984 of children who had been included in our first-grade sample, but now were in the fifth grade. Little change occurred in the children's performance during the four years. The mean score for the American children in 1984 on the mathematics test was 44.9, a score nearly identical to the average of 44.5 obtained by the fifth-graders 4 years earlier. The Japanese children remained ahead, with a mean score of 51.

Differences in the attitudes of mothers in the three countries were as strong as they had been 4 years earlier. In analyses of the 1984 data that have been completed, we have found, for example, that mothers of American fifth-graders were even more satisfied, and Chinese and Japanese mothers were just as dissatisfied with their child's performance in 1984 as mothers were in 1980. Nearly 60 percent of the American mothers, compared to 40 percent 4 years earlier, were "very satisfied" with their child's current academic performance. Fewer than 10 percent of the Chinese and Japanese mothers were "very satisfied."

CONCLUSIONS

Impetus for change often comes from dissatisfaction with the present state of affairs. Most American mothers interviewed in this study did not appear to be dissatisfied with their children's schools, and seem unlikely, therefore, to become advocates for reform. Moreover, the children, faced with parents who generally are satisfied and approving of what happens in school, must see little need to spend more time and effort on their schoolwork. The poor performance of American children in mathematics thus reflects a general failure to perceive that American elementary school children are performing ineffectively and that there is a need for improvement and change if the United States is to remain competitive with other countries in areas such as technology and science which require a solid foundation in mathematical skills.

The lack of time spent teaching mathematics may be a reflection of the view of American parents and teachers that education in elementary school is synonymous with learning to read. Large amounts of time are devoted to reading instruction, and if changes were to be made in the curriculum, both parents and teachers agreed that even greater proportions of time should be devoted to reading. Mathematics and science play a small role in Americans' conception of elementary education.

American mothers have unrealistically favorable evaluations of their children and what they are accomplishing in school. This optimism may lead to a sense of well-being but is unwarranted in the context of cross-national comparisons of children's scholastic achievement. When we look only within the United States, we may find cause to deplore the poor performance only of certain subgroups of our population. When we broaden our perspective to include children from other countries, we have cause for concern. Although a small proportion of American children perform superbly, the large majority appear to be falling behind their peers in other countries.

The data we have presented are from a single set of studies, conducted in particular locales and with particular methods. Nevertheless, the findings are directly in line with those from other cross-national studies of achievement in mathematics and science involving older children and adolescents (10–12). Preliminary results from the Second International Mathematics Study, for example, indicate that among eighth-graders from 20 countries, Japanese children received the highest scores in arithmetic, algebra, geometry, statistics, and measurement. The average scores of the American children on these tests ranged from 8th to 18th position. The poor performance of American children that begins in kindergarten is maintained through the later grades.

Regardless of the funds that may be allocated to the development and application of new methods of teaching, it seems obvious that children's success in mathematics and other subjects will depend on greater awareness and an increased willingness by American parents to be of direct assistance to their children. Schools may be improved, but the task of helping children reach higher levels of achievement cannot be accomplished without more cooperation and communication between the school and the home. Further, without greater acknowledgement of the importance of the elementary school years to children's education in mathematics and science, legislation to improve instruction in secondary schools may result in little more than exercises in remediation for most children.

REFERENCES AND NOTES

1 J. W. Stigler, S. Y. Lee, G. W. Lucker, H. W. Stevenson, *J. Educ. Psychol.* **74**, 315 (1982).
2 H. W. Stevenson *et al.*, *Child Devel.* **53**, 1164 (1982).
3 H. W. Stevenson *et al.*, *ibid.* **56**, 718 (1985).
4 H. W. Stevenson *et al.*, in *Advances in Instructional Psychology*, R. Glaser, Ed. (Erlbaum, Hillside, NJ, in press).
5 H. W. Stevenson, H. Azuma, K. Hakuta, Eds., *Child Development and Education in Japan* (Freeman, New York, in press).
6 Care was taken to develop procedures that would result in the selection of representative samples of children within each city. Selection was made after we discussed our goals with educational authorities in each city. We obtained a list of schools stratified by region and socioeconomic status of the families. Schools in Taipei and Sendai were then selected at random so that the ten elementary schools would constitute a representative sample of schools within each city. In the Minneapolis metropolitan area, where there are many different school districts, we sought to adopt a procedure that was as comparable to that used in Sendai and Taipei as possible. All elementary schools in Sendai were public schools, but one private school was chosen in both Taipei and Minneapolis to represent the proportion of children in those cities that attend private schools. All children in each of the classrooms in Japan and Taiwan were included as potential subjects. In Minneapolis, parental permission had to be obtained before we could test a child. Parents were very cooperative; only 4.5 percent failed to return slips giving us permission to test their children. Children with IQs below 70 were eliminated from the samples in all three cities.
7 Statistical analyses of the achievement tests indicated good reliability. Tests of the reliability of the mathematics test yielded values that ranged from 0.92 to 0.95 when the Cronbach α statistic was computed separately by grade and country. The coefficients of concordance for the three parts of the reading test ranged from 0.91 to 0.94 when computed separately for each country. Results for standardized tests of mathematics and reading were not obtained for purposes of comparison with our tests. The standardized achievement tests, if available, were not comparable among the three countries; the results often were not current; and they were group tests, rather than individually administered tests such as those used in this study.
8 R. Lynn, *Nature (London)* **297**, 222 (1982).
9 H. W. Stevenson and H. Azuma, *ibid.* **306**, 291 (1983).
10 T. Husén, *International Study of Achievement in Mathematics: A Comparison of Twelve Countries* (Wiley, New York, 1967).
11 L. C. Comber and J. Keeves, *Science Achievement in Nineteen Countries* (Wiley, New York, 1973).
12 "Preliminary report: Second International Mathematics Study" (University of Illinois, Urbana, 1984).
13 This article reports results from a collaborative study undertaken with S. Kitamura, S. Kimura, and T. Kato of Tohoku Fukushi College in Sendai, Japan, and C. C. Hsu of National Taiwan University in Taipei. Supported by NIMH grants MH 33259 and MH 30567.

CHAPTER 11

CHILDHOOD PSYCHOPATHOLOGY

Up to this point, we have focused on normal child development. We will now examine the development of children who exhibit atypical developmental patterns and will look at methods of intervention. Biological vulnerability, deleterious social factors, and a lack of personal and social resources all may interact to produce different types of psychopathology in children. In order to demonstrate the complex interactions among some of these factors, we have selected two articles dealing with the development of psychopathology. Both take a family systems approach to the problem. The article by Eric Mash and Charlotte Johnson examines the relations between parental perceptions of child behavior, parental self-esteem, and mother's reported stress in families of younger and older hyperactive and normal children. These relations differ for mothers and fathers and for parents of older and younger children. Since this is a correlational study, the authors emphasize that they are unable to conclude whether parental perceptions of the child as a problem precede or follow the deficits in parental self-esteem and reported maternal stress. They suggest that there is probably a bidirectional pattern of effects occurring where parental low self-esteem and maternal stress is a response to parents' perceiving their children as problematic and where the parental perceptions may influence parent-child interactions in ways that may exacerbate their children's problems.

The article by Zahn-Waxler and her colleagues also takes a systems approach to examining the effects on child development of the presence of a bipolar parent whose moods swing from manic agitation to acute depression. Growing up in such a family seems to have little impact on young children in their early understanding of the physical world or on their development of self-recognition. Developmental deviations in the first two years of life in such children are most likely to be in social and interpersonal problem-solving skills, as manifested in such things as atypical development of role-taking skills and insecure relationships with their mothers. Other research has demonstrated that these early interpersonal problems extend beyond the family system into later difficulties in peer relations. It should be noted that biological vulnerability and genetic factors, as well as social disturbances, may play a role in the transmission of affective problems.

One of the critical problems confronting the child clinical psychologist is how to intervene in the development of childhood psychopathology. Traditional methods of intervention have involved the treatment of psychopathology after it occurred. More recently, however, there is a new emphasis on prevention of disorders before they arise. Mindy Rosenberg and Dickon Reppucci review the results of primary prevention programs of child abuse and the methodological problems encountered in the evaluation of such programs.

Hicks Marlowe and his coinvestigators take a very different approach to intervention with a type of child who usually has proved very resistant to treatment—the chronic delinquent. They find that training parents of delinquents to use family management techniques involving consistent appropriate discipline and monitoring of the children's activities can reduce targeted delinquent or predelinquent activities in the children.

The criteria for the usefulness of an intervention program should include not only the effectiveness of the treatment but should also consider the costs and feasibility of large-scale utilization of the program. At this point even effective primary prevention and therapeutic programs are limited in application because of cost and utilization problems.

Parental Perceptions of Child Behavior Problems, Parenting Self-Esteem, and Mothers' Reported Stress in Younger and Older Hyperactive and Normal Children

Eric J. Mash
Charlotte Johnston

Recent writings have emphasized the need to consider both the social contexts for hyperactivity and the reciprocal influences inherent in these contexts (Routh, 1980; Whalen & Henker, 1980). Although parent characteristics as a "context" for hyperactivity have received some attention (see Paternite & Loney, 1980 and Werner, 1980 for reviews), the focus of this work has been on the identification of possible "causes" of the problem from a predominantly unidirectional perspective, that is, the effect of the parent on the child. Within such a framework, a greater incidence of problems for the parents of hyperactives has been reported, particularly paternal alcoholism and sociopathy and maternal hysteria (Cantwell, 1972; Morrison & Stewart, 1971). However, a pattern of disturbance *specific* to parents of hyperactives has not been identified, and a higher incidence of these problems may be characteristic of parents with disturbed children in general, rather than being specific to hyperactivity (Sandberg, Weiselberg, & Shaffer, 1980; Stewart, DeBlois, & Cummings, 1980).

The presence of maternal distress has been frequently noted in both clinical and empirical work with families of hyperactives (Ross & Ross, 1976; Safer & Allen, 1976). In fact, Sandberg et al. (1980) found that maternal reports of mental distress far outweighed the contribution of any other family-background variable (e.g., social class, family size, broken home) in predicting child behavior disturbance, accounting for 73% of the total variance in parental ratings of hyperactivity. Such findings suggest the need for further empirical work examining the types of distress reported by mothers of hyperactives, concomitant with the recognition that such distress may also be characteristic of other types of child disturbances.

Parenting itself can be a generally stressful life event (Gibaud-Wallston & Wandersman, Note 1), and the manifestation of major and persistent child problems may be the most significant dimension of stress across a range of unpleasant parental effects (Weinberg & Richardson, 1981). Mothers of children exhibiting hyperactivity (Barkley, 1981), conduct disorders (Patterson, 1976, 1980), and other types of handicapping conditions, such as cerebral palsy (Kogan, Tyler, & Turner, 1974), epilepsy (Long & Moore, 1979), and developmental delay (Kogan, 1980), participate in transactions with their children that are more stressful, are less rewarding, and provide considerably less positive feedback than is the case for mothers of normal children.

Many of the behaviors commonly exhibited by problem children are perceived by parents as annoying, noxious, and stressful (Jones, Reid, & Patterson, 1975) and result in a range of parental coping reactions encompassing overt behavior, cognitions, emotions, and physiological responses. For example, adults are likely to react harshly and use more severe forms of punishment in response to children who are overactive (Stevens-Long, 1973), unresponsive to discipline (Mulhern & Passman, 1981), or uncontrollable (Bugental, Caporeal, & Shennum, 1980). Child problems at a very early age are also related to mothers' emotions and perceptions. For example, Blumberg (1980) reported that mothers of infants at high levels of neonatal risk showed concomitantly higher levels of depression and anxiety and also perceived their children more negatively.

Parental perceptions of child problems have been shown to be correlated with observed child behavior (e.g., Barkley & Cunningham, 1980) and are also sensitive predictors in distinguishing clinic from non-clinic children (Griest, Forehand, Wells, & McMahon, 1980), even in some circumstances in which these groups may not differ in their social behavior (Lobitz & Johnson, 1975) or test performance (Cohen, Sullivan, Minde, Novak, & Helwig, 1981). Maternal perceptions of child deviancy are positively correlated with reports of maternal depression (Griest, Wells, & Forehand, 1979) and inversely related to marital satisfaction (Johnson & Lobitz, 1974). Patterson (1980) reported that mothers of aggressive boys have a negative self-image, low self-esteem, and experience feelings of depression, anxiety, fatigue, anger, and isolation. In a series of studies, Wahler (Wahler, 1980a, 1980b; Wahler, Leske, & Rogers, 1979) has suggested that mothers of problem children may be isolated from social support, such as contacts with friends, and that this insularity may be predictive of higher levels of maternal negativism and poorer treatment outcomes. Other studies have suggested that social support may be a particularly critical factor when a family is under a particular stress, such as that associated with an irritable child (e.g., Crockenberg, 1981).

The above findings suggest that having a handicapped or behavior-problem child creates ongoing stress for mothers that potentially undermines their self-esteem and confidence in their ability to care for their children (Block, 1969; Cummings, Bayley, & Rie, 1966; Patterson, 1980; Wolf & Acton, 1968). Having a "difficult child" may adversely affect the manner in which mothers perceive their child, their role as a parent, and themselves. These perceptions have not been empirically studied to any great extent in the parents of hyperactive children, even though stress in the families of

hyperactives is reported to be high (Delameter, Lahey, & Drake, 1981). The current investigation examined the relationships between both mothers' and fathers' perceptions of their hyperactive children's behavior, parenting self-esteem and reports of maternal stress.

In examining these relationships it is important to note at the outset that the correlational nature of this investigation, and many of those previously described, does not permit an assessment of the directionality of effects. However, as we have indicated elsewhere (Mash & Johnston, 1982), the question of whether hyperactivity produces parental disturbances, or vice versa, does not negate the need to describe the mutual influences in the parent-child relationship, with a view of hyperactivity and parental disturbance as both causes *and* outcomes (Patterson, 1976). This investigation obtained information from parents of younger and older hyperactive and normal children. Since previous research (Mash & Johnston, 1982) has shown the mother-child interactions of younger hyperactives to be more negative than those of older hyperactives, it was predicted that mothers of younger hyperactives might also report the highest levels of stress and lowest levels of parenting competence. It was also predicted that parental perceptions of child deviancy would be positively correlated with reports of maternal stress and inversely correlated with reports of parental self-esteem.

METHOD

Subjects

Forty families with a hyperactive child and 51 families with normal children participated. Hyperactive children were divided into "younger" ($n = 16$; M age = 5 years, 1 month) and "older" ($n = 24$; M age = 8 years, 4 months) age groups, for the purpose of making age comparisions. The parents of comparable groups of younger ($n = 26$; M age = 5 years, 1 month) and older ($N = 25$; M age = 8 years, 5 months) control children also participated. Two of the younger hyperactive children and one child in each of the other three groups were female. The inclusion of predominantly boys reflected the greater frequency of hyperactivity in boys and facilitated comparisons with other studies of hyperactive children.

Families of hyperactives were referred by family physicians, pediatricians, psychologists, psychiatrists, and other child-treatment professionals. Multiple criteria were used in designating a child as hyperactive, including a clinical diagnosis of hyperactivity by the referral agent, maternal report of a developmental history of hyperactivity, and maternal ratings at least two standard deviations above the normative mean on the Conners' Abbreviated Rating Scale (Conners, 1972) and the Werry-Weiss-Peters Activity Scale (WWP; Routh, Schroeder, & O'Tuama, 1974). Almost all children were of average or above-average intelligence (M IQ = 115.93; SD = 13.96; range = 76–143) as assessed by the Peabody Picture Vocabulary Test—Form A (Dunn, 1965) and were free from any gross neurological, sensory, or motor impairments.

Families of normal children were recruited through school notices and a door-to-door survey. None of the normal children were rated by their mothers as within the hyperactive range on either the Conners' or WWP scales, nor were they described as experiencing any serious medical or behavioral difficulties. All families were of middle- to upper-middle socioeconomic status (SES) as determined by the Hollingshead Four-Factor Index of Social Status (Hollingshead, 1975). A one-way analysis of variance (ANOVA) revealed no significant differences between groups in respect to family SES ($p > .05$).

Procedure

The measures included in this report were administered as part of an ongoing research project concerning hyperactivity and family in-

teractions (Mash & Johnston, 1982). Where possible, both parents completed the checklists concerning child behavior and parenting self-esteem. However, due to practical limitations, only mothers were requested to complete the measure of parenting stress. Instructions to parents emphasized that they were to complete the questionnaires independently.

Measures of Parental Perceptions of Child Behavior

Hyperactivity Rating Scales Parents completed two commonly used hyperactivity rating scales, the Conners' scale (Conners, 1972) and the WWP as adapted by Routh et al. (1974). The Conners' is a 10-item scale on which the parent rates the degree to which the "hyperactive behaviors" described are characteristic of their child. The WWP scale instructs the parent to indicate the degree of "hyperactive" behavior their child demonstrates in a variety of situations (e.g., mealtime, public places).

Child Behavior Checklist Parental perceptions of child behavior problems, including but not restricted to hyperactivity, were assessed using the Child Behavior Checklist (CBCL; Achenbach, 1978; Achenbach & Edelbrock, 1981). Norms for the CBCL have been reported for children of each sex at 4 to 5, 6 to 11, and 12 to 16 years of age. Empirically derived behavior-problem scales are available for each age and sex grouping, as are two broad band factors representing Internalizing and Externalizing problems (Achenbach, 1966). Since the factor structure (e.g., specific scales) of the CBCL is different across age groupings, and the age range of children in the current sample was wide, only the Internalizing and Externalizing Scale scores were considered in the current analyses. In order to assess parental perceptions of child competency, the Social scale from the CBCL was also examined. This scale includes items relating to the child's social involvement, including participation in organizations, contact with friends, and behavior alone and with others.

Measure of Parenting Self-Esteem

Parenting self-esteem was assessed using the Parenting Sense of Competence Scale (PSOC; Gibaud-Wallston & Wandersman, Note 1), which contains two subscales each assessing a different aspect of parenting competence. The first is labelled "Skill/Knowledge" and reflects the degree to which a parent feels he or she has acquired the skill and understanding necessary to be a good parent. The second subscale is "Valuing/Comfort" and assesses the amount of value a parent places on parenthood and how comfortable he or she feels in the parenting role. The PSOC has been shown to possess satisfactory internal consistency, appears reliable over time, and correlates moderately with other measures of self-esteem. Additionally, the PSOC has been shown to relate to both child characteristics (e.g., easy or difficult to manage) and to the availability of marital and social support systems (Gibaud-Wallston & Wandersman, Note 1).

Measure of Parenting Stress

Degree of stress in the mother-child relationship was assessed with the Parenting Stress Index (PSI; Abidin & Burke, Note 2). The assumption underlying the questionnaire is that stress within the mother-child relationship is multifaceted and originates from the mother, the child, and situational factors. The PSI contains 126 items, which are divided into four domains reflecting major areas of stress in the mother-child relationship. The first domain represents *child characteristics* and consists of five subscales measuring such things as child distractibility and degree of bother to the mother. The questions in the child domain are designed to reveal stresses a mother is likely to experience arising from the manner in which she perceives her child and the demands her child makes of her (e.g., "There are some things my

child does that really bother me a lot": "My child is much more active than I expected"). The second domain reflects properties of the *mother-child interaction*. This domain concerns the degree to which the mother feels reinforced by her interactions with her child (e.g., "When I do things for my child I get the feeling that my efforts are not appreciated very much.") The third domain concerns *mother characteristics* and includes eight subscales describing areas such as maternal depression and degree of attachment to the child. The mother domain reflects stress arising from the mother's perception of herself, including her feelings about herself and her functioning as a parent (e.g., "I often feel guilty about the way I feel toward my child"; "I enjoy being a parent"). The final domain encompasses stress arising from *situational characteristics,* including demographics (e.g., income and education level) and life events (e.g., divorce, illness).

The PSI has demonstrated acceptable levels of internal consistency in the four domains and satisfactory test-retest reliability. In addition, preliminary validity information has also been presented (Burke & Abidin, Note 3).

RESULTS

Parent Perceptions of Child Behavior

The mean mother and father ratings for each of the four groups on the three child behavior measures are presented in Table 1. Pearson correlation coefficients between mothers' and fathers' ratings are also presented. An analysis of the precise diagnostic category (hyperactive vs normal) and of age (younger vs older) on mother and father ratings for each measure was performed.

The differences between parental ratings of hyperactives and normals on the Conners' scale and the WWP scale reflect the use of these measures in subject selection. Mother and father ratings on both of these measures were highly, positively correlated. However, paired *t*

TABLE 1   MEAN PARENT RATINGS OF CHILD BEHAVIOR AND MOTHER-FATHER AGREEMENT

| Measures of child behavior | Hyperactives | | Normals | | |
	Younger	Older	Younger	Older	F(df)
Conners' Abbreviated Rating Scale (.71**)					
Mothers	2.47	2.26	.67	.59	442.27(1,80)D**
Fathers	2.04	1.85	.86	.68	70.49(1,63)D**
Werry-Weiss-Peters Activity Scale (.82**)					
Mothers	31.19	29.39	11.48	9.22	310.69(1,81)D**
Fathers	25.93	26.18	14.06	9.86	90.21(1,66)D**
Child Behavior Checklist[a,b]					
Externalizing score (.74**)					
Mothers	75.75	75.25	52.54	53.92	203.81(1,87)D**
Fathers	73.21	72.56	54.10	48.75	124.73(1,73)D**
Internalizing score (.67**)					
Mothers	69.88	69.25	49.69	56.72	98.45(1,87)D**
					5.46(1,87)A*
					5.60(1,87)D X A*
Fathers	68.21	65.28	53.62	51.25	49.80(1,73)D**
Social Scale score (.66**)					
Mothers	15.84	16.42	49.42	55.64	36.76(1,87)D**
Fathers	12.03	23.65	48.81	55.90	27.86(1,86)D**

Note: D = significant main effect for diagnosis; A = significant main effect for age; D x A = significant Diagnosis x Age interaction. Numbers in parentheses following each measure refer to the Pearson correlations between mother and father ratings.

[a] *Internalizing and Externalizing scores are expressed as T scores; the Social scale scores are percentiles.*

[b] *All Child Behavior Checklist scores are based on appropriate age and sex norms.*

*p<.05. **p<.01.

tests between mothers' and fathers' ratings revealed that fathers of hyperactives rated their children lower on these measures of hyperactivity than did mothers ($p < .01$).

There were also significant differences between the hyperactive and normal groups for both mother and father ratings on the CBCL. The Externalizing scale scores, which include behavior problems similar to those tapped by the hyperactivity scales, were highly correlated with both the Conners' and WWP scales, with correlation coefficients ranging from $+.82$ to $+.87$, $p < .01$. As with the hyperactivity scales, parents of hyperactives perceived their children as showing significantly more behavior problems on the Externalizing scale of the CBCL than did parents of normals. Parents of hyperactives also perceived their children as exhibiting significantly more of the behavior prob-

lems represented by the Internalizing scale of the CBCL, including items reflecting depression and social withdrawal. The correlations between the CBCL Internalizing scale scores and the Conners' and WWP scales, although significant, were generally lower ($r = +.62$ to $+.72$, $p < .01$) than those between the Externalizing Scale and the hyperactivity scales. A significant age effect and an Age x Diagnosis interaction were also found for mothers' ratings on the Internalizing scale. Multiple-range tests revealed that mothers of older normals reported more internalizing problems than mothers of younger normals, with mothers of both younger and older normals reporting fewer internalizing problems than mothers of hyperactives ($p < .05$). Finally, the group differences for mothers' and fathers' ratings on the Social scale were highly significant. Both younger and older hyperactive children were perceived as being well below the norms for their age on social involvement.

As with the hyperactivity scales, mothers' and fathers' ratings on the three CBCL scales were highly correlated. In general, the highest levels of interparent agreement were obtained for the externalizing scale of the CBCL and the two hyperactivity checklists, perhaps reflecting the overt and observable nature of the behaviors represented in these scales as compared to behaviors contained in the Internalizing or Social scales.

Parenting Self-Esteem

Mother and father ratings of their self-esteem as parents, expressed as standardized z scores, and the Pearson correlations between mothers' and fathers' ratings are presented in Table 2. Transformations to z scores were carried out in order to permit comparisons across the scales of the self-esteem measure and with the scales of the measure of maternal stress. The ANOVAS revealed that both mothers and fathers of hyperactives perceived themselves as significantly less skilled and knowledgeable as parents and as deriving less value and comfort from their parenting roles than the parents of normal children. An inspection of mean ratings indicated that for parents' perceptions of their skill and knowledge, parents of older hyperactives obtained the lowest scores, whereas mothers of

older normal children rated themselves as most skilled and knowledgeable (p < .05). Ratings of the amount of comfort and value derived from parenting were higher for fathers of older normal children relative to fathers of younger normals. In contrast, mothers in both groups displayed ratings for valuing/comfort that were equivalent at the two age levels.

In considering the relationship between mothers' and fathers' ratings of self-esteem, all but one of the correlations were statistically significant, although moderate. For the hyperactive children, mothers' and fathers' parenting self-esteem as reflected in ratings of both skill/ knowledge and valuing/comfort were significantly correlated. However, for the normal children, although there was a significant relationship between mothers' and fathers' ratings of their skill and knowledge as parents, their ratings of the degree of value and comfort derived from the parental role were unrelated.

Perceptions of Child Behavior and Parenting Self-Esteem

The correlations between parent ratings of their own self-esteem and their own and their spouses' perceptions of child behavior are presented in Table 3. Mothers' ratings of their own skill/knowledge were negatively correlated with both their own and their spouses' ratings of child behavior problems. These correlations were all low to moderate but

TABLE 2   MEAN SCORES FOR PARENTING SELF-ESTEEM AND MOTHER-FATHER AGREEMENT

| | Hyperactives | | Normals | | | Pearson correlations between mother and father | |
Parenting self-esteem measure	Younger	Older	Younger	Older	F(df)	Hyperactives	Normals
Skill/Knowledge						.43**	.37**
Mothers	−.15	−.70	.23	.52	14.45(1,79)**		
Fathers	−.06	−.53	.22	.23	4.61(1,68)*		
Valuing/Comfort						.37*	.07
Mothers	−.54	−.59	.40	.47	20.57(1,79)**		
Fathers	−.66	−.50	.13	.60	15.57(1,68)**		

Note: Scores are expressed as standardized z scores. All F values refer to a significant main effect for diagnosis.

*p<.05. **p<.01.

TABLE 3 CORRELATIONS BETWEEN PARENTING SELF-ESTEEM AND RATINGS OF CHILD BEHAVIOR

	Child behavior ratings									
	Mothers					Fathers				
		Child behavior checklist					Child behavior checklist			
Parenting self-esteem measure	Conners'	WWP	Externalizing	Internalizing	Social	Conners'	WWP	Externalizing	Internalizing	Social
Skill/Knowledge										
Mothers	−.35**	−.35**	−.30**	−.22*	.25*	−.37**	−.33**	−.49**	−.40**	.15
Fathers	−.17	−.23*	−.21	−.15	.19	−.17	−.34**	−.28**	−.29**	.29**
Valuing/Comfort										
Mothers	−.44**	−.43**	−.43**	−.39**	.44**	−.45**	−.42**	−.50**	−.40**	.26**
Fathers	−.36**	−.35**	−.35**	−.20*	.17	−.37**	−.34**	−.41**	−.26**	.35**

Note: Conners' = Conners' Abbreviated Rating Scale; WWP = Werry-Weiss-Peters Activity Scale.

*p<.05. **p<.01.

statistically significant. Interestingly, mothers' self-esteem in terms of having the skill/knowledge to be a "good parent" was more highly correlated with their husbands' ratings on both the Externalizing and Internalizing scales of the CBCL than with their own ratings. Mothers' ratings of their degree of value/comfort as parents were also correlated with both their own and their husbands' perceptions of the child as a problem.

Although fathers' reports of their own skill/knowledge were inconsistently related to their spouses' perceptions of the child as a problem, there was a relationship between these ratings and their own perceptions of child behavior. Additionally, fathers' reported value/comfort in the parental role was significantly and inversely correlated with both mother and father perceptions of child problems. In general, the relationships between parental self-esteem and perceived child problems were stronger for mothers than for fathers, and self-esteem related to the value/comfort derived from being a parent was more highly correlated with perceived child problems than self-esteem related to parents' skill/knowledge.

There were significant positive correlations between both mothers' and fathers' perceptions of their child's Social Scale score and their own reported self-esteem. However, parents' reports of their own self-esteem did not generally appear to be related to their spouses' view of the child's social involvement.

Mothers' Reported Stress

Table 4 presents the group means for mothers' self-reported stress, expressed as standardized *z* scores, for each subscale of the Parenting Stress Index. In considering maternal stress related to child characteristics, mothers of hyperactives reported significantly more stress on all subscales than mothers of normal children. Maternal stress associated with child distractibility was also significantly greater for mothers of younger children than for mothers of older children. Mothers of hyperactives also indicated significantly more stress associated with the mother-child interaction than did mothers of normals.

For subscales reflecting stress related to mother characteristics, mothers of hyperactives again rated themselves as significantly more stressed than did mothers of normals, with the exception of stress related to the marital relationship and maternal health. Mothers of younger hyperactives were significantly more depressed and more self-blaming than mothers in any of the other three groups. Comparisons of the stresses related to situational factors,

TABLE 4 MEAN SCORES FOR MOTHERS' REPORTED STRESS

Stress measure	Hyperactives		Normals	
	Younger	Older	Younger	Older
Child characteristics				
Adaptability	1.16	1.02	−.98	−.81
Acceptability	.72	.92	−.67	−.72
Degree of bother	1.46	1.57	−1.12	−1.40
Temperament	.57	.98	−.64	−.70
Distractibility	2.06	1.22	−1.07	−1.51
Total	1.70	1.61	−1.27	−1.46
Mother–child interaction	.88	.40	−.61	−.39
Mother characteristics				
Depression	.85	−.03	−.29	−.26
Attachment to child	.44	.44	−.46	−.28
Role restriction	.48	.16	−.11	−.37
Sense of competence	.72	.47	−.64	−.32
Social isolation	.73	.18	−.44	−.24
Self–blame	.74	−.03	−.31	−.17
Marital relationship	.53	−.05	−.11	−.21
Health	.30	.08	−.18	−.10
Total	.89	.25	−.46	−.39
Situational characteristics				
Demographic	.43	−.03	−.25	−.02
Life events	.13	.11	.04	−.23
Total	.43	.04	−.15	−.19
Grand total	1.38	.80	−.87	−.85

such as demographic characteristics and life events, showed no significant differences between mothers of hyperactives and mothers of normals. These findings suggested that the greatest differences in reported maternal stress for mothers of hyperactives versus mothers of normals were for stress arising from child characteristics.

The analyses of the subscale mean scores on the stress measure suggested that possible differences existed between mothers of younger and older hyperactives on the stress subscales associated with maternal characteristics. For these subscales, there were often only small mean differences between the mothers of older hyperactives and the mothers of normal children, compared with much greater mean differences between the mothers of younger hyperactives and the other three

groups. In contrast to the hyperactive versus normal comparisons previously described, this within group analysis of the hyperactive children revealed that subscales reflecting mother characteristics were the best discriminators between younger and older children. The mothers' depression subscale scores accounted for 13% of the variance between groups. Mothers' skill/knowledge scores from the parenting self-esteem measure accounted for an additional 8% of the variance, while child distractibility and acceptability subscale scores added 6% and 7%, respectively. Finally, mothers' valuing/comfort portion of the self-esteem ratings, mothers' competence, and the mother-child interaction subscales scores from the maternal stress measure accounted for 5%, 6%, and 5% of the variance, respectively.

Individual total scores for the mother characteristics scale of the maternal stress measure were also rank ordered from lowest to highest reported stress. This ordering revealed a strong pattern associated with the age of the child that was not revealed by the previous analyses. With the exception of four extreme and deviant scores, mothers of older hyperactive children reported less stress associated with maternal characteristics than mothers of younger hyperactive children. The four extreme scores in the reverse direction heavily influenced group means and obscured the otherwise clear division of mothers of younger hyperactives reporting high levels of stress relative to mothers of older hyperactives.

Reported Mothers' Stress and Parental Perceptions of Child Behavior

The correlations between reported maternal stress and mothers' and fathers' ratings of child behavior are presented in Table 5. In general, these correlations suggest that strong, positive relationships exist between parental perceptions of child deviancy and the degree of stress reported by mothers. Additionally, moderate but significant inverse relationships were re-

TABLE 5   CORRELATIONS BETWEEN MOTHERS' REPORTED STRESS AND RATINGS OF CHILD BEHAVIOR

	Child behavior ratings									
	Mothers					Fathers				
		Child behavior checklist					Child behavior checklist			
Stress measure	Conners'	WWP	Externalizing	Internalizing	Social	Conners'	WWP	Externalizing	Internalizing	Social
Child characteristics										
Adaptability	.73**	.67**	.69**	.62*	−.48**	.53**	.58**	.69**	.60**	−.45**
Acceptability	.63**	.53**	.66**	.56**	−.44**	.44**	.52**	.61**	.53**	−.42**
Degree of bother	.78**	.75**	.79**	.67**	−.54**	.67**	.73**	.80**	.64**	−.47**
Temperament	.58**	.48**	.60**	.55**	−.41**	.46**	.48**	.61**	.54**	−.34**
Distractibility	.82**	.76**	.73**	.53**	−.53**	.72**	.71**	.74**	.54**	−.48**
Total	.83**	.76**	.81**	.68**	−.56**	.67**	.72**	.82**	.66**	−.51**
Mother–child interaction	.45**	.31**	.50**	.47**	−.26**	.26**	.18**	.38**	.36**	−.22**
Mother characteristics										
Depression	.33**	.30**	.32**	.32**	−.26**	.16	.22*	.29**	.23*	−.26**
Attachment to child	.36**	.34**	.38**	.41**	−.21*	.15	.22*	.31**	.27**	−.26**
Role restriction	.21*	.24*	.22*	.26**	−.33**	.32**	.29**	.34**	.27**	−.23*
Sense of competence	.46**	.41**	.49**	.48**	−.41**	.37**	.40**	.51**	.46**	−.33**
Social isolation	.39**	.38**	.40**	.46**	−.44**	.27**	.28**	.34**	.37**	−.39**
Self-blame	.39**	.33**	.42**	.33**	−.21**	.20**	.18	.28**	.19	−.01
Marital relationship	.21*	.24*	.25**	.28**	−.25**	.12	.15	.15	.18	−.18
Health	.20*	.24*	.23*	.36**	−.29**	.15	.18	.14	.15	−.21*
Total	.45**	.43**	.48**	.51**	−.42**	.31**	.34**	.44**	.39**	−.35**
Situational characteristics										
Demographic	.17	.23*	.19*	.19*	−.05	.15	.18	.30**	.30**	−.09
Life events	.14	.17	.18*	.20*	−.08	.06	.01	−.03	−.08	.02
Total	.21*	.27**	.26**	.28*	−.10	.17	.14	.21*	.19*	−.08
Grand total	.70**	.65**	.71**	.67**	−.53**	.52**	.56**	.69**	.59**	−.47**

Note: Conners' = Conners' Abbreviated Rating Scale; WWP = Werry-Weiss-Peters Activity Scale.

*p<.05. **p<.01.

vealed for parent perceptions of their child's social involvement and reported maternal stress. Inspection of the correlation coefficients indicates that maternal stress associated with child characteristics correlates most highly with parent ratings of child behavior problems. Stress reflected in subscales from the mother domain showed generally significant but moderate relationships with parental ratings of child behavior, whereas maternal stress associated with situational characteristics was inconsistently related to mother and father reports of child behavior problems. Overall, mothers' ratings of child behavior were more strongly associated with maternal reports of stress than were fathers' ratings, particularly for stress related to mother characteristics.

DISCUSSION

The results of this study indicated that, in comparison to parents of normal children, parents of hyperactives reported lower levels of parenting self-esteem, reported greater maternal stress, and perceived their children as more problematic. Additionally, it was found that both mothers' and fathers' self-esteem as parents and reports of maternal stress were related to parental perceptions of child behavior.

Results from the Parenting Sense of Competence Scale (Gibaud-Wallston & Wandersman, Note 1) indicated that mothers and fathers of hyperactives see themselves as less competent than parents of normals in respect to both their skill/knowledge in being good parents and the degree of valuing/comfort derived from the parenting role. The results are also consistent with Gibaud-Wallston and Wandersman's (Note 1) view that the two scales of this measure are assessing different aspects of parenting competence, with the Valuing/Comfort scale being more a reflection of cultural norms and therefore being less influenced by variables associated with the passage of time than the Skill/ Knowledge scale. In our study, both mothers

and fathers of younger hyperactive children perceived themselves at levels of skill/knowledge that approached those reported by parents of normals. However, relative to parents of normals, parents of older hyperactives were markedly lower in their sense of competence related to skill/knowledge. Although correlational, these findings suggest a cumulative deficit in parenting self-esteem related to unsuccessful child-rearing experiences. In contrast to the findings for skill/knowledge, the valuing/ comfort dimension of parental self-esteem was unrelated to the age of the hyperactive child.

Consistent inverse relationships were found between parental perceptions of child behavior problems and parenting self-esteem. These relationships were generally stronger for mothers than for fathers. Parents' perceptions of the child as a problem were more highly correlated with the valuing/comfort dimension of parenting self-esteem than with the skill/knowledge dimension. It is interesting that fathers' perceptions of the child as a problem were consistently correlated with mothers' reported self-esteem for both skill/knowledge and valuing/comfort. In contrast, mothers' perceptions of the child as a problem correlated with fathers' valuing/comfort but were weakly and inconsistently correlated with fathers' skill/knowledge. It appears that mothers' feelings about themselves as parents are as much related to their husbands' perception of the child as problematic as to their own, whereas fathers' perceptions of their own skill/knowledge as parents do not appear to correlate with their spouses' views of the child as a problem.

For almost every dimension of stress assessed by the Parenting Stress Index (PSI, Abidin & Burke, Note 2) mothers of hyperactive children reported themselves as more severely stressed than mothers of normals. Child characteristics emerged as a major source of stress, especially the child's perceived degree of bother and distractibility. Mothers of hyperactives also reported more stress related to the parent-child interaction, as well as feelings of depression, social isolation, self-blame, role restriction and lack of attachment to their child. These findings are consistent with other reports describing maternal distress in mothers of both hyperactive (Sandberg et al., 1980) and conduct-disordered children (Patterson, 1980), although the findings are not necessarily specific to these types of child problems.

Further examination of the data revealed that most of the hyperactive versus normal differences in reported stress related to mother characteristics, such as depression, isolation, and self-blame, were for mothers of younger hyperactive children. Although mothers of older hyperactive children reported child-related stress, their reported stress related to feelings about themselves and their situation was not nearly as great as that of mothers of younger hyperactives. Although there were no statistically significant group differences related to maternal reports of stress for their marital relationships, health, or situation, the mothers of younger hyperactives again tended to report more stress on all of these dimensions. The failure to find group differences in respect to the marital relationship is inconsistent with findings from other investigations (e.g., Oltmanns, Broderick, & O'Leary, 1977) and may reflect the small number of items on the PSI that deal with this area.

The correlations between mothers' reported stress for child characteristics and both their own and their spouses' perceptions of the child as a problem were consistently high. As was the case for self-esteem, fathers' perceptions of the child as a problem were highly correlated with the degree of stress reported by mothers. For stress related to mother characteristics, there were consistent but weaker relationships between mothers' perceptions of child behavior and their reported feelings about themselves. Fathers' perceptions of child problems were again related to mothers' reported stress in the mother domain but to a lesser degree than for

the child domain. The relationships between perceived child problems and reports of situational stress tended to be weak and insignificant.

Current findings related to parental perceptions of hyperactive children are consistent with previous investigations in demonstrating that although agreement between parents may be high (Goyette, Conners, & Ulrich, 1978), fathers tend to view the problem as less severe than mothers (Firestone & Witt, Note 4). Parental ratings of their hyperactive children also indicated that in addition to the acting out, conduct, and attentional difficulties encompassed under the Externalizing scale of the CBCL, hyperactives were also perceived as exhibiting problems reflected on the Internalizing scale. Marked deficits in social involvement were also reported, and such deficits were characteristic of both younger and older hyperactives. This indication of the multidimensional nature of hyperactivity suggests the need for multifaceted assessment procedures. In this regard the CBCL demonstrated good interparent agreement, and its Externalizing scale correlated highly with the Conners' and WWP rating scales. This checklist also assesses internalizing problems and social competence and has the potential for profile analysis using individual scales.

The limited sample size in this study did not permit an extensive examination of the relationships between *specific* CBCL scales and the parent self-report measures. However, a preliminary examination of the data indicated that, relative to the other CBCL scales, the hyperactivity-related scales (hyperactive, aggressive, delinquent, and immature) correlated most highly with parent reports of self-esteem and maternal stress. Since the ratings of problems not associated with hyperactivity per se were being made for a group of children whose primary presenting problem was hyperactivity, the current findings are inconclusive concerning the specificity of the relationships between self-esteem, maternal stress, and hyperactivity. Further research comparing the responses on these measures by parents of hyperactives and parents of children exhibiting other types of primary deficits will be needed to clarify this question.

In summary, the present study supports the need for multidimensional assessments with families of hyperactive children that include measures tapping a wide range of child problems and examining closely the role of parental views regarding themselves and their family situations. Such an approach is consistent with currently converging viewpoints regarding the potential importance of parental cognitions and affects in moderating the effects of childhood disturbance (e.g., Wahler, Gordon, & Dumas, Note 5). The consistent age-related differences in parents' reports of stress and self-esteem suggest the need to consider different types of intervention targets in families with younger versus older hyperactive children, as well as the importance of early interventions. In addition, current findings related to fathers of hyperactive children, both in respect to their own deficits in self-esteem and to the relationship between their views of the child and their spouses' reported feelings about themselves, suggest the need to consider the role of the father in families of hyperactives in designing treatment programs. Interventions that are specific to the role that fathers may play in disturbed families (e.g. as a support system for mothers) may be as important as attempts to include fathers in ways that have been traditionally employed in treatment with mothers (e.g., training in child management) in influencing long-term outcomes (Cunningham, Note 6).

The current findings only begin to explore potentially important social factors related to hyperactivity, and there is a need to relate the findings regarding parent self-esteem and reported maternal stress to direct observations of parent-child interactions. In this regard,

some of our preliminary work (Mash & Johnston, in press) suggests that the parental-report measures used in this study are related to observational measures of both mother and child behaviors. As noted previously, the normal control groups in this study do not permit any conclusions regarding the specificity of the current findings to parents of hyperactive children versus parents of children with other types of problems. Similar investigations with parents of other populations of disturbed children may help to clarify this question. The correlational/cross-sectional findings related to age also point up the need to identify and treat families with younger hyperactive children and to explore some of the suggested age-related differences in parenting self-esteem and maternal stress within a longitudinal framework.

Finally, we would reemphasize that the current findings are correlational and therefore inconclusive in respect to whether parental perceptions of the child as a problem precede or follow deficits in parental self-esteem and reported maternal stress. In this regard, there is little question that the hyperactive children being rated by parents in this study were exhibiting observable behavior problems and that parental reports were a reflection of these difficulties. Reports of low self-esteem and maternal stress are likely to be, in part, a reaction to having a child who is perceived as difficult. However, such feelings are equally likely to influence the parent-child interaction in ways that may exacerbate the child's difficulties and the parent's subsequent perceptions of these difficulties. The purpose of the current study was to identify possible self-esteem deficits and the nature of stress reported by mothers of hyperactive children. Further research involving longitudinal designs or experimental manipulations may permit a better understanding of the causal network surrounding parental perceptions and child behaviors.

REFERENCE NOTES

1 Gibaud-Wallston, J., & Wandersman, L.P. *Development and utility of the Parenting Sense of Competence Scale*. Paper presented at the meeting of the American Psychological Association, Toronto, Canada, August 1978.
2 Abidin, R. R., & Burke, W. T. *Parenting Stress Index*. Unpublished manuscript, Department of Foundations of Education, University of Virginia, 1978.
3 Burke, W. T., & Abidin, R. R. *The development of a Parenting Stress Index*. Paper presented at the meeting of the American Psychological Association, Toronto, Canada, August 1978.
4 Firestone, P., & Witt, J. E. *Characteristics of families completing and prematurely discontinuing a behavioral parent training program*. Unpublished manuscript, School of Psychology, University of Ottawa, 1981.
5 Wahler, R. G., Gordon, J. S., & Dumas, J.E. *Improving the attentional tracking of insular mothers: Discriminative restructuring*. Paper presented at the meeting of the Association for the Advancement of Behavior Therapy, Toronto, Canada, 1981.
6 Cunningham, C. E. Personal communication, November, 1981.

REFERENCES

Achenbach, T. M. The classification of children's psychiatric symptoms: A factor analytic study. *Psychological Monographs,* 1966, *80* (7, Whole No. 615).
Achenbach, T. M. The Child Behavior Profile, I: Boys aged 6–11. *Journal of Consulting and Clinical Psychology,* 1978, *46,* 759–776.
Achenbach, T. M., & Edelbrock, C. S. Behavioral problems and competencies reported by parents of normal and disturbed children aged four through sixteen. *Monographs of the Society for Research in Child Development,* 1981, *46,*(1, Serial No. 188).
Barkley, R. A. Hyperactivity. In E. J. Mash & L. G. Terdal (Eds.), *Behavioral assessment of childhood disorders*. New York: Guilford Press, 1981.
Barkley, R. A., & Cunningham, C. E. The parent-child interactions of hyperactive children and their modification by stimulant drugs. In R. M. Knights & D. J. Bakker (Eds.), *Treatment of hyperactive and learning disordered children*. Baltimore, Md.: University Park Press, 1980.
Block, J. Parents of schizophrenic, neurotic, asthmatic, and congenitally ill children. *Archives of General Psychiatry,* 1969, *20,* 659–674.
Blumberg, N. L. Effects of neonatal risk, maternal attitude and cognitive style on early postpartum adjustment. *Journal of Abnormal Psychology,* 1980, *89,* 139–150.
Bugental, D. B. Caporeal, L., & Shennum, W. A. Experimentally produced child uncontrollability: Effects of the potency of adult communication patterns. *Child Development,* 1980, *51,* 520–528.
Cantwell, D. Psychiatric illness in the families of hyperactive children. *Archives of General Psychiatry,* 1972, *27,* 414–417.
Cohen, N. J., Sullivan, J., Minde, K., Novak, C., & Helwig, C. Evaluation of the relative effectiveness of methylphenidate and cognitive behavior modification in the treatment of kindergarten-aged hyperactive children. *Journal of Abnormal Child Psychology,* 1981, *9,* 43–54.
Conners, C. K. Pharmacotherapy of psychopathology in children. In H. C. Quay & J. S. Werry (Eds.), *Psychopathological disorders of childhood*. New York: Wiley, 1972.
Crockenberg, S. B. Infant irritability, mother responsiveness, and social-support influences on the security of infant-mother attachment. *Child Development,* 1981, *52,* 857–865.
Cummings, S. T., Bayley, H. C., & Rie, H. E. Effects of the child's deficiency on the mother: A study of mothers of mentally retarded, chronically ill, and neurotic children. *American Journal of Orthopsychiatry,* 1966, *36,* 595–608.
Delamater, A. M., Lahey, B. B., & Drake, L. Toward an empirical subclassification of "learning disabilities": A psychophysiological comparison of "hyperactive" and "nonhyperactive" subgroups. *Journal of Abnormal Child Psychology,* 1981, *9,* 65–77.
Dunn, L. M. *Peabody Picture Vocabulary Test*. Circle Pines, Minn.: American Guidance Service, 1965.
Goyette, C. H., Conners, C. K., & Ulrich, R. F. Normative data on Revised Conners Parent and Teacher Rating Scales. *Journal of Abnormal Child Psychology,* 1978, *6,* 221–236.

Griest, D. L., Forehand, R., Wells, K. C., & McMahon, R. J. An examination of differences between nonclinic and behavior-problem clinic-referred children and their mothers. *Journal of Abnormal Psychology, 1980, 89,* 497–500.

Griest, S., Wells, K. C., & Forehand, R. An examination of predictors of maternal perceptions of maladjustment in clinic-referred children. *Journal of Abnormal Psychology, 1979, 88,* 277–281.

Hollingshead, A. B. *Four Factor Index of Social Status.* New Haven, Conn.: Yale University, Department of Sociology, 1975.

Johnson, S. M., & Lobitz, G. K. The personal and marital adjustment of parents as related to observed child deviance and parenting behaviors. *Journal of Abnormal Child Psychology, 1974, 2,* 193–207.

Jones, R. R., Reid, J. B., & Patterson, G. R. Naturalistic observations in a clinical assessment. In P. McReynolds (Ed.,) *Advances in psychological assessment* (Vol. 3). San Francisco: Jossey-Bass, 1975.

Kogan, K. L. Interaction systems between preschool handicapped or developmentally delayed children and their parents. In T. M. Field, S. Goldberg, D. Stern, & A. M. Sostek (Eds.), *High-risk infants and children: Adult and peer interactions.* New York: Academic Press, 1980.

Kogan, K. L., Tyler, N., & Turner, P. The process of interpersonal adaptation between mothers and their cerebral palsied children. *Developmental Medicine and Child Neurology, 1974, 16,* 518–527.

Lobitz, G. K., & Johnson, S. M. Normal versus deviant children: A multimethod comparison. *Journal of Abnormal Child Psychology, 1975, 3,* 353–374.

Long, C. G., & Moore, J. R. Parental expectations for their epileptic children. *Journal of Child Psychology and Psychiatry, 1929, 20,* 299–312.

Mash, E. J., & Johnston, C. A comparison of the mother-child interactions of younger and older hyperactive and normal children. *Child Development, 1982, 53,* 1371–1381.

Mash, E. J., & Johnston, C. A note on the prediction of mothers' behavior with their hyperactive children during play and task situations. *Child and Family Behavior Therapy,* in press.

Morrison, J. R., & Stewart, M. A. A family study of the hyperactive syndrome. *Biological Psychiatry, 1971, 3,* 189–195.

Mulhern, R. K., & Passman, R. H. Parental discipline as affected by the sex of the parent, the sex of the child, and the child's apparent responsiveness to discipline. *Developmental Psychology, 1981, 17,* 604–613.

Oltmanns, T. F., Broderick, J. E., & O'Leary, K. D. Marital adjustment and the efficacy of behavior therapy with children. *Journal of Consulting and Clinical Psychology, 1977, 45,* 724–729.

Paternite, C. E., & Loney, J. Childhood hyperkinesis: Relationships between symptomatology and home environment. In C. K. Whalen & B. Henker (Eds.), *Hyperactive Children: The social ecology of identification and treatment.* New York: Academic Press, 1980.

Patterson, G. R. The aggressive child: Victim and architect of coercive system. In E. J. Mash, L. A. Hamerlynck, & L. C. Handy (Eds.), *Behavior modification and families.* New York: Brunner/Mazel, 1976.

Patterson, G. R. Mothers: The unacknowledged victims. *Monographs of the Society for Research in Child Development, 1980, 45*(5, Serial No. 186).

Ross, D. M., & Ross, S. A. *Hyperactivity.* New York: Wiley, 1976.

Routh, D. K. Developmental and social aspects of hyperactivity. In C. K. Whalen & B. Henker (Eds.), *Hyperactive children: The social ecology of identification and treatment.* New York: Academic Press, 1980.

Routh, D., K. Schroeder, C. S., & O'Tuama, L. C. Development of activity level in children. *Developmental Psychology, 1974, 10,* 163–168.

Safer, R., & Allen, D. *Hyperactive children: Diagnosis and management.* Baltimore, Md: University Park Press, 1976.

Sandberg, S. T., Weiselberg, M., & Shaffer, D. Hyperkinetic and conduct problem children in a primary school population: Some epidemiological considerations. *Journal of Child Psychology and Psychiatry, 1980, 21,* 293–311.

Stevens-Long, J. The effect of behavioral context on some aspects of adult disciplinary practice and effect. *Child Development, 1973, 44,* 476–484.

Stewart, M. A., DeBlois, C. S., & Cummings, C. Psychiatric disorder in the parents of hyperactive boys and those with conduct disorders. *Journal of Child Psychology and Psychiatry*, 1980, *21*, 283–292.

Wahler, R. G. The insular mother: Her problems in parent-child treatment. *Journal of Applied Behavior Analysis*, 1980, *13*, 207–219 (a).

Wahler, R. G. Parent insularity as a determinant of generalization success in family treatment. In S. Salzinger, J. Antrobus, & J. Glick (Eds.), *The ecosystem of the "sick" child*. New York: Academic Press, 1980 (b).

Wahler, R. G., Leske, G., & Rogers, E. S. The insular family: A deviance support system for oppositional children. In L. A. Hamerlynck (Ed.), *Behavioral systems for the developmentally dis-*abled: *I. School and family environment*. New York: Brunner/Mazel, 1979.

Weinberg, S. L., & Richardson, M. S. Dimensions of stress in early parenting. *Journal of Consulting and Clinical Psychology*, 1981, *49*, 686–693.

Werner, E. E. Environmental interaction in minimal brain dysfunction. In H. Rie & E. Rie (Eds.), *Handbook of minimal brain dysfunction*. New York: Wiley & Sons, 1980.

Whalen, C., & Henker, B. (Eds.). *Hyperactive children: The social ecology of identification and treatment*. New York: Academic Press, 1980.

Wolf, S., & Acton, W. P., Characteristics of parents of disturbed children. *British Journal of Psychiatry*, 1968, *114*, 593–601.

READING 53

Cognitive and Social Development in Infants and Toddlers with a Bipolar Parent

Carolyn Zahn-Waxler
Michael Chapman
E. Mark Cummings

Offspring of parents with a manic-depressive disorder may be at risk for a variety of affective disorders, including bipolar illness (illness where extremes of agitated manic behavior and of depressed behavior are experienced at different times). Both biological and environmental mechanisms have been implicated in the intergenerational patterns of bipolar illness commonly observed in families.[1] Psychoanalytic concepts of object relations (referring to interpersonal relationships with significant others) often have been used to explain the development of affective disorders. The focus has been either on the connection between early childhood disturbances in object relations and later depression,[2,3] or on the connection between depressed parenting and the development of poor object relations in children.[4] The processes hypothesized to influence the corresponding development of poor self-concept, poor interpersonal relations and affective dysregulation have included difficulties in coping with separation and loss, and disturbances in the stability and security of the child's attachment relationship to the caregiver. Related to these problems, in turn, are the presumed disruptions in processes of self-awareness and separation/individuation that occur in children from unstable caregiving environments.[5] Much of the research in these areas, however, has been derived from clinical studies, and findings from psychoanalytically oriented research have not been based on prospective data (i.e., data linking certain childhood disturbances to later affective illness).

Piaget broadened the concept of object relations to include analysis of the child's relationship to the physical, as well as the social world.[6] In his theory of cognitive development, attachment was viewed as representing not only a shift in the child's emotional energy from a narcissistic emphasis on self to a focus on another person (mother), but to a restructuring of the whole cognitive and affective universe. Within this framework, as physical objects become permanent, people too take on permanent existence in the child's mind. Thus, there is hypothesized to be reciprocal development of (a) permanence in the physical world (the world of objects), (b) permanence in the social world (the world of people) and (c) establishment of the self as an entity that participates in these worlds but is also separate from it. There are also considerable differences in the nature of the physical and social worlds of children.[7] Levels of functioning in one domain might not always correspond to performance in other arenas of functioning. The purpose of this research was to observe whether children from manic-depressive families showed disturbances in the early development of object relations in each of these three domains of cognitive and social development.

A fourth, related area of children's social-cognitive functioning was also examined. The development of role-taking abilities were assessed in the context of symbolic play. In the early stages of role-taking the child begins to learn that *others* have separate lives, needs and internal states that may differ from those of the child. The recent establishment of normed infant tests[8,9,10,11] with demonstratable reliability and validity makes it possible to begin to investigate empirically psychoanalytic and cognitive concepts of object relations using prospective research designs. Several of these tests were utilized here to compare the early cognitive and social problem solving abilities from a development perspective in young children from families with and without bipolar affective illness.

METHOD

Seven male infants with a bipolar parent were studied longitudinally beginning at age one and were compared with a control group of 20 children (ten males and ten females). Extensive recruitment efforts failed to yield any one-year females from bipolar families. Preliminary statistical analyses of data indicated that boys and girls from control families performed very similarly on all of the tasks. Therefore data from both sexes was combined and the bipolar sample was compared with the entire control sample in subsequent analyses. None of the children had physical health problems.

Parental Diagnoses

Seven families originally had been part of an inpatient research project on bipolar illness and, hence, had been clinically evaluated. In four of the index families, the mother was bipolar; the father was bipolar in the remaining three families. In five of the seven, spouses also had diagnoses of unipolar depression (depression not accompanied by intermittent periods of manic activity as is found in a bipolar or manic-depressive condition). A sixth spouse suffered from alcoholism and neurosis. Hence, multiple forms of depression and multiple problems, in fact, characterized these families. Bipolar patients were in remission at the time of the study; most were being treated with lithium. All of the mothers in the control group were diagnosed as currently normal and seven of the fathers from control families also were diagnosed as normal using the same criteria. It was not possible to screen the remaining 13 fathers with the same diagnostic tests.

However, clinical evaluation was used to ascertain that they did not have affective disorders and that they were not receiving medical or psychological treatment for emotional problems. The control families were part of the Normal Volunteer Program associated with the medical facility. Control and bipolar families were equated in terms of socio-economic status, race, religion, ethnicity and parental age. The samples were predominantly white and middle class with average ages in the early to mid thirties. Informed consent was obtained from all families.

Procedures

Object relations were assessed in the four tests of perceptual, cognitive and social functioning described below. The first three tasks were administered (in the order listed) in the home on three separate occasions when the child was 12 to 14, 18 and 24 months of age. The remaining assessment was made in the laboratory when children were two years old. For home assessments, testing typically took place in the family's living room. Mothers were told to respond to the child if the latter initiated interaction during testing but not to initiate interactions herself. Two observers were present at each visit: one administered and scored the assessments for all children and the second was present for reliability purposes. The observer whose scores were used for data analyses was not informed of the parental diagnoses.

1 *Self-other differentiation* was measured by the Agent Use Scale as described by Watson & Fischer.[8] This scale was designed to provide a measure of the development of the understanding of persons as independent agents in the context of pretend play. As such, it provides a measure of rudimentary, social role-taking skills. In this procedure, an experimenter models activities related to specified internal need states (eating/drinking; sleeping, cleaning self). These activities are either acted out by the experimenter or by inanimate agents controlled by the experimenter. Three different agents combined with three different actions were modeled in counterbalanced sequences. The agents were the examiner (self), a doll (other) and a wooden block (substitute other). The actions were eating/drinking from a cup, sleeping by lying on a pillow, and washing hands, face and arms with a wash cloth. In each case, the experimenter would perform the actions or have the doll or block perform them. There was

a seven minute free play period after the modeling period. Then the experimenter took the test materials in turn and asked the child to imitate the actions that had previously been modeled. The objects were presented in the same order as before.

Four types of imitations representing a previously identified developmental stage sequence in normal social-cognitive development[8] were coded, namely; (1) Self as Agent, (2) Passive Other Agent, (3) Passive Substitute Agent and (4) Active Other Agent. Here, only the first two forms of agent use occurred with any frequency. They represent a beginning transition from a self- to other-orientation. Coder reliabilities were $r = .88$ for coding Self as Agent (self-oriented play) and $r = .85$ for coding Passive Other Agent (other-oriented play).

2 *Self-awareness* was assessed using a test of visual self-recognition development by Bertenthal and Fischer (1978).[9] It measures the reaction of an infant to his/her own mirror image and the progressive ability to identify self and objects in the environment in relation to the mirror image of self on tasks graded in difficulty. To begin, the mother was requested to put a special vest on the child (to the back of which objects visible to the child only in the mirror were later attached). The mother also was asked to put a spot of rouge or lipstick on the child's nose as unobtrusively as possible. The latter procedure dates back to studies of self-concept in monkeys, in which rouge was put on the monkey's face and observers noted whether the monkey examined the rouge "on the other monkey in the mirror" or referred back to the self in exploring the location of the rouge.[14] The mother was requested to sit the child in front of a full length mirror and to stand to one side so that her image was not visible to the child. On the first task, the mother pointed to the child's reflection in the mirror and asked, "Who's that?" The critical response to this task was the child's use of his or her own name or an appropriate personal pronoun as a response to the mother's question. On the second task, the rouge task, observers determined whether or not the child after looking in the mirror either touched his/her nose or indicated verbally that something was different about it. The remaining tasks involved finding objects located behind the infant and visible to him/her only as reflected in the mirror. Observer reliability for coding the different stages of visual self-recognition was $r = .84$.

3 *Object permanence,* defined as the understanding that objects continue to exist even when they disappear from sight, was measured with the Uzgiris-Hunt object permanence scale.[10] This scale consists of a graded series of increasingly difficult tasks assessing the infant's progress through the last three stages in the development of the object concept according to Piaget.[15] Stage four tasks (Uzgiris-Hunt items four to seven) required infants to find objects hidden completely under a single screen; stage five tasks (items eight and nine) required objects to be found following one or more visible displacements between screens; and stage six tasks (items ten to fifteen) involved finding objects that had been invisibly displaced. According to Piaget, each successive stage represents the infant's increasing ability to remember a series of spatial displacements and, accordingly, to understand the object as independent of the action involved in its displacement. In addition to this stage-related sequence, the Uzgiris-Hunt scale includes within-stage items ordered by increasing complexity. For example, item four consists in finding an object completely covered in one place, whereas item five involves an object covered in two places. This scale may thus be interpreted as reflecting the child's gradual discovery of the permanence of physical objects across the first two years of life (cf. Cummings & Bjork).[16] Double scoring was not obtained because the inter-rater reli-

ability has previously been found to be extremely high (Uzgiris & Hunt).[10]

4 *Interpersonal object relations* were assessed in terms of the child's relationship to the mother. These laboratory assessments were made two times. Average age of children at time one was 25.6 months and at time two was 27.4 months. A variant of the Ainsworth paradigm was used in which the mother left the room and the child's behaviors during both the separation and reunion with the mother were coded.[11] These episodes had been preceded by a half-hour of peer interactions. Thus, in a departure from the usual separation studies, the child was left with a playmate during the mother's departure. Children's responses were scored according to Ainsworth's criteria for secure and insecure (ambivalent or avoidant) attachments.[11] Secure infants are defined as those who actively seek contact or interaction during reunion with the mother and are effectively quieted by contact with the mother. Insecure avoidant infants ignore and/or avoid the mother during reunion. Insecure-ambivalent infants are difficult to comfort during reunion and may mix contact seeking with pushing away. Reliability of attachment classifications was 92 percent. Coders were blind with regard to parental diagnoses.

RESULTS

Children from bipolar and control families performed very similarly on the Uzguris-Hunt test of understanding of the permanence of physical objects (Figure 1). By the second half of the second year of life children from both groups had attained stage six, the last stage of sensorimotor development described by Piaget on the test of object permanence. This ability to process information concerning the location of physical objects that have temporarily disappeared from view increases with age similarly for children from bipolar and normal families.

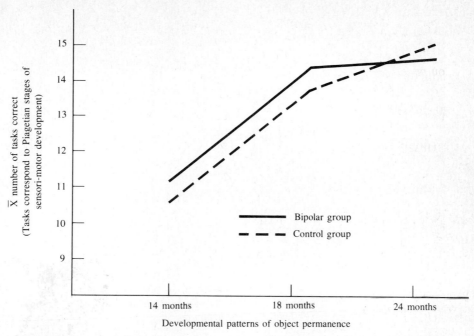

FIGURE 1 Performance on the Uzguris-Hunt object permanence task: Assessment of children's spatial/temporal memory for physical objects.

Stage six is characterized by the beginning of an ability to use symbols and representations of physical objects in conceptualizing the physical world. Hence, it marks a significant transition in cognitive development from concrete thought to the beginnings of abstract thought.

Children from both groups also followed the normal developmental sequences identified by Bertenthal & Fischer[9] on the attainment of self-awareness (Figure 2). The child's ability to coordinate complex behaviors pertaining to the spatial location of physical objects in relation to his/her mirror image was found to increase with age similarly for children from bipolar and control families. Thus, on the cognitive test of self-recognition as well, there were no deficits in the performance of children from bipolar families.

In contrast, on measures of object relations that pertain more to social and interpersonal problem solving abilities, disturbances in the functioning of infants and toddlers with a bipolar parent were identified. On the Agent-Use task, children from control families showed the normal developmental progression identified by Watson & Fischer.[8] Namely, there is a transition from a predominance of self-oriented imitation of the model during play (e.g., pretending to feed oneself) to a predominance of actions involving (symbolic) others in the environment (e.g., feeding the doll, or putting a doll to sleep). In the context of pretend play, these latter actions constitute the beginning of an understanding, awareness or interest in the need states of others. However, between the ages of one and two, children from control families decreased on the expression of self-oriented pretend play while children from bipolar families showed an increase. There was an increase with age in children from both groups in other-oriented pretend play, but children with a bipolar parent show less other-oriented pretend play

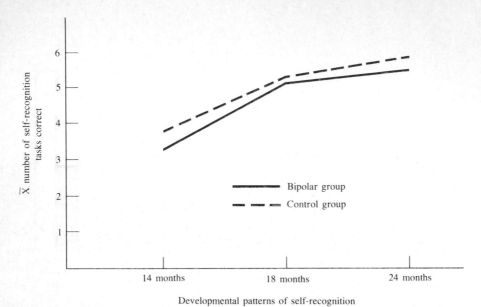

Developmental patterns of self-recognition

FIGURE 2   Performance on the Bertenthal-Fischer self-recognition task: Perceptual/cognitive test of children's attainment of a separate self image.

than controls (Figure 3). These data indicate that children from bipolar families show very early an atypical pattern of development in their role-taking abilities. Role-taking is defined here as the recognition that others are separate, independent agents with needs and feeling states (fatigue, hunger, etc.) of their own.

Impairments in object relations in the interpersonal realm were also identified in children from bipolar families in terms of their relationships with the primary caregiver. In the second laboratory assessment, children from bipolar homes were more frequently judged to have insecure (ambivalent or avoidant) relationships with their mothers while children from control families tended to have secure attachments. A similar but non-significant trend was present for the first session (Table 1).

DISCUSSION

Disturbances in object relations in the first years of life were found to occur in the social but not in the cognitive domain in children with a bipolar parent. A great majority of children

with a bipolar parent were judged not to have a secure relationship to the mother. And there was evidence in the symbolic play of these children of a lag in their ability or inclination to explore the emotions or internal states of others. The typical developmental course of such role-taking in the second year of life is the transition from a predominance of exploration of self-oriented actions to a preponderance of actions that begin to explore the inner worlds of others, albeit in the context of fantasy. In the child of a bipolar parent, the development of this latter capacity appears to be in active competition with the continuation and expansion of self-oriented behaviors.

Prior assessments of attachment patterns in the bipolar sample and a subsample of the control children using a more standard version of the Ainsworth paradigm suggested that the attachment problems of children from proband families develop and increase in severity during the second year of life.[17] The lack of a secure or trusting relationship with the primary caregiver coupled with apparent difficulties in self-other differentiation as seen

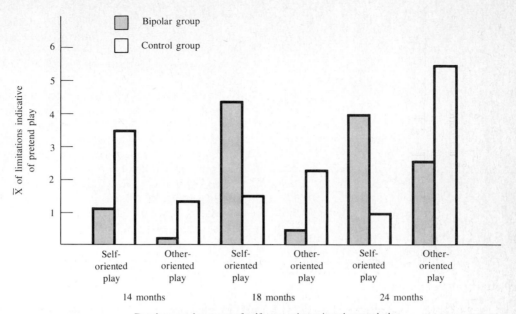

Developmental patterns of self – vs. other-oriented pretend play
following exposure to an adult model

FIGURE 3   Performance on the Watson-Fischer agent-use task. Assessment of children's social-cognitive role-taking abilities.

in these children's symbolic play do not portend well for the development of their future social relationships outside the family settings. There are already some indications that the early peer relations of these children are marred by emotion disregulation and an inability to share.[18] The pattern of findings in the present research with very young children parallels observations of clinicians who work with adult bipolar patients. Formal cognitive functioning is often intact except in psychotics: intellectual achievement and creative accomplishments often are not impaired. However, social relations of manic-depressives are marked by instability and insecurity. Anthony[4] has discussed the potential impact of related characteristics of manic-depressives on their parenting, e.g., (a) taking but refusing to give and (b) having little awareness of others as people and hence, little ability to empathize with them.

The similarity of patterns of disturbance in

childhood and adulthood in bipolar families may have implications for theories regarding intergenerational continuity of interpersonal problems associated with the disorder. Environmental disturbances, as well as biological vulnerability or predisposition, may play a causal role in the transmission of bipolar illness. The present research design does not permit an assessment of the mechanisms implicated in the problems. Nor can we infer that the problems identified in the children are uniquely a result of having a bipolar parent, for some of the mothers had unipolar depression. Further research on the specific rearing practices of these parents is needed to examine environmental influences. Initial explorations of parenting practices in these proband families suggest a variety of differences in the mothers from the bipolar and control groups.[19] The former mothers placed a great deal of emphasis on the control of emotions, both their own emotions and their children's feelings. They were simultaneously pro-

TABLE 1 ATTACHMENT PATTERNS OF TWO-YEAR-OLD CHILDREN FROM BIPOLAR AND CONTROL FAMILIES: NUMBER OF CHILDREN WHO EVIDENCE SECURE AND INSECURE ATTACHMENT, ASSESSED ON TWO SEPARATE OCCASIONS

Parental psychopathology	Attachment to mother	
	Secure	Insecure
Session I		
Bipolar	4	3
Control	15	5
Session II		
Bipolar	1	6
Control	15	5

tective and negative toward the child and they were viewed as unhappy, tense, disorganized, ineffective and inconsistent in their caregiving. It is reasonable to expect that this constellation of environmental disturbance will have some impact on the child's social and emotional development. Biological vulnerability needs to be viewed in this context.

Regardless of the etiology of the illness, the empirical data is unique in indicating that social-emotional problems in children of parents with affective illness may begin very early in life. Clinical observations of several of these children indicate that the disturbances are not subtle. Two of the children and their parents were referred for therapy. Thus, the early detection of problems have corresponding implications for early treatment and intervention. Further research is needed to identify those particular patterns of parent-child interaction which may contribute partially to the familial aggregation of affective disorders. There is also a need to continue to follow such families with longitudinal, prospective research designs in order to obtain more direct evidence on processes of transmission of psychopathology.[20,21]

REFERENCES

1 Davenport YB, Adland ML, Gold PW, et al: Manic-depressive illness: Psychodynamic features of multigenerational families. *Am J Orthopsychiat*. 49:24–35, 1979.

2 Cohen MB, Baker G, Cohen RA and Wiegert E: An intensive study of twelve cases of manic-depressive psychosis. *Psychiatry*. 17:103–107, 1954.

3 Bowlby L: *Attachment and Loss: Loss Sadness and Depression, vol. III*. New York: Basic Books, 1980.

4 Anthony EJ: The influence of a manic-depressive environment on the developing child, in Anthony EJ, Benedek T (eds.). *Depression and Human Existence*. Boston: Little, Brown & Co, 1975.

5 Mahler MS, Pine F and Bergman A: *The Psychological Birth of the Human Infant: Symbiosis and Individuation*. New York: Basic Books, 1975.

6 Cowan PA: *Piaget with Feeling: Cognitive, Social and Emotional Dimensions*. New York: Holt, Rinehart, & Winston, 1978.

7 Damon W: Five questions for research in social-cognitive development, in Higgins ET, Ruble N and Hartup WW (eds.). *Social Cognition and Social Development*. Cambridge: University Press, pp 371–393, 1983.

8 Watson MW and Fischer KW: A developmental sequence of agent use in late infancy. *Child Dev*. 48:828–836, 1977.

9 Bertenthal BI and Fischer KW: The development of self-recognition in the infant. *Dev. Psychol* 14:44–50, 1978.

10 Uzgiris IC and Hunt JMc: *Assessment in Infancy*. Urbana, Illinois: University of Illinois Press, 1975.

11 Ainsworth MDS, Blehar MC, Waters E et al: *Patterns of Attachment: A Psychological Study of the Strange Situation*. Hillsdale, New Jersey: Erlbaum, 1978.

12 Spitzer RL and Endicott J: Schedule for affective disorders and schizophrenia: Life-time version, in *Biometrics Research*. New York: New York State Psychiatric Institute, 1978.

13 Mazure C, Gershon ES: Blindness and reliability in lifetime psychiatric diagnosis. *Arch Gen Psychiatry*. 36:521–525, 1979.

14 Gallup CG Jr: Chimpanzees: self recognition. *Science*. 167:86–87, 1970.

15 Piaget J: *The Construction of Reality in the Child*. New York: Basic Books, 1954.

16 Cummings EM and Bjork EL: Search behavior in multi-choice hiding task. Evidence for an objective conception of space in infancy. *Int J Beh Dev. 6:*71–87, 1983.

17 Gaensbauer TJ, Harmon RJ, Cytryn L and McKnew DH: Social and affective development in infants with a manic-depressive parent. *American J Psychiatry. 141:*223–229, 1984.

18 Zahn-Waxler C, Cummings EM, McKnew DH and Radke-Yarrow M: Altruism, aggression and social interactions in young children with a manic-depressive parent. *Child Development. 55:*112–122, 1984.

19 Davenport YB, Zahn-Waxler C, Adland ML and Mayfield A: Early child-rearing practices in families with a manic-depressive parent. *American J Psychiatry. 14:*230–235, 1984.

20 Garmezy N: Children at risk. The search for the antecedents of schizophrenia. Part I. *Schizophr Bull. 8:*14–91, 1974.

21 Garmezy N: The search for the antecedents of schizophrenia. Part II. *Schizophr Bull. 8:*55–126, 1974.

READING 54

Treating Adolescent Multiple Offenders: A Comparison and Follow-up of Parent Training for Families of Chronic Delinquents

Hicks Marlowe
John B. Reid
Gerald R. Patterson
Mark R. Weinrott

The primary objective of this study was to test the hypothesis that parent training based on social learning principles can lower the offense rates of multiple-offending adolescent delinquents. A comparison design with follow-up measures was used in conducting the research.

The distinctiveness of this category of offenders and the challenge they represent is reflected in both their disproportionate contribution to offense rates and the stability of their delinquent behavior. Wolfgang, Figlio, and Sellin's (1972) study of 9,945 Philadelphia male adolescents is perhaps the classic documentation of these characteristics (see also Monahan, 1981; Polk, 1974; Wolfgang, 1977). They found that although chronic delinquents (i.e., five or more offenses) constituted only 18% of the offenders in their sample, they committed over half (51.9% of all reported offenses). Further, the risk of chronicity was cumulative, and a stable pattern of delinquency was established early in the sequence of offenses. Each of the first three offenses was associated with an increased probability of additional offenses, after which the probability stabilized at around 70% to 80%. The study also showed that the earlier the age of onset, the greater the risk for chronic offending, with the critical period for onset of a chronic pattern occurring between the ages of 12 and 16.

Chronicity adds significantly to the already formidable task of rehabilitation and prevention (Patterson, 1981). In fact, the results of a wide range of outcome evaluation studies of delinquency treatment programs have led many to conclude that "nothing works" (cf. Lipton, Martinson, & Wilks, 1975; Martinson, 1974; McCord, 1978; Sechrest, White, & Brown, 1979). In a report for the National Institute for Juvenile Justice and Delinquency Prevention, for example, Berleman (1980) reviewed what he considered to be the *best* delinquency prevention experiments done between 1937 and 1968. Approximately 2,400 youth between the ages of 5 and 21 were treated in the programs considered, which included such major studies as the Cambridge-Somerville Youth Study (Powers & Witmer, 1951), the Chicago Youth Development Project (Gold & Mattick, 1974), and the Seattle Atlantic Street Center Experiment (Berleman, Seaberg, & Steinburn, 1972). Of the 10 programs reviewed, only one—the Wincroft Youth Project in Manchester, England (Smith, Farrant, & Marchant, 1972)—produced data showing it to be effective in reducing delinquent behavior, a finding which was no longer statistically significant at one-year follow-up. Similarly, Empey and Erikson (1972), using a treatment approach which emphasized work and peer group discussions, did manage to significantly reduce offense rates during the first year following intervention, but the effect did not persist in the second or third year of follow-up.

Most of the studies above did not explicitly include the family in treatment. However, the results of both the Seattle Atlantic Street and Lane County Youth projects (Berleman, 1972; Polk, 1967) suggest that even when the family is included as the object of intervention, *conventional* treatment methods appear to have little positive effect on offense rates. In the former project, for instance, an average of 75 hours of intensive casework per family was provided over a two-year period. But in neither project did the experimental group have significantly lower rates of delinquent behavior than the comparison group at follow-up evaluation.

More recent research has attempted to specify which family variables are most directly associated with delinquency. Two parent behaviors appear to be of primary importance— tracking the behaviors in which the child engages and contingently applying positive and negative sanctions for behaviors considered to be appropriate or inappropriate. Ineffective use of these family management practices—*monitoring* and *discipline*—consistently has been

found to be associated with delinquency (McCord, 1979; Patterson & Loeber, 1981; West & Farrington, 1973, 1977).

A study of the families of seventh- and tenth-grade boys by Patterson and Stouthamer-Loeber (1984) provides several important findings in this regard. First, their data indicate that monitoring and discipline are significantly related to one another (.54, $p < .001$), suggesting that the two are part of an overall approach to parenting. Second, the variables were also highly correlated with both official records of police contacts and self-reports of delinquent life style (monitor, .55 and .54, $p < .0001$; discipline, .30 and .35, $p < .05$). Third, and directly relevant to our present concerns, parental monitoring differentiated effectively between moderate (one or two police contacts) and multiple offending (three or more contacts) delinquents on both measures ($x^2(2) = 18.03$ and 25.06, both $p < .0001$). Loeber and Dishion's (1983b) comparative review of factors assumed to contribute to delinquency and recidivism also demonstrates the strong effects of family management variables, particularly composite measures using monitoring and discipline as major components.

The study described here is an extension of an ongoing line of treatment research with families of antisocial preadolescent boys begun by investigators at the Oregon Social Learning Center (OSLC) nearly 20 years ago. The general model on which treatment is based is the application of social learning principles to family interaction (Cairns, 1979). The fundamental implications of this theoretical orientation for the development and treatment of delinquency are: (1) that disruptions in family management practices provide an environment that promotes socially unacceptable behaviors in the child; (2) over time, these behaviors escalate and generalize to contacts outside the family, increasing the probability that they will come to the attention of formal control agents; and (3) that training parents to use more effective control practices can significantly reduce the frequency and seriousness of these inappropriate behaviors, and the likelihood that they will have to be officially sanctioned by the community (Patterson, Reid, Jones, & Conger, 1975; Reid, 1978).

Evidence was cited earlier suggesting the importance of inadequate monitoring and discipline in development and maintenance of delinquency. Patterson's (1982) comprehensive summary of data of dysfunctional family processes and Kazdin's (1985) review of studies using parent management training provide further support for the usefulness of training parents to more effectively engage in the basic practices that make up the family management model.

In addition, a series of comparison studies using random assignment showed parent training procedures were not only effective, but significantly more effective in reducing antisocial child behavior than were either leaderless parent discussion groups (Walter & Gilmore, 1973) or traditional therapies provided by mental health facilities in the community (Patterson, Chamberlain, & Reid, 1982). And the positive effects of parent training have been found to persist for follow-up periods ranging from 12 months to 9 years (Baum & Forehand, 1981; Patterson & Fleischman, 1979; Strain, Steele, Ellis, & Timm, 1983), although persistence of effect appears to be affected considerably by family characteristics, such as socioeconomic status (Dumas & Wahler, 1983) and whether or not the training continues until parents feel competent in effecting management techniques (Fleischman & Szykula, 1981).

To briefly summarize: although recent research has shown ineffective parent practices to be significantly related to a variety of antisocial and delinquent behaviors and, although parent training has been found to be an effective means for reducing antisocial child behavior, there have been few attempts to incorporate this information in a systematic program for treating delinquency.

Regardless of the apparent success of parent training with the families of younger antisocial boys, however, it would be naive to presume that these same procedures could be used directly and with equal success with families of older youth who have already initiated a pattern of officially recognized delinquent behavior. There are at least two reasons for anticipating a possible difference in outcome effectiveness for the two groups. First, the family management practices of this latter group, and particularly families of youth who have been identified as multiple offenders, are more seriously disrupted (Patterson, 1981, 1982). Each passing year in such an environment increases the probability that the child's antisocial behavior will increase in frequency and stability, and eventually generalize to settings outside the family. Second, a high proportion of delinquent offenses are covert acts, predominantly some form of theft or burglary. FBI statistics cited by Galvin and Polk (1983) indicate that these two categories alone represent over a third of all arrests for youth under 18 years of age. Furthermore, the evasion of negative sanctions for these deviant behaviors strengthens the likelihood of their recurrence. Confirmation of the contribution of covert deviant acts to a subsequent pattern of chronic delinquency was provided by Moore, Chamberlain, and Mukai (1979). Following up a sample of preadolescents whose parents had documented at least four instances of stealing in the four-month period prior to intake, they found that, by age 17, 84% of these youth had been arrested and 67% of them ultimately became chronic offenders. This was in contrast to a comparison group of preadolescents referred for overt aggressive behavior, only 15% of whom became delinquent.

These characteristics of the behaviors of adolescent multiple offenders and their families suggest that these youth should be among those at greatest risk for a criminal career and among those most resistant to a parent training, or any other, program of rehabilitation. Even so, the incomparable costs they represent to the families and communities to which they belong make it impossible to ignore then as possible candidates for change. And their very intransigence offers the strongest possible test of treatment techniques. The procedures described below were an attempt to provide just such a stringent examination of the comparable effectiveness of our family management training program on a sample of this high-risk population of offenders, using both a randomly assigned control group to assess the relative effectiveness of treatment procedures and follow-up measures to determine the stability of treatment effects.

METHOD

Subjects

The initial pool from which our primary comparison samples were drawn consisted of the families of 64 boys referred by the Lane County Juvenile Court as being interested in treatment. Three major selection criteria were used. First, we required that the target child be a repeat offender by the time we began intake with him and his family. Specifically, he had to have at least two recorded offenses, at least one of which had to be a nonstatus offense. Second, the target child had to be no more than 16 years of age at intake. This requirement was based on the assumption that, given the independence and peer influence characterizing boys in later adolescence, any parent management training that began later than that would have little chance of being effective. It also placed the majority of our subjects in the age range at high risk for delinquency mentioned earlier. Finally, we required that the family or whomever had custody of the boy live within 20 miles of the Oregon Social Learning Center. This was necessary because of the direct contact with the family required for training parents in family management procedures.

Assignment of the 64 delinquent boys who met our criteria to the experimental ("Treated") or comparison ("Community Control") group was made by random selection procedures using a table of random numbers. Families of subjects assigned in this way to the Treated group received the OSLC program in family management, to be described below, while subjects in the Community Control group were referred to other community agencies that normally offer services for such cases. These two groups are used for all comparisons of the study. In addition, a second control group ("Yoked Control") was used in comparing baseline year offense rates. Subjects in this group were matched subject-by-subject with the boys assigned to the Treated group on the dimensions of age at intake, age at first offense, and seriousness of offenses. The Yoked Control group served as a check on the degree to which the delinquents assigned to the Treated and Community Control groups were representative of youth who came to the attention of the Lane County Juvenile Court.

Table 1 compares the families of the Treated and Community Control groups on a number of demographic characteristics. On none of the comparisons were the two groups significantly different. In general, however, both could be described as disadvantaged families, characterized by low education and income, and father absence was common.

Treatment

OSLC parent training was originally developed for use with families of preadolescent antisocial boys (Patterson & Forgatch, 1978; Patterson, Reid, Jones, & Conger, 1975). Its basic objective is teaching parents to engage more effectively in four major dimensions of family functioning: rule setting, monitoring, discipline, and problem-solving. Modifying the basic training procedures to deal with the problems of the families of older delinquent subjects required a change of emphasis and format. Specifically, parents were trained to

TABLE 1   DEMOGRAPHIC CHARACTERISTICS OF EXPERIMENTAL AND COMMUNITY CONTROL GROUPS AT INTAKE

	Mean	
	Experimental group (N = 28)	Comparison group (N = 27)
Age of target child at intake	13.8	14.2
Number of siblings in home	1.6	1.5
Family size	4.3	4.1
Father education	4.0	3.8
Mother education	4.0	3.3
Father occupation	3.7	3.5
Mother occupation	3.0	2.6
Father absent	(39%)	(38%)

concretely identify not only prosocial and antisocial behaviors, but also any other behaviors believed to put the child at risk for further delinquency. Parents and other family members were taught to track the occurrence of these behaviors systematically on a daily basis, and to record them in order to facilitate daily and weekly supervision. Parents were also taught to involve, when appropriate, the family as a unit in learning to construct and modify behavioral contracts. The contracts specify behavioral expectations of the youngster and prescribed reactions to both compliance and violation. Audiotape cassettes that demonstrate contracting procedures, as well as pinpointing and tracking procedures, were used to enhance this training. A shift was also made from the use of the Time Out procedures that were appropriate for preadolescent subjects, to work details, point loss, and restitution as punishment, and parents were taught to monitor carefully the whereabouts and activites of the target child. Since these families were much more disrupted than had been the families of the younger antisocial boys, and parents devoted more time to coping with external crises, marital discord, parental depression, and other adult adjustment problems, more therapist time was devoted to working on problems that were not directly related to delinquency.

The treatment was not time-limited, nor was it restricted to any particular set of training procedures or predefined goals. An attempt was made to work with the family until the parents were satisfied that they were able to work with the youngster's delinquent behavior in a productive way. Consistent with this approach to treatment, families were free to contact the OSLC for further assistance after they were formally terminated from the treatment program. That parents were willing to accept this invitation is indicated by the fact that over 40% of the Treated families received some treatment (mean, 15 hours) during the year following treatment.

Measures

Official Offense Reports   The basic measure of official delinquency for our two principal subject groups was official offense records collected from the Lane County Juvenile Court in the year prior to intake (baseline), the treatment year, and one follow-up year. We were also able to get somewhat less complete information for two additional follow-up years, and these will be presented as supplementary data. Comparable baseline data were obtained for the Yoked Control group as a check on the representativeness of the two main groups. Four offense categories corresponding to different dimensions of offending were analyzed separately: (1) total offenses, (2) status offenses, which are offenses that are dependent on the offender's age, such as curfew violation or runaway, (3) nonstatus offenses, excluding such less serious offenses as traffic and shoplifting, and (4) index offenses, which are included in the FBI list of more serious offenses. Time spent in a Lane County institution for boys in the Treated and Community Control groups was available for baseline through the first follow-up year, and these were used to correct offense records to reflect only time our subjects were free to commit delinquent acts.

Family Measures   As part of the agreement to participate in the study families in the Treated group consented to having OSLC collect three additional types of data. The first, direct observation and recording of family member behavior, was conducted by trained coders both shortly after intake and just prior to termination of treatment, using the Family Interaction Coding System (FICS) (Reid, 1978). FICS is made up of 29 coding categories which capture an extensive range of discrete positive, negative, and neutral behaviors of family members. Of particular interest for this study were the items making up the Total Aversive Behavior (TAB) and Abusive (AC) clusters. The second type of family behavior collected was a structured set of more global impressions formed by the coders during the family visits for direct behavioral observation. Third, Parent Daily Report (PDR) telephone interviews were conducted by trained interviewers for one week prior to the beginning of treatment, and again for one week just prior to termination. The PDR uses a structured checklist format, the items of which are designed for the particular subject group and problems targeted by the study design. For the parents in our Treated sample, targeted items were those behaviors of their child which they thought to be delinquent or which could increase the likelihood of delinquent behavior. Pretreatment and post-treatment scores on each of these three forms of family data were compared to test the effectiveness of the parent training program in reducing family dysfunctioning. These results, in turn, were compared to the subjects' offense records to see whether positive changes in family interaction were associated with decreased frequency of delinquent acts by the target boy.

RESULTS

Offense Rates

Prior research suggests that the probability that a youth will develop a pattern of chronic delinquency and later adult crime increases considerably after the first repeated offense. Our basic research question has been whether training parents to engage in more effective family management procedures can significantly reduce the offense rates of the multiple offending delinquents and perhaps prevent or slow the developing process of chronicity. More specifically, we have asked whether such training is significantly more effective than are traditional community approaches. Of course, although reduction of official offense rates is a major criterion, overall effectiveness should include other considerations, such as cost to the community and, particularly where adolescents are concerned, the long-term effects of the processes that lead to reduced offense rates. These also will be briefly discussed.

As a broad test of overall effects, an analysis of the mutually exclusive and exhaustive offense subcategories status and nonstatus was performed.

Figure 1 and Table 2 provide more specific information on the source of these group differences over time, as well as other comparative data. As the table indicates, the two groups were comparable in all offense categories at baseline. There were also no significant baseline differences between the various offense rates of either of them and those of the Yoked Control group mentioned earlier, suggesting that the random assignment procedures were effective and that these youth were generally representative of the repeated offenders the Lane County Juvenile Court encounters.

A comparison of baseline and subsequent year means also suggests that by the follow-up year, both approaches to prevention seem to have had a generally positive effect. The most striking feature of these data, however, is the difference in time required by the respective treatment approaches to have an effect on offense rates. For the OSLC Treated group, by the end of the treatment year all offense cate-

gories, with the exception of status offenses, had been significantly lowered. In contrast, the Community Control group rates had actually increased minimally during that same period. And although the rates for both groups are noticeably lower by the end of the follow-up year, a separate test of baseline versus an average of treatment and follow-up years for each group showed the offense rate reduction for *all* offense categories to be significant for the Treated group, while none of the similar tests for the Community Control group was statistically significant.

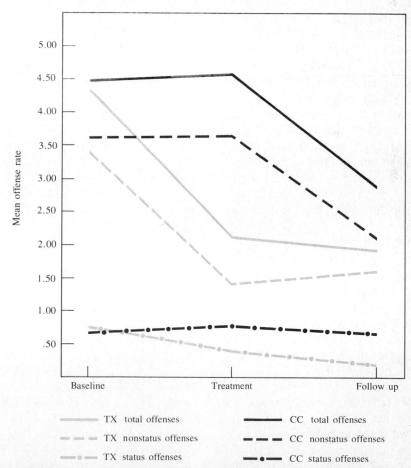

FIGURE 1 Total, nonstatus, and status offense rates for OSLC treated (TX) and community control (CC) groups. (Scores are corrected for institution time.)

TABLE 2 OFFENSE RATES AND INSTITUTION TIME FOR OSLC TREATED AND COMMU-
NITY CONTROL GROUPS. OFFENSE RATES FOR BASELINE THROUGH YEAR 2 FOLLOW-UP
CORRECTED FOR INSTITUTION TIME

	Mean		
Offense category	Baseline	Treatment year	Year 1 follow-up
Total			
OSLC Treatment	4.45	2.10**	1.98
Community Control	4.57	4.69	2.97
Status			
OSLC Treatment	.76	.42	.22
Community Control	.71	.82	.73
Nonstatus			
OSLC Treatment	3.47	1.48***	1.59
Community Control	3.72	3.75	2.16
Index			
OSLC Treatment	2.16	.77**	1.26
Community Control	2.68	2.76	1.73

*$p < .05$
**$p < .01$
***$p < .005$
OSLC Treated sample, $N = 28$ for baseline through Year 1 follow-up.
Community Control sample size, $N = 27, 26, 26$.

Of comparable importance, extended offense data suggest that reduction in the Treated group's rates persisted into the third follow-up year. It should be mentioned that this finding is based on an estimate of institution time-corrected offense scores. That is, although raw offense scores are complete for the extended period, complete institution time for Year 2 and Year 3 follow-up was not available. The estimate was calculated using a composite average of the ratio of corrected to uncorrected scores for the treatment year and Year 1 follow-up. For these scores, baseline versus Year 3 rates were significantly different for total, nonstatus, and index offenses. Given the absence of long-term stability of treatment effects typical in delinquency research, these results seem quite promising.

Institution Time

One very practical way to estimate the usefulness and efficacy of a prevention program is in terms of financial savings to the community. And institutionalization is very expensive. Greenwood and Zimring (1985), for example,

calculate that the average cost of keeping a youth in a correctional facility is approximately $60.00 per day. Clearly, then, any sizeable reduction in the time a youth spends in a community-supported treatment setting represents an important savings to the community.

Table 3 shows institution time for the OSLC Treated and Community Control groups. As with the offense categories, comparing the subjects in the two programs revealed no significant difference in institution time at baseline but a significant difference in both the treatment year and Year 1 follow-up. In the treatment year, Year 1 follow-up, and the institution time available to us for the following year, OSLC Treated subjects spent a total of 2,247 fewer days in institutional confinement. This meant a savings to the community of nearly $135,000 over the three-year period.

Implications for treatment effectiveness can also be inferred from these institutional time data. Given the differences noted, the Treated group had about 14% *more* time available to them to commit offenses during the treatment year through Year 2 follow-up period, yet com-

TABLE 3   INSTITUTION TIME FOR OSLC TREATED AND COMMUNITY CONTROL GROUPS.
THROUGH YEAR 2 FOLLOW-UP CORRECTED FOR INSTITUTION TIME

| | Mean | | |
	Baseline	Treatment year	Year 1 follow-up
OSLC Treatment	3.21	28.46*	33.89*
Community Control	.89	56.85	80.29

*p<.05

mitted about 24% *fewer* offenses. And given the similarities of Treated and Community Control group families and their comparable inability to control the delinquent behavior of their youth at baseline, a reasonable hypothesis would be that changes in the Treated families resulting from parent training were associated with this reduction in officially recorded delinquency, a possibility that we will now consider.

Family Management and Official Deliquency

As we suggested earlier, the families of the OSLC Treated subjects were extremely disrupted. In fact, the impression of our clinical staff was that these were probably the most difficult families with which we have worked in our two decades of treatment, and potential staff burn-out was a serious problem. In both of the family process evaluation clusters based on direct observation, for example, during the initial observation period they were significantly more dysfunctional than were a comparable group of normal families (Total Aversive Behavior, $p < .001$; Abusive Cluster, $p < .006$). In more concrete terms, this meant that they engaged more often in such negative behaviors as disapproval, humiliation, physical aggression, negativism, teasing, yelling, whining, destructiveness, and noncompliance. The structured observer impressions also indicated that family interaction was more chaotic and the parents more out of control in dealing with their children than were the normal group.

And, despite a rather heavy investment of treatment time by the OSLC clinicians (mean, 21.5 hours in treatment year), there were very few positive changes in family process per se.

None of the direct observation or impression measures suggested a significant improvement between intake and termination in the way members of these families dealt with one another.

Interestingly, though, even though general family interaction did not seem to improve, the procedures designed to help parents track and control specific behaviors that put the child at risk for further delinquency did seem to be effective, as shown by the Parent Daily Report data. Targeted delinquent or predelinquent behaviors were reported by the parents as significantly reduced and there were *no* stealing incidents reported at termination.

Even though there were no *overall* baseline-to-termination differences in the direct observation measures of family interaction in the Treated group, it is instructive to examine the possible relationship of offense frequency and rate of improvement in family process for those Treated families in which positive change *did* occur. These data should be considered as suggestive, due to small sample sizes. For both Total Aversive Behavior (TAB) and the Abusive Cluster (AC) measures, improvement in family interaction was associated with lower rates in all offense categories. The effect of positive changes in the items making up the Abuse Cluster was greatest, especially for nonserious offenses, correlating .42 with a lower frequency of nonstatus offenses, and .29 with fewer status offenses. Correlations between improved TAB and these same categories were .42 and .10.

Taken together, these results offer strong support for parent training as a means of reducing the offense rates of adolescent multiple offenders. This holds true whether one is comparing the Treated group's own post-treatment approach and that of conventional community prevention or rehabilitation procedures. From these data, family management treatment appears to have a significant positive effect more quickly and with less cost to the community. Finally, since the vehicle for offense reduction is the delinquent youth's own family and may well be a direct product of changes in family interaction, it seems reasonable to argue that this method of treatment is more humane and has greater potential for producing overall positive change in the youthful offender.

To say that parent training clearly reduces delinquent behavior is not tantamount to saying that this approach to treatment eliminates delinquency. Only five, or about 18%, of the OSLC Treated subjects completely dropped out of the delinquency process during the post-treatment period of data collection (i.e., no offenses for follow-up Years 1 through 3). It is interesting to note, however, that for four of these five, "dropping out" began in the treatment year, which was true for only one of the Community Control subjects, again providing evidence for the method's potential for early benefits. But, in view of the continued disrupted and chaotic state of these families, we would expect that most of our subjects will continue to commit offenses in the future. As an intervention for adolescent youth, parent training is, at best, a stopgap measure, and one which is much more likely to slow the path to chronicity, rather than to stop it.

DISCUSSION

Taken together, the results of this study show clearly that the family is a viable focus for intervention with delinquent youngsters. Not only was it possible to help the families in the experimental group exert quick and effective control over the official delinquency rates of their sons, relative to the families of the Juve-

nile Court treated group, they were able to do it with much less reliance on incarceration. Although it was not possible to get specific data on the amount of face-to-face treatment time spent by the counselors/parole officers on the control group youngsters, discussions with the administration at the court suggest that it was comparable. All control subjects were assigned to an intensive treatment program, averaging about five months with weekly individual sessions and group therapy focused on social skills and substance use. It should also be noted that this particular juvenile court offers excellent services, utilizing a combination of family therapy and behavioral interventions. And it should be emphasized that by two years after intake, the offense rates of the two groups were comparable.

Neither the home observational data nor the clinical impressions indicated that many significant changes in family function or dynamics were affected by the experimental treatment. These were severely distressed families with multiple problems, and they were certainly not normalized by the treatment. On the other hand, it was possible to assist the parents to negotiate, monitor, and enforce rules of conduct related to delinquency-related activities (e.g., going to school, not bringing drugs or stolen goods home, doing homework, coming home at reasonable hours), and to get parents in the intact families to cooperate to some extent during discipline confrontations. Perhaps the main outcome of the treatment was to help the parents remain actively involved and responsible for the conduct of their boys. Rather than helping the youngster conceal a delinquent event, they were taught to report him to the authorities and then come to the court hearing with a plan to rectify the problem (e.g., discipline and supervision tactics, plans for restitution). It seemed to us that this involvement was what convinced the judges, in many instances, to leave the child with his parents rather than to opt for an out-of-home placement. The offense data strongly suggest that the parents were able to curtail delinquent activity as well or better than the institutions.

Although the data from this study suggest that the experimental treatment was effective for intervention with families of delinquents, we have our doubts as to its feasiblity as a widely used approach. Our clinical work with these families was extraordinarily difficult; it took tremendous effort to prevent staff burn-out. Because the study was conducted at a research institute rather than in a service setting, our therapists had the luxury of small caseloads, solid staff support, and the added incentive that the work was interesting on theoretical as well as clinical grounds. In a line agency, extreme measures would have to be taken to keep case loads (of this type case) small, peer support and supervision high, and morale up. Without a clear commitment by an agency to protect the therapists, the proper execution of the clinical approach with these clients would be impossible. Beginning intervention in the delinquency process should be the focus of further work in this area.

REFERENCES

Baum, C. G., & Forehand, R. (1981). Long-term follow-up assessment of parent training by use of multiple outcome measures. *Behavior Therapy, 12,* 643–652.

Berleman, W. C. (1980). Juvenile delinquency prevention experiments: A review and analysis. *Reports of the National Juvenile Justice Assessment Centers.* U.S. Department of Justice.

Berleman, W. C., Seaberg, J. R., & Steinburn, T. W. (1972). The delinquency prevention experiment of the Seattle Atlantic Street Center: A final evaluation. *Social Science Review, 46,* 323–346.

Cairns, R. B. (1979). *Social development: The origins and plasticity of interchanges.* San Francisco: W. H. Freeman and Co.

Dumas, J. E., & Wahler, R. G. (1983). Predictors of treatment outcome in parent training: Mother insularity and socioeconomic disadvantage. *Behavioral Assessment, 5,* 301–313.

Empey, L. T., & Erickson, M. L. (1972). *The Provo Experiment.* Lexington, MA: D.C. Heath and Co.

Fleischman, M. J., & Szykula, S. A. (1981). A community setting replication of a social learning treatment for aggressive children. *Behavior Therapy, 12,* 115–122.

Galvin, J., & Polk, K. (1983). Juvenile justice: Time for a new direction? *Crime and Delinquency, 29,* 325–332.

Gold, M., & Mattick, H. W. (1974, March). *Experiment in the streets: The Chicago Youth Development Project.* Ann Arbor, MI: University of Michigan Institute of Social Research.

Greenwood, P. W., & Zimring, F. E. (1985, May). *One more chance: The pursuit of promising intervention strategies for chronic juvenile offenders.* Report #R-3214-OJJDP, prepared under a grant from the Office of Juvenile Justice and Delinquency Prevention, U.S. Department of Justice. Santa Monica, CA: Rand.

Kazdin, A. E. (1985). *Treatment of antisocial behavior in children and adolescents.* Homewood, IL: Dorsey.

Lipsey, M. W. (1984). Is delinquency prevention a cost-effective strategy? A California perspective. *Journal of Research in Crime and Delinquency, 21,* 279–302.

Lipton, D., Martinson, R., & Wilks, J. (1975). *The effectiveness of correctional treatment: A survey of treatment evaluation studies.* New York: Praeger.

Loeber, R., & Dishion, T. J. (1983). Early predictors of male delinquency: A review. *Psychological Bulletin, 94,* 68–99.

Martinson, R. (1974). What works? Questions and answers about prison reform. *Public Interest, 35,* 22–54.

McCord, J. (1978). A thirty-year follow-up of treatment effects. *American Psychologist, 33,* 284–289.

McCord, J. (1979). Some child-rearing antecedents of criminal behavior in adult men. *Journal of Personality and Social Psychology, 9,* 1477–1486.

Monahan, J. (1981, Oct.). *Childhood predictors of adult criminal behavior.* Invited testimony before the Subcommittee on Juvenile Justice Committee on the Judiciary, United States Senate.

Moore, D. R., Chamberlain, P., & Mukai, L. (1979). Children at risk for delinquency: A follow-up comparison of aggressive children and children who steal. *Journal of Abnormal Child Psychology, 7,* 345–355.

Patterson, G. R. (1981, Oct.). *Chronicity: Treatment, prediction, and prevention.* Invited testimony before the Subcommittee on Juvenile Justice Committee on the Judiciary, United States Senate.

Patterson, G. R. (1982). *Coercive family process.* Eugene, OR: Castalia Publishing Co.

Patterson, G. R., Chamberlain, P., & Reid, J. B. (1982). A comparative evaluation of a parent-training program. *Behavior Therapy, 13,* 638–650.

Patterson, G. R., & Fleischman, M. J. (1979). Maintenance of treatment effects: Some considerations concerning family systems and follow-up data. *Behavior Therapy, 10,* 168–185.

Patterson, G. R., & Forgatch, M. (1978). *Family living series.* Audio cassette tapes. Champaign, IL: Research Press.

Patterson, G. R., & Loeber, R. (1981, Aug.). *Family management skills and delinquency.* Paper presented at the meeting of the International Society for the Study of Behavioral Development, Toronto, Ontario, Canada.

Patterson, G. R., Reid, J. B., Jones, R. R., & Conger, R. E. (1975). *A social learning approach to family intervention. Vol. I. Families with aggressive children.* Eugene, OR: Castalia Publishing Co.

Patterson, G. R., & Stouthamer-Loeber, M. (1984). The correlation of family management practices and delinquency. *Child Development, 55,* 1299–1307.

Polk, K. (1967). *Lane County Youth Project: Final report.* Office of Juvenile Delinquency and Youth Development. U.S. Department of Health, Education, and Welfare.

Polk, K. (1974). Teenage delinquency in small-town America. *National Institute of Mental Health Research Report, 5.*

Powers, E., & Witmer, H. (1951). *An experiment in the prevention of delinquency: The Cambridge-Somerville Youth Study.* New York: Columbia University Press.

Reid, J. B. (Ed.). (1978). *A social learning approach to family intervention: Vol. II. Observation in home settings.* Eugene, OR: Castalia Publishing Co.

Sechrest, L., White, S. O., & Brown, E. D. (Eds.) (1979). *The rehabilitation of criminal offenders: Problems and prospects.* Washington, D.C.: National Academy of Sciences.

Smith, C. S., Farrant, M. R., & Marchant, M. J. (1972). *The Wincroft Youth Project: A social-work programme in a slum area.* London: Tavistock Publications, Ltd.

Strain, P. S., Steele, P., Ellis, T., & Timm, M. A. (1982). Long-term effects of oppositional child treatment with mothers as therapists and therapist trainers. *Journal of Applied Behavior Analysis, 15,* 163–169.

Walter, H. I., & Gilmore, S. K. (1974). Placebo versus social learning effects in parent training procedures designed to alter the behaviors of aggressive boys. *Behavior Therapy, 4,* 361–377.

West, D. J., & Farrington, D. T. (1973). *Who becomes delinquent?* New York: Crane, Russek, and Co.

West, D. J., & Farrington, D. T. (1977). *The delinquent way of life.* London: Heinemann.

Wiltz, N. A., Jr., & Patterson, G. R. (1974). An evaluation of parent training procedures designed to alter inappropriate aggressive behavior of boys. *Behavior Therapy, 5,* 215–221.

Wolfgang, M. E., Figlio, R., & Sellin, T. (1972). *Delinquency in a birth cohort.* Chicago: University of Chicago Press.

Wolfgang, M. E. (1977, Sept.). *From boy to man, from delinquency to crime.* Paper presented at the National Symposium on Serious Juvenile Offenders, Minneapolis.

Primary Prevention of Child Abuse

Mindy S. Rosenberg
N. Dickon Reppucci

The purpose of the present article is to provide a selective review of primary prevention activities in the area of child abuse, to discuss problems in methodology, and to highlight future program and research directions. Only examples of child abuse primary prevention programs with research components are included for discussion. Programs to prevent sexual abuse, severe neglect, and adolescent abuse are excluded because these forms of maltreatment are often associated with risk factors different from those related to child abuse (Finkelhor, 1979; Garbarino, 1984; Giovannoni, 1980; Polansky, Chalmers, Buttenwieser, & Williams, 1981). Although the original conception of prevention in mental health encompassed the three levels of primary, secondary, and tertiary prevention (Caplan, 1964), several researchers (Cowen, 1973, 1983; Felner, Jason, Moritsugu, & Farber, 1983; Zax & Spector, 1974) have argued against the inclusion of tertiary and certain forms of secondary prevention under the general prevention rubric because it increases the ambiguity of the concept and perpetuates a traditional mental health perspective (i.e., intervene with identified individuals after disorders are present).

Despite the identification and careful scrutiny of several thousand references from *Child Abuse and Neglect* (1977–1984), computerized data bases from The Child Abuse and Neglect Clearinghouse Project and from *Psychological Abstracts* (1973–1984), and two comprehensive overviews (National Center on Child Abuse and Neglect, 1983; Gray, 1983a, 1983b, 1983c, 1983d), only a relatively small number refer to actual primary prevention programs and even fewer refer to programs with research components. Furthermore, local prevention programs funded by state agencies typically do not publish final reports in journals, which contributes to the inaccessibility of many programs' results. Thus, this review is not meant to be exhaustive but rather to highlight innovative and/or prototypic efforts to prevent child abuse.

The article is divided into six major sections. The first section examines the ecological theory base for the study and design of child abuse prevention programs. The next three sections review programs with different preventive approaches including competency enhancement, preventing the onset of abusive behavior, and targeting high-risk groups. The fifth section outlines methodological problems in evaluating child abuse prevention programs. The final section provides suggestions for future program and research directions.

THEORETICAL BASE FOR PRIMARY PREVENTION IN CHILD ABUSE: THE ECOLOGICAL PERSPECTIVE

The development of effective primary preventive efforts in mental health is dependent on a sound, generative research base for program design, implementation, and evaluation (Cowen, 1980). Until recently, the generative base in child abuse consisted of several discrepant, unitary models to explain etiology, including models emphasizing psychiatric, sociological, and social-situational factors (Parke & Collmer, 1975). Whichever model is chosen is of concern for more than academic debate because the theoretical assumptions that underlie the definition of a social problem like child abuse have inherent approaches to its solution (Caplan & Nelson, 1973). With the emergence of an ecological model of child abuse (Belsky, 1980; Garbarino, 1977; Rosenberg & Reppucci,

671

1983b), these divergent etiological perspectives have been integrated into a coherent conceptual system.

Belsky (1980) summarized the ecological model of child abuse as follows:

> While abusing parents enter the...family with developmental histories that may predispose them to treat children in an abusive or neglectful manner, stress-promoting forces both within the immediate family...and beyond it...increase the likelihood that parent-child conflict will occur. The fact that a parent's response to such conflict and stress takes the form of child maltreatment is seen to be a consequence both of the parent's own experience as a child...and of the values and childrearing practices that characterize the society or subculture in which the individual, family, and community are embedded. (p. 330)

Because it is beyond the scope of this article to delineate the various causal factors, the reader is referred to several excellent reviews (e.g., Belsky, 1980; Cohen, Gray, & Wald, 1984; Garbarino, 1977; Gerbner, Ross, & Zigler, 1980; National Center on Child Abuse and Neglect, 1983). Based on these reviews, a brief listing of important factors at each level of analysis is presented to alert the reader to the types of causative agents addressed in preventive activities. Individual-level factors include parental personality variables and parents' socialization history such as experience with or exposure to violence, parental rejection, and inappropriate developmental expectations for children. Familial-level factors include dysfunctional interactions among family members, abuse-eliciting child characteristics, and conflictual spousal relationships. Community-level factors include isolation from formal and informal supports, unemployment, and unmanageable stress. Societal-level factors include the sanctioning of physical punishment to control children's behavior.

The ecological approach to child abuse has implications for the design of preventive programs as well as for the development of the field. First, the adoption of a multifactorial causation model to explain abuse is congruent with prevention ideology (Price, 1974). By conceptualizing prevention in terms of a multiple risk factor orientation, primary prevention programs can be implemented at a variety of different levels. Second, the potential to develop innovative interventions, such as enhancing social support systems, is encouraged. Third, an ecological perspective directs researchers and practitioners to the interrelation between variables from different ecological levels rather than focusing on single correlates of child abuse. Thus, the ecological approach provides those interested in primary prevention activities with a model that acknowledges the complexity of child abuse and the different critical factors needing attention.

PREVENTIVE APPROACHES

The goals of primary prevention can be categorized broadly as either (a) enhancing psychological health and strengthening competencies, resources, and coping skills as protection against dysfunction or (b) reducing the rate of occurrence of emotional disorders (Bloom, 1979; Cowen, 1980; Goldston, 1977). Primary prevention programs focus on populations of people, not individuals, and are directed toward "well" people who may or may not be at risk for adverse psychological outcomes as a result of life circumstances or recent experiences (Cowen, 1983). In the context of child abuse, examples of primary prevention strategies include (a) interventions that enhance competencies, resources, and coping skills, such as parent education programs in hospitals and communities; (b) interventions that prevent the onset of abusive behavior, such as media campaigns, crisis lines, and community enhancement of social networks; and (c) interventions that target vulnerable populations especially during periods of transition and stress, including programs that facilitate parent-child bonding, lay health visitors, and parent aides.

Competency Enhancement

One promising approach to the primary prevention of child abuse is to focus on enhancing competencies, personal resources, and coping skills in parents that contribute to the development of positive parent-child relationships and prevent the onset of dysfunctional interactions (Education Commission of the States, 1976). Programs with this philosophy usually incorporate parenting skills, child development information, and coping strategies to reduce stress in the parenting role into programs directed at a variety of audiences including the general public (Gray, 1983c), specific cultural groups (Alvy & Rosen, 1980), first-time parents (Cooper, Dreznicl, & Rowe, 1982; Weal, 1979), or young adults who may be future parents (Morris, 1977).

The use of live theater and television to communicate parenting information is a unique and exciting approach to child abuse prevention. Programs of this type use the creative arts to attract and engage audiences who would rather be entertained by dramatic portrayals of family crises and resolutions than receive traditional presentations of similar material. Inter-Act: Street Theater for Parents is an example of a live theater program that provides parenting skills in the form of entertaining skits to the general public, especially hard to reach parents who do not come into contact with traditional service systems (Gray, 1983c). Live performances or videotaped skits are shown in a variety of settings such as community service branch offices, well-child clinics, state fairs, alternative high school classes for teenage parents, military bases, shopping centers, and battered women's shelters. Parenting skills also form part of the family life curriculum at a community college. The content of the skits focuses on using natural support systems in times of stress, demonstrating assertive problem-solving skills, and providing alternatives to physical punishment and emotional abuse.

Pre-post attitudinal information obtained from questionnaires formed the basis for program evaluation. Audiences were divided into general, high-risk, and professional viewers by virtue of the predominant viewer type at each performance site and were assigned randomly to experimental, control, pretest, or posttest conditions to evaluate the five skits. The two skits that were related directly to child behavior management affected the high-risk group more than the other audiences. For example, the high-risk audience was the only group to demonstrate significant attitude change as a result of watching the skit on emotional abuse, and the skit demonstrating the use of time-out as an alternative to physical punishment had a significant, positive impact on all three audiences, but particularly for high-risk viewers. Overall, general audiences demonstrated the most pre-post attitude change across skits, followed by professionals and high-risk viewers. Interestingly, the attitudes of high-risk viewers changed most positively around child-rearing issues (as opposed to skits focusing on anger control or support systems), suggesting that these issues may be most relevant to their immediate situation. Although short-term impact on general audiences suggests that an entertainment format may be effective in helping people stop and reassess their attitudes or knowledge about common problems, actual behavior change remains unknown.

In contrast to programs directed at the general public are preventive efforts aimed at pockets of the population, for example, different cultural groups who, for a variety of reasons, could benefit from special attention. Project C.A.N. Prevent, part of the Advance Parent-Child Education Program, is a comprehensive program to decrease the prevalence of child abuse and improve children's school performance in a target population of low-income Hispanic families (Gray, 1983b).

One unique aspect of the program was the collection of needs assessment data (a) to match program curriculum with the cultural and socioeconomic needs of the population; (b) to identify factors associated with high punishment and those that buffer against the potential for abuse; and (c) to determine the similarity between target and control neighborhoods for the purpose of program evaluation. Program curriculum included parent education classes, toy making classes, a home visiting program with regular filming of parent-child interactions, and involvement in practicum where parents integrated practice and theory with children in the project's day care center.

Curriculum effectiveness was assessed by questionnaires in a two-group (experimental and control), pre-post, nonrandomized design. Relative to controls, program participants were significantly more knowledgeable about a variety of child-rearing areas, were more willing to utilize support systems during stress, and were more hopeful about the future. Differences in self-reported frequencies of emotional and physical punishment did not reach statistical significance, although trends were in the predicted direction. Given the extent of contact with the target population and access to controls, it is unfortunate that the formal evaluation was limited to self-report knowledge and attitude measures.

The Pan Asian Parent Education Project, under the auspices of the Union of Pan Asian Communities of San Diego, California, is another example of integrating culture-specific issues into a child abuse preventive program (Gray, 1983b). Four Asian-American ethnic communities (Samoan, Filipino, Japanese, and Vietnamese) were offered parent education groups to enhance parents' abilities to cope with child-rearing problems, to explore potential conflicts between mainstream and Asian child-rearing practices, and to identify sources of support to reduce isolation and confusion in the acculturation process. In-service training and cultural materials about each ethnic community were provided for agency personnel to increase their understanding of traditional cultural practices that could be misperceived as intentional child abuse (e.g., the practice of pinching the child to ward off bad spirits or that of rubbing the child's body with a coin to rid it of impurities while leaving bruises). Evaluation consisted of a single-group, pretest-posttest design where materials specific to each ethnic group were developed to assess changes in knowledge and attitudes toward child-rearing practices in traditional and mainstream cultures; knowledge of child development principles and child protection laws; and general satisfaction with the parent education experience. Individual group leaders' perceptions of parent involvement, group cohesiveness, quality of participation, and accomplishment of objectives were also recorded. Results indicated evidence of changes in awareness, attitudes, and beliefs across groups, although responses varied according to the level of acculturation and the cultural traditions of the individual groups. Participants uniformly found learning American child-rearing practices to be among the most valuable aspects of the experience, and consumer satisfaction was unanimously positive.

In summary, programs that adopt a competency orientation toward child abuse prevention focus on strengthening parenting skills and coping abilities as innoculation against stress. In general, these programs are innovative and cost-effective, with clearly specified program components directed at appropriate audiences. However, to be a viable strategy for child abuse prevention, parent educators must focus serious attention on program evaluation because these programs have not yet demonstrated that those individuals whose parenting knowledge and skills are strengthened become less vulnerable to the likelihood of abusing their children.

Preventing the Onset of Abusive Behavior

Programs with the goal of preventing the onset of abusive behavior typically involve media campaigns; information, crisis, and referral services; and efforts at the neighborhood and community levels to empower social networks in their ability to provide support and feedback to families (Cohn, 1982; Garbarino, Stocking, & Associates, 1980). These programs rest on the assumption that increased understanding of the problem and where and how to reach for help are the bases of any effort to prevent abuse. As a result of their community-wide focus, multiple goals, and multiple methods, these programs are often challenging to implement and difficult to evaluate.

Project Network, a community-based project at Atlanta University, targeted three census tracts in Atlanta's central city for a comprehensive community education and referral campaign that included efforts to strengthen formal and informal helping networks (Gray, 1983d). Community impact and consumer satisfaction were assessed by two rounds of interviews at different points in the project's history with representatives of collaborating agencies, community residents and leaders involved in the project, and service recipients. Consumer response was uniformly positive, painting a picture of an accessible project responsive to community and individual needs. However, interviewing community residents not affiliated with the project might have provided unbiased information about project visibility and the extent to which their needs were represented.

Another example of a multifaceted public awareness project is the Primary Prevention Partnership (PPP), located in the state of Washington (Gray, 1983d). Four rural counties presenting significant service delivery problems, including transportation, service location, and service cost were targeted for prevention activities. These counties were characterized by a high percentage of residents living in poverty and in social and physical isolation, with no available hot-line services, and with a lack of public awareness about child abuse.

In contrast to Project Network, the PPP evaluation was more extensive, including systematic assessment of program implementation, output, and impact. With the exception of one county's resistance, project goals of providing professional and community education, developing information and referral systems, and networking within the community system were realized successfully. In terms of community impact, PPP is one of the few programs of its type to compile child abuse reporting statistics for targeted counties. Over the grant period, sharp increases of child abuse reports were noted in each target county that matched the intensification of prevention activities in that county. Thus, efforts to prevent abusive behavior by increasing public awareness resulted in massive reporting of suspected cases, which may be a realistic, although paradoxical, first step toward the ultimate goal of reducing the incidence of abuse. Of course, overreporting may become a problem itself, and intrusiveness of the state, a questionable activity. (For a discussion of this concern about intrusiveness, see Goldstein, Freud, & Solnit, 1979).

Crisis services, usually an integral part of any media campaign on child abuse, are designed to provide immediate assistance to parents under stress and to function as a major referral source to long-term services as needed. These programs may be free-standing services or may operate as one component of a multiservice program.

Telephone hot lines, available since the 1960s as a crisis intervention service for a variety of mental health problems, have emerged recently as a viable preventive strategy for child maltreatment. The Parents Anonymous national hot line (Baker & Martin, 1976), Michigan's Warm-Line (Gray, 1983a), and Connecticut's Care-Line (Connecticut Child Welfare Association, 1978) are examples of three different telephone services focusing on family support and child maltreatment issues. Although these programs value the idea of reaching parents before abuse occurs, in reality, the number of calls classified as prevention-stress are low relative to calls from multiple-problem families or calls involving various forms of child maltreatment (Boratynaski, 1983). For example, of approximately 9,000 calls, 40% were reports of abuse or neglect, 59% were information and referral, and 1% were primary prevention-stress calls (Connecticut Child Welfare Association, 1978). The difficulties in operating a noncrisis, support and information service are exemplified by Michigan's Warm-Line, where volunteers revised the concept of a 24-hour line to an answering service format when the number of calls became too low to justify a more elaborate program (Gray, 1983a).

Evaluation procedures used with telephone services include tracking numbers of incoming and outgoing calls and categorizing calls by type of problem and/or type of service provided. Rarely is follow-up information collected due to the volume of calls needing immediate attention or the anonymity of many callers. One of the problems inherent in evaluating the usefulness of a telephone service as a preventive strategy in child abuse is the lack of coordinated information with other crisis lines whose services may also prevent abuse. For example, parents who call child health-related hot lines for medical advice may receive information and support that may reduce the stress of living with an ill child. In addition, by offering information and referral services to battered women and their families, safehouse crisis lines frequently aid in preventing child abuse by helping battered women protect their children when the perpetrators threaten to involve the children in the violence.

In summary, programs created to prevent the onset of abusive behavior have taken the form of community-wide media campaigns, crisis services, and enhancement of local networks. Although consumer satisfaction is generally positive and programs report large numbers of well-attended activities, we still know very little about the effect of increased public awareness and related services on the incidence of child abuse.

Targeting High-Risk Groups

The third type of child abuse prevention targets selected groups who, by virtue of psychological vulnerabilities alone or in combination with environmental stressors, show a higher probability of abusing children compared with the general population. Risk factors associated with child abuse include but are not limited to low socioeconomic status, single and teenage parenthood, isolation from support systems, and complicated pregnancies (Belsky, 1980).

Programs that encourage increased contact between parent and child following delivery are based on the assumption that prolonged separation of parent and newborn in the postnatal period may be detrimental to the formation of successful bonding in some cases (Klaus & Kennell, 1976). Researchers studying the relation of early/extended contact to improved parent-child attachment have found conflicting results. One study demonstrating the benefit of extended contact, or "rooming-in," was conducted with low-income, first-time mothers who had normal deliveries (O'Conner, Vietze, Sherrod, Sandler, & Altemeier, 1980). Three hundred and one women were assigned randomly to rooming-in ($n = 143$) or routine postpartum contact ($n = 158$). Within the first 48 hr. mothers in the rooming-in condition spent a mean of 11.4 daytime hr with their infant compared with 2.2 hr for control group mothers. Approximately 17 months after birth, 2 cases of child maltreatment were found in rooming-in families, whereas 10 cases were reported for control families.

Other studies (e.g., Cohen et al., 1984; Gray, 1983a) have found that the benefits of these interventions are neither confirmed nor disproved. Programs that focus on early bonding may be a useful child abuse prevention strategy, but more research is needed to clarify conceptual and methodological questions about the relation of bonding and attachment to child abuse.

A second category of family support programs includes home visitors and parent aides (e.g., Gray, 1983a). In their original study of lay health visitors, Gray, Culter, Dean, and Kempe (1976) identified 100 mothers at risk for dysfunctional parenting practices and randomly assigned half to routine procedures and half to a comprehensive pediatric follow-up by a health visitor. A third group of low-risk mothers who delivered at the same time served as controls. Five children from the high-risk, routine procedure group required hospitalization for serious injuries, whereas no hospitalizations occurred in the high-risk, intervention or low-risk groups. In a subsequent study of 550 high-risk families receiving health visitors for an 18-month period, no children were found seriously injured as a result of parental abuse or neglect (Gray & Kaplan, 1980). In fact, the majority of high-risk families no longer needed routine visitation by the end of their child's 3rd month, whereas one third of the families, characterized as the most chaotic and prone to violence, continued service past the 6th month.

The Prenatal/Early Infancy Project (Olds, 1984), one of the most sophisticatedly designed research projects in the field of child abuse prevention, targeted prospective mothers expecting a first child with particular emphasis on women under 19 years of age, single, and from low socioeconomic backgrounds. Families were assigned randomly to one of four treatment conditions: (a) no services during pregnancy with sensory and developmental screening at the 12th and 24th month of life; (b) free transportation for regular prenatal and well-child visits plus screening services; (c) nurse home visitation during pregnancy plus transportation plus screening; and (d) nurse home visitation through the child's first 2 years of life

plus all services offered to the other groups. Both the program intervention (which included parent education, enhancement of informal social support, and linkage of families with health and human services) and program evaluation followed the ecological model.

Results indicated a range of significant preventive effects in the nurse-visited conditions in contrast to the comparison groups, including reduced cigarette smoking during pregnancy, reduced number of premature births, and appropriate weight gain during pregnancy. In contrast to high-risk mothers in the first two conditions, high-risk mothers visited by a nurse completed or returned to school, viewed their infants' temperaments more positively, reported fewer instances of conflict with and scolding of infants, provided more appropriate play materials, and restricted and punished their infants less frequently. Social service records indicated that 6% of the nurse-visited high-risk mothers abused or neglected their children during the first 2 years of life in contrast to 20% of comparison group high-risk mothers. Incidents of child maltreatment rose even higher for comparison group mothers as their socioeconomic status declined over time, but the same trend did not occur for mothers in the nurse-visited group. In addition, 2-year-old children from nurse-visited mothers were seen less frequently in the emergency room for accidents or ingestions than were 2-year-old children of comparison group mothers. Both the findings from Olds (1984) and the work of Gray and her colleagues (Gray et al., 1976; Gray & Kaplan, 1980) indicate that well-designed home visitation services to appropriately targeted groups can prevent a range of problems including those resulting from poor prenatal health habits to dysfunctional and abusive parent-child relationships.

At least one additional project deserves comment even though the investigators have not yet engaged in primary prevention efforts. Lutzker, Wesch, and Rice (1984) have developed several services for identified clients that could be provided to high-risk groups by home visitors or parent aides. For example, they devised a comprehensive home safety training program because unsafe homes have been commonly found among child abuse and neglect families (Gelles, 1982). They also developed money management, job-finding, health maintenance and nutrition, and leisure time counseling programs, all of which focus on identified problem areas of abusive parents. Evaluation data of treated clients suggest that the likelihood of child abuse may be reduced by some of these programs. Dissemination to high-risk groups is a logical next step.

METHODOLOGICAL PROBLEMS WITH CHILD ABUSE PRIMARY PREVENTION PROGRAMS

Three methodological problems that cut across programs in each of the preventive approaches are highlighted briefly: (a) the lack of appropriate comparison groups; (b) poor choice of outcome measures; and (c) the failure to measure proximal programmatic objectives and distal prevention goals. The reader is referred to Lorian (1983) for an excellent review of methodological problems in prevention programs and to Mahoney (1978) for a similar review of problems relevant to outcome research.

First, the lack of appropriate comparison groups in the majority of child abuse programs, although no different from what exists in the etiological studies of child abuse (Rosenberg & Reppucci, 1983a), seriously undermines the quality of the conclusions or interpretations that can be made about program impact. For example, the use of posttest only (i.e., Project Network) or pretest-posttest designs (i.e., Pan Asian Parent Education Project) are weak and uninformative in contrast to designs using one or more control groups (i.e., Prenatal/Early Infancy Project). Community-wide programs should be targeting well-matched control communities on socioeconomic and demographic characteristics such as family income, percent-

age of single-parent households, and level of transience (Garbariono, 1982) to determine whether the intervention had the intended effect on the experimental communities. Time series analyses of child abuse reports before, during, and after public awareness campaigns in both target and control communities could be used to demonstrate program impact. The family support programs appeared to be most likely to use comparison groups and randomized assignment of participants.

The second methodological problem concerns the poor choice of outcome measures to document program impact. Most of the measures used in the programs were developed specifically for use with the individual program with no evidence of their psychometric properties. In fact, most programs had very little outcome data beyond the initial description of indicators for successful program implementation (e.g., number of participants, numbers of activities, and service delivery interviews).

However, the most important and glaring methodological weakness involves the failure to document proximal programmatic objectives (i.e., criterion tests of new skills, knowledge, attitudes, and behaviors of the target population) and distal prevention goals (i.e., decreased incidence of abuse: see e.g., Heller, Price, & Sher, 1980). For example, most parent education programs demonstrate short-term changes in attitude and knowledge but do not assess behavioral changes. In Project C.A.N. Prevent, for example, a variety of opportunities to collect behavioral and objective data existed including (a) adding a pretest videotaped parent-child interaction and pretest observations of parent-as-teacher in the day care setting to compare with parent-child videotapes and observations obtained later in the program; (b) coding both parental behavior and children's response in the videotapes and day care settings; (c) charting the use of formal and informal support systems over the program time period; and (d) documenting suspected or founded cases of child abuse. Unfortunately, there is no indication that these opportunities were exploited.

Determining the program's effects on behavior constitutes the first step toward realizing prevention goals. The second step is to link these proximal objectives with the distal goal of reducing the child abuse rates. Because it is unlikely that a single program component will influence child abuse reports, Heller et al. (1980) advocated the design of preventive programs that target a variety of risk factors, for example, patterns of stressful events and personal predispositional factors, and then determined what combination of preventive strategies are most effective in reducing the incidence of abuse.

CONCLUSION

The programs presented here offer unique, innovative, and exciting ideas for the primary prevention of child abuse. However, with the possible exception of the health visitor concept, the degree to which these approaches can actually prevent child abuse and/or enhance family functioning is an empirical question yet to be answered. Although we have come a long way in terms of child abuse research and operationalization of prevention approaches, we will go no further in our goal of eradicating child abuse until evaluation of prevention programs is taken as seriously as the ideas that formulate the programs. It is this task that confronts the serious prevention researcher and practitioner over the next decade.

REFERENCES

Alvy, K. T., & Rosen, L. D. (1980). *Personnel for parent development program, Report number Two. A controlled study of parent training effects with poverty-level Black and Mexican-American parents*. Studio City, CA: Center for the Improvement of Child Caring.

Baker, J. M., & Martin, M. (1976). *Parents anonymous self-help for child abusing parents project. Evaluation report for period May 1974–April 30, 1976*. Tucson, AZ: Behavior Associates.

Belsky, J. (1980). Child maltreatment: An ecological integration. *American Psychologist, 35,* 320–335.

Bloom, B. L. (1979), Prevention of mental disorders: Recent advances in theory and practice. *Community Mental Health Journal, 15.* 179–191.

Boratynski, M. (1983). *Final report: The child abuse primary prevention project*. New Haven, CT: Yale University, The Consultation Center.

Caplan, G. (1964). *Principles of preventive psychiatry*. New York: Basic Books.

Caplan, G., & Nelson, S. (1973). On being useful: The nature and consequences of psychological research on social problems. *American Psychologist, 28,* 199–211.

Cohen, S., Gray. E., & Wald, M. (1984). *What do we really know from research about preventing child abuse and neglect?* Chicago: National Committee for Prevention of Child Abuse.

Cohn, A. H. (1982). Stopping abuse before it occurs: Different solutions for different population groups. *Child Abuse and Neglect, 6,* 473–483.

Connecticut Child Welfare Association, Inc. (1978). *Fifth annual report of the call-line. July 1, 1977–June 30, 1978*. Hartford, CT: Author.

Cooper, H., Dreznick. J., & Rowe. B. (1982). Perinatal coaching: A new beginning. *Social Casework, 63,* 35–40.

Cowen, E. L. (1973). Social and community intervention. *Annual Review of Psychology, 24,* 423–472.

Cowen, E. L. (1980). The wooing of primary prevention. *American Journal of Community Psychology, 8,* 258–284.

Cowen, E. L. (1983). Primary prevention in mental health. Past, present and future. In F. D. Felner, L. A. Jason, J. N. Moritsugu, & S. S. Farber (Eds.), *Preventive psychology: Theory, research and practice* (pp. 11–25). New York: Pergamon Press.

Education Commission of the States, (1976). *Education for parenthood: A primary prevention strategy for child abuse and neglect*. Denver, CO: Author.

Felner, R. D., Jason, L. A., Moritsugu, J. N., & Farber, S. S. (Eds.), (1983). *Preventive psycholo-*

gy: Theory, research and practice. New York: Pergamon Press.

Finkelhor D. (1979) *Sexually victimized children*. New York: Free Press.

Garbarino, J. (1977). The human ecology of child maltreatment: A conceptual model for research. *Journal of Marriage and the Family, 39*, 721–726.

Garbarino, J. (1982). *Children and families in the social environment*. New York: Aldine.

Garbarino, J. (1984, August). *Adolescent abuse: Troubled youth, troubled families*. Paper presented at the 92nd annual convention of the American Psychological Association. Toronto, Canada.

Garbarino, J., Stocking. S. H., & Associates (Eds.). (1980). *Protecting children from abuse and neglect: Developing and maintaining effective support systems for families*. San Francisco: Jossey-Bass.

Gelles, R. J. (1982). Problems in defining and labeling child abuse. In R. H. Starr (Ed.). *Child abuse prediction: Policy implications* (pp. 1–30). Cambridge, Ballinger.

Gerbner, G., Ross. C. J., & Zigler. E. (Eds.). (1980) *Child abuse: An agenda for action*. New York: Oxford University Press.

Giovannoni, J. M. (1980. October). *Measuring success in child abuse and neglect prevention*. Paper presented at Conference on Primary Prevention sponsored by Region VII Resource Center on Child Abuse and Neglect Kansas City, KS.

Goldstein, J., Freud, A., & Solnit, A. J. (1979). *Before the best interests of the child*. New York: Free Press.

Goldston, S. E. (1977). Defining primary prevention. In G. W. Albee & J. M. Jaffee (Eds.). *Primary prevention of psychopathology. Vol. I: The issues* (pp. 18–23). Hanover, NH: University Press of New England.

Gray, E. B. (1983a). *Final report. Collaborative research of community and minority group action to prevent child abuse and neglect. Vol. I: Perinatal interventions*. Chicago: National Committee for Prevention of Child Abuse.

Gray, E. B. (1983b). *Final report: Collaborative research of community and minority group action to prevent child abuse and neglect. Vol. II: Culture-based parent education programs*. Chicago: National Committee for Prevention of Child Abuse.

Gray, E. B. (1983c). *Final report: Collaborative research of community and minority group action to prevent child abuse and neglect. Vol. III: Public awareness and education using the creative arts*. Chicago: National Committee for Prevention of Child Abuse.

Gray, E. B. (1983d). *Final report. Collaborative research of community and minority group action to prevent child abuse and neglect. Vol. IV: Information and referral programs*. Chicago: National Committee for Prevention of Child Abuse.

Gray, J., Cutler, C., Dean, J., & Kempe, C. H. (1976). Perinatal assessment of mother-baby interaction. In R. E. Helfer & C. H. Kempe (Eds.). *Child abuse and neglect: The family and the community* (pp. 377–392). Chicago: University of Chicago Press.

Gray, J., & Kaplan, B. (1980). The lay health visitor program: An eighteen-month experience. In C. H. Kempe & R. Helfer (Eds.). *The battered child* (pp. 373–378). Chicago: University of Chicago Press.

Helier, K., Price, R. H., & Sher, K. J. (1980). Research and evaluation on primary prevention. Issues and guidelines. In R. H. Price, R. F. Ketterer, B. C. Bader, & J. Monahan (Eds.). *Prevention in mental health: Research, policy and practice* (pp 285–313). Beverly Hills, CA: Sage.

Klaus, M. H., & Kennell, J. H. (1976) *Maternal-infant bonding*. St. Louis, MO: C. V. Mosby.

Lorian, R. P. (1983). Evaluating preventive interventions: Guidelines for serious social change agent. In R. D. Felner, L. A. Jason, J. N. Moritsugu, & S. S. Farber (Eds.). *Preventive psychology: Theory, research and practice* (pp. 251–268). New York: Pergamon Press.

Lutzker, J. R., Wesch. D., & Rice, J. M. (1984). A review of "Project 12-Ways": An ecobehavioral approach to the treatment and prevention of child abuse and neglect. *Advances in Behavior Research and Therapy, 6*, 63–73.

Mahoney, M. J. (1978). Experimental methods and outcome evaluation. *Journal of Consulting and Clinical Psychology, 46*, 660–672.

Morris, L. (1977). *Education for parenthood: A program curriculum and evaluation guide*. Washington, DC: Department of Health, Education and Welfare.

National Center on Child Abuse and Neglect. (1983). Special supplement: Overview of five years of research on prevention. In *1983 Review of child abuse and neglect research* (Report No. 62. HHS-105-81-C-012: pp. 123–157). Washington, DC: Department of Health and Human Services.

O'Connor, S., Vietze, P. M., Sherrod, K. B., Sandler, H. M., & Altemeier, W. A. (1980). Reduced incidence of parenting inadequacy following rooming-in. *Pediatrics, 66,* 176–182.

Olds, D. L. (1984). *Final report: Prenatal early infancy project.* Washington, DC: Maternal and Child Health Research. National Institute of Health.

Parke, R., & Collmer, C. (1975). Child abuse: An interdisciplinary review. In E. M. Hetherington (Ed.), *Review of child development research* (Vol. 5. pp. 509–590). Chicago: University of Chicago Press.

Polansky, N., Chalmers, M. A., Buttenwieser, E., &

Williams, D. P. (1981). *Damaged parents: An anatomy of child neglect.* Chicago: University of Chicago Press.

Price, R. H. (1974). Etiology, the social environment, and the prevention of psychological dysfunction. In P. Insel & R. H. Moos (Eds.). *Health and the social environment* (pp. 287–300). Lexington, MA: D. C. Heath.

Rosenberg, M. S., & Reppucci, N. D. (1983a). Abusive mothers: Perceptions of their own and their children's behavior. *Journal of Consulting and Clinical Psychology, 51,* 674–682.

Rosenberg, M. S., & Reppucci, N. D. (1983b). Child abuse: A review with special focus on an ecological approach in rural communities. In A. W. Childs & G. B. Melton (Eds.) *Rural psychology,* (pp. 305–336). New York: Plenum Press.

Weal, E. (1979). On-the-job training for new moms in need. *Innovations, 6,* 20–21.

Zax, M., & Spector, G. A. (1974). *An introduction to community psychology.* New York: Wiley.

ACKNOWLEDGMENTS

Chapter 1 The Biological Basis of Behavior

Sandra Scarr & Kathleen McCartney. How People make their own environments: A theory of genotype/environmental effects. *Child Development,* 1983, *54,* 424–435. Copyright © 1983 by the Society for Research in Child Development, Inc. Reprinted with permission of the author and publisher.

Greta G. Fein, Pamela M. Schwartz, Sandra W. Jacobson, & Joseph L. Jacobson. Environmental toxins and behavioral development. *American Psychologist,* 1983, *38,* 1188–1197. Copyright © 1983 by the American Psychological Association. Reprinted with permission of the author and publisher.

Susan Goldberg. Premature birth: Consequences for the parent-infant relationship. *American Scientist,* 1979, March. Reprinted with permission of the American Scientist, Journal of Sigma Xi, The Scientific Research Society, and the author.

Michael Rutter. Temperament: Concepts, issues and problems. *Temperamental differences in infants and young children.* London Foundations Symposium, *89,* 1982, 1–15. Copyright © J. W. Wiley & Son Ltd. Reprinted with permission of the publisher and the author.

Emmy E. Werner. Resilent children. *Young Children,* 1984, Nov., 68–72. Copyright © 1984, National Association for the Education of Young Children. Reprinted with permission of the author and publisher.

Chapter 2: Physical Growth and Maturation

Henry N. Ricciuti. Interaction of adverse environmental and nutritional influences on mental development. *Baroda Journal of Nutrition,* 1982, *9,* 327–335. Reprinted with permission of the author and publisher.

Ruth Striegel-Moore, Lisa R. Silberstein, & Judith Rodin. Toward an understanding of risk factors for bulimia. *American Psychologist,* 198, *3,* 246–263. Copyright © American Psychological Association. Reprinted with permission of author and publisher.

David Magnusson, Hakan Stattin, & Vernon Allen. Differential maturation among girls and its relations to social adjustment: A longitudinal perspective. *Life-span Development & Behavior,* vol. 7. Lawrence Erlbaum, Associates, Inc., pp. 136–172. Reprinted with permission of author and publisher.

Chapter 3: Infancy and Early Development

Andrew Meltzoff & Keith Moore. Newborn infants imitate adult facial gestures. *Child Development,* 1983, *54,* 702–709. Copyright © Society for Research in Child Development Inc. Reprinted with permission of author and publisher.

Renee Baillargeon, Elizabeth S. Spelke, & Stanley Wasserman. Object permanence in five-month-old infants. *Cognition,* 1985, *20,* 191–208. Copyright © North-Holland Publishing Co. Reprinted with permission of author and publisher.

Prentice Starkey, Elizabeth S. Spelke, & Rochel Gelman. Detection of intermodal numerical correspondences by human infants. *Science* 1983, *10,* 179–181. Copyright © American Association for the Advancement of Science. Reprinted with permission of author and publisher.

Bennett I. Bertenthal & Joseph J. Campos. An epigenetic perspective on the development of fear. *World Congress of Psychiatry,* vol. 7, *Developments in Psychiatry* 1986, 1281–1283. Copyright 1986 Elsevier Science Publishing Co. Reprinted with permission of author and publisher.

Jerome Kagan & Robert E. Klein. Cross-cultural perspectives on early development. *American Psychologist,* 1973, *28,* 947–961. Copyright © 1973 by the American Psychological Association. Reprinted with permission of author and publisher.

Chapter 4: Emotional Development

Susan B. Crockenberg. Infant irritability, mother responsiveness, and social support influences on the security of infant-mother attachment. *Child Development,* 1981, *52,* 857–865. Copyright © by the Society for Research in Child Development, Inc. Reprinted with permission of author and publisher.

Megan Gunnar-VonGnechten. Changing a frightening toy into a pleasant toy by allowing the infant to control its actions. *Developmental Psychology*, 1978, *14*, 157–162. Copyright © by the American Psychological Association. Reprinted with permission of author and publisher.

James F. Sorce, Robert N. Emde, Joseph J. Campos, & Mary D. Klinnert. Maternal emotional signaling: Its effect on the visual cliff behavior of 1-year- olds. *Developmental Psychology*, 1985, *21*, 195–200. Copyright © by the American Psychological Association. Reprinted with permission of author and publisher.

Barbara G. Melamed & Lawrence J. Siegal. Children's reactions to medical stressors: An ecological approach to the study of anxiety. *Anxiety and the anxiety disorders*, A. H. Tuma & J. Musor (Eds.), 1984. Copyright © by Lawrence Erlbaum Associates. Reprinted with permission of author and publisher.

Chapter 5: Language and Communication

Dan I. Slobin. Children and Language: They learn the same way all around the world. *Psychology Today*, July, 1972. Copyright © 1972 Ziff-Davis Publishing Co. Reprinted with permission of author and publisher.

Anne Fernald. Four-month-old infants prefer to listen to motherese. *Infant Behavior and Development*, 1985, *8*, 181–185. Copyright © Ablex Publishing Co. Reprinted with permission of author and publisher.

Susan Goldin-Meadow & Carolyn Mylander. Gestural communication in deaf children: Noneffect of parental input on language development. *Science*, 1983, *221*, 372–374. Copyright © American Association for the Advancement of Science. Reprinted with permission of author and publisher.

Francois Grosjean. The bilingual child. *Life with Two Languages*, 1982. Reprinted with permission of the author and Harvard University Press.

Catherine Garvey. The facilitation system. *Children's Talk*, 1984. Reprinted with permission of the author and Harvard University Press.

Chapter 6: Cognition and Learning

Henry M. Wellman. The foundations of knowledge: Concept development in the young child. *The Young Child*, 1983, *3*, 115–134. Copyright © National Association for the Education of Young Children. Reprinted with permission of the author and publisher.

Robert S. Siegler. Five generalizations about cognitive development. *American Psychologist*, 1983, *38*, 263–277. Copyright © *American Psychological Association*. Reprinted with permission of author and publisher.

John H. Flavell. The development of children's knowledge about the appearance-reality distinction. *American Psychologist*, 1986 *41*, 418–425. Copyright © American Psychological Association. Reprinted with permission of author and publisher.

Jennifer H. Cousins, Alexander W. Siegel, & Scott E. Maxwell. Way finding and cognitive mapping in large-scale environments: A test of a developmental model. *Journal of Experimental Child Psychology*, 1983, *35*, 1–20. Copyright © 1983 by Academic Press, Inc. Reprinted with permission of author and publisher.

Sheldon Cohen, Gary W. Evans, David S. Krantz & Daniel Stokols. Physiological, motivational, and cognition effects of aircraft noise on children. *American Psychologist*, 1980, *35*, 231–243. Copyright © American Psychological Association. Reprinted with permission of author and publisher.

Stephen J. Ceci & Urie Bronfenbrenner. "Don't forget to take the cupcakes out of the oven": Prospective memory, strategic time-monitoring, and context. *Child Development*, 1985, *56*, 152–164. Copyright © The Society for Research in Child Development, Inc. Reprinted with permission of author and publisher.

Sandra Scarr-Salapatek and Richard A. Weinberg. The war over race and IQ: When black children grow up in white homes. *Psychology Today*, December 1975. Copyright © 1975 Ziff Davis Publishing Company. Reprinted with permission of Psychology Today and the authors.

Chapter 7: Social Cognition

Jeanne-Brooks-Gunn & Michael Lewis. The development of early visual self-recognition. *Developmental Review*, 1984, *4*, 215–239. Copyright © Academic Press. Reprinted with permission of author and publisher.

William S. Rholes & Diane N. Ruble. Children's understanding of dispositional characteristics of others. *Child Development*, 1984, *55*, 550–560. Copyright © Society for Research in Child Development, Inc. Reprinted with permission of author and publisher.

Malcolm W. Watson. Development of social role understanding. *Developmental Review*, *4*, 192–213. Copyright © Academic Press. Reprinted with permission of author and publisher.

Chapter 8: The Family

Laurence Steinberg. The ABCs of transformations in the family at adolescence: Changes in affect, behavior, and cognition. Presented at the Third Biennial Conference on Adolescence Research, March 1985. Reprinted with permission of the author.

Robert B. Stewart & Robert S. Marvin. Sibling relations: The role of conceptual perspective-taking in the ontogeny of sibling caregiving. *Child Development*, 1984, *55*, 1322–1332. Copyright © Society for Research in Child Development, Inc. Reprinted with permission of author and publishers.

E. Mavis Hetherington. Family relations six years after divorce. *Remarriage and Stepparenting today: Research and Theory*, 1986. Copyright © Guilford Press. Reprinted with permission of author and publisher.

Glen H. Elder, Jr., A. Caspi, & T. Van Nguyen. Resoureful and vulnerable children: Family influences in hard times. *Development as action in context: Integrative perspectives on youth development*, 1986. Copyright © Springer-Verlag. Reprinted with permission of author and publisher.

Frank F. Furstenberg, Jr., Richard Lincoln, & Jane Menken. Teenage sexuality, pregnancy, and childbearing. *Teenage sexuality, pregnancy, and childbearing*, 1981, 1–17. Copyright © University of Pennsylvania Press. Reprinted with permission of author and publisher.

Chapter 9: Extra-Familial Agents of Socialization: Peers, Day Care, Schools, and Television

Mary Main & Carol George. Responses of abused and disadvantaged toddlers to distress in age-mates: A study in the day care setting. *Developmental Psychology*, 21, 407–412. Copyright © American Psychological Association. Reprinted with permission of author and publisher.

John D. Coie & Kenneth A. Dodge. Continuities and changes in children's social studies: A five-year longitudinal study. *Merrill Palmer Quarterly*, 1983, *29*, 261–281. Reprinted by permission of the Wayne State University Press and author.

Jay Belsky. Developmental effects of day care and conditions of quality. *Day Care: Report of the 16th Ross Roundtable on Critical Approaches to Pediatric Problems*, 1985. Reprinted with permission of author and publisher.

Victoria Seitz, Laurie K. Rosenbaum, & Nancy H. Apfel. Effects of family support intervention; a ten-year follow-up. *Child Development*, 1985, *56*, 376–391. Copyright © Society for Research in Child Development, Inc. Reprinted with permission of author and publisher.

Mark R. Lepper, Microcomputers in education: Motivational and social issues. *American Psychologist*, 1985, *40*, 1–18. Copyright © American Psychological Association. Reprinted with permission of author and publisher.

Elliot Aronson & Diane Bridgeman. Jigsaw groups and the desegregated classroom: In pursuit of common goals. *The Jigsaw Classroom*, 1978. Copyright © Sage. Reprinted with permission of author and publisher.

W. A. Collins. Social antecedents, cognitive processing, and comprehension of social portrayals on television. In T. Higgins, D. Ruble, & W. W. Hartup (Eds.), *Social Cognition and Social Development*, 1983, pp. 110–133. Reprinted with permission of author and Cambridge University Press.

Chapter 10: Targets of Socialization: Moral Development, Sex Typing, Aggression and Achievement

Martin L. Hoffman. Development of moral thought, feelings, and behavior. *American Psychologist*, 1979, *34*, 958–966. Copyright © 1979 by the American Psychological Association. Reprinted with permission of author and publisher.

Diane N. Ruble, Terry Balaban, & Joel Cooper. Gender constancy and the effects of sex-typed televised toy commercials. *Child Development*, 1981, *51*, 667–673. Copyright © Society for Research in Child Development, Inc. Reprinted with permission of author and publisher.

Harvey J. Ginsburg & Shirley M. Miller. Sex differences in children's risk-taking behavior. *Child De-*

velopment, 1982, *53*, 426–428. Copyright © Society for Research in Child Development, Inc. Reprinted with permission of author and publishers.

E. Mark Cummings, Ronald J. Iannotti, & Carolyn Zahn-Waxler. Influence of conflict between adults on the emotions and aggression of young children. *Developmental Psychology*, 1985, *21*, 495–507. Copyright © American Psychological Association, 1985.Rreprinted with permission of author and publisher.

Kenneth A. Dodge. Social cognition and children's aggressive behavior. *Child Development*, 1980, *51*, 162–170. Copyright © Society for Research in Child Development, Inc. Reprinted with permission of author and publisher.

Carol S. Dweck & Janine Bempechat. Children's theories of intelligence: Consequences for learning. *Learning and Motivation in the Classroom*, S. Paris, G. Olson, & H. Stevenson (Eds.), 1983, 239–256. Copyright © Academic Press, 1983. Reprinted with permission of author and publisher.

Harold W. Stevenson, Shin-Ying Lee, & James W. Stigler. Mathematics achievement of Chinese, Japanese, and American children. *Science*, 1986, *231*, 693–699. Copyright © American Association for the Advancement of Science. Reprinted with permission of author and publisher.

Chapter 11: Childhood Psychopathology

Eric J. Mash & Charlotte Johnston. Parental perceptions of child behavior problems, parenting self-esteem, and mothers' reported stress in younger and older hyperactive and normal children. *Journal of Consulting and Clinical Psychology*, 1983, *51*, 86–99. Copyright © American Psychological Association, 1983. Reprinted with permissiion of author and publisher.

Carolyn Zahn-Waxler, Michael Chapman, & E. Mark Cummings. Cognitive and social development in infants with a bipolar parent. *Child Psychiatry and Human Development*, 1984-85, 15, 75–85. Copyright © Human Services Press, Inc. Reprinted with permission of author and publisher.

Hicks Marlow, John B. Reid, Gerald R. Patterson, & Mark R. Weinrott. Treating adolescent multiple offenders: A comparison and follow-up of parent training for families of chronic delinquents. Reprinted with permission of the author, 1986, and the Oregon Social Learning Center.

Mindy S. Rosenberg & N. Dickon Reppucci. Primary prevention of child abuse. *Psychological Bulletin*, 1985, *98*, 576–585. Copyright © American Psychological Association. Reprinted with permission of author and publisher.